MEASURES for PSYCHOLOGICAL ASSESSMENT

Ki-Taek Chun
Sidney Cobb
John R. P. French, Jr.

with Foreword by
E. Lowell Kelly

A Guide to 3,000 Original Sources and Their Applications

SURVEY RESEARCH CENTER
INSTITUTE FOR SOCIAL RESEARCH

ISR Code No. 4014

Library of Congress Catalog Card No. 74-620127
ISBN 0-87944-168-2

Published by the Institute for Social Research
The University of Michigan, Ann Arbor, Michigan 48106

Table of Contents

Foreword

"Whatever exists, exists in some amount, and can be measured." This dictum, generally attributed to E.L. Thorndike (circa 1914), seems to have been accepted as a basic postulate by the literally thousands of individuals who have developed and published one or more of the even larger number of tests, inventories, scales, and other instruments purporting to assess some psychological variable presumed to be relevant to an issue of theoretical and/or practical concern to social scientists. At first blush, the development and availability of such a large number of assessment devices in the past 50 years would appear to reflect re-markable progress in the development of the social sciences. Unfortunately, this conclusion is not justified, since as the authors of this volume have found and reported elsewhere (Chun et al., 1973), nearly three out of four of the measures are used but once and often only by the developer of the instrument. Worse still, as these same authors have reported, the more popular instruments tend to be selected more frequently not because they are better measuring instruments but primarily because of their convenience.

Having taught courses in psychological measurement for over forty years, I have been asked by literally hundreds of graduate students and colleagues, in psychology and in related disciplines, to help them choose an instrument to assess one or more of the variables they believed were critical to a research project they were undertaking. Before 1938, I was forced to rely on my general knowledge of the field, available textbooks, and familiarity with psychological journals. The result, I am sure, was that my advice was often less than adequate. My role as a consultant on assessment was greatly facilitated by the publication of Buros' Mental Measurement Yearbook, the first of which appeared in 1938 and the seventh (in two volumes) in 1972. Thanks to this series of extremely valuable volumes, I could refer my students and colleagues to systematic and often multiple critical reviews of published tests of ability, aptitudes, educational

v

achievement, and personality. Unfortunately, however, the Buros Yearbooks did not cover the much greater number of less formal and often ad hoc assessment devices which were being developed and described in journal articles. Even the conscientious social science researcher was often baffled when confronted with the task of choosing the most appropriate tool available for assessing the variable or variables with which he was concerned. Given this situation, it is perhaps not too surprising to find that instead of using an existing instrument about which at least something was known, the investigator often elected to devise his own ad hoc measuring device, give it a name, and add it to the burgeoning array of instruments already available. Regretfully, the originator of each "new" instrument rarely felt constrained to determine and report its psychometric properties or to demonstrate its comparability or superiority to similar instruments used by others. Thus, an already chaotic situation was even further compounded.

Hopefully, the present volume will contribute greatly to the much needed correction of this state of affairs. Thanks to literally thousands of hours of systematic effort by nearly a dozen dedicated scholars, any conscientious investigator may now, with relatively little effort, be able to identify those measures which have been used by others to assess any of a large number of variables in which he may be interested, and to evaluate the known relative merits and limitations of those instruments. The investigator may be shocked to discover, however, that essential facts regarding psychometric aspects of the measures are simply not available.

The last 20 years have produced a large number of sophisticated developments in psychometrics, both theoretical and methodological. Regretfully, however, these developments appear to have had but little impact on too many investigators who still naively believe that the creation of a new assessment device is a relatively simple procedure. Anyone can specify a construct which he wishes to measure, compose a set of questions which he believes will assess it, develop a scoring key which will result in a distribution of scores, and then assert that the scores reflect the variables (or construct) which the instrument purports to assess. All too often, however, authors of these instruments fail to determine and report on the sources of the variance of the resulting scores. Obviously, variance in scores is a sine qua non of any instrument that purports to discriminate among respondents. Unfortunately, however, variance of scores alone does not assure us that the instrument is measuring anything: any set of questions requiring a yes/no or other dichotomous response scored using any set of arbitrarily assigned 0-1 weights will yield a distribution of scores. Even if the

questions should be written in a language unknown to the respondent, the scores would be distributed as predictable from the binomial theorem. The resulting scores, however, could not be expected to correlate even with themselves, much less with any other variable! Common sense as well as psychometric theory demands, as a minimum, that the author of an instrument tell us how well it measures whatever it measures: what proportion of the variance is replicable and how much only noise, i.e., non-replicable error variance?

But demonstration that the resulting measure has some reliability, i.e., replicates variance, is only the minimal requirement of any assessment device. Again, common sense as well as psychometric theory demands some basis for inferring what the instrument measures. From experience we have learned that several previously accepted bases for assuming validity simply dare not be trusted. These include the following varieties of what I call "psuedo-validity."

a) nominal validity -- i.e., the assumption that the instrument measures what its name implies.

b) validity by fiat -- e.g., assertion by the author (no matter how distinguished!) that the instrument measures variable x, y or z.

c) face validity -- inference that the instrument measures what it appears to measure as judged on the basis of the questions asked or the performance required by subjects.

In addition to having some replicable variance, one needs to know that the scores have some utility, e.g., that they will discriminate groups or subjects falling in clearly distinguishable categories or predict the future behavior of persons in training, undergoing treatment, or adapting to some defined life role. To the extent that scores on any instrument are shown to have either some discriminative or predictive validity, the instrument has some utility. But, this is not enough; one must next ask how well the scores discriminate or predict, i.e., how efficient is the discrimination or prediction as compared with that possible with alternative assessments sometimes far less sophisticated and less time consuming. Large samples may yield statistically significant t's or r's, but still the variance discriminated or predicted may be woefully small, too small to have any utility in the real life world.

Even if an instrument is shown to have useful discriminative or predictive validity, one cannot be at all sure that the instrument is measuring what it purports to measure or the construct that its author asserts that it measures. Experience has shown that the replicable variance of any set of scores is rarely attributable to any one variable; instead it is typically composed of a combination of variances associated with two (or even more) psychological variables

or constructs. In the domain of variables related to "mental health," it is especially difficult to construct an assessment device and not have the total replicable variance of its scores composed in part of "nuisance variables," i.e., variables which the investigator would prefer not to measure. Two of the most troublesome of these are: the tendency on the part of subjects to give "yes" or "no" responses regardless of the question asked and the tendency to give what are perceived as the more socially acceptable responses. And, when assessing variables related to mental health, investigators must always be on guard against the possibility that more intelligent and more sophisticated subjects are more able to perceive what the investigator is attempting to assess and to respond to the questions in a manner which they believe will raise or lower their scores.

Fortunately, thanks to the sophisticated post World War II contributions of Cronbach and Meehl especially, we now have a much better understanding of construct validity and of the necessary logical and experimental steps required to provide the kinds of evidence necessary to justify the conclusion that most, if not all, of the replicable variance of the scores yielded by any assessment device is in fact attributable to individual differences in variable X. The authors of many of the instruments listed in this volume, unfortunately, were either unaware of the importance of construct validity or, if aware, could not be bothered to undertake the complex and arduous task of establishing the construct validity of their devices. Given this state of affairs, it is not surprising that such a large proportion of the instruments developed have not been utilized by subsequent investigators.

I am not so naive as to believe that the publication of this volume will suddenly halt the continued production of inadequate assessment devices, created on an ad hoc basis by relatively unsophisticated researchers and published in one of our journals. Hopefully, however, by making readily available the facts regarding the usually brief life history and the fate of similar devices previously developed by others, this unique volume will contribute to a somewhat more systematic approach to the development of better assessment instruments so essential for real progress in the social sciences.

E. Lowell Kelly
Professor of Psychology
The University of Michigan

September 1974

Preface

     This volume is a compilation of annotated references to the measures of
mental health and related variables, and the uses of these measures. It has
the primary objectives of providing expedient access to all relevant measures
for an area of one's interest, helping in the selection of appropriate measures,
and providing a bibliography of all quantitative research which has used these
measures. We hope this book will contribute toward the improvement of measurement methodology in the social sciences. There presently exist at least two
dozen compilations of references to or descriptions of measures, and the appear-
ance of another one naturally calls for justification. In this Preface, then,
we will discuss the rationale for this volume, describe the services it can
perform or the needs it can serve, and indicate the intended readership of this
volume.
     We believe that the progress of research in the social sciences, particu-
larly in mental health and related fields, has been unduly impeded by the logis-
tic problem of information storage and retrieval. The difficulty of information
search and retrieval is indeed real and overwhelming. Think of the plight of a
research worker or student who wishes to have a reasonably good knowledge of the
empirical research in a given area. He needs to identify and be familiar with
the representative measures and the substantive studies which use these measures.
Any attempt at a thorough search becomes prohibitively time-consuming and costly
since the materials are numerous, scattered, and sometimes hidden in the methods
sections of substantive papers. Even a modest search requires a considerable
amount of time and labor that might be better spent for other purposes.
     If this alleged difficulty is not convincing, imagine a researcher who is
looking for a good measure of adjustment, for example. The definitional problem of the concept of adjustment aside, this researcher will immediately find
himself plagued by the problem of too many possibilities. There are too many

journals rather than too few: the topic is discussed in the literature of psychiatry, clinical psychology, personality and social psychology, counseling and guidance, education and educational psychology, sociology, and so on. In any particular source, there will be too many references rather than too few, so a conscientious researcher who uses the usual bibliographies and abstracts will dig up several dozen discussions on adjustment in order to find a single quantitative measure. The lack of efficient search mechanisms has adversely affected every student, teacher, and researcher, and this problem of tedious, inefficient digging will become even more severe in the future because of the exponential growth of relevant scientific literature.

At this point, some figures might add a sense of urgency. According to Bonjean, Hill, and McLemore (1967), of the 2,080 different measures used in four leading sociological journals during the twelve-year period of 1954-1965, only 2.5 percent of them were used with any appreciable frequency (six or more times) while 72 percent were inactive or dead (i.e., either published in the period covered but never used again, or published before 1954 but used only once during the period searched). We find that a similar situation prevails in psychology as well. The examination of a 20 percent sample of articles which appeared in 15 measurement-related journals from 1960 to 1969 revealed that approximately 2,500 different measures were in use and that only about 3 percent of these measures were used 10 or more times during this period and 63 percent were used only once (Chun, Barnowe, Wykowski, Cobb, and French, 1972; more fully reported in Chun, Barnowe, Cobb, and French, 1974). Although empirical research is often viewed as a continuous and integrated collective endeavor, these findings re-flect an individualistic process which is discontinuous, fragmented, and wasteful.

This astonishing rate of obsolescence of psychological measures may comfort those who feel that most of the measures are not worthy of repeated use and, as such, they might as well die out. However, evidence indicates that this is wish-ful thinking. For example, our comparison of the quality of three groups of measures used in psychology, matched for age but differing in their frequency of usage, shows that the more frequently used measures are not qualitatively any better than the less popular ones. That is to say, compared to the frequently used measures, the infrequently used ones are equally valid, equally reliable, have been developed on samples of comparable size, and provide norms that are equally extensive. Thus, the typical researcher chooses his measures not because of any of the conventional dimensions of qualitative evaluation but only because they were easy to find (Chun et al., 1972). A similar situation prevails regard-ing the measures used in sociology (Barnowe and Chun, 1974). Furthermore, when

a sample of psychological measures published in 1960 were examined for their quality and subsequent use through 1970, an essentially similar picture emerged indicating no relationship between a measure's quality and the frequency of its use (Chun et al., 1974). An obvious implication of these findings is that a researcher has much to gain from examining all relevant measures before making the final choice.

As proposed elsewhere (Chun et al., 1973), we believe that the most rational solution to this problem of information search and retrieval is to develop a comprehensive National Repository of Social Science Measures. Without the services of such a repository, it seems unrealistic to expect the future of social science research to be much different from its present situation. As an experimental prototype of such a system, we have developed a computerized repository under a grant from the Center for Epidemiological Studies, National Institute of Mental Health. Our original plan was to develop a usable system and to transfer the updating and servicing functions to an appropriate agency. Unfortunately, neither the long range plan of incorporating the system into the Psychological Abstracts nor the interim plan of continuously updating the system was funded. Our inference is that the need for such a centralized storage-retrieval system and its beneficial effects are not recognized fully. However, we predict (half wishfully, of course) that in the next ten years or so it will become possible to search the measurement literature more rapidly and efficiently by computer. Since the Repository is neither being updated nor processing retrieval requests, it was deemed essential that we make the data base of the Repository available to as many potential users as possible.

There are four objectives to this volume. The first objective is to provide a comprehensive bibliography relating to all measures of mental health and related concepts. Since inclusiveness is a most desirable feature here, an attempt has been made to cite all measures, whether they are popular or infamous, visible or obscure, and recent or old. The entries in this volume are based on our search of 26 measurement-related journals in psychology and sociology from the period 1960-1970 (see pp. xx-xxii for details on the search procedure). This volume obviates the need of duplicative searches of this literature by other researchers. The problem of oversupply (i.e., supplying information that is insufficiently differentiated) common to most of the information systems is also present in the fixed format of this volume, although an attempt has been made to avoid some degree of indiscriminate referencing by pairing or cross-referencing the retrieval terms (see pp. xix-xx). The flexibility of querying and requesting information at the desired level of differentiation which was possible with the

computerized Repository is no longer available in the fixed format of this volume. Consequently, the reader will have to select from a larger set that subset of measures which is specifically relevant to his interest.

The second of the four objectives is to aid the reader in selecting measures most appropriate to the intended use. This volume can be of use in two ways: (1) for each measure of interest the reader can now go directly to the original source where the measure was first described; and (2) the user can readily look up all the studies in which the measure was subsequently used. In so doing, the initial as well as the cumulative performance characteristics of any measure can be evaluated.

The third objective of this volume is to save time for those readers who wish to obtain a summary of all quantitative research in a given content area. One simply needs to identify the measures relevant to an area and follow through the uses of individual measures. Obtaining an appropriate summary is facilitated by the annotation that indicates the type of information to be found in each of the uses (see pp. xvii-xix), since the titles of journal articles seldom reflect the specific type of information that can be found in the articles regarding the use of a measure.

In addition, this volume will be useful in helping the reader select and use better measures, in preventing the creation of redundant measures, and in stimulating the needed methodological research. Information on the multiplicity of measures for a given concept will hopefully encourage many research workers to examine the nature of the interrelationships among the measures. Furthermore, when information on the multiplicity of measures is either known or readily retrievable, it may become a norm for the authors of new measures to demonstrate the incremental utility of the new measures. And, it would become reasonable for editors and referees to request such demonstrations. In this manner, we hope this volume will contribute toward improving the quality of measurement in mental health and in related social science fields.

As noted earlier in this Preface, there presently exist approximately two dozen compilations of measures. Most of these compilations consist of descriptions of individual measures with varying degrees of evaluative comments. The compiled measures are frequently those that are either visible or better known. There is no assurance that the list of measures assembled for a content area is either exhaustive or representative. Unless the listed measures are qualitatively better than the unlisted ones, the compilations would tend to perpetuate the use of popular measures rather than good ones. The compilations usually list a few, but rarely all, uses of individual measures. Although a listing of

some uses is admittedly better than none, it runs the risk both of biasing the evaluation of individual measures and of causing the frequently cited references to be cited with an even 'greater frequency, a phenomenon which Merton (1968) deplores as the "Matthew effect" in science. However, these compilations can be highly useful sources of information, and the reader of this volume should be aware of them. For the reader's convenience, the more useful ones are listed at the end of this Preface (p. xiii).

For those seeking additional sources, the survey by Backer (1973) of various storage-retrieval systems for measurement-related information should be mentioned. Also worthy of particular mention in this connection is the Compendia Reviews section of <u>Measuring Human Behavior</u> by Lake, Miles, and Earle (1973), which provides a brief description and critique of 20 compendia including 8 of those listed at the end of the Preface. We further note that the compilation by Comrey, Backer, and Glaser (1973) lists unpublished measures, while the present volume covers the published literature. The two volumes, then, should be used as a complementary set.

This volume should prove useful as a reference resource to all those who have occasion to make measurements of a wide range of variables. Social and community psychiatrists and their colleagues would find it of use whether they are interested in planning, evaluation, or research. Another obvious set of readers would be behavioral scientists who are interested in the quantitative assessment of their variables. And those who want access to the quantitative research literature on mental health will find this volume a great time-saver.

This volume consists of computer print-outs from the Repository, which in turn was the work of many staff members over a period of nearly three years. Credit naturally goes to these staff members and we gratefully acknowledge the steadfast contributions of Barbara B. Surovell, J. Thad Barnowe, Margaret S. Groncznack, Nina Gupta, Patricia A. Pecorella, Samuel R. Pinneau, Jr., Carolyn Smith, Jean Dingwall, Harriet Selin, Barbara R. Cox, and Catherine S. Wykowski. In addition, the indispensable aid of Margaret A. Sachs has made possible the preparation of this volume. Robert L. Kahn, Director of the Survey Research Center, and the staff of the ISR Publishing Division have been instrumental in making this volume available.

Finally, we acknowledge with appreciation the support of National Institute of Mental Health Grants R01-MH-16794, K5-MH-16709, and K6-MH-21844.

References

Backer, T. E. A Reference Guide for Psychological Measures. _Psychological_
Reports, 1972, _31_, 751-768.

Barnowe, J. T., and Chun, K. T. Discontinuity in Sociological Measurement:
Frequency of Usage and Quality. Unpublished manuscript, Institute for
Social Research, The University of Michigan, 1974.

Bonjean, C. M., Hill, R. J., and McLemore, S. D. _Sociological Measurement:_
An Inventory of Scales and Indices. San Francisco: Chandler, 1967.

Buros, O. K. (Ed.). _The Seventh Mental Measurements Yearbook_ (2 vols.).
Highland Park, N. J.: Gryphon Press, 1972.

Chun, K. T., Barnowe, J. T., Cobb, S., and French, J. R. P., Jr. Publication
and Uses of Psychological Measures in the 1960's. Unpublished manuscript,
Institute for Social Research, The University of Michigan, 1974.

Chun, K. T., Barnowe, J. T., Wykowski, K. S., Cobb, S., and French, J. R. P., Jr.
Selection of Psychological Measures: Quality or Convenience? _Proceedings_
of the 80th Annual Convention of the American Psychological Association,
1972, _7_, 15-16.

Chun, K. T., Cobb, S., French, J. R. P., Jr., and Seashore, S. E. Storage and
Retrieval of Information on Psychological Measures. _American Psychologist_,
1973, _28_, 592-599.

Merton, R. K. The Matthew Effect in Science. _Science_, 1968, _159_, 56-63.

Some Useful Compilations

1. Bonjean, C. M., Hill, R. J., and McLemore, S. D. Sociological Measurement: An Inventory of Scales and Indices. San Francisco: Chandler, 1967.

2. Comrey, A. L., Backer, T. E., and Glaser, E. M. A Sourcebook of Mental Health Measures. Los Angeles: Human Interaction Research Institute, 1973.

3. Johnson, O. G., and Bommarito, J. W. Tests and Measurements in Child Development: A Handbook. San Francisco: Jossey-Bass, 1971.

4. Lake, D. G., Miles, M. B., and Earle, R. B., Jr. Measuring Human Behavior: Tools for the Assessment of Social Functioning. New York: Teachers College Press, Columbia University, 1973.

5. McReynolds, P. (Ed.). Advances in Psychological Assessment. Vol. 1. Palo Alto, Calif.: Science and Behavior Books, 1968.

6. McReynolds, P. (Ed.). Advances in Psychological Assessment. Vol. 2. Palo Alto, Calif.: Science and Behavior Books, 1971.

7. McReynolds, P. (Ed.). Advances in Psychological Assessment. Vol. 3. San Francisco, Calif.: Jossey-Bass, 1975.

8. Miller, D. C. Handbook of Research Design and Social Measurement (2nd ed.). New York: David McKay, 1970.

9. Robinson, J. P., Athanasiou, R., and Head, K. B. Measures of Occupational Attitudes and Occupational Characteristics. Ann Arbor, Mich.: Institute for Social Research, The University of Michigan, 1969.

10. Robinson, J. P., Rusk, J. G., and Head, K. B. Measures of Political Attitudes. Ann Arbor, Mich.: Institute for Social Research, The University of Michigan, 1968.

11. Robinson, J. P., and Shaver, P. R. Measures of Social Psychological Attitudes (Rev. ed.). Ann Arbor, Mich.: Institute for Social Research, The University of Michigan, 1973.

12. Shaw, M. E., and Wright, J. M. Scales for the Measurement of Attitudes. New York: McGraw-Hill, 1967.

13. Straus, M. A. Family Measurement Techniques: Abstracts of Published Instruments, 1935-1965. Minneapolis: University of Minnesota Press, 1969.

Instructions for the Users

CONTENTS OF THIS VOLUME
This volume consists of two major sections, <u>Primary References</u> and
<u>Applications</u>, and two indexes. The section on Primary References lists approxi-
mately 3,000 references to the journal articles or other publications in which
the measures were first described. The Application section provides information
on about 6,600 instances in which the measures described in the 'Primary References
have been used. The <u>Author Index</u> and the <u>Descriptor Index</u> are designed to facilitate the use of these major sections.

<u>Primary References</u> (pp. 56-361)
Each Primary Reference is identified and referred to by a "scale number,"
an alpha-numeric code consisting of the initial of the first author's last name
hyphenated with a number (e.g., B-46). Scale numbers are used in both the Author
and Descriptor Indexes. Each Primary Reference contains: (a) a reference to the
first source which described the measure, (b) the title of the scale or measure,
and (c) several lines beginning with the symbol @ which list the descriptors,
i.e., keywords descriptive of the content of a measure. The following is an
example of a Primary Reference:

```
B-46      BYRNE, D.
            THE REPRESSION-SENSITIZATION SCALE: RATIONALE, RELIABILITY, AND VALIDITY.
            JOURNAL OF PERSONALITY, 1961, 29, 334-349.
          BYRNE, D., BARRY, J., & NELSON, D.
            RELATION OF THE REVISED REPRESSION-SENSITIZATION SCALE TO MEASURES OF SELF-
            DESCRIPTION.
            PSYCHOLOGICAL REPORTS, 1963, 13, 323-334.
            (REPRESSION-SENSITIZATION SCALE)*
         @B-46 REPRESSION SENSITIZATION ADJUSTMENT DEFENSIVENESS COPING-DEFENSE
         @RESPONSE-BIAS 1961M
            (APPLICATIONS:     34    151    202    253    259    271    276    280    289    437
                              462    467    480    482    491    910    954   1025   1034   1046
                             1053   1054   1063   1070   1432   1892   1899   1930   1971   2000
                             2008   2069   2082   2086   2100   2113   2122   2140   2163   2172
                             2177   2203   2246   2254   2315   2323   2328   2333   2405   2433
                             2512   2517   2567   2655   2660   2686   2738   2742   2824   2919)
```

This example illustrates occasional inclusion of a second citation in a Primary Reference entry. A second reference has been added as an aid to the user under certain circumstances: (a) when the original reference cited a relatively inaccessible publication (dissertation, out-of-print book, or unpublished manuscript), (b) when the measure appeared almost simultaneously in two different publications, or (c) when a second reference included vital information (e.g., a list of the scale's items).

The asterisk which follows the scale title in the example above indicates that the title of the measure was established by the author or is in general use in the literature. Titles which have no asterisk are descriptive names assigned by our staff.

Whenever there are known applications, Primary Reference entries are followed by an indented parenthesis which lists, by application numbers, all instances of known applications of a given measure. For example, the scale B46 has 60 applications, each of which can be looked up in the Applications section of this volume by means of the respective application numbers.

Applications (pp. 362-664)

Each entry in the Applications section consists of (a) an application number, a serial number, with which each application is identified, (b) a reference to an article in which a measure has been used, (c) a set of terms (set off in parentheses) indicating the types of information available in the article, and (d) one or more @APPLICATION lines that list scale numbers for measures used in the article. The following is an example of an Application entry:

```
34      MCDONALD, R.
        EGO-CONTROL PATTERNS AND ATTRIBUTION OF HOSTILITY TO SELF AND OTHERS.
        JOURNAL OF PERSONALITY AND SOCIAL PSYCHOLOGY, 1965, 2, 273-277.
           (MODIFICATION; CORRELATES:PSYCHOLOGICAL; USED AS CRITERION;
            NORMATIVE DATA; N=177 SINGLE WHITE PREGNANT FEMALES)
        @APPLICATION 1965 B-46 W-41 L-93
```

Note that the entries in the @APPLICATION line are scale numbers. These numbers refer to those scales (measures) that are used in the study. That is to say, this study by McDonald has used three measures, B-46, W-41, and L-93. If one's interest is in the relationship between the two measures B-46 and W-41, this application by McDonald would be worth examining. Again, a user could find out what each of these three measures is by looking in the Primary References section.

In each Application entry, the section in parentheses contains a description of the sample used and labels which describe the type of information available in the referenced article. Thus, each application is tagged with one or more of the

following labels, called application categories. Where appropriate, subcategories are used to further differentiate the information contained.

Application Categories

Description/Mention/Modification/Revision

Review article

Reliability: retest, internal consistency, interrater

Validity: content, criterion, construct, cross-validation

Correlates: behavioral, psychological, physiological, physical, demographic, environmental, intelligence

Used as criterion

Cross-cultural application

Dimensional analysis (factor analysis, cluster analysis, etc.)

Normative data

Bias: response, tester

Sample descriptions (size and characteristics)

The category of "used as a criterion" refers to those cases in which the measure was used as a criterion for the validation of other measures or theories.

There is one shortcoming in the present annotation system which needs to be pointed out. When a paper is an application of more than one measure, the Application Categories do not specify to which of the measures they are referring. As a consequence, the user may be misled to expect more than what is contained in the article. For example, in the above illustration of an application by McDonald, one cannot determine which of the three measures was "used as a criterion."

Author Index (pp. 1-17)

All the authors of primary references are listed alphabetically and each is followed by the scale number(s) that refers to the scale(s) he has contributed. For example, Aaronson, B. S. contributed the scale numbered A-1 and Aaronson, M. was a co-author of scale S-78 ("S" indicates that the first author's last name starts with S).

Descriptor Index (pp. 18-56)

This is a cross-referenced index of the main types of descriptors used for primary references. The great majority of the descriptors in the index describe the content of measures, i.e., the traits, characteristics, moods, attitudes, behaviors, and so forth, which they intend to assess. Knowledge of the terms

used as descriptors in this index is essential for an effective use of the primary references because not all relevant terms are used as descriptors. Often, only one of a group of synonymous or highly related terms has been used as a descriptor. For example, among the terms "job," "work," and "employment," only "job" is used as a descriptor.

In order to facilitate the use of descriptors and maximize the retrieval of relevant primary references, many descriptors are cross-referenced to other descriptors by "see also" (i.e., "s.a."), or paired (i.e., listed) with others. The pairing descriptors are indented five spaces on successive lines. For example, the first descriptor "abasement" is cross-referenced to "depreciation" and paired with "self." In this example, we find that listed in the volume are four measures of "self abasement" (C-82, H-11, H-216, and M-245) and ten measures of "abasement" (C-82, D-22, ..., Z-12).

For convenience, some frequently used terms or pairs which were not included in the descriptor index are listed in the Supplement to the Descriptor Index (pp. 54-55).

METHOD USED IN SEARCHING THE LITERATURE

The entries in this volume have been gathered primarily from the following sources:

a) Search of all articles (100% search) for the 1960-1969 period appearing in those 6 journals with the greatest proportion of high quality studies involving measurement.

b) Search of a systematic 20% random sample of articles appearing in 10 additional measurement-related journals from the 1960-1969 period.

c) Search of Psychological Abstracts for the 1965-1970 period.

d) Search of all articles (100% search) appearing in all 1970 and some 1971 issues of 26 measurement-related journals.

e) Other publications containing measures which were referenced by any of the above search strategies (a) through (d).

The table below indicates the extent of search for each of the 26 journals:

| Journals | 1960-1969 | | 1970 |
	100% search	20% search	100% search
1. Journal of Abnormal and Social Psychology	yes (60-64)		---
2. Journal of Abnormal Psychology	yes (65-69)		yes
3. Journal of Personality and Social Psychology	yes (65-69)		yes
4. Journal of Consulting and Clinical Psychology	yes		yes
5. Journal of Personality	yes		yes
6. Journal of Counseling Psychology	yes		yes
7. American Journal of Psychology	---	yes	yes
8. American Journal of Sociology	---	---	yes
9. American Sociological Review	---	---	yes
10. Developmental Psychology	---	---	yes
11. Educational and Psychological Measurement	---	yes	yes
12. Human Factors	---	---	yes
13. Journal of Applied Behavioral Science	---	yes	yes
14. Journal of Applied Psychology	---	yes	yes
15. Journal of Educational Psychology	---	yes	yes
16. Journal of General Psychology	---	---	yes
17. Journal of Projective Techniques and Personality Assessment	---	---	yes
18. Journal of Psychology	---	yes	yes
19. Journal of Social Psychology	---	yes	yes
20. Multivariate Behavioral Research	---	---	yes
21. Personnel Psychology	---	yes	yes
22. Psychological Bulletin	---	---	yes
23. Psychological Record	---	---	yes
24. Psychological Reports	---	yes	yes
25. Psychological Review	---	---	yes
26. Psychology in the Schools	---	yes	---
27. Public Opinion Quarterly	---	---	yes
28. Sociometry	---	---	yes

As can be seen, then, the information contained in this volume covers primarily the 1960-1970 period, and will need to be supplemented by searching the literature for the subsequent years.

As it was pointed out in the Preface, our search was primarily to identify the measures of mental health and related variables, and the uses of these measures. Since the term mental health does not represent a clearly circumscribed concept, our search has been inclusive both out of necessity and by design. Consequently, in addition to those measures obviously related to mental health, this volume includes (a) measures of individual moods, traits (other than intelligence or aptitude), behaviors, and some attitudes, (b) measures of interpersonal relationships or behavior, or (c) measures of characteristics of organizations, cultures, or social groups (e.g., norms, structures). Attitude measures have been included only for topics which were deemed to have relevance to general psychological or social phenomena (e.g., attitudes toward oneself, people in general, war, or racial differences, but not attitudes toward a particular political figure or issue). When in doubt as to whether attitudes toward a given topic have been included, it would be advisable to consult the Descriptor Index for related content terms. Measures of intelligence, aptitude, and most attitudinal measures were omitted, since they have been covered extensively by others (see references No. 1, 5, 6, 7, 9, 10, 11, and 12 given in the Preface).

Although multiscale inventories like the MMPI, CPI, and 16 PF were at first included only when individual scales were used for the assessment of specific content dimensions, this policy was later modified to include all uses of the inventories, thus resulting in an uneven coverage. For several inventories, handbooks are now available, and these handbooks, rather than applications listed herein, should serve as comprehensive resources. References to these handbooks are:

Butcher, J. N. MMPI: Research Developments and Clinical Applications. New York: McGraw-Hill, 1969.

Dahlstrom, W. G., Welsh, G. S., and Dahlstrom, L. E. An MMPI Handbook. Vol. 1: Clinical Interpretation (Rev. Ed.). Minneapolis: University of Minnesota Press, 1972.

Megargee, E. I. The California Psychological Inventory Handbook. San Francisco: Jossey-Bass, 1972.

Cattell, R. B., Eber, H. W., and Tatsuoka, M. M. Handbook for the Sixteen Personality Factor Questionnaire (16PF). Champaign, Ill.: Institute for Personality and Ability Testing, 1970.

With this kind of search strategy it is clear that very nearly all of the measures that have been used repeatedly in the period 1960-1970 have been included. However, there are undoubtedly many measures which were introduced and never used again that have been missed. This is unfortunate because there is no evidence that those measures that are used repeatedly are of any higher quality than those that die aborning.

ILLUSTRATIVE USES

We hope our description of the Primary References and Applications sections and the two indexes has been clear enough to enable the reader to think of various uses that would meet his needs. A few typical uses or questions that the user might ask are illustrated below:

(A) What measures are available for assessing a dimension of interest, for example "self abasmment"? One can find in the Descriptor Index the scale numbers of those measures that are related to the assessment of the desired dimension. For example, one finds on page 18 that there are four measures of "self abasement" (C-82, H-11, H-216, and M-245) and 30 measures of "self acceptance" (B-13, B-18, . . . T-61, and U-10). Another example: by examining the listings of both "global adjustment" (p. 19) and "marital satisfaction" (p. 38), one ginds that there are three measures (L-133, L-144, and T-4) relevant to the assessment of both "global adjustment" and "marital satisfaction."

(B) What is the current state of empirical research or overall knowledge on a dimension of interest? A search for such an overview can be facilitated by examining the applications of those measures that are pertinent to the assessment of this dimension. The amount of literature to be covered for such a review would often be considerable, but the task can be effectively organized and realistically planned through the use of application categories.

In the case of "self abasement," one finds that only H-216 has two applications, 1220 and 2091, while no applications have been identified for the remaining three measures. As for "self acceptance," the 30 measures together have a total of 72 applications (4 for B-13, 20 for B-18, ..., 1 for T-61, and 1 for U-10). In less than 10 minutes, then, a user of this volume discovers that there are at least 30 different measures of self acceptance and that they have been used at least 72 times in the period 1960-1970. In addition, the user knows exactly where to turn to read more about each of these measures and their applications.

The use of application categories will further help the user to identify a

particular subset of these 72 uses that might be of special relevance to his interest. For example, a user who is interested in the dimensional structure underlying the "self acceptance" measures needs to look up only those applications tagged with the application category of "dimensional analysis." He will discover that factor or cluster analysis was performed in six of these 72 uses (1287, 1058, 1373, 1221, 1450, and 1461).

(C) What empirical findings have been produced by the use of a given measure? Stated in a different way, what are the overall performance characteristics of a particular measure? A review of such findings can be accomplished by examining all applications of a measure.

(D) What is the reference to the original description of a measure? The answer to this question can be sought either via the Author Index if the author is known, or via the Descriptor Index using the characteristics of the measure.

(E) What additional information about a measure has been acquired since its publication? This question can be easily answered by evaluating the applications of the measure, particularly those applications which have relevant application categories (e.g., validity, cross-validation, etc.).

(F) Finally, teachers will find this volume a useful time-saver for the pedagogic chores of selecting and/or identifying either measures of a given concept or applications of a given measure. The fact that each application is annotated by descriptive labels (i.e., Application Categories) should help the user to generate differentiated lists of references.

1

AUTHOR INDEX

A

Aaronson, B. S., A-1
Aaronson, M., S-78
Aas, A., A-21 A-69
Abbey, D. S., W-140
Abe, C., A-2
Abbott, R. D., E-28
Abeles, N., A-61 K-116
 M-105
Abelson, R. P., A-67 A-68
 W-68
Abramoff, E., E-77
Achenbach, T. M., A-19
 A-59 A-73
Acker, C. W., C-209
Acker, M., M-12 M-138
Ackerman, J. M., J-41
Adams, C. K., P-140
Adams, C. R., A-41
Adams, J., S-22
Adcock, C. J., A-4
Adcock, N. V., A-4
Adelson, J., A-35
Adler, P. T., A-49
Adorno, T. W., A-5 A-15
 A-17
Agger, R. E., A-22
Agras, W. S., B-213
Ainsworth, L. H., A-85
Ainsworth, M. D., A-85
Albee, G. W., A-98
Albers, R., R-47
Albert, J., K-122 K-163
Albrecht, R. E., C-62
Albright, L. E., S-116
Albright, R. J., Z-30
Alcock, N. Z., E-27
Alcock, W., W-119
Alderfer, C. P., A-40
 A-100 A-101
Alexander, J. F., A-61
Alexander, S. A., A-26
 A-87
Alfert, E., L-47
Allen, S. A., S-180
Allen, T. W., A-49 A-77
 A-78 A-102
Allen, V. L., A-38
Allerhand, M. E., A-56
Allinsmith, W., A-71
Allison, R. B., Jr., A-57
Allkire, A. A., G-191
Allport, F. H., A-6 T-73
Allport, G. W., A-6 A-7
 A-23 A-24 G-68
Alpert, R., A-8 S-14
Altman, I., T-1
Altrocchi, J., A-10 A-54
Altucher, N., A-90 A-103
 M-59 M-60 M-61
Altus, W. D., A-37 A-43
Amon, A. H., M-133
Anant, S. S., A-9
Anastasi, A., S-118
Anastasiow, N. S., A-11
Anderson, C. V., A-84
Anderson, G. V., A-82
Anderson, J. C., C-141
Anderson, L. S., J-18

Anderson, N. H., A-12
 A-92
Anderson, R. P., A-82 A-84
Anderson, W. F., A-99 D-22
Andrews, F. M., A-34
Andrews, S. L., M-124
Anisfeld, M., A-36 A-64
 A-66 L-23
Anker, J. M., A-32 A-58
Annis, A. P., C-209
Antler, L., A-13 A-46
 A-47
Antonovsky, H., W-45
Anzel, A. S., A-50
Apfelbaum, B., A-83
Apostal, R. A., A-88
April, C., B-262 B-273
Appelbaum, S., A-60
Apperson, L. B., A-33
Applezweig, M. H., A-42
 A-63
Arenberg, D., F-1
Armer, M., A-86
Armitage, S. G., A-74
Armstrong, J. C., A-44
Arnoff, F. N., A-104
Arnold, D. L., A-30
Arnold, J., C-170
Aron, B., A-94
Aronfreed, J., A-14
Aronoff, J., A-97
Aronson, E., A-28 H-157
 H-158
Aronson, H., A-72
Arthur, G., E-54 E-55
 E-56
Arthur, R. J., G-27
As, A., H-99 H-100
Asch, M. J., A-16
Asch, S. E., A-93
Ashby, J. D., A-48
Asher, J. J., A-75
Astin, A. W., A-18 A-31
 A-39 A-70 M-161
Atkins, A. L., B-97
Atkinson, J. W., A-55
 H-150 M-7 0-3 V-23
 V-31
Attneave, F., A-25
Auld, F., A-27
Auld, F. Jr., D-35
Aumack, L., A-20
Ayres, B., W-45
Ayers, D., R-19

B

Bach, G. R., B-136
Backer, T. E., C-202
Badgley, R. F., B-38
Baehr, M. E., B-20
Baer, D. L., B-152
Baer, M., B-131
Baggaley, A. R., B-67 B-239
Bailey, K. G., B-241
Baird, L. L., H-19 H-218
 N-12
Baker, B. L., B-212
Baker, E., B-250 B-251
Baker, G., K-13
Baker, R., C-102
Baldridge, B., C-49

Baldwin, A. L., B-1 P-86
 P-87 P-90
Bales, R. F., B-2 B-120
Balla, D., 0-32
Ballachy, E. L., F-121
Balogh, B., S-3
Bandura, A., B-22
Bankes, J., L-74
Banta, T. J., B-100 B-231
 B-232 E-44 W-68
Barabasz, A. F., B-132
 B-141
Barber, T. X., B-3 B-92
Barclay, A. M., B-107
Barclay, J. R., B-244
Bardis, P. D., B-219
Barker, B., M-103
Barker, E. N., S-202
Barlow, D. H., B-213
Barndt, R. J., B-186
Barratt, E. S., B-61
 B-160
Barrell, R. P., B-290
 D-29 D-43 D-65 D-66
Barrett, L., J-46
Barrett-Lennard, G. T.,
 B-21 B-50
Barron, F., B-4 B-5 B-6
 B-76 B-78 B-79 B-150
 B-151 B-162 B-257
 B-282 B-283 B-284
Barry, J. R., B-46 M-70
Barthel, C. E., B-16
Barthol, R. P. B-235
Bartlett, C. J., S-218
 W-47
Bass, A. R., B-288
Bass, B. M., B-9 B-81
 B-83 B-105 B-192
 B-201 B-287 G-199
 W-119
Bassell, J. S., B-119
Basu, G. K., Z-32
Battle, E. S., B-114
Bauernfiend, R. H., R-48
Baughman, E. E., B-285
Bauman, M. K., B-104
Bavelas, A., B-237
Baxter, J. C., A-99 B-90
 B-286
Beach, D. R., C-108
Beach. L., B-194
Beall, H. S., B-123
Beattle, M., G-87
Beck, A. T., B-8
Becker, J. B-90 B-96
 B-286 F-136
Becker, M. H., B-140
Becker, S. W., H-146
Becker, W. C., B-82
 B-166 B-167 B-217
 B-242 B-275 F-122
Bee, H., R-72
Beer, M., B-87 B-88
Behrens, M. L., B-165
Beigel, A., F-59
Beitner, M. S., B-202
Bell, A. P., B-291
Bell, E. G., B-267
Bell, H. M., B-128 B-281
Bell, R. Q., S-9
Bellak, L., B-210 B-238
Bellak, S. S., B-210
 B-238
Beller, E. K., B-52
Belleville, R. E., H-25
Bellugi, U., C-41

C

Cairns, R. B., C-60 C-115
California Test Bureau,
  C-147
Callahan, R., E-48
Callahon, D. M., M-128
Calverly, D. S., B-92
Cameron, G. R., P-31
Cameron, J. S., W-42 W-69
Cameron, P., C-210
Campbell, A., C-109
Campbell, D. C., Q-3 Q-4
  Q-5
Campbell, D. P., C-7
  C-229
Campbell, D. T., C-30
  R-131
Campbell, E. Q., C-107
Campbell, J. D., Y-6 Y-7
Campbell, M. M., C-177
Campbell, R. C., C-231
Campbell, W. J., Y-1
Canavan, D., G-71
Cancro, R., C-201
Cannell, C. F., K-151
Canter, A., C-123
Cantril, H., C-2
Capaldi, E. J., B-173
  B-272
Caplovitz, D., B-236
Capps, H., C-233
Carey, G., C-175
Carkhuff, R. R., B-68
  C-105 C-106 C-243
  C-251 H-222 T-38
  T-74 T-75 T-105
Carlson, R., C-3 C-88
  C-176 C-199
Carnes, E. F., W-169
Carpenter, B., W-43 W-102
Carpenter, J. T., W-43
  W-102
Carr, J. E., C-77
Carrier, N. A., C-214
  C-215
Carter, A. R., T-52
Carter, H. D., C-54
Cartwright, D. S., C-12
  C-142 C-143 K-152
Cartwright, R. D., C-4
  C-138 C-139
Cash, L. M., C-211
Casky, O. L., C-219
Cassel, R. N., C-5 C-6
  C-101 C-212
Cassell, S., C-65
Castenada, A., C-55
Castiglione, L., K-100
Caston, J., C-99
Cataldo, J. F., C-67
Cattell, P., C-197
Cattell, R. B., C-8 C-9
  C-10 C-11 C-29 C-68
  C-89 C-102 C-116
  C-117 C-118 C-119
  C-120 C-121 C-122
  C-125 C-135 C-136
  C-141 C-151 C-158
  C-168 C-224 P-62
  S-10 S-68
Caudill, W., D-8
Cautela, J. R., C-213
  C-234
Cauthen, N. R., K-140
Cavan, R. S., B-227
Center for the Study of
  Higher Education, H-12
Centers, R., C-64

Centra, J. A., P-61
Cervin, V., C-79 C-111
Chalmers, D. K., C-239
Chambers, J. L., C-13
Chance, E., C-170
Chance, J., C-58
Chandler, K. A., G-86
Chang, J., C-140
Chapin, F. S., C-221
Chapman, A. W., C-245
Chapman, L. J., C-1 C-20
  C-30 C-203
Chapple, E. D., C-66
Charlens, A. M., M-244
Chasdi, E., W-45
Chase, P. H., C-149
Chave, E. J., T-23
Cheek, F. E., C-178
Chernow, H. M., C-223
Cherry, C. N., W-60
Cherry, H. O., E-66
Chesler, M., C-44
Child, I. L., C-35 C-45
  C-46 C-47 C-57 C-59
  C-61 C-73 C-74 C-75
  C-128 W-48 W-180
Childers, B., E-54 E-55
  E-56
Chodorkoff, B., C-104
Choungourian, A., C-86
Christal, R. E., T-34
Christensen, P. R., C-226
  G-50 G-51 G-80 G-107
  G-194 T-46 W-118
Christie, R., C-14 C-31
  C-48 C-81 C-137 C-152
  G-2 S-130
Chu, C. L., S-246
Chun, N., W-89
Ciarlo, J. A., L-28
Cicchetti, D. V., C-195
  C-196
Clapp, W. F., H-14 H-31
  H-77
Clark, C. A., C-249
Clark, E. T., C-113
Clark, J. A., M-105
Clark, J. H., C-246
Clark, J. R., C-148 C-173
Clark, K. E., C-52
Clark, R. A., C-126 C-242
  M-7
Clark, W. W., T-25
Clarke, A. R., G-55
Clarke, W. N., H-8
Clarke, W. V., C-15
Clarke, W. W. T-41
Clausen, J. D., G-104
Clayton, M. B., C-32
Clayton, W. H., E-20
Cleckley, H., C-189
Cleveland, S. E., F-75
  F-135
Clifford, C., W-99
Clifford, E., C-85 C-90
Clifford, M., C-85 C-90
Cline, V. B., C-33 C-146
  C-169 C-236
Clore, G. L., C-49
Clore, G. L., Jr., B-48
Clyde, D. J., C-16
Coan, R. W., C-102
Cobb, S., H-58
Cochrane, C. T., C-247
Coe, W. C., C-193 C-194
Coelho, G. V., C-17
Cofer, C. N., C-58 M-168

Cohen, A. R., C-34 C-112
  S-98
Cohen, J., C-69
Cohen, M., K-100 M-74
  M-178
Cohler, B. J., C-83
Cohn, T. S., C-18
Cole, C. W., C-53 C-91
Coleman, J. S., C-107
Collett, L. J., C-200
Collins, M. E., C-50
Colman, A. M., C-252
Colvin, R. W., C-254
Combs, A. W., T-113
Commoss, H. H., C-56
Comrey, A. L., C-19 C-72
  C-98 C-153 C-198
  C-202 C-207
Cone, J. D., Jr., C-28
Conlon, E. J., C-36
Conners, C. K., K-99
Conrad, H. S., S-2
Constantinople, A., C-37
  C-205 C-206
Converse, P., C-21
Cook, P. E., M-171
Cook, S. W., S-64 W-27
  W-195
Cooke, G., C-104
Coons, A. H., H-97
Cooper, J. B., C-22
Cooper, L. M., C-70 C-99
Cooperman, M., C-46
Coopersmith, S., C-38
  C-190
Coplan, A. S., L-66
Corah, N. L., F-77
Corey, J., G-56
Corsini, R., C-39
Costanzo, P. R., C-82
Costelein, J., D-12
Costello, C. G., C-198
  C-207
Cottle, T. J., C-84 C-87
  C-92 C-154 C-155
  C-156 C-164 C-166
Cottrell, L. S., B-42
Couch, A. S., C-23 C-171
  C-172 C-179 C-180
  C-181 C-182 C-183
  C-184 C-188 K-17
  K-130
Counts, R. N., S-224
Cowan, J. R., T-53
Cowen, E. L., C-24 C-51
  C-71 C-108 C-159
  C-173 L-77 L-78
Cowen, J. E., C-40 M-25
Cowitz, B., P-84
Coyle, F. A., Jr., F-57
Coyne, L., C-93
Craddick, R. A., W-149
Craik, K. H., S-195 S-196
Crandall, J. E., C-131
  C-132
Crandall, V. C., C-25
  C-42 K-56
Crandall, V. J., C-25
  C-41 C-42
Crary, W. G., C-160 C-161
Creaser, J. W., C-225
Creasy, M. A., F-86
Crissman, P., C-241
Crites, J. O., B-135
  C-26 C-217 S-155
Crockett, W. H., C-76
  M-227 M-228 R-34

Hardesty, A. S.,   B-41
  B-86 S-343
Harding, I., S-44
Harding, J., B-200 S-43
  S-266
Hardyck, C. D.,   S-37
Hardyck, J. A., S-52 S-55
Hargreaves, W. A., H-152
Harlan, G. E.,   D-89
Harleston, B. W., H-28
Harman, W. W., H-6
Harmon, L. W., H-219
Harren, V. A., H-201
Harris, D. B.,   G-111 H-29
  H-175 P-9
Harris, F. J., H-82 N-16
Harris, H., H-169
Harris, J. G., H-159
Harris, R. E., H-92
Harris, R. H., H-187
Harris, S., M-188 M-189
Harrison, G. J.,   W-157
Harrison, R. H., H-85
  H-202
Harrower, M. R.,   H-123
  H-173
Hart, J., L-136
Hartlage, L. C., H-90
Hartley, J. A., H-7
Hartley, R. E., H-61
Hartnett, R. T., P-61
Hartshorne, H., H-30
  H-197 H-198
Harvey, O. J., H-14 H-31
  H-32 H-77 H-98 H-112
Hasler, R., H-8
Hastdorf, A. H., B-9
  H-190
Hathaway, S. R., D-45
  H-71 M-38
Hatt, R. K., N-46
Haupt, E. J., C-50
Hauri, P., H-151
Hautlage, L. C., H-189
Havel, J., C-31 H-117
Havighurst, R. J.,   B-227
  N-9
Havron, M. D., H-211
Hawkins, L. G., C-145
Hawks, D. V., H-171
Haworth, M. R., H-121
  H-174
Haworth, M. S., B-210
Hax, H., L-4
Hays, L. W., H-137
Hays, W. L., H-9
Haywood, H. C., H-49
  H-148 H-149
Healey, C. C., H-193
Heath, D. E., H-139
Heath, D. H., H-76
Heath, R., H-33
Heathers, L. B.,   M-215
Hedegard, J., L-132
Heilbrun, A. B., H-10 H-11
  H-34 H-66 H-216
Heilbrun, A. B., Jr., G-21
  H-119 H-120 H-200
  H-216
Heilfron, M., R-142
Heilizer, F., H-84
Heine, R. W., H-215
Heineman, C. E., H-51
Heinicke, C. M., H-154
Heist, P., H-12
Helfand, A., N-11
Heller, K., H-118 H-212

Helm, D., H-155
Helmreich, R. L., H-111
  H-157 H-158
Helper, M. M., H-42 H-91
  H-143
Helson, R., H-45 H-50
  H-89 H-115 H-116
Hemphill, J. K., H-97
  H-161
Henderson, R. W., H-184
Hendrick, C., H-20 H-142
Henry, D. R., R-144
Hereford, C. F., H-13
Hermans, H. J. M., H-88
Herron, E. W., H-37
Herron, W. G., H-163
Hersen, M., F-23 F-105
Hershenson, D. B., H-186
Hertzka, A. F., G-107
Hertzman, M., W-19 W-73
  W-188
Herzberg, F., H-70
Hess, A. K., D-96 D-97
Hester, R., J-38 J-39
Hetherington, E. M., H-35
  H-41
Hetznecker, W., H-15
Hevner, K., M-237
Hewlett, J. H. G., P-108
Heyns, R. W., H-150
Hicks, J. M., W-23
Higgs, W. J., H-67
Hilden, A. H., H-52 H-57
Hildreth, H. M., H-54
Hiler, E. W., H-125
Hilgard, E. R., W-31 W-103
Hill, H. E., H-25
Hill, W. F., H-136 T-81
Hinckley, E. D., H-36
Hinkle, J. E., C-91
Hinrichs, J. R., H-16 H-56
Hinsey, W. C., P-27
Hirsh, E., M-50
Hirt, M., H-160
Hobart, C. W., H-17
Hobson, C. F., C-107
Hochberg, A. C., H-171
Hodges, W. F., H-95 N-6
Hoffman, A. E., H-199
Hoffman, M. L., H-59 H-60
Hoffmeister, J. K., H-98
Hofman, J. E., H-94
Hofstee, W. K. B., H-109
Hogan, H. W., H-108
Hogan, R., H-132 H-172
Hogge, J. H., H-18
Hokanson, J. E., H-140
Holder, R. H., D-83
Holder, T., H-222
Holland, B., S-126
Holland, C., M-30
Holland, J. L., A-2 A-31
  F-79 H-19 H-21 H-44
  H-46 H-47 H-207 H-218
  N-12 N-42
Hollander, E. P., H-166
Hollingshead, A. B., H-22
Holmes, D. S., B-196 B-230
  H-138 H-204
Holmes, J. E., H-208
Holmes, J. S., H-87
Holmes, T. H., H-23
Holsopple, J. Q., H-113
  L-88
Holt, R. R., H-117 H-156
Holtzman, P. S., G-5 G-153
Holtzman, W. H., B-74 D-24

(cont.) D-55 H-37 H-124
  K-29 M-42
Holzberg, J. D., H-24 H-53
  H-165
Holzman, P. H., C-93
Holzman, P. S., H-43 H-93
  H-147
Honigfeld, G., H-221
Honigmann, I., M-50
Hooke, J. F., H-101
Hooks, W., B-286
Hooper, H. E., H-220
Hope, K., C-28 F-10
Hopke, W. E., H-181
Hoppock, R., H-188
Horai, J., T-46
Horn, J. L., C-11
Hornaday, J. A., H-83
Hornstein, M. G., H-114
Horowitz, E., H-62
Horowitz, J. Z., C-8
Horowitz, S. L., H-79
Horrocks, J. E., L-21
House, W. C., L-60
Houts, P. S., H-180 M-15
Hover, G. L., L-12
Hovey, H. R., H-214
Hovland, C. I., H-144
Howard, K. I., H-65 O-12
Howe, E. S., H-127 H-128
Howell, M. A., H-55 N-16
Howell, R. J., C-70
Howells, L. T., H-146
Huebner, B., V-12
Huffman, P. E., L-161 O-23
Hulin, C. L., K-7
Hull, C. L., H-178
Hull, V., W-187
Hummel, R. C., S-155
Hunt, D. E., H-32 H-75
  H-167 S-76 S-177 S-345
Hunt, J. McV., E-16 E-17
  E-42 H-185 U-7
Hunt, R. G., H-213
Hunt, S. M., H-58
Hunt, W. A., A-104
Hunter, M., H-68
Huntley, C. W., H-129
Hurlbut, F. C., G-192
Hurley, J. R., H-74 H-106
  H-133 H-134 H-135
Hurley, R. B., P-60
Hurley, S. J., H-106 H-107
Hurvich, M. S., B-210
  B-238
Husband, R. W., D-77
Husek, T. R., A-26 H-38
  N-10 S-77
Huser, J., C-108
Hutchins, E. B., F-5
Huttner, L., H-78

Iambert, W. W., T-86
Ihilevich, D., G-30
Imber, S. D., F-84
Indik, B. P., I-2 I-5 I-8
Inkeles, A., S-163
Irvin, F. S., I-4
Isaacs, R. S., H-3
Isnor, C., L-142

10

Love, L. R.,   B-262 B-273
Lovibond, S. H.,   L-125
   L-157
Lovinger, E.,   K-112
Lowe, A.,   L-80
Lowe, C. A.,   L-131
Lowenherz, L.,   L-129
Loy, D. L.,   L-18
Lubin, B.,   L-19 L-20
   L-82 Z-4 Z-27
Luborsky, L.,   L-101 L-119
Lucas, C. M.,   L-21 L-42
Lucero, R. J.,   L-124
Luchins, A. S.,   L-45
Ludwig, D.,   M-106
Lumsden, E. A., Jr.,   L-65
Lunn, J. C. B.,   L-64
Lushene, R. E.,   S-147
Luther, B.,   T-39
Lutz, S. W.,   A-2
Lutzker, D.,   L-31
Lyerly, S. B.,   K-58
Lykken, D. T.,   L-22 L-164
Lyle, C.,   M-249
Lyle, F. A.,   R-135 R-136
   R-137
Lyle, W. H., Jr.,   L-55
   L-116 L-117 0-9
Lynn, R.,   L-145
Lyons, M.,   J-27
Lysgaard, S.,   S-160

M

Maccasland, B. W.,   M-235
Maccoby, E. E.,   M-157
   R-29 S-13
MacDonald, A. P., Jr.,   M-68
   M-185 M-186
MacDonald, J. M.,   K-99
MacDougall, E.,   N-23
Macfarlane, J. W.,   M-238
Machotka, P.,   M-182
Machover, K.,   M-58 W-19
   W-73 W-188
Mack, J.,   B-8
Mackay, C. K.,   M-111 M-254
Mackinney, A. C.,   M-49
Mackler, B.,   M-1
Mackworth, N.,   L-119
Madden, J. E.,   M-132
Maddi, D.,   M-244
Maddi, S. R.,   M-57 M-101
   M-124 M-126 M-127
   M-244
Madison, P.,   W-183
Madsen, C. H., Jr.,   M-34
Maehr, M. L.,   H-2 M-106
Maher, B. A.,   R-131
Maher, H.,   M-83
Mahl, G. F.,   K-161 M-35
Maholick, L. T.,   C-95
Mahrer, A. R.,   M-193
   M-236
Mainord, F. R.,   M-136
Mainord, W. A.,   G-10 M-2
Maldonado-Sierra, E. D.,
   T-32 T-61
Maley, R. F.,   M-155 M-233
Malinovsky, M. R.,   M-70
Maliver, B. L.,   M-23
Maltzman, I.,   M-72

Management Research Division,
   M-201
Mandell, E. E.,   M-24
Mandler, G.,   M-3 M-4 M-25
   M-248
Mandler, J. M.,   M-3
Mangione, T. W.,   Q-3 Q-4
   Q-5
Mann, D.,   M-74
Manning, W. H.,   M-79
Manosevitz, M.,   M-190
Marcia, J. E.,   H-166 M-5
   M-125
Marggraff, W. M.,   C-98
Margolis, R. A.,   F-37 M-74
Mark, J. C.,   M-71
Markel, N. N.,   M-226
Marks, C. S.,   Z-30
Marks, E.,   M-108 M-257
Marks, J.,   M-181 M-249
Marks, P. A.,   M-135 M-255
Marlowe, D.,   C-27 M-26
   M-259
Marrash, J.,   L-73
Marsh, M. M.,   G-165
Marshall, S.,   M-48
Marshell, G. R.,   M-168
Marston, A. R.,   B-32 M-184
   R-15
Martin, B.,   M-154
Martin, H. G.,   G-40 G-75
Martin, W. E.,   G-111
Martin, W. T.,   M-196
Martire, J. G.,   M-163
   P-29
Martuza, V. R.,   M-44
Marwell, G.,   M-183
Maryland Counseling Center,
   M-200
Masling, J.,   M-148 M-149
Maslow, A. H.,   M-50 M-197
Mason, R. E.,   M-6 M-67
Massimo, J. L.,   M-164
Masuda, M.,   M-93
Matarazzo, J. D.,   W-78
Mathewson, R. H.,   M-205
   M-206
Mathiew, P. L.,   K-42 K-83
Mathis, H. I.,   M-198
Matsumoto, G. H.,   M-93
Matsushima, J.,   M-51
Matteson, R. W.,   M-120
Matthews, E.,   M-208
Mattis, P.,   D-49 D-50
   D-51
Mattsson, P. O.,   M-243
Matulef, N. J.,   M-207
Maurer, O. H.,   D-56
Maw, E. W.,   M-258
Maw, W. H.,   M-258
May, J. G., Jr.,   L-154
May, M. A.,   H-30 H-197
   H-198
May, R.,   M-55
Mayer, D.,   G-89
Mayman, M.,   M-173
Mayo, C. W.,   M-227 M-228
Mayo, G. D.,   M-79
Mazer, G. E.,   M-202 S-202
McAdoo, W. G.,   S-147
McAdoo, W. G., Jr.,   A-33
McCandless, B. R.,   C-55
McCann, B.,   P-39 P-40
McCarthy, C. D.,   M-142
McClain, E. W.,   M-47
McClelland, D. C.,   D-28

(cont.) D-30 M-7 M-54
McClintock, C. G.,   K-44
   M-241
McClosky, H.,   G-19 G-36
   M-175
McClure, G.,   P-66
McConnell, T. R.,   E-78
McCord, J.,   M-162 M-231
McCord, W.,   M-162 M-231
McCraven, V. G.,   S-82
McCulloch, J. W.,   P-8
McDaniel, M.,   W-90
McDavid, J. W.,   M-8 S-316
McDonald, R. L.,   M-27
   M-102
McFall, R. M.,   M-184 M-220
McFarland, R. A.,   M-62
McFarland, R. L.,   U-8 U-9
McGaughran, L. S.,   M-170
   R-111
McGee, H. M.,   M-45
McGrath, J. E.,   H-211 M-28
   V-38 V-39 V-40 V-41
McGuire, C.,   M-77 M-78
   P-113
McGuire, W. J.,   M-219
McGurk, E.,   M-81
McInnis, T. L.,   M-166
McKeachie, W. J.,   L-132
McKee, M. G.,   D-36
McKinley, J. C.,   D-45 H-71
   M-38
McKinney, F.,   M-9
McLean, O. S.,   B-18
McNair, D. M.,   L-3 L-17
   L-49 M-128 M-146 M-156
   M-160
McNamara, W. J.,   D-88
McPartland, J.,   C-107
McPartland, T. S.,   K-21
McPhee, W. M.,   J-49
McQuary, J. P.,   M-89
McQuitty, L. L.,   M-10
   M-105 W-60
McReynolds, P.,   B-169
   F-121 G-28 M-11 M-12
   M-66 M-130 M-138 M-177
Meade, R. D.,   M-216
Meadow, A.,   M-239
Meadows, A.,   J-36
Medinnus, G. R.,   M-139
   M-140
Mednick, S. A.,   M-29
Meehl, P. E.,   G-19 G-39
   M-141
Meeker, F. O.,   M-137
Meeker, M.,   W-160
Meer, B.,   M-133
Mees, H. L.,   M-160
Megargee, E. I.,   M-171
Megas, J.,   Z-20
Mehrabian, A.,   M-13 M-97
   M-98
Meier, N. C.,   M-252 M-253
Meissner, P. B.,   W-19 W-73
   W-188
Meissner, R.,   J-18
Melamed, B. G.,   L-136
Meltzoff, J.,   B-205
Mendelsohn, G. A.,   M-171
   M-174 P-136 R-121
Mendelson, M.,   B-8
Menges, R. J.,   M-69 M-129
Mensing, J.,   M-106
Meredith, G. M.,   M-93
Merrell, D. W.,   K-112
Merrifield, P. R.,   C-226

T

Y

Z

2

DESCRIPTOR INDEX

Depression -- s.a. affective-states/nega-
  tive

B-8	B-17	C-9	C-105	C-123
C-207	D-3	F-6	F-84	F-137
G-4	G-37	G-39	G-133	H-4
H-58	L-11	L-134	M-37	M-52
M-80	M-196	M-199	M-260	O-1
P-21	S-20	S-156	S-170	S-243
S-286	S-324	T-56	W-6	W-15
W-52	W-122	W-172	Z-4	Z-5

  Symptom

F-84	G-4	H-4	L-134	S-156
T-56	W-6		

Deprivation

M-55	Z-18	Z-32

  Sensory

Z-32

Description

B-26	B-164	B-177	B-194	B-248
C-66	C-85	C-86	C-96	C-176
D-11	D-31	D-46	D-47	E-33
G-3	G-59	H-50	H-55	H-89
H-112	J-10	K-20	K-28	K-84
K-137	L-3	L-12	M-1	M-28
M-39	M-58	M-74	M-77	M-81
M-83	M-193	N-18	N-19	Q-2
R-138	R-144	S-1	S-18	S-23
S-48	S-75	S-103	S-104	S-112
S-113	S-114	S-142	S-180	S-206
S-231	S-290	T-22	T-41	T-58
T-60	U-5	V-11	V-12	V-25
V-41	W-1	W-13	W-42	W-69
W-71	W-85	W-96	W-108	W-169

  Job

G-3	H-50	H-55	N-18	R-138
W-13				

  Role

M-77	S-113	V-11	W-85

  Self

B-26	B-248	C-66	C-85	D-11
D-31	G-3	G-59	H-55	H-89
H-112	J-10	K-28	K-84	K-137
L-3	L-12	M-1	M-58	M-77
M-81	M-83	M-193	N-18	N-19
Q-2	R-144	S-1	S-48	S-23
S-75	S-103	S-104	S-142	S-290
T-22	W-1	W-13	W-42	W-69
W-71	W-169			

Desegregation -- s.a. Negro, racial

B-195	K-19	K-29	W-27	W-75

  Racial

K-19	K-29	W-27	W-75

Desirability

A-92	A-101	B-7	B-27	B-164
B-183	B-280	C-24	C-27	C-41
C-42	C-43	C-71	C-121	C-171
C-172	D-11	D-26	D-86	E-1
E-21	E-28	E-79	F-9	F-43
F-77	F-113	G-67	G-77	G-103
G-105	G-115	G-116	G-127	G-131
H-5	H-10	H-72	H-109	H-122
H-195	J-2	J-3	J-49	K-45
K-59	K-63	K-88	L-8	M-196
P-120	Q-1	S-66	S-107	S-123
S-183	S-259	S-337	T-77	T-78
T-79	V-27	W-1	W-14	W-47
W-108	W-164			

  Personal

A-101	K-45	P-120

  Social

B-7	B-27	C-24	C-27	C-41
C-42	C-43	C-71	D-11	D-26
E-1	E-21	E-79	F-9	F-43
F-77	G-67	G-77	G-103	G-105
G-115	G-116	G-127	G-131	H-5
H-10	H-72	H-109	H-122	J-2
K-45	K-59	K-88	L-8	Q-1

Desirability
  Social (cont.)

S-66	S-107	S-123	S-183	W-1
W-14	W-47			

Development -- s.a. actualization, enhancement, growth

A-7	A-14	B-35	B-53	B-120
C-73	C-104	C-205	C-217	C-233
C-241	D-4	F-24	G-14	G-43
G-99	G-173	H-29	H-59	H-163
H-169	K-27	K-39	K-40	L-16
L-37	M-6	M-9	M-32	P-38
P-64	R-32	R-70	S-23	S-122
S-162	S-334	T-55	T-98	U-7
W-3				

  Conceptual -- see Conceptual/Development
  Moral

A-14	C-73	C-241	G-99	H-29
H-59	H-169	K-27	K-39	L-16
L-37	R-70	S-122	T-55	

  Personal

G-14	G-173	L-16	P-38	S-334

  Self

B-35	B-53	C-205	G-43	H-59
K-27	L-37	M-9	P-38	S-23
T-98	W-3			

Deviance

A-59	A-63	A-70	B-213	C-208
C-209	C-246	E-74	F-112	G-166
N-45	P-105	P-109	P-128	P-138
R-106	R-158	S-174	S-239	S-242
S-303	S-305	T-62		

Diagnosis

A-63	A-74	A-88	A-104	B-30
B-41	B-49	B-82	B-85	B-94
B-119	B-127	B-199	B-239	B-266
C-98	C-203	D-90	E-19	E-54
E-55	E-56	F-1	F-10	F-37
F-82	F-86	F-122	G-4	G-8
G-27	G-83	G-150	G-203	H-4
H-8	H-15	H-24	H-34	H-54
H-105	H-154	H-214	K-13	K-51
K-81	L-1	L-39	L-106	L-137
L-164	M-62	M-75	M-252	M-258
O-7	O-22	P-36	P-108	P-114
P-145	R-27	R-36	R-40	R-56
R-111	R-139	S-84	S-110	S-156
S-224	S-243	T-41	T-61	T-81
T-82	U-1	V-22	V-35	W-6
W-10	W-44	W-49	W-50	W-59
W-111	W-143	Z-5	Z-20	

  Psychiatric

A-88	A-104	B-41	B-85	B-94
B-119	B-127	B-190	B-239	E-19
F-1	F-37	F-82	F-122	G-4
G-8	G-83	G-150	G-203	H-4
H-8	H-15	H-54	H-214	K-51
K-81	L-1	L-39	L-137	M-75
M-252	M-258	O-22	P-108	R-27
R-36	R-40	R-56	S-84	S-156
S-224	S-243	T-81	T-82	V-22
W-6	W-10	W-143		

  Schizophrenia

A-104	B-49	B-82	B-94	B-119
C-203	F-122	K-51	L-164	M-252
P-108	S-84	S-156	V-35	W-44
W-49	W-50	W-111	W-143	

Differences

C-241	E-73	E-74	F-123	G-162
G-180	H-53	H-202	K-15	K-111
M-54	M-55	M-113	P-13	R-29
S-316	S-330	W-45	W-46	W-56

Culture -- see Culture/Differences
  Racial

E-73	F-123	H-202

  Sex

C-241	H-53	K-15	K-111	M-54

E

Extraversion (cont.)
H-99	H-204	J-31	K-130	N-19
P-4	P-18	S-279	T-34	V-27
V-45	W-86			

Extrinsic -- s.a. autonomy, intrinsic
A-24	B-102	C-26	F-17	H-69
H-70	L-9	N-11	R-44	S-59
S-168	T-33	W-33		

Motive
A-24	B-102	C-26	F-17	H-69
H-70	N-11	S-168	W-33	

F

F-scale -- s.a. authoritarianism, dogmatism
A-37	B-14	B-190	B-192	C-30
C-31	J-4	J-13	K-8	K-43
L-25	L-162	M-45	M-241	P-46
S-60	S-108	W-55		

Facilitation
H-102	U-4

Failure -- s.a. performance, success
A-55	B-81	B-98	B-115	C-70
C-126	D-70	D-114	G-28	H-95
J-21	K-87	M-4	N-24	R-134
R-146	R-152	S-25	S-76	S-148
V-30	W-13	W-116		

Fear
B-81	B-98	C-70	C-126	G-28
H-95	J-21	K-87	M-4	S-148
V-30	W-116			

Faking -- s.a. enhancement, malingering, response-bias
B-27	C-58	E-66	F-132	H-30
H-197	H-198	P-40	S-263	

Family -- s.a. child, home, marital, parental, parent-child, paternal, sibling (Not included here are Family/Activities, Family/Counseling, Family/Ideology, and Family/Interaction)
A-30	A-85	B-42	B-43	B-152
B-205	B-219	C-195	D-88	E-67
G-54	G-109	G-173	H-83	H-121
I-6	K-126	K-141	K-142	M-71
P-31	R-87	R-104	R-105	R-149
T-4	T-42	T-86	W-13	W-51
Z-18				

Activities -- see Activities/Family
Counseling -- see Counseling/Family
Ideology
L-161	S-69	T-64

Interaction
A-33	A-36	B-1	B-28	B-29
B-38	B-100	B-122	B-128	B-130
B-135	B-165	B-166	B-167	B-262
C-22	C-65	C-83	C-84	C-101
C-108	C-129	C-178	D-34	D-41
E-15	E-51	F-2	F-12	F-15
F-22	F-49	F-62	G-9	G-34
G-35	G-55	G-82	G-167	H-13
H-27	H-35	H-50	H-52	H-60
H-66	H-100	H-133	H-134	L-63
M-42	M-60	M-61	N-15	O-5
P-12	P-27	P-44	P-50	R-23
R-29	R-35	R-41	S-8	S-9
S-13	S-45	S-50	S-91	S-131
S-199	S-230	S-297	S-298	T-19
T-31	T-44	T-64	T-68	V-2
V-6	V-11	V-12	W-18	W-29
W-36	W-54	W-76	W-93	W-138
Y-6	Y-7			

Fantasy -- s.a. imagination
A-27	B-207	B-234	B-238	C-99

Fantasy (cont.)
D-68	E-8	E-12	E-23	E-26
E-52	F-76	F-88	F-89	F-92
F-104	G-144	G-155	G-197	H-151
H-174	J-41	K-113	L-52	M-46
M-55	M-173	M-235	M-244	P-14
P-127	R-148	S-38	S-51	S-67
S-82	S-83	S-221	S-256	S-303
T-54	T-70	T-81	U-8	W-30
W-106	W-120	W-124	Z-2	

Fear -- s.a. phobia
B-41	B-81	B-98	B-112	B-273
C-11	C-70	C-126	C-164	C-200
C-211	D-49	D-50	D-51	D-64
D-75	D-98	E-43	F-42	F-75
F-109	F-110	G-28	G-41	G-133
H-79	H-95	J-21	K-79	K-87
K-129	L-24	L-46	L-59	L-135
L-136	M-4	M-37	P-104	R-39
R-80	S-147	S-148	S-256	S-259
T-96	V-30	W-37	W-116	W-135

Death -- see Death/Fear
Failure -- see Failure/Fear
Feeling
A-72	D-57	D-58	D-68	F-120
K-146	K-153	M-197	M-257	R-124
R-126	R-132	S-216	S-223	S-274
V-40				

Achievement
V-40

Competence -- see Competence/Feeling
Subjective
D-58	K-153

Feminity -- s.a. masculinity, sex/role
A-1	A-11	A-103	B-10	B-35
C-92	C-247	D-2	D-24	E-67
F-3	F-11	F-98	F-145	G-20
G-23	G-30	G-35	G-40	H-21
H-34	H-45	H-115	H-180	J-20
J-25	K-3	K-11	M-54	M-55
M-208	N-20	N-21	N-22	O-2
P-15	R-1	R-11	R-22	R-24
R-96	S-3	S-14	S-33	S-34
S-136	S-165	S-248	S-336	T-3
W-5	W-28	W-46	W-149	Z-2

Field
Dependence -- see Dependence/Field
Figure -- s.a. graphic
A-49	A-98	B-125	B-155	B-175
B-231	B-284	C-62	D-100	E-9
F-52	F-53	F-56	F-138	G-33
G-139	G-150	H-165	H-168	H-173
H-175	J-17	J-54	K-46	K-60
K-90	K-114	L-11	L-154	M-113
M-240	M-248	R-79	R-152	S-57
S-107	S-237	S-252	S-327	S-329
S-330	S-341	T-20	T-84	V-1
W-9	W-19	W-28	W-46	W-72
W-102	W-136	W-142	W-193	W-199

Preference -- s.a. projective
B-155	E-9	G-165	M-240	S-57
S-107	S-327	S-341	V-1	W-9
W-28	W-46	W-72		

Flexibility -- s.a. ambiguity/tolerance, authoritarianism, dogmatism, openness, overexclusive, overinclusive, rigidity seeking/sensation
A-5	A-60	B-6	B-37	B-72
B-73	B-78	B-79	B-93	B-106
B-116	B-125	B-155	B-220	B-231
B-277	C-47	C-57	C-59	C-75
C-111	C-226	D-6	D-21	E-9
E-38	E-41	F-4	F-19	F-52
F-53	F-72	F-141	G-76	G-84
G-113	G-194	H-6	H-63	H-108
H-167	K-8	K-81	K-120	K-155
L-6	L-45	L-162	M-186	M-196
M-248	O-27	P-16	P-24	P-47

G

J

L

M

Moral (cont.)
    Development -- see Development/Moral
    Judgment -- see Judgment/Moral
    Responsibility

A-71	H-29	H-172	M-48	S-74
S-100	S-122	T-64	T-91	

    Values

A-14	A-71	B-168	B-235	B-237
C-11	C-73	C-92	G-99	G-114
G-141	H-165	J-41	K-27	K-39
K-70	K-140	L-16	L-37	M-48
R-26	R-115	S-74	S-100	S-246
T-64	T-91			

Morale

C-123	D-88	F-61	G-81	L-53
R-33	R-104	S-12	T-114	Y-2

Mortality -- s.a. death

B-112	C-200	C-211	D-64	F-105
T-96				

Motive -- s.a. drive, incentive, need,
    press

A-24	A-28	A-43	A-55	B-48
B-70	B-87	B-102	B-110	B-117
C-11	C-26	C-47	C-211	C-242
D-28	D-30	D-35	E-34	E-43
E-68	F-17	F-20	F-25	F-117
F-129	G-48	G-71	G-92	G-93
G-94	G-105	G-187	G-198	H-48
H-69	H-70	H-120	H-150	H-180
J-21	K-136	K-149	L-31	L-145
M-7	M-13	M-47	M-63	M-79
M-87	M-232	M-235	M-259	N-11
N-42	O-3	O-9	P-28	P-39
R-17	R-17	R-83	R-140	S-18
S-83	S-121	S-131	S-138	S-168
S-281	S-283	S-286	S-300	T-21
T-52	T-67	T-73	V-4	V-23
W-7	W-33	W-45	W-74	W-81
W-151	W-165	Z-8	Z-19	

    Achievement -- see Achievement/Motive
    Extrinsic -- see Extrinsic/Motive
    Integration -- see Integration/Motive
    Intrinsic -- see Intrinsic/Motive
Multitrait

A-41	A-43	B-11	B-24	B-26
B-30	B-47	B-63	B-99	B-121
B-126	C-6	C-10	C-11	C-15
C-19	C-41	C-46	C-72	C-86
C-89	C-125	D-33	D-36	D-45
E-2	E-5	E-6	E-7	E-20
E-30	F-16	F-21	F-50	F-54
F-59	G-12	G-14	G-21	G-22
G-26	G-39	G-40	G-43	G-57
G-58	G-59	G-61	G-70	G-74
G-75	G-78	G-79	G-84	G-89
H-9	H-12	H-14	H-21	H-37
H-45	H-47	H-55	H-83	H-213
J-1	J-2	J-9	J-10	J-18
K-14	K-42	K-63	K-64	K-70
K-82	K-84	L-2	L-52	M-20
M-41	M-42	M-58	M-77	M-78
M-81	M-196	N-2	N-18	N-19
P-4	P-37	R-31	R-52	S-4
S-56	S-65	S-85	S-103	S-104
S-110	S-111	S-118	S-138	S-140
S-142	S-277	S-295	T-7	T-17
T-22	T-25	T-27	T-34	V-28
W-51	W-65	W-67	W-71	W-80
W-86				

N

National

A-13	A-46	T-17	T-46

    Attitude -- see Attitude/National
    Awareness -- see Awareness/National
Nationalism -- s.a. internationalism, pac-
    ifism, political

A-13	A-17	F-51	T-8	W-157

Need -- s.a. drive, incentive, motive,
    press
    (Not included here are Need/Achievement,
    Need/Affection, Need/Affiliation, Need/
    Approval, Need/Belongingness, Need/De-
    pendence, Need/Dominance, Need/Inte-
    gration, Need/Novelty, Need/Nurturance,
    Need/Order, Need/Power, Need/Satisfac-
    tion, Need/Security, and Need/Social
    Approval)

B-48	B-139	B-168	B-177	B-272
C-139	C-150	C-177	C-242	E-2
E-43	G-21	G-40	G-93	G-129
G-132	H-11	H-99	H-148	K-33
K-155	P-28	P-30	S-56	S-184
S-231	S-232	S-271	S-281	T-91
W-97	W-148	Z-3		

    Achievement -- see Achievement/Need
    Affection -- see Affection/Need
    Affiliation -- see Affiliation/Need
    Approval -- see Approval/Need
    Belongingness -- see Belongingness/Need
    Dependence -- see Dependence/Need
    Dominance -- see Dominance/Need
    Integration -- see Integration/Need
    Novelty

G-129	H-148	K-155	S-271

    Nurturance

C-6	D-22	F-20	H-61	H-119
H-120	H-216	K-100	M-245	W-58

    Order

D-22	G-14	G-61	H-61

    Power

S-16	S-179	T-90	V-4	V-45

    Satisfaction

A-40	A-97	B-87	B-88	B-105
G-11	G-176	H-61	K-97	P-49
S-125	T-6			

    Security

A-97	B-87	B-116	G-94	H-74
H-95	H-194	M-50	P-5	R-80
V-45	W-94			

    Social Approval

B-4	B-32	B-83	B-87	C-6
C-13	E-1	E-21	F-43	F-146
F-147	G-77	G-81	G-103	K-20
M-24	R-54	R-80	S-11	S-16
S-31	S-98	V-45		

Negative
    (Not included here are Negative/Affec-
    tive-states, Negative/Evaluation, Neg-
    ative/Image, and Negative/Self-identity)

C-113	C-131	C-170	C-220	F-106
W-103	W-116			

    Affective-states -- see Affective-
    states/Negative
    Evaluation -- see Evaluation/Negative
    Image -- see Image/Negative
    Self-identity

B-17	H-11	J-7	L-16

Negro -- s.a. desegregation, ethnic, racial
C-50 C-252 F-123 G-87 G-91
G-93 G-94 G-95 G-96 G-97
H-36 H-202 K-19 K-29 K-44
K-92 M-23 O-4 S-43 S-54
S-64 S-95 S-178 S-182 S-274
S-276 W-27 W-62 W-75 W-150
W-195
Prejudice
C-50 F-123 G-97 H-36 K-19
K-29 K-44 K-92 M-23 O-4
S-43 S-54 S-64 S-95 S-178
S-182 S-274 S-276 W-27 W-62
W-75 W-150
Nervousness
C-147 G-40 V-5
Neuroticism
B-80 B-147 B-174 B-176 B-199
B-239 C-19 C-35 C-135 C-153
C-188 E-5 E-6 E-7 E-29
E-62 F-10 F-111 G-8 G-203
K-81 K-129 M-62 M-258 M-260
O-7 P-4 P-31 R-121 S-10
S-155 S-156 S-249 S-317 S-324
T-49 T-61 W-8 W-41 W-61
Z-1
Normality -- s.a. adjustment
A-63 B-24 S-201
Norms -- s.a. ideals, values
D-13 G-162 O-31 R-147 S-74
S-106 T-3 W-141 Y-1
Culture -- see Culture/Norms
Group -- see Group/Norms
Social
D-13 S-106 Y-1
Novelty
A-86 G-129 H-148 K-155 M-244
S-209 S-271 S-327 Z-21
Need -- see Need/Novelty
Nurturance
C-6 D-22 F-20 H-61 H-66
H-119 H-120 H-216 K-63 K-64
K-100 M-245 W-58
Need -- see Need/Nurturance

O

Openness -- s.a. ambiguity/tolerance, authoritarianism, dogmatism, flexibility, rigidity, seeking/sensation
A-67 A-68 A-86 A-102 B-220
C-57 C-59 C-75 F-19 F-72
H-18 H-130 J-50 L-60 M-170
P-142 R-128 R-141 S-163 S-290
T-105 W-147 W-148
Experience -- see Experience/Openness
Opinion -- s.a. attitude, belief
B-292 C-195 C-210 C-214 C-215
C-234 D-29 E-31 F-21 F-38
F-71 G-61 G-117 G-136 H-36
H-59 H-64 H-190 K-133 M-54
M-219 P-122 R-50 R-104 R-133
R-146 S-126 S-137 S-146 S-280
S-309 V-38 Z-37
Change -- see Change/Opinion
Leadership -- see Leadership/Opinion
Political
K-133
Student
C-214 C-215 H-64 R-146 S-280
S-309
Opponent -- s.a. competition
M-26
Opportunity -- s.a. aspiration
J-28
Optimism -- s.a. pessimism
D-37 G-57 R-134 S-2
Orality -- s.a. compulsiveness, neuroticism, orderliness
B-176 B-272 L-158 R-121 S-249
W-182
Order
B-19 D-22 E-31 G-14 G-61
G-173 H-61 K-63 K-64 L-63
Birth -- see Birth/Order
Need -- see Need/Order
Organization -- s.a. college, job, school
B-71 B-105 B-221 B-222 B-271
F-115 G-122 H-32 H-70 H-83
J-45 M-114 M-183 M-229 P-34
S-105 S-119 S-218 S-309 Z-37
Effectiveness -- see Effectiveness/Organization
Environment -- see Environment/Organization
Goals -- see Goals/Organization
Structure
B-222 G-122 H-32 M-114 Z-37
Orientation
Future -- see Future/Orientation
Interpersonal -- see Interpersonal/Orientation
Others
A-9 B-9 B-21 B-83 B-136
B-200 B-267 D-10 E-10 E-12
E-67 F-14 F-46 G-13 H-17
H-171 K-9 K-35 K-130 M-41
R-2 R-10 R-46 S-7 S-37
S-55 S-85 S-87 T-24 T-29
T-30 T-55 T-64 T-90 W-24
Z-6 Z-9
Personal
C-3 C-94 C-95 C-117 C-118
C-119 D-61 E-13 G-14 G-66
H-47 J-6 L-16 L-147 S-21
S-163 S-175 T-76 T-90 T-91
V-3 V-28 W-34 W-167 W-174
Z-9 Z-10 Z-11
Political
A-7 A-22 A-29 C-7 C-64
C-72 C-92 C-109 D-18 E-27
E-41 E-59 G-98 K-12 K-133
L-31 L-54 O-6 P-10 R-10
S-69 S-81 S-163 W-23
Rational
S-259
Religion
A-7 A-24 B-111 C-33 C-184
D-84 E-74 F-17 F-116 K-36
L-16 L-56 P-42 S-69 S-163
T-23 T-90 T-91 W-33 W-51
W-141
Sensory
B-189 M-1 S-245 S-258 Z-32
Originality -- s.a. creativity, imagination
B-76 B-78 B-232 B-257 B-283
B-284 D-52 F-21 F-97 G-12
G-52 G-53 G-80 G-107 G-113
G-129 G-134 G-165 G-192 G-194
H-187 H-218 K-76 L-6 M-43
M-72 N-12 R-27 R-56 S-116
S-205 S-209 S-245 S-277 T-16
T-28 T-39 T-57 W-118
Others
Awareness -- see Awareness/Others
Esteem -- see Esteem/Others
Orientation -- see Orientation/Others

Others (cont.)
   Respect
      G-171   S-167
Overexclusive -- s.a. flexibility, rigidity
      B-250   C-20
   Thinking
      C-20
Overinclusive -- s.a. flexibility, rigidity
      B-250   C-1   E-38   H-171   P-137
   Thinking
      C-1   E-38   H-171   P-137

P

Pacifism -- s.a. internationalism, mili-
   tarism, nationalism, political
      D-18
Pain
   Tolerance
      S-197
Parental -- s.a. family, maternal, parent-
   child, paternal, punitiveness
   (Not included here are Parental/Accep-
   tance, Parental/Affection, Parental/
   Approval, Parental/Attitude, Parental/
   Behavior, Parental/Dominance, Parental/
   Identification, Parental/Punitiveness,
   and Parental/Strictness)
      A-36   B-122   B-166   B-219   B-262
      C-11   C-22   C-56   C-129   C-130
      C-158   C-183   D-83   E-36   E-80
      G-173   G-191   H-27   H-66   H-115
      H-116   S-199   S-211   S-230   S-253
      T-68   T-86   W-93   W-133
   Acceptance -- see Acceptance/Parental
   Affection -- see Affection/Parental
   Approval -- see Approval/Parental
   Attitude -- see Attitude/Parental
   Behavior -- see Behavior/Parental
   Dominance -- see Dominance/Parental
   Identification -- see Identification/
      Parental
   Punitiveness
      E-15   H-60   H-134   P-63   W-126
   Strictness
      B-174   G-9   G-34
Parent-child -- s.a. child, family, home,
   maternal, parental, paternal
   (Not included here are Parent-child/
   Interaction, Parent-child/Problem,
   Parent-child/Relationships, and Par-
   ent-child/Similarity)
      B-133   B-198   C-176   D-72   D-88
      G-56   G-114   G-141   G-193   H-115
      H-116   H-159   L-55   M-71   T-67
      W-133   Z-18
   Interaction -- see Interaction/Parent-
      child
   Problem
      C-108   C-178   J-44   R-87
   Relationships
      F-15   H-42   H-66   H-133   H-134
      M-42   N-15   P-27   P-50   R-41
      R-87   S-16   S-230   T-31   T-59
      T-86   V-12   W-29   W-36   W-54
   Similarity
      B-204   C-22   D-42   H-35
Participation -- s.a. activities
      B-142   D-99   F-140   H-85   H-86
      J-27   L-56   M-198   P-123   S-222
      T-19   T-31   V-20

Participation (cont.)
   Group -- see Group/Participation
Passive -- s.a. active, autonomy, initia-
   tive
      B-178   C-170   C-178   R-149   S-195
      S-211   S-294   W-174   W-182
Past
      A-86   B-259   C-154   C-155   C-156
      C-202   K-127   M-190   M-216
Paternal -- s.a. family, parental, parent-
   child
      A-90   B-202   B-204   B-256   B-264
      C-140   C-195   G-196   H-27   O-5
      P-48   P-63   S-9   S-199   S-253
   Identification -- see Identification/
      Paternal
   Role
      A-90   O-5   S-199
Patient
      A-20   A-32   A-48   A-50   A-56
      A-72   A-77   A-78   A-84   A-99
      B-22   B-50   B-82   B-86   B-119
      B-127   B-143   B-147   B-183   B-191
      B-214   B-230   B-251   B-260   B-261
      B-290   B-292   C-135   C-136   C-138
      C-139   C-143   C-148   C-149   C-170
      C-230   C-233   C-243   D-8   D-29
      D-35   D-38   D-41   D-43   D-65
      D-66   D-89   E-19   E-49   E-50
      E-56   E-57   E-81   F-1   F-71
      F-81   F-84   F-90   F-101   F-104
      F-133   F-137   F-144   G-31   G-54
      G-55   G-130   G-132   G-136   G-156
      G-166   G-176   G-178   G-181   G-184
      G-185   G-187   H-8   H-38   H-54
      H-67   H-145   H-176   H-215   H-220
      H-221   J-16   J-19   J-59   J-60
      K-32   K-42   K-51   K-58   K-83
      K-99   K-112   K-134   K-136   K-158
      K-162   L-11   L-17   L-39   L-138
      L-140   L-143   L-153   M-12   M-52
      M-74   M-179   M-192   M-199   M-233
      N-43   O-22   P-114   P-115   P-119
      P-124   R-36   R-45   R-130   R-135
      R-140   R-141   R-160   S-31   S-72
      S-121   S-143   S-198   S-200   S-202
      S-214   S-215   S-216   S-222   S-227
      S-267   S-269   S-289   S-299   S-322
      S-326   S-337   S-339   T-37   T-38
      T-48   T-69   T-74   T-75   T-80
      T-82   T-98   T-105   V-8   V-22
      V-26   V-34   V-38   W-10   W-44
      W-89   W-110   W-155   W-187   Y-4
      Z-5   Z-20
PE-fit -- s.a. environment, press, well-
   being
      A-18   A-31   A-39   A-40   B-20
      B-48   B-87   B-88   B-128   B-189
      B-210   B-212   C-2   C-21   C-37
      C-178   C-193   D-31   D-40   F-27
      F-38   G-11   G-17   G-73   G-82
      G-84   H-16   H-23   H-56   H-65
      H-70   H-82   H-95   H-102   J-16
      K-2   K-6   K-7   K-52   K-54
      K-55   K-57   K-71   L-9   L-53
      M-15   M-70   N-11   P-11   P-30
      P-33   P-34   P-49   Q-3   Q-4
      R-23   R-33   R-48   R-126   S-12
      S-56   S-148   S-151   S-169   S-233
      T-14   T-33   W-38   W-81   W-159
      W-180   Y-2   Z-8
   Job -- see Job/PE-fit
Peer -- s.a. sociometric
      B-16   B-25   B-133   B-152   B-168
      B-178   B-235   B-237   B-244   B-267
      C-56   C-161   E-36   E-44   E-80
      F-146   G-23   G-36   G-66   G-78

Primary-process
  A-27   B-180 B-226 B-271 F-88
  F-92   G-144 H-117 H-151 H-156
  H-170 H-218 J-43   R-148 S-194
  S-255 S-257 T-54   T-92   T-94
  U-5
 Thinking
  A-27   F-88   F-92   G-144 H-117
  H-151 H-156 J-43   R-148 S-194
  S-257
Privacy -- s.a. accessibility, disclosure
  B-272 W-148
Private -- s.a. public
  M-170
Problem
  A-30   A-44   A-88   B-109 B-212
  B-251 C-108 C-178 C-219 F-123
  H-186 J-41   J-44   K-50   L-45
  L-117 M-62   M-193 M-199 M-236
  P-31   P-114 P-142 Q-8   R-28
  R-49   R-87   R-139 W-49   W-50
 Adolescent -- see Adolescent/Problem
 Checklist -- see Checklist/Problem
 Parent-child -- see Parent-child/Problem
 Racial
  F-123
Prognosis
  B-41   B-82   B-242 B-275 C-4
  C-233 D-35   D-38   D-114 E-57
  F-37   F-80   F-136 G-27   G-172
  G-201 H-15   H-34   K-13   K-116
  K-136 K-152 L-39   M-233 M-255
  N-46   O-22   P-36   P-126 R-32
  R-36   R-146 S-31   S-72   S-187
  V-22   W-44
 Psychiatric
  B-41   B-82   B-275 C-4   C-233
  D-35   D-38   E-57   F-37   F-80
  G-201 H-15   K-152 L-39   M-233
  M-255 O-22   P-126 R-36   S-31
  S-72   V-22
 Rating
  B-41   F-136 G-172 H-15   K-13
  K-152 L-39   N-46   O-22   R-36
  S-187 V-22   W-44
Projective -- s.a. figure/preference,
 Rorschach, TAT
  A-14   A-94   A-98   B-32   B-34
  B-81   B-82   B-90   B-98   B-113
  B-114 B-162 B-175 B-207 B-209
  B-210 B-238 B-254 B-264 C-4
  C-6   C-17   C-60   C-134 C-154
  C-242 D-4   D-25   D-30   D-46
  D-47   D-68   D-72   D-100 D-111
  D-112 E-13   E-36   E-43   E-52
  E-76   E-80   F-8   F-11   F-40
  F-75   F-97   F-122 F-135 F-138
  G-6   G-16   G-56   G-77   G-78
  G-105 G-133 G-134 G-135 G-142
  G-143 G-153 G-155 G-163 G-169
  G-188 G-197 H-24   H-37   H-73
  H-74   H-84   H-93   H-100 H-113
  H-117 H-121 H-123 H-130 H-150
  H-168 H-173 H-175 I-4   J-21
  J-41   K-10   K-13   K-14   K-31
  K-43   K-46   K-47   K-48   K-55
  K-56   K-68   K-69   K-81   K-86
  K-96   K-98   K-113 K-117 K-125
  K-149 L-11   L-18   L-26   L-57
  L-58   M-7   M-14   M-19   M-20
  M-46   M-47   M-55   M-58   M-79
  M-235 M-241 M-244 P-28   P-64
  P-126 P-127 P-138 R-5   R-12
  R-31   R-113 R-134 R-137 R-145
  R-159 S-19   S-27   S-41   S-57
  S-67   S-73   S-83   S-88   S-92
  S-97   S-99   S-103 S-110 S-128

Projective (cont.)
  S-179 S-181 S-188 S-190 S-221
  S-232 S-235 S-275 S-281 S-283
  S-286 S-294 S-317 T-26   T-68
  T-70   T-81   U-4   V-4   V-14
  V-23   V-29   V-31   V-32   W-30
  W-45   W-56   W-59   W-76   W-104
  W-106 W-113 W-120 W-127 W-131
  W-147 Z-14   Z-20   Z-29   Z-34
Protectiveness
  T-67   V-2   V-6
Psychiatric -- s.a. therapy
 (Not included here are Psychiatric/Di-
  agnosis, Psychiatric/Prognosis, Psy-
  chiatric/Rating, and Psychiatric/Symp-
  tom)
  A-32   A-63   A-74   B-50   B-191
  B-205 B-214 B-245 B-292 C-123
  C-145 C-148 C-149 C-150 C-170
  C-201 C-208 C-209 D-41   E-49
  E-50   E-81   F-6   F-71   F-80
  F-99   F-104 F-112 F-137 G-55
  G-132 G-150 G-156 G-159 G-160
  G-166 G-176 G-178 H-125
  H-173 H-189 H-215 H-221 K-6
  K-99   L-17   M-12   M-15   M-52
  M-179 M-236 N-41   N-45   P-41
  P-144 R-135 R-140 R-160 S-165
  S-173 S-198 S-222 S-267 S-289
  S-299 S-304 S-305 T-80   T-105
  W-114 W-155 Y-8
 Diagnosis -- see Diagnosis/Psychiatric
 Prognosis -- see Prognosis/Psychiatric
 Rating
  A-20   B-41   C-243 F-82   F-121
  G-4   H-4   H-15   H-127 J-38
  J-39   K-32   K-58   K-82   K-112
  K-152 K-162 L-1   L-39   M-74
  M-202 O-22   R-36   R-130 S-210
  S-214 S-243 S-268 S-269 S-324
  V-22   V-35   W-6   W-155 Z-18
 Symptom
  A-59   A-99   F-84   G-4   H-4
  H-15   J-38   J-39   K-58   L-1
  L-122 L-134 L-137 L-138 L-152
  L-153 M-193 S-156 S-190 S-224
  T-47   W-6   W-10
Psychosomatic
  C-153 G-151 H-23   H-145 L-134
  M-62   S-224 W-10   Z-30
 Illness -- see Illness/Psychosomatic
 Symptom
  C-153 G-151 L-134 S-224 W-10
  Z-30
Psychopathy -- s.a. acculturation, mental-
 illness, therapy
  A-42   A-63   C-98   C-189 C-246
  H-24   K-81   K-112 M-201 N-46
  P-31   P-41   T-62   V-5
Public -- s.a. private
  C-208 C-209 C-234 F-16   F-48
  F-112 G-81   G-82   G-93   G-176
  H-7   H-30   H-38   K-161 L-29
  M-8   M-24   M-170 P-29   P-147
  P-149 S-305
 Esteem -- see Esteem/Public
Punitiveness -- s.a. attribution/guilt,
 direction/hostility
  C-134 E-15   E-50   F-23   F-86
  G-188 H-60   H-134 K-10   L-55
  P-63   R-5   R-12   S-67   S-146
  S-181 W-104 W-126 W-180
 Parental -- see Parental/Punitiveness
Purpose -- s.a. goals
  C-95   K-151 S-277

Religion (cont.)
    Conformity -- see Conformity/Religion
    Conviction -- see Conviction/Religion
    Orientation -- see Orientation/Religion
Repression -- s.a. defense, sensitization
    A-10   B-32   B-46   C-179   G-153
    G-157   L-26   L-47   M-27   P-95
    P-96   R-5   R-12   R-151   W-41
    W-43   W-147   W-183
    Sensitization
    A-10   B-46   M-27   R-5   R-12
    W-43
Resentment -- s.a. affective-states/nega-
    tive, Hostility, irritability
    B-44   B-66   B-81   C-9   C-28
    C-80   D-37   E-17   F-18   F-23
    F-50   G-16   G-25   G-63   H-24
    H-73   K-4   K-5   K-10   L-18
    L-42   L-51   M-14   M-46   P-35
    R-5   R-12   S-24   S-36   S-47
    S-67   S-96   T-15   T-56   W-68
    Z-7
Resistance
    B-251   G-141   P-142   S-168
Respect
    G-171   P-3   S-167
    Others -- see Others/Respect
    Self
    S-167
Response -- s.a. behavior
    A-49   A-77   A-78   B-12   B-118
    B-147   B-169   C-67   C-79   C-188
    C-213   D-53   D-65   E-17   E-42
    E-46   E-48   F-55   G-105   G-142
    G-156   H-43   H-57   H-77   K-43
    K-60   K-69   L-45   L-135   M-232
    M-239   0-27   P-16   P-46   P-70
    P-94   P-95   P-96   P-97   P-98
    P-99   P-130   R-40   R-43   R-82
    R-100   S-65   S-66   S-107   S-129
    S-235   S-294   S-342   S-344   T-99
    U-8   U-9   W-4   W-48   W-162
    W-163   W-170   W-180   W-190   W-202
    Y-4   Z-40
    Intensity -- see Intensity/Response
    Set
    B-12   B-118   C-188   D-53   F-55
    K-43   L-45   P-16   P-46   P-70
    R-100   S-129   S-235   W-4
    Specificity
    S-294
    Stimulus
    C-213   E-17   L-135   P-94   P-95
    P-96   P-97   P-98   P-99   S-344
Response-bias -- s.a. acquiescence, defen-
    siveness, enhancement, experimenter/in-
    fluence, faking, malingering
    A-10   A-12   A-16   A-25   B-7
    B-12   B-27   B-32   B-46   B-59
    B-118   B-183   B-192   B-280   C-18
    C-23   C-27   C-30   C-32   C-42
    C-43   C-58   C-71   C-116   C-121
    C-122   C-171   C-172   C-175   C-188
    D-26   D-53   E-1   E-6   E-21
    E-28   E-66   E-79   F-9   F-13
    F-34   F-55   F-77   F-95   F-113
    F-131   F-132   G-1   G-88   G-103
    G-104   G-127   G-202   H-5   H-10
    H-30   H-72   H-122   H-197   H-198
    J-2   J-3   J-4   J-14   J-15
    J-24   K-43   K-59   K-75   L-4
    L-12   L-20   L-25   L-26   L-47
    N-10   N-41   P-6   P-16   P-40
    P-46   P-70   P-120   Q-1   R-5
    R-12   R-20   R-100   S-65   S-66
    S-79   S-107   S-123   S-129   S-263
    T-77   T-79   W-1   W-4   W-14

Response-bias (cont.)
    W-25   W-39   W-41   W-43   W-47
    W-101   W-108   W-123   W-164
Responsibility -- s.a. acculturation, au-
    tonomy
    A-71   B-26   B-54   C-25   C-82
    C-109   D-76   E-37   F-44   F-107
    F-123   G-36   G-60   G-70   G-140
    H-12   H-29   H-172   K-28   K-133
    L-138   M-48   M-188   M-189   P-105
    R-106   R-124   S-42   S-73   S-74
    S-100   S-122   S-181   T-42   T-64
    T-91   V-27   V-45   W-107
    Acceptance -- see Acceptance/Responsi-
    bility
    Attribution -- see Attribution/Respon-
    sibility
    Moral -- see Moral/Responsibility
    Political -- see Political/Responsibil-
    ity
    Social
    B-54   F-44   G-36   G-140   H-12
    H-29   R-106   S-73   S-100   V-45
Rigidity -- s.a. ambiguity/tolerance, au-
    thoritarianism, dogmatism, flexibility,
    openness, overexclusive, overinclusive,
    seeking/sensation
    A-5   A-56   A-60   B-6   B-37
    B-72   B-73   B-93   B-106   B-116
    B-125   B-155   B-192   C-47   C-57
    C-59   C-75   C-79   C-111   D-6
    D-21   E-9   E-38   E-41   F-4
    F-19   G-76   G-84   H-6   H-63
    H-108   H-167   K-8   K-81   K-96
    K-120   K-155   L-6   L-45   L-162
    M-45   M-186   M-196   0-27   P-16
    P-24   P-47   R-8   R-25   R-46
    R-50   R-121   R-128   S-60   S-69
    S-88   S-108   S-109   S-171   S-182
    S-226   S-235   T-18   T-20   V-26
    W-11   W-55   W-70   W-141   W-161
    W-162   W-176   Z-1   Z-38
Risk-taking
    B-69   H-194   K-87   K-94   L-28
    L-30   M-13   M-31   M-85   0-3
    P-25   R-26   T-11   W-2   W-38
    Z-42
Rivalry -- s.a. competition
    Sibling
    B-174   H-121
Role
    (Not included here are Role/Acceptance,
    Role/Conflict, Role/Consistency, Role/
    Demands, Role/Description, Role/Enact-
    ment, Role/Maternal, Role/Marital,
    Role/Paternal, Role/Perception, Role/
    Preference, Role/Sex, and Role/Struc-
    ture)
    A-69   A-83   B-70   B-159   B-185
    B-193   B-260   B-261   C-92   C-140
    C-193   C-194   D-54   D-55   D-57
    D-58   E-68   F-38   G-72   G-82
    G-84   H-13   H-193   H-199   J-55
    K-11   K-54   K-147   M-113   M-183
    N-41   0-25   R-6   R-127   S-102
    S-106   S-131   S-239   S-299   W-168
    W-174
    Acceptance -- see Acceptance/Role
    Conflict -- see Conflict/Role
    Consistency -- see Consistency/Role
    Demands -- see Demands/Role
    Description -- see Description/Role
    Enactment -- see Enactment/Role
    Maternal -- see Maternal/Role
    Marital -- see Marital/Role
    Paternal -- see Paternal/Role
    Perception -- see Perception/Role

S

Subjective -- s.a. perceived
   (Not included here is Subjective/Stress)
      A-21   A-69   C-166   D-58   D-66
      G-199   J-36   K-153   L-33   R-105
      S-51   S-82   S-83   T-6   T-37
      W-30   W-37
   Stress -- see Stress/Subjective
Submission -- s.a. ascendence, dominance
      A-6   B-190   C-195   C-196   D-33
      F-58   G-7   G-19   G-40   G-84
      W-3   Z-27
Success -- s.a. failure, performance
      A-55   A-75   B-43   B-105   B-115
      D-70   D-114   F-47   F-80   G-28
      G-89   H-83   H-185   H-195   H-200
      H-215   J-21   J-46   K-14   K-87
      K-134   K-136   L-145   M-31   M-52
      M-87   M-203   M-254   N-42   R-134
      R-152   R-159   R-160   S-25   S-72
      S-104   W-13   W-110   Z-19   Z-28
   Academic -- see Academic/Success
   Hope -- see Hope/ Success
   Marital -- see Marital/Success
   Prediction -- see Prediction/Success
Succorance
      C-6   M-245   S-281   S-283
Suggestibility
      A-21   A-69   B-3   B-92   B-171
      C-194   D-61   D-77   F-87   F-132
      H-178   L-33   M-34   P-23   R-97
      S-51   S-90   S-258   T-94   W-31
      W-63   W-103   W-124
   Hypnosis -- see Hypnosis/Suggestibility
Suicide -- s.a. depression, mental-illness
      D-15   E-19   F-137   K-127   L-59
      M-233   P-21
Supervisor -- s.a. employee, job, manage-
   ment
      A-34   A-47   B-20   B-221   B-222
      B-252   F-38   F-46   F-47   F-48
      F-61   G-58   G-59   G-73   H-78
      H-81   I-2   K-7   K-53   L-53
      M-56   M-70   M-84   N-1   O-10
      P-20   R-42   R-160   S-12   S-209
      S-285   T-33   T-111   U-6   V-19
      W-60   W-83   W-121   Y-2
   Rating -- see Rating/Supervisor
   Relationships -- see Relationships/Sup-
      ervisor-employee
Support
      B-174   C-176   G-13   G-193   H-135
      K-74   P-105   P-116   R-80   S-199
      T-60
Symptom
      A-59   A-72   A-99   C-153   E-56
      F-10   F-84   G-4   G-151   G-172
      H-4   H-15   H-171   J-38   J-39
      K-58   L-1   L-122   L-134   L-137
      L-138   L-152   L-153   M-193   N-46
      O-29   P-110   S-156   S-190   S-224
      T-47   T-56   T-94   V-34   W-6
      W-10   W-111   W-165   Z-30   Z-33
   Depression -- see Depression/Symptom
   Mental-illness -- see Mental-illness/
      Symptom
   Psychiatric -- see Psychiatric/Symptom
   Psychosomatic -- see Psychosomatic/Symp-
      tom
   Withdrawal
      V-34

T

TAT -- s.a. projective
      A-94   B-32   B-90   B-98   B-107
      B-207   B-210   B-238   B-254   B-264
      C-17   C-242   D-25   D-30   D-68
      E-13   E-36   E-43   E-48   E-52
      E-80   F-8   F-74   F-97   G-85
      G-163   G-197   H-73   H-74   H-84
      H-93   H-100   H-130   H-140   H-150
      J-21   K-31   K-48   K-68   K-113
      K-149   L-165   M-7   M-19   M-20
      M-46   M-47   M-55   M-235   M-244
      P-28   P-127   P-138   S-19   S-27
      S-67   S-92   S-99   S-179   S-188
      S-232   S-256   S-303   T-107   U-4
      U-8   U-9   V-4   V-23   V-31
      W-7   W-30   W-56   W-76   W-106
      W-127   W-131   W-138
Taylor-MA -- s.a. anxiety/manifest
      B-182   B-184   H-49   H-51   T-2
Teacher -- s.a. college, school, student
      B-145   C-159   E-71   F-29   F-41
      F-58   F-59   F-114   G-86   G-109
      H-59   H-64   H-102   J-46   K-40
      K-62   M-33   M-228   O-9   R-33
      S-16   S-77   S-78   S-242   S-243
      S-302   S-310   T-40   V-9   W-67
   Attitude -- see Attitude/Teacher
   Rating -- see Rating/Teacher
Temperament
      B-272   C-61   G-26   S-191   T-7
      T-27
Tension -- s.a. anxiety
      B-171   B-174   B-184   C-152   C-198
      D-56   D-74   D-80   E-42   E-70
      F-92   G-206   H-88   H-118   I-5
      I-8   K-71   K-161   M-30   M-194
      M-243   M-260   P-121   P-147   P-149
      S-177   S-262   T-15   T-56   T-65
      W-65   W-135   W-166   Z-33
   Job -- see Job/Tension
Test
      A-8   C-40   E-70   H-28   H-96
      H-122   L-50   M-4   M-25   M-30
      M-200   O-29   P-22   P-121   P-130
      S-4   S-5   S-35   S-170   S-313
      W-7   W-94
   Anxiety -- see Anxiety/Test
Therapy -- s.a. counseling, psychiatric,
   psychopathy
   (Not included here are Therapy/Group,
   and Therapy/Relationships)
      A-48   A-50   A-61   A-72   B-22
      B-143   B-147   B-148   B-180   B-214
      B-241   B-251   B-253   C-4   C-12
      C-105   C-106   C-138   C-139   C-142
      C-143   C-148   C-170   C-213   D-35
      D-38   D-56   E-37   E-39   F-70
      F-71   F-80   F-101   F-133   F-144
      G-8   G-126   G-181   G-200   H-4
      H-34   H-38   H-68   H-105   H-127
      H-131   H-185   J-19   J-59   K-112
      K-116   K-134   K-136   L-39   L-96
      L-143   M-19   M-181   M-203   N-43
      P-41   P-110   P-114   P-116   P-124
      Q-9   R-36   R-75   R-130   R-141
      R-159   S-187   S-210   S-300   S-322
      S-337   S-339   S-342   T-24   T-37
      T-38   T-74   T-89   T-98   T-105

Ward (cont.)
    Behavior -- see Behavior/Ward
Well-being -- s.a. affective-states, hap-
    piness, PE-fit, positive, satisfaction
        B-5   C-206   K-146   W-160
Withdrawal
        B-123   B-178   C-9   H-60   H-84
        R-13   S-201   S-222   S-306   T-62
        V-34   W-15   W-122
    Symptom -- see Symptom/Withdrawal

3

SUPPLEMENT TO THE DESCRIPTOR INDEX

ACL........see Checklist
Adequacy...see Competence
Adjective checklist
         ...see Checklist
Affect.....see Affective-states
Anger......see Aggression, Hostility, Ir-
              ritability
Anti-interoceptive
         ...see Interoceptive
Anxiousness
         ...see Anxiety
Assessment
         ...see Evaluation

Black......see Negro

Card-sort
         ...see Q-sort
Child rearing
         ...see Family, Parental, Parent-
              child
Client.....see Patient
Compulsivity
         ...see Compulsiveness
Congruity
         ...see Consistency, Dissonance
Conscientiousness
         ...see Conscientious
Control/External
         ...see IE-control
Control/Internal
         ...see IE-control
Credibility
         ...see Trust
Crime......see Delinquency
Criminal...see Delinquency
Crowne-Marlowe
         ...see Desirability/Social
Cultural...see Cross-cultural, Culture

Daydreaming
         ...see Fantasy
Deliberation
         ...see Impulsiveness
Differential
         ...see Differentiation, Sem-differ-
              ential
Disabled...see Disability
Discriminability
         ...see Differentiation
Disease....see Illness
Disorders
         ...see Illness
Disparity
         ...see Discrepancy
Distrust...see Trust
Doctor-patient-relations
         ...see Relationship/Therapy

Dream......see Fantasy, Primary-process/
              Thinking

Education
         ...see Academic, College, School,
              Student, Teacher
Effects....see Influence
Efficacy...see Competence/Feeling, IE-con-
              trol
Embedded...see Figure
Emotional states
         ...see Affective-states, Emotion
Emotionality
         ...see Emotion
Exhibition
         ...see Expression, Expressiveness
Experimenter/Bias
         ...see Experimenter/Influence
Experimenter/Effects
         ...see Experimenter/Influence
Exploitation
         ...see Machaivellianism
External...see IE-control
Extropunitive
         ...see Punitiveness

Father.....see Paternal
Feelings...see Affective-states, Emotion
Future-oriented
         ...see Future/Orientation

Helplessness
         ...see Alienation, Anomie, Power-
              lessness
Hidden.....see Figure
Homicide...see Delinquency
Honesty....see Conscience, Guilt, Respon-
              sibility/Social
Hopelessness
         ...see Alienation, Anomie, Power-
              lessness
Hypnotizability
         ...see Hypnosis/Suggestibility

Ideological
         ...see Ideology
Impoverishment
         ...see Deprivation
Impulsivity
         ...see Impulsiveness
Incongruence
         ...see Consistency, Discrepancy
Inconsistency
         ...see Consistency
Independence
         ...see Autonomy, Dependence
Inner-life
         ...see Fantasy

Insecurity
          ...see Security
Instrumentality
          ...see Control/Locus
Integrative
          ...see Integration
Internal...see IE-control
Internalization
          ...see Acculturation, Autonomy
Intolerance
          ...see Tolerance
Intropunitive
          ...see Punitiveness
Inventiveness
          ...see Creativity, Originality
Irritation
          ...see Affective-states/Negative,
              Aggression, Hostility, Ir-
              ritability, Resentment

Loneliness
          ...see Alienation, Belongingness
Love.......see Affection
Loyalty....see Affiliation, Autonomy, Sup-
              port

Manic......see Mental-illness, Neuroticism
Marlowe-Crowne
          ...see Desirability/Social
Marriage...see Marital
Mental.....see Cognitive, Mental-health,
              Mental-illness, Thinking
Mirth......see Humor
Monetary...see Financial
Mores......see Norms, Values
Mother.....see Maternal
Motivation
          ...see Motive, Need

Neurosis...see Neuroticism
Non-conformity
          ...see Conformity

Obligation
          ...see Responsibility
Occupational
          ...see Job
Open-mindedness
          ...see Authoritarianism, Dogmatism,
              Flexibility, Openness, Rig-
              idity
Other-oriented
          ...see Orientation/Others

Patriotism
          ...see Internationalism, Nationalism
Person-environment fit
          ...see PE-fit
Playing....see Behavior, Enactment
Politico-economic
          ...see Political
Position...see Order, Power, Status
Pride......see Esteem/Self, Evaluation/Self
Primary....see Elementary, Primary-process
Process....see Interaction, Primary-process
Psychiatric/Diagnostic categories
          ...see Mental-illness

Rating-scale
          ...see Rating
Rejection
          ...see Affiliation, Support
Relations
          ...see Relationship
Religiousity
          ...see Orientation/Religion
Religious
          ...see Religion
Role-playing
          ...see Enactment/Role

Safety.....see Security
Scholastic
          ...see Academic
Semantic...see Sem-differential
Sense of...
          ...see Feeling
Separation
          ...see Affiliation, Distance
Simplicity
          ...see Complexity
Social/Class
          ...see Status
Socialization
          ...see Acculturation
State......see Affective-states
Stereotyping
          ...see Stereotype
Strength...see Intensity
Superego...see Conscience
Supportiveness
          ...see Affiliation, Support
Susceptibility
          ...see Suggestibility

Underachievement
          ...see Achievement

Width......see Breadth
Wit........see Humor
Work.......see Job, Vocational
Worth......see Esteem, Evaluation

4

PRIMARY REFERENCES

A-1   AARONSON, B. S.
             A COMPARISON OF TWO MMPI MEASURES OF MASCULINITY-FEMININITY.
             JOURNAL OF CLINICAL PSYCHOLOGY, 1959, 15, 48-50.
             (AARONSON MF INDEX)*
         @A-1 MASCULINITY FEMININITY SELF-IDENTITY SUB-IDENTITY ROLE PERCEPTION SEX 1959M
             (APPLICATIONS: 2540)

A-2   ABE, C., HOLLAND, J. L., LUTZ, S. W., & RICHARDS, J. M., JR.
             A DESCRIPTION OF AMERICAN COLLEGE FRESHMAN.
             IOWA CITY: AMERICAN COLLEGE TESTING PROGRAM, 1965.
             (LIFE GOALS: 35 ITEMS FROM AMERICAN COLLEGE SURVEY)
         @A-2 LIFE GOALS SELF-IDENTITY VALUES IDEALS COLLEGE 1965M
             (APPLICATIONS: 1433   1466   1515   2750)

A-4   ADCOCK, N. V., & ADCOCK, C. J.
             A FACTORIAL STUDY OF THE EGO REFERENCE SYSTEM.
             JOURNAL OF GENETIC PSYCHOLOGY, 1967, 110, 105-115.
             (EGO-INTEGRATION QUESTIONNAIRE)*
         @A-4 SELF CONCEPT EGO INTEGRATION CONTROL COPING-DEFENSE EGO-STRENGTH IDEAL
         @A-4 EGO-RESILIENCY OTHER-CATEGORY SELF-IDENTITY IMAGE 1967M

A-5   ADORNO, T. W., FRENKEL-BRUNSWICK, E., LEVINSON, D. J., & SANFORD, R. N.
             THE AUTHORITARIAN PERSONALITY. NEW YORK: HARPER, 1950.
             (CALIFORNIA F-SCALE)*
         @A-5 AUTHORITARIANISM COPING-DEFENSE OTHER-CATEGORY AFFECTIVE-STATES DOGMATISM
         @A-5 RIGIDITY FLEXIBILITY 1950M
             (APPLICATIONS: See page 361)

A-6   ALLPORT, G. W., & ALLPORT, F. H.
             THE A-S REACTION STUDY: A SCALE FOR MEASURING ASCENDENCE-SUBMISSION IN
             PERSONALITY.
             BOSTON:HOUGHTON MIFFLIN, 1928.
             (A-S REACTION STUDY)*
         @A-6 1928M DOMINANCE ASCENDENCE SUBMISSION AUTONOMY NEED
             (APPLICATIONS: 56   170   398   521)

A-7   ALLPORT, G. W., VERNON, P. E., & LINDZEY, G.
             STUDY OF VALUES (REV. ED.).
             CAMBRIDGE, MASSACHUSETTS:RIVERSIDE PRESS, 1951.
             (ALLPORT-VERNON-LINDZEY SCALE OF VALUES)*
         @A-7 VALUES SELF IDENTITY IDEALS LIFE GOALS ORIENTATION POLITICAL RELIGION
         @DEVELOPMENT 1951M
             (APPLICATIONS: 96   102   320   355   398   430   587   603   790   823
                              943   1170   1225   1244   1282   1289   1302   1339   1354   1380
                             1400   1841   2336   2356   2589   2651   2810   2903   2924)

A-8   ALPERT, R., & HABER, R. N.
             ANXIETY IN ACADEMIC ACHIEVEMENT SITUATIONS.
             JOURNAL OF ABNORMAL AND SOCIAL PSYCHOLOGY, 1960, 61, 207-215.
             (ACHIEVEMENT-ANXIETY TEST)*
         @A-8 ACHIEVEMENT ANXIETY AFFECTIVE-STATES SUBJECTIVE STRESS AUTONOMY NEED
         @A-8 TEST ACADEMIC 1960M
             (APPLICATIONS: 156   160   185   285   384   399   461   512   559   584
                              766   783   908   913   1484   1507   1531   1744   2171   2329
                             2345   2528   2761   2862   2879   2931)

A-9   ANANT, S. S.
             BELONGINGNESS AND MENTAL HEALTH: SOME RESEARCH FINDINGS.
             ACTA PSYCHOLOGICA, 1967, 26, 391-396.
             (MEASURE OF BELONGINGNESS)
         @A-9 BELONGINGNESS AUTONOMY AFFILIATION NEED OTHERS ORIENTATION AFFECTIVE-STATES
         @A-9 OTHER-CATEGORY 1967M

A-10   ALTROCCHI, J., PARSONS, O. A., & DICKOFF, H.
            CHANGES IN SELF-IDEAL DISCREPANCY IN REPRESSORS AND SENSITIZERS.
            JOURNAL OF ABNORMAL AND SOCIAL PSYCHOLOGY, 1960, 61, 67-72.
            (MEASURE OF REPRESSION-SENSITIZATION)
        @A-10 REPRESSION SENSITIZATION COPING-DEFENSE GLOBAL ADJUSTMENT RESPONSE-BIAS
        @A-10 1960M

A-11   ANASTASIOW, N. S.
            SUCCESS IN SCHOOL AND BOYS' SEX ROLE PATTERNS.
            CHILD DEVELOPMENT, 1965, 36, 1053-1066.
            (GROUP TOY PREFERENCE TEST)*
        @A-11 SEX ROLE SELF-IDENTITY AFFECTIVE-STATES ALIENATION ROLE PERCEPTION
        @A-11 SUB-IDENTITY CHILD MASCULINITY FEMININITY 1965M

A-12   ANDERSON, N. H.
            LIKEABLENESS RATINGS OF 555 PERSONALITY TRAIT ADJECTIVES.
            UNPUBLISHED MIMEO, UNIVERSITY OF CALIFORNIA, LOS ANGELES, 1964.
        ANDERSON, N. H.
            LIKEABLENESS RATINGS OF 555 PERSONALITY-TRAIT WORDS.
            JOURNAL OF PERSONALITY AND SOCIAL PSYCHOLOGY, 1968, 9, 272-279.
            (LIKEABLENESS RATINGS OF TRAIT TERMS)
        @A-12 RATING TRAIT-TERMS RESPONSE-BIAS OTHER-CATEGORY 1968M
            (APPLICATIONS: 2497 2521 2786)

A-13   ANTLER, L., & ZARETSKY, H. H.
            NATIONAL CONSCIOUSNESS AMONG FOREIGN PHYSICIANS IN THE UNITED STATES: COR-
            RELATES IN ATTITUDE, ADJUSTMENT, PERSONALITY, AND DEMOGRAPHIC VARIABLES.
            JOURNAL OF SOCIAL PSYCHOLOGY, 1967, 71, 209-220.
            (AFFILIATE SCALE)*
        @A-13 NATIONAL ADJUSTMENT SELF-IDENTITY OTHER-CATEGORY AWARENESS NATIONALISM
        @A-13 IDENTIFICATION CULTURE ATTITUDE AFFILIATION NEED 1967M

A-14   ARONFREED, J.
            THE NATURE, VARIETY, AND SOCIAL PATTERNING OF MORAL RESPONSES TO TRANS-
            GRESSION.
            JOURNAL OF ABNORMAL AND SOCIAL PSYCHOLOGY, 1961, 63, 223-240.
            (PROJECTIVE STORY COMPLETION TEST OF MORAL RESPONSES)
        @A-14 VALUES MORAL SELF-IDENTITY IDEALS LIFE GOALS PROJECTIVE ORIENTATION
        @A-14 AFFECTIVE-STATES DEVELOPMENT 1961M
            (APPLICATIONS: 2179)

A-15   ADORNO, T. W., FRENKEL-BRUNSWICK, E., LEVINSON, D. J., & SANFORD, R. N.
            THE AUTHORITARIAN PERSONALITY. NEW YORK: HARPER, 1950.
            (ANTI-SEMITISM SCALE)*
        @A-15 AUTHORITARIANISM RACIAL PREJUDICE ATTITUDE COPING-DEFENSE OTHER-CATEGORY
        @A-15 1950M
            (APPLICATIONS: 115   119   163   197   590   637   671   747   770   872)

A-16   ASCH, M. J.
            THE RELATIONSHIP OF NEGATIVE RESPONSE BIAS TO PERSONALITY.
            DISSERTATION ABSTRACTS, 1957, 17, 1704.
            (SPEED OF DECISION TEST)*
        @A-16 RESPONSE-BIAS MALINGERING DECISION 1957M
            (APPLICATIONS: 26)

A-17   ADORNO, T. W., FRENKEL-BRUNSWICK, E., LEVINSON, D. J., & SANFORD, R. N.
            THE AUTHORITARIAN PERSONALITY. NEW YORK: HARPER, 1950.
            (ETHNOCENTRISM SCALE)*
        @A-17 ETHNOCENTRISM AUTHORITARIANISM COPING-DEFENSE ATTITUDE NATIONALISM 1950M
            (APPLICATIONS: 53   144   218   571   647   670   752 2830 2960)

A-18   ASTIN, A. W.
            THE INVENTORY OF COLLEGE ACTIVITIES (ICA): ASSESSING THE COLLEGE ENVIRON-
            MENT THROUGH OBSERVABLE EVENTS.
            PAPER PRESENTED AT THE MEETING OF THE AMERICAN PSYCHOLOGICAL ASSOCIATION,
            CHICAGO, SEPTEMBER, 1965.
            (INVENTORY OF COLLEGE ACTIVITIES)*
        @A-18 PE-FIT COLLEGE ENVIRONMENT ACTIVITIES 1965M
            (APPLICATIONS: 2702)

A-19   ACHENBACH, T., & ZIGLER, E.
              SOCIAL COMPETENCE AND SELF-IMAGE DISPARITY IN PSYCHIATRIC AND NON-PSYCHIA-
              TRIC PATIENTS.
              JOURNAL OF ABNORMAL AND SOCIAL PSYCHOLOGY, 1963, 67, 197-205.
              (SELF IMAGE DISPARITY SCORE)
          aA-19 ADJUSTMENT SOCIAL COMPETENCE SELF-IDENTITY SELF IMAGE DISCREPANCY CONCEPT
          aA-19 PERCEPTION 1963M

A-20   AUMACK, L.
              A SOCIAL ADJUSTMENT BEHAVIOR RATING SCALE.
              JOURNAL OF CLINICAL PSYCHOLOGY, 1962, 18, 436-441.
              (SOCIAL ADJUSTMENT BEHAVIOR RATING SCALE)*
          aA-20 ADJUSTMENT RATING SOCIAL COMPETENCE BEHAVIOR INTERPERSONAL PSYCHIATRIC
          aA-20 PATIENT RELATIONSHIPS MENTAL-ILLNESS 1962M
              (APPLICATIONS: 2741)

A-21   AAS, A., O'HARA, J. W., & MUNGER, M. P.
              THE MEASUREMENT OF SUBJECTIVE EXPERIENCES PRESUMABLY RELATED TO HYPNOTIC
              SUSCEPTIBILITY.
              SCANDINAVIAN JOURNAL OF PSYCHOLOGY, 1962, 3, 47-64.
              (SUBJECTIVE EXPERIENCES INVENTORY)*
          aA-21 SELF PERCEPTION ESTEEM SELF-IDENTITY HYPNOTIC SUGGESTIBILITY SUBJECTIVE
          aA-21 EXPERIENCE 1962M
              (APPLICATIONS: 178)

A-22   AGGER, R. E., GOLDSTEIN, M. N., & PEARL, S. A.
              POLITICAL CYNICISM: MEASUREMENT AND MEANING.
              JOURNAL OF POLITICS, 1961, 23, 477-506.
              (POLITICAL CYNICISM SCALE)*
          aA-22 POLITICAL CYNICISM AFFECTIVE-STATES ALIENATION OTHER-CATEGORY ORIENTATION
          aA-22 GLOBAL 1961M
              (APPLICATIONS: 111)

A-23   ALLPORT, G. W., & KRAMER, B. M.
              SOME ROOTS OF PREJUDICE.
              JOURNAL OF PSYCHOLOGY, 1946, 22, 9-39.
              (PREJUDICE SCALE)*
          aA-23 PREJUDICE AFFECTIVE-STATES OTHER-CATEGORY RACIAL ETHNIC 1946M
              (APPLICATIONS: 119)

A-24   ALLPORT, G. W., & ROSS, J. M.
              PERSONAL RELIGIOUS ORIENTATION AND PREJUDICE.
              JOURNAL OF PERSONALITY AND SOCIAL PSYCHOLOGY, 1967, 5, 432-443.
              (RELIGIOUS ORIENTATION MEASURE)
          aA-24 EXTRINSIC INTRINSIC RELIGION PREJUDICE AUTONOMY MOTIVE ORIENTATION 1967M

A-25   ATTNEAVE, F.
              APPLICATIONS OF INFORMATION THEORY TO PSYCHOLOGY.
              NEW YORK: HOLT, 1959.
              (DISCRIMINABILITY MEASURE)
          aA-25 OTHER-CATEGORY ADJUSTMENT ENVIRONMENT PERCEPTION RESPONSE-BIAS BREADTH
          aA-25 DIFFERENTIATION CONCEPTUAL COGNITIVE STRUCTURE FUNCTIONING 1959M

A-26   ALEXANDER, S., & HUSEK, T. R.
              THE ANXIETY DIFFERENTIAL: INITIAL STEPS IN THE DEVELOPMENT OF A MEASURE OF
              SITUATIONAL ANXIETY.
              EDUCATIONAL AND PSYCHOLOGICAL MEASUREMENT, 1962, 22, 325-348.
              (ALEXANDER-HUSEK ANXIETY DIFFERENTIAL)*
          aA-26 ANXIETY SITUATIONAL AFFECTIVE-STATES SUBJECTIVE STRESS 1962M
              (APPLICATIONS: 252   820   990   1012   1072   1100   1139   1143   2082   2931)

A-27   AULD, F., GOLDENBERG, G. M., & WEISS, J. V.
              MEASUREMENT OF PRIMARY-PROCESS THINKING IN DREAM REPORTS.
              JOURNAL OF PERSONALITY AND SOCIAL PSYCHOLOGY, 1968, 8, 418-426.
              (PRIMARY-PROCESS THINKING RATING SCALE)
          aA-27 PRIMARY-PROCESS THINKING GLOBAL ADJUSTMENT RATING FANTASY IMAGERY 1968M

A-28   ARONSON, E.
              THE NEED FOR ACHIEVEMENT AS MEASURED BY GRAPHIC EXPRESSION.
              IN J. W. ATKINSON (ED.), MOTIVES IN FANTASY, ACTION, AND SOCIETY. PRINCE-
              TON: VAN NOSTRAND, 1958.
              (DOODLES: A GRAPHIC MEASURE OF NEED ACHIEVEMENT)
          aA-28 ACHIEVEMENT AUTONOMY NEED GRAPHIC EXPRESSION MOTIVE SELF 1958M
              (APPLICATIONS: 285   1368)

A-29   ADORNO, T. W., FRENKEL-BRUNSWIK, E., LEVINSON, D. J., & SANFORD, R. N.
             THE AUTHORITARIAN PERSONALITY.
             NEW YORK: HARPER, 1950.
             (POLITICAL AND ECONOMIC CONSERVATISM SCALE--PEC)*
         @A-29 LIBERALISM CONSERVATISM POLITICAL ORIENTATION 1950M
             (APPLICATIONS: 197   349   872   2489   2887)

A-30   ARNOLD, D. L., & MOONEY, R. L.
             A STUDENTS' PROBLEM CHECK LIST FOR JUNIOR HIGH SCHOOL.
             EDUCATIONAL RESEARCH BULLETIN, 1943, 22, 42-48.
             (MOONEY PROBLEM CHECK LIST)*
         @A-30 AFFECTIVE-STATES GLOBAL ADJUSTMENT SATISFACTION OTHER-CATEGORY PERCEPTION
         @A-30 SELF FAMILY TIME STUDENT PROBLEM CHECKLIST SECONDARY SCHOOL 1943M

A-31   ASTIN, A. W., & HOLLAND, J. L.
             THE ENVIRONMENTAL ASSESSMENT TECHNIQUE: A WAY TO MEASURE COLLEGE ENVIRON-
             MENTS.
             JOURNAL OF EDUCATIONAL PSYCHOLOGY, 1961, 52, 308-316.
             (ENVIRONMENTAL ASSESSMENT TECHNIQUE)*
         @A-31 ENVIRONMENT ADJUSTMENT PE-FIT COLLEGE 1961M
             (APPLICATIONS: 1305   2801)

A-32   ANKER, J. M.
             CHRONICITY OF NEUROPSYCHIATRIC HOSPITALIZATION: A PREDICTIVE SCALE.
             JOURNAL OF CONSULTING PSYCHOLOGY, 1961, 25, 425-432.
             (NEUROPSYCHIATRIC CHRONICITY SCALE)*
         @A-32 MMPI WARD HOSPITALIZATION PATIENT PREDICTION PSYCHIATRIC ADJUSTMENT
         @A-32 MENTAL-ILLNESS MENTAL-HEALTH 1961M
             (APPLICATIONS: 1844   2266)

A-33   APPERSON, L. B., & MCADOO, W. G., JR.
             PARENTAL FACTORS IN THE CHILDHOOD OF HOMOSEXUALS.
             JOURNAL OF ABNORMAL PSYCHOLOGY, 1968, 73, 201-206.
             (PERCEPTION OF PARENT BEHAVIOR SCALE)*
         @A-33 FAMILY INTERACTION ADJUSTMENT PERCEPTION PARENT-CHILD PARENTAL BEHAVIOR
         @A-33 1968M
             (APPLICATIONS: 1078)

A-34   ANDREWS, F. M., & FARRIS, G. F.
             SUPERVISORY PRACTICES AND INNOVATION IN SCIENTIFIC TEAMS.
             PERSONNEL PSYCHOLOGY, 1967, 20, 497-515.
             (MEASURES OF SUPERVISORY BEHAVIOR)
         @A-34 BEHAVIOR JOB ADJUSTMENT SUPERVISOR LEADERSHIP MANAGEMENT EMPLOYEE
         @A-34 SATISFACTION 1967M

A-35   ADELSON, J.
             A STUDY OF MINORITY GROUP AUTHORITARIANISM.
             JOURNAL OF ABNORMAL AND SOCIAL PSYCHOLOGY, 1953, 48, 477-485.
             (JEWISH AUTHORITARIANISM SCALE)*
         @A-35 AUTHORITARIANISM OTHER-CATEGORY COPING-DEFENSE AFFECTIVE-STATES
         @A-35 MINORITY GROUP ETHNIC ETHNOCENTRISM 1953M
             (APPLICATIONS: 770)

A-36   ANISFELD, M., MUNOZ, S., & LAMBERT, W.
             THE STRUCTURE AND DYNAMICS OF THE ETHNIC ATTITUDES OF JEWISH ADOLESCENTS.
             JOURNAL OF ABNORMAL AND SOCIAL PSYCHOLOGY, 1963, 66, 31-36.
             (EVALUATIONS OF SELF, MOTHER, FATHER)
         @A-36 SELF CONCEPT PARENTAL FAMILY INTERACTION ADJUSTMENT SELF-IDENTITY
         @A-36 EVALUATION PERCEPTION ESTEEM SEM-DIFFERENTIAL ETHNIC 1963M

A-37   ALTUS, W. D., & TAFEJIAN, T. T.
             MMPI CORRELATES OF THE CALIFORNIA E-F SCALE.
             JOURNAL OF SOCIAL PSYCHOLOGY, 1953, 38, 145-149.
             (MMPI ITEMS ASSOCIATED WITH AUTHORITARIANISM-ETHNOCENTRISM)
         @A-37 AUTHORITARIANISM ETHNOCENTRISM AFFECTIVE-STATES OTHER-CATEGORY MMPI
         @A-37 F-SCALE 1953M
             (APPLICATIONS: 821   2824)

A-38   ALLEN, V. L., & LEVINE, J. M.
             CREATIVITY AND CONFORMITY.
             JOURNAL OF PERSONALITY, 1968, 36, 405-419.
             (TEST OF CONFORMITY FOR CHILDREN)
         @A-38 CONFORMITY AUTONOMY CREATIVITY CHILD 1968M

A-39   ASTIN, A. W.
               DIMENSIONS OF WORK SATISFACTION IN THE OCCUPATIONAL CHOICES OF COLLEGE
               FRESHMEN.
               JOURNAL OF APPLIED PSYCHOLOGY, 1958, 42, 187-190.
               (WORK SATISFACTION QUESTIONNAIRE)*
          @A-39 AFFECTIVE-STATES GLOBAL JOB SATISFACTION PE-FIT ADJUSTMENT 1958M

A-40   ALDERFER, C. P.
               DIFFERENTIAL IMPORTANCE OF HUMAN NEEDS AS A FUNCTION OF SATISFACTION
               OBTAINED IN THE ORGANIZATION.
               UNPUBLISHED DOCTORAL DISSERTATION, YALE UNIVERSITY, 1966.
          ALDERFER, C. P.
               CONVERGENT AND DISCRIMINATE VALIDATION OF SATISFACTION AND DESIRE
               MEASURES BY INTERVIEWS AND QUESTIONNAIRES.
               JOURNAL OF APPLIED PSYCHOLOGY, 1967, 51, 509-520.
               (JOB SATISFACTION SCALES)
          @A-40 1967M GLOBAL JOB SATISFACTION ADJUSTMENT NEED ENVIRONMENT PE-FIT

A-41   ADAMS, C. R.
               MANUAL OF DIRECTIONS FOR THE ADAMS PERSONAL AUDIT (FORM LL). CHICAGO:
               SCIENCE RESEARCH ASSOCIATION. 1945.
               (ADAMS PERSONAL AUDIT (FORM LL))*
          @A-41 MULTITRAIT EMOTION IRRITABILITY STABILITY TOLERANCE IMPULSE SATISFACTION
          @A-41 1945M

A-42   APPLEZWEIG, M. H., DIBNER, A. S., & OSBORNE, R. L.
               PEAQ: A MEASURE OF PSYCHOPATHIC BEHAVIOR.
               JOURNAL OF CLINICAL PSYCHOLOGY, 1958, 14, 26-30.
               (PERSONAL EXPERIENCE AND ATTITUDE QUESTIONNAIRE)*
          @A-42 PSYCHOPATHY GLOBAL ADJUSTMENT EXPERIENCE ATTITUDE PERSONAL MENTAL-ILLNESS
          @A-42 MENTAL-HEALTH EMOTION STABILITY SOCIAL COMPETENCE 1958M
               (APPLICATIONS: 1614 1766)

A-43   ALTUS, W. D.
               A COLLEGE ACHIEVER AND NON-ACHIEVER SCALE FOR THE MMPI.
               JOURNAL OF APPLIED PSYCHOLOGY, 1948, 32, 385-397.
               (HUMAN TRAIT INVENTORY)*
          @A-43 MULTITRAIT MMPI ACHIEVEMENT NEED AUTONOMY MOTIVE 1948M

A-44   ARMSTRONG, J. C.
               PERCEIVED INTIMATE FRIENDSHIP AS A QUASI-THERAPEUTIC AGENT.
               JOURNAL OF COUNSELING PSYCHOLOGY, 1969, 16, 137-141.
               (PROBLEM AREA INVENTORY)*
          @A-44 PROBLEM INVENTORY INTERPERSONAL SOCIAL ADJUSTMENT COMPETENCE 1969M

A-46   ANTLER, L.
               CORRELATES OF HOME AND HOST COUNTRY ACQUAINTANCESHIP AMONG FOREIGN MEDICAL
               RESIDENTS IN THE UNITED STATES.
               JOURNAL OF SOCIAL PSYCHOLOGY. 1970, 80, 49-57.
               (PERSONAL CONTACTS SCALES--UNITED STATES AND HOME COUNTRY)*
          @A-46 1970M NATIONAL AWARENESS RELATIONSHIPS PERSONAL

A-47   ANTLER, L.
               CORRELATES OF HOME AND HOST COUNTRY ACQUAINTANCESHIP AMONG FOREIGN MEDICAL
               RESIDENTS IN THE UNITED STATES.
               JOURNAL OF SOCIAL PSYCHOLOGY. 1970, 80, 49-57.
               (SATISFACTION SCALES)
          @A-47 1970M SATISFACTION ACADEMIC SUPERVISOR

A-48   ASHBY, J. D., FORD, D. H., GUERNEY, B. G., JR., GUERNEY, L. F., & SNYDER, W. U.
               EFFECTS ON CLIENTS OF A REFLECTIVE AND A LEADING TYPE OF PSYCHOTHERAPY.
               PSYCHOLOGICAL MONOGRAPHS, 1957, 71, (24 WHOLE NO. 453).
               (POST THERAPY RATING SCALE)
          @A-48 1957M THERAPY PATIENT COUNSELING EFFECTIVENESS
               (APPLICATIONS: 2310 2544 2935)

A-49   ADLER, P. T.
               EVALUATION OF THE FIGURE DRAWING TECHNIQUE: RELIABILITY, FACTORIAL
               STRUCTURE, AND DIAGNOSTIC USEFULNESS.
               JOURNAL OF CONSULTING AND CLINICAL PSYCHOLOGY, 1970, 35, 52-57.
               (FIGURE DRAWING TECHNIQUE)
          @A-49 1970M FIGURE GRAPHIC PERSON PERCEPTION BODY IMAGE MATURITY ADJUSTMENT

A-50   ALLEN, T. W.
            COUNSELORS IN TRAINING: A STUDY OF ROLE EFFECTIVENESS AS A FUNCTION OF
            PSYCHOLOGICAL OPENNESS.
            UNPUBLISHED DOCTORAL DISSERTATION, HARVARD UNIVERSITY, 1966.
            (SCORING SYSTEM FOR COUNSELOR RESPONSES)
        aA-50 1966M COUNSELING RESPONSE BEHAVIOR THERAPIST INTERACTION VERBAL

A-51   ANZEL, A. S.
            A-B TYPING AND PATIENT SOCIOECONOMIC AND PERSONALITY CHARACTERISTICS
            IN A QUASI-THERAPEUTIC SITUATION.
            JOURNAL OF CONSULTING AND CLINICAL PSYCHOLOGY, 1970, 35, 102-115.
            (MEASURE OF FAVORABILITY)
        aA-51 1970M PATIENT THERAPY ATTITUDE RELATIONSHIPS

A-54   ALTROCCHI, J., & PERLITSH, H.
            EGO CONTROL PATTERNS AND ATTRIBUTION OF HOSTILITY.
            PSYCHOLOGICAL REPORTS, 1963, 12, 811-818.
            (EXPRESSOR INDEX)
        aA-54 1963M HOSTILITY EXPRESSION IMPULSE CONTROL MMPI INTERPERSONAL PERCEPTION
            (APPLICATIONS: 462   467)

A-55   ATKINSON, J. W., & O'CONNOR, P.
            EFFECTS OF ABILITY GROUPINGS IN SCHOOLS RELATED TO INDIVIDUAL DIFFERENCES
            IN ACHIEVEMENT-RELATED MOTIVATION.
            COOPERATIVE RESEARCH PROJECT NO. 1283. ANN ARBOR: UNIVERSITY OF
            MICHIGAN, 1963.
            (ACHIEVEMENT RISK PREFERENCE SCALE)
        aA-55 1963M ACHIEVEMENT RISK SUCCESS FAILURE MOTIVE PREFERENCE
            (APPLICATIONS: 504)

A-56   ALLERHAND, M. E., GOUGH, H. G., & GRAIS, M. L.
            PERSONALITY FACTORS IN NEURODERMATITIS: A PRELIMINARY STUDY.
            PSYCHOSOMATIC MEDICINE, 1950, 12, 386-390.
            (MEASURE OF MANIFEST HOSTILITY: NE SCALE)
        aA-56 1950M AFFECTIVE-STATES HOSTILITY PATIENT MANIFEST
        aA-56 RIGIDITY SEX AGGRESSION
            (APPLICATIONS: 1576)

A-57   ALLISON, R. B., JR.
            A TWO DIMENSIONAL SEMANTIC DIFFERENTIAL.
            JOURNAL OF CONSULTING PSYCHOLOGY, 1963, 27, 18-23.
            (TWO DIMENSIONAL SEMANTIC DIFFERENTIAL)
        aA-57 1963M SEM-DIFFERENTIAL PSYCHOPATHOLOGY

A-58   ANKER, J. M.
            CHRONICITY OF NEUROPSYCHIATRIC HOSPITALIZATION: A PRÉDICTIVE SCALE.
            JOURNAL OF CONSULTING PSYCHOLOGY, 1961, 25, 425-432.
            (SCALE TO PREDICT LENGTH OF HOSPITALIZATION FOR PSYCHIATRIC PATIENTS)
        aA-58 1961M MENTAL-ILLNESS PATIENT HOSPITALIZATION PROGNOSIS
        aA-58 PSYCHOPATHOLOGY MMPI

A-59   ACHENBACH, T. M.
            THE CLASSIFICATION OF CHILDREN'S PSYCHIATRIC SYMPTOMS: A FACTOR ANALYTIC
            STUDY.
            PSYCHOLOGICAL MONOGRAPHS, 1966, 80 (7, WHOLE NO. 615).
            (CHILD PSYCHIATRIC SYMPTOM CHECKLIST)
        aA-59 1966M SYMPTOM CHECKLIST CHILD PSYCHIATRIC BEHAVIOR ATTITUDE DEVIANCE
            (APPLICATIONS: 2303)

A-60   APPELBAUM, S.
            AUTOMATIC AND VOLITIONAL PROCESSES IN THE VERBAL RESPONSES OF BRAIN-
            DAMAGED AND NORMAL SUBJECTS.
            UNPUBLISHED DOCTORAL DISSERTATION, BOSTON UNIVERSITY, 1958.
            (MENTAL SET SHIFTING TEST)
        aA-60 1958M COGNITIVE FLEXIBILITY RIGIDITY SET
            (APPLICATIONS: 565)

A-61   ALEXANDER, J. F., & ABELES, N.
            DEPENDENCY CHANGES IN PSYCHOTHERAPY AS RELATED TO INTERPERSONAL
            RELATIONSHIPS.
            JOURNAL OF CONSULTING AND CLINICAL PSYCHOLOGY, 1968, 32, 685-689.
            (THERAPY INTERVIEWS SCORED FOR DEPENDENCY)
        aA-61 1968M THERAPY COUNSELING DEPENDENCE INTERPERSONAL RELATIONSHIPS

A-63   APPLEZWEIG, M. H., DIBNER, A. S., & OSBORNE, R. L.
                PEAQ: A MEASURE OF PSYCHOPATHIC BEHAVIOR.
                JOURNAL OF CLINICAL PSYCHOLOGY, 1958, 14, 26-30.
                (BEHAVIOR DISTURBANCE INVENTORY)
            @A-63 1958M BEHAVIOR NORMALITY PSYCHOPATHY MENTAL-ILLNESS
            @A-63 DEVIANCE PSYCHIATRIC DIAGNOSIS
                (APPLICATIONS: 726)

A-64   ANISFELD, M., & LAMBERT, W. E.
                SOCIAL AND PSYCHOLOGICAL VARIABLES IN LEARNING HEBREW.
                JOURNAL OF ABNORMAL AND SOCIAL PSYCHOLOGY, 1961, 63, 524-529.
                (JEWISH ORIENTATION INDEX)
            @A-64 1961M ORIENTATION ETHNIC RACIAL INTEGRATION CULTURE
            @A-64 RELIGION

A-66   ANISFELD, M., MUNOZ, S. R., & LAMBERT, W. E.
                THE STRUCTURE AND DYNAMICS OF THE ETHNIC ATTITUDES OF JEWISH ADOLESCENTS.
                JOURNAL OF ABNORMAL AND SOCIAL PSYCHOLOGY, 1963, 66, 31-36.
                (ANTI-GENTILISM SCALE)
            @A-66 1963M PREJUDICE RACIAL ETHNIC
            @A-66 RELIGION

A-67   ABELSON, R. P., & LESSER, G. S.
                THE MEASUREMENT OF PERSUASIBILITY IN CHILDREN.
                IN C. I. HOVLAND & I. L. JANIS (EDS.), PERSONALITY AND PERSUASIBILITY.
                NEW HAVEN: YALE UNIVERSITY PRESS, 1959, 141-166.
                (PERSUASIBILITY BOOKLET MEASURE)
            @A-67 1959M PERSUABILITY INFLUENCE GRAPHIC OPENNESS ATTITUDE CHANGE
                (APPLICATIONS: 796)

A-68   ABELSON, R. P., & LESSER, G. S.
                THE MEASUREMENT OF PERSUASIBILITY IN CHILDREN.
                IN C. I. HOVLAND & I. L. JANIS (EDS.), PERSONALITY AND PERSUASIBILITY.
                NEW HAVEN: YALE UNIVERSITY PRESS, 1959, 141-166.
                (MOTHER PERSUASIBILITY MEASURE)
            @A-68 1959M PERSUASIBILITY CONFORMITY OPENNESS ATTITUDE CHANGE
                (APPLICATIONS: 796)

A-69   AS, A., O'HARA, J. W., & MUNGER, M. P.
                THE MEASUREMENT OF SUBJECTIVE EXPERIENCES PRESUMABLY RELATED TO HYPNOTIC
                SUSCEPTIBILITY.
                SCANDINAVIAN JOURNAL OF PSYCHOLOGY, 1962, 3, 47-64.
                (EXPERIENCE INVENTORY)
            @A-69 1962M HYPNOTIC SUGGESTIBILITY EXPERIENCE SUBJECTIVE INTERPERSONAL
            @A-69 RELATIONSHIPS TRUST EGO CONTROL ROLE PLAYING
                (APPLICATIONS: 777)

A-70   ASTIN, A. W.
                A FACTOR STUDY OF THE MMPI PSYCHOPATHIC DEVIATE SCALE.
                JOURNAL OF CONSULTING PSYCHOLOGY, 1959, 23, 550-554.
                (SOCIAL MALADAPTATION SCALE)
            @A-70 1959M SOCIAL ADJUSTMENT COMPETENCE
            @A-70 DEVIANCE
                (APPLICATIONS: 680)

A-71   ALLINSMITH, W.
                THE LEARNING OF MORAL STANDARDS.
                IN D. R. MILLER & G. E. SWANSON (EDS.), INNER CONFLICT AND DEFENSE,
                NEW YORK: HOLT, 1960, PP. 141-176.
                (MEASURE OF GUILT)
            @A-71 1960M ATTRIBUTION GUILT ACCEPTANCE RESPONSIBILITY
            @A-71 STORY-COMPLETION MORAL VALUES
                (APPLICATIONS: 806   2179)

A-72   ARONSON, H., & WEINTRAUB, W.
                PATIENT CHANGES DURING CLASSICAL PSYCHOANALYSIS AS A FUNCTION OF
                INITIAL STATUS AND DURATION OF TREATMENT.
                PSYCHIATRY, 1968, 31, 369-379.
                (MEASURES OF SYMPTOMATIC STATUS AND LEVEL OF FUNCTIONING)
            @A-72 1968M THERAPY COUNSELING PATIENT SYMPTOM CHANGE ADJUSTMENT INTERPERSONAL
            @A-72 RELATIONSHIPS FEELING EMOTION FUNCTIONING SOCIAL
                (APPLICATIONS: 1147)

A-73   ACHENBACH, T.
            CUE LEARNING, ASSOCIATIVE RESPONDING, AND SCHOOL PERFORMANCE IN CHILDREN.
            DEVELOPMENTAL PSYCHOLOGY, 1969, 1, 717-725.
            (CHILDREN'S ASSOCIATIVE RESPONDING TEST (CART))*
        aA-73 1969M CHILD INTELLIGENCE THINKING STYLE FREE ASSOCIATION COGNITIVE
            (APPLICATIONS: 2788)

A-74   ARMITAGE, S. G.
            AN ANALYSIS OF CERTAIN PSYCHOLOGICAL TESTS USED FOR THE EVALUATION OF BRAIN
            INJURY. ‘
            PSYCHOLOGICAL MONOGRAPHS, 1946, 60, (1 WHOLE NO. 277).
        REITAN, R. M.
            THE VALIDITY OF THE TRAIL MAKING TEST AS AN INDICATOR OF ORGANIC BRAIN
            DAMAGE.
            PERCEPTUAL AND MOTOR SKILLS, 1958, 8, 271-276.
            (TRAIL MAKING TEST)*
        aA-74 1946M MENTAL-ILLNESS DIAGNOSIS PSYCHIATRIC
            (APPLICATIONS: 939)

A-75   ASHER, J. J.
            RELIABILITY OF A NOVEL FORMAT FOR THE SELECTION INTERVIEW.
            PSYCHOLOGICAL REPORTS, 1970, 26, 451-456.
            (Q BY Q SELECTION INTERVIEW)
        aA-75 1970M INTERVIEW JOB SUCCESS PREDICTION ADJUSTMENT ABILITY ACHIEVEMENT

A-77   ALLEN, T. W.
            EFFECTIVENESS OF COUNSELOR TRAINNEES AS A FUNCTION OF PSYCHOLOGICAL
            OPENNESS.
            JOURNAL OF COUNSELING PSYCHOLOGY, 1967, 14, 35-40.
            (RESPONSE TO CLIENT AFFECT SCALE)
        aA-77 1967M COUNSELING THERAPY RELATIONSHIPS SENSITIVITY EMOTION

A-78   ALLEN, T. W.
            EFFECTIVENESS OF COUNSELOR TRAINNEES AS A FUNCTION OF PSYCHOLOGICAL
            OPENNESS.
            JOURNAL OF COUNSELING PSYCHOLOGY, 1967, 14, 35-40.
            (RESPONSIVENESS TO FEELING SCALE)
        aA-78 1967M COUNSELING THERAPY RELATIONSHIPS SENSITIVITY EMOTION
        aPATIENT RESPONSE EXPRESSION THERAPIST

A-82   ANDERSON, R. P., & ANDERSON, G. V.
            THE DEVELOPMENT OF AN INSTRUMENT FOR MEASURING RAPPORT.
            TESTING AND GUIDANCE BUREAU, UNIVERSITY OF TEXAS, 1954, 1, 1-15.
            (COMMUNICATION RATING SCALE)
        aA-82 1954M COMMUNICATION RATING COUNSELING THERAPY RELATIONSHIPS INTERACTION
            (APPLICATIONS: 1191)

A-83   APFELBAUM, B.
            DIMENSIONS OF TRANSFERENCE IN PSYCHOTHERAPY.
            BERKELEY: UNIVERSITY OF CALIFORNIA PRESS, 1958.
            (COUNSELOR ROLE PERCEPTION Q-SORT)
        aA-83 1958M COUNSELING ROLE PERCEPTION Q-SORT THERAPIST
            (APPLICATIONS: 1318)

A-84   ANDERSON, R. P., & ANDERSON, C. V.
            DEVELOPMENT OF AN INSTRUMENT FOR MEASURING RAPPORT.
            PERSONNEL AND GUIDANCE JOURNAL, 1962, 41, 18-24.
            (INTERVIEW RATING SCALE)*
        aA-84 1962M RATING COUNSELING PATIENT RELATIONSHIPS COMMUNICATION INTERVIEW
            (APPLICATIONS: 1330 1398)

A-85   AINSWORTH, M. D., & AINSWORTH, L. H.
            MEASURING SECURITY IN PERSONAL ADJUSTMENT.
            TORONTO: UNIVERSITY OF TORONTO, 1958.
            (TEST OF SECURITY IN PERSONAL ADJUSTMENT)
        aA-85 1958M SECURITY ADJUSTMENT GLOBAL PERSONAL FAMILY DEPENDENCE MATURITY
            (APPLICATIONS: 1263)

A-86   ARMER, M., & YOUTZ, R.
            FORMAL EDUCATION AND INDIVIDUAL MODERNITY IN AN AFRICAN SOCIETY.
            AMERICAN JOURNAL OF SOCIOLOGY, 1971, 76, 604-626.
            (MEASURE OF MODERN VALUE ORIENTATIONS)
        aA-86 1971M VALUES ORIENTATION BELIEF TRUST FUTURE FAMILY DEPENDENCE RACIAL SEX
        aOPENNESS NOVELTY PRESENT PAST

A-87   ALEXANDER, S. A., & DRUCKER, E. H.
            THE EFFECTS OF EXPERIMENTALLY MODIFIED INTERPERSONAL PERCEPTIONS ON SOCIAL
            BEHAVIOR AND ADJUSTMENT.
            (INTERIM TECHNICAL REPORT NO. 9. INTERPERSONAL PERCEPTION AND THE
            PSYCHOLOGICAL ADJUSTMENT OF GROUP MEMBERS. CONTRACT DA-49-193-MD-2060.)
            URBANA: CENTER FOR RESEARCH IN SOCIAL PSYCHOLOGY, GROUP EFFECTIVENESS
            RESEARCH LABORATORY, DEPARTMENT OF PSYCHOLOGY, UNIVERSITY OF ILLINOIS,
            1960.
            (MEASURE OF LIKING FOR EXPERIMENTAL PARTNER)
            ƏA-87 1960M INTERPERSONAL PERCEPTION ATTRACTION

A-88   APOSTAL, R. A., & MILLER, J. C.
            A MANUAL FOR USE OF A SET OF DIAGNOSTIC CATEGORIES.
            (UNIVERSITY TESTING AND COUNSELING SERVICE REPORT NO. 21)
            COLUMBIA: UNIVERSITY OF MISSOURI, 1959.
            (DIAGNOSTIC CLASSIFICATION SYSTEM)
            ƏA-88 1959M DIAGNOSIS COUNSELING PROBLEM GOALS PSYCHIATRIC
                (APPLICATIONS: 1154)

A-90   ALTUCHER, N.
            CONFLICT IN SEX IDENTIFICATION IN BOYS.
            UNPUBLISHED DOCTORAL DISSERTATION, UNIVERSITY OF MICHIGAN, 1956.
            (MEASURE OF DOMINANCE IN DISCIPLINE)
            ƏA-90 1956M PARENTAL DOMINANCE SEX MATERNAL PATERNAL CHILD IDENTIFICATION ROLE
                (APPLICATIONS: 97)

A-92·   ANDERSON, N. H.
            LIKEABLENESS RATINGS OF 555 PERSONALITY-TRAIT ADJECTIVES.
            UNPUBLISHED MANUSCRIPT, UNIVERSITY OF CALIFORNIA, LOS ANGELES, 1964.
            (PERSONALITY-TRAIT ADJECTIVES RATED FOR LIKEABLENESS)
            ƏA-92 1964M TRAIT-TERMS EVALUATION ATTITUDE DESIRABILITY RATING
                (APPLICATIONS: 273)

A-93   ASCH, S. E.
            FORMING IMPRESSIONS OF PERSONALITY.
            JOURNAL OF ABNORMAL AND SOCIAL PSYCHOLOGY, 1946, 41, 258-290.
            (TRAIT CHECK LISTS)
            ƏA-93 1946M INTERPERSONAL PERCEPTION TRAIT-TERMS CHECKLIST
                (APPLICATIONS: 882)

A-94   ARON, B.
            A MANUAL FOR ANALYSIS OF THE THEMATIC APPERCEPTION TEST.
            BERKELEY, CALIFORNIA: WILLIS E. BERG, 1949.
            (TAT SCORING SYSTEM)
            ƏA-94 1949M TAT PROJECTIVE
                (APPLICATIONS: 894 1774)

A-97   ARONOFF, J.
            PSYCHOLOGICAL NEEDS AND CULTURAL SYSTEMS.
            PRINCETON, N. J.: VAN NOSTRAND, 1967.
            ARONOFF, J.
            PSYCHOLOGICAL NEEDS AS A DETERMINANT IN THE FORMATION OF ECONOMIC
            STRUCTURES: A CONFIRMATION.
            HUMAN RELATIONS, 1970, 23, 123-138.
            (SENTENCE COMPLETION PERSONALITY TEST OF MASLOW'S NEED LEVELS)
            ƏA-97 1967M SENTENCE-COMP ESTEEM ORIENTATION SECURITY
            ƏSELF AFFECTION ACTUALIZATION INVENTORY NEED SATISFACTION

A-98   ALBEE, G. W., & HAMLIN, R. M.
            AN INVESTIGATION OF THE RELIABILITY AND VALIDITY OF JUDGMENTS OF
            ADJUSTMENT INFERRED FROM DRAWINGS.
            JOURNAL OF CLINICAL PSYCHOLOGY, 1949, 5, 389-392.
            (SCORING OF DRAW-A-PERSON TEST FOR ADJUSTMENT)
            ƏA-98 1949M ADJUSTMENT PROJECTIVE FIGURE GRAPHIC MENTAL-HEALTH MENTAL-ILLNESS

A-99   ANDERSON, W., KUNCE, J., & BAXTER, J.
            MAZE SCORE AND JOB PERFORMANCE IN PSYCHIATRIC PATIENTS.
            JOURNAL OF COUNSELING PSYCHOLOGY, 1962, 9, 173-175.
            (JOB PERFORMANCE RATING SCALE)*
            ƏA-99 1962M JOB PERFORMANCE SOCIAL RELATIONSHIPS INTERPERSONAL
            ƏJUDGMENT PSYCHIATRIC SYMPTOM PATIENT

A-100   ALDERFER, C. P.
              DIFFERENTIAL IMPORTANCE OF HUMAN NEEDS AS A FUNCTION OF SATISFACTIONS
              OBTAINED IN THE ORGANIZATION.
              UNPUBLISHED DOCTORAL DISSERTATION, YALE UNIVERSITY, 1966.
          ALDERFER, C. P.
              CONVERGENT AND DISCRIMINANT VALIDATION OF SATISFACTION AND DESIRE
              MEASURES BY INTERVIEWS AND QUESTIONNAIRES.
              JOURNAL OF APPLIED PSYCHOLOGY, 1967, 51, 509-520.
              (JOB SATISFACTION INTERVIEW)
          @A-100 1966M JOB SATISFACTION VALUES VOCATIONAL INTERVIEW

A-101   ALDERFER, C. P.
              CONVERGENT AND DISCRIMINANT VALIDATION OF SATISFACTION AND DESIRE
              MEASURES BY INTERVIEWS AND QUESTIONNAIRES.
              JOURNAL OF APPLIED PSYCHOLOGY, 1967, 51, 509-520.
              (DESIRE SCALES)
          @A-101 1967M JOB SATISFACTION PERSONAL VOCATIONAL DESIRABILITY

A-102   ALLEN, T. W.
              EMPATHY IS A CRUCIAL VARIABLE IN THE COUNSELING RELATIONSHIP.
              UNPUBLISHED QUALIFYING PAPER, HARVARD UNIVERSITY, 1964.
              (GROUP SUPERVISION REPORT SCALE)
          @A-102 1964M COUNSELING OPENNESS BEHAVIOR

A-103   ALTUCHER, N.
              CONFLICT IN SEX IDENTIFICATION IN BOYS.
              UNPUBLISHED DOCTORAL DISSERTATION, UNIVERSITY OF MICHIGAN, 1956.
              (MEASURE OF SEX TYPING)
          @A-103 1956M MASCULINITY FEMININITY SEX IDENTIFICATION PARENT CHILD

A-104   ARNOFF, F. N.
              SOME FACTORS INFLUENCING THE UNRELIABILITY OF CLINICAL JUDGEMENTS.
              JOURNAL OF CLINICAL PSYCHOLOGY, 1954, 10, 272-275.
          HUNT, W. A., & JONES, N. F.
              THE EXPERIMENTAL INVESTIGATION OF CLINICAL JUDGMENT.
              IN A. BACHRACH (ED.), EXPERIMENTAL FOUNDATIONS OF CLINICAL PSYCHOLOGY.
              NEW YORK: BASIC BOOKS, 1962, PP. 26-51.
              (SCHIZOPHRENIC VOCABULARY TEST RESPONSES)
          @A-104 1954M DIAGNOSIS PSYCHIATRIC SCHIZOPHRENIA

B-1   BALDWIN, A., KALHORN, J., & BREESE, F.
              THE APPRAISAL OF PARENT BEHAVIOR.
              PSYCHOLOGICAL MONOGRAPHS, 1949, 63, (WHOLE NO. 299).
              (PARENT BEHAVIOR RATING SCALES)*
          @B-1 ADJUSTMENT FAMILY INTERACTION PARENTAL BEHAVIOR RATING PARENT-CHILD 1949M
              (APPLICATIONS: 1225 2843)

B-2   BALES, R. F.
              INTERACTION PROCESS ANALYSIS: A METHOD FOR THE STUDY OF SMALL GROUPS.
              READING, MASS.: ADDISON-WESLEY, 1951.
              (INTERACTION PROCESS ANALYSIS)*
          @B-2 INTERACTION INTERPERSONAL ANALYTIC BEHAVIOR RELATIONSHIPS GROUP 1951M
              (APPLICATIONS: 63   76   129   280   656   759 1167 1598 2373 2826)

B-3   BARBER, T. X., & GLASS, L. B.
              SIGNIFICANT FACTORS IN HYPNOTIC BEHAVIOR.
              JOURNAL OF ABNORMAL AND SOCIAL PSYCHOLOGY, 1962, 64, 222-228.
              (BARBER SUGGESTIBILITY SCALE)*
          @B-3 1962M HYPNOTIC SUGGESTIBILITY
              (APPLICATIONS: 420   447   808   847   896   958   988   995 1886 1922
                              2372)

B-4   BARRON, F.
              SOME PERSONALITY CORRELATES OF INDEPENDENCE OF JUDGMENT.
              JOURNAL OF PERSONALITY, 1953, 21, 287-297.
              (BARRON INDEPENDENCE OF JUDGMENT SCALE)*
          @B-4 AUTONOMY CONFORMITY DEPENDENCE APPROVAL JUDGMENT NEED SOCIAL 1953M
              (APPLICATIONS: 26   190   191   281   386   423   430   480   498   672
                              761   859 1299 1548 1634 1912 1933 1951 2143 2323
                             2647)

B-5   BARRON, F.
              AN EGO STRENGTH SCALE WHICH PREDICTS RESPONSE TO PSYCHOTHERAPY.
              JOURNAL OF CONSULTING PSYCHOLOGY, 1953, 17, 327-333.
              (BARRON EGO STRENGTH SCALE)*
        ƏB-5 COPING-DEFENSE EGO-STRENGTH WELL-BEING EGO-RESILIENCY EGO ADJUSTMENT 1953M
              (APPLICATIONS: 40   82   128   232   378   407   413   451   480   634
                                726   757   792   929   967   970   1032   1060   1086   1140
                               1172   1282   1284   1299   1560   1582   1587   1606   1610   1614
                               1622   1656   1672   1680   1708   1719   1727   1738   1746   1807
                               1835   1843   1844   1856   1873   1889   1899   1924   1926   1932
                               2019   2071   2073   2105   2107   2108   2109   2123   2126   2140
                               2147   2163   2239   2243   2297   2312   2324   2371   2386   2420
                               2580   2655   2660   2663   2739   2780   2875)

B-6   BARRON, F.
              COMPLEXITY-SIMPLICITY AS A PERSONALITY DIMENSION.
              JOURNAL OF ABNORMAL AND SOCIAL PSYCHOLOGY, 1953, 48, 163-172.
           BARRON, F.
              DISCOVERING THE CREATIVE PERSONALITY.
              PRINCETON: COLLEGE ENTRANCE EXAMINATION BOARD EDUCATIONAL TESTING
              SERVICE, 1963.
              (BARRON COMPLEXITY SCALE)*
        ƏB-6 COPING-DEFENSE AUTONOMY CONFORMITY DEPENDENCE COMPLEXITY FLEXIBILITY
        ƏB-6 RIGIDITY DOGMATISM COGNITIVE STRUCTURE FUNCTIONING COPING BEHAVIOR 1963M
              (APPLICATIONS: 498   1282   1299   1764   1933   2639)

B-7   BASS, B. M.
              DEVELOPMENT AND EVALUATION OF A SCALE FOR MEASURING SOCIAL ACQUIESCENCE.
              JOURNAL OF ABNORMAL AND SOCIAL PSYCHOLOGY, 1956, 53, 296-299.
              (SOCIAL ACQUIESCENCE SCALE)*
        ƏB-7 RESPONSE-BIAS ACQUIESCENCE SOCIAL DESIRABILITY 1956M
              (APPLICATIONS: 51   190   398   724   1270   2140   2213   2324   2495   2605)

B-8   BECK, A. T., WARD, C. H., MENDELSON, M., MACK, J., & ERBAUGH, J.
              AN INVENTORY FOR MEASURING DEPRESSION.
              ARCHIVES OF GENERAL PSYCHIATRY, 1961, 4, 561-571.
              (BECK DEPRESSION INVENTORY)*
        ƏB-8 AFFECTIVE-STATES GLOBAL NEGATIVE DEPRESSION 1961M
              (APPLICATIONS: 899   1721   2084)

B-9   BENDER, I. E., & HASTORF, A. H.
              ON MEASURING GENERALIZED EMPATHIC ABILITY (SOCIAL SENSITIVITY).
              JOURNAL OF ABNORMAL AND SOCIAL PSYCHOLOGY, 1953, 48, 503-506.
              (REFINED EMPATHY SCORE)
        ƏB-9 AFFECTIVE-STATES EMPATHY SENSITIVITY SOCIAL OTHERS ORIENTATION 1953M
              (APPLICATIONS: 1176)

B-10   BERDIE, R. F.
              A FEMININITY ADJECTIVE CHECK LIST.
              JOURNAL OF APPLIED PSYCHOLOGY, 1959, 43, 327-333.
              (FEMININITY ADJECTIVE CHECKLIST)*
        ƏB-10 SELF-IDENTITY SUB-IDENTITY ROLE PERCEPTION MASCULINITY FEMININITY
        ƏB-10 CHECKLIST SEX 1959M
              (APPLICATIONS: 1807)

B-11   BERDIE, R. F., & LAYTON, W. L.
              MANUAL, MINNESOTA COUNSELING INVENTORY.
              NEW YORK: PSYCHOLOGICAL CORPORATION, 1957.
              (MINNESOTA COUNSELING INVENTORY)*
        ƏB-11 MULTITRAIT STABILITY MOOD ADJUSTMENT COUNSELING FAMILY
        ƏB-11 RELATIONSHIPS SOCIAL INTERPERSONAL EMOTION CONFORMITY LEADERSHIP SECONDARY
        ƏB-11 SCHOOL STUDENT ADOLESCENT 1957M
              (APPLICATIONS: 114   1002   1159   1310   1455   1456   2104   2147   2306   2751
                               2764)

B-12   BERG, I. A., & RAPPAPORT, G. M.
              RESPONSE BIAS IN AN UNSTRUCTURED QUESTIONNAIRE.
              JOURNAL OF PSYCHOLOGY, 1954, 38, 475-481.
              (NO QUESTIONS SCALE)*
        ƏB-12 RESPONSE-BIAS ACQUIESCENCE RESPONSE SET 1954M

B-13   BERGER, E. M.
              THE RELATION BETWEEN EXPRESSED ACCEPTANCE OF SELF AND EXPRESSED ACCEPTANCE
              OF OTHERS.
              JOURNAL OF ABNORMAL AND SOCIAL PSYCHOLOGY, 1952, 47, 778-782.
              (SCALES FOR SELF-ACCEPTANCE AND ACCEPTANCE OF OTHERS)
        ƏB-13 SELF-IDENTITY AFFECTIVE-STATES OTHERS SELF EVALUATION ESTEEM
        ƏPERCEPTION ACCEPTANCE 1952M
              (APPLICATIONS: 114   1206   1625   1690)

B-14   BERKOWITZ, N. H., & WOLKON, G. H.
        A FORCED CHOICE FORM OF THE F SCALE--FREE OF ACQUIESCENT RESPONSE SET.
        SOCIOMETRY, 1964, 27, 54-65.
        (FORCED CHOICE FORM OF THE F SCALE)
        @B-14 COPING-DEFENSE OTHER-CATEGORY F-SCALE AUTHORITARIANISM 1964M
        (APPLICATIONS: 2448)

B-15   BERNBERG, R. E.
        A MEASURE OF SOCIAL CONFORMITY.
        JOURNAL OF PSYCHOLOGY, 1955, 39, 89-96.
        (HUMAN RELATIONS INVENTORY)*
        @B-15 AUTNONOMY CONFORMITY PERSUASIBILITY SOCIAL INFLUENCE INTERPERSONAL
        @B-15 RELATIONSHIPS 1955M
        (APPLICATIONS: 1586   2798)

B-16   BARTHEL, .C. E.
        THE EFFECTS OF THE APPROVAL MOTIVE, GENERALIZED EXPECTANCY, AND SITUATIONAL
        CUES UPON GOAL-SETTING AND SOCIAL DEFENSIVENESS.
        ANN ARBOR, MICHIGAN: UNIVERSITY MICROFILMS, INC., 1963.
        (SOCIOMETRIC MEASURE OF SOCIAL DEFENSIVENESS)
        @B-16 SOCIAL DEFENSIVENESS PEER RATING ADJUSTMENT COMPETENCE 1963M

B-17   BILLS, R. E.
        SELF CONCEPTS AND RORSCHACH SIGNS OF DEPRESSION.
        JOURNAL OF CONSULTING PSYCHOLOGY, 1954, 18, 135-137.
        (SELF CONCEPT AND DEPRESSION MEASURE)
        @B-17 AFFECTIVE-STATES SELF CONCEPT GLOBAL DEPRESSION NEGATIVE IDEAL
        @B-17 DISCREPANCY RORSCHACH SELF-IDENTITY IMAGE 1954M

B-18   BILLS, R. E., VANCE, E. L., & MCLEAN, O. S.
        AN INDEX OF ADJUSTMENT AND VALUES.
        JOURNAL OF CONSULTING PSYCHOLOGY, 1951, 15, 257-261.
        BILLS, R. E.
        MANUAL FOR THE INDEX OF ADJUSTMENT AND VALUES.
        AUBURN, ALABAMA: ALABAMA POLYTECHNICAL INSTITUTE, 1958.
        (INDEX OF ADJUSTMENT AND VALUES)*
        @B-18 ADJUSTMENT VALUES GLOBAL SELF ESTEEM SELF-IDENTITY PERCEPTION EVALUATION
        @IDEAL IMAGE ACCEPTANCE CONCEPT DISCREPANCY 1951M
        (APPLICATIONS: 264   535   1191 1206 1216   1221   1222   1248   1270 1276
                        1325   1350   1371 1430 1450   1461   1596   1827   1935 2245)

B-19   BJERSTEDT, A.
        THE "AUTONOMOUS" PERSONALITY AND THE NEED FOR SYSTEMATIZATION.
        EDUCATIONAL AND PSYCHOLOGICAL INTERACTIONS, 1966, NO. 10.
        (AUTONOMY ORIENTATION AND ATTITUDE SCALE)
        @B-19 AUTONOMY ORDER ORIENTATION ATTITUDE 1966M

B-20   BURNS, R. K., THURSTONE, L. L., MOORE, D. G., & BAEHR, M. E.
        SCIENCE RESEARCH ASSOCIATES, INC. 259 E. ERIE STREET, CHICAGO, ILL. 1951,
        1958.
        (SRA EMPLOYEE INVENTORY)*
        @B-20 JOB SATISFACTION SUPERVISOR EMPLOYEE DEMANDS PE-FIT
        @B-20 AFFECTIVE-STATES GLOBAL 1958M

B-21   BARRETT-LENNARD, G. T.
        REFERENCE UNAVAILABLE, (FOR REFERENCE TO THE SCALE, SEE PIERCE, W. D., &
        MOSHER, D. L., JOURNAL OF CONSULTING PSYCHOLOGY, 1967, 31, 101.)
        (PERCEIVED EMPATHY QUESTIONNAIRE)*
        @B-21 PERCEPTION EMPATHY SOCIAL INTERACTION AFFECTIVE-STATES ADJUSTMENT OTHERS
        @COMPETENCE ORIENTATION
        (APPLICATIONS: 1486)

B-22   BANDURA, A., LIPSHER, D. H., & MILLER, P. E.
        PSYCHOTHERAPISTS' APPROACH-AVOIDANCE REACTIONS TO PATIENTS' EXPRESSION OF
        HOSTILITY.
        JOURNAL OF CONSULTING PSYCHOLOGY, 1960, 24, 1-8.
        (METHOD FOR SCORING PATIENT-THERAPIST INTERACTIONS)
        @B-22 1960M PATIENT THERAPY INTERACTION HOSTILITY
        @B-22 RELATIONSHIPS
        (APPLICATIONS: 2161)

B-23   BLOCK, J.
            EGO IDENTITY, ROLE VARIABILITY, AND ADJUSTMENT.
            JOURNAL OF CONSULTING PSYCHOLOGY, 1961, 25, 392-397.
            (ROLE CONSISTENCY MEASURE)
        @B-23 ROLE CONSISTENCY SELF EGO PERCEPTION ADJUSTMENT BEHAVIOR
        @B-23 COPING-DEFENSE EGO-STRENGTH EGO-RESILIENCY SELF-IDENTITY SUB-IDENTITY
        @B-23 INTERPERSONAL IDENTITY 1961M

B-24   BONNEY, M. E.
            SOME CORRELATES OF A SOCIAL DEFINITION OF NORMAL PERSONALITY.
            JOURNAL OF CLINICAL PSYCHOLOGY, 1964, 20, 415-422.
            (PERSONALITY SELF-RATING SCALE)*
        @B-24 ADJUSTMENT SELF CONCEPT NORMALITY RATING MENTAL-HEALTH GLOBAL MULTITRAIT
        @B-24 1964M

B-25   BORGATTA, E. F.
            A SYSTEMATIC STUDY OF INTERACTION PROCESS SCORES, PEER AND SELF-ASSESS-
            MENTS, PERSONALITY AND OTHER VARIABLES.
            GENETIC PSYCHOLOGY MONOGRAPHS, 1961, 63, 3-65.
            (CLASSIFICATION SYSTEM FOR SOCIAL INTERACTION)
        @B-25 COPING-DEFENSE ADJUSTMENT INTERACTION SOCIAL COMPETENCE GLOBAL PEER SELF
        @B-25 INTERPERSONAL 1961M

B-26   BORGATTA, E. F.
            A VERY SHORT TEST OF PERSONALITY: THE BEHAVIORAL SELF-RATING (BSR) FORM.
            PSYCHOLOGICAL REPORTS, 1964, 14, 275-284.
            (BEHAVIORAL SELF-RATING FORM)*
        @B-26 MULTITRAIT ASSERTIVENESS EMOTION RESPONSIBILITY SELF RATING BEHAVIOR
        @B-26 DESCRIPTION 1964M
            (APPLICATIONS: 557)

B-27   BORISLAW, B.
            THE EPPS AND FAMILIARITY.
            JOURNAL OF APPLIED PSYCHOLOGY, 1958, 42, 22-27.
            ("PERFECT PERSON" MEASURE)
        @B-27 RESPONSE-BIAS SOCIAL DESIRABILITY FAKING 1958M
            (APPLICATIONS: 1221)

B-28   BORKE, H.
            THE COMMUNICATION OF INTENT: A SYSTEMATIC APPROACH TO THE OBSERVATION OF
            FAMILY INTERACTION.
            HUMAN RELATIONS, 1967, 20, 13-28.
            (CLASSIFICATION SYSTEM FOR FAMILY INTERACTION)
        @B-28 ADJUSTMENT INTERACTION FAMILY COMMUNICATION 1967M

B-29   BORKE, H.
            THE COMMUNICATION OF INTENT: A REVISED PROCEDURE FOR ANALYZING FAMILY
            INTERACTION FROM VIDEO TAPES.
            UNPUBLISHED MANUSCRIPT, 1967.
            (ANALYSIS OF FAMILY INTERACTION)
        @B-29 ADJUSTMENT COMMUNICATION FAMILY INTERACTION VIDEO-TAPE 1967M

B-30   BOWN, O. H., & RICHEK, H. G.
            THE BOWN SELF-REPORT INVENTORY (SRI): A QUICK SCREENING INSTRUMENT FOR
            MENTAL HEALTH PROFESSIONALS.
            COMPREHENSIVE PSYCHIATRY, 1967, 8, 45-52.
            (BOWN SELF-REPORT INVENTORY)*
        @B-30 MULTITRAIT MENTAL-HEALTH SELF GLOBAL ADJUSTMENT REALITY HOPE DIAGNOSIS
        @AUTHORITY MENTAL-ILLNESS 1967M
            (APPLICATIONS: 2242   2978)

B-31   BOYD, J. E., & JACKSON, D. N.
            THE PERCEIVED STRUCTURE OF SOCIAL ATTITUDES AND PERSONALITY: A MULTI-
            DIMENSIONAL SCALING APPROACH.
            MULTIVARIATE BEHAVIORAL RESEARCH, 1967, 2, 281-297.
            (MEASURE OF AUTHORITARIANISM)
        @B-31 COPING-DEFENSE AUTHORITARIANISM SOCIAL ATTITUDE POWER OTHER-CATEGORY 1967M

B-32   BREGER, L.
                CONFORMITY AS A FUNCTION OF THE ABILITY TO EXPRESS HOSTILITY.
                JOURNAL OF PERSONALITY, 1963, 31, 245-255.
                (TAT MEASURE OF HOSTILITY)
          aB-32 RESPONSE-BIAS HOSTILITY CONFORMITY REPRESSION SOCIAL APPROVAL
          aCOPING-DEFENSE PERCEPTICN DENIAL DEFENSIVENESS TAT PROJECTIVE NEED NEGATIVE
          aB-32 AFFECTIVE-STATES 1963M
                (APPLICATIONS: 372   2010)

B-33   BRONSON, W. C.
                ADULT DERIVATIVES OF EMOTICNAL EXPRESSIVENESS AND REACTIVITY-CONTROL:
                DEVELOPMENTAL CONTINUITIES FROM CHILDHOOD TO ADULTHOOD.
                CHILD DEVELOPMENT, 1967, 38, 801-817.
                (MEASURE OF EMOTIONAL EXPRESSIVENESS AND REACTIVITY-CONTROL)
          aB-33 AFFECTIVE-STATES EXPRESSIVENESS REACTIVITY CONTROL OTHER-CATEGORY EMOTION
          aB-33 SELF EXPRESSION 1967M

B-34   BROWN, D. G., & TOLOR, A.
                HUMAN FIGURE DRAWINGS AS INDICATORS OF SEXUAL IDENTIFICATION AND INVERSION.
                PERCEPTUAL AND MOTOR SKILLS, 1957, 7, 199-211.
                (INDICATORS OF SEXUAL IDENTIFICATION AND INVERSION)
          aB-34 SELF-IDENTITY SUB-IDENTITY ROLE PERCEPTION SEX IDENTIFICATION
          aB-34 PROJECTIVE 1957M
                (APPLICATIONS: 1461)

B-35   BROWN, D. G.
                SEX ROLE PREFERENCE IN YOUNG CHILDREN.
                PSYCHOLOGICAL MONOGRAPHS, 1956, 70 (14, WHOLE NO. 421).
                (IT SCALE FOR CHILDREN)*
          aB-35 SELF IDENTITY SUB-IDENTITY ROLE PERCEPTION MASCULINITY FEMININITY SEX
          aCHILD DEVELOPMENT 1956M
                (APPLICATIONS: 18   117   1594   1808   2971)

B-36   BROWNFAIN, J. J.
                STABILITY OF THE SELF-CONCEPT AS A DIMENSION OF PERSONALITY.
                JOURNAL OF ABNORMAL AND SOCIAL PSYCHOLOGY, 1952, 47, 597-607.
                (SELF-RATING INVENTORY)*
          aB-36 SELF CONCEPT STABILITY SELF-IDENTITY SOCIAL CONFLICT EVALUATION ROLE
          aB-36 PERCEPTION ESTEEM SUB-IDENTITY RATING 1952M
                (APPLICATIONS: 1206 1423)

B-37   BUDNER, S.
                INTOLERANCE OF AMBIGUITY AS A PERSONALITY VARIABLE.
                JOURNAL OF PERSONALITY, 1962, 30, 29-50.
                (MEASURE OF INTOLERANCE OF AMBIGUITY)
          aB-37 COPING-DEFENSE DOGMATISM TOLERANCE AMBIGUITY FLEXIBILITY RIGIDITY 1962M
                (APPLICATIONS: 26   156   293   386   496   502   509   529 1299 2319
                        2666)

B-38   BUERKLE, J. V., & BADGLEY, R. F.
                COUPLE ROLE-TAKING: THE YALE MARITAL INTERACTION BATTERY.
                MARRIAGE AND FAMILY LIVING, 1959, 21, 53-58.
                (YALE MARITAL INTERACTICN BATTERY)*
          aB-38 ADJUSTMENT ROLE MARITAL INTERACTION FAMILY INTERPERSONAL 1959M

B-39   BUGENTAL, J. F. T., & ZELLER, S. L.
                INVESTIGATION INTO THE 'SELF-CONCEPT': THE W-A-Y TECHNIQUE.
                JOURNAL OF PERSONALITY, 1950, 18, 483-498.
                (W-A-Y: WHO ARE YOU?)*
          aB-39 SELF PERCEPTION CONCEPT EVALUATION ESTEEM SELF-IDENTITY IMAGE 1950M
                (APPLICATIONS: 1206 2189 2651)

B-40   BURCH, I. A.
                THE SELF-INFLATION HYPOTHESIS: A STUDY IN CONSTRUCT VALIDATION.
                PENNSYLVANIA STATE UNIVERSITY, 1956.
                (SELF-ESTEEM MULTIPLE CHOICE INVENTORY)
          aB-40 SELF ESTEEM PERCEPTION EVALUATION SELF-IDENTITY ENHANCEMENT 1956M

B-41   BURDOCK, E. I., & HARDESTY, A. S.
                PSYCHOLOGICAL TEST FOR PSYCHOPATHOLOGY.
                JOURNAL OF ABNORMAL PSYCHOLOGY, 1968, 73, 62-69.
                (STRUCTURED CLINICAL INTERVIEW)*
          aB-41 FEAR HOSTILITY SELF DEPRECIATION GLOBAL ADJUSTMENT MENTAL-ILLNESS
          aB-41 PSYCHIATRIC RATING DIAGNOSIS PROGNOSIS 1968M
                (APPLICATIONS: 2728)

B-42   BURGESS, E. W., & COTTRELL, L. S.
                PREDICTING SUCCESS OR FAILURE IN MARRIAGE.
                NEW YORK: PRENTICE-HALL, 1939.
                (BURGESS-COTTRELL MARITAL ADJUSTMENT TEST)*
            @B-42 ADJUSTMENT MARITAL SATISFACTION FAMILY INTERPERSONAL RELATIONSHIPS 1939M

B-43   BURGESS, E. W., & WALLIN, P.
                ENGAGEMENT AND MARRIAGE.
                PHILADELPHIA: LIPPINCOTT, 1953.
                (BURGESS-WALLIN MARITAL-SUCCESS SCHEDULE)*
            @B-43 MARITAL ADJUSTMENT SUCCESS SATISFACTION FAMILY 1953M

B-44   BUSS, A. H., & DURKEE, A.
                AN INVENTORY FOR ASSESSING DIFFERENT KINDS OF HOSTILITY.
                JOURNAL OF CONSULTING PSYCHOLOGY, 1957, 21, 343-349.
                (HOSTILITY-GUILT INVENTORY)*
            @B-44 AFFECTIVE-STATES RESENTMENT IRRITABILITY HOSTILITY NEGATIVE GUILT 1957M
                (APPLICATIONS: 111   163   206   397   1600   1705   1712   1720   1753   2065
                             2104   2164   2650   2882)

B-45   BUXTON, C. E.
                EVALUATIONS OF FORCED-CHOICE AND LIKERT-TYPE TESTS OF MOTIVATION TO ACA-
                DEMIC ACHIEVEMENT.
                BRITISH JOURNAL OF EDUCATIONAL PSYCHOLOGY, 1966, 36, 192-201.
                (FORCED-CHOICE AND LIKERT-TYPE TESTS OF ACADEMIC ACHIEVEMENT)
            @B-45 ACHIEVEMENT AUTONOMY NEED ACADEMIC STUDENT SCHOOL 1966M

B-46   BYRNE, D.
                THE REPRESSION-SENSITIZATION SCALE: RATIONALE, RELIABILITY, AND VALIDITY.
                JOURNAL OF PERSONALITY, 1961, 29, 334-349.
            BYRNE, D., BARRY, J., & NELSON, D.
                RELATION OF THE REVISED REPRESSION-SENSITIZATION SCALE TO MEASURES OF SELF-
                DESCRIPTION.
                PSYCHOLOGICAL REPORTS, 1963, 13, 323-334.
                (REPRESSION-SENSITIZATION SCALE)*
            @B-46 REPRESSION SENSITIZATION ADJUSTMENT DEFENSIVENESS COPING-DEFENSE
            @RESPONSE-BIAS 1961M
                (APPLICATIONS: 34   151   202   253   259   271   276   280   289   437
                              462   467   480   482   491   910   954   1025   1034   1046
                             1053   1054   1063   1070   1432   1892   1899   1930   1971   2000
                             2008   2069   2082   2086   2100   2113   2122   2140   2163   2172
                             2177   2203   2246   2254   2315   2323   2328   2333   2405   2433
                             2512   2517   2567   2655   2660   2686   2738   2742   2824   2919)

B-47   BOGARD, H. M.
                UNION AND MANAGEMENT TRAINEES--A COMPARATIVE STUDY OF PERSONALITY AND
                OCCUPATIONAL CHOICE.
                JOURNAL OF APPLIED PSYCHOLOGY, 1960, 44, 56-63.
                (BIOGRAPHICAL INVENTORY)*
            @B-47 MULTITRAIT COPING-DEFENSE STYLE HISTORY SOCIAL VOCATIONAL JOB INTEREST
            @AUTHORITY CONFORMITY 1960M

B-48   BYRNE, D., & CLORE, G. L., JR.
                EFFECTANCE AROUSAL AND ATTRACTION.
                JOURNAL OF PERSONALITY AND SOCIAL PSYCHOLOGY, 1967, 6 (4, WHOLE NO. 638).
                (EFFECTANCE AROUSAL SCALE)*
            @B-48 PE-FIT ADJUSTMENT EFFECTANCE APPROACH AVOIDANCE INTERPERSONAL MOTIVE
            @B-48 NEED AROUSAL 1967M
                (APPLICATIONS: 278)

B-49   BRAATZ, G. A.
                PREFERENCE INTRANSITIVITY AS AN INDICATOR OF COGNITIVE SLIPPAGE IN SCHIZO-
                PHRENIA.
                JOURNAL OF ABNORMAL PSYCHOLOGY, 1970, 75, 1-6.
                (SCALE TO DETECT THOUGHT DISORDER OR COGNITIVE SLIPPAGE BY MEANS OF
                PREFERENCE INTRANSITIVITY)
            @B-49 SCHIZOPHRENIA COGNITIVE THINKING FUNCTIONING DIAGNOSIS MENTAL-HEALTH
            @B-49 MENTAL-ILLNESS 1970M

B-50   BARRETT-LENNARD, G. T.
            DIMENSIONS OF THERAPIST RESPONSE AS CAUSAL FACTORS IN THERAPEUTIC CHANGE.
            PSYCHOLOGICAL MONOGRAPHS, 1962, 76, NO. 7 (WHOLE NO. 562).
            (BARRETT-LENNARD RELATIONSHIP INVENTORY)*
        aB-50 THERAPY ADJUSTMENT OTHER-CATEGORY INTERACTION RELATIONSHIPS COUNSELING
        aB-50 PSYCHIATRIC PATIENT MENTAL-ILLNESS CHANGE 1962M
            (APPLICATIONS: 1006 1187 1273 1345 1360 1367 1404 1467 1505 1520
                            1534 1538 1918 2117 2137 2854 2950)

B-51   BOSSART, P., & DIVESTA, F. J.
            EFFECTS OF CONTEXT, FREQUENCY, AND ORDER OF PRESENTATION OF EVALUATIVE
            ASSERTIONS ON IMPRESSION FORMATION.
            JOURNAL OF PERSONALITY AND SOCIAL PSYCHOLOGY, 1966, 4, 538-544.
            (SEMANTIC -DIFFERENTIAL MEASURE OF IMPRESSIONS)
        aB-51 IMPRESSION FORMATION CREDIBILITY SEM-DIFFERENTIAL COMMUNICATION 1966M

B-52   BELLER, E. K.
            DEPENDENCY AND AUTONOMOUS ACHIEVEMENT-STRIVING RELATED TO ORALITY AND
            ANALITY IN EARLY CHILDHOOD.
            (MEASURES OF DEPENDENCE AND INDEPENDENCE)
            CHILD DEVELOPMENT, 1957, 28, 287-315.
        aB-52 AUTONOMY DEPENDENCE CHILD 1957M
            (APPLICATIONS: 117)

B-53   BEREITER, C. E.
            THE DIFFERENTIAL CHANGE SCALES.
            POUGHKEEPSIE, N. Y.: MARY CONOVER MELLON FOUNDATION, VASSAR COLLEGE, 1960,
            MIMEO.
            (DIFFERENTIAL CHANGE SCALES)*
        aB-53 SELF-IDENTITY SELF ACTUALIZATION DEVELOPMENT ASSERTION PERSONALITY CHANGE
        aB-53 ATTITUDE STRESS 1960M

B-54   BERKOWITZ, L., & DANIELS, L. R.
            AFFECTING THE SALIENCE OF THE SOCIAL RESPONSIBILITY NORM: EFFECTS OF PAST
            HELP ON THE RESPONSE TO DEPENDENCY RELATIONSHIPS.
            JOURNAL OF ABNORMAL AND SOCIAL PSYCHOLOGY, 1964, 68, 275-281.
            (SOCIAL RESPONSIBILITY SCALE)*
        aB-54 SOCIAL RESPONSIBILITY ADJUSTMENT OTHER-CATEGORY DEPENDENCE TRUST
        aB-54 COLLEGE STUDENT INTERPERSONAL RELATIONSHIPS 1964M
            (APPLICATIONS: 50 111 490 2903)

B-55   BIRNEY, R. C., & TAYLOR, M. J.
            SCHOLASTIC BEHAVIOR AND ORIENTATION TO COLLEGE.
            JOURNAL OF EDUCATIONAL PSYCHOLOGY, 1959, 50, 266-274.
            (ORIENTATION TO COLLEGE INVENTORY)*
        aB-55 ORIENTATION COLLEGE BEHAVIOR ACADEMIC 1959M

B-56   BLANCHARD, W. A.
            ASSIMILATION AND CONTRAST IN INTERPERSONAL PREDICTION WITH CONTROL FOR THE
            INTERACTION OF REAL SIMILARITY AND DIFFERENTIAL ACCURACY.
            JOURNAL OF PERSONALITY AND SOCIAL PSYCHOLOGY, 1966, 3, 567-573.
            (RATING SCALE FOR JUDGMENTS OF SIMILARITY)
        aB-56 INTERPERSONAL PREDICTION ADJUSTMENT OTHER-CATEGORY SELF SIMILARITY
        aB-56 RATING VOCATIONAL JUDGMENT 1966M

B-58   BOGARDUS, E. S.
            MEASURING SOCIAL DISTANCE.
            JOURNAL OF APPLIED SOCIOLOGY, 1925, 9, 299-308.
            (SOCIAL DISTANCE SCALE)*
        aB-58 1925M OTHERS RELATIONSHIPS ATTITUDE RACIAL ETHNIC SOCIAL DISTANCE
        aMINORITY
            (APPLICATIONS: 2 144 1168 2154 2887)

B-59   BREGER, L., & RUIZ, C.
            THE ROLE OF EGO-DEFENSE IN CONFORMITY.
            JOURNAL OF SOCIAL PSYCHOLOGY, 1966, 69, 73-85.
            (MEASURE OF CONFORMITY)
        aB-59 CONFORMITY EGO DEFENSE COPING-DEFENSE GLOBAL AUTONOMY RESPONSE-BIAS
        aDEFENSIVENESS 1966M

B-60   BUTLER, J. M., & HAIGH, G. V.
            CHANGES IN THE RELATION BETWEEN SELF-CONCEPTS AND IDEAL CONCEPTS
            CONSEQUENT UPON CLIENT-CENTERED COUNSELING.
            IN C. R. ROGERS & R. F. DYMOND (EDS.) PSYCHOTHERAPY AND PERSONALITY
            CHANGE. CHICAGO: UNIVERSITY OF CHICAGO PRESS, 1954.
            (Q-SORT MEASURE FOR SELF AND IDEAL-SELF CONCEPTS)
        @B-60 SELF-IDENTITY SELF ESTEEM PERCEPTION EVALUATION IDEAL IMAGE Q-SORT CONCEPT
        @1954M
            (APPLICATIONS: 226   558   779   1002   1006   1117   1176   1190   1196   1197
                             1206   1221   1223   1224   1247   1260   1270   1313   1353   1431
                             1461   1572   1648   1952   1953   2024   2035   2147   2269   2297
                             2417   2777   2878)

B-61   BARRATT, E. S.
            THE SPACE-VISUALIZATION FACTORS RELATED TO TEMPERAMENT TRAITS.
            JOURNAL OF PSYCHOLOGY, 1955, 39, 279-287.
            (BARRATT-FRUCHTER CHAIR-WINDOW TEST)*
        @B-61 FIELD DEPENDENCE AUTONOMY PERCEPTION 1955M
            (APPLICATIONS: 2324)

B-62   BERKUN, M. M., BIALEK, H. M., KERN, R. P., & YOGI, K.
            EXPERIMENTAL STUDIES OF PSYCHOLOGICAL STRESS IN MAN.
            PSYCHOLOGICAL MONOGRAPHS, 1962, 76, (15, WHOLE NO. 534).
            (SUBJECTIVE STRESS SCALE)*
        @B-62 AFFECTIVE-STATES ANXIETY SUBJECTIVE STRESS NEGATIVE 1962M
            (APPLICATIONS: 271   282   1009   1076   1096   1132)

B-63   BLOCK, J.
            BERKELEY PSYCHOLOGICAL INVENTORY.
            NO REFERENCE--CITED IN:
            OPTON, E. M., JR., & LAZARUS, R. S.
            PERSONALITY DETERMINANTS OF PSYCHOPHYSIOLOGICAL RESPONSE TO STRESS:
            A THEORETICAL ANALYSIS AND AN EXPERIMENT.
            JOURNAL OF PERSONALITY AND SOCIAL PSYCHOLOGY, 1967, 6, 291-303.
            (BERKELEY PSYCHOLOGICAL INVENTORY)*
        @B-63 MULTITRAIT INTROSPECTION INVENTORY PERSONALITY
            (APPLICATIONS: 178)

B-64   BREWER, M. B.
            DETERMINANTS OF SOCIAL DISTANCE AMONG EAST AFRICAN TRIBAL GROUPS.
            JOURNAL OF PERSONALITY AND SOCIAL PSYCHOLOGY, 1968, 10, 279-289.
            (MEASURE OF SOCIAL DISTANCE)
        @B-64 SOCIAL DISTANCE AFFECTIVE-STATES OTHER-CATEGORY CROSS-CULTURAL 1968M

B-65   BYRNE, D.
            INTERPERSONAL ATTRACTION AND ATTITUDE SIMILARITY.
            JOURNAL OF ABNORMAL AND SOCIAL PSYCHOLOGY, 1961, 62, 713-715.
            (INTERPERSONAL JUDGMENT SCALE)*
        @B-65 INTERPERSONAL JUDGMENT ADJUSTMENT OTHER-CATEGORY AFFECTIVE-STATES POSITIVE
        @ATTRACTION SOCIAL INTERACTION 1961M
            (APPLICATIONS: 132   151   267   278   353   449   484   751   2337   2488
                            2512   2520   2646   2909)

B-66   BERKUN, M. M., BURDICK, H. A., & WOODRING, T. M.
            A CHECK LIST FOR FEELINGS OF HOSTILITY.
            (NO REFERENCE AVAILABLE)
            (BERKUN HOSTILITY SCALE)
        @B-66 HOSTILITY AFFECTIVE-STATES RESENTMENT CHECKLIST NEGATIVE
            (APPLICATIONS: 182)

B-67   BAGGALEY, A. R.
            DEVELOPMENT OF A PREDICTIVE ACADEMIC INTEREST INVENTORY.
            JOURNAL OF COUNSELING PSYCHOLOGY, 1963, 10, 41-46.
            (MILWAUKEE ACADEMIC INTEREST INVENTORY)*
        @B-67 ACADEMIC INTEREST PREDICTION COLLEGE 1963M

B-68   BERENSON, B. G., CARKHUFF, R. R., & MYRUS, P.
            THE INTERPERSONAL FUNCTIONING AND TRAINING OF COLLEGE STUDENTS.
            JOURNAL OF COUNSELING PSYCHOLOGY, 1966, 13, 441-446.
            (MEASURE OF INTERPERSONAL FUNCTIONING)
        @B-68 INTERPERSONAL FUNCTIONING SOCIAL COMPETENCE ADJUSTMENT EMPATHY SELF
        @EXPLORATION ESTEEM CONCRETENESS RELATIONSHIPS 1966M

B-69   BERGER, E. M.
            WILLINGNESS TO ACCEPT LIMITATIONS AND COLLEGE ACHIEVEMENT.
            JOURNAL OF COUNSELING PSYCHOLOGY, 1961, 8, 140-146.
            (WILLINGNESS TO ACCEPT LIMITATIONS SCALE)*
        aB-69 AUTONOMY ACHIEVEMENT NEED RISK-TAKING SELF ACCEPTANCE PERCEPTION 1961M
            (APPLICATIONS: 1201   1287   1514)

B-70   BEZDEK, W., & STRODTBECK, F. L.
            SEX-ROLE IDENTITY AND PRAGMATIC ACTION.
            AMERICAN SOCIOLOGICAL REVIEW, 1970, 35, 491-502.
            (WILLINGNESS TO ACT MEASURE)
        aB-70 1970M ACTIVITIES SEX ROLE IDENTITY SELF-IDENTITY MOTIVE

B-71   BRAUNSTEIN, D. N.
            INTERPERSONAL BEHAVIOR IN A CHANGING ORGANIZATION.
            JOURNAL OF APPLIED PSYCHOLOGY, 1970, 54, 184-191.
            (ORGANIZATIONAL BEHAVIOR SURVEY)*
        aB-71 1970M JOB ORGANIZATION BEHAVIOR PERFORMANCE

B-72   BEREITER, C. E.
            VERBAL AND IDEATIONAL FLUENCY IN SUPERIOR TENTH-GRADE STUDENTS.
            UNPUBLISHED DOCTORAL DISSERTATION, UNIVERSITY OF WISCONSIN, 1959.
            (TESTS OF IDEATIONAL FLUENCY)
        aB-72 CREATIVITY AUTONOMY COGNITIVE STRUCTURE FLEXIBILITY RIGIDITY THINKING
        aB-72 FUNCTIONING 1959M

B-73   BERLAK, H.
            RIGIDITY SCALE.
            UNPUBLISHED MANUSCRIPT. CAMBRIDGE: HARVARD GRADUATE SCHOOL OF EDUCATION,
            1959.
            (COMPULSIVITY SCALE)*
        aB-73 COPING-DEFENSE FLEXIBILITY RIGIDITY COMPULSIVENESS DOGMATISM 1959M

B-74   BROWN, W. F., & HOLTZMAN, W. H.
            SURVEY OF STUDY HABITS AND ATTITUDES: FORM S.
            NEW YORK: PSYCHOLOGICAL CORPORATION, 1967.
            (SURVEY OF STUDY HABITS AND ATTITUDES)*
        aB-74 STUDY HABITS ATTITUDE ACADEMIC STUDENT SECONDARY COLLEGE SCHOOL 1967M
            (APPLICATIONS: 1208   1252   1297   1328   1395   1507   2761   2766)

B-76   BARRON, F., & WELSH, G. S.
            ARTISTIC PERCEPTION AS A POSSIBLE FACTOR IN PERSONALITY STYLE.
            JOURNAL OF PSYCHOLOGY, 1952, 33, 199-203.
            (BARRON-WELSH ART SCALE)*
        aB-76 ORIGINALITY AUTONOMY CREATIVITY ESTHETIC PREFERENCE JUDGMENT 1952M
            (APPLICATIONS: 339   357   423   430   498   2259   2568   2807   2829   2868
                            2902   2924)

B-77   BULLEY, M. H.
            ART AND EVERYMAN.
            VOL. 1. LONDON: BATSFORD, 1951.
            (MEASURE OF ESTHETIC JUDGMENT)
        aB-77 PREFERENCE ESTHETIC JUDGMENT 1951M
            (APPLICATIONS: 357)

B-78   BARRON, F.
            THE MEASUREMENT OF CREATIVITY.
            IN D. WHITLA (ED.), HANDBOOK OF MEASUREMENT AND ASSESSMENT IN BEHAVIORAL
            SCIENCES. NEW YORK: ADDISON-WESLEY, 1968.
            (ORIGINALITY SCALE)
        aB-78 FLEXIBILITY AUTONOMY ORIGINALITY CREATIVITY 1968M
            (APPLICATIONS: 409   430   498   1282   1933   2336   2924)

B-79   BARRON, F.
            COMPLEXITY-SIMPLICITY AS A PERSONALITY DIMENSION.
            JOURNAL OF ABNORMAL AND SOCIAL PSYCHOLOGY, 1953, 48, 163-172.
            (SELF-REPORT QUESTIONNAIRE MEASURE OF COMPLEXITY-SIMPLICITY)
        aB-79 COMPLEXITY SIMPLICITY CONFORMITY FLEXIBILITY DEPENDENCE CREATIVITY VALUES
        aB-79 AUTONOMY COPING-DEFENSE COGNITIVE STRUCTURE FUNCTIONING 1953M
            (APPLICATIONS: 386   430   1299)

B-80   BROWN, F.
          A PSYCHONEUROTIC INVENTORY FOR CHILDREN BETWEEN NINE AND FOURTEEN YEARS OF
          AGE.
          JOURNAL OF APPLIED PSYCHOLOGY, 1934, 18, 566-577.
          (PSYCHONEUROTIC INVENTORY)
          @B-80 NEUROTICISM GLOBAL ADJUSTMENT ANXIETY SENSITIVITY INFERIORITY CHILD 1934M

B-81   BASS, B. M.
          FAMOUS SAYINGS TEST: GENERAL MANUAL.
          PSYCHOLOGICAL REPORTS, 1958, 4, 479-497.
          (FAMOUS SAYINGS TEST)*
          @B-81 PERSUASIBILITY SOCIAL INFLUENCE CONFORMITY COPING-DEFENSE APPROACH
          @AVOIDANCE AUTONOMY RESENTMENT HOSTILITY FEAR FAILURE PROJECTIVE
          @ACQUIESCENCE AFFECTIVE-STATES 1958M
              (APPLICATIONS: 701   724   2631)

B-82   BECKER, W. C.
          A GENETIC APPROACH TO THE INTERPRETATION AND EVALUATION OF THE PROCESS-
          REACTIVE DISTINCTION IN SCHIZOPHRENIA.
          JOURNAL OF ABNORMAL AND SOCIAL PSYCHOLOGY, 1956, 53, 229-236.
          BECKER, W. C.
          THE RELATIONSHIP OF SEVERITY OF THINKING DISORDER TO THE PROCESS-REACTIVE
          CONCEPT OF SCHIZOPHRENIA.
          UNPUBLISHED DOCTURAL DISSERTATION, STANFORD UNIVERSITY, 1955.
          (RORSCHACH MEASURE OF DIFFERENTIATION AND INTEGRATION)
          @B-82 PROGNOSIS SCHIZOPHRENIA PSYCHIATRIC DIAGNOSIS PATIENT EGO MENTAL-ILLNESS
          @EGO-STRENGTH EGO-RESILIENCY RORSCHACH DIFFERENTIATION INTEGRATION PROJECTIVE
          @B-82 PERSONALITY 1956M
              (APPLICATIONS: 780   1665   2243)

B-83   BASS, B. M.
          THE ORIENTATION INVENTORY.
          PALO ALTO, CALIFORNIA: CONSULTING PSYCHOLOGISTS PRESS, 1962.
          (ORIENTATION INVENTORY)*
          @B-83 NEED ORIENTATION INTERACTION SOCIAL ADJUSTMENT COMPETENCE SELF OTHERS
          @B-83 INTERPERSONAL RELATIONSHIPS 1962M
              (APPLICATIONS: 1450   1897   2490)

B-84   BENDIG, A. W.
          THE PITTSBURGH SCALES OF SOCIAL EXTRAVERSION-INTROVERSION AND EMOTIONALITY.
          JOURNAL OF PSYCHOLOGY, 1962, 53, 199-209.
          BENDIG, A. W.
          COLLEGE NORMS FOR AND CONCURRENT VALIDITY OF THE PITTSBURGH REVISIONS OF
          THE MAUDSLEY PERSONALITY INVENTORY.
          JOURNAL OF PSYCHOLOGICAL STUDIES, 1959, 11, 12-17.
          (PITTSBURGH SCALES OF SOCIAL EXTRAVERSION-INTROVERSION)
          @B-84 EXTRAVERSION INTROVERSION EMOTION ADJUSTMENT AUTONOMY OTHER-CATEGORY 1962M
              (APPLICATIONS: 885   990   1012   1072   1740   2095   2438   2748)

B-85   BRIGGS, P. F.
          PRELIMINARY VALIDATION OF A STANDARD PERSONAL HISTORY FOR PSYCHIATRIC
          DIAGNOSIS.
          UNPUBLISHED DOCTORAL DISSERTATION, UNIVERSITY OF MINNESOTA, 1955.
          (M-B HISTORY RECORD)*
          @B-85 GLOBAL ADJUSTMENT PERSONAL HISTORY DIAGNOSIS PSYCHIATRIC MENTAL-ILLNESS
          @B-85 1955M
              (APPLICATIONS: 655   695   1038)

B-86   BURDOCK, E. I., HAKEREM, G., HARDESTY, A. S., & ZUBIN, J.
          A WARD BEHAVIOR RATING SCALE FOR MENTAL HOSPITAL PATIENTS.
          JOURNAL OF CLINICAL PSYCHOLOGY, 1960, 16, 246-247.
          (WARD BEHAVIOR INVENTORY)*
          @B-86 WARD BEHAVIOR GLOBAL ADJUSTMENT PATIENT MENTAL-ILLNESS HOSPITALIZATION
          @B-86 1960M
              (APPLICATIONS: 1805   2075   2081   2728)

B-87   BEER, M.
          LEADERSHIP, EMPLOYEE NEEDS AND MOTIVATION.
          COLUMBUS: OHIO STATE UNIVERSITY, BUREAU OF BUSINESS RESEARCH, MONOGRAPH
          NO. 129, 1966.
          (PREFERENCE INVENTORY)
          @B-87 NEED ADJUSTMENT AUTONOMY OTHER-CATEGORY ESTEEM SELF ACTUALIZATION
          @B-87 SECURITY SOCIAL LEADERSHIP MOTIVE JOB SATISFACTION PE-FIT EMPLOYEE 1966M

B-88   BEER, M.
             LEADERSHIP, EMPLOYEE NEEDS AND MOTIVATION.
             COLUMBUS: OHIO STATE UNIVERSITY, BUREAU OF BUSINESS RESEARCH, MONOGRAPH
             NO. 129, 1966.
             (JOB INVENTORY)
         @B-88 JOB SATISFACTION AFFECTIVE-STATES GLOBAL NEED PE-FIT 1966M

B-89   BONNEY, M. E.
             UNPUBLISHED MANUSCRIPT. (SEE MMH TEST LIBRARY)
             (SENTENCE COMPLETION TEST OF COPING-AVOIDANCE REGARDING SEX AND AGGRESSION)
         @B-89 COPING-DEFENSE AVOIDANCE SELF ESTEEM CONFIDENCE AUTONOMY SOCIABILITY
         @B-89 COPING BEHAVIOR SEX AGGRESSION

B-90   BAXTER, J. C., & BECKER, J.
             ANXIETY AND AVOIDANCE BEHAVIOR IN SCHIZOPHRENICS IN RESPONSE TO PARENTAL
             FIGURES.
             JOURNAL OF ABNORMAL AND SOCIAL PSYCHOLOGY, 1962, 64, 432-437.
             (TAT MEASURE OF ANXIETY AND AVOIDANCE)
         @B-90 ANXIETY AVOIDANCE BEHAVIOR COPING-DEFENSE APPROACH AFFECTIVE-STATES STRESS
         @B-90 SUBJECTIVE TAT PROJECTIVE IMAGERY 1962M

B-91   BLOCK, J.
             THE DEVELOPMENT OF AN MMPI-BASED SCALE TO MEASURE EGO CONTROL.
             MIMEOGRAPHED MATERIALS. BERKELEY: INSTITUTE OF PERSONALITY ASSESSMENT
             AND RESEARCH, UNIVERSITY OF CALIFORNIA, 1953.
             (EC3)*: (MEASURE OF EGO CONTROL)
         @B-91 COPING-DEFENSE EGO CONTROL OTHER-CATEGORY ADJUSTMENT MMPI 1953M
             (APPLICATIONS: 459   876   1847 1948 1982)

B-92   BARBER, T. X., & CALVERLY, D. S.
             AN EXPERIMENTAL STUDY OF "HYPNOTIC" (AUDITORY AND VISUAL) HALLUCINATIONS.
             JOURNAL OF ABNORMAL AND SOCIAL PSYCHOLOGY, 1964, 68, 13-20.
             (RATING SCALES A AND B OF HYPNOTIC SUGGESTIBILITY)
         @B-92 HYPNOTIC SUGGESTIBILITY HALLUCINATION 1964M

B-93   BRENGELMANN, J. C.
             EXTREME RESPONSE SET, DRIVE LEVEL AND ABNORMALITY IN QUESTIONNAIRE RIGIDITY
             JOURNAL OF MENTAL SCIENCE, 1960, 106, 171-186.
             (MEASURES OF RIGIDITY)
         @B-93 RIGIDITY FLEXIBILITY DOGMATISM COPING-DEFENSE 1960M
             (APPLICATIONS: 711   866)

B-94   BENJAMIN, J. D.
             A METHOD FOR DISTINGUISHING AND EVALUATING FORMAL THINKING DISORDERS IN
             SCHIZOPHRENIA.
             IN J. S. KASANIN (ED.) LANGUAGE AND THOUGHT IN SCHIZOPHRENIA. BERKELEY:
             UNIVERSITY OF CALIFORNIA PRESS, 1944.
             (BENJAMIN'S PROVERBS TEST)*
         @B-94 SCHIZOPHRENIA THINKING PSYCHIATRIC MENTAL-ILLNESS DIAGNOSIS ADJUSTMENT
         @B-94 1944M
             (APPLICATIONS: 888 1026 1048 1151 1864 2018 2111 2272 2404 2592
                              2630)
B-95   BORGATTA, E. F., & FORD, R. N.
             A NOTE ON TASK AND SITUATIONAL FACTORS IN WORK ORIENTATION AND
             SATISFACTION.
             JOURNAL OF PSYCHOLOGY, 1970, 74, 125-130.
             ("REACTIONS TO YOUR JOB" FORM)
         @B-95 1970M JOB SATISFACTION

B-96   BECKER, J., & NICHOLS, C. H.
             COMMUNALITY OF MANIC-DEPRESSIVE AND "MILD" CYCLOTHYMIC CHARACTERISTICS.
             JOURNAL OF ABNORMAL AND SOCIAL PSYCHOLOGY, 1964, 69, 531-538.
             (MOOD INVENTORY - SELF/OTHERS, FOR CYCLOTHYMIA)
         @B-96 MOOD AFFECTIVE-STATES GLOBAL SATISFACTION NEGATIVE ADJUSTMENT SELF OTHERS
         @B-96 1964M

B-97   BIERI, J., ATKINS, A. L., BRIAR, S., LEAMAN, R. L., MILLER, H., & TRIPODI, T.
             CLINICAL AND SOCIAL JUDGMENT: THE DISCRIMINATION OF BEHAVIORAL INFORMATION.
             NEW YORK: WILEY, 1966.
             (MEASURE OF COGNITIVE COMPLEXITY)
         @B-97 COGNITIVE COMPLEXITY AUTONOMY CREATIVITY DIFFERENTIATION STRUCTURE
         @B-97 FUNCTIONING THINKING JUDGMENT 1966M
             (APPLICATIONS: 219   510 2180 2775)

B-98   BIRNEY, R. C., BURDICK, H., & TEEVAN, R. C.
                ANALYSIS OF TAT STORIES FOR HOSTILE PRESS THEMA.
                PAPER PRESENTED AT THE MEETING OF THE EASTERN PSYCHOLOGICAL ASSOCIATION,
                PHILADELPHIA, APRIL, 1961.
                (TAT MEASURES OF HOSTILE PRESS AND FEAR OF FAILURE)
            aB-98 PRESS ADJUSTMENT OTHER-CATEGORY FEAR FAILURE TAT HOSTILITY
            aB-98 PROJECTIVE ENVIRONMENT IMAGERY 1961M
                (APPLICATIONS: 213   395)

B-99   BERNREUTER, R. G.
                THE THEORY AND CONSTRUCTION OF THE PERSONALITY INVENTORY.
                JOURNAL OF SOCIAL PSYCHOLOGY, 1933, 4, 387-405.
            BERNREUTER, R. G.
                THE PERSONALITY INVENTORY.
                STANFORD: STANFORD UNIVERSITY PRESS, 1935.
                (BERNREUTER PERSONALITY INVENTORY)*
            aB-99 1933M MULTITRAIT GLOBAL PERSONALITY INVENTORY
                (APPLICATIONS: 521   591   748   2911)

B-100   BANTA, T. J., WALDER, L. O., & ERON, L. D.
                CONVERGENT AND DISCRIMINANT VALIDATION OF A CHILD-REARING SURVEY
                QUESTIONNAIRE.
                JOURNAL OF SOCIAL PSYCHOLOGY, 1963, 60, 115-125.
                (CHILD-REARING SURVEY QUESTIONNAIRE)*
            aB-100 PARENT-CHILD ADJUSTMENT FAMILY INTERACTION BEHAVIOR PARENTAL 1963M

B-101   BUEL, W. D.
                THE VALIDITY OF BEHAVIORAL RATING SCALE ITEMS FOR THE ASSESSMENT OF INDIVI-
                DUAL CREATIVITY.
                JOURNAL OF APPLIED PSYCHOLOGY, 1960, 44, 407-412.
                (MEASURE OF INDIVIDUAL CREATIVITY)
            aB-101 CREATIVITY AUTONOMY RATING CHECKLIST 1960M

B-102   BENDIG, A. W., & STILLMAN, E. L.
                DIMENSIONS OF JOB INCENTIVES AMONG COLLEGE STUDENTS.
                JOURNAL OF APPLIED PSYCHOLOGY, 1958, 42, 367-371.
                (JOB INCENTIVE RANKINGS)*
            aB-102 JOB INCENTIVE ADJUSTMENT AUTONOMY MOTIVE INTRINSIC EXTRINSIC STUDENT
            aB-102 1958M

B-103   BRAINARD, P. P., & BRAINARD, R. I.
                BRAINARD OCCUPATIONAL PREFERENCE INVENTORY MANUAL, FORM R.
                NEW YORK: PSYCHOLOGICAL CORPORATION, 1956.
                (BRAINARD OCCUPATIONAL PREFERENCE INVENTORY)*
            aB-103 PREFERENCE ADJUSTMENT JOB VOCATIONAL INTEREST 1956M

B-104   BAUMAN, M. K.
                A MANUAL OF NORMS FOR TESTS USED IN COUNSELING BLIND PERSONS.
                NEW YORK: AMERICAN FOUNDATION FOR THE BLIND, 1958.
                (EMOTIONAL FACTORS INVENTORY)*
            aB-104 ADJUSTMENT COUNSELING DISABILITY EMOTION AFFECTIVE-STATES MENTAL-HEALTH
            aB-104 1958M

B-105   BASS, B. M.
                HOW TO SUCCEED IN BUSINESS ACCORDING TO BUSINESS STUDENTS AND MANAGERS.
                JOURNAL OF APPLIED PSYCHOLOGY, 1968, 52, 254-262.
                (ORGANIZATIONAL SUCCESS QUESTIONNAIRE)*
            aB-105 NEED ADJUSTMENT JOB ORGANIZATION SUCCESS SATISFACTION 1968M

B-106   BRAEN, B. B.
                DEVELOPMENT OF A THEORETICALLY-BASED MANIFEST RIGIDITY INVENTORY.
                PSYCHOLOGICAL REPORTS, 1960, 6, 75-88.
                (SELF DESCRIPTION INVENTORY)*
            aB-106 COPING-DEFENSE RIGIDITY DOGMATISM FLEXIBILITY IMPULSIVENESS MANIFEST
            aB-106 1960M

B-107   BARCLAY, A. M., & HABER, R. N.
                THE RELATION OF AGGRESSIVE TO SEXUAL MOTIVATION.
                JOURNAL OF PERSONALITY, 1965, 33, 462-475.
                (TAT SCORED FOR AGGRESSION AND SEXUALITY)
            aB-107 1965M TAT IMAGERY AGGRESSION SEX DEFENSIVENESS

B-108   BLOOMER, R. H.
               IDENTIFICATION FIGURES OF BOYS AND GIRLS UNDER VARYING DEGREES OF IMPLIED
               STRESS.
               PSYCHOLOGICAL REPORTS, 1964, 15, 635-642.
               (QUESTIONNAIRE MEASURE OF IDENTIFICATION IN CHILDREN)
           @B-108 IDENTIFICATION SELF-IDENTITY IDEAL SELF IMAGE. CHILD ADJUSTMENT 1964M

B-109   BLUMBERG, R. W.
               A SCALE FOR "PROBLEMS-IN-LIVING" RESEARCH.
               PSYCHOLOGICAL REPORTS, 1968, 22, 161-162.
               (PROBLEM PATHOLOGICAL POTENTIAL SCALE)*
           @B-109 GLOBAL ADJUSTMENT COPING-DEFENSE PROBLEM LIFE COPING ADAPTABILITY 1968M

B-110   BORGATTA, E. F., FORD, R. N., & BOHRNSTEDT, G. W.
               THE WORK COMPONENTS STUDY (WCS): A REVISED SET OF MEASURES FOR WORK
               MOTIVATION.
               MULTIVARIATE BEHAVIORAL RESEARCH, 1968, 3, 403-414.
               (WORK COMPONENTS STUDY)*
           @B-110 1968M JOB MOTIVE ADJUSTMENT ENVIRONMENT
               (APPLICATIONS: 2871)

B-111   BROWN, C. M., & FERGUSON, L. W.
               SELF-CONCEPT AND RELIGIOUS BELIEF.
               PSYCHOLOGICAL REPORTS, 1968, 22, 266.
               (RELIGIOUS ATTITUDE SCALE)
           @B-111 RELIGION ATTITUDE SELF CONCEPT ORIENTATION 1968M

B-112   BOYAR, J.
               THE CONSTRUCTION AND PARTIAL VALIDATION OF A SCALE FOR THE MEASUREMENT OF
               THE FEAR OF DEATH.
               DISSERTATION ABSTRACTS, 1964, 25, 2041.
               (FEAR OF DEATH SCALE)*
           @B-112 AFFECTIVE-STATES FEAR DEATH ANXIETY STRESS SUBJECTIVE PHOBIA NEGATIVE
           @B-112 MORTALITY 1964M

B-113   BRODSKY, S. L.
               THE WAYTE METHOD OF INVESTIGATING SELF-PERCEPTIONS.
               JOURNAL OF PROJECTIVE TECHNIQUES AND PERSONALITY ASSESSMENT, 1967, 31, 60-
               64.
               (WHO-ARE-YOU-TIME-EXTENSION: WAYTE)*
           @B-113 SELF-IDENTITY SELF ROLE PERCEPTION TIME GROUP AFFILIATION SUB-IDENTITY
           @ESTEEM PROJECTIVE PERSPECTIVE FUTURE 1967M

B-114   BATTLE, E. S., & ROTTER, J. B.
               CHILDREN'S FEELINGS OF PERSONAL CONTROL AS RELATED TO SOCIAL CLASS AND
               ETHNIC GROUP.
               JOURNAL OF PERSONALITY, 1963, 31, 482-490.
               (CHILDREN'S PICTURE TEST OF INTERNAL-EXTERNAL CONTROL)
           @B-114 LOCUS CONTROL AUTONOMY IE-CONTROL CHILD PROJECTIVE 1963M

B-115   BIALER, I.
               CONCEPTUALIZATION OF SUCCESS AND FAILURE IN MENTALLY RETARDED AND NORMAL
               CHILDREN.
               JOURNAL OF PERSONALITY, 1961, 29, 303-320.
               (LOCUS OF CONTROL SCALE)*
           @B-115 SUCCESS FAILURE AFFECTIVE-STATES ALIENATION AUTONOMY LOCUS CONTROL
           @IE-CONTROL CHILD 1961M
               (APPLICATIONS: 343   380   878 2803)

B-116   BRIM, O. G., JR.
               ATTITUDE CONTENT-INTENSITY AND PROBABILITY EXPECTATIONS.
               AMERICAN SOCIOLOGICAL REVIEW, 1955, 20, 68-76.
               ("DESIRE FOR CERTAINTY" OR "NEED FOR SECURITY" TEST)
           @B-116 NEED SECURITY FLEXIBILITY RIGIDITY DOGMATISM COPING-DEFENSE 1955M
               (APPLICATIONS: 190)

B-117   BRIGGS, L. J.
               DEVELOPMENT AND APPRAISAL OF A MEASURE OF STUDENT MOTIVATION.
               RESEARCH BULLETIN, AIR FORCE PERSONNEL AND TRAINING RESEARCH CENTER,
               LACKLAND AIR FORCE BASE, SAN ANTONIO, NO. TR-54-31, 1954. (FOR REFERENCE
               TO THIS SCALE, SEE MAYO, G. D., & MANNING, W. H.   EDUCATIONAL AND
               PSYCHOLOGICAL MEASUREMENT, 1961, 21, 73-83.)
               (BEHAVIOR CHECKLIST OF ACHIEVEMENT MOTIVATION)
           @B-117 AUTONOMY NEED ACHIEVEMENT MOTIVE CHECKLIST BEHAVIOR 1954M

B-118   BERG, I. A.
              THE RELIABILITY OF EXTREME POSITION RESPONSE SETS IN TWO TESTS.
              JOURNAL OF PSYCHOLOGY, 1953, 36, 3-9.
              (PERCEPTUAL REACTION TEST)*
          ∂B-118 RESPONSE-BIAS PERCEPTION RESPONSE SET 1953M
              (APPLICATIONS: 724   834   1308   1737   1777   2143)

B-119   BASSELL, J. S.
              A STUDY OF THE ATTITUDES OF SCHIZOPHRENIC PATIENTS TOWARD MENTAL ILLNESS:
              AN INVESTIGATION OF THE DIFFERENCES IN CERTAIN STEREOTYPED ATTITUDES
              REGARDING MENTAL ILLNESS IN SCHIZOPHRENIC PATIENTS REFERRED FOR RELEASE
              FROM THE HOSPITAL, AND IN THOSE WHO HAD TO REMAIN IN THE HOSPITAL.
              UNPUBLISHED DOCTORAL DISSERTATION, NEW YORK UNIVERSITY, 1955.
              (QUESTIONNAIRE MEASURE OF BELIEFS CONCERNING MENTAL ILLNESS)
          ∂B-119 ADJUSTMENT PATIENT PSYCHIATRIC MENTAL-HEALTH MENTAL-ILLNESS ATTITUDE
          ∂B-119 BELIEF DIAGNOSIS SCHIZOPHRENIA 1955M
              (APPLICATIONS: 827)

B-120   BALES, R. F.
              THE VALUE PROFILE, FORM E.
              UNPUBLISHED, UNDATED MANUSCRIPT. (FOR REFERENCE TO THE MEASURE, SEE
              HOROWITZ, H., JOURNAL OF PSYCHOLOGY, 1966, 63, 235-247.)
              (VALUE PROFILE)*
          ∂B-120 VALUES SELF-IDENTITY IDEALS LIFE GOALS DEVELOPMENT ORIENTATION 1966M
              (APPLICATIONS: 867)

B-121   BORGATTA, E. F.
              THE MULTI-LEVEL PERSONALITY INVENTORY.
              UNPUBLISHED MANUSCRIPT, 1961. (FOR REFERENCE TO THIS SCALE, SEE HOROWITZ,
              H. JOURNAL OF PSYCHOLOGY, 1966, 63, 235-247.)
              (MULTI-LEVEL PERSONALITY INVENTORY)*
          ∂B-121 MULTITRAIT 1961M

B-122   BREZNITZ, S., & KUGLEMASS, S.
              THE PERCEPTION OF PARENTS BY ADOLESCENTS: CONSIDERATION OF THE
              INSTRUMENTALITY-EXPRESSIVITY DIFFERENTIATION.
              HUMAN RELATIONS, 1965, 18, 103-113.
              (MEASURE OF PERCEPTION OF PARENTS BY ADOLESCENTS)
          ∂B-122 1965M FAMILY INTERACTION PARENT-CHILD PERSON PERCEPTION EXPRESSIVENESS
          ∂B-122 PARENTAL CONTROL ADOLESCENT
              (APPLICATIONS: 2876)

B-123   BEALL, H. S., & PANTON, J. H.
              USE OF THE MINNESOTA MULTIPHASIC PERSONALITY INVENTORY AS AN INDEX TO
              "ESCAPISM".
              JOURNAL OF CLINICAL PSYCHOLOGY, 1956, 12, 392-394.
              (ESCAPISM SCALE FROM MMPI)
          ∂B-123 1956M MMPI WITHDRAWAL ADJUSTMENT
              (APPLICATIONS: 2386)

B-125   BUSSE, T. V.
              ESTABLISHMENT OF THE FLEXIBLE THINKING FACTOR IN FIFTH-GRADE BOYS.
              JOURNAL OF PSYCHOLOGY, 1968, 69, 93-100.
              (INSIGHT PROBLEMS: MEASURE OF "FIGURAL ADAPTIVE FLEXIBILITY" OR "DIVERGENT
              FIGURAL TRANSFORMATIONS")
          ∂B-125 CREATIVITY FLEXIBILITY RIGIDITY DOGMATISM COPING-DEFENSE FIGURE COGNITIVE
          ∂B-125 STRUCTURE FUNCTIONING 1968M

B-126   BLOCK, J.
              THE Q-SORT METHOD IN PERSONALITY ASSESSMENT AND PSYCHIATRIC RESEARCH.
              SPRINGFIELD, ILLINOIS: C. C. THOMAS, 1961.
              CALIFORNIA Q-SORT DECK. PALO ALTO, CALIFORNIA: CONSULTING PSYCHOLOGISTS
              PRESS, 1961.
              (CALIFORNIA Q-SORT DECK)*
          ∂B-126 Q-SORT MULTITRAIT SELF-IDENTITY SELF CONCEPT EVALUATION ACCEPTANCE ESTEEM
          ∂B-126 OTHERS IMAGE PERCEPTION 1961M
              (APPLICATIONS: 424   1058   1373   1481   1564   2146   2326   2576   2943)

B-127   BRODMAN, K., ERDMANN, A. J., JR., LORGE, I., & WOLFF, H. G.
              THE CORNELL MEDICAL INDEX: AN ADJUNCT TO THE MEDICAL INTERVIEW.
              JOURNAL OF THE AMERICAN MEDICAL ASSOCIATION, 1949, 140, 530-534.
              (CORNELL MEDICAL INDEX HEALTH QUESTIONNAIRE)*
          ∂B-127 ADJUSTMENT GLOBAL MENTAL-ILLNESS MENTAL-HEALTH PATIENT PSYCHIATRIC
          ∂DIAGNOSIS 1949M
              (APPLICATIONS: 614   1039   1122   2225   2235   2697)

B-128   BELL, H. M.
          MANUAL FOR THE ADJUSTMENT INVENTORY: ADULT FORM.
          PALO ALTO, CALIF.: CONSULTING PSYCHOLOGISTS PRESS, 1938.
          (BELL ADJUSTMENT INVENTORY)*
       aB-128 ADJUSTMENT HOME OCCUPATIONAL GLOBAL JOB FAMILY INTERACTION
       aB-128 SATISFACTION PE-FIT 1938M
          (APPLICATIONS: 760   1347)

B-129   BUNNEY, W. E., & HAMBURG, D. A.
          METHODS FOR RELIABLE LONGITUDINAL OBSERVATION OF BEHAVIOR.
          ARCHIVES OF GENERAL PSYCHIATRY, 1963, 9, 280-294.
          (MOOD AND BEHAVIOR RATING SCALE)
        B-129 AFFECTIVE-STATES BEHAVIOR PHYSICAL ILLNESS DEPRESSION ANXIETY DENIAL
       aB-129 1963M MOOD OFFENSIVENESS
          (APPLICATIONS: 2435   2938)

B-130   BROWN, G. W., & RUTTER, M.
          THE MEASUREMENT OF FAMILY ACTIVITIES AND RELATIONSHIPS.
          HUMAN RELATIONS, 1966, 19, 241-263.
          (INTERVIEW MEASURE OF FAMILY ACTIVITIES AND RELATIONSHIPS)
       aB-130 FAMILY ACTIVITIES RELATIONSHIPS INTERACTION ADJUSTMENT 1966M

B-131   BUSS, A. H., & GERJUOY, H.
          THE SCALING OF TERMS USED TO DESCRIBE PERSONALITY.
          JOURNAL OF CONSULTING PSYCHOLOGY, 1957, 21, 361-369.
          ZUCKERMAN, M., BAER, M., & MONASHKIN, I.
          ACCEPTANCE OF SELF, PARENTS AND PEOPLE IN PATIENTS AND NORMALS.
          JOURNAL OF CLINICAL PSYCHOLOGY, 1956, 12, 327-332.
          (MEASURE OF SELF AND IDEAL-SELF)
       aB-131 SELF-IDENTITY SELF PERCEPTION EVALUATION ESTEEM IDEAL IMAGE CONCEPT 1956M
          (APPLICATIONS: 2670)

B-132   BARABASZ, A. F.
          TIME ESTIMATION AND TEMPORAL ORIENTATION IN DELINQUENTS AND NONDELINQUENTS:
          A RE-EXAMINATION.
          JOURNAL OF GENERAL PSYCHOLOGY, 1970, 82, 265-267.
          (TIME-ESTIMATION INSTRUMENT)
       aB-132 1970M GOALS ORIENTATION FUTURE TIME PERSPECTIVE PERCEPTION

B-133   BRONFENBRENNER, U.
          RESPONSE TO PRESSURE FROM PEERS VERSUS ADULTS AMONG SOVIET AND AMERICAN
          SCHOOLCHILDREN.
          INTERNATIONAL JOURNAL OF PSYCHOLOGY, 1962, 2, 199-207.
          (MEASURE OF RESPONSE TO PRESSURE FROM PEERS VERSUS ADULTS)
       aB-133 1967M SOCIAL PRESSURE CONFORMITY PARENT-CHILD PEER RELATIONSHIPS
          (APPLICATIONS: 2453)

B-134   BODDEN, J. L.
          COGNITIVE COMPLEXITY AS A FACTOR IN APPROPRIATE VOCATIONAL CHOICE.
          UNPUBLISHED DOCTORAL DISSERTATION, OHIO STATE UNIVERSITY, 1969.
          (MEASURE OF VOCATIONAL COMPLEXITY)
       aB-134 1969M COMPLEXITY VOCATIONAL PREFERENCE RATING

B-135   BRUNKAN, R. J., & CRITES, J. O.
          AN INVENTORY TO MEASURE THE PARENTAL ATTITUDE VARIABLES IN ROE'S THEORY
          OF VOCATIONAL CHOICE.
          JOURNAL OF COUNSELING PSYCHOLOGY, 1964, 11, 3-12.
          (FAMILY RELATIONS INVENTORY)*
       aB-135 1964M PARENTAL ACCEPTANCE APPROVAL DOMINANCE AUTHORITY APPROACH AVOIDANCE
       aB-135 PARENT-CHILD FAMILY INTERACTION RELATIONSHIPS
          (APPLICATIONS: 1301   1364   1463   1528   2853)

B-136   BACH, G. R.
          MARATHON GROUP DYNAMICS: II. DIMENSIONS OF HELPFULNESS: THERAPEUTIC
          AGGRESSION.
          PSYCHOLOGICAL REPORTS, 1967, 20, 1147-1158.
          (QUESTIONNAIRE MEASURE OF HELPFULNESS IN T-GROUPS)
       aB-136 1967M OTHERS ORIENTATION ALTRUISM INTERPERSONAL INTERACTION
       aB-136 1967M RELATIONSHIPS SOCIAL GROUP
          (APPLICATIONS: 2693)

B-138   BORGATTA, E. F.
          AN ANALYSIS OF THREE LEVELS OF RESPONSE: AN APPROACH TO SOME RELATIONSHIPS
          AMONG DIMENSIONS OF PERSONALITY.
          SOCIOMETRY, 1951, 14, 267-316.
          (SITUATIONAL TEST OF REACTIONS TO FRUSTRATION)
       aB-138 1951M SITUATIONAL DEPENDENCE GRAPHIC FRUSTRATION ROLE ENACTMENT COPING
          (APPLICATIONS: 1647)

B-139   BROOKS, G. W., & MUELLER, E. F.
                 SERUM URATE CONCENTRATIONS AMONG UNIVERSITY PROFESSORS.
                 JAMA, 1966, 195, 415-418.
                 (TOTAL ACHIEVEMENT ORIENTATION BEHAVIOR SCORE)
           @B-139 1966M ACHIEVEMENT ORIENTATION BEHAVIOR NEED AUTONOMY
                 (APPLICATIONS: 2913)

B-140   BECKER, M. H.
                 SOCIOMETRIC LOCATION AND INNOVATIVENESS: REFORMULATION AND EXTENSION
                 OF THE DIFFUSION MODEL.
                 AMERICAN SOCIOLOGICAL REVIEW, 1970, 35, 267-282.
                 (MEASURE OF COSMOPOLITANISM)
           @B-140 1970M SOCIAL ORIENTATION LIFE STYLE ATTITUDE

B-141   BARABASZ, A. F.
                 TEMPORAL ORIENTATION AND ACADEMIC ACHIEVEMENT IN COLLEGE.
                 JOURNAL OF SOCIAL PSYCHOLOGY, 1970, 80, 231-232.
                 (MEASURE OF TEMPORAL ORIENTATION)
           @B-141 1970M TIME PERSPECTIVE ORIENTATION FUTURE

B-142   BLANKENSHIP, L. V., & MILES, R. E.
                 ORGANIZATION STRUCTURE AND MANAGERIAL DECISION BEHAVIOR.
                 ADMINISTRATIVE SCIENCE QUARTERLY, 1968, 13, 106-120.
                 (MEASURE OF PERCEIVED PARTICIPATION IN JOB DECISIONS)
           @B-142 1968M PERCEIVED PARTICIPATION JOB DECISION MANAGEMENT EMPLOYEE
           @B-142 BEHAVIOR
                 (APPLICATIONS: 2469)

B-143   BERZINS, J. I., SEIDMAN, E., & WELCH, R. D.
                 A-B THERAPIST "TYPES" AND RESPONSES TO PATIENT-COMMUNICATED HOSTILITY:
                 AN ANALOGUE STUDY.
                 JOURNAL OF CONSULTING AND CLINICAL PSYCHOLOGY, 1970, 34, 27-32.
                 (STRESS-REACTION CHECKLIST)
           @B-143 1970M THERAPY PATIENT HOSTILITY STRESS CHECKLIST SITUATIONAL
           @B-143 INTERACTION RELATIONSHIPS

B-144   BOWER, E. M.
                 EARLY IDENTIFICATION OF EMOTIONALLY HANDICAPPED CHILDREN.
                 SPRINGFIELD, ILLINOIS: CHARLES C. THOMAS, 1960.
                 (THINKING ABOUT YOURSELF MEASURE)
           @B-144 1960M CHILD MALADJUSTMENT IDEAL SELF DISCREPANCY
           @B-144 SELF-IDENTITY
                 (APPLICATIONS: 2050 2199 2545)

B-145   BOWER, E. M.
                 EARLY IDENTIFICATION OF EMOTIONALLY HANDICAPPED CHILDREN.
                 SPRINGFIELD ILLINOIS: CHARLES C. THOMAS, 1960.
                 (CLASS PLAY SCALE)
           @B-145 1960M CHILD BEHAVIOR MALADJUSTMENT TEACHER
                 (APPLICATIONS: 2050 2199 2545)

B-147   BERZINS, J. I., & SEIDMAN, E.
                 SUBJECTIVE REACTIONS OF A AND B QUASI-THERAPISTS TO SCHIZOID AND
                 NEUROTIC COMMUNICATIONS: A REPLICATION AND EXTENSION.
                 JOURNAL OF CONSULTING AND CLINICAL PSYCHOLOGY, 1968, 32, 342-347.
                 (MEASURE OF THERAPISTS' SUBJECTIVE REACTIONS)
           @B-147 1968M NEUROTICISM SCHIZOPHRENIA RESPONSE PATIENT COUNSELING THERAPY
           @B-147 INTERACTION RELATIONSHIPS

B-148   BERGIN, A. E., & SOLOMON, S.
                 PERSONALITY AND PERFORMANCE CORRELATES OF EMPATHY UNDERSTANDING IN
                 PSYCHOTHERAPY.
                 PAPER PRESENTED AT THE MEETING OF THE AMERICAN PSYCHOLOGICAL ASSOCIATION,
                 PHILADELPHIA, SEPTEMBER, 1963.
                 (REVISED ACCURATE EMPATHY SCALE)
           @B-148 1963M EMPATHY THERAPY INTERACTION RELATIONSHIPS
                 (APPLICATIONS: 1006 1153 2950)

B-151   BARRON, F.
                 SOME PERSONALITY CORRELATES OF INDEPENDENCE OF JUDGMENT.
                 JOURNAL OF PERSONALITY, 1953, 21, 287-297.
                 (MEASURE OF INDEPENDENCE-YIELDING)
           @B-151 1953M JUDGMENT DEPENDENCE AUTONOMY CONFORMITY BEHAVIOR

B-152   BAER, D. L.
             TAXONOMIC CLASSIFICATION OF MALE DELINQUENTS FROM AUTOBIOGRAPHICAL DATA AND
             SUBSEQUENT RECIDIVISM.
             JOURNAL OF PSYCHOLOGY, 1970, 76, 27-31.
             (BIOGRAPHICAL QUESTIONNAIRE)
         @B-152 1970M DELINQUENCY HOME FAMILY PEER HABITS BEHAVIOR

B-153   BIERI, J., & BLACKER, E.
             EXTERNAL AND INTERNAL STIMULUS FACTORS IN RORSCHACH PERFORMANCE.
             JOURNAL OF CONSULTING PSYCHOLOGY, 1956, 20, 1-7.
             (RORSCHACH MEASURE OF COGNITIVE COMPLEXITY)
         @B-153 1956M COGNITIVE COMPLEXITY STRUCTURE FUNCTIONING
         @B-153 RORSCHACH
             (APPLICATIONS: 339)

B-154   BIERI, J.
             COGNITIVE COMPLEXITY-SIMPLICITY AND PREDICTIVE BEHAVIOR.
             JOURNAL OF ABNORMAL AND SOCIAL PSYCHOLOGY, 1955, 51, 263-268.
             (MEASURE OF COGNITIVE COMPLEXITY)
         @B-154 1955M COGNITIVE COMPLEXITY STRUCTURE FUNCTIONING
             (APPLICATIONS: 339)

B-155   BRESKIN, S.
             MEASUREMENT OF RIGIDITY, A NON VERBAL TEST.
             PERCEPTUAL AND MOTOR SKILLS, 1968, 27, 1203-1206.
             (BRESKIN RIGIDITY TEST)*
         @B-155 1968M RIGIDITY BEHAVIOR FLEXIBILITY STIMULUS FIGURE PREFERENCE
             (APPLICATIONS: 2886)

B-159   BERGIN, A. E.
             THE EFFECT OF DISSONANT PERSUASIVE COMMUNICATION UPON CHANGES IN A
             SELF-REFERRING ATTITUDE.
             JOURNAL OF PERSONALITY, 1962, 30, 423-438.
             (MASCULINITY-FEMINITY SCALE)
         @B-159 1962M MASCULINITY FEMINITY SEX ROLE SELF-IDENTITY SUB-IDENTITY

B-160   BARRATT, E. S.
             ANXIETY AND IMPULSIVENESS RELATED TO PSYCHOMOTOR EFFICIENCY.
             PERCEPTUAL AND MOTOR SKILLS, 1959, 9, 191-198.
             (IMPULSIVENESS SCALE)
         @B-160 1959M IMPULSE BEHAVIOR CONTROL INHIBITION EXPRESSION
             (APPLICATIONS: 386)

B-161   BODIN, A. M., & GEER, J. H.
             ASSOCIATION RESPONSES OF DEPRESSED AND NON-DEPRESSED PATIENTS TO WORDS
             OF THREE HOSTILITY LEVELS.
             JOURNAL OF PERSONALITY, 1965, 33, 392-408.
             (MEASURE OF ASSOCIATIVE DISRUPTIONS DUE TO PERSONAL CONFLICT)
         @B-161 1965M AFFECTIVE-STATES HOSTILITY COGNITIVE FUNCTIONING
         @B-161 CONFLICT

B-162   BARRON, F.
             THRESHOLDS FOR THE PERCEPTION OF HUMAN MOVEMENT IN INKBLOTS.
             JOURNAL OF CONSULTING PSYCHOLOGY, 1955, 19, 33-38.
             (MEASURE OF FREQUENCY OF HUMAN MOVEMENT RESPONSES IN INKBLOTS)
         @B-162 1955M PROJECTIVE PERCEPTION RORSCHACH INTROSPECTION INTELLIGENCE
         @B-162 EXTRAVERSION COGNITIVE STRUCTURE FUNCTIONING
             (APPLICATIONS: 423 1959 2246)

B-163   BUTERBAUGH, R. L.
             PREFERENCE FOR DELAYED REWARD AS A FUNCTION OF DELINQUENCY AND RACE.
             UNPUBLISHED MASTERS THESIS, KENT STATE UNIVERSITY, 1962.
             (DELAY OF GRATIFICATION SCALE)
         @B-163 1962M GOALS PREFERENCE DELINQUENCY

B-164   BLOCK, J.
             THE IPAR CLINICAL Q-SET (FORM II), 115 PERSONALITY DESCRIPTIVE ITEMS.
             BERKELEY: INSTITE OF PERSONALITY ASSESSMENT AND RESEARCH, 1954.
             (IPAR CLINICAL Q-SET (FORM II))
         @B-164 1954M Q-SORT PERSONALITY DESCRIPTION STEREOTYPE ADOLESCENT DESCRIPTION
         @B-164 SOCIAL DESIRABILITY NEUROTIC

B-165   BLOCH, D. A., BEHRENS, M. L., GUTTENBERG, H., KING, F. G., & TENDLER, D.
               A STUDY OF CHILDREN REFERRED FOR RESIDENTIAL TREATMENT IN NEW YORK STATE.
               ALBANY: NEW YORK STATE INTERDEPARTMENTAL HEALTH RESOUCES BOARD, 1959.
               (MULTIPROBLEM FAMILY INDEX)*
            @B-165 1959M FAMILY INTERACTION PARENT-CHILD ADJUSTMENT
            @B-165 MARITAL RELATIONSHIPS PHYSICAL MENTAL-HEALTH
               (APPLICATIONS: 1615)

B-166   BECKER, W. C.
               THE RELATIONSHIP OF FACTORS IN PARENTAL RATINGS OF SELF AND EACH OTHER
               TO THE BEHAVIOR OF KINDERGARTEN CHILDREN AS RATED BY MOTHERS, FATHERS, AND
               TEACHERS.
               JOURNAL OF CONSULTING PSYCHOLOGY, 1960, 24, 507-527.
               (PARENT RATING SCHEDULE)
            @B 166 1960M PARENTAL RATING BEHAVIOR PARENT-CHILD FAMILY INTERACTION
            @B-166 SEM-DIFFERENTIAL

B-167   BECKER, W. C.
               THE RELATIONSHIP OF FACTORS IN PARENTAL RATINGS OF SELF AND EACH OTHER
               TO THE BEHAVIOR OF KINDERGARTEN CHILDREN AS RATED BY MOTHERS, FATHERS, AND
               TEACHERS.
               JOURNAL OF CONSULTING PSYCHOLOGY, 1960, 24, 507-527.
               (CHILD RATING SCHEDULE)
            @B-167 1960M CHILD RATING BEHAVIOR PARENT-CHILD FAMILY INTERACTION
            @B-167 SEM-DIFFERENTIAL
               (APPLICATIONS: 43)

B-168   BOLDUC, T. E.
               SOCIAL VALUE-NEED PATTERNS IN MENTAL RETARDATES.
               JOURNAL OF CONSULTING PSYCHOLOGY, 1960, 24, 472-479.
               (SOCIAL VALUE-NEED SCALE)*
            @B-168 1960M NEED VALUES CONFLICT SOCIAL AUTONOMY PEER MORAL CONFLICT

B-169   BYRNE, D.
               RESPONSE TO HUMOR AS A FUNCTION OF DRIVE AROUSAL AND PSYCHOLOGICAL
               DEFENSES.
               UNPUBLISHED DOCTORAL DISSERTATION, STANFORD UNVISERSITY, 1957.
            BYRNE, D., TERRILL, J., & MCREYNOLDS, P.
               INCONGRUENCY AS A PREDICTOR OF RESPONSE TO HUMOR.
               JOURNAL OF ABNORMAL AND SOCIAL PSYCHOLOGY, 1961, 62, 435-438.
               (CARTOON TEST)
            @B-169
               (APPLICATIONS: 644   1713)

B-171   BRANCA, A. A., & PODOLNICK, E. E.
               NORMAL, HYPNOTICALLY INDUCED, AND FEIGNED ANXITY AS REFLECTED AND DETECTED
               BY THE MMPI.
               JOURNAL OF CONSULTING PSYCHOLOGY, 1961, 25, 165-170.
               (ANXIETY RATING SCALE)
            @B-171 1961M ANXIETY HYPNOTIC SUGGESTIBILITY TENSION EMOTION SITUATIONAL

B-173   BYRNE, D., GOLIGHTLY, C., & CAPALDI, E. J.
               CONSTRUCTION AND VALIDATION OF THE FOOD ATTITUDE SCALE.
               JOURNAL OF CONSULTING PSYCHOLOGY, 1963, 27, 215-222.
               (FOOD ATTITUDE SCALE)*
            @B-173 1963M ATTITUDE HABITS PREFERENCE

B-174   BROWN, F.
               A PSYCHONEUROTIC INVENTORY FOR CHILDREN BETWEEN NINE AND FOURTEEN YEARS
               OF AGE.
               JOURNAL OF APPLIED PSYCHOLOGY, 1934, 18, 566-577.
               (BROWN PERSONALITY INVENTORY)*
            @B-174 1934M CHILD NEUROTICISM PARENTAL SUPPORT STRESS STRICTNESS SIBLING
            @B-174 RIVALRY COMPETENCE PHYSICAL ANXIETY SECURITY TENSION EMOTION
               (APPLICATIONS: 1641)

B-175   BUCK, J. N.
               THE H-T-P TECHNIQUE: A QUALITATIVE AND QUANTITATIVE SCORING MANUAL.
               JOURNAL OF CLINICAL PSYCHOLOGY, 1948, MONOGRAPH SUPPLEMENT NO. 5.
               (HOUSE-TREE-PERSON TEST)*
            @B-175 1948M PROJECTIVE GRAPHIC FIGURE
               (APPLICATIONS: 1701   2953)

B-176   BLUM, G. S.
         THE BLACKY PICTURES: A TECHNIQUE FOR THE EXPLORATION OF PERSONALITY
         DYNAMICS (MANUAL).   NEW YORK: THE PSYCHOLOGICAL CORPORATION, 1950.
         (THE BLACKY TEST)*
         @B-176 1950M PSYCHOPATHOLOGY ORALITY MENTAL-HEALTH MENTAL-ILLNESS NEUROTICISM

B-177   BLATT, S. J.
         AN ATTEMPT TO DEFINE MENTAL HEALTH.
         JOURNAL OF CONSULTING PSYCHOLOGY, 1964, 28, 146-153.
         STEIN, M. I.
         EXPLORATION IN TYPOLOGY. IN R. W. WHITE (ED.). THE STUDY OF LIVES.
         NEW YORK: ATHERTON PRESS, 1964, 280-303.
         (SELF DESCRIPTION TEST)
         @B-177 1964M NEED SELF DESCRIPTION SELF EVALUATION
         (APPLICATIONS: 1969)

B-178   BUTCHER, J. N.
         MANIFEST AGGRESSION: MMPI CORRELATES IN NORMAL BOYS.
         JOURNAL OF CONSULTING PSYCHOLOGY, 1965, 29, 446-454.
         (PEER NOMINATION RATINGS FOR CHILDREN)
         @B-178 1965M EXPRESSION AGGRESSION PEER RATING HOSTILITY WITHDRAWAL PASSIVE
         @B-178 PERCEPTION CHILD

B-179   BREGER, L., & LIVERANT, S.
         HOMOSEXUAL PREJUDICE AND PERCEPTUAL DEFENSE
         JOURNAL OF CONSULTING PSYCHOLOGY, 1961, 25, 459.
         (SCALE OF MANIFEST ATTITUDES TOWARDS HOMOSEXUALITY)
         @B-179 1961M MANIFEST ATTITUDE HOMOSEXUALITY PREJUDICE DEFENSE
         @B-179 PERCEPTION

B-180   BORDIN, E. S.
         PERSONALITY AND FREE ASSOCIATION.
         JOURNAL OF CONSULTING PSYCHOLOGY, 1966, 30, 30-38.
         BORDIN, E. S.
         FREE ASSOCIATION: AN EXPERIMENTAL ANALOGUE OF THE PSYCHOANALYTIC SITUATION.
         IN L. A. GOTTSCHALK & A. H. AUERBACK (ED.), METHODS OF RESEARCH IN
         PSYCHOTHERAPY. NEW YORK: APPLETON-CENTURY-CROFTS, 1966.
         (RATING SCALES OF FREE ASSOCIATION)
         @B-180 1966M PERSONALITY THERAPY PRIMARY-PROCESS SPONTANEITY INVOLVEMENT
         (APPLICATIONS: 1017)

B-182   BENDIG, A. W.
         THE PITTSBURGH SCALES OF SOCIAL EXTRAVERSION-INTROVERSION AND
         EMOTIONALITY.
         JOURNAL OF PSYCHOLOGY, 1962, 53, 199-209.
         (PITTSBURGH SCALE OF EMOTIONALITY)
         @B-182 1962M EMOTION TAYLOR-MA AFFECTIVE-STATES
         (APPLICATIONS: 2008 2095)

B-183   BRAGINSKY, B. M., GROSSE, M., & RING, K.
         CONTROLLING OUTCOMES THROUGH IMPRESSION-MANAGEMENT: AN EXPERIMENTAL
         STUDY OF THE MANIPULATIVE TACTICS OF MENTAL PATIENTS.
         JOURNAL OF CONSULTING PSYCHOLOGY, 1966, 30, 295-300.
         (MENTAL STATUS TEST OF PATIENT'S FAKING GOOD OR BAD)
         @B-183 1966M MENTAL-HEALTH STATUS SELF PATIENT RESPONSE-BIAS SOCIAL
         @B-183 DESIRABILITY

B-184   BENDIG, A. W.
         THE DEVELOPMENT OF A SHORT FORM OF THE MANIFEST ANXIETY SCALE.
         JOURNAL OF CONSULTING PSYCHOLOGY, 1956, 20, 384.
         (SHORT FORM OF MANIFEST ANXIETY SCALE)
         @B-184 1956M ANXIETY AFFECTIVE-STATES MANIFEST TAYLOR-MA
         @B-184 TENSION STRESS NEGATIVE AFFECTIVE-STATES
         (APPLICATIONS: 193   252   536   631   633   1061   1514   1613   1677   2126
                          2379   2570)

B-185   BUXBAUM, J.
         EFFECT OF NURTURANCE ON WIVES' APPRAISALS OF THEIR MARITAL SATISFACTION AND
         THE DEGREE OF THEIR HUSBANDS' APHASIA.
         JOURNAL OF CONSULTING PSYCHOLOGY, 1967, 31, 240-243.
         (MEASURE OF MARITAL ROLES AND ATTITUDES)
         @B-185 1967M MARITAL ROLE ADJUSTMENT RELATIONSHIPS ATTITUDE
         @B-185 COMPATIBILITY SATISFACTION

B-186   BARNDT, R. J., & JOHNSON, D. M.
              TIME ORIENTATION IN DELINQUENTS.
              JOURNAL OF ABNORMAL AND SOCIAL PSYCHOLOGY, 1955, 51, 343-345.
              (STORY COMPLETION MEASURE OF FUTURE TIME PERSPECTIVE)
          aB-186 1955M TIME ORIENTATION FUTURE PERSPECTIVE DELINQUENT
              (APPLICATIONS: 487   639   2074   2133)

B-187   BUSS, A.
              THE PSYCHOLOGY OF AGGRESSION.
              NEW YORK: WILEY, 1961.
              (BUSS AGGRESSION MACHINE)*
          aB-187 1961M AGGRESSION AGGRESSIVENESS CONTROL INHIBITION HOSTILITY
          aB-187 EXPRESSION
              (APPLICATIONS: 2164)

B-188   BENDIG, A. W.
              FACTOR ANALYTIC SCALES OF COVERT AND OVERT HOSTILITY.
              JOURNAL OF CONSULTING PSYCHOLOGY, 1962, 26, 200.
              (COVERT AND OVERT HOSTILITY SCALES)
          aB-188 1962M HOSTILITY AGGRESSION EXPRESSION INHIBITION CONTROL
              (APPLICATIONS: 2302)

B-189   BUSH, M.
              A STUDY OF REALITY-CLOSENESS-REALITY-DISTANCE: A DIRECTIONAL DETERMINANT
              OF ATTENTION DEPLOYMENT.
              UNPUBLISHED DOCTORAL DISSERTATION, UNIVERSITY OF MICHIGAN, 1968.
              (REALITY-ATTENTIVENESS-REALITY-INATTENTIVENESS (RA-RI) QUESTIONNAIRE)*
          aB-189 1968M BREADTH ATTENTION AWARENESS SENSORY INTENSITY ORIENTATION PE-FIT
          aB-189 REALITY PERCEPTION
              (APPLICATIONS: 2250)

B-190   BIERI, J., & LOBECK, R.
              ACCEPTANCE OF AUTHORITY AND PARENTAL IDENTIFICATION.
              JOURNAL OF PERSONALITY, 1959, 27, 74-86.
              (ACCEPTANCE OF AUTHORITY SCALE)
          aB-190 1959M ACCEPTANCE AUTHORITY AUTHORITARIANISM DOGMATISM DOMINANCE F-SCALE
          aATTITUDE NEED AUTONOMY SUBMISSION
              (APPLICATIONS: 546)

B-191   BERGER, D. G., RICE, C. E., SEWALL, L. G., & LEMKAU, P. V.
              POSTHOSPITAL EVALUATION OF PSYCHIATRIC PATIENTS: THE SOCIAL ADJUSTMENT
              INVENTORY.
              PSYCHIATRIC STUDIES AND PROJECTS, 1964, 2, NO. 15.
              (SOCIAL ADJUSTMENT INVENTORY)
          aB-191 1964M RATING PATIENT ADJUSTMENT SOCIAL COMPETENCE
          aB-191 PSYCHIATRIC

B-192   BASS, B. M.
              AUTHORITARIANISM OR ACQUIESCENCE?
              JOURNAL OF ABNORMAL AND SOCIAL PSYCHOLOGY, 1955, 51, 616-623.
              (REVERSED FASCISM SCALE (G SCALE))
          aB-192 1955M AUTHORITARIANISM RIGIDITY F-SCALE DOGMATISM SEM-DIFFERENTIAL
          aACQUIESCENCE RESPONSE-BIAS
              (APPLICATIONS: 77   560)

B-193   BIEBER, I., DAIN, H. J., DINCE, P. R., DRELLICH, M. G., GRAND, H. G.,
          GUNDLACH, R. H., KREMER, M. W., RIFKIN, A. H., WILBUR, C. B., & BIEBER, T. B.
              HOMOSEXUALITY: A PSYCHOANALYTIC STUDY.
              NEW YORK: BASIC BOOKS, 1962.
              (MEASURE OF SEX-ROLE RELATED CHILDHOOD EXPERIENCES)
          aB-193 1962M SEX ROLE IDENTITY SELF-IDENTITY SUB-IDENTITY MASCULINITY
          aB-193 HOMOSEXUALITY CHILD EXPERIENCE
              (APPLICATIONS: 2262)

B-194   BEACH, L., & WERTHEIMER, M.
              A FREE RESPONSE APPROACH TO THE STUDY OF PERSON COGNITION.
              JOURNAL OF ABNORMAL AND SOCIAL PSYCHOLOGY, 1961, 62, 367-374.
              (METHOD FOR CONTENT ANALYSIS OF PERSON DESCRIPTIONS)
          aB-194 1961M OTHERS DESCRIPTION PERSON PERCEPTION
          aB-194 SOCIAL INTERACTION BEHAVIOR CONTENT-ANALYSIS

B-195   BYRNE, D.
              INTERPERSONAL ATTRACTION AND ATTITUDE SIMILARITY.
              JOURNAL OF ABNORMAL AND SOCIAL PSYCHOLOGY, 1961, 62, 713-715.
              (SURVEY OF ATTITUDES)
          aB-195 1961M ATTITUDE DESEGREGATION RELIGION POLITICAL SEX BEHAVIOR
              (APPLICATIONS: 278   353   751   2449   2646)

B-196   BERKOWITZ, L., & HOLMES, D. S.
              A FURTHER INVESTIGATION OF HOSTILITY GENERALIZATION TO DISLIKED OBJECTS.
              JOURNAL OF PERSONALITY, 1960, 28, 427-442.
              (SEMANTIC DIFFERENTIAL FOR EVALUATING OTHERS)
          @B-196 1960M HOSTILITY DIRECTION SEM-DIFFERENTIAL OTHERS EVALUATION ATTITUDE
              (APPLICATIONS: 721)

B-197   BRAMEL, D.
              A DISSONANCE THEORY APPROACH TO DEFENSIVE PROJECTION.
              JOURNAL OF ABNORMAL AND SOCIAL PSYCHOLOGY, 1962, 64, 121-129.
              (SELF-CONCEPT MEASURE)
          @B-197 1962M CONCEPT IMAGE SELF SELF-IDENTITY CHECKLIST

B-198   BLANTON, R. L., & NUNNALLY, J. C.
              SEMANTIC HABITS AND COGNITIVE STYLE PROCESSES IN THE DEAF.
              JOURNAL OF ABNORMAL AND SOCIAL PSYCHOLOGY, 1964, 68, 397-402.
              (SEMANTIC MEASURES OF ADJUSTMENT, EVALUATION, UNDERSTANDABILITY, AND
              POTENCY)
          @B-198 1964M SEM-DIFFERENTIAL SELF-IDENTITY SELF CONCEPT ATTITUDE DISABILITY
          @B-198 PARENT-CHILD EVALUATION POWER ADJUSTMENT

B-199   BLOCK, J.
              THE DEVELOPMENT OF AN MMPI-BASED SCALE TO MEASURE EGO CONTROL.
              MIMEOGRAPHED MATERIALS. BERKELEY: INSTITUTE OF PERSONALITY ASSESSMENT AND
              RESEARCH, UNIVERSITY OF CALIFORNIA, 1953.
              (PSYCHONEUROTIC TENDENCY SCALE FROM MMPI)
          @B-199 1953M NEUROTICISM MMPI ADJUSTMENT DIAGNOSIS MENTAL-ILLNESS
              (APPLICATIONS: 876 1671)

B-200   BRONFENBRENNER, U., HARDING, J., & GALLWEY, M.
              THE MEASUREMENT OF SKILL IN SOCIAL PERCEPTION.
              IN D. C. MCCLELLAND, A. L. BALDWIN, U. BRONFENBRENNER, & F. L. STRODTBECK
              (EDS.), TALENT AND SOCIETY. PRINCETON, N. J.: VAN NOSTRAND, 1958.
              (MEASURE OF INTERPERSONAL SENSITIVITY)
          @B-200 1958M INTERPERSONAL RELATIONSHIPS SENSITIVITY ORIENTATION OTHERS
          @B-200 GROUP INTERACTION SOCIAL

B-201   BASS, B. M.
              AN EVALUATION OF THE USE OF OBJECTIVE SOCIAL DATA FOR TRAINING PROBLEM-
              SOLVING DISCUSSANTS.
              TECHNICAL REPORT NO. 22, 1960, LOUISIANA STATE UNIVERSITY, CONTRACT N7 ONR
              35609.
              (MEASURE OF PROBLEM-SOLVING ABILITY)
          @B-201 1960M COGNITIVE ABILITY GROUP INFLUENCE MORAL
          @B-201 BEHAVIOR FUNCTIONING
              (APPLICATIONS: 685)

B-202   BEITNER, M. S.
              WORD MEANING AND SEXUAL IDENTIFICATION IN PARANOID SCHIZOPHRENICS AND
              ANXIETY NEUROTICS.
              JOURNAL OF ABNORMAL AND SOCIAL PSYCHOLOGY, 1961, 63, 289-293.
              (SEMANTIC DIFFERENTIAL MEASURE OF IDENTIFICATION)
          @B-202 1961M SEM-DIFFERENTIAL IDENTIFICATION INTERPERSONAL RELATIONSHIPS
          @B-202 MATERNAL PATERNAL

B-204   BIERI, J., LOBECK, R., & GALINSKY, M. D.
              A COMPARISON OF DIRECT, INDIRECT, AND FANTASY MEASURES OF IDENTIFICATION.
              JOURNAL OF ABNORMAL AND SOCIAL PSYCHOLOGY, 1959, 58, 253-258.
              (MEASURE OF CHILD'S IDENTIFICATION WITH MOTHER AND FATHER)
          @B-204 1959M PARENT-CHILD SIMILARITY PATERNAL MATERNAL PARENTAL IDENTIFICATION
          @B-204 CHILD
              (APPLICATIONS: 615)

B-205   BLUMENTHAL, R. L.
              SOCIOMETRIC CHOICE PATTERNS IN OUTPATIENT SCHIZOPHRENICS.
              NEWSLETTER FOR RESEARCH IN PSYCHOLOGY, 1964, 6, 41-43.
          BLUMENTHAL, R., MELTZOFF, J., & ROSENBERG, S.
              SOME DETERMINANTS OF PERSISTENCE IN CHRONIC SCHIZOPHRENIC SUBJECTS.
              JOURNAL OF ABNORMAL PSYCHOLOGY, 1965, 70, 246-250.
              (ADJUSTMENT RATING SCALE)
          @B-205 1964M ADJUSTMENT MALADJUSTMENT PSYCHIATRIC INTERPERSONAL RELATIONSHIPS
          @B-205 SELF CONCEPT FAMILY DEPENDENCE MOOD
              (APPLICATIONS: 962)

B-207   BORENSTEIN, B.
          A STUDY OF THE RELATIONSHIP BETWEEN THEMATIC APPERCEPTION TEST FANTASY AND
          OVERT BEHAVIOR.
          UNPUBLISHED DOCTORAL DISSERTATION, UNIVERSITY OF CALIFORNIA, 1954.
          (TAT SCORED FOR EGO AND DRIVE VARIABLES)
          aB-207 1954M TAT EGO-STRENGTH DRIVE INTENSITY FANTASY
          aB-207 IMAGERY PROJECTIVE
          (APPLICATIONS: 1018)

B-208   BRONSON, W. C.
          CENTRAL ORIENTATIONS: A STUDY OF BEHAVIOR ORGANIZATION FROM CHILDHOOD TO
          ADOLESCENCE.
          CHILD DEVELOPMENT, 1966, 37, 125-155.
          (BEHAVIOR RATING SCALES FOR CHILDREN)
          aB-208 1966M BEHAVIOR RATING CHILD
          (APPLICATIONS: 1018)

B-209   BLUM, G. S.
          DEFENSE PREFERENCES IN FOUR COUNTRIES.
          JOURNAL OF PROJECTIVE TECHNIQUES, 1956, 20, 33-41.
          (DEFENSE PREFERENCE INQUIRY)*
          aB-209 1956M PROJECTIVE COPING-DEFENSE CONFLICT EGO DEFENSE
          (APPLICATIONS: 984)

B-210   BELLAK, L., BELLAK, S. S., & HAWORTH, M. S.
          A SCHEDULE OF ADAPTIVE MECHANISMS IN CAT RESPONSES.
          NEW YORK: C.P.S., INC., 1949. REVISED EDITION, 1961.
          BELLAK, L., & HURVICH, M. S.
          A HUMAN MODIFICATION OF THE CHILDRENS APPERCEPTION TEST (CAT-H).
          JOURNAL OF PROJECTIVE TECHNIQUES AND PERSONALITY ASSESSMENT, 1966, 30, 228-
          242.
          (CHILDRENS APPERCEPTION TEST)*
          aB-210 1949M TAT PROJECTIVE PE-FIT PERSONALITY STRUCTURE CHILD
          aB-210 PERCEPTION
          (APPLICATIONS: 1059)

B-212   BAKER, B. L.
          SYMPTOM TREATMENT AND SYMPTOM SUBSTITUTION IN ENURESIS.
          JOURNAL OF ABNORMAL PSYCHOLOGY, 1969, 74, 42-49.
          (SELF-IMAGE QUESTIONNAIRE)
          aB-212 1969M SELF IMAGE RATING CONCEPT DEPRECIATION BEHAVIOR PROBLEM
          aB-212 GLOBAL ADJUSTMENT PE-FIT CHILD

B-213   BARLOW, D. H., LEITENBERG, H., & AGRAS, W. S.
          EXPERIMENTAL CONTROL OF SEXUAL DEVIATION THROUGH MANIPULATION OF THE
          NOXIOUS SCENE IN COVERT SENSITIZATION.
          JOURNAL OF ABNORMAL PSYCHOLOGY, 1969, 74, 597-601.
          (MEASURE OF SEXUALLY AROUSING SCENES)
          aB-213 1969M AROUSAL SEX ATTRACTION HOMOSEXUALITY DEVIANCE ADJUSTMENT

B-214   BERZINS, J. I.
          THE BEHAVIORAL VALIDATION OF A PSYCHOTHERAPY PATIENT ROLE-EXPECTANCY
          INVENTORY.
          UNPUBLISHED DOCTORAL DISSERTATION, UNIVERSITY OF CONNECTICUT, 1966.
          (PSYCHOTHERAPY EXPECTANCY SCALE)*
          aB-214 1966M PATIENT THERAPY RELATIONSHIPS PSYCHIATRIC RATING
          (APPLICATIONS: 1118)

B-215   BRAYFIELD, A. H., & ROTHE, H. F.
          AN INDEX OF JOB SATISFACTION.
          JOURNAL OF APPLIED PSYCHOLOGY, 1951, 35, 307-311.
          (MEASURE OF JOB SATISFACTION)
          aB-215 1951M JOB SATISFACTION EMPLOYEE ATTITUDE
          (APPLICATIONS: 1349   2358)

B-216   BLOCH, A. A.
          REMEMBRANCE OF FEELINGS PAST: A STUDY OF PHENOMENOLOGICAL GENETICS.
          JOURNAL OF ABNORMAL PSYCHOLOGY, 1969, 74, 340-347.
          (METHOD FOR CATEGORIZING DESCRIBED EMOTIONAL EXPERIENCES)
          aB-216 1969M EMOTION AFFECTIVE-STATES ADJUSTMENT EXPERIENCE

B-217   BECKER, W. C., & KRUG, R. S.
          A CIRCUMPLEX MODEL FOR SOCIAL BEHAVIOR IN CHILDREN.
          CHILD DEVELOPMENT, 1964, 35, 371-396.
          (BEHAVIOR RATING SCHEDULE)
          aB-217 1964M CHILD BEHAVIOR RATING
          (APPLICATIONS: 1051   1101)

B-219   BARDIS, P. D.
               A FAMILISM SCALE.
               MARRIAGE AND FAMILY LIVING, 1959, 21, 340-341.
               (FAMILISM SCALE)*
           @B-219 1970M FAMILY RELATIONSHIPS CHILD PARENTAL
               (APPLICATIONS: 2843)

B-220   BOLMAN, L.
               LABORATORY VERSUS LECTURE IN TRAINING EXECUTIVES.
               JOURNAL OF APPLIED BEHAVIORAL SCIENCE, 1970, 6, 323-335.
               (ANALYSIS OF PERSONAL BEHAVIOR IN GROUPS QUESTIONNAIRE)
           @B-220 1970M PERSONAL BEHAVIOR ANALYTIC THINKING AFFECTIVE-STATES OPENNESS
           @AUTHORITARIANISM FLEXIBILITY GROUP

B-221   BOLMAN, L.
               LABORATORY VERSUS LECTURE IN TRAINING EXECUTIVES.
               JOURNAL OF APPLIED BEHAVIORAL SCIENCE, 1970, 6, 323-335.
               (MANAGERIAL EXPERIENCES QUESTIONNAIRE)
           @B-221 1970M MANAGEMENT SUPERVISOR INTERPERSONAL INTERACTION BEHAVIOR
           @ORGANIZATION EXPERIENCE JOB

B-222   BOLMAN, L.
               LABORATORY VERSUS LECTURE IN TRAINING EXECUTIVES.
               JOURNAL OF APPLIED BEHAVIORAL SCIENCE, 1970, 6, 323-335.
               (MANAGERIAL BEHAVIOR QUESTIONNAIRE)
           @B-222 1970M MANAGEMENT SUPERVISOR INTERPERSONAL INTERACTION CONFRONTATION
           @POWER STRUCTURE ORGANIZATION BEHAVIOR JOB

B-223   BERNE, E. V. C.
               AN EXPERIMENTAL INVESTIGATION OF SOCIAL BEHAVIOR PATTERNS IN YOUNG
               CHILDREN.
               UNIVERSITY OF IOWA STUDIES IN CHILD WELFARE, VOL. 4, IOWA CITY: IOWA
               UNIVERSITY PRESS, 1930.
               (NURSERY SCHOOL BEHAVIOR RATING SCALE)
           @B-223 1930M CHILD BEHAVIOR RATING SOCIAL SCHOOL
               (APPLICATIONS: 2457)

B-225   BURKE, R. L., & BENNIS, W. G.
               CHANGES IN PERCEPTION OF SELF AND OTHERS DURING HUMAN RELATIONS TRAINING.
               HUMAN RELATIONS, 1961, 14, 165-182.
               (GROUP SEMANTIC DIFFERENTIAL)*
           @B-225 1961M SEM-DIFFERENTIAL SELF PERCEPTION EVALUATION GROUP
               (APPLICATIONS: 2896)

B-226   BETTS, G. H.
               THE DISTRIBUTION AND FUNCTIONS OF MENTAL IMAGERY.
               TEACHERS COLLEGE CONTRIBUTIONS TO EDUCATION, 1909, NO. 26.
               (QUESTIONNAIRE UPON MENTAL IMAGERY)*
           @B-226 1909M PRIMARY-PROCESS IMAGERY SENSORY
               (APPLICATIONS: 2413)

B-227   BURGESS, E. W., CAVAN, R. S., & HAVIGHURST, R. J.
               ADULT ATTITUDE INVENTORY.
               CHICAGO, ILL.: SCIENCE RESEARCH ASSOCIATION, 1949.
               (ADULT ATTITUDE INVENTORY)*
           @B-227 1949M ATTITUDE ADJUSTMENT PERSONAL
               (APPLICATIONS: 2644)

B-230   BOULWARE, D. W., & HOLMES, D. S.
               PREFERENCES FOR THERAPISTS AND RELATED EXPECTANCIES.
               JOURNAL OF CONSULTING AND CLINICAL PSYCHOLOGY, 1970, 35, 269-277.
               (MEASURE OF THERAPIST PREFERENCE)
           @B-230 1970M THERAPY PATIENT RELATIONSHIPS PREFERENCE

B-231   BANTA, T. J.
               TESTS FOR THE EVALUATION OF EARLY CHILDHOOD EDUCATION.
               THE CINCINNATI AUTONOMY TEST BATTERY.
               IN J. HELLMUTH (ED.), COGNITIVE STUDIES, VOL. 1.
               NEW YORK: BRUNNER/MAZEL, 1970.
               (EARLY CHILDHOOD EMBEDDED FIGURES TEST)
           @B-231 1970M CHILD FIGURE GRAPHIC COGNITIVE FLEXIBILITY ABILITY PERCEPTION
           @FUNCTIONING
               (APPLICATIONS: 2462)

B-232   BANTA, T. J.
              TESTS FOR THE EVALUATION OF EARLY CHILDHOOD EDUCATION.
              THE CINCINNATI AUTONOMY TEST BATTERY.
              IN J. HELLMUTH (ED.), COGNITIVE STUDIES, VOL. 1.
              NEW YORK: BRUNNER/MAZEL, 1970.
              (DOG AND BONE TEST OF INNOVATIVE BEHAVIOR)
          @B-232 1970M CHILD IMAGINATION ORIGINALITY CREATIVITY AUTONOMY
              (APPLICATIONS: 2462)

B-233   BLOCK, J.
              THE CHILD-REARING PRACTICES REPORT.
              BERKELEY: UNIVERSITY OF CALIFORNIA, INSTITUTE OF HUMAN DEVELOPMENT, 1965.
              (MIMEO).
              (CHILD-REARING PRACTICES REPORT)*
          @B-233 1965M CHILD Q-SORT RELATIONSHIPS MATERNAL ATTITUDE PARENTAL
              (APPLICATIONS: 2460)

B-234   BRENNEIS, B.
              MALE AND FEMALE EGO MODALITIES IN MANIFEST DREAM CONTENT.
              JOURNAL OF ABNORMAL PSYCHOLOGY, 1970, 76, 434-442.
              (METHOD FOR ANALYSIS OF MANIFEST DREAM CONTENT)
          @B-234 1970M FANTASY CONTENT ANALYSIS BEHAVIOR DREAM

B-235   BARTHOL, R. P., & BRIDGE, R. G.
              THE ECHO MULTI-RESPONSE METHOD FOR SURVEYING VALUE AND INFLUENCE PATTERNS
              IN GROUPS.
              PSYCHOLOGICAL REPORTS, 1968, 22, 1345-1354.
              (ECHO VALUE SURVEY)*
          @B-235 1968M SOCIAL ACCEPTANCE AUTHORITY GROUP PEER VALUES IDEALS MORAL GLOBAL
          @RELIGION BEHAVIOR APPROVAL SELF IDEOLOGY
              (APPLICATIONS: 2681)

B-236   BRADBURN, N. M., & CAPLOVITZ, D.
              REPORTS ON HAPPINESS.
              CHICAGO: ALDINE, 1965.
              (3-ITEM JOB ADJUSTMENT INDEX)
          @B-236 1965M JOB ATTITUDE SATISFACTION EMPLOYEE MANAGEMENT

B-237   BAVELAS, A.
              A METHOD FOR INVESTIGATING INDIVIDUAL AND GROUP IDEOLOGY.
              SOCIOMETRY, 1942, 5, 371-377.
              (BAVELAS MORAL IDEOLOGY TECHNIQUE)
          @B-237 1942M APPROVAL ACCEPTANCE PEER SOCIAL RELIGION VALUES IDEALS IDEOLOGY
          @GROUP AUTHORITY GLOBAL BEHAVIOR MORAL
              (APPLICATIONS: 2681)

B-238   BELLAK, L., & BELLAK, S.
              THE CAT-H.
              NEW YORK: C. P. S. CO., 1965.
              BELLAK, L., & HURVICH, M. S.
              MANUAL FOR THE CAT-H.
              NEW YORK: C. P. S. CO., 1965.
              (HUMAN FORM OF CHILDRENS APPERCEPTION TEST)
          @B-238 1965M CHILD PROJECTIVE FANTASY IMAGINATION TAT

B-239   BAGGALEY, A. R., & RIEDEL, W. W.
              A DIAGNOSTIC ASSEMBLY OF MMPI ITEMS BASED ON COMREY'S FACTOR ANALYSES.
              JOURNAL OF CLINICAL PSYCHOLOGY, 1966, 22, 306-308.
              (TEST FOR PSYCHIATRIC DIAGNOSIS)
          @B-239 1966M DIAGNOSIS PSYCHIATRIC MMPI NEUROTICISM MENTAL-ILLNESS INVENTORY

B-240   BRAGINSKY, D.
              MACHIAVELLIANISM AND MANIPULATIVE INTERPERSONAL BEHAVIOR IN CHILDREN: TWO
              EXPLORATORY STUDIES.
              UNPUBLISHED DOCTORAL DISSERTATION, UNIVERSITY OF CONNECTICUT, 1966.
              ANN ARBOR: UNIVERSITY MICROFILMS, NO. 67-3847.
              (MACH IV SCALE FOR CHILDREN)
          @B-240 1966M CHILD BEHAVIOR MACHIAVELLIANISM DECEPTIVENESS EXPLOITATION
          @ATTITUDE PEOPLE BELIEF

B-241   BAILEY, K. G.
              AUDIOTAPE SELF-CONFRONTATION IN GROUP PSYCHOTHERAPY.
              PSYCHOLOGICAL REPORTS, 1970, 27, 439-444.
              (Q-SORT MEASURE OF THERAPEUTIC CHANGE)
          @B-241 1970M CHANGE THERAPY Q-SORT

B-242   BECKER, W. C.
         ELGIN PROGNOSTIC SCALE.
         MIMEOGRAPH, 1956.
         (MODIFIED ELGIN PROGNOSTIC SCALE)
@B-242 1956M PROGNOSIS INTERPERSONAL RELATIONSHIPS ACTIVITIES INTEREST JOB
@PREFERENCE SATISFACTION
         (APPLICATIONS: 1148   1574   2077   2604)

B-244   BARCLAY, J. R.
         EFFECTING BEHAVIOR CHANGE IN THE ELEMENTARY CLASSROOM: AN EXPLORATORY
         STUDY.
         JOURNAL OF COUNSELING PSYCHOLOGY, 1967, 14, 240-247.
         (SEMANTIC DIFFERENTIAL MEASURE OF ATTITUDES TO PEERS AND AUTHORITY)
@B-244 1967M SEM-DIFFERENTIAL ATTITUDE AUTHORITY PEER

B-245   BERRY, K. L., KEIL, E. C., & ROBIN, S. S.
         ROLE EXPECTATIONS OF THE VOCATIONAL REHABILITATION COUNSELOR IN A
         THERAPEUTIC MILIEU.
         JOURNAL OF COUNSELING PSYCHOLOGY, 1969, 16, 203-208.
         (ROLE EXPECTATIONS QUESTIONNAIRE)
@B-245 1969M ROLE DEMANDS THERAPY PSYCHIATRIC RELATIONSHIPS COUNSELING
@PERCEPTION THERAPIST

B-247   BOROW, H.
         THE MEASUREMENT OF ACADEMIC ADJUSTMENT.
         JOURNAL OF THE AMERICAN ASSOCIATION OF COLLEGE REGISTRARS, 1947, 22,
         274-286.
         BOROW, H.
         MANUAL FOR THE COLLEGE INVENTORY OF ACADEMIC ADJUSTMENT.
         PALO ALTO: STANFORD UNIVERSITY PRESS AND CONSULTING PSYCHOLOGISTS PRESS,
         1949.
         (COLLEGE INVENTORY OF ACADEMIC ADJUSTMENT)*
@B-247 1947M COLLEGE ADJUSTMENT ACADEMIC PERFORMANCE GOALS MATURITY PERSONAL
@EFFECTIVENESS ASPIRATION MENTAL-HEALTH INTERPERSONAL RELATIONSHIPS STUDY HABITS
         (APPLICATIONS: 1155   1297)

B-248   BLOCHER, D. H., & SCHUTZ, R. A.
         RELATIONSHIPS AMONG SELF-DESCRIPTIONS, OCCUPATIONAL STEREOTYPES, AND
         VOCATIONAL PREFERENCES.
         JOURNAL OF COUNSELING PSYCHOLOGY, 1961, 8, 314-317.
         (DESCRIPTIVE CHECK LIST)
@B-248 1961M CHECKLIST SELF IDEAL IDENTITY RATING DESCRIPTION VOCATIONAL
@CONCEPT
         (APPLICATIONS: 1472)

B-249   BONTRAGER, H. L.
         SOME PSYCHOLOGICAL CORRELATES OF DISABLED PERSONS' CONSCIOUS ATTITUDES
         TOWARD THEIR DISABILITIES.
         UNPUBLISHED MASTER'S THESIS, UNIVERSITY OF KANSAS, 1965.
         (DISABILITY EFFECTS SCALE)*
@B-249 1965M ATTITUDE HEALTH DISABILITY PHYSICAL PERCEPTION BELIEF
         (APPLICATIONS: 1543)

B-250   BAKER, E.
         THE DIFFERENTIAL EFFECTS OF TWO PSYCHOTHERAPEUTIC APPROACHES ON CLIENT
         PERCEPTIONS.
         JOURNAL OF COUNSELING PSYCHOLOGY, 1960, 7, 46-50.
         (INDEX OF INDISCRIMINATION)
@B-250 1960M PERCEPTION OVEREXCLUSIVE OVERINCLUSIVE COGNITIVE FUNCTIONING

B-251   BAKER, E.
         THE DIFFERENTIAL EFFECTS OF TWO PSYCHOTHERAPEUTIC APPROACHES ON CLIENT
         PERCEPTIONS.
         JOURNAL OF COUNSELING PSYCHOLOGY, 1960, 7, 46-50.
         (MEASURE OF RESISTANCE TO ANALYZING PROBLEMS)
@B-251 1960M PROBLEM ANALYTIC THINKING RESISTANCE THERAPY COUNSELING PATIENT

B-252   BUEL, W. D.
         SUPERVISOR'S EVALUATION OF RESEARCH PERSONNEL.
         SCIENCE RESEARCH ASSOCIATES, INC., CHICAGO, 1960.
         (SUPERVISOR'S EVALUATION OF RESEARCH PERSONNEL)
@B-252 1960M EVALUATION BEHAVIOR SUPERVISOR JOB RATING EMPLOYEE COMPETENCE
@ABILITY
         (APPLICATIONS: 1242)

B-253   BROEDEL, J., OHLSEN, M., PROFF, F., & SOUTHARD, C.
         THE EFFECTS OF GROUP COUNSELING ON GIFTED UNDERACHIEVING ADOLESCENTS.
         JOURNAL OF COUNSELING PSYCHOLOGY, 1960, 7, 163-170.
         (BEHAVIOR INVENTORY)
         @B-253 1960M BEHAVIOR SELF PERCEPTION OTHERS ADJUSTMENT COUNSELING CHANGE
         @THERAPY ADOLESCENT

B-254   BROEDEL, J., OHLSEN, M., PROFF, F., & SOUTHARD, C.
         THE EFFECTS OF GROUP COUNSELING ON GIFTED UNDERACHIEVING ADOLESCENTS.
         JOURNAL OF COUNSELING PSYCHOLOGY, 1960, 7, 163-170.
         (PICTURE STORY TEST)
         @B-254 1960M PROJECTIVE GRAPHIC TAT CONTENT-ANALYSIS SELF OTHERS
         @ACCEPTANCE COUNSELING CHANGE

B-256   BIERI, J., LOBECK, R., & GALINSKY, M. D.
         A COMPARISON OF DIRECT, INDIRECT, AND FANTASY MEASURES OF IDENTIFICATION.
         JOURNAL OF ABNORMAL AND SOCIAL PSYCHOLOGY, 1959, 58, 253-258.
         (SEMANTIC DIFFERENTIAL MEASURE OF CHILD'S IDENTIFICATION WITH MOTHER AND
         FATHER)
         @B-256 1959M SIMILARITY PATERNAL MATERNAL IDENTIFICATION CHILD PARENTAL
         @SEM-DIFFERENTIAL

B-257   BARRON, F.
         THE DISPOSITION TOWARD ORIGINALITY.
         JOURNAL OF ABNORMAL AND SOCIAL PSYCHOLOGY, 1955, 51, 478-485.
         (ANAGRAMS TEST)*
         @B-257 1955M ABILITY CREATIVITY ORIGINALITY IMAGINATION
         (APPLICATIONS: 1355)

B-259   BROCK, T. C., & DEL GIUDICE, C.
         STEALING AND TEMPORAL ORIENTATION.
         JOURNAL OF ABNORMAL AND SOCIAL PSYCHOLOGY, 1963, 66, 91-94.
         (MEASURE OF USE OF TEMPORAL CONCEPTS)
         @B-259 1963M TIME FUTURE PERSPECTIVE CONCEPT PAST PRESENT
         (APPLICATIONS: 1293)

B-260   BRIGANTE, T. R., HAEFNER, D. P., & WOODSON, W. B.
         CLINICAL AND COUNSELING PSYCHOLOGISTS' PERCEPTIONS OF THEIR SPECIALTIES.
         JOURNAL OF COUNSELING PSYCHOLOGY, 1962, 9, 225-231.
         (MEASURE OF PERCEPTION OF CLINICAL AND COUNSELOR ROLES)
         @B-260 1962M COUNSELING THERAPY ROLE PERCEPTION PATIENT RELATIONSHIPS ACTIVITIES
         @ABILITY THERAPIST

B-261   BUXTON, W. S., & SMALL, J. J.
         COUNSELING ATTITUDES OF CORRECTIONAL CASEWORKERS IN NEW ZEALAND.
         JOURNAL OF COUNSELING PSYCHOLOGY, 1966, 13, 348-351.
         (MEASURE OF DIRECTIVENESS/NONDIRECTIVENESS IN COUNSELING)
         @B-261 1966M COUNSELING THERAPY RELATIONSHIPS ATTITUDE ROLE AUTHORITY
         @COMMUNICATION STYLE THERAPIST PATIENT INTERACTION

B-262   BUGENTAL, D. E., LOVE, L. R., KASWAN, J. W., AND APRIL, C.
         VERBAL-NONVERBAL CONFLICT IN PARENTAL MESSAGES TO NORMAL AND DISTURBED
         CHILDREN.
         JOURNAL OF ABNORMAL PSYCHOLOGY, 1971, 77, 6-10.
         (MEASURE OF CONFLICTING CONTENT IN PARENT-CHILD COMMUNICATION)
         @B-262 1971M FAMILY CHILD INTERACTION CONFLICT VERBAL COMMUNICATION CONSISTENCY
         @PARENTAL CONTENT-ANALYSIS

B-264   BIERI, J., LOBECK, R., & GALINSKY, M. D.
         A COMPARISON OF DIRECT, INDIRECT, AND FANTASY MEASURES OF IDENTIFICATION.
         JOURNAL OF ABNORMAL AND SOCIAL PSYCHOLOGY, 1959, 58, 253-258.
         (TAT FANTASY MEASURE OF CHILD'S IDENTIFICATION WITH MOTHER AND FATHER)
         @B-264 1959M SIMILARITY PATERNAL MATERNAL IDENTIFICATION CHILD PARENTAL TAT
         @PROJECTIVE

B-266   BEREZIN, A. G.
         THE DEVELOPMENT AND USE OF A SYSTEM OF DIAGNOSTIC CATEGORIES IN
         COUNSELING.
         UNPUBLISHED DOCTORAL DISSERTATION, UNIVERSITY OF MISSOURI, 1957.
         (DIAGNOSTIC CLASSIFICATION SYSTEM)
         @B-266 1957M DIAGNOSIS COUNSELING ADJUSTMENT PERSONAL
         (APPLICATIONS: 1154)

B-267   BELL, E. G.
                 INNER-DIRECTED AND OTHER-DIRECTED ATTITUDES.
                 UNPUBLISHED DOCTORAL DISSERTATION, YALE UNIVERSITY, 1955.
                 (BELL QUESTIONNAIRE FOR INNER- AND OTHER-DIRECTEDNESS)
           @B-267 1955M IE-CONTROL SELF OTHERS ORIENTATION VALUES ATTITUDE BEHAVIOR PEER
           @AUTONOMY
                 (APPLICATIONS: 102)

B-270   BLOCK, J. R., & YUKER, H. E.
                 CORRELATES OF AN INTELLECTUAL ORIENTATION AMONG COLLEGE STUDENTS.
                 IN PROCEEDINGS OF THE 73RD ANNUAL CONVENTION OF THE AMERICAN PSYCHOLOGICAL
                 ASSOCIATION.
                 WASHINGTON, D. C.: AMERICAN PSYCHOLOGICAL ASSOCIATION, 1965.
                 (INTELLECTUAL-PRAGMATISM SCALE)
           @B-270 1965M INTELLECTUAL ORIENTATION STUDENT COLLEGE
                 (APPLICATIONS: 2766)

B-271   BURSTEIN, A. G.
                 SOME VERBAL ASPECTS OF PRIMARY PROCESS THOUGHT IN SCHIZOPHRENIA.
                 JOURNAL OF ABNORMAL AND SOCIAL PSYCHOLOGY, 1961, 62, 155-157.
                 (MEASURE OF CONCEPTUAL DISORDER)
           @B-271 1961M CONCEPTUAL ORGANIZATION PRIMARY-PROCESS SCHIZOPHRENIA
           @MENTAL-ILLNESS COGNITIVE FUNCTIONING
                 (APPLICATIONS: 1815)

B-272   BYRNE, D., GOLIGHTLY, C., & CAPALDI, E. J.
                 CONSTRUCTION AND VALIDATION OF THE FOOD ATTITUDE SCALE.
                 JOURNAL OF CONSULTING PSYCHOLOGY, 1963, 27, 215-222.
                 (TEMPERAMENT SCALE MEASURING VISCEROTONIA, SOMATOTONIA AND CEREBROTONIA)
           @B-272 1963M TEMPERAMENT SOMATOTYPE BODY ORALITY SOCIABILITY EXTRAVERSION
           @ INTROVERSION ASSERTIVENESS AGGRESSIVENESS NEED PRIVACY

B-273   BUGENTAL, D. E., LOVE, L. R., KASWAN, J. W., & APRIL, C.
                 VERBAL-NONVERBAL CONFLICT IN PARENTAL MESSAGES TO NORMAL AND DISTURBED
                 CHILDREN.
                 JOURNAL OF ABNORMAL PSYCHOLOGY, 1971, 77, 6-10.
                 (CHILDREN'S BEHAVIOR RATING SCALE)
           @B-273 1971M CHILD BEHAVIOR RATING AGGRESSION HOSTILITY HABITS MATURITY
           @EXPRESSION PHYSICAL ATTENTION BREADTH FEAR ANXIETY DEPENDENCY AGGRESSIVENESS
           @SELF CONFIDENCE SPAN

B-274   BLAUFARB, H.
                 A DEMONSTRATION OF VERBAL ABSTRACTING ABILITY IN CHRONIC SCHIZOPHRENICS
                 UNDER ENRICHED STIMULUS AND INSTRUCTIONAL CONDITIONS.
                 JOURNAL OF CONSULTING PSYCHOLOGY, 1962, 26, 471-475.
                 (PROVERBS TEST)
           @B-274 1962M SCHIZOPHRENIA FUNCTIONING COGNITIVE ABSTRACTNESS
                 (APPLICATIONS: 977)

B-275   BECKER, W. C.
                 UNPUBLISHED DOCTORAL DISSERTATION, 1955.
                 BECKER, W. C.
                 THE PROCESS-REACTIVE DESTINCTION: A KEY TO THE PROBLEM OF
                 SCHIZOPHRENIA?
                 JOURNAL OF NERVOUS AND MENTAL DISEASE, 1959, 129, 442-449.
                 (REVISION OF THE ELGIN PROGNOSTIC SCALE)
           @B-275 1959M REVISION OF W-44 SCHIZOPHRENIA PROGNOSIS PSYCHIATRIC
                 (APPLICATIONS: 982 1934)

B-276   BRODBECK, A. J., & PERLMUTTER, H. V.
                 SELF-DISLIKE AS A DETERMINANT OF MARKED INGROUP-OUTGROUP PREFERENCES.
                 JOURNAL OF PSYCHOLOGY, 1954, 38, 271-280.
                 (SELF-DISLIKE SCALE)
           @B-276 1954M SELF EVALUATION DEPRECIATION ESTEEM CONCEPT IMAGE
                 (APPLICATIONS: 613)

B-277   BERG, E. A.
                 A SIMPLE OBJECTIVE TECHNIQUE FOR MEASURING FLEXIBILITY IN THINKING.
                 JOURNAL OF GENERAL PSYCHOLOGY, 1948, 39, 15-22.
                 (THE WISCONSIN CARD SORTING TEST)
           @B-277 1948M COGNITIVE FLEXIBILITY FUNCTIONING THINKING
                 (APPLICATIONS: 1047)

B-280   BUSS, A.
               THE EFFECT OF ITEM STYLE ON SOCIAL DESIRABILITY AND FREQUENCY OF
               ENDORSEMENT.
               JOURNAL OF CONSULTING PSYCHOLOGY, 1959, 23, 510-513.
               (MEASURE OF ITEM STYLE EFFECT ON SOCIAL DESIRABILITY)
           @B-280 1959M SOCIAL DESIRABILITY RESPONSE-BIAS
               (APPLICATIONS: 1706)

B-281   BELL, H. M.
               MANUAL -- BELL ADJUSTMENT INVENTORY REVISED (1962) STUDENT FORM.
               PALO ALTO: CONSULTING PSYCHOLOGIST PRESS, 1963.
               (REVISED STUDENT FORM OF BELL ADJUSTMENT INVENTORY)
           @B-281 1963M ADJUSTMENT MENTAL-HEALTH B-128R
               (APPLICATIONS: 1558   2289)

B-282   BARRON, F.
               SOME PERSONALITY CORRELATES OF INDEPENDENCE OF JUDGMENT.
               JOURNAL OF PERSONALITY, 1953, 21, 287-297.
               (INVENTORY OF PERSONAL PHILOSOPHY)
           @B-282 1953M PERSONAL VALUES IDEALS BELIEF ATTITUDE INVENTORY
               (APPLICATIONS: 1299)

B-283   BARRON, F.
               THE DISPOSITION TOWARD ORIGINALITY.
               JOURNAL OF ABNORMAL AND SOCIAL PSYCHOLOGY, 1955, 51, 478-485.
               (WORD REARRANGEMENT TEST FOR ORIGINALITY)
           @B-283 1955M ABILITY CREATIVITY ORIGINALITY IMAGINATION

B-284   BARRON, F.
               THE DISPOSITION TOWARD ORIGINALITY.
               JOURNAL OF ABNORMAL AND SOCIAL PSYCHOLOGY, 1955, 51, 478-485.
               (ACHROMATIC INKBLOTS TEST FOR ORIGINALITY)
           @B-284 1955M CREATIVITY ORIGINALITY IMAGINATION FIGURE

B-285   BAUGHMAN, E. E.
               A COMPARATIVE ANALYSIS OF RORSCHACH FORMS WITH ALTERED STIMULUS
               CHARACTERISTICS.
               JOURNAL OF PROJECTIVE TECHNIQUES, 1954, 18, 151-164.
               (MEASURE OF ROLE OF STIMULUS ATTRIBUTES IN RORSCHACH RESPONSE)
           @B-285 1954M RORSCHACH STIMULUS PROJECTIVE PERCEPTION BEHAVIOR
               (APPLICATIONS: 1561)

B-286   BAXTER, J. C., BECKER, J., & HOOKS, W.
               DEFENSIVE STYLE IN THE FAMILIES OF SCHIZOPHRENICS AND CONTROLS.
               JOURNAL OF ABNORMAL AND SOCIAL PSYCHOLOGY, 1963, 66, 512.
               (DEFENSIVE STYLE SCALE)*
           @B-286 1963M DEFENSE STYLE

B-287   BASS, B. M., GAIER, E. L., FLINT, A. W., & FARESE, F. J.
               AN OBJECTIVE METHOD FOR STUDYING GROUP BEHAVIOR.
               PSYCHOLOGICAL REPORT MONOGRAPHS, 1957, 3, 265-280.
               (OBJECTIVE MEASURES OF SOCIAL INTERACTION)
           @B-287 1957M SOCIAL INTERACTION GROUP BEHAVIOR
               (APPLICATIONS: 685)

B-288   BASS, A. R., & FIEDLER, F. E.
               INTERPERSONAL PERCEPTION SCORES: A COMPARISON OF D SCORES AND THEIR
               COMPONENTS.
               TECHNICAL REPORT NO. 5, 1959, GROUP EFFECTIVENESS RESEARCH LABORATORY,
               UNIVERSITY OF ILLINOIS, U.S. PUBLIC HEALTH PROJECT M-1774.
               BASS, A. R., & FIEDLER, F. E.
               INTERPERSONAL PERCEPTION SCORES AND THEIR COMPONENTS AS PREDICTORS OF
               PERSONAL ADJUSTMENT.
               JOURNAL OF ABNORMAL AND SOCIAL PSYCHOLOGY, 1961, 62, 442-445.
               (MEASURE OF ASSUMED SIMILARITY TO OTHERS)
           @B-288 1959M OTHERS SIMILARITY INTERPERSONAL PERCEPTION

B-289   BERLEW, D.
               A STUDY OF INTERPERSONAL SENSITIVITY.
               UNPUBLISHED DOCTORAL DISSERTATION, HARVARD UNIVERSITY, 1959.
               BERLEW, D. E.
               INTERPERSONAL SENSITIVITY AND MOTIVE STRENGTH.
               JOURNAL OF ABNORMAL AND SOCIAL PSYCHOLOGY, 1961, 63, 390-394.
               (MEASURE OF INTERPERSONAL SENSITIVITY)
           @B-289 1959M INTERPERSONAL SENSITIVITY OTHERS AWARENESS

B-290   BARRELL, R. P., DEWOLFE, A. S., & CUMMINGS, J. W.
             A MEASURE OF STAFF ATTITUDES TOWARD CARE OF PHYSICALLY ILL PATIENTS.
             JOURNAL OF CONSULTING PSYCHOLOGY, 1965, 29, 218-222.
             (MEASURE OF STAFF ATTITUDES TOWARD CARE OF PHYSICALLY ILL PATIENTS)
         aB-290 1965M ATTITUDE DISABILITY PATIENT PHYSICAL HOSPITALIZATION HEALTH
             (APPLICATIONS: 1981)

B-291   BELL, A. P.
             ROLE MODELSHIP AND INTERACTION IN ADOLESCENCE AND YOUNG ADULTHOOD.
             DEVELOPMENTAL PSYCHOLOGY, 1970, 2, 123-128.
             (ROLE MODELSHIP AND INTERACTION MEASURE)
         aB-291 1970M ROLE INTERACTION ENACTMENT

B-292   BERGER, D., "& OTHERS."
             STAFF OPINION SURVEY: AN UNPUBLISHED FACTOR ANALYSED ATTITUDE SCALE ARISING
             OUT OF THE MEDICAL AUDIT RESEARCH.
             VETERANS ADMINISTRATION HOSPITAL, PERRY POINT, MARYLAND, 1962
             (STAFF OPINION SURVEY)*
         aB-292 1962M OPINION ATTITUDE STAFF MENTAL-ILLNESS PSYCHIATRIC PATIENT

C-1   CHAPMAN, L. J. & TAYLOR, J. A.
             BREADTH OF DEVIATE CONCEPTS USED BY SCHIZOPHRENICS.
             JOURNAL OF ABNORMAL AND SOCIAL PSYCHOLOGY, 1957, 24, 118-132.
             (CARD-SORT MEASURE OF OVER-INCLUSIVENESS)
         aC-1 CONCEPTUAL OVERINCLUSIVE BREADTH THINKING COGNITIVE 1961M STRUCTURE
         aC-1 FUNCTIONING
             (APPLICATIONS: 1858)

C-2   CANTRIL, H.
             THE PATTERN OF HUMAN CONCERNS.
             NEW BRUNSWICK, N. J.: RUTGERS UNIVERSITY PRESS, 1965.
             (SELF-ANCHORING SCALE)
         aC-2 LIFE SATISFACTION AFFECTIVE-STATES GLOBAL 1965M PERCEPTION PE-FIT
             (APPLICATIONS: 355)

C-3   CARLSON, R., & LEVY, N.
             BRIEF METHOD FOR ASSESSING SOCIAL-PERSONAL ORIENTATION.
             PSYCHOLOGICAL REPORTS, 1968, 23, 911-914.
             (CARLSON ADJECTIVE CHECK LIST)*
         aC-3 SOCIAL PERSONAL ORIENTATION SELF-IDENTITY EVALUATION SELF PERCEPTION ESTEEM
         aC-3 1968M
             (APPLICATIONS: 2525)

C-4   CARTWRIGHT, R. D.
             PREDICTING RESPONSE TO CLIENT-CENTERED THERAPY WITH THE RORSCHACH
             PROGNOSTIC RATING SCALE.
             JOURNAL OF COUNSELING PSYCHOLOGY, 1958, 5, 11-15.
             (MODIFICATION OF KLOPFER'S RORSCHACH PROGNOSTIC RATING SCALE)
         aC-4 EGO-STRENGTH COPING-DEFENSE EGO-RESILIENCY RORSCHACH PROJECTIVE PROGNOSIS
         aC-4 THERAPY PSYCHIATRIC 1958M
             (APPLICATIONS: 1250)

C-5   CASSEL, R. N.
             THE EGO STRENGTH Q-SORT TEST.
             CHICAGO: PSYCHOMETRIC AFFILIATES, 1958.
             (EGO STRENGTH Q-SORT)*
         aC-5 Q-SORT HAPPINESS EGO-STRENGTH MENTAL-HEALTH SOCIAL STRESS PHYSICAL STATUS
         aEGORESILIENCY COPING-DEFENSE EGO ADJUSTMENT 1958M

C-6   CASSEL, R. N., & KAHN, T. C.
             THE GROUP PERSONALITY PROJECTIVE TEST.
             PSYCHOLOGICAL REPORTS, 1961, 8, 23-41.
             (GROUP PERSONALITY PROJECTIVE TEST)*
         aC-6 MULTITRAIT NEED SUCCORANCE ANXIETY NURTURANCE AFFILIATION MENTAL-HEALTH
         aC-6 PROJECTIVE GROUP ADJUSTMENT SOCIAL COMPETENCE 1961M

C-7   CAMPBELL, D. P.
             A STUDY OF COLLEGE FRESHMEN -- TWENTY-FIVE YEARS LATER. (COOPERATIVE
             RESEARCH PROJECT NO. 2160, OFFICE OF EDUCATION, UNITED STATES DEPARTMENT OF
             HEALTH, EDUCATION & WELFARE) MINNEAPOLIS: UNIVERSITY OF MINNESOTA, 1965.
             (CAMPBELL LIBERALISM-CONSERVATISM SCALE)*
         aC-7 1965M LIBERALISM CONSERVATISM POLITICAL ORIENTATION
             (APPLICATIONS: 2489)

C-8   CATTELL, R. B., & HOROWITZ, J. Z.
               OBJECTIVE PERSONALITY TESTS INVESTIGATING THE STRUCTURE OF ALTRUISM IN
               RELATION TO SOURCE TRAITS A, H, AND L.
               JOURNAL OF PERSONALITY, 1952, 21, 103-117.
               (OBJECTIVE PERSONALITY TESTS OF ALTRUISM IN RELATION TO SOURCE TRAITS)
           @C-8 ALTRUISM AFFECTIVE-STATES TRAIT 1952M

C-9   CATTELL, R. B., & BJERSTEDT, A.
               THE STRUCTURE OF DEPRESSION, AS REVEALED IN Q-DATA: FINDINGS, THEORY AND
               RELATION TO GENERAL PERSONALITY TRAITS OF NORMAL AND PATHOLOGICAL SUBJECTS.
               UNIVERSITY OF ILLINOIS, PSYCHOLOGY DEPARTMENT, LABORATORY OF PERSONALITY
               AND GROUP ANALYSIS, 1966, ADVANCED PUBLICATION #3.
               (PROTO DEPRESSION SCALE QUESTIONNAIRE)*
           @C-9 1966M DEPRESSION Q-SORT ANXIETY GUILT RESENTMENT WITHDRAWAL SELF
           @INTELLIGENCE

C-10   CATTELL, R. B., SAUNDERS, D. R., & STICE, G. F.
               SIXTEEN PERSONALITY FACTOR QUESTIONNAIRE. INSTITUTE FOR PERSONALITY AND
               ABILITY TESTING, 1602 CORONADO DRIVE, CHAMPAIGN, ILL., 1949.
           CATTELL, R. B., & EBER, H. W.
               SPECIMEN SET FOR THE SIXTEEN PERSONALITY FACTOR QUESTIONNAIRE. "THE 16 PF"
               FORMS A AND B, YOUNG ADULTS AND ADULTS. INSTITUTE FOR PERSONALITY AND
               ABILITY TESTING, 1602 CORONADO DRIVE, CHAMPAIGN, ILL., 1962.
               (SIXTEEN PERSONALITY FACTOR QUESTIONNAIRE)*
           @C-10 MULTITRAIT DOMINANCE MATURITY HAPPINESS CONSCIENTIOUS SELF CONTROL
           @C-10 ANXIETY 1949M
               (APPLICATIONS: 9   37   164   223   398   414   451   452   521   576
                                 792   1231   1299   1363   1390   1393   1440   1488   1492   1534
                                1743   1759   1888   1907   1958   2046   2149   2158   2241   2514
                                2536   2624   2639   2642   2752   2912   2913   2930   2936   2963
                                2980)

C-11   CATTELL, R. B., & HORN, J. L.
               THE MOTIVATION ANALYSIS TEST.
               CHAMPAIGN, ILLINOIS: INSTITUTE FOR PERSONALITY AND ABILITY TESTING, 1964.
               (MOTIVATION ANALYSIS TEST)*
           @C-11 SELF CONCEPT INTEGRATION COPING-DEFENSE CONFLICT PARENTAL 1964M
           @MOTIVE OTHER-CATEGORY SELF-IDENTITY ESTEEM PERCEPTION EVALUATION FEAR LOVE
           @VALUES MORAL MULTITRAIT ASSERTION HOME

C-12   CARTWRIGHT, D. S., KIRTNER, W. L., & FISKE, D. W.
               METHOD FACTORS IN CHANGES ASSOCIATED WITH PSYCHOTHERAPY.
               JOURNAL OF ABNORMAL AND SOCIAL PSYCHOLOGY, 1963, 66, 164-175.
               (BEHAVIORAL ADEQUACY SCALES)
           @C-12 ADJUSTMENT SOCIAL COMPETENCE SELF SATISFACTION AFFECTIVE-STATES BEHAVIOR
           @C-12 1963M THERAPY PERSONALITY CHANGE
               (APPLICATIONS: 950)

C-13   CHAMBERS, J. L., & LIEBERMAN, L. R.
               DIFFERENCES BETWEEN NORMAL AND CLINICAL GROUPS IN JUDGING, EVALUATING,
               AND ASSOCIATING NEEDS.
               JOURNAL OF CLINICAL PSYCHOLOGY, 1965, 21, 145-149.
               (PICTURE IDENTIFICATION TEST)*
           @C-13 SOCIAL ADJUSTMENT EFFECTIVENESS AUTONOMY OTHER-CATEGORY NEED
           @C-13 JUDGMENT 1965M
               (APPLICATIONS: 1453   1668)

C-14   CHRISTIE, R., & MERTON, R. K.
               PROCEDURES FOR THE SOCIOLOGICAL STUDY OF THE VALUES CLIMATE OF MEDICAL
               SCHOOLS.
               JOURNAL OF MEDICAL EDUCATION, 1958, 33, 125-153.
               (MACHIAVELLIANISM SCALE)*
           @C-14 VALUES MACHIAVELLIANISM COPING-DEFENSE OTHER-CATEGORY ENVIRONMENT 1958M
               (APPLICATIONS: 111   262   294   346   496   499   2841)

C-15   CLARKE, W. V.
               THE CONSTRUCTION OF AN INDUSTRIAL SELECTION PERSONALITY TEST.
               JOURNAL OF PSYCHOLOGY, 1956, 41, 379-394.
               (ACTIVITY VECTOR ANALYSIS)*
           @C-15 MULTITRAIT EMOTION CONTROL SOCIAL ADAPTABILITY AGGRESSIVENESS SOCIABILITY
           @C-15 1956M JOB ADJUSTMENT EMPLOYEE

C-16   CLYDE, D. J.
            CLYDE MOOD SCALE MANUAL.
            CORAL GABLES, FLORIDA: UNIVERSITY OF MIAMI, BIOMETRICS LABORATORY, 1963.
            (CLYDE MOOD SCALE)*
        @C-16 AFFECTIVE-STATES MOOD OTHER-CATEGORY 1963M POSITIVE NEGATIVE
            (APPLICATIONS: 243   871   874   2239 2387 2673 2730)

C-17   COELHO, G. V., SILBER, E., & HAMBURG, D. A.
            USE OF THE STUDENT-TAT TO ASSESS COPING BEHAVIOR IN HOSPITALIZED, NORMAL,
            AND EXCEPTIONALLY COMPETENT COLLEGE FRESHMEN.
            PERCEPTUAL AND MOTOR SKILLS, 1962, 14, 355-365.
            (STUDENT TAT)
        @C-17 COPING-DEFENSE GLOBAL TAT COMPETENCE COPING STUDENT BEHAVIOR 1962M
        @C-17 PROJECTIVE

C-18   COHN, T. S.
            FACTORS RELATED TO SCORES ON THE F (PREDISPOSITION TO FASCISM) SCALE.
            UNPUBLISHED DOCTORAL DISSERTATION, UNIVERSITY OF MICHIGAN, ANN ARBOR, 1953.
            (PLUS SCALE)*
        @C-18 RESPONSE-BIAS ACQUIESCENCE 1953M

C-19   COMREY, A. L.
            FACTORED HOMOGENEOUS ITEM DIMENSIONS IN PERSONALITY RESEARCH.
            EDUCATIONAL AND PSYCHOLOGICAL MEASUREMENT, 1961, 21, 417-431.
            (COMREY PERSONALITY INVENTORY)*
        @C-19 MULTITRAIT DEPENDENCE EMPATHY HOSTILITY SHYNESS COMPULSIVENESS
        @C-19 NEUROTICISM SELF CONTROL 1961M
            (APPLICATIONS: 13   2974)

C-20   CHAPMAN, L. J. & TAYLOR, J. A.
            BREADTH OF DEVIATE CONCEPTS USED BY SCHIZOPHRENICS.
            JOURNAL OF ABNORMAL AND SOCIAL PSYCHOLOGY, 1957, 24, 118-132.
            (CARD-SORT MEASURE OF OVEREXCLUSIVENESS)
        @C-20 CONCEPTUAL OVEREXCLUSIVE BREADTH THINKING COGNITIVE 1961M STRUCTURE
        @C-20 FUNCTIONING
            (APPLICATIONS: 1114 1815 1858)

C-21   CONVERSE, P., & ROBINSON, J.
            THE USE OF TIME IN AMERICAN SOCIETY, IN PRESS.
            ANN ARBOR: UNIVERSITY OF MICHIGAN, SURVEY RESEARCH CENTER POST ELECTION
            STUDY OF POLITICAL BEHAVIOR, 1968.
            (MEASURE OF LIFE SATISFACTION)
        @C-21 LIFE SATISFACTION AFFECTIVE-STATES GLOBAL HAPPINESS 1968M TIME PE-FIT

C-22   COOPER, J. B.
            TWO SCALES FOR PARENT EVALUATION.
            JOURNAL OF GENETIC PSYCHOLOGY, 1966, 108, 49-53.
        COOPER, J. B., & BLAIR, M.A.
            PARENT EVALUATION AS A DETERMINER OF IDEOLOGY.
            JOURNAL OF GENETIC PSYCHOLOGY, 1959, 94, 93-100.
            (PARENT EVALUATION SCALES)*
        @C-22 PARENTAL EVALUATION FAMILY ADJUSTMENT INTERACTION PARENT-CHILD 1959M
        @C-22 SIMILARITY
            (APPLICATIONS   1207)

C-23   COUCH, A., & KENISTON, K.
            YEASAYERS AND NAYSAYERS: AGREEING RESPONSE SET AS A PERSONALITY VARIABLE.
            JOURNAL OF ABNORMAL AND SOCIAL PSYCHOLOGY, 1960, 60, 151-174.
            (AGREEMENT RESPONSE SCALE)*
        @C-23 RESPONSE-BIAS ACQUIESCENCE 1960M
            (APPLICATIONS: 26   95   190   193   214   386   531   619   620   623
                             629   724   728   789   1044   1065   1270   1732   1807   1899
                            2100   2140   2213   2448   2489   2605   2742   2829   2830   2836)

C-24   COWEN, E. L., BUDIN, W., WOLITSKY, D. L., & STILLER, A.
            THE SOCIAL DESIRABILITY OF TRAIT DESCRIPTIVE TERMS: A FACTOR IN THE PREDIC-
            TION OF Q SORT.
            JOURNAL OF PERSONALITY, 1960, 28, 530-544.
            (SELF-ACCEPTANCE Q SORT)
        @C-24 SOCIAL DESIRABILITY CONCEPT IDEAL COMPETENCE ADJUSTMENT SELF-IDENTITY SELF
        @EVALUATION PERCEPTION ESTEEM Q-SORT ACCEPTANCE 1960M
            (APPLICATIONS: 2742)

C-25   CRANDALL, V. C., KATKOVSKY, W., & CRANDALL, V. J.
          CHILDREN'S BELIEFS IN THEIR OWN CONTROL OF REINFORCEMENTS IN INTELLECTUAL-
          ACADEMIC ACHIEVEMENT SITUATIONS.
          CHILD DEVELOPMENT, 1965, 36, 91-109.
          (INTELLECTUAL ACHIEVEMENT RESPONSIBILITY QUESTIONNAIRE)*
       ƏC-25 AUTONOMY LOCUS CONTROL IE-CONTROL CHILD ACADEMIC ELEMENTARY SCHOOL 1965M
       ƏC-25 INTELLECTUAL ACHIEVEMENT RESPONSIBILITY
          (APPLICATIONS: 2501   2805)

C-26   CRITES, J. O.
          FACTOR ANALYTIC DEFINITIONS OF VOCATIONAL MOTIVATION.
          JOURNAL OF APPLIED PSYCHOLOGY, 1961, 45, 330-337.
          (CRITES VOCATION SURVEY)*
       ƏC-26 VOCATION JOB ADJUSTMENT AUTONOMY MOTIVE INTRINSIC EXTRINSIC 1961M
          (APPLICATIONS: 1430   2858)

C-27   CROWNE, D. P., & MARLOWE, D.
          A NEW SCALE OF SOCIAL DESIRABILITY INDEPENDENT OF PSYCHOPATHOLOGY.
          JOURNAL OF CONSULTING PSYCHOLOGY, 1960, 24, 349-354.
          (MARLOWE-CROWNE SOCIAL DESIRABILITY SCALE)*
       ƏC-27 RESPONSE-BIAS SOCIAL DESIRABILITY 1960M
          (APPLICATIONS: 5   11   21   26   50   52   98   111   125   131
                              163   190   203   214   219   236   248   250   252   255
                              262   281   285   289   304   347   364   385   394   404
                              407   423   448   451   457   461   462   473   499   502
                              507   509   512   514   531   532   686   761   772   811
                              832   904   931   1103   1270   1368   1384   1450   1634   1694
                             1760   1769   1807   1831   1890   1892   1897   1899   2005   2010
                             2015   2042   2085   2086   2099   2100   2102   2120   2136   2164
                             2174   2178   2181   2213   2232   2246   2247   2274   2280   2287
                             2324   2328   2329   2338   2345   2378   2422   2484   2489   2505
                             2506   2509   2526   2529   2551   2558   2567   2571   2575   2577
                             2646   2647   2658   2660   2673   2703   2742   2840   2848   2878
                             2900   2903   2910   2936   2946)

C-28   CAINE, T. M., FOULDS, G. A., & HOPE, K.
          MANUAL OF THE HOSTILITY AND DIRECTION OF HOSTILITY QUESTIONNAIRE (HDHQ).
          LONDON: UNIVERSITY OF LONDON PRESS, 1967.
          (HOSTILITY AND DIRECTION OF HOSTILITY QUESTIONNAIRE)*
       ƏC-28 AFFECTIVE-STATES HOSTILITY RESENTMENT NEGATIVE DIRECTION 1967M

C-29   CATTELL, R. B.
          THE O-A PERSONALITY TEST PATTERNS: YOUTH AND ADULT.
          CHAMPAIGN, ILLINOIS: INSTITUTE FOR PERSONALITY AND ABILITY TESTING, 1955.
          (GOODNESS OF WORK TEST)*
       ƏC-29 JOB SATISFACTION EVALUATION ADJUSTMENT 1955M
          (APPLICATIONS: 30)

C-30   CHAPMAN, L. J., & CAMPBELL, D. T.
          RESPONSE SET IN THE F SCALE.
          JOURNAL OF ABNORMAL AND SOCIAL PSYCHOLOGY, 1957, 54, 129-132.
          (SHORT FORM OF F-SCALE)
       ƏC-30 1957M ETHNOCENTRISM RESPONSE-BIAS ACQUIESCENCE F-SCALE AUTHORITARIANISM
          (APPLICATIONS: 201)

C-31   CHRISTIE, R., HAVEL, J., & SEIDENBERG, B.
          IS THE F-SCALE REVERSIBLE?
          JOURNAL OF ABNORMAL AND SOCIAL PSYCHOLOGY, 1958, 56, 143-159.
          (MODIFIED F-SCALE)
       ƏC-31 AUTHORITARIANISM COPING-DEFENSE OTHER-CATEGORY F-SCALE 1958M
          (APPLICATIONS: 346   362   463   531   668   670   761   789   834   2830
                          2946)

C-32   CLAYTON, M. B., & JACKSON, D. N.
          EQUIVALENCE RANGE, ACQUIESCENCE, AND OVERGENERALIZATION.
          EDUCATIONAL AND PSYCHOLOGICAL MEASUREMENT, 1961, 21, 371-382.
          (ACQUIESCENCE AND AUTHORITARIANISM SCALES)
       ƏC-32 RESPONSE-BIAS ACQUIESCENCE AUTHORITARIANISM COPING-DEFENSE OTHER-CATEGORY
       ƏC-32 1961M
          (APPLICATIONS: 190)

C-33   CLINE, V. B., & RICHARDS, J. M., JR.
          A FACTOR-ANALYTIC STUDY OF RELIGIOUS BELIEF AND BEHAVIOR.
          JOURNAL OF PERSONALITY AND SOCIAL PSYCHOLOGY, 1965, 1, 569-578.
          (RELIGIOUS BELIEF-BEHAVIOR QUESTIONNAIRE)*
       ƏC-33 RELIGION BELIEF BEHAVIOR ORIENTATION 1965M

C-34   COHEN, A. R.
                A REPORT ON SOME EXPLORATIONS OF SELF-ESTEEM.
                UNPUBLISHED REPORT, 1954.
                (SELF-ESTEEM AND DEFENSE PREFERENCE SCALE)
            @C-34 SELF ESTEEM COPING DEFENSE STYLE HISTORY SELF-IDENTITY EVALUATION
            @PERCEPTION 1954M IMAGE
                (APPLICATIONS: 214)

C-35   CHILD, I. L.
                PERSONALITY CORRELATES OF ESTHETIC JUDGMENT IN COLLEGE STUDENTS.
                JOURNAL OF PERSONALITY, 1965, 33, 476-511.
                (AWARENESS OF ANXIETY SCALE)
            @C-35 AFFECTIVE-STATES SUBJECTIVE AWARENESS ANXIETY NEUROTICISM STRESS GLOBAL
            @ADJUSTMENT COPING-DEFENSE HISTORY STYLE COPING 1965M
                (APPLICATIONS: 480)

C-36   CONLON, E. J.
                PERFORMANCE AS DETERMINED BY EXPECTATION OF SUCCESS OR FAILURE.
                UNPUBLISHED DOCTORAL DISSERTATION, COLUMBIA UNIVERSITY, 1965.
                (FEELINGS OF GENERAL SELF CONFIDENCE)
            @C-36 SELF ESTEEM SELF-IDENTITY PERCEPTION EVALUATION CONFIDENCE 1965M MMPI

C-37   CONSTANTINOPLE, A.
                PERCEIVED INSTRUMENTALITY OF THE COLLEGE AS A MEASURE OF ATTITUDES TOWARD
                COLLEGE.
                JOURNAL OF PERSONALITY AND SOCIAL PSYCHOLOGY, 1967, 5, 196-201.
                (PERCEIVED INSTRUMENTALITY OF THE COLLEGE TEST)*
            @C-37 GOALS PE-FIT ADJUSTMENT COLLEGE ENVIRONMENT 1967M STUDENT
                (APPLICATIONS: 2968)

C-38   COOPERSMITH, S.
                A METHOD FOR DETERMINING TYPES OF SELF ESTEEM.
                JOURNAL OF ABNORMAL AND SOICAL PSYCHOLOGY, 1959, 59, 87-94.
                (SELF-ESTEEM INVENTORY)*
            @C-38 SELF ESTEEM SELF-IDENTITY EVALUATION PERCEPTION 1959M IMAGE CONCEPT
                (APPLICATIONS: 553   2245   2460   2463   2637)

C-39   CORSINI, R.
                SAQS, CHICAGO Q-SORT. CHICAGO: PSYCHOMETRIC AFFILIATES, 1956.
                (SELF-IDEAL SELF MEASURE)
            @C-39 SELF CONCEPT SELF-IDENTITY ESTEEM EVALUATION PERCEPTION IDEAL IMAGE
            @C-39 1956M Q-SORT
                (APPLICATIONS: 48)

C-40   COWEN, J.
                TEST ANXIETY IN HIGH SCHOOL STUDENTS AND ITS RELATIONSHIP TO PERFORMANCE ON
                GROUP TESTS.
                UNPUBLISHED DOCTORAL DISSERTATION, HARVARD UNIVERSITY, 1957.
                (TEST ANXIETY QUESTIONNAIRE)*
            @C-40 TEST ANXIETY AFFECTIVE-STATES SUBJECTIVE STRESS NEGATIVE 1957M
                (APPLICATIONS: 257)

C-41   CRANDALL, V. J., & BELLUGI, U.
                SOME RELATIONSHIPS OF INTERPERSONAL AND INTRAPERSONAL CONCEPTUALIZATIONS TO
                PERSONAL-SOCIAL ADJUSTMENT.
                JOURNAL OF PERSONALITY, 1954, 23, 224-232.
                (SOCIAL DESIRABILITY AND WORD FAMILIARITY ADJECTIVE CHECKLIST)
            @C-41 MULTITRAIT SOCIAL COMPETENCE ADJUSTMENT CHECKLIST DESIRABILITY 1954M
                (APPLICATIONS: 107)

C-42   CRANDALL, V. C., CRANDALL, V. J., & KATKOVSKY, W.
                A CHILDREN'S SOCIAL DESIRABILITY QUESTIONNAIRE.
                JOURNAL OF CONSULTING PSYCHOLOGY, 1965, 29, 27-36.
                (CHILDREN'S SOCIAL DESIRABILITY SCALE)*
            @C-42 SOCIAL DESIRABILITY RESPONSE-BIAS CHILD 1965M
                (APPLICATIONS: 38   139   149   266   270   2248   2261   2802   2903)

C-43   CRUSE, D. B.
                SOCIALLY DESIRABLE RESPONSES IN RELATION TO GRADE LEVEL.
                CHILD DEVELOPMENT, 1963, 34, 777-789.
                (SOCIAL DESIRABILITY SCALE)
            @C-43 RESPONSE-BIAS SOCIAL DESIRABILITY CHILD 1963M
                (APPLICATIONS: 138)

C-44   CHESLER, M.
                ETHNOCENTRISM AND ATTITUDES TOWARD THE PHYSICALLY DISABLED.
                JOURNAL OF PERSONALITY AND SOCIAL PSYCHOLOGY, 1965, 2, 877-882.
                (INTERGROUP RELATIONS SCALE)*
            aC-44 COPING-DEFENSE ETHNOCENTRISM OTHER-CATEGORY DISABILITY PHYSICAL ATTITUDE
            aC-44 1965M GROUP PREJUDICE

C-45   CHILD, I. L.
                PERSONALITY CORRELATES OF ESTHETIC JUDGMENT IN COLLEGE STUDENTS.
                JOURNAL OF PERSONALITY, 1965, 33, 476-511.
                (ESTHETIC SENSITIVITY MEASURE)
            aC-45 ESTHETIC PREFERENCE SENSITIVITY 1965M JUDGMENT
                (APPLICATIONS: 298   2816)

C-46   CHILD, I. L., COOPERMAN, M., & WOLOWITZ, H. M.
                ESTHETIC PREFERENCE AND OTHER CORRELATES OF ACTIVE VERSUS PASSIVE FOOD
                PREFERENCE.
                JOURNAL OF PERSONALITY AND SOCIAL PSYCHOLOGY, 1969, 11, 75-84.
                (PERSONALITY QUESTIONNAIRE: INDEPENDENCE, SELF-ASSERTION, INTROVERSION,
                ANXIETY)
            aC-46 ANXIETY INTROVERSION SELF ASSERTION DEPENDENCE MULTITRAIT ESTHETIC
            aPREFERENCE 1969M

C-47   CHILD, I. L. & IWAO, S.
                PERSONALITY AND ESTHETIC SENSITIVITY: EXTENSION OF FINDINGS TO YOUNGER AGE
                AND TO DIFFERENT CULTURE.
                JOURNAL OF PERSONALITY AND SOCIAL PSYCHOLOGY, 1968, 8, 308-312.
                (MEASURES OF ESTHETIC SENSITIVITY-RELATED VARIABLES)
            aC-47 ESTHETIC SENSITIVITY DEPENDENCE TOLERANCE COMPLEXITY REGRESSION CONFLICT
            aCOPING-DEFENSE INTEGRATION RESOLUTION MOTIVE FLEXIBILITY RIGIDITY DOGMATISM
            aC-47 FIELD AUTONOMY 1968M

C-48   CHRISTIE, R.
                THE PREVALENCE OF MACHIAVELLIAN ORIENTATIONS.
                PAPER PRESENTED AT THE MEETING OF THE AMERICAN PSYCHOLOGICAL ASSOCIATION,
                LOS ANGELES, 1964.
                (MACHIAVELLIANISM, ANOMIE, AND AUTHORITARIANISM SCALES)
            aC-48 MACHIAVELLIANISM ANOMIE AUTHORITARIANISM COPING-DEFENSE OTHER-CATEGORY
            aAFFECTIVE-STATES ALIENATION 1964M
                (APPLICATIONS: 687)

C-49   CLORE, G. L., & BALDRIDGE, B.
                INTERPERSONAL ATTRACTION: THE ROLE OF AGREEMENT AND TOPIC INTEREST.
                JOURNAL OF PERSONALITY AND SOCIAL PSYCHOLOGY, 1968, 9, 340-346.
                (INTERPERSONAL BEHAVIOR SCALE)*
            aC-49 SOCIAL DISTANCE ATTRACTION INTERPERSONAL COMPETENCE ADJUSTMENT 1968M
            aC-49 BEHAVIOR

C-50   COLLINS, M. E., & HAUPT, E. J.
                UNPUBLISHED RESEARCH, RESEARCH CENTER FOR HUMAN RELATIONS, NEW YORK
                UNIVERSITY. (NO REFERENCE AVAILABLE)
                (MEASURES OF ATTITUDES TOWARD NEGROES)
            aC-50 ATTITUDE RACIAL NEGRO AFFECTIVE-STATES OTHER-CATEGORY PREJUDICE
            aC-50 SOCIAL DISTANCE
                (APPLICATIONS: 179)

C-51   COWEN, E. L., BOBROVE, P. H., ROCKWAY, A. M., & STEVENSON, J.
                DEVELOPMENT AND EVALUATION OF AN ATTITUDES TO DEAFNESS SCALE.
                JOURNAL OF PERSONALITY AND SOCIAL PSYCHOLOGY, 1967, 6, 183-191.
                (MEASURE OF ATTITUDES TOWARD DEAFNESS)
            aC-51 ATTITUDE DEAFNESS SOCIAL DISTANCE 1967M OTHERS

C-52   CLARK, K. E.
                A VOCATIONAL INTEREST TEST AT THE SKILLED TRADES LEVEL.
                JOURNAL OF APPLIED PSYCHOLOGY, 1949, 33, 291-303.
                (MINNESOTA VOCATIONAL INTEREST INVENTORY)*
            aC-52 VOCATIONAL INTEREST JOB PREFERENCE ACTIVITIES 1949M
                (APPLICATIONS: 1171   1298   1396   1402   2352)

C-53   COLE, C. W., & MILLER, C. D.
                RELEVANCE OF EXPRESSED VALUES TO ACADEMIC PERFORMANCE.
                JOURNAL OF COUNSELING PSYCHOLOGY, 1967, 14, 272-276.
                (SEMANTIC-DIFFERENTIAL MEASURE OF EXPRESSED VALUES)
            aC-53 SEM-DIFFERENTIAL VALUES IDEALS SELF-IDENTITY LIFE GOALS 1967M

C-54   CARTER, H. D.
               CALIFORNIA STUDY METHODS SURVEY. LOS ANGELES: CALIFORNIA TEST BUREAU, 1958
               (CALIFORNIA STUDY METHODS SURVEY)*
          aC-54 STUDENT ATTITUDE SELF SECONDARY SCHOOL 1958M ACADEMIC
               (APPLICATIONS: 1500)

C-55   CASTENADA, A., MCCANDLESS, B. R., & PALERMO, D. S.
               THE CHILDREN'S FORM OF THE MANIFEST ANXIETY SCALE.
               CHILD DEVELOPMENT, 1956, 27, 317-325.
               (CHILDREN'S MANIFEST ANXIETY SCALE)*
          aC-55 MANIFEST ANXIETY AFFECTIVE-STATES SUBJECTIVE STRESS CHILD
          aC-55 NEGATIVE 1956M
               (APPLICATIONS: 323   713   739   746   822   1575   1590   1619   1638   1641
                                1837   1893   2050   2199   2330   2519   2545   2752)

C-56   COMMOSS, H. H.
               SOME CHARACTERISTICS RELATED TO SOCIAL ISOLATION OF SECOND GRADE CHILDREN.
               JOURNAL OF EDUCATIONAL PSYCHOLOGY, 1962, 53, 38-42.
               (SOCIOMETRIC PEER-RATING OF SOCIAL ISOLATION/ACCEPTANCE)
          aC-56 SOCIOMETRIC PEER RATING SOCIAL ISOLATION ACCEPTANCE AFFECTIVE-STATES CHILD
          aALIENATION ADJUSTMENT COMPETENCE INTERACTION ELEMENTARY SCHOOL 1962M

C-57   CHILD, I. L.
               PERSONALITY CORRELATES OF ESTHETIC JUDGMENT IN COLLEGE STUDENTS.
               JOURNAL OF PERSONALITY, 1965, 33, 476-511.
               (TOLERANCE OF AMBIGUITY)
          aC-57 OPENNESS EXPERIENCE COGNITIVE STYLE COPING-DEFENSE RIGIDITY FLEXIBILITY
          aDOGMATISM TOLERANCE AMBIGUITY COMPLEXITY 1965M
               (APPLICATIONS: 480   562   1274   2323   2513)

C-58   COFER, C. N., CHANCE, J., & JUDSON, A. J.
               A STUDY OF MALINGERING ON THE MINNESOTA MULTIPHASIC PERSONALITY INVENTORY.
               JOURNAL OF PSYCHOLOGY, 1949, 27, 491-499.
               (FAKING-GOOD INDEX OF MMPI)
          aC-58 MMPI RESPONSE-BIAS FAKING MALINGERING 1949M
               (APPLICATIONS: 757   1414   1626   1872   1899   2085   2910)

C-59   CHILD, I. L.
               PERSONALITY CORRELATES OF ESTHETIC JUDGMENT IN COLLEGE STUDENTS.
               JOURNAL OF PERSONALITY, 1965, 33, 476-511.
               (TOLERANCE OF COMPLEXITY)
          aC-59 OPENNESS EXPERIENCE COGNITIVE STYLE COPING-DEFENSE RIGIDITY FLEXIBILITY
          aDOGMATISM TOLERANCE AMBIGUITY COMPLEXITY 1965M
               (APPLICATIONS: 480   2513)

C-60   CAIRNS, R. B.
               THE INFLUENCE OF DEPENDENCY INHIBITION ON THE EFFECTIVENESS OF SOCIAL REIN-
               FORCEMENT.
               JOURNAL OF PERSONALITY, 1961, 29, 466-488.
               (PROJECTIVE MEASURE OF DEPENDENCY INHIBITION)
          aC-60 DEPENDENCE INHIBITION AUTONOMY CONFORMITY PROJECTIVE 1961M

C-61   CHILD, I. L.
               THE RELATION OF SOMATOTYPE TO SELF-RATINGS ON SHELDON'S TEMPERAMENTAL
               TRAITS.
               JOURNAL OF PERSONALITY, 1950, 18, 440-453.
               (MEASURES OF SOMATOTYPE-RELATED TRAITS)
          aC-61 SOMATOTYPE TRAIT TEMPERAMENT BODY 1950M
               (APPLICATIONS: 357   423   480)

C-62   CRUTCHFIELD, R. S., WOODWORTH, D. G., & ALBRECHT, R. E.
               PERCEPTUAL PERFORMANCE AND THE EFFECTIVE PERSON.
               LACKLAND AIR FORCE BASE, TEXAS: WRIGHT AIR DEVELOPMENT CENTER, PERSONNEL
               LABORATORY, APRIL, 1958. TECHNICAL NOTE WADC-TN-58-60; ASTIA DOCUMENT NO.
               AD 210 219.
               (GOTTSCHALDT FIGURES TEST)*
          aC-62 AUTONOMY PERCEPTION CREATIVITY FIGURE 1958M PERCEPTION
               (APPLICATIONS: 430)

C-63   CRUTCHFIELD, R. S.
               CONFORMITY AND CREATIVE THINKING.
               IN H. E. GRUBER, S. TERRELL, & M. WERTHEIMER (EDS.), CONTEMPORARY
               APPROACHES TO CREATIVE THINKING. NEW YORK: ATHERTON PRESS, 1962.
               (MEASURE OF CONFORMITY)
          aC-63 AUTONOMY CREATIVITY CONFORMITY 1962M THINKING COGNITIVE STRUCTURE
          aC-63 FUNCTIONING
               (APPLICATIONS: 386   430)

C-64   CENTERS, R.
            THE PSYCHOLOGY OF SOCIAL CLASSES: A STUDY OF CLASS CONSCIOUSNESS.
            PRINCETON, N. J.: PRINCETON UNIVERSITY PRESS, 1949.
            ALSO: NEW YORK: RUSSELL AND RUSSELL, 1961.
            (LIBERALISM-CONSERVATISM SCALE)
        @C-64 LIBERALISM CONSERVATISM POLITICAL ORIENTATION 1949M
            (APPLICATIONS: 2489)

C-65   CASSELL, S.
            EFFECT OF BRIEF PUPPET THERAPY UPON THE EMOTIONAL RESPONSES OF CHILDREN
            UNDERGOING CARDIAC CATHETERIZATION.
            JOURNAL OF CONSULTING PSYCHOLOGY, 1965, 29, 1-8.
            (PARENTAL EVALUATION OF CHILD'S BEHAVIOR)
        @C-65 EVALUATION RATING PARENT-CHILD BEHAVIOR FAMILY INTERACTION ADJUSTMENT
        @C-65 CHILD 1965M

C-66   CHAPPLE, E. D.
            THE INTERACTION CHRONOGRAPH; ITS EVOLUTION AND PRESENT APPLICATION.
            PERSONNEL, 1949, 25, 295-307.
            (INTERACTION CHRONOGRAPH)*
        @C-66 SELF DESCRIPTION ADJUSTMENT OTHER-CATEGORY INTERACTION INTERPERSONAL 1949M
            (APPLICATIONS: 1034 1598 1662)

C-67   CATALDO, J. F., SILVERMAN, I., & BROWN, J. M.
            DEMAND CHARACTERISTICS ASSOCIATED WITH SEMANTIC DIFFERENTIAL RATINGS OF
            NOUNS AND VERBS.
            EDUCATIONAL AND PSYCHOLOGICAL MEASUREMENT, 1967, 27, 83-87.
            (MEASURE OF COMPLIANCE WITH DEMAND CHARACTERISTICS)
        @C-67 1967M SEM-DIFFERENTIAL DEMANDS RESPONSE
            (APPLICATIONS: 2483)

C-68   CATTELL, R. B.
            HANDBOOK FOR THE OBJECTIVE-ANALYTIC PERSONALITY TEST BATTERIES.
            CHAMPAIGN, ILLINOIS: INSTITUTE FOR PERSONALITY AND ABILITY TESTING, 1955.
            (ANXIETY TO ACHIEVE BATTERY)*
        @C-68 AFFECTIVE-STATES ANXIETY SUBJECTIVE STRESS ACHIEVEMENT NEED 1955M

C-69   COHEN, J., & STRUENING, E. L.
            OPINIONS ABOUT MENTAL ILLNESS IN THE PERSONNEL OF TWO LARGE MENTAL
            HOSPITALS.
            JOURNAL OF ABNORMAL AND SOCIAL PSYCHOLOGY, 1962, 64, 349-360.
            (MEASURE OF ATTITUDES TOWARD MENTAL ILLNESS)
        @C-69 ATTITUDE MENTAL-ILLNESS IDEOLOGY 1962M

C-70   COOPER, L. M., & HOWELL, R. J.
            A REFORMULATION OF THE "FEAR OF FAILURE" AND "HOPE OF SUCCESS" CONCEPTS,
            AS MEASURED BY MCCLELLAND'S NEED ACHIEVEMENT TEST.
            JOURNAL OF SOCIAL PSYCHOLOGY, 1961, 53, 81-85.
            (RATIONAL STRESS SCALE)*
        @C-70 AFFECTIVE-STATES ANXIETY STRESS MMPI SUBJECTIVE RATIONAL 1961M FEAR
        @C-70 FAILURE

C-71   COWEN, E. L., BUDIN, W., & BUDIN, F. A.
            THE SOCIAL DESIRABILITY OF TRAIT-DESCRIPTIVE TERMS: A PAIRED-COMPARISON
            APPROACH.
            JOURNAL OF SOCIAL PSYCHOLOGY, 1964, 63, 265-279.
            (FOUR PAIRED-COMPARISON ADJECTIVE LISTS)
        @C-71 TRAIT-TERMS SOCIAL DESIRABILITY RESPONSE-BIAS PERCEIVED 1964M
            (APPLICATIONS: 2236)

C-72   COMREY, A. L., & NEWMEYER, J. A.
            MEASUREMENT OF RADICALISM-CONSERVATISM.
            JOURNAL OF SOCIAL PSYCHOLOGY, 1965, 67, 357-369.
            (RADICALISM-CONSERVATISM QUESTIONNAIRE)
        @C-72 RADICALISM CONSERVATISM MULTITRAIT 1965M VALUES POLITICAL ORIENTATION

C-73   CHILD, I. L.
            PERSONALITY CORRELATES OF ESTHETIC JUDGMENT IN COLLEGE STUDENTS.
            JOURNAL OF PERSONALITY, 1965, 33, 476-511.
            (SUPEREGO SCALE: MEASURE OF STRENGTH OF INNER SANCTIONS)
        @C-73 SELF-IDENTITY VALUES CONSCIENCE AUTONOMY MORAL OTHER-CATEGORY 1965M
        @C-73 DEVELOPMENT
            (APPLICATIONS: 480 2513)

C-74   CHILD, I. L.
            PERSONALITY CORRELATES OF ESTHETIC JUDGMENT IN COLLEGE STUDENTS.
            JOURNAL OF PERSONALITY, 1965, 33, 476-511.
            (SCANNING SCALE)
        aC-74 PERCEPTION WIDTH SCANNING ESTHETIC JUDGMENT ATTENTION 1965M
            (APPLICATIONS: 480   2513)

C-75   CHILD, I. L.
            PERSONALITY CORRELATES OF ESTHETIC JUDGMENT IN COLLEGE STUDENTS.
            JOURNAL OF PERSONALITY, 1965, 33, 476-511.
            (TOLERANCE OF UNREALISTIC EXPERIENCES)
        aC-75 OPENNESS EXPERIENCE COGNITIVE STYLE COPING-DEFENSE RIGIDITY FLEXIBILITY
        aDOGMATISM TOLERANCE AMBIGUITY COMPLEXITY 1965M
            (APPLICATIONS: 480   2323   2513)

C-76   CROCKETT, W. H.
            COGNITIVE COMPLEXITY AND IMPRESSION FORMATION.
            IN B. A. MAHER (ED.), PROGRESS IN EXPERIMENTAL PERSONALITY RESEARCH. VOL.
            2. NEW YORK: ACADEMIC PRESS, 1965.
            (MEASURE OF COGNITIVE COMPLEXITY)
        aC-76 STRUCTURE COGNITIVE COMPLEXITY 1965M IMPRESSION FORMATION
            (APPLICATIONS: 510   534   2780)

C-77   CARR, J. E.
            THE ROLE OF CONCEPTUAL ORGANIZATION IN INTERPERSONAL DISCRIMINATION.
            JOURNAL OF PSYCHOLOGY, 1965, 59, 159-176.
            (INTERPERSONAL DISCRIMINATION TEST)*
        aC-77 DIFFERENTIATION PERSON COGNITIVE COMPLEXITY INTERPERSONAL 1965M
        aC-77 SELF-IDENTITY SUB-IDENTITY ROLE PERCEPTION
            (APPLICATIONS: 518   2420)

C-78   CALIFORNIA PICTURE INTEREST INVENTORY.
            PRIMARY SOURCE UNKNOWN. SEE: BLAKE, P. COMPARATIVE RELIABILITY OF PIC-
            TURE FORM AND VERBAL FORM INTEREST INVENTORIES.
            JOURNAL OF APPLIED PSYCHOLOGY, 1969, 53, 42-44.
            (CALIFORNIA PICTURE INTEREST INVENTORY)*
        aC-78 INTEREST VOCATIONAL JOB 1969M

C-79   CERVIN, V.
            PERSONALITY DIMENSIONS OF EMOTIONAL RESPONSIVENESS AND RIGIDITY, AND SCALES
            FOR MEASURING THEM.
            JOURNAL OF PERSONALITY, 1957, 25, 626-642.
            (MEASURE OF EMOTIONAL RESPONSIVENESS)
        aC-79 RIGIDITY EMOTION RESPONSE AFFECTIVE-STATES OTHER-CATEGORY 1957M

C-80   CAINE, T. M.
            THE EXPRESSION OF HOSTILITY AND GUILT IN MELANCHOLIC AND PARANOID WOMEN.
            JOURNAL OF CONSULTING PSYCHOLOGY, 1960, 24, 18-22.
            (WORD SCRAMBLE TEST OF HOSTILITY AND GUILT)
        aC-80 HOSTILITY GUILT AFFECTIVE-STATES RESENTMENT GLOBAL NEGATIVE 1960M

C-81   CHRISTIE, R., LANE, H., SANFORD, N., STERN, G., & WEBSTER, H.
            SSRC S-A SCHEDULE, FORM 186C (UNPUBLISHED INVENTORY, NO DATE AVAILABLE).
            (SSRC S-A SCHEDULE, FORM 186O)*
        aC-81 AUTHORITARIANISM ACQUIESCENCE STEREOTYPE

C-82   COSTANZO, P. R.
            CONFORMITY DEVELOPMENT AS A FUNCTION OF SELF-BLAME.
            JOURNAL OF PERSONALITY AND SOCIAL PSYCHOLOGY, 1970, 14, 366-374.
            (SELF-BLAME SCALE)
        aC-82 1970M RESPONSIBILITY ACCEPTANCE SELF APPROVAL ABASEMENT DEPRECIATION

C-83   COHLER, B. J., WOOLSEY, S. H., WEISS, J. L., & GRUNEBAUM, H. H.
            CHILDREARING ATTITUDES AMONG MOTHERS VOLUNTEERING AND REVOLUNTEERING FOR A
            PSYCHOLOGICAL STUDY.
            PSYCHOLOGICAL REPORTS, 1968, 23, 603-612.
            (MATERNAL ATTITUDE SCALE)
        aC-83 MATERNAL CHILD ATTITUDE FAMILY INTERACTION ADJUSTMENT 1968M PARENT-CHILD

C-84   COTTLE, T. J.
          FAMILY PERCEPTIONS, SEX ROLE IDENTITY AND THE PREDICTION OF SCHOOL PERFOR-
          MANCE.
          EDUCATIONAL AND PSYCHOLOGICAL MEASUREMENT, 1968, 28, 861-886.
          (FAMILY INTERACTION ATTITUDES)
          @C-84 FAMILY ADJUSTMENT INTERACTION SEX ROLE SUB-IDENTITY INTERPERSONAL 1968M

C-85   CLIFFORD, E., & CLIFFORD, M.
          SELF-CONCEPTS BEFORE AND AFTER SURVIVAL TRAINING.
          BRITISH JOURNAL OF SOCIAL AND CLINICAL PSYCHOLOGY, 1967, 6, 241-248.
          (SELF DESCRIPTION SCALE)
          @C-85 SELF CONCEPT SELF-IDENTITY EVALUATION ESTEEM PERCEPTION DESCRIPTION 1967M

C-86   GHOUNGOURIAN, A.
          LEBANESE AND AMERICAN ASPECTS OF PERSONALITY: A CROSS-CULTURAL COMPARISON.
          JOURNAL OF SOCIAL PSYCHOLOGY, 1970, 81, 117-118.
          (MEASURE OF SIX ASPECTS OF PERSONALITY)
          @C-86 1970M MULTITRAIT SELF DESCRIPTION CROSS-CULTURAL PERSONALITY

C-87   COTTLE, T. J.
          FAMILY PERCEPTIONS, SEX ROLE IDENTITY AND THE PREDICTION OF SCHOOL
          PERFORMANCE.
          EDUCATIONAL AND PSYCHOLOGICAL MEASUREMENT, 1968, 28, 861-886.
          (SEMANTIC-DIFFERENTIAL MEASURE OF SELF-CONCEPT)
          @C-87 SELF CONCEPT SUB-IDENTITY SEX ROLE SCHOOL PERFORMANCE SELF-IDENTITY
          @C-87 EVALUATION PERCEPTION SEM-DIFFERENTIAL 1968M

C-88   CARLSON, R.
          STABILITY AND CHANGE IN THE ADOLESCENT'S SELF-IMAGE.
          CHILD DEVELOPMENT , 1965, 36, 659-666.
          (MEASURE OF SOCIAL ORIENTATION AND SELF-ESTEEM)
          @C-88 SELF IMAGE SELF-IDENTITY ESTEEM PERCEPTION EVALUATION SOCIAL ORIENTATION
          @C-88 ADOLESCENT 1965M
          (APPLICATIONS: 2695)

C-89   CATTELL, R. B., & BELOFF, H.
          HANDBOOK FOR THE JUNIOR-SENIOR HIGH SCHOOL PERSONALITY QUESTIONNAIRE.
          CHAMPAIGN, ILLINOIS: INSTITUTE FOR PERSONALITY AND ABILITY TESTING, 1962.
          (JUNIOR-SENIOR HIGH SCHOOL PERSONALITY QUESTIONNAIRE)*
          @C-89 MULTITRAIT PERSONALITY SCHOOL SECONDARY STUDENT 1962M
          (APPLICATIONS: 460   554   911   919   1792   2619   2797)

C-90   CLIFFORD, E., & CLIFFORD, M.
          SELF-CONCEPTS BEFORE AND AFTER SURVIVAL TRAINING.
          BRITISH JOURNAL OF SOCIAL AND CLINICAL PSYCHOLOGY, 1967, 6, 241-248.
          (SELF-RATING SCALE)
          @C-90 SELF CONCEPT SELF-IDENTITY EVALUATION ESTEEM PERCEPTION RATING 1967M

C-91   COLE, C. W., OETTING, E. R., & HINKLE, J. E.
          NON-LINEARITY OF SELF-CONCEPT DISCREPENCY--THE VALUE DIMENSION.
          PSYCHOLOGICAL REPORTS, 1967, 21, 58-60.
          (SEMANTIC DIFFERENTIAL MEASURE OF SELF AND IDEAL SELF)
          @C-91 CONCEPT DISCREPANCY GLOBAL ADJUSTMENT SELF-IDENTITY SELF ESTEEM PERCEPTION
          @EVALUATION IDEAL IMAGE VALUES SEM-DIFFERENTIAL 1967M
          (APPLICATIONS: 1139)

C-92   COTTLE, T. J., EDWARDS, C. N., & PLECK, J.
          THE RELATIONSHIP OF SEX ROLE IDENTITY AND SOCIAL AND POLITICAL ATTITUDES.
          JOURNAL OF PERSONALITY, 1970, 38, 435-452.
          (SOCIAL-POLITICAL INVENTORY)
          @C-92 1970M SEX ROLE MASCULINITY FEMININITY POLITICAL MORAL VALUES PREJUDICE
          @C-92 SOCIAL ORIENTATION ATTITUDE

C-93   COYNE, L., & HOLZMAN, P. H.
          THREE EQUIVALENT FORMS OF A SEMANTIC DIFFERENTIAL INVENTORY.
          EDUCATIONAL AND PSYCHOLOGICAL MEASUREMENT, 1966, 26, 665-674.
          (SEMANTIC DIFFERENTIAL FORMS)
          @C-93 SEM-DIFFERENTIAL SELF-IDENTITY ESTEEM SELF PERCEPTION EVALUATION 1966M

C-94   CRUMBAUGH, J. C.
            CROSS-VALIDATION OF PURPOSE-IN-LIFE TEST BASED ON FRANKL'S CONCEPTS.
            JOURNAL OF INDIVIDUAL PSYCHOLOGY, 1968, 24, 74-81.
            (MINISTERS' RATING SCALE FOR PARISHIONERS)*
            ƏC-94 LIFE GOALS SELF-IDENTITY IDEALS VALUES RATING 1968M ORIENTATION PERSONAL

C-95   CRUMBAUGH, J. C., & MAHOLICK, L. T.
            AN EXPERIMENTAL STUDY IN EXISTENTIALISM: THE PSYCHOMETRIC APPROACH TO
            FRANKL'S CONCEPT OF NOOGENIC NEUROSIS.
            JOURNAL OF CLINICAL PSYCHOLOGY, 1964, 20, 200-207.
            (PURPOSE-IN-LIFE TEST)*
            ƏC-95 LIFE GOALS SELF-IDENTITY VALUES IDEALS PURPOSE 1964M PERSONAL ORIENTATION

C-96   CUTICK, R. A.
            SELF-EVALUATION OF CAPACITIES AS A FUNCTION OF SELF-ESTEEM AND THE
            CHARACTERISTICS OF A MODEL.
            UNPUBLISHED DOCTORAL DISSERTATION, UNIVERSITY OF PENNSYLVANIA, 1962.
            (SELF DESCRIPTION INVENTORY)
            ƏC-96 1962M SELF EVALUATION SELF ESTEEM DESCRIPTION SELF-IDENTITY
                 (APPLICATIONS: 932   2340)

C-98   COMREY, A. L., & MARGGRAFF, W. M.
            A FACTOR ANALYSIS OF ITEMS ON THE MMPI SCHIZOPHRENIA SCALE.
            EDUCATIONAL AND PSYCHOLOGICAL MEASUREMENT, 1958, 18, 301-311.
            (PSYCHOTIC TENDENCIES FACTOR OF MMPI)
            ƏC-98 1958M MMPI MENTAL-ILLNESS PSYCHOPATHY DIAGNOSIS
                 (APPLICATIONS: 2386)

C-99   COOPER, L., & CASTON, J.
            PHYSICAL ACTIVITY AND INCREASES IN M RESPONSE.
            JOURNAL OF PROJECTIVE TECHNIQUES AND PERSONALITY ASSESSMENT, 1970, 34,
            295-301.
            (COGNITIVE PROCESS INVENTORY)
            ƏC-99 1970M COGNITIVE FUNCTIONING IMAGERY FANTASY

C-101   CASSEL, R. N.
            TEST OF SOCIAL INSIGHT MANUAL.
            NEW ROCHELLE, N.Y.: BRUCE, 1959.
            (TEST OF SOCIAL INSIGHT)
            ƏC-101 1959M SOCIAL BEHAVIOR ATTITUDE INTEREST AUTHORITY FAMILY INTERACTION
                 (APPLICATIONS: 2696)

C-102   COAN, R. W., & CATTELL, R. B.
            THE DEVELOPMENT OF THE EARLY SCHOOL PERSONALITY QUESTIONNAIRE.
            JOURNAL OF EXPERIMENTAL EDUCATION, 1959, 28, 143-152.
            COAN, R. W., BAKER, R., & CATTELL, R. B.
            THE EARLY SCHOOL PERSONALITY QUESTIONNAIRE.
            CHAMPAIGN, ILLINOIS: INSTITUTE OF PERSONALITY AND ABILITY TESTING, 1966.
            (EARLY SCHOOL PERSONALITY QUESTIONNAIRE)*
            ƏC-102 1959 SCHOOL PERSONALITY STRUCTURE CHILD
                 (APPLICATIONS: 1011   2797)

C-104   CHODORKOFF, B., & COOKE, G.
            DEVELOPMENT OF AN INVENTORY TO MEASURE PSYCHOSEXUAL DEVELOPMENT.
            PSYCHOLOGICAL REPORTS, 1970, 27, 186.
            (PSYCHOSEXUAL STAGES INVENTORY)*
            ƏC-104 1970M SEX DEVELOPMENT ADJUSTMENT SOCIAL

C-105   CARKHUFF, R. R.
            CRITICAL VARIABLES IN EFFECTIVE COUNSELOR TRAINING.
            JOURNAL OF COUNSELING PSYCHOLOGY, 1969, 16, 238-245.
            (INDEX OF COMMUNICATION)
            ƏC-105 1969M INTERPERSONAL COUNSELING AFFECTIVE-STATES DEPRESSION AGGRESSION
            ƏC-105 HOSTILITY VOCATIONAL RACIAL ATTITUDE THERAPY COMMUNICATION
                 (APPLICATIONS: 2860)

C-106   CARKHUFF, R. R.
            CRITICAL VARIABLES IN EFFECTIVE COUNSELOR TRAINING.
            JOURNAL OF COUNSELING PSYCHOLOGY, 1969, 16, 238-245.
            (INDEX OF DISCRIMINATION)
            ƏC-106 1969M RACIAL STIMULUS EXPRESSION COMMUNICATION THERAPY
                 (APPLICATIONS: 2860)

C-107   COLEMEN, J. S., CAMPBELL, E. Q., HOBSON, C. F., MCPARTLAND, J., & MOOD, A. M.
               EQUALITY OF EDUCATIONAL OPPORTUNITY,
               WASHINGTON: U.S. OFFICE OF EDUCATION, 1966.
               (MEASURE OF FATE CONTROL/PERSONAL EFFICACY)
           @C-107 1966M LOCUS CONTROL PERSONAL COMPETENCE IE-CONTROL
               (APPLICATIONS: 2720)

C-108   COWEN, E. L., HUSER, J., BEACH, D. R., & RAPPAPORT, J.
               PARENTAL PERCEPTIONS OF YOUNG CHILDREN AND THEIR RELATION TO INDEXES OF
               ADJUSTMENT.
               JOURNAL OF CONSULTING AND CLINICAL PSYCHOLOGY, 1970, 34, 97-103.
               (PARENT ATTITUDES TEST)
           @C-108 1970M ATTITUDE PARENT-CHILD ADJUSTMENT CHECKLIST BEHAVIOR PROBLEM
           @C-108 FAMILY INTERACTION

C-109   CAMPBELL, A., GURIN, G., & MILLER, W. E.
               THE VOTER DECIDES. EVANSTON, ILLINOIS: ROW, PETERSON, 1954.
               (POLITICAL EFFICACY SCALE)
           @C-109 ANOMIE ALIENATION INFLUENCE POWER 1954M POLITICAL ORIENTATION SOCIAL
           @C-109 CYNICISM RESPONSIBILITY POWERLESSNESS
               (APPLICATIONS: 2334)

C-110   CRUTCHFIELD, R. S.
               CONFORMITY AND CHARACTER.
               AMERICAN PSYCHOLOGIST, 1955, 10, 191-198.
               (MEASURE OF INDEPENDENCE YIELDING)
           @C-110 1955M DEPENDENCE AUTONOMY CONFORMITY JUDGMENT
               (APPLICATIONS: 63   190)

C-111   CERVIN, V.
               PERSONALITY DIMENSIONS OF EMOTIONAL RESPONSIVENESS AND RIGIDITY, AND
               SCALES FOR MEASURING THEM.
               JOURNAL OF PERSONALITY, 1957, 25, 626-642.
               (MEASURE OF RIGIDITY)
           @C-111 1957M RIGIDITY IE-CONTROL AUTONOMY STIMULUS FLEXIBILITY

C-112   COHEN, A. R.
               COGNITIVE TUNING AS A FACTOR AFFECTING IMPRESSION FORMATION.
               JOURNAL OF PERSONALITY, 1961, 29, 235-245.
               (METHOD FOR ASSESSING SUSPENSION-POLARIZATION IN IMPRESSION FORMATION)
           @C-112 1961M IMPRESSION FORMATION PERCEPTION COGNITIVE FUNCTIONING

C-113   CLARK, E. T., & OZEHOSKY, R.
               PRELIMINARY MANUAL FOR THE U SCALE.
               UNPUBLISHED MANUAL, DEPARTMENT OF PSYCHOLOGY, ST. JOHNS UNIVERSITY,
               N. Y., 1966.
               (U-SCALE FOR MEASURING SELF-CONCEPT)
           @C-113 1966M SELF CONCEPT IMAGE CHILD POSITIVE NEGATIVE
           @C-113 SELF-IDENTITY
               (APPLICATIONS: 2889)

C-115   CAIRNS, R. B.
               THE INFLUENCE OF DEPENDENCY INHIBITION ON THE EFFECTIVENESS OF SOCIAL
               REINFORCEMENT.
               JOURNAL OF PERSONALITY, 1961, 29, 466-488.
               (MEASURE OF DEPENDENCY INHIBITION IN OVERT BEHAVIOR)
           @C-115 1961M DEPENDENCE INHIBITION ADOLESCENT COUNSELOR
           @C-115 NEED EXPRESSION BEHAVIOR

C-116   CATTELL, R. B.
               PERSONALITY AND MOTIVATION STRUCTURE AND MEASUREMENT.
               YONKERS-ON-HUDSON, N. Y.: WORLD BOOK, 1957.
               (MEASURE OF AGREEMENT WITH MAJORITY)
           @C-116 1957M AUTONOMY CONFORMITY BEHAVIOR GROUP RESPONSE-BIAS
               (APPLICATIONS: 386)

C-117   CATTELL, R. B.
               PERSONALITY AND MOTIVATION STRUCTURE AND MEASUREMENT.
               YONKERS-ON-HUDSON, N. Y.: WORLD BOOK, 1957.
               (MEASURE OF PERSONAL VS. INSTITUTIONAL VALUES)
           @C-117 1957M VALUES ORIENTATION PERSONAL SOCIAL AUTONOMY
               (APPLICATIONS: 386)

C-118   CATTELL, R. B.
          PERSONALITY AND MOTIVATION STRUCTURE AND MEASUREMENT.
          YONKERS-ON-HUDSON, N. Y.: WORLD BOOK, 1957.
          (MEASURE OF REALITY VS. PLEASURE PRINCIPLE)
          aC-118 1957M PERSONAL ORIENTATION REALITY
             (APPLICATIONS: 386)

C-119   CATTELL, R. B.
          PERSONALITY AND MOTIVATION STRUCTURE AND MEASUREMENT.
          YONKERS-ON-HUDSON, N. Y.: WORLD BOOK, 1957.
          (MEASURE OF SEVERITY-HOSTILITY VS. SENTIMENTALISM)
          aC-119 1957M PERSONAL ORIENTATION AFFECTIVE-STATES HOSTILITY
             (APPLICATIONS: 386)

C-120   CATTELL, R. B.
          PERSONALITY AND MOTIVATION STRUCTURE AND MEASUREMENT.
          YONKERS-ON-HUDSON, N. Y.: WORLD BOOK, 1957.
          (GOOD AND BAD PERSONAL VALUES SCALE)
          aC-120 1957M AUTHORITARIANISM VALUES ORIENTATION
             (APPLICATIONS: 386)

C-121   CATTELL, R. B.
          PERSONALITY AND MOTIVATION STRUCTURE AND MEASUREMENT.
          YONKERS-ON-HUDSON, N. Y.: WORLD BOOK, 1957.
          (COMMON FRAILTIES MEASURE)
          aC-121 1957M SOCIAL DESIRABILITY RESPONSE-BIAS
             (APPLICATIONS: 386)

C-122   CATTELL, R. B.
          PERSONALITY AND MOTIVATION STRUCTURE AND MEASUREMENT.
          YONKERS-ON-HUDSON, N. Y.: WORLD BOOK, 1957.
          (MEASURE OF EXTREMITY OF VIEWPOINT/ TENDENCY TO AGREE)
          aC-122 1957M RESPONSE-BIAS ACQUIESCENCE
          aC-122 GROUP CONFORMITY
             (APPLICATIONS: 386)

C-123   CANTER, A.
          THE EFFICACY OF A SHORT FORM OF THE MMPI TO EVALUATE DEPRESSION AND MORALE
          LOSS.
          JOURNAL OF CONSULTING PSYCHOLOGY, 1960, 24, 14-17.
          (MORALE LOSS SCALE)
          aC-123 1960M MORALE MMPI DEPRESSION NEGATIVE AFFECTIVE-STATES
          aC-123 MENTAL-ILLNESS PSYCHIATRIC
             (APPLICATIONS: 371)

C-125   CATTELL, R. B.
          HANDBOOK FOR THE OBJECTIVE-ANALYTIC PERSONALITY TEST MATRICES.
          CHAMPAIGN, ILLINOIS: IPAT, 1955.
          (OBJECTIVE-ANALYTIC TEST BATTERY)*
          aC-125 1955M ANALYTIC MULTITRAIT EVALUATION
          aC-125 SELF PERSONALITY BEHAVIOR
             (APPLICATIONS: 398   549   1126)

C-126   CLARK, R. A., TEEVAN, R., & RICIUTTI, H. N.
          HOPE OF SUCCESS AND FEAR OF FAILURE AS ASPECTS OF NEED FOR ACHIEVEMENT.
          JOURNAL OF ABNORMAL AND SOCIAL PSYCHOLOGY, 1956, 53, 182-190.
          (LEVEL OF ASPIRATION MEASURE)
          aC-126 1956M ACADEMIC ACHIEVEMENT ANXIETY ATTITUDE SCHOOL COLLEGE FEAR FAILURE
          aC-126 SATISFACTION SELF EVALUATION ASPIRATION
             (APPLICATIONS: 399   642)

C-128   CHILD, I. L.
          PERSONALITY CORRELATES OF ESTHETIC JUDGMENT IN COLLEGE STUDENTS.
          JOURNAL OF PERSONALITY, 1965, 33, 476-511.
          (MEASURE OF SOCIAL INTROVERSION VS. EXTRAVERSION)
          aC-128 1965M AUTONOMY EXTRAVERSION INTROVERSION SOCIAL ORIENTATION
             (APPLICATIONS: 423   2631)

C-129   CROSS, H. J.
          THE RELATION OF PARENTAL TRAINING CONDITIONS TO CONCEPTUAL LEVEL
          IN ADOLESCENT BOYS.
          JOURNAL OF PERSONALITY, 1966, 34, 348-365.
          (INTERVIEW ASSESSMENT OF PARENTAL TRAINING CONDITIONS)
          aC-129 1966M FAMILY INTERACTION ADJUSTMENT PARENTAL BEHAVIOR PARENT-CHILD
          aC-129 DEPENDENCE

C-130   CROSS, H. J.
         THE RELATION OF PARENTAL TRAINING CONDITIONS TO CONCEPTUAL LEVEL
         IN ADOLESCENT BOYS.
         JOURNAL OF PERSONALITY, 1966, 34, 348-365.
         (SENTENCE COMPLETION MEASURE OF CONCEPTUAL LEVEL)
         @C-130 1966M CONCEPTUAL COGNITIVE STRUCTURE FUNCTIONING
         @C-130 PARENTAL ADOLESCENT

C-131   CRANDALL, J. E.
         SOME RELATIONSHIPS AMONG SEX, ANXIETY, AND CONSERVATISM OF JUDGMENT.
         JOURNAL OF PERSONALITY, 1965, 33, 99-107.
         (TEST OF EVALUATIVE CONSERVATISM)
         @C-131 1965M CONSERVATISM JUDGMENT SEX ANXIETY EVALUATION
         @C-131 POSITIVE NEGATIVE AMBIGUITY

C-132   CRANDALL, J. E.
         SELF-PERCEPTION AND INTERPERSONAL ATTRACTION AS RELATED TO TOLERANCE-
         INTOLERANCE OF AMBIGUITY.
         JOURNAL OF PERSONALITY, 1969, 37, 127-140.
         (MEASURE OF TOLERANCE-INTOLERANCE OF DISAGREEMENT)
         @C-132 1969M TOLERANCE AMBIGUITY SELF-PERCEPTION INTERPERSONAL ATTRACTION
         @C-132 CONFLICT

C-134   CAINE, T. M.
         THE EXPRESSION OF HOSTILITY AND GUILT IN MELANCHOLIC AND PARANOID WOMEN.
         JOURNAL OF CONSULTING PSYCHOLOGY, 1960, 24, 18-22.
         (MEASURE OF EXTRAPUNITIVE AND INTROPUNITIVE ATTITUDES)
         @C-134 1960M HOSTILITY AFFECTIVE-STATES PUNITIVENESS
         @C-134 GUILT PROJECTIVE MMPI

C-135   CATTELL, R. B.
         THE NEUROTIC PERSONALITY FACTOR QUESTIONNAIRE.
         CHAMPAIGN, ILL.: INSTITUTE FOR PERSONALITY AND ABILITY TESTING, 1955.
         (NEUROTIC PERSONALITY FACTOR QUESTIONNAIRE)*
         @C-135 1955M NEUROTICISM MENTAL-HEALTH MENTAL-ILLNESS PATIENT
         (APPLICATIONS: 1568)

C-136   CATTELL, R. B.
         HANDBOOK FOR THE IPAT ANXIETY SCALE.
         CHAMPAIGN, ILL.: INSTITUTE FOR PERSONALITY AND ABILITY TESTING, 1957.
         (IPAT ANXIETY SCALE)*
         @C-136 1957M ANXIETY GLOBAL PATIENT
         (APPLICATIONS: 301   363   915   990   1012   1072   1165   1307   1475   1505
                         1568   1620   1744   1863   1958   2095   2138   2313   2438   2514
                         2517   2656)

C-137   CHRISTIE, R.
         MEDICAL SCHOOL VALUE CLIMATES AND MACHIAVELLIAN ORIENTATIONS OF STUDENTS.
         UNPUBLISHED MANUSCRIPT, COLUMBIA UNIVERSITY, N. Y., 1960.
         (MEASURE OF INTOLERANCE OF AMBIGUITY)
         @C-137 1960M TOLERANCE AMBIGUITY MACHIAVELLIANISM
         (APPLICATIONS: 531)

C-138   CARTWRIGHT, R. D., & LERNER, B.
         EMPATHY, NEED TO CHANGE, AND IMPROVEMENT WITH PSYCHOTHERAPY.
         JOURNAL OF CONSULTING PSYCHOLOGY, 1963, 27, 138-144.
         (MEASURE OF IMPROVEMENT IN PSYCHOTHERAPY)
         @C-138 1963M MENTAL-ILLNESS THERAPY PATIENT RATING CHANGE PERSONALITY STABILITY
         @C-138 EFFECTIVENESS

C-139   CARTWRIGHT, R. D., & LERNER, B.
         EMPATHY, NEED TO CHANGE, AND IMPROVEMENT WITH PSYCHOTHERAPY.
         JOURNAL OF CONSULTING PSYCHOLOGY, 1963, 27, 138-144.
         (MEASURE OF PERSONAL CONSTRUCTS IN THERAPY)
         @C-139 1963M SELF IDEAL DISCREPANCY MENTAL-ILLNESS THERAPY RATING PATIENT
         @C-139 RELATIONSHIPS NEED CHANGE EMPATHY SENSITIVITY

C-140   CHANG, J., & BLOCK, J.
         A STUDY OF IDENTIFICATION IN MALE HOMOSEXUALS.
         JOURNAL OF CONSULTING PSYCHOLOGY, 1960, 24, 307-310.
         (MEASURE OF IDENTIFICATION WITH PARENTS)
         @C-140 1960M PARENTAL IDENTIFICATION HOMOSEXUALITY SEX ROLE SELF IDEAL
         @C-140 MATERNAL PATERNAL

C-141   CATTELL, R. B., & ANDERSON, J. C.
        THE I.P.A.T. MUSIC PREFERENCE TEST OF PERSONALITY.
        CHAMPAIGN, ILLINOIS: I.P.A.T., 1953.
        CATTELL, R. B., & ANDERSON, J. C.
        THE MEASUREMENT OF PERSONALITY AND BEHAVIOR DISORDERS BY THE I.P.A.T. MUSIC
        PREFERENCE TEST.
        JOURNAL OF APPLIED PSYCHOLOGY, 1953, 37, 446-454.
        (MUSIC PREFERENCE TEST)*
        aC-141 1953M ESTHETIC PREFERENCE MENTAL-ILLNESS DRIVE SCHIZOPHRENIA ANXIETY
        aINTROVERSION SOCIAL RELATIONSHIPS ADJUSTMENT
              (APPLICATIONS: 1608)

C-142   CARTWRIGHT, D. S., ROBERTSON, R. J., FISKE, D. W., & KIRTNER, W. L.
        LENGTH OF THERAPY IN RELATION TO OUTCOME AND CHANGE IN PERSONAL INTEGRATION
        JOURNAL OF CONSULTING PSYCHOLOGY, 1961, 25, 84-88.
        (DIFFERENCE MEASURE OF CHANGE IN INTEGRATION OVER THERAPY)
        aC-142 1961M PERSONALITY CHANGE INTEGRATION THERAPY COUNSELING ADJUSTMENT
        aC-142 MALADJUSTMENT EFFECTIVENESS

C-143   CARTWRIGHT, D. S., ROBERTSON, R. J., FISKE, D. W., & KIRTNER, W. L.
        LENGTH OF THERAPY IN RELATION TO OUTCOME AND CHANGE IN PERSONAL INTEGRATION
        JOURNAL OF CONSULTING PSYCHOLOGY, 1961, 25, 84-88.
        (POSTTHERAPY ESTIMATE OF CHANGE IN INTEGRATION)
        aC-143 1961M THERAPY COUNSELING PERSONAL INTEGRATION PERSONALITY CHANGE PATIENT
        aC-143 MALADJUSTMENT EFFECTIVENESS
              (APPLICATIONS: 779)

C-145   CAINE, T. M., & HAWKINS, L. G.
        QUESTIONNAIRE MEASURE OF THE HYSTEROID/OBSESSOID COMPONENT OF PERSONALITY:
        THE HOQ.
        JOURNAL OF CONSULTING PSYCHOLOGY, 1963, 27, 206-209.
        (HYSTEROID/OBSESSOID QUESTIONNAIRE)*
        aC-145 1963M PERSONALITY TYPOLOGY RATING SELF PSYCHIATRIC BEHAVIOR

C-146   CLINE, V. B.
        ABILITY TO JUDGE PERSONALITY ASSESSED WITH A STRESS INTERVIEW AND
        SOUND-FILM TECHNIQUE.
        JOURNAL OF ABNORMAL AND SOCIAL PSYCHOLOGY, 1955, 50, 183-187.
        CLINE, V. B.
        THE ASSESSMENT OF GOOD AND POOR JUDGES OF PERSONALITY USING A STRESS
        INTERVIEW AND SOUND -FILM TECHNIQUE.
        UNPUBLISHED DOCTORAL DISSERTATION, UNIV. OF CALIFORNIA, BERKELEY, 1953.
        (TESTS OF PERSONALITY JUDGING ABILITY)
        aC-146 1955M JUDGMENT ABILITY PREDICTION STRESS BEHAVIOR PERSONALITY
              (APPLICATIONS: 1639)

C-147   CALIFORNIA TEST BUREAU.
        MANUAL FOR MENTAL HEALTH ANALYSIS (REVISED ED.).
        LOS ANGELES: C.T.B., 1959.
        (MENTAL HEALTH ANALYSIS)*
        aC-147 1959M MENTAL-HEALTH STATUS SELF RATING MATURITY STABILITY ADEQUACY
        aC-147 NERVOUSNESS PERSONAL RELATIONSHIPS SOCIAL JOB GOALS

C-148   CLARK, J. R., KOCH, B., & NICHOLS. R. C.
        A FACTOR ANALYTICALLY DERIVED SCALE FOR RATING PSYCHIATRIC PATIENTS IN
        OCCUPATIONAL THERAPY: I. DEVELOPMENT.
        AMERICAN JOURNAL OF OCCUPATIONAL THERAPY, 1965, 19, 14-18.
        (BEHAVIOR IN OCCUPATIONAL THERAPY)
        aC-148 1965M THERAPY PSYCHIATRIC RELATIONSHIPS PATIENT
              (APPLICATIONS: 1958)

C-149   CHASE, P. H.
        SELF-CONCEPT IN ADJUSTED AND MALADJUSTED HOSPITAL PATIENTS.
        JOURNAL OF CONSULTING PSYCHOLOGY, 1957, 21, 495-497.
        (SELF-CONCEPT ADJUSTMENT Q-SORT)
        aC-149 1957M Q-SORT SELF CONCEPT IMAGE ADJUSTMENT MALADJUSTMENT PSYCHIATRIC
        aC-149 PATIENT
              (APPLICATIONS: 1962)

C-150   CUADRA, C. A.
        A SCALE FOR CONTROL IN PSYCHOLOGICAL ADJUSTMENT (CH).
        IN G. S. WELSH AND W. G. DAHLSTROM (ED.), BASIC READINGS ON THE MMPI IN
        PSYCHOLOGY AND MEDICINE.
        MINNEAPOLIS: UNIVERSITY OF MINNESOTA PRESS, 1956.
        (CONTROL SCALE (CH) FROM MMPI)
        aC-150 1956M CONTROL MMPI ADJUSTMENT
        aC-150 HOSPITALIZATION NEED IE-CONTROL PSYCHIATRIC
              (APPLICATIONS: 792 1140 1844)

C-151   CATTELL, R. B.
               THE IPAT SELF-ANALYSIS FORM.
               CHAMPAIGN, ILL.: INSTITUTE FOR PERSONALITY AND ABILITY TESTING, 1957.
               (IPAT SELF-ANALYSIS FORM)
           @C-151 1957M SELF TRAIT ANXIETY EVALUATION
               (APPLICATIONS: 1971 1981)

C-152   CHRISTIE, R., & BUDNITZKY, S. A.
               A SHORT FORCED-CHOICE ANXIETY SCALE.
               JOURNAL OF CONSULTING PSYCHOLOGY, 1957, 218, 501.
               (SHORT FORCED-CHOICE ANXIETY SCALE)
           @C-152 1957M ANXIETY TENSION
               (APPLICATIONS: 1423 1979)

C-153   COMREY, A. L.
               A FACTOR ANALYSIS OF ITEMS ON THE MMPI HYPOCHONDRIASIS SCALE.
               EDUCATIONAL AND PSYCHOLOGICAL MEASUREMENT, 1957, 17, 568-577.
               (POOR PHYSICAL HEALTH SCALE)*
           @C-153 1957M NEUROTICISM PHYSICAL HEALTH ILLNESS PSYCHOSOMATIC SYMPTOM
               (APPLICATIONS: 528)

C-154   COTTLE, T. J.
               THE CIRCLES TEST: AN INVESTIGATION OF PERCEPTIONS OF TEMPORAL RELATEDNESS
               AND DOMINANCE.
               JOURNAL OF PROJECTIVE TECHNIQUES AND PERSONALITY ASSESSMENT, 1967, 31(5),
               58-71.
               (CIRCLES TEST OF TEMPORAL DOMINANCE AND RELATEDNESS)
           @C-154 1967M TIME PERSPECTIVE FUTURE ORIENTATION PAST
           @RELATIONSHIPS INTEGRATION PROJECTIVE
               (APPLICATIONS: 530 2301)

C-155   COTTLE T. J.
               THE LOCATION OF EXPERIENCE: A MANIFEST TIME ORIENTATION.
               ACTA PSYCHOLOGICA, 1968, 28, 129-149.
               (MEASURE OF EXPERIENTIAL TIME ORIENTATION)
           @C-155 1968M TIME PERSPECTIVE FUTURE ORIENTATION PAST
           @C-155 EXPERIENCE
               (APPLICATIONS: 530 2301)

C-156   COTTLE, T. J.
               THE MONEY GAME: NOTES ON FANTASIES OF TEMPORAL RECOVERY AND PREKNOWLEDGE.
               DIOGENES, 1969, 65, 110-134.
               COTTLE, T. J.
               TEMPORAL CORRELATES OF THE ACHIEVEMENT VALUE AND MANIFEST ANXIETY.
               JOURNAL OF CONSULTING AND CLINICAL PSYCHOLOGY, 1969, 33, 541-550.
               (THE MONEY GAME)*
           @C-156 1969M TIME PERSPECTIVE FUTURE ORIENTATION PAST
               (APPLICATIONS: 530 2301)

C-158   CATTELL, R. B.
               PERSONALITY AND MOTIVATION STRUCTURE AND MEASUREMENT.
               NEW YORK: WORLD BOOK, 1957.
               (IDEAL-SELF-PARENT-PROFILE SIMILARITY MEASURES)
           @C-158 1957M IDEAL SELF PARENTAL SIMILARITY SEM-DIFFERENTIAL
               (APPLICATIONS: 2051)

C-159   COWEN, E. L., IZZO, L. D., MILES, H., TELSCHOW, E. F., TROST, M. A., & ZAK, M.
               A PREVENTIVE MENTAL HEALTH PROGRAM IN THE SCHOOL SETTING: DESCRIPTION AND
               EVALUATION.
               JOURNAL OF PSYCHOLOGY, 1963, 56, 307-356.
               (TEACHERS' BEHAVIOR RATING SCALE)
           @C-159 1963M RATING TEACHER BEHAVIOR CHILD DEPENDENCE MOOD
               (APPLICATIONS: 2050 2199)

C-160   CRARY, W. G.
               UNPUBLISHED DOCTORAL DISSERTATION, UNIVERSITY OF COLORADO, 1963.
               CRARY, W. G.
               REACTIONS TO INCONGRUENT SELF-EXPERIENCES
               JOURNAL OF CONSULTING PSYCHOLOGY, 1966, 30, 246-252.
               (MEASURE OF INTELLECTUAL SELF-ESTEEM)
           @C-160 1963M INTELLECTUAL SELF ESTEEM CONCEPT

C-161   CRARY, W. G.
               UNPUBLISHED DOCTORAL DISSERTATION, UNIVERSITY OF COLORADO, 1963.
               CRARY, W. G.
               REACTIONS TO INCONGRUENT SELF-EXPERIENCES
               JOURNAL OF CONSULTING PSYCHOLOGY, 1966, 30, 246-252.
               (MEASURE OF STABILITY OF SELF-CONCEPT)
           @C-161 1963M SELF CONCEPT STABILITY PEER RELATIONSHIPS

C-164   COTTLE, T. J.
         TEMPORAL CORRELATES OF THE ACHIEVEMENT VALUE AND MANIFEST ANXIETY.
         JOURNAL OF CONSULTING AND CLINICAL PSYCHOLOGY, 1969, 33, 541-550.
         (MEASURE OF TEMPORAL ANXIETY)
         aC-164 1969M ANXIETY TIME ORIENTATION FEAR FUTURE
            (APPLICATIONS: 2301)

C-166   COTTLE, T. J.
         THE DURATION INVENTORY: SUBJECTIVE EXTENSION OF TEMPORAL ZONES.
         ACTA PSYCHOLOGICA, IN PRESS, 1969.
         (DURATION INVENTORY)
         aC-166 1969M TIME SUBJECTIVE FUTURE PERSPECTIVE ORIENTATION
            (APPLICATIONS: 530 2301)

C-168   CATTELL, R. B., & KING, J.
         THE CONTACT PERSONALITY FACTOR QUESTIONNAIRE.
         CHAMPAIGN, ILL.: INSTITUTE FOR PERSONALITY AND ABILITY TESTING, 1955.
         (THE CONTACT PERSONALITY FACTOR QUESTIONNAIRE)*
         aC-168 1955M PERSONALITY EXTRAVERSION

C-169   CLINE, V. B., & RICHARDS, J. M., JR.
         THE GENERALITY OF ACCURACY OF INTERPERSONAL PERCEPTION.
         JOURNAL OF ABNORMAL AND SOCIAL PSYCHOLOGY, 1961, 62, 446-449.
         (MEASURE OF INTERPERSONAL PERCEPTION)
         aC-169 1961M PERSON PERCEPTION OTHERS
         aC-169 INTERPERSONAL RELATIONSHIPS SOCIAL INTERACTION
            (APPLICATIONS: 815)

C-170   CHANCE, E., & ARNOLD, J.
         THE EFFECT OF PROFESSIONAL TRAINING, EXPERIENCE, AND PREFERENCE FOR A
         THEORETICAL SYSTEM UPON CLINICAL CASE DESCRIPTION.
         HUMAN RELATIONS, 1960, 13, 195-213.
         CHANCE, E., & ARNOLD, J., & TYRRELL, S.
         COMMUNALITY AND STABILITY OF MEANING IN CLINICAL CASE DESCRIPTION.
         JOURNAL OF ABNORMAL AND SOCIAL PSYCHOLOGY, 1962, 64, 389-406.
         (RATING SCALE FOR DESCRIBING PATIENTS VERBALIZATIONS)
         aC-170 1960M RATING PATIENT THERAPY INTERPERSONAL EXPERIENCE ACTIVE PASSIVE
         aC-170 POSITIVE NEGATIVE PSYCHIATRIC

C-171   COUCH, A., & KENISTON, K.
         AGREEING RESPONSE SET AND SOCIAL DESIRABILITY.
         JOURNAL OF ABNORMAL AND SOCIAL PSYCHOLOGY, 1961, 62, 175-179.
         (LOW-MEAN AGREEMENT SCALE)
         aC-171 1961M RESPONSE-BIAS SOCIAL DESIRABILITY ACQUIESCENCE

C-172   COUCH, A., & KENISTON, K.
         AGREEING RESPONSE SET AND SOCIAL DESIRABILITY.
         JOURNAL OF ABNORMAL AND SOCIAL PSYCHOLOGY, 1961, 62, 175-179.
         (HIGH-MEAN AGREEMENT SCALES)
         aC-172 1961M RESPONSE-BIAS SOCIAL DESIRABILITY ACQUIESCENCE
            (APPLICATIONS: 629)

C-173   COWEN, E. L., UNDERBERG, R. P., & VERRILLO, R. T.
         THE DEVELOPMENT AND TESTING OF AN ATTITUDE TO BLINDNESS SCALE.
         JOURNAL OF SOCIAL PSYCHOLOGY, 1958, 48, 297-304.
         (ATTITUDE TOWARD BLINDNESS)
         aC-173 1958M ATTITUDE DISABILITY PHYSICAL
            (APPLICATIONS: 613)

C-175   CAREY, G., ROGOW, A. A., & FARRELL, C.
         THE RELATIONSHIP BETWEEN THE F SCALE AND APHORISM USAGE AND AGREEMENT.
         JOURNAL OF PSYCHOLOGY, 1957, 43, 163-167.
         (APHORISM QUESTIONNAIRE FOR ACQUIESCENCE)
         aC-175 1957M RESPONSE-BIAS ACQUIESCENCE

C-176   CARLSON, R.
         IDENTIFICATION AND PERSONALITY STRUCTURE IN PREADOLESCENTS.
         JOURNAL OF ABNORMAL AND SOCIAL PSYCHOLOGY, 1963, 67, 566-573.
         (SELF-DESCRIPTION MEASURE FOR CHILDREN)
         aC-176 1963M CHILD PARENT-CHILD SELF-IDENTITY SELF ESTEEM PARENTAL IDEAL SOCIAL
         aC-176 IDENTIFICATION ORIENTATION SUPPORT DESCRIPTION PERCEPTION

C-177   CAMPBELL, M. M.
                 THE PRIMARY DIMENSIONS OF ITEM RATINGS ON SCALES DESIGNED TO MEASURE 24 OF
                 MURRAY'S MANIFEST NEEDS.
                 UNPUBLISHED DOCTORAL DISSERTATION, UNIVERSITY OF WASHINGTON, 1959.
                 (MEASURES OF PERSONAL NEEDS)
            aC-177 1959M NEED AUTONOMY SELF
                 (APPLICATIONS: 818)

C-178   CHEEK, F. E.
                 A SERENDIPITOUS FINDING: SEX ROLES AND SCHIZOPHRENIA.
                 JOURNAL OF ABNORMAL AND SOCIAL PSYCHOLOGY, 1964, 69, 392-400.
                 (FAMILY PROBLEMS QUESTIONNAIRE)
            aC-178 1964M PARENT-CHILD PROBLEM INTERACTION FAMILY DEPENDENCE PERCEPTION
            aC-178 REALITY PASSIVE ACTIVE PE-FIT MENTAL-HEALTH

C-179   COUCH, A. S.
                 PSYCHOLOGICAL DETERMINANTS OF INTERPERSONAL BEHAVIOR.
                 UNPUBLISHED DOCTORAL DISSERTATION, HARVARD UNIVERSITY, 1960.
                 (REPRESSION OF HOSTILITY SCALE)
            aC-179 1960M REPRESSION HOSTILITY AGGRESSION
                 (APPLICATIONS: 897)

C-180   COUCH, A. S.
                 PSYCHOLOGICAL DETERMINANTS OF INTERPERSONAL BEHAVIOR.
                 UNPUBLISHED DOCTORAL DISSERTATION, HARVARD UNIVERSITY, 1960.
                 (ACCEPTANCE OF VIOLENCE SCALE)
            aC-180 1960M ACCEPTANCE AGGRESSION EXPRESSION
                 (APPLICATIONS: 897)

C-181   COUCH, A. S.
                 PSYCHOLOGICAL DETERMINANTS OF INTERPERSONAL BEHAVIOR.
                 UNPUBLISHED DOCTORAL DISSERTATION, HARVARD UNIVERSITY, 1960.
                 (RACIAL MILITANCY SCALE)
            aC-181 1960M RACIAL ATTITUDE AGGRESSION HOSTILITY
                 (APPLICATIONS: 897)

C-182   COUCH, A. S.
                 PSYCHOLOGICAL DETERMINANTS OF INTERPERSONAL BEHAVIOR.
                 UNPUBLISHED DOCTORAL DISSERTATION, HARVARD UNIVERSITY, 1960.
                 (FEELINGS OF INTERNAL VERSUS EXTERNAL CONTROL OF FATE SCALE)
            aC-182 1960M LOCUS CONTROL IE-CONTROL
            aC-182 AUTONOMY PERCEIVED
                 (APPLICATIONS: 897)

C-183   COUCH, A. S.
                 PSYCHOLOGICAL DETERMINANTS OF INTERPERSONAL BEHAVIOR.
                 UNPUBLISHED DOCTORAL DISSERTATION, HARVARD UNIVERSITY, 1960.
                 (AUTHORITARIAN CHILD TRAINING ATTITUDES SCALE)
            aC-183 1960M AUTHORITARIANISM PARENT-CHILD INTERACTION
            aC-183 PARENTAL CHILD
                 (APPLICATIONS: 897)

C-184   COUCH, A. S.
                 PSYCHOLOGICAL DETERMINANTS OF INTERPERSONAL BEHAVIOR.
                 UNPUBLISHED DOCTORAL DISSERTATION, HARVARD UNIVERSITY, 1960.
                 (RELIGIOUS CONVENTIONALISM VERSUS ATHEISTIC RATIONALISM SCALE)
            aC-184 1960M RELIGION BELIEF CONFORMITY
            aC-184 RATIONALISM ORIENTATION
                 (APPLICATIONS: 897)

C-188   COUCH, A., & KENISTON, K.
                 YEASAYERS AND NAYSAYERS: AGREEING RESPONSE SET AS A PERSONALITY VARIABLE.
                 JOURNAL OF ABNORMAL AND SOCIAL PSYCHOLOGY, 1960, 60, 151-174.
                 (OVERALL AGREEMENT SCORE)*
            aC-188 1960M EMOTION CONTROL EXPRESSIVENESS EXCITEMENT NEUROTICISM MENTAL-HEALTH
            aMENTAL-ILLNESS RESPONSE STRUCTURE ANXIETY IMPULSE IE-CONTROL EGO INTEGRATION
            aSET COMPETITION TRUST INTELLECTUAL RESPONSE-BIAS STYLE
                 (APPLICATIONS: 620)

C-189   CLECKLEY, H.
                 PSYCHOPATHIC STATES.
                 IN S. ARIETI (ED.), AMERICAN HANDBOOK OF PSYCHIATRY, VOL. 1, NEW YORK:
                 BASIC BOOKS, 1959, PP. 567-588.
                 (CHECKLIST MEASURE OF PSYCHOPATHY)
            aC-189 1959M CHECKLIST MENTAL-ILLNESS PSYCHOPATHY
                 (APPLICATIONS: 978 2421)

C-190   COOPERSMITH, S.
          A METHOD OF DETERMINING TYPES OF SELF ESTEEM.
          JOURNAL OF ABNORMAL AND SOCIAL PSYCHOLOGY, 1959, 59, 87-94.
          (SELF-ESTEEM BEHAVIOR RATING FORM)
          aC-190 1959M SELF ESTEEM BEHAVIOR RATING SELF-IDENTITY
               (APPLICATIONS: 553)

C-193   COE, W. C., & SARBIN, T. R.
          AN EXPERIMENTAL DEMONSTRATION OF HYPNOSIS AS ROLE ENACTMENT.
          JOURNAL OF ABNORMAL PSYCHOLOGY, 1966, 71, 400-406.
          (CONGRUENCE QUESTIONNAIRE)
          aC-193 1966M ROLE STRUCTURE SELF-IDENTITY PE-FIT HYPNOSIS CONGRUENCE CHANGE
          aC-193 ACCEPTANCE

C-194   COE, W. C., & SARBIN, T. R.
          AN EXPERIMENTAL DEMONSTRATION OF HYPNOSIS AS ROLE ENACTMENT.
          JOURNAL OF ABNORMAL PSYCHOLOGY, 1966, 71, 400-406.
          (ROLE EXPECTATION QUESTIONNAIRE)
          aC-194 1966M HYPNOTIC SUGGESTIBILITY ROLE PERCEPTION DEMANDS COGNITIVE
          aC-194 FUNCTIONING IE-CONTROL SELF-IDENTITY SUB-IDENTITY

C-195   CICCHETTI, D. V.
          REPORTED FAMILY DYNAMICS AND PSYCHOPATHOLOGY: I. THE TIME REACTIONS OF
          SCHIZOPHRENICS AND NORMALS TO PARENTAL DIALOGUES.
          JOURNAL OF ABNORMAL PSYCHOLOGY, 1967, 72, 282-289.
          (OPINIONS ABOUT PARENTS MEASURE)
          aC-195 1967M PARENTAL SCHIZOPHRENIA OPINION FAMILY
          aC-195 MATERNAL PATERNAL DOMINANCE ASCENDENCE CONFLICT IMPRESSION FORMATION
          aC-195 SUBMISSION

C-196   CICCHETTI, D. V., KLEIN, E. B., FONTANA, A. F., & SPOHN, H. E.
          A TEST OF THE CENSURE-DEFICIT MODEL IN SCHIZOPHRENIA, EMPLOYING THE
          RODNICK-GARMEZY VISUAL DISCRIMINATION TASK.
          JOURNAL OF ABNORMAL PSYCHOLOGY, 1967, 72, 326-334.
          (MEASURE OF PARENTAL DOMINANCE AND CONFLICT)
          aC-196 1967M PARENTAL DOMINANCE ASCENDENCE SUBMISSION CONFLICT SCHIZOPHRENIA

C-197   CATTELL, P.
          THE MEASUREMENT OF INTELLIGENCE OF INFANTS AND YOUNG CHILDREN.
          NEW YORK: PSYCHOLOGICAL CORPORATION, 1940.
          (CATTELL INFANT SCALE)*
          aC-197 1940M ACHIEVEMENT ABILITY CHILD
               (APPLICATIONS: 1062)

C-198   COSTELLO, C. G., & COMREY, A. L.
          SCALES FOR MEASURING DEPRESSION AND ANXIETY.
          JOURNAL OF PSYCHOLOGY, 1967, 66, 303-313.
          (ANXIETY SCALE)
          aC-198 1967M ANXIETY TENSION
               (APPLICATIONS: 1082)

C-199   CARLSON, R., & LEVY, N.
          SELF, VALUES, AND AFFECTS: DERIVATIONS FROM TOMKINS' POLARITY THEORY.
          JOURNAL OF PERSONALITY AND SOCIAL PSYCHOLOGY, 1970, 16, 338-345.
          (MEASURE OF INDIVIDUALISTIC-INTERPERSONAL VALUE HIERARCHY)
          aC-199 1970M VALUES INTERPERSONAL NEED AFFILIATION COMPETENCE LIFE GOALS

C-200   COLLETT, L. J., & LESTER, D.
          THE FEAR OF DEATH AND THE FEAR OF DYING.
          JOURNAL OF PSYCHOLOGY, 1969, 72, 179-181.
          (FEAR OF DEATH SCALE)
          aC-200 1969M DEATH MORTALITY FEAR ANXIETY

C-201   CANCRO, R.
          A COMPARISON OF PROCESS AND REACTIVE SCHIZOPHRENIA.
          DOCTORAL DISSERTATION, STATE UNIVERSITY OF NEW YORK, BROOKLYN.
          ANN ARBOR, MICH.: UNIVERSITY MICROFILMS, 1962, NO. 5166.
          (MEASURE OF DEGREE OF REALITY DISRUPTION)
          aC-201 1962M SCHIZOPHRENIA MENTAL-ILLNESS PSYCHIATRIC PERCEPTION REALITY
          aC-201 DISCREPANCY
               (APPLICATIONS: 1151)

C-202   COMREY, A. L., & BACKER, T. E.
               CONSTRUCT VALIDATION OF THE COMREY PERSONALITY SCALES.
               MULTIVARIATE BEHAVIORAL RESEARCH, 1970, 5, 469-477.
               (BIOGRAPHICAL DATA INVENTORY)
          aC-202 1970M LIFE BEHAVIOR PAST HISTORY INVENTORY

C-203   CHAPMAN, L. J.
               CONFUSION OF FIGURATIVE AND LITERAL USAGES OF WORDS BY SCHIZOPHRENICS AND
               BRAIN DAMAGED PATIENTS.
               JOURNAL OF ABNORMAL AND SOCIAL PSYCHOLOGY, 1960, 60, 412-416.
               (LITERAL-FIGURATIVE MEANING TEST)
          aC-203 1960M SCHIZOPHRENIA MENTAL-ILLNESS MENTAL-HEALTH COGNITIVE UNCONSCIOUS
          aDIFFERENTIATION WORD STRUCTURE DIAGNOSIS FUNCTIONING
               (APPLICATIONS: 2734)

C-205   CONSTANTINOPLE, A.
               AN ERIKSONIAN MEASURE OF PERSONALITY DEVELOPMENT IN COLLEGE STUDENTS.
               DEVELOPMENTAL PSYCHOLOGY, 1969, 1, 357-372.
               (INVENTORY OF PSYCHOSOCIAL DEVELOPMENT)*
          aC-205 1969M DEVELOPMENT PERSONALITY MATURITY GROWTH SELF ACTUALIZATION
               (APPLICATIONS: 2968)

C-206   CONSTANTINOPLE, A.
               AN ERIKSONIAN MEASURE OF PERSONALITY DEVELOPMENT IN COLLEGE STUDENTS.
               DEVELOPMENTAL PSYCHOLOGY, 1969, 1, 357-372.
               (MEASURE OF HAPPINESS)
          aC-206 1969M HAPPINESS POSITIVE AFFECTIVE-STATES WELL-BEING ELATION LIFE
          aSATISFACTION SENSE
               (APPLICATIONS: 2968)

C-207   COSTELLO, C. G., & COMREY, A. L.
               SCALES FOR MEASURING DEPRESSION AND ANXIETY.
               JOURNAL OF PSYCHOLOGY, 1967, 66, 303-313.
               (DEPRESSION SCALE)
          aC-207 1967M DEPRESSION MOOD EMOTION NEGATIVE AFFECTIVE-STATES

C-208   CUMMING, E., & CUMMING, J.
               CLOSED RANKS.
               CAMBRIDGE: HARVARD UNIVERSITY PRESS, 1957.
               (SOCIAL DISTANCE MEASURE OF MENTALLY ILL FROM PUBLIC)
          aC-208 1957M SOCIAL DISTANCE MENTAL-ILLNESS PUBLIC ATTITUDE DISABILITY
          aPSYCHIATRIC DEVIANCE
               (APPLICATIONS: 2559)

C-209   CRUMPTON, E., WEINSTEIN, A. D., ACKER, C. W., & ANNIS, A. P.
               HOW PATIENTS AND NORMALS SEE THE MENTAL PATIENT.
               JOURNAL OF CLINICAL PSYCHOLOGY, 1967, 23, 46-49.
               (SEMANTIC DIFFERENTIAL MEASURE OF PUBLIC ATTITUDE TOWARD DEVIANTS AND
               NORMALS)
          aC-209 1967M SEM-DIFFERENTIAL PUBLIC ATTITUDE MENTAL-ILLNESS DEVIANCE BEHAVIOR
          aPSYCHIATRIC DISABILITY
               (APPLICATIONS: 2559)

C-210   CAMERON, P.
               THE GENERATION GAP: BELIEFS ABOUT SEXUALITY AND SELF-REPORTED SEXUALITY.
               DEVELOPMENTAL PSYCHOLOGY, 1970, 3, 272.
               (MEASURE OF BELIEFS ABOUT SEXUALITY)
          aC-210 1970M SEX BELIEF ATTITUDE OPINION SELF OTHERS

C-211   CASH, L. M., & KOOKER, E. W.
               ATTITUDES TOWARD DEATH OF NP PATIENTS WHO HAVE ATTEMPTED SUICIDE.
               PSYCHOLOGICAL REPORTS, 1970, 26, 879-882.
               (MEASURE OF ATTITUDES TOWARD DEATH)
          aC-211 1970M ATTITUDE DEATH FEAR MORTALITY MOTIVE SELF CONCEPT SATISFACTION LIFE

C-212   CASSELL, R. N.
               THE CASSELL GROUP LEVEL OF ASPIRATION TEST.
               LOS ANGELES: WESTERN PSYCHOLOGICAL SERVICES, 1957.
               (CASSELL GROUP LEVEL OF ASPIRATION TEST)
          aC-212 1957M GROUP ASPIRATION
               (APPLICATIONS: 2970)

C-213   CAUTELA, J. R., & KASTENBAUM, R.
           A REINFORCEMENT SURVEY SCHEDULE FOR USE IN THERAPY, TRAINING, AND RESEARCH.
           PSYCHOLOGICAL REPORTS, 1967, 20, 1115-1130.
           (REINFORCEMENT SURVEY SCHEDULE)
           aC-213 1967M BEHAVIOR THERAPY ADJUSTMENT CHANGE STIMULUS ATTITUDE RESPONSE
           aSEEKING PREFERENCE
                (APPLICATIONS: 2616)

C-214   CARRIER, N. A.
           EVALUATING THE INTRODUCTORY PSYCHOLOGY COURSE.
           READING, MASS.: ADDISON-WESLEY, 1966.
           (ATTITUDE-TOWARD-PSYCHOLOGY SCALE)
           aC-214 1966M ATTITUDE COLLEGE ACADEMIC SCHOOL STUDENT OPINION

C-215   CARRIER, N. A.
           EVALUATING THE INTRODUCTORY PSYCHOLOGY COURSE.
           READING, MASS.: ADDISON-WESLEY, 1966.
           (ATTITUDE-TOWARD-SCIENCE SCALE)
           aC-215 1966M ATTITUDE COLLEGE ACADEMIC SCHOOL STUDENT OPINION

C-217   CRITES, J. O.
           THE INTERNAL CONSISTENCY AND STABILITY OF THE ATTITUDE TEST OF THE
           VOCATIONAL DEVELOPMENT INVENTORY.
           PAPER PRESENTED AT MEETING OF THE AMERICAN PERSONNEL AND GUIDANCE
           ASSOCIATION, SAN FRANCISCO, APRIL 1963.
           CRITES, J. O.
           THE MEASUREMENT OF VOCATIONAL MATURITY IN ADOLESCENCE: I. THE ATTITUDE
           TEST OF THE VOCATIONAL DEVELOPMENT INVENTORY.
           PSYCHOLOGICAL MONOGRAPHS, 1965, 79 (2, WHOLE NO. 595).
           (ATTITUDE SCALE FROM THE VOCATIONAL DEVELOPMENT INVENTORY)*
           aC-217 1963M VOCATIONAL DEVELOPMENT ATTITUDE ADOLESCENT ADJUSTMENT
           aCHOICE MATURITY
                (APPLICATIONS: 1308)

C-219   CASKY, O. L.
           TEACHER INCONSISTENCY AND GUIDANCE READINESS.
           JOURNAL OF COUNSELING PSYCHOLOGY, 1960, 7, 58-61.
           (MEASURE OF INCONSISTENCY AND PROBLEM MISPLACEMENT IN COUNSELING)
           aC-219 1960M STUDENT PROBLEM COUNSELING

C-220   CAHOON, D. D.
           A COMPARISON OF THE EFFECTIVENESS OF VERBAL REINFORCEMENT APPLIED IN
           GROUP AND INDIVIDUAL INTERVIEWS.
           JOURNAL OF COUNSELING PSYCHOLOGY, 1965, 12, 121-126.
           (WORD RATING CHECKLIST)
           aC-220 1965M CHECKLIST WORD ASSOCIATION RATING JOB ORIENTATION POSITIVE

C-221   CHAPIN, F. S.
           PRELIMINARY STANDARDIZATION OF A SOCIAL INSIGHT SCALE.
           AMERICAN SOCIOLOGICAL REVIEW, 1942, 7, 214-225.
           (CHAPIN SOCIAL INSIGHT SCALE)*
           aC-221 1942M SOCIAL AWARENESS BEHAVIOR INTERPERSONAL SITUATIONAL SENSITIVITY
                (APPLICATIONS: 1309)

C-223   CHERNOW, H. M.
           THE EFFECTS OF PERSONAL ADJUSTMENT COUNSELING UPON THE REALITY OF
           VOCATIONAL CHOICE.
           UNPUBLISHED DOCTORAL DISSERTATION, NEW YORK UNIVERSITY, 1956.
           (RATING SCALE OF REALITY OF VOCATIONAL CHOICE)
           aC-223 1956M VOCATIONAL RATING IDEAL DISCREPANCY REALITY PERCEPTION INTEREST
           aABILITY
                (APPLICATIONS: 1304)

C-224   CATTELL, R. B., & SCHEIER, I. H.
           OBJECTIVE-ANALYTIC (O-A) ANXIETY BATTERY.
           CHAMPAIGN, ILLINOIS: THE INSTITUTE FOR PERSONALITY AND ABILITY TESTING,
           1960.
           (OBJECTIVE ANALYTIC ANXIETY BATTERY)*
           aC-224 1960M ANXIETY STRESS BEHAVIOR ATTITUDE
                (APPLICATIONS: 1165)

C-225   CREASER, J. W.
           FACTOR ANALYSIS OF A STUDY-HABITS Q-SORT TEST.
           JOURNAL OF COUNSELING PSYCHOLOGY, 1960, 7, 298-300.
           (STUDY HABITS Q-SORT TEST)
           aC-225 1960M STUDENT STUDY HABITS Q-SORT TYPOLOGY ATTITUDE ABILITY

C-226   CHRISTENSEN, P. R., MERRIFIELD, P. R., & GUILFORD, J. P.
               CONSEQUENCES TEST.
               BEVERLY HILLS: SHERIDAN SUPPLY, 1962.
               (CONSEQUENCES TEST)*
          aC-226 1962M ORIGNIALITY COGNITIVE ABILITY CREATIVITY FLEXIBILITY
               (APPLICATIONS: 933 1355)

C-229   CAMPBELL, D. P., & JOHANSSON, C. B.
               ACADEMIC INTERESTS, SCHOLASTIC ACHIEVEMENTS AND EVENTUAL OCCUPATIONS.
               JOURNAL OF COUNSELING PSYCHOLOGY, 1966, 13, 416-424.
               (ACADEMIC ACHIEVEMENT SCALE FOR SVIB)
          aC-229 1966M ACHIEVEMENT VOCATIONAL INTEREST ACADEMIC JOB PREFERENCE

C-230   CUNDICK, B.
               THE RELATION OF STUDENT AND COUNSELOR EXPECTATIONS TO RATED COUNSELING
               SATISFACTION.
               UNPUBLISHED DOCTORAL DISSERTATION, OHIO STATE UNIVERSITY, 1962.
               (SATISFACTION QUESTIONNAIRE)
          aC-230 1962M SATISFACTION COUNSELING RELATIONSHIPS STUDENT PATIENT
               (APPLICATIONS: 1367)

C-231   CAMPBELL, R. C.
               DEVELOPMENT AND VALIDATION OF A MULTIPLE-CHOICE SCALE TO MEASURE
               AFFECTIVE SENSITIVITY (EMPATHY).
               UNPUBLISHED DOCTORAL DISSERTATION, MICHIGAN STATE UNIVERSITY, 1967.
          DANISH, S. J., & KAGAN, N.
               MEASUREMENT OF AFFECTIVE SENSITIVITY: TOWARD A VALID MEASURE OF
               INTERPERSONAL PERCEPTION.
               JOURNAL OF COUNSELING PSYCHOLOGY, 1971, 18, 51-54.
               (AFFECTIVE SENSITIVITY SCALE)*
          aC-231 1967M SENSITIVITY AWARENESS EMPATHY VIDEO-TAPE INTERPERSONAL PERCEPTION
          aOTHERS

C-233   CAPPS, H.
               VOCABULARY CHANGES IN MENTAL DETERIORATION.
               ARCHIVES OF PSYCHOLOGY, 1939. 34, NO. 242.
          ZUBIN, J., & WINDLE, C.
               THE PROGNOSTIC VALUE OF THE METENYM TEST IN A FOLLOW-UP STUDY OF
               PSYCHOSURGERY PATIENTS AND THEIR CONTROLS.
               JOURNAL OF CLINICAL PSYCHOLOGY, 1951, 7, 221-223.
               (METENYM TEST OF MEANING SHIFT)
          aC-233 1939M PSYCHIATRIC PROGNOSIS CONCEPTUAL DEVELOPMENT PATIENT
          aCOGNITIVE FUNCTIONING ADJUSTMENT PREDICTION

C-234   CAUTELA, J. R., WALSH, K. J., & WISH, P. A.
               THE USE OF COVERT REINFORCEMENT IN THE MODIFICATION OF ATTITUDES TOWARD
               THE MENTALLY RETARDED.
               JOURNAL OF PSYCHOLOGY, 1971, 77, 257-260.
               (MENTAL RETARDATION OPINIONNAIRE)
          aC-234 1971M PUBLIC ATTITUDE RETARDATION OPINION

C-236   CLINE, V. B.
               ABILITY TO JUDGE PERSONALITY ASSESSED WITH A STRESS INTERVIEW AND
               SOUND-FILM TECHNIQUE.
               JOURNAL OF ABNORMAL AND SOCIAL PSYCHOLOGY, 1955, 50, 183-187.
               (PERSONALITY WORD CARD)*
          aC-236 1955M CHECKLIST PERSONALITY JUDGMENT SOCIAL INTERPERSONAL PREDICTION
          aABILITY SENSITIVITY EMPATHY VERBAL BEHAVIOR
               (APPLICATIONS: 1639)

C-239   CHALMERS, D. K.
               REPETITION AND ORDER EFFECTS IN ATTITUDE FORMATION.
               JOURNAL OF PERSONALITY AND SOCIAL PSYCHOLOGY, 1971, 17, 219-228.
               (MEASURE OF IMPRESSION-FORMATION)
          aC-239 1971M IMPRESSION FORMATION PERSON PERCEPTION INTERPERSONAL ATTRACTION

C-241   CRISSMAN, P.
               TEMPORAL CHANGE AND SEXUAL DIFFERENCE IN MORAL JUDGMENTS.
               JOURNAL OF SOCIAL PSYCHOLOGY, 1942, 16, 29-38.
               (MORAL JUDGMENT QUESTIONNAIRE)
          aC-241 JUDGMENT MORAL SEX DIFFERENCES ORIENTATION DEVELOPMENT 1942M

C-242   CLARK, R. A.
             THE PROJECTIVE MEASUREMENT OF EXPERIMENTALLY INDUCED LEVELS OF SEXUAL
             MOTIVATION.
             JOURNAL OF EXPERIMENTAL PSYCHOLOGY, 1952, 44, 391-399.
             (TAT MEASURE OF NEED FOR SEX)
         aC-242 1952M NEED SEX PROJECTIVE TAT MOTIVE INTENSITY
             (APPLICATIONS: 2014)

C-243   CARKHUFF, R. R., & DEBURGER, R.
             GROSS RATINGS OF PATIENT BEHAVIOR.
             UNIVERSITY OF MASSACHUSETTS, 1964 (MIMEO).
             (GROSS RATINGS OF PATIENT BEHAVIOR)*
         aC-243 1964M PSYCHIATRIC RATING BEHAVIOR ADJUSTMENT PATIENT
             (APPLICATIONS: 1953)

C-245   CHAPMAN, A. W.
             ATTITUDES TOWARD LEGAL AGENCIES OF AUTHORITY FOR JUVENILES: A
             COMPARATIVE STUDY OF 133 DELINQUENT AND 133 NONDELINQUENT BOYS IN DAYTON,
             OHIO.
             DISSERTATION ABSTRACTS, 1960, 20, 2943-2946.
             (ATTITUDES TOWARD LEGAL AGENCIES SCALE)
         aC-245 1960M ATTITUDE AUTHORITY ADOLESCENT DELINQUENCY
             (APPLICATIONS: 2423)

C-246   CLARK, J. H.
             APPLICATION OF THE MMPI IN DIFFERENTIATING AWOL RECIDIVISTS FROM
             NON-RECIDIVISTS.
             JOURNAL OF PSYCHOLOGY, 1948, 26, 229-234.
             (MMPI SCALE TO PREDICT AWOL RECIDIVISM)
         aC-246 1948M MMPI PSYCHOPATHY DELINQUENCY SOCIAL DEVIANCE
             (APPLICATIONS: 970)

C-247   COCHRANE, C. T., STRODTBECK, F. L., & PARKMAN, M. A.
             A MASCULINITY-FEMININITY MEASURE TO PREDICT DEFENSIVE BEHAVIOR.
             SOCIAL PSYCHOLOGY LABORATORY, UNIVERSITY OF CHICAGO, 1965 (MIMEOGRAPHED).
             (ABBREVIATED GOUGH SCALE OF MASCULINITY-FEMININITY)
         aC-247 1965M MASCULINITY FEMININITY SEX ROLE SOCIAL PREFERENCE G-20R IDENTITY
             (APPLICATIONS: 2346)

C-249   CLARK, C. A.
             A STUDY OF THE ADOLESCENT'S CONCEPTION OF THE NATURE OF SCIENTIFIC
             KNOWLEDGE.
             UNPUBLISHED DOCTORAL DISSERTATION, STATE UNIVERSITY OF IOWA, 1953.
             (PHYSICAL CAUSAL TEST)
         aC-249 1953M COGNITIVE FUNCTIONING STRUCTURE
             (APPLICATIONS: 323)

C-251   CARKHUFF, R. R., & BERENSON, B. G.
             BEYOND COUNSELING AND PSYCHOTHERAPY.
             NEW YORK: HOLT, RINEHART AND WINSTON, 1967.
             (EMPATHY SCALE)
         aC-251 1967M EMPATHY

C-252   COLMAN, A. M.
             PERSONALITY AND ATTITUDE CHANGE THROUGH NORMATIVE PRESSURE.
             UNPUBLISHED THESIS, UNIVERSITY OF CAPE TOWN, 1968.
         ORPEN, C.
             AUTHORITARIANISM AND RACIAL ATTITUDES AMONG ENGLISH-SPEAKING SOUTH
             AFRICANS.
             JOURNAL OF SOCIAL PSYCHOLOGY, 1971, 84, 301-302.
             (MEASURE OF ANTI-AFRICAN PREJUDICE)
         aC-252 1970M RACIAL PREDJUDICE ETHNIC NEGRO ATTITUDE

C-254   COLVIN, R. W.
             A STUDY IN FAMILY DIAGNOSIS AND TREATMENT FOR PRESCHOOL RETARDED CHILDREN
             AND THEIR PARENTS.
             INTERNATIONAL COPENHAGEN CONGRESS ON SCIENTIFIC STUDY OF MENTAL
             RETARDATION, 1964, NO. 125
             (CHILD'S SELF CONCEPT MEASURE)
         aC-254 1964M CHILD SELF CONCEPT

D-1   DEAN, D. G.
             CAN EMOTIONAL MATURITY BE MEASURED?
             PSYCHOLOGICAL REPORTS, 1967, 20, 60.
             (MEASURE OF EMOTIONAL MATURITY)
         aD-1 EMOTION MATURITY GLOBAL ADJUSTMENT COMPETENCE COPING-DEFENSE 1967M
         aD-1 AFFECTIVE-STATES

D-2   DELUCIA, L. A.
                THE TOY PREFERENCE TEST: A MEASURE OF SEX-ROLE IDENTIFICATION.
                CHILD DEVELOPMENT, 1963, 34, 107-117.
                (PICTURE CHOICE MEASURE OF SEX-ROLE PREFERENCE)
                (TOY PREFERENCE TEST)*
           @D-2 SEX ROLE SELF-IDENTITY PERCEPTION IDENTIFICATION MASCULINITY
           @D-2 FEMININITY 1963M IDENTITY

D-3   DEMPSEY, P.
                A UNIDIMENSIONAL DEPRESSION SCALE FOR THE MMPI.
                JOURNAL OF CONSULTING PSYCHOLOGY, 1964, 28, 364-370.
                (DEPRESSION SCALE: D30)*
           @D-3 DEPRESSION AFFECTIVE-STATES NEGATIVE 1964M

D-4   DENNIS, W.
                GROUP VALUES THROUGH CHILDREN'S DRAWINGS. NEW YORK: WILEY, 1966.
                (MEASURES OF GROUP VALUES)
           @D-4 VALUES IDEALS LIFE SELF-IDENTITY GOALS GROUP PROJECTIVE CHILD 1966M
           @D-4 DEVELOPMENT

D-5   DICKOFF, H.
                REACTIONS TO EVALUATIONS BY ANOTHER PERSON AS A FUNCTION OF SELF-EVALUATION
                AND THE INTERACTION CONTEXT.
                UNPUBLISHED DOCTORAL THESIS, DUKE UNIVERSITY, 1961.
                (SELF EVALUATION TRIADS TEST)*
           @D-5 SELF EVALUATION SELF-IDENTITY PERCEPTION CONCEPT IMAGE 1961M
                (APPLICATIONS: 304)

D-6   DITTES, J. E.
                EFFECT OF CHANGES IN SELF-ESTEEM UPON IMPULSIVENESS AND DELIBERATION IN
                MAKING JUDGMENTS.
                JOURNAL OF ABNORMAL AND SOCIAL PSYCHOLOGY, 1959, 58, 348-356.
                (MEASURE OF GENERAL DESIRE FOR CLARITY)
           @D-6 COPING-DEFENSE FLEXIBILITY RIGIDITY DOGMATISM TOLERANCE AMBIGUITY 1959M

D-7   DOLL, E. A.
                VINELAND SOCIAL MATURITY SCALE MANUAL. MINNEAPOLIS: EDUCATIONAL TEST
                BUREAU, 1947.
                (VINELAND SOCIAL MATURITY SCALE)*
           @D-7 ADJUSTMENT SOCIAL MATURITY GLOBAL 1947M COMPETENCE
                (APPLICATIONS: 1062 1688 1985 2561 2664)

D-8   DRAGUNS, J. G., PHILLIPS, L., BROVERMAN, I. K., & CAUDILL, W.
                SOCIAL COMPETENCE AND PSYCHIATRIC SYMPTOMATOLOGY IN JAPAN: A CROSS-CULTURAL
                EXTENSION OF EARLIER AMERICAN FINDINGS.
                JOURNAL OF ABNORMAL PSYCHOLOGY, 1970, 75, 68-83.
                (GLOBAL SOCIAL COMPETENCE RATING)
           @D-8 SOCIAL COMPETENCE PATIENT MENTAL-HEALTH MENTAL-ILLNESS RATING 1970M

D-9   DUNCAN, C. B.
                A REPUTATION TEST OF PERSONALITY INTEGRATION.
                JOURNAL OF PERSONALITY AND SOCIAL PSYCHOLOGY, 1966, 3, 516-524.
                PERSONALITY INTEGRATION SCALE. UNPUBLISHED TEST. NASHVILLE, TENNESSEE,
                GEORGE PEABODY COLLEGE, 1963.
                (PERSONALITY INTEGRATION REPUTATION TEST)*
           @D-9 INTEGRATION SOCIAL ADJUSTMENT GLOBAL COPING-DEFENSE CONFLICT PERSONALITY
           @D-9 1963M
                (APPLICATIONS: 177 2466)

D-10   DYMOND, R. F.
                A SCALE FOR THE MEASUREMENT OF EMPATHIC ABILITY.
                JOURNAL OF CONSULTING PSYCHOLOGY, 1949, 13, 127-133.
                (EMPATHY RATING TEST)
           @D-10 EMPATHY AFFECTIVE-STATES 1949M OTHERS ORIENTATION

D-11   DABBS, J. M., JR.
                SELF-ESTEEM, COMMUNICATOR CHARACTERISTICS, AND ATTITUDE CHANGE.
                JOURNAL OF ABNORMAL AND SOCIAL PSYCHOLOGY, 1964, 69, 173-181.
                (MEASURE OF SELF-ESTEEM)
           @D-11 SELF ESTEEM EVALUATION ATTITUDE CHANGE 1964M DESCRIPTION SOCIAL
           @D-11 DESIRABILITY

D-12   DAVIS, J. H., WRIGLEY, C. F., & COSTELEIN, J.
         FACTOR ANALYSIS OF SOCIAL ATTITUDES: A PRELIMINARY COMPARISON OF AMERICAN
         AND ENGLISH RESULTS.
         PAPER READ AT MIDWESTERN PSYCHOLOGICAL ASSOCIATION, ST. LOUIS, 1960.
         (MEASURE OF SOCIAL ATTITUDES)
      @D-12 SOCIAL ATTITUDE CROSS-CULTURAL 1960M
         (APPLICATIONS: 10   26)

D-13   DEAN, D. G.
         ALIENATION: ITS MEANING AND MEASUREMENT.
         AMERICAN SOCIOLOGICAL REVIEW. 1961, 26, 753-758.
         (MEASURE OF ALIENATION: POWERLESSNESS, NORMLESSNESS, AND SOCIAL ISOLATION)
      @D-13 ALIENATION POWERLESSNESS AFFECTIVE-STATES NEGATIVE NORMS GLOBAL
      @D-13 1961M ANOMIE SOCIAL
         (APPLICATIONS: 24 2765)

D-14   DECHARMS, R., & ROSENBAUM, M. E.
         STATUS VARIABLES AND MATCHING BEHAVIOR.
         JOURNAL OF PERSONALITY, 1960, 28, 492-502.
         (THE SELF-ESTEEM SCALE)*.
      @D-14 SELF ESTEEM EVALUATION CONFIDENCE 1960M
         (APPLICATIONS: 326   464   797   855 2332)

D-15   DEVRIES, A. G.
         A POTENTIAL SUICIDE PERSONALITY INVENTORY.
         PSYCHOLOGICAL REPORTS, 1966, 18, 731-738.
         (POTENTIAL SUICIDE PERSONALITY INVENTORY)*
      @D-15 SUICIDE ADJUSTMENT OTHER-CATEGORY MENTAL-HEALTH MENTAL-ILLNESS 1966M
      @D-15 EMOTION STABILITY
         (APPLICATIONS: 2288 2588)

D-16   DIGNAN, M. H.
         EGO IDENTITY AND MATERNAL IDENTIFICATION.
         JOURNAL OF PERSONALITY AND SOCIAL PSYCHOLOGY, 1965, 1, 476-483.
         DIGNAN, M. H.
         EGO IDENTITY, MATERNAL IDENTIFICATION, AND ADJUSTMENT IN COLLEGE WOMEN.
         UNPUBLISHED DOCTORAL DISSERTATION, FORDHAM UNIVERSITY, 1963.
         (EGO IDENTITY SCALE)*
      @D-16 STABILITY INTERPERSONAL RELATIONSHIPS MATERNAL IDENTIFICATION EGO IDENTITY
      @D-16 SELF-IDENTITY SELF GOAL ACCEPTANCE GLOBAL ADJUSTMENT ESTEEM 1965M
         (APPLICATIONS: 2966)

D-17   DORRIS, R. J., LEVINSON, D. J., & HANFMANN, E.
         AUTHORITARIAN PERSONALITY STUDIED BY A NEW VARIATION OF THE SENTENCE. COM-
         PLETION TECHNIQUE.
         JOURNAL OF ABNORMAL AND SOCIAL PSYCHOLOGY, 1954, 49, 99-108.
         (SENTENCE COMPLETION MEASURE OF AUTHORITARIANISM)
      @D-17 AUTHORITARIANISM ADJUSTMENT GLOBAL COPING-DEFENSE 1954M DOGMATISM
         (APPLICATIONS: 196)

D-18   DROBA, D. D.
         A SCALE OF MILITARISM-PACIFISM.
         JOURNAL OF EDUCATIONAL PSYCHOLOGY, 1931, 22, 96-111.
         (MILITARISM-PACIFISM SCALE)
      @D-18 MILITARISM PACIFISM POLITICAL 1931M ORIENTATION
         (APPLICATIONS: 69)

D-20   DITTES, J. E.
         EFFECT OF CHANGES IN SELF-ESTEEM UPON IMPULSIVENESS AND DELIBERATION IN
         MAKING JUDGMENTS.
         JOURNAL OF ABNORMAL AND SOCIAL PSYCHOLOGY, 1959, 58, 348-356.
         (SELF-ESTEEM)
      @D-20 SELF-IDENTITY SELF EVALUATION PERCEPTION ESTEEM CONCEPT IMAGE 1959M

D-21   DRUCKMAN, D.
         DOGMATISM, PRENEGOTIATION EXPERIENCE AND SIMULATED GROUP REPRESENTATION AS
         DETERMINANTS OF DYADIC BEHAVIOR IN A BARGAINING SITUATION.
         JOURNAL OF PERSONALITY AND SOCIAL PSYCHOLOGY, 1967, 6, 279-290.
         (DOGMATISM SCALE)
      @D-21 DOGMATISM ATTITUDE COPING-DEFENSE FLEXIBILITY RIGIDITY 1967M

D-22   DIPBOYE, W. J., & ANDERSON, W. F.
         OCCUPATIONAL STEREOTYPES AND MANIFEST NEEDS OF HIGH SCHOOL STUDENTS.
         JOURNAL OF COUNSELING PSYCHOLOGY, 1961, 8, 296-304.
         (MEASURES OF MANIFEST NEEDS)
      @D-22 INTEROCEPTIVE JOB STEREOTYPE AUTONOMY OTHER-CATEGORY NEED AFFILIATION
      @D-22 AGGRESSION ORDER EXHIBITION 1961M MANIFEST STUDENT ABASEMENT NURTURANCE
      @D-22 CHANGE VOCATIONAL DOMINANCE ACHIEVEMENT
         (APPLICATIONS: 1174)

D-23   DIGNAN, M. H.
            EGO IDENTITY AND MATERNAL IDENTIFICATION.
            JOURNAL OF PERSONALITY AND SOCIAL PSYCHOLOGY, 1965, 1, 476-483.
            (RATING SCALE FOR IDENTITY TRAITS)
        @D-23 IDENTIFICATION EGO IDENTITY MATERNAL GLOBAL ADJUSTMENT SELF-IDENTITY SELF
        @D-23 ESTEEM EVALUATION PERCEPTION TRAIT 1965M RATING

D-24   DOIDGE, W. T., & HOLTZMAN, W. H.
            IMPLICATIONS OF HOMOSEXUALITY AMONG AIR FORCE TRAINEES.
            JOURNAL OF CONSULTING PSYCHOLOGY, 1960, 24, 9-13.
            (SEXUAL IDENTIFICATION SURVEY)*
        @D-24 SEX ROLE IDENTIFICATION SELF-IDENTITY 1960M MASCULINITY FEMININITY

D-25   DYMOND, R. F.
            ADJUSTMENT CHANGES OVER THERAPY FROM THEMATIC APPERCEPTION TEST RATINGS.
            IN C. R. ROGERS & R. F. DYMOND (EDS.) PSYCHOTHERAPY AND PERSONALITY CHANGE.
            CHICAGO: UNIVERSITY CHICAGO PRESS, 1954.
            (METHOD FOR SCORING TAT STORIES FOR ADJUSTMENT)
        @D-25 ADJUSTMENT TAT GLOBAL MENTAL-ILLNESS INTEGRATION PROJECTIVE 1954M IMAGERY
            (APPLICATIONS: 1190 1461 1572 1659)

D-26   DIERS, C. J.
            SOCIAL DESIRABILITY AND ACQUIESCENCE IN RESPONSE TO PERSONALITY ITEMS.
            JOURNAL OF CONSULTING PSYCHOLOGY, 1964, 28, 71-77.
            (SOCIAL DESIRABILITY SCALES)
        @D-26 SOCIAL DESIRABILITY RESPONSE-BIAS 1964M

D-27   DIBNER, A. S.
            AMBIGUITY AND ANXIETY.
            JOURNAL OF ABNORMAL AND SOCIAL PSYCHOLOGY, 1958, 56, 165-174.
            (ANXIETY CARDS)*
        @D-27 AFFECTIVE-STATES ANXIETY AMBIGUITY SUBJECTIVE STRESS NEGATIVE 1958M
            (APPLICATIONS: 1947)

D-28   DE CHARMS, R., MORRISON, H. W., REITMAN, W., & MCCLELLAND, D. C.
            BEHAVIORAL CORRELATES OF DIRECTLY AND INDIRECTLY MEASURED ACHIEVEMENT
            MOTIVATION.
            IN D. C. MCCLELLAND (ED.) STUDIES IN MOTIVATION. NEW YORK: APPLETON-
            CENTURY-CROFTS, 1955.
            (VALUE ACHIEVEMENT (V ACH) SCALE)
        @D-28 VALUES ACHIEVEMENT AUTONOMY NEED MOTIVE 1955M
            (APPLICATIONS: 433   436   596   934 1014 1087)

D-29   DEWOLFE, A. S., BARRELL, R. P., & CUMMINGS, J. W.
            PATIENT VARIABLES IN EMOTIONAL RESPONSE TO HOSPITALIZATION FOR PHYSICAL
            ILLNESS.
            JOURNAL OF CONSULTING PSYCHOLOGY, 1966, 30, 68-72.
            (PATIENT'S OPINION FORM)*
        @D-29 PATIENT ATTITUDE ILLNESS ADJUSTMENT GLOBAL SATISFACTION PHYSICAL 1966M
        @D-29 HOSPITALIZATION OPINION

D-30   DE CHARMS, R., MORRISON, H. W., REITMAN, W., & MCCLELLAND, D. C.
            BEHAVIORAL CORRELATES OF DIRECTLY AND INDIRECTLY MEASURED ACHIEVEMENT
            MOTIVATION.
            IN D. C. MCCLELLAND (ED.) STUDIES IN MOTIVATION. NEW YORK: APPLETON-
            CENTURY-CROFTS, 1955.
            (PICTURE INTERPRETATION TEST FOR N ACH / N AFF)
        @D-30 MOTIVE NEED ACHIEVEMENT AFFILIATION TAT PROJECTIVE 1955M
            (APPLICATIONS: 129   934 1087)

D-31   DUNNETTE, M. D.
            A SELF DESCRIPTION ADJECTIVE CHECKLIST AS AN INDICATOR OF BEHAVIORAL
            MODALITIES. PAPER PRESENTED AT THE MEETING OF THE AMERICAN PSYCHOLOGICAL
            ASSOCIATION, 1960.
            (MEASURE OF BEHAVIORAL TENDENCIES RELEVANT TO INDUSTRIAL SETTINGS)
        @D-31 SELF DESCRIPTION PERFORMANCE JOB ASSERTIVENESS COOPERATION IMAGINATION
        @D-31 CHECKLIST BEHAVIOR 1960M ADJUSTMENT PE-FIT

D-32   DIVESTA, F. J., & MERWIN, J. C.
            THE EFFECTS OF NEED-ORIENTED COMMUNICATIONS ON ATTITUDE CHANGE.
            JOURNAL OF ABNORMAL AND SOCIAL PSYCHOLOGY, 1960, 60, 80-85.
            (PERCEIVED INSTRUMENTALITY SCALES)
        @D-32 DOMINANCE AFFILIATION ACHIEVEMENT PERCEIVED ADJUSTMENT EFFECTIVENESS
        @D-32 AUTONOMY LOCUS CONTROL IE-CONTROL 1960M

D-33   DIVESTA, F. J., & MERWIN, J. C.
            THE EFFECTS OF NEED-ORIENTED COMMUNICATIONS ON ATTITUDE CHANGE.
            JOURNAL OF ABNORMAL AND SOCIAL PSYCHOLOGY, 1960, 60, 80-85.
            (MEASURES OF NEED ACHIEVEMENT, AFFILIATION, DOMINANCE, AND EXHIBITION)
         @D-33 ADJUSTMENT AUTONOMY NEED ACHIEVEMENT OTHER-CATEGORY AFFILIATION DOMINANCE
         @D-33 SUBMISSION MULTITRAIT EXHIBITION 1960M

D-34   DIEN, D. S., & VINACKE, W. E.
            SELF-CONCEPT AND PARENTAL IDENTIFICATION OF YOUNG ADULTS WITH MIXED
            CAUCASIAN-JAPANESE PARENTAGE.
            JOURNAL OF ABNORMAL AND SOCIAL PSYCHOLOGY, 1964, 69, 463-466.
            (RATING FOR SELF, IDEAL-SELF, MOTHER, AND FATHER)
         @D-34 CONCEPT SELF-IDENTITY EVALUATION SELF ESTEEM FAMILY INTERACTION ADJUSTMENT
         @D-34 IDEAL IMAGE IDENTIFICATION 1964M

D-35   DOLLARD, J., & AULD, F., JR.
            SCORING HUMAN MOTIVES. NEW HAVEN: YALE UNIVERSITY PRESS, 1959.
            (CONTENT-ANALYSIS MEASURE OF CONVERSATION IN THERAPY)
         @D-35 EGO-STRENGTH COPING-DEFENSE ADJUSTMENT MOTIVE OTHER-CATEGORY PATIENT
         @D-35 EGO-RESILIENCY THERAPY PROGNOSIS PSYCHIATRIC 1959M CHANGE
            (APPLICATIONS: 1017)

D-36   DENELSKY, G. Y., & MCKEE, M. G.
            PREDICTION OF JOB PERFORMANCE FROM ASSESSMENT REPORTS: USE OF A MODIFIED
            Q-SORT TECHNIQUE TO EXPAND PREDICTOR AND CRITERION VARIANCE.
            JOURNAL OF APPLIED PSYCHOLOGY, 1969, 53, 439-445.
            (Q-SORT MEASURES OF PERFORMANCE AND PERSONALITY TRAITS)
         @D-36 JOB ADJUSTMENT PERFORMANCE Q-SORT 1969M PREDICTION MULTITRAIT

D-37   DAVIDS, A.
            ALIENATION, SOCIAL APPERCEPTION, AND EGO STRUCTURE.
            JOURNAL OF CONSULTING PSYCHOLOGY, 1955, 19, 21-27.
            (AFFECT QUESTIONNAIRE)*
         @D-37 PESSIMISM TRUST ANXIETY RESENTMENT AFFECTIVE-STATES OPTIMISM SOCIAL EGO
         @D-37 ALIENATION ENVIRONMENT PERCEPTION ADJUSTMENT STRUCTURE SELF-IDENTITY
         @D-37 1955M
            (APPLICATIONS: 2682   2867)

D-38   DINGMAN, H. F., PAULSON, M. J., EYMAN, R. K., & MILLER, C. R.
            THE SEMANTIC DIFFERENTIAL AS A TOOL FOR MEASURING PROGRESS IN THERAPY.
            PSYCHOLOGICAL REPORTS, 1969, 25, 271-279.
            (SEMANTIC DIFFERENTIAL MEASURE OF AFFECTIVE CHANGES IN THERAPY)
         @D-38 SEM-DIFFERENTIAL THERAPY PATIENT MENTAL-ILLNESS ADJUSTMENT GLOBAL CHANGE
         @D-38 OTHER-CATEGORY PSYCHIATRIC AFFECTIVE-STATES 1969M PROGNOSIS

D-39   DUNN, J. A.
            THE THEORETICAL RATIONALE UNDERLYING THE DEVELOPMENT OF THE SCHOOL ANXIETY
            QUESTIONNAIRE.
            PSYCHOLOGY IN THE SCHOOLS, 1968, 5, 204-210.
            (SCHOOL ANXIETY QUESTIONNAIRE)*
         @D-39 AFFECTIVE-STATES SCHOOL ANXIETY SUBJECTIVE STRESS NEGATIVE 1968M

D-40   DUTTON, E.
            TALENT-FLAIR-ENDOGENOUS FASCINATION: A THEORY AND SOME ATTEMPTS TO MEASURE
            PREFERRED GENERAL RESPONSE MODALITIES.
            IN M. KATZ (ED.) NINETEENTH YEARBOOK OF THE NATIONAL COUNCIL ON MEASUREMENT
            IN EDUCATION. AMES, IOWA: NATIONAL COUNCIL ON MEASUREMENT IN EDUCATION,
            1962.
            (PREFERENCE ASSOCIATION SURVEY)*
         @D-40 SELF PE-FIT ENVIRONMENT EXPRESSION STYLE LIFE ADJUSTMENT 1962M PREFERENCE
            (APPLICATIONS: 1397   1518)

D-41   DWORIN, J., AND WYANT, O.
            AUTHORITARIAN PATTERNS IN THE MOTHERS OF SCHIZOPHRENICS.
            JOURNAL OF CLINICAL PSYCHOLOGY, 1957, 13, 332-338.
            (MEASURE OF AUTHORITARIANISM)
         @D-41 COPING-DEFENSE OTHER-CATEGORY AUTHORITARIANISM PATIENT SCHIZOPHRENIA
         @D-41 DOGMATISM ADJUSTMENT PSYCHIATRIC MENTAL-ILLNESS FAMILY INTERACTION 1957M
         @D-41 MATERNAL

D-42   DANESINO, A., & LAYMAN, W. A.
            CONTRASTING PERSONALITY PATTERNS OF HIGH AND LOW ACHIEVERS AMONG COLLEGE
            STUDENTS OF ITALIAN AND IRISH DESCENT.
            JOURNAL OF PSYCHOLOGY, 1969, 72, 71-83.
            (SIMILIARITY PERCEPTION QUESTIONNAIRE)*
        aD-42 SUB-IDENTITY PERCEPTION IDENTIFICATION PARENTAL 1969M PARENT-CHILD
        aD-42 CROSS-CULTURAL ACHIEVEMENT SCHOOL PERCEIVED SIMILARITY ROLE SELF-IDENTITY

D-43   DEWOLFE, A. S., BARRELL, R. P., & CUMMINGS, J. W.
            PATIENT VARIABLES IN EMOTIONAL RESPONSE TO HOSPITALIZATION FOR PHYSICAL
            ILLNESS.
            JOURNAL OF CONSULTING PSYCHOLOGY, 1966, 30, 68-72.
            (HOSPITAL ADJUSTMENT INVENTORY)*
        aD-43 PATIENT ATTITUDE ILLNESS ADJUSTMENT GLOBAL SATISFACTION
        aD-43 AFFECTIVE-STATES 1966M HOSPITALIZATION

D-44   DRUCKMAN, D.
            DOGMATISM, PRENEGOTIATION EXPERIENCE, AND SIMULATED GROUP REPRESENTATION AS
            DETERMINANTS OF DYADIC BEHAVIOR IN A BARGAINING SITUATION.
            JOURNAL OF PERSONALITY AND SOCIAL PSYCHOLOGY, 1967, 6, 279-290.
            (LABOR-MANAGEMENT SCALE)
        aD-44 JOB MANAGEMENT ROLE ENACTMENT ATTITUDE ADJUSTMENT LABOR 1967M
        aD-44 RELATIONSHIPS

D-45   DAHLSTROM, W. G., & WELSH, G. S.
            AN MMPI HANDBOOK: A GUIDE TO USE IN CLINICAL PRACTICE AND RESEARCH.
            MINNEAPOLIS, MINNESOTA: UNIVERSITY OF MINNESOTA, 1968.
            (MINNESOTA MULTIPHASIC PERSONALITY INVENTORY)*
        HATHAWAY, S. R., & MCKINLEY, J. C.
            MINNESOTA MULTIPHASIC PERSONALITY INVENTORY: MANUAL, REVISED 1951.
            NEW YORK: PSYCHOLOGICAL CORPORATION, 1951.
        aD-45 1968M MMPI MULTITRAIT
            (APPLICATIONS:

19	21	29	43	50	82	95	114	138	141
154	178	180	183	188	222	228	232	241	271
328	339	342	367	371	378	428	430	444	452
460	467	480	528	531	538	551	568	569	577
605	606	607	609	614	619	620	629	644	650
652	657	663	666	667	680	688	689	706	711
715	719	730	738	757	767	769	779	789	792
793	809	821	824	826	827	829	838	852	859
861	866	876	886	895	910	918	919	929	934
945	949	950	958	959	964	967	970	972	975
990	993	994	1000	1003	1014	1032	1038	1039	1060
1063	1067	1079	1080	1086	1092	1118	1121	1124	1125
1126	1127	1131	1134	1135	1140	1153	1157	1158	1165
1166	1168	1169	1173	1187	1189	1191	1200	1203	1208
1227	1235	1240	1243	1249	1251	1253	1280	1282	1307
1337	1338	1341	1351	1357	1360	1372	1379	1383	1414
1415	1417	1418	1421	1422	1432	1441	1454	1457	1475
1482	1489	1492	1512	1551	1553	1555	1564	1566	1568
1570	1587	1588	1595	1596	1600	1606	1610	1614	1622
1624	1626	1627	1640	1643	1644	1645	1651	1654	1658
1669	1674	1678	1679	1682	1687	1695	1696	1698	1702
1703	1709	1713	1723	1727	1737	1739	1740	1741	1743
1746	1752	1756	1763	1764	1770	1771	1775	1776	1779
1780	1784	1785	1787	1788	1789	1791	1793	1794	1795
1797	1800	1810	1811	1813	1819	1822	1825	1830	1835
1841	1843	1844	1845	1847	1854	1855	1859	1860	1861
1866	1872	1880	1889	1891	1895	1897	1899	1903	1909
1914	1921	1924	1926	1932	1933	1945	1946	1948	1949
1950	1953	1955	1958	1961	1963	1964	1965	1967	1972
1973	1982	1988	1991	1995	1996	2002	2003	2004	2011
2017	2019	2030	2034	2036	2040	2041	2042	2043	2044
2047	2048	2052	2053	2058	2063	2066	2067	2073	2076
2080	2085	2097	2099	2103	2105	2107	2112	2117	2123
2124	2126	2129	2134	2140	2147	2158	2160	2168	2172
2175	2185	2186	2188	2200	2208	2213	2220	2224	2227
2234	2239	2241	2266	2275	2283	2285	2294	2297	2299
2300	2302	2303	2309	2312	2323	2336	2361	2371	2376
2386	2395	2415	2416	2418	2420	2421	2422	2425	2429
2430	2443	2444	2470	2482	2495	2517	2519	2533	2538
2540	2544	2554	2562	2563	2569	2572	2574	2581	2597
2603	2604	2611	2627	2632	2636	2671	2673	2675	2692
2697	2704	2725	2726	2729	2732	2739	2742	2743	2781
2815	2845	2863	2875	2887	2904	2910	2911	2924	2928
2935	2937	2947	2959	2975	2977	2979)			

D-46   DAVIDS, A., & PILDNER, H.
               COMPARISON OF DIRECT AND PROJECTIVE METHODS OF PERSONALITY ASSESSMENT
               UNDER DIFFERENT CONDITIONS OF MOTIVATION.
               PSYCHOLOGICAL MONOGRAPHS, 1958, 72 (11, WHOLE NO. 464).
          DAVIDS, A.
               THE INFLUENCE OF PERSONALITY ON AUDITORY APPERCEPTION AND MEMORY.
               UNPUBLISHED DOCTORAL DISSERTATION, HARVARD UNIVERSITY, 1953.
               (SENTENCE COMPLETION TEST)
          @D-46 1953M SELF DESCRIPTION RATING ALIENATION AFFECTIVE-STATES ADJUSTMENT
          @D-46 PROJECTIVE
               (APPLICATIONS: 2682 2867)

D-47   DAVIDS, A., & PILDNER, H.
               COMPARISON OF DIRECT AND PROJECTIVE METHODS OF PERSONALITY ASSESSMENT
               UNDER DIFFERENT CONDITIONS OF MOTIVATION.
               PSYCHOLOGICAL MONOGRAPHS, 1958, 72 (11, WHOLE NO. 464).
          DAVIDS, A.
               THE INFLUENCE OF PERSONALITY ON AUDITORY APPERCEPTION AND MEMORY.
               UNPUBLISHED DOCTORAL DISSERTATION, HARVARD UNIVERSITY, 1953.
               (SELF-RATING SCALE)
          @D-47 1953M PROJECTIVE SELF DESCRIPTION ALIENATION AFFECTIVE-STATES ADJUSTMENT
               (APPLICATIONS: 2682 2867)

D-48   DESOTO, C. B., & KEUTHE, J. L.
               SUBJECTIVE PROBABILITIES OF INTERPERSONAL RELATIONSHIPS.
               JOURNAL OF ABNORMAL AND SOCIAL PSYCHOLOGY, 1959, 59, 290-294.
               (MEASURE OF SYMMETRY/ASYMMETRY IN INTERPERSONAL RELATIONSHIPS)
          @D-48 1959M INTERPERSONAL RELATIONSHIPS SOCIAL ADJUSTMENT
          @D-48 COMPETENCE
               (APPLICATIONS: 2341)

D-49   DOLGAN, J.
               THE EFFICACY OF SYSTEMATIC DESENSITIZATION PROCEDURES AND A RATIONAL
               THERAPY IN THE MODIFICATION OF PHOBIC BEHAVIOR.
               UNPUBLISHED DOCTORAL DISSERTATION, OHIO STATE UNIVERSITY, 1967.
          MATTIS, P.
               THE LEARNING TO LEARN PHENOMENON AS A CRITERION FOR TESTING THE EFFECTS OF
               DESENSITIZATION WITH A "SELF" AND AN "OTHER" SET.
               UNPUBLISHED DOCTORAL DISSERTATION, OHIO STATE UNIVERSITY, 1968.
               (FEAR BEHAVIOR CHECKLIST)
          @D-49 1967M FEAR BEHAVIOR CHECKLIST
               (APPLICATIONS: 2432)

D-50   DOLGAN, J.
               THE EFFICACY OF SYSTEMATIC DESENSITIZATION PROCEDURES AND A RATIONAL
               THERAPY IN THE MODIFICATION OF PHOBIC BEHAVIOR.
               UNPUBLISHED DOCTORAL DISSERTATION, OHIO STATE UNIVERSITY, 1967.
          MATTIS, P.
               THE LEARNING TO LEARN PHENOMENON AS A CRITERION FOR TESTING THE EFFECTS OF
               DESENSITIZATION WITH A "SELF" AND AN "OTHER" SET.
               UNPUBLISHED DOCTORAL DISSERTATION, OHIO STATE UNIVERSITY, 1968.
               (LOOK-TOUCH-HOLD TEST)
          @D-50 1967M PHOBIA FEAR BEHAVIOR APPROACH AVOIDANCE
               (APPLICATIONS: 2432)

D-51   DOLGAN, J.
               THE EFFICACY OF SYSTEMATIC DESENSITIZATION PROCEDURES AND A RATIONAL
               THERAPY IN THE MODIFICATION OF PHOBIC BEHAVIOR.
               UNPUBLISHED DOCTORAL DISSERTATION, OHIO STATE UNIVERSITY, 1967.
          MATTIS, P.
               THE LEARNING TO LEARN PHENOMENON AS A CRITERION FOR TESTING THE EFFECTS OF
               DESENSITIZATION WITH A "SELF" AND AN "OTHER" SET.
               UNPUBLISHED DOCTORAL DISSERTATION, OHIO STATE UNIVERSITY, 1968.
               (FEAR THERMOMETER)
          @D-51 1967M PHOBIA FEAR STIMULUS
               (APPLICATIONS: 2432)

D-52   DOMINO, G.
               IDENTIFICATION OF POTENTIALLY CREATIVE PERSONS FROM THE ADJECTIVE
               CHECK LIST.
               JOURNAL OF CONSULTING AND CLINICAL PSYCHOLOGY, 1970, 35, 48-51.
               (CREATIVITY SCALE)
          @D-52 1970M CREATIVITY CHECKLIST RATING ORIGINALITY

D-53   DAMARIN, F., & MESSICK, S.
          RESPONSE STYLES AS PERSONALITY VARIABLES: A THEORETICAL INTEGRATION OF
          MULTIVARIATE RESEARCH.
          RESEARCH BULLETIN, 65-10, PRINCETON, N.J.: EDUCATIONAL TESTING SERVICE,
          1965.
          (MEASURE OF EXTREMENESS OF RESPONSE STYLES)
          @D-53 1965M RESPONSE STYLE INTENSITY SET RESPONSE-BIAS

D-54   DEAUX, K. K., & BIERI, J.
          LATITUDE OF ACCEPTANCE IN JUDGEMENTS OF MASCULINITY-FEMININITY.
          JOURNAL OF PERSONALITY, 1967, 35, 109-117.
          (MEASURE OF LATITUDE OF ACCEPTANCE OF MASCULINE-FEMININE CHARACTERISTICS)
          @D-54 1967M MASCULINITY FEMININTY SELF-IDENTITY SEX ROLE IDENTITY
          @D-54 SUB-IDENTITY

D-55   DOIDGE, W. T., & HOLTZMAN, W. H.
          IMPLICATIONS OF HOMOSEXUALITY AMONG AIR FORCE TRAINEES.
          JOURNAL OF CONSULTING PSYCHOLOGY, 1960, 24, 9-13.
          (HOMOSEXUAL HOMONYMS TEST)
          @D-55 1960M SEX IDENTITY ROLE SELF-IDENTITY MASCULINITY HOMOSEXUALITY
          @D-55 SUB-IDENTITY

D-56   DOLLARD, J., & MAURER, O. H.
          A METHOD OF MEASURING TENSION IN WRITTEN DOCUMENTS.
          JOURNAL OF ABNORMAL AND SOCIAL PSYCHOLOGY, 1947, 42, 3-32.
          (DISCOMFORT-RELIEF QUOTIENT)*
          @D-56 1947M AFFECTIVE-STATES ANXIETY SUBJECTIVE STRESS TENSION THERAPY
          (APPLICATIONS: 4 1307 1596)

D-57   DICKEY, B. A.
          ATTITUDE TOWARDS SEX ROLES AND FEELINGS OF ADEQUACY IN HOMOSEXUAL MALES.
          JOURNAL OF CONSULTING PSYCHOLOGY, 1961, 25, 116-122.
          (MEASURE OF FEELINGS OF ADEQUACY AMONG HOMOSEXUALS)
          @D-57 1961M COMPETENCE HOMOSEXUALITY SEX ROLE CONFLICT SELF IDEAL TRAIT
          @D-57 ESTEEM INADEQUACY FEELING
          (APPLICATIONS: 1624 1932)

D-58   DICKEY, B. A.
          ATTITUDE TOWARDS SEX ROLES AND FEELINGS OF ADEQUACY IN HOMOSEXUAL MALES.
          JOURNAL OF CONSULTING PSYCHOLOGY, 1961, 25, 116-122.
          (MEASURE OF SUBJECTIVE ROLE CONFLICT)
          @D-58 1961M SUBJECTIVE ROLE CONFLICT TRAIT HOMOSEXUALITY STEREOTYPE
          @D-58 INADEQUACY FEELING

D-61   DERMEN, D., & LONDON, P.
          CORRELATES OF HYPNOTIC SUSCEPTIBILITY.
          JOURNAL OF CONSULTING PSYCHOLOGY, 1965, 29, 537-545.
          (PERSONAL EXPERIENCES QUESTIONNAIRE)
          @D-61 1965M HYPNOTIC SUGGESTIBILITY PERSONAL ORIENTATION EXPERIENCE IE-CONTROL

D-62   DREGER, R. M., LEWIS, P. M., RICH, T. A., MILLER, K. S., REID, M. P., OVERLADE,
          D. C., TAFFEL, C., & FLEMMING, E. L.
          BEHAVIORAL CLASSIFICATION PROJECT.
          JOURNAL OF CONSULTING PSYCHOLOGY, 1964, 28, 1-13.
          (SYSTEM FOR CLASSIFICATION OF CHILDREN'S EMOTIONAL DISORDERS)
          @D-62 1964M CHILD BEHAVIOR ADJUSTMENT MENTAL-ILLNESS EMOTION

D-63   DIBNER, A. S.
          CUE-COUNTING: A MEASURE OF ANXIETY IN INTERVIEWS.
          JOURNAL OF CONSULTING PSYCHOLOGY, 1956, 20, 475-478.
          (MEASURE OF ANXIETY BY SPEECH DISRUPTION)
          @D-63 1956M ANXIETY AFFECTIVE-STATES SUBJECTIVE STRESS VOICE
          (APPLICATIONS: 1650 1663)

D-64   DICKSTEIN, L. S., & BLATT, S. J.
          DEATH CONCERN, FUTURITY, AND ANTICIPATION.
          JOURNAL OF CONSULTING PSYCHOLOGY, 1966, 30, 11-17.
          (MEASURE OF PREOCCUPATION WITH DEATH)
          @D-64 1966M DEATH FEAR FUTURE ORIENTATION MANIFEST
          @D-64 MORTALITY ANXIETY
          (APPLICATIONS: 2074)

D-65   DEWOLFE, A. S., BARRELL, R. P., & CUMMINGS, J. W.
          PATIENT VARIABLES IN EMOTIONAL RESPONSE TO HOSPITALIZATION FOR PHYSICAL
          ILLNESS.
          JOURNAL OF CONSULTING PSYCHOLOGY, 1966, 30, 68-72.
          (PATIENTS' PHILOSOPHY OF TREATMENT FORM)
      @D-65 1966M PATIENT HOSPITALIZATION PHYSICAL ILLNESS EMOTION RESPONSE
      @D-65 AUTHORITY AWARENESS NEGATIVE AFFECTIVE-STATES

D-66   DEWOLFE, A. S., BARRELL, R. P., & CUMMINGS, J. W.
          PATIENT VARIABLES IN EMOTIONAL RESPONSE TO HOSPITALIZATION FOR PHYSICAL
          ILLNESS.
          JOURNAL OF CONSULTING PSYCHOLOGY, 1966, 30, 68-72.
          (PLEASURE-DISPLEASURE QUOTIENT)
      @D-66 1966M PATIENT HOSPITALIZATION PHYSICAL ILLNESS POSITIVE NEGATIVE
      @D-66 AFFECTIVE-STATES SUBJECTIVE EMOTION

D-67   DOMINO, G., GOLDSCHMID, M. L., & KAPLAN, M.
          PERSONALITY TRAITS OF INSTITUTIONALIZED MONGOLOID GIRLS.
          AMERICAN JOURNAL OF MENTAL DEFICIENCY, 1964, 68, 498-502.
          (SONOMA CHECK LIST)*
      @D-67 1964M RATING ADJUSTMENT PERSONALITY MENTAL-ILLNESS
          (APPLICATIONS: 2121)

D-68   DANA, R. H.
          PROPOSAL FOR OBJECTIVE SCORING OF THE TAT.
          PERCEPTUAL AND MOTOR SKILLS, 1959, 9, 27-43.
          (TAT SCORED FOR ADAPTIVE ADEQUACY)
      @D-68 1959M TAT ADAPTABILITY COMPETENCE FANTASY PROJECTIVE FUTURE FEELING
      @D-68 THINKING
          (APPLICATIONS: 2238 2963)

D-70   DITTES, J. E.
          IMPULSIVE CLOSURE AS REACTION TO FAILURE INDUCED-THREAT.
          JOURNAL OF ABNORMAL AND SOCIAL PSYCHOLOGY, 1961, 63, 562-569.
          (MEASURE OF VALUATION ON ACHIEVEMENT)
      @D-70 1961M ACHIEVEMENT VALUES SELF ESTEEM SUCCESS FAILURE

D-71   DAVIDS, A., & LAWTON, M. J.
          SELF-CONCEPT, MOTHER CONCEPT, AND FOOD AVERSIONS IN EMOTIONALLY DISTURBED
          AND NORMAL CHILDREN.
          JOURNAL OF ABNORMAL AND SOCIAL PSYCHOLOGY, 1961, 62, 309-314.
          (MEASURE OF SELF-CONCEPT IN CHILDREN)
      @D-71 1961M CHECKLIST SELF-IDENTITY CHILD SELF CONCEPT IMAGE EVALUATION

D-72   DAVIDS, A., & LAWTON, M. J.
          SELF-CONCEPT, MOTHER CONCEPT, AND FOOD AVERSIONS IN EMOTIONALLY DISTURBED
          AND NORMAL CHILDREN.
          JOURNAL OF ABNORMAL AND SOCIAL PSYCHOLOGY, 1961, 62, 309-314.
          (SENTENCE COMPLETION MEASURE OF CHILD'S SELF AND MOTHER CONCEPTS)
      @D-72 1961M SELF-IDENTITY CHILD PROJECTIVE SELF CONCEPT PARENT-CHILD IMAGE
      @D-72 RELATIONSHIPS CONCEPT SENTENCE-COMP MATERNAL

D-73   DAVIDS, A., & LAWTON, M. J.
          SELF-CONCEPT, MOTHER CONCEPT, AND FOOD AVERSIONS IN EMOTIONALLY DISTURBED
          AND NORMAL CHILDREN.
          JOURNAL OF ABNORMAL AND SOCIAL PSYCHOLOGY, 1961, 62, 309-314.
          (PICTURE SELF-RATING MEASURE OF CHILD'S SELF-CONCEPT)
      @D-73 1961M SELF-IDENTITY SELF CONCEPT CHILD GRAPHIC

D-74   DEESE, J., LAZARUS, R. S., & KEENAN, J.
          ANXIETY, ANXIETY REDUCTION, AND STRESS IN LEARNING.
          JOURNAL OF EXPERIMENTAL PSYCHOLOGY, 1953, 46, 55-60.
          (WINNIE ANXIETY SCALE)
      @D-74 1953M ANXIETY TENSION STRESS PRESSURE MMPI

D-75   DIGGORY, J. C., & ROTHMAN, D. Z.
          VALUES DESTROYED BY DEATH.
          JOURNAL OF ABNORMAL AND SOCIAL PSYCHOLOGY, 1961, 63, 205-210.
          (MEASURE OF CONCERN FOR CONSEQUENCES OF DEATH)
      @D-75 1961M DEATH FEAR ATTITUDE FUTURE

D-76   DABBS, J. M., JR.
         SELF-ESTEEM, COMMUNICATOR CHARACTERISTICS, AND ATTITUDE CHANGE.
         JOURNAL OF ABNORMAL AND SOCIAL PSYCHOLOGY, 1964, 69, 173-181.
         (MEASURE OF ATTRIBUTION OF RESPONSIBILITY)
         @D-76 1964M RESPONSIBILITY ACCEPTANCE IE-CONTROL LOCUS
         @D-76 ATTRIBUTION

D-77   DAVIS, L. W., & HUSBAND, R. W.
         A STUDY OF HYPNOTIC SUSCEPTIBILITY IN RELATION TO PERSONALITY TRAITS.
         JOURNAL OF ABNORMAL AND SOCIAL PSYCHOLOGY, 1931, 26, 175-182.
         (DAVIS-HUSBAND HYPNOTIC SUSCEPTIBILITY TEST)
         @D-77 1931M HYPNOTIC SUGGESTIBILITY
         (APPLICATIONS: 29   95   939)

D-78   DINOLA, A. J., KIMINSKY, B. P., & STERNFELD, A. E.
         TMR PERFORMANCE PROFILE TEST.
         RIDGEFIELD, N.J.: REPORTING SERVICE FOR EXCEPTIONAL CHILDREN, 1965.
         (TMR PERFORMANCE PROFILE TEST)*
         @D-78 1965M PERFORMANCE
         (APPLICATIONS: 1128)

D-80   DUTT, N. K.
         PSYCHOLOGICAL AND EDUCATIONAL IMPLICATIONS OF THE CONCEPT OF MENTAL HEALTH
         IN INDIAN THOUGHT.
         UNPUBLISHED DOCTORAL THESIS, PUNJAB UNIVERSITY LIBRARY, CHANDIGARH, 1964.
         (DUTTS' ANXIETY QUESTIONNAIRE)
         @D-80 1964M ANXIETY TENSION CROSS-CULTURAL MENTAL-ILLNESS
         (APPLICATIONS: 2656)

D-81   DENNIS, W.
         ANIMISTIC THINKING AMONG COLLEGE AND UNIVERSITY STUDENTS.
         SCIENTIFIC MONTHLY, 1953, 76, 247-249.
         (ANIMISM QUESTIONNAIRE)
         @D-81 1953M ATTRIBUTION LIFE
         (APPLICATIONS: 2666)

D-83   DAVIDS, A., & HOLDER, R. H.
         CONSISTENCY OF MATERNAL ATTITUDES AND PERSONALITY FROM PREGNANCY TO
         EIGHT MONTHS FOLLOWING CHILDBIRTH.
         DEVELOPMENTAL PSYCHOLOGY, 1970, 2, 364-366.
         (MEASURE OF MATERNAL PERSONALITY AND MOTHER-CHILD INTERACTION)
         @D-83 1970M MATERNAL CHILD TRAIT RELATIONSHIPS PARENTAL INTERACTION PERSONALITY

D-84   DEMERATH, N. J.
         SOCIAL CLASS AND AMERICAN PROTESTANTISM.
         CHICAGO: RAND, MCNALLY, 1965.
         (MEASURE OF FELT BENEFIT FROM ONE'S RELIGION)
         @D-84 1965M RELIGION SATISFACTION EVALUATION EXPERIENCE ORIENTATION ATTITUDE
         (APPLICATIONS: 2700)

D-85   DYNES, R. R.
         CHURCH-SECT TYPOLOGY AND SOCIO-ECONOMIC STATUS.
         AMERICAN SOCIOLOGICAL REVIEW, 1955, 20, 555-560.
         (MEASURE OF LIBERALISM-CONSERVATISM OF RELIGIOUS VIEWS)
         @D-85 1955M RELIGION ATTITUDE BELIEF CONSERVATISM LIBERALISM
         (APPLICATIONS: 2700)

D-86   DOLE, A. A., NOTTINGHAM, J., & WRIGHTSMAN, L. S., JR.
         BELIEFS ABOUT HUMAN NATURE HELD BY COUNSELING, CLINICAL, AND
         REHABILITATION STUDENTS.
         JOURNAL OF COUNSELING PSYCHOLOGY, 1969, 16, 197-202.
         (ASPIRATIONS INVENTORY)
         @D-86 1969M ASPIRATION ALTRUISM TRUST COMPLEXITY AWARENESS AUTONOMY INVENTORY
         @GOALS DESIRABILITY

D-87   DOLE, A. A.
         A STUDY OF VALUES AS DETERMINANTS OF EDUCATIONAL VOCATIONAL CHOICE
         IN HAWAII.
         COOPERATIVE RESEARCH PROJECT NO. 757, HAWAII STATE DEPT OF EDUCATION, 1961.
         DOLE, A. A., & DIGMAN, J. M.
         FACTORS IN COLLEGE ATTENDANCE.
         JOURNAL OF APPLIED PSYCHOLOGY, 1967, 51, 247-253.
         (REASONS FOR GOING TO COLLEGE INVENTORY)
         @D-87 1967M COLLEGE VOCATIONAL SOCIAL CONFORMITY ACADEMIC VALUES ALTRUISM SCHOOL
         @EXPERIENCE INTEREST INFLUENCE
         (APPLICATIONS: 1447)

D-88   DARLEY, J. G., & MCNAMARA, W. J.
            FACTOR ANALYSIS IN THE ESTABLISHMENT OF NEW PERSONALITY TESTS.
            JOURNAL OF EDUCATIONAL PSYCHOLOGY, 1940, 31, 321-334.
        DARLEY, J. G., & MCNAMARA, W. J.
            MANUAL OF DIRECTIONS.
            NEW YORK, PSYCHOLOGICAL CORPORATION, 1941.
            (MINNESOTA PERSONALITY SCALE: MPS)*
        ƏD-88 1940M PERSONALITY STRUCTURE SOCIAL ADJUSTMENT FAMILY RELATIONSHIPS MORALE
        ƏCONSERVATISM EMOTION PARENT-CHILD ATTITUDE AFFECTIVE-STATES STUDENT
            (APPLICATIONS: 95   2766)

D-89   DONNAN, H. H., HARLAN, G. E., & THOMPSON, S. A.
            COUNSELOR PERSONALITY AND LEVEL OF FUNCTIONING AS PERCEIVED BY COUNSELEES.
            JOURNAL OF COUNSELING PSYCHOLOGY, 1969, 16, 482-485.
            (RELATIONSHIP INVENTORY)
        ƏD-89 1969M COUNSELING PATIENT THERAPY RELATIONSHIPS THERAPIST PERCEPTION
        ƏSATISFACTION

D-90   DOMBROSE, L. A., & SLOBIN, M. S.
            THE IFS TEST.
            MISSOULA, MONTANA: PSYCHOLOGICAL TEST SPECIALISTS, 1958.
            (ID EGO SUPEREGO TEST - IFS)*
        ƏD-90 1958M EGO CONSCIENCE ADJUSTMENT DIAGNOSIS CONTROL IMPULSE
            (APPLICATIONS: 1239)

D-91   DOLE, A. A.
            SELECTION OF STUDENT COUNSELORS IN HAWAII.
            HONOLULU: PSYCHOLOGICAL RESEARCH CENTER, UNIVERSITY OF HAWAII, 1963
            (MIMEO).
        DOLE, A. A.
            THE PREDICTION OF EFFECTIVENESS IN SCHOOL COUNSELING.
            JOURNAL OF COUNSELING PSYCHOLOGY, 1964, 11, 112-121.
            (COUNSELOR APPRAISAL BATTERY)
        ƏD-91 1963M COUNSELING EVALUATION EFFECTIVENESS PREDICTION ABILITY THERAPIST

D-92   DOLE, A. A.
            SELECTION OF STUDENT COUNSELORS IN HAWAII.
            HONOLULU: PSYCHOLOGICAL RESEARCH CENTER, UNIVERSITY OF HAWAII, 1963
            (MIMEO).
            (COUNSELOR RATING SCALE)
        ƏD-92 1963M COUNSELING RATING EFFECTIVENESS PERSONAL TRAIT RELATIONSHIPS
        ƏTHERAPIST ABILITY
            (APPLICATIONS: 1274)

D-96   DIES, R. R., & HESS, A. K.
            AN EXPERIMENTAL INVESTIGATION OF COHESIVENESS IN MARATHON AND CONVENTIONAL
            GROUP THERAPY.
            JOURNAL OF ABNORMAL AND SOCIAL PSYCHOLOGY, 1971, 77, 258-262.
            (SEMANTIC DIFFERENTIAL MEASURE OF INTERPERSONAL BEHAVIOR IN GROUPS)
        ƏD-96 1971M SEM-DIFFERENTIAL INTERPERSONAL BEHAVIOR GROUP COHESIVENESS

D-97   DIES, R. R., & HESS, A. K.
            AN EXPERIMENTAL INVESTIGATION OF COHESIVENESS IN MARATHON AND CONVENTIONAL
            GROUP THERAPY.
            JOURNAL OF ABNORMAL AND SOCIAL PSYCHOLOGY, 1971, 77, 258-262.
            (MEASURE OF COHESIVENESS IN GROUPS)
        ƏD-97 1971M INTERPERSONAL BEHAVIOR GROUP COHESIVENESS

D-98   DEWOLFE, A. S., & GOVERNALE, C. N.
            FEAR AND ATTITUDE CHANGE.
            JOURNAL OF ABNORMAL AND SOCIAL PSYCHOLOGY, 1964, 69, 119-123.
            (FEAR OF TUBERCULOSIS QUESTIONNAIRE)
        ƏD-98 1964M FEAR ANXIETY ILLNESS HEALTH

D-99   DRAKE, L. E.
            A SOCIAL I-E SCALE.
            JOURNAL OF APPLIED PSYCHOLOGY, 1946, 30, 51-54.
        DRAKE, L. E.
            SCALE 0 (SOCIAL INTROVERSION).
            IN G. S. WELSH, & W. G. DAHLSTROM (EDS.).
            BASIC READINGS ON THE MMPI IN PSYCHOLOGY AND MEDICINE.
            MINNEAPOLIS: UNIVERSITY OF MINNESOTA PRESS, 1956, 181-183.
            (SOCIAL INTROVERSION SCALE (MMPI BASIC SCALE))
        ƏD-99 1956M SOCIAL INTROVERSION MMPI PARTICIPATION ACTIVITIES
        ƏEXTRAVERSION INTERACTION OTHERS COMPETENCE
            (APPLICATIONS: 1282)

D-100   DUNN, M., & LORGE, I.
               A GESTALT SCALE FOR THE APPRAISAL OF HUMAN FIGURE DRAWINGS.
               AMERICAN PSYCHOLOGIST, 1954, 9, 357 (ABSTRACT).
               (SCORING OF DRAW-A-PERSON TEST FOR MATURITY)
          @D-100 1954M FIGURE GRAPHIC PROJECTIVE MATURITY
               (APPLICATIONS: 1701)

D-111   DAVIDSON, H. H.
               A MEASURE OF ADJUSTMENT OBTAINED FROM THE RORSCHACH PROTOCOL.
               JOURNAL OF PROJECTIVE TECHNIQUES, 1950, 14, 31-38.
               (DAVIDSON SIGNS OF ADJUSTMENT)
          @D-111 1950M ADJUSTMENT RORSCHACH PROJECTIVE
               (APPLICATIONS: 1182)

D-112   DEVOS, G.
               A QUANTITATIVE APPROACH TO AFFECTIVE SYMBOLISM IN RORSCHACH RESPONSES.
               JOURNAL OF PROJECTIVE TECHNIQUES, 1952, 16, 133-150.
               (INDEX FOR SCORING AFFECTIVE SYMBOLISM IN RORSCHACH)
          @D-112 1952M RORSCHACH CONTENT-ANALYSIS HOSTILITY
          @ANXIETY DEPENDENCE BODY AWARENESS POSITIVE PROJECTIVE
               (APPLICATIONS: 1705)

D-114   DOLE, A. A.
               PREDICTION OF ACADEMIC SUCCESS UPON READMISSION TO COLLEGE.
               JOURNAL OF COUNSELING PSYCHOLOGY, 1963, 10, 169-175.
               (SCALE TO PREDICT SUCCESS FOLLOWING READMISSION TO SCHOOL)
          @D-114 1963M COLLEGE PROGNOSIS FAILURE SUCCESS ACADEMIC SCHOOL STUDENT

D-115   DITTES, J. E.
               VOCATIONAL GUIDANCE OF THEOLOGICAL STUDENTS--A MANUAL FOR THE USE OF THE
               THEOLOGICAL SCHOOL INVENTORY.
               DAYTON: MINISTRY STUDIES BOARD, 1964.
               (THEOLOGICAL SCHOOL INVENTORY)
          @D-115 1964M RELIGION ATTITUDE BELIEF
               (APPLICATIONS: 2073)

E-1   EDWARDS, A. L.
               THE SOCIAL DESIRABILITY VARIABLE IN PERSONALITY ASSESSMENT AND RESEARCH.
               NEW YORK: DRYDEN, 1957.
               (EDWARDS SOCIAL DESIRABILITY SCALE)*
          @E-1 SOCIAL DESIRABILITY GLOBAL ADJUSTMENT RESPONSE-BIAS NEED APPROVAL 1957M
               (APPLICATIONS: 26   50   111   138   158   190   204   226   346   450
                                   502   619   620   623   629   666   689   733   757   789
                                   792   950   967   986   1014   1063   1189   1374   1414   1568
                                  1587   1626   1634   1640   1692   1695   1765   1767   1771   1807
                                  1811   1816   1859   1860   1861   1866   1872   1896   1899   1909
                                  1914   1920   1948   1979   2042   2044   2048   2085   2126   2147
                                  2162   2232   2287   2297   2339   2489   2506   2555   2563   2605
                                  2673   2848   2910   2975   2977   2979)

E-2   EDWARDS, A. L.
               MANUAL FOR THE EDWARDS PERSONAL PREFERENCE SCHEDULE. NEW YORK: PSYCHO-
               LOGICAL CORPORATION, 1959.
               (EDWARDS PERSONAL PREFERENCE SCHEDULE)*
          @E-2 MULTITRAIT AUTONOMY NEED PREFERENCE 1959M
               (APPLICATIONS: 72   77   118   130   140   152   192   195   228   285
                                   315   322   341   363   371   389   408   422   491   521
                                   544   555   556   569   575   587   597   612   641   700
                                   701   720   733   776   788   802   812   819   826   829
                                   843   875   883   902   904   920   958   1104   1109   1127
                                  1153   1160   1163   1165   1166   1185   1192   1212   1214   1216
                                  1222   1228   1231   1235   1276   1304   1308   1329   1337   1338
                                  1340   1344   1359   1371   1379   1386   1394   1434   1439   1463
                                  1540   1566   1578   1584   1600   1604   1605   1611   1621   1636
                                  1647   1657   1684   1707   1733   1736   1740   1742   1750   1751
                                  1753   1800   1818   1840   1841   1884   1957   2001   2088   2149
                                  2181   2182   2188   2213   2226   2285   2294   2355   2398   2476
                                  2546   2618   2635   2646   2658   2665   2713   2752   2766   2770
                                  2779   2844   2846   2851   2894   2897   2903   2936)

E-3   EDWARDS, C. N.
            CULTURAL DISSONANCE AND DISSIMULATION: A STUDY IN ROLE CONFLICT.
            JOURNAL OF CONSULTING AND CLINICAL PSYCHOLOGY, 1968, 32, 6C7-610.
            (ROLE CONFLICT AND DISSONANCE QUESTIONNAIRE)
         aE-3 CONFLICT ADJUSTMENT SELF-IDENTITY SUB-IDENTITY ROLE PERCEPTION SOCIAL 1968M

E-4   EDWARDS, C. N.
            THE SITUATION PREFERENCE INVENTORY: AN OBJECTIVE APPROACH TO THE ASSESS-
            MENT OF INTERACTIVE STYLE. UNPUBLISHED MANUSCRIPT, HARVARD UNIVERSITY,
            1968.
            (SITUATION PREFERENCE INVENTORY)*
         aE-4 INTERPERSONAL ROLE ORIENTATION PREFERENCE SOCIAL COMPETENCE ADJUSTMENT
         aE-4 SELF-IDENTITY SUB-IDENTITY PERCEPTION INTERACTION STYLE SITUATIONAL 1968M

E-5   EYSENCK, H. J.
            THE QUESTIONNAIRE MEASUREMENT OF NEUROTICISM AND EXTRAVERSION.
            REVISTA DI PSICOLOGIA, 1956, 50, 113-140.
         EYSENCK, H. J.
            MANUAL OF MAUDSLEY PERSONALITY INVENTORY, LONDON: UNIVERSITY OF LONDON
            PRESS, 1959.
         EYSENCK, H. J.
            THE MAUDSLEY PERSONALITY INVENTORY. SAN DIEGO: EDUCATIONAL AND
            INDUSTRIAL TESTING SERVICE, 1962.
            (MAUDSLEY PERSONALITY INVENTORY)*
         aE-5 EXTRAVERSION NEUROTICISM GLOBAL ADJUSTMENT AUTONOMY MULTITRAIT 1956M
         aE-5 INTROVERSION
            (APPLICATIONS: 11   222   237   297   312   371   375   435   451   478
                              576   602   664   674   697   698   711   718   778   817
                              853   864   866   958   998   1102   1568   1591   1776   1801
                             1870   1923   1982   2061   2110   2140   2158   2225   2517   2542
                             2656   2667   2706)

E-6   EYSENCK, H. J., & EYSENCK, S. B. G.
            THE EYSENCK PERSONALITY INVENTORY.   SAN DIEGO, CALIFORNIA: EDUCATIONAL
            & INDUSTRIAL TESTING SERVICE, 1963.
            (EYSENCK PERSONALITY INVENTORY)*
         aE-6 MULTITRAIT EXTRAVERSION NEUROTICISM GLOBAL ADJUSTMENT AUTONOMY 1963M
         aE-6 RESPONSE-BIAS INTROVERSION
            (APPLICATIONS: 105   303   1055   1446   1937   2079   2140   2179   2183   2188
                             2219   2228   2276   2364   2474   2606   2615   2622   2684   2804
                             2810)

E-7   EYSENCK, S. B. G.
            MANUAL OF THE JUNIOR EYSENCK PERSONALITY INVENTORY.   LONDON: UNIVERSITY OF
            LONDON PRESS, 1965.
            (JUNIOR EYSENCK PERSONALITY INVENTORY)*
         aE-7 EXTRAVERSION NEUROTICISM GLOBAL ADJUSTMENT AUTONOMY MULTITRAIT CHILD
         aE-7 INTROVERSION 1965M

E-8   ELMS, A. C.
            INFLUENCE OF FANTASY ABILITY ON ATTITUDE CHANGE THROUGH ROLE PLAYING.
            JOURNAL OF PERSONALITY AND SOCIAL PSYCHOLOGY, 1966, 4, 36-43.
            (REWARD-ORIENTED FANTASY SCALE)*
         aE-8 FANTASY COPING-DEFENSE APPROACH AVOIDANCE 1966M ADAPTABILITY
            (APPLICATIONS: 2140   2804)

E-9   EISENMAN, R.
            PERSONALITY AND DEMOGRAPHY IN COMPLEXITY-SIMPLICITY.
            JOURNAL OF CONSULTING AND CLINICAL PSYCHOLOGY, 1968, 32, 140-143.
            (MEASURE OF RIGIDITY-FLEXIBILITY)
         aE-9 COMPLEXITY FIGURE PREFERENCE RIGIDITY COPING-DEFENSE FLEXIBILITY 1968M
         aE-9 DOGMATISM COGNITIVE STRUCTURE FUNCTIONING

E-10   EKMAN, P.
            BODY POSITION, FACIAL EXPRESSION, AND VERBAL BEHAVIOR DURING INTERVIEWS.
            JOURNAL OF ABNORMAL AND SOCIAL PSYCHOLOGY, 1964, 68, 295-301.
            (MEASURE OF VERBAL AND NONVERBAL BEHAVIOR DURING INTERVIEWS)
         aE-10 BEHAVIOR COPING COPING-DEFENSE EMPATHY GLOBAL AFFECTIVE-STATES OTHERS
         aE-10 ORIENTATION 1964M INTERPERSONAL
            (APPLICATIONS: 1054)

E-11   ELMORE, T. M.
                 THE DEVELOPMENT OF A SCALE TO MEASURE PSYCHOLOGICAL ANOMIE AND ITS IMPLI-
                 CATIONS FOR COUNSELING PSYCHOLOGY.
                 PROCEEDINGS OF THE 73RD ANNUAL AMERICAN PSYCHOLOGICAL ASSOCIATION CONVEN-
                 TION, 1965, 359-360.
                 (MEASURE OF DIMENSIONS OF ANOMIE)
            ƏE-11 ANOMIE AFFECTIVE-STATES ALIENATION SOCIAL ADJUSTMENT 1965M

E-12   ELMS, A. C.
                 INFLUENCE OF FANTASY ABILITY ON ATTITUDE CHANGE THROUGH ROLE PLAYING.
                 JOURNAL OF PERSONALITY AND SOCIAL PSYCHOLOGY, 1966, 4, 36-43.
                 (EMPATHIC FANTASY SCALE)*
            ƏE-12 AFFECTIVE-STATES FANTASY OTHERS ORIENTATION EMPATHY COPING-DEFENSE 1966M
            ƏE-12 ADAPTABILITY
                 (APPLICATIONS: 2825)

E-13   EPLEY, D., & RICKS, D. F.
                 FORESIGHT AND HINDSIGHT IN THE TAT.
                 JOURNAL OF PROJECTIVE TECHNIQUES, 1963, 27, 51-59.
                 (TAT SCORED FOR EXTENSION OF PERSONAL TIME)
            ƏE-13 PERSONAL TIME PERSPECTIVE AFFECTIVE-STATES TAT FUTURE ORIENTATION
            ƏE-13 PROJECTIVE 1963M
                 (APPLICATIONS: 112   912   2317)

E-14   EPSTEIN, R., & KOMORITA, S. S.
                 PARENTAL DISCIPLINE, STIMULUS CHARACTERISTICS OF OUTGROUPS, AND SOCIAL
                 DISTANCE IN CHILDREN.
                 JOURNAL OF PERSONALITY AND SOCIAL PSYCHOLOGY, 1965, 2, 416-420.
                 (SOCIAL DISTANCE SCALE)
            ƏE-14 SOCIAL DISTANCE AFFECTIVE-STATES CHILD OTHER-CATEGORY 1965M OTHERS
            ƏE-14 RELATIONSHIPS

E-15   EPSTEIN, R., & KOMORITA, S. S.
                 THE DEVELOPMENT OF A SCALE OF PARENTAL PUNITIVENESS TOWARDS AGGRESSION.
                 CHILD DEVELOPMENT, 1965, 36, 129-142.
                 (PARENTAL PUNITIVENESS SCALE)*(PPS)
            ƏE-15 PARENTAL PUNITIVENESS PARENT-CHILD AGGRESSION FAMILY 1965M CHILD
            ƏE-15 INTERACTION ADJUSTMENT PERCEPTION
                 (APPLICATIONS: 135   136)

E-16   ENDLER, N. S., HUNT, J. MCV., & ROSENSTEIN, A. J.
                 AN S-R INVENTORY OF ANXIOUSNESS.
                 PSYCHOLOGICAL MONOGRAPHS, 1962, 76, (17, WHOLE NO. 536).
                 (S-R INVENTORY OF ANXIOUSNESS)
            ƏE-16 ANXIETY AFFECTIVE-STATES SUBJECTIVE STRESS NEGATIVE 1962M
                 (APPLICATIONS: 503   990   1012   1072   1134   2095   2429   2438   2852)

E-17   ENDLER, N. S., & HUNT, J. MCV.
                 S-R INVENTORIES OF HOSTILITY AND COMPARISONS OF THE PROPORTIONS OF VARIANCE
                 FROM PERSONS, RESPONSES, AND SITUATIONS FOR HOSTILITY AND ANXIOUSNESS.
                 JOURNAL OF PERSONALITY AND SOCIAL PSYCHOLOGY, 1968, 9, 309-315.
                 (STIMULUS-RESPONSE INVENTORY OF HOSTILITY)*
            ƏE-17 AFFECTIVE-STATES HOSTILITY NEGATIVE RESENTMENT STIMULUS RESPONSE 1968M
                 (APPLICATIONS: 400)

E-18   ENGELMANN, H. O.
                 THE EVALUATION MODALITY TEST. CHICAGO: PSYCHOMETRIC AFFILIATES, 1956.
                 (EVALUATION MODALITY TEST)*
            ƏE-18 BEHAVIOR SELF EVALUATION SELF-IDENTITY PERCEPTION ESTEEM 1956M
                 (APPLICATIONS: 1266)

E-19   EFRON, H. Y.
                 AN ATTEMPT TO EMPLOY A SENTENCE COMPLETION TEST FOR THE DETECTION OF
                 PSYCHIATRIC PATIENTS WITH SUICIDAL IDEAS.
                 JOURNAL OF CONSULTING PSYCHOLOGY, 1960, 24, 156-160.
                 (SENTENCE COMPLETION MEASURE OF CHARACTERISTICS ASSOCIATED WITH SUICIDE)
            ƏE-19 AFFECTIVE-STATES ALIENATION SUICIDE NEGATIVE GLOBAL ADJUSTMENT GUILT
            ƏE-19 OTHER-CATEGORY PSYCHIATRIC PATIENT DIAGNOSIS 1960M

E-20   ` ELLSWORTH, R. B.
                THE MACC BEHAVIORAL ADJUSTMENT SCALE. LOS ANGELES: WESTERN PSYCHOLOGICAL
                SERVICES, 1957.
           ELLSWORTH, R. B., & CLAYTCN, W. H.
                MEASUREMENT OF IMPROVEMENT IN "MENTAL ILLNESS."
                JOURNAL OF CONSULTING PSYCHOLOGY, 1959, 23, 15-20.
                (MOTILITY, AFFECT, CCOPERATION AND COMMUNICATION TEST)*
           aE-20 AFFECTIVE-STATES BEHAVIOR ADJUSTMENT GLOBAL COMMUNICATION MULTITRAIT
           aE-20 COOPERATION 1957M
                (APPLICATIONS: 792 1675 1875 1900 2157 2562 2933 2935)

E-21   EPSTEIN, R.
                NEED FOR APPROVAL AND VERBAL CONDITIONING.
                UNPUBLISHED MANUSCRIPT, OHIO STATE UNIVERSITY, 1960.
           EPSTEIN, R.
                NEED FOR APPROVAL AND THE CONDITIONING OF VERBAL HOSTILITY IN ASTHMATIC
                CHILDREN.
                JOURNAL OF ABNORMAL AND SOCIAL PSYCHOLOGY, 1964, 69, 105-109.
           aE-21 NEED APPROVAL RESPONSE-BIAS SELF-IDENTITY SOCIAL CHILD ESTEEM AUTONOMY
           aE-21 DESIRABILITY 1960M
                (APPLICATIONS: 916 2942)

E-22   EISENMAN, R., & ROBINSON, N.
                COMPLEXITY-SIMPLICITY, CREATIVITY, INTELLIGENCE, AND CTHER CORRELATES.
                JOURNAL OF PSYCHOLOGY, 1967, 67, 331-334.
                (PERSONAL OPINION SURVEY)*
           aE-22 CREATIVITY AUTONOMY DEPENDENCE JUDGMENT REGRESSION EGO TOLERANCE 1967M
           aE-22 SCANNING AMBIGUITY COMPLEXITY
                (APPLICATIONS: 2459 2548 2816)

E-23   EVANS, F. J., & THORN, W. F.
                QUESTIONNAIRE SCALES CORRELATING WITH FACTORS OF HYPNOSIS: A PRELIMINARY
                REPORT.
                PSYCHOLOGICAL REPORTS, 1964, 14, 67-70.
                (QUESTIONNAIRE MEASURE OF EVERYDAY TRANCE-LIKE EXPERIENCES)
           aE-23 HYPNOTIC SUGGESTIBILTY FANTASY HALLUCINATION 1964M EXPERIENCE

E-24   ELLIOTT, R.
                USE OF A "CONFORMITY" SCALE TO ASSESS VOCATIONAL INTERESTS OF UNDER-
                GRADUATES.
                PSYCHOLOGICAL REPORTS, 1965, 16, 969-975.
                (EMPIRICALLY DERIVED MEASURE OF CONFORMITY)
           aE-24 CONFORMITY AUTONOMY 1965M VOCATIONAL INTEREST PREFERENCE

E-25   ESON, M. E.
                AN ANALYSIS OF TIME PERSPECTIVES AT FIVE AGE LEVELS. UNPUBLISHED DOCTORAL
                DISSERTATION, UNIVERSITY OF CHICAGO, 1951.
                (MEASURE OF TIME PERSPECTIVE)
           aE-25 TIME FUTURE ORIENTATION AFFECTIVE-STATES PERSPECTIVE 1951M

E-26   ELMS, A. C.
                INFLUENCE OF FANTASY ABILITY ON ATTITUDE CHANGE THROUGH ROLE PLAYING.
                JOURNAL OF PERSONALITY AND SOCIAL PSYCHOLOGY, 1966, 4, 36-43.
                (GENERAL FANTASY SCALE)*
           aE-26 FANTASY COPING-DEFENSE 1966M ADJUSTMENT ADAPTABILITY

E-27   ECKHARDT, W., & ALCOCK, N. Z.
                IDEOLOGY AND PERSONALITY IN WAR/PEACE ATTITUDES.
                JOURNAL OF SOCIAL PSYCHOLOGY, 1970, 81, 105-116.
                (QUESTIONNAIRE MEASURE OF IDEO-PERSONAL FACTOR IN WAR/PEACE ATTITUDES)
           aE-27 1970M PERSONALITY PCLITICAL IDEOLOGY ATTITUDE ORIENTATION

E-28   EDWARDS, A. L., CONE, J. D., JR., & ABBOTT, R. D.
                ANXIETY, STRUCTURE, OR SOCIAL DESIRABILITY?
                JOURNAL OF CONSULTING AND CLINICAL PSYCHOLOGY, 1970, 34, 236-238.
                (CONTROL SCALE)
           aE-28 1970M SOCIAL DESIRABILITY ANXIETY RESPONSE-BIAS

E-29   EYSENCK, H. J.
                THE QUESTIONNAIRE MEASUREMENT OF NEUROTICISM AND EXTRAVERSION.
                REVISTA DI PSICOLOGIA, 1956, 50, 113-140.
                (NEUROTICISM INVENTORY)
           aE-29 NEUROTICISM ADJUSTMENT 1956M MENTAL-HEALTH
                (APPLICATIONS: 664 1740 2378 2725)

E-30   EDWARDS, A. L.
               EDWARDS PERSONALITY INVENTORY MANUAL.
               CHICAGO: SCIENCE RESEARCH ASSOCIATES, 1967.
               (EDWARDS PERSONALITY INVENTORY)*
           @E-30 1967M MULTITRAIT PERSONALITY SOCIAL BEHAVIOR COMPETENCE INTERPERSONAL
           @E-30 RELATIONSHIPS
               (APPLICATIONS: 2535 2599)

E-31   EISENMAN, R., & SMITH, J. F.
               MORAL JUDGEMENT AND EFFORT IN HUMAN FIGURE DRAWINGS.
               PERCEPTUAL AND MOTOR SKILLS, 1966, 23, 951-954.
               (TEST OF MORAL JUDGMENT IN MITIGATING CIRCUMSTANCES)
           @E-31 1966M AUTHORITARIANISM MORAL JUDGMENT BIRTH ORDER SEX-DIFFERENCES
           @E-31 OPINION CHANGE
               (APPLICATIONS: 2631 2783)

E-32   EISENMAN, R., & TOWNSEND, T. D.
               STUDIES IN ACQUIESCENCE: 1. SOCIAL DESIRABILITY: 2. SELF-ESTEEM:
               3. CREATIVITY; AND 4. PREJUDICE.
               JOURNAL OF PROJECTIVE TECHNIQUES AND PERSONALITY ASSESSMENT, 1970, 34,
               45-54.
               (MEASURE OF SELF-ESTEEM)
           @E-32 1970M SELF ESTEEM SELF-IDENTITY CONCEPT IMAGE
               (APPLICATIONS: 2888)

E-33   EDWARDS, B. C., & EDGERLY, J. W.
               EFFECTS OF COUNSELOR-CLIENT COGNITIVE CONGRUENCE ON COUNSELING OUTCOME
               IN BRIEF COUNSELING.
               JOURNAL OF COUNSELING PSYCHOLOGY, 1970, 17, 313-318.
               (SEMANTIC DIFFERENTIAL MEASURE OF COLLEGE ADJUSTMENT)
           @E-33 1970M SEM-DIFFERENTIAL SELF-IDENTITY SUB-IDENTITY SELF CONCEPT EVALUATION
           @E-33 DESCRIPTION COLLEGE ADJUSTMENT

E-34   EXLINE, R. V.
               EFFECTS OF SEX, NORMS, AND AFFILIATION MOTIVATION UPON ACCURACY OF
               PERCEPTION OF INTERPERSONAL PREFERENCE.
               JOURNAL OF PERSONALITY, 1960, 28, 397-412.
               (MEASURE OF AFFILIATION MOTIVATION)
           @E-34 1960M AFFILIATION NEED MOTIVE INTERPERSONAL RELATIONSHIPS APPROACH
           @E-34 AVOIDANCE

E-35   EPSTEIN, R.
               (NO REFERENCE AVAILABLE)
           SALTZ, G. B.
               THE RELATIONSHIP BETWEEN OVERCONTROLLED AND UNDERCONTROLLED HOSTILITY AMD
               RESPONSES TO A TAT-LIKE TEST WITH A BUILT-IN STIMULUS DIMENSION OF
               HOSTILITY.
               UNPUBLISHED DOCTORAL DISSERTATION, UNIVERSITY OF MASSACHUSETTS, 1962.
               (MEASURE OF OVERCONTROLLED AND UNDERCONTROLLED HOSTILE BEHAVIOR)
           @E-35 1962M AFFECTIVE-STATES BEHAVIOR AGGRESSION
           @E-35 HOSTILITY CONTROL INHIBITION EXPRESSION
               (APPLICATIONS: 471)

E-36   ERON, L. D.
               RESPONSES OF WOMEN TO THE THEMATIC APPERCEPTION TEST.
               JOURNAL OF CONSULTING PSYCHOLOGY, 1953, 17, 269-282.
               (CHECKLIST OF TAT THEMES FOR WOMEN)
           @E-36 1953M TAT HOSTILITY AGGRESSION PROJECTIVE EMOTION CHECKLIST PARENTAL
           @MARITAL PEER INTERPERSONAL RELATIONSHIPS
               (APPLICATIONS: 516)

E-37   EWING, T. N.
               THERAPEUTIC COUNSELING RESEARCH PROJECT REPORT NO. I. UNIVERSITY OF
               ILLINOIS: STUDENT COUNSELING SERVICE AND DEPARTMENT OF PSYCHOLOGY, 1957.
               (GILBERT SELF-INTERVIEW TEST)*
           @E-37 1957M RESPONSIBILITY ADJUSTMENT COUNSELING
           @E-37 THERAPY
               (APPLICATIONS: 1602)

E-38   EPSTEIN, S.
             A STUDY OF OVER-INCLUSION IN A SCHIZOPHRENIC AND CONTROL GROUP.
             UNPUBLISHED MASTER'S THESIS, UNIVERSITY OF WISCONSIN, 1951.
         EPSTEIN, S.
             OVERINCLUSIVE THINKING IN A SCHIZOPHRENIC AND A CONTROL GROUP.
             JOURNAL OF CONSULTING PSYCHOLOGY, 1953, 17, 384-388.
             (INCLUSION TEST)
         aE-38 1951M OVERINCLUSIVE FLEXIBILITY RIGIDITY CONCEPTUAL CONCRETENESS
         aE-38 THINKING
             (APPLICATIONS: 947   1047   1908   2111   2630)

E-39   EWING, T. N.
             CHANGES IN ATTITUDE DURING COUNSELING.
             JOURNAL OF COUNSELING PSYCHOLOGY, 1954, 1, 232-239.
             (RATING OF SELF, IDEAL SELF, PARENTS, COUNSELOR)
         aE-39 1954M COUNSELING THERAPY ATTITUDE TRAIT CHANGE SELF RATING IDEAL PARENTAL
         aDISCREPANCY ESTEEM EVALUATION
             (APPLICATIONS: 1206   1278)

E-41   EYSENCK, H. J.
             THE PSYCHOLOGY OF POLITICS.
             LONDON: ROUTLEDGE AND KEGAN PAUL LTD., 1954.
         EYSENCK, H. J.
             THE PSYCHOLOGY OF POLITICS.
             NEW YORK: PRAEGER, 1955.
             (RADICALISM-CONSERVATISM SCALE)
         aE-41 1954M INTOLERANCE AMBIGUITY RIGIDITY FLEXIBILITY CONSERVATISM POLITICAL
         aE-41 ORIENTATION
             (APPLICATIONS: 346   647)

E-42   ENDLER, N. S., & HUNT, J. MCV.
             GENERALISABILITY OF CONTRIBUTIONS FROM SOURCES OF VARIANCE IN THE S-R
             INVENTORIES OF ANXIOUSNESS.
             JOURNAL OF PERSONALITY, 1969, 37, 1-24.
             (5 NEW FORMS OF S-R INVENTORY OF ANXIOUSNESS)
         aE-42 1969M ANXIETY SITUATIONAL STRESS TENSION RESPONSE

E-43   EPSTEIN, S.
             NO REFERENCE AVAILABLE--CITED IN:
             SHORE, M. F., MASSIMO, J. L., & MACK, R.
             CHANGES IN THE PERCEPTION OF INTERPERSONAL RELATIONSHIPS IN
             SUCCESSFULLY TREATED ADOLESCENT DELINQUENT BOYS.
             JOURNAL OF CONSULTING PSYCHOLOGY, 1965, 29, 213-217.
             (EMOTIONS AND MOTIVATIONS TAT TEST)
         aE-43 PROJECTIVE AFFECTIVE-STATES EMOTION MOTIVE NEED TAT
         aPERSONALITY FUNCTIONING HOSTILITY AGGRESSION CONTROL FEAR
             (APPLICATIONS: 1916)

E-44   ERON, E. D., BANTA, T. J., WALDER, L. O., & LAULICHT, J. H.
             COMPARISON OF DATA OBTAINED FROM MOTHERS AND FATHERS ON CHILDREARING
             PRACTICES AND THEIR RELATION TO CHILD AGGRESSION.
             CHILD DEVELOPMENT, 1961, 32, 457-472.
             (PEER NOMINATION RATINGS)*
         aE-44 1961M EXPRESSION AGGRESSION PEER RATING SOCIOMETRIC AGGRESSIVENESS
             (APPLICATIONS: 1955)

E-45   EPSTEIN, S.
             UNCONSCIOUS SELF-EVALUATION IN A NORMAL AND A SCHIZOPHRENIC GROUP.
             JOURNAL OF ABNORMAL AND SOCIAL PSYCHOLOGY, 1955, 50, 65-70.
             (MEASURE OF SIMILARITY-RECOGNITION)
         aE-45 1955M SIMILARITY SELF EVALUATION SCHIZOPHRENIA MENTAL-ILLNESS
         aE-45 RATING VOICE
             (APPLICATIONS: 1819)

E-46   EHRLICH, H. J., & LIPSEY, C.
             AFFECTIVE STYLE AS A VARIABLE IN PERSONALITY PERCEPTION.
             JOURNAL OF PERSONALITY, 1969, 37, 522-540.
             (AFFECTIVE STYLE SCALE)
         aE-46 1969M INTENSITY EMOTION AFFECTIVE-STATES PERSON PERCEPTION RESPONSE OTHERS

E-47   EAGLY, A. H.
                 INVOLVEMENT AS A DETERMINANT OF RESPONSE TO FAVORABLE AND UNFAVORABLE
                 INFORMATION.
                 JOURNAL OF PERSONALITY AND SOCIAL PSYCHOLOGY, 1967, 7 (WHOLE NO. 643).
                 (MEASURE OF SELF ESTEEM)
            aE-47 1967M SELF ESTEEM EVALUATION CONCEPT PERCEPTION CONFIDENCE
                 (APPLICATIONS: 527)

E-48   ERON, L. D., TERRY, D., & CALLAHAN, R.
                 THE USE OF RATING SCALES FOR EMOTIONAL TONE OF TAT STORIES.
                 JOURNAL OF CONSULTING PSYCHOLOGY, 1950, 14, 473-478.
                 (EMOTIONAL TONE RATING SCALE)
            aE-48 1950M ANXIETY EMOTION AFFECTIVE-STATES RESPONSE TAT
                 (APPLICATIONS: 1729 2021)

E-49   ELSTEIN, A. S., & VAN PELT, J. D.
                 DIMENSIONS IN THE PERCEPTION OF PSYCHIATRIC PATIENTS BY HOSPITAL STAFF.
                 JOURNAL OF CONSULTING PSYCHOLOGY, 1966, 30, 213-218.
                 (BEHAVIOR Q-SORT)
            aE-49 1966M Q-SORT BEHAVIOR PATIENT PSYCHIATRIC MANAGEMENT MENTAL-ILLNESS

E-50   ELSTEIN, A. S., & VAN PELT, J. D.
                 DIMENSIONS IN THE PERCEPTION OF PSYCHIATRIC PATIENTS BY HOSPITAL STAFF.
                 JOURNAL OF CONSULTING PSYCHOLOGY, 1966, 30, 213-218.
                 (INTERPERSONAL CHARACTERISTICS Q-SORT)
            aE-50 1966M INTERPERSONAL TRAIT PSYCHIATRIC PATIENT Q-SORT PUNITIVENESS

E-51   ERON, L. D., WALDER, L. O., TOIGO, R., & LEFKOWITZ, M. M.
                 SOCIAL CLASS, PARENTAL PUNISHMENT FOR AGGRESSION, AND CHILD AGGRESSION.
                 CHILD DEVELOPMENT, 1963, 34, 849-867.
                 (PUNISHMENT SCALE)
            aE-51 1963M PARENT-CHILD RELATIONSHIPS FAMILY INTERACTION AGGRESSION BEHAVIOR
                 (APPLICATIONS: 2072)·

E-52   EISLER, R. M.
                 THEMATIC EXPRESSION OF SEXUAL CONFLICT UNDER VARYING STIMULUS CONDITIONS.
                 JOURNAL OF CONSULTING AND CLINICAL PSYCHOLOGY, 1968, 32, 216-220.
                 (TAT SCORED FOR VERBAL SEX APPROACH)
            aE-52 1968M TAT SELF RATING SEX APPROACH AVOIDANCE FANTASY IMAGINATION CONFLICT
            aE-52 PROJECTIVE

E-54   ELLSWORTH, R. B., FOSTER, L., CHILDERS, B., ARTHUR, G., & KROEKER, D.
                 HOSPITAL AND COMMUNITY ADJUSTMENT AS PERCEIVED BY PSYCHIATRIC PATIENTS,
                 THEIR FAMILIES, AND STAFF.
                 JOURNAL OF CONSULTING AND CLINICAL PSYCHOLOGY MONOGRAPH SUPPLEMENT, 1968,
                 32, 1-41.
                 (COMMUNITY ADJUSTMENT SCALE)
            aE-54 1968M COMMUNITY ADJUSTMENT RATING SOCIAL BEHAVIOR COMPETENCE INTERPERSONAL
            aE-54 RELATIONSHIPS DIAGNOSIS

E-55   ELLSWORTH, R. B., FOSTER, L., CHILDERS, B., ARTHUR, G., & KROEKER, D.
                 HOSPITAL AND COMMUNITY ADJUSTMENT AS PERCEIVED BY PSYCHIATRIC PATIENTS,
                 THEIR FAMILIES, AND STAFF.
                 JOURNAL OF CONSULTING AND CLINICAL PSYCHOLOGY MONOGRAPH SUPPLEMENT, 1968,
                 32, 1-41.
                 (SOCIAL WORK SCALE)
            aE-55 1968M ADJUSTMENT SOCIAL COMPETENCE RATING BEHAVIOR INTERPERSONAL
            aE-55 RELATIONSHIPS DIAGNOSIS

E-56   ELLSWORTH, R. B., FOSTER, L., CHILDERS, B., ARTHUR, G., & KROEKER, D.
                 HOSPITAL AND COMMUNITY ADJUSTMENT AS PERCEIVED BY PSYCHIATRIC PATIENTS,
                 THEIR FAMILIES, AND STAFF.
                 JOURNAL OF CONSULTING AND CLINICAL PSYCHOLOGY MONOGRAPH SUPPLEMENT, 1968,
                 32, 1-41.
                 (PATIENT SELF-RATING SCALE)
            aE-56 1968M PATIENT ADJUSTMENT SELF RATING SYMPTOM MENTAL-ILLNESS DIAGNOSIS

E-57   ELSTEIN, A. S., & VAN PELT, J. D.
                 STRUCTURE OF STAFF PERCEPTIONS OF PSYCHIATRIC PATIENTS.
                 JOURNAL OF CONSULTING AND CLINICAL PSYCHOLOGY, 1968, 32, 550-559.
                 (RATING SCALE TO MEASURE PERCEPTION OF PSYCHIATRIC PATIENTS)
            aE-57 1968M RATING PSYCHIATRIC PATIENT INTERPERSONAL RELATIONSHIPS PROGNOSIS
            aE-57 COGNITIVE FUNCTIONING EMOTION PERCEPTION

E-59   EYSENCK, H. J.
              THE PSYCHOLOGY OF POLITICS.
              NEW YORK: PRAEGER, 1955.
              (RADICALISM-CONSERVATISM SCALE)
         aE-59 1955M POLITICAL ORIENTATION CONSERVATISM RADICALISM

E-60   EPSTEIN, S., & SMITH, R.
              THEMATIC APPERCEPTION, RORSCHACH CONTENT, AND RATINGS OF SEXUAL
              ATTRACTIVENESS OF WOMEN AS MEASURES OF THE SEX DRIVE.
              JOURNAL OF CONSULTING PSYCHOLOGY, 1957, 21, 473-478.
              (SEX DRIVE QUESTIONNAIRE)
         aE-60 1957M SEX BEHAVIOR GUILT ADJUSTMENT INHIBITION DRIVE
              (APPLICATIONS: 683)

E-61   ELLIOTT, R.
              INTERRELATIONSHIPS AMONG MEASURES OF FIELD DEPENDENCE, ABILITY, AND
              PERSONALITY TRAITS.
              JOURNAL OF ABNORMAL AND SOCIAL PSYCHOLOGY, 1961, 63, 27-36.
              (MEASURE OF SELF-CONCEPT DIFFERENTIATION)
         aE-61 1961M SELF-IDENTITY SELF CONCEPT SEM-DIFFERENTIAL
         aE-61 DIFFERENTIATION

E-62   EYSENCK, H. J.
              A SHORT QUESTIONNIARE FOR THE MEASUREMENT OF TWO DIMENSIONS OF PERSONALITY.
              JOURNAL OF APPLIED PSYCHOLOGY, 1958, 42, 14-17.
              (SHORT QUESTIONNAIRE MEASURE OF INTROVERSION-EXTRAVERSION AND NEUROTICISM)
         aE-62 1958M INTROVERSION EXTRAVERSION NEUROTICISM SOCIABILITY ADJUSTMENT
         aMENTAL-HEALTH
              (APPLICATIONS: 1033   2700   2725)

E-66   EISENMAN, R., & CHERRY, H. O.
              CREATIVITY, AUTHORITARIANISM, AND BIRTH ORDER.
              JOURNAL OF SOCIAL PSYCHOLOGY, 1970, 80, 233-235.
              (RESPONSE ACQUIESCENCE MEASURE)
         aE-66 1970M RESPONSE-BIAS ACQUIESCENCE AUTHORITARIANISM FAKING
              (APPLICATIONS: 2631)

E-67   EDWARDS, C. N.
              CLUTURAL VALUES AND ROLE DECISIONS: A STUDY OF EDUCATED WOMEN.
              JOURNAL OF COUNSELING PSYCHOLOGY, 1969, 16, 36-40.
              (VALUES QUESTIONNAIRE)
         aE-67 1969M MARITAL FAMILY SEX ROLE IDENTIFICATION FEMININITY MASCULINITY
         a ORIENTATION JOB VALUES PREFERENCE SELF OTHERS ACADEMIC IDENTITY CONCEPT

E-68   EYDE, L. D.
              WORK VALUES AND BACKGROUND FACTORS AS PREDICTORS OF WOMEN'S DESIRE TO WORK.
              OHIO STUDIES IN PERSONNEL RESEARCH MONOGRAPH NO. 108, THE OHIO STATE
              UNIVERSITY, BUREAU OF BUSINESS RESEARCH, 1962.
              (DESIRE TO WORK SCALE)
         aE-68 1962M JOB INVOLVEMENT VOCATIONAL ATTITUDE INTEREST MOTIVE VALUES ROLE
              (APPLICATIONS: 1437)

E-69   EYDE, L. D.
              WORK VALUES AND BACKGROUND FACTORS AS PREDICTORS OF WOMEN'S DESIRE TO WORK.
              OHIO STUDIES IN PERSONNEL RESEARCH MONOGRAPH NO. 108, THE OHIO STATE
              UNIVERSITY, BUREAU OF BUSINESS RESEARCH, 1962.
         EYDE, L. D.
              WORK MOTIVATION OF WOMEN COLLEGE GRADUATES: 5 YEAR FOLLOW-UP.
              JOURNAL OF COUNSELING PSYCHOLOGY, 1968, 15, 199-202.
              (RANKED WORK VALUE SCALE)
         aE-69 1962M JOB VOCATIONAL VALUES INTEREST PREFERENCE ATTITUDE
              (APPLICATIONS: 1437)

E-70   EMERY, J. R.
              AN EVALUATION OF STANDARD VERSUS INDIVIDUALIZED HIERARCHIES IN
              DESENSITIZATION TO REDUCE TEST ANXIETY.
              UNPUBLISHED DOCTORAL DISSERTATION, STANFORD UNIVERSITY, 1966.
              (TEST ANXIETY SCALE)
         aE-70 1966M TEST ANXIETY PERFORMANCE TENSION
              (APPLICATIONS: 1406)

E-71   ENGLANDER, M. E.
              A PSYCHOLOGICAL ANALYSIS OF VOCATIONAL CHOICE: TEACHING.
              JOURNAL OF COUNSELING PSYCHOLOGY, 1960, 7, 257-264.
              (Q-SORT MEASURE OF SELF CONCEPT AND PERCEPTION OF TEACHING)
          ∂E-71 1960M SELF CONCEPT Q-SORT PERCEPTION TEACHER ROLE CONSISTENCY
          ∂DISCREPANCY

E-73   EHRLICH, H. J., & VAN TUBERGEN, G. N.
              EXPLORING THE STRUCTURE AND SALIENCE OF STEREOTYPES.
              JOURNAL OF SOCIAL PSYCHOLOGY, 1971, 83, 113-127.
              (JEWISH STEREOTYPE CHECKLIST)
          ∂E-73 1971M STEREOTYPE PREJUDICE RACIAL ETHNIC MINORITY BELIEF DIFFERENCES
          ∂ATTITUDE CHECKLIST RELIGION

E-74   EHRLICH, H. J., & VAN TUBERGEN, G. N.
              EXPLORING THE STRUCTURE AND SALIENCE OF STEREOTYPES.
              JOURNAL OF SOCIAL PSYCHOLOGY, 1971, 83, 113-127.
              (ATHEIST STEREOTYPE CHECKLIST)
          ∂E-74 1971M STEREOTYPE PREJUDICE MINORITY BELIEF DIFFERENCES ATTITUDE RELIGION
          ∂ORIENTATION CONFORMITY CHECKLIST DEVIANCE

E-76   ELIZUR, A.
              CONTENT ANALYSIS OF THE RORSCHACH WITH REGARD TO ANXIETY AND HOSTILITY.
              RORSCHACH RESEARCH EXCHANGE, 1949, 13, 247-283.
              (RORSCHACH HOSTILE CONTENT TEST)
          ∂E-76 1949M RORSCHACH PROJECTIVE HOSTILITY ANXIETY
              (APPLICATIONS: 1592 1699 1704 1705)

E-77   ENDICOTT, N. A., JORTNER, S., & ABRAMOFF, E.
              OBJECTIVE MEASURES OF SUSPICIOUSNESS.
              JOURNAL OF ABNORMAL PSYCHOLOGY, 1969, 74, 26-32.
              (SUSPICIOUSNESS RATING SCALE)
          ∂E-77 1969M TRUST

E-78   EVANS, C., & MCCONNELL, T. R.
              A NEW MEASURE OF INTROVERSION-EXTRAVERSION.
              JOURNAL OF PSYCHOLOGY, 1941, 12, 111-124.
              (THINKING INTROVERSION SCALE)
          ∂E-78 1941M INTROVERSION EXTRAVERSION SOCIAL THINKING COGNITIVE INVOLVEMENT
              (APPLICATIONS: 1282)

E-79   EDWARDS, A. L., DIERS, C. J., & WALKER, J. N.
              RESPONSE SETS AND FACTOR LOADINGS ON SIXTY-ONE PERSONALITY SCALES.
              JOURNAL OF APPLIED PSYCHOLOGY, 1962, 46, 220-225.
              (EXPERIMENTAL FORCED-CHOICE MMPI SOCIAL DESIRABILITY SCALE)
          ∂E-79 1962M SOCIAL DESIRABILITY MMPI RESPONSE-BIAS
              (APPLICATIONS: 1899)

E-80   ERON, L. D.
              FREQUENCIES OF THEMES AND IDENTIFICATIONS IN THE STORIES OF SCHIZOPHRENIC
              PATIENTS AND NONHOSPITALIZED COLLEGE STUDENTS.
              JOURNAL OF CONSULTING PSYCHOLOGY, 1948, 12, 387-395.
              (CHECKLIST OF TAT THEMES FOR MEN)
          ∂E-80 1948M TAT HOSTILITY AGGRESSION PROJECTIVE EMOTION CHECKLIST PARENTAL
          ∂MARITAL PEER INTERPERSONAL RELATIONSHIPS

E-81   ELLSWORTH, R. B.
              A BEHAVIORAL STUDY OF STAFF ATTITUDES TOWARDS MENTAL ILLNESS.
              JOURNAL OF ABNORMAL PSYCHOLOGY, 1965,70,194-200.
              (INTERPERSONAL BEHAVIOR INVENTORY)
          ∂E-81 1965M PATIENT BEHAVIOR PERCEPTION ATTITUDE PSYCHIATRIC

F-1   FARINA, A., ARENBERG, D., & GUSKIN, S.
              A SCALE FOR MEASURING MINIMAL SOCIAL BEHAVIOR.
              JOURNAL OF CONSULTING PSYCHOLOGY, 1957, 21, 265-268.
              (MINIMAL SOCIAL BEHAVIOR SCALE)*
          ∂F-1 SOCIAL ADJUSTMENT BEHAVIOR COMPETENCE PATIENT DIAGNOSIS 1957M PSYCHIATRIC
          ∂F-1 MENTAL-ILLNESS MENTAL-HEALTH
              (APPLICATIONS: 581 1998 2039 2101 2623 2668 2694)

F-2   FARQUHAR, W. W.
             A COMPREHENSIVE STUDY OF MOTIVATIONAL FACTORS UNDERLYING THE ACHIEVEMENT OF
             ELEVENTH GRADE HIGH SCHOOL STUDENTS.
             RESEARCH PROJECT NO. 846 (8458), U. S. OFFICE OF EDUCATION, 1959.
             (PERCEIVED PARENTAL ATTITUDE INVENTORY)*
         aF-2 PARENTAL ATTITUDE DEPENDENCE PARENT-CHILD SOCIALIZATION FAMILY INTERACTION
         aF-2 ADJUSTMENT CHILD PERCEPTION 1959M PERCEIVED

F-3   FAULS, L. B., & SMITH, W. D.
             SEX-ROLE LEARNING OF FIVE-YEAR-OLDS.
             JOURNAL OF GENETIC PSYCHOLOGY, 1956, 89, 105-117.
             (MEASURE OF SEX-ROLE PREFERENCE)
         aF-3 SEX ROLE IDENTITY SELF-IDENTITY SUB-IDENTITY PERCEPTION MASCULINITY
         aF-3 FEMININITY 1956M

F-4   FELKER, D. W., & SMITH, P. G.
             THE MEASUREMENT OF PHILOSOPHIC-MINDEDNESS ON THE CRITERION OF FLEXIBILITY.
             BULLETIN OF THE SCHOOL OF EDUCATION. INDIANA UNIVERSITY, 1966, 42, PP. 138.
             (PHILOSOPHIC-MINDEDNESS SCALE)*
         aF-4 COPING-DEFENSE FLEXIBILITY TOLERANCE RIGIDITY DOGMATISM AMBIGUITY
         aF-4 ORIENTATION THINKING COGNITIVE FUNCTIONING 1966M

F-5   FIEDLER, F. E.
             LEADER ATTITUDES AND GROUP EFFECTIVENESS.
             URBANA: U. ILLINOIS PRESS, 1958.
             FIEDLER, F. E., HUTCHINS, E. B., & DODGE, J. S.
             QUASI-THERAPEUTIC RELATIONS IN SMALL COLLEGE AND MILITARY GROUPS.
             PSYCHOLOGICAL MONOGRAPHS, 1959, 73, WHOLE NO. 473.
             (MEASURE OF ASSUMED SIMILARITY)
         aF-5 SEM-DIFFERENTIAL SELF ESTEEM GLOBAL ADJUSTMENT IDENTITY EVALUATION
         aIDEAL PERCEPTION IMAGE RATING 1959M CONCEPT OTHERS
             (APPLICATIONS: 1209)

F-6   FISHER, S.
             DEPRESSIVE AFFECT AND PERCEPTION OF UP-DOWN.
             JOURNAL OF PSYCHIATRIC RESEARCH, 1964, 2, 25-30.
             (MEASURE OF PERCEPTUAL DISTORTIONS ASSOCIATED WITH DEPRESSION)
         aF-6 PERCEPTION DEPRESSION AFFECTIVE-STATES GLOBAL PSYCHIATRIC 1964M

F-7   FITTS, W. H.
             TENNESSEE (DEPARTMENT OF MENTAL HEALTH) SELF-CONCEPT SCALE: MANUAL.
             NASHVILLE, TENN.: COUNSELOR RECORDINGS AND TESTS (BOX 6184-ACKLEN STA.),
             1965.
             (TENNESSEE SELF-CONCEPT SCALE)*
         aF-7 CONCEPT IMAGE SELF ESTEEM SELF-IDENTITY EVALUATION PERCEPTION 1965M
             (APPLICATIONS: 127 1333 1530 1690 2149 2209 2523 2822 2865)

F-8   FITZGERALD, B. J.
             SOME RELATIONSHIPS AMONG PROJECTIVE TEST, INTERVIEW, AND SOCIOMETRIC
             MEASURES OF DEPENDENT BEHAVIOR.
             JOURNAL OF ABNORMAL AND SOCIAL PSYCHOLOGY, 1958, 56, 199-203.
             (METHOD OF SCORING TAT FOR DEPENDENCY CONFLICTS)
         aF-8 DEPENDENCE CONFLICT AUTONOMY TAT PROJECTIVE 1958M
             (APPLICATIONS: 129)

F-9   FORD, L. H., JR.
             A FORCED-CHOICE, ACQUIESCENCE-FREE, SOCIAL DESIRABILITY (DEFENSIVENESS)
             SCALE.
             JOURNAL OF CONSULTING PSYCHOLOGY, 1964, 28, 475.
             (FORD SOCIAL DESIRABILITY SCALE)*
         aF-9 SOCIAL DESIRABILITY DEFENSIVENESS RESPONSE-BIAS MMPI 1964M
             (APPLICATIONS: 158 448 450)

F-10   FOULDS, G. A.
             PERSONALITY AND PERSONAL ILLNESS. LONDON: TAVISTOCK, 1965.
             FOULDS, G. A.
             SOME DIFFERENCES BETWEEN NEUROTICS AND CHARACTER DISORDERS.
             BRITISH JOURNAL OF SOCIAL AND CLINICAL PSYCHOLOGY, 1967, 6, 52-59.
             FOULDS, G. A., & HOPE, K.
             MANUAL OF THE SYMPTOM SIGN INVENTORY.
             LONDON: UNIVERSITY OF LONDON PRESS, 1968.
             (SYMPTOM SIGN INVENTORY)*
         aF-10 ADJUSTMENT GLOBAL NEUROTICISM MENTAL-ILLNESS SYMPTOM 1967M DIAGNOSIS
             APPLICATIONS: 2437 2920)

F-11   FRANCK, D., & ROSEN, F.
              A PROJECTIVE TEST OF MASCULINITY-FEMININITY.
              JOURNAL OF CONSULTING PSYCHOLOGY, 1949, 13, 247-256.
              (FRANCK DRAWING COMPLETION TEST)*
           aF-11 PROJECTIVE SEX IDENTITY SELF-IDENTITY SUB-IDENTITY ROLE PERCEPTION
           aF-11 MASCULINITY FEMININITY 1949M
              (APPLICATIONS: 205   423 1101 1113 2043 2173 2346 2572 2648 2718)

F-12   FOLEY, J. M.
              CHILDREN'S RESPONSES TO FRUSTRATION: RELATIONSHIP WITH CHILD-REARING
              PRACTICES AND INFANT REACTION PATTERNS.
              UNPUBLISHED DOCTORAL DISSERTATION. NORTHWESTERN UNIVERSITY, 1962.
              (CRITICAL INCIDENTS INTERVIEW)*
           aF-12 MATERNAL PARENT-CHILD FAMILY BEHAVIOR INTERACTION ADJUSTMENT ORIENTATION
           aF-12 AFFECTION RATING

F-13   FRICKE, B. G.
              A RESPONSE BIAS (B) SCALE FOR THE MMPI.
              JOURNAL OF COUNSELING PSYCHOLOGY, 1957, 4, 149-153.
              (B SCALE: MEASURE OF MMPI RESPONSE-BIAS)
           aF-13 ACQUIESCENCE MMPI RESPONSE-BIAS CORRECTIVE-USE 1957M
              (APPLICATIONS: 1414 1626 1899)

F-14   FRIEDRICHS, R. W.
              ALTER VERSUS EGO: AN EXPLORATORY ASSESSMENT OF ALTRUISM.
              AMERICAN SOCIOLOGICAL REVIEW, 1960, 25, 496-508.
              (MEASURE OF ALTRUISM)
           aF-14 ALTRUISM AFFECTIVE-STATES OTHERS ORIENTATION 1960M SOCIAL RELATIONSHIPS
           aF-14 INTERPERSONAL
              (APPLICATIONS: 2903)

F-15   FARINA, A.
              PATTERNS OF ROLE DOMINANCE AND CONFLICT IN PARENTS OF SCHIZOPHRENIC
              PATIENTS.
              JOURNAL OF ABNORMAL AND SOCIAL PSYCHOLOGY, 1960, 61, 31-38.
              (MEASURE OF PARENTAL DOMINANCE)
           aF-15 PARENTAL AUTONOMY DOMINANCE FAMILY INTERACTION ADJUSTMENT CHILD BEHAVIOR
           aPARENT-CHILD RELATIONSHIPS 1960M
              (APPLICATIONS: 18   574 1049)

F-16   FAUCHEUX, C., & MOSCOVICI, S.
              SELF-ESTEEM AND EXPLOITATIVE BEHAVIOR IN A GAME AGAINST CHANCE AND NATURE.
              JOURNAL OF PERSONALITY AND SOCIAL PSYCHOLOGY, 1968, 8, 83-88.
              (SELF-ESTEEM SCALE)
           aF-16 SELF ESTEEM SELF-IDENTITY EVALUATION PERCEPTION MULTITRAIT SOCIAL PUBLIC
           aF-16 RATING 1968M

F-17   FEAGIN, J. R.
              PREJUDICE AND RELIGIOUS TYPES: A FOCUSED STUDY OF SOUTHERN FUNDAMENTALISTS.
              JOURNAL FOR THE SCIENTIFIC STUDY OF RELIGION, 1964, 4, 3-13.
              (MEASURE OF RELIGIOUS ORIENTATION)
           aF-17 EXTRINSIC INTRINSIC ORIENTATION RELIGION AUTONOMY MOTIVE 1964M

F-18   FISHMAN, C. G.
              NEED FOR APPROVAL AND THE EXPRESSION OF AGGRESSION UNDER VARYING CONDITIONS
              OF FRUSTRATION.
              JOURNAL OF PERSONALITY AND SOCIAL PSYCHOLOGY, 1965, 2, 809-816.
              (MEASURE OF AGGRESSION TOWARD THE EXPERIMENTER)
           aF-18 AGGRESSION HOSTILITY AFFECTIVE-STATES NEGATIVE RESENTMENT RATING
           aF-18 EXPERIMENTER 1965M

F-19   FITZGERALD, E. T.
              MEASUREMENT OF OPENNESS TO EXPERIENCE: A STUDY OF REGRESSION IN THE SERVICE
              OF THE EGO.
              JOURNAL OF PERSONALITY AND SOCIAL PSYCHOLOGY, 1966, 4, 655-663.
              (EXPERIENCE INQUIRY)*
           aF-19 OPENNESS EXPERIENCE COPING-DEFENSE FLEXIBILITY RIGIDITY DOGMATISM GLOBAL
           aTOLERANCE ADJUSTMENT 1966M
              (APPLICATIONS: 2655)

F-20   FRENCH, E. G.
              DEVELOPMENT OF A MEASURE OF COMPLEX MOTIVATION.
              IN J. W. ATKINSON (ED.) MOTIVES IN FANTASY, ACTION, AND SOCIETY. PRINCETON:
              VAN NOSTRAND, 1958.
              (FRENCH TEST OF INSIGHT)*
           aF-20 AUTONOMY NEED ACHIEVEMENT MOTIVE 1958M NURTURANCE
              (APPLICATIONS: 22   78   195   285   359   361   376   384   405   542
                               544   722   862   879   889   913   922 1164 2369)

F-21   FRICKE, B. G.
            OPINION, ATTITUDE, AND INTEREST SURVEY HANDBOOK.
            ANN ARBOR: UNIVERSITY OF MICHIGAN, EVALUATION AND EXAMINATION DIVISION,
            1963.
            (OPINION ATTITUDE AND INTEREST SURVEY)*
            (CREATIVE PERSONALITY SCALE)
        aF-21 OPINION PERSONALITY ATTITUDE INTEREST AUTONOMY MULTITRAIT CREATIVITY
        aF-21 ORIGINALITY 1963M
            (APPLICATIONS: 2281)

F-22   FELD, S. C.
            LONGITUDINAL STUDY OF THE ORIGINS OF ACHIEVEMENT STRIVINGS.
            JOURNAL OF PERSONALITY AND SOCIAL PSYCHOLOGY, 1967, 7, 408-414.
            (ADOLESCENT MATERNAL PRACTICES CHECK LIST)*
        aF-22 CHECKLIST DEPENDENCE ACHIEVEMENT MATERNAL FAMILY INTERACTION ADJUSTMENT
        aPARENT-CHILD ADOLESCENT ATTITUDE 1967M

F-23   FORD, L. H., JR., & HERSEN, M.
            NEED APPROVAL, DEFENSIVE DENIAL, AND DIRECTION OF AGGRESSION IN A FAILURE-
            FRUSTRATION SITUATION.
            JOURNAL OF PERSONALITY AND SOCIAL PSYCHOLOGY, 1967, 6, 228-232.
            (MEASURE OF DIRECTION OF AGGRESSION)
        aF-23 DIRECTION AGGRESSION AFFECTIVE-STATES RESENTMENT PUNITIVENESS
        aF-23 NEGATIVE 1967M

F-24   FRIENDLY, M. L., & GLUCKSBERG, S.
            ON THE DESCRIPTION OF SUBCULTURAL LEXICONS: A MULTIDIMENSIONAL APPROACH.
            JOURNAL OF PERSONALITY AND SOCIAL PSYCHOLOGY, 1970, 14, 55-65.
            (METHOD FOR DETERMINING DIFFERENCES IN MULTIDIMENSIONAL STRUCTURE OF TRAIT
            TERMS)
        aF-24 GROUP EXPERIENCE TRAIT-TERMS ACCULTURATION DEVELOPMENT COGNITIVE STRUCTURE
        aF-24 1970M

F-25   FARQUHAR, W. W.
            AN INTEGRATED RESEARCH ATTACK ON ACADEMIC MOTIVATION.
            JOURNAL OF COUNSELING PSYCHOLOGY, 1962, 9, 84-86.
            (PREFERRED JOB CHARACTERISTICS SCALE)*
        aF-25 MOTIVE VALUES ASPIRATION ACADEMIC JOB SELF-IDENTITY IDEALS LIFE GOALS
        aAUTONOMY NEED ACHIEVEMENT 1962M
            (APPLICATIONS: 1217)

F-26   FARBER, I. E., & GOODSTEIN, L. D.
            STUDENT ORIENTATION SURVEY.
            PRELIMINARY REPORT, PHS RESEARCH GRANT M-226. UNIVERSITY OF IOWA, IOWA
            CITY, IOWA, 1964.
            (STUDENT ORIENTATION SURVEY)*
        aF-26 ORIENTATION GOALS AUTONOMY CONFORMITY VOCATIONAL SELF-IDENTITY VALUES
        aIDEALS LIFE STUDENT ACADEMIC COLLEGE 1964M
            (APPLICATIONS: 1375)

F-27   FORD, R. N., & BORGATTA, E. F.
            JOB TYPE AND THE STRUCTURE OF SATISFACTION. (TENTATIVE TITLE)
            UNPUBLISHED MANUSCRIPT, 1969.
        FORD, R. N., & BORGATTA, E. F.
            SATISFACTION WITH THE WORK ITSELF.
            JOURNAL OF APPLIED PSYCHOLOGY, 1970, 54, 128-134.
            (MEASURE OF SATISFACTION WITH THE NATURE OF WORK)
        aF-27 1969M JOB SATISFACTION PE-FIT

F-29   FLANDERS, N. A.
            INTERACTION ANALYSIS IN THE CLASSROOM: A MANUAL FOR OBSERVERS.
            MINNEAPOLIS: COLLEGE OF EDUCATION, UNIVERSITY OF MINNESOTA, 1960.
            (SCALE OF NEED INTEGRATION)
        aF-29 NEED INTERACTION INTEGRATION STUDENT AUTONOMY TEACHER RATING
        aF-29 BEHAVIOR INTERPERSONAL 1960M

F-30   FLANAGAN, J. C., DAVIS, F. B., DAILEY, J. T., SHAYCOFT, M. F., ORR, D. B.,
        GOLDBERG, I., & NEWMAN, C. A., JR.
            THE AMERICAN HIGH SCHOOL STUDENT.
            UNITED STATES OFFICE OF EDUCATION COOPERATIVE RESEARCH BRANCH TECHNICAL
            REPORT NO. 635. PITTSBURGH: UNIVERSITY OF PITTSBURGH, 1964.
            (SOCIABILITY SCALE)
        aF-30 SOCIABILITY ADJUSTMENT SOCIAL COMPETENCE ADOLESCENT STUDENT SECONDARY
        aSCHOOL PREDICTION 1964M

F-31   FLANAGAN, J. C., DAVIS, F. B., DAILEY, J. T., SHAYCOFT, M. F., ORR, D. B.,
          GOLDBERG, I., & NEWMAN, C. A., JR.
                  THE AMERICAN HIGH SCHOOL STUDENT.
                  UNITED STATES OFFICE OF EDUCATION COOPERATIVE RESEARCH BRANCH TECHNICAL
                  REPORT NO. 635. PITTSBURGH: UNIVERSITY OF PITTSBURGH, 1964.
                  (IMPULSIVENESS SCALE)
          @F-31 IMPULSE AFFECTIVE-STATES OTHER-CATEGORY SELF EXPRESSION ADOLESCENT STUDENT
          @F-31 SECONDARY SCHOOL PREDICTION 1964M BEHAVIOR

F-32   FLANAGAN, J. C., DAVIS, F. B., DAILEY, J. T., SHAYCOFT, M. F., ORR, D. B.,
          GOLDBERG, I., & NEWMAN, C. A., JR.
                  THE AMERICAN HIGH SCHOOL STUDENT.
                  UNITED STATES OFFICE OF EDUCATION COOPERATIVE RESEARCH BRANCH TECHNICAL
                  REPORT NO. 635. PITTSBURGH: UNIVERSITY OF PITTSBURGH, 1964.
                  (LEADERSHIP SCALE)
          @F-32 LEADERSHIP ADJUSTMENT SOCIAL COMPETENCE AUTONOMY ADOLESCENT STUDENT SCHOOL
          @SECONDARY PREDICTION 1964M

F-33   FISHER, S.
                  BODY AWARENESS AND SELECTIVE MEMORY FOR BODY VERSUS NON-BODY REFERENCES.
                  JOURNAL OF PERSONALITY, 1964, 32, 138-144.
                  (BODY AWARENESS MEASURE)
          @F-33 BODY AWARENESS SELF-IDENTITY IMAGE PERCEPTION 1964M
                  (APPLICATIONS: 2298)

F-34   FULKERSON, S. C.
                  AN ACQUIESCENCE KEY FOR THE MMPI.
                  USAF SCHOOL OF AVIATION MEDICINE REPORT, 1958, NO. 58-71, 1-11.
                  (ACQUIESCENCE KEY)
          @F-34 RESPONSE-BIAS ACQUIESCENCE MMPI 1958M
                  APPLICATIONS: 190   386   757   859   1654   1807)

F-35   FREEMAN, M. J.
                  THE DEVELOPMENT OF A TEST FOR THE MEASUREMENT OF ANXIETY: A STUDY OF ITS
                  RELIABILITY AND VALIDITY.
                  PSYCHOLOGICAL MONOGRAPHS, 1953, 6 (3, WHOLE NO. 353).
                  (MEASURE OF GENERALIZED OR MANIFEST ANXIETY)
          @F-35 AFFECTIVE-STATES ANXIETY SUBJECTIVE STRESS MANIFEST NEGATIVE 1953M
                  (APPLICATIONS: 584   1856   1969)

F-37   FREEDMAN, N., ROSEN, B., ENGELHARDT, D. M., & MARGOLIS, R.
                  PREDICTION OF PSYCHIATRIC HOSPITALIZATION: I. THE MEASUREMENT OF
                  HOSPITALIZATION PRONENESS.
                  JOURNAL OF ABNORMAL PSYCHOLOGY, 1967, 72, 468-477.
                  (HOSPITALIZATION PRONENESS SCALE)*
          @F-37 HOSPITALIZATION PSYCHIATRIC GLOBAL ADJUSTMENT DIAGNOSIS MENTAL-ILLNESS
          @SOCIAL BEHAVIOR INTERACTION PROGNOSIS 1967M

F-38   FLEISHMAN, E. A.
                  LEADERSHIP CLIMATE AND SUPERVISORY BEHAVIOR.
                  COLUMBUS, OHIO: PERSONNEL RESEARCH BOARD, OHIO STATE UNIVERSITY, 1951.
          FLEISHMAN, E. A.
                  MANUAL FOR ADMINISTERING THE LEADERSHIP OPINION QUESTIONNAIRE.   CHICAGO:
                  SCIENCE RESEARCH ASSOCIATES, 1960.
                  (LEADERSHIP OPINION QUESTIONNAIRE)*
          @F-38 LEADERSHIP OPINION SUPERVISOR JOB ADJUSTMENT BEHAVIOR ROLE ORIENTATION
          @F-38 PE-FIT 1951M
                  (APPLICATIONS: 2365   2470   2478)

F-39   FOA, U. G.
                  CROSS-CULTURAL SIMILARITY AND DIFFERENCE IN INTERPERSONAL BEHAVIOR.
                  JOURNAL OF ABNORMAL AND SOCIAL PSYCHOLOGY, 1964, 68, 517-522.
                  (MEASURE OF EIGHT TYPES OF INTERPERSONAL BEHAVIOR)
          @F-39 INTERPERSONAL BEHAVIOR SOCIAL COMPETENCE ADJUSTMENT INTERACTION 1964M
                  (APPLICATIONS: 1355)

F-40   FRIEDMAN, H.
                  THE STRUCTURAL ASPECTS OF SCHIZOPHRENIC RESPONSES TO AUDITORY STIMULI.
                  JOURNAL OF GENETIC PSYCHOLOGY, 1956, 89, 221-230.
                  (TEST OF COGNITIVE INTEGRATION)
          @F-40 COGNITIVE INTEGRATION STRUCTURE DIFFERENTIATION PROJECTIVE
          @F-40 1956M FUNCTIONING THINKING

F-41   FINNEY, B. C., & VAN DALSEM, E.
            GROUP COUNSELING FOR GIFTED UNDERACHIEVING HIGH SCHOOL STUDENTS.
            JOURNAL OF COUNSELING PSYCHOLOGY, 1969, 16, 87-94.
            (STUDENT BEHAVIOR QUESTIONNAIRE)*
        aF-41 STUDENT BEHAVIOR TEACHER ATTITUDE 1969M

F-42   FENZ, W. D. & EPSTEIN, S.
            MANIFEST ANXIETY: UNIFACTORIAL OR MULTIFACTORIAL COMPOSITION?
            PERCEPTUAL AND MOTOR SKILLS, 1965, 20, 773-780.
        FENZ, W. D.
            SPECIFICITY IN SOMATIC RESPONSE TO ANXIETY.
            PERCEPTUAL AND MOTOR SKILLS, 1967, 24, 1183-1190.
            (EPSTEIN-FENZ MANIFEST ANXIETY SCALE)*
        aF-42 AFFECTIVE-STATES ANXIETY SUBJECTIVE STRESS FEAR AUTONOMIC INFERIORITY
        aF-42 NEGATIVE 1967M
            (APPLICATIONS: 2399)

F-43   FONTANA, A. F., KLEIN, E. B., LEWIS, E., & LEVINE, L.
            PRESENTATION OF SELF IN MENTAL ILLNESS.
            JOURNAL OF CONSULTING AND CLINICAL PSYCHOLOGY, 1968, 32, 110-119.
            (MEASURE OF PRESENTATION OF SELF AS HEALTHY-UNHEALTHY)
        aF-43 SELF GLOBAL ADJUSTMENT COMPETENCE PERCEPTION NEED SOCIAL APPROVAL
        aDESIRABILITY MENTAL-HEALTH MENTAL-ILLNESS 1968M
            (APPLICATIONS: 2266)

F-44   FONTANA, A. F., & GESSNER, T.
            PATIENTS' GOALS AND THE MANIFESTATION OF PSYCHOPATHOLOGY.
            JOURNAL OF CONSULTING AND CLINICAL PSYCHOLOGY, 1969, 33, 247-253.
            (ADEQUACY-RESPONSIBILITY SCALE)
        aF-44 APPROVAL IMPRESSION MANAGEMENT PERCEPTION SELF-IDENTITY EVALUATION SELF
        aEXPRESSION RESPONSIBILITY SOCIAL COMPETENCE ADJUSTMENT ESTEEM 1969M

F-45   FINNEY, B. C.
            A SCALE TO MEASURE INTERPERSONAL RELATIONSHIPS IN GROUP PSYCHOTHERAPY.
            GROUP PSYCHOTHERAPY, 1954, 7, 52-66.
            (PALO ALTO GROUP THERAPY SCALE)*
        aF-45 ADJUSTMENT THERAPY INTERPERSONAL RELATIONSHIPS COMPETENCE OTHER-CATEGORY
        aSOCIAL BEHAVIOR INTERACTION 1954M GROUP
            (APPLICATIONS: 617   657 2297 2417)

F-46   FOA, U. G.
            A TEST OF THE FOREMAN-WORKER RELATIONSHIP.
            PERSONNEL PSYCHOLOGY, 1956, 9, 469-486.
            (TEST OF FOREMAN-WORKER RELATIONSHIP)
        aF-46 INTERPERSONAL RELATIONSHIPS JOB ADJUSTMENT AFFECTIVE-STATES OTHERS
        aSUPERVISOR INTERACTION EMPLOYEE 1956M LEADERSHIP ORIENTATION

F-47   FILE, Q. W., & REMMERS, H. H.
            HOW SUPERVISE?
            NEW YORK: PSYCHOLOGICAL CORPORATION, 1948.
            (HOW SUPERVISE? SCALE)*
        aF-47 BEHAVIOR TRAIT PREDICTION SUPERVISOR SUCCESS JOB ADJUSTMENT
        aF-47 1948M LEADERSHIP

F-48   FIEDLER, F. E.
            A CONTINGENCY MODEL OF LEADERSHIP EFFECTIVENESS.
            IN L. BERKOWITZ (ED.), ADVANCES IN EXPERIMENTAL SOCIAL PSYCHOLOGY. NEW
            YORK: ACADEMIC PRESS, 1964.
            (MEASURE OF THE LEADER'S ESTEEM FOR LEAST PREFERRED CO-WORKER)
        aF-48 LEADERSHIP STYLE PUBLIC ESTEEM JOB SUPERVISOR INTERPERSONAL INTERACTION
        aF-48 EMPLOYEE 1964M
            (APPLICATIONS: 76   284 2322 2365 2478 2480 2813 2819)

F-49   FUNKENSTEIN, D. H., KING, S. H., & DROLETTE, M. E.
            MASTERY OF STRESS.
            CAMBRIDGE, MASSACUSSETTS: HARVARD UNIVERSITY PRESS, 1957.
            (MEASURE OF PERCEPTION OF PARENTAL ROLES)
        aF-49 ADJUSTMENT FAMILY INTERACTION PERCEPTION PARENT-CHILD PARENTAL ROLE
        aAUTHORITY AFFECTION CHILD 1957M PERCEIVED

F-50   FIEDLER, F. E.
              LEADER ATTITUDES AND GROUP EFFECTIVENESS.
              URBANA: UNIVERSITY OF ILLINOIS PRESS, 1958.
              (ASSUMED DISSIMILARITY BETWEEN OPPOSITES TEST)*
          aF-50 MULTITRAIT JOB ADJUSTMENT INTERACTION PERCEPTION INTERPERSONAL BEHAVIOR
          aAFFECTIVE-STATES RESENTMENT GLOBAL NEGATIVE ATTITUDE SEM-DIFFERENTIAL 1958M
              (APPLICATIONS: 42   180   408   2478)

F-51   FERGUSON, L. W.
              A REVISION OF THE PRIMARY SOCIAL ATTITUDE SCALES.
              JOURNAL OF PSYCHOLOGY, 1944, 17, 229-241.
              (PRIMARY SOCIAL ATTITUDES SCALES)
          aF-51 INTERPERSONAL FUNCTIONING ADJUSTMENT SOCIAL COMPETENCE ATTITUDE RELIGION
          aF-51 NATIONALISM 1944M

F-52   FULGOSI, A., & GUILFORD, J. P.
              FLUCTUATION OF AMBIGUOUS FIGURES AND INTELLECTUAL FLEXIBILITY.
              AMERICAN JOURNAL OF PSYCHOLOGY, 1966, 79, 602-607.
              (HIDDEN FIGURES TEST)*
          aF-52 FIGURE AUTONOMY FLEXIBILITY FIELD DEPENDENCE COGNITIVE STRUCTURE
          aF-52 1966M PERCEPTION

F-53   FULGOSI, A., & GUILFORD, J. P.
              FLUCTUATION OF AMBIGUOUS FIGURES AND INTELLECTUAL FLEXIBILITY.
              AMERICAN JOURNAL OF PSYCHOLOGY, 1966, 79, 602-607.
              (MEASURE OF DIVERGENT PRODUCTION OF FIGURAL CLASSES.)
          aF-53 DIFFERENTIATION INTELLECTUAL FLEXIBILITY AUTONOMY CREATIVITY COGNITIVE
          aSTRUCTURE COMPLEXITY FIGURE 1966M PERCEPTION FUNCTIONING

F-54   FRENCH, J. W.
              COMPARATIVE PREDICTION OF COLLEGE MAJOR-FIELD GRADES BY PURE-FACTOR
              APTITUDE, INTEREST, AND PERSONALITY MEASURES.
              EDUCATIONAL AND PSYCHOLOGICAL MEASUREMENT, 1963, 23, 767-774.
              (12 MULTITRAIT PERSONALITY SCALES)
          aF-54 SELF CONFIDENCE SOCIABILITY ORIENTATION MULTITRAIT AUTONOMY DOMINANCE
          aTOLERANCE SOCIAL COMPETENCE ADJUSTMENT AFFECTIVE-STATES EMOTION 1963M

F-55   FREDERIKSEN, N., & MESSICK, S.
              RESPONSE SET AS A MEASURE OF PERSONALITY.
              EDUCATIONAL AND PSYCHOLOGICAL MEASUREMENT, 1959, 19, 137-157.
              (SCALE OF ACQUIESCENCE RESPONSE SET)
          aF-55 RESPONSE-BIAS RESPONSE SET ACQUIESCENCE 1959M

F-56   FRENCH, J. W., EKSTROM, R. B., & PRICE, L. A.
              KIT OF REFERENCE TESTS FOR COGNITIVE FACTORS.
              PRINCETON, N. J.: EDUCATIONAL TESTING SERVICE, 1963.
              (CF-1 HIDDEN FIGURES TEST)*
          aF-56 AUTONOMY FIELD DEPENDENCE PERCEPTION COGNITIVE STRUCTURE FIGURE 1963M
              (APPLICATIONS: 520   2531)

F-57   FOWLER, R. D., JR., COYLE, F. A., JR., REED, P. C., & WHITE, C. A.
              THE MMPI MEASUREMENT OF PHENOTYPIC ANXIETY: I. EXPLORATORY STUDY.
              JOURNAL OF PSYCHOLOGY, 1968, 68, 305-312.
              (PHENOTYPIC ANXIETY SCALE)
          aF-57 STATE SITUATIONAL ANXIETY AFFECTIVE-STATES SUBJECTIVE STRESS MMPI
          aF-57 NEGATIVE 1968M

F-58   FLANDERS, N. A.
              INTERACTION ANALYSIS IN THE CLASSROOM: A MANUAL FOR OBSERVERS.
              MINNEAPOLIS: COLLEGE OF EDUCATION, UNIVERSITY OF MINNESOTA, 1960.
              (SCALE OF NEED DOMINANCE)
          aF-58 NEED AUTONOMY DOMINANCE SUBMISSION INTERACTION STUDENT TEACHER
          aF-58 BEHAVIOR INTERPERSONAL 1960M

F-59   FESHBACH, N. D., & BEIGEL, A.
              A NOTE ON THE USE OF THE SEMANTIC DIFFERENTIAL IN MEASURING TEACHER
              PERSONALITY AND VALUES.
              EDUCATIONAL AND PSYCHOLOGICAL MEASUREMENT, 1968, 28, 923-929.
              (SEMANTIC DIFFERENTIAL FOR SELF, IDEAL SELF, IDEAL CHILD)
          aF-59 TEACHER CHILD SEM-DIFFERENTIAL SELF-IDENTITY SELF IDEAL IMAGE PERCEPTION
          aF-59 CONCEPT MULTITRAIT VALUES 1968M

F-60   FIEDLER, F. E.
              A THEORY OF LEADERSHIP EFFECTIVENESS.
              NEW YORK: MCGRAW-HILL, 1967.
              (MEASURE OF BEHAVIOR AND OPINION OF INDIVIDUAL TEAM MEMBERS)
          aF-60 1967M GROUP BEHAVIOR LEADERSHIP STYLE ORIENTATION
              (APPLICATIONS: 2365)

F-61   FLEISHMAN, E. A.
              THE DESCRIPTION OF SUPERVISORY BEHAVIOR.
              JOURNAL OF APPLIED PSYCHOLOGY, 1953, 36, 1-6.
          FLEISHMAN, E. A.
              A LEADER BEHAVIOR DESCRIPTION FOR INDUSTRY. IN LEADER BEHAVIOR: ITS
              DESCRIPTION AND MEASUREMENT, STOGDILL, R. M., & COONS, A. F. (EDS.)
              COLUMBUS, OHIO: BUREAU OF BUSINESS RESEARCH, OHIO STATE UNIVERSITY, 1957.
              (SUPERVISORY BEHAVIOR DESCRIPTION)*
          aF-61 JOB BEHAVIOR SUPERVISOR LEADERSHIP 1953M MORALE EMPLOYEE RELATIONSHIPS
          aF-61 MANAGEMENT
              (APPLICATIONS: 2473)

F-62   FERREIRA, A. J., & WINTER, W. D.
              FAMILY INTERACTION AND DECISION MAKING.
              ARCHIVES OF GENERAL PSYCHIATRY, 1965, 13, 214-223.
              ("UNREVEALED DIFFERENCES" TECHNIQUE: MEASURE OF FAMILY INTERACTION)
          aF-62 1965M FAMILY INTERACTION RELATIONSHIPS

F-63   FIEDLER, F. E.
              LEADER ATTITUDES, GROUP CLIMATE, AND GROUP CREATIVITY.
              JOURNAL OF ABNORMAL AND SOCIAL PSYCHOLOGY, 1962, 65, 308-318.
              (GROUP ATMOSPHERE SCALE)
          aF-63 1962M GROUP SITUATIONAL ENVIRONMENT EVALUATION ATTITUDE SATISFACTION
          aINTERACTION
              (APPLICATIONS: 2808)

F-64   FLANAGAN, J. C., DAILEY, J. T., SHAYCOFT, M. F., GORHAM, W. A., ORR, D. B., &
          GOLDBERG, I.
              DESIGN FOR A STUDY OF AMERICAN YOUTH.
              BOSTON: HOUGHTON MIFFLIN, 1962.
              (PROJECT TALENT INTEREST INVENTORY)*
          aF-64 1962M ACTIVITIES JOB PREFERENCE INTEREST
              (APPLICATIONS: 2759)

F-65   FREEBERG, N. E.
              ASSESSMENT OF DISADVANTAGED ADOLESCENTS: A DIFFERENT APPROACH TO
              RESEARCH AND EVALUATION MEASURES.
              JOURNAL OF EDUCATIONAL PSYCHOLOGY, 1970, 61, 229-240.
              (VOCATIONAL ASPIRATION MEASURE)
          aF-65 1970M VOCATIONAL ASPIRATION JOB STATUS ADOLESCENT

F-66   FREEBERG, N. E.
              ASSESSMENT OF DISADVANTAGED ADOLESCENTS: A DIFFERENT APPROACH TO
              RESEARCH AND EVALUATION MEASURES.
              JOURNAL OF EDUCATIONAL PSYCHOLOGY, 1970, 61, 229-240.
              (VOCATIONAL PLANS SCALE)
          aF-66 1970M VOCATIONAL PLANNING JOB STATUS ADOLESCENT

F-67   FREEBERG, N. E.
              ASSESSMENT OF DISADVANTAGED ADOLESCENTS: A DIFFERENT APPROACH TO
              RESEARCH AND EVALUATION MEASURES.
              JOURNAL OF EDUCATIONAL PSYCHOLOGY, 1970, 61, 229-240.
              (MEASURE OF INTEREST IN VOCATIONAL TASKS)
          aF-67 1970M VOCATIONAL INTEREST JOB ADOLESCENT

F-68   FREEBERG, N. E.
              ASSESSMENT OF DISADVANTAGED ADOLESCENTS: A DIFFERENT APPROACH TO
              RESEARCH AND EVALUATION MEASURES.
              JOURNAL OF EDUCATIONAL PSYCHOLOGY, 1970, 61, 229-240.
              (MEASURE OF ATTITUDE TOWARDS AUTHORITY)
          aF-68 1970M ATTITUDE AUTHORITY ADOLESCENT

F-69   FREEBERG, N. E.
              ASSESSMENT OF DISADVANTAGED ADOLESCENTS: A DIFFERENT APPROACH TO
              RESEARCH AND EVALUATION MEASURES.
              JOURNAL OF EDUCATIONAL PSYCHOLOGY, 1970, 61, 229-240.
              (MEASURE OF SELF-ESTEEM)
          aF-69 1970M SELF-ESTEEM ADOLESCENT SOCIAL COMPETENCE ACTION ENVIRONMENT

F-70   FISH, J. M.
                EMPATHY AND THE REPORTED EMOTIONAL EXPERIENCES OF BEGINNING
                PSYCHOTHERAPISTS.
                JOURNAL OF CONSULTING AND CLINICAL PSYCHOLOGY, 1970, 35, 64-69.
                (MEASURE OF EMPATHIC STYLE OF EMOTIONAL SELF-REPORT)
            aF-70 1970M EMPATHY THERAPY COUNSELING SELF EMOTION THERAPIST

F-71   FISCHER, E. H., & TURNER, J. LEB.
                ORIENTATION TO SEEKING PROFESSIONAL HELP: DEVELOPMENT AND RESEARCH
                UTILITY OF AN ATTITUDE SCALE.
                JOURNAL OF CONSULTING AND CLINICAL PSYCHOLOGY, 1970, 35, 79-90.
                (ATTITUDES TOWARD SEEKING PROFESSIONAL PSYCHOLOGICAL HELP SCALE)
            aF-71 ORIENTATION 1970M ATTITUDE OPINION BELIEF MENTAL-ILLNESS THERAPY
            aF-71 PSYCHIATRIC COUNSELING PATIENT

F-72   FRENCH, J. W., EKSTROM, R. B., & PRICE, L. A.
                KIT OF REFERENCE TESTS FOR COGNITIVE FACTORS. (REVISED EDITION).
                PRINCETON, N.J.: EDUCATIONAL TESTING SERVICE, 1963.
                (MEASURE OF SPONTANEOUS FLEXIBILITY)
            aF-72 1963M FLEXIBILITY OPENNESS SPONTANEITY CHANGE COGNITIVE FUNCTIONING
                (APPLICATIONS: 520)

F-74   FRIEDMAN, C. J., JOHNSON, C. A., & FODE, K.
                SUBJECTS' DESCRIPTIONS OF SELECTED TAT CARDS VIA THE SEMANTIC DIFFERENTIAL.
                JOURNAL OF CONSULTING PSYCHOLOGY, 1964, 28, 317-325.
                (MEASURE OF STIMULUS PROPERTIES FOR TAT)
            aF-74 1964M TAT SEM-DIFFERENTIAL STIMULUS IMAGERY

F-75   FISHER, S., & CLEVELAND, S. E.
                BODY RANGE AND PERSONALITY.
                PRINCETON: VAN NOSTRAND, 1958.
                (PENETRATION SCORE)
            aF-75 1958M BODY IMAGE PROJECTIVE SECURITY PHYSICAL ANXIETY FEAR
                (APPLICATIONS: 425   857   1016   1579   1697   1764   1834   2233   2298)

F-76   FEFFER, M. H.
                THE COGNITIVE IMPLICATIONS CF ROLE-TAKING BEHAVIOR.
                JOURNAL OF PERSONALITY, 1959, 27, 152-168.
                (ROLE TAKING TASK)*
            aF-76 1959M ROLE ENACTMENT PRESTIGE IMAGE CONSISTENCY
            aF-76 COGNITIVE FANTASY IMAGINATION EMPATHY
                (APPLICATIONS: 570   2194)

F-77   FELDMAN, M. J., & CORAH, N. L.
                SOCIAL DESIRABILITY AND THE FORCED CHOICE METHOD.
                JOURNAL OF CONSULTING PSYCHOLOGY, 1960, 24, 480-482.
                (MEASURE OF EFFICACY OF FORCED-CHOICE FORMAT IN CONTROLLING SOCIAL
                DESIRABILITY)
            aF-77 1960M SOCIAL DESIRABILITY RESPONSE-BIAS
                (APPLICATIONS: 438)

F-78   FRANCHER, R. E., JR.
                EXPLICIT PERSONALTIY THEORIES AND ACCURACY IN PERSON PERCEPTION.
                JOURNAL OF PERSONALITY, 1966, 34, 252-261.
                (JUDGMENT OF PERSON PERCEPTION TEST)
            aF-78 1966M JUDGMENT PERSON PERCEPTION BEHAVIOR SITUATIONAL

F-79   FAIRWEATHER, G. W., SIMON, R., GEBHARD, M. E., WEINGARTEN, E., HOLLAND, J. L.,
            SANDERS, R., STONE, G. B., & REAHL, J. E.
                RELATIVE EFFECTIVENESS OF PSYCHOTHERAPEUTIC PROGRAMS: A MULTICRITERIA
                COMPARISON FOR FOUR PROGRAMS FOR THREE DIFFERENT PATIENT GROUPS.
                PSYCHOLOGICAL MONOGRAPHS, 1960, 74 (5, WHOLE NO. 492).
                (MEASURE OF EFFECTIVENESS CF PSYCHOTHERAPEUTIC PROGRAMS)
            aF-79 1960M PSYCHOPATHOLOGY THERAPY EVALUATION INTERPERSONAL RELATIONSHIPS
            aF-79 BEHAVIOR SOCIAL COMMUNICATION

F-80   FELDMAN, M. J.
                A PROGNOSTIC SCALE FOR SHOCK THERAPY.
                PSYCHOLOGICAL MONOGRAPHS, 1951, 65, (10, WHOLE NO. 327).
                (MEASURE OF PROGNOSIS FOR SHOCK THERAPY)
            PRINT 1473...
            aF-80 1951M MMPI PROGNOSIS PSYCHIATRIC THERAPY· SUCCESS
                (APPLICATIONS: 1654)

F-81   FIEDLER, F. E.
            THE CONCEPT OF AN IDEAL THERAPEUTIC RELATIONSHIP.
            JOURNAL OF CONSULTING PSYCHOLOGY, 1950, 14, 239-245.
            (IDEAL THERAPEUTIC RELATIONSHIP Q-SORT)
        aF-81 1950M IDEAL THERAPY COUNSELING RELATIONSHIPS Q-SORT PATIENT STATUS
        aF-81 BEHAVIOR
            (APPLICATIONS: 29   1628)

F-82   FOULDS, G. A., & CAINE, T. M.
            PSYCHONEUROTIC SYMPTOM CLUSTERS, TRAIT CLUSTERS AND PSYCHOLOGICAL TESTS.
            JOURNAL OF MENTAL SCIENCE, 1958, 104 ,722-731.
            (MEASURE OF HYSTERICAL/OBSESSOID COMPONENT)
        aF-82 1958M PERSONALITY TYPOLOGY RATING PSYCHIATRIC BEHAVIOR
        aF-82 DIAGNOSIS
            (APPLICATIONS: 1776)

F-83   FESHBACH, S.
            THE DRIVE-REDUCING FUNCTION OF FANTASY BEHAVIOR.
            JOURNAL OF ABNORMAL AND SOCIAL PSYCHOLOGY, 1955, 50, 3-11.
            (QUESTIONNAIRE TO EVALUATE THE EFFECTIVENESS OF AN EXPERIMENTAL
            AGGRESSION MANIPULATION)
        aF-83 1955M AGGRESSION HOSTILITY EXPRESSION EXPERIMENTER INFLUENCE
            (APPLICATIONS: 204   536   693)

F-84   FRANK, J. D., GLIEDMAN, L. H., IMBER, S. D., NASH, E. H., JR., & STONE, A. R.
            WHY PATIENTS LEAVE PSYCHOTHERAPY.
            A. M. A. ARCHIVES OF NEUROLOGY AND PSYCHIATRY, 1957, 77, 283-299.
            (SYMPTOM DISTRESS SCALE)
        aF-84 1957M SYMPTOM PSYCHIATRIC DEPRESSION MENTAL-ILLNESS PATIENT
            (APPLICATIONS: 2081)

F-85   FANCHER, R. E.
            EXPLICIT PERSONALITY THEORIES AND ACCURACY IN PERSON PERCEPTION.
            JOURNAL OF PERSONALITY, 1966, 34, 252-261.
            (MEASURE OF ACCURACY AND VALIDITY IN PERSON PERCEPTION)
        aF-85 1966M PERSON PERCEPTION PREDICTION CONCEPTUAL LIFE HISTORY
            (APPLICATIONS: 2083)

F-86   FOULDS, G. A., CAINE, J. M., & CREASY, M. A.
            ASPECTS OF EXTRA- AND INTROPUNITIVE EXPRESSION IN MENTAL ILLNESS.
            JOURNAL OF MENTAL SCIENCE, 1960, 106, 599-610.
            (HOSTILITY BATTERY)
        aF-86 1960M HOSTILITY PUNITIVENESS MENTAL-ILLNESS EXPRESSION
        aF-86 DIAGNOSIS
            (APPLICATIONS   2302)

F-87   FIELD, P. B.
            AN INVENTORY SCALE OF HYPNOTIC DEPTH.
            INTERNATIONAL JOURNAL OF CLINICAL AND EXPERIMENTAL HYPNOSIS, 1965, 13, 238-
            249.
            (HYPNOSIS INVENTORY)
        aF-87 1965M HYPNOTIC SUGGESTIBILITY
            (APPLICATIONS: 2196)

F-88   FOULKES, D., SPEAR, P. S., & SYMONDS, J. D.
            INDIVIDUAL DIFFERENCES IN MENTAL ACTIVITY AT SLEEP ONSET.
            JOURNAL OF ABNORMAL PSYCHOLOGY, 1966, 71, 280-286.
            (DREAMLIKE FANTASY SCALE)
        aF-88 1966M FANTASY IMAGINATION PRIMARY-PROCESS THINKING
            (APPLICATIONS: 2163)

F-89   FOULKES, D., SPEAR, P. S., & SYMONDS, J. D.
            INDIVIDUAL DIFFERENCES IN MENTAL ACTIVITY AT SLEEP ONSET.
            JOURNAL OF ABNORMAL PSYCHOLOGY, 1966, 71, 280-286.
            (PICTURE-STORY TEST)
        aF-89 1966M GRAPHIC FANTASY IMAGINATION
            (APPLICATIONS: 2163)

F-90   FREEMAN, H. E., & SIMMONS, D. G.
            THE MENTAL PATIENT COMES HOME.
            NEW YORK: WILEY, 1963.
            (QUESTIONNAIRE MEASURE OF SOCIAL ADJUSTMENT)
        aF-90 1963M ADJUSTMENT SOCIAL COMPETENCE MENTAL-ILLNESS PATIENT

F-92   FRAMO, J. L., OSTERWEIL, J., & BOSZORMENYI-NAGI, I.
                A RELATIONSHIP BETWEEN THREAT IN THE MANIFEST CONTENT OF DREAMS AND ACTIVE-
                PASSIVE BEHAVIOR IN PSYCHOTICS.
                JOURNAL OF ABNORMAL AND SOCIAL PSYCHOLOGY, 1962, 65, 41-47.
                (DREAM THREAT SCALE)*
            aF-92 1962M PRIMARY-PROCESS THINKING FANTASY IMAGINATION ANXIETY TENSION
            aF-92 MANIFEST

F-93   FRIJDA, N. H., & PHILIPSZOON, E.
                DIMENSIONS OF RECOGNITION OF EXPRESSION.
                JOURNAL OF ABNORMAL AND SOCIAL PSYCHOLOGY, 1963, 66, 45-51.
                (MEASURE OF PERCEIVED FACIAL EXPRESSIONS IN PHOTOGRAPHS)
            aF-93 1963M GRAPHIC EXPRESSION FUGURE RATING PERCEIVED

F-95   FOSTER, R. J.
                ACQUIESCENT RESPONSE SET AS A MEASURE OF ACQUIESCENCE.
                JOURNAL OF ABNORMAL AND SOCIAL PSYCHOLOGY, 1961, 63, 155-160.
                (APHORISM QUESTIONNAIRE FOR ACQUIESCENCE)
            aF-95 1961M RESPONSE-BIAS ACQUIESCENCE
            aF-95 SUBMISSIVE CONFORMITY

F-96   FISHBEIN, M., & RAVEN, B. H.
                AN OPERATIONAL DISTINCTION BETWEEN BELIEF AND ATTITUDE.
                TECHNICAL REPORT NO. 2, 1959, UNIVERSITY OF CALIFORNIA, LOS ANGELES,
                CONTRACT NONR 233(54).
                (AB SCALES TO MEASURE BELIEF IN EXTRASENSORY PERCEPTION)
            aF-96 1959M PERCEPTION COMMUNICATION BELIEF
                (APPLICATIONS: 694   776   940   1403)

F-97   FIEDLER, F. E., & MEUWESE, W. A. T.
                LEADER'S CONTRIBUTION TO TASK PERFORMANCE IN COHESIVE AND UNCOHESIVE
                GROUPS.
                JOURNAL OF ABNORMAL AND SOCIAL PSYCHOLOGY, 1963, 67, 83-87.
                (TAT MEASURE OF CREATIVITY)
            @F-97 1963M TAT IMAGERY AUTONOMY CREATIVITY ORIGINALITY PROJECTIVE

F-98   FRENCH, E. G., & LESSER, G. S.
                SOME CHARACTERISTICS OF THE ACHIEVEMENT MOTIVE IN WOMEN.
                JOURNAL OF ABNORMAL AND SOCIAL PSYCHOLOGY, 1964, 68, 119-128.
                (STUDENT ATTITUDE SCALE)
            @F-98 1964M STUDENT ATTITUDE INTELLECTUAL VALUES FEMINITY SEX ROLE

F-99   FORSYTH, R. P.
                MMPI AND DEMOGRAPHIC CORRELATES OF POST-HOSPITAL ADJUSTMENT IN
                NEUROPSYCHIATRIC PATIENTS.
                (DOCTORAL DISSERTATION, UNIVERSITY OF NORTH CAROLINA.)
                ANN ARBOR, MICH.: UNIVERSITY MICROFILMS, 1960, NO. 378-756F 735M.
                (RECOVERY SCALE)
            aF-99 1960M MMPI PSYCHIATRIC MENTAL-ILLNESS ADJUSTMENT MALADJUSTMENT
                (APPLICATIONS: 959)

F-100   FARNHAM-DIGGORY, S.
                SELF-EVALUATION AND SUBJECTIVE LIFE EXPECTANCY AMONG SUICIDAL AND
                NONSUICIDAL PSYCHOTIC MALES.
                JOURNAL OF ABNORMAL AND SOCIAL PSYCHOLOGY, 1964, 69, 628-634.
                (SELF-EVALUATION QUESTIONNAIRE)
            aF-100 1964M SELF-IDENTITY SELF EVALUATION SELF CONCEPT ATTITUDE ACHIEVEMENT

F-102   FONG, S. L. M.
                ASSIMILATION OF CHINESE IN AMERICA: CHANGES IN ORIENTATION AND SOCIAL
                PERCEPTION.
                AMERICAN JOURNAL OF SOCIOLOGY, 1965, 71, 265-273.
                (PERSONAL DATA FORM)*
            aF-102 1965M PERSONAL LIFE HISTORY
                (APPLICATIONS: 1137)

F-103   FULLAN, M.
              INDUSTRIAL TECHNOLOGY AND WORKER INTEGRATION IN THE ORGANIZATION.
              AMERICAN SOCIOLOGICAL REVIEW, 1970, 35, 1028-1039.
              (WORKER INTEGRATION QUESTIONNAIRE)
          ƏF-103 1970M INTEGRATION JOB ADJUSTMENT PERCEPTION EMPLOYEE RELATIONSHIPS
          ƏF-103 VOCATIONAL INTEREST SATISFACTION

F-104   FORGUS, R. H., & DEWOLFE, A. S.
              PERCEPTUAL SELECTIVITY IN HALLUCINATORY SCHIZOPHRENICS.
              JOURNAL OF ABNORMAL PSYCHOLOGY, 1969, 74, 288-292.
              (METHOD FOR CATEGORIZING HALLUCINATION THEMES)
          ƏF-104 1969M FANTASY PERCEPTION DISTORTION PSYCHIATRIC PATIENT HALLUCINATION

F-105   FELDMAN, M. J., & HERSEN, M.
              ATTITUDES TOWARDS DEATH IN NIGHTMARE SUBJECTS.
              JOURNAL OF ABNORMAL PSYCHOLOGY, 1967, 72, 421-425.
              (DEATH SCALE)
          ƏF-105 1967M DEATH MORTALITY ATTITUDE

F-106   FERGUSON, L. W.
              AN INDEX OF SELF-ALLOCATION ON A COLD-WARM PERSONALITY DIMENSION.
              PERCEPTUAL AND MOTOR SKILLS, 1970, 30, 787-793.
              (SELF-RATING OF COLDNESS/WARMTH IN PERSONALITY)
          ƏF-106 1970M SELF RATING POSITIVE NEGATIVE TRAITS PERSONALITY

F-107   FITCH, G.
              EFFECTS OF SELF-ESTEEM, PERCEIVED PERFORMANCE, AND CHOICE ON CAUSAL
              ATTRIBUTIONS.
              JOURNAL OF PERSONALITY AND SOCIAL PSYCHOLOGY, 1970, 16, 311-315.
              (MEASURE OF INTERNAL-EXTERNAL CAUSAL ATTRIBUTION)
          ƏF-107 1970M IE-CONTROL LOCUS CONTROL ATTRIBUTION RESPONSIBILITY

F-108   FRIEDMAN, C. J., SIBINGA, M. S., STEISEL, I. M., & SINNAMON, H. M.
              SENSORY RESTRICTION AND ISOLATION EXPERIENCES IN CHILDREN WITH
              PHENYLKETONURIA.
              JOURNAL OF ABNORMAL PSYCHOLOGY, 1968, 73, 294-303.
              (MEASURE OF CHILD'S INTERACTIVE EFFORTS)
          ƏF-1C8 1968M INTERACTION CHILD BEHAVIOR NEED AFFILIATION

F-109   FAZIO, A. F.
              BEHAVIORAL AND OVERT-BEHAVIORAL ASSESSMENT OF A SPECIFIC FEAR.
              JOURNAL OF CONSULTING AND CLINICAL PSYCHOLOGY, 1969, 33, 705-709.
              (OVERT BEHAVIORAL ANXIETY TEST)
          ƏF-109 1969M BEHAVIOR FEAR ANXIETY STIMULUS MANIFEST
              (APPLICATIONS: 2429)

F-110   FAZIO, A. F.
              TREATMENT COMPONENTS IN IMPLOSIVE THERAPY.
              JOURNAL OF ABNORMAL PSYCHOLOGY, 1970, 76, 211-219.
              (INVENTORY OF REPORTED FEARS)
          ƏF-110 1970M FEAR SITUATIONAL BEHAVIOR RATING SELF STIMULUS ANXIETY
              (APPLICATIONS: 2429)

F-111   FURNEAUX, W. D., & GIBSON, H. B.
              THE NEW JUNIOR MAUDSLEY INVENTORY, MANUAL.
              LONDON: UNIVERSITY OF LONDON PRESS, 1966.
              (NEW JUNIOR MAUDSLEY INVENTORY)*
          ƏF-111 1966M PERSONALITY CHILD EXTRAVERSION NEUROTICISM INVENTORY E-7R
              (APPLICATIONS: 2643)

F-112   FREEMAN, H. E., & KASSEBAUM, G. E.
              RELATIONSHIP OF EDUCATION AND KNOWLEDGE TO OPINIONS ABOUT MENTAL ILLNESS.
              MENTAL HYGIENE, 1960, 44, 43-47.
              (MEASURE OF PUBLIC ATTITUDE TO MENTAL DISORDER)
          ƏF-112 1960M MENTAL-ILLNESS DEVIANCE ATTITUDE PUBLIC BEHAVIOR
          ƏPSYCHIATRIC DISABILITY
              (APPLICATIONS: 2559)

F-113   FORD, L. H., JR., & RUBIN, B. M.
              A SOCIAL DESIRABILITY QUESTIONNAIRE FOR YOUNG CHILDREN.
              JOURNAL OF CONSULTING AND CLINICAL PSYCHOLOGY, 1970, 35, 195-204.
              (YOUNG CHILDREN'S SOCIAL DESIRABILITY SCALE)*
          ƏF-113 1970M SOCIAL DESIRABILITY CHILD MMPI RESPONSE-BIAS

F-114   FLANDERS, N. A.
                INTERACTION ANALYSIS IN THE CLASSROOM: A MANUAL FOR OBSERVERS.
                UNPUBLISHED MANUSCRIPT, UNIVERSITY OF MICHIGAN, 1960.
                (VERBAL INTERACTION ANALYSIS SCALE)*
           ∂F-114 1960M VERBAL INTERACTION SCHOOL STUDENT TEACHER INTERPERSONAL
                (APPLICATIONS: 1535)

F-115   FRIEDMAN, H.
                PERCEPTUAL REGRESSION IN SCHIZOPHRENIA: AN HYPOTHESIS SUGGESTED BY THE USE
                OF THE RORSCHACH TEST.
                JOURNAL OF GENETIC PSYCHOLOGY, 1952, 81, 63-98.
                (RORSCHACH SCORED FOR W (WHOLE) RESPONSES)
           ∂F-115 1952M RORSCHACH PERCEPTION ORGANIZATION COGNITIVE FUNCTIONING

F-116   FAGAN, J., & BREED, G.
                A GOOD, SHORT MEASURE OF RELIGIOUS DOGMATISM.
                PSYCHOLOGICAL REPORTS, 1970, 26, 533-534.
                (RELIGIOUS DOGMATISM MEASURE)
           ∂F-116 1970 DOGMATISM AUTHORITARIANISM ATTITUDE PEOPLE RELIGION CONVICTION
           ∂BELIEF ORIENTATION CONSERVATISM

F-117   FARQUHAR, W. W.
                A COMPREHENSIVE STUDY OF THE MOTIVATIONAL FACTORS UNDERLYING
                ACHIEVEMENT OF ELEVENTH GRADE HIGH SCHOOL STUDENTS.
                OFFICE OF RESEARCH AND PUBLICATIONS, MICHIGAN STATE UNIVERSITY, 1963.
                (HUMAN TRAIT INVENTORY)*
           ∂F-117 1963M TRAIT ACADEMIC ACHIEVEMENT MOTIVE STUDENT INVENTORY
           ∂ADOLESCENT PERSONALITY

F-118   FROELICH, H. P.
                FACTOR ANALYSIS OF AN ENGINEERING ATTITUDE SURVEY.
                UNPUBLISHED MASTER'S THESIS, IOWA STATE UNIVERSITY, 1958.
                (MEASURE OF JOB ATTITUDE)
           ∂F-118 1958M JOB SATISFACTION ATTITUDE EMPLOYEE HAPPINESS
                (APPLICATIONS: 1183)

F-119   FLORENCE, E. DE C.
                MOTIVATIONAL FACTORS IN INDIVIDUAL AND GROUP PRODUCTIVITY. II. VALIDATION
                AND STANDARDIZATION OF THE STUDENT BEHAVIOR DESCRIPTION.
                COLUMBUS: THE OHIO STATE UNIVERSITY RESEARCH FOUNDATION, 1956.
                (STUDENT BEHAVIOR DESCRIPTION)*
           ∂F-119 1956M STUDENT BEHAVIOR COLLEGE GOALS LEADERSHIP ACHIEVEMENT SELF
           ∂ADJUSTMENT SOCIAL ACCEPTANCE CONFORMITY MORAL
                (APPLICATIONS: 1209)

F-120   FRETZ, B. R.
                POSTURAL MOVEMENTS IN A COUNSELING DYAD.
                JOURNAL OF COUNSELING PSYCHOLOGY, 1966, 13, 335-343.
                (MEASURE OF THERAPIST CHARISMA)
           ∂F-120 1966M THERAPY COUNSELING RELATIONSHIPS BELIEF CONVICTION FEELING
           ∂IMPRESSION FORMATION

F-121   FERGUSON, J. T., MCREYNOLDS, P., & BALLACHY, E. L.
                HOSPITAL ADJUSTMENT SCALE.
                PALO ALTO, CALIF.: STANFORD UNIVERSITY, 1953.
                (HOSPITAL ADJUSTMENT SCALE)*
           ∂F-121 1953M HOSPITALIZATION ADJUSTMENT WARD BEHAVIOR RATING PSYCHIATRIC
           ∂MENTAL-ILLNESS

F-122   FRIEDMAN, H.
                PERCEPTUAL REGRESSION IN SCHIZOPHRENIA: AN HYPOTHESIS SUGGESTED BY
                THE USE OF THE RORSCHACH TEST.
                JOURNAL OF PROJECTIVE TECHNIQUES, 1953, 17, 171-185.
           BECKER, W. C.
                A GENETIC APPROACH TO THE INTERPRETATION AND EVALUATION OF THE
                PROCESS-REACTIVE DISTINCTION IN SCHIZOPHRENIA.
                JOURNAL OF ABNORMAL AND SOCIAL PSYCHOLOGY, 1956, 53, 229-236.
                (RORSCHACH GENETIC-LEVEL SCALE)
           ∂F-122 1953M RORSCHACH PROJECTIVE MATURITY SCHIZOPHRENIA DIAGNOSIS PSYCHIATRIC
                (APPLICATIONS: 1719)

F-123   FORBES, G. B., & MITCHELL, S.
             ATTRIBUTION OF BLAME, FEELINGS OF ANGER, AND DIRECTION OF AGGRESSION IN
             RESPONSE TO INTERRACIAL FRUSTRATION AMONG POVERTY-LEVEL FEMALE NEGRO
             ADULTS.
             JOURNAL OF SOCIAL PSYCHOLOGY, 1971, 83, 73-78.
             (MEASURE OF REACTIONS TO INTERRACIAL FRUSTRATION)
         aF-123 1971M RACIAL ETHNIC MINORITY NEGRO ATTITUDE HOSTILITY FRUSTRATION
         aPREJUDICE BELIEF DIFFERENCES PROBLEM AGGRESSION EXPRESSION ATTRIBUTION
         aRESPONSIBILITY GUILT

F-126   FEATHER, N. T.
             PERSISTENCE IN RELATION TO ACHIEVEMENT MOTIVATION, ANXIETY ABOUT FAILURE,
             AND TASK DIFFICULTY.
             PAPER READ AT MIDWESTERN PSYCHOLOGICAL ASSOCIATION, CHICAGO, MAY 1960.
             (PERCEPTUAL REASONING)
         aF-126 1960M PERCEPTION FRUSTRATION
             (APPLICATIONS: 20)

F-127   FULKERSON, S. C.
             ADAPTABILITY SCREENING OF FLYING PERSONNEL: RESEARCH ON THE MINNESOTA
             MULTIPHASIC PERSONALITY INVENTORY.
             USAF SCHOOL OF AVIATION MEDICAL REPORT, 1957, NO. 57-106.
             (ADJUSTMENT KEY FOR MMPI)
         aF-127 1957M MMPI ADJUSTMENT MENTAL-HEALTH MENTAL-ILLNESS GLOBAL
             (APPLICATIONS: 1654)

F-128   FITTING, E. A.
             EVALUATION OF ADJUSTMENT TO BLINDNESS.
             NEW YORK: AMERICAN FOUNDATION FOR THE BLIND, 1953.
             (ATTITUDES TOWARD BLINDNESS SCALE)
         aF-128 1953M ATTITUDE DISABILITY PHYSICAL
             (APPLICATIONS: 1656)

F-129   FARQUHAR, W. W.
             THE MICHIGAN STATE M SCALES.
             EAST LANSING: MICHIGAN STATE UNIVERSITY OF AGRICULTURE AND APPLIED
             SCIENCE, 1961. (MIMEO.)
             (MICHIGAN M SCALES)
         aF-129 1961M MOTIVE INCENTIVE DRIVE
             (APPLICATIONS: 1402)

F-131   FOSTER, R. J., & GRIGG, A. E.
             ACQUIESCENT RESPONSE SET AS A MEASURE OF ACQUIESCENCE: FURTHER EVIDENCE.
             JOURNAL OF ABNORMAL AND SOCIAL PSYCHOLOGY, 1963, 67, 304-306.
             (ACTIVITIES SCALE)
         aF-131 1963M ACQUIESCENCE RESPONSE-BIAS ACTIVITIES

F-132   FORER, B. R.
             THE FALLACY OF PERSONAL VALIDATION: A CLASSROOM DEMONSTRATION OF
             GULLIBILITY.
             JOURNAL OF ABNORMAL AND SOCIAL PSYCHOLOGY, 1949, 44, 118-123.
             (MEASURE OF GULLIBILITY SCALE)
         aF-132 1949M DECEPTIVENESS PERSONAL RESPONSE-BIAS FAKING PERSUASIBILITY
         aSUGGESTIBILITY

F-133   FISKE, D. W., & GOODMAN, G.
             THE POSTTHERAPY PERIOD.
             JOURNAL OF ABNORMAL PSYCHOLOGY, 1965, 70, 169-179.
             (BEHAVIORAL ADEQUACY SCALES)*
         aF-133 1965M BEHAVIOR CHECKLIST CHANGE COUNSELING THERAPY PATIENT

F-135   FISHER, S., & CLEVELAND, S. E.
             BODY IMAGE AND PERSONALITY.
             PRINCETON, N. J.: VAN NOSTRAND, 1958.
             (BARRIER INDEX)*
         aF-135 1958M RORSCHACH PROJECTIVE BODY IMAGE

F-136   FARINA, A., GARMEZY, N., ZALUSKY, M., & BECKER, J.
             PREMORBID BEHAVIOR AND PROGNOSIS IN FEMALE SCHIZOPHRENIC PATIENTS.
             JOURNAL OF CONSULTING PSYCHOLOGY, 1962, 26, 56-60.
             (REVISED PHILLIPS PREMORBID SCALE)
         aF-136 1962M P-32R SCHIZOPHRENIA RATING PROGNOSIS
             (APPLICATIONS: 1042 1045 1113 1149)

F-137   FARBEROW, N. L., & DEVRIES, A. G.
               AN ITEM DIFFERENTIATION ANALYSIS OF MMPIS OF SUICIDAL NEUROPSYCHIATRIC
               HOSPITAL PATIENTS.
               PSYCHOLOGICAL REPORTS, 1967, 20, 601-617.
               (SUICIDE THREAT SCALE)
           ƏF-137 1967M SUICIDE DEPRESSION MMPI MENTAL-ILLNESS PSYCHIATRIC PATIENT
           ƏPREDICTION
               (APPLICATIONS: 2288 2299)

F-138   FISHER, S.
               BODY REACTIVITY GRADIENTS AND FIGURE DRAWING VARIABLES.
               JOURNAL OF CONSULTING PSYCHOLOGY, 1959, 23, 54-59.
               (BODY IMAGE SCALE FOR DRAW-A-PERSON TEST)
           ƏF-138 1959M BODY IMAGE FIGURE GRAPHIC PROJECTIVE
               (APPLICATIONS: 1701)

F-140   FOREMAN, M. E.
               SOME EMPIRICAL CORRELATES OF PSYCHOLOGICAL HEALTH.
               JOURNAL OF COUNSELING PSYCHOLOGY, 1966, 13, 3-11.
               (ACTIVITIES PARTICIPATION QUESTIONNAIRE)
           ƏF-140 1966M ACTIVITIES PARTICIPATION

F-141   FOREMAN, M. E.
               SOME EMPIRICAL CORRELATES OF PSYCHOLOGICAL HEALTH.
               JOURNAL OF COUNSELING PSYCHOLOGY, 1966, 13, 3-11.
               (MEASURE OF SPONTANEITY BY REFLEX-RESERVE METHOD)
           ƏF-141 1966M SPONTANEITY FLEXIBILITY BEHAVIOR

F-142   FRANKFURT, L. P.
               THE ROLE OF SOME INDIVIDUAL AND INTERPERSONAL FACTORS ON THE
               ACQUAINTANCE PROCESS.
               UNPUBLISHED DOCTORAL DISSERTATION, AMERICAN UNIVERSITY, 1965.
               (PROBING SCALE)
           ƏF-142 1965M SELF DISCLOSURE
               (APPLICATIONS: 91)

F-143   FARBER, B.
               AN INDEX OF MARITAL INTEGRATION.
               SOCIOMETRY, 1957, 20, 117-134.
               (INDEX OF MARITAL INTEGRATION)
           ƏF-143 1957M MARITAL RELATIONSHIPS INTEGRATION ROLE COMPATIBILITY
               (APPLICATIONS: 2449)

F-144   FRANK, G. H., & SWEETLAND, A.
               A STUDY OF THE PROCESS OF PSYCHOTHERAPY: THE VERBAL INTERACTION.
               JOURNAL OF CONSULTING PSYCHOLOGY, 1962, 26, 135-138.
               (MODIFIED SNYDER CATEGORIZATION OF CLIENT-THERAPIST VERBAL INTERACTION)
           ƏF-144 1962M PATIENT THERAPY RELATIONSHIPS STYLE INTERACTION ACCEPTANCE APPROVAL
               (APPLICATIONS: 2091)

F-145   FARD, A. B.
               SEX ROLE AND SELF CONCEPT.
               UNPUBLISHED DOCTORAL DISSERTATION, CORNELL UNIVERSITY, 1955.
               (FEMININE ROLE RATING INVENTORY)*
           ƏF-145 1955M FEMININITY ROLE CONCEPT SEX IDENTIFICATION

F-146   FITZGERALD, B. J.
               SOME RELATIONSHIPS AMONG PROJECTIVE TEST, INTERVIEW, AND SOCIOMETRIC
               MEASURES OF DEPENDENT BEHAVIOR.
               JOURNAL OF APPLIED SOCIAL PSYCHOLOGY, 1958,56,199-203.
               (SOCIOMETRIC MEASURE OF DEPENDENT BEHAVIOR)
           ƏF-146 1958M DEPENDENCE BEHAVIOR SOCIOMETRIC PEER RATING NEED AUTONOMY
           ƏINTERPERSONAL SOCIAL

F-147   FITZGERALD, B. J.
               SOME RELATIONSHIPS AMONG PROJECTIVE TEST, INTERVIEW, AND SOCIOMETRIC
               MEASURES OF DEPENDENT BEHAVIOR.
               JOURNAL OF APPLIED SOCIAL PSYCHOLOGY, 1958, 56, 199-203.
               (INTERVIEW MEASURE: DEPENDENT BEHAVIOR, N. DEP., AND FREEDOM OF MOVEMENT
               TOWARD DEPENDENCE)
           ƏF-147 1958M DEPENDENCE BEHAVIOR NEED INTERPERSONAL SOCIAL INTERVIEW AUTONOMY

G-1   GAGE, N. L., LEAVITT, G. S., & STONE, G. C.
            THE PSYCHOLOGICAL MEANING OF ACQUIESCENCE SET FOR AUTHORITARIANISM.
            JOURNAL OF ABNORMAL AND SOCIAL PSYCHOLOGY, 1957, 55, 98-103.
            (INFORMATION TRUE TEST)*
        aG-1 ACQUIESCENCE RESPONSE-BIAS 1957M
            (APPLICATIONS: 190   682)

G-2   GEIS, L., CHRISTIE, R., & NELSON, C.
            ON MACHIAVELLIANISM.
            UNPUBLISHED MANUSCRIPT, COLUMBIA UNIVERSITY, 1963.
            (MACH V SCALE)*
        aG-2 AUTONOMY DOMINANCE MACHIAVELLIANISM COPING-DEFENSE STYLE OTHER-CATEGORY
        aINTERPERSONAL RELATIONSHIPS 1963M OTHERS
            (APPLICATIONS: 2149)

G-3   GERGEN, K. J., & MORSE, S. J.
            SELF-CONSISTENCY: MEASUREMENT AND VALIDATION.
            PROCEEDINGS OF THE 75TH ANNUAL CONVENTION OF THE AMERICAN PSYCHOLOGICAL
            ASSOCIATION, 1967, 207-208.
            (MEASURE OF SELF-CONSISTENCY)
        aG-3 SELF CONSISTENCY PERCEPTION ADJUSTMENT SELF-IDENTITY EVALUATION ESTEEM
        aDESCRIPTION 1967M

G-4   GERSHON, E. S., CROMER, M., & KLERMAN, G. L.
            HOSTILITY AND DEPRESSION.
            PSYCHIATRY, 1968, 31, 224-235.
            (DEPRESSIVE SYMPTOM SCALE)*
        aG-4 AFFECTIVE-STATES GLOBAL NEGATIVE DEPRESSION MOOD RATING GUILT HOPE SYMPTOM
        aG-4 PSYCHIATRIC 1968M DIAGNOSIS MENTAL-ILLNESS

G-5   GARDNER, R. W., HOLTZMAN, P. S., KLEIN, G. S., LINTON, H. B., & SPENCE, D. P.
            COGNITIVE CONTROL: A STUDY OF INDIVIDUAL CONSISTENCIES IN COGNITIVE
            BEHAVIOR.
            PSYCHOLOGICAL ISSUES, 1959, 1, NO. 4.
            (FREE ASSOCIATION TEST)
        aG-5 1959M CREATIVITY AUTONOMY COGNITIVE CONTROL FUNCTIONING
            (APPLICATIONS: 2485)

G-6   GLESER, G. C., GOTTSCHALK, L. A., & SPRINGER, K. J.
            AN ANXIETY SCALE APPLICABLE TO VERBAL SAMPLES.
            ARCHIVES OF GENERAL PSYCHIATRY, 1961, 5, 103-115.
            (MEASURE OF ANXIETY THROUGH VERBAL CONTENT ANALYSIS)
        aG-6 ANXIETY SUBJECTIVE AFFECTIVE-STATES STRESS NEGATIVE 1961M PROJECTIVE
            (APPLICATIONS: 2141   2198)

G-7   GOLD, S., DELEON, P., & SWENSEN, C.
            BEHAVIORAL VALIDATION OF A DOMINANCE-SUBMISSION SCALE.
            PSYCHOLOGICAL REPORTS, 1966, 19, 735-739.
            (DOMINANCE-SUBMISSION SCALE)
        aG-7 DOMINANCE AUTONOMY SUBMISSION MMPI 1966M

G-8   GOLDBERG, L. R.
            DIAGNOSTICIANS VS. DIAGNOSTIC SIGNS. THE DIAGNOSIS OF PSYCHOSIS VS.
            NEUROSIS FROM THE MMPI.
            PSYCHOLOGICAL MONOGRAPHS, 1965, 79 (9, WHOLE NO. 602).
            (MEASURE OF PSYCHOTIC TENDENCY)
        aG-8 MENTAL-ILLNESS EGO-STRENGTH DIAGNOSIS THERAPY STYLE HISTORY COPING-DEFENSE
        aG-8 EGO-RESILIENCY MMPI NEUROTICISM PSYCHIATRIC 1965M

G-9   GORDON, J. E., & SMITH, E.
            CHILDREN'S AGGRESSION, PARENTAL ATTITUDES, AND THE EFFECTS OF AN
            AFFILIATION-AROUSING STORY.
            JOURNAL OF PERSONALITY AND SOCIAL PSYCHOLOGY, 1965, 1, 654-659.
            (PERMISSIBLE AGGRESSION SCALE)
        aG-9 PARENT-CHILD PARENTAL ATTITUDE STRICTNESS AGGRESSION FAMILY INTERACTION
        aADJUSTMENT MATERNAL 1965M

G-10   GOLDSTEIN, M. J.
                THE RELATIONSHIP BETWEEN COPING AND AVOIDING BEHAVIOR AND ATTITUDE
                MODIFICATION.
                UNPUBLISHED DOCTORAL DISSERTATION, UNIVERSITY OF WASHINGTON, 1957.
            MAINORD, W. A.
                EXPERIMENTAL REPRESSION RELATED TO COPING AND AVOIDANCE BEHAVIORS IN THE
                RECALL AND RELEARNING OF NONSENSE SYLLABLES.
                UNPUBLISHED DOCTORAL DISSERTATION, UNIVERSITY OF WASHINGTON, 1956.
                (MEASURE OF COPING-AVOIDANCE TRAITS)
            aG-10 COPING-DEFENSE COPING AVOIDANCE APPROACH BEHAVIOR TRAIT 1957M
                (APPLICATIONS: 1015 1661 2511)

G-11   GORDON, L. V.
                WORK ENVIRONMENT PREFERENCE SCHEDULE - WEPS. ALBANY: AUTHOR, 1968.
            GORDON, L. V.
                MEASUREMENT OF BUREAUCRATIC ORIENTATION.
                PERSONNEL PSYCHOLOGY, 1970, 23, 1-11.
                (WORK ENVIRONMENT PREFERENCE SCHEDULE)*
            aG-11 NEED ENVIRONMENT PE-FIT JOB SATISFACTION AFFECTIVE-STATES GLOBAL
            aG-11 ADJUSTMENT PREFERENCE 1968M
                (APPLICATIONS: 2475 2591)

G-12   GORDON, L. V.
                MANUAL, GORDON PERSONAL INVENTORY.
                YONKERS, NEW YORK: WORLD BOOK, 1956.
            GORDON, L. V.
                REVISED MANUAL FOR THE GORDON PERSONAL INVENTORY.
                NEW YORK: HARCOURT, BRACE & WORLD, 1963.
                (GORDON PERSONAL INVENTORY)*
            aG-12 MULTITRAIT THINKING ORIGINALITY INTERPERSONAL RELATIONSHIPS SOCIAL
            a1956M
                (APPLICATIONS: 306 1817 2495 2602)

G-13   GORDON, L. V.
                SRA MANUAL FOR SURVEY OF INTERPERSONAL VALUES.
                CHICAGO: SCIENCE RESEARCH ASSOCIATES, 1960.
                (SURVEY OF INTERPERSONAL VALUES)*
            aG-13 OTHERS SOCIAL ALTRUISM VALUES ORIENTATION ADJUSTMENT DEPENDENCE AUTONOMY
            aSUPPORT CONFORMITY SELF-IDENTITY IDEALS LIFE GOALS INTERPERSONAL LEADERSHIP
            aG-13 1960M
                (APPLICATIONS: 1233 1494 2367 2476 2589 2829 2838)

G-14   GORDON, L. V.
                MANUAL, SURVEY OF PERSONAL VALUES.
                CHICAGO: SCIENCE RESEARCH ASSOCIATES, 1967.
                (SURVEY OF PERSONAL VALUES)*
            aG-14 MULTITRAIT ORIENTATION SELF-IDENTITY IDEALS VALUES LIFE GOALS ACHIEVEMENT
            aORDER NEED PERSONAL 1967M DEVELOPMENT

G-15   GORDON, E. M., & SARASON, S. B.
                THE RELATIONSHIP BETWEEN "TEST ANXIETY" AND "OTHER ANXIETIES."
                JOURNAL OF PERSONALITY, 1955, 13, 317-323.
                (GENERALIZED ANXIETY SCALE)
            aG-15 ANXIETY SUBJECTIVE STRESS AFFECTIVE-STATES NEGATIVE 1955M

G-16   GOTTSCHALK, L. A., GLESER, G. C., & SPRINGER, K. J.
                THREE HOSTILITY SCALES APPLICABLE TO VERBAL SAMPLES.
                ARCHIVES OF GENERAL PSYCHIATRY, 1963, 9, 254-279.
                (MEASURE OF HOSTILITY THROUGH VERBAL CONTENT ANALYSIS)
            aG-16 HOSTILITY DIRECTION AFFECTIVE-STATES RESENTMENT NEGATIVE 1963M PROJECTIVE
            aG-16 CONTENT-ANALYSIS

G-17   GIEBINK, J. W., STOVER, D. O., & FAHL, M. A.
                TEACHING ADAPTIVE RESPONSES TO FRUSTRATION TO EMOTIONALLY DISTURBED BOYS.
                JOURNAL OF CONSULTING AND CLINICAL PSYCHOLOGY, 1968, 32, 366-368.
                (FRUSTRATION QUESTIONNAIRE)
            aG-17 COPING COPING-DEFENSE ADJUSTMENT ADAPTABILITY PE-FIT FRUSTRATION
            aSITUATIONAL ADOLESCENT DELINQUENCY 1968M

G-18   GOUGH, H. G.
                STUDIES OF SOCIAL INTOLERANCE: II. A PERSONALITY SCALE FOR ANTI-SEMITISM.
                JOURNAL OF SOCIAL PSYCHOLOGY, 1951, 33, 247-255.
                (PREJUDICE SCALE)
            aG-18 AUTHORITARIANISM COPING-DEFENSE OTHER-CATEGORY MMPI PREJUDICE RACIAL
            aG-18 MINORITY GROUP ETHNIC SOCIAL DISTANCE 1951M
                (APPLICATIONS: 709   821 1191 1587 2140 2824)

G-19   GOUGH, H. G., MCCLOSKY, H., & MEEHL, P.
             A PERSONALITY SCALE OF DOMINANCE.
             JOURNAL OF ABNORMAL AND SOCIAL PSYCHOLOGY, 1951, 46, 360-366.
             (DOMINANCE SCALE)
          aG-19 DOMINANCE SUBMISSION AUTONOMY 1951M
             (APPLICATIONS: 521   653   743   950   1191   1334   1899   1932   2312) *

G-20   GOUGH, H. G.
             IDENTIFYING PSYCHOLOGICAL FEMININITY.
             EDUCATIONAL AND PSYCHOLOGICAL MEASUREMENT, 1952, 12, 427-439.
             (SCALE OF PSYCHOLOGICAL FEMININITY)*
          aG-20 SEX ROLE IDENTITY SELF SELF-IDENTITY SUB-IDENTITY PERCEPTION FEMININITY
          aG-20 1952M
             (APPLICATIONS: 97   205   413   423   430   506   527   1683   1987   2043
                              2173   2312   2346   2463   2467   2718   2815)

G-21   GOUGH, H. G.
             THE ADJECTIVE CHECKLIST AS A PERSONALITY ASSESSMENT RESEARCH TECHNIQUE.
             PSYCHOLOGICAL REPORTS, 1960, 6, 107-122.
          GOUGH, H. G., & HEILBRUN, A. B., JR.
             THE ADJECTIVE CHECK LIST MANUAL.
             PALO ALTO, CALIFORNIA: CONSULTING PSYCHOLOGISTS PRESS, 1965.
             (ADJECTIVE CHECK LIST)*
          aG-21 CHECKLIST NEED TRAIT-TERMS AUTONOMY OTHER-CATEGORY MULTITRAIT 1960M
             (APPLICATIONS: 29   128   141   213   342   378   419   430   443   456
                               481   482   507   537   538   669   801   967   970   996
                              1034   1071   1073   1116   1165   1192   1220   1237   1290   1309
                              1343   1523   1565   1669   1715   1733   1778   1800   1807   1866
                              1985   2026   2054   2091   2099   2134   2142   2155   2170   2188
                              2197   2206   2247   2311   2336   2450   2483   2528   2553   2555
                              2568   2573   2601   2641   2651   2655   2726   2734   2738   2755
                              2804   2902   2924   2925   2978)

G-22   GOUGH, H. G.
             THE CALIFORNIA PSYCHOLOGICAL INVENTORY.
             PALO ALTO, CALIFORNIA: CONSULTING PSYCHOLOGISTS PRESS, 1957.
             (CALIFORNIA PSYCHOLOGICAL INVENTORY)*
          aG-22 MULTITRAIT AUTONOMY SELF-IDENTITY ADJUSTMENT COPING-DEFENSE
          aG-22 AFFECTIVE-STATES 1957M
             (APPLICATIONS: 109   139   141   148   271   285   378   430   472   495
                               498   507   538   653   691   711   719   838   859   863
                               866   891   933   944   967   970   996   1004   1055   1063
                              1101   1109   1113   1137   1152   1165   1166   1185   1192   1202
                              1211   1219   1237   1272   1279   1291   1299   1307   1334   1387
                              1402   1421   1443   1446   1448   1461   1475   1492   1500   1519
                              1544   1559   1593   1599   1671   1728   1732   1755   1783   1798
                              1800   1839   1855   1881   1930   1933   1948   2020   2022   2031
                              2049   2134   2139   2163   2205   2216   2219   2228   2246   2247
                              2253   2254   2295   2336   2422   2451   2517   2555   2572   2628
                              2647   2657   2692   2697   2778   2872   2874   2912   2924   2949)

G-23   GRAY, S. W.
             MASCULINITY-FEMININITY IN RELATION TO ANXIETY AND SOCIAL ACCEPTANCE.
             CHILD DEVELOPMENT, 1957, 28, 203-214.
             (PEER RATINGS OF MASCULINITY-FEMININITY)
          aG-23 SEX ROLE IDENTITY SELF-IDENTITY SUB-IDENTITY PERCEPTION MASCULINITY PEER
          aFEMININITY RATING CHILD 1957M

G-24   GREEN, R. F., & NOWLIS, V. A.
             A FACTOR ANALYTIC STUDY OF THE DOMAIN OF MOOD WITH INDEPENDENT VALIDATION
             OF THE FACTORS.
             AMERICAN PSYCHOLOGIST, 1957, 12, 438. (ABSTRACT)
             (GREEN AND NOWLIS MOOD SCALE)
          aG-24 MOOD STATE AFFECTIVE-STATES OTHER-CATEGORY 1957M EMOTION
             (APPLICATIONS: 71)

G-25   GREEN, R. T., & STACEY, B.
             THE DEVELOPMENT OF A QUESTIONNAIRE MEASURE OF HOSTILITY AND AGGRESSION.
             ACTA PSYCHOLOGICA, 1967, 26, 265-285.
             (MEASURE OF HOSTILITY AND AGGRESSION)
          aG-25 HOSTILITY AGGRESSION AFFECTIVE-STATES RESENTMENT NEGATIVE 1967M

G-26   GUILFORD, J. P., & ZIMMERMAN, W. S.
             THE GUILFORD-ZIMMERMAN TEMPERAMENT SURVEY: MANUAL OF INSTRUCTIONS AND
             INTERPRETATIONS.
             BEVERLY HILLS, CALIFORNIA: SHERIDAN SUPPLY CO., 1949.
             (GUILFORD-ZIMMERMAN TEMPERAMENT SURVEY)*
         aG-26 TEMPERAMENT MULTITRAIT AUTONOMY SELF-IDENTITY ADJUSTMENT 1949M
             (APPLICATIONS: 16   37   120   227   250   363   429   576   648   658
                              664   726   958   1104   1168   1215   1251   1306   1347   1492
                             1557   1573   1595   1614   1637   1766   1800   1825   1832   2119
                             2281   2398   2470   2514   2580   2582   2674   2852   2912   2980)

G-27   GUNDERSON, E. K. E., & ARTHUR, R. J.
             A BRIEF MENTAL HEALTH INDEX.
             JOURNAL OF ABNORMAL PSYCHOLOGY, 1969, 74, 100-104.
             (BRIEF MENTAL HEALTH INDEX)*
         aG-27 MENTAL-HEALTH GLOBAL ADJUSTMENT MENTAL-ILLNESS DIAGNOSIS 1969M PROGNOSIS

G-28   GUEVARA, C. I.
             THE EFFECTS OF SUCCESS AND FAILURE EXPERIENCES ON SCHIZOPHRENICS' RATE OF
             LEARNING UNDER CONDITIONS OF HIGH AND LOW EXPECTANCY OF SUCCESS.
             UNPUBLISHED DOCTORAL DISSERTATION, STANFORD UNIVERSITY, 1965.
         MCREYNOLDS, P., & GUEVARA, C. I.
             ATTITUDES OF SCHIZOPHRENICS AND NORMALS TOWARD SUCCESS AND FAILURE.
             JOURNAL OF ABNORMAL PSYCHOLOGY, 1967, 72, 303-310.
             (SUCCESS-FAILURE INVENTORY)*
         aG-28 HOPE SUCCESS FEAR FAILURE COPING-DEFENSE APPROACH AVOIDANCE ORIENTATION
         aG-28 SCHIZOPHRENIA 1965M
             (APPLICATIONS: 1043   2925)

G-30   GLESER, G. C., & IHILEVICH, D.
             AN OBJECTIVE INSTRUMENT FOR MEASURING DEFENSE MECHANISMS.
             JOURNAL OF CONSULTING AND CLINICAL PSYCHOLOGY, 1969, 33, 51-60.
             (DEFENSE MECHANISM INVENTORY)*
         aG-30 ADJUSTMENT COPING-DEFENSE GLOBAL STYLE HISTORY DEPENDENCE MASCULINITY
         aFEMININITY AUTHORITY DEFENSE 1969M
             (APPLICATIONS: 2313)

G-31   GILBERT, D. C., & LEVINSON, D. J.
             IDEOLOGY, PERSONALITY, AND INSTITUTIONAL POLICY IN THE MENTAL HOSPITAL.
             JOURNAL OF ABNORMAL AND SOCIAL PSYCHOLOGY, 1956, 53, 263-271.
             (CUSTODIAL MENTAL ILLNESS IDEOLOGY SCALE)*
         aG-31 ADJUSTMENT MENTAL-ILLNESS IDEOLOGY AFFECTIVE-STATES OTHER-CATEGORY
         a HOSPITALIZATION PATIENT ATTITUDE PREJUDICE 1956M WARD
             (APPLICATIONS: 169   613   1314   2153   2613)

G-32   GOLDSTEIN, M. J., JONES, R. B., & KINDER, M. I.
             A METHOD FOR THE EXPERIMENTAL ANALYSIS OF PSYCHOLOGICAL DEFENSES THROUGH
             PERCEPTION.
             JOURNAL OF PSYCHIATRIC RESEARCH, 1964, 2, 135-146.
             (PERCEPTUAL DEFENSE BATTERY)
         aG-32 COPING STYLE COPING-DEFENSE GLOBAL PERCEPTION AVOIDANCE SENSITIZATION
         aG-32 DEFENSE 1964M
             (APPLICATIONS: 58)

G-33   GOODENOUGH, D. R., & EAGLE, C. J.
             A MODIFICATION OF THE EMBEDDED-FIGURES TEST FOR USE WITH YOUNG CHILDREN.
             JOURNAL OF GENETIC PSYCHOLOGY, 1963, 103, 67-74.
             (CHILDREN'S EMBEDDED FIGURES TEST)*
         aG-33 FIELD DEPENDENCE FIGURE AUTONOMY PERCEPTION COGNITIVE STRUCTURE STYLE
         aCHILD 1963M
             (APPLICATIONS: 23   181   673)

G-34   GORDON, J. E., & SMITH, E.
             CHILDREN'S AGGRESSION, PARENTAL ATTITUDES, AND THE EFFECTS OF AN
             AFFILIATION-AROUSING STORY.
             JOURNAL OF PERSONALITY AND SOCIAL PSYCHOLOGY, 1965, 1, 654-659.
             (GENERAL STRICTNESS SCALE)
         aG-34 PARENT-CHILD PARENTAL ATTITUDE STRICTNESS AGGRESSION FAMILY INTERACTION
         aADJUSTMENT MATERNAL 1965M

G-35   GOTTS, E. E., & PHILLIPS, B. N.
               THE RELATION BETWEEN PSYCHOMETRIC MEASURES OF ANXIETY AND MASCULINITY-
               FEMININITY.
               JOURNAL OF SCHOOL PSYCHOLOGY, 1968, 6, 123-130.
               (PUPIL PERCEPTIONS TEST)*
           aG-35 ELEMENTARY SCHOOL STUDENT SOCIAL COMPETENCE MASCULINITY FEMININITY FAMILY
           aG-35 INTERACTION ADJUSTMENT SELF-IDENTITY SELF PERCEPTION EVALUATION ESTEEM
           aG-35 SUB-IDENTITY 1968M SEX ROLE IDENTITY

G-36   GOUGH, H. G., MCCLOSKY, H., & MEEHL, P. E.
               A PERSONALITY SCALE FOR SOCIAL RESPONSIBILITY.
               JOURNAL OF ABNORMAL AND SOCIAL PSYCHOLOGY, 1952, 47, 73-80.
               (MEASURE OF SOCIAL RESPONSIBILITY)
           aG-36 ADOLESCENT PEER SOCIAL RESPONSIBILITY VALUES IDEALS ADJUSTMENT
           aG-36 OTHER-CATEGORY 1952M
               (APPLICATIONS: 653   738   1191   1282   1899   2312)

G-37   GRINKER, R. R., SR., MILLER, J., SABSHIN, M., NUNN, R., & NUNNALLY, J. C.
               THE PHENOMENA OF DEPRESSION.
               NEW YORK: HOEBER, 1961.
               (CHECKLIST MEASURE OF DEPRESSION)
           aG-37 AFFECTIVE-STATES DEPRESSION NEGATIVE MOOD CHECKLIST 1961M

G-38   GROSS, L.
               A BELIEF PATTERN SCALE FOR MEASURING ATTITUDES TOWARD ROMANTICISM.
               AMERICAN SOCIOLOGICAL REVIEW, 1944, 9, 463-472.
               (BELIEF PATTERN SCALE FOR ROMANTICISM)
           aG-38 ATTITUDE ROMANTICISM BELIEF ORIENTATION LIFE GOALS IDEALS VALUES
           aG-38 SELF-IDENTITY 1944M

G-39   GUILFORD, J. P.
               AN INVENTORY OF FACTORS STDCR.
               BEVERLY HILLS, CALIFORNIA: SHERIDAN SUPPLY COMPANY, 1940.
               (INVENTORY OF FACTORS STDCR)
           aG-39 POSITIVE AFFECTIVE-STATES ADJUSTMENT GLOBAL MULTITRAIT INTROVERSION SOCIAL
           aEXTRAVERSION DEPRESSION THINKING STYLE 1940M
               (APPLICATIONS: 190   549   593   649   664   666   785   1704   1748   2059)

G-40   GUILFORD, J. P., & MARTIN, H. G.
               GUILFORD-MARTIN INVENTORY OF FACTORS GAMIN: MANUAL.
               BEVERLY HILLS, CALIFORNIA: SHERIDAN SUPPLY, 1948.
               (GUILFORD-MARTIN INVENTORY OF FACTORS: GAMIN)*
           aG-40 ACTIVITY NERVOUSNESS SELF-IDENTITY NEED COMPATIBILITY ASCENDENCE
           aG-40 MASCULINITY FEMININITY INFERIORITY MULTITRAIT SUBMISSION AUTONOMY IDENTITY
           aG-40 ESTEEM ADJUSTMENT SUB-IDENTITY 1948
               (APPLICATIONS: 77   190   1262   1975   2128   2213   2807)

G-41   GEER, J. H.
               DEVELOPMENT OF A SCALE TO MEASURE FEAR.
               BEHAVIOR RESEARCH AND THERAPY, 1965, 3, 45-53.
               (FEAR SURVEY SCHEDULE II)*
           aG-41 AFFECTIVE-STATES FEAR NEGATIVE 1965M
               (APPLICATIONS: 172   989   999   2383   2616   2736   2737)

G-42   GOLDRICH, J. M.
               A STUDY IN TIME ORIENTATION: THE RELATION BETWEEN MEMORY FOR PAST
               EXPERIENCE AND ORIENTATION TO THE FUTURE.
               JOURNAL OF PERSONALITY AND SOCIAL PSYCHOLOGY, 1967, 6, 216-221.
               (MEASURES OF TEMPORAL ORIENTATION)
           aG-42 TIME ORIENTATION AFFECTIVE-STATES FUTURE 1967M

G-43   GRYGIER, T. G.
               DYNAMIC PERSONALITY INVENTORY.
               LONDON: NATIONAL FOUNDATION FOR EDUCATIONAL RESEARCH IN ENGLAND AND WALES,
               1956.
               (DYNAMIC PERSONALITY INVENTORY)*
           aG-43 MULTITRAIT SEX PERSONALITY SELF-IDENTITY SELF ACTUALIZATION DEVELOPMENT
           aG-43 1956M IDENTITY ROLE
               (APPLICATIONS: 165   2023   2125   2256)

G-45   GORDON, L. V.
               GORDON OCCUPATIONAL CHECK LIST.
               NEW YORK: HARCOURT, 1961. (REV., 1963).
               (OCCUPATIONAL CHECK LIST)*
           aG-45 VOCATIONAL JOB PREFERENCE ACTIVITIES INTEREST CHECKLIST 1961M

G-46   GRIBBONS, W. D., & LOHNES, P. R.
              RELATIONSHIPS AMONG MEASURES OF READINESS FOR VOCATIONAL PLANNING.
              JOURNAL OF COUNSELING PSYCHOLOGY, 1964, 11, 13-19.
              (READINESS FOR VOCATIONAL PLANNING SCALES)
         @G-46 SELF-IDENTITY INTEREST JOB VOCATIONAL PLANNING ADJUSTMENT SELF RATING
         @VALUES IDEALS LIFE GOALS DEPENDENCE 1964M
              (APPLICATIONS: 1547)

G-47   GRATER, H. A.
              CLIENT PREFERENCES FOR AFFECTIVE OR COGNITIVE COUNSELOR CHARACTERISTICS AND
              FIRST INTERVIEW BEHAVIOR.
              JOURNAL OF COUNSELING PSYCHOLOGY, 1964, 11, 248-250.
              (COGNITIVE-AFFECTIVE INVENTORY)*
         @G-47 AFFECTIVE-STATES COGNITIVE TRAIT PREFERENCE THERAPY RELATIONSHIPS
         @G-47 COUNSELING 1964M

G-48   GOLDBERG, L. R., & SLOVIC, P.
              IMPORTANCE OF TEST ITEM CONTENT: AN ANALYSIS OF A COROLLARY OF THE
              DEVIATION HYPOTHESIS.
              JOURNAL OF COUNSELING PSYCHOLOGY, 1967, 14, 462-472.
              (MEASURE OF ACHIEVEMENT MOTIVATION)
         @G-48 NEED ACHIEVEMENT AUTONOMY MOTIVE 1967M

G-49   GIBSON, R. L., SNYDER, W. U., & RAY, W. S.
              A FACTOR ANALYSIS OF MEASURES OF CHANGE FOLLOWING CLIENT-CENTERED THERAPY.
              JOURNAL OF COUNSELING PSYCHOLOGY, 1955, 2, 83-89.
              (MEASURE OF ATTITUDES TOWARD SELF AND OTHERS)
         @G-49 ATTITUDE SELF IMAGE SELF-IDENTITY ESTEEM EVALUATION PERCEPTION OTHERS
         @G-49 1955M
              (APPLICATIONS: 1514)

G-50   GUILFORD, J. P., WILSON, R. C., CHRISTENSEN, P. R., & LEWIS, D. J.
              A FACTOR-ANALYTIC STUDY OF CREATIVE THINKING, I. HYPOTHESES AND DESCRIPTION
              OF TESTS.
              REPORTS FROM PSYCHOLOGICAL LABORATORY, NO. 4. LOS ANGELES: UNIVERSITY OF
              SOUTHERN CALIFORNIA, 1951.
              (GUILFORD TESTS OF CREATIVITY)*
         @G-50 AUTONOMY CREATIVITY COGNITIVE STRUCTURE FUNCTIONING THINKING 1951M
              (APPLICATIONS: 430   469   588   933   2568   2639   2866   2899   2902   2912)

G-51   GUILFORD, J. P., KETTNER, N. W., & CHRISTENSEN, P. R.
              A FACTOR-ANALYTIC STUDY ACROSS THE DOMAINS OF REASONING CREATIVITY AND
              EVALUATION.
              UNIVERSITY OF SOUTHERN CALIFORNIA, PSYCHOLOGICAL LABORATORY REPORTS, 1956,
              NO. 16.
              (TESTS OF IDEATIONAL FLUENCY)
         @G-51 SELF EXPRESSION COGNITIVE STRUCTURE FUNCTIONING CREATIVITY EVALUATION
         @G-51 1956M

G-52   GOUGH, H. G.
              PREDICTING SUCCESS IN GRADUATE TRAINING: A PROGRESS REPORT.
              (REV. ED.). IPAR RESEARCH BULLETIN, 1952.
              (IPAR ORIGINALITY SCALE)*
         @G-52 AUTONOMY CREATIVITY ORIGINALITY IMAGINATION 1952M
              (APPLICATIONS: 430   1933)

G-53   GOUGH, H. G.
              IMAGINATION--UNDEVELOPED RESOURCE.
              IN PROCEEDINGS, FIRST ANNUAL CONFERENCE ON RESEARCH DEVELOPMENTS IN
              PERSONNEL MANAGEMENT. LOS ANGELES: UNIVERSITY OF CALIFORNIA, INSTITUTE
              OF INDUSTRIAL RELATIONS, 1956, PP. 4-10.
              (DIFFERENTIAL REACTION SCHEDULE)*
         @G-53 AUTONOMY ORIGINALITY CREATIVITY IMAGINATION 1956M
              (APPLICATIONS: 430   933   1299   1933   2336)

G-54   GOUCHER, E. L., RIGGS, L. E., EFRON, H. Y., MYERS, R. F., & SCANLAN, E. R. G-97
              LYONS RELATIONSHIP SCALES: A STUDY OF RELIABILITY.
              JOURNAL OF CONSULTING PSYCHOLOGY, 1961, 25, 556.
              (LYONS RELATIONSHIP SCALES)*
         @G-54 RELATIONSHIPS THERAPY PATIENT FAMILY INTERPERSONAL BEHAVIOR SOCIAL
         @COMPETENCE ADJUSTMENT 1961M

G-55   GARMEZY, N., CLARKE, A. R., & STOCKNER, C.
               CHILD-REARING ATTITUDES OF MOTHERS AND FATHERS AS REPORTED BY
               SCHIZOPHRENIC AND NORMAL PATIENTS.
               JOURNAL OF ABNORMAL AND SOCIAL PSYCHOLOGY, 1961, 63, 176-182.
               (CHILD REARING ATTITUDE SCALE)
          aG-55 ADJUSTMENT PARENT-CHILD ATTITUDE FAMILY INTERACTION SCHIZOPHRENIA PATIENT
          aG-55 PSYCHIATRIC 1961M PARENTAL BEHAVIOR
               (APPLICATIONS: 1042   1044   1049   1065   1113   2731)

G-56   GOTTHEIL, E., COREY, J., & PAREDES, A.
               PSYCHOLOGICAL AND PHYSICAL DIMENSIONS OF PERSONAL SPACE.
               JOURNAL OF PSYCHOLOGY, 1968, 69, 7-9.
               (MAGNET TEST OF INTERPERSONAL DISTANCE)
          aG-56 PROJECTIVE PERSONAL SPACE SOCIAL INTERPERSONAL DISTANCE AFFECTIVE-STATES
          aOTHER-CATEGORY SELF PARENTAL PARENT-CHILD 1968M
               (APPLICATIONS: 2739)

G-57   GOLDMAN-EISLER, F.
               BREASTFEEDING AND CHARACTER FORMATION.
               IN C. KLUCKHOHN AND H. A. MURRAY (EDS.), PERSONALITY IN NATURE, SOCIETY,
               AND CULTURE. NEW YORK: KNOPF, 1953.
               (MULTITRAIT RATING SCALES)
          aG-57 OPTIMISM PESSIMISM MULTITRAIT AUTONOMY AFFECTIVE-STATES ADJUSTMENT RATING
          aG-57 1953M
               (APPLICATIONS: 2740)

G-58   GHISELLI, E. E.
               INDIVIDUALITY AS A FACTOR IN THE SUCCESS OF MANAGEMENT PERSONNEL.
               PERSONNEL PSYCHOLOGY, 1960, 13, 1-10.
               (RATINGS OF MANAGERS)
          aG-58 MULTITRAIT SUPERVISOR MANAGEMENT TRAIT JOB ADJUSTMENT LEADERSHIP ABILITY
          aRATING 1960M

G-59   GHISELLI, E. E.
               THE FORCED-CHOICE TECHNIQUE IN SELF-DESCRIPTION.
               PERSONNEL PSYCHOLOGY, 1954, 7, 201-208.
               (SELF-DESCRIPTION INVENTORY)*
          aG-59 SUPERVISOR MULTITRAIT BEHAVIOR MANAGEMENT TRAIT JOB ADJUSTMENT LEADERSHIP
          aABILITY INTELLIGENCE SELF CONFIDENCE 1954M DESCRIPTION
               (APPLICATIONS: 244   2362   2470)

G-60   GOUGH, H. G.
               THE PERSONNEL REACTION BLANK.
               BERKELEY, CALIFORNIA: AUTHOR, 1954.
               (PERSONNEL REACTION BLANK)*
          aG-60 RESPONSIBILITY CONSCIENTIOUS JOB ADJUSTMENT 1954M

G-61   GUILFORD, J. P.
               OPINION INVENTORY.
               SAN ANTONIO, TEXAS: AIR RESEARCH AND DEVELOPMENT COMMAND, 1951.
               (GUILFORD OPINION INVENTORY)*
          aG-61 ATTENTION AUTONOMY INTEREST OPINION MULTITRAIT NEED ORDER VARIETY PHYSICAL
          aDRIVE AGGRESSION CONFORMITY DEPENDENCE 1951M
               (APPLICATIONS: 549)

G-62   GETZELS, J. W., & JACKSON, P. W.
               OCCUPATIONAL CHOICE AND COGNITIVE FUNCTIONING: CAREER ASPIRATIONS OF HIGHLY
               INTELLIGENT AND OF HIGHLY CREATIVE ADOLESCENTS.
               JOURNAL OF ABNORMAL AND SOCIAL PSYCHOLOGY, 1960, 61, 119-123.
               (BATTERY FOR MEASURE OF CREATIVITY)
          aG-62 CREATIVITY AUTONOMY COGNITIVE FUNCTIONING 1960M
               (APPLICATIONS: 588   2970   2976)

G-63   GELLERMAN, S.
               THE EFFECTS OF EXPERIMENTALLY INDUCED AGGRESSION AND INHIBITION ON WORD
               ASSOCIATION RESPONSE SEQUENCES.
               UNPUBLISHED DOCTORAL DISSERTATION, UNIVERSITY OF PENNSYLVANIA, 1956.
               (WORD ASSOCIATION TEST OF AROUSED AGGRESSION)
          aG-63 HOSTILITY AGGRESSION AFFECTIVE-STATES RESENTMENT NEGATIVE 1956M
               (APPLICATIONS: 52   204   693   2500)

G-64   GOLDINGS, H. J.
               ON THE AVOWAL AND PROJECTION OF HAPPINESS.
               JOURNAL OF PERSONALITY, 1954, 23, 30-47.
               (SELF-RATING MEASURE OF HAPPINESS)
          aG-64 SELF RATING HAPPINESS SATISFACTION AFFECTIVE-STATES GLOBAL POSITIVE 1954M

G-65   GLICKSMAN, M., & WOHL, J.
                 EXPRESSED VALUES OF BURMESE AND AMERICAN UNIVERSITY STUDENTS.
                 JOURNAL OF SOCIAL PSYCHOLOGY, 1965, 65, 17-25.
                 (MEASURE OF EXPRESSED VALUES)
            aG-65 ORIENTATION EXPRESSION SELF SELF-IDENTITY VALUES IDEALS LIFE GOALS
            aG-65 1965M

G-66   GOTTHEIL, E., & VIELHABER, D. P.
                 INTERACTION OF LEADER AND SQUAD ATTRIBUTES RELATED TO PERFORMANCE OF
                 MILITARY SQUADS.
                 JOURNAL OF SOCIAL PSYCHOLOGY, 1966, 68, 113-127.
                 (RATINGS OF TASK ORIENTATION AND PERSONNEL ORIENTATION)
            aG-66 SOCIOMETRIC ORIENTATION SOCIAL COMPETENCE ADJUSTMENT JOB AUTONOMY PEER
            aPERSONAL CREATIVITY RATING LEADERSHIP 1966M EMPLOYEE

G-67   GOTTHEIL, E., & VIELHABER, D. P.
                 INTERACTION OF LEADER AND SQUAD ATTRIBUTES RELATED TO PERFORMANCE OF
                 MILITARY SQUADS.
                 JOURNAL OF SOCIAL PSYCHOLOGY, 1966, 68, 113-127.
                 (INDEX OF SELF-SATISFACTION AND SELF-ESTEEM)
            aG-67 SOCIAL DESIRABILITY COOPERATION APPROVAL SELF SATISFACTION ESTEEM
            aAFFECTIVE-STATES GLOBAL IMAGE CONCEPT SELF-IDENTITY PERCEPTION EVALUATION
            aG-67 1966M

G-68   GILLESPIE, J. M., & ALLPORT, G. W.
                 YOUTH'S OUTLOOK ON THE FUTURE.
                 NEW YORK: DOUBLEDAY, 1955.
                 (YOUTH OUTLOOK SURVEY)*
            aG-68 AFFECTIVE-STATES JOB PREFERENCE VOCATIONAL FUTURE ORIENTATION ADOLESCENT
            aLIFE GOALS VALUES IDEALS ADJUSTMENT 1955M

G-69   GORLOW, L., & NOLL, G. A.
                 A STUDY OF EMPIRICALLY DERIVED VALUES.
                 JOURNAL OF SOCIAL PSYCHOLOGY, 1967, 73, 261-IL9.
                 (MEASURE OF VALUES)
            aG-69 ORIENTATION IDEALS VALUES SELF-IDENTITY LIFE GOALS Q-SORT 1967M

G-70   GORDON, L. V.
                 MANUAL, GORDON PERSONAL PROFILE.
                 NEW YORK: HARCOURT, 1963.
                 (GORDON PERSONAL PROFILE)*
            aG-70 MULTITRAIT SOCIABILITY RESPONSIBILITY ASCENDANCE EMOTION MATURITY
            aG-70 1963M
                 (APPLICATIONS: 561   875   1274   1494   2349   2368   2602   2812)

G-71   GLASS, D. C. CANAVAN, D., & SCHIAVO, S.
                 ACHIEVEMENT MOTIVATION, DISSONANCE, AND DEFENSIVENESS.
                 JOURNAL OF PERSONALITY, 1968, 36, 474-492.
                 (MEASURE OF ACHIEVEMENT MOTIVATION)
            aG-71 MOTIVE ACHIEVEMENT AUTONOMY NEED SELF RATING 1968M

G-72   GONYEA, G. G.
                 DIMENSIONS OF JOB PERCEPTIONS.
                 JOURNAL OF COUNSELING PSYCHOLOGY, 1961, 8, 305-312.
                 (JOB PERCEPTION BLANK)*
            aG-72 1961M ADJUSTMENT JOB PERCEPTION ROLE VOCATIONAL

G-73   GRUENFELD, L. W., & FOLTMAN, F. F.
                 RELATIONSHIP AMONG SUPERVISORS' INTEGRATION, SATISFACTION, AND ACCEPTANCE
                 OF A TECHNOLOGICAL CHANGE.
                 JOURNAL OF APPLIED PSYCHOLOGY, 1967, 51, 74-77.
                 (MEASURE OF SUPERVISOR ATTITUDES TOWARD TECHNOLOGICAL CHANGE)
            aG-73 SUPERVISOR ADJUSTMENT ATTITUDE JOB CHANGE SATISFACTION INTEGRATION
            aADAPTABILITY ACCEPTANCE PE-FIT 1967M

G-74   GEIST, H.
                 THE GEIST PICTURE INTEREST INVENTORY: GENERAL FORM: MALE.
                 PSYCHOLOGICAL REPORTS, 1959, 5, 413-438.
                 (GEIST PICTURE INTEREST INVENTORY)*
            aG-74 ACTIVITIES INTEREST MULTITRAIT VOCATIONAL ORIENTATION 1959M

G-75   GUILFORD, J. P. & MARTIN, H. G.
          PERSONNEL INVENTORY: MANUAL OF DIRECTIONS AND NORMS.
          BEVERLY HILLS, CALIFORNIA: SHERIDAN SUPPLY COMPANY, 1943.
          (PERSONNEL INVENTORY)*
     aG-75 MULTITRAIT JOB ADJUSTMENT EMPLOYEE COOPERATION SATISFACTION BEHAVIOR 1943M

G-76   GOUGH, H. G., & SANFORD, R. N.
          RIGIDITY AS A PSYCHOLOGICAL VARIABLE.
          UNPUBLISHED MANUSCRIPT. UNIVERSITY OF CALIFORNIA, INSTITUTE OF PERSONALITY
          ASSESSMENT AND RESEARCH, 1952.
          (CALIFORNIA RIGIDITY SCALE)*
     aG-76 RIGIDITY FLEXIBILITY COPING-DEFENSE DOGMATISM 1952M
          (APPLICATIONS: 386   392   537   2605   2647)

G-77   GETZELS, J. W.
          THE ASSESSMENT OF PERSONALITY AND PREJUDICE BY THE METHOD OF PAIRED DIRECT
          AND PROJECTIVE QUESTIONS.
          UNPUBLISHED DOCTORAL DISSERTATION, HARVARD UNIVERSITY, 1951.
          (PAIRED DIRECT AND PROJECTIVE QUESTIONS TEST>*
     aG-77 SOCIAL DESIRABILITY PREJUDICE APPROVAL NEED AFFECTIVE-STATES PROJECTIVE
     aOTHER-CATEGORY 1951M

G-78   GOODENOUGH, F. L.
          MEASUREMENT OF INTELLIGENCE THROUGH DRAWINGS.
          YONKERS, NEW YORK: WORLD BOOK, 1926.
          (DRAW-A-PERSON TEST)*
     aG-78 MULTITRAIT CHILD PEER INTERACTION GROUP ENVIRONMENT ADJUSTMENT
     aG-78 INTELLIGENCE OTHER-CATEGORY PROJECTIVE 1926M
          (APPLICATIONS: 528   754   1126   1136   1168   1415   1450   1617   1629   1649
                      1681   1701   1711   1731   1747   1818   1822   1828   1850   1985
                      1990   2070   2110   2877   2967)

G-79   GRAY, H., & WHEELWRIGHT, J. B.
          JUNG'S PSYCHOLOGICAL TYPES, THEIR FREQUENCY OF OCCURRENCE.
          JOURNAL OF GENERAL PSYCHOLOGY, 1946, 34, 3-17.
          (GRAY-WHEELWRIGHT PSYCHOLOGICAL TYPE QUESTIONNAIRE)*
     aG-79 MULTITRAIT TYPOLOGY INTROVERSION EXTRAVERSION THINKING ORIENTATION STYLE
     aHISTORY 1949M

G-80   GUILFORD, J. P.
          PERSONALITY. NEW YORK: MCGRAW-HILL, 1959.
     CHRISTENSEN, P. R., MERRIFIELD, P. R., & GUILFORD, J. P.
          CONSEQUENCES: MANUAL OF ADMINISTRATION, SCORING, AND INTERPRETATION.
          (2ND ED.) BEVERLY HILLS, CALIFORNIA: SHERIDAN SUPPLY, 1958.
          (CONSEQUENCES TEST)*
     aG-80 1958M CREATIVITY AUTONOMY ORIGINALITY
          (APPLICATIONS: 109   609   2485   2486   2912)

G-81   GARDNER, E. F., & THOMPSON, G. G.
          SOCIAL RELATIONS AND MORALE IN SMALL GROUPS. NEW YORK: APPLETON-
          CENTURY-CROFTS, 1956.
          SYRACUSE SCALES OF SOCIAL RELATIONS: ELEMENTARY LEVEL: MANUAL OF
          DIRECTIONS. NEW YORK: HARCOURT, BRACE AND WORLD, 1959.
          (SYRACUSE SCALES OF SOCIAL RELATIONS)*
     aG-81 SELF-IDENTITY APPROVAL PUBLIC ADJUSTMENT SOCIOMETRIC SOCIAL INTERACTION
     aG-81 NEED COMPETENCE ESTEEM MORALE GROUP PEER RATING 1959M
          (APPLICATIONS: 563   1609)

G-82   GOUGH, H. G., & PETERSON, D. R.
          THE IDENTIFICATION AND MEASUREMENT OF PREDISPOSITIONAL FACTORS IN CRIME AND
          DELINQUENCY.
          JOURNAL OF CONSULTING PSYCHOLOGY, 1952, 16, 207-212.
          (DELINQUENCY SCALE)*
     aG-82 AFFECTIVE-STATES INTERACTION ALIENATION FAMILY PARENT-CHILD BEHAVIOR
     aPUBLIC IDENTITY DELINQUENCY PE-FIT ADJUSTMENT OTHER-CATEGORY SOCIAL COMPETENCE
     aG-82 ROLE SELF-IDENTITY SUB-IDENTITY SELF EVALUATION ESTEEM IMAGE 1952M
          (APPLICATIONS: 1372   2312)

G-83   GORHAM, D. R.
          A PROVERBS TEST FOR CLINICAL AND EXPERIMENTAL USE.
          PSYCHOLOGICAL REPORTS MONOGRAPH SUPPLEMENT, 1956, NO. 1.
          (PROVERBS TEST)*
     aG-83 CONCRETENESS ABSTRACTNESS PSYCHIATRIC DIAGNOSIS CONCEPTUAL ADJUSTMENT
     aOTHER-CATEGORY GLOBAL SCHIZOPHRENIC COGNITIVE FUNCTIONING 1956M
          (APPLICATIONS: 814   927   961   1029   1047   1958   2138   2441)

G-84   GITTINGER, J. W.
                INTRODUCTION TO THE PERSONALITY ASSESSMENT SYSTEM.
                PAPER PRESENTED AT THE AMERICAN COLLEGE PERSONNEL ASSOCIATION, DALLAS,
                MARCH, 1967.
                (PERSONALITY ASSESSMENT SYSTEM)*
          aG-84 MULTITRAIT ROLE FLEXIBILITY RIGIDITY COPING-DEFENSE DOGMATISM AUTONOMY
          aDOMINANCE SOCIAL GLOBAL COMPETENCE ADJUSTMENT SUBMISSION PE-FIT 1967M

G-85   GRANOFSKY, J.
                MODIFICATION OF ATTITUDES TOWARD THE PHYSICALLY DISABLED.
                UNPUBLISHED DOCTORAL DISSERTATION, YESHIVA UNIVERSITY, 1955.
                (GRANOFSKY PICTURES TEST)*
          aG-85 ATTITUDE DISABILITY ACCEPTANCE TAT 1955M
                (APPLICATIONS: 2324)

G-86   GOWIN, D. B., NEWSOME, G. L., & CHANDLER, K. A.
                A SCALE TO STUDY LOGICAL CONSISTENCY OF IDEAS ABOUT EDUCATION.
                JOURNAL OF PSYCHOLOGY, 1961, 51, 443-455.
                (GNC SCALE)*
          aG-86 RATIONALISM EMPIRICISM TEACHER ATTITUDE ORIENTATION 1961M

G-87   GURIN, P., & KATZ, D.
                MOTIVATION AND ASPIRATION IN THE NEGRO COLLEGE. (FINAL REPORT, OFFICE OF
                EDUCATION, DEPARTMENT OF HEALTH, EDUCATION, AND WELFARE) WASHINGTON, D. C.:
                UNITED STATES GOVERNMENT PRINTING OFFICE, 1966.
                GURIN, P., GURIN, G., LAO, R. C., & BEATTIE, M.
                INTERNAL-EXTERNAL CONTROL IN THE MOTIVATIONAL DYNAMICS OF NEGRO YOUTH.
                JOURNAL OF SOCIAL ISSUES, 1969, 25, 29-53.
                (EXTENDED I-E SCALE)
          aG-87 1969M IE-CONTROL LOCUS CONTROL PERSONAL COMPETENCE RACIAL NEGRO
                (APPLICATIONS: 2487)

G-88   GILBERT, A. R.
                TOWARD AN AUTOMATED TECHNIQUE OF PROBING INTO EMOTIONAL BLOCKS.
                JOURNAL OF PSYCHOLOGY, 1963, 56, 385-404.
                (AUTOMATED TECHNIQUE OF MEASURING EMOTIONAL BLOCKS)
          aG-88 AFFECTIVE-STATES ADJUSTMENT STYLE DEFENSIVENESS HISTORY EMOTION
          aGLOBAL RESPONSE-BIAS COPING-DEFENSE 1963M

G-89   GREENBERG, H., & MAYER, D.
                A NEW APPROACH TO THE SCIENTIFIC SELECTION OF SUCCESSFUL SALESMEN.
                JOURNAL OF PSYCHOLOGY, 1964, 57, 113-123.
                (MULTIPLE PERSONAL INVENTORY)*
          aG-89 MULTITRAIT EMPATHY EGO DRIVE VOCATIONAL PREDICTION SUCCESS 1964M JOB

G-90   GOUGH, H. G., & WOODWORTH, D. G.
                STYLISTIC VARIATIONS AMONG PROFESSIONAL RESEARCH SCIENTISTS.
                JOURNAL OF PSYCHOLOGY, 1960, 49, 87-98.
                (RESEARCH SCIENTIST Q SORT)*
          aG-90 1960M SELF CONCEPT Q-SORT
                (APPLICATIONS: 2336)

G-91   GURIN, P.
                MOTIVATION AND ASPIRATIONS OF SOUTHERN NEGRO COLLEGE YOUTH.
                AMERICAN JOURNAL OF SOCIOLOGY, 1970, 75, 607-631.
                (OCCUPATIONAL ASPIRATIONS MEASURE)
          aG-91 1970M ASPIRATION VOCATIONAL JOB NEGRO COLLEGE STUDENT

G-92   GURIN, P.
                MOTIVATION AND ASPIRATIONS OF SOUTHERN NEGRO COLLEGE YOUTH.
                AMERICAN JOURNAL OF SOCIOLOGY, 1970, 75, 607-631.
                (ACHIEVEMENT ORIENTATION MEASURE)
          aG-92 1970M CONTENT-ANALYSIS ACHIEVEMENT ORIENTATION MOTIVE APPROACH AUTONOMY
          aG-92 SELF-IDENTITY NEED

G-93   GURIN, P.
                MOTIVATION AND ASPIRATIONS OF SOUTHERN NEGRO COLLEGE YOUTH.
                AMERICAN JOURNAL OF SOCIOLOGY, 1970, 75, 607-631.
                (DESIRE FOR RECOGNITION MEASURE)
          a-93 1970M CONTENT-ANALYSIS MOTIVE APPROACH NEED PUBLIC ESTEEM AUTONOMY
          aG-93 SELF-IDENTITY NEGRO

G-94　　GURIN, P.
　　　　　MOTIVATION AND ASPIRATIONS OF SOUTHERN NEGRO COLLEGE YOUTH.
　　　　　AMERICAN JOURNAL OF SOCIOLOGY, 1970, 75, 607-631.
　　　　　(DESIRE FOR SECURITY MEASURE)
　　　aG-94 1970M NEED SECURITY CONTENT ANALYSIS MOTIVE AVOIDANCE AUTONOMY NEGRO

G-95　　.GURIN, P.
　　　　　MOTIVATION AND ASPIRATIONS OF SOUTHERN NEGRO COLLEGE YOUTH.
　　　　　AMERICAN JOURNAL OF SOCIOLOGY, 1970, 75, 607-631.
　　　　　(MEASURE OF PERSONAL CONTROL)
　　　aG-95 LOCUS CONTROL IE-CONTROL AUTONOMY PERSONAL COMPETENCE SELF PERCEPTION
　　　aG-95 1970M NEGRO

G-96　　GURIN, P.
　　　　　MOTIVATION AND ASPIRATIONS OF SOUTHERN NEGRO COLLEGE YOUTH.
　　　　　AMERICAN JOURNAL OF SOCIOLOGY, 1970, 75, 607-631.
　　　　　(MEASURE OF CONTROL IDEOLOGY)
　　　aG-96 1970M CONTROL IDEOLOGY OTHERS NEGRO

G-97　　GURIN, P.
　　　　　MOTIVATION AND ASPIRATIONS OF SOUTHERN NEGRO COLLEGE YOUTH.
　　　　　AMERICAN JOURNAL OF SOCIOLOGY, 1970, 75, 607-631.
　　　　　(MEASURE OF INDIVIDUAL-SYSTEM BLAME)
　　　aG-97 NEGRO RACIAL PREJUDICE 1970M IE-CONTROL AUTONOMY

G-98　　GOLD, J. A., & MODRICK, J. A.
　　　　　ATTITUDE TOWARD THE FEDERAL GOVERNMENT.
　　　　　JOURNAL OF SOCIAL PSYCHOLOGY, 1970, 81, 25-30.
　　　　　(MEASURE OF ATTITUDES TOWARD FEDERAL GOVERNMENT)
　　　aG-98 1970M POLITICAL ATTITUDE ORIENTATION

G-99　　GIANNELL, A. S.
　　　　　THE ROLE OF INTERNAL INHIBITION IN CRIME CAUSATION.
　　　　　JOURNAL OF SOCIAL PSYCHOLOGY, 1970, 81, 31-36.
　　　　　(MEASURE OF INTERNAL INHIBITION IN CRIME CAUSATION)
　　　aG-99 1970M LOCUS CONTROL IMPULSE AUTONOMY VALUES MORAL DEVELOPMENT IE-CONTROL
　　　aG-99 DELINQUENCY

G-100　　GOODMAN, I. Z.
　　　　　INFLUENCE OF PARENTAL FIGURES ON SCHIZOPHRENIC PATIENTS.
　　　　　JOURNAL OF ABNORMAL PSYCHOLOGY, 1968, 73, 503-512.
　　　　　(SOCIO-SEXUAL ADJUSTMENT SCALE)
　　　aG-100 1968M ADJUSTMENT SOCIAL COMPETENCE SEX BEHAVIOR INTERPERSONAL
　　　aG-100 RELATIOSHIPS
　　　　　(APPLICATIONS:　1103　2390)

G-101　　GREEN, R., & BERKOWITZ, L.
　　　　　NAME-MEDIATED AGGRESSIVE CUE PROPERTIES.
　　　　　JOURNAL OF PERSONALITY, 1966, 34, 456-465.
　　　　　(MEASURE OF EMOTIONAL STATE)
　　　aG-101 1966M AFFECTIVE-STATES EMOTION AGGRESSION HOSTILITY MOOD
　　　　　(APPLICATIONS:　2837)

G-103　　GREENWALD, H. J., & SATOW, Y.
　　　　　A SHORT SOCIAL DESIRABILITY SCALE.
　　　　　PSYCHOLOGICAL REPORTS, 1970, 27, 131-135.
　　　　　(SHORT MEASURE OF SOCIAL DESIRABILITY)
　　　aG-103 1970M SOCIAL DESIRABILITY NEED APPROVAL RESPONSE-BIAS

G-104　　GREENWALD, H. J., & CLAUSEN, J. D.
　　　　　TEST OF RELATIONSHIP BETWEEN YEASAYING AND SOCIAL DESIRABILITY.
　　　　　PSYCHOLOGICAL REPORTS, 1970, 27, 139-141.
　　　　　(MEASURE OF YEASAYING TENDENCY)
　　　aG-104 1970M RESPONSE-BIAS ACQUIESCENCE

G-105   GALBRAITH, G. G., HAHN, K., & LEIBERMAN, H.
                PERSONALITY CORRELATES OF FREE-ASSOCIATIVE SEX RESPONSES TO DOUBLE-ENTENDRE
                WORDS.
                JOURNAL OF CONSULTING AND CLINICAL PSYCHOLOGY, 1968, 32, 193-197.
                (DOUBLE ENTENDRE WORD ASSOCIATION TEST)
           @G-105 1968M PROJECTIVE SEX VERBAL RESPONSE SOCIAL DESIRABILITY GUILT MOTIVE
           @G-105 WORD ASSOCIATION
                (APPLICATIONS: 2221   2567   2916)

G-107   GUILFORD, J. P., HERTZKA, A. F., & CHRISTENSEN, P. R.
                A FACTOR-ANALYTIC STUDY OF EVALUATIVE ABILITIES: II. ADMINISTRATION
                OF TESTS AND ANALYSIS OF RESULTS.
                REPORTS OF THE PSYCHOLOGICAL LABORATORY, UNIVERSITY OF SOUTHERN
                CALIFORNIA., LOS ANGELES, JULY 1953, NO. 9
                (CARTOONS TEST OF CLEVERNESS)
           @G-107 1953M ORIGINALITY HUMOR CREATIVITY IMAGINATION

G-108   GARDNER, R. W.
                COGNITIVE STYLES IN CATEGORIZING BEHAVIOR.
                JOURNAL OF PERSONALITY, 1953, 22, 214-233.
                (MEASURE OF CATEGORIZING PREFERENCE)
           @G-108 1953M PREFERENCE STYLE COGNITIVE CONCEPTUAL BREADTH DIFFERENTIATION

G-109   GOLIGHTLY, C., NELSON, D., & JOHNSON, J.
                CHILDREN'S DEPENDENCY SCALE.
                DEVELOPMENTAL PSYCHOLOGY, 1970, 3, 114-118.
                (CHILDREN'S DEPENDENCY SCALE)*
           @G-109 1970M CHILD DEPENDENCE SCHOOL HOME FAMILY BEHAVIOR
           @G-109 PARENT TEACHER RELATIONSHIPS

G-111   GOUGH, H. G., HARRIS, D. B., MARTIN, W. E., & EDWARDS, M.
                CHILDREN'S ETHNIC ATTITUDES: I. RELATIONSHIP TO CERTAIN **PERSONALITY**
                FACTORS.
                CHILD DEVELOPMENT, 1950, 21, 83-91.
                (CHILDREN'S RACIAL ATTITUDE SCALE)*
           @G-111 1950M ATTITUDE CHILD PREJUDICE ETHNIC RACIAL
                (APPLICATIONS: 323)

G-113   GUILFORD, J. P.
                CREATIVE ABILITY IN THE ARTS.
                PSYCHOLOGICAL REVIEW, 1957, 64, 110-118.
                (MEASURE OF SPONTANEOUS FLEXIBILITY)
           @G-113 1957M SPONTANEITY FLEXIBILITY CREATIVITY ORIGINALITY
                (APPLICATIONS: 409)

G-114   GRATER, H.
                IMPULSE EXPRESSION AND EMOTIONAL ADJUSTMENT.
                JOURNAL OF CONSULTING PSYCHOLOGY, 1960, 24, 144-149.
                (MORAL ETHICAL VALUES SCALES)*.
           @G-114 1960M MORAL VALUES ORIENTATION
           @G-114 MATERNAL PARENT-CHILD CONFLICT

G-115   GOLDSTEIN, J. W.
                EFFECT OF SECURITY ON ATTRACTION TO A DISSIMILAR PERSON.
                (DOCTORAL DISSERTATION, UNIVERSITY OF KANSAS) ANN ARBOR, MICHIGAN:
                UNIVERSITY MICROFILMS, 1967, NO. 67-10, 807.
                GOLDSTEIN, J. W., & ROSENFELD, H. M.
                INSECURITY AND PREFERENCE FOR PERSONS SIMILAR TO ONESELF.
                JOURNAL OF PERSONALITY, 1969, 37, 253-268.
                (COLLEGE SOCIAL RESOURCES SURVEY)
           @G-115 1967M SOCIAL DESIRABILITY ACCEPTANCE PEER SECURITY
           @G-115 STUDENT COLLEGE ACTIVITIES
                (APPLICATIONS: 514)

G-116   GOLDSTEIN, J. W.
            EFFECT OF SECURITY ON ATTRACTION TO A DISSIMILAR PERSON.
            (DOCTORAL DISSERTATION, UNIVERSITY OF KANSAS) ANN ARBOR, MICHIGAN:
            UNIVERSITY MICROFILMS, 1967, NO. 67-10, 807.
         GOLDSTEIN, J. W., & ROSENFELD, H. M.
            INSECURITY AND PREFERENCE FOR PERSONS SIMILAR TO ONESELF.
            JOURNAL OF PERSONALITY, 1969, 37, 253-268.
            (PERSONAL CHARACTERISTICS SURVEY)
         aG-116 1967M INTEREST TRAIT SOCIAL DESIRABILITY
         aG-116 OTHERS PERCEPTION
            (APPLICATIONS: 514)

G-117   GOLDSTEIN, J. W., & ROSENFELD, H. M.
            INSECURITY AND PREFERENCE FOR PERSONS SIMILAR TO ONESELF.
            JOURNAL OF PERSONALITY, 1969, 37, 253-268.
            (INTERPERSONAL-RELATIONS MEASURE)
         aG-117 1969M INTERPERSONAL RELATIONSHIPS OTHERS PREFERENCE SECURITY OPINION
         aG-117 INTEREST SIMILARITY SOCIAL

G-118   GOUGH, H. G.
            IMAGINATION - UNDEVELOPED RESOURCE.
            IN PROCEEDINGS, FIRST ANNUAL CONFERENCE ON RESEARCH DEVELOPMENT IN PER-
            SONNEL MANAGEMENT.
            LOS ANGELES: UNIVERSITY OF CALIFORNIA, INSTITUTE OF INDUSTRIAL RELATIONS-
            1956, 4-10.
            (GENERAL EFFECTIVENESS SCALE)*
         aG-118 1956M EFFECTIVENESS COMPETENCE ABILITY GLOBAL
            (APPLICATIONS: 378   498)

G-120   GRUEN, W.
            REJECTION OF FALSE INFORMATION ABOUT ONESELF AS AN INDICATION OF EGO
            IDENTITY.
            JOURNAL OF CONSULTING PSYCHOLOGY, 1960, 24, 231-233.
            (MEASURE OF EGO IDENTITY VERSUS EGO DIFFUSION)
         aG-120 1960M EGO IDENTITY IDEAL ADOLESCENT OTHER SELF EVALUATION

G-121   GOUGH, H. G.
            A NEW DIMENSION OF STATUS: 1. DEVELOPMENT OF A PERSONALITY SCALE.
            AMERICAN SOCIOLOGICAL REVIEW, 1948, 13, 401-409.
            (MEASURE OF STATUS)
         aG-121 1948M STATUS PRESTIGE MMPI SOCIAL SECURITY CONFIDENCE SELF MORAL
         aG-121 ATTITUDES DOGMATISM ANXIETY DENIAL
            (APPLICATIONS: 1186 1191 1587 1899)

G-122   GOLLIN, E. S.
            ORGANIZATIONAL CHARACTERISTICS OF SOCIAL JUDGMENT: A DEVELOPMENTAL
            INVESTIGATION.
            JOURNAL OF PERSONALITY, 1958, 26, 139-154.
            (IMPRESSION FORMATION TASK)
         aG-122 1958M IMPRESSION FORMATION CONCEPT SOCIAL JUDGMENT ORGANIZATION
         aG-122 STRUCTURE INTERPERSONAL PERCEPTION OTHERS
            (APPLICATIONS: 366)

G-124   GUERTIN, W. H.
            A FACTOR ANALYSIS OF GERIATRIC ATTITUDES.
            JOURNAL OF CONSULTING PSYCHOLOGY, 1961, 25, 39-42.
            (GERIATRIC ATTITUDE SCALE)
         aG-124 1961M ATTITUDE ADJUSTMENT ANXIETY ALIENATION PHYSICAL ILLNESS INTEREST
         aG-124 GERIATRIC

G-125   GRIGG, A. E., & THORPE, J. S.
            DEVIANT RESPONSE IN COLLEGE ADJUSTMENT CLIENTS: A TEST OF BERG'S DEVIATION
            HYPOTHESIS.
            JOURNAL OF CONSULTING PSYCHOLOGY, 1960, 24, 92-94.
            (MEASURE OF DEVIANCE)
         aG-125 1960M COLLEGE ADJUSTMENT MALADJUSTMENT CHECKLIST
            (APPLICATIONS: 1565 1807)

G-126   GOLDSTEIN, A. P.
            THERAPIST AND CLIENT EXPECTATIONS OF PERSONALITY CHANGE IN PSYCHOTHERAPY.
            JOURNAL OF COUNSELING PSYCHOLOGY, 1960, 7, 180-184.
            (MEASURE OF THERAPIST EXPECTATIONS)
         aG-126 1960M THERAPY CLIENT PERSONALITY CHANGE Q-SORT
            (APPLICATIONS: 1647)

G-127   GOUGH, H. G.
             SOME COMMON MISCONCEPTIONS ABOUT NEUROTICISM.
             JOURNAL OF CONSULTING PSYCHOLOGY, 1954, 18, 287-292.
             (DISSIMULATION SCALE FROM MMPI)
         aG-127 1954M RESPONSE-BIAS MMPI SOCIAL DESIRABILITY
             (APPLICATIONS: 1414 1626 1899 2085)

G-129   GETZELS, J. W., & JACKSON, P. W.
             CREATIVITY AND INTELLIGENCE.
             NEW YORK: WILEY, 1962.
             (USES TEST)
         aG-129 1962M NOVELTY NEED VARIETY ORIGINALITY CREATIVITY INTELLIGENCE
             (APPLICATIONS: 2015 2074 2976)

G-130   GORDON, C. M.
             SOME EFFECTS OF INFORMATION, SITUATION, AND PERSONALITY ON DECISION MAKING
             IN A CLINICAL SETTING.
             JOURNAL OF CONSULTING PSYCHOLOGY, 1966, 30, 219-224.
             (INTERPRETIVE DECISION SCALE)
         aG-130 1966M RORSCHACH DECISION THERAPY COUNSELING SITUATIONAL PERSONALITY
         aG-130 PATIENT RELATIONSHIPS
             (APPLICATIONS: 2125)

G-131   GOLDMAN, I. J.
             THE WILLINGNESS OF MUSIC AND VISUAL ART STUDENTS TO ADMIT TO SOCIALLY
             UNDESIRABLE AND PSYCHOPATHOLOGICAL CHARACTERISTICS.
             UNPUBLISHED DOCTORAL DISSERTATION, COLUMBIA UNIVERSITY, 1962.
             (FORCED CHOICE SOCIAL DESIRABILITY MEASURE)
         aG-131 1962M SOCIAL DESIRABILITY TRAIT
             (APPLICATIONS: 1868)

G-132   GARD, J. G.
             FUNDAMENTAL INTERPERSONAL RELATIONS ORIENTATIONS IN CLINICAL GROUPS.
             UNPUBLISHED DOCTORAL DISSERTATION, UNIVERSITY OF PITTSBURGH, 1961.
         GARD, J. G., & BENDIG, A. W.
             A FACTOR ANALYTIC STUDY OF E.SENCK'S AND SCHUTZ'S PERSONALITY DIMENSIONS
             AMONG PSYCHIATRIC GROUPS.
             JOURNAL OF CONSULTING PSYCHOLOGY, 1964, 28, 252-258.
             (BEHAVIOR CHECK LIST)
         aG-132 1961M BEHAVIOR CHECKLIST PSYCHIATRIC PATIENT NEED
             (APPLICATIONS: 1870)

G-133   GARMIZE, L. M., & RYCHLAK, J. F.
             ROLE-PLAY VALIDATION OF A SOCIOCULTURAL THEORY OF SYMBOLISM.
             JOURNAL OF CONSULTING PSYCHOLOGY, 1964, 28, 107-115.
             (RORSCHACH SCORED FOR TYPICAL MOOD INTERPRETATIONS)
         aG-133 1964M RORSCHACH MOOD AFFECTIVE-STATES ROLE ENACTMENT PROJECTIVE
         aG-133 AGGRESSION DEPRESSION FEAR SECURITY

G-134   GAYLIN, N. L.
             PSYCHOTHERAPY AND PSYCHOLOGICAL HEALTH: A RORSCHACH FUNCTION AND STRUCTURE
             ANALYSIS.
             JOURNAL OF CONSULTING PSYCHOLOGY, 1966, 30, 494-500.
             (RORSCHACH FUNCTION SCORE)*
         aG-134 1966M RORSCHACH MENTAL-HEALTH MENTAL-ILLNESS SELF ESTEEM ADJUSTMENT
         aG-134 1966M ORIGINALITY CREATIVITY COGNITIVE COMPLEXITY FUNCTIONING PROJECTIVE

G-135   GAYLIN, N. L.
             PSYCHOTHERAPY AND PSYCHOLOGICAL HEALTH: A RORSCHACH FUNCTION AND STRUCTURE
             ANALYSIS.
             JOURNAL OF CONSULTING PSYCHOLOGY, 1966, 30, 494-500.
             (RORSCHACH STRUCTURE SCORE)*
         aG-135 1966M RORSCHACH MENTAL-HEALTH MENTAL-ILLNESS ADJUSTMENT PROJECTIVE

G-136   GREENBERG, R. P.
             EFFECTS OF PRESESSION INFORMATION ON PERCEPTION OF THE THERAPIST AND
             RECEPTIVITY TO INFLUENCE IN A PSYCHOTHERAPY ANALOGUE.
             JOURNAL OF CONSULTING AND CLINICAL PSYCHOLOGY, 1969, 33, 425-429.
             (MEASURE OF PATIENT PERSUASIBILITY)
         aG-136 1969M PERSUASIBILITY ATTITUDE CHANGE CONFORMITY INFLUENCE OPINION
         aG-136 RELATIONSHIPS CLIENT THERAPIST COUNSELOR PATIENT
             (APPLICATIONS: 2310)

G-137   GIEDT, F. H., & DOWNING, L.
                AN EXTRAVERSION SCALE FOR THE MMPI.
                JOURNAL OF CLINICAL PSYCHOLOGY, 1961, 17, 156-159.
                (EXTRAVERSION SCALE)
           @G-137 1961M EXTRAVERSION INTROVERSION MMPI
                (APPLICATIONS: 2302)

G-138   GOULD, L. J.
                THE ALIENATION SYNDROME: PSYCHOSOCIAL CORRELATES AND BEHAVIORAL
                CONSEQUENCES.
                DOCTORAL DISSERTATION, UNIVERSITY OF CONNECTICUT, ANN ARBOR, MICH.,
                UNIVERSITY MICROFILMS, 1964, NO. 66-848.
                (ALIENATION SCALE)
           @G-138 1964M ALIENATION BEHAVIOR SOCIAL ANOMIE
                (APPLICATIONS: 2174)

G-139   GOTTSCHALDT, K.
                GESTALT FACTORS AND REPETITION.
                IN W. D. ELLIS (ED.), A SOURCEBOOK OF GESTALT PSYCHOLOGY. NEW YORK:
                HARCOURT, BRACE & WORLD, 1938.
                (EMBEDDED FIGURES TEST)
           @G-139 1938M FIGURE GRAPHIC FIELD DEPENDENCE PERCEPTION COGNITIVE FUNCTIONING
                (APPLICATIONS: 1764   2239)

G-140   GOUGH, H. G.
                APPRAISAL OF SOCIAL MATURITY BY MEANS OF THE CPI.
                JOURNAL OF ABNORMAL PSYCHOLOGY, 1966, 71, 189-195.
                (SOCIAL MATURITY SCALE)
           @G-140 1966M SOCIAL MATURITY ADJUSTMENT RESPONSIBILITY
                (APPLICATIONS: 2150   2949)

G-141   GRINDER, R. E.
                PARENTAL CHILD REARING PRACTICES, GUILT, AND RESISTANCE TO TEMPTATION OF
                SIXTH GRADE CHILDREN.
                AMERICAN PSYCHOLOGIST, 1960, 15, 399. (ABSTRACT)
                (MEASURE OF RESISTANCE TO TEMPTATION)
           @G-141 1960M RESISTANCE VALUES MORAL ORIENTATION BEHAVIOR GUILT PARENT-CHILD
           @G-141 IDENTIFICATION CHILD
                (APPLICATIONS: 691   928   1194   2460)

G-142   GOLDBERGER, L.
                INDIVIDUAL DIFFERENCES IN THE EFFECTS OF PERCEPTUAL ISOLATION AS RELATED
                TO RORSCHACH MANIFESTATIONS OF THE PRIMARY PROCESS.
                UNPUBLISHED DOCTORAL DISSERTATION, NEW YORK UNIVERSITY, 1958.
                (RORSCHACH SCORED FOR DEFENSE-DEMAND AND DEFENSE-EFFECTIVENESS)
           @G-142 1958M RORSCHACH PROJECTIVE DEFENSE DEMANDS EFFECTIVENESS PERSONAL
           @G-142 RESPONSE
                (APPLICATIONS: 609)

G-143   GOLDBERGER, L.
                INDIVIDUAL DIFFERENCES IN THE EFFECTS OF PERCEPTUAL ISOLATION AS RELATED
                TO RORSCHACH MANIFESTATIONS OF THE PRIMARY PROCESS.
                UNPUBLISHED DOCTORAL DISSERTATION, NEW YORK UNIVERSITY, 1958.
                (RORSCHACH SCORED FOR ADAPTIVE VS. MALADAPTIVE REGRESSION)
           @G-143 1958M RORSCHACH PROJECTIVE EFFECTIVENESS DEFENSE ADAPTABILITY EXPRESSION
           @G-143 CONTROL
                (APPLICATIONS: 609)

G-144   GOLDHIRSH, M. I.
                MANIFEST CONTENT OF DREAMS OF CONVICTED SEX OFFENDERS.
                JOURNAL OF ABNORMAL AND SOCIAL PSYCHOLOGY, 1961, 63, 643-645.
                (DREAMS SCORED FOR SEX CONTENT)
           @G-144 1961M FANTASY PRIMARY-PROCESS THINKING SEX DELINQUENCY

G-145   GIBB, J. R.
                FACTORS PRODUCING DEFENSIVE BEHAVIOR WITHIN GROUPS.
                QUARTERLY STATUS REPORT, FEB. 15, 1954, CONTRACT NONR-1147 (03) NR 170-226.
                (MEASURE OF SATISFACTION WITH GROUP EXPERIENCE)
           @G-145 1954M SATISFACTION GROUP BEHAVIOR FUNCTIONING EXPERIENCE
                (APPLICATIONS: 599)

G-146   GERARD, H. B.
                SOME DETERMINANTS OF SELF-EVALUATION.
                JOURNAL OF ABNORMAL AND SOCIAL PSYCHOLOGY, 1961, 62, 288-293.
                (MEASURE OF DEPENDENCY ON OTHERS FOR SELF EVALUATION)
           @G-146 1961M SELF-IDENTITY SELF EVALUATION DEPENDENCE AUTONOMY CONCEPT
           @G-146 OTHERS

G-147   GERGEN, K. J., & JONES, E. E.
                MENTAL ILLNESS, PREDICTABILITY AND AFFECTIVE CONSEQUENCES AS STIMULUS
                FACTORS IN PERSON PERCEPTION.
                JOURNAL OF ABNORMAL AND SOCIAL PSYCHOLOGY, 1963, 67, 95-104.
                (IMPRESSION RATING SCALE)
            aG-147 1963M RATING IMPRESSION PERSON PERCEPTION AFFECTION AFFILIATION
            aG-147 INTELLIGENCE PREDICTION

G-148   GARDNER, R. W.
                COGNITIVE CONTROLS OF ATTENTION DEPLOYMENT AS DETERMINANTS OF VISUAL
                ILLUSIONS.
                JOURNAL OF ABNORMAL AND SOCIAL PSYCHOLOGY, 1961, 62, 120-127.
                (SIZE ESTIMATION TESTS A AND B)
            aG-148 1961M STIMULUS PERCEPTION

G-149   GARDNER, R. W.
                COGNITIVE CONTROLS OF ATTENTION DEPLOYMENT AS DETERMINANTS OF VISUAL
                ILLUSIONS.
                JOURNAL OF ABNORMAL AND SOCIAL PSYCHOLOGY, 1961, 62, 120-127.
                (KINESTHETIC AFTEREFFECTS TEST)
            aG-149 1961M STIMULUS PERCEPTION

G-150   GRAHAM, F. K., & KENDALL, B. S.
                MEMORY-FOR-DESIGNS TEST: REVISED GENERAL MANUAL.
                PERCEPTUAL AND MOTOR SKILLS, 1960, 11, 147-188.
                (MEMORY-FOR-DESIGNS TEST)
            aG-150 1960M PSYCHIATRIC DIAGNOSIS GRAPHIC FIGURE
                (APPLICATIONS: 939   1787)

G-151   GURIN, G., VEROFF, J., & FELD, S.
                AMERICANS VIEW THEIR MENTAL HEALTH.
                NEW YORK: BASIC BOOKS, 1960.
                (INDEX OF PSYCHOSOMATIC SYMPTOMS (PS))
            aG-151 1960M SYMPTOM PSYCHOSOMATIC MENTAL-HEALTH ADJUSTMENT
                (APPLICATIONS: 906)

G-153   GARDNER, R. W., HOLTZMAN, P. S., KLEIN, G. S., LINTON, H. B., & SPENCE, D. P.
                COGNITIVE CONTROL: A STUDY OF INDIVIDUAL CONSISTENCIES IN COGNITIVE
                BEHAVIOR.
                PSYCHOLOGICAL ISSUES, 1959, 1, NO. 4.
                (RORSCHACH SCORED FOR DEFENSIVE CONTENT)
            aG-153 1959M RORSCHACH PROJECTIVE REPRESSION DEFENSE
                (APPLICATIONS: 969)

G-154   GOLDMAN, A. R.
                DIFFERENTIAL EFFECTS OF SOCIAL REWARD AND PUNISHMENT ON DEPENDENT AND
                DEPENDENCY-ANXIOUS SCHIZOPHRENICS.
                JOURNAL OF ABNORMAL PSYCHOLOGY, 1965, 70, 412-418.
                (WARD BEHAVIOR MEASURE OF DEPENDENCE)
            aG-154 1965M WARD BEHAVIOR SCHIZOPHRENIA MENTAL-ILLNESS AVOIDANCE DEPENDENCE

G-155   GOLDMAN, A. R.
                DIFFERENTIAL EFFECTS OF SOCIAL REWARD AND PUNISHMENT ON DEPENDENT AND
                DEPENDENCY-ANXIOUS SCHIZOPHRENICS.
                JOURNAL OF ABNORMAL PSYCHOLOGY, 1965, 70, 412-418.
                (INCOMPLETE STORY TEST: MEASURE OF DEPENDENCY)
            aG-155 1965M FANTASY IMAGINATION DEPENDENCE AUTONOMY NEED ATTENTION
            aG-155 PROJECTIVE STORY-COMPLETION

G-156   GROSZ, H. J., & GROSSMAN, K. G.
                THE SOURCES OF OBSERVER VARIATION AND BIAS IN CLINICAL JUDGMENTS: THE ITEM
                OF PSYCHIATRIC HISTORY.
                JOURNAL OF NERVOUS AND MENTAL DISEASE, 1964, 138, 105-113.
            GROSZ, H. J., & GROSSMAN, K. G.
                CLINICIAN'S RESPONSE STYLE: A SOURCE OF VARIATION AND BIAS IN CLINICAL
                JUDGMENTS.
                JOURNAL OF ABNORMAL PSYCHOLOGY, 1968, 73, 207-214.
                (MEASURE OF RESPONSE BIAS IN PSYCHIATRIC ASSESSMENT)
            aG-156 1968M PSYCHIATRIC PATIENT EVALUATION RESPONSE BIAS JUDGMENT
                (APPLICATIONS: 1074)

G-157   GOLDSTEIN, S.
        A PROJECTIVE STUDY OF PSYCHOANALYTIC MECHANISMS OF DEFENSE.
        UNPUBLISHED DOCTORAL DISSERTATION, UNIVERSITY OF MICHIGAN, 1952.
        (DEFENSE PREFERENCE INQUIRY)
      aG-157 1952M DENIAL DEFENSE COPING COPING-DEFENSE REPRESSION PROJECTION
      aSTYLE
        (APPLICATIONS: 2726)

G-158   GROAT, H. T., & NEAL, A. G.
        SOCIAL PSYCHOLOGICAL CORRELATES OF URBAN FERTILITY.
        AMERICAN SOCIOLOGICAL REVIEW, 1967, 32, 945-959.
        (ALIENATION SCALE)
      aG-158 1967M ALIENATION POWERLESSNESS SOCIAL INVOLVEMENT
        (APPLICATIONS: 2723)

G-159   GULLER, I. B.
        STABILITY OF SELF-CONCEPT IN SCHIZOPHRENIA.
        JOURNAL OF ABNORMAL PSYCHOLOGY, 1966, 71, 275-279.
        (SELF-CONCEPT MEASURE).
      aG-159 1966M SELF CONCEPT SCHIZOPHRENIA EVALUATION MENTAL-ILLNESS PSYCHIATRIC

G-160   GULLER, I. B.
        STABILITY OF SELF-CONCEPT IN SCHIZOPHRENIA.
        JOURNAL OF ABNORMAL PSYCHOLOGY, 1966, 71, 275-279.
        (HEALTH-CONCEPT SCALE)
      aG-160 1966M HEALTH SCHIZOPHRENIA CONCEPT SELF MENTAL-ILLNESS PSYCHIATRIC

G-161   GOLDBERG, L. R., & RORER, L. G.
        AN INTENSIVE STUDY OF SOCIOMETRIC MEASURES.
        UNPUBLISHED MANUSCRIPT, OREGON RESEARCH INSTITUTE, 1963.
        (MEASURES OF SELF AWARENESS AND SELF ACCEPTANCE)
      @G-161 1963M SELF AWARENESS ACCEPTANCE PEER TRAIT RATING
        (APPLICATIONS: 1055)

G-162   GORDON, L. V., & KIKUCHI, A.
        RESPONSE SETS OF JAPANESE AND AMERICAN STUDENTS.
        JOURNAL OF SOCIAL PSYCHOLOGY, 1970, 82, 143-148.
        (SCHOOL ENVIRONMENT PREFERENCE SCHEDULE)
      @G-162 1970M SCHOOL ENVIRONMENT PREFERENCE VALUES NORMS ACCEPTANCE DIFFERENCES
      @CROSS-CULTURAL

G-163   GRISSO, J. T.
        VERBAL BEHAVIOR AND THE ACTION-THOUGHT DIMENSION.
        JOURNAL OF ABNORMAL PSYCHOLOGY, 1970, 76, 265-269.
        (TAT SCORED FOR VERBAL BEHAVIOR STYLE)
      aG-163 1970M TAT BEHAVIOR ORIENTATION THINKING ACTIVITY STYLE PROJECTIVE

G-164   GURIN, G., VEROFF, J., & FELD, S.
        AMERICANS VIEW THEIR MENTAL HEALTH.
        NEW YORK: BASIC BOOKS, 1960.
        (SELF-RATING OF HAPPINESS SCALE)
      aG-164 1960M HAPPINESS SELF RATING ELATION POSITIVE AFFECTIVE-STATES
      aSATISFACTION LIFE
        (APPLICATIONS: 2559)

G-165   GROSS, R. B., & MARSH, M. M.
        AN INSTRUMENT FOR MEASURING CREATIVITY IN YOUNG CHILDREN: THE GROSS
        GEOMETRIC FORMS.
        DEVELOPMENTAL PSYCHOLOGY, 1970, 3, 267.
        (GROSS GEOMETRIC FORMS)*
      aG-165 1970M CREATIVITY ORIGINALITY IMAGINATION FIGURE CHILD PREFERENCE

G-166   GREENBERG, I. M.
        CLINICAL CORRELATES OF FOURTEEN- AND SIX-CYCLES-PER-SECOND POSITIVE EEG
        SPIKING AND FAMILY PATHOLOGY.
        JOURNAL OF ABNORMAL PSYCHOLOGY, 1970, 76, 403-412.
        (CLINICAL QUESTIONNAIRE FOR ADJUSTMENT)
      aG-166 1970M ADJUSTMENT INTERVIEW AFFECTIVE-STATES DEVIANCE AGGRESSION PATIENT
      aDEPENDENCE PSYCHIATRIC MENTAL-ILLNESS

G-167   GREENBERG, I. M., & ROSENBERG, G.
              FAMILIAL CORRELATES OF THE 14 AND 6 C/SEC. EEG POSITIVE SPIKE PATTERN.
              (PSYCHIATRIC RESEARCH REPORT NO. 20), WASHINGTON, D.C.: AMERICAN
              PSYCHIATRIC ASSOCIATION, 1966.
          GREENBERG, I. M.
              CLINICAL CORRELATES OF FOURTEEN- AND SIX-CYCLES-PER-SECOND POSITIVE EEG
              SPIKING AND FAMILY PATHOLOGY.
              JOURNAL OF ABNORMAL PSYCHOLOGY, 1970, 76, 403-412.
              (FAMILY INTERACTION QUESTIONNAIRE)*
          aG-167 1966M FAMILY INTERACTION SOCIAL ADJUSTMENT MENTAL-ILLNESS ALIENATION
          aRELATIONSHIPS
              (APPLICATIONS: 2445)

G-169   GILBERT, A. R.
              SUPERIORITY OF LATENCY-WEIGHTED SCORES OVER UNWEIGHTED SCORES IN THE
              ASSESSMENT OF PROFESSIONAL INTERESTS.
              PSYCHOLOGICAL REPORTS, 1970, 26, 93-94.
              (UNWEIGHTED AND LATENCY-WEIGHTED VOCATIONAL INTEREST FORMS)
          aG-169 1970M VOCATIONAL INTEREST PREFERENCE JOB PROJECTIVE SENTENCE-COMP

G-170   GREENWALD, H. J., & SELLE, E. D.
              RESPONSES TO INTACT AND INTERMIXED PERSONALITY INVENTORIES.
              PSYCHOLOGICAL REPORTS, 1970, 27, 365-366.
              (MEASURE OF SELF-CONFIDENCE)
          aG-170 SELF CONFIDENCE COMPETENCE ESTEEM EVALUATION

G-171   GREENWALD, H. J., & SELLE, E. D.
              RESPONSES TO INTACT AND INTERMIXED PERSONALITY INVENTORIES.
              PSYCHOLOGICAL REPORTS, 1970, 27, 365-366.
              (MEASURE OF RESPECT FOR OTHERS)
          aG-171 RESPECT OTHERS ATTITUDE PEOPLE

G-172   GUREL, L. (ED.)
              A MANUAL FOR STUDIES OF FACTORS AFFECTING THE POST-HOSPITAL EMPLOYMENT
              OF FUNCTIONALLY PSYCHOTIC VETERANS.
              WASHINGTON, D.C.: VA PSYCHIATRIC EVALUATION PROJECT, 1961.
              (SYMPTOM, HISTORY, AND VOCATIONAL EXPECTATION RATINGS)
          aG-172 1961M ALIENATION ANOMIE RATING ADJUSTMENT PROGNOSIS SYMPTOM VOCATIONAL
          aINTEREST PREFERENCE HISTORY LIFE HOSPITALIZATION
              (APPLICATIONS: 2604)

G-173   GREENE, R. L., & CLARK, J. R.
              ADLER'S THEORY OF BIRTH ORDER.
              PSYCHOLOGICAL REPORTS, 1970, 26, 387-390.
              (MEASURE OF BIRTH ORDER EFFECT ON PERSONALITY)
          aG-173 1970M PARENTAL CHILD DEVELOPMENT PERSONAL PERSONALITY BIRTH ORDER
          aRELATIONSHIPS HOME FAMILY ENVIRONMENT

G-176   GOLDBERG, R. T.
              NEED SATISFACTION AND REHABILITATION PROGRESS OF PSYCHOTIC PATIENTS.
              JOURNAL OF COUNSELING PSYCHOLOGY, 1967, 14, 253-257.
              (INTERVIEW MEASURE OF NEED FOR BELONGINGNESS AND ESTEEM)
          aG-176 1967M NEED ESTEEM BELONGINGNESS JOB VOCATIONAL PSYCHIATRIC PATIENT
          aSATISFACTION INTERVIEW AFFILIATION SELF PUBLIC

G-177   GOLDBERG, R. T.
              NEED SATISFACTION AND REHABILITATION PROGRESS OF PSYCHOTIC PATIENTS.
              JOURNAL OF COUNSELING PSYCHOLOGY, 1967, 14, 253-257.
              (WARD BEHAVIOR RATING SCALE)
          aG-177 1967M WARD BEHAVIOR ADJUSTMENT RATING

G-178   GOLDBERG, R. T.
              NEED SATISFACTION AND REHABILITATION PROGRESS OF PSYCHOTIC PATIENTS.
              JOURNAL OF COUNSELING PSYCHOLOGY, 1967, 14, 253-257.
              (MEASURE OF WORK ABILITY)
          aG-178 1967M ADJUSTMENT COMPETENCE JOB PSYCHIATRIC PATIENT

G-180   GILBREATH, S. H.
              GROUP COUNSELING WITH MALE UNDERACHIEVING COLLEGE VOLUNTEERS.
              PERSONNEL AND GUIDANCE JOURNAL, 1967, 45, 469-476.
              (MEASURE OF DEGREE OF PERCEIVED STRUCTURE)
          aG-180 1967M STRUCTURE PERCEPTION GROUP COUNSELING DIFFERENCES
              (APPLICATIONS: 1514)

G-181   GREENBERG, B. S., KAGAN, N., & BOWES, J.
          DIMENSIONS OF EMPATHETIC JUDGEMENT OF CLIENTS BY COUNSELORS.
          JOURNAL OF COUNSELING PSYCHOLOGY, 1969, 16, 303-308.
          (SEMANTIC DIFFERENTIAL MEASURE OF EMPATHY)
          aG-181 1969M SEM-DIFFERENTIAL COUNSELING THERAPY PATIENT SENSITIVITY
          aJUDGMENT EMPATHY HOSTILITY AVOIDANCE DEPENDENCE AWARENESS

G-182   GOLDBERG, L. R., & SLOVIC, P.
          IMPORTANCE OF TEST ITEM CONTENT: AN ANALYSIS OF A COROLLARY OF THE
          DEVIATION HYPOTHESIS.
          JOURNAL OF COUNSELING PSYCHOLOGY, 1967, 14, 462-472.
          (STATEMENT REACTION TEST)*
          aG-182 1967M SOCIAL AFFILIATION ABASEMENT AUTONOMY DOMINANCE ACHIEVEMENT

G-183   GONYEA, G. G.
          JOB PERCEPTIONS IN RELATION TO VOCATIONAL PREFERENCE.
          JOURNAL OF COUNSELING PSYCHOLOGY, 1963, 10, 20-26.
          (JOB PREFERENCE SCALE)
          aG-183 1963M JOB PREFERENCE VOCATIONAL INTEREST ATTITUDE EVALUATION
          (APPLICATIONS: 1258)

G-184   GRIGG, A. E.
          CLIENT RESPONSE TO COUNSELORS AT DIFFERENT LEVELS OF EXPERIENCE.
          JOURNAL OF COUNSELING PSYCHOLOGY, 1961, 8, 217-222.
          (CLIENT OBSERVATION REPORT)
          aG-184 1961M COUNSELING EXPERIENCE INTERACTION RELATIONSHIPS PATIENT THERAPIST

G-185   GUSTAV, A.
          EVALUATION OF DENTIST-PATIENT RELATIONSHIP BY MEANS OF A PSYCHOLOGICAL
          TEST.
          IN J. L. BLASS, MOTIVATING PATIENTS FOR MORE EFFECTIVE DENTAL SERVICE.
          PHILADELPHIA: LIPPINCOTT, 1958, PP. 5-11.
          (SENTENCE-COMPLETION MEASURE OF DENTIST-PATIENT RELATIONSHIP)
          aG-185 1958M SENTENCE-COMP PHYSICAL ILLNESS PATIENT RELATIONSHIPS
          (APPLICATIONS: 1160)

G-186   GARDNER, R. W., & SCHOEN, R. A.
          DIFFERENTIATION AND ABSTRACTION IN CONCEPT FORMATION.
          PSYCHOLOGICAL MONOGRAPHS, 1962, 76 (41, WHOLE NO. 560).
          (CONCEPTUAL DIFFERENTIATION AS MEASURED BY CATEGORY SORTING)
          aG-186 1962M COGNITIVE COMPLEXITY
          (APPLICATIONS: 286)

G-187   GLADIS, M., & MINTON, H.
          JOB INCENTIVE PREFERENCES OF EMOTIONALLY DISTURBED PATIENTS.
          JOURNAL OF COUNSELING PSYCHOLOGY, 1962, 9, 54-57.
          (MEASURE OF JOB INCENTIVE PREFERENCES)
          aG-187 1962M JOB INCENTIVE PREFERENCE MOTIVE PSYCHIATRIC PATIENT ATTRACTION

G-188   GRINDER, R. E.
          NEW TECHNIQUES FOR RESEARCH IN CHILDREN'S TEMPTATION BEHAVIOR.
          CHILD DEVELOPMENT, 1961, 32, 679-688.
          (MEASURE OF GUILT)
          aG-188 GUILT MORAL BEHAVIOR SELF PUNITIVENESS STORY-COMPLETION PROJECTIVE
          (APPLICATIONS: 493 1194)

G-190   GRINDER, R. E.
          NEW TECHNIQUES FOR RESEARCH IN CHILDREN'S TEMPTATION BEHAVIOR.
          CHILD DEVELOPMENT, 1961, 32, 679-688.
          (MEASURE OF COGNITIVE MORAL BEHAVIOR)
          aG-190 COGNITIVE MORAL BEHAVIOR JUDGMENT MATURITY SUPEREGO
          (APPLICATIONS: 1194)

G-191   GOLDSTEIN, M. J., JUDD, L. L., RODRICK, E. H., ALLKIRE, A. A., & GOULD, E.
          A METHOD FOR STUDYING SOCIAL INFLUENCE AND COPING PATTERNS WITHIN FAMILIES
          OF DISTURBED ADOLESCENTS.
          JOURNAL OF NERVOUS AND MENTAL DISEASE, 1968, 147, 233-251.
          (SOCIAL INFLUENCE-COUNTERINFLUENCE CODING SYSTEM)
          aG-191 1968M SOCIAL INFLUENCE CHILD PARENTAL ADOLESCENT INTERACTION
          aRELATIONSHIPS

G-192   GOUGH, H., HURLBUT, F. C., & WOODWORTH, D.
                SCIENTIFIC WORD ASSOCIATION TEST.
                BERKELEY: UNIVERSITY OF CALIFORNIA, INSTITUTE OF PERSONALITY ASSESSMENT
                AND RESEARCH, 1957.
                (SCIENTIFIC WORD ASSOCIATION TEST)*
           aG-192 1957M WORD ASSOCIATION CREATIVITY ORIGINALITY
                (APPLICATIONS: 933)

G-193   GRIGG, A. E.
                CHILDHOOD EXPERIENCE WITH PARENTAL ATTITUDES: A TEST OF ROE'S HYPOTHESIS.
                JOURNAL OF COUNSELING PSYCHOLOGY, 1959, 6, 153-156.
                (MEASURE OF PARENT-CHILD RELATIONSHIPS)
           aG-193 1959M AFFILIATION SUPPORT PARENT-CHILD RELATIONSHIPS VOCATIONAL
           aPREFERENCE
                (APPLICATIONS: 1546)

G-194   GUILFORD, J. P., FRICK, J. W., CHRISTENSEN, P. R., & MERRIFIELD, P. R.
                A FACTOR ANALYTIC STUDY OF FLEXIBILITY IN THINKING.
                REPORTS FROM THE PSYCHOLOGY LABORATORY, NO. 18.
                LOS ANGELES: UNIVERSITY OF SOUTHERN CALIFORNIA, 1957.
                (MEASURE OF DIVERGENT THINKING)
           aG-194 1957M COGNITIVE STYLE THINKING ORIGINALITY FLEXIBILITY
                (APPLICATIONS: 609   2074)

G-195   GHEI, S.
                VOCATIONAL INTERESTS, ACHIEVEMENT AND SATISFACTION.
                JOURNAL OF COUNSELING PSYCHOLOGY, 1960, 7, 132-136.
                (SCORING KEYS FOR VOCATIONAL INTEREST INVENTORY)
           aG-195 1960M VOCATIONAL INTEREST INVENTORY

G-196   GREENSTEIN, J. M.
                FATHER CHARACTERISTICS AND SEX TYPING.
                JOURNAL OF PERSONALITY AND SOCIAL PSYCHOLOGY, 1966, 3, 271-277.
                (RATING SCALE OF FATHER'S DOMINANCE, CLOSENESS, WARMTH)
           aG-196 1966M PATERNAL TRAIT RATING DOMINANCE DISTANCE INTERPERSONAL
           aSENSITIVITY RELATIONSHIPS CHILD PARENTAL

G-197   GREENSTEIN, J. M.
                FATHER CHARACTERISTICS AND SEX TYPING.
                JOURNAL OF PERSONALITY AND SOCIAL PSYCHOLOGY, 1966, 3, 271-277.
                (TAT HERO CHOICE MEASURE OF FANTASY IDENTIFICATION)
           aG-197 1966M TAT FANTASY IDENTIFICATION ROLE IDENTITY SEX PROJECTIVE

G-198   GERARD, H. B., & RABIE, J. M.
                FEAR AND SOCIAL COMPARISON.
                UNPUBLISHED MANUSCRIPT, BELL TELEPHONE RESEARCH LABORATORIES, 1960.
                (SCALE OF REASONS FOR AFFILIATIVE CHOICE)
           aG-198 1960M AFFILIATION MOTIVE
                (APPLICATIONS: 625)

G-199   GURMAN, E. B., & BASS, B. M.
                OBJECTIVE COMPARED WITH SUBJECTIVE MEASURES OF THE SAME BEHAVIOR IN GROUPS.
                JOURNAL OF ABNORMAL AND SOCIAL PSYCHOLOGY, 1961, 63, 368-374.
                (SUBJECTIVE MEASURES OF SOCIAL INTERACTION)
           aG-199 1961M SUBJECTIVE SOCIAL INTERACTION GROUP BEHAVIOR

G-200   GARDNER, E. F., & THOMPSON, G. G.
                SOCIAL RELATIONS AND MORALE IN SMALL GROUPS.
                NEW YORK: APPLETON CENTURY CROFTS, 1956.
                (SOCIOMETRIC MEASURE OF THERAPY RELATIONSHIPS)
           aG-200 1956M SOCIOMETRIC THERAPY RELATIONSHIPS

G-201   GEIDT.
                NO REFERENCE--CITED IN:
                JOHNSTON, R., & MCNEAL, G. F.
                COMBINED MMPI AND DEMOGRAPHIC DATA IN PREDICTING LENGTH OF NEUROPSYCHIATRIC
                HOSPITAL STAY.
                JOURNAL OF CONSULTING PSYCHOLOGY, 1964, 28, 64-70.
                (DISCHARGE POTENTIAL SCALE)
           aG-201 PROGNOSIS PSYCHIATRIC CHANGE MENTAL-ILLNESS MENTAL-HEALTH ADJUSTMENT
                (APPLICATIONS: 1844)

G-202   GOUGH, H. G.
               THE F MINUS K DISSIMULATION INDEX FOR THE MMPI.
               JOURNAL OF CONSULTING PSYCHOLOGY, 1950, 14, 408-413.
               (MEASURE OF MALINGERING ON MMPI)
           aG-202 1950M MMPI RESPONSE-BIAS
               (APPLICATIONS: 2085)

G-203   GILBERSTADT, H., & DUKER, J.
               A HANDBOOK FOR CLINICAL AND ACTUARIAL MMPI INTERPRETATION.
               PHILADELPHIA: SAUNDERS, 1965.
               (PROFILE CLASSIFICATION SYSTEM FOR MMPI)
           aG-203 1965M MMPI DIAGNOSIS PSYCHIATRIC INVENTORY MENTAL-HEALTH MENTAL-ILLNESS
           aNEUROTICISM
               (APPLICATIONS: 2227)

G-205   GUERNEY, B. G., STOVER, L., & DEMERITT, S.
               A MEASUREMENT OF EMPATHY IN PARENT-CHILD INTERACTION.
               JOURNAL OF GENETIC PSYCHOLOGY, 1968, 112, 49-55.
               (BEHAVIORAL MEASURE OF EMPATHY)
           aG-205 1968M PARENT-CHILD RELATIONSHIPS INTERACTION EMPATHY BEHAVIOR

H-1   HAAN, N.
               COPING AND DEFENSE MECHANISMS RELATED TO PERSONALITY INVENTORIES.
               JOURNAL OF CONSULTING PSYCHOLOGY, 1965, 29, 373-378.
               (INTERVIEW MEASURE OF COPING AND DEFENSE MECHANISMS)
           aH-1 COPING-DEFENSE GLOBAL STYLE HISTORY 1965M EGO DEFENSE EGO-STRENGTH
               (APPLICATIONS: 1054   2127)

H-2   HAAS, H. I., & MAEHR, M. L.
               TWO EXPERIMENTS ON THE CONCEPT OF SELF AND THE REACTION OF OTHERS.
               JOURNAL OF PERSONALITY AND SOCIAL PSYCHOLOGY, 1965, 1, 100-105.
               (RATING OF PHYSICAL SELF-ADEQUACY)
           aH-2 PHYSICAL SELF RATING SELF-IDENTITY ESTEEM BODY IMAGE PERCEPTION CONCEPT
           aH-2 1965M

H-3   HAGGARD, L. A., & ISAACS, R. S.
               MICROMOMENTARY FACIAL EXPRESSIONS AS INDICATORS OF EGO MECHANISMS IN
               PSYCHOTHERAPY. IN L. A. GOTTSCHALK & A. H. AUERBACH (EDS.) METHODS OF
               RESEARCH IN PSYCHOTHERAPY. NEW YORK: APPLETON-CENTURY-CROFTS, 1966.
               (MEASURE OF AFFECTIVE STATES THROUGH FACIAL EXPRESSIONS)
           aH-3 EMPATHY AFFECTIVE-STATES ORIENTATION OTHER-CATEGORY PERCEPTION 1966M

H-4   HAMILTON, M.
               A RATING SCALE FOR DEPRESSION.
               JOURNAL OF NEUROLOGICAL AND NEUROSURGICAL PSYCHIATRY, 1960, 23, 56-62.
               (HAMILTON RATING SCALE)*
           aH-4 DEPRESSION AFFECTIVE-STATES GLOBAL NEGATIVE PSYCHIATRIC DIAGNOSIS THERAPY
           aH-4 RATING SYMPTOM 1960M

H-5   HAND, J.
               MEASUREMENT OF RESPONSE SETS.
               PSYCHOLOGICAL REPORTS, 1964, 14, 907-913.
               (HAND ACQUIESCENCE SCALE)*
           aH-5 ACQUIESCENCE SOCIAL DESIRABILITY RESPONSE-BIAS 1964M

H-6   HARMAN, W. W., FADIMAN, J., & MOGAR, R.
               THE VALUE-BELIEF Q-SORT. (MANUSCRIPT IN PREPARATION, 1966)
               (VALUE-BELIEF Q-SORT)*
           aH-6 VALUES ORIENTATION BELIEF SELF-IDENTITY IDEALS LIFE GOALS Q-SORT DOGMATISM
           aH-6 AUTHORITARIANISM COPING-DEFENSE RIGIDITY FLEXIBILITY 1966M

H-7   HARTLEY, J. A.
               A SEMANTIC DIFFERENTIAL SCALE FOR ASSESSING GROUP PROCESS CHANGES.
               JOURNAL OF CLINICAL PSYCHOLOGY, 1968, 24, 74.
               (SEMANTIC DIFFERENTIAL MEASURE OF GROUP PROCESS CHANGE)
           aH-7 SEM-DIFFERENTIAL SOCIAL GROUP CHANGE INTERACTION JOB ADJUSTMENT RATING SELF
           aH-7 EVALUATION SELF-IDENTITY IMAGE ESTEEM PUBLIC IDENTITY 1968M

H-8   HASLER, R., & CLARKE, W. N.
              AN EXPERIMENTAL MEASURE OF PERSONAL ADJUSTMENT FROM A SELF CONCEPT
              ANALYSIS.
              JOURNAL OF CLINICAL PSYCHOLOGY, 1967, 23, 467-469.
              (PERSONAL ADJUSTMENT FORM)*
           aH-8 ADJUSTMENT GLOBAL PSYCHIATRIC DIAGNOSIS MENTAL-ILLNESS MENTAL-HEALTH
           aH-8 PATIENT 1967M PERSONAL

H-9   HAYS, W. L.
              AN APPROACH TO THE STUDY OF TRAIT IMPLICATION AND TRAIT SIMILARITY. IN R.
              TAGIURI AND L. PETRULLO (EDS.) PERSON PERCEPTION AND INTERPERSONAL
              BEHAVIOR. STANFORD: STANFORD UNIVERSITY PRESS, 1958.
              (METHOD FOR GROUPING TRAITS BY SIMILARITY)
           aH-9 MULTITRAIT TRAIT-TERMS 1958M TRAIT SIMILARITY

H-10   HEILBURN, A. B.
              THE PSYCHOLOGICAL SIGNIFICANCE OF THE MMPI K SCALE IN A NORMAL POPULATION.
              JOURNAL OF CONSULTING PSYCHOLOGY, 1961, 25, 486-491.
              (DEFENSIVENESS SCALE)*
           aH-10 SOCIAL DESIRABILITY DEFENSIVENESS COPING-DEFENSE GLOBAL RESPONSE-BIAS
           aH-10 1961M

H-11   HEILBRUN, A. B.
              VALIDATION OF A NEED SCALING TECHNIQUE FOR THE ADJECTIVE CHECK LIST.
              JOURNAL OF CONSULTING PSYCHOLOGY, 1959, 23, 347-351.
              (ABASEMENT SCALE)*
           aH-11 ABASEMENT GUILT AFFECTIVE-STATES GLOBAL NEGATIVE SELF-IDENTITY EVALUATION
           aH-11 PERCEPTION SELF ESTEEM DEPRECIATION CHECKLIST NEED 1959M

H-12   HEIST, P., & WILLIAMS, P.
              MANUAL FOR THE OMNIBUS PERSONALITY INVENTORY. UNIVERSITY OF CALIFORNIA,
              BERKELEY, CENTER FOR STUDY OF HIGHER EDUCATION, 1957 (MIMEO).
           CENTER FOR THE STUDY OF HIGHER EDUCATION.
              OMNIBUS PERSONALITY INVENTORY--RESEARCH MANUAL.
              BERKELEY: UNIVERSITY OF CALIFORNIA, CENTER FOR THE STUDY OF HIGHER
              EDUCATION, 1962.
              (OMNIBUS PERSONALITY INVENTORY)*
           aH-12 MULTITRAIT SOCIAL MATURITY RESPONSIBILITY EGO-STRENGTH AUTONOMY ADJUSTMENT
           aH-12 COPING-DEFENSE 1957M
              (APPLICATIONS: 537   1170   1205   1282   1299   1324   1336   1366   1388   1401
                                1421   1425   1460   1491   1501   1521   1527   1549   1954   2286
                                2339   2343   2390   2768   2856   2902   2954)

H-13   HEREFORD, C. F.
              CHANGING PARENTAL ATTITUDES THROUGH GROUP DISCUSSION. UNIVERSITY OF TEXAS
              PRESS, 1963.
              (HEREFORD PARENT ATTITUDE SURVEY)*
           aH-13 PARENTAL ATTITUDE FAMILY INTERACTION ADJUSTMENT PARENT-CHILD ROLE BEHAVIOR
           aH-13 TRUST 1963M

H-14   HARVEY, O. J., & CLAPP, W. F.
              HOPE, EXPECTANCY AND REACTIONS TO THE UNEXPECTED.
              JOURNAL OF PERSONALITY AND SOCIAL PSYCHOLOGY, 1965, 2, 45-52.
              (GRAPHIC RATINGS OF PERSONAL CHARACTERISTICS)
           aH-14 MULTITRAIT MATURITY COMPETENCE ADJUSTMENT SELF-IDENTITY GRAPHIC RATING
           aH-14 1965M

H-15   HETZNECKER, W., GARDNER, E. A., ODOROFF, C. L., & TURNER, R. J.
              FIELD SURVEY METHODS IN PSYCHIATRY: A SYMPTOM CHECK LIST, MENTAL STATUS AND
              CLINICAL STATUS SCALES FOR EVALUATION OF PSYCHIATRIC IMPAIRMENT.
              ARCHIVES OF GENERAL PSYCHIATRY, 1966, 15, 427-438.
              (PSYCHIATRIC SYMPTOM CHECK LIST)
           aH-15 SYMPTOM CHECKLIST PSYCHIATRIC RATING GLOBAL ADJUSTMENT BEHAVIOR DIAGNOSIS
           aH-15 MENTAL-ILLNESS EVALUATION 1966M PROGNOSIS
              (APPLICATIONS: ⁻2434)

H-16   HINRICHS, J. R., & MISCHKIND, L. A.
              EMPIRICAL AND THEORETICAL LIMITATIONS OF THE TWO-FACTOR HYPOTHESIS OF JOB
              SATISFACTION.
              JOURNAL OF APPLIED PSYCHOLOGY, 1967, 51, 191-200.
              (MEASURE OF JOB SATISFACTION)
           aH-16 JOB SATISFACTION AFFECTIVE-STATES GLOBAL RATING POSITIVE PE-FIT 1967M

H-17   HOBART, C. W., & FAHLBERG, N.
             THE MEASUREMENT OF EMPATHY.
             AMERICAN JOURNAL OF SOCIOLOGY, 1965, 70, 595-603.
             (EMPATHY RATIO SCORE)*
         aH-17 EMPATHY AFFECTIVE-STATES TYPOLOGY 1965M OTHERS ORIENTATION

H-18   HOGGE, J. H., & FRIEDMAN, S. T.
             THE OPENNESS AND AFFECT DENIAL SCALES: A PRELIMINARY REPORT.
             JOURNAL OF PSYCHOLOGY, 1967, 66, 281-286.
             (AFFECT DENIAL SCALE)
         aH-18 OPENNESS EMOTION DENIAL AFFECTIVE-STATES OTHER-CATEGORY 1967M

H-19   HOLLAND, J. L.
             A PSYCHOLOGICAL CLASSIFICATION SCHEME FOR VOCATIONS AND MAJOR FIELDS.
             JOURNAL OF COUNSELING PSYCHOLOGY, 1966, 13, 278-288.
         HOLLAND, J. L., & BAIRD, L. .L.
             AN INTERPERSONAL COMPETENCY SCALE.
             EDUCATIONAL AND PSYCHOLOGICAL MEASUREMENT, 1968, 28, 503-510.
             (INTERPERSONAL COMPETENCY SCALE)*
         aH-19 1966M INTERPERSONAL SOCIAL COMPETENCE INTERACTION RELATIONSHIPS
         aBEHAVIOR ADJUSTMENT
             (APPLICATIONS: 1515)

H-20   HENDRICK, C., & LILLY, R. S.
             THE STRUCTURE OF MOOD: A COMPARISON BETWEEN SLEEP DEPRIVATION AND
             NORMAL WAKEFULNESS CONDITIONS.
             JOURNAL OF PERSONALITY, 1970. 38, 453-465.
             (HENDRICK AND LILLY MOOD CHECKLIST FORM)
         aH-20 1970M MOOD CHECKLIST AFFECTIVE-STATES
             (APPLICATIONS: 1515   2912)

H-21   HOLLAND, J. L.
             MANUAL FOR THE HOLLAND VOCATIONAL PREFERENCE INVENTORY.   PALO ALTO, CALIF.:
             CONSULTING PSYCHOLOGISTS PRESS, 1959.
             (HOLLAND VOCATIONAL PREFERENCE INVENTORY)*
         aH-21 MULTITRAIT SELF-IDENTITY SUB-IDENTITY ROLE PERCEPTION MASCULINITY
         aH-21 FEMININITY VOCATIONAL PREFERENCE 1959M INTEREST
             (APPLICATIONS: 657   1181   1299   1375   1402   1515   1539   1548   2585   2750
                              2775   2779   2859   2958)

H-22   HOLLINGSHEAD, A. B.
             TWO-FACTOR INDEX OF SOCIAL POSITION. NEW HAVEN: YALE UNIVERSITY, 1957.
             (INDEX OF SOCIAL POSITION)
         aH-22 ROLE SOCIAL STATUS SELF-IDENTITY SUB-IDENTITY PERCEPTION 1957M
             (APPLICATIONS: 255   512   531   615   691   1443   1769   1870   2021   2249
                             2464   2724)

H-23   HOLMES, T. H., & RAHE, R. H.
             THE SOCIAL READJUSTMENT RATING SCALE.
             JOURNAL OF PSYCHOSOMATIC RESEARCH, 1967, 11, 213-218.
             (SOCIAL READJUSTMENT RATING SCALE)*
         aH-23 SOCIAL ADJUSTMENT RATING COMPETENCE ADAPTABILITY ENVIRONMENT PE-FIT
         aH-23 MENTAL-ILLNESS MENTAL-HEALTH PSYCHOSOMATIC 1967M

H-24   HOLZBERG, J. D., & HAHN, F.
             THE PICTURE FRUSTRATION TECHNIQUE AS A MEASURE OF HOSTILITY AND GUILT
             REACTIONS IN ADOLESCENT PSYCHOPATHS.
             AMERICAN JOURNAL OF ORTHOPSYCHIATRY, 1952, 22, 776-796.
             (PICTURE FRUSTRATION TEST)*
         aH-24 HOSTILITY AGGRESSION NEGATIVE AFFECTIVE-STATES RESENTMENT FRUSTRATION
         aH-24 PROJECTIVE DIAGNOSIS MENTAL-ILLNESS PSYCHOPATHY GUILT 1952M

H-25   HAERTZEN, C. A., HILL, H. E., & BELLEVILLE, R. E.
             DEVELOPMENT OF THE ADDICTION RESEARCH CENTER INVENTORY (ARCI): SELECTION
             OF ITEMS THAT ARE SENSITIVE TO THE EFFECTS OF VARIOUS DRUGS.
             PSYCHOPHARMACOLOGIA, 1963, 4, 155-166.
             (ADDICTION RESEARCH CENTER INVENTORY)*
         aH-25 DRUG INFLUENCE IMPULSE PHYSIOLOGICAL DEPENDENCE 1963M ADDICTION

H-26   HALLER, A. O. & MILLER, I. W.
                THE OCCUPATIONAL ASPIRATION SCALE.
                MICHIGAN STATE UNIVERSITY, TECHNICAL BULLETIN, 1963, NO. 288.
                (OCCUPATIONAL ASPIRATION SCALE)*
            ∂H-26 VOCATIONAL INTEREST ASPIRATION SELF-IDENTITY SUB-IDENTITY ROLE PERCEPTION
            ∂H-26 JOB SATISFACTION ADJUSTMENT GOALS 1963M
                (APPLICATIONS: 1430   2757)

H-27   HARBURG, E.
                COVERT HOSTILITY: ITS SOCIAL ORIGINS AND RELATIONSHIP WITH OVERT COMPLIANCE
                UNPUBLISHED DOCTORAL DISSERTATION, UNIVERSITY OF MICHIGAN, 1962.
                (PARENT IMAGE DIFFERENTIAL)*
            ∂H-27 PARENT-CHILD PARENTAL IMAGE FAMILY INTERACTION ADJUSTMENT SEM-DIFFERENTIAL
            ∂H-27 CONCEPT EVALUATION PATERNAL MATERNAL 1962M
                (APPLICATIONS: 28)

H-28   HARLESTON, B. W.
                TEST ANXIETY AND PERFORMANCE IN PROBLEM-SOLVING SITUATIONS.
                JOURNAL OF PERSONALITY, 1962, 30, 557-573.
                (QUESTIONNAIRE MEASURE OF TEST ANXIETY)
            ∂H-28 TEST ANXIETY AFFECTIVE-STATES SUBJECTIVE STRESS NEGATIVE SITUATIONAL 1962M
                (APPLICATIONS: 47)

H-29   HARRIS, D. B.
                A SCALE FOR MEASURING ATTITUDES OF SOCIAL RESPONSIBILITY IN CHILDREN.
                JOURNAL OF ABNORMAL AND SOCIAL PSYCHOLOGY, 1957, 55, 322-326.
                (MEASURE OF SOCIAL RESPONSIBILITY IN CHILDREN)
            ∂H-29 ATTITUDE CHILD SOCIAL RESPONSIBILITY ADJUSTMENT OTHER-CATEGORY MORAL PEER
            ∂H-29 ORIENTATION DEVELOPMENT INTERACTION INTERPERSONAL RELATIONSHIPS 1957M
                (APPLICATIONS: 610   654   858   2803)

H-30   HARTSHORNE, H., & MAY, M. A.
                STUDIES IN THE NATURE OF CHARACTER.
                VOL. I, NEW YORK: MACMILLAN, 1928.
                (LIE TEST)
            ∂H-30 BEHAVIOR DECEPTIVENESS RESPONSE-BIAS FAKING SELF IMAGE PUBLIC IDENTITY
            ∂1928M
                (APPLICATIONS: 263 1890)

H-31   HARVEY, O. J., & CLAPP, W. F.
                HOPE, EXPECTANCY AND REACTIONS TO THE UNEXPECTED.
                JOURNAL OF PERSONALITY AND SOCIAL PSYCHOLOGY, 1965, 2, 45-52.
                (SELF-ESTEEM RATING SCALE)
            ∂H-31 SELF-IDENTITY EVALUATION SELF PERCEPTION ESTEEM IMAGE 1965M RATING

H-32   HARVEY, O. J., HUNT, D. E., & SCHRODER, H. M.
                CONCEPTUAL SYSTEMS AND PERSONALITY ORGANIZATION.
                NEW YORK: WILEY, 1961.
                (THIS I BELIEVE TEST)*
            ∂H-32 COGNITIVE STRUCTURE FUNCTIONING ORGANIZATION CONCEPT CONCRETENESS ATTITUDE
            ∂H-32 ABSTRACTNESS CONCEPTUAL 1961M
                (APPLICATIONS: 17   186   225   272)

H-33   HEATH, R.
                THE REASONABLE ADVENTURER AND OTHERS. PITTSBURGH: UNIVERSITY OF PITTSBURGH
                PRESS, 1964.
                (RATING SCALES FOR SATISFACTION AND SELF-ACCEPTANCE)
            ∂H-33 ADJUSTMENT SATISFACTION GLOBAL SELF ACCEPTANCE SOCIAL RELATIONSHIPS
            ∂H-33 INTERPERSONAL ACADEMIC PERFORMANCE CONCEPT IMAGE EVALUATION SELF-IDENTITY
            ∂H-33 1964M

H-34   HEILBRUN, A. B., & SULLIVAN, D. J.
                THE PREDICTION OF COUNSELING READINESS.
                PERSONNEL AND GUIDANCE JOURNAL, 1962, 41, 112-117.
                ("FEMININITY" TEST)
            ∂H-34 CHECKLIST COUNSELING THERAPY ADJUSTMENT GLOBAL OTHER-CATEGORY
            ∂H-34 MENTAL-ILLNESS FEMININITY MENTAL-HEALTH 1962M DIAGNOSIS PROGNOSIS
                (APPLICATIONS: 145 1073)

H-35   HETHERINGTON, E. M.
                A DEVELOPMENTAL STUDY OF THE EFFECTS OF SEX OF THE DOMINANT PARENT ON SEX-
                ROLE PREFERENCE, IDENTIFICATION, AND IMITATION IN CHILDREN.
                JOURNAL OF PERSONALITY AND SOCIAL PSYCHOLOGY, 1965, 2, 188-194.
                (PARENT-CHILD SIMILARITY MEASURE)
            ∂H-35 PARENT-CHILD SIMILARITY FAMILY INTERACTION ADJUSTMENT SELF-IDENTITY
            ∂H-35 PERCEPTION CHECKLIST DOMINANCE AUTONOMY RATING 1965M

H-36   HINCKLEY, E. D.
               THE INFLUENCE OF INDIVIDUAL OPINION ON CONSTRUCTION OF AN ATTITUDE SCALE.
               JOURNAL OF SOCIAL PSYCHOLOGY, 1932, 3, 283-296.
               (MEASURE OF ATTITUDES TOWARD NEGROES)
          aH-36 ATTITUDE NEGRO RACIAL PREJUDICE OPINION SOCIAL DISTANCE 1932M
               (APPLICATIONS: 59   69   288   833)

H-37   HOLTZMAN, W. H., THORPE J. S., SWARTZ, J. D., & HERRON, E. W.
               INKBLOT PERCEPTION AND PERSONALITY.
               AUSTIN: UNIVERSITY OF TEXAS PRESS, 1961.
               (HOLTZMAN INKBLOT TECHNIQUE)*
          aH-37 COGNITIVE MULTITRAIT PROJECTIVE PERCEPTION PERSONALITY 1961M RORSCHACH
               (APPLICATIONS: 49   275   345   446   869   913   927   965   987   1092
                               1126   1476   1579   1616   1665   1764   1852   1939   2006   2057
                               2089   2177   2214   2239   2294   2314   2391   2436   2485   2508
                               2531   2561   2899   2912   2915   2944)

H-38   HUSEK, T. R.
               PERSUASIVE IMPACTS OF EARLY, LATE, OR NO MENTION OF A NEGATIVE SOURCE.
               JOURNAL OF PERSONALITY AND SOCIAL PSYCHOLOGY, 1965, 2, 125-128.
               (SEMANTIC DIFFERENTIAL FOR RATING SELF AND MENTALLY ILL OTHERS)
          aH-38 SEM-DIFFERENTIAL SELF EVALUATION ATTITUDE MENTAL-ILLNESS PATIENT OTHERS
          aH-38 SELF-IDENTITY IMAGE PUBLIC ESTEEM SUB-IDENTITY RATING THERAPY 1965M

H-41   HETHERINGTON, E. M.
               EFFECTS OF PATERNAL ABSENCE ON SEX-TYPED BEHAVIORS IN NEGRO AND WHITE PRE-
               ADOLESCENT MALES.
               JOURNAL OF PERSONALITY AND SOCIAL PSYCHOLOGY, 1966, 4, 87-91.
               (RATING SCALES FOR CHILD BEHAVIOR)
          aH-41 ADULT ADOLESCENT RATING DEPENDENCE AGGRESSION PEER CHILD BEHAVIOR SOCIAL
          aH-41 COMPETENCE AFFECTIVE-STATES ADJUSTMENT INTERPERSONAL RELATIONSHIPS
          aH-41 1966M AUTONOMY

H-42   HELPER, M. M., & GARFIELD, S. L.
               USE OF THE SEMANTIC DIFFERENTIAL TO STUDY ACCULTURATION IN AMERICAN INDIAN
               ADOLESCENTS.
               JOURNAL OF PERSONALITY AND SOCIAL PSYCHOLOGY, 1965, 2, 817-822.
               (SEMANTIC DIFFERENTIAL FOR ACCULTURATION CONCEPTS)
          aH-42 ACCULTURATION CONCEPT SELF TIME SEM-DIFFERENTIAL PARENT-CHILD INTERACTION
          aH-42 SCHOOL EVALUATION IMAGE RELATIONSHIPS 1965M

H-43   HOLZMAN, P. S., & ROUSEY, C.
               THE VOICE AS A PERCEPT.
               JOURNAL OF PERSONALITY AND SOCIAL PSYCHOLOGY, 1966, 4, 79-86.
               (VOICE CONFRONTATION RESPONSES)*
          aH-43 AFFECTIVE-STATES PERCEIVED PERCEPTION VOICE RESPONSE INTERPERSONAL
          aH-43 INTERACTION 1966M
               (APPLICATIONS: 221)

H-44   HOLLAND, J. L.
               A PSYCHOLOGICAL CLASSIFICATION SCHEME FOR VOCATIONS AND MAJOR FIELDS.
               JOURNAL OF COUNSELING PSYCHOLOGY, 1966, 13, 278-288.
               (RANGE OF COMPETENCIES SCALE)*
          aH-44 ACTIVITIES PERSONAL COMPETENCE OTHER-CATEGORY CHECKLIST ACHIEVEMENT
          aH-44 ABILITY SOCIAL ADJUSTMENT GLOBAL VOCATIONAL 1966M PREFERENCE
               (APPLICATIONS: 1515)

H-45   HELSON, R.
               PERSONALITY OF WOMEN WITH IMAGINATIVE AND ARTISTIC INTERESTS: THE ROLE OF
               MASCULINITY, ORIGINALITY, AND OTHER CHARACTERISTICS IN THEIR CREATIVITY.
               JOURNAL OF PERSONALITY, 1966, 34, 1-25.
               (CHILDHOOD ACTIVITIES LIST)*
          aH-45 AUTONOMY CREATIVITY MASCULINITY FEMININITY MULTITRAIT SELF-IDENTITY
          aH-45 ROLE PERCEPTION CHILD ACTIVITIES IMAGINATION SUB-IDENTITY 1966M
               (APPLICATIONS: 430)

H-46   HOLLAND, J. L., & NICHOLS, R. C.
               THE DEVELOPMENT AND VALIDATION OF AN INDECISION SCALE: THE NATURAL HISTORY
               OF A PROBLEM IN BASIC RESEARCH.
               JOURNAL OF COUNSELING PSYCHOLOGY, 1964, 11, 27-34.
               (INDECISION SCALE)*
          aH-46 DECISION ADJUSTMENT VOCATIONAL EFFECTIVENESS JOB LIFE GOALS IDEALS
          aH-46 PLANNING AUTONOMY 1964M
               (APPLICATIONS: 1433   1515)

H-47   HOLLAND, J. L.
               THE PSYCHOLOGY OF VOCATIONAL CHOICE: A THEORY OF PERSONALITY TYPES AND
               MODEL ENVIRONMENTS.
               WALTHAM, MASS.: BLAISDELL, 1966.
               (PERSONAL SURVEY)*
          @H-47 SELF-IDENTITY GOALS LIFE PERSONAL ORIENTATION VOCATIONAL SELF TRAIT
          @H-47 MULTITRAIT ENVIRONMENT IDEALS ABILITY 1966M
               (APPLICATIONS: 1524   2758)

H-48   HAMLIN, R. M., & NEMO, R. S.
               SELF-ACTUALIZATION IN CHOICE SCORES OF IMPROVED SCHIZOPHRENICS.
               JOURNAL OF CLINICAL PSYCHOLOGY, 1962, 18, 51-54.
               (MEASURE OF MOTIVATICNAL ORIENTATION)
          @H-48 SELF ACTUALIZATION ORIENTATION AUTONOMY MOTIVE SCHIZOPHRENIA ADJUSTMENT
          @H-48 SELF-IDENTITY 1962M
               (APPLICATIONS: 400)

H-49   HAYWOOD, H. C.
               SOME RELATIONSHIPS BETWEEN ANXIETY LEVEL AND ABILITY TO PREDICT THE
               ANXIETY LEVEL OF PEERS.
               UNPUBLISHED MASTER'S THESIS, SAN DIEGO STATE COLLEGE, 1957.
               HAYWOOD, H. C.
               NOVELTY-SEEKING BEHAVIOR AS A FUNCTION OF MANIFEST ANXIETY AND
               PHYSIOLOGICAL AROUSAL.
               JOURNAL OF PERSONALITY, 1962, 30, 63-74.
               (ANXIETY QUESTIONNAIRE)*
          @H-49 MMPI ANXIETY AFFECTIVE-STATES STRESS SUBJECTIVE TAYLOR-MA NEGATIVE 1957M

H-50   HELSON, R.
               PERSONALITY OF WOMEN WITH IMAGINATIVE AND ARTISTIC INTERESTS: THE ROLE OF
               MASCULINITY, ORIGINALITY, AND CTHER CHARACTERISTICS IN THEIR CREATIVITY.
               JOURNAL OF PERSONALITY, 1966, 34, 1-25.
               (QUESTIONNAIRE FOR PARENTS' DESCRIPTION OF CHILD)
          @H-50 ADJUSTMENT FAMILY INTERACTION PARENT-CHILD RELATICNSHIP BEHAVIOR
          @H-50 DESCRIPTION PARENTAL 1966M CHILD

H-51   HEINEMAN, C. E.
               A FORCED-CHOICE FORM OF THE TAYLOR ANXIETY SCALE.
               JOURNAL OF CONSULTING PSYCHOLOGY, 1953, 17, 447-454.
               (FORCED-CHOICE VERSICN OF TAYLOR MAS)
          @H-51 TAYLOR-MA MMPI MANIFEST ANXIETY AFFECTIVE-STATES SUBJECTIVE STRESS
          @H-51 NEGATIVE 1953M
               (APPLICATIONS: 566   643   803   1566   1685   2869)

H-52   HILDEN, A. H.
               MANUAL FOR Q-SORT AND RANDOM SETS OF PERSONAL CONCEPTS.
               ST. LOUIS: AUTHOR, 1954, (MIMEO).
               (Q-SORT MEASURE OF SELF AND PARENTAL ACCEPTANCE)
          @H-52 PARENT-CHILD SELF-IDENTITY PERCEPTION IMAGE ESTEEM Q-SORT IDEAL EVALUATION
          @H-52 SELF ACCEPTANCE PARENTAL FAMILY INTERACTION ADJUSTMENT 1954M
               (APPLICATIONS: 1021)

H-53   HOLZBERG, J., & PLUMMER, J.
               SEX DIFFERENCES IN SCHIZOPHRENICS: SATISFACTIONS WITH BODY PARTS.
               UNPUBLISHED PAPER, WESLEYAN UNIVERSITY, 1964.
               (MEASURE OF BODY-PARTS SATISFACTION)
          @H-53 SEX DIFFERENCES SATISFACTION SELF-IDENTITY SUB-IDENTITY RCLE PERCEPTION
          @H-53 BODY IMAGE ACCEPTANCE SELF 1964M SCHIZOPHRENIA
               (APPLICATIONS: 1079)

H-54   HILDRETH, H. M.
               A BATTERY OF FEELING AND ATTITUDE SCALES FOR CLINICAL USE.
               JOURNAL OF CLINICAL PSYCHOLOGY, 1946, 2, 214-221.
               (FEELING AND ATTITUDE BATTERY)
          @H-54 DIAGNOSIS ADJUSTMENT PATIENT EMOTION PSYCHIATRIC ATTITUDE AFFECTIVE-STATES
          @H-54 OTHER-CATEGORY GLOBAL 1946M
               (APPLICATIONS: 596   934 1087)

H-55   HOWELL, M. A., & NEWMAN, S. H.
               PREDICTION OF WORK AREA SPECIALIZATION AMONG PROFESSIONAL HEALTH PERSONNEL.
               PERSONNEL PSYCHOLOGY, 1967, 20, 89-110.
               (BIOGRAPHICAL-PERSONAL INVENTORY)*
          @H-55 MULTITRAIT SELF DESCRIPTION VOCATIONAL INTEREST PREDICTION JOB 1967M

H-56   HINRICHS, J. R.
           A REPLICATED STUDY OF JOB SATISFACTION DIMENSIONS.
           PERSONNEL PSYCHOLOGY, 1968, 21, 479-503.
           (GENERAL JOB ATTITUDE QUESTIONNAIRE)
      aH-56 JOB SATISFACTION ATTITUDE PE-FIT ADJUSTMENT EMPLOYEE AFFECTIVE-STATES
      aH-56 GLOBAL ENVIRONMENT 1968M

H-57   HILDEN, A. H.
           Q-SORT CORRELATION: STABILITY AND RANDOM CHOICE OF STATEMENTS.
           JOURNAL OF CONSULTING PSYCHOLOGY, 1958, 22, 45-50.
           (Q-SORT TECHNIQUE FOR IDENTIFICATION)
      aH-57 Q-SORT RESPONSE IDENTIFICATION SELF-IDENTITY SELF ESTEEM EVALUATION
      aH-57 PERCEPTION IDEAL 1958M
           (APPLICATIONS: 826   952   1962)

H-58   HUNT, S. M., SINGER, K., & COBB, S.
           COMPONENTS OF DEPRESSION: IDENTIFIED FROM A SELF-RATING DEPRESSION
           INVENTORY FOR SURVEY USE.
           ARCHIVES OF GENERAL PSYCHIATRY, 1967, 16, 441-447.
           (DEPRESSION INVENTORY)*
      aH-58 DEPRESSION AFFECTIVE-STATES NEGATIVE SELF RATING 1967M

H-59   HOFFMAN, M. L., & SALTZSTEIN, H. D.
           PARENT DISCIPLINE AND THE CHILD'S MORAL DEVELOPMENT.
           JOURNAL OF PERSONALITY AND SOCIAL PSYCHOLOGY, 1967, 5, 45-57.
           (CHILD MORALITY INDEXES)
      aH-59 IDENTIFICATION ADJUSTMENT CHILD JUDGMENT TEACHER MORAL DEVELOPMENT SELF
      aH-59 SELF-IDENTITY ACTUALIZATION CONSCIENCE GUILT PARENTAL OPINION RATING 1967M

H-60   HOFFMAN, M. L., & SALTZSTEIN, H. D.
           PARENT DISCIPLINE AND THE CHILD'S DEVELOPMENT.
           JOURNAL OF PERSONALITY AND SOCIAL PSYCHOLOGY, 1967, 5, 45-57.
           (MEASURES OF PARENT PRACTICES)
      aH-60 PARENT-CHILD PUNITIVENESS WITHDRAWAL AFFECTION POWER BEHAVIOR PARENTAL
      aH-60 FAMILY INTERACTION ADJUSTMENT 1967M

H-61   HARTLEY, R. E.
           PERSONAL NEEDS AND THE ACCEPTANCE OF A NEW GROUP AS A REFERENCE GROUP.
           JOURNAL OF SOCIAL PSYCHOLOGY, 1960, 51, 349-358.
           (PERSONAL NEEDS QUESTIONNAIRE)*
      aH-61 PERSONAL NEED SATISFACTION AUTONOMY ACHIEVEMENT DOMINANCE AFFILIATION
      aH-61 ORDER OTHER-CATEGORY CHANGE ABASEMENT NURTURANCE AGGRESSION 1960M

H-62   HOROWITZ, E.
           REPORTED EMBARRASSMENT MEMORIES OF ELEMENTARY SCHOOL, HIGH SCHOOL, AND
           COLLEGE STUDENTS.
           JOURNAL OF SOCIAL PSYCHOLOGY, 1962, 56, 317-325.
           (EMBARRASSMENT QUESTIONNAIRE)*
      aH-62 ELEMENTARY SECONDARY COLLEGE STUDENT EMBARRASSMENT AFFECTIVE-STATES
      aH-62 GLOBAL NEGATIVE 1962M SELF AWARENESS

H-63   HANSON, D. J.
           DOGMATISM AND AUTHORITARIANISM.
           JOURNAL OF SOCIAL PSYCHOLOGY, 1968, 76, 89-95.
           (STEREOPATHY-ACQUIESCENCE SCALE)*
      aH-63 DOGMATISM ACQUIESCENCE AUTHORITARIANISM COPING-DEFENSE FLEXIBILITY
      aH-63 RIGIDITY STEREOTYPE 1968M

H-64   HAND, H. C., FINLAY, G. C., & DOLIO, A. J.
           ILLINOIS INVENTORY OF PUPIL OPINION (SECONDARY-SCHOOL FORM).
           NEW YORK: HARCOURT, BRACE AND WORLD, 1948.
           (ILLINOIS INVENTORY OF PUPIL OPINION)*
      aH-64 STUDENT OPINION TEACHER SATISFACTION ATTITUDE GLOBAL AFFECTIVE-STATES
      aH-64 SECONDARY SCHOOL 1948M

H-65   HOWARD, K. I.
           A TEST OF STIMULUS-SEEKING BEHAVIOR.
           PERCEPTUAL AND MOTOR SKILLS, 1961, 13, 416.
           (TEST OF STIMULUS- OR CHANGE-SEEKING BEHAVIOR)
      aH-65 STIMULUS SEEKING CHANGE BEHAVIOR ADJUSTMENT ENVIRONMENT PE-FIT COPING
      aH-65 STYLE COPING-DEFENSE 1961M SENSATION
           (APPLICATIONS: 1820)

H-66   HEILBRUN, A. B.
                 PARENT MODEL ATTRIBUTES, NURTURANT REINFORCEMENT AND CONSISTENCY OF
                 BEHAVIOR IN ADOLESCENTS.
                 CHILD DEVELOPMENT, 1964, 35, 151-167.
                 (PARENT-CHILD INTERACTION RATING SCALES)*
            @H-66 FAMILY ADJUSTMENT PARENT-CHILD INTERACTION PARENTAL RATING NURTURANCE
            @H-66 ADOLESCENT 1964M INTERPERSONAL RELATIONSHIPS
                 (APPLICATIONS: 1523 1984 2200 2263 2280 2465)

H-67   HIGGS, W. J.
                 THE EFFECTS OF AN ENVIRONMENTAL CHANGE UPON BEHAVIOR OF SCHIZOPHRENICS.
                 UNPUBLISHED MASTER'S THESIS, UNIVERSITY OF ILLINOIS, 1964.
                 (PATIENT ACTIVITY CHECKLIST)*
            @H-67 ADJUSTMENT PATIENT BEHAVIOR GLOBAL SOCIAL COMPETENCE MENTAL-ILLNESS
            @H-67 CHECKLIST SCHIZOPHRENIA WARD RATING 1964M
                 (APPLICATIONS: 2212)

H-68   HUNTER, M., SCHOOLER, C., & SPOHN, H. E.
                 THE MEASUREMENT OF CHARACTERISTIC PATTERNS OF WARD BEHAVIOR IN CHRONIC
                 SCHIZOPHRENICS.
                 JOURNAL OF CONSULTING PSYCHOLOGY, 1962, 26, 69-73.
                 (LOCATION ACTIVITY INVENTORY)*
            @H-68 SCHIZOPHRENIA WARD BEHAVIOR ACTIVITIES ADJUSTMENT GLOBAL OTHER-CATEGORY
            @H-68 MENTAL-ILLNESS THERAPY HOSPITALIZATION 1962M
                 (APPLICATIONS: 881)

H-69   HAMMOND, M.
                 OCCUPATIONAL ATTITUDE RATING SCALES.
                 PERSONNEL GUIDANCE JOURNAL, 1954, 32, 470-474.
                 (OCCUPATIONAL ATTITUDE RATING SCALES)*
            @H-69 VOCATIONAL INTEREST ATTITUDE RATING JOB SATISFACTION ADJUSTMENT INTRINSIC
            @H-69 EXTRINSIC AUTONOMY MOTIVE 1954M PREFERENCE

H-70   HERZBERG, F., MAUSNER, B., & SNYDERMAN, B.
                 THE MOTIVATION TO WORK.
                 NEW YORK: WILEY, 1959.
                 (MEASURE OF MOTIVATION TO WORK)
            @H-70 INTRINSIC EXTRINSIC PERFORMANCE ORGANIZATION SATISFACTION PE-FIT JOB
            @H-70 MOTIVE EMPLOYEE ADJUSTMENT ENVIRONMENT 1959M JOB-HYGIENE

H-71   HATHAWAY, S. R., & MCKINLEY, J. C.
                 MANUAL FOR THE MINNESOTA MULTIPHASIC PERSONALITY INVENTORY.
                 (REV. ED.) NEW YORK: PSYCHOLOGICAL CORPORATION, 1943.
                 (EGO FUNCTIONING SCALE)
            @H-71 ADJUSTMENT EGO-STRENGTH GLOBAL FUNCTIONING MMPI COPING-DEFENSE EGO
            @H-71 EGO-RESILIENCY 1943M
                 (APPLICATIONS: 122)

H-72   HAND, J.
                 MEASUREMENT OF RESPONSE SETS.
                 PSYCHOLOGICAL REPORTS, 1964, 14, 907-913.
                 (HAND SOCIAL DESIRABILITY SCALE)*
            @H-72 ACQUIESCENCE SOCIAL DESIRABILITY RESPONSE-BIAS 1964M
                 (APPLICATIONS: 1637)

H-73   HAFNER, A. J., & KAPLAN, A. M.
                 HOSTILITY CONTENT ANALYSIS OF THE RORSCHACH AND TAT.
                 JOURNAL OF PROJECTIVE TECHNIQUES, 1960, 24, 137-143.
                 (METHOD FOR SCORING TAT FOR HOSTILITY)
            @H-73 RORSCHACH TAT HOSTILITY RESENTMENT AFFECTIVE-STATES PROJECTIVE 1960M
                 (APPLICATIONS: 1910 2191)

H-74   HURLEY, J. R.
                 THE IOWA PICTURE INTERPRETATION TEST: A MULTIPLE-CHOICE VARIATION OF THE
                 TAT.
                 JOURNAL OF CONSULTING PSYCHOLOGY, 1955, 19, 372-376.
                 (IOWA PICTURE INTERPRETATION TEST)*
            @H-74 PROJECTIVE TAT ADJUSTMENT GLOBAL SECURITY HOSTILITY AUTONOMY NEED
            @H-74 ACHIEVEMENT 1955M
                 (APPLICATIONS: 328   922 1705)

H-75   HUNT, D. E., & HALVERSON, C. F.
                 MANUAL FOR SCORING SENTENCE COMPLETION RESPONSES FOR ADOLESCENTS.
                 UNPUBLISHED MANUSCRIPT, SYRACUSE UNIVERSITY, 1964.
                 (SENTENCE COMPLETION MEASURE OF CONCEPTUAL LEVEL)
            @H-75 SOCIAL COMPETENCE INTERPERSONAL COGNITIVE COMPLEXITY CONCEPTUAL MATURITY
            @H-75 ADOLESCENT STRUCTURE FUNCTIONING 1964M

H-76   HEATH, D. H.
            EXPLORATIONS OF MATURITY: STUDIES OF MATURE AND IMMATURE COLLEGE MEN.
            NEW YORK: APPLETON-CENTURY-CROFTS, 1965.
            (SELF-IMAGE QUESTIONNAIRE)*
        @H-76 SELF ESTEEM IMAGE SELF-IDENTITY PERCEPTION EVALUATION SEM-DIFFERENTIAL
        @H-76 CONCEPT RATING 1965M

H-77   HARVEY, O. J., & CLAPP, W. F.
            HOPE, EXPECTANCY AND REACTIONS TO THE UNEXPECTED.
            JOURNAL OF PERSONALITY AND SOCIAL PSYCHOLOGY, 1965, 2, 45-52.
            (AFFECTIVE RESPONSE MEASURE)
        @H-77 AFFECTIVE-STATES OTHER-CATEGORY POSITIVE NEGATIVE GLOBAL RESPONSE 1965M
        @H-77 EMOTION

H-78   HUTTNER, L., & KATZELL, R. A.
            DEVELOPING A YARDSTICK OF SUPERVISORY PERFORMANCE.
            PERSONNEL, 1957, 33, 371-378.
            (RATINGS OF OVERALL MANAGEMENT EFFECTIVENESS)
        @H-78 MANAGEMENT EFFECTIVENESS RATING JOB SUPERVISOR PERFORMANCE 1957M
        @H-78 LEADERSHIP

H-79   HOROWITZ, S. L.
            STRATEGIES WITHIN HYPNOSIS FOR REDUCING PHOBIC BEHAVIOR.
            JOURNAL OF ABNORMAL PSYCHOLOGY, 1970, 75, 104-112.
            (FEAR CHECK LIST)*
        @H-79 PHOBIA FEAR CHECKLIST AFFECTIVE-STATES NEGATIVE 1970M

H-81   HAIRE, M., GHISELLI, E. E., & PORTER, L. W.
            MANAGERIAL THINKING.
            NEW YORK: WILEY, 1966.
            (QUESTIONNAIRE MEASURE OF BELIEF STRUCTURE IN MANAGERS)
        @H-81 JOB LEADERSHIP ORIENTATION SUPERVISOR MANAGEMENT BELIEF VALUES 1966M
            (APPLICATIONS: 2360)

H-82   HARRIS, F. J.
            THE QUANTIFICATION OF AN INDUSTRIAL EMPLOYEE SURVEY. I. METHOD.
            JOURNAL OF APPLIED PSYCHOLOGY, 1949, 33, 103-111.
            (MORALE SCALE)
        @H-82 JOB SATISFACTION EMPLOYEE PE-FIT 1949M
            (APPLICATIONS: 2369)

H-83   HORNADAY, J. A., & BUNKER, C. S.
            THE NATURE OF THE ENTREPRENEUR.
            PERSONNEL PSYCHOLOGY, 1970, 23, 47-54.
            (INTERVIEW GUIDESHEET)*
        @H-83 LIFE HISTORY EXPERIENCE FAMILY ORGANIZATION MULTITRAIT SUCCESS JOB 1970M

H-84   HEILIZER, F.
            AN EXPLORATION OF THE RELATIONSHIP BETWEEN HYPNOTIZABILITY AND ANXIETY
            AND/OR NEUROTICISM.
            JOURNAL OF CONSULTING PSYCHOLOGY, 1960, 24, 432-436.
            (TAT SCORED FOR EMOTIONALITY, DISTANCE, CONSTRICTION, AND TIME/PHRASE)
        @H-84 1960M TAT PROJECTIVE IMAGERY EMOTION WITHDRAWAL AFFECTIVE-STATES DISTANCE
        @H-84 TIME ORIENTATION

H-85   HARRISON, R., & OSHRY, B.
            (NO REFERENCE AVAILABLE)
            (GROUP PERCEPTION QUESTIONNAIRE)*
        @H-85 GROUP PERCEPTION SOCIOMETRIC RATING PARTICIPATION SOCIAL INFLUENCE
        @H-85 EFFECTIVENESS PERSONAL INTERPERSONAL
            (APPLICATIONS: 2477)

H-86   HACKMAN, J. R., & VIDMAR, N.
            EFFECTS OF SIZE AND TASK TYPE ON GROUP PERFORMANCE AND MEMBER REACTIONS.
            SOCIOMETRY, 1970, 33, 37-54.
            (MEMBER REACTION QUESTIONNAIRE)
        @H-86 1970M GROUP PARTICIPATION INTERPERSONAL INTERACTION RELATIONSHIPS

H-87   HOLMES, J. S.
            COMPARISON OF GROUP LEADER AND NON-PARTICIPANT OBSERVER JUDGMENTS OF
            CERTAIN OBJECTIVE INTERACTION VARIABLES.
            PSYCHOLOGICAL REPORTS, 1969, 24, 655-659.
            (GROUP INTERACTION RECORDING SYSTEM)*
        @H-87 1969M GROUP THERAPY INTERACTION BEHAVIOR
            (APPLICATIONS: 2831)

H-88   HERMANS, H. J. M.
                A QUESTIONNAIRE MEASURE OF ACHIEVEMENT MOTIVATION.
                JOURNAL OF APPLIED PSYCHOLOGY, 1970, 4, 353-363.
                (MEASURE OF ACHIEVEMENT MOTIVATION)
            @H-88 1970M NEED ACHIEVEMENT MOTIVATION ANXIETY ASPIRATION TENSION
            @H-88 AUTONOMY

H-89   HELSON, R.
                SEX DIFFERENCES IN CREATIVE STYLE.
                JOURNAL OF PERSONALITY, 1967, 35, 214-233.
                (MATHEMATICIANS Q SORT)*
            @H-89 1967M Q-SORT SELF DESCRIPTION
                (APPLICATIONS: 2336 2924)

H-90   HARTLAGE, L. C., & HALE, P.
                SELF-CONCEPT DECLINE FROM PSYCHIATRIC HOSPITALIZATION.
                JOURNAL OF INDIVIDUAL PSYCHOLOGY, 1968, 24, 174-176.
                (MEASURE OF SELF CONCEPT)
            @H-90 1968M SELF-IDENTITY SELF CONCEPT ESTEEM IMAGE EVALUATION
                (APPLICATIONS: 2922)

H-91   HELPER, M. M.
                MESSAGE PREFERENCES: AN APPROACH TO THE ASSESSMENT OF INTERPERSONAL
                STANDARDS.
                JOURNAL OF PROJECTIVE TECHNIQUES AND PERSONALITY ASSESSMENT, 1970, 34,
                64-70.
                (MESSAGE PREFERENCE MEASURE OF INTERPERSONAL STANDARDS)
            @H-91 1970M INTERPERSONAL RELATIONSHIPS COMMUNICATION PREFERENCE

H-92   HARRIS, R. E., & LINGOES, J. C.
                SUBSCALES FOR THE MMPI: AN AID TO PROFILE INTERPRETATION,.
                SAN FRANCISCO: UNIVERSITY OF CALIFORNIA, DEPARTMENT OF PSYCHIATRY, 1955.
                (MIMEO)
                (SOCIAL ALIENATION INDEX FROM MMPI)
            @H-92 1955M ADJUSTMENT SOCIAL COMPETENCE ALIENATION MMPI
                (APPLICATIONS: 122 2386)

H-93   HOLZMAN, P. S., & ROUSEY, C.
                MONITORING, ACTIVATION, AND DISINHIBITION: EFFECTS OF WHITE NOISE MASKING
                ON SPOKEN THOUGHT.
                JOURNAL OF ABNORMAL PSYCHOLOGY, 1970, 75, 227-241.
                (TAT SCORED FOR DEFENSIVENESS/IMPULSE EXPRESSION)
            @H-93 1970M TAT DEFENSIVENESS IMPULSE EXPRESSION PROJECTIVE IMAGERY
            @H-93 COPING-DEFENSE

H-94   HOFMAN, J. E.
                THE MEANING OF BEING A JEW IN ISRAEL: AN ANALYSIS OF ETHNIC IDENTITY.
                JOURNAL OF PERSONALITY AND SOCIAL PSYCHOLOGY, 1970, 15, 196-202.
                (SEMANTIC DIFFERENTIAL MEASURE OF ETHNIC IDENTITY)
            @H-94 1970M SEM-DIFFERENTIAL ETHNIC IDENTITY SELF-IDENTITY SUB-IDENTITY

H-95   HODGES, W. F., & FELLING, J. P.
                TYPES OF STRESSFUL SITUATIONS AND THEIR RELATION TO TRAIT ANXIETY AND
                SEX.
                JOURNAL OF CONSULTING AND CLINICAL PSYCHOLOGY, 1970, 34, 333-337.
                (STRESSFUL SITUATIONS QUESTIONNAIRE)*
            @H-95 1970M ANXIETY FAILURE FEAR STRESS PE-FIT NEED SECURITY
            @H-95 SITUATIONAL

H-97   HEMPHILL, J. K., & COONS, A. H.
                DEVELOPMENT OF THE LEADER BEHAVIOR DESCRIPTION QUESTIONNAIRE.
                BUREAU OF BUSINESS RESEARCH MONOGRAPH NO. 88.
                COLUMBUS, OHIO: OHIO STATE UNIVERSITY, 1957.
                (LEADER BEHAVIOR DESCRIPTION QUESTIONNAIRE)*
            @H-97 1957M LEADERSHIP ABILITY STYLE BEHAVIOR INTERPERSONAL COMPETENCE
                (APPLICATIONS: 2808)

H-98   HARVEY, O. J., & HOFFMEISTER, J. K.
                THE CONCEPTUAL SYSTEMS TEST AND NINE CRITERION FACTORS (REVISED).
                BOULDER: UNIVERSITY OF COLORADO, 1967.
                (CONCEPTUAL SYSTEMS TEST)
            @H-98 1967M CONCEPTUAL COGNITIVE STRUCTURE FUNCTIONING AFFILIATION NEED
            @H-98 INTERPERSONAL AGGRESSION ABSTRACTNESS
                (APPLICATIONS: 2423)

H-99   HAGGARD, E. A., AS, A., & BORGEN, C. M.
        SOCIAL ISOLATES AND URBANITES IN PERCEPTUAL ISOLATION.
        JOURNAL OF ABNORMAL PSYCHOLOGY, 1970, 76, 1-9.
        (INVENTORY OF PERSONALITY TRAITS)
        aH-99 1970M TRAIT EXTRAVERSION INTENSITY NEED SENSATION SEEKING INTROVERSION

H-100   HAGGARD, E. A., AS, A., & BORGEN, C.
        SOCIAL ISOLATES AND URBANITES IN PERCEPTUAL ISOLATION.
        JOURNAL OF ABNORMAL PSYCHOLOGY, 1970, 76, 1-9.
        (MEASURE OF APARTNESS-TOGETHERNESS)
        aH-100 1970M ALIENATION BELONGINGNESS AFFILIATION FAMILY INTERACTION TAT
        aH-100 PROJECTIVE IMAGERY

H-101   HOOKE, J. F.
        RATING DELINQUENT BEHAVIOR.
        PSYCHOLOGICAL REPORTS, 1970, 27, 155-158.
        (SYSTEM FOR CLASSIFYING DELINQUENT BEHAVIORS)
        aH-101 1970M DELINQUENCY BEHAVIOR AGGRESSION DIRECTION

H-102   HALL, D. T.
        THE EFFECT OF TEACHER-STUDENT CONGRUENCE UPON STUDENT LEARNING IN COLLEGE
        CLASSES.
        JOURNAL OF EDUCATIONAL PSYCHOLOGY, 1970, 61, 205-213.
        (MEASUREMENT OF IDEAL TEACHER STYLE)
        aH-102 1970M PE-FIT TEACHER STUDENT LEADERSHIP INTERACTION FACILITATION
        aH-102 STYLE

H-104   HALVERSON, C. F., JR.
        INTERPERSONAL PERCEPTION: COGNITIVE COMPLEXITY AND TRAIT IMPLICATION.
        JOURNAL OF CONSULTING AND CLINICAL PSYCHOLOGY, 1970, 34, 86-90.
        (TRAIT IMPLICATION INSTRUMENT)
        aH-104 1970M INTERPERSONAL PERCEPTION COGNITIVE COMPLEXITY TRAIT-TERMS
        aH-104 JUDGMENT

H-105   HAMMOND, L. K.
        COGNITIVE STRUCTURE AND CLINICAL INFERENCE.
        JOURNAL OF GENERAL PSYCHOLOGY, 1970, 83, 107-118.
        (MEASURE OF COGNITIVE STRUCTURE)
        aH-105 1970M COGNITIVE STRUCTURE FUNCTIONING DIAGNOSIS THERAPY THINKING

H-106   HURLEY, J. R., & HURLEY, S. J.
        TOWARD AUTHENTICITY IN MEASURING SELF-DISCLOSURE.
        JOURNAL OF COUNSELING PSYCHOLOGY, 1969, 16, 271-274.
        (DIRECT DISCLOSURE RATING SCALE)
        aH-106 1969M SELF DISCLOSURE GROUP RATING OTHERS
            (APPLICATIONS: 1517)

H-107   HURLEY, S. J.
        SELF-DISCLOSURE IN COUNSELING GROUPS AS INFLUENCED BY STRUCTURED
        CONFRONTATION AND INTERPERSONAL PROCESS RECALL.
        UNPUBLISHED DOCTORAL DISSERTATION, MICHIGAN STATE UNIVERSITY, 1967.
        (SELF-DISCLOSURE RATING)
        aH-107 1967M SELF DISCLOSURE GROUP INTERACTION COUNSELING RATING
            (APPLICATIONS: 1517)

H-108   HOGAN, H. W.
        A SYMBOLIC MEASURE OF AUTHORITARIANISM: AN EXPLORATORY STUDY.
        JOURNAL OF SOCIAL PSYCHOLOGY, 1970, 82, 215-219.
        (SYMBOLIC TOLERANCE-OF-AMBIGUITY TEST)
        aH-108 1970M AUTHORITARIANISM AMBIGUITY TOLERANCE DOGMATISM RIGIDITY FLEXIBILITY
            (APPLICATIONS: 2818 2883)

H-109   HOFSTEE, W. K. B.
        METHODS EFFECTS IN ABSOLUTE AND COMPARATIVE JUDGMENTS.
        UNPUBLISHED DISSERTATION, 1967.
        (ABSOLUTE AND COMPARATIVE RATINGS OF TRAIT DESIRABILITY)
        aH-109 1967M TRAIT DESIRABILITY SOCIAL JUDGMENT
            (APPLICATIONS: 2709)

H-111   HELMREICH, R. L.
           PROLONGED STRESS IN SEA LAB II: A FIELD STUDY OF INDIVIDUAL AND GROUP
           REACTIONS.
           UNPUBLISHED DOCTORAL DISSERTATION, YALE UNIVERSITY, 1966.
           (MOOD-ADJECTIVE CHECK LIST)
         aH-111 1966M MOOD AFFECTIVE-STATES CHECKLIST
         aH-111 STRESS
           (APPLICATIONS: 494)

H-112   HARVEY, O. J., KELLY, H. H., & SHAPIRO, M. M.
           REACTIONS TO UNFAVOURABLE EVALUATIONS OF THE SELF MADE BY OTHER PERSONS.
           JOURNAL OF PERSONALITY, 1957, 25, 393-411.
           (SCALE OF SOCIAL CHARACTERISTICS)
         aH-112 1957M SOCIAL SELF INTERPERSONAL DESCRIPTION
         aH-112 EVALUATION PEER PERCEPTION OTHERS
           (APPLICATIONS: 62   379)

H-113   HOLSOPPLE, J. Q., & MIALE, F. R.
           SENTENCE COMPLETION: A PROJECTIVE METHOD FOR THE STUDY OF PERSONALITY.
           SPRINGFIELD, ILLINOIS: THOMAS, 1954.
           (MIALE-HOLSOPPLE SENTENCE COMPLETION TASK)*
         aH-113 1954M PROJECTIVE PERSONALITY STRUCTURE
         aH-113 SENTENCE-COMP
           (APPLICATIONS: 349   390)

H-114   HORNSTEIN, M. G.
           ACCURACY OF EMOTIONAL COMMUNICATION AND INTERPERSONAL COMPATIBILITY.
           JOURNAL OF PERSONALITY, 1967, 35, 20-28.
           (MEASURE OF SENSITIVITY TO EMOTIONAL EXPRESSIONS)
         aH-114 1967M EMOTION SENSITIVITY COMMUNICATION INTERPERSONAL INTERACTION
         aH-114 RELATIONSHIPS AFFECTIVE-STATES PERCEIVED EMPATHY

H-115   HELSON, R.
           PERSONALITY OF WOMEN WITH IMAGINATIVE AND ARTISTIC INTERESTS: THE ROLE OF
           MASCULINITY, ORIGINALITY, AND OTHER CHARACTERISTICS IN THEIR CREATIVITY
           JOURNAL OF PERSONALITY, 1966, 34, 1-25.
           (TRAIT DESCRIPTION OF DAUGHTERS)
         aH-115 1966M TRAIT PARENT-CHILD FEMININITY
         aH-115 MASCULINITY CHILD PARENTAL PERCEPTION

H-116   HELSON, R.
           PERSONALITY OF WOMEN WITH IMAGINATIVE AND ARTISTIC INTERESTS: THE ROLE OF
           MASCULINITY, ORIGINALITY, AND OTHER CHARACTERISTICS IN THEIR CREATIVITY
           JOURNAL OF PERSONALITY, 1966, 34, 1-25.
           (CHECK LIST FOR DESCRIPTION OF PARENTS)
         aH-116 1966M PARENT-CHILD TRAIT PARENTAL CHILD PERCEPTION

H-117   HOLT, R. R., & HAVEL, J.
           A METHOD FOR ASSESSING PRIMARY AND SECONDARY PROCESS IN THE RORSCHACH.
           IN MARIA A. RICKERS-OUSANKINA (ED.), RORSCHACH PSYCHOLOGY. NEW YORK:
           WILEY, 1960, 263-315.
           HOLT, R. R.
           MANUAL FOR THE SCORING OF PRIMARY PROCESS MANIFESTATIONS IN RORSCHACH
           RESPONSES (8TH. ED.).
           NEW YORK: RESEARCH CENTER FOR MENTAL HEALTH, 1962
           (RORSCHACH SCORED FOR PRIMARY PROCESS THINKING)
         aH-117 RORSCHACH PROJECTIVE PRIMARY-PROCESS THINKING DEFENSE DEMANDS DEFENSIVE
         aH-117 1960M EFFECTIVENESS DRIVE
           (APPLICATIONS: 515   609   1007   1130   1994)

H-118   HELLER, K., MYERS, R. A., & KLINE, L. V.
           INTERVIEWER BEHAVIOR AS A FUNCTION OF STANDARDIZED CLIENT ROLES.
           JOURNAL OF CONSULTING PSYCHOLOGY, 1963, 27, 117-122.
           (BEHAVIORAL ANXIETY CHECK LIST)
         aH-118 1963M BEHAVIOR CHECKLIST INTERPERSONAL ANXIETY TENSION PERFORMANCE
         aH-118 INTERVIEW

H-119   HEILBRUN, A. B., JR.
           EVIDENCE REGARDING THE EQUIVALENCE OF IPSATIVE AND NORMATIVE PERSONALITY
           SCALES.
           JOURNAL OF CONSULTING PSYCHOLOGY, 1963, 27, 152-156.
           (Q-SORT MEASURE OF NEED ACHIEVEMENT AND NURTURANCE)
         aH-119 1963M ACHIEVEMENT NEED NURTURANCE Q-SORT

H-120   HEILBRUN, A. B., JR.
          EVIDENCE REGARDING THE EQUIVALENCE OF IPSATIVE AND NORMATIVE PERSONALITY
          SCALES.
          JOURNAL OF CONSULTING PSYCHOLOGY, 1963, 27, 152-156.
          (FORCED-CHOICE MEASURE OF NEED ACHIEVEMENT AND NURTURANCE)
          @H-120 1963M NEED ACHIEVEMENT NURTURANCE MOTIVE

H-121   HAWORTH, M. R.
          THE USE OF A FILMED PUPPET SHOW AS A GROUP PROJECTIVE TECHNIQUE FOR
          CHILDREN.
          GENETIC PSYCHOLOGY MONOGRAPHS, 1957, 56, 257-296.
          (CHILDRENS' PERSONALITY MEASURES FROM PROJECTIVE FILM)
          @H-121 1957M CHILD PROJECTIVE FAMILY AGGRESSION SIBLING RIVALRY GUILT ANXIETY
          (APPLICATIONS: 1631)

H-122   HANLEY, C.
          DERIVING A MEASURE OF TEST-TAKING DEFENSIVENESS.
          JOURNAL OF CONSULTING PSYCHOLOGY, 1957, 21, 391-397.
          (MEASURE OF DEFENSIVENESS)
          @H-122 1957M MMPI DEFENSIVENESS RESPONSE-BIAS TEST ANXIETY
          @H-122 SOCIAL DESIRABILITY
          (APPLICATIONS: 757 1414 1626 1899 2085)

H-123   HARROWER, M. R., & STEINER, M. F.
          LARGE SCALE RORSCHACH TECHNIQUES.
          SPRINGFIELD, ILLINOIS: CHARLES C. THOMAS, 1945.
          (HARROWER MULTIPLE-CHOICE RORSCHACH TEST)*
          @H-123 1945M PROJECTIVE RORSCHACH
          (APPLICATIONS: 1823 2085)

H-124   HOLTZMAN, W. H.
          TENTATIVE MANUAL: THE HOLTZMAN FORM-RECOGNITION TEST.
          AUSTIN: UNIVERSITY OF TEXAS, 1955 (MIMEO).
          (FORM RECOGNITION TEST)*
          @H-124 1955M FIELD DEPENDENCE PERCEPTION COGNITIVE FUNCTIONING
          (APPLICATIONS: 720 1786)

H-125   HILER, E. W., & NESVIG, D.
          CHANGES IN INTELLECTUAL FUNCTIONS OF CHILDREN IN A PSYCHIATRIC HOSPITAL.
          JOURNAL OF CONSULTING PSYCHOLOGY, 1961, 25, 288-292.
          (MEASURE OF CHANGE IN CONDITION)
          @H-125 1961M CHANGE FUNCTIONING INTELLECTUAL CHILD PSYCHIATRIC COGNITIVE STYLE
          (APPLICATIONS: 1990)

H-127   HOWE, E. S., & POPE, B.
          THE DIMENSIONALITY OF RATINGS OF THERAPIST VERBAL RESPONSES.
          JOURNAL OF CONSULTING PSYCHOLOGY, 1961, 25, 296-303.
          (MEASURE OF DIMENSIONALITY OF THERAPIST RATINGS)
          @H-127 1961M THERAPY RATING PSYCHIATRIC AMBIGUITY STRESS EVALUATION
          @H-127 ACTIVITIES SUBJECTIVE

H-128   HOWE, E. S., & POPE, B.
          AN EMPIRICAL SCALE OF THERAPIST VERBAL ACTIVITY LEVEL IN THE INITIAL
          INTERVIEW.
          JOURNAL OF CONSULTING PSYCHOLOGY, 1961, 25, 510-520.
          (THERAPIST VERBAL ACTIVITY SCALES)
          @H-128 1961M THERAPY COUNSELING INTERPERSONAL RELATIONSHIPS INTERACTION
          @H-128 ACTIVITY VOICE

H-129   HUNTLEY, C. W.
          JUDGMENTS OF SELF BASED UPON RECORDS OF EXPRESSIVE BEHAVIOR.
          JOURNAL OF ABNORMAL SOCIAL PSYCHOLOGY, 1940, 35, 398-427.
          (MEASURE OF UNCONSCIOUS SELF-JUDGMENT)
          @H-129 1940M SELF JUDGMENT BEHAVIOR EXPRESSIVENESS GRAPHIC RATING VOICE
          @H-129 CONCEPT
          (APPLICATIONS: 1819)

H-130   HAMSHER, J. H., & FARINA, A.
          "OPENNESS" AS A DIMENSION OF PROJECTIVE TEST RESPONSES.
          JOURNAL OF CONSULTING PSYCHOLOGY, 1967, 31, 525-528.
          (TAT MEASURE OF OPENNESS IN COMMUNICATION OF PERSONAL INFORMATION)
          @H-130 1967M TAT PROJECTIVE OPENNESS COMMUNICATION SELF DISCLOSURE

H-131   HALKIDES, G.
               AN INVESTIGATION OF THERAPEUTIC SUCCESS AS A FRACTION OF FOUR VARIABLES.
               UNPUBLISHED DOCTORAL DISSERTATION, UNIVERSITY OF CHICAGO, 1958.
               (THERAPIST CONDITION SCALES)
           @H-131 1958M THERAPY CONSISTENCY DISSONANCE EMPATHY SENSITIVITY PERSONALITY
               (APPLICATIONS: 2117)

H-132   HOGAN, R.
               DEVELOPMENT OF AN EMPATHY SCALE.
               JOURNAL OF CONSULTING AND CLINICAL PSYCHOLOGY, 1969, 33, 307-316.
               (EMPATHY SCALE)
           @H-132 1969M EMPATHY INTROCEPTIVE SENSITIVITY INTERPERSONAL RELATIONSHIPS
           @H-132 OTHERS AWARENESS PERSON PERCEPTION MMPI
               (APPLICATIONS: 2628)

H-133   HURLEY, J. R.
               PARENTAL MALEVOLENCE AND CHILDREN'S INTELLIGENCE.
               JOURNAL OF CONSULTING PSYCHOLOGY, 1967, 31, 199-204.
               (PARENTAL REJECTION SCALE)
           @H-133 1967M PARENT-CHILD RELATIONSHIPS INTERACTION FAMILY ACCEPTANCE

H-134   HURLEY, J. R.
               PARENTAL ACCEPTANCE-REJECTION AND CHILDREN'S INTELLIGENCE.
               MERRILL-PALMER QUARTERLY, 1965, 11, 19-31.
               (JUDGMENT OF PUNISHMENT INDEX)
           @H-134 1965M PUNITIVENESS PARENTAL PARENT-CHILD RELATIONSHIPS FAMILY INTERACTION

H-135   HURLEY, J. R.
               PARENTAL ACCEPTANCE-REJECTION AND CHILDREN'S INTELLIGENCE.
               MERRILL-PALMER QUARTERLY, 1965, 11, 19-31.
               (MANIFEST REJECTION SCALE)
           @H-135 1965M PARENTAL ACCEPTANCE MANIFEST SUPPORT CHILD
               (APPLICATIONS: 2316)

H-136   HILL, W. F.
               HILL INTERACTION MATRIX: A METHOD OF STUDYING INTERACTIONS IN
               PSYCHOTHERAPY GROUPS.
               LOS ANGELES: UNIVERSITY OF SOUTHERN CALIFORNIA, YOUTH STUDY CENTER, 1965.
           HILL, W. F.
               HILL INTERACTION MATRIX SCORING MANUAL.
               LOS ANGELES: UNIVERSITY OF SOUTHERN CALIFORNIA, YOUTH STUDY CENTER, 1966.
               (HILL INTERACTION MATRIX)*
           @H-136 1965M INTERACTION GROUP THERAPY INTERPERSONAL RELATIONSHIPS
               (APPLICATIONS: 2144)

H-137   HAYS, L. W., & WORELL, L.
               ANXIETY DRIVE, ANXIETY HABIT, AND ACHIEVEMENT: A THEORETICAL REFORMULATION
               IN TERMS OF OPTIMAL MOTIVATION.
               JOURNAL OF PERSONALITY, 1967, 35, 145-163.
               (PREFERENCE-BEHAVIOR DIFFERENTIAL)
           @H-137 1967M BEHAVIOR PREFERENCE CONFLICT
               (APPLICATIONS: 2290)

H-138   HOLMES, D. S., & TYLER, J. D.
               DIRECT VERSUS PROJECTIVE MEASUREMENT OF ACHIEVEMENT MOTIVATION.
               JOURNAL OF CONSULTING AND CLINICAL PSYCHOLOGY, 1968, 32, 712-717.
               (OBJECTIVE RATINGS OF NEED FOR ACHIEVEMENT)
           @H-138 1968M NEED ACHIEVEMENT SELF PEER RATING

H-139   HEATH, D. E.
               THE PHRASE ASSOCIATION TEST: A RESEARCH MEASURE OF ANXIETY THRESHOLDS AND
               DEFENSE TYPE.
               JOURNAL OF GENERAL PSYCHOLOGY, 1960, 62, 165-176.
               (PHRASE ASSOCIATION TEST)
           @H-139 1960M ANXIETY DEFENSE MASCULINITY HOSTILITY DEPENDENCE
               (APPLICATIONS: 2211 2726)

H-140   HOKANSON, J. E., & GORDON, J. E.
               THE EXPRESSION AND INHIBITION OF HOSTILITY IN IMAGINATIVE AND OVERT
               BEHAVIOR.
               JOURNAL OF ABNORMAL AND SOCIAL PSYCHOLOGY, 1958, 57, 327-333.
               (TAT SCORED FOR HOSTILITY)
           @H-140 1958M TAT HOSTILITY AGGRESSION AROUSAL
           @H-140 EXPRESSION
               (APPLICATIONS: 708   735)

H-141   HALPIN, A. W., & WINER, B. J.
             STUDIES IN AIRCREW COMPOSITION III: THE LEADERSHIP BEHAVIOR OF THE
             AIRPLANE COMMANDER.
             HRRL CONTRACT TECHNICAL REPORT NO. 3, PERSONNEL RESEARCH BOARD, OHIO STATE
             UNIVERSITY, MAY 1952.
             (LEADERSHIP STYLE INVENTORY)*
         aH-141 LEADERSHIP STYLE STRUCTURE PLANNING INTERPERSONAL RELATIONSHIPS
         aH-141 1952M
             (APPLICATIONS: 2705 2819)

H-142   HENDRICK, C., & PAGE, H. A.
             SELF-ESTEEM, ATTITUDE SIMILARITY, AND ATTRACTION.
             JOURNAL OF PERSONALITY, 1970, 38, 588-601.
             (INTERPERSONAL PREDICTION FORM)
         aH-142 1970M INTERPERSONAL RELATIONSHIPS ATTITUDE SIMILARITY ATTRACTION
         aH-142 PREDICTION

H-143   HELPER, M. M., GARFIELD, S. L., & WILCOTT, R. C.
             ELECTRODERMAL REACTIVITY AND RATED BEHAVIOR IN EMOTIONALLY DISTURBED
             CHILDREN.
             JOURNAL OF ABNORMAL AND SOCIAL PSYCHOLOGY, 1963, 66, 600-603.
             (CHILD WARD BEHAVIOR RATING SCALES)
         aH-143 1963M CHILD WARD BEHAVIOR RATING ACTIVE AGGRESSION HOSTILITY
         aH-143 ANXIETY MOOD AFFECTIVE-STATES

H-144   HOVLAND, C. I., & JANIS, I. L. (EDS.)
             PERSONALITY AND PERSUASABILITY. NEW HAVEN: YALE UNIVERSITY PRESS, 1959.
             (FEELINGS OF SOCIAL INADEQUACY SCALE)
         aH-144 1959M COMPETENCE SOCIAL MALADJUSTMENT ANXIETY SELF RATING SITUATIONAL
         aH-144 ESTEEM
             (APPLICATIONS: 770)

H-145   HANVIK, L. J.
             MMPI PROFILES IN PATIENTS WITH LOW BACK PAIN.
             JOURNAL OF CONSULTING PSYCHOLOGY, 1951, 15, 350-353.
             (FUNCTIONAL LOW BACK PAIN SCALE)
         aH-145 1951M MMPI PHYSICAL ILLNESS PATIENT PSYCHOSOMATIC
             (APPLICATIONS: 792)

H-146   HOWELLS, L. T., & BECKER, S. W.
             SEATING ARRANGEMENT AND LEADERSHIP EMERGENCE.
             JOURNAL OF ABNORMAL AND SOCIAL PSYCHOLOGY, 1962, 64, 148-150.
             (MEASURE OF LEADERSHIP)
         aH-146 1962M LEADERSHIP PEER RATING PERSONALITY
         aH-146 GROUP

H-147   HOLZMAN, P. S.
             THE RELATION OF ASSIMILATION TENDENCIES IN VISUAL, AUDITORY, AND
             KINESTHETIC TIME-ERROR TO COGNITIVE ATTITUDES OF LEVELING AND SHARPENING.
             JOURNAL OF PERSONALITY, 1954, 22, 375-394.
             (SCHEMATIZING TEST)
         aH-147 1954M COGNITIVE FUNCTIONING THINKING CONCEPTUAL PERCEPTION
             (APPLICATIONS: 723)

H-148   HAYWOOD, H. C.
             NOVELTY-SEEKING BEHAVIOR AS A FUNCTION OF MANIFEST ANXIETY AND
             PHYSIOLOGICAL AROUSAL.
             JOURNAL OF PERSONALITY, 1962, 30, 63-74.
             (MEASURE OF NOVELTY PREFERENCE)
         aH-148 1962M NOVELTY NEED PREFERENCE GRAPHIC DRUG INFLUENCE
             (APPLICATIONS: 831)

H-149   HAYWOOD, H. C.
             NOVELTY-SEEKING BEHAVIOR AS A FUNCTION OF MANIFEST ANXIETY AND
             PHYSIOLOGICAL AROUSAL.
             UNPUBLISHED DOCTORAL DISSERTATION, UNIVERSITY OF ILLINOIS, 1961.
             (BIOGRAPHICAL INVENTORY)
         aH-149 1961M INTELLIGENCE ANXIETY MANIFEST
             (APPLICATIONS: 850)

H-150   HEYNS, R. W., VEROFF, J., & ATKINSON, J. W.
             A SCORING MANUAL FOR THE AFFILIATION MOTIVE.
             IN J. W. ATKINSON (ED.), MOTIVES IN FANTASY, ACTION, AND SOCIETY.
             PRINCETON, N.J.: VAN NOSTRAND, 1958.
             (TAT SCORED FOR AFFILIATION)
         aH-150 1958M PROJECTIVE NEED AFFILIATION AUTONOMY TAT IMAGERY MOTIVE
             (APPLICATIONS: 20   213   214   353   665   887   893   934)

H-151   HAURI, P., SAWYER, J., & RECHTSCHAFFEN, A.
               DIMENSIONS OF DREAMING: A FACTORED SCALE FOR RATING DREAM REPORTS.
               JOURNAL OF ABNORMAL PSYCHOLOGY, 1967, 72, 16-22.
               (FACTORED SCALE FOR RATING DREAM CONTENT)
          aH-151 1967M FANTASY IMAGINATION PRIMARY-PROCESS THINKING
               (APPLICATIONS: 2427)

H-152   HARGREAVES, W. A., STARKWEATHER, J. A., & BLACKER, K. H.
               VOICE QUALITY IN DEPRESSION.
               JOURNAL OF ABNORMAL PSYCHOLOGY, 1965, 70, 218-220.
               (INVENTORY OF MOOD, CONFUSION, AND MEMORY LOSS)
          H-152 1965M DEPRESSION MOOD RETARDATION

H-154   HEINICKE, C. M.
               FREQUENCY OF PSYCHOTHERAPEUTIC SESSION AS A FACTOR AFFECTING THE CHILD'S
               DEVELOPMENTAL STATUS.
               PSYCHOANALYTIC STUDY OF THE CHILD, 1965, 20, 42-98.
               (DIAGNOSTIC PROFILE)
          aH-154 1965M DIAGNOSIS EGO-STRENGTH DEFENSE COPING DEPENDENCE PEER AUTONOMY
          aCHILD
               (APPLICATIONS: 1136)

H-155   HELM, D.
               MOTORIC-IDEATIONAL INTEREST PATTERNS CF DELINQUENT AND NONDELINQUENT
               ADOLESCENT BOYS.
               UNPUBLISHED M.A. THESIS, UNIVERSITY OF CALIFORNIA, BERKELEY, 1968.
               (MEASURE OF MOTORIC AND IDEATIONAL EXPRESSION)
          aH-155 1968M DELINQUENT BEHAVIOR SELF EXPRESSION THINKING

H-156   HOLT, R. R.
               MANUAL FOR THE SCORING OF PRIMARY PROCESS MANIFESTATIONS IN RORSCHACH
               RESPONSES.
               DRAFT 7, RESEARCH CENTER FOR MENTAL HEALTH, NEW YORK UNIVERSITY, APRIL
               1959.
               (RORSCHACH SCORED FOR MEAN DEFENSE EFFECTIVENESS)
          aH-156 1959M RORSCHACH DEFENSE EFFECTIVENESS PRIMARY-PROCESS THINKING
               (APPLICATIONS: 1007)

H-157   HELMREICH, R., ARONSON, E., AND LEFAN, J.
               TO ERR IS HUMANIZING--SOMETIMES: EFFECTS OF SELF-ESTEEM, COMPETENCE, AND A
               PRATFALL ON INTERPERSONAL ATTRACTION.
               JOURNAL OF PERSONALITY AND SOCIAL PSYCHOLOGY, 1970, 16, 259-264.
               (MEASURE OF INTERPERSONAL ATTRACTIVENESS)
          aH-157 1970M ATTRACTION INTERPERSONAL SOCIAL

H-158   HELMREICH, R., ARONSON, E., AND LEFAN, J.
               TO ERR IS HUMANIZING--SOMETIMES: EFFECTS OF SELF-ESTEEM, COMPETENCE, AND A
               PRATFALL ON INTERPERSONAL ATTRACTION.
               JOURNAL OF PERSONALITY AND SOCIAL PSYCHOLOGY, 1970, 16, 259-264.
               (TEXAS SOCIAL BEHAVIOR INVENTORY)*
          aH-158 1970M GLOBAL SOCIAL BEHAVIOR COMPETENCE SELF CONFIDENCE ESTEEM
          aINVENTORY

H-159   HARRIS, J. G.
               A STUDY OF THE MOTHER-SON RELATIONSHIP IN SCHIZOPHRENIA.
               UNPUBLISHED DOCTORAL DISSERTATION, DUKE UNIVERSITY, 1955.
               (MEASURE OF PERCEPTION OF MOTHER'S CHILD REARING ATTITUDES)
          aH-159 1955M PERCEPTION ATTITUDE MATERNAL CHILD PARENT-CHILD
          aH-159 DOMINANCE
               (APPLICATIONS: 1152)

H-160   HIRT, M., ROSS, W. D., KURTZ, R., & GLESER, G. C.
               ATTITUDES TO BODY PRODUCTS AMONG NORMAL SUBJECTS.
               JOURNAL OF ABNORMAL PSYCHOLOGY, 1969, 74, 486-489.
               (SEMANTIC DIFFERENTIAL MEASURE OF ATTITUDE TOWARDS BODY PRODUCTS)
          aH-160 1969M SEM-DIFFERENTIAL BODY ATTITUDE

H-161   HEMPHILL, J. K., & WESTIE, C. M.
               GROUP DIMENSIONS DESCRIPTIONS QUESTIONNAIRE.
               COLUMBUS: OHIO STATE UNIVERSITY, 1965.
               (GROUP DIMENSIONS DESCRIPTIONS QUESTIONNAIRE)*
          aH-161 1965M GROUP BEHAVIOR INTERPERSONAL RELATIONSHIPS INTERACTION
               (APPLICATIONS: 2961)

H-163   HERRON, W. G.
         ABSTRACT ABILITY IN THE PROCESS-REACTIVE CLASSIFICATION OF SCHIZOPHRENIA.
         JOURNAL OF GENERAL PSYCHOLOGY, 1962, 67, 147-154.
         (HERRON CATEGORY TEST)*
     aH-163 CONCEPT CONCEPTUAL DEVELOPMENT ABSTRACTNESS 1962M FUNCTIONING COGNITIVE
     aSCHIZOPHRENIA
         (APPLICATIONS: 2578)

H-165   HOLZBERG, J. D., GEWIRTZ, H., & EBNER, E.
         CHANGES IN MORAL JUDGMENT AND SELF-ACCEPTANCE IN COLLEGE STUDENTS AS A
         FUNCTION OF COMPANIONSHIP WITH HOSPITALIZED MENTAL PATIENTS.
         JOURNAL OF CONSULTING PSYCHOLOGY, 1964, 28, 299-303.
         (MORAL JUDGMENT QUESTIONNAIRE)
     aH-165 1964M MORAL VALUES BELIEF CONVICTION ATTITUDE SEX AGGRESSION JUDGMENT
         (APPLICATIONS: 2940)

H-166   HOLLANDER, E. P., & MARCIA, J. E.
         PARENTAL DETERMINANTS OF PEER-ORIENTATION AND SELF-ORIENTATION AMONG
         PREADOLESCENTS.
         DEVELOPMENTAL PSYCHOLOGY, 1970, 2, 292-302.
         (SOCIOMETRIC RATING SCALES)
     aH-166 1970M SOCIOMETRIC CONFORMITY DEPENDENCE AUTONOMY CONTROL RATING
     aSELF PEER OTHER ORIENTATION

H-167   HUNT, D. E.
         PERSONALITY PATTERNS OF ADOLESCENT BOYS.
         (NATIONAL INSTITUTE OF MENTAL HEALTH PROGRESS REPORT), WASHINGTON, D. C.:
         UNITED STATES GOVERNMENT PRINTING OFFICE, 1964.
         (INTERPERSONAL FLEXIBILITY SCALE)
     aH-167 1964M INTERPERSONAL RIGIDITY FLEXIBILITY RELATIONSHIPS SOCIAL ADOLESCENT
         (APPLICATIONS: 2789)

H-168   HANDLER, L., & REYHER, J.
         THE EFFECTS OF STRESS ON THE DRAW-A-PERSON TEST.
         JOURNAL OF CONSULTING PSYCHOLOGY, 1964, 28, 259-264.
         (DRAW-A-PERSON TEST SCORED FOR ANXIETY)
     aH-168 1964M GRAPHIC FIGURE IMAGINATION ANXIETY STRESS PROJECTIVE
         (APPLICATIONS: 2893)

H-169   HARRIS, H.
         DEVELOPMENT OF MORAL ATTITUDES IN WHITE AND NEGRO BOYS.
         DEVELOPMENTAL PSYCHOLOGY, 1970, 2, 376-383.
         (MEASURE OF MORAL ATTITUDES IN CHILDREN)
     aH-169 1970M CHILD DEVELOPMENT MORAL ATTITUDE BELIEF JUDGMENT MATURITY

H-170   .HALL, C. S., & VAN DE CASTLE, R. L.
         THE CONTENT ANALYSIS OF DREAMS.
         NEW YORK: APPLETON-CENTURY-CROFTS, 1966.
         (SCALES FOR RATING DREAM CONTENT)
     aH-170 1966M PRIMARY-PROCESS ACTIVITIES SOCIAL INTERACTION CONTENT-ANALYSIS
     aDREAM
         (APPLICATIONS: 2427)

H-171   HAWKS, D. V.
         OVERINCLUSIVE THOUGHT DISORDER IN PSYCHIATRIC PATIENTS.
         UNPUBLISHED DOCTORAL THESIS, QUEEN'S UNIVERSITY, ONTARIO, 1967.
         PAYNE, R. W., HOCHBERG, A. C., & HAWKS, D. V.
         DICHOTIC STIMULATION AS A METHOD OF ASSESSING DISORDER OF ATTENTION IN
         OVERINCLUSIVE SCHIZOPHRENIC PATIENTS.
         JOURNAL OF ABNORMAL PSYCHOLOGY, 1970, 76, 185-193.
         (SYMPTOM RATING SCALE)
     aH-171 1967M SYMPTOM RATING OVERINCLUSIVE THINKING PERCEPTION OTHERS ORIENTATION
         (APPLICATIONS: 2404)

H-172   HOGAN, R.
         A DIMENSION OF MORAL JUDGMENT.
         JOURNAL OF CONSULTING AND CLINICAL PSYCHOLOGY, 1970, 35, 205-212.
         (SURVEY OF ETHICAL ATTITUDES)*
     aH-172 1970M MORAL ATTITUDE SITUATIONAL CONSCIENCE SOCIAL RESPONSIBILITY
     aJUDGMENT

H-173   HARROWER, M. R.
         THE MOST UNPLEASANT CONCEPT TEST: A GRAPHIC PROJECTIVE INSTRUMENT.
         JOURNAL OF CLINICAL PSYCHOLOGY, 1950, 6, 212-233.
         (MOST UNPLEASANT CONCEPT TEST)*
     aH-173 1950M FIGURE GRAPHIC CONCEPT PROJECTIVE PSYCHIATRIC ATTITUDE SEX REALITY

H-174   HAWORTH, M. R.
              A SCHEDULE OF ADAPTIVE MECHANISMS IN CAT RESPONSES.
              NEW YORK: C. P. S. CO., 1965.
              (SCHEDULE OF ADAPTIVE MECHANISMS CRITICAL SCORES)*
           @H-174 1965M CHILD PROJECTIVE FANTASY ADAPTABILITY DEFENSIVENESS COPING DEFENSE

H-175   HARRIS, D. B.
              GOODENOUGH-HARRIS DRAWING TEST MANUAL.
              NEW YORK: HARCOURT, BRACE & WORLD, 1963.
              (QUALITY SCALE AND METHOD OF SCORING DAP)
           @H-175 1963M GRAPHIC PROJECTIVE FIGURE

H-176   HALEY, H. B., JUAN, I. R., & GAGAN, J. F.
              FACTOR-ANALYTIC APPROACH TO ATTITUDE SCALE CONSTRUCTION.
              JOURNAL OF MEDICAL EDUCATION, 1968, 43, 331-336.
              (CANCER ATTITUDE SURVEY)
           @H-176 1968M ATTITUDE PATIENT ILLNESS PHYSICAL DEATH ACCEPTANCE AUTHORITARIANISM
              (APPLICATIONS: 2589)

H-177   HANFMANN, E., & KASANIN, J.
              A METHOD FOR THE STUDY OF CONCEPT FORMATION.
              JOURNAL OF PSYCHOLOGY, 1937, 3, 521-540.
              (CONCEPT FORMATION TEST)
           @H-177 1937M COGNITIVE FUNCTIONING SCHIZOPHRENIC MENTAL-ILLNESS CONCEPTUAL
           @BREADTH CONCEPT FORMATION

H-178   HULL, C. L.
              QUANTITATIVE METHODS OF INVESTIGATING WAKING SUGGESTION.
              JOURNAL OF ABNORMAL AND SOCIAL PSYCHOLOGY, 1929, 24, 153-169.
              (HULL BODY SWAY TEST)
           @H-178 1929M HYPNOTIC SUGGESTIBILITY

H-180   HOUTS, P. S., & ENTWISLE, D. R.
              ACADEMIC ACHIEVEMENT AMONG FEMALES: ACHIEVEMENT ATTITUDES AND SEX-ROLE
              ORIENTATION.
              JOURNAL OF COUNSELING PSYCHOLOGY, 1968, 15, 284-286.
              (MEASURE OF ATTITUDES TOWARD FEMALE SEX-ROLE AND ACHIEVEMENT)
           @H-180 1968M FEMININITY SEX ROLE ACHIEVEMENT ACADEMIC COMPETITION MOTIVE
           @INHIBITION EXPRESSION ACCEPTANCE ATTITUDE

H-181   HOPKE, W. E.
              THE MEASUREMENT OF COUNSELOR ATTITUDES.
              JOURNAL OF COUNSELING PSYCHOLOGY, 1955, 2, 212-216.
              (REVISED TEST OF COUNSELOR ATTITUDES)
           @H-181 1955M ATTITUDE COUNSELING THERAPY RELATIONSHIPS THERAPIST
              (APPLICATIONS: 1464)

H-183   HABBE, S.
              JOB ATTITUDES OF LIFE INSURANCE AGENTS.
              JOURNAL OF APPLIED PSYCHOLOGY, 1947, 31, 111-128.
              (SHORTENED JOB SATISFACTION SCALE)
           @H-183 1947M JOB SATISFACTION GLOBAL ATTITUDE HAPPINESS
              (APPLICATIONS: 1482)

H-184   HENDERSON, R. W.
              MANUAL FOR THE COLLEGE INTEREST INVENTORY.
              BEREA, OHIO: PERSONAL GROWTH PRESS, 1967.
              (COLLEGE INTEREST INVENTORY)*
           @H-184 1967M ACADEMIC INTEREST COLLEGE STUDENT SCHOOL VOCATIONAL PREFERENCE
           @INVENTORY
              (APPLICATIONS: 1542)

H-185   HUNT, J. MCV., & KOGAN, L. S.
              MEASURING RESULTS IN SOCIAL CASEWORK.
              NEW YORK: FAMILY SERVICE ASSOCIATION, 1952.
              (MOVEMENT SCALE)*
           @H-185 1952M THERAPY CHANGE EFFECTIVENESS ADJUSTMENT SUCCESS
              (APPLICATIONS: 1198 1199 1250 1278)

H-186   HERSHENSON, D. B.
                ERIKSON'S "SENSE OF IDENTITY," OCCUPATIONAL FIT, AND ENCULTURATION IN
                ADOLESCENCE.
                UNPUBLISHED DOCTORAL DISSERTATION, BOSTON UNIVERSITY, 1964.
                (OCCUPATIONAL PLANS QUESTIONNAIRE)
         @H-186 1964M ADOLESCENT PROBLEM IDENTITY SELF-IDENTITY SUB-IDENTITY VOCATIONAL
         @PREFERENCE
                (APPLICATIONS: 1312 1423)

H-187   HARRIS, R. H., & SIMBERG, A. L.
                MANUAL FOR THE AC TEST OF CREATIVE ABILITY.
                CHICAGO: EDUCATION-INDUSTRY SERVICE, 1959.
                (THE AC TEST OF CREATIVE ABILITY)*
         @H-187 1959M ABILITY CREATIVITY ORIGINALITY IMAGINATION
                (APPLICATIONS: 1355)

H-188   HOPPOCK, R.
                JOB SATISFACTION.
                NEW YORK: HARPER, 1935.
                (JOB SATISFACTION BLANK)*
         @H-188 1935M JOB SATISFACTION VOCATIONAL ATTITUDE INTEREST PRESTIGE
                (APPLICATIONS: 1342 1349 1482)

H-189   HAUTLAGE, L. C.
                COMMUNITY EXPECTATIONS AND PSYCHIATRIC REHABILITATION.
                AMERICAN JOURNAL OF PSYCHIATRY, 1964, 121, 67-69.
                (CHECKLIST OF EMPLOYER ATTITUDES TOWARD FORMER MENTAL PATIENTS)
         @H-189 1964M ATTITUDE MENTAL-HEALTH MENTAL-ILLNESS DISABILITY
         @JOB PERFORMANCE PSYCHIATRIC
                (APPLICATIONS: 1348)

H-190   HASTORF, A. H., & PIPER, G. W.
                A NOTE ON THE EFFECT OF EXPLICIT INSTRUCTIONS ON PRESTIGE SUGGESTION.
                JOURNAL OF SOCIAL PSYCHOLOGY, 1951, 33, 289-293.
                (OPINION QUESTIONNAIRE)*
         @H-190 1951M SOCIAL INFLUENCE PRESSURE ATTITUDE CHANGE CONFORMITY OPINION BELIEF
         @AUTONOMY DEPENDENCE
                (APPLICATIONS: 190   527)

H-192   HALL, L. G.
                COUNSELOR'S MANUAL -- HALL OCCUPATIONAL ORIENTATION INVENTORY.
                CHICAGO: FOLLETT, 1968.
                (HALL OCCUPATIONAL ORIENTATION INVENTORY)*
         @H-192 1968M VOCATIONAL PREFERENCE JOB INTEREST

H-193   HEALEY, C. C.
                RELATION OF OCCUPATIONAL CHOICE TO THE SIMILARITY BETWEEN SELF RATINGS AND
                OCCUPATIONAL RATINGS.
                JOURNAL OF COUNSELING PSYCHOLOGY, 1968, 15, 317-323.
                (SELF RATING SCALE OF VOCATIONAL TRAITS)
         @H-193 1968M SELF RATING VOCATIONAL TRAIT SEM-DIFFERENTIAL PERCEPTION SIMILARITY
         @ROLE

H-194   HALL, W. S.
                DIFFERENTIAL PRODUCTIVE INVOLVEMENT IN THE CULTURE AMONG YOUNG MEN--A
                PILOT STUDY.
                UNPUBLISHED MANUSCRIPT, UNIVERSITY OF CHICAGO, CHICAGO, ILLINOIS, 1966.
                (MEASURE OF RISK-TAKING BEHAVIOR)
         @H-194 1966M RISK-TAKING BEHAVIOR SECURITY NEED

H-195   HAKEL, M. D., & DUNNETT, M. D.
                CHECKLISTS FOR DESCRIBING JOB APPLICANTS.
                MINNEAPOLIS: UNIVERSITY OF MINNESOTA INDUSTRIAL RELATIONS CENTER, 1970.
            HAKEL, M. D., & SCHUH, A. J.
                JOB APPLICANT ATTRIBUTES JUDGED IMPORTANT ACROSS SEVEN DIVERSE OCCUPATIONS.
                PERSONNEL PSYCHOLOGY, 1971, 24, 45-52.
                (MEASURE FOR EVALUATION OF JOB APPLICANTS)
         @H-195 1970M RATING DESIRABILITY EMPLOYEE EVALUATION PREDICTION SUCCESS
         @JOB TRAIT

H-197   HARTSHORNE, H., & MAY, M. A.
               STUDIES IN THE NATURE OF CHARACTER.   VOL. 1.
               NEW YORK: MACMILLAN, 1928.
               (PEEPING TEST FROM IMPROBABLE ACHIEVEMENT TESTS)
           @H-197 1928M ACHIEVEMENT DECEPTIVENESS FAKING RESPONSE-BIAS
               (APPLICATIONS: 263)

H-198   HARTSHORNE, H., & MAY, M. A.
               STUDIES IN THE NATURE OF CHARACTER.   VOL. 1.
               NEW YORK: MACMILLAN, 1928.
               (BLOCKS TEST FROM IMPROBABL ACHIEVEMENT SPEED TESTS)
           @H-198 1928M ACHIEVEMENT DECEPTIVENESS FAKING RESPONSE-BIAS
               (APPLICATIONS: 263)

H-199   HOFFMAN, A. E.
               AN ANALYSIS OF COUNSELOR SUB-ROLES.
               JOURNAL OF COUNSELING PSYCHOLOGY, 1959, 6, 61-68.
               (CHECKLIST OF SUB-ROLES)
           @H-199 1959M COUNSELING BEHAVIOR ROLE RELATIONSHIPS THERAPIST CHECKLIST
           @INTERPERSONAL
               (APPLICATIONS: 28)

H-200   HEILBRUN, A. B., JR., & SULLIVAN, D. J.
               THE PREDICTION OF COUNSELING READINESS.
               PERSONNEL AND GUIDANCE JOURNAL, 1962, 41, 112-122.
               (MEASURE OF COUNSELING READINESS)
           @H-200 COUNSELING ADJUSTMENT PERSONAL EFFECTIVENESS
           @CHECKLIST VOCATIONAL ACADEMIC PREDICTION SUCCESS
               (APPLICATIONS: 121   1237   1290   1309)

H-201   HARREN, V. A.
               THE VOCATIONAL DECISION-MAKING PROCESS AMONG COLLEGE MALES.
               JOURNAL OF COUNSELING PSYCHOLOGY, 1966, 13, 271-277.
               (VOCATIONAL DECISION-MAKING Q-SORT)
           @H-201 VOCATIONAL DECISION 1966M COLLEGE STUDENT Q-SORT

H-202   HARRISON, R. H., & KASS, E. H.
               DIFFERENCES BETWEEN NEGRO AND WHITE PREGNANT WOMEN ON THE MMPI.
               JOURNAL OF CONSULTING PSYCHOLOGY, 1967, 31, 454-463.
               (RACIAL DIFFERENTIATION SCALE)
           @H-202 1967M NEGRO RACIAL MMPI DIFFERENCES DIFFERENTIATION
               (APPLICATIONS: 232)

H-204   HOLMES, D. S.
               PUPILLARY RESPONSE, CONDITIONING, AND PERSONALITY.
               JOURNAL OF PERSONALITY AND SOCIAL PSYCHOLOGY, 1967, 5, 98-103.
               (EXTRAVERSION-INTROVERSION PERSONALITY RATING FORM)
           @H-204 1967M INTROVERSION EXTRAVERSION RATING

H-207   HOLLAND, J. L., & NICHOLS, R. C.
               THE PREDICTION OF ACADEMIC AND EXTRACURRICULAR ACHIEVEMENT IN COLLEGE.
               JOURNAL OF EDUCATIONAL PSYCHOLOGY, 1964, 55, 55-65.
               (MEASURES TO PREDICT EXTRACURRICULAR ACHIEVEMENT IN COLLEGE)
           @H-207 ACHIEVEMENT COLLEGE PREDICTION LEADERSHIP ABILITY BEHAVIOR ACADEMIC

H-208   HOLMES, J. E.
               THE PRESENTATION OF TEST INFORMATION TO COLLEGE FRESHMEN.
               JOURNAL OF COUNSELING PSYCHOLOGY, 1964, 11, 54-58.
               (COUNSELOR-INTERVIEW RATING SCALE)
           @H-208 1964M COUNSELING RATING EVALUATION EFFECTIVENESS INTERVIEW THERAPIST
           @H-208 1964M COUNSELING RATING EVALUATION EFFECTIVENESS

H-211   HAVRON, M. D., MCGRATH, J. E., & FAY, R. J.
               THE EFFECTIVENESS OF SMALL MILITARY UNITS: PARTS I-III.
               PRS REPORT NO. 980.
               1961, DEPT. OF ARMY, THE ADJUTANT GENERAL'S OFFICE, PERSONNEL RESEARCH
               SECTION, INSTITUTE FOR RESEARCH IN HUMAN RELATIONS.
               (INVENTORY OF INTERPERSONAL KNOWLEDGE)
           @H-211 1961M INTERPERSONAL INTERACTION DISTANCE RELATIONSHIPS
           @SENSITIVITY AWARENESS

H-212   HELLER, K.
              DEPENDENCY CHANGES IN PSYCHOTHERAPY AS A FUNCTION OF THE DISCREPANCY
              BETWEEN CONSCIOUS SELF-DESCRIPTION AND PROJECTIVE TEST PERFORMANCE.
              UNPUBLISHED DOCTORAL DISSERTATION, PENNSYLVANIA STATE UNIVERSITY, 1959.
          HELLER, K., & GOLDSTEIN, A. P.
              CLIENT DEPENDENCY AND THERAPIST EXPECTANCY AS RELATIONSHIP MAINTAINING
              VARIABLES IN PSYCHOTHERAPY.
              JOURNAL OF CONSULTING PSYCHOLOGY, 1961, 25, 371-375.
              (SITUATIONAL TEST OF DEPENDENCY)*
          @H-212 1959M DEPENDENCE ROLE PERCEPTION ENACTMENT NEED AUTONOMY
          @THERAPY RELATIONSHIPS

H-213   HUNT, R. G., AND LIN, T. K.
              ACCURACY OF JUDGMENTS OF PERSONAL ATTRIBUTES FROM SPEECH.
              JOURNAL OF PERSONALITY AND SOCIAL PSYCHOLOGY, 1967, 6, 450-453.
              (PERSONALITY CHECK LIST)
          @H-213 1967M CHECKLIST PERSONALITY MULTITRAIT

H-214   HOVEY, H. R.
              BRAIN LESIONS AND 5 MMPI ITEMS.
              JOURNAL OF CONSULTING PSYCHOLOGY, 1964, 28, 78-79.
              (MEASURE FOR DIAGNOSIS OF PATIENTS WITH CENTRAL NERVOUS SYSTEM DAMAGE)
          @H-214 1964M MMPI DIAGNOSIS PHYSIOLOGICAL ILLNESS PSYCHIATRIC DISABILITY

H-215   HEINE, R. W., & TROSMAN, H.
              INITIAL EXPECTATIONS OF THE DOCTOR-PATIENT INTERACTION AS A FACTOR
              IN CONTINUANCE IN PSYCHOTHERAPY.
              PSYCHIATRY, 1960, 23, 275-278.
              (EXPECTANCY QUESTIONNAIRE)
          @H-215 1960M PSYCHIATRIC PATIENT SELF PERCEPTION PREDICTION SUCCESS
              (APPLICATIONS: 1945 1947)

H-216   HEILBRUN, A. B.
              RELATIONSHIPS BETWEEN THE ADJECTIVE CHECK LIST, PERSONAL PREFERENCE
              SCHEDULE AND DESIRABILITY FACTORS UNDER VARYING DEFENSIVENESS CONDITIONS.
              JOURNAL OF CLINICAL PSYCHOLOGY, 1958, 14, 283-287.
          GOUGH, H. G., & HEILBRUN, A. B., JR.
              ADJECTIVE CHECK LIST MANUAL.
              PALO ALTO: CONSULTING PSYCHOLOGISTS PRESS, 1965.
              (HEILBRUN NEED SCALES)
          @H-216 1959M NEED ACHIEVEMENT EXPRESSION AFFILIATION AUTONOMY DOMINANCE
          @NURTURANCE CHANGE AGGRESSION SEX SELF ABASEMENT
              (APPLICATIONS: 1220 2091)

H-218   HOLLAND, J. L., & BAIRD, L. L.
              THE PRECONSCIOUS ACTIVITY SCALE: THE DEVELOPMENT AND VALIDATION OF AN
              ORIGINALITY MEASURE.
              JOURNAL OF CREATIVE BEHAVIOR, 1968, 2, 217-225.
              (PRECONSCIOUS ACTIVITY SCALE)*
          @H-218 1968M ORIGINALITY CREATIVITY IMAGINATION PRIMARY-PROCESS
              (APPLICATIONS: 1515)

H-219   HARMON, L. W.
              OCCUPATIONAL SATISFACTION - A BETTER CRITERION?
              JOURNAL OF COUNSELING PSYCHOLOGY, 1966, 13, 295-299.
              (OCCUPATIONAL AND JOB SATISFACTION BLANKS)
          @H-219 1966M JOB SATISFACTION

H-220   HOOPER, H. E.
              NO REFERENCE
              (HOSPITAL ADJUSTMENT INVENTORY)
          @H-220 ANXIETY ADJUSTMENT HOSPITALIZATION PATIENT
              (APPLICATIONS: 1981)

H-221   HONIGFELD, G., & KLETT, C. J.
              THE NURSES' OBSERVATION SCALE FOR INPATIENT EVALUATION: A NEW SCALE FOR
              MEASURING IMPROVEMENT IN CHRONIC SCHIZOPHRENIA.
              JOURNAL OF CLINICAL PSYCHOLOGY, 1965, 21, 65-71.
              (NURSES' OBSERVATION SCALE FOR INPATIENT EVALUATION (NOSIE))*
          @H-221 1965M PATIENT PSYCHIATRIC EVALUATION WARD SCHIZOPHRENIA BEHAVIOR CHANGE

H-222   HOLDER, T., CARKHUFF, R. R., & BERENSON, B. G.
              DIFFERENTIAL EFFECTS OF THE MANIPULATION OF THERAPEUTIC CONDITIONS UPON
              HIGH- AND LOW-FUNCTIONING CLIENTS.
              JOURNAL OF COUNSELING PSYCHOLOGY, 1967, 14. 63-66.
          CARKHUFF, R. R. (ED.)
              THE COUNSELOR'S CONTRIBUTION TO FACILITATIVE PROCESSES.
              URBANA, ILL.: PARKINSON (FOLLETT), IN PRESS 1967.
              (MEASURE OF INTERPERSONAL FUNCTIONING IN THERAPY)
          @H-222 1967M THERAPY COUNSELING RELATIONSHIPS INTERACTION BEHAVIOR SELF
          @EXPLORATION INTERPERSONAL FUNCTIONING COUNSELING THERAPIST

I-1   IZARD, C. E., & NUNNALLY, J. C.
              EVALUATIVE RESPONSES TO AFFECTIVELY POSITIVE AND NEGATIVE FACIAL
              PHOTOGRAPHS: FACTOR STRUCTURE AND CONSTRUCT VALIDITY.
              EDUCATIONAL AND PSYCHOLOGICAL MEASUREMENT, 1965, 25, 1061-1071.
              (FIRST IMPRESSION RATING SCALE)*
          @I-1 AFFECTIVE-STATES EVALUATION PERCEPTION POSITIVE NEGATIVE IMPRESSION RATING
          @I-1 1965M OTHERS

I-2   INDIK, B. P., GEORGOPOULOS, B. S., & SEASHORE, S. E.
              SUPERIOR-SUBORDINATE RELATIONSHIPS AND PERFORMANCE.
              PERSONNEL PSYCHOLOGY, 1961, 14, 357-374.
              (ATTITUDE QUESTIONNAIRE MEASURING SUPERIOR-SUBORDINATE RELATIONSHIPS)
          @I-2 ATTITUDE PERFORMANCE SUPERVISOR EMPLOYEE RELATIONSHIPS JOB ADJUSTMENT
          @I-2 INTERPERSONAL LEADERSHIP AUTHORITY 1961M

I-3   IVEY, A. E., MILLER, C. D., MORRILL, W. H., & NORMINGTON, C. J.
              THE COUNSELOR EFFECTIVENESS SCALE. UNPUBLISHED REPORT, COLORADO STATE
              UNIVERSITY, 1967. (MIMEO)
              (COUNSELOR EFFECTIVENESS SCALE)*
          @I-3 1967M THERAPY RELATIONSHIPS INTERPERSONAL COUNSELING EVALUATION
          @I-3 EFFECTIVENESS
              (APPLICATIONS: 2772)

I-4   IRVIN, F. S.
              EFFECTS OF STEM REFERENCE ON SENTENCE-COMPLETION RESPONSES.
              PSYCHOLOGICAL REPORTS, 1967, 21, 679-680.
          IRVIN, F. S.
              SENTENCE-COMPLETION RESPONSES AND SCHOLASTIC SUCCESS OR FAILURE.
              JOURNAL OF COUNSELING PSYCHOLOGY, 1967, 14, 269-271.
              (SENTENCE COMPLETION MEASURE OF SELF-CONCEPT, NEED FOR
              ACHIEVEMENT AND LEARNING ATTITUDE)
          @I-4 1967M ATTITUDE NEED ACHIEVEMENT ACCEPTANCE REJECTION SELF CONCEPT
          @I-4 PROJECTIVE
              (APPLICATIONS: 1479 2926)

I-5   INDIK, B., SEASHORE, S. E., & SLESINGER, J.
              DEMOGRAPHIC CORRELATES OF PSYCHOLOGICAL STRAIN.
              JOURNAL OF ABNORMAL AND SOCIAL PSYCHOLOGY, 1964, 69, 26-38.
              (INDEX OF JOB-RELATED STRAIN)*
          @I-5 1964M JOB TENSION ANXIETY STRESS
              (APPLICATIONS: 2369)

I-6   ITKIN, W.
              SOME RELATIONSHIPS BETWEEN INTRA-FAMILY ATTITUDES AND PRE-PARENTAL
              ATTITUDES TOWARD CHILDREN.
              UNPUBLISHED DOCTORAL DISSERTATION, NORTHWESTERN UNIVERSITY, 1949.
          ITKIN, W.
              SOME RELATIONSHIPS BETWEEN INTRA-FAMILY ATTITUDES AND PRE-PARENTAL
              ATTITUDES TOWARD CHILDREN.
              JOURNAL OF GENETIC PSYCHOLOGY, 1952, 80, 221-252.
              (PARENTAL AND INTRA-FAMILY ATTITUDE SCALES)
          @I-6 1970M FAMILY ATTITUDE PARENTAL CHILD
              (APPLICATIONS: 2843)

I-8   INDIK, B., SEASHORE, S. E., & SLESINGER, J.
              DEMOGRAPHIC CORRELATES OF PSYCHOLOGICAL STRAIN.
              JOURNAL OF ABNORMAL AND SOCIAL PSYCHOLOGY, 1964, 69, 26-38.
              (INDEX OF ECONOMIC STRAIN)
          @I-8 1964M STRESS SITUATIONAL PRESS ENVIRONMENT PRESSURE TENSION

J-1   JACKSON, D. N.
            A MODERN STRATEGY FOR PERSONALITY ASSESSMENT: THE PERSONALITY RESEARCH
            FORM.
            RESEARCH BULLETIN NO. 33C, OCTOBER, 1966. LONDON, CANADA: UNIVERSITY OF
            WESTERN ONTARIO DEPARTMENT OF PSYCHOLOGY.
            MANUAL FOR THE PERSONALITY RESEARCH FORM.
            LONDON, CANADA: UNIVERSITY OF WESTERN ONTARIO PRESS, 1967.
            (PERSONALITY RESEARCH FORM)*
        aJ-1 PERSONALITY MULTITRAIT 1967M
            (APPLICATIONS: 310   521   1120   1511   2535   2617   2691   2716   2773   2793
                            2799   2864   2891)

J-2   JACKSON, D. N.
            DESIRABILITY JUDGMENT AS A METHOD OF PERSONALITY ASSESSMENT.
            EDUCATIONAL AND PSYCHOLOGICAL MEASUREMENT, 1964, 24, 223-238.
            (PREDICTOR INVENTORY)*
        aJ-2 SOCIAL DESIRABILITY RESPONSE-BIAS MMPI JUDGMENT MULTITRAIT 1964M PREDICTION
            (APPLICATIONS: 190)

J-3   JACKSON, D. N., & MESSICK, S.
            ACQUIESCENCE AND DESIRABILITY AS RESPONSE DETERMINANTS ON THE MMPI.
            EDUCATIONAL AND PSYCHOLOGICAL MEASUREMENT, 1961, 21, 771-790.
            (DESIRABILITY SCALES FROM MMPI)
        aJ-3 ACQUIESCENCE RESPONSE-BIAS ADJUSTMENT GLOBAL MENTAL-ILLNESS 1962M SOCIAL
        aJ-3 DESIRABILITY

J-4   JACKSON, D. N., & MESSICK, S. J.
            A NOTE ON ETHNOCENTRISM AND ACQUIESCENCE RESPONSE SET.
            JOURNAL OF ABNORMAL AND SOCIAL PSYCHOLOGY, 1957, 54, 132-134.
            (REVERSED FASCISM SCALE)*
        aJ-4 AUTHORITARIANISM COPING-DEFENSE OTHER-CATEGORY F-SCALE ETHNOCENTRISM
        aRESPONSE-BIAS ACQUIESCENCE 1957M
            (APPLICATIONS: 26   560   613   690)

J-5   JACOBSON, A. H.
            CONFLICT OF ATTITUDES TOWARD THE ROLES OF HUSBAND AND THE WIFE IN MARRIAGE.
            AMERICAN SOCIOLOGICAL REVIEW. 1952, 17, 146-150.
            (ATTITUDES TOWARD MARITAL ROLE SCALE)
        aJ-5 MARITAL ADJUSTMENT SELF-IDENTITY SUB-IDENTITY ROLE PERCEPTION CONFLICT
        aATTITUDE 1952M

J-6   JAMES, W. H.
            INTERNAL VS. EXTERNAL CONTROL OF REINFORCEMENTS AS A BASIC VARIABLE IN
            LEARNING THEORY.
            UNPUBLISHED DOCTORAL DISSERTATION, OHIO STATE UNIVERSITY, 1957.
            (JAMES INTERNAL-EXTERNAL CONTROL SCALE)*
        aJ-6 IE-CONTROL AUTONOMY LOCUS CONTROL ORIENTATION PERSONAL 1957M
            (APPLICATIONS: 335   343   1368   1384   2148   2369)

J-7   JANIS, I. L., & FIELD, P. B.
            SEX DIFFERENCES AND PERSONALITY FACTORS RELATED TO PERSUASIBILITY.
            IN C. I. HOVLAND AND I. L. JANIS (EDS.), PERSONALITY AND PERSUASIBILITY.
            NEW HAVEN: YALE UNIVERSITY PRESS, 1959.
            (PERSONALITY INVENTORY QUESTIONNAIRE)*
        aJ-7 SOCIAL COMPETENCE SELF ESTEEM AFFECTIVE-STATES GLOBAL NEGATIVE
        aJ-7 IMAGE EVALUATION PERCEPTION SELF-IDENTITY 1959M
            (APPLICATIONS: 131   150   173   180   223   291   369   448   457   520
                            527   548   914   942   2195   2490   2823)

J-8   JANIS, I. L., & RIFE, D.
            PERSUASIBILITY AND EMOTIONAL DISORDER.
            IN C. I. HOVLAND AND I. L. JANIS (EDS.), PERSONALITY AND PERSUASIBILITY.
            NEW HAVEN: YALE UNIVERSITY PRESS, 1959.
            (MEASURE OF PERSUASIBILITY, SOCIAL INFLUENCE)
        aJ-8 PERSUASIBILITY AUTONOMY SOCIAL INFLUENCE COMMUNICATION ATTITUDE CHANGE
        aJ-8 1959M
            (APPLICATIONS: 448   520   859   942)

J-9   JENKINS, T. N.
            HOW WELL DO YOU KNOW YOURSELF? GLOBAL FORM A42.
            NEW YORK: T. N. JENKINS, 21 WASHINGTON PLACE, NEW YORK, 10003, 1962.
            (JENKINS GLOBAL PERSONALITY INVENTORY)*
        aJ-9 GLOBAL PERSONALITY MULTITRAIT MMPI 1962M

J-10   JACKSON, D. N., & MINTON, H. L.
     A FORCED-CHOICE ADJECTIVE PREFERENCE SCALE FOR PERSONALITY ASSESSMENT.
     PSYCHOLOGICAL REPORTS, 1963, 12, 515-520.
     (ADJECTIVE PREFERENCE SCALE)*
   aJ-10 PERCEPTION CONCEPT SELF-IDENTITY IMAGE MULTITRAIT SELF TRAIT-TERMS
   aJ-10 PERSONALITY SEM-DIFFERENTIAL DESCRIPTION COGNITIVE COMPLEXITY FUNCTIONING
   aJ-10 STRUCTURE 1963M

J-11   JAQUES, M. E., GAIER. E. L., & LINKOWSKI, D. C.
     COPING-SUCCUMBING ATTITUDES TOWARD PHYSICAL AND MENTAL DISABILITIES.
     JOURNAL OF SOCIAL PSYCHOLOGY, 1967, 71, 295-307.
     (MEASURE OF COPING-SUCCUMBING ATTITUDES TOWARD DISABILITY)
   aJ-11 ADAPTABILITY COPING-DEFENSE GLOBAL ATTITUDE DISABILITY MENTAL-ILLNESS
   aCOPING PHYSICAL 1967M

J-12   JOHNSON, L. C.
     BODY CATHEXIS AS A FACTOR IN SOMATIC COMPLAINTS.
     JOURNAL OF CONSULTING PSYCHOLOGY, 1956, 20, 145-149.
     (MEASURE OF BODY CATHEXIS)
   aJ-12 SELF SELF-IDENTITY BODY IMAGE PERCEPTION CATHEXIS SUB-IDENTITY ADJUSTMENT
   aJ-12 1956M
     (APPLICATIONS: 36)

J-13   JONES, M. B.
     THE PENSACOLA Z SURVEY: A STUDY IN THE MEASUREMENT OF AUTHORITARIAN
     TENDENCY.
     PSYCHOLOGICAL MONOGRAPHS, 1957, 71 (23, WHOLE NO. 452), 1-19.
     (PENSACOLA Z SCALE)*
   aJ-13 AUTHORITARIANISM AUTONOMY COPING-DEFENSE STYLE OTHER-CATEGORY F-SCALE
   aJ-13 1957M

J-14   JOURARD, S. M.
     SELF-DISCLOSURE PATTERNS IN BRITISH AND AMERICAN COLLEGE FEMALES.
     JOURNAL OF SOCIAL PSYCHOLOGY, 1961, 54, 315-320.
     (SHORTENED VERSION OF THE SELF-DISCLOSURE INVENTORY (SD-25))*
   aJ-14 ADJUSTMENT ACCESSIBILITY SELF DISCLOSURE SOCIAL RESPONSE-BIAS
   aCOMMUNICATION INTERPERSONAL RELATIONSHIPS INTERACTION 1961M
     (APPLICATIONS: 91   1314   2571)

J-15   JOURARD, S. M., & LASAKOW, P.
     SOME FACTORS IN SELF-DISCLOSURE.
     JOURNAL OF ABNORMAL AND SOCIAL PSYCHOLOGY, 1958, 56, 91-98.
     (SELF-DISCLOSURE INVENTORY (SD-60))*
   aJ-15 ADJUSTMENT ACCESSIBILITY INTERACTION SELF DISCLOSURE SOCIAL RESPONSE-BIAS
   aCOMMUNICATION INTERPERSONAL RELATIONSHIPS 1958M
     (APPLICATIONS: 244   499   1263   1510   1517   2179   2271   2280   2849)

J-16   JACKSON, J.
     TOWARD THE COMPARATIVE STUDY OF MENTAL HOSPITALS: CHARACTERISTICS OF THE
     TREATMENT ENVIRONMENT. IN A. F. WESSON (ED.), THE PSYCHIATRIC HOSPITAL AS
     A SOCIAL STYSTEM. SPRINGFIELD, ILLINOIS: THOMAS, 1964.
     (CHARACTERISTICS OF THE TREATMENT ENVIRONMENT SCALE)*
   aJ-16 HOSPITALIZATION PERCEPTION ENVIRONMENT PATIENT ADJUSTMENT OTHER-CATEGORY
   aJ-16 PE-FIT SELF-IDENTITY MENTAL-ILLNESS SELF ESTEEM AUTONOMY CREATIVITY
   aJ-16 ANXIETY AFFECTIVE-STATES 1964M

J-17   JACKSON, D. N., MESSICK, S., & MYERS, C. T.
     THE ROLE OF MEMORY AND COLOR IN GROUP AND INDIVIDUAL EMBEDDED-FIGURES
     MEASURES OF FIELD INDEPENDENCE. (RESEARCH BULLETIN 62-34) PRINCETON,
     NEW JERSEY: EDUCATIONAL TESTING SERVICE, 1962.
     (EMBEDDED-FIGURES TEST FOR DETERMINING MODE OF FIELD ORIENTATION)
   aJ-17 FIELD PERCEPTION ORIENTATION AUTONOMY DEPENDENCE FIGURE COGNITIVE
   aJ-17 STRUCTURE FUNCTIONING 1962M
     (APPLICATIONS: 101   386   921   2405)

J-18   JACOBS, M. A., KNAPP, P. H., ANDERSON, L. S., KARUSH, N., MEISSNER, R., &
     RICHMAN, S. J.
     RELATIONSHI. OF ORAL FRUSTRATION FACTORS WITH HEAVY CIGARETTE SMOKING IN
     MALES.
     JOURNAL OF NERVOUS AND MENTAL DISEASE, 1965, 141, 161-171.
     (BOSTON UNIVERSITY PERSONALITY INVENTORY)*
   aJ-18 PERSONALITY GLOBAL MULTITRAIT 1965M

J-19   JACOBS, M. A., MULLER, J. J., EISMAN, H. D., KNITZER, J., & SPILKEN, A.
           THE ASSESSMENT OF CHANGE IN DISTRESS LEVEL AND STYLES OF ADAPTATION AS A
           FUNCTION OF PSYCHOTHERAPY.
           JOURNAL OF NERVOUS AND MENTAL DISEASE, 1968, 145, 392-404.
           (MANIFEST DISTRESS SCALE)
        aJ-19 EMOTION ADJUSTMENT MANIFEST AFFECTIVE-STATES ANXIETY SUBJECTIVE STRESS
        aJ-19 ADAPTABILITY THERAPY PATIENT MENTAL-ILLNESS NEGATIVE 1968M

J-20   JENKINS, J. J., RUSSELL, W. A., & SUCI, G. J.
           AN ATLAS OF SEMANTIC PROFILES FOR 360 WORDS.
           AMERICAN JOURNAL OF PSYCHOLOGY, 1958, 71, 688-699.
           (SEMANTIC DIFFERENTIAL MEASURE OF MASCULINITY-FEMININITY)
        aJ-20 SELF-IDENTITY SELF CONCEPT IMAGE EVALUATION SUB-IDENTITY SEM-DIFFERENTIAL
        aJ-20 FEMININITY MASCULINITY SEX ROLE 1958M IDENTITY
           (APPLICATIONS: 973)

J-21   JORDAN, T. E., & DECHARMS, R.
           THE ACHIEVEMENT MOTIVE IN NORMAL AND MENTALLY RETARDED CHILDREN.
           AMERICAN JOURNAL OF MENTAL DEFICIENCY, 1959, 64, 457-466.
           (TAT SCORED FOR HOPE FOR SUCCESS/FEAR OF FAILURE)
        aJ-21 HOPE SUCCESS PERFORMANCE TAT FEAR FAILURE AUTONOMY COPING-DEFENSE APPROACH
        aJ-21 AVOIDANCE ACHIEVEMENT MOTIVE NEED PROJECTIVE 1959M

J-22   JOURARD, S. M.
           AN EXPLORATORY STUDY OF BODY ACCESSIBILITY.
           BRITISH JOURNAL OF SOCIAL AND CLINICAL PSYCHOLOGY, 1966, 5, 221-231.
           (BODY CONTACT QUESTIONNAIRE)*
        aJ-22 BODY PERSONAL SPACE SELF-IDENTITY IMAGE OTHER-CATEGORY ACCESSIBILITY
        aJ-22 1966M
           (APPLICATIONS: 295)

J-23   JACKSON, D. N.
           INDEPENDENCE AND RESISTANCE TO PERCEPTUAL FIELD FORCES.
           JOURNAL OF ABNORMAL AND SOCIAL PSYCHOLOGY, 1958, 56, 279-281.
           (INDEPENDENCE-CONFORMITY INVENTORY)
        aJ-23 DEPENDENCE CONFORMITY AUTONOMY 1958M
           (APPLICATIONS: 1737)

J-24   JACKSON, D. N., & MESSICK, S.
           DIFFERENTIAL PERSONALITY INVENTORY.   PENNSYLVANIA STATE UNIVERSITY:
           AUTHORS, 1964.
           (DEFENSIVENESS SCALE)*
        aJ-24 JUDGMENT ORIENTATION DEFENSIVENESS COPING-DEFENSE GLOBAL RESPONSE-BIAS
        aJ-24 1964M

J-25   JENKIN, N., & VROEGH, K.
           CONTEMPORARY CONCEPTS OF MASCULINITY AND FEMININITY.
           PSYCHOLOGICAL REPORTS, 1969, 25, 679-697.
           (ADJECTIVE CHECKLIST MEASURE OF MASCULINITY-FEMININITY)
        aJ-25 SELF-IDENTITY MASCULINITY FEMININITY SUB-IDENTITY ROLE PERCEPTION
        aJ-25 CHECKLIST 1969M SEX IDENTITY

J-26   JACOBSON, L. I., BERGER, S. E., & MILLHAM, J.
           INDIVIDUAL DIFFERENCES IN CHEATING DURING A TEMPTATION PERIOD WHEN CON-
           FRONTING FAILURE.
           JOURNAL OF PERSONALITY AND SOCIAL PSYCHOLOGY, 1970, 15, 48-56.
           (SELF-SATISFACTION MEASURE)
        aJ-26 1970M SELF ESTEEM SATISFACTION ASPIRATION

J-27   JACKSON, D. & LYONS, M.
           A FACTOR ANALYTIC DESCRIPTION OF EXCITEMENT.
           UNPUBLISHED PAPER, UNIVERSITY OF WISCONSIN, 1969.
           (DESIRE FOR EXCITEMENT TEST)
        aJ-27 1969M PREFERENCE PARTICIPATION EXCITEMENT ACTIVITIES
           (APPLICATIONS: 2335)

J-28   JESSOR, R., GRAVES, T. D., HANSON, R. C. & JESSOR, S. L.
           SOCIETY, PERSONALITY, AND DEVIANT BEHAVIOR: A STUDY OF A TRI-ETHNIC
           COMMUNITY.
           NEW YORK: HOLT, RINEHART, & WINSTON, 1968.
           (MEASURE OF EXPECTATION OF GOAL ATTAINMENT)
        aJ-28 1968M GOALS   PERCEIVED OPPORTUNITY ASPIRATION
           (APPLICATIONS: 2510)

J-29   JESSOR, R., GRAVES, T. D., HANSEN, R. C. & JESSOR, S. L.
              SOCIETY, PERSONALITY, AND DEVIANT BEHAVIOR: A STUDY OF A TRI-ETHNIC
              COMMUNITY.
              NEW YORK: HOLT, RINEHART, & WINSTON, 1968.
              (MEASURE OF ALIENATION)
            aJ-29 1968M ALIENATION ANOMIE ADJUSTMENT
              (APPLICATIONS: 2510)

J-31   JOHANSSON, C. B.
              STRONG VOCATIONAL INTEREST BLANK INTROVERSION-EXTRAVERSION AND
              OCCUPATIONAL MEMBERSHIP.
              JOURNAL OF COUNSELING PSYCHOLOGY, 1970, 17, 451-455.
              (OCCUPATIONAL INTROVERSION-EXTRAVERSION SCALE)
            aJ-31 1970M JOB EXTRAVERSION INTROVERSION MMPI SOCIAL VOCATIONAL INTEREST
              (APPLICATIONS: 2863)

J-32   JACKSON, J.
              ANALYSIS OF INTERPERSONAL RELATIONS IN A FORMAL ORGANIZATION.
              UNPUBLISHED DOCTORAL DISSERTATION, UNIVERSITY OF MICHIGAN, 1953.
              (MEASURE OF GROUP ATTRACTIVENESS)
            aJ-32 1953M ATTRACTION GROUP OTHERS INTERPERSONAL SOCIAL
              (APPLICATIONS: 325)

J-34   JANIS, I. L., & FIELD, P. B.
              C. L. HOVLAND, AND I. C. JANIS (EDS.) PERSONALITY AND PERSUASABILITY.
              NEW HAVEN: YALE UNIVERSITY PRESS, 1959, 55-68.
              (SCALE OF SOCIAL INHIBITION)
            aJ-34 1959M SEX PERSONALITY SOCIAL INHIBITION CONTROL EXPRESSION IMPULSE
              (APPLICATIONS: 369)

J-35   JONES, E. E., JONES, R. G., & GERGEN, K. J.
              SOME CONDITIONS AFFECTING THE EVALUATION OF A CONFORMIST.
              JOURNAL OF PERSONALITY, 1963, 31, 270-288.
              (MEASURE OF EVALUATION OF A CONFORMIST)
            aJ-35 1963M CONFORMITY EVALUATION RATING
            aJ-35 JUDGMENT SOCIAL ATTITUDE

J-36   JOHNSON, M. H., & MEADOWS, A.
              PARENTAL IDENTIFICATION AMONG MALE SCHIZOPHRENICS.
              JOURNAL OF PERSONALITY, 1966, 34, 300-309.
              (MEASURE OF PARENTAL IDENTIFICATION)
            aJ-36 1966M PARENTAL IDENTIFICATION SCHIZOPHRENIA MENTAL-ILLNESS
            aJ-36 SELF IDEAL IMPRESSION SUBJECTIVE Q-SORT

J-37   JOURARD, S. M.
              IDENTIFICATION, PARENT-CATHEXIS, AND SELF-ESTEEM.
              JOURNAL OF CONSULTING PSYCHOLOGY, 1957, 21, 375-380.
              (REAL-SELF-IDEAL-SELF DISCREPANCY SCALE)
            aJ-37 1957M SELF CONCEPT IDEAL SELF EVALUATION ESTEEM DISCLOSURE
            aJ-37 DISCREPANCY
              (APPLICATIONS: 1206 1718)

J-38   JENKINS, R. L., STAUFFACHER, J., & HESTER, R.
              A SYMPTOM RATING SCALE FOR USE WITH PSYCHOTIC PATIENTS.
              A. M. A. ARCHIVES OF GENERAL PSYCHIATRY, 1959, 1, 197-204.
              (SYMPTOM RATING SCALE)
            aJ-38 1959M SYMPTOM PSYCHIATRIC MENTAL-ILLNESS SCHIZOPHRENIA RATING

J-39   JENKINS, R. L., STAUFFACHER, J., & HESTER, R.
              SYMPTOM RATING SCALE FOR USE WITH PSYCHOTIC PATIENTS.
              A. M. A. ARCHIVES OF GENERAL PSYCHIATRY, 1959, 1, 197-204.
              (SYMPTOM RATING SHEET)*
            aJ-39 1959M SYMPTOM RATING SCHIZOPHRENIA PSYCHIATRIC MENTAL-ILLNESS
              (APPLICATIONS: 792 1719 1873)

J-40   JACKSON, D. N.
              THE DEVELOPMENT AND EVALUATION OF THE PERSONALITY RESEARCH FORM.
              UNPUBLISHED MANUSCRIPT, UNIVERSITY OF WESTERN ONTARIO, 1965.
              (JACKSON NEED-ACHIEVEMENT SCALE)
            aJ-40 1965M NEED ACHIEVEMENT AUTONOMY
              (APPLICATIONS: 2108)

J-41   JOHNSON, R. C., ACKERMAN, J. M., FRANK, H., & FIONDA, A. J.
        RESISTANCE TO TEMPTATION, GUILT FOLLOWING YIELDING, AND PSYCHOPATHOLOGY.
        JOURNAL OF CONSULTING AND CLINICAL PSYCHOLOGY, 1968, 32, 169-175.
        (STORY COMPLETION MEASURE OF TEMPTATION RESISTANCE AND GUILT FOLLOWING
        YIELDING)
        aJ-41 1968M GUILT PROJECTIVE MORAL VALUES BELIEF PROBLEM FANTASY IMAGINATION
        aJ-41 INHIBITION IMPULSE CONTROL EXPRESSION

J-42   JACKSON, D. N., & PAYNE, I. R.
        PERSONALITY SCALE FOR SHALLOW AFFECT.
        PSYCHOLOGICAL REPORTS, 1963, 13, 687-698.
        (SHALLOW AFFECT SCALE)*
        aJ-42 1963M AFFECTIVE-STATES INTENSITY HOSTILITY IRRITABILITY
        (APPLICATIONS: 924)

J-43   JOHNSON, H., & ERIKSEN, C. W.
        PRECONSCIOUS PERCEPTION: A RE-EXAMINATION OF THE POETZL PHENOMENON.
        JOURNAL OF ABNORMAL AND SOCIAL PSYCHOLOGY, 1961, 62, 497-503.
        (MEASURE OF DISTORTION IN DREAMING)
        aJ-43 1961M PRIMARY-PROCESS COGNITIVE THINKING FUNCTIONING STYLE

J-44   JACKSON, P. W.
        VERBAL SOLUTIONS TO PARENT-CHILD PROBLEMS.
        CHILD DEVELOPMENT, 1956, 27, 339-349.
        (JACKSON PROBLEM QUESTIONNAIRE (JPQ))*
        aJ-44 1956M PARENT-CHILD AGGRESSION HOSTILITY COPING STYLE PROBLEM CHILD
        aJ-44 BEHAVIOR PEER
        (APPLICATIONS: 1101 1113)

J-45   JENKS, R. S.
        AN ACTION-RESEARCH APPROACH TO ORGANIZATIONAL CHANGE.
        JOURNAL OF APPLIED BEHAVIORAL SCIENCE, 1970, 6, 131-150.
        (ORGANIZATIONAL Q-SORT)
        aJ-45 1970M Q-SORT GROUP ORGANIZATION JOB INTERPERSONAL RELATIONSHIPS
        aINTERACTION

J-46   JACOBS, P. D., MUNZ, D. C., BARRETT, L., & EVERETT, F.
        ACADEMIC SURVIVAL: SUCCESS INDICATORS IN INTRODUCTORY PSYCHOLOGY.
        PSYCHOLOGICAL REPORTS, 1970, 26, 231-233.
        (SEMANTIC DIFFERENTIAL APPLIED TO STUDENT ATTITUDES AND VALUES)
        aJ-46 1970M INTEREST ORIENTATION PERFORMANCE TEACHER STUDENT TEXT ACADEMIC
        aSEM-DIFFERENTIAL SUCCESS ATTITUDE SCHOOL COLLEGE VALUES

J-47   JACKSON, D. N., & MESSICK, S.
        DIFFERENTIAL PERSONALITY INVENTORY (FORM L).
        COLLEGE PARK, PENNSYLVANIA: AUTHORS, 1964.
        (DIFFERENTIAL PERSONALITY INVENTORY)*
        aJ-47 1964M PERSONALITY STRUCTURE INVENTORY MULTI-TRAIT

J-49   JORGENSEN, G. Q., JANSEN, F. V., SAMUELSON, C. O., & MCPHEE, W. M.
        INTERPERSONAL RELATIONSHIPS: FACTORS IN JOB PLACEMENT.
        (BULLETIN NO. 3), SALT LAKE CITY, UTAH: REGIONAL REHABILITATION RESEARCH
        INSTITUTE, UNIVERSITY OF UTAH (IN PRESS -- 1969?).
        (SOCIAL VOCABULARY INDEX)*
        aJ-49 SELF CONCEPT ACCEPTANCE IDEAL SOCIAL DESIRABILITY ESTEEM PERCEPTION OTHERS
        (APPLICATIONS: 1506)

J-50   JANIS, I. L., & FIELD, P. B.
        A BEHAVIORAL ASSESSMENT OF PERSUASIBILITY: CONSISTENCY OF INDIVIDUAL
        DIFFERENCES.
        SOCIOMETRY, 1956, 19, 241-259.
        (PERSUASIBILITY TEST)
        aJ-50 1956M PERSUASIBILITY ATTITUDE CHANGE CONFORMITY OPENNESS
        (APPLICATIONS: 1529 2483)

J-51   JAFFE, J.
        ATTITUDES OF ADOLESCENTS TOWARD PERSONS WITH DISABILITIES.
        UNPUBLISHED DOCTORAL PROJECT, TEACHERS COLLEGE, COLUMBIA UNIVERSITY, 1965.
        JAFFE, J.
        ATTITUDES AND INTERPERSONAL CONTACT: RELATIONSHIPS BETWEEN CONTACT WITH
        THE MENTALLY RETARDED AND DIMENSIONS OF ATTITUDE.
        JOURNAL OF COUNSELING PSYCHOLOGY, 1967, 14, 482-484.
        (SEMANTIC DIFFERENTIAL MEASURE OF ATTITUDES TOWARD THE MENTALLY RETARDED)
        aJ-51 1965M SEM-DIFFERENTIAL ATTITUDE MENTAL-ILLNESS PERCEPTION DISABILITY
        aRETARDATION

J-52   JACOBS, D. F.
                MANUAL FOR JACOBS SELF-ATTITUDE SCALE.
                BRECKVILLE, OHIO: VETERANS ADMINISTRATION HOSPITAL, 1961.
                (JACOBS SELF-ATTITUDE SCALE)*
            aJ-52 1961M SELF ATTITUDE CONCEPT ESTEEM EVALUATION PERCEPTION
                (APPLICATIONS: 1283)

J-53   JOHNSON, G.
                AN INSTRUMENT FOR THE MEASUREMENT OF JOB SATISFACTION.
                PERSONNEL PSYCHOLOGY, 1955, 8, 27-37.
                (JOB SATISFACTION INVENTORY)
            aJ-53 1955M JOB SATISFACTION COUNSELING RELATIONSHIPS INTEREST EVALUATION
            aGOALS LIFE FUTURE
                (APPLICATIONS: 1275)

J-54   JACKSON, D. N.
                A SHORT FORM OF WITKIN'S EMBEDDED FIGURES TEST.
                JOURNAL OF ABNORMAL AND SOCIAL PSYCHOLOGY, 1956, 53, 254-255.
                (EMBEDDED FIGURES TEST)*
            aJ-54 1956M FIGURE COGNITIVE STYLE DIFFERENTIATION W-19R FIELD DEPENDENCE
                (APPLICATIONS: 191   880)

J-55   JULIAN, J. W., BISHOP, D. W., & FIEDLER, F. E.
                QUASI-THERAPEUTIC EFFECTS OF INTERGROUP COMPETITION.
                JOURNAL OF PERSONALITY AND SOCIAL PSYCHOLOGY, 1966, 3, 321-327.
                (PERSONAL REACTION FORM--PRF)
            aJ-55 1966M PERCEPTION ROLE JOB

J-59   JOHNSON, R. W., & FREDRICKSON, R. H.
                EFFECT OF FINANCIAL REMUNERATION AND CASE DESCRIPTION ON COUNSELOR
                PERFORMANCE.
                JOURNAL OF COUNSELING PSYCHOLOGY, 1968, 15, 130-135.
                (CLIENT SATISFACTION SCALE)
            aJ-59 1968M COUNSELING THERAPY SATISFACTION INTEREST ATTITUDE SEM-DIFFERENTIAL
            aPATIENT

J-60   JACOBS, D. F., & DOWNIE, N. M.
                THE JOB PREFERENCE RECORD: A NEW TEST FOR PLACING PATIENTS IN INSTITUTIONAL
                WORK ASSIGNMENTS.
                PAPER READ AT MIDWESTERN PSYCHOLOGICAL ASSOCIATION, ST. LOUIS, APRIL, 1960.
                (JOB PREFERENCE RECORD)
            aJ-60 1960M JOB PREFERENCE PATIENT COUNSELING INTEREST VOCATIONAL
                (APPLICATIONS: 1306)

J-70   JESSOR, R., GRAVES, T. D., HANSON, R. C. & JESSOR, S. L.
                SOCIETY, PERSONALITY, AND DEVIANT BEHAVIOR: A STUDY OF A TRI-ETHNIC
                COMMUNITY.
                NEW YORK: HOLT, RINEHART, & WINSTON, 1968.
                (MEASURE OF INTERNAL CONTROL)
            aJ-70 1968M CONTROL LOCUS IE-CONTROL AUTONOMY
                (APPLICATIONS: 2510)

K-1   KAGAN, J., MOSS, H. A., & SIGEL, I. E.
                PSYCHOLOGICAL SIGNIFICANCE OF STYLES OF CONCEPTUALIZATION.
                MONOGRAPHS OF THE SOCIETY FOR RESEARCH IN CHILD DEVELOPMENT, 1963, 28,
                (SERIAL NO. 86, WHOLE NO. 2), 73-112.
                (MEASURE OF CONCEPTUAL STYLE)
            aK-1 ANALYTIC GLOBAL COGNITIVE STYLE STRUCTURE CONCEPTUAL CONCEPT THINKING
            aK-1 FUNCTIONING 1963M
                (APPLICATIONS: 386)

K-2   KORMAN, A. K.
                RELEVANCE OF PERSONAL NEED SATISFACTION FOR OVERALL SATISFACTION AS A
                FUNCTION OF SELF-ESTEEM.
                JOURNAL OF APPLIED PSYCHOLOGY, 1967, 51, 533-538.
                (JOB SATISFACTION QUESTIONNAIRE)
            aK-2 AFFECTIVE-STATES GLOBAL JOB SATISFACTION ADJUSTMENT PE-FIT 1967M

K-3   KAMMEYER, K.
                THE FEMININE ROLE: AN ANALYSIS OF ATTITUDE CONSISTENCY.
                JOURNAL OF MARRIAGE AND THE FAMILY, 1964, 26, 295-305.
                (MEASURE OF ATTITUDES TOWARD FEMININE ROLE)
            aK-3 SEX ATTITUDE IDENTITY SELF-IDENTITY SUB-IDENTITY ROLE PERCEPTION FEMININITY
            aK-3 BEHAVIOR 1964M

K-4   KARLSSON, G.
            ADAPTABILITY AND COMMUNICATION IN MARRIAGE: A SWEDISH PREDICTION STUDY
            OF MARITAL SATISFACTION. UPPSALA, SWEDEN: ALMQVIST AND WIKSELLS,
            BOKTRYCHERI AKTIEBOLAG, 1951. 95-99.
            (KARLSSON INDEX OF MARITAL SATISFACTION)*
        aK-4 MARITAL SATISFACTION ADJUSTMENT AFFECTIVE-STATES GLOBAL RESENTMENT
        aK-4 COMMUNICATION ADAPTABILITY 1951M

K-5   KAUFMANN, H.
            CORRELATIONS AMONG VERBAL RESPONSE HOSTILITY MEASURES.
            PERCEPTUAL AND MOTOR SKILLS, 1965, 20, 258.
            (SHORT HOSTILITY SCALE)
        aK-5 AFFECTIVE-STATES HOSTILITY NEGATIVE RESENTMENT MANIFEST 1965M

K-6   KELLAM, S. G., SCHMELZER, J. L., & BERMAN, A.
            VARIATION IN THE ATMOSPHERES OF PSYCHIATRIC WARDS.
            ARCHIVES OF GENERAL PSYCHIATRY, 1966, 14, 561-570.
            (WARD INFORMATION FORM)*
        aK-6 PE-FIT WARD ADJUSTMENT HOSPITALIZATION ENVIRONMENT PSYCHIATRIC 1966M
            (APPLICATIONS: 1083)

K-7   KENDALL, L. M., SMITH, P. C., HULIN, C. L., & LOCKE, E. A.
            CORNELL STUDIES OF JOB SATISFACTION: IV. THE RELATIVE VALIDITY OF THE JOB
            DESCRIPTIVE INDEX ND OTHER METHODS OF MEASUREMENT OF JOB SATISFACTION.
            ITHACA: CORNELL UNIVERSITY, 1963. (MIMEO)
            (JOB DESCRIPTIVE INDEX)*
        aK-7 JOB SATISFACTION ADJUSTMENT AFFECTIVE-STATES GLOBAL ATTITUDES EMPLOYEE
        aK-7 SUPERVISOR 1963M PE-FIT
            (APPLICATIONS: 2480)

K-8   KERLINGER, F., & ROKEACH, M.
            THE FACTORIAL NATURE OF THE F AND D SCALES.
            JOURNAL OF PERSONALITY AND SOCIAL PSYCHOLOGY, 1966, 4, 391-399.
            (F + D SCALE)*
        aK-8 AUTHORITARIANISM COPING-DEFENSE OTHER-CATEGORY F-SCALE DOGMATISM RIGIDITY
        aK-8 FLEXIBILITY 1966M

K-9   KERR, W. A., & SPEROFF, B. J.
            THE EMPATHY TEST: MANUAL. CHICAGO: PSYCHOMETRIC AFFILIATES, 1955.
            (EMPATHY TEST)*
        aK-9 EMPATHY AFFECTIVE-STATES ORIENTATION POSITIVE 1951M OTHERS
            (APPLICATIONS: 485)

K-10   KINZIE, W., & ZIMMER, H.
            ON THE MEASUREMENT OF HOSTILITY, AGGRESSION ANXIETY, PROJECTION AND
            DEPENDENCY.
            JOURNAL OF PROJECTIVE TECHNIQUES AND PERSONALITY ASSESSMENT, 1968, 32, 388-
            391.
            (PEER RATING SCALE OF EXTRAPUNITIVE-INTROPUNITIVE OTHERS)
        aK-10 HOSTILITY PROJECTIVE DEPENDENCE PEER RATING AFFECTIVE-STATES RESENTMENT
        aK-10 ANXIETY AGGRESSION PUNITIVENESS OTHERS NEGATIVE DIRECTION 1968M

K-11   KIRKPATRICK, C.
            THE CONSTRUCTION OF A BELIEF-PATTERN SCALE FOR MEASURING ATTITUDES TOWARD
            FEMINISM.
            JOURNAL OF SOCIAL PSYCHOLOGY, 1936, 7, 421-437.
            (KIRKPATRICK FEMINIST ATTITUDE SCALE)*
        aK-11 FEMININITY ATTITUDE BELIEF SUB-IDENTITY SELF-IDENTITY ROLE ADJUSTMENT
        aK-11 IMAGE EVALUATION CONCEPT
            (APPLICATIONS: 2498)

K-12   KERR, W. A.
            TULANE FACTORS OF LIBERALISM-CONSERVATISM. CHICAGO: PSYCHOMETRIC
            AFFILIATES, 1946.
            (LIBERALISM-CONSERVATISM SCALE)
        aK-12 1946M LIBERALISM CONSERVATISM POLITICAL ORIENTATION
            (APPLICATIONS: 2489)

K-13   KLOPFER, B., KIRKNER, F. J., WISHAM, W., & BAKER, G.
            RORSCHACH PROGNOSTIC RATING SCALE.
            JOURNAL OF PROJECTIVE TECHNIQUES AND PERSONALITY ASSESSMENT, 1951, 15,
            425-428.
            (RORSCHACH PROGNOSTIC RATING SCALE)*
        aK-13 PROJECTIVE RORSCHACH ADJUSTMENT EGO-STRENGTH COPING-DEFENSE EGO-RESILIENCY
            (APPLICATIONS: 929 1182 1250 1562 1676 1880 1982 2135)

K-14   KNAPP, R. H.
                A STUDY OF THE METAPHOR.
                JOURNAL OF PROJECTIVE TECHNIQUES, 1960, 24, 389-395.
                (SCALES USING METAPHORS TO MEASURE ATTITUDES)
            @K-14 MULTITRAIT CONSCIENCE PROJECTIVE DEATH TIME METAPHOR SUCCESS IMAGE 1960M
            @K-14 SELF SELF-IDENTITY EVALUATION ESTEEM PERCEPTION
                (APPLICATIONS: 926   1823   2336   2607   2898)

K-15   KOCH, H. L.
                SISSINESS AND TOMBOYISHNESS IN RELATION TO SIBLING CHARACTERISTICS.
                JOURNAL OF GENETIC PSYCHOLOGY, 1956, 88, 231-244.
                (POINT RATING SCALE OF MASCULINITY)
            @K-15 SEX DIFFERENCES IDENTITY SELF-IDENTITY SUB-IDENTITY ROLE PERCEPTION
            @K-15 MASCULINITY RATING 1956M

K-16   KOGAN, N.
                ATTITUDES TOWARD OLD PEOPLE: THE DEVELOPMENT OF A SCALE AND AN EXAMINATION
                OF CORRELATES.
                JOURNAL OF ABNORMAL AND SOCIAL PSYCHOLOGY, 1961, 62, 44-54.
                (ATTITUDES TOWARD OLD PEOPLE SCALE)*
            @K-16 INTERPERSONAL ATTITUDE OTHERS 1961M
                (APPLICATIONS: 660)

K-17   KASSEBAUM, G. G., COUCH, A. S., & SLATER, P. E.
                THE FACTORIAL DIMENSIONS OF THE MMPI.
                JOURNAL OF CONSULTING PSYCHOLOGY, 1959, 23, 226-236.
                (ADMISSION OF WEAKNESS SCALE)
            @K-17 DISCLOSURE SELF MMPI SELF-IDENTITY EVALUATION EGO-STRENGTH MENTAL-ILLNESS
            @DISABILITY COPING-DEFENSE EGO 1959M

K-18   KATZ, P., & ZIGLER, E.
                SELF-IMAGE DISPARITY: A DEVELOPMENTAL APPROACH.
                JOURNAL OF PERSONALITY AND SOCIAL PSYCHOLOGY, 1967, 5, 186-195.
                (ADJECTIVE LIST MEASURE OF SELF-IMAGE DISPARITY)
            @K-18 DISCREPANCY SELF IMAGE CONCEPT PERCEPTION ADJUSTMENT SELF-IDENTITY
            @K-18 EVALUATION 1967M

K-19   KOMORITA, S. S.
                ATTITUDE CONTENT, INTENSITY, AND THE NEUTRAL POINT ON A LIKERT-TYPE SCALE.
                JOURNAL OF SOCIAL PSYCHOLOGY, 1963, 61, 327-334.
                (SEGREGATIONISM SCALE)*
            @K-19 AUTHORITARIANISM COPING-DEFENSE OTHER-CATEGORY RACIAL PREJUDICE ATTITUDE
            @K-19 DESEGREGATION NEGRO 1963M

K-20   KORMAN, A. K.
                RELEVANCE OF PERSONAL NEED SATISFACTION FOR OVERALL SATISFACTION AS A
                FUNCTION OF SELF-ESTEEM.
                JOURNAL OF APPLIED PSYCHOLOGY, 1967, 51, 533-538.
                (MEASURE OF IDEAL AND FAVORITE GROUP)
            @K-20 SOCIAL NEED INTERACTION GROUP DESCRIPTION ADJUSTMENT PREFERENCE IDEAL
            @K-20 1967M

K-21   KUHN, M. H., & MCPARTLAND, T. S.
                AN EMPIRICAL INVESTIGATION OF SELF-ATTITUDES.
                AMERICAN SOCIOLOGICAL REVIEW, 1954, 19, 68-76.
                (TWENTY STATEMENTS TEST)*
            @K-21 SELF ATTITUDE SELF-IDENTITY PERCEPTION EVALUATION ESTEEM 1954M IMAGE
            @K-21 CONCEPT
                (APPLICATIONS: 1195)

K-22   KATZ, P., & ZIGLER, E.
                SELF-IMAGE DISPARITY: A DEVELOPMENTAL APPROACH.
                JOURNAL OF PERSONALITY AND SOCIAL PSYCHOLOGY, 1967, 5, 186-195.
                (QUESTIONNAIRE MEASURE OF SELF-IMAGE DISPARITY)
            @K-22 DISCREPANCY SELF IMAGE CONCEPT PERCEPTION ADJUSTMENT SELF-IDENTITY
            @K-22 1967M EVALUATION

K-23   KELLY, G. A.
         THE PSYCHOLOGY OF PERSONAL CONSTRUCTS. NEW YORK: NORTON, 1955.
         (ROLE CONSTRUCT REPERTORY (REP) TEST)*
         @K-23 PERSONAL ROLE SELF-IDENTITY SUB-IDENTITY PERCEPTION 1955M
                  (APPLICATIONS: 214   260   355   391   396   438   439   453   611   672
                                    882   892   1168   1292   1331   1352   1461   1462   1646   1700
                                   1773   1938   2038   2083   2180   2629   2760   2775   2861)

K-24   KERLE, R. H., & BIALEK, H. M.
         THE CONSTRUCTION, VALIDATION, AND APPLICATION OF A SUBJECTIVE STRESS SCALE.
         STAFF MEMORANDUM, UNITED STATES ARMY LEADERSHIP HUMAN RESEARCH UNIT,
         PRESIDIO OF MONTEREY, FEBRUARY 1958.
         (SUBJECTIVE STRESS SCALE)*
         @K-24 SUBJECTIVE STRESS ANXIETY AFFECTIVE-STATES NEGATIVE 1958M
                  (APPLICATIONS: 243   245   1071)

K-25   KIPNIS, D.
         STUDIES IN CHARACTER STRUCTURE.
         JOURNAL OF PERSONALITY AND SOCIAL PSYCHOLOGY, 1968, 8, 217-227.
         (SCALE OF VALUES)
         @K-25 SOCIAL VALUES SELF-IDENTITY IDEALS LIFE GOALS BELIEF BEHAVIOR ORIENTATION
         @K-25 1968M

K-26   KLINEBERG, S. L.
         FUTURE TIME PERSPECTIVE AND THE PREFERENCE FOR DELAYED REWARD.
         JOURNAL OF PERSONALITY AND SOCIAL PSYCHOLOGY, 1968, 8, 253-257.
         (MEASURE OF TEMPORAL COHERENCE)
         @K-26 COHERENCE TIME PERSPECTIVE AFFECTIVE-STATES FUTURE ORIENTATION REALITY
         @PERCEPTION 1968M

K-27   KOHLBERG, L.
         THE DEVELOPMENT OF MODES OF MORAL THINKING IN THE YEARS TEN TO SIXTEEN.
         UNPUBLISHED DOCTORAL DISSERTATION, UNIVERSITY OF CHICAGO, 1958.
         (MORAL JUDGMENT INTERVIEW)
         @K-27 CHILD ADOLESCENT DEVELOPMENT MORAL JUDGMENT ADJUSTMENT OTHER-CATEGORY SELF
         @SELF-IDENTITY ACTUALIZATION VALUES IDEALS LIFE GOALS ORIENTATION THINKING 1958M
                  (APPLICATIONS: 90   504   513   1028   2966)

K-28   KOTCHEN, T.
         EXISTENTIAL MENTAL HEALTH: AN EMPIRICAL APPROACH.
         JOURNAL OF INDIVIDUAL PSYCHOLOGY, 1960, 16, 174-181.
         (MEASURE OF EXISTENTIAL MENTAL HEALTH)
         @K-28 EXISTENTIAL MENTAL-HEALTH GLOBAL ADJUSTMENT SELF DESCRIPTION RATING
         @RESPONSIBILITY TRANSCENDENCE 1960M

K-29   KELLY, J. G., FERSON, J. E., & HOLTZMAN, W. H.
         THE MEASUREMENT OF ATTITUDES TOWARD THE NEGRO IN THE SOUTH.
         JOURNAL OF ABNORMAL AND SOCIAL PSYCHOLOGY, 1958, 48, 305-317.
         (DESEGREGATION SCALE)*
         @K-29 DESEGREGATION RACIAL NEGRO AFFECTIVE-STATES OTHER-CATEGORY ATTITUDE
         @PREJUDICE MINORITY GROUP 1958M
                  (APPLICATIONS: 224   725   751)

K-30   KATZ, D., & BRALY, K. W.
         RACIAL STEROTYPES OF ONE HUNDRED COLLEGE STUDENTS.
         JOURNAL OF ABNORMAL AND SOCIAL PSYCHOLOGY, 1933, 28, 280-290.
         (MEASURE OF MULTINATIONAL TRAIT STEREOTYPES)
         @K-30 STEREOTYPE AFFECTIVE-STATES OTHER-CATEGORY TRAIT ATTITUDE PREJUDICE RACIAL
         @K-30 1933M ETHNIC
                  (APPLICATIONS: 309   1764)

K-31   KLINEBERG, S. L.
         CHANGES IN OUTLOOK ON THE FUTURE BETWEEN CHILDHOOD AND ADOLESCENCE.
         JOURNAL OF PERSONALITY AND SOCIAL PSYCHOLOGY, 1967, 7, 185-193.
         (QUESTIONNAIRE MEASURE OF FUTURE TIME PERSPECTIVE)
         @K-31 TAT PROJECTIVE FUTURE TIME PERSPECTIVE AFFECTIVE-STATES ORIENTATION
         @CHILD ADOLESCENT 1967M

K-32   KELMAN, H. C., & PARLOFF, M. B.
         INTERRELATIONS AMONG THREE CRITERIA OF IMPROVEMENT IN GROUP THERAPY:
         COMFORT, EFFECTIVENESS, AND SELF-AWARENESS.
         JOURNAL OF ABNORMAL AND SOCIAL PSYCHOLOGY, 1957, 54, 281-288.
         (MEASURES OF THERAPIST-PATIENT RELATIONSHIPS)
         @K-32 EFFECTIVENESS THERAPY ADJUSTMENT PATIENT OTHER-CATEGORY RELATIONSHIPS
         @PSYCHIATRIC MENTAL-ILLNESS Q-SORT INTERACTION RATING 1957M
                  (APPLICATIONS: 1628)

K-33   KIBRICK, A. K.
         DROP-OUTS FROM SCHOOLS OF NURSING: THE EFFECT OF SELF AND ROLE PERCEPTION.
         UNPUBLISHED DOCTORAL DISSERTATION, HARVARD GRADUATE SCHOOL OF EDUCATION,
         1958.
         (QUESTIONNAIRE OF PERSONALITY CHARACTERISTICS AND BEHAVIORS)
     @K-33 NEED SELF-IDENTITY SELF IDEAL ROLE PERCEPTION ESTEEM EVALUATION AUTONOMY
     @OTHER-CATEGORY IMAGE 1961M
         (APPLICATIONS: 1184)

K-34   KUDER, G. F.
         EXAMINER MANUAL FOR KUDER PREFERENCE RECORD-PERSONAL, FORM A (4TH ED.)
         CHICAGO: SCIENCE RESEARCH ASSOCIATES, 1953.
         (KUDER PREFERENCE RECORD)*
     @K-34 VOCATIONAL PREFERENCE INTEREST JOB 1934M
         (APPLICATIONS: 100   826   1162   1183   1186   1208   1215   1246   1251   1255
                          1271   1294   1313   1315   1323   1372   1389   1470   1540   1541
                          1551   1552   1553   1556   1595   2604   2674   2865   2945)

K-35   KASSARJIAN, W. M.
         A STUDY OF RIESMAN'S THEORY OF SOCIAL CHARACTER.
         SOCIOMETRY, 1962, 25, 213-230.
         (I-O SCALE)*
     @K-35 ORIENTATION DIRECTION LOCUS CONTROL AUTONOMY IE-CONTROL 1962M OTHERS
         (APPLICATIONS: 1302)

K-36   KIRKPATRICK, C.
         RELIGION AND HUMANITARIANISM: A STUDY OF INSTITUTIONAL IMPLICATIONS.
         PSYCHOLOGICAL MONOGRAPHS, 1949, 63 (4, WHOLE NO. 304).
         (KIRKPATRICK RELIGIOSITY SCALE)*
     @K-36 RELIGION ATTITUDE ORIENTATION BELIEF 1964M
         (APPLICATIONS: 1434)

K-37   KESSLER, S.
         AN EXPERIMENTAL COMPARISON OF ELECTROENCEPHALOGRAPHIC PATTERNS OF NORMAL
         AND PASSIVE-DEPENDENT INDIVIDUALS.
         UNPUBLISHED DOCTORAL DISSERTATION, UNIVERSITY OF SOUTHERN CALIFORNIA, 1952.
         (KESSLER PASSIVE-DEPENDENCY SCALE)*
     @K-37 AUTONOMY DEPENDENCE ADULT 1952M

K-38   KOOKER, E.
         AN INVESTIGATION OF SECURITY, INSECURITY, ACHIEVEMENT, AND BOREDOM IN
         ELEMENTARY SCHOOL CHILDREN.
         UNPUBLISHED DOCTORAL DISSERTATION, STATE UNIVERSITY OF IOWA, 1951.
         (KOOKER SECURITY-INSECURITY SCALE)*
     @K-38 ADJUSTMENT GLOBAL SECURITY CHILD BEHAVIOR SCHOOL RATING ELEMENTARY CHILD
     @K-38 1951M
         (APPLICATIONS: 323)

K-39   KLAUSMEIER, H. J., & RIPPLE, R. E.
         EFFECTS OF ACCELERATING BRIGHT OLDER PUPILS FROM SECOND TO FOURTH GRADE.
         JOURNAL OF EDUCATIONAL PSYCHOLOGY, 1962, 53, 93-100.
         (MEASURE OF ETHICAL VALUES)
     @K-39 MORAL AUTONOMY VALUES GROUP CONFORMITY SELF-IDENTITY DEVELOPMENT CHILD
     @ORIENTATION 1962M

K-40   KLAUSMEIER, H. J., & RIPPLE, R. E.
         EFFECTS OF ACCELERATING BRIGHT OLDER PUPILS FROM SECOND TO FOURTH GRADE.
         JOURNAL OF EDUCATIONAL PSYCHOLOGY, 1962, 53, 93-100.
         (TEACHER RATING SCALE)*
     @K-40 INTELLIGENCE TEACHER RATING AFFECTIVE-STATES GLOBAL STUDENT BEHAVIOR
     @SOCIAL DEVELOPMENT 1962M

K-41   KLAUSMEIER, H. J., & RIPPLE, R. E.
         EFFECTS OF ACCELERATING BRIGHT OLDER PUPILS FROM SECOND TO FOURTH GRADE.
         JOURNAL OF EDUCATIONAL PSYCHOLOGY, 1962, 53, 93-100.
         (SOCIOMETRIC INSTRUMENT OF PEER ACCEPTANCE)
     @K-41 ELEMENTARY SCHOOL SOCIOMETRIC INTERPERSONAL RELATIONSHIPS STUDENT CHILD
     @PEER ACCEPTANCE SOCIAL COMPETENCE ADJUSTMENT OTHER-CATEGORY 1962M

K-42   KIESLER, D. J., MATHIEW, P. L., & KLEIN, M. H.
              SAMPLING FROM THE RECORDED THERAPY INTERVIEW: A COMPARATIVE STUDY OF
              DIFFERENT SEGMENT LENGTHS.
              JOURNAL OF CONSULTING PSYCHOLOGY, 1964, 28, 349-357.
              (EXPERIENCING SCALE)*
         aK-42 MULTITRAIT THERAPY ADJUSTMENT EXPERIENCE PATIENT MENTAL-ILLNESS
         aRELATIONSHIPS 1964M
              (APPLICATIONS: 1034)

K-43   KUETHE, J. L.
              THE POSITIVE RESPONSE SET AS RELATED TO TASK PERFORMANCE.
              JOURNAL OF PERSONALITY, 1959, 27, 87-94.
              (POSITIVE RESPONSE SET MEASURE)
         aK-43 RORSCHACH RESPONSE SET RESPONSE-BIAS ACQUIESCENCE PROJECTIVE F-SCALE 1959M
              (APPLICATIONS: 606)

K-44   KATZ, D., SARNOFF, I., & MCCLINTOCK, C.
              EGO-DEFENSE AND ATTITUDE CHANGE.
              HUMAN RELATIONS, 1956, 9, 27-45.
              (MEASURE OF NEGRO STEREOTYPES)
         aK-44 NEGRO RACIAL ATTITUDE PREJUDICE STEROTYPE AFFECTIVE-STATES OTHER-CATEGORY
         aK-44 1956M
              (APPLICATIONS: 640)

K-45   KLEIN, M. H.
              COMPLIANCE, CONSISTENT CONFORMITY, AND PERSONALITY.
              JOURNAL OF PERSONALITY AND SOCIAL PSYCHOLOGY, 1967, 5, 239-245.
              (PERSONALITY GOALS TEST)*
         aK-45 SELF-IDENTITY COLLEGE PERSONALITY GOALS IDEALS PERSONAL STUDENT LIFE
         aSOCIAL DESIRABILITY 1967M

K-46   KUETHE, J. L.
              SOCIAL SCHEMAS.
              JOURNAL OF ABNORMAL AND SOCIAL PSYCHOLOGY, 1962, 64, 31-38.
              (FELT FIGURES TEST)*
         aK-46 PROJECTIVE RELATIONSHIPS INTERPERSONAL OTHERS FIGURE DISTANCE SOCIAL
         aAFFECTIVE-STATES OTHER-CATEGORY 1962M
              (APPLICATIONS: 388   974 1103)

K-47   KNAPP, R. H.
              PERCEPTUAL INTERPRETATION OF THE SOCIAL DIAD: II. CHARACTER OF RELATIONSHIP
              JOURNAL OF SOCIAL PSYCHOLOGY, 1964, 64, 89-100.
              (DIADIC PROFILE TEST)*
         aK-47 INTERPERSONAL RELATIONSHIPS INTERACTION BEHAVIOR SOCIAL PERCEPTION
         aADJUSTMENT PROJECTIVE 1964M

K-48   KORNER, I. N.
              THE MECHANICS OF SUPPRESSION: AN EXPERIMENTAL INVESTIGATION.
              JOURNAL OF CONSULTING PSYCHOLOGY, 1966, 30, 269-272.
              (PROJECTIVE MEASURE OF SUPPRESSION)
         aK-48 GLOBAL PROJECTIVE COPING-DEFENSE TAT REALITY PERCEPTION DENIAL
         aSTIMULUS 1966M
              (APPLICATIONS: 2132)

K-49   KULIK, J. A., STEIN, K. B., & SARBIN, T. R.
              DIMENSIONS AND PATTERNS OF ADOLESCENT ANTISOCIAL BEHAVIOR.
              JOURNAL OF CONSULTING AND CLINICAL PSYCHOLOGY, 1968, 32, 375-382.
              (DELINQUENCY CHECKLIST)
         aK-49 CHECKLIST OTHER-CATEGORY ADJUSTMENT BEHAVIOR DELINQUENCY COMPETENCE SOCIAL
         aK-49 1968M
              (APPLICATIONS: 2205)

K-50   KULIK, J. A.
              INTERRELATIONSHIPS AND SOURCES OF BIAS IN SEVERAL CRITERIA OF DELINQUENCY.
              UNPUBLISHED DOCTORAL DISSERTATION, UNIVERSITY OF CALIFORNIA, BERKELEY,
              1966.
              (TEENAGE DIFFICULTIES SCALE)*
         aK-50 ADJUSTMENT DELINQUENCY BEHAVIOR SOCIAL COMPETENCE GLOBAL ADOLESCENT SCHOOL
         aPROBLEM 1966M
              (APPLICATIONS: 2205)

K-51   KANTOR, R. E., WALLNER, J. M., & WINDER, C. L.
              PROCESS AND REACTIVE SCHIZOPHRENIA.
              JOURNAL OF CONSULTING PSYCHOLOGY, 1953, 17, 157-162.
              (FRAME OF REFERENCE FOR ANALYSIS OF PSYCHIATRIC PATIENTS' CASE HISTORIES)
         aK-51 DIAGNOSIS SCHIZOPHRENIA PATIENT PSYCHIATRIC MENTAL-ILLNESS LIFE HISTORY
              (APPLICATIONS: 1802 1978 2060 2064 2578)

K-52   KOLSTAD ASSOCIATES, 1956. NO REFERENCE. FOR DESCRIPTION SEE: KATZELL, R. A.,
          BARRETT, R. S., & PARKER, T. C. JOB SATISFACTION, JOB PERFORMANCE, AND
          SITUATIONAL CHARACTERISTICS. JOURNAL OF APPLIED PSYCHOLOGY, 1961, 45, 65-
          72.
          (JOB SATISFACTION ATTITUDE SURVEY)
          aK-52 PE-FIT ADJUSTMENT GLOBAL JOB SATISFACTION ATTITUDE AFFECTIVE-STATES

K-53   KAY, E., MEYER, H. H., & FRENCH, J. R. P., JR.
          EFFECTS OF THREAT IN A PERFORMANCE APPRAISAL INTERVIEW.
          JOURNAL OF APPLIED PSYCHOLOGY, 1965, 49, 311-317.
          (MEASURE OF MAN-MANAGER RELATIONS)
          aK-53 INTERPERSONAL PERFORMANCE RELATIONSHIPS MANAGEMENT SUPERVISOR EMPLOYEE
          aSOCIAL COMPETENCE ADJUSTMENT INTERACTION 1965M JOB SATISFACTION

K-54   KAY, F., MEYER, H. H., & FRENCH, J. R. P., JR.
          EFFECTS OF THREAT IN A PERFORMANCE APPRAISAL INTERVIEW.
          JOURNAL OF APPLIED PSYCHOLOGY, 1965, 49, 311-317.
          (MEASURE OF OCCUPATIONAL SELF-ESTEEM)
          aK-54 SUB-IDENTITY EVALUATION ROLE VOCATIONAL ENVIRONMENT PE-FIT SATISFACTION
          aSELF ESTEEM JOB SELF-IDENTITY AFFECTIVE-STATES GLOBAL ADJUSTMENT 1965M

K-55   KUNIN, T.
          THE CONSTRUCTION OF A NEW TYPE OF ATTITUDE MEASURE.
          PERSONNEL PSYCHOLOGY, 1955, 8, 65-77.
          (GENERAL MOTORS FACES SCALE)*
          aK-55 ENVIRONMENT PE-FIT ADJUSTMENT ATTITUDE JOB SATISFACTION AFFECTIVE-STATES
          aGLOBAL PROJECTIVE 1955M

K-56   KATKOVSKY, W., CRANDALL, V. C., & ROTTER, J. B.
          NO REFERENCE. SEE GRANT, D. L., KATKOVSKY, W., & BRAY, D. W. CONTRIBU-
          TIONS OF PROJECTIVE TECHNIQUES TO ASSESSMENT OF MANAGEMENT POTENTIAL.
          JOURNAL OF APPLIED PSYCHOLOGY, 1967, 51, 226-232.
          (MANAGEMENT INCOMPLETE SENTENCES TEST)*
          aK-56 INTERPERSONAL ACHIEVEMENT ORIENTATION PROJECTIVE PREDICTION MANAGEMENT
          aATTITUDE PERFORMANCE JOB ADJUSTMENT LEADERSHIP

K-57   KALLICK, M.
          ORGANIZATIONAL DETERMINANTS OF CREATIVE PRODUCTIVITY.
          UNPUBLISHED DOCTORAL DISSERTATION, PURDUE UNIVERSITY, 1964.
          (JOB ENVIRONMENT SURVEY)*
          aK-57 JOB-HYGIENE JOB ENVIRONMENT PE-FIT ADJUSTMENT 1964M

K-58   KATZ, M. M., & LYERLY, S. B.
          METHODS FOR MEASURING ADJUSTMENT AND SOCIAL BEHAVIOR IN THE COMMUNITY: I.
          RATIONALE, DESCRIPTION, DISCRIMINATIVE VALIDITY AND SCALE DEVELOPMENT.
          PSYCHOLOGICAL REPORTS, 1963, 13, 503-535.
          (KATZ ADJUSTMENT SCALE)*
          aK-58 ADJUSTMENT SOCIAL BEHAVIOR GLOBAL RATING COMPETENCE PATIENT SYMPTOM
          aPSYCHIATRIC MENTAL-HEALTH MENTAL-ILLNESS 1963M
          (APPLICATIONS: 2270)

K-59   KLEIN, E. B., & SOLOMON, L. F.
          A FACTOR ANALYTIC STUDY OF RESPONSE SETS IN NORMAL AND SCHIZOPHRENIC
          SAMPLES.
          UNPUBLISHED MANUSCRIPT, IN PREPARATION, 1966.
          (SD CONVENTIONALITY SCALE)*
          aK-59 RESPONSE-BIAS SOCIAL DESIRABILITY 1966M

K-60   KAGAN, J., PEARSON, L., & WELCH, L.
          MODIFIABILITY OF AN IMPULSIVE TEMPO.
          JOURNAL OF EDUCATIONAL PSYCHOLOGY, 1966, 57, 359-365.
          (MATCHING FAMILIAR FIGURES SCALE FROM THE WECHSLER INTELLIGENCE SCALE FOR
          CHILDREN)
          aK-60 IMPULSE CHILD BEHAVIOR STYLE SELF EXPRESSION PERCEPTION TIME RESPONSE
          aK-60 FIGURE 1966M
          (APPLICATIONS: 434   983   2452   2456   2962)

K-61   KRAUSS, H. H., & RUIZ, R. A.
          ANXIETY AND TEMPORAL PERSPECTIVE.
          JOURNAL OF CLINICAL PSYCHOLOGY, 1967, 23, 454-455.
          (INCOMPLETE THOUGHTS TEST)*
          aK-61 AFFECTIVE-STATES ORIENTATION TIME PERSPECTIVE COGNITIVE FUTURE THINKING
          aK-61 1967M

K-62   KERLINGER, F. N.
          THE FIRST- AND SECOND-ORDER FACTOR STRUCTURES OF ATTITUDES TOWARD EDUCATION
          AMERICAN EDUCATIONAL RESEARCH JOURNAL, 1967, 4, 191-205.
          (EDUCATION SCALE VII)*
       ƏK-62 EDUCATION ATTITUDE ORIENTATION RATING TEACHER BEHAVIOR 1967M

K-63   KUSYSZYN, I., & JACKSON, D. N.
          A MULTIMETHOD FACTOR ANALYTIC APPRAISAL OF ENDORSEMENT AND JUDGMENT METHODS
          IN PERSONALITY ASSESSMENT.
          EDUCATIONAL AND PSYCHOLOGICAL MEASUREMENT, 1968, 28, 1047-1061.
          (MULTITRAIT PERSONALITY INVENTORY)
       ƏK-63 MULTITRAIT DESIRABILITY DEFENSIVENESS NURTURANCE AUTONOMY AGGRESSION
       ƏACHIEVEMENT IMPULSE ORDER 1968M

K-64   KUSYSZYN, I., & JACKSON, D. N.
          A MULTIMETHOD FACTOR ANALYTIC APPRAISAL OF ENDORSEMENT AND JUDGMENT METHODS
          IN PERSONALITY ASSESSMENT.
          EDUCATIONAL AND PSYCHOLOGICAL MEASUREMENT, 1968, 28, 1047-1061.
          (PEER BEHAVIOR RATINGS)
       ƏK-64 ORDER MULTITRAIT PEER BEHAVIOR RATING NURTURANCE AUTONOMY AGGRESSION
       ƏACHIEVEMENT IMPULSE 1968M

K-65   KAMANO, D. K.
          SELF-SATISFACTION AND PSYCHOLOGICAL ADJUSTMENT IN SCHIZOPHRENICS.
          JOURNAL OF CONSULTING PSYCHOLOGY, 1961, 25, 492-496.
          (SEMANTIC DIFFERENTIAL MEASURE OF SELF-SATISFACTION)
       ƏK-65 SEM-DIFFERENTIAL SELF SATISFACTION AFFECTIVE-STATES GLOBAL SELF-IDENTITY
       ƏK-65 EVALUATION PERCEPTION ESTEEM IMAGE IDEAL 1961M ADJUSTMENT SCHIZOPHRENIA

K-67   KLINEBERG, S. L.
          FUTURE TIME PERSPECTIVE AND THE PREFERENCE FOR DELAYED REWARD.
          JOURNAL OF PERSONALITY AND SOCIAL PSYCHOLOGY, 1968, 8, 253-257.
          (MEASURE OF "PREDOMINANCE")
       ƏK-67 TIME PERSPECTIVE FUTURE ORIENTATION 1968M

K-68   KAGAN, J., & MUSSEN, P. H.
          DEPENDENCY THEMES ON THE TAT AND GROUP CONFORMITY.
          JOURNAL OF CONSULTING PSYCHOLOGY, 1956, 20, 29-32.
          (TAT SCORED FOR DEPENDENCY)
       ƏK-68 TAT IMAGERY AUTONOMY DEPENDENCE CONFORMITY PROJECTIVE 1956M
          (APPLICATIONS: 1689)

K-69   KAGAN, J., PEARSON, L., & WELCH, L.
          MODIFIABILITY OF AN IMPULSIVE TEMPO.
          JOURNAL OF EDUCATIONAL PSYCHOLOGY, 1966, 57, 359-365.
          (PICTURE COMPLETION REASONING TEST FROM THE WECHSLER INTELLIGENCE SCALE FOR
          CHILDREN)
       ƏK-69 IMPULSE CHILD BEHAVIOR STYLE SELF EXPRESSION PERCEPTION TIME RESPONSE
       ƏK-69 PROJECTIVE THINKING 1966M

K-70   KLEIN, G. S., & WOLITZKY, D. L.
          VOCAL ISOLATION: EFFECTS OF OCCLUDING AUDITORY FEEDBACK FROM ONE'S OWN
          VOICE.
          JOURNAL OF ABNORMAL PSYCHOLOGY, 1970, 75, 50-56.
          (METHOD OF CONTENT ANALYSIS OF VERBAL BEHAVIOR)
       ƏK-70 CONTENT-ANALYSIS MULTITRAIT AFFECTIVE-STATES DRIVE SENSORY INTENSITY
       ƏK-70 MORAL VALUES 1970M

K-7.I   KAHN, R. L., WOLFE, D. M., QUINN, R. P., SNOCK, J. D., & ROSENTHAL, R. A.
          ORGANISATIONAL STRESS: STUDIES IN ROLE CONFLICT AND AMBIGUITY.
          NEW YORK: WILEY, 1964.
          (JOB RELATED TENSION INDEX)
       ƏK-71 1964M JOB STRESS ANXIETY ADJUSTMENT SATISFACTION PE-FIT TENSION
          (APPLICATIONS: 2369)

K-72   KUDER, G. F.
          GENERAL MANUAL, OCCUPATIONAL INTEREST SURVEY. CHICAGO: SCIENCE RESEARCH
          ASSOCIATES, 1968.
          (OCCUPATIONAL INTEREST SURVEY)*
       ƏK-72 INTEREST VOCATIONAL JOB 1968M
          (APPLICATIONS: 2476 2701 2774)

K-73   KAGAN, N., & KRATHWOHL, D.
              STUDIES IN HUMAN INTERACTION.
              (RESEARCH REPORT NO. 20) MICHIGAN STATE UNIVERSITY, EDUCATIONAL
              PUBLICATION SERVICES, 1967.
              (AFFECTIVE SENSITIVITY SCALE)*
          @K-73 1967M INTERACTION AFFECTIVE-STATES COMMUNICATION SELF DISCLOSURE INTER-
          @K-73 PERSONAL RELATIONSHIPS SENSITIVITY
              (APPLICATIONS: 2772)

K-74   KLEIN, S. M., & RITTI, R. R.
              WORK PRESSURE, SUPERVISORY BEHAVIOR, AND EMPLOYEE ATTITUDES: A FACTOR
              ANALYSIS.
              PERSONNEL PSYCHOLOGY, 1970, 23, 153-167.
              (MEASURE OF EMPLOYEE ATTITUDES)
          @K-74 1970M EMPLOYEE MANAGEMENT ATTITUDE SATISFACTION SOCIAL SUPPORT PRESSURE
          @K-74 POWER

K-75   KIMBLE, G. A., & POSNICK, G. M.
              ANXIETY?
              JOURNAL OF PERSONALITY AND SOCIAL PSYCHOLOGY, 1967, 7, 108-110.
              (ANXIETY CONTENT-FREE MATCHED VERSION OF TAYLOR MAS)
          @K-75 1967M ANXIETY AFFECTIVE-STATES RESPONSE-BIAS
              (APPLICATIONS: 2538)

K-76   KUUSINEN, S.
              EVIDENCE FOR A CURVILINEAR RELATIONSHIP BETWEEN COMPLEXITY AND ORIGINALITY.
              JOURNAL OF PERSONALITY, 1970, 38, 329-343.
              (INVENTION OF HYPOTHESES TEST)
          @K-76 1970M COMPLEXITY ORIGINALITY FLUENCY AUTONOMY

K-77   KELLERMAN, H., & PLUTCHIK, R.
              MANUAL FOR EMOTION PROFILE INDEX.
              HEMPSTEAD, N.Y.: HOFSTA UNIVERSITY PRESS, 1966.
          KELLERMAN, H., & PLUTCHIK, R.
              EMOTION-TRAIT INTERRELATIONS AND THE MEASUREMENT OF PERSONALITY.
              PSYCHOLOGICAL REPORTS, 1968, 23, 1107-1114.
              (EMOTION PROFILE INDEX)
          @K-77 1966M AFFECTIVE-STATES EMOTION CONFLICT
              (APPLICATIONS: 2875)

K-78   KEMP, D. E.
              PERSONALITY AND BEHAVIOR IN PSYCHOTHERAPEUTIC RELATIONSHIPS, CORRELATES
              OF A SCALE OF THERAPEUTIC EFFECTIVENESS.
              UNPUBLISHED DOCTORAL DISSERTATION, DUKE UNIVERSITY, 1963.
              (MEASURE OF THERAPEUTIC EFFECTIVENESS)
          @K-78 1963M THERAPY RELATIONSHIPS STYLE EFFECTIVENESS
              (APPLICATIONS: 1904   2190   2393)

K-79   KRAPEL, J. E., & NAWAS, M. M.
              CLIENT-THERAPIST RELATIONSHIP FACTOR IN SYSTEMATIC DESENSITIZATION.
              JOURNAL OF CONSULTING AND CLINICAL PSYCHOLOGY, 1969, 33, 435-439.
              (BEHAVIORAL AVOIDANCE TEST)*
          @K-79 1969M BEHAVIOR CHANGE FEAR PHOBIA AFFECTIVE-STATES AVOIDANCE

K-81   KAHN, T. C.
              MANUAL FOR THE KAHN TEST OF SYMBOL ARRANGEMENT.
              BEVERLY HILLS: WESTERN PSYCHOLOGICAL SERVICES, 1953.
          KAHN, T. C.
              THE KAHN TEST OF SYMBOL ARRANGEMENT: CLINICAL MANUAL.
              PERCEPTUAL AND MOTOR SKILLS, 1957, 7, 97-168.
              (KAHN TEST OF SYMBOL ARRANGEMENT)*
          @K-81 1953M PROJECTIVE SYMBOL PERCEPTION PSYCHIATRIC DIAGNOSIS MENTAL-ILLNESS
          @K-81 NEUROTICISM PSYCHOPATHY ADJUSTMENT FLEXIBILITY RIGIDITY
              (APPLICATIONS: 1754)

K-82   KINCANNON, J. C.
              PREDICTIONS OF THE STANDARD MMPI SCALE SCORES FROM 71 ITEMS: THE MINI-MULT.
              JOURNAL OF CONSULTING AND CLINICAL PSYCHOLOGY, 1968, 32, 319-325.
              (MINI-MULT)*
          @K-82 1968M MMPI GLOBAL RATING PSYCHIATRIC MENTAL-HEALTH MENTAL-ILLNESS
          @K-82 INVENTORY MULTITRAIT
              (APPLICATIONS: 2937)

K-83   KLEIN, M. H., MATHIEU, P. L., & KIESLER, D. T.
         THE EXPERIENCING SCALE: A RESEARCH AND TRAINING MANUAL.
         MADISON: UNIVERSITY OF WISCONSIN, BUREAU OF AUDIO-VISUAL INSTRUCTION, 1969.
         (EXPERIENCING SCALE)*
         @K-83 1969M EXPERIENCE THERAPY PATIENT RELATIONSHIPS INTERACTION
         (APPLICATIONS: 2939)

K-84   KAGAN, J., & MOSS, H. A.
         THE AVAILABILITY OF CONFLICTUAL IDEAS: A NEGLECTED PARAMETER IN ASSESSING
         PROJECTIVE TEST RESPONSES.
         JOURNAL OF PERSONALITY, 1961, 29, 217-234.
         (SELF-RATING SCALE)
         @K-84 1961M SELF RATING DESCRIPTION MULTITRAIT AGGRESSION HOSTILITY
         @K-84 AFFECTIVE STATES NEGATIVE

K-85   KAGAN, J., & MOSS, H. A.
         THE AVAILABILITY OF CONFLICTUAL IDEAS: A NEGLECTED PARAMETER IN ASSESSING
         PROJECTIVE TEST RESPONSES.
         JOURNAL OF PERSONALITY, 1961. 29, 217-234.
         (INTERVIEW MEASURE OF AGGRESSION)
         @K-85 1961M AGGRESSION AFFECTIVE-STATES NEGATIVE HOSTILITY INTROSPECTION RATING
         @K-85 AUTHORITY ANGER INTERVIEW

K-86   KAGAN, J.
         THE LONG TERM STABILITY OF SELECTED RORSCHACH RESPONSES.
         JOURNAL OF CONSULTING PSYCHOLOGY, 1960, 24, 67-73.
         (RORSCHACH MEASURE OF AGGRESSIVE ACTIVITY)
         @K-86 1960M AGGRESSION AFFECTIVE-STATES HOSTILITY NEGATIVE
         @K-86 RORSCHACH PROJECTIVE
         (APPLICATIONS: 345)

K-87   KOGAN, N., & WALLACH, M. A.
         RISK-TAKING: A STUDY IN COGNITION AND PERSONALITY.
         NEW YORK: HOLT, RINEHART AND WINSTON, 1964.
         (TEST OF SOCIAL RISK PREFERENCES)
         @K-87 1964M SOCIAL RISK-TAKING PREFERENCE SUCCESS
         @K-87 ACCEPTANCE FEAR FAILURE
         (APPLICATIONS: 274   296   307   308   840   2614   2885)

K-88   KIPNIS, D. M.
         CHANGES IN SELF-CONCEPTS IN RELATION TO PERCEPTIONS OF OTHERS.
         JOURNAL OF PERSONALITY, 1961. 29, 449-465.
         (PERSONALITY DESCRIPTION SCALE)
         @K-88 1961M SELF CONCEPT OTHERS PERCEPTION PERSONALITY TRAIT ESTEEM
         @K-88 SOCIAL DESIRABILITY GROUP

K-89   KING, H. E.
         PSYCHOMOTOR ASPECTS OF MENTAL DISEASES: AN EXPERIMENTAL STUDY.
         CAMBRIDGE: HARVARD UNIVERSITY PRESS, 1954.
         (KING TEST BEHAVIOR SCALE)
         @K-89 1954M BEHAVIOR MENTAL-ILLNESS
         (APPLICATIONS: 354)

K-90   KARP, S. A., & KONSTADT, N. L.
         CHILDREN'S EMBEDDED FIGURE TEST.
         NEW YORK: COGNITIVE TESTS, 1963.
         (CHILDREN'S EMBEDDED FIGURES TEST)*
         @K-90 1963M CHILD FIGURE GRAPHIC COGNITIVE FUNCTIONING FIELD DEPENDENCE STYLE
         (APPLICATIONS: 416)

K-91   KASL, S. V., SAMPSON, E. E., & FRENCH, J. R. P., JR.
         THE DEVELOPMENT OF A PROJECTIVE MEASURE OF THE NEED FOR INDEPENDENCE: A
         THEORETICAL STATEMENT AND SOME PRELIMINARY EVIDENCE.
         JOURNAL OF PERSONALITY, 1964, 32, 566-586.
         (PROJECTIVE MEASURE OF DEPENDENCE-INDEPENDENCE)
         @K-91 1964M DEPENDENCE AUTONOMY NEED SELF RATING

K-92   KLEIN, E. B.
         STYLISTIC COMPONENTS OF RESPONSE AS RELATED TO ATTITUDE CHANGE.
         (UNPUBLISHED DOCTORAL DISSERTATION, COLUMBIA UNIVERSITY, 1960.)
         JOURNAL OF PERSONALITY, 1963, 31, 38-51.
         (NEGRO ATTITUDE SCALE)*
         @K-92 1963M NEGRO ATTITUDE PREJUDICE SEM-DIFFERENTIAL RACIAL STEREOTYPE
         (APPLICATIONS: 362)

K-94   KOGAN, N., & WALLACH, M. A.
              RISK TAKING.
              NEW YORK: HOLT, RINEHART AND WINSTON, 1964.
              (CHANCE BETS INSTRUMENT)
            @K-94 1964M RISK-TAKING BEHAVIOR PREFERENCE
              (APPLICATIONS: 256   274   283   307   461   499   537   2329)

K-95   KLABER, M. M.
              MANIFESTATIONS OF HOSTILITY IN NEURODERMATITIS.
              JOURNAL OF CONSULTING PSYCHOLOGY, 1960, 24, 116-120.
              (SENTENCE FORMATION TASK)
            @K-95 1960M HOSTILITY EXPRESSION AFFECTIVE-STATES THERAPY

K-96   KING, G. F.
              A SCALE FOR MEASURING 'DEFENSIVENESS' IN PROBLEM DRIVERS.
              EAST LANSING: HIGHWAY TRAFFIC SAFETY CENTER, MICHIGAN STATE UNIVERSITY,
              1957.
              (DRIVERS' DEFENSIVENESS BEHAVIOR INVENTORY)
            @K-96 1957M DEFENSIVENESS BEHAVIOR DENIAL PROJECTIVE RIGIDITY
              (APPLICATIONS: 1582)

K-97   KATZ, I., GLUCKSBERG, S., & KRAUSS, R.
              NEED SATISFACTION AND EDWARDS PPS SCORES IN MARRIED COUPLES.
              JOURNAL OF CONSULTING PSYCHOLOGY, 1960, 24, 205-208.
              (QUESTIONNAIRE MEASURE OF NEED GRATIFICATION AFFORDED BY SPOUSE)
            @K-97 1960M NEED MARITAL SATISFACTION COMPATIBILITY
            @K-97 RELATIONSHIPS
              (APPLICATIONS: 816   2088)

K-98   KOHEN-RAZ, R.
              EINE KOLLEKTIVE RORSCHACH METHODE MIT 20 TAFELN.
              SCHWEIZERISCHE ZEITSCHRIFT FUER PSYCHOLOGIE UND THRE ANWENDUNGEN, 1962, 21,
              329-338.
              (GROUP RORSCHACH METHOD)
            @K-98 1962M PROJECTIVE GROUP RORSCHACH
              (APPLICATIONS: 1931)

K-99   KAHN, M. W., JONES, N. F., MACDONALD, J. M., CONNERS, C. K., & BURCHARD, J.
              A FACTORIAL STUDY OF PATIENT ATTITUDES TOWARD MENTAL ILLNESS AND
              PSYCHIATRIC HOSPITALIZATION.
              JOURNAL OF CLINICAL PSYCHOLOGY, 1963, 19, 235-241.
              (MEASURE OF PATIENT ATTITUDES TOWARD HOSPITALIZATION AND MENTAL ILLNESS)
            @K-99 1963M ATTITUDE PATIENT ADJUSTMENT MENTAL-ILLNESS HOSPITALIZATION
            @K-99 PSYCHIATRIC
              (APPLICATIONS: 1906   2559)

K-100   KATZ, I., COHEN, M., & CASTIGLIONE, L.
              EFFECT OF ONE TYPE OF NEED COMPLEMENTARITY ON MARRIAGE PARTNERS' CONFORMITY
              TO ONE ANOTHER'S JUDGMENTS.
              JOURNAL OF ABNORMAL AND SOCIAL PSYCHOLOGY, 1963, 67, 8-14.
              (MEASURE OF STRENGTH OF NURTURANT AND SUCCORANT TENDENCIES)
            @K-100 1963M PERSONAL PREFERENCE NEED NURTURANCE MARITAL RELATIONSHIPS AUTONOMY
              (APPLICATIONS: 2088)

K-111   KURTZ, R. M.
              SEX DIFFERENCES AND VARIATIONS IN BODY ATTITUDES.
              JOURNAL OF CONSULTING AND CLINICAL PSYCHOLOGY, 1969, 33, 625-629
              (SEMANTIC DIFFERENTIAL MEASURE OF BODY ATTITUDE)
            @K-111 1969M SEM-DIFFERENTIAL BODY ATTITUDE SEX DIFFERENCES ACTIVE POWER
            @K-111 EVALUATION

K-112   KING, G. F., MERRELL, D. W., LOVINGER, E., DENNY, M. R.
              OPERANT MOTOR BEHAVIOR IN ACUTE SCHIZOPHRENICS.
              JOURNAL OF PERSONALITY, 1957, 25, 317-326.
              (CLINICAL IMPROVEMENT SCALE)
            @K-112 1957M PSYCHOPATHY THERAPY PATIENT RATING PSYCHIATRIC
            @K-112 CHANGE
              (APPLICATIONS: 581)

K-113   KAGAN, J., & MOSS, H. A.
              BIRTH TO MATURITY: A STUDY IN PSYCHOLOGICAL DEVELOPMENT.
              NEW YORK: WILEY, 1962
              (TAT SCORED FOR AFFECT)
            @K-113 1962M TAT AFFECTIVE-STATES FANTASY PROJECTIVE IMAGERY
              (APPLICATIONS: 2008   2238)

K-114   KAGAN, J., & MOSS, H. A.
             BIRTH TO MATURITY: A STUDY IN PSYCHOLOGICAL DEVELOPMENT.
             NEW YORK: WILEY, 1962.
             (FIGURE SORTING TASK)
         @K-114 1962M FIGURE GROUP CONCEPT GRAPHIC
             (APPLICATIONS: 488   2238)

K-115   KULIK, J. A.
             INTERRELATIONSHIPS AND SOURCES OF BIAS IN SEVERAL CRITERIA OF DELINQUENCY.
             UNPUBLISHED DOCTORAL DISSERTATION, UNIVERSITY OF CALIFORNIA, BERKELEY,
             1966.
             (TWO-ITEM MEASURE OF DELINQUENT SELF-IMAGE)
         @K-115 1966M DELINQUENCY ADOLESCENT SELF IMAGE PERCEPTION EVALUATION
             (APPLICATIONS: 2205)

K-116   KARL, N. J., & ABELES, N.
             PSYCHOTHERAPY PROCESS AS A FUNCTION OF THE TIME SEGMENT SAMPLED.
             JOURNAL OF CONSULTING AND CLINICAL PSYCHOLOGY, 1969, 33, 207-212.
             (METHOD FOR CONTENT ANALYSIS OF THERAPY TAPES)
         @K-116 1969M THERAPY INTERACTION PROGNOSIS ADJUSTMENT

K-117   KELLY, E. L., & FISKE, D. W.
             THE PREDICTION OF PERFORMANCE IN CLINICAL PSYCHOLOGY.
             ANN ARBOR: UNIVERSITY OF MICHIGAN, 1951.
             (MICHIGAN SENTENCE COMPLETION TEST)*
         @K-117 1951M PROJECTIVE ANXIETY AFFECTIVE-STATES MANIFEST
         @K-117 SENTENCE-COMP
             (APPLICATIONS: 636)

K-118   KOSON, D., KITCHEN, C., KOCHEN, M., & STODOLSKY, D.
             PSYCHOLOGICAL TESTING BY COMPUTER: EFFECT ON RESPONSE BIAS.
             EDUCATIONAL AND PSYCHOLOGICAL MEASUREMENT, 1970, 30, 803-810.
             (THREAT SCALE)
         @K-118 1970M MMPI STRESS DEFENSIVENESS EMBARRASSMENT

K-120   KLEIN, G. S.
             NEED AND REGULATION.
             IN M. R. JONES (ED.), NEBRASKA SYMPOSIUM ON MOTIVATION. LINCOLN: UNIVERSITY
             OF NEBRASKA PRESS, 1954.
             (TESTS OF CONSTRICTED-FLEXIBLE CONTROL)
         @K-120 1954M FIELD DEPENDENCE PERCEPTION CONTROL COGNITIVE INHIBITION STIMULUS
         @K-120 FLEXIBILITY RIGIDITY
             (APPLICATIONS: 616)

K-121   KRASNER, L., ULLMANN, L. P., & FISHER, D.
             CHANGES IN PERFORMANCE AS RELATED TO VERBAL CONDITIONING OF ATTITUDES
             TOWARD THE EXAMINER.
             PERCEPTUAL AND MOTOR SKILLS, 1964, 19, 811-816.
             (MEDICAL SCIENCE QUESTIONNAIRE)
         @K-121 1964M ATTITUDE HEALTH BELIEF ILLNESS PHYSICAL
             (APPLICATIONS: 11)

K-122   KAGAN, J., ROSMAN, B., DAY, D., ALBERT, J., & PHILLIPS, W.
             INFORMATION PROCESSING IN THE CHILD: SIGNIFICANCE OF ANALYTIC AND
             REFLECTIVE ATTITUDES.
             PSYCHOLOGICAL MONOGRAPHS, 1964, 78 (1, WHOLE NO. 578).
             (CONCEPTUAL STYLES TEST)*
         @K-122 1964M COGNITIVE STYLE THINKING ANALYTIC
         @K-122 CONCEPTUAL
             (APPLICATIONS: 1016)

K-123   KAUFMAN, L. N.
             THE DEVELOPMENT OF A PROVERBS SCALE FOR THE MEASUREMENT OF THINKING
             PATHOLOGY IN SCHIZOPHRENIA AND A FURTHER INVESTIGATION OF THE PROCESS
             REACTIVE DIMENSION.
             UNPUBLISHED DOCTORAL DISSERTATION, UNIVERSITY OF ILLINOIS, 1960.
             (PROVERB SCALES TO MEASURE LEVEL OF ABSTRACT THOUGHT)
         @K-123 1960M COGNITIVE ABSTRACTNESS THINKING SCHIZOPHRENIA MENTAL-ILLNESS
             (APPLICATIONS: 1010   1993)

K-125   KATZ, M. M., WASKOW, I. E., & OLSSON, J.
             CHARACTERIZING THE PSYCHOLOGICAL STATE PRODUCED BY LSD.
             JOURNAL OF ABNORMAL PSYCHOLOGY, 1968, 73, 1-14.
             (PICTURE RATING TECHNIQUE)*
         @K-125 1968M PROJECTIVE RATING SELF MOOD PERCEPTION OTHERS PERCEIVED SIMILARITY
         @PERSON

K-126   KAGITCIBASI, C.
                SOCIAL NORMS AND AUTHORITARIANISM: A TURKISH-AMERICAN COMPARISON.
                JOURNAL OF PERSONALITY AND SOCIAL PSYCHOLOGY, 1970, 16, 444-451.
                (MEASURE OF AUTHORITARIANISM)
          aK-126 1970M AUTHORITARIANISM AUTHORITY ATTITUDE FAMILY CROSS-CULTURAL

K-127   KRAUSS, H. H., & KRAUSS, B. J.
                CROSS-CULTURAL STUDY OF THE THWARTING DISORIENTATION THEORY OF SUICIDE.
                JOURNAL OF ABNORMAL PSYCHOLOGY, 1968, 73, 353-357.
                (CASE HISTORY QUESTIONNAIRE OF SUICIDE CASES)
          aK-127 1968M SUICIDE HISTORY PAST LIFE

K-129   KAMIL, L. J.
                PSYCHODYNAMIC CHANGES THROUGH SYSTEMATIC DESENSITIZATION.
                JOURNAL OF ABNORMAL PSYCHOLOGY, 1970, 76, 199-205.
                (RORSCHACH SCORED FOR CASTRATION ANXIETY)
          aK-129 1970M RORSCHACH SEX ANXIETY PHOBIA NEUROTICISM FEAR BODY

K-130   KASSEBAUM, G. G., COUCH, A. S., & SLATER, P. E.
                THE FACTORIAL DIMENSIONS OF THE MMPI.
                JOURNAL OF CONSULTING PSYCHOLOGY, 1959, 23, 226-236.
                (FACTOR SCALE OF INTROVERSION/EXTRAVERSION)
          aK-130 1959M MMPI INTROVERSION EXTRAVERSION SOCIAL RELATIONSHIPS OTHERS
          aORIENTATION

K-133   KERPELMAN, L. C.
                STUDENT POLITICAL ACTIVISM AND IDEOLOGY: COMPARATIVE CHARACTERISTICS OF
                ACTIVISTS AND NONACTIVISTS.
                JOURNAL OF COUNSELING PSYCHOLOGY, 1969, 16, 8-13.
                (ACTIVISM SCALE)*
          aK-133 1969M ACTIVE POLITICAL ORIENTATION INVOLVEMENT SOCIAL CHANGE ATTITUDE

K-134   KELZ, J. W.
                THE DEVELOPMENT AND EVALUATION OF A MEASURE OF COUNSELOR EFFECTIVENESS.
                DOCTORAL DISSERTATION, PENNSYLVANIA STATE UNIVERSITY.
                ANN ARBOR, MICH.: UNIVERSITY MICROFILMS, 1961.   NO. 62-1723.
          KELZ, J. W.
                THE DEVELOPMENT AND EVALUATION OF A MEASURE OF COUNSELOR EFFECTIVENESS.
                PERSONNEL AND GUIDANCE JOURNAL, 1966, 44, 511-516.
                (DIMENSIONS OF COUNSELING EFFECTIVENESS)
          aK-134 1961M COUNSELING THERAPY EFFECTIVENESS PERCEPTION PATIENT THERAPIST
          aSUCCESS RATING CONSISTENCY INTERVIEW EVALUATION SENSITIVITY AWARENESS
                (APPLICATIONS: 1429)

K-136   KRAUSE, M. S.
                BEHAVIORAL INDEXES OF MOTIVATION FOR TREATMENT.
                JOURNAL OF COUNSELING PSYCHOLOGY, 1967, 14, 426-435.
                (CLIENT BEHAVIOR INVENTORY)*
          aK-136 1967M COUNSELING THERAPY BEHAVIOR MOTIVE PATIENT PREDICTION SUCCESS
          aCHANGE PROGNOSIS

K-137   KIRCHNER, J. H., & NICHOLS, R. C.
                THE UTILITY OF COUNSELOR, TEACHER, PEER AND SELF RATINGS FOR THE PREDICTION
                OF STUDENT BEHAVIOR.
                JOURNAL OF COUNSELING PSYCHOLOGY, 1965, 12, 192-195.
                (ADJECTIVE RATING SCALE)
          aK-137 1965M RATING SEM-DIFFERENTIAL PERSONALITY SELF CONCEPT IDEAL DESCRIPTION
          aESTEEM

K-138   KLEINMUNTZ, B.
                IDENTIFICATION OF MALADJUSTED COLLEGE STUDENTS.
                JOURNAL OF COUNSELING PSYCHOLOGY, 1960, 7, 209-211.
                (MALADJUSTMENT SCALE FOR MMPI)
          aK-138 1960M MMPI ADJUSTMENT MENTAL-HEALTH MENTAL-ILLNESS
          aGLOBAL COLLEGE STUDENT
                (APPLICATIONS: 1180 1932)

K-139   KERR, W. A.
                THE TEAR BALLOT FOR INDUSTRY.
                CHICAGO: PSYCHOMETRIC AFFILIATES, 1962.
                (TEAR BALLOT)*
          aK-139 1962M JOB SATISFACTION VOCATIONAL INTEREST PRESTIGE ATTITUDE
                (APPLICATIONS: 1349)

K-140   KILPATRICK, D. G., & CAUTHEN, N. R.
          THE RELATIONSHIP OF ORDINAL POSITION, DOGMATISM AND PERSONAL SEXUAL
          ATTITUDES.
          JOURNAL OF PSYCHOLOGY, 1969, 73, 115-120.
     KILPATRICK, D. G., CAUTHEN, N. R., SANDMAN, C. A., & QUATTLEBAUM, L. F.
          DOGMATISM AND PERSONAL SEXUAL ATTITUDES.
          PSYCHOLOGICAL REPORTS, IN PRESS.
          (SEXUAL ATTITUDES SURVEY (SAS))*
     @K-140 1969M SEX ATTITUDE VALUES MORAL IDEALS
          (APPLICATIONS: 2652)

K-141   KINNANE, J. F., & PABLE, M. W.
          FAMILY BACKGROUND AND WORK VALUE ORIENTATION.
          JOURNAL OF COUNSELING PSYCHOLOGY, 1962, 9, 320-325.
          (MATERIALISTIC ATMOSPHERE SCALE)*
     @K-141 1962M FAMILY VALUES HOME ENVIRONMENT LIFE STYLE ORIENTATION

K-142   KINNANE, J. F., & PABLE, M. W.
          FAMILY BACKGROUND AND WORK VALUE ORIENTATION.
          JOURNAL OF COUNSELING PSYCHOLOGY, 1962, 9, 320-325.
          (WORK VALUES INVENTORY)*
     @K-142 1962M JOB VALUES FAMILY ENVIRONMENT SOCIAL STATUS

K-143   KUDER, G. F.
          KUDER GENERAL INTEREST SURVEY, (FORM E).
          CHICAGO: SCIENCE RESEARCH ASSOCIATES, 1964.
          (KUDER GENERAL INTEREST SURVEY)*
     @K-143 1964M INTEREST ACADEMIC VOCATIONAL PREFERENCE ACTIVITIES ENVIRONMENT

K-145   KAR, S. B.
          INDIVIDUAL ASPIRATIONS AS RELATED TO ACCEPTANCE OF FAMILY PLANNING.
          DOCTORAL DISSERTATION, UNIVERSITY OF CALIFORNIA, BERKELEY, 1966.
          (MEASURE OF FUTURE ORIENTATION)
     @K-145 1966M FUTURE TIME ORIENTATION PERSPECTIVE

K-146   KNUTSON, A. L.
          PERSONAL SECURITY AS RELATED TO STATION IN LIFE.
          PSYCHOLOGICAL MONOGRAPHS, 1952, 66 (WHOLE NO. 336).
          (SCALE OF AREAS OF SATISFACTION IN LIFE)
     @K-146 1952M LIFE SATISFACTION FEELING HAPPINESS WELL-BEING SECURITY

K-147   KAGAN, J.
          THE CHILD'S PERCEPTION OF THE PARENT.
          JOURNAL OF ABNORMAL AND SOCIAL PSYCHOLOGY, 1956, 53, 257-258.
          (PARENT ROLE PERCEPTION QUESTIONNAIRE)
     @K-147 1956M PERCEPTION ROLE CHILD PARENTAL ATTITUDE RELATIONSHIPS
          (APPLICATIONS: 43)

K-149   KLINGER, E., & WILSON, R.
          A REFERENCE MANUAL FOR SCORING THEMATIC APPERCEPTIVE STORIES.
          UNPUBLISHED PAPER, 1965.
          (HERO AND NONHERO SCORING OF THE TAT)
     @K-149 1965M TAT NEED ACHIEVEMENT PROJECTIVE MOTIVE
          (APPLICATIONS: 213)

K-151   KAHN, R. L., & CANNELL, C. F.
          THE DYNAMICS OF INTERVIEWING.
          NEW YORK: WILEY, 1957.
          (AWARENESS OF PURPOSE QUESTIONNAIRE)
     @K-151 1957M AWARENESS PURPOSE EXPERIMENTER INTERVIEW
          (APPLICATIONS: 48)

K-152   KIRTNER, W. L., & CARTWRIGHT, D. S.
          SUCCESS AND FAILURE IN CLIENT-CENTERED THERAPY AS A FUNCTION OF INITIAL
          IN-THERAPY BEHAVIOR.
          JOURNAL OF CONSULTING PSYCHOLOGY, 1958, 22, 329-333.
          (THE KIRTNER TYPOLOGY)
     @K-152 1958M MENTAL-HEALTH RATING PROGNOSIS PSYCHIATRIC
          (APPLICATIONS: 929)

K-153   KATZ, M. M., WASKOW, I. E., & OLSSON, J.
          CHARACTERIZING THE PSYCHOLOGICAL STATE PRODUCED BY LSD.
          JOURNAL OF ABNORMAL PSYCHOLOGY, 1968, 73, 1-14.
          (SUBJECTIVE DRUG EFFECTS QUESTIONNAIRE)*
     @K-153 1968M DRUG INFLUENCE SUBJECTIVE FEELING

K-155   KLEIN, G. S., GARDNER, R. W., & SCHLESINGER, H. J.
               TOLERANCE FOR UNREALISTIC EXPERIENCES: A STUDY OF THE GENERALITY OF
               COGNITIVE CONTROL.
               BRITISH JOURNAL OF PSYCHOLOGY, 1962, 53, 41-45.
               (RORSCHACH MEASURE OF TOLERANCE FOR UNREALISTIC EXPERIENCES)
           aK-155 1962M CONTROL COGNITIVE FLEXIBILITY RIGIDITY STRUCTURE RORSCHACH
           aNOVELTY REALITY NEED
               (APPLICATIONS: 1928)

K-156   KATKIN, E. S., SASMOR, D. B., & TAN, R.
               CONFORMITY AND ACHIEVEMENT-RELATED CHARACTERISTICS OF DEPRESSED PATIENTS.
               JOURNAL OF ABNORMAL PSYCHOLOGY, 1966, 71, 407-412.
               (CONFORMITY SCALE)
           aK-156 1966M CONFORMITY INFLUENCE OTHERS SOCIAL

K-158   KELLY, E. L., & FISKE, D. W.
               THE PREDICTION OF PERFORMANCE IN CLINICAL PSYCHOLOGY.
               ANN ARBOR, MICHIGAN: UNIVERSITY OF MICHIGAN PRESS, 1951.
               (RELATIONSHIP INDEX)*
           aK-158 1951M RELATIONSHIPS INTERPERSONAL THERAPY COUNSELING PATIENT THERAPIST
               (APPLICATIONS: 1259)

K-161   KASL, S. V., & MAHL, G. F.
               THE RELATIONSHIP OF DISTURBANCES AND HESITATIONS IN SPONTANEOUS SPEECH TO
               ANXIETY.
               JOURNAL OF PERSONALITY AND SOCIAL PSYCHOLOGY, 1965, 1, 425-433.
               (SPEECH DISRUPTIONS CHECKLIST)
           aK-161 1965M ANXIETY PUBLIC PERFORMANCE TENSION
               (APPLICATIONS: 2932)

K-162   KNIGHT, R. P.
               EVALUATION OF THE RESULTS OF PSYCHOANALYTIC THERAPY.
               AMERICAN JOURNAL OF PSYCHIATRY, 1941, 98, 487-492.
               (PSYCHIATRIC PATIENT EVALUATION CRITERIA)
           aK-162 1941M PSYCHIATRIC EVALUATION RATING PATIENT ADJUSTMENT MENTAL-HEALTH
           aMENTAL-ILLNESS
               (APPLICATIONS: 2922)

K-163   KAGAN, J., ROSMAN, B. L., DAY, D., ALBERT, J., & PHILLIPS, W.
               INFORMATION PROCESSING IN THE CHILD: SIGNIFICANCE OF ANALYTIC & REFLECTIVE
               ATTITUDES.
               PSYCHOLOGICAL MONOGRAPHS, 1964, 78 (1, WHOLE NO. 578).
               (DESIGN RECALL TEST) USED AS MEASURE OF REFLECTION IMPULSIVITY.
           aK-163 1964M GRAPHIC IMPULSIVENESS CHILD ANALYTIC THINKING

L-1   ·LANGNER, T. S.
               A 22-ITEM SCREENING SCORE FOR PSYCHIATRIC SYMPTOMS.
               JOURNAL OF HEALTH AND HUMAN BEHAVIOR, 1962, 3, 269-276.
               (SCREENING MEASURE FOR PSYCHIATRIC SYMPTOMS)
           aL-1 ADJUSTMENT GLOBAL PSYCHIATRIC SYMPTOM DIAGNOSIS MENTAL-ILLNESS RATING 1962M
               (APPLICATIONS: 949 2719 2766)

L-2   LANYON, R. I.
               MEASUREMENT OF SOCIAL COMPETENCE IN COLLEGE MALES.
               JOURNAL OF CONSULTING PSYCHOLOGY, 1967, 31, 495-498.
               (BIOGRAPHICAL SURVEY III SCALE)*
           aL-2 SOCIAL COMPETENCE MULTITRAIT STUDENT COLLEGE BEHAVIOR INTERPERSONAL
           aL-2 RELATIONSHIPS 1967M LIFE HISTORY

L-3   LORR, M., MCNAIR, D. M., MICHAUX, W. W., & RASKIN, A.
               FREQUENCY OF TREATMENT AND CHANGE IN PSYCHOTHERAPY.
               JOURNAL OF ABNORMAL AND SOCIAL PSYCHOLOGY, 1962, 64, 281-292.
               (SELF-RATING SCALE)*
           aL-3 AFFECTIVE-STATES ADJUSTMENT SELF-IDENTITY SELF SATISFACTION ACCEPTANCE
           aL-3 RATING DESCRIPTION ESTEEM 1962M
               (APPLICATIONS: 1118 2580)

L-4   LEAVITT, H. J., HAX, H., & ROCHE, J. H.
               AUTHORITARIANISM AND AGREEMENT WITH THINGS AUTHORITATIVE.
               JOURNAL OF PSYCHOLOGY, 1955, 40, 215-221.
               (CONTRADICTORY MAXIMS)*
           aL-4 ACQUIESCENCE RESPONSE-BIAS AUTHORITARIANISM PERSONAL STYLE AUTHORITY 1955M

L-6   LESTER, D.
                 THE SHAW TEST: SIMULTANEOUS MEASURES OF INTELLIGENCE, ORIGINALITY, AND
                 RIGIDITY.
                 .PERCEPTUAL AND MOTOR SKILLS, 1967, 24, 1106.
         LESTER, D.
                 THE SHAW TEST: A DESCRIPTION.
                 JOURNAL OF CLINICAL PSYCHOLOGY, 1967, 23, 88-89.
                 (SHAW TEST)*
         aL-6 STRUCTURE FUNCTIONING RIGIDITY ORIGINALITY COPING-DEFENSE FLEXIBILITY
         aL-6 DOGMATISM AUTONOMY CREATIVITY INTELLIGENCE COGNITIVE 1967M

L-7   LEVENTHAL, A. M.
                 AN ANXIETY SCALE FOR THE CPI.
                 JOURNAL OF CLINICAL PSYCHOLOGY, 1966, 22, 459-461.
                 (ANXIETY SCALE)
         aL-7 ANXIETY AFFECTIVE-STATES SUBJECTIVE STRESS NEGATIVE 1966M
                 (APPLICATIONS: 1475)

L-8   LEVENTHAL, H., & PERLOE, S. I.
                 A RELATIONSHIP BETWEEN SELF-ESTEEM AND PERSUASIBILITY.
                 JOURNAL OF ABNORMAL AND SOCIAL PSYCHOLOGY, 1962, 64, 385-388.
                 (MEASURE OF SELF-ESTEEM)
         aL-8 SELF-IDENTITY EVALUATION IMAGE SELF ESTEEM CONCEPT SOCIAL PERSUASIBILITY
         aL-8 DESIRABILITY PERCEPTION 1962M

L-9   LEVINE, E. L., & WEITZ, J.
                 JOB SATISFACTION AMONG GRADUATE STUDENTS: INTRINSIC VERSUS EXTRINSIC
                 VARIABLES.
                 JOURNAL OF APPLIED PSYCHOLOGY, 1968, 52, 263-271.
                 (GRADUATE STUDENT QUESTIONNAIRE)*
         aL-9 INTRINSIC EXTRINSIC JOB SATISFACTION AFFECTIVE-STATES GLOBAL STUDENT
         aL-9 SELF-IDENTITY EVALUATION SELF PERCEPTION ESTEEM COLLEGE ENVIRONMENT PE-FIT
         aL-9 1968M

L-11   LEWINSOHN, P. M.
                 RELATIONSHIP BETWEEN HEIGHT OF FIGURE DRAWINGS AND DEPRESSION IN
                 PSYCHIATRIC PATIENTS.
                 JOURNAL OF CONSULTING PSYCHOLOGY, 1964, 28, 380-381.
                 (FIGURE DRAWING MEASURE OF DEPRESSION)
         aL-11 PROJECTIVE ADJUSTMENT DEPRESSION AFFECTIVE-STATES NEGATIVE FIGURE 1964M
         aL-11 PATIENT MENTAL-ILLNESS

L-12   LICHTENSTEIN, E., QUINN, R. P., & HOVER, G. L.
                 DOGMATISM AND ACQUIESCENCE IN RESPONSE SET.
                 JOURNAL OF ABNORMAL AND SOCIAL PSYCHOLOGY, 1961, 63, 636-638.
                 (DIFFERENCE SCORE)*
         aL-12 ACQUIESCENCE RESPONSE-BIAS SELF DESCRIPTION 1961M

L-14   LEHMANN, S.
                 PERSONALITY AND COMPLIANCE: A STUDY OF ANXIETY AND SELF-ESTEEM IN OPINION
                 AND BEHAVIOR CHANGE.
                 JOURNAL OF PERSONALITY AND SOCIAL PSYCHOLOGY, 1970, 15, 76-86.
                 (GENERAL SELF-ESTEEM SCALE)
         aL-14 1970M SELF ESTEEM IMAGE CONCEPT SELF-IDENTITY EVALUATION

L-15   LOCKE, H. J., & WALLACE, K. M.
                 SHORT MARITAL-ADJUSTMENT AND PREDICTION TESTS: THEIR RELIABILITY AND
                 VALIDITY.
                 MARRIAGE AND FAMILY LIVING, 1959, 251-255.
                 (LOCKE SHORT MARITAL PREDICTION TEST)*
         aL-15 MARITAL ADJUSTMENT AFFECTIVE-STATES SATISFACTION PREDICTION 1959M
                 (APPLICATIONS: 701 1577 2088 2955)

L-16   LONDON, P., SCHULMAN, R. E., & BLACK, M. S.
                 RELIGION, GUILT, AND ETHICAL STANDARDS.
                 JOURNAL OF SOCIAL PSYCHOLOGY, 1964, 63, 145-159.
                 (MEASURE OF ETHICAL STANDARDS)
         aL-16 RELIGION PERCEPTION MORAL GUILT PERSONAL ORIENTATION AFFECTIVE-STATES
         aL-16 GLOBAL NEGATIVE SELF-IDENTITY VALUES IDEALS LIFE GOALS DEVELOPMENT 1964M

L-17   LORR, M., MCNAIR, D. M., WEINSTEIN, G. J., MICHAUX, W. W., & RASKIN, A.
            MEPROBAMATE AND CHLORPROMAZINE IN PSYCHOTHERAPY.
            AMERICAN MEDICAL ASSOCIATION ARCHIVES OF GENERAL PSYCHIATRY, 1961, 4, 381-
            389.
            (PSYCHIATRIC OUTPATIENT MOOD SCALE)*
        @L-17 STATE ADJUSTMENT MOOD PSYCHIATRIC PATIENT MENTAL-ILLNESS MENTAL-HEALTH
        @L-17 CHANGE 1961M EMOTION
            (APPLICATIONS: 931 1118 2145)

L-18   LOY, D. L., & TURNBULL, J. W.
            INDIRECT ASSESSMENT OF ANGER DISPOSITIONS.
            JOURNAL OF PROJECTIVE TECHNIQUES AND PERSONALITY ASSESSMENT, 1964, 28, 314-
            321.
            (MEASURE OF ANGER DISPOSITION)
        @L-18 PROJECTIVE AGGRESSION NEGATIVE HOSTILITY AFFECTIVE-STATES RESENTMENT
        @L-18 FRUSTRATION SITUATIONAL 1964M

L-19   LUBIN, B.
            ADJECTIVE CHECKLISTS FOR MEASUREMENT OF DEPRESSION.
            ARCHIVES OF GENERAL PSYCHIATRY, 1965, 12, 57-62.
        LUBIN, B.
            DEPRESSION ADJECTIVE CHECK LISTS: MANUAL.
            SAN DIEGO, CALIFORNIA: EDUCATIONAL AND INDUSTRIAL TESTING SERVICE, 1967.
            (DEPRESSION ADJECTIVE CHECK LISTS)*
        @L-19 DEPRESSION AFFECTIVE-STATES NEGATIVE CHECKLIST 1965M

L-20   LUBIN, B.
            A MODIFIED VERSION OF THE SELF-DISCLOSURE INVENTORY.
            PSYCHOLOGICAL REPORTS, 1965, 17, 498.
            (LUBIN SELF-DISCLOSURE INVENTORY)*
        @L-20 SELF DISCLOSURE RESPONSE-BIAS COMMUNICATION ADJUSTMENT ACCESSIBILITY
        @L-20 INTERPERSONAL RELATIONSHIPS INTERACTION 1965M

L-21   LUCAS, C. M.
            AN EMERGENT CATEGORY APPROACH TO THE ANALYSIS OF ADOLESCENT NEEDS.
            UNPUBLISHED DOCTORAL DISSERTATION, OHIO STATE UNIVERSITY, 1951.
        LUCAS, C. M., & HORROCKS, J. E.
            AN EXPERIMENTAL APPROACH TO THE ANALYSIS OF ADOLESCENT NEEDS.
            CHILD DEVELOPMENT, 1960, 31, 479-487.
            (SOCIAL ATTITUDES INVENTORY)
        @L-21 INTERPERSONAL SOCIAL RELATIONSHIPS ATTITUDE NEED COPING STYLE ADOLESCENT
        @L-21 COGNITIVE CONTROL COPING-DEFENSE GLOBAL ENVIRONMENT COMPETENCE 1960M
            (APPLICATIONS: 2873)

L-22   LYKKEN, D. T.
            A STUDY OF ANXIETY IN THE SOCIOPATHIC PERSONALITY.
            JOURNAL OF ABNORMAL AND SOCIAL PSYCHOLOGY, 1957, 55, 6-10.
            (ACTIVITY PREFERENCE QUESTIONNAIRE MEASURE OF ANXIETY)
        @L-22 ANXIETY ACTIVITIES SITUATIONAL PREFERENCE AFFECTIVE-STATES SUBJECTIVE
        @L-22 STRESS NERVOUSNESS PSYCHOPATHY NEGATIVE 1957M
            (APPLICATIONS: 188   240   711 2294 2339 2418 2556)

L-23   LAMBERT, W. E., ANISFELD, M., & YENI-KOMSHIAN, G.
            EVALUATIONAL REACTIONS OF JEWISH AND ARAB ADOLESCENTS TO DIALECT AND
            LANGUAGE VARIATIONS.
            JOURNAL OF PERSONALITY AND SOCIAL PSYCHOLOGY, 1965, 2, 84-90.
            (MEASURES OF JEWISH-ARAB ATTITUDES)
        @L-23 ETHNIC ATTITUDE COPING-DEFENSE OTHER-CATEGORY AFFECTIVE-STATES RACIAL
        @L-23 PREJUDICE EVALUATION SOCIAL DISTANCE CULTURE 1965M

L-24   LAZOVIK, A. D., & LANG, P. J.
            A LABORATORY DEMONSTRATION OF SYSTEMATIC DESENSITIZATION PSYCHOTHERAPY.
            JOURNAL OF PSYCHOLOGICAL STUDIES, 1960, 11, 238-247.
            (FEAR QUESTIONNAIRE)
        @L-24 FEAR AFFECTIVE-STATES ANXIETY STRESS SUBJECTIVE NEGATIVE 1960M
            (APPLICATIONS: 240   809 2383 2416)

L-25   LEE, R. E., III, & WARR, P. B.
            THE DEVELOPMENT AND STANDARDIZATION OF A BALANCED F-SCALE.
            JOURNAL OF GENERAL PSYCHOLOGY, 1969, 81, 109-129.
            (BALANCED F-SCALE)
        @L-25 F-SCALE AUTHORITARIANISM COPING-DEFENSE OTHER-CATEGORY RESPONSE-BIAS
        @L-25 ACQUIESCENCE 1969M

L-26   LEVINE, M., & SPIVAK, G.
        THE RORSCHACH INDEX OF REPRESSIVE STYLE. SPRINGFIELD, ILLINOIS: CHARLES C.
        THOMAS, 1964.
        (RORSCHACH INDEX OF REPRESSIVE STYLE)*
     aL-26 RORSCHACH REPRESSION STYLE ADJUSTMENT RESPONSE-BIAS DEFENSIVENESS
     aL-26 COPING-DEFENSE PROJECTIVE 1964M
        (APPLICATIONS: 969 1378 1862 2686)

L-27   LEVINSON, P. K.
        THE EFFECT OF SENSORY DEPRIVATION UPON STIMULATION SEEKING BEHAVIOR, MOOD,
        AND ATTITUDE STRUCTURE. UNPUBLISHED DOCTORAL DISSERTATION, UNIVERSITY OF
        ROCHESTER, 1959.
        (MOOD ADJECTIVE CHECK LIST)*
     aL-27 MOOD CHECKLIST AFFECTIVE-STATES OTHER-CATEGORY 1964M EMOTION
        (APPLICATIONS: 101)

L-28   LITWIN, G. H., & CIARLO, J. A.
        ACHIEVEMENT MOTIVATION AND RISK-TAKING IN A BUSINESS SETTING, TECHNICAL
        REPORT. OSSINING, NEW YORK: GENERAL ELECTRIC COMPANY, BEHAVIORAL
        RESEARCH SERVICE, 1961.
        (LITWIN-CIARLO BUSINESS GAME)*
     aL-28 ADAPTABILITY ADJUSTMENT RISK-TAKING COPING-DEFENSE APPROACH AVOIDANCE
     aL-28 INTERPERSONAL RELATIONSHIPS INTERACTION PERFORMANCE 1961M BEHAVIOR
        (APPLICATIONS: 22)

L-29   LIVERANT, S.
        THE USE OF ROTTER'S SOCIAL LEARNING THEORY IN DEVELOPING A PERSONALITY
        INVENTORY.
        PSYCHOLOGICAL MONOGRAPHS, 1958, 72 (28, WHOLE NO. 455).
        (GOAL PREFERENCE INVENTORY)*
     aL-29 ACADEMIC SELF-IDENTITY SOCIAL APPROVAL PUBLIC ESTEEM VALUES IDEALS LIFE,
     aL-29 GOALS SELF PREFERENCE AFFECTION AUTONOMY COPING-DEFENSE 1958M
        (APPLICATIONS: 9   129   787 2488)

L-30   LIVERANT, S., & SCODEL, A.
        INTERNAL AND EXTERNAL CONTROL AS DETERMINANTS OF DECISION MAKING UNDER
        CONDITIONS OF RISK.
        PSYCHOLOGICAL REPORTS, 1960, 7, 59-67.
        (SOCIAL REACTION INVENTORY)*
     aL-30 LOCUS CONTROL AUTONOMY IE-CONTROL SOCIAL REACTIVITY RISK-TAKING DECISION
     aL-30 1960M BEHAVIOR
        (APPLICATIONS: 127   399)

L-31   LUTZKER, D.
        INTERNATIONALISM AS A PREDICTOR OF COOPERATIVE BEHAVIOR.
        JOURNAL OF CONFLICT RESOLUTION, 1960, 4, 426-430.
        (INTERNATIONALISM-ISOLATIONISM SCALE)*
     aL-31 INTERNATIONALISM LIBERALISM COPING-DEFENSE CONFLICT MOTIVE
     aL-31 POLITICAL ORIENTATION BEHAVIOR COOPERATION 1960M
        (APPLICATIONS: 32   840)

L-32   LEVINSON, P. J., & SANFORD, R. N.
        A SCALE FOR THE MEASUREMENT OF ANTI-SEMITISM.
        JOURNAL OF PSYCHOLOGY, 1944, 17, 339-370.
        (MEASURE OF ANTI-SEMITISM)
     aL-32 AFFECTIVE-STATES OTHER-CATEGORY RACIAL PREJUDICE ATTITUDE ETHNOCENTRISM
     aL-32 COPING-DEFENSE ETHNIC MINORITY SOCIAL DISTANCE GROUP 1944M
        (APPLICATIONS: 53   552   646   662   791)

L-33   LONDON, P.
        THE CHILDREN'S HYPNOTIC SUSCEPTIBILITY SCALE. PALO ALTO, CALIF.:
        CONSULTING PSYCHOLOGISTS PRESS, 1963.
        (CHILDREN'S HYPNOTIC SUSCEPTIBILITY SCALE)*
     aL-33 HYPNOTIC SUGGESTIBILITY CHILD SUBJECTIVE BEHAVIOR INVOLVEMENT 1963M
        (APPLICATIONS: 231)

L-34   LONDON, P., & BOWERS, P.
        THE DRAMATIC ACTING TEST: A ROLE PLAYING TEST FOR CHILDREN. LOS ANGELES:
        UNIVERSITY OF SOUTHERN CALIFORNIA, 1964.
        (DRAMATIC ACTING TEST)*
     aL-34 ROLE ENACTMENT ABILITY AFFECTIVE-STATES CHILD 1964M
        (APPLICATIONS: 231)

L-35   LAFORGE, R., & SUCZEK, R. F.
            THE INTERPERSONAL DIMENSIONS OF PERSONALITY: III. AN INTERPERSONAL CHECK
            LIST.
            JOURNAL OF PERSONALITY, 1955, 24, 94-112.
            (INTERPERSONAL CHECK LIST)*
        LEARY, T.
            MULTILEVEL MEASUREMENT OF INTERPERSONAL BEHAVIOR. BERKELEY, CALIFORNIA:
            PSYCHOLOGICAL CONSULTATION SERVICE, 1956.
            (LEARY INTERPERSONAL CHECKLIST)*
        aL-35 CHECKLIST RELATIONSHIPS INTERACTION INTERPERSONAL BEHAVIOR STYLE SOCIAL
        aL-35 COMPETENCE ADJUSTMENT 1955M
            (APPLICATIONS: 35   191   289   437   467   509   577   615   652   653
                              726   743   760   818   933   958   1206   1257   1277   1577
                             1614   1623   1684   1692   1698   1772   1806   1840   1958   2036
                             2046   2116   2213   2274   2327   2328   2341   2598   2646   2911
                             2917   2955   2956   2957   2963)

L-36   LEVONIAN, E.
            PERSONALITY MEASUREMENT WITH ITEMS SELECTED FROM THE 16 PF QUESTIONNAIRE.
            EDUCATIONAL AND PSYCHOLOGICAL MEASUREMENT, 1961, 21, 937-946.
            (SELF ESTEEM MEASURE)
        aL-36 SELF ESTEEM EVALUATION IDENTITY IMAGE CONCEPT SELF-IDENTITY IDEAL 1961M
            (APPLICATIONS: 251)

L-37   LE FURGY, W. G., & WOLOSHIN, G. W.
            IMMEDIATE AND LONG-TERM EFFECTS OF EXPERIMENTALLY INDUCED SOCIAL INFLUENCE
            IN THE MODIFICATION OF ADOLESCENTS' MORAL JUDGMENTS.
            JOURNAL OF PERSONALITY AND SOCIAL PSYCHOLOGY, 1969, 12, 104-110.
            (MORAL RELATIVISM SCALE)
        aL-37 MORAL ORIENTATION ADJUSTMENT OTHER-CATEGORY SELF-IDENTITY SELF DEVELOPMENT
        aL-37 VALUES IDEALS LIFE GOALS 1969M

L-38   LESSER, W. M.
            THE RELATIONSHIP BETWEEN COUNSELING PROGRESS AND EMPATHIC UNDERSTANDING.
            JOURNAL OF COUNSELING PSYCHOLOGY, 1961, 8, 330-336.
            (EMPATHIC UNDERSTANDING SCALE)*
        aL-38 AFFECTIVE-STATES EMPATHY RATING INTERPERSONAL SOCIAL COUNSELING 1961M
        aL-38 THERAPY RELATIONSHIPS
            (APPLICATIONS: 1241)

L-39   LORR, M.
            MULTIDIMENSIONAL SCALE FOR RATING PSYCHIATRIC PATIENTS, HOSPITAL FORM.
            U. S. VETERANS ADMINISTRATION TECHNICAL BULLETIN, WASHINGTON, 1953.
            (MULTIDIMENSIONAL SCALE FOR RATING PSYCHIATRIC PATIENTS (1953))*(MSRPP)
            MANUAL FOR THE INPATIENT MULTIDIMENSIONAL PSYCHIATRIC SCALE. PALO ALTO,
            CALIF.: CONSULTING PSYCHOLOGISTS PRESS, 1962.
            (INPATIENT MULTIDIMENSIONAL PSYCHIATRIC SCALE (1962))*
        aL-39 ADJUSTMENT BEHAVIOR WARD RATING PSYCHIATRIC PATIENT MENTAL-ILLNESS GLOBAL
        aL-39 DIAGNOSIS PROGNOSIS THERAPY 1962M
            (APPLICATIONS: 581   704   719   744   1007   1023   1029   1084   1145   1150
                             1286   1579   1653   1675   1690   1764   1800   1805   1829   1878
                             1879   1942   1958   1976   2075   2138   2396)

L-40   LEE, E. A., & THORPE, L. P.
            MANUAL: OCCUPATIONAL INTEREST INVENTORY, ADVANCED. LOS ANGELES:
            CALIFORNIA TEST BUREAU, 1956.
            (OCCUPATIONAL INTEREST INVENTORY)*
        aL-40 VOCATIONAL INTEREST LIFE GOALS PREFERENCE JOB 1956M
            (APPLICATIONS: 1271   1502)

L-41   LEHMANN, S.
            PERSONALITY AND COMPLIANCE: A STUDY OF ANXIETY AND SELF-ESTEEM IN OPINION
            AND BEHAVIOR CHANGE.
            JOURNAL OF PERSONALITY AND SOCIAL PSYCHOLOGY, 1970, 15, 76-86.
            (SITUATIONAL ANXIETY SCALE)
        aL-41 1970M SITUATIONAL ANXIETY AFFECTIVE-STATES NEGATIVE MATERNAL

L-42   LUCAS, C.
            FRUSTRATION AND THE PERCEPTION OF AGGRESSIVE ANIMALS.
            JOURNAL OF CONSULTING PSYCHOLOGY, 1962, 26, 287.
            (MEASURE OF AGGRESSION IN RESPONSE TO FRUSTRATION)
        aL-42 ATTITUDE RESENTMENT AGGRESSION HOSTILITY AFFECTIVE-STATES FRUSTRATION
        aL-42 1962M

L-43   LORR, M.
              CLIENT PERCEPTIONS OF THERAPISTS: A STUDY OF THE THERAPEUTIC RELATION.
              JOURNAL OF CONSULTING PSYCHOLOGY, 1965, 29, 146-149.
              (MEASURE OF CLIENT PERCEPTION OF CLIENT-THERAPIST INTERPERSONAL BEHAVIOR
              PATTERNS)
          aL-43 INTERPERSONAL THERAPY ADJUSTMENT PERCEPTION OTHER-CATEGORY BEHAVIOR
          aL-43 RELATIONSHIPS COUNSELING ACCEPTANCE DEPENDENCE INTERACTION 1965M
              (APPLICATIONS: 2145)

L-44   LOTT, A. J., & LOTT, B. E.
              GROUP COHESIVENESS, COMMUNICATION LEVEL, AND CONFORMITY.
              JOURNAL OF ABNORMAL AND SOCIAL PSYCHOLOGY, 1961, 62, 408-412.
              (GROUP COHESIVENESS INDEX)*
          aL-44 INTERPERSONAL RELATIONSHIPS GROUP COHESIVENESS COMMUNICATION RATING SOCIAL
          aL-44 INTERACTION ADJUSTMENT 1961M

L-45   LUCHINS, A. S.
              MECHANIZATION IN PROBLEM SOLVING.
              PSYCHOLOGICAL MONOGRAPHS, 1942, 54 (6, WHOLE NO. 248).
              (WATER JAR TEST OF RIGIDITY)*
          aL-45 COPING-DEFENSE ADAPTABILITY BEHAVIOR COGNITIVE FUNCTIONING RIGIDITY
          aL-45 FLEXIBILITY PROBLEM SET RESPONSE 1942M
              (APPLICATIONS: 601   678   782   2239   2332)

L-46   LANG, P. J., & LAZOVIK, A. D.
              EXPERIMENTAL DESENSITIZATION OF A PHOBIA.
              JOURNAL OF ABNORMAL AND SOCIAL PSYCHOLOGY, 1963, 66, 519-525.
              (FEAR SURVEY SCHEDULE)*
          aL-46 FEAR ANXIETY STRESS SUBJECTIVE PHOBIA ADJUSTMENT OTHER-CATEGORY 1963M
          aL-46 AFFECTIVE-STATES
              (APPLICATIONS: 972   2416   2432)

L-47   LAZARUS, R. S., & ALFERT, E.
              SHORT-CIRCUITING OF THREAT BY EXPERIMENTALLY ALTERING COGNITIVE APPRAISAL.
              JOURNAL OF ABNORMAL AND SOCIAL PSYCHOLOGY, 1964, 69, 195-205.
              (MEASURE OF BELIEFS CONCERNING ANXIETY-RELATED EVENTS)
          aL-47 ANXIETY DEFENSE BELIEF COPING-DEFENSE GLOBAL DENIAL REPRESSION REALITY
          aL-47 PERCEPTION RESPONSE-BIAS DEFENSIVENESS 1964M

L-48   LEHMANN, S.
              PERSONALITY AND COMPLIANCE: A STUDY OF ANXIETY AND SELF-ESTEEM IN OPINION
              AND BEHAVIOR CHANGE.
              JOURNAL OF PERSONALITY AND SOCIAL PSYCHOLOGY, 1970, 15, 76-86.
              (SITUATIONAL SELF-ESTEEM SCALE)
          aL-48 SITUATIONAL SELF ESTEEM SELF-IDENTITY CONCEPT IMAGE EVALUATION MATERNAL
          aL-48 1970M

L-49   LORR, M., & MCNAIR, D. M.
              AN INTERPERSONAL BEHAVIOR CIRCLE.
              JOURNAL OF ABNORMAL AND SOCIAL PSYCHOLOGY, 1963, 67, 68-75.
              (INTERPERSONAL BEHAVIOR INVENTORY)*
          aL-49 ADJUSTMENT RATING INTERACTION SOCIAL RELATIONSHIPS STYLE INTERPERSONAL
          aL-49 BEHAVIOR AFFECTIVE-STATES ALIENATION 1963M
              (APPLICATIONS: 981   2543)

L-50   LIEBERT, R. M., & MORRIS, L. W.
              COGNITIVE AND EMOTIONAL COMPONENTS OF TEST ANXIETY: A DISTINCTION AND
              SOME INITIAL DATA.
              PSYCHOLOGICAL REPORTS, 1967, 20, 975-978.
              (SHORT FORM OF MANDLER-SARASON TEST ANXIETY QUESTIONNAIRE)
          aL-50 ANXIETY TEST SELF SUBJECTIVE STRESS AFFECTIVE-STATES SITUATIONAL
          aL-50 NEGATIVE 1967M

L-51   LINDGREN, H. C., & LINDGREN, F.
              EXPRESSED ATTITUDES OF AMERICAN AND CANADIAN TEACHERS TOWARD AUTHORITY.
              PSYCHOLOGICAL REPORTS, 1960, 7, 51-54.
              (MEASURE OF ATTITUDES TOWARD AUTHORITY)
          aL-51 AUTONOMY ATTITUDE AUTHORITY AFFECTIVE-STATES RESENTMENT ANXIETY ACCEPTANCE
          aL-51 1960M

L-52   LITTLE, K. B., & SHNEIDMAN, E. S.
                CONGRUENCIES AMONG INTERPRETATIONS OF PSYCHOLOGICAL TEST AND ANAMNESTIC
                BEHAVIOR.
                PSYCHOLOGICAL MONOGRAPHS, 1959, 73, (6, WHOLE NO. 476).
                (MEASURE OF PERSONALITY FUNCTIONING)
            @L-52 COPING-DEFENSE MULTITRAIT EVALUATION PERSONALITY FUNCTIONING FANTASY
            @L-52 INTERPERSONAL RELATIONSHIPS PERCEPTION DEFENSE 1959M
                (APPLICATIONS: 1903)

L-53   LAHIRI, D. K., & SRIVASTVA, S.
                DETERMINANTS OF SATISFACTION IN MIDDLE-MANAGEMENT PERSONNEL.
                JOURNAL OF APPLIED PSYCHOLOGY, 1967, 51, 254-265.
                (QUESTIONNAIRE MEASURE OF JOB SATISFACTION)
            @L-53 MORALE MANAGEMENT SUPERVISOR BEHAVIOR ADJUSTMENT JOB SATISFACTION GLOBAL
            @L-53 AFFECTIVE-STATES PE-FIT 1967M

L-54   LENTZ, T. F.
                THE CONSERVATISM-RADICALISM QUESTIONNAIRE. ST. LOUIS: WASHINGTON UNIVER-
                SITY, CHARACTER RESEARCH ASSOCIATION, 1946.
                (CONSERVATISM-RADICALISM QUESTIONNAIRE)*
            @L-54 CONSERVATISM RADICALISM POLITICAL ORIENTATION 1946M

L-55   LYLE, W. H., JR., & LEVITT, E. E.
                SITUATIONAL DIFFERENCES IN PUNITIVENESS OF IOWA SCHOOL CHILDREN.
                PROCEEDINGS OF THE IOWA ACADEMY OF SCIENCE, 1954, 61, 378-381.
                (MEASURE OF PUNITIVENESS)
            @L-55 PUNITIVENESS CHILD PARENT-CHILD SCHOOL SITUATIONAL ELEMENTARY 1954M
            @L-55 AGGRESSION DIRECTION

L-56   LIGON, L.
                PHILOSOPHIES OF HUMAN NATURE AND RELIGIOUS BACKGROUNDS. PAPER READ AT
                SOUTHEASTERN PSYCHOLOGICAL ASSOCIATION, ATLANTA, APRIL, 1965.
                (RELIGIOUS PARTICIPATION SCALE)*
            @L-56 RELIGION ORIENTATION ATTITUDE PARTICIPATION ACTIVITIES BEHAVIOR 1965M

L-57   LESHAN, L. L.
                TIME ORIENTATION AND SOCIAL CLASS.
                JOURNAL OF ABNORMAL AND SOCIAL PSYCHOLOGY, 1952, 47, 589-592.
                (PROJECTIVE MEASURE OF TEMPORAL PERSPECTIVE)
            @L-57 CHILD TIME PERSPECTIVE AFFECTIVE-STATES FUTURE ORIENTATION PROJECTIVE
            @L-57 1952M
                (APPLICATIONS: 1293   2062   2133)

L-58   LESHAN, L. L.
                TIME ORIENTATION AND SOCIAL CLASS.
                JOURNAL OF ABNORMAL AND SOCIAL PSYCHOLOGY, 1952, 47, 589-592.
                (INCOMPLETE SENTENCE MEASURE OF TEMPORAL ORIENTATION OF CHILDREN)
            @L-58 AFFECTIVE-STATES TIME ORIENTATION FUTURE PERSPECTIVE PROJECTIVE CHILD
            @L-58 1952M

L-59   LESTER, D.
                FEAR OF DEATH OF SUICIDAL PERSONS.
                PSYCHOLOGICAL REPORTS, 1967, 20, 1077-1078.
                (FEAR OF DEATH SCALE)*
            @L-59 ATTITUDE SUICIDE FEAR DEATH AFFECTIVE-STATES ANXIETY SUBJECTIVE STRESS
            @L-59 NEGATIVE 1967M

L-60   LEVY, L. H., & HOUSE, W. C.
                PERCEIVED ORIGINS OF BELIEFS AS DETERMINANTS OF EXPECTANCY OF THEIR CHANGE.
                JOURNAL OF PERSONALITY AND SOCIAL PSYCHOLOGY, 1970, 14, 329-334.
                (QUESTIONNAIRE OF PERCEIVED ORIGINS AND EXPECTED CHANGE OF BELIEFS)
            @L-60 1970M PREDICTION OPENNESS CHANGE BELIEF ATTITUDE

L-61   LAWLER, E. E., III, & HALL, D. T.
                RELATIONSHIP OF JOB CHARACTERISTICS TO JOB INVOLVEMENT, SATISFACTION,
                AND INTRINSIC MOTIVATION.
                JOURNAL OF APPLIED PSYCHOLOGY, 1970, 54, 305-312.
                (MEASURE OF JOB INVOLVEMENT, SATISFACTION, AND MOTIVATION)
            @L-61 1970M JOB INVOLVEMENT SATISFACTION MOTIVATION BEHAVIOR

L-62   LEFCOURT, H. M., & STEFFY, R. A.
            LEVEL OF ASPIRATION, RISK-TAKING, AND PROJECTIVE TEST PERFORMANCE:
            A SEARCH FOR COHERENCE.
            JOURNAL OF CONSULTING AND CLINICAL PSYCHOLOGY. 1970, 34, 193-198.
            (TAT SCORED FOR ABILITY TO HANDLE SEXUAL STIMULI)
        @L-62 1970M PROJECTIVE TAT SEX IMAGERY ADJUSTMENT

L-63   LARSEN, K. S., & SCHWENDIMAN, G.
            PERCEIVED AGGRESSION TRAINING AS A PREDICTOR OF TWO ASSESSMENTS OF
            AUTHORITARIANISM.
            JOURNAL OF PEACE RESEARCH, 1970, 1, 69-71.
            (MEASURE OF PERCEPTION OF PARENTAL AGGRESSION TRAINING)
        @L-63 1970M AGGRESSION AUTHORITARIANISM DOGMATISM BIRTH ORDER PARENT-CHILD
        @L-63 FAMILY INTERACTION CHILD
            (APPLICATIONS: 2782)

L-64   LUNN, J. C. B.
            CHILDREN'S ATTITUDE SCALES.
            UNPUBLISHED PAPER, 1967.
        LUNN, J. C. B.
            THE DEVELOPMENT OF SCALES TO MEASURE JUNIOR SCHOOL CHILDREN'S ATTITUDES.
            BRITISH JOURNAL OF EDUCATIONAL PSYCHOLOGY, 1969, 39, 64-7 .
            (MEASURE OF CHILDREN'S ATTITUDES AND ADJUSTMENT IN SCHOOL)
        @L-64 1967M CHILD SCHOOL ATTITUDE ADJUSTMENT SOCIAL AUTONOMY SELF-IDENTITY
            (APPLICATIONS: 2795)

L-65   LUMSDEN, E. A., JR.
            PERSON PERCEPTION AS A FUNCTION OF THE DEVIATION OF THE VISUAL AXES OF
            THE OBJECT-PERSON.
            JOURNAL OF SOCIAL PSYCHOLOGY. 1970, 80, 71-78.
            (MEASURE OF PERSON PERCEPTION)
        @L-65 1970M PERSON PERCEPTION OTHERS PEOPLE

L-66   LIEBERMAN, M. A., & COPLAN, A. S.
            DISTANCE FROM DEATH AS A VARIABLE IN THE STUDY OF AGING.
            DEVELOPMENTAL PSYCHOLOGY, 1970, 2, 71-84.
            (MEASURE OF BODY PREOCCUPATION)
        @L-66 1970M BODY IMAGE ORIENTATION

L-67   LINDGREN, H. C., & LINDGREN, F.
            BRAINSTORMING AND ORNERINESS AS FACILITATORS OF CREATIVITY.
            PSYCHOLOGICAL REPORTS, 1965, 16, 577-583.
            (ASYMMETRICAL PREFERENCE TEST)
        @L-67 1965M CREATIVITY ORIGINALITY CONFORMITY
            (APPLICATIONS: 2912)

L-68   L'ABATE, L.
            MMPI SCATTER AS A SINGLE INDEX OF MALADJUSTMENT.
            JOURNAL OF CLINICAL PSYCHOLOGY, 1962, 18, 142-143.
            (L'ABATE'S MALADJUSTMENT INDEX)
        @L-68 1962M ADJUSTMENT MMPI MENTAL-ILLNESS
            (APPLICATIONS: 1417 1739 2845)

L-69   LORR, M., & VESTRE, N. D.
            THE PSYCHOTIC INPATIENT PROFILE MANUAL.
            LOS ANGELES: WESTERN PSYCHOLOGICAL SERVICES, 1968.
            (PSYCHOTIC INPATIENT PROFILE)*
        @L-69 1968M PSYCHOPATHY MENTAL-HEALTH MENTAL-ILLNESS DIAGNOSIS PROGNOSIS
        @L-69 WARD PSYCHIATRIC PATIENT BEHAVIOR
            (APPLICATIONS: 2604)

L-70   LORR, M., O'CONNOR, J. P., & STAFFORD, J. W.
            THE PSYCHOTIC REACTION PROFILE.
            JOURNAL OF CLINICAL PSYCHOLOGY, 1960, 16, 241-245.
            (PSYCHOTIC REACTION PROFILE)*
        @L-70 1960M PSYCHOPATHY MENTAL-HEALTH MENTAL-ILLNESS DIAGNOSIS PROGNOSIS
        @L-70 WARD PSYCHIATRIC PATIENT BEHAVIOR
            (APPLICATIONS: 977 1825 1997 2270 2561 2630 2951)

L-72   LOEVINGER, J.
            MEASURING PERSONALITY PATTERNS OF WOMEN,
            GENETIC PSYCHOLOGY MONOGRAPHS, 1962, 65, 53-136.
            (AUTHORITARIAN FAMILY IDEOLOGY SCALE)
        @L-72 1962M AUTHORITARIANISM FAMILY INTERACTION PARENT-CHILD IDEOLOGY
            (APPLICATIONS: 2973)

L-73   LINDGREN, H. C., & MARRASH, J.
         A COMPARATIVE STUDY OF INTERCULTURAL INSIGHT AND EMPATHY.
         JOURNAL OF SOCIAL PSYCHOLOGY, 1970, 80, 135-141.
         (INTERCULTURAL INSIGHT QUESTIONNAIRE)
         @L-73 1970M PERCEPTION CROSS-CULTURAL TRAIT

L-74   ZILLER, R. C. & GROSSMAN, S. A.
         A DEVELOPMENTAL STUDY OF THE SELF-SOCIAL CONSTRUCTS OF NORMALS AND THE
         NEUROTIC PERSONALITY.
         JOURNAL OF CLINICAL PSYCHOLOGY, 1967, 23, 15-1.
         LONG, B. H., ZILLER, R. C., & BANKES, J.
         SELF-OTHER ORIENTATIONS OF INSTITUTIONALIZED BEHAVIOR-PROBLEM ADOLESCENTS.
         JOURNAL OF CONSULTING AND CLINICAL PSYCHOLOGY, 1970, 34, 43-47.
         (SELF-SOCIAL SYMBOLS TASK)
         @L-74 1970M SELF SOCIAL RELATIONSHIPS PARENT TEACHER PEER IDENTIFICATION
         @L-74 ESTEEM POWER
             (APPLICATIONS: 2744)

L-75   LOREI, T. W.
         STAFF RATINGS OF THE RELATIVE IMPORTANCE OF THE CONSEQUENCES OF RELEASE
         FROM OR RETENTION IN A PSYCHIATRIC HOSPITAL.
         JOURNAL OF CONSULTING AND CLINICAL PSYCHOLOGY, 1970, 34, 48-55.
         (RELEASE-RETENTION OUTCOME INVENTORY)
         @L-75 1970M MENTAL-ILLNESS PSYCHIATRIC HOSPITALIZATION PATIENT

L-76   LINDER, J. D., STONE, S. C., & SHERTZER, B.
         DEVELOPMENT AND EVALUATION OF AN INVENTORY FOR RATING COUNSELING.
         PERSONNEL AND GUIDANCE JOURNAL, 1965, 44, 267-276.
         (COUNSELING EVALUATION INVENTORY)
         @L-76 1965M THERAPY COUNSELING PATIENT SATISFACTION
             (APPLICATIONS: 1385 1435 1459 2544)

L-77   LIEM, G. R., YELLOTT, A. W., COWEN, E. L., TROST, M. A., & IZZO, L. D.
         SOME CORRELATES OF EARLY-DETECTED EMOTIONAL DYSFUNCTION IN THE SCHOOLS.
         AMERICAN JOURNAL OF ORTHOPSYCHIATRY, 1969, 39, 619-626.
         (TEACHER'S BEHAVIOR CHECKLIST)
         @L-77 1969M CHILD BEHAVIOR ADJUSTMENT TEACHER MATURITY
             (APPLICATIONS: 2545)

L-78   LIEM, G. R., YELLOTT, A. W., COWEN, E. L., TROST, M. A., & IZZO, L. D.
         SOME CORRELATES OF EARLY-DETECTED EMOTIONAL DYSFUNCTION IN THE SCHOOLS.
         AMERICAN JOURNAL OF ORTHOPSYCHIATRY, 1969, 39, 619-626.
         (ADJECTIVE CHECKLIST FOR JUDGING CHILD PERSONALITY)
         @L-78 1969M CHECKLIST TEACHER PERSONALITY CHILD
         @L-78 ADJUSTMENT MENTAL-ILLNESS MENTAL-HEALTH MATURITY

L-80   LOWE, A.
         INDIVIDUAL DIFFERENCE IN REACTION TO FAILURE: MODE OF COPING WITH ANXIETY
         AND INTERFERENCE PRONENESS.
         JOURNAL OF ABNORMAL AND SOCIAL PSYCHOLOGY, 1961, 62, 303-308.
         (INTERFERENCE PRONENESS SCALE)
         @L-80 1961M ANXIETY INTERFERENCE COGNITIVE
             (APPLICATIONS: 370)

L-81   LESSER, W.
         THE RELATIONSHIP BETWEEN COUNSELING PROGRESS AND EMPATHETIC UNDERSTANDING.
         UNPUBLISHED DOCTORAL DISSERTATION, MICHIGAN STATE UNIVERSITY, 1958.
         LESSER, W.
         THE RELATIONSHIP BETWEEN COUNSELING PROGRESS AND EMPATHETIC UNDERSTANDING.
         JOURNAL OF COUNSELING PSYCHOLOGY, 1961, 8, 330-336.
         (SELF-ACCEPTANCE QUESTIONNAIRE)
         @L-81 1958M SELF SELF-IDENTITY ACCEPTANCE CONCEPT IMAGE
             (APPLICATIONS: 1884)

L-82   LEVITT, E. E., LUBIN, B., & ZUCKERMAN, M.
         A SIMPLIFIED METHOD OF SCORING RORSCHACH CONTENT FOR DEPENDENCY.
         JOURNAL OF PROJECTIVE TECHNIQUES, 1962, 26, 234-236.
         (RORSCHACH SCORED FOR DEPENDENCY)
         @L-82 1962M RORSCHACH DEPENDENCE NEED PROJECTIVE
             (APPLICATIONS: 363)

L-83   LEVENTHAL, H., & TREMBLY, G.
         NEGATIVE EMOTIONS AND PERSUASION.
         JOURNAL OF PERSONALITY, 1968, 36, 154-168.
         (SELF-ESTEEM ADJECTIVE CHECKLIST)
         @L-83 1968M SELF ESTEEM CHECKLIST PHYSICAL SOCIAL EMOTION COPING MORAL VALUES
         @L-83 BELIEF CONVICTION DESIRABILITY

L-84   LESSING, E. E.
            DEMOGRAPHIC, DEVELOPMENTAL, AND PERSONALITY CORRELATES OF LENGTH OF FUTURE
            TIME PERSPECTIVE (FTP).
            JOURNAL OF PERSONALITY, 1968, 36, 183-201.
            (INCOMPLETE SENTENCES TEST)*
        aL-84 1968M FUTURE PERSPECTIVE ORIENTATION FANTASY PROJECTIVE
        aL-84 SENTENCE-COMP TIME

L-85   LEVY, L. H.
            THE EFFECTS OF VARIANCE ON PERSONALITY IMPRESSION FORMATION.
            JOURNAL OF PERSONALITY, 1967, 35, 179-193.
            (MEASURE OF OTHER-PERSONALITY IMPRESSION FORMATION)
        aL-85 1967M IMPRESSION FORMATION PERCEPTION OTHERS
        aL-85 GRAPHIC FIGURE SOCIAL

L-86   LIBERTY, P. G., JR., BURNSTEIN, E., & MOULTON, R. W.
            CONCERN WITH MASTERY AND OCCUPATIONAL ATTRACTION.
            JOURNAL OF PERSONALITY, 1966, 34, 105-117.
            (MEASURE OF PRESTIGE, ATTRACTIVENESS, AND COMPETENCE REQUIRED BY
            OCCUPATIONS)
        aL-86 1966M PRESTIGE ATTRACTION COMPETENCE JOB
        aL-86 ACHIEVEMENT ORIENTATION VOCATIONAL PERCEPTION

L-87   LANGER, J., & ROSENBERG, B. G.
            NONVERBAL REPRESENTATION OF VERBAL REFERENTS.
            PERCEPTUAL AND MOTOR SKILLS, 1964, 19, 663-670.
        LANGER, J., & ROSENBERG, B. G.
            SYMBOLIC MEANING AND COLOR NAMING.
            JOURNAL OF PERSONALITY AND SOCIAL PSYCHOLOGY, 1966, 4, 364-373.
            (COLOR PHONETIC SYMBOL TEST)
        aL-87 1964M COGNITIVE STYLE FUNCTIONING STRUCTURE PERCEPTION
            (APPLICATIONS: 443)

L-88   LORR, M., HOLSOPPLE, J. Q., & TURK, E.
            A MEASURE OF SEVERITY OF ILLNESS.
            JOURNAL OF CLINICAL PSYCHOLOGY, 1956, 12, 384-386.
            (SEVERITY RATING)
        aL-88 1956M THERAPY MENTAL-ILLNESS ADJUSTMENT PSYCHIATRIC DIAGNOSIS PROGNOSIS
            (APPLICATIONS: 726   1614   1738)

L-90   LONDON, P.
            SUBJECT CHARACTERISTICS IN HYPNOSIS RESEARCH: PART I. A SURVEY OF
            EXPERIENCE, INTEREST, AND OPINION.
            INTERNATIONAL JOURNAL OF CLINICAL AND EXPERIMENTAL HYPNOSIS, 1961, 9,
            151-161.
            (HYPNOSIS SURVEY)
        aL-90 1961M HYPNOTIC SUGGESTIBILITY
            (APPLICATIONS: 850   1975)

L-91   LONDON, P., & LARSEN, D. E.
            TEACHERS' USE OF LEISURE.
            TEACHERS COLLEGE RECORD, 1964, 65, 538-545.
            (LEISURE ACTIVITIES INVENTORY)
        aL-91 1964M ACTIVITIES PARTICIPATION INTEREST PREFERENCE BEHAVIOR
            (APPLICATIONS: 1959)

L-92   LESSLER, K.
            CULTURAL AND FREUDIAN DIMENSIONS OF SEXUAL SYMBOLS.
            JOURNAL OF CONSULTING PSYCHOLOGY, 1964, 28, 46-53.
            (SET OF FREUDIAN AND CULTURAL SEX SYMBOLS)
        aL-92 1964M SEX MASCULINITY FEMININITY MEANING PERCEPTION
            (APPLICATIONS: 2192)

L-93   LITTLE, K. B., & FISHER, J.
            TWO NEW EXPERIMENTAL SCALES OF THE MMPI.
            JOURNAL OF CONSULTING PSYCHOLOGY, 1958, 22, 305-306.
            (HYSTERIA DENIAL SCALE FROM MMPI)
        aL-93 1958M ADJUSTMENT DIAGNOSIS COPING-DEFENSE
        aL-93 MMPI MENTAL-HEALTH MENTAL-ILLNESS
            (APPLICATIONS: 34   876   910   1307   1847   2085)

L-94   LEVY, B. I., & MINSKI, R.
               INTELLIGENCE AND ADJUSTMENT IN RELATION TO THE PROPORTIONAL ACCURACY OF
               DRAWINGS OF HUMAN FIGURES.
               UNPUBLISHED STUDY, UNIVERSITY OF MARYLAND, 1961.
          LEVY, B. I., & MINSKY, R.
               MANUAL FOR THE ASSESSMENT OF THE ACCURACY OF DRAWINGS OF HUMAN FIGURES.
               WASHINGTON: B. I. LEVY, 1962.
               (CLINICAL MEASURE OF ADJUSTMENT)
          aL-94 1961M ADJUSTMENT MALADJUSTMENT GRAPHIC AGGRESSION DEPENDENCE INTELLIGENCE
          aL-94 SEX PROBLEM FIGURE
               (APPLICATIONS: 1812)

L-95   LIBO, L.
               PICTURE IMPRESSIONS: A PROJECTIVE TECHNIQUE FOR INVESTIGATING THE PATIENT-
               THERAPIST RELATIONSHIP.
               (DEPARTMENT OF PSYCHIATRY PUBLICATION SERIES) BALTIMORE: UNIVERSITY OF
               MARYLAND MEDICAL SCHOOL, 1956.
               (PICTURE IMPRESSIONS TEST)*
          aL-95 1956M PROJECTIVE PATIENT THERAPY RELATIONSHIPS ATTRACTION GRAPHIC
          aL-95 IMPRESSION
               (APPLICATIONS: 1647 2215)

L-96   LAXER, R. M.
               RELATION OF REAL SELF-RATING TO MOOD AND BLAME AND THEIR INTERACTION IN
               DEPRESSION.
               JOURNAL OF CONSULTING PSYCHOLOGY, 1964, 28, 538-546.
               (BLAME ASSIGNMENT SCALE)
          aL-96 1964M THERAPY ADJUSTMENT MENTAL-ILLNESS OTHERS
          aL-96 GUILT ATTRIBUTION

L-98   LEHMAN, H., & DORKEN, H.
               THE CLINICAL APPLICATION OF THE VERDUN PROJECTIVE BATTERY.
               CANADIAN JOURNAL OF PSYCHOLOGY, 1952, 6, 164-172.
          SIGAL, J. J. & DORKEN, H.
               WORD-ASSOCIATION COMMONALITY: A STANDARDIZED TEST AND A THEORY.
               JOURNAL OF CONSULTING PSYCHOLOGY, 1966, 30, 402-407.
               (VERDUN PROJECTIVE BATTERY)
          aL-98 1952M PROJECTIVE
               (APPLICATIONS: 2013)

L-99   LEWIS, M. K.
               COUNSELOR PREDICTION AND PROJECTION IN CLIENT-CENTERED PSYCHOTHERAPY.
               UNPUBLISHED DOCTORAL DISSERTATION, UNIVERSITY OF CHICAGO, 1959.
               ('EXPERT' Q-SORT)
          aL-99 1959M Q-SORT IDEAL COUNSELING ADJUSTMENT THERAPY
               (APPLICATIONS: 2024)

L-100   LAXER, R. M.
               SELF-CONCEPT CHANGES OF DEPRESSIVE PATIENTS IN GENERAL HOSPITAL
               TREATMENT.
               JOURNAL OF CONSULTING PSYCHOLOGY, 1964, 28, 214-219.
               (SEMANTIC DIFFERENTIAL MEASURE OF SELF-CONCEPT)
          aL-100 1964M SEM-DIFFERENTIAL SELF CONCEPT IDEAL EVALUATION POWER
          aL-100 ACTIVITIES BEHAVIOR

L-101   LUBORSKY, L.
               CLINICIANS' JUDGMENTS OF MENTAL HEALTH.
               A. M. A. ARCHIVES OF GENERAL PSYCHIATRY, 1962, 1, 407-417.
               (MENNINGER HEALTH-SICKNESS SCALE)*
          aL-101 1962M MENTAL-HEALTH MENTAL-ILLNESS JUDGMENT DIAGNOSIS
               (APPLICATIONS: 1873)

L-102   LOREI, T. W.
               PREDICTION OF COMMUNITY STAY AND EMPLOYMENT FOR RELEASED PSYCHIATRIC
               PATIENTS.
               JOURNAL OF CONSULTING PSYCHOLOGY, 1967, 31, 349-357.
               (SURVEY OF OPINION QUESTIONNAIRE)*
          aL-102 1967M PSYCHIATRIC GLOBAL ADJUSTMENT OPINION

L-103   LITTLE, K. B., & FISHER, J.
               TWO NEW EXPERIMENTAL SCALES OF THE MMPI.
               JOURNAL OF CONSULTING PSYCHOLOGY, 1958, 22, 305-306.
               (ADMISSION OF SYMPTOM SCALE FROM MMPI)
          aL-103 1958M MMPI ADJUSTMENT OPENNESS MENTAL-ILLNESS SYMPTOM
          aL-103 MMPI COPING-DEFENSE
               (APPLICATIONS: 122 1307 2085)

L-105   LEIMAN, A. H.
         RELATIONSHIP OF TAT SEXUAL RESPONSES TO SEXUAL DRIVE, SEXUAL GUILT,
         AND SEXUAL CONFLICT.
         UNPUBLISHED DOCTORAL DISSERTATION, UNIVERSITY OF MASSACHUSETTS, 1961.
         (LEIMAN SEX CONFLICT SCALE)
     @L-105 1961M SEX CONFLICT DRIVE INTENSITY GUILT
         (APPLICATIONS: 2186)

L-106   LANYUN, R. I.
         DEVELOPMENT AND VALIDATION OF A PSYCHOLOGICAL SCREENING MEASURE.
         JOURNAL OF CONSULTING AND CLINICAL PSYCHOLOGY MONOGRAPH, 1970, 35, 1-24.
         (PSYCHOLOGICAL SCREENING INVENTORY)*
     @L-106 1970M ADJUSTMENT MENTAL-HEALTH MENTAL-ILLNESS DIAGNOSIS ALIENATION
     @L-106 ANXIETY CONFORMITY SOCIAL EXPRESSION SELF

L-109   LIPSITT, L. P.
         A SELF-CONCEPT SCALE FOR CHILDREN AND ITS RELATIONSHIP TO THE CHILDREN'S
         FORM OF THE MANIFEST ANXIETY SCALE.
         CHILD DEVELOPMENT, 1958, 29, 463-472.
         (SELF-CONCEPT SCALE FOR CHILDREN)
     @L-109 1958M CHILD SELF-IDENTITY SELF CONCEPT IDEAL
         (APPLICATIONS: 638   746)

L-110   LEWIT, D. W., BRAYER, A. R., & LEIMAN, A. H.
         EXTERNALIZATION IN PERCEPTUAL DEFENSE.
         JOURNAL OF ABNORMAL AND SOCIAL PSYCHOLOGY, 1962, 65, 6-13.
         (EXTERNALIZATION SCALE)
     @L-110 1962M PE-FIT ATTRIBUTION RESPONSIBILITY PUNITIVENESS GUILT
     @L-110 EGO DEFENSE EXPRESSION AGGRESSION.

L-112   LIKERT, R.
         A TECHNIQUE FOR THE MEASUREMENT OF ATTITUDES.
         ARCHIVES OF PSYCHOLOGY, NEW YORK, 1932, NO. 140.
         (MURPHY-LIKERT SCALE OF ATTITUDES TOWARD THE NEGRO)*
     @L-112 1932M ATTITUDE BELIEF OPINION RACIAL NEGRO
         (APPLICATIONS: 714)

L-113   LESSER, G. S.
         CONFLICT ANALYSIS OF FANTASY AGGRESSION.
         JOURNAL OF PERSONALITY, 1958, 26, 29-41.
         (MODIFIED TAT MEASURE OF AGGRESSION)
     @L-113 1958M TAT PROJECTIVE DIRECTION AGGRESSION EXPRESSION INHIBITION **FANTASY**
         (APPLICATIONS: 796   842)

L-114   LEIMAN, A. H., & EPSTEIN, S.
         THEMATIC SEXUAL RESPONSES AS RELATED TO SEXUAL DRIVE AND GUILT.
         JOURNAL OF ABNORMAL AND SOCIAL PSYCHOLOGY, 1961, 63, 169-175.
         (PROJECTIVE MEASURE OF SEXUAL NEEDS AND GUILT)
     @L-114 1961M PROJECTIVE NEED SEX GUILT TAT IMAGERY

L-115   LIRO, L. M.
         MEASURING GROUP COHESIVENESS.
         ANN ARBOR, RESEARCH CENTER FOR GROUP DYNAMICS, 1953.
         (MEASURE OF ATTRACTION TO THE GROUP)
     @L-115 1953M GROUP COHESIVENESS
         (APPLICATIONS: 716)

L-116   LEVITT, E. E.
         STUDIES IN INTOLERANCE OF AMBIGUITY: I. THE DECISION-LOCATION TEST WITH
         GRADE SCHOOL CHILDREN.
         CHILD DEVELOPMENT, 1953, 24, 263-268.
         (DECISION-LOCATION TEST)
     @L-116 1953M PERCEPTION COGNITIVE FUNCTIONING INTEGRATION
         (APPLICATIONS: 323)

L-117   LEVITT, E. E.
         PUNITIVENESS AND "CAUSALITY" IN GRADE SCHOOL CHILDREN.
         JOURNAL OF EDUCATIONAL PSYCHOLOGY, 1955, 46, 494-498.
         LYLE, W. H., & LEVITT, E. E.
         PUNITIVENESS, AUTHORITARIANISM AND PARENTAL DISCIPLINE OF GRADE SCHOOL
         CHILDREN.
         JOURNAL OF ABNORMAL AND SOCIAL PSYCHOLOGY, 1955, 51, 42-46.
         (PROBLEM SITUATIONS TEST)
     @L-117 1955M PUNITIVENESS EXPRESSION HOSTILITY AGGRESSION SITUATIONAL
         (APPLICATIONS: 323)

L-118   LERNER, M. J., & FAIRWEATHER, G. W.
          SOCIAL BEHAVIOR OF CHRONIC SCHIZOPHRENICS IN SUPERVISED AND UNSUPERVISED
          WORK GROUPS.
          JOURNAL OF ABNORMAL AND SOCIAL PSYCHOLOGY, 1963, 67, 219-225.
          (MEASURE OF GROUP BEHAVIOR)
          aL-118 1963M GROUP BEHAVIOR SCHIZOPHRENIA SUPERVISOR COHESIVENESS LEADER
          aL-118 ATTITUDE DEPENDENCY

L-119   LUBORSKY, L., BLINDER, B., & MACKWORTH, N.
          EYE FIXATION AND RECALL OF PICTURES AS A FUNCTION OF GSR RESPONSIVITY.
          PERCEPTUAL AND MOTOR SKILLS, 1963, 16, 469-483.
          (PICTURE RECALL MEASURE OF DEFENSES OF ISOLATION AND REPRESSION)
          aL-119 1963M DEFENSE REPRESSION SEX PROJECTIVE AGGRESSION ANXIETY
          aL-119 COPING-DEFENSE
             (APPLICATIONS: 969)

L-120   LEE-TENG, E.
          TRANCE-SUSCEPTIBILITY, INDUCTION-SUSCEPTIBILITY, AND ACQUIESCENCE AS
          FACTORS IN HYPNOTIC PERFORMANCE.
          JOURNAL OF ABNORMAL PSYCHOLOGY, 1965, 70, 383-389.
          (HYPNOTIC CHARACTERISTICS INVENTORY)
          aL-120 1965M HYPNOTIC SUGGESTIBILITY AUTONOMY CONFORMITY ROLE ENACTMENT
          aL-120 IMPULSIVENESS RATIONALISM

L-121   LEVIN, R. B.
          AN EMPIRICAL TEST OF THE FEMALE CASTRATION COMPLEX.
          JOURNAL OF ABNORMAL PSYCHOLOGY, 1966, 71, 181-188.
          (RORSCHACH FEMALE CASTRATION COMPLEX MEASURE
          aL-121 1966M PROJECTIVE RORSCHACH SEX IDENTIFICATION IE-CONTROL FEMININITY
          aL-121 MASCULINITY ROLE ANXIETY COPING-DEFENESE FRUSTRATION INFERIORITY CONFLICT
          aL-121 AFFECTIVE-STATES

L-122   LAPOUSE, R., & MONK, M. A.
          FEARS AND WORRIES IN A REPRESENTATIVE SAMPLE OF CHILDREN.
          AMERICAN JOURNAL OF ORTHOPSYCHIATRY, 1959, 29, 803-818.
          (BEHAVIOR RATING SCALE)
          aL-122 1959M BEHAVIOR MENTAL-HEALTH PSYCHIATRIC SYMPTOM
             (APPLICATIONS: 1011)

L-124   LUCERO, R. J., & MEYER, W. T.
          A BEHAVIOR RATING SCALE SUITABLE FOR USE IN MENTAL HOSPITALS.
          JOURNAL OF CLINICAL PSYCHOLOGY, 1951, 7, 250-254.
          (LUCERO-MEYER FERGUS FALLS BEHAVIOR RATING SCALE)
          aL-124 1951M BEHAVIOR WARD RATING
          aL-124 DIAGNOSIS PSYCHIATRIC MENTAL-HEALTH MENTAL-ILLNESS
             (APPLICATIONS: 1027 1065)

L-125   LOVIBOND, S. H.
          CONDITIONING AND ENURESIS.
          OXFORD: PERGAMON PRESS, 1964.
          (BEHAVIOR PROBLEM RECORD)*
          aL-125 1964M CHILD BEHAVIOR PROBLEM
             (APPLICATIONS: 1094)

L-128   LODAHL, T. M., & KEJNER, M.
          THE DEFINITION AND MEASUREMENT OF JOB INVOLVEMENT.
          JOURNAL OF APPLIED PSYCHOLOGY, 1965, 49, 24-33.
          (JOB INVOLVEMENT SCALE)
          aL-128 1965M JOB INVOLVEMENT SATISFACTION INTEREST
             (APPLICATIONS: 1402 2354)

L-129   LOWENHERZ, L., & FEFFER, M.
          COGNITIVE LEVEL AS A FUNCTION OF DEFENSIVE ISOLATION.
          JOURNAL OF ABNORMAL PSYCHOLOGY, 1969, 74, 352-357.
          (TAT MEASURE OF DEFENSIVE ISOLATION AND ROLE-TAKING)
          aL-129 1969M TAT DEFENSE COPING-DEFENSE PROJECTIVE IMAGERY ROLE ENACTMENT
          aL-129 DENIAL

L-130   LIVINGTON, P. B., & ZIMET, C. N.
          DEATH ANXIETY, AUTHORITARIANISM, AND CHOICE OF SPECIALITY IN MEDICAL
          STUDENTS.
          JOURNAL OF NERVOUS AND MENTAL DISEASE, 1965, 140, 222-230.
          (DEATH ANXIETY SCALE)
          aL-130 1965M DEATH MORTALITY ANXIETY FEAR
             (APPLICATIONS: 1053)

L-131   LOWE, C. A., AND GOLDSTEIN, J. W.
         RECIPROCAL LIKING AND ATTRIBUTIONS OF ABILITY: MEDIATING EFFECTS OF
         PERCEIVED INTENT AND PERSONAL INVOLVEMENT.
         JOURNAL OF PERSONALITY AND SOCIAL PSYCHOLOGY, 1970, 16, 291-297.
         (LIKING SCALE)
         aL-131 1970M SOCIAL INTERPERSONAL ATTRACTION RELATIONSHIPS

L-132   LIN, Y., MCKEACHIE, W. J., WERNANDER, M., & HEDEGARD, J.
         THE RELATIONSHIP BETWEEN STUDENT-TEACHER COMPATIBILITY OF COGNITIVE
         STRUCTURE AND STUDENT PERFORMANCE.
         PSYCHOLOGICAL RECORD, 1970, 20, 513-522.
         (MEASURE OF COMPATIBILITY OF COGNITIVE STRUCTURE)
         aL-132 1970M COGNITIVE STRUCTURE COMPATIBILITY STUDENT TEACHER

L-133   LOCKE, H. J., & WALLACE, K. M.
         SHORT MARITAL-ADJUSTMENT AND PREDICTION TESTS: THEIR RELIABILITY AND
         VALIDITY.
         MARRIAGE AND FAMILY LIVING, 1959, 21, 251-255.
         (LOCKE-WALLACE MARITAL ADJUSTMENT TEST)*
         aL-133 1959M MARITAL SATISFACTION ADJUSTMENT COMPATIBILITY RELATIONSHIPS
         (APPLICATIONS: 2580)

L-134   LORR, M., SONN, T. M., & KATZ, M. M.
         TOWARD A DEFINITION OF DEPRESSION.
         ARCHIVES OF GENERAL PSYCHIATRY, 1967, 17, 183-186.
         (MEASURES OF FUNCTIONAL IMPAIRMENT AND SOMATIC COMPLAINTS)
         aL-134 1967M PSYCHOSOMATIC SYMPTOM DEPRESSION PSYCHIATRIC
         (APPLICATIONS: 1150)

L-135   LANG, P. J., & LAZOVIK, A. D.
         EXPERIMENTAL DESENSITIZATION OF A PHOBIA.
         JOURNAL OF ABNORMAL AND SOCIAL PSYCHOLOGY, 1963, 66, 519-525.
         LANG, P. J., LAZOVIK, A. D., & REYNOLDS, D. J.
         DESENSITIZATION, SUGGESTIBILITY, AND PSYCHOTHERAPY.
         JOURNAL OF ABNORMAL AND SOCIAL PSYCHOLOGY, 1965, 70, 395-402.
         (SNAKE AVOIDANCE TEST)
         aL-135 1963M FEAR PHOBIA ANXIETY STIMULUS APPROACH AVOIDANCE RESPONSE BEHAVIOR
         (APPLICATIONS: 972 1134 2416)

L-136   LANG, P. J., MELAMED, B. G., & HART, J.
         A PSYCHOPHYSIOLOGICAL ANALYSIS OF FEAR MODIFICATION USING AN AUTOMATED
         DESENSITIZATION PROCEDURE.
         JOURNAL OF ABNORMAL PSYCHOLOGY, 1970, 76, 220-234.
         (SPECIFIC FEAR ITEM QUESTIONNAIRE)
         aL-136 1970M FEAR PHOBIA SITUATIONAL AROUSAL SENSITIZATION STIMULUS AVOIDANCE

L-137   LEVINE, D.
         RELATIONS AMONG CRITERIA OF IMPROVEMENT IN FUNCTIONAL PSYCHOSES.
         PROCEEDINGS OF THE AMERICAN PSYCHOLOGICAL ASSOCIATION, 1965, 1, 233-234.
         (MEASURES OF IMPROVEMENT AMONG FUNCTIONALLY PSYCHOTIC)
         aL-137 1965M PSYCHIATRIC DIAGNOSIS MENTAL-ILLNESS CHANGE SYMPTOM BEHAVIOR
         (APPLICATIONS: 2633)

L-138   LEVINE, D., & WITTENBORN, J. R.
         RELATION OF EXPRESSED ATTITUDES TO IMPROVEMENT IN FUNCTIONAL PSYCHOTICS.
         PSYCHOLOGICAL REPORTS, 1970, 26, 275-277.
         (SELF-REPORT SCALE OF PSYCHIATRIC PATIENTS' ATTITUDES)
         aL-138 1970M RESPONSIBILITY LOCUS SELF CONCEPT NEED AFFILIATION TRUST
         aPSYCHIATRIC PATIENT INTERPERSONAL RELATIONSHIPS SOCIAL INTERACTION
         aBEHAVIOR ATTITUDE ILLNESS MENTAL-ILLNESS HOSPITALIZATION SYMPTOM WARD
         aATTRIBUTION

L-139   LEVINSON, D. J.
         T.A.P. SOCIAL ATTITUDE BATTERY.
         CAMBRIDGE, MASS.: HARVARD UNIVERSITY, 1959. (MIMEO).
         (REVISED POLITICAL-ECONOMIC CONSERVATISM SCALES)
         aL-139 1959M POLITICAL IDEOLOGY CONSERVATISM LIBERALISM RADICALISM A-29R
         (APPLICATIONS: 1494)

L-140   LEMERT, J.
         DIMENSIONS OF SOURCE CREDIBILITY.
         PAPER PRESENTED AT THE MEETING OF THE ASSOCIATION FOR EDUCATION IN
         JOURNALISM, AUGUST, 1963.
         (COUNSELOR RATING SCALE (CRS))*
         aL-140 1963M COUNSELING TRUST SEM-DIFFERENTIAL THERAPY RELATIONSHIPS PATIENT
         aTHERAPIST EVALUATION SATISFACTION
         (APPLICATIONS: 1498)

L-142   LAXER, R. M., QUARTER, J. J., ISNOR, C., & KENNEDY, D. R.
               COUNSELING SMALL GROUPS OF BEHAVIOR PROBLEM STUDENTS IN JUNIOR HIGH
               SCHOOLS.
               JOURNAL OF COUNSELING PSYCHOLOGY, 1967, 14, 454-457.
               (Q-SORT MEASURE OF SELF AND IDEAL SELF)
           aL-142 1967M Q-SORT SELF IDEAL PERCEPTION SATISFACTION ESTEEM
           aDISCREPANCY CONCEPT

L-143   LESSER, W. M.
               THE RELATIONSHIP BETWEEN COUNSELING PROGRESS AND EMPATHETIC UNDERSTANDING.
               JOURNAL OF COUNSELING PSYCHOLOGY, 1961, 8, 330-336.
               (SCALE OF FELT SIMILARITY TO CLIENTS)
           aL-143 1961M SIMILARITY THERAPY PATIENT RELATIONSHIPS COUNSELING

L-144   LOCKE, H. J.
               PREDICTING ADJUSTMENT IN MARRIAGE.
               NEW YORK: HOLT, 1951.
               (MARITAL ADJUSTMENT SCALE)*
           aL-144 1951M MARITAL ADJUSTMENT RELATIONSHIPS SATISFACTION HAPPINESS
               (APPLICATIONS: 1277)

L-147   LERNER, M. J., DILLEHAY, R. C., & SHERER, W. C.
               SIMILARITY AND ATTRACTION IN SOCIAL CONTEXTS.
               JOURNAL OF PERSONALITY AND SOCIAL PSYCHOLOGY, 1967, 5, 481-486.
               (PERSONAL ITEMS QUESTIONNAIRE)
           aL-147 1967M PERSONAL ORIENTATION BEHAVIOR SOCIAL

L-149   LERNER, M. J., DILLEHAY, R. C., & SHERER, W. C.
               SIMILARITY AND ATTRACTION IN SOCIAL CONTEXTS.
               JOURNAL OF PERSONALITY AND SOCIAL PSYCHOLOGY, 1967, 5, 481-486.
               (MEASURE OF INTERPERSONAL ATTRACTION)
           aL-149 1967M ATTRACTION INTERPERSONAL SOCIAL VALUES

L-151   LEHMANN, S.
               PERSONALITY AND COMPLIANCE: A STUDY OF ANXIETY AND SELF-ESTEEM IN OPINION
               AND BEHAVIOR CHANGE.
               JOURNAL OF PERSONALITY AND SOCIAL PSYCHOLOGY, 1970, 15, 76-86.
               (GENERAL ANXIETY SCALE)
           aL-151 1970M ANXIETY AFFECTIVE-STATES NEGATIVE

L-152   LEWINSOHN, P. M.
               UNPUBLISHED MATERIAL, OBTAINABLE FROM AUTHOR (S. ILLINOIS UNIVERSITY).
           LEWINSOHN, P. M.
               PSYCHOLOGICAL CORRELATES OF OVERALL QUALITY OF FIGURE DRAWING.
               JOURNAL OF CONSULTING PSYCHOLOGY, 1965, 29, 504-512.
               (MEASURE OF SOCIAL HISTORY AND PREMORBID ADJUSTMENT)
           aL-152 1965M ADJUSTMENT SYMPTOM PSYCHIATRIC MENTAL-ILLNESS SOCIAL HISTORY

L-153   LEWINSOHN, P. M., & NICHOLS, R. C.
               THE EVALUATION OF CHANGES IN PSYCHIATRIC PATIENTS DURING AND AFTER
               HOSPITALIZATION.
               JOURNAL OF CLINICAL PSYCHOLOGY, 1964, 20, 272-279.
               (FOLLOW-UP MEASURE OF ADJUSTMENT IN PSYCHIATRIC PATIENTS)
           aL-153 1964M PSYCHIATRIC ADJUSTMENT SYMPTOM PATIENT CHANGE
               (APPLICATIONS: 1958)

L-154   LEWINSOHN, P. M., & MAY, J. G., JR.
               A TECHNIQUE FOR THE JUDGMENT OF EMOTION FROM FIGURE DRAWINGS.
               JOURNAL OF PROJECTIVE TECHNIQUES, 1963, 27, 79-85.
           NICHOLS, R. L. & LEWINSOHN, P. M.
               BEHAVIORAL CORRELATES OF THE DRAW-A-PERSON TEST.
               UNPUBLISHED.
               (MEASURE OF OVERALL QUALITY OF FIGURE DRAWINGS)
           aL-154 1963M QUALITY GLOBAL PROJECTIVE GRAPHIC FIGURE
               (APPLICATIONS: 1958)

L-157   LOVIBOND, S. H.
               THE OBJECT SORTING TEST AND CONCEPTUAL THINKING IN SCHIZOPHRENIA.
               AUSTRALIAN JOURNAL OF PSYCHIATRY, 1954, 5, 52-70.
               (OBJECT SORTING TEST SCORED FOR PSYCHOTIC IMPAIRMENT)
           aL-157 1954M SCHIZOPHRENIA DIAGNOSIS PSYCHOSIS
               (APPLICATIONS: 1106)

L-158   LEWIS, J. M., GRIFFITH, E. C., RIEDEL, A. F., & SIMMONS, B. A.
             STUDIES IN ABSTRACTION: SCHIZOPHRENIA AND ORALITY: PRELIMINARY RESULTS.
             JOURNAL OF NERVOUS AND MENTAL DISEASES, 1959, 129, 564-567.
             (PROVERBS TEST)
         aL-158 1959M ORALITY ANALITY ABSTRACTNESS
             (APPLICATIONS: 744)

L-159   LIVERANT, S., & SCODEL, A.
             INTERNAL AND EXTERNAL CONTROL AS DETERMINANTS OF DECISION MAKING UNDER
             CONDITIONS OF RiSK.
             PSYCHOLOGICAL REPORTS, 1960, 7, 59-67.
             (I-E SCALE)*
         aL-159 1960M IE-CONTROL COMPETENCE CONTROL LOCUS SELF
             (APPLICATIONS: 343   811)

L-160   LORR
             REFERENCE UNKNOWN.
             (ANXIETY RATING SCALE)*
         aL-160 ANXIETY RATING
             (APPLICATIONS: 595)

L-161   LEVINSON, D., & HUFFMAN, P. E.
             TRADITIONAL FAMILY IDEOLOGY AND ITS RELATION TO PERSONALITY.
             JOURNAL OF PERSONALITY, 1955, 23, 251-273.
             (FERPT SCALE)
         aL-161 1955M FAMILY IDEOLOGY

L-162   LEVINSON, D.
             PERSONAL COMMUNICATION, 1956.
             BLATT, S. J.
             AN ATTEMPT TO DEFINE MENTAL HEALTH.
             JOURNAL OF CONSULTING PSYCHOLOGY, 1964, 28, 146-153.
             (ABBREVIATED F-SCALE)
         aL-162 1956M AUTHORITARIANISM COPING-DEFENSE DOGMATISM RIGIDITY FLEXIBILITY
         aF-SCALE
             (APPLICATIONS: 1856)

L-164   LYKKEN, D. T.
             A STUDY OF ANXIETY IN THE SOCIOPATHIC PERSONALITY.
             JOURNAL OF ABNORMAL AND SOCIAL PSYCHOLOGY, 1957, 55, 6-10.
             (MEASURE OF PSYCHOPATHY)
         aL-164 1957M PSYCHOPATHY MENTAL-ILLNESS

L-165   LIEBERMAN, M. A., & LAKIN, M.
             ON BECOMING AN AGED INSTITUTIONALIZED INDIVIDUAL.
             IN W. DONAHUE, C. TIBBITS, AND R. WILLIAMS (EDS.) SOCIAL AND PSYCHOLOGICAL
             PROCESSES OF AGING, NEW YORK: ATHERTON, 1963.
             (THE OLD AGE TAT) CARDS 1, 2, 4, 5, 27.
         aL-165 1963M TAT GERIATRIC

M-1   MACKLER, B., & SHONTZ, F. C.
             AN ASSESSMENT OF SENSORY STYLE.
             PERCEPTUAL AND MOTOR SKILLS, 1964, 18, 841-848.
             (LIFE STYLE SCALE)*
         aM-1 LIFE STYLE SELF DESCRIPTION SENSORY ORIENTATION 1964M

M-2   MAINORD, W. A.
             EXPERIMENTAL REPRESSION RELATED TO COPING AND AVOIDANCE BEHAVIORS IN THE
             RECALL AND RELEARNING OF NONSENSE SYLLABLES.
             UNPUBLISHED DOCTORAL DISSERATION, UNIVERSITY OF WASHINGTON, 1956.
             (MEASURE OF COPER-AVOIDER TRAITS)
         aM-2 COPING BEHAVIOR COPING-DEFENSE GLOBAL STYLE APPROACH AVOIDANCE TRAIT SEX
         aM-2 AGGRESSION 1956M
             (APPLICATIONS: 792   1630)

M-3   MANDLER, G., MANDLER, J. M., & UVILLER, E. T.
             AUTONOMIC FEEDBACK: THE PERCEPTION OF AUTONOMIC ACTIVITY.
             JOURNAL OF ABNORMAL AND SOCIAL PSYCHOLOGY, 1958, 56, 367-373.
             (AUTONOMIC PERCEPTION QUESTIONNAIRE)*
         aM-3 ANXIETY POSITIVE AUTONOMIC PERCEPTION AFFECTIVE-STATES SUBJECTIVE STRESS
         aM-3 1958M NEGATIVE BODY
             (APPLICATIONS: 178   1672)

M-4   MANDLER, G., & SARASON, S. B.
              A STUDY OF ANXIETY AND LEARNING.
              JOURNAL OF ABNORMAL AND SOCIAL PSYCHOLOGY, 1952, 47, 166-173.
              (MANDLER-SARASON TEST ANXIETY QUESTIONNAIRE)*
           @M-4 ANXIETY TEST AFFECTIVE-STATES SUBJECTIVE STRESS SOCIAL FEAR FAILURE
           @M-4 ADJUSTMENT NEGATIVE 1952M
              (APPLICATIONS: 20   39   46   113   134   146   159   167   194   235
                               285   303   319   356   374   383   415   417   418   431
                               433   436   455   475   517   523   544   567   584   692
                               720   722   755   795   813   836   846   879   886   889
                               893   1068   1882   2141   2339   2501   2503   2579   2646   2722
                              2757   2805   2897   2908)

M-5   MARCIA, J. E
              DEVELOPMENT AND VALIDATION OF EGO-IDENTITY STATUS.
              JOURNAL OF PERSONALITY AND SOCIAL PSYCHOLOGY, 1966, 3, 551-558.
              (EGO-IDENTITY INCOMPLETE SENTENCES BLANK)*
           @M-5 EGO IDENTITY SELF COPING STYLE IMAGE CONFLICT COPING-DEFENSE GLOBAL 1966M
           @M-5 EGO-RESILIENCY SELF-IDENTITY EVALUATION PERCEPTION ESTEEM EGO-STRENGTH

M-6   MASON, R. E.
              VALUE ORIENTATION SCALE DEVELOPMENT.
              PSYCHOLOGICAL REPORTS, 1968, 22, 184.
              (VALUE ORIENTATION SCALE)*
           @M-6 VALUES IDEALS LIFE ORIENTATION GOALS SELF-IDENTITY ADJUSTMENT BEHAVIOR
           @M-6 INTERPERSONAL PERSONALITY DEVELOPMENT 1966M

M-7   MCCLELLAND, D. C., CLARK, R. A., ROBY, T. B., & ATKINSON, J. W.
              THE EFFECT OF THE NEED FOR ACHIEVEMENT ON THEMATIC APPERCEPTION.
              IN J. W. ATKINSON (ED.) MOTIVES IN FANTASY, ACTION, AND SOCIETY. PRINCETON,
              NEW JERSEY: VAN NOSTRAND, 1958. ALSO IN:
              JOURNAL OF EXPERIMENTAL PSYCHOLOGY, 1949, 37, 242-255.
              (TAT SCORED FOR NEED ACHIEVEMENT)
           @M-7 ACHIEVEMENT NEED AUTONOMY MOTIVE TAT PROJECTIVE 1949M IMAGERY
              (APPLICATIONS: 31   41   46   100   134   156   157   159   160   174
                               213   268   344   374   383   415   417   433   436   512
                               517   539   553   559   600   628   636   642   651   654
                               684   692   702   745   771   783   795   813   828   836
                               846   860   867   879   889   893   894   897   922   926
                               928   934   1168   1612   1624   1824   1857   1968   2014   2016
                              2031   2032   2033   2131   2165   2230   2290   2357   2447   2470
                              2501   2503   2722   2757)

M-8   MCDAVID, J. W.
              IMMEDIATE EFFECTS OF GROUP THERAPY UPON RESPONSE TO SOCIAL REINFORCEMENT
              AMONG JUVENILE DELINQUENTS.
              JOURNAL OF CONSULTING PSYCHOLOGY, 1964, 28, 409-412.
              (SOCIAL REINFORCEMENT INTERPRETATION TEST)*
           @M-8 SOCIAL APPROVAL SELF IDENTITY PUBLIC ESTEEM NEED ADJUSTMENT
           @AUTONOMY INTERACTION INTERPERSONAL RELATIONSHIPS 1964M
              (APPLICATIONS: 8   2840)

M-9   MCKINNEY, F.
              THE SENTENCE COMPLETION BLANK IN ASSESSING STUDENT SELF-ACTUALIZATION.
              PERSONNEL AND GUIDANCE JOURNAL, 1967, 709-713.
              (SENTENCE COMPLETION BLANK)*
           @M-9 STUDENT SELF ACTUALIZATION CONCEPT COPING-DEFENSE GLOBAL SELF-IDENTITY
           @M-9 DEVELOPMENT 1967M
              (APPLICATIONS: 1369)

M-10   MCQUITTY, L. L.
              A MEASURE OF PERSONALITY INTEGRATION IN RELATION TO THE CONCEPT OF SELF.
              JOURNAL OF PERSONALITY, 1950, 18, 461-482.
              (MEASURE OF PERSONALITY INTEGRATION)
           @M-10 PERSONALITY INTEGRATION GLOBAL SELF-IDENTITY IMAGE SELF CONCEPT ESTEEM
           @M-10 1950M

M-11   MCREYNOLDS, P.
              ON THE ASSESSMENT OF ANXIETY: I. BY A BEHAVIOR CHECKLIST.
              PSYCHOLOGICAL REPORTS, 1965, 16, 805-808.
              (ANXIETY BEHAVIOR CHECKLIST)*
           @M-11 BEHAVIOR CHECKLIST ANXIETY AFFECTIVE-STATES SUBJECTIVE STRESS NEGATIVE
           @M-11 1965M
              (APPLICATIONS: 2725)

M-12   MCREYNOLDS, P., & ACKER, M.
        ON THE ASSESSMENT OF ANXIETY: II. BY A SELF-REPORT INVENTORY.
        PSYCHOLOGICAL REPORTS, 1966, 19, 231-237.
        (ASSIMILATION SCALE)*
    aM-12 ANXIETY ADJUSTMENT AFFECTIVE-STATES SUBJECTIVE STRESS HOSPITALIZATION
    aM-12 PSYCHIATRIC PATIENT MENTAL-ILLNESS NEGATIVE 1966M

M-13   MEHRABIAN, A.
        MALE AND FEMALE SCALES OF THE TENDENCY TO ACHIEVE.
        EDUCATIONAL AND PSYCHOLOGICAL MEASUREMENT, 1968, 28, 493-502.
        (MEHRABIAN ACHIEVEMENT RISK-PREFERENCE SCALE)*
    aM-13 ACHIEVEMENT NEED AUTONOMY MOTIVE 1968M RISK-TAKING
        (APPLICATIONS: 2501 2805)

M-14   MINTURN, L.
        THE DIMENSIONS OF AGGRESSION: A DESCRIPTIVE SCALING STUDY OF THE
        CHARACTERISTICS OF AGGRESSIVE PICTURES.
        JOURNAL OF EXPERIMENTAL RESEARCH IN PERSONALITY, 1967, 2, 86-99.
        (MEASURE OF CHARACTERISTICS OF AGGRESSIVE PICTURES)
    aM-14 AGGRESSION AFFECTIVE-STATES RESENTMENT HOSTILITY NEGATIVE INTERACTION
    aM-14 PROJECTIVE 1967M PERCEIVED

M-15   MOOS, R. H., & HOUTS, P. S.
        ASSESSMENT OF THE SOCIAL ATMOSPHERES OF PSYCHIATRIC WARDS.
        JOURNAL OF ABNORMAL PSYCHOLOGY, 1968, 73, 595-604.
        (WARD ATMOSPHERE SCALE)*
    aM-15 MENTAL-ILLNESS WARD ENVIRONMENT PE-FIT ADJUSTMENT PSYCHIATRIC
    aM-15 HOSPITALIZATION 1968M

M-16   MOSHER, D. L.
        THE DEVELOPMENT AND VALIDATION OF A SENTENCE COMPLETION MEASURE OF GUILT.
        UNPUBLISHED DOCTORAL DISSERTATION, OHIO STATE UNIVERSITY, 1961.
        (MOSHER INCOMPLETE SENTENCES TEST)*
    aM-16 GUILT AFFECTIVE-STATES NEGATIVE SEX HOSTILITY MORAL CONSCIENCE 1961M
        (APPLICATIONS: 230   248   292 1936 1979 2009 2229 2232 2743)

M-17   MOSHER, D. L.
        THE DEVELOPMENT AND MULTITRAIT-MULTIMETHOD MATRIX ANALYSIS OF THREE
        ASPECTS OF GUILT.
        JOURNAL OF CONSULTING PSYCHOLOGY, 1966, 30, 25-29.
        (TRUE-FALSE GUILT INVENTORY)*
    aM-17 GUILT HOSTILITY AFFECTIVE-STATES NEGATIVE MORAL SEX CONSCIENCE 1966M
        (APPLICATIONS: 1979 2443)

M-18   MOSHER, D. L.
        MEASUREMENT OF GUILT IN FEMALES BY SELF-REPORT INVENTORIES.
        JOURNAL OF CONSULTING AND CLINICAL PSYCHOLOGY, 1968, 32, 690-695.
        (TRUE-FALSE MEASURE OF GUILT IN FEMALES)
    aM-18 GUILT AFFECTIVE-STATES NEGATIVE SEX MORAL CONSCIENCE HOSTILITY 1968M

M-19   MOWRER, O.
        PSYCHOTHERAPY: THEORY AND RESEARCH.
        NEW YORK: RONALD, 1953.
        (DISCOMFORT-RELIEF QUOTIENT)*
    aM-19 MENTAL-ILLNESS TAT ADJUSTMENT THERAPY AFFECTIVE-STATES ANXIETY SUBJECTIVE
    aM-19 STRESS PROJECTIVE POSITIVE NEGATIVE 1953M

M-20   MURRAY, H. A.
        THEMATIC APPERCEPTION TEST MANUAL.
        CAMBRIDGE: HARVARD UNIVERSITY PRESS, 1943.
        (THEMATIC APPERCEPTION TEST)*
    aM-20 MULTITRAIT PROJECTIVE ADJUSTMENT 1943M TAT

```
(APPLICATIONS:     44     52     95    105    110    112    129    140    146    150
                  157    166    168    181    204    247           253    255    268
                  314    331    342    345    350    360    395    397    403    430
                  493    505    519    532    536    540    541    545    572    582
                  583    609    617    628    635    651    654    657    665    683
                  692    705    727    737    750    759    779    798    799    813
                  821    826    829    830    842    867    874    894    919    929
                  933    936    945    947    950    969   1004   1006   1018   1061
                 1079   1090   1093   1094   1133   1136   1138   1142   1168   1249
                 1252   1332   1408   1415   1452   1461   1507   1567   1576   1586
                 1596   1602   1648   1659   1661   1667   1673   1689   1717   1729
                 1774   1791   1804   1814   1821   1831   1871   1903   1910   1913
                 1968   1985   2008   2010   2015   2016   2021   2028   2031   2032
```

M-20   APPLICATIONS: cont. 2033 2087 2117 2141 2194 2238 2252 2255 2309
                              2316 2317 2321 2391 2401 2406 2426 2433 2482 2508
                              2534 2671 2676 2688 2867 2893 2908 2912 2913 2956
                              2963)

M-21   MURRAY, E. N., & BUSS, A. H.
            MEDIATED STIMULUS GENERALIZATION AND WORDS CONNOTING MOOD.
            JOURNAL OF ABNORMAL AND SOCIAL PSYCHOLOGY, 1963, 67, 586-593.
            (METHOD FOR SCALING WORDS ACCORDING TO INTENSITY OF MOOD)
         @M-21 MOOD INTENSITY AFFECTIVE-STATES OTHER-CATEGORY 1963M

M-22   MYERS, I. B.
            TYPE AS THE INDEX TO PERSONALITY.
            SWARTHMORE, PA.: AUTHOR, 1945.
         MYERS, I. B.
            MANUAL FOR THE MYERS-BRIGGS TYPE INDICATOR.
            PRINCETON, NEW JERSEY: EDUCATIONAL TESTING SERVICE, 1962.
            (MYERS-BRIGGS TYPE INDICATOR)*
            (COUNSELING EVALUATION INVENTORY)
         @M-22 PERSONAL PERSONALITY ORIENTATION TYPOLOGY MULTITRAIT THINKING EMOTION
         @M-22 EXTRAVERSION INTROVERSION JUDGMENT PERCEPTION 1945M
            (APPLICATIONS: 357   423   430   498   519   852 1236 1261 1269 1299
                            1358 1368 1384 1407 1421 1452 1492 1499 1526 1911
                            1933 2189 2336 2555 2584 2639 2912)

M-23   MALIVER, B. L.
            ANTI-NEGRO BIAS AMONG NEGRO COLLEGE STUDENTS.
            JOURNAL OF PERSONALITY AND SOCIAL PSYCHOLOGY, 1965, 2, 770-775.
            (MEASURE OF ANTI-NEGRO BIAS)
         @M-23 COLLEGE STUDENT PREJUDICE RACIAL NEGRO AFFECTIVE-STATES OTHER-CATEGORY
         @M-23 MINORITY GROUP ATTITUDE 1965M

M-24   MANDELL, E. E.
            CONSTRUCT VALIDATION OF A PSYCHOMETRIC MEASURE OF EXPECTANCY.
            UNPUBLISHED MASTER'S THESIS, UNIVERSITY OF COLORADO, 1959.
            (INVENTORY OF EXPECTATIONS)*
         @M-24 ACADEMIC AFFECTION AUTONOMY GOALS AFFILIATION SOCIAL NEED ADJUSTMENT
         @M-24 SELF-IDENTITY APPROVAL PUBLIC ESTEEM 1959M
            (APPLICATIONS: 129)

M-25   MANDLER, G., & COWEN, J. E.
            TEST ANXIETY QUESTIONNAIRES.
            JOURNAL OF CONSULTING PSYCHOLOGY, 1958, 22, 228-229.
            (HIGH SCHOOL FORM OF THE MANDLER-SARASON TAQ)
         @M-25 AFFECTIVE-STATES ANXIETY SUBJECTIVE STRESS TEST SECONDARY SCHOOL STUDENT
         @M-25 ADOLESCENT NEGATIVE 1958M
            (APPLICATIONS: 41   44   100   195)

M-26   MARLOWE, D., GERGEN, K. J., & DOOB, A. N.
            OPPONENT'S PERSONALITY, EXPECTATION OF SOCIAL INTERACTION, AND
            INTERPERSONAL BARGAINING.
            JOURNAL OF PERSONALITY AND SOCIAL PSYCHOLOGY, 1966, 3, 206-213.
            (SEMANTIC-DIFFERENTIAL PERSONALITY IMPRESSION QUESTIONNAIRE)
         @M-26 SEM-DIFFERENTIAL IMPRESSION OPPONENT ADJUSTMENT OTHER-CATEGORY SOCIAL
         @M-26 INTERACTION INTERPERSONAL PERSONALITY RATING 1966M

M-27   MCDONALD, R. L.
            EGO-CONTROL PATTERNS AND ATTRIBUTION OF HOSTILITY TO SELF AND OTHERS.
            JOURNAL OF PERSONALITY AND SOCIAL PSYCHOLOGY, 1965, 2, 273-277.
            (EXPRESSOR SCALE)
         @M-27 COPING-DEFENSE REPRESSION SENSITIZATION EGO CONTROL SELF EXPRESSIVENESS
         @M-27 EXPRESSION BEHAVIOR MMPI 1965M

M-28   MCGRATH, J. E., & JULIAN, J. W.
            NEGOTIATION AND CONFLICT: AN EXPERIMENTAL STUDY.
            TECHNICAL REPORT NO. 16, JULY 1962, UNIVERSITY OF ILLINOIS GROUP
            EFFECTIVENESS RESEARCH LABORATORY, U. S. PUBLIC HEALTH GRANT M1174 AND SGO
            CONTRACT MD2060.
            (BEHAVIORAL DESCRIPTION QUESTIONNAIRE)*
         @M-28 BEHAVIOR DESCRIPTION EVALUATION ADJUSTMENT INTERPERSONAL PERCEPTION RATING
         @M-28 1962M
            (APPLICATIONS: 42)

M-29   MEDNICK, S.
              AN ORIENTATION TO RESEARCH IN CREATIVITY.
              (RESEARCH MEMO NO. 2), BERKELEY, CALIF.: UNIVERSITY OF CALIFORNIA,
              INSTITUTE OF PERSONALITY ASSESSMENT AND RESEARCH, 1958.
          MEDNICK, S. A.
              THE ASSOCIATIVE BASIS OF THE CREATIVE PROCESS.
              PSYCHOLOGICAL REVIEW, 1962, 69, 220-232.
              (REMOTE ASSOCIATES TEST)*
          aM-29 CREATIVITY AUTONOMY COGNITIVE STRUCTURE FUNCTIONING CONCEPTUAL CONCEPT
          aM-29 FORMATION THINKING 1958M
              (APPLICATIONS: 171   208   217   239   249   269   411   794   873   907
                                946   1005   1355   1799   2253   2458   2528   2568   2645   2676
                               2767   2912   2976)

M-30   MULRY, R., & HOLLAND, C.
              THE DEVELOPMENT OF AN INSTRUMENT FOR THE MEASUREMENT OF REFLECTIVE EFFORT.
              (RESEARCH MEMORANDUM) PRINCETON, N. J.: EDUCATIONAL TESTING SERVICE, 1967.
              (REFLECTIVE EFFORT INDEX)*
          aM-30 1967M MOTIVE RESPONSE TIME REACTIVITY
              (APPLICATIONS: 2482)

M-31   MORRIS, J. L.
              PROPENSITY FOR RISK-TAKING AS A DETERMINANT OF VOCATIONAL CHOICE: AN
              EXTENSION OF THE THEORY OF ACHIEVEMENT MOTIVATION.
              JOURNAL OF PERSONALITY AND SOCIAL PSYCHOLOGY, 1966, 3, 328-335.
              (LEVEL OF DIFFICULTY SCALE)*
          aM-31 DECISION RISK-TAKING BEHAVIOR SUCCESS INTEREST VOCATIONAL NEED ACHIEVEMENT
          aM-31 AUTONOMY 1966M

M-32   MORRIS, C., & JONES, L. V.
              VALUE SCALES AND DIMENSIONS.
              JOURNAL OF ABNORMAL AND SOCIAL PSYCHOLOGY, 1955, 51, 523-535.
              ("WAYS TO LIVE" SCALE)*
          aM-32 VALUES SELF-IDENTITY IDEALS LIFE GOALS STYLE ORIENTATION 1955M DEVELOPMENT
              (APPLICATIONS: 210   1450   2056)

M-33   MUSSEN, P. H., & PARKER, A. L.
              MOTHER NURTURANCE AND GIRLS' INCIDENTAL IMITATIVE LEARNING.
              JOURNAL OF PERSONALITY AND SOCIAL PSYCHOLOGY, 1965, 2, 94-97.
              (TEACHER RATINGS OF DEPENDENCY IN CHILDREN)
          aM-33 DEPENDENCE AUTONOMY CHILD RATING TEACHER SCHOOL BEHAVIOR NEED APPROVAL
          aM-33 1965M

M-34   MADSEN, C. H., JR., & LONDON, P.
              ROLE PLAYING AND HYPNOTIC SUSCEPTIBILITY IN CHILDREN.
              JOURNAL OF PERSONALITY AND SOCIAL PSYCHOLOGY, 1966, 3, 13-19.
              (HYPNOTIC SIMULATION TEST)*
          aM-34 ENACTMENT ROLE HYPNOTIC SUGGESTIBILITY CHILD BEHAVIOR 1966M

M-35   MAHL, G. F.
              DISTURBANCES AND SILENCES IN PATIENT'S SPEECH IN PSYCHOTHERAPY.
              JOURNAL OF ABNORMAL AND SOCIAL PSYCHOLOGY, 1956, 53, 1-15.
              (SPEECH DISTURBANCE CATEGORIES)*
          aM-35 PATIENT DEFENSE ANXIETY VOICE RESPONSE COPING-DEFENSE SELF EXPRESSION
          aM-35 AFFECTIVE-STATES SUBJECTIVE STRESS 1956M
              (APPLICATIONS: 221   1017   1642   1650   1663   1758   2021   2141   2215   2403)

M-37   MYERS, T. I., JOHNSON, E., III, & SMITH, S.
              UNPUBLISHED RESEARCH, NAVAL MEDICAL RESEARCH INSTITUTE.
              (PRIMARY AFFECT SCALE)*
          aM-37 MOOD AFFECTIVE-STATES POSITIVE NEGATIVE FEAR DEPRESSION HAPPINESS GLOBAL
              (APPLICATIONS: 182)

M-38   MCKINLEY, J. C., & HATHAWAY, S. R.
              THE MMPI: V. HYSTERIA, HYPOMANIA AND PSYCHOPATHIC DEVIATE.
              JOURNAL OF APPLIED PSYCHOLOGY, 1944, 28, 153-174.
              (ALSO REPRINTED IN G. S. WELSH AND W. G. DAHLSTROM (EDS.) BASIC READINGS ON
              THE MMPI IN PSYCHOLOGY AND MEDICINE. MINNEAPOLIS: UNIVERSITY OF MINNESOTA
              PRESS, 1956).
              (PSYCHOPATHIC DEVIATE (PD) SCALE OF MMPI)
          aM-38 PSYCHOPATHY MENTAL-ILLNESS MENTAL-HEALTH MMPI 1944M

M-39   MORRIS, C. G., & HACKMAN, J. R.
                BEHAVIORAL CORRELATES OF PERCEIVED LEADERSHIP.
                JOURNAL OF PERSONALITY AND SOCIAL PSYCHOLOGY, 1969, 13, 350-361.
                (BEHAVIORAL DESCRIPTION QUESTIONNAIRE)*
            aM-39 LEADERSHIP BEHAVIOR DESCRIPTION PERCEIVED RATING GROUP INTERPERSONAL
            aM-39 RELATIONSHIPS 1969M

M-40   MORRISON, R. L.
                SELF-CONCEPT IMPLEMENTATION IN OCCUPATIONAL CHOICES.
                JOURNAL OF COUNSELING PSYCHOLOGY, 1962, 9, 255-260.
                (Q-SORT MEASURE OF SELF-CONCEPT)
            aM-40 VOCATIONAL INTEREST Q-SORT IMAGE SELF CONCEPT SELF-IDENTITY EVALUATION
            aM-40 PERCEPTION ESTEEM 1962M

M-41   MORMAN, R. R.
                TAV SELECTION SYSTEM.
                NORTH HOLLYWOOD, CALIFORNIA: JOHN P. SMITH PRESS, 1968.
                (TAV SELECTION SYSTEM)*
            aM-41 MULTITRAIT ADJUSTMENT SOCIAL COMPETENCE INTERPERSONAL INTERACTION OTHERS
            aM-41 ORIENTATION APPROACH AVOIDANCE 1968M
                (APPLICATIONS: 1511)

M-42   MOORE, B. M., & HOLTZMAN, W. H.
                WHAT TEXAS KNOWS ABOUT YOUTH.
                NATIONAL PARENT-TEACHER, 1958, 53, 22-24.
                (TEXAS COOPERATIVE YOUTH STUDY)*
            aM-42 PARENT-CHILD COMPETENCE RELATIONSHIPS INTERACTION MULTITRAIT FAMILY
            aM-42 ADJUSTMENT SOCIAL ORIENTATION ADOLESCENT 1958M
                (APPLICATIONS: 911)

M-43   MINNESOTA TESTS OF CREATIVE THINKING.
                NO REFERENCE AVAILABLE, (1959 OR 1960).
            aM-43 FUNCTIONING COGNITIVE STRUCTURE ATUONOMY CREATIVITY THINKING ORIGINALITY
                (APPLICATIONS: 286)

M-44   MARTUZA, V. R.
                AN INVESTIGATION OF THE EFFECTS OF STRATEGY AVAILABILITY, BANKROLL, AND SEX
                ON RISK-TAKING BEHAVIOR MEASURED IN A PSYCHOMETRIC CONTEXT.
                JOURNAL OF PERSONALITY, 1970, 38, 146-160.
                (PROGRESSIVE VOCABULARY INDEX)*
            aM-44 AUTONOMY RESPONSE STYLE RISK-TAKING PREFERENCE 1970M

M-45   MCGEE, H. M.
                MEASUREMENT OF AUTHORITARIANISM AND ITS RELATION TO TEACHERS' CLASSROOM
                BEHAVIOR.
                GENETIC PSYCHOLOGY MONOGRAPHS, 1955, 52, 89-146.
                (MCGEE REVISED F-SCALE)
            aM-45 COPING-DEFENSE AUTHORITARIANISM RIGIDITY F-SCALE TOLERANCE AMBIGUITY
            aM-45 THINKING PERCEPTION 1955M

M-46   MUSSEN, P. H., & NAYLOR, H. K.
                THE RELATIONSHIPS BETWEEN OVERT AND FANTASY AGGRESSION.
                JOURNAL OF ABNORMAL AND SOCIAL PSYCHOLOGY, 1954, 49, 235-240.
                (TAT SCORED FOR HOSTILITY)
            aM-46 PROJECTIVE TAT IMAGERY AUTHORITY AGGRESSION FANTASY HOSTILITY RESENTMENT
            aM-46 AFFECTIVE-STATES NEGATIVE 1954M

M-47   MCCLAIN, E. W.
                THE RELATIONSHIP BETWEEN STUDENT TEACHERS' SELF-REPORTED PERCEPTIONS AND
                PUPIL EVALUATIONS.
                UNPUBLISHED DOCTORAL DISSERTATION, UNIVERSITY OF TEXAS, 1961.
                (TAT SCORED FOR INTERPERSONAL AFFECT)
            aM-47 AUTONOMY AFFECTIVE-STATES COPING-DEFENSE INTERPERSONAL APPROACH AVOIDANCE
            aM-47 AFFILIATION MOTIVE EMOTION TAT PROJECTIVE 1961M RELATIONSHIPS IMAGERY
                (APPLICATIONS: 20   27   68   84   113   235   257   285   360   734
                            735 2374)

M-48   MARSHALL, S.
                PERSONALITY CORRELATES OF PEPTIC ULCER PATIENTS.
                JOURNAL OF CONSULTING PSYCHOLOGY, 1960, 24, 218-223.
                (PEPTIC ULCER INDEX)*
            aM-48 DOMINANCE AGGRESSION RESPONSIBILITY MORAL VALUES CONFORMITY AUTONOMY IDEAL
            aM-48 IMAGE EMOTION SELF-IDENTITY PERCEPTION EVALUATION GLOBAL ADJUSTMENT 1960M

M-49   MACKINNEY, A. C.
        THE LONGITUDINAL STUDY OF MANAGER PERFORMANCE: PHASE I VARIABLES.
        UNPUBLISHED MANUSCRIPT. AMES: IOWA STATE UNIVERSITY OF SCIENCE AND
        TECHNOLOGY, DEPARTMENT OF PSYCHOLOGY, 1967.
        (QUESTIONNAIRE MEASURE OF JOB SATISFACTION)
        @M-49 1967M JOB SATISFACTION PE-FIT SUPERVISOR PERFORMANCE
        (APPLICATIONS: 2366)

M-50   MASLOW, A. H., HIRSH, E., STEIN, M., & HONIGMANN, I.
        A CLINICALLY DERIVED TEST FOR MEASURING PSYCHOLOGICAL SECURITY-INSECURITY.
        JOURNAL OF GENERAL PSYCHOLOGY, 1945, 33, 21-41.
        MASLOW, A. H.
        MANUAL FOR THE SECURITY-INSECURITY INVENTORY.
        STANFORD, CALIFORNIA: STANFORD UNIVERSITY PRESS, 1952.
        (SECURITY-INSECURITY INVENTORY)*
        @M-50 ADJUSTMENT SECURITY GLOBAL AFFECTIVE-STATES AUTONOMY NEED 1945M
        @ANXIETY
        (APPLICATIONS: 514 1321 1589 1807 1902 2828 2874)

M-51   MATSUSHIMA, J.
        A COMPARISON OF ADULT AND PEER AUTHORITY IN THE CONTROL OF IMPULSIVITY
        AMONG BOYS.
        UNPUBLISHED DOCTORAL DISSERTATION, WESTERN RESERVE UNIVERSITY, 1963.
        (IMPULSE CONTROL CATEGORIZATION INSTRUMENT)*
        @M-51 ADJUSTMENT SELF IMPULSE CONTROL OTHER-CATEGORY AUTONOMY LOCUS IE-CONTROL
        @M-51 EXPRESSION AGGRESSION BEHAVIOR 1963M
        (APPLICATIONS: 1842)

M-52   MITCHELL, K. R.
        REPEATED MEASURES AND THE EVALUATION OF CHANGE IN THE INDIVIDUAL CLIENT
        DURING COUNSELING.
        JOURNAL OF COUNSELING PSYCHOLOGY, 1969, 16, 522-527.
        (QUESTIONNAIRE TECHNIQUE FOR MEASURING CHANGE DUE TO COUNSELING)
        @M-52 COUNSELING EVALUATION ADJUSTMENT PATIENT RELATIONSHIPS PSYCHIATRIC GLOBAL
        @M-52 THERAPY SUCCESS AFFECTIVE-STATES DEPRESSION CHANGE 1969M

M-53   MYERS, T. I., MURPHY, D. B., SMITH, S., & GOFFARD, S. J.
        EXPERIMENTAL STUDIES OF SENSORY DEPRIVATION AND SOCIAL ISOLATION.
        UNPUBLISHED MANUSCRIPT.
        (MEASURE OF OVERALL MOOD)
        @M-53 CHECKLIST GLOBAL STATE MOOD AFFECTIVE-STATES OTHER-CATEGORY
        (APPLICATIONS: 1009 1076 1096 1132)

M-54   MCCLELLAND, D. C., & WATT, N. F.
        SEX-ROLE ALIENATION IN SCHIZOPHRENIA.
        JOURNAL OF ABNORMAL PSYCHOLOGY, 1968, 73, 226-239.
        (MEASURE OF SEX-ROLE DIFFERENCES IN ATTITUDES, INTERESTS AND OPINIONS)
        @M-54 DIFFERENCES ATTITUDE INTEREST OPINION MASCULINITY FEMININITY ALIENATION
        @M-54 SEX IDENTITY MMPI SELF-IDENTITY SUB-IDENTITY ROLE PERCEPTION 1968M

M-55   MAY, R.
        SEX DIFFERENCES IN FANTASY PATTERNS.
        JOURNAL OF PROJECTIVE TECHNIQUES, 1966, 30, 576-586.
        (TAT SCORED FOR DEPRIVATION/ENHANCEMENT)
        @M-55 DEPRIVATION ENHANCEMENT MASCULINITY FEMININITY TAT FANTASY SELF-IDENTITY
        @M-55 SUB-IDENTITY ROLE PERCEPTION IMAGERY PROJECTIVE SEX DIFFERENCES 1966M
        (APPLICATIONS: 1079)

M-56   MINER, J. B.
        THE KUDER PREFERENCE RECORD IN MANAGEMENT APPRAISAL.
        PERSONNEL PSYCHOLOGY, 1960, 13, 187-196.
        (MEASURE OF INTEREST IN DIRECTING ACTIVITIES OF OTHERS)
        @M-56 MACHIAVELLIANISM SUPERVISOR PREFERENCE MANAGEMENT INTEREST JOB ADJUSTMENT
        @M-56 LEADERSHIP ACTIVITIES DECISION INTERPERSONAL RELATIONSHIPS INTERACTION
        @M-56 1960M

M-57   MADDI, S. R.
        AFFECTIVE TONE DURING ENVIRONMENTAL REGULARITY AND CHANGE.
        JOURNAL OF ABNORMAL AND SOCIAL PSYCHOLOGY, 1961, 62, 338-345.
        (MEASURE OF AFFECTIVE TONE)
        @M-57 GLOBAL INTENSITY ORIENTATION AFFECTIVE-STATES OTHER-CATEGORY 1961M

M-58   MACHOVER, K.
              PERSONALITY PROJECTION.
              SPRINGFIELD, ILLINOIS: CHARLES C. THOMAS, 1950.
              (DRAW-A-PERSON TEST)*
         @M-58 IMAGE CONCEPT SELF-IDENTITY SELF IDEAL MULTITRAIT PROJECTIVE ADJUSTMENT
         @M-58 DESCRIPTION 1950M
              (APPLICATIONS: 83   381   416   869   939   1035   1094   1126   1450   1617
                              1623   1629   1666   1701   1710   1711   1869   1871   1876   1877
                              1879   1901   1958   1974   1980   2046   2070   2130   2257   2258
                              2374   2734   2893   2953)

M-59   MOULTON, R. W., BURNSTEIN, E., LIBERTY, P. G., JR., & ALTUCHER, N.
              PATTERNING OF PARENTAL AFFECTION AND DISCIPLINARY DOMINANCE AS A
              DETERMINANT OF GUILT AND SEX TYPING.
              JOURNAL OF PERSONALITY AND SOCIAL PSYCHOLOGY, 1966, 4, 356-363.
              (MEASURE OF GUILT FEELINGS)
         @M-59 GUILT AFFECTIVE-STATES NEGATIVE 1966M

M-60   MOULTON, R. W., BURNSTEIN, E., LIBERTY, P. G., JR., & ALTUCHER, N.
              PATTERNING OF PARENTAL AFFECTION AND DISCIPLINARY DOMINANCE AS A
              DETERMINANT OF GUILT AND SEX TYPING.
              JOURNAL OF PERSONALITY AND SOCIAL PSYCHOLOGY, 1966, 4, 356-363.
              (INDEX OF PARENTAL RESPONSE TO REQUESTS FOR POSITIVE INTERACTION)
         @M-60 PARENT-CHILD INTERACTION PARENTAL AFFECTION FAMILY ADJUSTMENT 1966M

M-61   MOULTON, R. W., BURNSTEIN, E., LIBERTY, P. G., JR., & ALTUCHER, N.
              PATTERNING OF PARENTAL AFFECTION AND DISCIPLINARY DOMINANCE AS A
              DETERMINANT OF GUILT AND SEX TYPING.
              JOURNAL OF PERSONALITY AND SOCIAL PSYCHOLOGY, 1966, 4, 356-363.
              (MEASURE OF PARENTAL DOMINANCE IN DISCIPLINE)
         @M-61 PARENTAL DOMINANCE FAMILY INTERACTION ADJUSTMENT PARENT-CHILD 1966M

M-62   MCFARLAND, R. A., & SEITZ, C. P.
              A PSYCHO-SOMATIC INVENTORY.
              JOURNAL OF APPLIED PSYCHOLOGY, 1938, 22, 327-339.
              (PSYCHOSOMATIC INVENTORY)*
         @M-62 NEUROTICISM STATE PROBLEM PSYCHOSOMATIC GLOBAL ADJUSTMENT DIAGNOSIS
         @M-62 MENTAL-ILLNESS ILLNESS 1938M

M-63   A FORCED-CHOICE TEST OF ACHIEVEMENT MOTIVATION.
              JOURNAL OF THE INDIAN ACADEMY OF APPLIED PSYCHOLOGY, 1965, 2, 85-92.
              (MUKHERJEE SENTENCE COMPLETION TEST)*
         @M-63 ACHIEVEMENT MOTIVE NEED AUTONOMY ORIENTATION 1965M

M-64   MOSHER, D. L.
              THE DEVELOPMENT AND MULTITRAIT-MULTIMETHOD MATRIX ANALYSIS OF THREE
              ASPECTS OF GUILT.
              JOURNAL OF CONSULTING PSYCHOLOGY, 1966, 30, 25-29.
              (FORCED-CHOICE GUILT INVENTORY)*
         @M-64 GUILT HOSTILITY AFFECTIVE-STATES NEGATIVE MORAL SEX CONSCIENCE 1966M
              (APPLICATIONS: 230   1028   1979   2181   2184   2612   2735   2743   2916)

M-66   MCREYNOLDS, P., & FERGUSON, J. T.
              CLINICAL MANUAL FOR THE HOSPITAL ADJUSTMENT SCALE.
              PALO ALTO: CONSULTING PSYCHOLOGISTS PRESS, 1946.
              (PALO ALTO HOSPITAL ADJUSTMENT SCALE)*
         @M-66 ADJUSTMENT PATIENT HOSPITALIZATION WARD MENTAL-HEALTH MENTAL-ILLNESS
         @M-66 THERAPY RELATIONSHIPS PSYCHIATRIC 1946M
              (APPLICATIONS: 1024   1958   2734   2922)

M-67   MASON, R. E.
              INTERNAL PERCEPTION AND BODILY FUNCTIONING.
              NEW YORK: INTERNATIONAL UNIVERSITY PRESS, 1961.
              (SELF-RATING INVENTORY OF INTERNAL PERCEPTION AND BODILY FUNCTIONING)
         @M-67 SELF CONCEPT SELF-IDENTITY PERCEPTION ESTEEM EVALUATION BODY PERSONALITY
         @M-67 FUNCTIONING RATING 1961M

M-68   MACDONALD, A. P., JR., & AL, J.
              PERCEPTION OF DISABILITY BY THE NONDISABLED.
              JOURNAL OF CONSULTING AND CLINICAL PSYCHOLOGY, 1969, 33, 654-660.
              (DISABILITY SCALE)
         @M-68 PERSONAL EMOTION PHYSICAL ADJUSTMENT SOCIAL PERCEPTION DISABILITY
         @M-68 SELF-IDENTITY BODY IMAGE ATTITUDE PERCEIVED 1969M

M-69   MENGES, R. J.
             STUDENT-INSTRUCTOR COGNITIVE COMPATIBILITY IN THE LARGE LECTURE CLASS: AN
             EXPLORATORY STUDY.
             UNPUBLISHED DOCTORAL DISSERTATION. TEACHERS COLLEGE, COLUMBIA UNIVERSITY.
             ANN ARBOR, MICHIGAN: UNIVERSITY MICROFILMS, 1967, NO. 67-12, 699.
             (COGNITIVE STRUCTURE QUESTIONNAIRE)*
         @M-69 COGNITIVE STRUCTURE FUNCTIONING COMPATIBILITY 1967M

M-70   MALINOVSKY, M. R., & BARRY, J. R.
             DETERMINANTS OF WORK ATTITUDES.
             JOURNAL OF APPLIED PSYCHOLOGY, 1965, 49, 446-451.
             (WORK ATTITUDE SURVEY)*
         @M-70 SUPERVISOR EMPLOYEE ENVIRONMENT PE-FIT ATTITUDE JOB-HYGIENE JOB GLOBAL
         @M-70 SATISFACTION ADJUSTMENT AFFECTIVE-STATES 1965M
             (APPLICATIONS: 2358)

M-71   MARK, J. C.
             THE ATTITUDES OF THE MOTHERS OF MALE SCHIZOPHRENICS TOWARD CHILD BEHAVIOR.
             JOURNAL OF ABNORMAL AND SOCIAL PSYCHOLOGY, 1953, 48, 185-189.
             (MEASURE OF ATTITUDE TOWARD CHILD-REARING)
         @M-71 ADJUSTMENT FAMILY PARENT-CHILD MATERNAL ATTITUDE BEHAVIOR SCHIZOPHRENIA
         @M-71 1953M

M-72   MALTZMAN, I.
             ON THE TRAINING OF ORIGINALITY.
             PSYCHOLOGICAL REVIEW, 1960, 67, 229-242.
             (FREE ASSOCIATION TEST FOR MEASURING ORIGINALITY)
         @M-72 AUTONOMY ORIGINALITY CREATIVITY 1960M
             (APPLICATIONS: 1355)

M-73   MORGAN, C. T.
             STUDENTS' WORKBOOK.
             NEW YORK: MCGRAW-HILL, 1956.
             (MODIFICATION OF BOGARDUS SOCIAL DISTANCE SCALE)
         @M-73 INTERPERSONAL ATTITUDE RELATIONSHIPS SOCIAL DISTANCE AFFECTIVE-STATES
         @M-73 OTHER-CATEGORY 1956M

M-74   MANN, D., COHEN, M., ENGELHARDT, D. M., FREEDMAN, N., & MARGOLIS, R. A.
             A METHOD FOR MEASURING SOCIAL BEHAVIOR OF PSYCHIATRIC OUTPATIENTS.
             PSYCHOLOGICAL REPORTS, 1966, 18, 371-378.
             (CODING SYSTEM TO CHARACTERIZE PATIENTS' BEHAVIOR FROM REPORTS OF
             RELATIVES)
         @M-74 MENTAL-ILLNESS MENTAL-HEALTH DESCRIPTION SOCIAL COMPETENCE BEHAVIOR TRAIT
         @M-74 ADJUSTMENT AFFILIATION HOSTILITY AGGRESSION PSYCHIATRIC PATIENT ILLNESS
         @M-74 RATING 1966M

M-75   MILLER, L. C.
             LOUISVILLE BEHAVIOR CHECK LIST FOR MALES, 6-12 YEARS OF AGE.
             PSYCHOLOGICAL REPORTS, 1967, 21, 885-896.
             (LOUISVILLE BEHAVIOR CHECK LIST)*
         @M-75 CHECKLIST BEHAVIOR CHILD EMOTION GLOBAL ADJUSTMENT MENTAL-ILLNESS
         @M-75 PSYCHIATRIC DIAGNOSIS 1967M

M-77   MCGUIRE, C.
             MODELS FOR Q REPRESENTATION OF SAMPLE POPULATIONS.
             RESEARCH MEMO NO. 7, LABORATORY OF HUMAN BEHAVIOR, DEPARTMENT OF
             EDUCATIONAL PSYCHOLOGY, THE UNIVERSITY OF TEXAS, APRIL, 1957.
             (MCGUIRE Q-CHECK)*
         @M-77 ROLE SOCIAL COMPETENCE AUTHORITY REALITY MENTAL-HEALTH SELF-IDENTITY
         @M-77 MULTITRAIT EVALUATION SELF PERCEPTION ESTEEM DESCRIPTION IMAGE CONCEPT
         @M-77 ORIENTATION INTERPERSONAL 1957M Q-SORT

M-78   MCGUIRE, C.
             THE TEXTOWN STUDY OF ADOLESCENCE.
             TEXAS JOURNAL OF SCIENCE, 1956, 8, 264-274.
             (SOCIOMETRIC PEER RATINGS)
         @M-78 SOCIAL EFFECTIVENESS ACCEPTANCE ADOLESCENT MULTITRAIT PEER RATING
         @M-78 SOCIOMETRIC BEHAVIOR DEPENDENCE 1956M

M-79   MAYO, G. D., & MANNING, W. H.
                MOTIVATION MEASUREMENT.
                EDUCATIONAL AND PSYCHOLOGICAL MEASUREMENT, 1961, 21, 73-83.
                (PROJECTIVE MEASURE OF ACHIEVEMENT MOTIVATION)
            aM-79 AUTONOMY NEED MOTIVE ACHIEVEMENT IMAGERY PROJECTIVE 1961M

M-80   MURAWSKI, B., SAPIR, P., SHULMAN, N., RYAN, G., & STURGIS, S.
                AN INVESTIGATION OF MOOD STATES IN WOMEN TAKING ORAL CONTRACEPTIVES.
                FERTILITY AND STERILITY, 1968, 19, 50-63.
                (MIRROR PICTURE TEST)*
            aM-80 MOOD STATE DEPRESSION AFFECTIVE-STATES NEGATIVE 1968M CHANGE

M-81   MCGURK, E.
                SUSCEPTIBILITY TO VISUAL ILLUSIONS.
                JOURNAL OF PSYCHOLOGY, 1965, 61, 127-143.
                (SELF-RATING SHEET)
            aM-81 PERCEPTION LEADERSHIP ABILITY COMMUNICATION ESTEEM AUTONOMY DOMINANCE
            aM-81 MULTITRAIT RATING SELF DESCRIPTION EVALUATION DEPENDENCE JUDGMENT DRIVE
            aM-81 INTELLIGENCE 1965M

M-83   MAHER, H.
                CONSTRUCTION OF A FORCED-CHOICE COOPERATION TEST AND AN INVESTIGATION OF
                MATCHING INDICES OF POTENTIAL VALUE TO FORCED-CHOICE QUESTIONNAIRES.
                UNDATED PUBLICATION, IOWA STATE COLLEGE, AMES, IOWA.
                (COOPERATION SCALE)*
            aM-83 COOPERATION DESCRIPTION SELF CONCEPT IDEAL IMAGE EVALUATION SELF-IDENTITY
            aM-83 PERCEPTION ESTEEM LEADERSHIP INTERPERSONAL INTERACTION ADJUSTMENT

M-84   MOORE, J. V.
                FACTOR ANALYTIC COMPARISON OF SUPERIOR AND SUBORDINATE RATINGS OF THE SAME
                NCO SUPERVISORS.
                TECHNILOGICAL REPORT NO. 53-24, HUMAN RESOURCES RESEARCH CENTER, RANDOLPH
                AIR FORCE BASE, SAN ANTONIO, TEXAS, 1953.
                (LEADERSHIP ORIENTATION SCALE)*
            aM-84 LEADERSHIP ORIENTATION ADJUSTMENT JOB SUPERVISOR MANAGEMENT STYLE 1953M

M-85   MEYER, H. H., & WALKER, W. B.
                NEED FOR ACHIEVEMENT AND RISK PREFERENCES AS THEY RELATE TO ATTITUDES
                TOWARD REWARD SYSTEMS AND PERFORMANCE APPRAISAL IN AN INDUSTRIAL SETTING.
                JOURNAL OF APPLIED PSYCHOLOGY, 1961, 45, 251-256.
                (RISK PREFERENCE QUESTIONNAIRE)*
            aM-85 RISK-TAKING PREFERENCE COPING-DEFENSE APPROACH AVOIDANCE NEED ACHIEVEMENT
            aM-85 AUTONOMY PERFORMANCE JOB 1961M

M-86   MOSHER, D. L.
                MEASUREMENT OF GUILT IN FEMALES BY SELF-REPORT INVENTORIES.
                JOURNAL OF CONSULTING AND CLINICAL PSYCHOLOGY, 1968, 32, 690-695.
                (FORCED-CHOICE MEASURE OF GUILT IN FEMALES)
            aM-86 GUILT AFFECTIVE-STATES NEGATIVE SEX MORAL CONSCIENCE HOSTILITY 1968M
                (APPLICATIONS: 2287)

M-87·   MORRIS, J. L.
                PROPENSITY FOR RISK-TAKING AS A DETERMINANT OF VOCATIONAL CHOICE: AN
                EXTENSION OF THE THEORY OF ACHIEVEMENT MOTIVATION.
                JOURNAL OF PERSONALITY AND SOCIAL PSYCHOLOGY, 1966, 3, 328-335.
                (PROBABILITY OF SUCCESS SCALE)*
            aM-87 SUCCESS PREDICTION VOCATIONAL ACHIEVEMENT MOTIVE AUTONOMY 1966M

M-89   MCQUARY, J. P., & TRUAX, W. E., JR.
                AN UNDERACHIEVEMENT SCALE.
                JOURNAL OF EDUCATIONAL RESEARCH, 1955, 48, 393-399.
                (UNDERACHIEVEMENT SCALE FROM MMPI)
            aM-89 1955M MMPI ACHIEVEMENT NEED AUTONOMY MOTIVE ORIENTATION
                (APPLICATIONS: 2386)

M-93   MASUDA, M., MATSUMOTO, G. H., & MEREDITH, G. M.
                ETHNIC IDENTITY IN THREE GENERATIONS OF JAPANESE AMERICANS.
                JOURNAL OF SOCIAL PSYCHOLOGY, 1970, 81, 199-207.
                (ETHNIC IDENTITY QUESTIONNAIRE)
            aM-93 1970M ETHNIC IDENTITY TIME SELF-IDENTITY SUB-IDENTITY

M-94   MYERS, T. I., MURPHY, D. B., & TERRY, D. F.
              THE ROLE OF EXPECTANCY IN SUBJECTS' RESPONSES TO SUSTAINED SENSORY
              DEPRIVATION.
              PAPER READ AT AMERICAN PSYCHOLOGICAL ASSOCIATION, ST. LOUIS,
              SEPTEMBER, 1962.
         MYERS, T. I., MURPHY, D. B., SMITH, S., & GOFFARD, J.
              EXPERIMENTAL STUDIES OF SENSORY DEPRIVATION AND SOCIAL ISOLATION.
              (HUM RRO TECHNICAL REPORTS, 66-88.)
              WASHINGTON, D. C.: GEORGE WASHINGTON UNIVERSITY, HUMAN RESOURCES RESEARCH
              OFFICE, JUNE 1966.
              (ISOLATION SYMPTOM QUESTIONNAIRE)
         @M-94 1962M AFFECTIVE-STATES SUBJECTIVE STRESS DEPRIVATION SOCIAL SENSORY
              (APPLICATIONS: 1030   1064   1132   2430)

M-97   MEHRABIAN, A.
              THE DEVELOPMENT AND VALIDATION OF MEASURES OF AFFILIATIVE TENDENCY AND
              SENSITIVITY TO REJECTION,
              EDUCATIONAL AND PSYCHOLOGICAL MEASUREMENT, 1970, 30, 417-428.
              (MEASURE OF SENSITIVITY TO REJECTION)
         @M-97 1970M NEED AFFILIATION AUTONOMY SENSITIVITY SUPPORT

M-98   MEHRABIAN, A.
              THE DEVELOPMENT AND VALIDATION OF MEASURES OF AFFILIATIVE TENDENCY AND
              SENSITIVITY TO REJECTION,
              EDUCATIONAL AND PSYCHOLOGICAL MEASUREMENT, 1970, 30, 417-428.
              (MEASURE OF AFFILIATIVE TENDENCY)
         @M-98 1970M NEED AFFILIATION AUTONOMY SUPPORT SENSITIVITY

M-99   MIDDLETON, W. C.
              SOME REACTIONS TOWARD DEATH AMONG COLLEGE STUDENTS.
              JOURNAL OF ABNORMAL AND SOCIAL PSYCHOLOGY, 1936, 31, 165-173.
              (MEASURE OF ATTITUDES TOWARD DEATH)
         @M-99 1936M FEAR DEATH AFFECTIVE-STATES ATTITUDE
              (APPLICATIONS: 1056)

M-100   MUSSEN, P. H.
              DIFFERENCES BETWEEN THE TAT RESPONSES OF NEGRO AND WHITE BOYS.
              JOURNAL OF CONSULTING PSYCHOLOGY, 1953, 17, 373-376.
              (SYSTEM OF NEEDS/PRESSES FOR SCORING TAT)
         @M-100 1953M TAT IMAGERY NEED STRUCTURE PROJECTIVE PRESS
              (APPLICATIONS: 2688)

M-101   MADDI, S. R.
              MOTIVATIONAL ASPECTS OF CREATIVITY
              JOURNAL OF PERSONALITY, 1965, 33, 330-347.
              (SIMILES PREFERENCE TEST)*
         @M-101 1965M CREATIVITY ORIGINALITY AUTONOMY
              (APPLICATIONS: 414   532   2912)

M-102   MCDONALD, S. L.
              ALTRUISM: A STUDY IN MEANS AND ENDS.
              UNPUBLISHED HONORS THESIS, HARVARD UNIVERSITY, APRIL 1966.
              (RATING-SCALE MEASURE OF ALTRUISM)
         @M-102 1966M ALTRUISM SOCIAL RESPONSIBILITY MORAL DEVELOPMENT INTERPERSONAL
         @M-102 RELATIONSHIPS
              (APPLICATIONS: 2903)

M-103   MILLER, A. R., WOO-SAM, J., ZAVOS, H., & BARKER, B.
              AN OBJECTIVE MEASURE OF INDUCED AGGRESSION.
              PSYCHOLOGICAL REPORTS, 1970, 26, 11-14.
              (OBJECTIVE MEASURE OF INDUCED AGGRESSION)
         @M-103 1970M AGGRESSION HOSTILITY

M-105   MCQUITTY, L. L., ABELES, N., & CLARK, J. A.
              A STUDY OF THE RELIABILITY OF INTRA-INDIVIDUAL PERSONALITY STRUCTURE
              BY ITERATIVE, INTERCOLUMNAR CORRELATIONAL ANALYSIS.
              MULTIVARIATE BEHAVIORAL RESEARCH, 1970, 5, 159-175.
              (MEASURE OF PSYCHOLOGICAL WELL-BEING)
         @M-105 1970M WELL-BEING EMOTION CONCEPT CONTROL SELF ACHIEVEMENT DEPENDENCE
         @M-105 RELIGION AFFECTIVE-STATES ANGER ANXIETY DEPRESSION

M-106   MAEHR, M. L., MENSING, J., & NAFZGER, S.
        CONCEPT OF SELF AND THE REACTION OF OTHERS.
        SOCIOMETRY, 1962, 25, 353-357.
    LUDWIG, D., & MAEHR, M.
        CHANGES IN SELF CONCEPT AND STATED BEHAVIORAL PREFERENCES.
        CHILD DEVELOPMENT, 1967, 38, 453-467.
        (PHYSICAL-SELF TEST)
    @M-106 1962M SELF-IDENTITY SELF BODY IMAGE CONCEPT PHYSICAL
        (APPLICATIONS: 2820)

M-107   MILLER, G. W.
        FACTORS IN SCHOOL ACHIEVEMENT AND SOCIAL CLASS.
        JOURNAL OF EDUCATIONAL PSYCHOLOGY, 1970, 61, 260-269.
        (MEASURE OF CHILDREN'S PERCEPTION OF ENVIRONMENT)
    @M-107 1970M SCHOOL ENVIRONMENT CHILD ADJUSTMENT PERCEPTION ACHIEVEMENT SOCIAL

M-108   MARKS, E.
        INDIVIDUAL DIFFERENCES IN PERCEPTIONS OF THE COLLEGE ENVIRONMENT)
        JOURNAL OF EDUCATIONAL PSYCHOLOGY, 1970, 61, 270-279.
        (MEASURE OF PERCEIVED COLLEGE ENVIRONMENT)
    @M-108 1970M PE-FIT COLLEGE ENVIRONMENT PERCEPTION

M-109   MITCHELL, V. F.
        THE RELATIONSHIP OF EFFORT, ABILITIES AND ROLE PERCEPTIONS TO MANAGERIAL
        PERFORMANCE.
        UNPUBLISHED DOCTORAL DISSERTATION, UNIVERSITY OF CALIFORNIA, BERKELEY, 1966
        (MEASURE OF EFFORT ON JOB PERFORMANCE)
    @M-109 1966M JOB PERFORMANCE EMPLOYEE
        (APPLICATIONS: 2468)

M-110   MILES, R. E.
        CONFLICTING ELEMENTS IN MANAGERIAL IDEOLOGIES.
        INDUSTRIAL RELATIONS, 1964, 4, 77-91.
        (MEASURE OF ATTITUDE OF SUPERIOR TO SUBORDINATE'S CAPABILITIES)
    @M-110 1964M MANAGEMENT EMPLOYEE ATTITUDE JOB LEADERSHIP
    @M-110 ABILITY PERFORMANCE EVALUATION
        (APPLICATIONS: 2469)

M-111   MACKAY, C. K., & BROWN, W. P.
        METAPHOR PREFERENCE VS. SEMANTIC RATINGS AS MEASURES OF ATTITUDES TOWARD
        TIME.
        JOURNAL OF GENERAL PSYCHOLOGY, 1970, 83, 207-212.
        (MEASURE OF ATTITUDES TOWARD TIME)
    @M-111 1970M ORIENTATION TIME ATTITUDE RATING FUTURE PAST

M-112   MISKIMINS, R. W., & SIMMONS, W. L.
        GOAL PREFERENCE AS A VARIABLE IN INVOLUTIONAL PSYCHOSIS.
        JOURNAL OF CONSULTING PSYCHOLOGY, 1966, 30, 73-77.
    MISKIMINS, R. W.
        THE CONCEPT OF SELF AND PSYCHOPATHOLOGY.
        (DOCTORAL DISSERTATION, UNIVERSITY OF COLORADO) ANN ARBOR, MICHIGAN:
        UNIVERSITY MICROFILMS, 1967, NO.67-422.
        (SELF-GOAL-OTHER DISCREPANCY SCALE)*
    @M-112 1966M SELF DISCREPANCY OTHERS IDEAL PATIENT
        (APPLICATIONS: 2308 2948)

M-113   MESSICK, S., & KOGAN, N.
        PERSONALITY CONSISTENCIES IN JUDGMENT: DIMENSIONS OF ROLE CONSTRUCTS.
        MULTIVARIATE BEHAVIORAL RESEARCH, 1966, 1, 165-175.
    MESSICK, S., & KOGAN, N.
        CATEGORIZING STYLES AND COGNITIVE STRUCTURE.
        PRINCETON, N.J.: EDUCATIONAL TESTING SERVICE, RESEARCH BULLETIN (IN
        PREPARATION IN 1966).
        (SCALE OF JUDGMENTS OF ROLE SIMILARITIES AND DIFFERENCES)
    @M-113 1966M JUDGMENT ROLE SIMILARITY FIGURE STIMULUS INTERPERSONAL FUNCTIONING
    @DIFFERENCES

M-114   MESSICK, S., & KOGAN, N.
        DIFFERENTIATION AND COMPARTMENTALIZATION IN OBJECT-SORTING MEASURES OF
        CATEGORIZING STYLE.
        PERCEPTUAL AND MOTOR SKILLS, 1963, 16, 47-51.
        (MEASURE OF CATEGORIZING PREFERENCES)
    @M114 1963M PREFERENCE STYLE COGNITIVE STRUCTURE THINKING ORGANIZATION
    @STIMULUS PERCEPTION RELATIONSHIPS

M-120   MATTESON, R. W.
             SELF-ESTIMATES OF COLLEGE FRESHMEN.
             PERSONNEL GUIDANCE JOURNAL, 1956, 34, 280-284.
         MATTESON, R. W.
             SELF-PERCEPTIONS OF STUDENTS SEEKING COUNSELING.
             PERSONNEL GUIDANCE JOURNAL, 1958, 36, 545-548.
             (SELF-EVALUATION SCALE)
         aM-120 1956M SELF EVALUATION ASPIRATION OTHERS PERCEPTION FUTURE
         aIDEAL DISCREPANCY ESTEEM
             (APPLICATIONS: 1206)

M-121   MICHAEL, W. B., MICHAEL, J. J., & ZIMMERMAN, W. S.
             STUDY ATTITUDES AND METHODS SURVEY, (EXPERIMENTAL FORM).
             SAN DIEGO: EDUCATIONAL AND.INDUSTRIAL TESTING SERVICE, 1969.
         ZIMMERMAN, W. S., MICHAEL, J. J., & MICHAEL, W. B.
             THE FACTORED DIMENSIONS OF THE STUDY ATTITUDES AND METHODS SURVEY TEST -
             EXPERIMENTAL FORM.
             EDUCATIONAL AND PSYCHOLOGICAL MEASUREMENT, 1970, 30, 433-436.
             (STUDY ATTITUDES AND METHODS SURVEY)*
         aM-121 1969M STUDENT ATTITUDE BEHAVIOR COLLEGE SCHOOL
         aM-121 INTELLECTUAL

M-123   MURRAY, H. A.
             EXPLORATIONS IN PERSONALITY.
             NEW YORK: OXFORD UNIVERSITY PRESS, 1938.
             (MURRAY AFFILIATION QUESTIONNAIRE)
         aM-123 1938M AFFILIATION APPROACH MOTIVE NEED INTERPERSONAL RELATIONSHIPS
             (APPLICATIONS: 360)

M-124   MADDI, S. R., & ANDREWS, S. L.
             THE NEED FOR VARIETY IN FANTASY AND SELF DESCRIPTION.
             JOURNAL OF PERSONALITY, 1966, 34, 610-625.
             (EXTEROCEPTION QUESTIONNAIRE)
         aM-124 1966M PERSONAL ORIENTATION EXPERIENCE LIFE STYLE
         aM-124 EXTERNAL
             (APPLICATIONS: 2015)

M-125   MARCIA, J. E.
             DETERMINATION AND CONSTRUCT VALIDITY OF EGO IDENTITY STATUS.
             UNPUBLISHED DOCTORAL DISSERTATION, OHIO STATE UNIVERSITY, 1964.
         MARCIA, J. E.
             DEVELOPMENT AND VALIDATION OF EGO IDENTITY STATUS.
             JOURNAL OF PERSONALITY AND SOCIAL PSYCHOLOGY, 1966, 3, 551-558.
             (INTERVIEW MEASURE OF EGO IDENTITY STATUS)
         aM-125 1964M EGO IDENTITY SELF-IDENTITY IDIOLOGY ADJUSTMENT INTERVIEW
             (APPLICATIONS: 464)

M-126   MADDI, S. R., PROPST, B. S., & FELDINGER, I.
             THREE EXPRESSIONS OF THE NEED FOR VARIETY.
             JOURNAL OF PERSONALITY, 1965, 33, 82-98.
             (MEASURE OF COMPLEXITY OF PRODUCTIONS)
         aM-126 1965M COGNITIVE COMPLEXITY GRAPHIC FIGURE NEED VARIETY

M-127   MADDI, S. R., PROPST, B. S., & FELDINGER, I.
             THREE EXPRESSIONS OF THE NEED FOR VARIETY.
             JOURNAL OF PERSONALITY, 1965, 33, 82-98.
             (MEASURE OF INTERNAL-EXTERNAL EXPLORATION OF THE ENVIRONMENT)
         aM-127 1965M EXPLORATION ENVIRONMENT ACTIVITIES INTROSPECTION
         aM-127 COMPETENCE CONFIDENCE
             (APPLICATIONS: 2015)

M-128   MCNAIR, D. M., LORR, M., & CALLAHON, D. M.
             PATIENT AND THERAPIST INFLUENCE ON QUITTING PSYCHOTHERAPY.
             JOURNAL OF CONSULTING PSYCHOLOGY, 1963, 27, 10-17.
             (IDEAL-ACTUAL SELF DISCREPANCY)
         aM-128 1963M RATING SELF IDEAL DISCREPANCY

M-129   MENGES, R. J.
               STUDENT-INSTRUCTOR COGNITIVE COMPATABILITY IN THE LARGE LECTURE CLASS:
               AN EXPLORATORY STUDY.
               DOCTORAL DISSERTATION, TEACHERS COLLEGE, COLUMBIA UNIVERSITY.
               ANN ARBOR, MICHIGAN: UNIVERSITY MICROFILMS, 1967, NO. 67-12, 699.
           MENGES, R. J.
               STUDENT-INSTRUCTOR COGNITIVE COMPATABILITY IN THE LARGE LECTURE CLASS:
               JOURNAL OF PERSONALITY, 1969, 37, 444-459.
               (MEASURE OF ATTITUDE TOWARDS INSTRUCTOR)
           @M-129 1967M STUDENT TEACHER COLLEGE COMPATIBILITY
           @M-129 ATTITUDE
               (APPLICATIONS: 524)

M-130   MCREYNOLDS, P.
               ANXIETY AS RELATED TO INCONGRUENCIES BETWEEN VALUES AND FEELINGS.
               PSYCHOLOGICAL RECORDS, 1958, 8, 57-66.
               (INCONGRUENCY TEST)
           @M-130 1958M COGNITIVE CONSISTENCY DISSONANCE
           @M-130 VALUES ANXIETY
               (APPLICATIONS: 644   1713)

M-132   MADDEN, J. F.
               SEMANTIC DIFFERENTIAL RATING OF SELF AND OF SELF-REPORTED PERSONAL
               CHARACTERISTICS.
               JOURNAL OF CONSULTING PSYCHOLOGY, 1961, 25, 183.
               (SEMANTIC DIFFERENTIAL RATING OF PERSONAL CHARACTERISTICS)
           @M-132 1961M SEM-DIFFERENTIAL SELF MMPI ACTIVITY EVALUATION SELF-CONCEPT

M-133   MEER, B., & AMON, A. H.
               PHOTO PREFERENCE TEST (PPT) AS A MEASURE OF MENTAL STATUS FOR HOSPITALIZED
               PSYCHIATRIC PATIENTS.
               JOURNAL OF CONSULTING PSYCHOLOGY, 1963, 27, 283-293.
               (PHOTOS PREFERENCE TEST)*
           @M-133 1963M PREFERENCE PSYCHOPATHY MENTAL-ILLNESS GRAPHIC FIGURE STATUS
           @M-133 HOSPITALIZED PSYCHIATRIC PATIENT

M-134   MURSTEIN, B. I., DAVID, C., FISHER, D., & FURTH, H. G.
               THE SCALING OF THE TAT FOR HOSTILITY BY A VARIETY OF SCALING METHODS.
               JOURNAL OF CONSULTING PSYCHOLOGY, 1961, 25, 497-504.
               (TAT SCORED FOR HOSTILITY VALUE)
           @M-134 1961M TAT IMAGERY HOSTILITY AFFECTIVE-STATES
               (APPLICATIONS: 1910 2191)

M-135   MARKS, P. A.
               AN ASSESSMENT OF THE DIAGNOSTIC PROCESS IN A CHILD GUIDANCE SETTING.
               PSYCHOLOGICAL MONOGRAPHS, 1961, 75, (3, WHOLE NO. 507).
               (Q-SORT PERSONALITY MEASURE)
           @M-135 1961M Q-SORT PERSONALITY STRUCTURE
               (APPLICATIONS: 1752)

M-136   MAINORD, F. R.
               PARENTAL ATTITUDES IN SCHIZOPHRENIA.
               DOCTORAL DISSERTATION, UNIVERSITY OF WASHINGTON, 1956, PUBLICATION NO. 20,
               388, MISC. 57-1427.
               (CHILD STUDY QUESTIONNAIRE)*
           @M-136 1956M PARENTAL STRICTNESS PARENT-CHILD RELATIONSHIPS MATERNAL ROLE
           @M-136 CHILD
               (APPLICATIONS: 1919)

M-137   MEEKER, F. O.
               AN EXPLORATORY STUDY OF SPECIFIC AND GENERAL PERSONALITY DIMENSIONS
               RELATED TO LENGTH OF HOSPITALIZATION AMONG PSYCHIATRIC PATIENTS.
               UNPUBLISHED MASTER'S THESIS, UNIVERSITY OF CALIFORNIA, 1958.
               (MEEKER CHRONICITY SCALE)*
           @M-137 1958M ADJUSTMENT MENTAL-ILLNESS DIAGNOSIS PSYCHIATRIC HOSPITALIZATION
               (APPLICATIONS: 1651 1844)

M-138   MCREYNOLDS, P., & ACKER, M.
               A PRELIMINARY REPORT ON THE DEVELOPMENT OF A TECHNIQUE FOR ASSESSING
               ANXIETY.
               RESEARCH REPORT, NO. 27, BEHAVIORAL RESEARCH LABORATORY, PALO ALTO
               VETERANS ADMINISTRATION HOSPITAL.
               (MEASURE OF ANXIETY)
           @M-138 ANXIETY TENSION STRESS
               (APPLICATIONS: 1820)

M-139   MEDINNUS, G. R., & CURTIS, F. J.
           THE RELATION BETWEEN MATERNAL SELF-ACCEPTANCE AND CHILD-ACCEPTANCE.
           JOURNAL OF CONSULTING PSYCHOLOGY, 1963, 27, 542-544.
           (MEASURE OF SELF-ACCEPTANCE)
      aM-139 1963M SELF-ACCEPTANCE SEM-DIFFERENTIAL DISCREPANCY MATERNAL CHILD
      aM-139 PARENT-CHILD

M-140   MEDINNUS, G. R., & CURTIS, F. J.
           THE RELATION BETWEEN MATERNAL SELF-ACCEPTANCE AND CHILD-ACCEPTANCE.
           JOURNAL OF CONSULTING PSYCHOLOGY, 1963, 27, 542-544.
           (MEASURE OF CHILD ACCEPTANCE)
      aM-140 1963M CHILD ACCEPTANCE MATERNAL SELF SEM-DIFFERENTIAL

M-141   MEEHL, P. E.
           PROFILE ANALYSIS OF THE MINNESOTA MULTIPHASIC PERSONALITY INVENTORY IN
           DIFFERENTIAL DIAGNOSIS.
           JOURNAL OF APPLIED PSYCHOLOGY, 1946, 30, 517-524.
           (PROGNOSTIC INDEX FROM MMPI)
      aM-141 1946M MMPI MENTAL-ILLNESS ADJUSTMENT PROGNOSIS
           (APPLICATIONS: 1889)

M-142   MCCARTHY, C. D.
           DEVELOPMENT OF THE MULTIPLE CHOICE FORM OF THE HOSPITAL SITUATION STUDY.
           V. A. NEWSLETTER FOR COOPERATIVE RESEARCH IN PSYCHOLOGY, 1960, 817, 207-
           229.
           (HOSPITAL SITUATION STUDY)
      aM-142 1960M HOSPITALIZATION SITUATIONAL GRAPHIC PROJECTIVE
           (APPLICATIONS: 1981)

M-144   MUELLER, W. J., & GRATER, H. A.
           AGGRESSION CONFLICT, ANXIETY, AND EGO STRENGTH.
           JOURNAL OF CONSULTING PSYCHOLOGY, 1965, 29, 130-134.
           (AGGRESSION CONFLICT SCALE)
      aM-144 1965M AGGRESSION CONFLICT ANXIETY EGO-STRENGTH SEM-DIFFERENTIAL ACTIVE
      aM-144 EVALUATION
           (APPLICATIONS: 2027)

M-145   MURRAY, H. A.
           EXPLORATIONS IN PERSONALITY.
           NEW YORK: OXFORD, 1938.
           (MURRAY ADJECTIVE CHECK LIST)*
      aM-145 1938M ADJECTIVE CHECKLIST PERSONALITY GLOBAL NEED
           (APPLICATIONS: 575)

M-146   MCNAIR, D., & LORR, M.
           AN ANALYSIS OF PROFESSED PSYCHOTHERAPEUTIC TECHNIQUES.
           JOURNAL OF CONSULTING PSYCHOLOGY, 1964, 28, 265-271.
           (ANALYSIS OF THERAPEUTIC DIMENSIONS MEASURE)
      aM-146 1964M THERAPY COUNSELING DIRECTION

M-148   MASLING, J., RABIE, L., & BLONDHEIM, J. H.
           OBESITY, LEVEL OF ASPIRATION, AND RORSCHACH AND TAT MEASURES OF ORAL
           DEPENDENCE.
           JOURNAL OF CONSULTING PSYCHOLOGY, 1967, 31, 233-239
           (RORSCHACH SCORED FOR ORAL DEPENDENCE AND ORAL SADISM)
      aM-148 1967M RORSCHACH ORALITY DEPENDENCE NURTURANCE DEPRIVATION
           (APPLICATIONS: 2151)

M-149   MASLING, J., RABIE, L., & BLONDHEIM, J. H.
           OBESITY, LEVEL OF ASPIRATION, AND RORSCHACH AND TAT MEASURES OF ORAL
           DEPENDENCE.
           JOURNAL OF CONSULTING PSYCHOLOGY, 1967, 31, 233-239.
           (TAT SCORED FOR ORAL DEPENDENCE AND ORAL SADISM)
      aM-149 1967M TAT DEPENDENCE ORALITY NURTURANCE DEPRIVATION

M-150   MEYER, R.
           A STUDY OF THE SCHIZOPHREGENIC MOTHER CONCEPT BY MEANS OF THE TAT.
           UNPUBLISHED MASTERS THESIS, MICHIGAN STATE UNIVERSITY, 1964.
      MEYER, R. G., & KARON, B. P.
           THE SCHIZOPHREGENIC MOTHER CONCEPT AND THE TAT.
           PSYCHIATRY, 1967, 30, 173-179.
           (PATHOGENIC INDEX FROM TAT)
      aM-150 1964M TAT SCHIZOPHRENIA MATERNAL
           (APPLICATIONS: 2316)

M-153   MURSTEIN, B.
              EFFECT OF STIMULUS, BACKGROUND, PERSONALITY, AND SCORING SYSTEM ON THE
              *MANIFESTATION OF HOSTILITY IN THE TAT.
              JOURNAL OF CONSULTING AND CLINICAL PSYCHOLOGY, 1968, 32, 355-365.
              (SOCIOMETRIC PEER RATING OF HOSTILITY-FRIENDLINESS)
         aM-153 1968M SOCIOMETRIC PEER RATING HOSTILITY STUDENT GROUP

M-154   MARTIN, B.
              THE VALIDITY OF A SELF REPORT MEASURE OF ANXIETY AS A FUNCTION OF THE TIME
              INTERVAL COVERED BY THE INSTRUCTIONS.
              JOURNAL OF CONSULTING PSYCHOLOGY, 1959, 23, 468.
              (FEELING INVENTORY)
         aM-154 1959M AFFECTIVE-STATES FEELING ANXIETY IE-CONTROL POSITIVE NEGATIVE
         aM-154 SUBJECTIVE STRESS
              (APPLICATIONS: 566)

M-155   MISKIMINS, R. W., DECOOK, R., WILSON, L. T., & MALEY, R. F.
              PREDICTION OF SUICIDE IN A PSYCHIATRIC HOSPITAL.
              JOURNAL OF CLINICAL PSYCHOLOGY, 1967, 23, 296-301.
         MISKIMINS, R. W., & WILSON, L. T.
              REVISED SUICIDE POTENTIAL SCALE.
              JOURNAL OF CONSULTING AND CLINICAL PSYCHOLOGY, 1969, 33, 258.
              (REVISED SUICIDE POTENTIAL SCALE)
         aM-155 1967M SUICIDE ADJUSTMENT MENTAL-ILLNESS DIAGNOSIS
              (APPLICATIONS: 2279   2941)

M-156   MCNAIR, D. M., & LORR, M.
              TWO THERAPIST MEASURES OF PATIENT CHANGE IN PSYCHOTHERAPY.
              AMERICAN PSYCHOLOGIST, 1960, 15, 386 (ABSTRACT) (B).
         MCNAIR, D. M., & LORR, M.
              THERAPIST JUDGMENTS OF APPROPRIATENESS OF PSYCHOTHERAPY FREQUENCY
              SCHEDULES.
              JOURNAL OF CONSULTING PSYCHOLOGY, 1960, 24, 500-506.
              (CHANGE INVENTORY)
         aM-156 1960M PATIENT THERAPY CHANGE PARTICIPATION RESISTANCE INTERPERSONAL
         aM-156 RELATIONSHIPS INTERVIEW INTERACTION MENTAL-HEALTH MENTAL-ILLNESS
              (APPLICATIONS: 726   1738)

M-157   MACCOBY, E. E.
              THE TAKING OF ADULT ROLES IN MIDDLE CHILDHOOD.
              JOURNAL OF ABNORMAL AND SOCIAL PSYCHOLOGY, 1961, 63, 493-503.
              (ROLE TAKING QUESTIONNAIRE)*
         aM-157 1961M ROLE ENACTMENT NURTURANCE
         aM-157 PARENT-CHILD ATTITUDE AUTHORITY MATURITY PREFERENCE CHILD PARENTAL
         aM-157 RELATIONSHIPS INTERACTION FAMILY

M-158   MEYER, H. H., WALKER, W. B., & LITWIN, G. H.
              MOTIVE PATTERNS AND RISK PREFERENCES ASSOCIATED WITH ENTREPRENEURSHIP.
              JOURNAL OF ABNORMAL AND SOCIAL PSYCHOLOGY, 1961, 63, 570-574.
              (MANAGEMENT RATING OF "ACHIEVEMENT DRIVE")
         aM-158 1961M ACHIEVEMENT NEED MOTIVE DRIVE MANAGEMENT SUPERVISOR JOB
         aM-158 RATING

M-159   MISCHEL, W., & METZNER, R.
              PREFERENCE FOR DELAYED REWARD AS A FUNCTION OF AGE, INTELLIGENCE, AND
              LENGTH OF DELAY INTERVAL.
              JOURNAL OF ABNORMAL AND SOCIAL PSYCHOLOGY, 1962, 64, 425-431.
              (MEASURE OF FUTURE TIME PERSPECTIVE)
         aM-159 1962M FUTURE TIME PERSPECTIVE CHILD
         aM-159 ORIENTATION PREFERENCE PRESENT
              (APPLICATIONS: 247)

M-160   MEES, H. L.
              PRELIMINARY STEPS IN THE REPRESENTATION OF FACTOR SCALES FOR THE MMPI.
              UNIVERSITY OF WASHINGTON, DIVISION OF COUNSELING AND TESTING, JULY 1959.
              (FACTOR SCALES FROM MMPI)
         aM-160 1959M MMPI NEUROTICISM MENTAL-ILLNESS PSYCHIATRIC DIAGNOSIS MULTITRAIT
         aM-160 INVENTORY
              (APPLICATIONS: 792)

M-161   MONROE, J. J., & ASTIN, A. W.
              IDENTIFICATION PROCESSES IN HOSPITALIZED NARCOTIC DRUG ADDICTS.
              JOURNAL OF ABNORMAL AND SOCIAL PSYCHOLOGY, 1961, 63, 215-218.
              (MEASURE OF IDENTIFICATION WITH NARCOTICS ADDICTS)
         aM-161 1961M DRUG ADDICTION IDENTIFICATION

M-162   MCCORD, W., & MCCORD, J.
               ORIGINS OF ALCOHOLISM.
               STANFORD: STANFORD UNIVERSITY PRESS, 1960.
               (RATING OF OBSERVED SOCIAL DEVIANCE)
          @M-162 1960M SOCIAL DELINQUENCY ADOLESCENT VOCATIONAL
          @M-162 DEVIANCE BEHAVIOR AFFECTION PARENT-CHILD INTERACTION RELATIONSHIPS JOB
               (APPLICATIONS: 784)

M-163   MARTIRE, J. G.
               RELATIONSHIPS BETWEEN THE SELF CONCEPT AND DIFFERENCES IN THE STRENGTH
               AND GENERALITY OF ACHIEVEMENT MOTIVATION.
               JOURNAL OF PERSONALITY, 1956, 24, 364-375.
               (SELF-IDEAL-SELF DIFFERENCE)
          @M-163 1956M SELF IDEAL ESTEEM CONCEPT MENTAL-HEALTH SATISFACTION ADJUSTMENT
          @M-163 ACTUALIZATION DISCREPANCY
               (APPLICATIONS: 922)

M-164   MASSIMO, J. L., & SHORE, M. F.
               THE EFFECTIVENESS OF A COMPREHENSIVE, VOCATIONALLY ORIENTED PSYCHOTHERAPY
               PROGRAM FOR ADOLESCENT DELINQUENT BOYS.
               AMERICAN JOURNAL OF ORTHOPSYCHIATRY, 1963, 33, 634-642.
               (THEMATIC APPERCEPTION TEST)
          @M-164 1963M TAT PROJECTIVE ATTITUDE AUTHORITY CONTROL INHIBITION AGGRESSION
          @M-164 HOSTILITY SELF CONCEPT
               (APPLICATIONS: 912)

M-165   MISCHEL, W.
               DELAY OF GRATIFICATION, NEED FOR ACHIEVEMENT, AND ACQUIESCENCE IN ANOTHER
               CULTURE.
               JOURNAL OF ABNORMAL AND SOCIAL PSYCHOLOGY, 1961, 62, 543-552.
               (PREFERENCE FOR DELAYED REINFORCEMENT MEASURES)
          @M-165 1961M DELAY GRATIFICATION FUTURE ORIENTATION PRESENT INHIBITION CONTROL
          @M-165 IMPULSE PREFERENCE
               (APPLICATIONS: 928)

M-166   MCINNIS, T. L.
               POSITIVE AND NEGATIVE REINFORCEMENT WITH SHORT- AND LONG-TERM HOSPITALIZED
               SCHIZOPHRENICS IN A PROBABILITY LEARNING SITUATION.
               UNPUBLISHED MASTERS THESIS, UNIVERSITY OF ILLINOIS, 1965.
          MCINNIS, T. L., & ULLMANN, L. P.
               POSITIVE AND NEGATIVE REINFORCEMENT WITH SHORT- AND LONG-TERM HOSPITALIZED
               SCHIZOPHRENICS IN A PROBABILITY LEARNING SITUATION.
               JOURNAL OF ABNORMAL PSYCHOLOGY, 1967, 72, 157-162.
               (PARANOIA SCALES)
          @M-166 1967M SCHIZOPHRENIA MMPI MENTAL-ILLNESS
          @M-166 PARANOIA DENIAL REPRESSION PSYCHIATRIC DIAGNOSIS
               (APPLICATIONS: 1033)

M-167   MINKOWICH, A.
               CORRELATES OF SUPEREGO FUNCTIONS.
               UNPUBLISHED DOCTORAL DISSERTATION, UNIVERSITY OF MICHIGAN, 1960.
          WEINGARTEN, L. L.
               CORRELATES OF AMBIVALENCE TOWARD PARENTAL FIGURES.
               UNPUBLISHED DOCTORAL DISSERTATION, UNIVERSITY OF MICHIGAN, 1962,
               (MEASURE OF AMBIVALENT FEELINGS)
          @M-167 1960M GLOBAL ADJUSTMENT PARENT-CHILD INTERACTION FAMILY POSITIVE
          @M-167 NEGATIVE AFFECTIVE-STATES AMBIGUITY TOLERANCE RIGIDITY DOGMATISM
               (APPLICATIONS: 984)

M-168   MARSHALL, G. R., & COFER, C. N.
               ASSOCIATIVE INDICES AS MEASURES OF WORD RELATEDNESS: A SUMMARY AND
               COMPARISON OF TEN METHODS.
               JOURNAL OF VERBAL LEARNING AND VERBAL BEHAVIOR, 1963, 1, 408-421.
               (INDEX OF TOTAL ASSOCIATION)
          @M-168 1963M THINKING COGNITIVE ACTIVITIES
          @M-168 ASSOCIATION WORD FUNCTIONING
               (APPLICATIONS: 1008)

M-169   MONROE, L. J.
               PSYCHOLOGICAL AND PHYSIOLOGICAL DIFFERENCES BETWEEN GOOD AND POOR SLEEPERS.
               JOURNAL OF ABNORMAL PSYCHOLOGY, 1967, 72, 255-264.
               (SLEEP HABITS QUESTIONNAIRE)
          @M-169 1967M BEHAVIOR HABITS
          @M-169 PATHOLOGY PERSONALITY PSYCHOSOMATIC

M-170   MCGAUGHRAN, L. S., & MORAN, L. J.
              "CONCEPTUAL LEVEL" VS. "CONCEPTUAL AREA" ANALYSIS OF OBJECT SORTING
              BEHAVIOR OF SCHIZOPHRENIC AND NONPSYCHIATRIC GROUPS.
              JOURNAL OF ABNORMAL AND SOCIAL PSYCHOLOGY, 1956, 52, 43-50.
          MCGAUGHRAN, L. S., & MORAN, L. J.
              REVISED (1956) SUPPLEMENTARY INSTRUCTIONS FOR SCORING CONCEPTUAL AREA ON
              THE GOLDSTEIN-GELB-WEIGL OBJECT SORTING TEST.
              DITTO, AUTHOR, UNIVERSITY OF HOUSTON, 1956.
              (MEASURE OF OPEN-CLOSED AND PUBLIC-PRIVATE DIMENSIONS OF OBJECT-SORTING
              PERFORMANCE)
          @M-170 1956M CONCEPT ABSTRACTNESS CONCRETENESS PRIVATE PUBLIC OPENNESS SELF
          @DISCLOSURE

M-171   MEGARGEE, E. I., COOK, P. E., & MENDELSOHN, G. A.
              DEVELOPMENT AND VALIDATION OF AN MMPI SCALE OF ASSAULTIVENESS IN
              OVERCONTROLLED INDIVIDUALS.
              JOURNAL OF ABNORMAL PSYCHOLOGY, 1967, 72, 519-528.
              (OVERCONTROLLED HOSTILITY SCALE)
          @M-171 1967M AGGRESSION HOSTILITY CONTROL EXPRESSION INHIBITION MMPI ALIENATION
          @M-171 IE-CONTROL LOCUS

M-172   MOONEY, R. L., & GORDON, L. V.
              MOONEY PROBLEM CHECK LISTS. (COLLEGE FORM).
              PSYCHOLOGICAL CORPORATION, 1950.
              (MOONEY PROBLEM CHECKLIST)
          @M-172 1950M PROBLEM CHECKLIST
          @M-172 BEHAVIOR PSYCHIATRIC MOOD
              (APPLICATIONS: 1118   1289   1303   1319   1335   1439   2036)

M-173   MAYMAN, M., & VOTH, H. M.
              REALITY CLOSENESS, PHANTASY, AND AUTOKINESIS: A DIMENSION OF COGNITIVE
              STYLE.
              JOURNAL OF ABNORMAL PSYCHOLOGY, 1969, 74, 635-641.
              (MEASURE OF REALITY CLOSENESS AND PHANTASY EMBELLISHMENT)
          @M-173 1969M COGNITIVE STYLE REALITY PERCEPTION FANTASY IMAGINATION THINKING

M-174   MENDELSOHN, G. A., & GELLER, M. H.
              STRUCTURE OF CLIENT ATTITUDES TOWARD COUNSELING AND THEIR RELATION TO
              CLIENT-COUNSELOR SIMILARITY.
              JOURNAL OF CONSULTING PSYCHOLOGY, 1965, 29, 63-72.
              (OUTCOME QUESTIONNAIRE)
          @M-174 1965M THERAPY RELATIONSHIPS COUNSELING PATIENT MENTAL-HEALTH
          @M-174 MENTAL-ILLNESS INTERACTION SATISFACTION SUCCESS
              (APPLICATIONS: 1115)

M-175   MCCLOSKY, H.
              CONSERVATISM AND PERSONALITY.
              THE AMERICAN POLITICAL SCIENCE REVIEW, 1958, 52, 27-45.
              (CONSERVATISM-LIBERALISM SCALE)*
          @M-175 1958M CONSERVATISM LIBERALISM POLITICAL IDEOLOGY ATTITUDE
              (APPLICATIONS: 2353)

M-177   MCREYNOLDS, P.
              THE RORSCHACH CONCEPT EVALUATION TECHNIQUE.
              AMERICAN PSYCHOLOGIST, 1949, 4, 270. ABSTRACT.
          MCREYNOLDS, P.
              THE RORSCHACH CONCEPT EVALUATION TEST.
              JOURNAL OF PROJECTIVE TECHNIQUES, 1954, 18, 60-74.
              (RORSCHACH CONCEPT EVALUATION TEST)
          @M-177 1949M RORSCHACH CONCEPT EVALUATION
              (APPLICATIONS: 1054)

M-178   MURRAY, E. J., & COHEN, M.
              MENTAL ILLNESS, MILIEU THERAPY, AND SOCIAL ORGANIZATION IN WARD GROUPS.
              JOURNAL OF ABNORMAL AND SOCIAL PSYCHOLOGY, 1959, 58, 48-54.
              (SOCIOMETRIC QUESTIONNAIRE)
          @M-178 1959M SOCIOMETRIC PEER PSYCHIATRIC PATIENT WARD
              (APPLICATIONS: 1000)

M-179   MOOS, R. H.
              SOURCES OF VARIANCE IN RESPONSES TO QUESTIONNAIRES AND IN BEHAVIOR.
              JOURNAL OF ABNORMAL PSYCHOLOGY, 1969, 74, 405-412.
              (MEASURE OF EFFECTS OF BEHAVIOR SETTINGS)
          @M-179 1969M BEHAVIOR SITUATIONAL PSYCHIATRIC PATIENT EXPERIENCE MOOD
          @ENVIRONMENT INFLUENCE SITUATIONAL

M-180   MILLER, K. M., & BIGGS, J. B.
             ATTITUDE CHANGE THROUGH UNDIRECTED GROUP DISCUSSION.
             JOURNAL OF EDUCATIONAL PSYCHOLOGY, 1958, 49, 224-228.
             (CHILDREN'S SOCIAL DISTANCE SCALE)
         aM-180 1958M CHILD SOCIAL DISTANCE ATTITUDE OTHERS
             (APPLICATIONS: 2518)

M-181   MARKS, J., SONODA, B., & SCHALOCK, R.
             REINFORCEMENT VERSUS RELATIONSHIP THERAPY FOR SCHIZOPHRENICS.
             JOURNAL OF ABNORMAL PSYCHOLOGY, 1968, 73, 397-402.
             (RATING SCALES FOR WORK, SOCIAL AND CONCEPTUAL COMPETENCE)
         aM-181 1968M MENTAL-ILLNESS COMPETENCE EFFECTANCE CHANGE THERAPY SCHIZOPHRENIC
         aEVALUATION JOB SOCIAL CONCEPTUAL ABILITY

M-182   MACHOTKA, P.
             DEFENSIVE STYLE AND ESTHETIC DISTORTION.
             JOURNAL OF PERSONALITY, 1967, 35, 600-622.
             (MEASURE OF SEXUAL GUILT)*
         aM-182 SEX GUILT AFFECTIVE-STATES 1967M
             (APPLICATIONS: 480)

M-183   MARWELL, G., & HAGE, J.
             THE ORGANIZATION OF ROLE-RELATIONSHIPS: A SYSTEMATIC DESCRIPTION.
             AMERICAN SOCIOLOGICAL REVIEW. 1970, 35, 884-900.
             (MEASURE OF ROLE RELATIONSHIPS)
         aM-183 1970M ROLE RELATIONSHIPS ORGANIZATION

M-184   MCFALL, R. M., & MARSTON, A. R.
             AN EXPERIMENTAL INVESTIGATION OF BEHAVIOR REHEARSAL IN ASSERTIVE TRAINING.
             JOURNAL OF ABNORMAL PSYCHOLOGY, 1970, 76, 295-303.
             (ROLE-PLAYING TEST OF ASSERTIVE BEHAVIOR)
         aM-184 1970M ROLE ENACTMENT BEHAVIOR ASSERTIVENESS ANXIETY SITUATIONAL
         aSECURITY CONFIDENCE SELF

M-185   MACDONALD, A. P., JR.
             REVISED SCALE FOR AMBIGUITY TOLERANCE: RELIABILITY AND VALIDITY.
             PSYCHOLOGICAL REPORTS, 1970, 26, 791-798.
             (SCRAMBLED WORDS TEST)
         aM-185 1970M COGNITIVE STYLE THINKING
             (APPLICATIONS: 2647)

M-186   MACDONALD, A. P., JR.
             REVISED SCALE FOR AMBIGUITY TOLERANCE: RELIABILITY AND VALIDITY.
             PSYCHOLOGICAL REPORTS, 1970, 26, 791-798.
             (AMBIGUITY TOLERANCE SCALE)*
         aM-186 1970M TOLERANCE AMBIGUITY RIGIDITY FLEXIBILITY AUTHORITARIANISM
         aDOGMATISM COGNITIVE STYLE PERSONALITY STRUCTURE

M-188   MUSSEN, P., HARRIS, S., RUTHERFORD, E., & KEASEY, C. B.
             HONESTY AND ALTRUISM AMONG PREADOLESCENTS.
             DEVELOPMENTAL PSYCHOLOGY, 1970, 3, 169-194.
             (SITUATIONAL MEASURES OF ALTRUISM AND HONESTY)
         aM-188 1970M SITUATIONAL ALTRUISM CHILD CONSCIENCE SOCIAL RESPONSIBILITY HONESTY

M-189   MUSSEN, P., HARRIS, S., RUTHERFORD, E., & KEASEY, C. B.
             HONESTY AND ALTRUISM AMONG PREADOLESCENTS.
             DEVELOPMENTAL PSYCHOLOGY, 1970, 3, 169-194.
             (SOCIOMETRIC MEASURE OF ALTRUISM AND HONESTY)
         aM-189 1970M SOCIOMETRIC PEER ALTRUISM CONSCIENCE SOCIAL RESPONSIBILITY
         aCHILD HONESTY

M-190   MANOSEVITZ, M.
             EARLY SEXUAL BEHAVIOR IN ADULT HOMOSEXUAL AND HETEROSEXUAL MALES.
             JOURNAL OF ABNORMAL PSYCHOLOGY, 1970, 76, 396-402.
             (LIFE HISTORY QUESTIONNAIRE)*
         aM-190 1970M SEX ROLE HOMOSEXUALITY IDENTITY LIFE HISTORY SELF PAST

M-192   MILLS, D. H.
             ADJECTIVES PERTINENT TO PSYCHOTHERAPY FOR USE WITH THE SEMANTIC
             DIFFERENTIAL: AN HEURISTIC NOTE.
             PSYCHOLOGICAL REPORTS, 1970, 26, 211-213.
             (SEMANTIC DIFFERENTIAL ADJECTIVE-PAIRS FOR PSYCHOTHERAPY RATING)
         @M-192 1970M SEM-DIFFERENTIAL TRAIT-TERMS MULTI-TRAIT COUNSELING THERAPY
         @RELATIONSHIPS RATING PATIENT

M-193   MAHRER, A. R.
             THE PSYCHOLOGICAL PROBLEM INVENTORY.
             PSYCHOLOGICAL REPORTS, 1967, 20, 711-714.
             (PSYCHOLOGICAL PROBLEM INVENTORY)*
         @M-193 1967M PSYCHIATRIC PROBLEM SYMPTOM SELF DESCRIPTION ADJUSTMENT PERSONAL

M-194   MILLIMET, C. R.
             MANIFEST ANXIETY-DEFENSIVENESS SCALE: FIRST FACTOR OF THE MMPI REVISITED.
             PSYCHOLOGICAL REPORTS, 1970, 27, 603-616.
             (MANIFEST ANXIETY-DEFENSIVENESS SCALE)*
         @M-194 1970M ANXIETY MANIFEST TENSION DEFENSIVENESS ADJUSTMENT COPING DEFENSE

M-196   MARTIN, W. T.
             SELF-PERCEPTION INVENTORY: A NEW TEST OF PERSONALITY.
             PSYCHOLOGICAL REPORTS, 1968, 23, 961-962.
         MARTIN, W. T.
             MANUAL FOR THE SELF-PERCEPTION INVENTORY.
             JACKSONVILLE, ILLINOIS: PSYCHOLOGISTS AND EDUCATORS PRESS, 1969.
             (SELF-PERCEPTION INVENTORY)*
         @M-196 1968M PERSONALITY MULTITRAIT INVENTORY CONSISTENCY SOCIAL DESIRABILITY
         @RIGIDITY FLEXIBILITY DOGMATISM MENTAL-HEALTH MENTAL-ILLNESS SELF GLOBAL
         @ADJUSTMENT PARANOIA ANXIETY DEPRESSION AUTHORITARIANISM ACTUALIZATION
         @PERCEPTION
             (APPLICATIONS: 2610 2679)

M-197   MASLOW, A. H.
             A TEST FOR DOMINANCE-FEELING (SELF-ESTEEM) IN COLLEGE WOMEN.
             JOURNAL OF SOCIAL PSYCHOLOGY, 1940, 12, 255-270.
             (SOCIAL PERSONALITY INVENTORY)*
         @M-197 1940M DOMINANCE FEELING SELF ESTEEM SATISFACTION POWERLESSNESS POWER
             (APPLICATIONS: 2598)

M-198   MATHIS, H. I.
             RELATING ENVIRONMENTAL FACTORS TO APTITUDE AND RACE.
             JOURNAL OF COUNSELING PSYCHOLOGY, 1968, 15, 563-568.
             (ENVIRONMENTAL PARTICIPATION INDEX)
         @M-198 1968M ENVIRONMENT HOME ACTIVITIES PARTICIPATION CHECKLIST
         @CULTURE EXPERIENCE INVOLVEMENT FAMILY

M-199   MITCHELL, K. R.
             REPEATED MEASURES AND THE EVALUATION OF CHANGE IN THE INDIVIDUAL CLIENT
             DURING COUNSELING.
             JOURNAL OF COUNSELING PSYCHOLOGY, 1969, 16, 522-527.
             (PROBLEMS QUESTIONNAIRE)
         @M-199 1969M PROBLEM ANXIETY DEPRESSION PATIENT PERSONAL ADJUSTMENT COUNSELING

M-200   MARYLAND COUNSELING CENTER.
             A CHECK LIST FOR RECORDING TEST TAKING BEHAVIOR.
             JOURNAL OF COUNSELING PSYCHOLOGY, 1960, 7, 116-119.
             (MARYLAND TEST BEHAVIOR CHECKLIST)*
         @M-200 1960M TEST BEHAVIOR COUNSELING CHECKLIST

M-201   MANAGEMENT RESEARCH DIVISION.
             INDUSTRIAL RELATIONS CENTER.   UNIVERSITY OF CHICAGO.   (DATE NOT GIVEN).
             (CLOSURE FLEXIBILITY TEST)*
         @M-201 FIGURE PERCEPTION FLEXIBILITY FIELD DEPENDENCE
             (APPLICATIONS: 1539)

M-202   MAZER, G. E.
             THE FACTORIAL DIMENSIONS OF SCHOOL COUNSELOR PRACTICES.
             JOURNAL OF COUNSELING PSYCHOLOGY, 1965, 12, 127-132.
             (INVENTORY OF COUNSELING PRACTICES)*
         @M-202 1965M RATING PSYCHIATRIC COUNSELING THERAPIST

M-203   MICHAUX, W. W., & LORR, M.
                 PSYCHOTHERAPISTS' TREATMENT GOALS.
                 JOURNAL OF COUNSELING PSYCHOLOGY, 1961, 8, 250-254.
                 (CHECKLIST OF CHANGES DUE TO THERAPY)
             @M-203 1961M THERAPY EFFECTIVENESS ADJUSTMENT BEHAVIOR CHANGE SUCCESS

M-204   MICHAUX, W. W., & LORR, M.
                 PSYCHOTHERAPISTS' TREATMENT GOALS.
                 JOURNAL OF COUNSELING PSYCHOLOGY, 1961, 8, 250-254.
                 (MEASURE OF PSYCHOTHERAPIST TREATMENT GOALS)
             @M-204 1961M GOALS THERAPY BEHAVIOR RELATIONSHIPS THERAPIST

M-205   MATHEWSON, R. H., & ORTON, J. W.
                 VOCATIONAL IMAGERY AND VOCATIONAL MATURITY OF HIGH SCHOOL STUDENTS.
                 JOURNAL OF COUNSELING PSYCHOLOGY, 1963, 10, 384-388.
                 (MEASURE OF VOCATIONAL IMAGERY)
             @M-205 1963M VOCATIONAL IMAGERY INTEREST PERCEPTION JOB

M-206   MATHEWSON, R. H., & ORTON, J. W.
                 VOCATIONAL IMAGERY AND VOCATIONAL MATURITY OF HIGH SCHOOL STUDENTS.
                 JOURNAL OF COUNSELING PSYCHOLOGY, 1963, 10, 384-388.
                 (VOCATIONAL MATURITY SCALE)
             @M-206 1963M VOCATIONAL MATURITY JOB INTEREST PERCEPTION

M-207   MATULEF, N. J.
                 THE EFFECTS OF SHORT-TERM VOCATIONAL COUNSELING ON TEMPORAL ORIENTATION.
                 UNPUBLISHED MASTER'S THESIS, IOWA STATE UNIVERSITY, 1963.
                 (MEASURE OF PROJECTED SELF)
             @M-207 1963M TIME FUTURE PERSPECTIVE ORIENTATION
                 (APPLICATIONS: 1293)

M-208   MATTHEWS, E.
                 THE MARRIAGE-CAREER CONFLICT IN THE CAREER DEVELOPMENT OF GIRLS AND YOUNG
                 WOMEN.
                 UNPUBLISHED DOCTORAL DISSERTATION, HARVARD GRADUATE SCHOOL OF EDUCATION,
                 1960.
                 (SCALE FOR ATTITUDES TOWARD CAREER AND MARRIAGE)
             @M-208 1960M MARITAL ROLE SATISFACTION FEMININITY JOB VOCATIONAL
             @ATTITUDE CONFLICT SELF IDENTITY CONCEPT SEX
                 (APPLICATIONS: 1296)

M-209   MUTHARD, J. E., & MILLER, L. A.
                 CRITERIA FOR REHABILITATION COUNSELOR PERFORMANCE IN STATE VOCATIONAL
                 REHABILITATION AGENCIES.
                 JOURNAL OF COUNSELING PSYCHOLOGY, 1964, 11, 123-128.
                 (CO-WORKER RATING BLANK)*
             @M-209 1964M RATING PERFORMANCE EVALUATION COUNSELING IDEAL PEER EFFECTIVENESS
             @THERAPIST

M-215   MERRILL, R. M., & HEATHERS, L. B.
                 THE USE OF AN ADJECTIVE CHECKLIST AS A MEASURE OF ADJUSTMENT.
                 JOURNAL OF COUNSELING PSYCHOLOGY, 1954, 1, 137-143.
                 (SELF CONCEPT CHECKLIST)
             @M-215 1954M SELF CONCEPT COUNSELING CHECKLIST ADJUSTMENT
             @PERCEPTION ATTITUDE IDENTITY
                 (APPLICATIONS: 1206)

M-216   MEADE, R. D.
                 FUTURE TIME PERSPECTIVES OF COLLEGE STUDENTS IN AMERICA AND IN INDIA.
                 JOURNAL OF SOCIAL PSYCHOLOGY, 1971, 83, 175-182.
                 (STORY COMPLETION MEASURE OF FUTURE TIME PERSPECTIVE)
             @M-216 1971M STORY-COMPLETION FUTURE TIME PERSPECTIVE ACTIVITIES PAST
             @PRESENT

M-218   MILLER, J. O.
                 THE CHILDREN'S LOCUS OF EVALUATION AND CONTROL SCALE.
                 IN H. C. HAYWOOD, & R. W. WOODCOCK (EDS.), ABSTRACTS OF PEABODY STUDIES IN
                 MENTAL RETARDATION. VOL. 3.
                 NASHVILLE: GEORGE PEABODY COLLEGE, 1965.
                 (CHILDREN'S LOCUS OF EVALUATION AND CONTROL SCALE)
             @M-218 1965M CHILD LOCUS CONTROL IE-CONTROL EVALUATION

M-219   MCGUIRE, W. J.
             RESISTANCE TO PERSUASION CONFERRED BY ACTIVE AND PASSIVE PRIOR
             REFUTATION OF THE SAME AND ALTERNATIVE COUNTERARGUMENTS.
             JOURNAL OF ABNORMAL AND SOCIAL PSYCHOLOGY, 1961, 63, 326-332.
             (OPINION QUESTIONNAIRE)
         @M-219 1961M HEALTH ATTITUDE BELIEF OPINION
             (APPLICATIONS: 180   233   305)

M-220   MCFALL, R., & LILLESAND, D. B.
             BEHAVIOR REHEARSAL WITH MODELING AND COACHING IN ASSERTION TRAINING.
             JOURNAL OF ABNORMAL PSYCHOLOGY, 1971, 77, 313-323.
             (CONFLICT RESOLUTION INVENTORY)
         @M-220 1971M CONFLICT ASSERTIVENESS BEHAVIOR SOCIAL SITUATIONAL ROLE DEMANDS
         @RESPONSE

M-226   MARKEL, N. N., & ROBLIN, G. L.
             THE EFFECT OF CONTENT AND SEX-OF-JUDGE ON JUDGMENT OF PERSONALITY FROM
             VOICE.
             INTERNATIONAL JOURNAL OF SOCIAL PSYCHIATRY, 1965, 11, 295-300.
             (EMOTIONAL CONTENT PASSAGES)
         @M-226 1965M EMOTION SEM-DIFFERENTIAL RATING EMOTION CONTENT VOICE PASSAGE
         @EVALUATION
             (APPLICATIONS: 220)

M-227   MAYO, C. W., & CROCKETT, W. H.
             COGNITIVE COMPLEXITY AND PRIMACY-RECENCY EFFECTS IN IMPRESSION
             FORMATION.
             JOURNAL OF ABNORMAL AND SOCIAL PSYCHOLOGY, 1964, 68, 335-338.
             (TRAIT CHECK LIST)
         @M-227 1964M TRAIT CHECKLIST IMPRESSION FORMATION STIMULUS PERSON PERCEPTION

M-228   MAYO, C. W., & CROCKETT, W. H.
             COGNITIVE COMPLEXITY AND PRIMACY-RECENCY EFFECTS IN IMPRESSION
             FORMATION.
             JOURNAL OF ABNORMAL AND SOCIAL PSYCHOLOGY, 1964, 68, 335-338.
             (CONFLICT SITUATIONS QUESTIONNAIRE)
         @M-228 1964M MORAL CONFLICT SITUATIONAL CONSCIENCE JUDGMENT

M-229   MOONEY, C. M., & FERGUSON, G. A.
             A NEW CLOSURE TEST.
             CANADIAN JOURNAL OF PSYCHOLOGY, 1951, 5, 129-133.
             (MCGILL CLOSURE TEST)*
         @M-229 1951M COGNITIVE INTEGRATION COMPLEXITY DIFFERENTIATION ORGANIZATION
         @AMBIGUITY INTEGRATION
             (APPLICATIONS: 923)

M-230   MONROE, J., & MILLER, J.
             EXPERIMENTAL TEST MANUAL.
             UNPUBLISHED MANUSCRIPT, NATIONAL INSTITUTE OF MENTAL HEALTH CLINICAL
             RESEARCH CENTER, LEXINGTON, KENTUCKY, 1968.
             (LEXINGTON PERSONALITY INVENTORY)*
         @M-230 1968M PERSONALITY SOCIAL DESIRABILITY ACQUIESCENCE MMPI INVENTORY
         @MULTITRAIT
             (APPLICATIONS: 2563)

M-231   MCCORD, W., & MCCORD, J.
             ORIGINS OF ALCOHOLISM.
             STANFORD: STANFORD UNIVERSITY PRESS, 1960.
             (RATING OF AGGRESSIVE BEHAVIORS)
         @M-231 1960M AGGRESSION BEHAVIOR ADOLESCENT FRUSTRATION ASSERTIVENESS DOMINANCE
         @AGGRESSIVENESS
             (APPLICATIONS: 784)

M-232   MURPHY, D. B., & HAMPTON, G. L.
             A TECHNIQUE FOR STUDYING ATTITUDE CHANGE.
             IN COLLECTED PAPERS RELATED TO THE STUDY OF THE EFFECTS OF SENSORY
             DEPRIVATION AND SOCIAL ISOLATION. (TASK PIONEER VI-ENDORSE) ALEXANDRIA, VA.
             HUMAN RESOURCES RESEARCH OFFICE, 1962.
             MYERS, T. I., MURPHY, D. B., & SMITH, S.
             THE EFFECT OF SENSORY DEPRIVATION AND SOCIAL ISOLATION ON SELF-
             EXPOSURE OT PROPAGANDA AND ATTITUDE CHANGE.
             AMERICAN PSYCHOLOGIST, 1963, 18, 440. (ABSTRACT).
             (TURK ATTITUDE SCALE)
         @M-232 1962M SEM-DIFFERENTIAL ETHNIC PREJUDICE ATTITUDE CHANGE
             (APPLICATIONS: 856)

M-233   MISKIMINS, R. W., DECOOK, R., WILSON, C. T., & MALEY, R. F.
                PREDICTION OF SUICIDE IN A PSYCHIATRIC HOSPITAL.
                JOURNAL OF CLINICAL PSYCHOLOGY, 1967, 23, 296-301.
                (SUICIDE POTENTIAL SCALE)*
          @M-233 1967M SUICIDE PSYCHIATRIC PATIENT HISTORY PROGNOSIS PREDICTION
                (APPLICATIONS: 2279)

M-234   MORSE, W. C., BLOOM, R. D., & DUNN, J. A.
                A STUDY OF SCHOOL CLASSROOM BEHAVIOR FROM DIVERSE EVALUATIVE
                FRAMEWORKS.
                UNITES STATES OFFICE OF EDUCATION, CONTRACT SAE 8414.
                ANN ARBOR, MICHIGAN: UNIVERSITY OF MICHIGAN, 1961.
                (REVISED CHILDREN'S TEST ANXIETY SCALE)
          @M-234 1961M S-35R CHILD TEST ANXIETY COLLEGE STUDENT ACADEMIC TENSION
          @PERFORMANCE EVALUATION
                (APPLICATIONS: 2237)

M-235   MACCASLAND, B. W.
                THE RELATION OF AGGRESSIVE FANTASY TO AGGRESSIVE BEHAVIOR IN CHILDREN.
                UNPUBLISHED DOCTORAL DISSERTATION, SYRACUSE UNIVERSITY, 1961.
                (TAT MEASURE OF AGGRESSION MOTIVATION)
          @M-235 1961M AGGRESSION MOTIVE TAT PROJECTIVE AGGRESSIVENESS FANTASY
                (APPLICATIONS: 2249)

M-236   MAHRER, A. R., & KATZ, G.
                PSYCHIATRIC SYMPTOMS AT ADMISSION TO HOSPITALIZATION.
                PSYCHIATRY DIGEST, 1963, 24, 23-30.
                (PSYCHOLOGICAL PROBLEM CHECKLIST)
          @M-236 1963M CHECKLIST PSYCHIATRIC ADJUSTMENT PERSONAL PROBLEM
                (APPLICATIONS: 1962)

M-237   MUELLER, J. H., MILL, E. G., ZANE, N. B., & HEVNER, K.
                STUDIES IN APPRECIATION AND ART.
                UNIVERSITY OF OREGON PUBLICATION, 1934, 4(6), 1-151.
          FARNSWORTH, P. R.
                HAS THE STATUS OF MUSIC CHANGED IN 30 YEARS?
                JOURNAL OF PSYCHOLOGY, 1963, 56, 269-272.
                (MUSIC ATTITUDE SCALE)
          @M-237 1963M ATTITUDE VALUE HOSTILE ESTHETIC
                (APPLICATIONS: 2486)

M-238   MACFARLANE, J. W.
                STUDIES IN CHILD GUIDANCE: I. METHODOLOGY OF DATA COLLECTION AND
                ORGANIZATION.
                MONOGRAPHS OF THE SOCIETY FOR RESEARCH IN CHILD DEVELOPMENT, 1938, 3, WHOLE
                NO. 6.
                (CHILDHOOD AND ADOLESCENT PERSONALITY SCALES)
          @M-238 1938M PERSONALITY RATING CHILD ADOLESCENT
                (APPLICATIONS: 1058)

M-239   MEADOW, A., GREENBLATT, M., FUNKENSTEIN, D. H., & SOLOMON, H. C.
                RELATIONSHIP BETWEEN CAPACITY FOR ABSTRACTION IN SCHIZOPHRENIA AND
                PHYSIOLOGIC RESPONSE TO AUTONOMIC DRUGS.
                JOURNAL OF NERVOUS AND MENTAL DISEASE, 1953, 118, 332-338.
                (ABSTRACTION SCALE FOR BENJAMIN'S PROVERB LIST)
          @M-239 1953M ABSTRACTNESS SCHIZOPHRENIA THINKING PSYCHIATRIC MENTAL-ILLNESS
          @DIAGNOSIS ADJUSTMENT ABSTRACTNESS COGNITIVE STYLE
                (APPLICATIONS: 1151)

M-240   MUNSINGER, H., & KESSEN, W.
                UNCERTAINTY, STRUCTURE, AND PREFERENCE.
                PSYCHOLOGICAL MONOGRAPHS, 1964, 78 (9, WHOLE NO. 586).
                (MEASURE OF SHAPE PREFERENCE)
          @M-240 1964M PREFERENCE FIGURE ENVIRONMENT VARIETY COGNITIVE STRUCTURE STIMULUS
                (APPLICATIONS: 1100)

M-241   MCCLINTOCK, C. G.
                PERSONALITY SYNDROMES AND ATTITUDE CHANGE.
                JOURNAL OF PERSONALITY, 1958, 479-493.
                (DEFENSIVENESS SUBSCALE OF F SCALE)
          @M-241 1958M EGO DEFENSIVENESS F-SCALE AUTHORITARIANISM ANTI-INTRACEPTIVE SEX
          @GUILT STEREOTYPE PROJECTIVE
                (APPLICATIONS: 640)

M-243   MATTSSON, P. O.
                COMMUNICATED ANXIETY IN A TWO-PERSON SITUATION.
                JOURNAL OF CONSULTING PSYCHOLOGY, 1960, 24, 488-495.
                (SELF-RATING ANXIETY SCALE)
          @M-243 1960M ANXIETY AWARENESS SITUATIONAL TENSION SELF RATING

M-244   MADDI, S. R., CHARLENS, A. M., MADDI, D., & SMITH, A. J.
               EFFECTS OF MONOTONY AND NOVELTY ON IMAGINATIVE PRODUCTS.
               JOURNAL OF PERSONALITY, 1962, 30, 513-527.
               (TAT SCORED FOR NEED FOR NOVELTY)
           aM-244 1962M PROJECTIVE FANTASY IMAGE PREFERENCE NOVELTY CONTENT-ANALYSIS TAT
               (APPLICATIONS: 409   414   2535   2676)

M-245   MUELLER, W. J.
               THE INFLUENCE OF SELF INSIGHT ON SOCIAL PERCEPTION SCORES.
               JOURNAL OF COUNSELING PSYCHOLOGY, 1963, 10, 185-191.
               (ADAPTATION OF STERN'S ACTIVITIES INDEX)
           aM-245 1963M NEED SELF EVALUATION ABASEMENT ACHIEVEMENT AGGRESSIVENESS DOMINANCE
           aNURTURANCE SUCCORANCE S-56R ACTIVITIES

M-246   MUUSS, R. E.
               THE EFFECTS OF A ONE- AND TWO-YEAR CAUSAL-LEARNING PROGRAM.
               JOURNAL OF PERSONALITY, 1960, 28, 479-491.
               (PHYSICAL CAUSAL TEST)
           aM-246 1960M COGNITIVE FUNCTIONING COMPLEXITY

M-247   MILGRAM, N.
               COGNITIVE AND EMPATHIC FACTORS IN THE ROLE ATTITUDES OF SCHIZOPHRENIC AND
               BRAIN DAMAGED PATIENTS.
               UNPUBLISHED DOCTORAL DISSERTATION, BOSTON UNIVERSITY, 1958.
           MILGRAM, N.
               COGNITIVE AND EMPATHIC FACTORS IN THE ROLE ATTITUDES OF SCHIZOPHRENIC AND
               BRAIN DAMAGED PATIENTS.
               JOURNAL OF ABNORMAL AND SOCIAL PSYCHOLOGY, 1960, 60, 219-224.
               (ABSTRACT-CONCRETE WORD ASSOCIATION TEST)
           aM-247 1958M WORD ASSOCIATION ABSTRACTNESS CONCRETENESS
               (APPLICATIONS: 333)

M-248   MANDLER, G., & WATSON, D. L.
               ANXIETY AND THE INTERRUPTION OF BEHAVIOR.
               IN C. SPIELSBERGER (ED.), ANXIETY AND BEHAVIOR.
               NEW YORK: ACADEMIC PRESS, 1966.
               (MEASURE OF FEELINGS ABOUT EXPERIMENT)
           aM-248 1966M SITUATIONAL STRESS FEELING
               (APPLICATIONS: 483)

M-249   MARKS, J., STAUFFACHER, J. C., & LYLE, C.
               PREDICTING OUTCOME IN SCHIZOPHRENIA.
               JOURNAL OF ABNORMAL AND SOCIAL PSYCHOLOGY, 1963, 66, 117-127.
               (HOSPITAL PROGNOSTIC SCALE)
           aM-249 1963M PROGNOSIS PSYCHIATRIC MENTAL-ILLNESS MENTAL-HEALTH ADJUSTMENT
               (APPLICATIONS: 1844)

M-252   MEIER, N. C.
               AESTHETIC PERCEPTION.
               IOWA CITY: BUREAU OF EDUCATIONAL RESEARCH AND SERVICE, UNIVERSITY OF IOWA,
               1963.
               (AESTHETIC PERCEPTION TEST)*
           aM-252 1963M ESTHETIC PERCEPTION SENSITIVITY
               (APPLICATIONS: 1558)

M-253   MEIER, N. C.
               NO REFERENCE--CITED IN:
               SIEGEL, L.
               TEST REVIEWS: THE AESTHETIC PERCEPTION TEST.
               JOURNAL OF COUNSELING PSYCHOLOGY, 1964, 11, 98.
               (ART JUDGMENT TEST)
           aM-253 ESTHETIC JUDGMENT
               (APPLICATIONS: 1558)

M-254   MACKAY, C. K., & BROWN, W. P.
               METAPHOR PREFERENCE VS SEMANTIC RATINGS AS MEASURES OF ATTITUDE TOWARD
               TIME.
               JOURNAL OF GENERAL PSYCHOLOGY, 1970, 83, 207-212.
               (SEMANTIC DIFFERENTIAL SCALES FOR MEASURING ABSTRACT TIME CONCEPTS)
           aM-254 1970M SEM-DIFFERENTIAL SUCCESS CONSCIENCE ATTITUDE TIME PERCEPTION
           aCONCEPT

M-255   MARKS, P. A., & SEEMAN, W.
              THE ACTUARIAL DESCRIPTION OF ABNORMAL PERSONALITY.
              BALTIMORE: WILLIAMS AND WILKINS, 1963.
              (PROFILE CLASSIFICATION SYSTEM FOR MMPI)
           @M-255 1963M MMPI DIAGNOSIS PSYCHIATRIC INVENTORY MENTAL-HEALTH MENTAL-ILLNESS
           @NEUROTICISM
              (APPLICATIONS: 2227)

M-257   MARKS, E., WEBB, S. C., & STRICKLAND, J. A.
              INTRAINSTITUTE TRANSFER REPORT: 1. EDUCATIONAL AND CAREER GOALS AND
              PERCEPTIONS OF CHOICE OF MAJOR.
              RESEARCH MEMORANDUM 67-6, JUNE 1967, EVALUATION STUDIES, GEORGIA
              INSTITUTE OF TECHNOLOGY.
              (TRANSFER QUESTIONNAIRE)
           @M-257 1967M COLLEGE STUDENT
              (APPLICATIONS: 2793)

M-258   MAW, W. H., & MAW, E. W.
              AN EXPLORATORY INVESTIGATION INTO THE MEASUREMENT OF CURIOSITY IN
              ELEMENTARY SCHOOL CHILDREN.
              COOPERATIVE RESEARCH PROJECT NO. 801, UNIVERSITY OF DELAWARE, 1964.
              (MEASURE OF CURIOSITY IN CHILDREN)
           @M-258 1964M CHILD PEER RATING TEACHER EXPLORATION SEEKING

M-259   MARLOWE, D.
              RELATIONSHIPS AMONG DIRECT AND INDIRECT MEASURES OF THE ACHIEVEMENT
              MOTIVE AND OVERT BEHAVIOR.
              JOURNAL OF CONSULTING PSYCHOLOGY, 1959, 23, 329-332.
              (SOCIOMETRIC MEASURE OF OVERT ACHIEVEMENT BEHAVIOR)
           @M-259 1959M SOCIOMETRIC ACHIEVEMENT BEHAVIOR NEED MOTIVE

M-260   MCNAIR, D. M., & LORR, M.
              AN ANALYSIS OF MOOD IN NEUROTICS.
              JOURNAL OF ABNORMAL AND SOCIAL PSYCHOLOGY, 1964, 69, 620-627.
              (REVISION OF PSYCHIATRIC OUTPATIENT MOOD SCALES)
           @M-260 1964M NEUROTICISM MOOD L-17R HOSTILITY ACTIVE TENSION ANXIETY
           @DEPRESSION AFFILIATION SOCIABILITY RETARDATION

N-1   NASH, A. N.
              DEVELOPMENT OF AN SVIB KEY FOR SELECTING MANAGERS.
              JOURNAL OF APPLIED PSYCHOLOGY, 1966, 50, 250-254.
              (NASH MANAGERIAL EFFECTIVENESS SCALE)*
           @N-1 MANAGEMENT SUPERVISOR EFFECTIVENESS JOB ADJUSTMENT PERFORMANCE VOCATIONAL
           @N-1 INTEREST LEADERSHIP 1966M

N-2   NELSON, A. R.
              EXAMINER'S MANUAL, TRAIT EVALUATION INDEX.
              NEW ROCHELLE, NEW YORK: MARTIN M. BRUCE, 1968.
              (TRAIT EVALUATION INDEX)*
           @N-2 TRAIT EVALUATION MULTITRAIT 1968M

N-3   NETTLER, G.
              A MEASURE OF ALIENATION.
              AMERICAN SOCIOLOGICAL REVIEW, 1957, 22, 670-677.
              (MEASURE OF ALIENATION)
           @N-3 ANOMIE ALIENATION AFFECTIVE-STATES 1957M

N-4   NADLER, E.
              YIELDING, AUTHORITARIANISM, AND AUTHORITARIAN IDEOLOGY REGARDING GROUPS.
              JOURNAL OF ABNORMAL AND SOCIAL PSYCHOLOGY, 1959, 58, 408-410.
              (MEASURE OF RUGGED INDIVIDUALIST IDEOLOGY)
           @N-4 1959M AUTONOMY CONFORMITY DEPENDENCE IDEOLOGY
              (APPLICATIONS: 2960)

N-5   NOWLIS, V., & NOWLIS, H. H.
              THE DESCRIPTION AND ANALYSIS OF MOOD.
              ANNALS OF THE NEW YORK ACADEMY OF SCIENCES, 1956, 65, 345-355.
              (NOWLIS ADJECTIVE CHECK LIST OF MOOD)*
           @N-5 AFFECTIVE-STATES OTHER-CATEGORY MOOD STATE CHECKLIST 1956M
              (APPLICATIONS: 122   178   271   821   876   910   941 1847 2344 2491
                       2730)

N-6   NUNNALLY, J. C., FLAUGHER, R. L., & HODGES, W. F.
                MEASUREMENT OF SEMANTIC HABITS.
                EDUCATIONAL AND PSYCHOLOGICAL MEASUREMENT, 1963, 23, 419-434.
                (MEASURE OF SEMANTIC HABITS)
           aN-6 HABITS EVALUATION COMMUNICATION STYLE COGNITIVE FUNCTIONING 1963M
                (APPLICATIONS: 371   878)

N-7   NATIONAL OPINION RESEARCH CENTER.
                JOBS AND OCCUPATIONS: A POPULAR EVALUATION.
                IN R. BENDIX AND S. M. LIPSET (EDS.), CLASS, STATUS AND POWER: A READER IN
                SOCIAL STRATIFICATION. GLENCOE, ILLINOIS: FREE PRESS, 1953, PP. 411-426.
                (OCCUPATIONAL PRESTIGE SCALE)*
           aN-7 VOCATIONAL PRESTIGE STATUS JOB SOCIAL 1953M SELF ESTEEM

N-8   NADLER, E.
                YIELDING, AUTHORITARIANISM, AND AUTHORITARIAN IDEOLOGY REGARDING GROUPS.
                JOURNAL OF ABNORMAL AND SOCIAL PSYCHOLOGY, 1959, 58, 408-410.
                (MEASURE OF IDEOLOGY OF CONFORMITY)
           aN-8 1959M AUTONOMY CONFORMITY IDEOLOGY
                (APPLICATIONS: 2960)

N-9   NEUGARTEN, B. L., HAVIGHURST, R. J., & TOBIN, S. S.
                THE MEASUREMENT OF LIFE SATISFACTION.
                JOURNAL OF GERONTOLOGY, 1961, 16, 134-143.
                (INTERVIEW-RATING MEASURE OF LIFE SATISFACTION)
           aN-9 1961M LIFE SATISFACTION GLOBAL ADJUSTMENT AFFECTIVE-STATES
                (APPLICATIONS: 2698   2963)

N-10   NUNNALLY, J. C., & HUSEK, T. R.
                THE PHONY LANGUAGE EXAMINATION: AN APPROACH TO THE MEASUREMENT OF RESPONSE
                BIAS.
                EDUCATIONAL AND PSYCHOLOGICAL MEASUREMENT, 1958, 18, 275-282.
                (GERMAN LANGUAGE RECOGNITION FORM)
           aN-10 ACQUIESCENCE RESPONSE-BIAS 1958M
                (APPLICATIONS: 233   724)

N-11   NEFF, W. S., & HELFAND, A.
                A Q-SORT INSTRUMENT TO ASSESS THE MEANING OF WORK.
                JOURNAL OF COUNSELING PSYCHOLOGY, 1963, 10, 139-145.
                (MEANING OF WORK Q-SORT)
           aN-11 Q-SORT SATISFACTION JOB ADJUSTMENT AUTONOMY MOTIVE INTRINSIC EXTRINSIC
           aN-11 SELF OTHERS 1963M SATISFACTION PE-FIT

N-12   NICHOLS, R. C., & HOLLAND, J. L.
                PREDICTION OF THE FIRST YEAR COLLEGE PERFORMANCE OF HIGH APTITUDE STUDENTS.
                PSYCHOLOGICAL MONOGRAPHS, 1963, 77 (7, WHOLE NO. 570).
           HOLLAND, J. L., & BAIRD, L. L.
                THE PRECONSCIOUS ACTIVITY SCALE: THE DEVELOPMENT AND VALIDATION OF AN
                ORIGINALITY MEASURE.
                JOURNAL OF CREATIVE BEHAVIOR, 1968, 2, 217-225.
                (PRECONSCIOUS ACTIVITY SCALE)*
           aN-12 AUTONOMY CREATIVITY ORIGINALITY 1963M
                (APPLICATIONS: 1375   1433   1515)

N-13   NEWTON, P. M.
                RECALLED DREAM CONTENT AND THE MAINTENANCE OF BODY IMAGE.
                JOURNAL OF ABNORMAL PSYCHOLOGY, 1970, 76, 134-139.
                (MEASURE OF ACTIVITY IN DREAMS)
           aN-13 1970M FANTASY BODY IMAGE

N-14   NAVRAN, L.
                A RATIONALLY DERIVED MMPI SCALE TO MEASURE DEPENDENCE.
                JOURNAL OF CONSULTING PSYCHOLOGY, 1954, 18, 192.
                (DEPENDENCE SCALE)*
           aN-14 MMPI EMOTION DEPENDENCE AUTONOMY AFFILIATION NEED 1954M
                (APPLICATIONS: 792   950   1622   1761)

N-15   NATHANSON, I. A.
                A SEMANTIC DIFFERENTIAL ANALYSIS OF PARENT-SON RELATIONSHIPS IN
                SCHIZOPHRENIA.
                JOURNAL OF ABNORMAL PSYCHOLOGY, 1967, 72, 277-281.
                (RATING FOR PARENT-SON RELATIONSHIPS)
           aN-15 SEM-DIFFERENTIAL SCHIZOPHRENIA PARENT-CHILD RELATIONSHIPS FAMILY
           aN-15 INTERACTION ADJUSTMENT 1967M

N-16   NEWMAN, S. H., HOWELL, M. A., & HARRIS, F. J.
           FORCED CHOICE AND OTHER METHODS FOR EVALUATING PROFESSIONAL HEALTH
           PERSONNEL.
           PSYCHOLOGICAL MONOGRAPHS, 1957, 71 (10, WHOLE NO. 439).
           (RATING SCALE OF WORK PERFORMANCE)
       aN-16 RATING GRAPHIC EVALUATION EMPLOYEE PERFORMANCE JOB ADJUSTMENT PEER 1957M

N-17   NOWLIS, V., & GREEN, R. F.
           THE EXPERIMENTAL ANALYSIS OF MOOD.
           IN PROCEEDINGS OF THE FIFTEENTH INTERNATIONAL CONGRESS OF PSYCHOLOGY.
           AMSTERDAM, NORTH HOLLAND, 1959, PP. 426-427.
           (MOOD ADJECTIVE CHECK LIST)*
       aN-17 POSITIVE NEGATIVE CHECKLIST STATE MOOD AFFECTIVE-STATES OTHER-CATEGORY
       aN-17 1959M
           (APPLICATIONS: 67   161   209   223   299   347   370   468   486 1019
                           1066 1672 2184 2287 2512 2515)

N-18   NORMAN, W. T.
           PERSONALITY MEASUREMENT, FAKING, AND DETECTION: AN ASSESSMENT METHOD FOR
           USE IN PERSONNEL SELECTION.
           JOURNAL OF APPLIED PSYCHOLOGY, 1963, 47, 225-241.
           (DESCRIPTIVE ADJECTIVE INVENTORY)*
       aN-18 JOB EMPLOYEE MULTITRAIT SELF-IDENTITY EVALUATION SELF PERCEPTION ESTEEM
       aN-18 DESCRIPTION 1953M

N-19   NORMAN, W. T.
           DEVELOPMENT OF SELF-REPORT TESTS TO MEASURE PERSONALITY FACTORS IDENTIFIED
           FROM PEER NOMINATIONS.
           USAF ASD TECHNICAL NOTE, 1961, NO. 61-44.
           (FORCED-CHOICE SELF-REPORT INVENTORIES)*
       aN-19 MULTITRAIT PERSONALITY SELF-IDENTITY PEER EVALUATION SELF ESTEEM EMOTION
       aN-19 PERCEPTION DESCRIPTION EXTRAVERSION STABILITY CONSCIENTIOUS 1961M

N-20   NICHOLS, R. C.
           SUBTLE, OBVIOUS AND STEREOTYPE MEASURES OF MASCULINITY-FEMININITY.
           EDUCATIONAL AND PSYCHOLOGICAL MEASUREMENT, 1962, 22, 449-461.
           (STEROTYPE SCALE)*
       aN-20 MASCULINITY FEMININITY STEREOTYPE SELF-IDENTITY SUB-IDENTITY SEX IDENTITY
       aN-20 1962M ROLE

N-21   NICHOLS, R. C.
           SUBTLE, OBVIOUS AND STEREOTYPE MEASURES OF MASCULINITY-FEMININITY.
           EDUCATIONAL AND PSYCHOLOGICAL MEASUREMENT, 1962, 22, 449-461.
           (SUBTLE SCALE)*
       aN-21 MASCULINITY FEMININITY STEREOTYPE SELF-IDENTITY SUB-IDENTITY SEX IDENTITY
       aN-21 1962M ROLE

N-22   NICHOLS, R. C.
           SUBTLE, OBVIOUS AND STEREOTYPE MEASURES OF MASCULINITY-FEMININITY.
           EDUCATIONAL AND PSYCHOLOGICAL MEASUREMENT, 1962, 22, 449-461.
           (OBVIOUS SCALE)*
       aN-22 MASCULINITY FEMININITY STEREOTYPE SELF-IDENTITY SUB-IDENTITY SEX IDENTITY
       aN-22 1962M ROLE

N-23   NYE, F. I., & MACDOUGALL, E.
           THE DEPENDENT VARIABLE IN MARITAL RESEARCH.
           PACIFIC SOCIOLOGICAL REVIEW, 1959, 2, 67-70.
           (NYE MARITAL ADJUSTMENT SCALE)*
       aN-23 MARITAL ADJUSTMENT SATISFACTION INTERPERSONAL RELATIONSHIPS MATURITY
       aN-23 EMOTION 1959M

N-24   NORDSTROM, C., FRIEDENBERG, E. Z., & GOLD, H. A.
           SOCIETY'S CHILDREN: A STUDY OF RESSENTIMENT IN THE SECONDARY SCHOOL.
           NEW YORK: RANDOM HOUSE, 1967.
           (FRIEDENBERG-NORDSTROM RESSENTIMENT INDEX)*
       aN-24 ORIENTATION VALUES AFFECTIVE-STATES GLOBAL HOSTILITY FAILURE ENVIRONMENT
       aN-24 PRESS 1967M

N-25   NUNNALLY, J. C., JR.
                POPULAR CONCEPTIONS ABOUT MENTAL HEALTH.
                NEW YORK: HOLT, RINEHART, & WINSTON, 1961.
                (MEASURE OF KNOWLEDGE ABOUT MENTAL ILLNESS)
            @N-25 1961M MENTAL-ILLNESS MENTAL-HEALTH ATTITUDE

N-26   NEILL, J. A., & JACKSON, D. N.
                AN EVALUATION OF ITEM SELECTION STRATEGIES IN PERSONALITY SCALE
                CONSTRUCTION.
                EDUCATIONAL AND PSYCHOLOGICAL MEASUREMENT, 1970, 30, 647-661.
                (MEASURE OF EVALUATION SENSITIVITY)
            @N-26 1970M EVALUATION SENSITIVITY JUDGMENT PERFORMANCE ATTITUDE PARENT TEACHER
            @N-26 PEER

N-27   NEWMAN, F. B.
                THE ADOLESCENT IN SOCIAL GROUPS: STUDIES IN THE OBSERVATION OF PERSONALITY.
                APPLIED PSYCHOLOGY MONOGRAPHS, 1946, NO. 9.
                (MEASURE OF ADOLESCENT VARIABLES)
            @N-27 1946M ADOLESCENT LEADERSHIP INHIBITION TENSION POSITIVE AFFECTIVE-STATES
                (APPLICATIONS: 1775)

N-28   NICHOLS, R. C., & SCHNELL, R. R.
                FACTOR SCALES FOR THE CALIFORNIA PSYCHOLOGICAL INVENTORY.
                JOURNAL OF CONSULTING PSYCHOLOGY, 1963, 27, 228-235.
                (VALUE ORIENTATION TEST)*
            @N-28 1963M VALUES ORIENTATION EMOTION AFFECTIVE-STATES STABILITY DENIAL
            @N-28 TEMPERAMENT HOSTILITY ANXIETY TENSION BODY WELL-BEING HOME RESPECTABLE

N-29   NICHOLS, R. C., & SCHNELL, R. R.
                FACTOR SCALES FOR THE CALIFORNIA PSYCHOLOGICAL INVENTORY.
                JOURNAL OF CONSULTING PSYCHOLOGY, 1963, 27, 228-235.
                (PERSON ORIENTATION TEST)*
            @N-29 1963M INTROVERSION EXTRAVERSION SHYNESS ORIENTATION INTERPERSONAL
            @N-29 INTERACTION SOCIAL DOMINANCE SUBMISSION LEADERSHIP FEAR RESPONSE
            @N-29 EMBARASSMENT

N-30   NEURINGER, C.
                DICHOTOMOUS EVALUATIONS IN SUICIDAL INDIVIDUALS.
                JOURNAL OF CONSULTING PSYCHOLOGY, 1961, 25, 445-449.
                (SEMANTIC DIFFERENTIAL MEASURE OF DICHOTOMOUS EVALUATIVE THINKING)
            @N-30 1961M SEM-DIFFERENTIAL EVALUATION THINKING SUICIDE

N-31   NOVICK, J., ROSENFELD, E., BLOCH, D. A., & DAWSON, D.
                ASCERTAINING DEVIANT BEHAVIOR IN CHILDREN.
                JOURNAL OF CONSULTING PSYCHOLOGY, 1966, 30, 230-238.
                (DEVIANT BEHAVIOR INVENTORY)*
            @N-31 1966M CHILD BEHAVIOR Q-SORT PARENT-CHILD SOCIAL

N-32   NUNNALLY, J. C.
                THE COMMUNICATION OF MENTAL HEALTH INFORMATION: A COMPARISON OF THE
                OPINIONS OF EXPERTS AND THE PUBLIC WITH MASS MEDIA PRESENTATIONS.
                BEHAVIORAL SCIENCE, 1957, 2, 222-230.
                (MENTAL HEALTH QUESTIONNAIRE)
            @N-32 1957M MENTAL-HEALTH MENTAL-ILLNESS ATTITUDE GLOBAL
                (APPLICATIONS: 827   2559)

N-34   NAYLOR, H. K.
                NO REFERENCE.
                CITED IN: MEGARGEE, E. I.
                RELATION BETWEEN BARRIER SCORES AND AGGRESSIVE BEHAVIOR.
                JOURNAL OF ABNORMAL PSYCHOLOGY, 1965, 70, 307-311.
                (CHECKLIST MEASURE OF AGGRESSIVE BEHAVIOR)
            @N-34 AGGRESSION BEHAVIOR CHECKLIST AGGRESSIVENESS HOSTILITY
                (APPLICATIONS: 965)

N-35   NATIONAL INSTITUTE OF MENTAL HEALTH PSYCHOPHARMACOLOGY SERVICE CENTER
                COLLABORATIVE STUDY GROUP.
                PHENOTHIAZINE TREATMENT IN ACUTE SCHIZOPHRENIA.
                ARCHIVES OF GENERAL PSYCHIATRY, 1964, 10, 246-261.
                (RATING OF SEVERITY OF MENTAL ILLNESS)
            @N-35 1964M MENTAL-ILLNESS MENTAL-HEALTH RATING PSYCHIATRIC
            @N-35 GLOBAL ADJUSTMENT DIAGNOSIS
                (APPLICATIONS: 1029)

N-36   NASH, M. M., & ZIMRING, F. M.
        PREDICTION OF REACTION TO PLACEBO.
        JOURNAL OF ABNORMAL PSYCHOLOGY, 1969, 74, 568-573.
        (INTERVIEWER PERSONALITY JUDGMENTS MEASURE)
        @N-36 1969M PERSONALITY STRUCTURE COOPERATION TRUST ANXIETY INTERVIEW RATING
            (APPLICATIONS: 1138)

N-37   NYE, F. I.
        FAMILY RELATIONSHIPS AND DELINQUENT BEHAVIOR.
        NEW YORK: WILEY, 1958.
        (FAMILY RELATIONS SCALES)
        @N-37 1958M FAMILY RELATIONSHIPS INTERACTION
        @N-37 PARENT-CHILD

N-40   NEIGER, S., SLEMON, A. G., & QUIRK, D. A.
        RORSCHACH SCALES OF REGRESSION IN PSYCHOSIS.
        GENETIC PSYCHOLOGY MONOGRAPHS, 1965, 71, 93-136.
        (MEASURE OF REGRESSION IN PSYCHOSIS)
        @N-40 1965N RORSCHACH PSYCHOPATHY PSYCHOSIS PROGNOSIS RATING SYMPTOM

N-41   NOE, F. P.
        A DENOTATIVE DIMENSION OF MEANING FOR THE MENTALLY ILL-HEALTHY ROLE IN
        SOCIETY.
        PSYCHOLOGICAL REPORTS, 1970, 26, 519-531.
        (SEMANTIC DIFFERENTIAL SCALES RELEVANT TO THE MENTALLY ILL ROLE)
        @N-41 1970M MENTAL-HEALTH EVALUATION RESPONSE-BIAS ROLE DISABILITY PSYCHIATRIC
        @SEM-DIFFERENTIAL PERCEPTION MENTAL-ILLNESS ATTITUDE.

N-42   NICHOLS, R. C., & HOLLAND, J. L.
        PREDICTION OF THE FIRST YEAR COLLEGE PERFORMANCE OF HIGH APTITUDE STUDENTS.
        PSYCHOLOGICAL MONOGRAPHS, 1963, 77 (7, WHOLE NO. 570).
        (POTENTIAL ACHIEVEMENT SCALES)
        @N-42 1963M ACHIEVEMENT ACTIVITIES NEED MOTIVE ACADEMIC LEADERSHIP PREDICTION
        @SUCCESS SCHOOL COLLEGE
            (APPLICATIONS: 1299 1515)

N-43   NOBLE, F., OHLSEN, M., & PROFF, F.
        A METHOD FOR THE QUANTIFICATION OF PSYCHOTHERAPEUTIC INTERACTION IN
        COUNSELING GROUPS.
        JOURNAL OF COUNSELING PSYCHOLOGY, 1961, 8, 54-61.
        (METHOD FOR QUANTIFYING INTERACTION IN THERAPY)
        @N-43 1961M THERAPY COUNSELING BEHAVIOR INTERACTION VERBAL CONTENT-ANALYSIS
        @THERAPIST PATIENT

N-44   NEURINGER, C., MYERS, R., & NORDMARK, T., JR.
        THE TRANSFER OF A VERBALLY CONDITIONED RESPONSE CLASS.
        JOURNAL OF COUNSELING PSYCHOLOGY, 1966, 13, 208-213.
        (VOCATIONAL PREFERENCE INVENTORY)*
        @N-44 1966M PREFERENCE VOCATIONAL JOB ATTITUDE ACTIVITIES

N-45   NUNNALLY, J., JR.
        POPULAR CONCEPTIONS OF MENTAL HEALTH.
        NEW YORK: HOLT, RINEHART AND WINSTON, 1961.
        (MEASURE OF ATTITUDES TOWARD THE MENTALLY ILL)
        @N-45 1961M ATTITUDE DISABILITY MENTAL-ILLNESS DEVIANCE PSYCHIATRIC SOCIAL
        @BELIEF PERCEPTION

N-46   NORTH, C. C., & HATT, R. K.
        THE NORC SCALES.
        IN A. J. REISS, JR., D. D. DUNCAN, P. K. HATT AND C. C. NORTH.
        OCCUPATIONS AND SOCIAL STRESS.
        GLENCOE, ILL.: THE FREE PRESS, 1961.
        (OCCUPATIONAL PRESTIGE SCALE)
        @N-46 1961M JOB PRESTIGE VOCATIONAL
            (APPLICATIONS: 2757)

O-1   OVERALL, J. E.
        DIMENSIONS OF MANIFEST DEPRESSION.
        JOURNAL OF PSYCHIATRIC RESEARCH, 1963, 1, 239-245.
        (RATING SCALE OF MANIFEST DEPRESSION)
        @O-1 RATING MOOD DEPRESSION GUILT AFFECTIVE-STATES GLOBAL NEGATIVE ANXIETY
        @O-1 DEFENSE STRESS SUBJECTIVE 1963M

0-2   OVERALL, J. E.
              A MASCULINITY-FEMININITY SCALE FOR THE KUDER PREFERENCE RECORD.
              JOURNAL OF GENERAL PSYCHOLOGY, 1963, 69, 209-216.
              (MASCULINITY-FEMININITY INDEX FOR KUDER PREFERENCE RECORD)
          @0-2 MASCULINITY FEMININITY SELF-IDENTITY SUB-IDENTITY SEX IDENTITY IMAGE
          @0-2 EVALUATION VOCATIONAL PREFERENCE INTEREST 1963M ROLE

0-3   O'CONNOR, P. A., & ATKINSON, J. W.
              AN ACHIEVEMENT RISK PREFERENCE SCALE: A PRELIMINARY REPORT.
              AMERICAN PSYCHOLOGIST, 1962, 17, 317. (ABSTRACT)
              (ACHIEVEMENT RISK-PREFERENCE SCALE)*
          @0-3 RISK-TAKING PREFERENCE NEED ACHIEVEMENT MOTIVE AUTONOMY APPROACH AVOIDANCE
          @0-3 ORIENTATION 1962M

0-4   OSTROM, T. M
              PERSPECTIVE AS AN INTERVENING CONSTRUCT IN THE JUDGMENT OF ATTITUDE
              STATEMENTS.
              JOURNAL OF PERSONALITY AND SOCIAL PSYCHOLOGY, 1966, 3, 135-144.
              (MEASURE OF ATTITUDE TOWARD NEGROES)
          @0-4 MINORITY GROUP RACIAL PREJUDICE ATTITUDE NEGRO AFFECTIVE-STATES 1966M
          @0-4 OTHER-CATEGORY SOCIAL DISTANCE

0-5   OLINER, M. H.
              SEX ROLE ACCEPTANCE AND PERCEPTION OF PARENTS.
              UNPUBLISHED DOCTORAL DISSERTATION, TEACHERS COLLEGE, COLUMBIA UNIVERSITY,
              1958.
              (MEASURE OF PARENTAL IDENTIFICATION)
          @0-5 MATERNAL PATERNAL ACCEPTANCE ADJUSTMENT SEX ROLE PARENTAL SELF PERCEPTION
          @0-5 SIMILARITY FAMILY IDEAL INTERACTION SELF-IDENTITY IMAGE IDENTIFICATION
          @0-5 1958M SUB-IDENTITY
              (APPLICATIONS: 1624)

0-6   OLSEN, M. E.
              TWO CATEGORIES OF POLITICAL ALIENATION.
              SOCIAL FORCES, 1969, 47, 288-299.
              (MEASURE OF POLITICAL ALIENATION)
          @0-6 ALIENATION POLITICAL AFFECTIVE-STATES NEGATIVE GLOBAL 1969M ORIENTATION
          @0-6 SATISFACTION

0-7   O'NEILL, M.
              VALIDITY OF HYSTERICAL PERSONALITY AS A CLINICAL CATEGORY.
              UNPUBLISHED MASTER'S THESIS, EMORY UNIVERSITY, 1965.
          O'NEILL, M.
              VALIDATION STUDY FOR HYSTERICAL PERSONALITY SCALES.
              UNPUBLISHED STUDY, EMORY UNIVERSITY, 1966.
              (MEASURE OF HYSTERICAL PERSONALITY)
          @0-7 PERSONALITY ADJUSTMENT GLOBAL NEUROTICISM DEFENSE 1965M MENTAL-ILLNESS
          @0-7 DIAGNOSIS MENTAL-HEALTH
              (APPLICATIONS: 1104 2398)

0-8   O'CONNELL, W.
              AN ITEM ANALYSIS OF THE WIT AND HUMOR APPRECIATION TEST.
              JOURNAL OF SOCIAL PSYCHOLOGY, 1962, 56, 271-276.
              (WIT AND HUMOR APPRECIATION TEST)*
          @0-8 AFFECTIVE-STATES HUMOR OTHER-CATEGORY POSITIVE HOSTILITY 1962M

0-9   OJEMANN, R. H., LEVITT, E. E., LYLE, W. H., JR., & WHITESIDE, M. F.
              THE EFFECTS OF A "CAUSAL" TEACHER-TRAINING PROGRAM AND CERTAIN CURRICULAR
              CHANGES ON GRADE SCHOOL CHILDREN.
              JOURNAL OF EXPERIMENTAL EDUCATION, 1955, 24, 95-114.
              (CAUSAL TEST)
          @0-9 STRUCTURE FUNCTIONING CHILD ORIENTATION COGNITIVE MOTIVE COMPLEXITY
          @0-9 1955M TEACHER
              (APPLICATIONS: 323)

0-10   OETTEL, A.
              LEADERSHIP: A PSYCHOLOGICAL ANALYSIS.
              UNPUBLISHED DOCTORAL DISSERTATION, UNIVERSITY OF CALIFORNIA, 1952.
              (LEADERSHIP SCALE)
          @0-10 MMPI LEADERSHIP JOB MANAGEMENT SUPERVISOR INTERPERSONAL RELATIONSHIPS
          @0-10 1952M

O-11   OBRADOVIC, J.
        MODIFICATION OF THE FORCED-CHOICE METHOD AS A CRITERION OF JOB PROFICIENCY.
        JOURNAL OF APPLIED PSYCHOLOGY, 1970, 54, 228-233.
        (FORCED-CHOICE JOB MERIT-RATING SYSTEM)
        aO-11 1970M EMPLOYEE RATING JOB

O-12   ORLINSKY, D. E., & HOWARD, K. I.
        THERAPY SESSION REPORTS, FORMS P AND T.
        CHICAGO: INSTITUTE FOR JUVENILE RESEARCH, 1966.
        (THERAPY SESSION REPORTS, FORMS P AND T)*
        aO-12 1966M THERAPY INTERACTION AFFECTIVE-STATES PATIENT
        aO-12 EFFECTIVENESS RELATIONSHIPS
        (APPLICATIONS: 2305 2389 2981)

O-16   OSGOOD, C. E.
        THE NATURE AND MEASUREMENT OF MEANING.
        PSYCHOLOGICAL BULLETIN, 1952, 49, 197-237.
        (SEMANTIC DIFFERENTIAL TECHNIQUE)
        aO-16 1952M SEM-DIFFERENTIAL ACTIVE EVALUATION POWER
        (APPLICATIONS: 2   10   15   71   106   121   153   226   228   242
                          317   410   546   560   611   618   621   624   659   661
                          694   740   770   791   805   823   856   895   943   956
                          968   973   984   1041   1042   1082   1093   1139   1146   1168
                         1198   1301   1329   1339   1361   1364   1399   1764   1797   1875
                         1894   1904   1926   1935   2169   2301   2309   2380   2488   2559
                         2573   2587   2594   2607   2613   2619   2625   2680   2772   2776
                         2777   2780   2785   2807   2883   2951   2958   2963   2966   2982)

O-17   O'NEIL, W. M., & LEVINSON, D. J.
        A FACTORIAL EXPLORATION OF AUTHORITARIANISM AND SOME OF ITS IDEOLOGICAL
        CONCOMITANTS.
        JOURNAL OF PERSONALITY, 1954, 22, 449-463.
        (RELIGIOUS CONVENTIONALISM SCALE)
        aO-17 1954M RELIGION ATTITUDE IDEOLOGY AUTHORITARIANISM CONSERVATISM
        (APPLICATIONS: 552 660 779)

O-18   O'NEIL, W. M., & LEVINSON, D. J.
        A FACTORIAL EXPLORATION OF AUTHORITARIANISM AND SOME OF ITS IDEOLOGICAL
        CONCOMITANTS.
        JOURNAL OF PERSONALITY, 1954, 22, 449-463.
        (ETHNOCENTRISM SCALE)
        aO-18 1954M AUTHORITARIANISM ETHNOCENTRISM IDEOLOGY ATTITUDE ETHNIC
        (APPLICATIONS: 779)

O-20   ORGEL, S. A.
        DIFFERENTIAL CLASSIFICATION OF HEBEPHRENIC AND PARANOID SCHIZOPHRENICS
        FROM CASE MATERIAL.
        JOURNAL OF CLINICAL PSYCHOLOGY, 1957, 13, 159-161.
        (SCALE FOR CLASSIFICATION OF SCHIZOPHRENIC PATIENTS)
        aO-20 1957M SCHIZOPHRENIA MENTAL-ILLNESS DIFFERENTIATION DIAGNOSIS PSYCHIATRIC
        (APPLICATIONS: 957 1020)

O-22   OVERALL, J. E., & GORHAM, D. R.
        THE BRIEF PSYCHIATRIC RATING SCALE.
        PSYCHOLOGICAL REPORTS, 1962, 10, 799-812.
        (BRIEF PSYCHIATRIC RATING SCALE)*
        aO-22 1962M PSYCHIATRIC RATING MENTAL-ILLNESS ADJUSTMENT DIAGNOSIS PROGNOSIS
        aPATIENT
        (APPLICATIONS: 957 2440 2636)

O-23   O'NEIL, W. M., & LEVINSON, D. J.
        A FACTORIAL EXPLORATION OF AUTHORITARIANISM AND SOME OF ITS IDEOLOGICAL
        CORRELATES.
        JOURNAL OF PERSONALITY, 1954, 449-463.
        LEVINSON, D. J., & HUFFMAN, P. E.
        TRADITIONAL FAMILY IDEOLOGY AND ITS RELATION TO PERSONALITY.
        JOURNAL OF PERSONALITY, 1955, 23, 251-273.
        (TRADITIONAL FAMILY IDEOLOGY SCALE)*
        aO-23 FAMILY IDEOLOGY COPING-DEFENSE INTERACTION ADJUSTMENT RELATIONSHIPS
        aO-23 PARENT-CHILD
        (APPLICATIONS: 389   393   424   596   779   934 1014 1087)

O-25   OLIVE, L. E.
        RELATIONSHIP OF VALUES AND PREFERRED ACTIVITIES TO THE PERCEPTION OF
        ACTIVITIES INVOLVED IN AN OCCUPATION.
        UNPUBLISHED DOCTORAL DISSERTATION, UNIVERSITY OF NEBRASKA, 1962.
        (OCCUPATIONAL ROLE PERCEPTIONS INVENTORY)*
        aO-25 1962M JOB PERCEPTION VOCATIONAL INVENTORY ROLE ATTITUDE ACTIVITIES

0-26   OSIPOW, S. H.
               COGNITIVE STYLES AND EDUCATIONAL-VOCATIONAL PREFERENCES AND SELECTION.
               JOURNAL OF COUNSELING PSYCHOLOGY, 1969, 16, 534-546.
               (WORD SIMILARITY TEST)
          aO-26 1969M WORD ASSOCIATION COGNITIVE STYLE SIMILARITY

0-27   OSIPOW, S. H.
               COGNITIVE STYLES AND EDUCATIONAL-VOCATIONAL PREFERENCES AND SELECTION.
               JOURNAL OF COUNSELING PSYCHOLOGY, 1969, 16, 534-546.
               (MEASURE OF TENDENCY FOR EXTREME RESPONSES)
          aO-27 1969M COGNITIVE STYLE AUTHORITARIANISM DOGMATISM RIGIDITY FLEXIBILITY
          aRESPONSE INTENSITY

0-28   OSIPOW, S. H.
               COGNITIVE STYLES AND EDUCATIONAL-VOCATIONAL PREFERENCES AND SELECTION.
               JOURNAL OF COUNSELING PSYCHOLOGY, 1969, 16, 534-546.
               (WORD SORT TEST)
          aO-28 1969M WORD ASSOCIATION Q-SORT COGNITIVE STYLE DIFFERENTIATION SIMILARITY

0-29   OSTERHOUSE, R. A.
               A COMPARISON OF DESENSITIZATION AND STUDY-SKILLS TRAINING FOR THE TREATMENT
               OF TWO KINDS OF TEST-ANXIOUS STUDENTS.
               UNPUBLISHED DOCTORAL DISSERTATION, OHIO STATE UNIVERSITY, 1969.
               (TEST ANXIETY SCALE)
          aO-29 1969M TEST ANXIETY STRESS EMOTION PHYSIOLOGICAL SYMPTOM PERFORMANCE

0-31   ORPEN, C.
               PREJUDICE AND ADJUSTMENT TO CULTURAL NORMS AMONG ENGLISH-SPEAKING SOUTH
               AFRICANS.
               JOURNAL OF PSYCHOLOGY, 1971, 77, 217-218.
               (MEASURE OF AGREEMENT WITH SOUTH AFRICAN VALUES)
          aO-31 1971M CROSS-CULTURAL VALUES CULTURE SOCIAL NORMS

0-32   OLLENDICK, T., BALLA, D., & ZIGLER, E.
               EXPECTANCY OF SUCCESS AND THE PROBABILITY LEARNING OF RETARDED CHILDREN.
               JOURNAL OF ABNORMAL PSYCHOLOGY, 1971, 77, 275-281.
               (COTTAGE RATING SCALES)*
          aO-32 1971M RATING CHILD MENTAL-ILLNESS JOB ACTIVITIES PEER RELATIONSHIPS
          aGLOBAL ATTITUDE LEADERSHIP ABILITY

0-33   OHIO STATE UNIVERSITY PSYCHOLOGICAL TEST.
               NO AUTHOR, NO REFERENCE, CITED IN:
               JOURNAL OF CONSULTING PSYCHOLOGY, 1967, 31, 213-215.
               (OHIO STATE UNIVERSITY PSYCHOLOGICAL TEST)*
          aO-33 PERSONALITY INVENTORY
               (APPLICATIONS: 2073)

P-1   PRUITT, D. G., & JOHNSON, D. F.
               MEDIATION AS AN AID TO FACE SAVING IN NEGOTIATION.
               JOURNAL OF PERSONALITY AND SOCIAL PSYCHOLOGY, 1970, 14, 239-246.
               (INDEX OF PERCEIVED PERSONAL STRENGTH)
          aP-1 INTERACTION COMPETITION PERSONAL PERCEIVED SEM-DIFFERENTIAL SELF RATING
          aP-1 COMPETENCE EVALUATION ESTEEM SOCIAL INTERPERSONAL 1970M

P-3   PECK, R. F., & DIAZ-GUERRERO, R.
               TWO CORE-CULTURE PATTERNS AND THE DIFFUSION OF VALUES ACROSS THEIR BORDER.
               INTERNATIONAL JOURNAL OF PSYCHOLOGY, 1967, 2, 275-282.
               (MEASURE OF CULTURAL VALUES THROUGH SEMANTIC MEANING)
          aP-3 CHECKLIST CULTURE RESPECT SELF-IDENTITY VALUES IDEALS LIFE GOALS
          aP-3 CROSS-CULTURAL 1967M

P-4   PEDERSEN, D. M.
               THE MEASUREMENT OF INDIVIDUAL DIFFERENCES IN PERCEIVED PERSONALITY TRAIT
               RELATIONSHIPS AND THEIR RELATION TO CERTAIN DETERMINANTS. URBANA: UNIVER-
               SITY OF ILLINOIS PRESS, 1962. ALSO IN JOURNAL OF SOCIAL PSYCHOLOGY, 1965,
               65, 233-258.
               (MEASURE OF SIX PERSONALITY TRAITS)
          aP-4 PERSONALITY MULTITRAIT EXTRAVERSION NEUROTICISM INTROVERSION THINKING
          aP-4 COOPERATION EMOTION STABILITY 1962M TRAIT

P-5   PEDERSEN, D. M.
               EGO STRENGTH AND DISCREPANCY BETWEEN CONSCIOUS AND UNCONSCIOUS
               SELF-CONCEPTS.
               PERCEPTUAL AND MOTOR SKILLS, 1965, 20, 691-692.
               (SELF-CONSISTENCY TEST)*
           ∂P-5 NEED AUTONOMY ACHIEVEMENT SECURITY SELF CONSISTENCY GLOBAL ADJUSTMENT
           ∂P-5 SELF-IDENTITY EVALUATION ESTEEM PERCEPTION OTHERS 1965M ROLE

P-6   PEDERSEN, D. M., & BREGLIO, V. J.
               THE CORRELATION OF TWO SELF-DISCLOSURE INVENTORIES WITH ACTUAL SELF-
               DISCLOSURE: A VALIDITY STUDY.
               JOURNAL OF PSYCHOLOGY, 1968, 68, 291-298.
               (SELF-DISCLOSURE QUESTIONNAIRE)*
           ∂P-6 SELF DISCLOSURE RESPONSE-BIAS COMMUNICATION PERSONAL ACCESSIBILITY 1968M

P-7   PETTIGREW, T.
               THE MEASUREMENT AND CORRELATES OF CATEGORY WIDTH AS A COGNITIVE VARIABLE.
               JOURNAL OF PERSONALITY, 1958, 26, 532-544.
               (CATEGORY WIDTH SCALE)*
           ∂P-7 COGNITIVE COMPLEXITY STRUCTURE FUNCTIONING STYLE CONCEPT CONCEPTUAL BREADTH
           ∂P-7 THINKING 1958M
               (APPLICATIONS: 73   103   156   410   466   529   533   537   677   878
                                921   1054   1145   1887)

P-8   PHILIP, A. E., & MCCULLOCH, J. W.
               SOCIAL PATHOLOGY AND PERSONALITY IN ATTEMPTED SUICIDE.
               BRITISH JOURNAL OF PSYCHIATRY, 1967, 113, 1405-1406.
               (SOCIAL PATHOLOGY SCALE)*
           ∂P-8 ADJUSTMENT GLOBAL SOCIAL COMPETENCE MENTAL-ILLNESS 1967M

P-9   PIERS, E. V., & HARRIS, D. B.
               AGE AND OTHER CORRELATES OF SELF-CONCEPT IN CHILDREN.
               JOURNAL OF EDUCATIONAL PSYCHOLOGY, 1964, 55, 91-95.
               (MEASURE OF SELF-CONCEPT IN CHILDREN)
           ∂P-9 CHILD IMAGE SELF CONCEPT SELF-IDENTITY EVALUATION PERCEPTION ESTEEM 1964M

P-10   PILISUK, M., POTTER, P., RAPOPORT, A., & WINTER, J. A.
               WAR HAWKS AND PEACE DOVES: ALTERNATE RESOLUTIONS OF EXPERIMENTAL CONFLICTS.
               JOURNAL OF CONFLICT RESOLUTION, 1965, 9, 491-508.
               (INTERNATIONALISM MEASURE)
           ∂P-10 INTERNATIONALISM COOPERATION GROUP CONFLICT COPING-DEFENSE GLOBAL STYLE
           ∂P-10 HISTORY INTERPERSONAL ATTITUDE POLITICAL ORIENTATION 1965M

P-11   PODELL, L.
               SEX AND ROLE CONFLICT.
               JOURNAL OF MARRIAGE AND THE FAMILY, 1966, 28, 163-165.
               (MEASURE OF OCCUPATIONAL ATTITUDES)
           ∂P-11 ATTITUDE JOB VOCATIONAL ADJUSTMENT ROLE IDENTITY ENVIRONMENT PE-FIT SEX
           ∂P-11 CONFLICT SELF-IDENTITY SUB-IDENTITY 1966M

P-12   PODELL, L.
               OCCUPATIONAL AND FAMILIAL ROLE-EXPECTATIONS.
               JOURNAL OF MARRIAGE AND THE FAMILY, 1967, 29, 492-493.
               (MEASURE OF FAMILIAL ATTITUDES)
           ∂P-12 ROLE FAMILY INTERACTION ADJUSTMENT MARITAL BEHAVIOR ATTITUDE 1967M

P-13   PRESSEY, A. W.
               GROUP DIFFERENCES ON THE POGGENDORFF ILLUSION.
               CANADIAN PSYCHOLOGIST, 1965, 6, 224.(ABSTRACT)
               (POGGENDORFF ILLUSION)*
           ∂P-13 FIELD DEPENDENCE PERCEPTION AUTONOMY GROUP PERFORMANCE DIFFERENCES 1965M

P-14   PAGE, H. A., & EPSTEIN, S.
               FANTASY SCALE.
               KENT: KENT STATE UNIVERSITY, 1959.(MIMEO)
               (FANTASY SCALE)*
           ∂P-14 FANTASY IMAGERY 1959M EXPERIENCE IMAGINATION

P-15   PANTON, J. H.
            A NEW MMPI SCALE FOR THE IDENTIFICATION OF HOMOSEXUALITY.
            JOURNAL OF CLINICAL PSYCHOLOGY, 1960, 16, 17-20.
            (HSX SCALE FOR HOMOSEXUALITY)
         aP-15 HOMOSEXUALITY MMPI SELF-IDENTITY SEX IDENTITY ROLE MASCULINITY FEMININITY
         aP-15 ADJUSTMENT 1960M
            (APPLICATIONS: 2067 2540)

P-16   PEABODY, D.
            ATTITUDE CONTENT AND AGREEMENT SET IN SCALES OF AUTHORITARIANISM, DOGMATISM
            ANTI-SEMITISM, AND ECONOMIC CONSERVATISM.
            JOURNAL OF ABNORMAL AND SOCIAL PSYCHOLOGY, 1961, 63, 1-11.
            (NEGATIVELY KEYED DOGMATISM SCALE)
         aP-16 DOGMATISM ACQUIESCENCE RESPONSE SET COPING-DEFENSE FLEXIBILITY RIGIDITY
         aP-16 OTHER-CATEGORY RESPONSE-BIAS 1961M
            (APPLICATIONS: 203)

P-17   PERKINS, C. W., & SHANNON, D. T.
            THREE TECHNIQUES FOR OBTAINING SELF-PERCEPTIONS IN PREADOLESCENT BOYS.
            JOURNAL OF PERSONALITY AND SOCIAL PSYCHOLOGY, 1965, 2, 443-447.
            (MEASURE OF SELF AND IDEAL SELF)
         aP-17 SELF IDEAL CONCEPT SELF-IDENTITY EVALUATION PERCEPTION ESTEEM IMAGE
         aP-17 CHILD 1965M
            (APPLICATIONS: 2460)

P-18   PETERSON, D. R. & CATTELL, R. B.
            PERSONALITY FACTORS IN NURSERY SCHOOL CHILDREN AS DERIVED
            FROM TEACHER RATINGS.
            JOURNAL OF CONSULTING PSYCHOLOGY, 1959, 23, 562.
            PETERSON, D. R.
            THE AGE OF GENERALITY OF PERSONALITY FACTORS DERIVED FROM RATINGS.
            EDUCATIONAL AND PSYCHOLOGICAL MEASUREMENT, 1960, 20, 461-474.
            (CHILD BEHAVIOR RATING SCHEDULE)
         aP-18 BEHAVIOR RATING ADJUSTMENT INTROVERSION EXTRAVERSION GLOBAL AUTONOMY 1960M
            (APPLICATIONS: 83)

P-19   PHILIPS, E. L.
            ATTITUDES TOWARD SELF AND OTHERS: A BRIEF QUESTIONNAIRE REPORT.
            JOURNAL OF CONSULTING PSYCHOLOGY, 1951, 15, 79-81.
            (PHILIP'S SELF-ACCEPTANCE INVENTORY)*
         aP-19 SELF ACCEPTANCE SELF-IDENTITY EVALUATION PERCEPTION ESTEEM CONCEPT IMAGE
         aP-19 ATTITUDE 1951M
            (APPLICATIONS: - 1206 1853)

P-20   PORTER, L. W.
            PERCEIVED TRAIT REQUIREMENTS IN BOTTOM AND MIDDLE MANAGEMENT JOBS.
            JOURNAL OF APPLIED PSYCHOLOGY, 1961, 45, 232-236.
            (MEASURE OF PERCEIVED TRAIT REQUIREMENTS IN MANAGEMENT JOBS)
         aP-20 SUPERVISOR LEADERSHIP MANAGEMENT JOB TRAIT ADJUSTMENT INTERPERSONAL
         aP-20 BEHAVIOR STYLE 1961M DEMANDS
            (APPLICATIONS: 2472)

P-21   PILOWSKY, I., LEVINE, S., & BOULTON, D. M.
            THE CLASSIFICATION OF DEPRESSION BY NUMERICAL TAXONOMY.
            BRITISH JOURNAL OF PSYCHIATRY, 1969, 115, 937-945.
            (DEPRESSION QUESTIONNAIRE)
         aP-21 DEPRESSION AFFECTIVE-STATES GLOBAL NEGATIVE SUICIDE REACTIVITY 1968M

P-22   PORTEUS, S. D.
            THE PORTEUS MAZE TEST AND INTELLIGENCE.
            PALO ALTO, CALIFORNIA: PACIFIC BOOKS, 1950.
            (PORTEUS MAZE TEST)*
         aP-22 INTELLIGENCE CHILD ADULT 1950M PERFORMANCE TEST
            (APPLICATIONS: 528   749 1061 1688 1837 1850 2045)

P-23   POWELL, F. A.
            SOURCE CREDIBILITY AND BEHAVIORAL COMPLIANCE AS DETERMINANTS OF ATTITUDE
            CHANGE.
            JOURNAL OF PERSONALITY AND SOCIAL PSYCHOLOGY, 1965, 2, 669-676.
            (MEASURE OF ATTITUDES TOWARD HEALTH AND MEDICINE)
         aP-23 ATTITUDE CHANGE HEALTH PERSUASIBILITY 1965M PRESTIGE SUGGESTIBILITY

P-24   PYRON, B.
            A FACTOR-ANALYTIC STUDY OF SIMPLICITY-COMPLEXITY OF SOCIAL ORDERING.
            PERCEPTUAL AND MOTOR SKILLS, 1966, 22, 259-272.
            (CHANGE INVENTORY)*
         aP-24 SOCIAL ORIENTATION CHANGE RIGIDITY COPING-DEFENSE FLEXIBILITY DOGMATISM
         aP-24 1966M
            (APPLICATIONS: 200)

P-25   PILISUK, M., POTTER, P., RAPAPORT, A., & WINTER, J. A.
        WAR HAWKS AND PEACE DOVES: ALTERNATE RESOLUTIONS OF EXPERIMENTAL CONFLICTS.
        JOURNAL OF CONFLICT RESOLUTION, 1965, 9, 491-508.
        (MONETARY RISK PREFERENCE MEASURE)
        aP-25 INTERPERSONAL COOPERATION GROUP CONFLICT ATTITUDE RISK-TAKING 1965M
        aP-25 GLOBAL STYLE HISTORY COPING-DEFENSE PREFERENCE

P-26   PETTIT, T. F.
        ANALITY AND TIME.
        JOURNAL OF CONSULTING AND CLINICAL PSYCHOLOGY, 1969, 33, 170-174.
        (TIME SCALE)
        aP-26 1969M TIME ORIENTATION PERSPECTIVE PERSONALITY

P-27   PATTERSON, G. R., LITTMAN, R. A., & HINSEY, W. C.
        PARENTAL EFFECTIVENESS AS REINFORCERS IN THE LABORATORY AND ITS RELATION TO
        CHILD REARING PRACTICES AND CHILD ADJUSTMENT IN THE CLASSROOM.
        JOURNAL OF PERSONALITY, 1964, 32, 180-199.
        (INTERVIEW FOR RATING PARENTAL BEHAVIOR AND ATTITUDES)
        aP-27 PARENTAL BEHAVIOR ATTITUDE FAMILY INTERACTION ADJUSTMENT INTERPERSONAL
        aP-27 RELATIONSHIPS RATING 1964M PARENT-CHILD
        (APPLICATIONS: 43)

P-28   PINE, F.
        A MANUAL FOR RATING DRIVE CONTENT IN THE THEMATIC APPERCEPTION TEST.
        JOURNAL OF PROJECTIVE TECHNIQUES AND PERSONALITY ASSESSMENT, 1960, 24, 32-
        45.
        (TAT SCORED FOR DRIVE INTENSITY)
        aP-28 DRIVE INTENSITY TAT IMAGERY MOTIVE AUTONOMY NEED PROJECTIVE 1960M
        (APPLICATIONS: 403   2238)

P-29   PALERMO, D. S., & MARTIRE, J. G.
        THE INFLUENCE OF ORDER OF ADMINISTRATION ON SELF-CONCEPT MEASURES.
        JOURNAL OF CONSULTING PSYCHOLOGY, 1960, 24, 372.
        (MEASURES OF ACTUAL, SOCIAL, AND IDEAL-SELF CONCEPTS)
        aP-29 SELF-IDENTITY SELF IDEAL CONCEPT IMAGE SOCIAL EVALUATION PERCEPTION PUBLIC
        aP-29 ESTEEM IDENTITY 1960M

P-30   PACE, C. R., & STERN, G. C.
        AN APPROACH TO THE MEASUREMENT OF PSYCHOLOGICAL CHARACTERISTICS OF COLLEGE
        ENVIRONMENTS.
        JOURNAL OF EDUCATIONAL PSYCHOLOGY, 1958, 49, 269-277.
        STERN, G. C.
        SCORING INSTRUCTIONS AND COLLEGE NORMS: ACTIVITIES INDEX, COLLEGE
        CHARACTERISTICS INDEX. SYRACUSE: PSYCHOLOGICAL RESEARCH CENTER, 1963.
        STERN, G. C., & PACE, C. R.
        COLLEGE CHARACTERISTICS INDEX, FORM 1158. SYRACUSE, N. Y.: PSYCHOLOGICAL
        RESEARCH CENTER, SYRACUSE UNIVERSITY, 1958.
        (COLLEGE CHARACTERISTICS INDEX)*
        aP-30 ENVIRONMENT ADJUSTMENT NEED COLLEGE PE-FIT 1958M STUDENT
        (APPLICATIONS: 1416)

P-31   PETERSON, D. R., QUAY, H. C., & CAMERON, G. R.
        PERSONALITY AND BACKGROUND FACTORS IN JUVENILE DELINQUENCY AS INFERRED FROM
        QUESTIONNAIRE RESPONSES.
        JOURNAL OF CONSULTING PSYCHOLOGY, 1959, 23, 395-399.
        (FACTOR SCALES FROM DELINQUENCY SCALES)
        aP-31 SCHOOL PROBLEM FAMILY NEUROTICISM PSYCHOPATHY DELINQUENCY
        aP-31 ADJUSTMENT OTHER-CATEGORY ADOLESCENT SOCIAL ALIENATION 1959M
        (APPLICATIONS: 994 1100 1619 1715 1716 1923)

P-32   PHILLIPS, L.
        CASE HISTORY DATA AND PROGNOSIS IN SCHIZOPHRENIA.
        JOURNAL OF NERVOUS AND MENTAL DISEASE, 1953, 117, 515-525.
        (PHILLIPS PROGNOSTIC RATING SCALE)*
        (PHILLIPS SCALE OF PREMORBID SOCIAL AND SEXUAL ADJUSTMENT)*
        aP-32 SOCIAL SEX ADJUSTMENT GLOBAL DIAGNOSIS SCHIZOPHRENIA MENTAL-ILLNESS
        aP-32 PSYCHIATRIC 1953M PROGNOSIS
        (APPLICATIONS: 337   442   676   732   734   763   765   804   845   884
                         941   947   966   973 1027 1041 1042 1044 1049 1050
                        1052 1057 1069 1081 1084 1091 1097 1111 1145 1148
                        1151 1562 1691 1802 1851 1934 1978 1981 2018 2060
                        2064 2068 2078 2080 2092 2193 2243 2263 2265 2272
                        2380 2393 2396 2403 2408 2727)

P-33   PATCHEN, M.
                ABSENCE AND EMPLOYEE FEELINGS ABOUT FAIR TREATMENT.
                PERSONNEL PSYCHOLOGY, 1960, 13, 349-360.
                (JOB SATISFACTION QUESTIONNAIRE)
            @P-33 JOB SATISFACTION ATTITUDE EMPLOYEE AFFECTIVE-STATES GLOBAL ENVIRONMENT
            @P-33 PE-FIT ADJUSTMENT 1960M

P-34   PICKLE, H., & FRIEDLANDER, F.
                SEVEN SOCIETAL CRITERIA OF ORGANIZATIONAL SUCCESS.
                PERSONNEL PSYCHOLOGY, 1967, 20, 165-177.
                (COMMUNITY SATISFACTION MEASURE)
            @P-34 GROUP SATISFACTION ENVIRONMENT PE-FIT ORGANIZATION 1967M

P-35   PALMER, S.
                FRUSTRATION, AGGRESSION, AND MURDER.
                JOURNAL OF ABNORMAL AND SOCIAL PSYCHOLOGY, 1960, 60, 430-432.
                (INDICES OF FRUSTRATION AND AGGRESSION)
            @P-35 FRUSTRATION AGGRESSION AFFECTIVE-STATES RESENTMENT HOSTILITY NEGATIVE
            @P-35 1960M

P-36   PALACIOS, M. H., NEWBERRY, L. A., & BOOTZIN, R. R.
                PREDICTIVE VALIDITY OF THE INTERVIEW.
                JOURNAL OF APPLIED PSYCHOLOGY, 1966, 50, 67-72.
                (DIAGNOSTIC INTERVIEW)*
            @P-36 DIAGNOSIS MENTAL-ILLNESS ADJUSTMENT GLOBAL OTHER-CATEGORY 1966M PROGNOSIS

P-37   PRELINGER, E., ZIMET, C., & LEVIN, M.
                AN EGO-PSYCHOLOGICAL SCHEME FOR PERSONALITY ASSESSMENT.
                PSYCHOLOGICAL REPORTS, 1960, 7, 182.
                (OVERALL PERSONALITY ASSESSMENT MEASURE)
            @P-37 MULTITRAIT PERSONALITY GLOBAL RATING EGO 1960M

P-38   PYRON, B.
                AN ATTEMPT TO TEST THE THEORY OF PSYCHOLOGICAL DEVELOPMENT.
                PSYCHOLOGICAL REPORTS, 1959, 5, 685-698.
                (BELIEF Q-SORT)*
            @P-38 GROWTH PERSONAL Q-SORT BELIEF CREATIVITY DEVELOPMENT SELF-IDENTITY SELF
            @P-38 ACTUALIZATION 1959M

P-39   PENNEY, R. K., & MCCANN, B.
                THE CHILDREN'S REACTIVE CURIOSITY SCALE.
                PSYCHOLOGICAL REPORTS, 1964, 15, 323-334.
                (CHILDREN'S REACTIVE CURIOSITY SCALE)*
            @P-39 ADJUSTMENT COMPETENCE ENVIRONMENT AUTONOMY APPROACH CHILD AVOIDANCE MOTIVE
            @P-39 OTHER-CATEGORY NEED ACHIEVEMENT VARIETY STIMULUS SEEKING 1964M

P-40   PENNEY, R. K., & MCCANN, B.
                THE CHILDREN'S REACTIVE CURIOSITY SCALE.
                PSYCHOLOGICAL REPORTS, 1964, 15, 323-334.
                (LIE SCALE)*
            @P-40 FAKING RESPONSE-BIAS MANIFEST ANXIETY CHILD 1964M

P-41   PERSONS, R. W.
                DEGREE OF AFFECT EXPRESSION IN PSYCHOTHERAPY AND DEGREE OF PSYCHOPATHY.
                PSYCHOLOGICAL REPORTS, 1965, 16, 1157-1162.
                (CLIENT AND THERAPIST AFFECT SCALES)
            @P-41 PSYCHOPATHY AFFECTIVE-STATES THERAPY OTHER-CATEGORY EXPRESSION COUNSELING
            @P-41 EXPRESSIVENESS EMOTION PSYCHIATRIC INTENSITY 1965M

P-42   PANG, H.
                RELIGIOUS ATTITUDES OF STUDENTS.
                PSYCHOLOGICAL REPORTS, 1968, 22, 344.
            PANG, H.
                RELIGIOUS ATTITUDES OF STUDENT DENOMINATIONAL GROUPS.
                UNPUBLISHED MASTER'S THESIS, UNIVERSITY OF ARKANSAS, 1961.
                (QUESTIONNAIRE MEASURE OF RELIGIOUS ATTITUDES)
            @P-42 ATTITUDE RELIGION ORIENTATION STUDENT ALTRUISM CONFORMITY 1961M

P-43   PLUTCHIK, R.
                  MULTIPLE RATING SCALES FOR THE MEASUREMENT OF AFFECTIVE STATES.
                  JOURNAL OF CLINICAL PSYCHOLOGY, 1966, 22, 423-425.
                  (MEASURE OF EIGHT BASIC EMOTIONS)
            @P-43 MOOD EMOTION GLOBAL AFFECTIVE-STATES OTHER-CATEGORY 1966M
                  (APPLICATIONS: 2636)

P-44   PEDERSEN, D. M., & STANFORD, G. H.
                  PERSONALITY CORRELATES OF CHILDREN'S SELF-ESTEEM AND PARENTAL
                  IDENTIFICATION.
                  PSYCHOLOGICAL REPORTS, 1969, 25, 41-42.
                  (IDENTIFICATION INVENTORY)*
            @P-44 CHILD PARENTAL IDENTIFICATION SEM-DIFFERENTIAL ADJUSTMENT FAMILY
            @P-44 INTERACTION PARENT-CHILD 1969M

P-45   PHILLIPS, L., & ZIGLER, E.
                  SOCIAL COMPETENCE: THE ACTION-THOUGHT PARAMETER AND VICARIOUSNESS IN NORMAL
                  AND PATHOLOGICAL BEHAVIORS.
                  JOURNAL OF ABNORMAL AND SOCIAL PSYCHOLOGY, 1961, 63, 137-146.
            ZIGLER, E., & PHILLIPS, L.
                  SOCIAL COMPETENCE AND THE PROCESS-REACTIVE DISTINCTION IN PSYCHOPATHOLOGY.
                  JOURNAL OF ABNORMAL AND SOCIAL PSYCHOLOGY, 1962, 65, 215-222.
                  (METHOD OF ASSESSING ROLE ORIENTATION)
            @P-45 ROLE ORIENTATION SYMPTOM PATIENT PSYCHIATRIC 1961M
                  (APPLICATIONS: 877 1113 1149 2268 2381)

P-46   PEDERSEN, D. M.
                  THE MEASUREMENT OF INDIVIDUAL DIFFERENCES IN PERCEIVED PERSONALITY-TRAIT
                  RELATIONSHIPS AND THEIR RELATION TO CERTAIN DETERMINANTS.
                  JOURNAL OF SOCIAL PSYCHOLOGY, 1965, 65, 233-258.
                  (NEGATIVE CALIFORNIA F SCALE)*
            @P-46 RESPONSE-BIAS F-SCALE ACQUIESCENCE RESPONSE SET PERCEPTION TRAIT
            @P-46 AUTHORITARIANISM 1965M

P-47   PILISUK, M., POTTER, P., RAPOPORT, A., & WINTER, J. A.
                  WAR HAWKS AND PEACE DOVES: ALTERNATE RESOLUTIONS OF EXPERIMENTAL CONFLICTS.
                  JOURNAL OF CONFLICT RESOLUTION, 1965, 9, 491-508.
                  (MEASURE OF TOLERANCE FOR AMBIGUITY)
            @P-47 TOLERANCE AMBIGUITY COGNITIVE STYLE STRUCTURE 1965M RIGIDITY FLEXIBILITY
                  (APPLICATIONS: 2885)

P-48   PEDERSEN, D. M.
                  THE RELATIONSHIP BETWEEN EGO-STRENGTH AND THE DISCREPANCY BETWEEN CONSCIOUS
                  AND UNCONSCIOUS SELF-SCHEMA.   UNPUBLISHED MASTER'S THESIS, BRIGHAM YOUNG
                  UNIVERSITY, (DATE UNKNOWN).
            PEDERSEN, D. M.
                  EVALUATION OF SELF AND OTHERS AND SOME PERSONALITY CORRELATES.
                  JOURNAL OF PSYCHOLOGY, 1969, 71, 225-244.
                  (SELF AND OTHERS RATING SCALE)*
            @P-48 SEM-DIFFERENTIAL SELF-IDENTITY SELF CONCEPT IMAGE SUB-IDENTITY EVALUATION
                  (APPLICATIONS: 2601)

P-49   PORTER, L. W.
                  A STUDY OF PERCEIVED NEED SATISFACTIONS IN BOTTOM AND MIDDLE MANAGEMENT
                  JOBS.
                  JOURNAL OF APPLIED PSYCHOLOGY, 1961, 45, 1-10.
                  (MEASURE OF PERCEIVED MANAGEMENT NEED SATISFACTIONS)
            @P-49 MANAGEMENT LEADERSHIP PE-FIT PERCEIVED NEED SATISFACTION JOB ADJUSTMENT
            @P-49 1961M
                  (APPLICATIONS: 2358   2370   2468   2472   2474   2479)

P-50   PUMROY, D. K.
                  REVISED PRELIMINARY MANUAL FOR THE MARYLAND PARENT ATTITUDE SURVEY.
                  UNPUBLISHED MANUSCRIPT, UNIVERSITY OF MARYLAND, 1960.
            PUMROY, D. K.
                  MARYLAND PARENT ATTITUDE SURVEY: A RESEARCH INSTRUMENT WITH SOCIAL
                  DESIRABILITY CONTROLLED.
                  JOURNAL OF PSYCHOLOGY, 1966, 64, 73-78.
                  (MARYLAND PARENT ATTITUDE SURVEY)*
            @P-50 PARENT-CHILD PARENTAL ATTITUDE FAMILY INTERACTION ADJUSTMENT INTERPERSONAL
            @P-50 RELATIONSHIPS 1960M
                  (APPLICATIONS: 55)

P-51   PHILLIPS, L., & ZIGLER, E.
                SOCIAL COMPETENCE: THE ACTION-THOUGHT PARAMETER AND VICARIOUSNESS IN NORMAL
                AND PATHOLOGICAL BEHAVIORS.
                JOURNAL OF ABNORMAL AND SOCIAL PSYCHOLOGY, 1961, 63, 137-146.
                (CATEGORIZATION OF PSYCHIATRIC SYMPTOMS)
        aP-51 PERSONAL ORIENTATION SYMPTOM PSYCHIATRIC PATIENT 1961M
                (APPLICATIONS: 877   2381   2412   2426)

P-52   PARTINGTON, J. T.
                DR. JEKYLL AND MR. HIGH: MULTIDIMENSIONAL SCALING OF ALCOHOLICS'
                SELF-EVALUATIONS.
                JOURNAL OF ABNORMAL PSYCHOLOGY, 1970, 75, 131-138.
                (SELF-EVALUATION MEASURE FOR ALCOHOLICS)
        aP-52 SELF EVALUATION SELF-IDENTITY ALCOHOLISM PERCEIVED SIMILARITY 1970M

P-53   POLAND, W. D.
                AN EXPLORATION OF THE RELATIONSHIP BETWEEN SELF-ESTIMATED AND MEASURED
                PERSONALITY CHARACTERISTICS IN THE OPEN AND CLOSED MIND.
                UNPUBLISHED DOCTORAL DISSERTATION, OHIO STATE UNIVERSITY, 1963.
                (SELF-RATING ON PERSONALITY CHARACTERISTICS)
        aP-53 1963M SELF RATING MULTITRAIT DESCRIPTION
                (APPLICATIONS: 2770   2851)

P-54   POLAN, C. G., & SPENCER, B. L.
                CHECK LIST OF SYMPTOMS OF AUTISM OF EARLY LIFE.
                WEST VIRGINIA MEDICAL JOURNAL, 1959, 55, 198-204.
                (CHECK LIST OF SYMPTOMS OF EARLY INFANTILE AUTISM)*
        aP-54 1959M CHILD MENTAL-ILLNESS ADJUSTMENT SYMPTOM
                (APPLICATIONS: 2907)

P-55   PERRUCCI, C. C., & PERRUCCI, R.
                SOCIAL ORIGINS, EDUCATIONAL CONTEXTS, AND CAREER MOBILITY.
                AMERICAN SOCIOLOGICAL REVIEW. 1970, 35, 451-463.
                (SCALE OF OCCUPATIONAL VALUES)
        aP-55 1970M ROLE JOB VALUES VOCATIONAL MOTIVE

P-56   PEARSON, P. H.
                RELATIONSHIPS BETWEEN GLOBAL AND SPECIFIED MEASURES OF NOVELTY SEEKING.
                JOURNAL OF CONSULTING AND CLINICAL PSYCHOLOGY, 1970, 34, 199-204.
                (NOVELTY EXPERIENCING SCALE)*
        aP-56 1970M EXPERIENCE SENSATION SEEKING OPENNESS NOVELTY VARIETY

P-57   PEARSON, P. H.
                RELATIONSHIPS BETWEEN GLOBAL AND SPECIFIED MEASURES OF NOVELTY SEEKING.
                JOURNAL OF CONSULTING AND CLINICAL PSYCHOLOGY, 1970, 34, 199-204.
                (DESIRE-FOR-NOVELTY SCALE)*
        aP-57 1970M EXPERIENCE SENSATION SEEKING OPENNESS NOVELTY VARIETY

P-58   PARLOFF, M. B., KELMAN, H. C., & FRANK, J. D.
                COMFORT, EFFECTIVENESS, AND SELF-AWARENESS AS CRITERIA OF IMPROVEMENT IN
                PSYCHOTHERAPY.
                AMERICAN JOURNAL OF PSYCHIATRY, 1954, 111, 343-351.
                (SYMPTOM DISTRESS CHECKLIST)*
        aP-58 1954M NEUROTICISM SYMPTOM CHECKLIST PSYCHIATRIC PATIENT AFFECTIVE-STATES
        aP-58 ADJUSTMENT THERAPY MENTAL-ILLNESS PROGNOSIS DIAGNOSIS
                (APPLICATIONS: 2921)

P-59   PEABODY, D.
                SYMMETRY AND ASYMMETRY IN INTERPERSONAL RELATIONS - WITH IMPLICATIONS FOR
                THE CONCEPT OF PROJECTION.
                JOURNAL OF PERSONALITY, 1970, 38, 426-434.
                (MEASURE OF SYMMETRY IN INTERPERSONAL RELATIONS)
        aP-59 1970M INTERPERSONAL RELATIONSHIPS SOCIAL ADJUSTMENT COMPETENCE

P-60   PALLONE, N. J., RICKARD, F. S., HURLEY, R. B., & TIRMAN, R. J.
                WORK VALUES AND SELF-MEANING.
                JOURNAL OF COUNSELING PSYCHOLOGY, 1970, 17, 376-377.
                (MEASURE OF SEMANTIC MEANING OF SELF)
        aP-60 1970M SELF-IDENTITY SELF-DESCRIPTION SEM-DIFFERENTIAL CONCEPT IMAGE

P-61   PETERSON, R. E., CENTRA, J. A., HARTNETT, R. T., & LINN, R. L.
            INSTITUTIONAL FUNCTIONING INVENTORY TECHNICAL MANUAL.
            PRINCETON, N. J.: EDUCATIONAL TESTING SERVICE, 1970.
        CENTRA, J. A., HARTNETT, R. T., & PETERSON, R. E.
            FACULTY VIEWS OF INSTITUTIONAL FUNCTIONING: A NEW MEASURE OF COLLEGE
            ENVIRONMENTS.
            EDUCATIONAL AND PSYCHOLOGICAL MEASUREMENT, 1970, 30, 405-416.
            (INSTITUTIONAL FUNCTIONING INVENTORY)*
        @P-61 1970M COLLEGE ENVIRONMENT PE-FIT FUNCTIONING
        @P-61 STUDENT TEACHER
            (APPLICATIONS: 2714)

P-62   PORTER, R. B., SCHEIER, I. H., & CATTELL, R. B.
            CHILD PERSONALITY QUESTIONNAIRE HANDBOOK (2ND. ED.).
            CHAMPAIGN, ILLINOIS: INSTITUTE OF PERSONALITY AND ABILITY TESTING, 1965.
            (CHILDREN'S PERSONALITY QUESTIONNAIRE)*
        @P-62 1965M SCHOOL PERSONALITY STRUCTURE CHILD
            (APPLICATIONS: 2797)

P-63   PASCAL, G. R., & JENKINS, W. O.
            SYSTEMATIC OBSERVATION OF GROSS HUMAN BEHAVIOR.
            NEW YORK: GRUNE & STRATTON, 1961.
            (PASCAL-JENKINS BEHAVIORAL SCALE)
        @P-63 1961M BEHAVIOR PARENTAL CHILD RELATIONSHIPS INTERACTION
        @MATERNAL PATERNAL AFFECTION RELIGION PHYSICAL HEALTH PUNITIVENESS
        @COMPATIBILITY ACTIVITIES
            (APPLICATIONS: 2565)

P-64   PHILLIPS, L., KADEN, S., & WALDMAN, M.
            RORSCHACH INDICES OF DEVELOPMENTAL LEVEL.
            JOURNAL OF GENETIC PSYCHOLOGY, 1959, 94, 267-285.
            (RORSCHACH DEVELOPMENTAL SCORING SYSTEM)
        @P-64 1959M RORSCHACH ADJUSTMENT DEVELOPMENT PROJECTIVE
            (APPLICATIONS: 1561 1563 2912)

P-66   PIM, J., & MCCLURE, G.
            BEHAVIOR OBSERVATIONS OF GRADE ONE PUPILS.
            OTTAWA, CANADA: OTTAWA CITY SCHOOL DISTRICT, 1966.
            (OTTAWA SCALE FOR MEASURING MALADAPTIVE BEHAVIORS)
        @P-66 1966M CHILD ADJUSTMENT BEHAVIOR TEACHER RATING
            (APPLICATIONS: 2545)

P-67   PACE, C. R.
            COLLEGE AND UNIVERSITY ENVIRONMENT SCALES.
            PRINCETON: EDUCATIONAL TESTING SERVICE, 1963.
            (COLLEGE AND UNIVERSITY ENVIRONMENT SCALES)*
        @P-67 1963M COLLEGE ENVIRONMENT PE-FIT
        @P-67 STUDENT
            (APPLICATIONS: 2712 2714 2801)

P-68   PETERSON, R. E.
            COLLEGE STUDENT QUESTIONNAIRES: TECHNICAL MANUAL.
            PRINCETON, N. J.: EDUCATIONAL TESTING SERVICE, 1965.
            (COLLEGE STUDENT QUESTIONNAIRES)*
        @P-68 1965M COLLEGE STUDENT ATTITUDE ADJUSTMENT
            (APPLICATIONS: 1468 1516 2712)

P-70   PEABODY, D.
            TWO COMPONENTS IN BIPOLAR SCALES: DIRECTION AND EXTREMENESS.
            PSYCHOLOGICAL REVIEW, 1962, 69, 65-73.
            (MEASURE OF EXTREMENESS OF RESPONSE STYLE)
        @P-70 1962M JUDGMENT RESPONSE BEHAVIOR INTENSITY STYLE RESPONSE-BIAS SET

P-72   PASTORE, N.
            THE ROLE OF ARBITRARINESS IN THE FRUSTRATION-AGGRESSION HYPOTHESIS.
            JOURNAL OF ABNORMAL AND SOCIAL PSYCHOLOGY, 1952, 47, 728-731.
            (FRUSTRATION-AGGRESSION QUESTIONNAIRE)
        @P-72 1952M FRUSTRATION AGGRESSION AFFECTIVE-STATES EMOTION AROUSAL ADJUSTMENT
        @P-72 SITUATIONAL STRESS
            (APPLICATIONS: 327)

P-73   PETTIT, T. F.
            ANALITY AND TIME.
            JOURNAL OF CONSULTING AND CLINICAL PSYCHOLOGY, 1969, 33, 170-174.
            (COMPOSITE ANALITY SCALE)
        @P-73 1969M RIGIDITY ORDERLINESS COMPULSIVENESS PERSONALITY
        @P-73 ANALITY ORALITY

P-74   PIROJNIKOFF, L.
          CATHARSIS AND THE ROLE OF PERCEPTUAL CHANGE IN THE REDUCTION OF HOSTILITY.
          UNPUBLISHED DOCTORAL DISSERTATION, UNIVERSITY OF TEXAS, 1958.
          (SOCIAL SENSITIVITY SCALE)*
          aP-74 1958M ATTITUDE SOCIAL SENSITIVITY EMPATHY OTHERS INTERPERSONAL
          (APPLICATIONS: 397)

P-75   PATCHEN, P.
          IN M. E. BROWN, IDENTIFICATION, INTEGRATION, AND THE CONDITIONS OF
          ORGANIZATIONAL INVOLVEMENT.
          UNPUBLISHED DOCTORAL DISSERTATION, UNIVERSITY OF MICHIGAN, 1964.
          (INDEX OF N AFFILIATION)
          aP-75 1564M AFFILIATION NEED TRAIT SOCIAL RELATIONSHIPS IDENTIFICATION
          aP-75 INTEGRATION INTERPERSONAL
          (APPLICATIONS: 504)

P-76   PERVIN, L. A., & RUBIN, D. B.
          STUDENT DISSATISFACTION WITH COLLEGE AND THE COLLEGE DROPOUT: A
          TRANSACTIONAL APPROACH.
          JOURNAL OF SOCIAL PSYCHOLOGY, 1967, 72, 285-295.
          (INSTRUMENT FOR THE TRANSACTIONAL ANALYSIS OF PERSCNALITY AND ENVIRONMENT)*
          aP-76 1967M PE-FIT SEM-DIFFERENTIAL SELF COLLEGE SELF-IDENTITY ENVIRONMENT
          (APPLICATIONS: 479)

P-77   PASCALL, G. R., & SUTTELL, B.
          THE BENDER-GESTALT TEST.
          NEW YORK: GRUNE & STRATTON, 1951.
          BENDER, L. A.
          A VISUAL MOTOR GESTALT TEST AND ITS CLINICAL USE.
          AMERICAN ORTHOPSYCHIATRIC RESEARCH MONOGRAPH, 1938, NO. 3.
          (BENDER-GESTALT SCORED FOR EGO STRENGTH)
          aP-77 1951M GRAPHIC PROJECTIVE EGO-STRENGTH EGO DEVELOPMENT SELF ACTUALIZATION
          (APPLICATIONS: 1603)

P-78   PEARSON, P. H.
          A CONCEPTUAL AND METHODOLOGICAL STUDY OF THREE ROGERIAN CONSTRUCTS.
          UNPUBLISHED DOCTORAL DISSERTATION, UNIVERSITY OF CHICAGO, 1968.
          (DECISION IMPLEMENTATION TEST)
          aP-78 1968M DECISION COMPLEXITY IE-CONTROL OTHERS
          (APPLICATIONS: 532)

P-79   PEARSON, P. H.
          A CONCEPTUAL AND METHODOLOGICAL STUDY OF THREE ROGERIAN CONSTRUCTS.
          UNPUBLISHED DOCTORAL DISSERTATION, UNIVERSITY OF CHICAGO, 1968.
          (DECISION MAKING INVENTORY)
          aP-79 1968M DECISION IE-CONTROL OTHERS
          (APPLICATIONS: 532 1662)

P-80   PEARSON, P. H.
          A CONCEPTUAL AND METHODOLOGICAL STUDY OF THREE ROGERIAN CONSTRUCTS.
          UNPUBLISHED DOCTORAL DISSERTATION, UNIVERSITY OF CHICAGO, 1968.
          (INDIVIDUAL REACTION INVENTORY)
          aP-80 1968M EXPERIENCE ENVIRONMENT SITUATIONAL
          (APPLICATIONS: 532   585 1881)

P-81   PEARSON, P. H.
          A CONCEPTUAL AND METHODOLOGICAL STUDY OF THREE ROGERIAN CONSTRUCTS.
          UNPUBLISHED DOCTORAL DISSERTATION, UNIVERSITY OF CHICAGO, 1968.
          (WORD REACTION TEST)
          aP-81 1968M AFFECTIVE-STATES FEELING
          (APPLICATIONS: 532 2021)

P-82   PAUL, G. L.
          INSIGHT VS. DESENSITIZATION IN PSYCHOTHERAPY: AN EXPERIMENT IN ANXIETY
          REDUCTION.
          STANFORD: STANFORD UNIVERSITY PRESS, 1966.
          (SCALE OF SPECIFIC ANXIETY IN SPEECH PERFORMANCE)
          aP-82 1966M ANXIETY PERFORMANCE TENSION STRESS VOICE
          (APPLICATIONS: 990 1012 1072 2095 2725)

P-83   PEARSON, P. H.
          A CONCEPTUAL AND METHODOLOGICAL STUDY OF THREE ROGERIAN CONSTRUCTS.
          UNPUBLISHED DOCTORAL DISSERTATION, UNIVERSITY OF CHICAGO, 1968.
          (MEASURE OF EMPATHY)
          aP-83 1968M EMPATHY SENSITIVITY FEELING OTHERS
          (APPLICATIONS: 532 2094)

P-84   PHILLIPS, L., & COWITZ, B.
                SOCIAL ATTAINMENT AND REACTIONS TO STRESS.
                JOURNAL OF PERSONALITY, 1953, 22, 270-283.
                (WORCESTER SCALE OF SOCIAL ATTAINMENT)*
            aP-84 1953M SOCIAL STATUS SELF ENHANCEMENT
                (APPLICATIONS: 570   1284)

P-85   PORTER, L. W., & LAWLER, E. E., 111.
                MANAGERIAL ATTITUDES AND PERFORMANCE.
                BEHAVIORAL SCIENCE, RICHARD D. IRWIN, INC., 1968.
                (JOB ATTITUDES QUESTIONNAIRE)
            aP-85 1968M ATTITUDE JOB SATISFACTION FINANCIAL
                (APPLICATIONS: 2481)

P-86   PAIVIO, A., BALDWIN, A. L., & BERGER, S.
                MEASUREMENT OF CHILDREN'S SENSITIVITY TO AUDIENCES.
                CHILD DEVELOPMENT, 1961, 32, 721-730.
                (MEASURE OF EXHIBITIONISM)
            aP-86 CHILD BEHAVIOR SOCIAL DEVELOPMENT COMPETENCE
            aP-86 1961M ATTRACTION ATTENTION SEEKING
                (APPLICATIONS: 594)

P-87   PAIVIO, A., BALDWIN, A. L., & BERGER, S.
                MEASUREMENT OF CHILDREN'S SENSITIVITY TO AUDIENCES.
                CHILD DEVELOPMENT, 1961, 32, 721-730.
                (MEASURE OF SELF-CONSCIOUSNESS)
            aP-87 1961M AWARENESS SELF SOCIAL
                (APPLICATIONS: 594)

P-88   PAGE, H. A., & PETTANATO, C.
                SOME PERSONALITY CHARACTERISTICS OF "GOOD" AND "POOR" TEST INTERPRETERS.
                PAPER PRESENTED AT MEETING OF THE EASTERN PSYCHOLOGICAL ASSOCIATION,
                NEW YORK, 1963.
                (SELF ESTEEM Q-SORT)
            aP-88 1963M SELF ESTEEM Q-SORT IDEAL JUDGMENT THERAPY
                (APPLICATIONS: 2318)

P-89   PEABODY, D.
                ATTITUDE CONTENT AND AGREEMENT SET IN SCALES OF AUTHORITARIANISM,
                DOGMATISM, ANTI-SEMITISM, AND ECONOMIC CONSERVATISM.
                JOURNAL OF ABNORMAL AND SOCIAL PSYCHOLOGY, 1961, 63, 1-11.
                (CONSERVATISM SCALE)
            aP-89 1961M POLITICAL ORIENTATION ATTITUDE CONSERVATISM

P-90   PAIVIO, A., BALDWIN, A. L., & BERGER, S. M.
                MEASUREMENT OF CHILDREN'S SENSITIVITY TO AUDIENCES.
                CHILD DEVELOPMENT, 1961, 32, 721-730.
                (CHILDREN'S AUDIENCE SENSITIVITY INVENTORY)*
            aP-90 1961M CHILD SENSITIVITY ATTRACTION SEEKING SITUATIONAL ANXIETY
                (APPLICATIONS: 822)

P-91   PAYNE, D. E., & MUSSEN, P. H.
                PARENT-CHILD RELATIONS AND FATHER IDENTIFICATION AMONG ADOLESCENT BOYS.
                JOURNAL OF ABNORMAL AND SOCIAL PSYCHOLOGY, 1956, 52, 358-362.
                (STORY COMPLETION TEST OF PERCEIVED PARENTAL POWER)
            aP-91 1956M PARENTAL POWER INTERPERSONAL RELATIONSHIPS PARENT-CHILD NURTURANCE
            aP-91 PUNITIVENESS IDENTIFICATION PROJECTIVE TAT PATERNAL

P-94   PALMER, R. D.
                PATTERNS OF DEFENSIVE RESPONSE TO THREATENING STIMULI: ANTECEDENTS AND
                CONSISTENCY.
                JOURNAL OF ABNORMAL PSYCHOLOGY, 1968, 73, 30-36.
                (PERCEPTION TEST OF VIGILANCE-DEFENSIVE BEHAVIOR)
            aP-94 1968M DEFENSE STIMULUS BEHAVIOR RESPONSE

P-95   PALMER, R. D.
                PATTERNS OF DEFENSIVE RESPONSE TO THREATENING STIMULI: ANTECEDENTS AND
                CONSISTENCY.
                JOURNAL OF ABNORMAL PSYCHOLOGY, 1968, 73, 30-36.
                (RECALL TEST OF VIGILANCE-DEFENSIVE BEHAVIOR)
            aP-95 1968M DEFENSE STIMULUS BEHAVIOR RESPONSE REPRESSION

P-96   PALMER, R. D.
                PATTERNS OF DEFENSIVE RESPONSE TO THREATENING STIMULI: ANTECEDENTS AND
                CONSISTENCY.
                JOURNAL OF ABNORMAL PSYCHOLOGY, 1968, 73, 30-36.
                (LEARNING TEST OF VIGILANCE-DEFENSIVE BEHAVIOR)
            @P-96 1968M DEFENSE STIMULUS BEHAVIOR RESPONSE REPRESSION

P-97   PALMER, R. D.
                PATTERNS OF DEFENSIVE RESPONSE TO THREATENING STIMULI: ANTECEDENTS AND
                CONSISTENCY.
                JOURNAL OF ABNORMAL PSYCHOLOGY, 1968, 73, 30-36.
                (PHRASE REVERSAL TEST OF VIGILANCE-DEFENSIVE BEHAVIOR)
            @P-97 1968M DEFENSE STIMULUS BEHAVIOR RESPONSE

P-98   PALMER, R. D.
                PATTERNS OF DEFENSIVE RESPONSE TO THREATENING STIMULI: ANTECEDENTS AND
                CONSISTENCY.
                JOURNAL OF ABNORMAL PSYCHOLOGY, 1968, 73, 30-36.
                (PREFERENCE TEST OF VIGILANCE-DEFENSIVE BEHAVIOR)
            @P-98 1968M DEFENSE STIMULUS BEHAVIOR RESPONSE PREFERENCE

P-99   PALMER, R. D.
                PATTERNS OF DEFENSIVE RESPONSE TO THREATENING STIMULI: ANTECEDENTS AND
                CONSISTENCY.
                JOURNAL OF ABNORMAL PSYCHOLOGY, 1968, 73, 30-36.
                (MOTOR PERFORMANCE TEST OF VIGILANCE-DEFENSIVE BEHAVIOR)
            @P-99 1968M DEFENSE STIMULUS BEHAVIOR RESPONSE PERFORMANCE

P-101   PHILLIS, J. A.
                CHILDREN'S JUDGMENTS OF PERSONALITY ON THE BASIS OF VOICE QUALITY.
                DEVELOPMENTAL PSYCHOLOGY, 1970, 3, 411.
                (MEASURE OF PERSONALITY JUDGMENTS OF CHILDREN ON BASIS OF VOICE)
            @P-101 1970M CHILD VOICE JUDGMENT PERSONALITY SEM-DIFFERENTIAL
            @OTHERS INTERPERSONAL EVALUATION

P-102   PETERS, D. R.
                IDENTIFICATION AND PERSONAL CHANGE IN LABORATORY TRAINING GROUPS.
                DOCTORAL DISSERTATION, SLOAN SCHOOL OF MANAGEMENT, MASSACHUSETTS INSTITUTE
                OF TECHNOLOGY, CAMBRIDGE, MASS.: MICROREPRODUCTION LABORATORY, M.I.T.
                LIBRARIES, 1966.
            PETERS, D. R.
                SELF-IDEAL CONGRUENCE AS A FUNCTION OF HUMAN RELATIONS TRAINING.
                JOURNAL OF PSYCHOLOGY, 1970, 76, 199-207.
                (SEMANTIC DIFFERENTIAL MEASURE OF SELF-CONCEPT)
            @P-102 1966M SEM-DIFFERENTIAL SELF CONCEPT INTERPERSONAL PERCEPTION GROUP IDEAL
                (APPLICATIONS: 2896)

P-104   PAUL, G. L.
                INSIGHT VERSUS DESENSITIZATION IN PSYCHOTHERAPY: AN EXPERIMENT IN ANXIETY
                REDUCTION.
                STANFORD, CALIFORNIA: STANFORD UNIVERSITY PRESS, 1966.
                (CHECKLIST OF OVERT BEHAVIORAL MANIFESTATIONS OF FEAR)
            @P-104 1966M CHECKLIST PERFORMANCE ANXIETY BEHAVIOR FEAR MANIFEST
                (APPLICATIONS: 2429)

P-105   P.HILLIPS, D. L.
                REJECTION: A POSSIBLE CONSEQUENCE OF SEEKING HELP FOR MENTAL DISORDERS.
                AMERICAN SOCIOLOGICAL REVIEW, 1963, 28, 963-972.
                (MEASUREMENT OF ACCEPTANCE OR REJECTION OF PERSONS SEEKING HELP)
            @P-105 1963M MENTAL-ILLNESS ACCEPTANCE SUPPORT DEVIANCE BEHAVIOR
            @SOCIAL RESPONSIBILITY REJECTION
                (APPLICATIONS: 1410   2559)

P-106   POPE, B., SIEGMAN, A. W., & BLASS, T.
                ANXIETY AND SPEECH IN THE INITIAL INTERVIEW.
                JOURNAL OF CONSULTING AND CLINICAL PSYCHOLOGY, 1970, 35, 233-238.
                (TEMPORAL MEASURES OF VERBAL FLUENCY)
            @P-106 1970M TIME ANXIETY VOICE COMMUNICATION

P-108   PAYNE, R. W., & HEWLETT, J. H. G.
         THOUGHT DISORDER IN PSYCHOTIC PATIENTS.
         IN H. J. EYSENCK (ED.), EXPERIMENTS IN PERSONALITY. VOL. II.
         ROUTLEDGE & KEGAN PAUL, 1960.
         (GOLDSTEIN OBJECT SORTING TEST)*
         @P-108 1960M MENTAL-ILLNESS PSYCHIATRIC SYMPTOMS DIAGNOSIS OVERINCLUSION
         @OVEREXCLUSION COGNITIVE FUNCTIONING STYLE SCHIZOPHRENIA
         (APPLICATIONS: 2404 2592 2630)

P-109.   PHILLIPS, L. A.
         A STUDY OF THE RELATIONSHIP BETWEEN ANOMIE AND ALCOHOLISM.
         UNPUBLISHED MASTER'S THESIS, OKLAHOMA STATE UNIVERSITY, 1967.
         (ALCOHOLISM SCALE)
         @P-109 1967M ALCOHOLISM BEHAVIOR DEVIANCE SOCIAL

P-110   POMERANZ, D. M., & GOLDFRIED, M. R.
         AN INTAKE REPORT OUTLINE FOR BEHAVIOR MODIFICATION.
         PSYCHOLOGICAL REPORTS, 1970, 26, 447-450.
         (ASSESSMENT QUESTIONNAIRE FOR BEHAVIOR THERAPY)
         @P-110 1970M COUNSELING BEHAVIOR THERAPY ADJUSTMENT SYMPTOM MENTAL-HEALTH
         @MENTAL-ILLNESS

P-111   PRINCE, R.
         A STUDY OF THE RELATIONSHIP BETWEEN INDIVIDUAL AND ADMINISTRATIVE
         EFFECTIVENESS IN THE SCHOOL SITUATION.
         UNPUBLISHED DOCTORAL DISSERTATION, UNIVERSITY OF CHICAGO, 1957.
         (DIFFERENTIAL VALUES INVENTORY)
         @P-111 1957M VALUES ORIENTATION

P-112   POE, W. A.
         DIFFERENTIAL VALUE PATTERNS OF COLLEGE STUDENTS.
         UNPUBLISHED DOCTORAL DISSERTATION, UNIVERSITY OF NEBRASKA, 1954.
         (POE INVENTORY OF VALUES (PIV))*
         @P-112 1954M VALUES INTELLECTUAL RELIGION POWER SOCIAL INVENTORY
         (APPLICATIONS: 1285 1503)

P-113   PECK, R. F., & MCGUIRE, C.
         MEASURING CHANGES IN MENTAL HEALTH WITH THE SENTENCE COMPLETION TECHNIQUE.
         PSYCHOLOGICAL REPORTS, 1959, 5, 151-160.
         (SENTENCE COMPLETION TEST)
         @P-113 1959M SENTENCE-COMP MENTAL-HEALTH ADJUSTMENT GLOBAL CHANGE
         (APPLICATIONS: 1411)

P-114   PALLONE, N. J., & GRANDE, P. P.
         FACILITATION OF COMMUNICATION OF PROBLEM RELATED CONTENT IN THE SCHOOL
         COUNSELING INTERVIEW.
         RESEARCH MONOGRAPH SERIES, NO. 2, 1964, UNIVERSITY OF NOTRE DAME,
         DEPARTMENT OF EDUCATION.
         (MEASURE OF CLIENT PROBLEM-RELATED CONTENT)
         @P-114 1964M PROBLEM COMMUNICATION THERAPY COUNSELING
         @INTERVIEW CONTENT-ANALYSIS PATIENT SCHOOL COLLEGE DIAGNOSIS
         (APPLICATIONS: 1398)

P-115   PALLONE, N. J., & GRANDE, P. P.
         FACILITATION OF COMMUNICATION OF PROBLEM RELATED CONTENT IN THE SCHOOL
         COUNSELING INTERVIEW.
         RESEARCH MONOGRAPH SERIES, NO. 2, 1964, UNIVERSITY OF NOTRE DAME,
         DEPARTMENT OF EDUCATION.
         (COUNSELOR VERBAL BEHAVIOR CLASSIFICATION SCHEDULE)
         @P-115 1964M COUNSELING COMMUNICATION BEHAVIOR THERAPIST PATIENT VERBAL
         @INTERACTION
         (APPLICATIONS: 1398)

P-116   PORTER, E. H., JR.
         A SIMPLE MEASURE OF COUNSELOR ATTITUDES.
         IN E. S. WILLIAMSON (ED.), TRENDS IN STUDENT PERSONNEL WORK.
         MINNEAPOLIS: UNIVERSITY OF MINNESOTA PRESS, 1949.
         (TEST OF COUNSELOR ATTITUDES)*
         @P-116 1949M COUNSELING THERAPY ATTITUDE SUPPORT EVALUATION EMPATHY THERAPIST
         (APPLICATIONS: 1214 1232 1400 1464)

P-118   PIERCE-JONES, J.
         VOCATIONAL INTEREST CORRELATES OF SOCIO-ECONOMIC STATUS IN ADOLESCENCE.
         EDUCATIONAL AND PSYCHOLOGICAL MEASUREMENT, 1959, 19, 65-71.
         (INTEREST STATUS SCALES FOR KUDER PREFERENCE RECORD)
         @P-118 1959M INTEREST STATUS VOCATIONAL SOCIAL JOB PERCEPTION ATTITUDE
         @PREFERENCE
         (APPLICATIONS: 1186)

P-119   PATTERSON, C. H.
            EFFECTS OF COUNSELOR EDUCATION ON PERSONALITY.
            JOURNAL OF COUNSELING PSYCHOLOGY, 1967, 14, 444-448.
            (COUNSELING ATTITUDE SCALE)
         aP-119 1967M COUNSELING ATTITUDE ADJUSTMENT SELF SOCIETY PATIENT THERAPIST

P-120   PODELL, J. E.
            A COMPARISON OF GENERALIZATION AND ADAPTATION LEVEL AS THEORIES OF
            CONNOTATION.
            JOURNAL OF ABNORMAL AND SOCIAL PSYCHOLOGY, 1961, 62, 593-597.
            (FAVORABLENESS SCALE)
         aP-120 1961M TRAIT EVALUATION DESIRABILITY SOCIAL PERSONAL RESPONSE-BIAS
            (APPLICATIONS: 1533)

P-121   PRESSY, S. L.
            A GROUP SCALE FOR INVESTIGATING THE EMOTIONS.
            JOURNAL OF ABNORMAL PSYCHOLOGY, 1921, 16, 55-64.
            (PRESSY X-O TESTS)
         aP-121 1921M ANXIETY TENSION TEST INTEREST CHECKLIST EMOTION GROUP
            (APPLICATIONS: 1268)

P-122   PETTIGREW, T. F.
            PERSONALITY AND SOCIOCULTURAL FACTORS IN INTERGROUP ATTITUDES: A
            CROSS-NATIONAL COMPARISON.
            JOURNAL OF CONFLICT RESOLUTION, 1958, 2, 29-42.
            (MEASURE OF ANTI-AFRICAN ATTITUDES)
         aP-122 1958M RACIAL PREJUDICE CROSS-CULTURAL ETHNOCENTRISM ETHNIC ATTITUDE
         aBELIEF OPINION

P-123   PEPINSKY, H. B., SIEGEL, L., & VAN ATTA, E. L.
            THE CRITERION IN COUNSELING: A GROUP PARTICIPATION SCALE.
            JOURNAL OF ABNORMAL AND SOCIAL PSYCHOLOGY, 1952, 47, 415-419.
            (GROUP PARTICIPATION SCALE)*
         aP-123 1952M GROUP PARTICIPATION COUNSELING
         aINVOLVEMENT INTERACTION SOCIABILITY SECURITY SOCIAL COMPETENCE
            (APPLICATIONS: 1164)

P-124   PAUL, G. L.
            INSIGHT VERSUS DESENSITIZATION IN PSYCHOTHERAPY.
            STANFORD, CALIFORNIA: STANFORD UNIVERSITY PRESS, 1966.
            (THERAPIST RATING FORMS)
         aP-124 1956M THERAPY RATING COUNSELING PATIENT ORIENTATION
         aTHERAPIST EFFECTIVENESS

P-125   PETTIGREW, T. F.
            PERSONALITY AND SOCIOCULTURAL FACTORS IN INTERGROUP ATTITUDES: A
            CROSS-NATIONAL COMPARISON.
            JOURNAL OF CONFLICT RESOLUTION, 1958, 2, 29-42.
            (MEASURE OF SOCIAL CONFORMITY)
         aP-125 1958M CROSS-CULTURAL SOCIAL CONFORMITY

P-126   PIOTROWSKI, Z. A., & BRICKLIN, B.
            A LONG-TERM PROGNOSTIC CRITERION FOR SCHIZOPHRENICS BASED ON RORSCHACH
            DATA.
            PSYCHIATRIC QUARTERLY SUPPLEMENT, 1958, 32, 315-329.
            (RORSCHACH PROGNOSTIC INDEX FOR SCHIZOPHRENICS)
         aP-126 1958M MENTAL-HEALTH MENTAL-ILLNESS SCHIZOPHRENIA ADJUSTMENT PROGNOSIS
         aPSYCHIATRIC PREDICTION FUTURE RORSCHACH PROJECTIVE
            (APPLICATIONS: 1561 1563 1635)

P-127   PYTKOWICZ, A. R., WAGNER, N. N., & SARASON, I. G.
            AN EXPERIMENTAL STUDY OF THE REDUCTION OF HOSTILITY THROUGH FANTASY.
            JOURNAL OF PERSONALITY AND SOCIAL PSYCHOLOGY, 1967, 5, 295-303.
            (DIRECT AND INDIRECT AGGRESSION SCALES FOR THE TAT)
         aP-127 1967M AGGRESSION TAT FANTASY BEHAVIOR HOSTILITY PROJECTIVE EXPRESSION

P-128   PARK, P.
            PROBLEM DRINKING AND SOCIAL ORIENTATION.
            UNPUBLISHED DOCTORAL DISSERTATION, YALE UNIVERSITY, 1958.
            (PROBLEM-DRINKING SCALE)
         aP-128 1958M BEHAVIOR DEVIANCE ALCOHOLISM SOCIAL
            (APPLICATIONS: 88)

P-130   PROCHASKA, J. O.
               SYMPTOM AND DYNAMIC CUES IN THE IMPLOSIVE TREATMENT OF TEST ANXIETY.
               JOURNAL OF ABNORMAL PSYCHOLOGY, 1971, 77, 133-142.
               (TREATMENT SCORES FOR TEST ANXIETY THERAPY)
           aP-130 1971M TEST ANXIETY RESPONSE SITUATIONAL STRESS CHANGE

P-131   PHILLIPS, J. S.
               THE RELATIONSHIP BETWEEN TWO MEASURES OF INTERVIEW BEHAVIOR COMPARING
               VERBAL CONTENT AND VERBAL TEMPORAL PATTERNS OF INTERACTION.
               UNPUBLISHED DOCTORAL DISSERTATION, WASHINGTON UNIVERSITY, 1957.
               (INTERPERSONAL SYSTEM)
           aP-131 1957M INTERPERSONAL INTERACTION GLOBAL PERSONALITY AFFECTIVE-STATES
           aDOMINANCE SUBMISSION

P-132   PINCHAK, L. E., & ROLLINS, G. W.
               A SOCIAL ADEQUACY RATING SCALE: PRELIMINARY REPORT.
               SOCIAL WORK, 1960, 5, 71-78.
               (WACO SOCIAL ADEQUACY SCALE)*
           aP-132 1960M ADJUSTMENT SOCIAL COMPETENCE BEHAVIOR INTERPERSONAL RELATIONSHIPS

P-133   POPE, B., & SIEGMAN, A. W.
               AN INTERCORRELATIONAL STUDY OF SOME INDICES OF VERBAL FLUENCY.
               PSYCHOLOGICAL REPORTS, 1964, 15, 303-310.
               (INDEXES OF VERBAL FLUENCY)
           aP-133 1964M VOICE ABILITY BEHAVIOR

P-134   PEARSON, P. H.
               A CONCEPTUAL AND METHODOLOGICAL STUDY OF THREE ROGERIAN CONSTRUCTS.
               UNPUBLISHED DOCTORAL DISSERTATION, UNIVERSITY OF CHICAGO, 1968.
               (MEASURE OF EXPERIENCE OF GUILT)
           aP-134 1968M GUILT EXPERIENCE APPROVAL OTHERS ESTEEM

P-136   PITTEL, S. M., & MENDELSOHN, G. A.
               SITUATIONAL APPRAISAL INVENTORY: DEVELOPMENT AND VALIDATION OF A MEASURE OF
               EVALUATIVE ATTITUDES.
               JOURNAL OF CONSULTING AND CLINICAL PSYCHOLOGY, 1969, 33, 396-405.
               (SITUATIONAL APPRAISAL INVENTORY)* (SAI)
           aP-136 1969M SITUATIONAL ATTITUDE BELIEF OPINION SOCIAL EVALUATION MORAL
           aRESPONSIBILITY VALUES

P-137   PAYNE, R. W., & FRIEDLANDER, D.
               A SHORT BATTERY OF SIMPLE TESTS FOR MEASURING OVERINCLUSIVE THINKING.
               JOURNAL OF MENTAL SCIENCE, 1962, 108, 362-367.
               (MEASURES OF OVERINCLUSIVE THINKING: OBJECT CLASSIFICATION, MODIFIED
               PROVERBS, MODIFIED OBJECT SORTING)
           aP-137 1962M OVERINCLUSIVE THINKING COGNITIVE FUNCTIONING SCHIZOPHRENIA

P-138   PURCELL, K.
               THE TAT AND ANTISOCIAL BEHAVIOR.
               JOURNAL OF CONSULTING PSYCHOLOGY, 1956, 20, 449-456.
               (TAT SCORED FOR HOSTILE CONTENT AND LOCUS OF PUNISHMENT)
           aP-138 1956M HOSTILITY AGGRESSION IMPULSIVENESS IMPULSE CONTROL TAT DELINQUENCY
           aDEVIANCE BEHAVIOR LOCUS PROJECTIVE
               (APPLICATIONS: 2191)

P-139   PEARSON, P. H.
               A CONCEPTUAL AND METHODOLOGICAL STUDY OF THREE ROGERIAN CONSTRUCTS.
               UNPUBLISHED DOCTORAL DISSERTATION, UNIVERSITY OF CHICAGO, 1968.
               (ARROWS TEST)*
           aP-139 1968M GRAPHIC PRESSURE OTHERS RESISTANCE
               (APPLICATIONS: 970)

P-140   PHARES, E. J., & ADAMS, C. K.
               THE CONSTRUCT VALIDITY OF THE EDWARDS PPS HETEROSEXUALITY SCALE.
               JOURNAL OF CONSULTING PSYCHOLOGY, 1961, 25, 341-344.
               (MEASURE OF ESTHETIC VALUES OF SEXUAL PHOTOGRAPHS)
           aP-140 1961M ESTHETIC PREFERENCE VALUES SEX GRAPHIC EVALUATION

P-142   POPE, B., SIEGMAN, A. W., & BLASS, T.
               ANXIETY AND SPEECH IN THE INITIAL INTERVIEW.
               JOURNAL OF CONSULTING AND CLINICAL PSYCHOLOGY, 1970, 35, 233-238.
               (INDEXES OF RESISTIVENESS AND SUPERFICIALITY)
           aP-142 1970M COMMUNICATION RESISTANCE DEFENSIVENESS DENIAL PROBLEM PERSONAL
           aDEFENSE OPENNESS

P-144   PETERS, H. N.
               CIRCULAR PENCIL MAZE PERFORMANCE IN CHRONIC SCHIZOPHRENICS.
               JOURNAL OF CLINICAL PSYCHOLOGY, 1956, 12, 170-173.
           PETERS, H. N.
               MANUAL FOR PETERS' CIRCULAR MAZES.
               GLENDALE, MO., PRIVATELY CIRCULATED BY AUTHOR, 1958.
               (PETERS' CIRCULAR MAZES)*
           aP-144 1956M COGNITIVE FUNCTIONING ADJUSTMENT PSYCHIATRIC PERFORMANCE
               (APPLICATIONS: 1306)

P-145   PORTER, E. H., JR.
               THE DEVELOPMENT AND EVALUATION OF A MEASURE OF COUNSELING INTERVIEW
               PROCEDURES. PART I.
               EDUCATION AND PSYCHOLOGICAL MEASUREMENT, 1943, 3, 105-125.
               (MEASURE OF COUNSELING INTERVIEW PROCEDURES)
           aP-145 1943M COUNSELING INTERACTION THERAPY RELATIONSHIPS

P-147   PAUL, G. L.
               INSIGHT VERSUS DESENSITIZATION IN PSYCHOTHERAPY: AN EXPERIMENT IN ANXIETY
               REDUCTION.
               STANFORD, CALIF.: STANFORD UNIVERSITY PRESS, 1966.
               (TIMED BEHAVIORAL CHECKLIST)
           aP-147 1966M ANXIETY BEHAVIOR RATING PERFORMANCE TENSION SECURITY SELF
           aCONFIDENCE PUBLIC
               (APPLICATIONS: 2932)

P-148   PAUL, G. L.
               INSIGHT VERSUS DESENSITIZATION IN PSYCHOTHERAPY: AN EXPERIMENT IN ANXIETY
               REDUCTION.
               STANFORD, CALIF.: STANFORD UNIVERSITY PRESS, 1966.
               (SHORT FORM OF GILKENSON'S PERSONAL REPORT OF CONFIDENCE AS SPEAKER)
           aP-148 1966M ANXIETY TENSION SELF CONFIDENCE PERFORMANCE PUBLIC
               (APPLICATIONS: 2932)

P-149   PIOTROWSKI, Z.
               THE RORSCHACH INK-BLOT METHOD IN ORGANIC DISTURBANCE OF THE CENTRAL
               NERVOUS SYSTEM.
               JOURNAL OF NERVOUS AND MENTAL DISEASES, 1937, 86, 525-537.
               (PIOTROWSKI'S SIGNS FOR ORGANIC BRAIN DAMAGE)
           aP-149 1937M RORSCHACH DIAGNOSIS

P-153   PSYCHIATRIC EVALUATION PROJECT.
               INTRAMURAL REPORT 63-1: DIMENSIONS OF PSYCHIATRIC PATIENT WARD BEHAVIOR.
               WASHINGTON, D.C.: VETERANS ADMINISTRATION PSYCHIATRIC EVALUATION PROJECT,
               1963.
               (BEHAVIOR RATING SCALE)
           aP-153 1963M RATING BEHAVIOR WARD PATIENT PSYCHIATRIC

Q-1   QUINN, R. P., & LICHTENSTEIN, E.
               CONVERGENT AND DISCRIMINANT VALIDITIES OF ACQUIESCENCE MEASURES.
               JOURNAL OF GENERAL PSYCHOLOGY, 1965, 73, 93-104.
               (ACQUIESCENCE-FREE SOCIAL DESIRABILITY SCALE)*
           aQ-1 SOCIAL DESIRABILITY RESPONSE-BIAS ACQUIESCENCE MMPI 1965M

Q-2   QUARTER, J., KENNEDY, D. R., & LAXER, R. M.
               EFFECT OF ORDER AND FORM IN THE Q-SORT.
               PSYCHOLOGICAL REPORTS, 1967, 20, 893-894.
               (Q-SORT MEASURE OF SELF, IDEAL-SELF)
           aQ-2 SELF IDEAL IMAGE Q-SORT SELF-IDENTITY CONCEPT EVALUATION TRAIT DESCRIPTION
           aQ-2 ESTEEM 1967M

Q-3   QUINN, R. P., CAMPBELL, D. C., MANGIONE, T. W., & STAINES, G.
               UNPUBLISHED STUDY. INSTITUTE FOR SOCIAL RESEARCH, ANN ARBOR, MICH., 1970.
               (CONTENT-FREE MEASURE OF JOB SATISFACTION)
           aQ-3 JOB SATISFACTION PE-FIT AFFECTIVE-STATES 1970M GLOBAL

Q-4   QUINN, R. P., CAMPBELL, D. C., MANGIONE, T. W., & STAINES, G.
         UNPUBLISHED STUDY. INSTITUTE FOR SOCIAL RESEARCH, ANN ARBOR, MICH., 1970.
         (MEASURE OF JOB SATISFACTION)
       @Q-4 JOB SATISFACTION PE-FIT AFFECTIVE-STATES 1970M GLOBAL

Q-5   QUINN, R. P., CAMPBELL, D. C., MANGIONE, T. W., & STAINES, G.
         UNPUBLISHED STUDY. INSTITUTE FOR SOCIAL RESEARCH, ANN ARBOR, MICH., 1970.
         (MEASURE OF MENTAL HEALTH)
       @Q-5 MENTAL-HEALTH ADJUSTMENT JOB 1970M

Q-7   QUAY, H. C., & PETERSON, D. R.
         THE QUESTIONNAIRE MEASUREMENT OF PERSONALITY DIMENSIONS ASSOCIATED WITH
         JUVENILE DELINQUENCY.
         UNPUBLISHED MANUSCRIPT, UNIVERSITY OF ILLINOIS, 1964.
         (MEASURE OF PERSONALITY DIMENSIONS ASSOCIATED WITH DELINQUENCY)
       @Q-7 1964M DELINQUENCY NEUROTICISM PSYCHOPATHY ACCULTURATION SUB-IDENTITY
       @Q-7 CULTURE
         (APPLICATIONS: 1022 1095)

Q-8   QUAY, H. C.
         PERSONALITY DIMENSION IN DELINQUENT MALES AS INFERRED FROM THE FACTOR
         ANALYSIS OF BEHAVIOR RATINGS.
         JOURNAL OF RESEARCH IN CRIME AND DELINQUENCY, 1964, 1, 33-37.
    QUAY, H. C., & PETERSON, D. R.
         MANUAL FOR THE BEHAVIOR PROBLEM CHECKLIST.
         URBANA: UNIVERSITY OF ILLINOIS, 1968. (MIMEO.)
         (BEHAVIOR PROBLEM CHECKLIST)*
       @Q-8 1964M BEHAVIOR PROBLEM CHECKLIST DELINQUENCY ADOLESCENT
         (APPLICATIONS: 1515 2556)

Q-9   QUAY, H. C., & PETERSON, D. R.
         A BRIEF SCALE FOR JUVENILE DELINQUENCY.
         JOURNAL OF CLINICAL PSYCHOLOGY, 1958, 14, 139-142.
         (BRIEF JUVENILE DELINQUENCY SCALE)
       @Q-9 1958M DELINQUENCY ADOLESCENT SOCIAL ADJUSTMENT BEHAVIOR ACTIVITIES
       @ATTITUDE DEVIANCE RESPONSIBILITY

R-1   RABBAN, M.
         SEX-ROLE IDENTIFICATION IN YOUNG CHILDREN IN TWO DIVERSE SOCIAL GROUPS.
         GENETIC PSYCHOLOGY MONOGRAPHS, 1950, 42, 81-158.
         (MEASURE OF SEX-ROLE IDENTIFICATION)
       @R-1 SEX ROLE IDENTIFICATION SELF-IDENTITY IDENTITY SUB-IDENTITY MASCULINITY
       @R-1 FEMININITY CHILD ADJUSTMENT 1950M

R-2   RETTIG, S.
         AN EXPLORATORY STUDY OF ALTRUISM.
         UNPUBLISHED DOCTORAL DISSERTATION, OHIO STATE UNIVERSITY, 1956.
         (MEASURE OF ALTRUISM)
       @R-2 ALTRUISM AFFECTIVE-STATES GLOBAL SATISFACTION POSITIVE 1956M OTHERS
       @R-2 AWARENESS ORIENTATION

R-3   REYNOLDS, E.
         VARIATIONS OF MOOD AND RECALL IN THE MENSTRUAL CYCLE.
         JOURNAL OF PSYCHOSOMATIC RESEARCH, 1969, 13, 163-166.
         (MOOD CHART)*
       @R-3 AFFECTIVE-STATES OTHER-CATEGORY MOOD POSITIVE NEGATIVE GRAPHIC 1969M
       @R-3 EMOTION

R-4   RICKERS-OVSIANKINA, M. A., & KUSMIN, A. A.
         INDIVIDUAL DIFFERENCES IN SOCIAL ACCESSIBILITY.
         PSYCHOLOGICAL REPORTS, 1958, 4, 391-406.
         (SOCIAL ACCESSIBILITY SCALE)*
       @R-4 PERSONAL SOCIAL ACCESSIBILITY SELF DISCLOSURE COMMUNICATION INTERPERSONAL
       @R-4 RELATIONSHIPS 1958M

R-5   ROSENZWEIG, S., FLEMING, E. E., & ROSENZWEIG, L.
         THE CHILDREN'S FORM OF THE ROSENZWEIG PICTURE-FRUSTRATION STUDY.
         JOURNAL OF PSYCHOLOGY, 1948, 26, 141-191.
         (CHILDREN'S FORM, ROSENZWEIG PICTURE-FRUSTRATION STUDY)
       @R-5 PROJECTIVE PUNITIVENESS DIRECTION REPRESSION SENSITIZATION AGGRESSION
       @R-5 FRUSTRATION COPING-DEFENSE AFFECTIVE-STATES RESENTMENT HOSTILITY
       @R-5 EGO DEFENSE CHILD RESPONSE-BIAS 1948M

R-6   RING, K., BRAGINSKY, B., & BRAGINSKY, B.
         PERFORMANCE STYLES IN INTERPERSONAL RELATIONS: A TYPOLOGY.
            PSYCHOLOGICAL REPORTS, 1966, 18, MONOGRAPH SUPPLEMENT 1-V18, 203-220.
         RING, K., & WALLSTON, K.
            A TEST TO MEASURE PERFORMANCE STYLES IN INTERPERSONAL RELATIONS.
            PSYCHOLOGICAL REPORTS, 1968, 22, 147-154.
            (PERFORMANCE STYLE TEST)*
         @R-6 TYPOLOGY INTERPERSONAL BEHAVIOR PERFORMANCE STYLE ROLE SOCIAL COMPETENCE
         @R-6 ADJUSTMENT 1966M RELATIONSHIPS INTERACTION

R-7   ROKEACH, M., & EGLASH, A.
            A SCALE FOR MEASURING INTELLECTUAL CONVICTION.
            JOURNAL OF SOCIAL PSYCHOLOGY, 1956, 44, 135-141.
            (INTELLECTUAL CONVICTION SCALE)*
         @R-7 BELIEF INTELLECTUAL CONVICTION COPING-DEFENSE OTHER-CATEGORY COGNITIVE
         @R-7 STRUCTURE 1956M

R-8   ROKEACH, M.
            THE OPEN AND CLOSED MIND.
            NEW YORK: BASIC BOOKS. 1960.
            (ROKEACH DOGMATISM SCALE)*
         @R-8 AUTHORITARIANISM DOGMATISM COPING-DEFENSE FLEXIBILITY RIGIDITY
         @R-8 OTHER-CATEGORY 1960M
            (APPLICATIONS: 48   66   200   215   218   220   254   287   289   293
                            386   398   457   508   525   529   622   671   675   706
                            707   711   740   742   774   841   866   872   900   1175
                           1216   1232   1245   1274   1299   1368   1375   1381   1384   1515
                           1530   1536   1809   2019   2022   2149   2166   2319   2328   2337
                           2446   2526   2555   2589   2593   2605   2647   2669   2672   2684
                           2711   2766   2782   2814   2821   2829   2836   2854   2866   2900
                           2936)

R-9   ROSENBERG, M.
            PARENTAL INTEREST AND CHILDREN'S SELF-CONCEPTIONS.
            SOCIOMETRY, 1963, 26, 35-49.
            (MEASURE OF CHILD'S SELF-ESTEEM)
         @R-9 SELF ESTEEM CHILD CONCEPT SELF-IDENTITY IMAGE EVALUATION PERCEPTION 1963M

R-10   ROSENBERG, M.
            MISANTHROPY AND POLITICAL IDEOLOGY.
            AMERICAN SOCIOLOGICAL REVIEW, 1956, 21, 690-695.
            (FAITH IN PEOPLE SCALE)
         @R-10 INTERPERSONAL TRUST ORIENTATION OTHERS MISANTHROPY AFFECTIVE-STATES
         @R-10 ALIENATION GLOBAL NEGATIVE POLITICAL IDEOLOGY 1956M
            (APPLICATIONS: 2789)

R-11   ROSENBERG, B. G., & SUTTON-SMITH, B.
            THE MEASUREMENT OF MASCULINITY AND FEMININITY IN CHILDREN.
            CHILD DEVELOPMENT, 1959, 30, 373-380.
            (MEASURE OF SEX ROLE IDENTITY)
         @R-11 PREFERENCE CHILD SEX ROLE IDENTITY SELF SELF-IDENTITY CONCEPT SUB-IDENTITY
         @R-11 MASCULINITY FEMININITY 1959M
            (APPLICATIONS: 1641   2051)

R-12   ROSENZWEIG, S.
            THE PICTURE-ASSOCIATION METHOD AND ITS APPLICATION IN A STUDY OF REACTIONS
            TO FRUSTRATION.
            JOURNAL OF PERSONALITY, 1945, 14, 3-23.
            (ROSENZWEIG PICTURE-FRUSTRATION STUDY)*
         @R-12 PROJECTIVE PUNITIVENESS DIRECTION REPRESSION SENSITIZATION AGGRESSION
         @R-12 FRUSTRATION COPING-DEFENSE AFFECTIVE-STATES RESENTMENT HOSTILITY
         @R-12 EGO DEFENSE CHILD RESPONSE-BIAS 1945M
            (APPLICATIONS: 62   67   95   329   550   897   1061   1068   1168   1412
                             1592   1640   1757   1758   1790   1814   1846   2745   2798   2820)

R-13   ROSS, A. O., LACEY, H. M., & PARTON, D. A.
            THE DEVELOPMENT OF A BEHAVIOR CHECKLIST FOR BOYS.
            CHILD DEVELOPMENT, 1965, 36, 1013-1027.
            (PITTSBURGH ADJUSTMENT SURVEY SCALES)*
         @R-13 ELEMENTARY WITHDRAWAL AGGRESSION SOCIAL ADJUSTMENT SCHOOL GLOBAL
         @R-13 COMPETENCE CHILD BEHAVIOR CHECKLIST 1965M

R-14   ROTHMAN, F.
            A STUDY IN THE MEASUREMENT, AND AN ATTEMPTED MODIFICATION OF, ATTITUDES
            TOWARD ACADEMIC ACHIEVEMENT AMONG GIFTED STUDENTS IN TWO INDEPENDENT
            SCHOOLS.
            UNPUBLISHED DOCTORAL DISSERTATION, TEMPLE UNIVERSITY, SCHOOL OF EDUCATION,
            1961.
            (MULTIDIMENSIONAL ACHIEVEMENT ORIENTATION SCALE)*
          aR-14 ACHIEVEMENT ATTITUDE MOTIVE AUTONOMY NEED ORIENTATION
          aR-14 ACADEMIC 1961M

R-15   REHM, L. P., & MARSTON, A. R.
            REDUCTION OF SOCIAL ANXIETY THROUGH MODIFICATION OF SELF-REINFORCEMENT: AN
            INSTIGATION THERAPY TECHNIQUE.
            JOURNAL OF CONSULTING AND CLINICAL PSYCHOLOGY, 1968, 32, 565-574.
            (SITUATION TEST)*
          aR-15 ADJUSTMENT AFFECTIVE-STATES SOCIAL COMPETENCE ANXIETY SUBJECTIVE STRESS
          aR-15 INTERACTION INTERPERSONAL RELATIONSHIPS MENTAL-HEALTH MENTAL-ILLNESS
          aR-15 1968M SITUATIONAL

R-16   ROTTER, J. B.
            A NEW SCALE FOR THE MEASUREMENT OF INTERPERSONAL TRUST.
            JOURNAL OF PERSONALITY, 1967, 35, 651-665.
            (INTERPERSONAL TRUST SCALE)*
          aR-16 INTERPERSONAL TRUST ORIENTATION SOCIAL INTERACTION ADJUSTMENT AUTONOMY
          aR-16 1967M RELATIONSHIPS
            (APPLICATIONS: 258 2509 2586 2600 2621 2946)

R-17   ROTTER, J. B.
            LEVEL OF ASPIRATION AS A METHOD OF STUDYING PERSONALITY II. DEVELOPMENT
            AND EVALUATION OF A CONTROLLED METHOD.
            JOURNAL OF EXPERIMENTAL PSYCHOLOGY, 1942, 31, 410-422.
            (LEVEL OF ASPIRATION BOARD)*
          aR-17 ASPIRATION MOTIVE SELF-IDENTITY VALUES IDEALS LIFE GOALS AUTONOMY NEED
          aR-17 ACHIEVEMENT 1942M
            (APPLICATIONS: 24   25   87   211   506   608   705   712   792   811
                           1168 2534)

R-18   ROTTER, J. B., LIVERANT, S., & SEEMAN, M. R.
            INTERNAL VERSUS EXTERNAL CONTROL OF REINFORCEMENT: A MAJOR
            VARIABLE IN BEHAVIOR THEORY.
            IN WASHBURNE (ED.), DECISIONS, VALUES, AND GROUPS. VOL.2. LONDON
            PERGAMON PRESS, 1962.
          ROTTER, J. B.
            GENERALIZED EXPECTANCIES FOR INTERNAL VERSUS EXTERNAL CONTROL OF
            REINFORCEMENT.
            PSYCHOLOGICAL MONOGRAPHS, 1966, 80 (1, WHOLE NO. 609).
            (INTERNAL-EXTERNAL CONTROL SCALE: I-E SCALE)*
          aR-18 IE-CONTROL CONTROL COPING AUTONOMY LOCUS ORIENTATION ENVIRONMENT 1966M
            (APPLICATIONS: 5   24   25   80   160   163   184   185   211   238
                             253   258   261   281   285   364   433   458   477   500
                             501   522   811 1053 1127 1424 1940 1959 2134 2174
                            2178 2179 2201 2236 2247 2260 2266 2282 2288 2304
                            2334 2338 2369 2382 2405 2487 2490 2523 2524 2526
                            2533 2534 2537 2563 2566 2590 2609 2614 2620 2638
                            2660 2669 2685 2687 2690 2722 2748 2752 2784 2789
                            2846 2864 2869 2901 2903 2946)

R-19   ROYCE, J. R., & SMITH, W. A. S.
            A NOTE ON THE DEVELOPMENT OF THE PSYCHOEPISTEMOLOGICAL PROFILE.
            PSYCHOLOGICAL REPORTS, 1964, 14, 297-298.
          SMITH, W. A. S., ROYCE, J. R., AYERS, D., & JONES, B.
            DEVELOPMENT OF AN INVENTORY TO MEASURE WAYS OF KNOWING.
            PSYCHOLOGICAL REPORTS, 1967, 21, 529-535.
            (PSYCHO-EPISTEMOLOGICAL PROFILE)*
          aR-19 ENVIRONMENT REALITY RELATIONSHIPS RATIONALISM EMPIRICISM EMOTION BELIEF
          aR-19 ORIENTATION AUTHORITARIANISM 1964M THINKING COGNITIVE STYLE STRUCTURE
          aR-19 FUNCTIONING

R-20   RUDIN, S. A.
            THE RELATIONSHIP BETWEEN RATIONAL AND IRRATIONAL AUTHORITARIANISM.
            JOURNAL OF PSYCHOLOGY, 1961, 52, 179-183.
            (MEASURE OF RATIONAL/IRRATIONAL AUTHORITARIANISM)
          aR-20 AUTHORITARIANISM ACQUIESCENCE RATIONAL IRRATIONAL COPING-DEFENSE
          aR-20 RESPONSE-BIAS OTHER-CATEGORY 1961M

R-21   RUST, R. M., & RYAN, F. J.
                 THE STRONG VOCATIONAL INTEREST BLANK AND COLLEGE ACHIEVEMENT.
                 JOURNAL OF APPLIED PSYCHOLOGY, 1954, 38, 341-345.
                 (MEASURE OF COLLEGE ACHIEVEMENT)
            @R-21 ACADEMIC ACHIEVEMENT NEED AUTONOMY VOCATIONAL INTEREST COLLEGE 1954M
                 (APPLICATIONS: 1300)

R-22   RYCHLAK, J. F., & LEGERSKI, A. T.
                 A SOCIOCULTURAL THEORY OF APPROPRIATE SEXUAL ROLE IDENTIFICATION AND LEVEL
                 OF PERSONAL ADJUSTMENT.
                 JOURNAL OF PERSONALITY, 1967, 35, 31-49.
                 (MEASURE OF SEX-ROLE IDENTIFICATION)
            @R-22 MASCULINITY FEMININITY SEX ROLE IDENTIFICATION SELF-IDENTITY SUB-IDENTITY
            @R-22 PERCEPTION ADJUSTMENT PARENTAL 1967M IDENTITY

R-23   RADKE, M.
                 THE RELATION OF PARENTAL AUTHORITY TO CHILDREN'S BEHAVIOR AND ATTITUDES.
                 UNIVERSITY OF MINNESOTA, INSTITUTE OF CHILD WELFARE MONOGRAPH, 1946, NO.22.
                 (QUESTIONNAIRE MEASURE OF PARENTAL ATTITUDES AND BEHAVIOR)
            @R-23 AUTHORITY PARENTAL ATTITUDE BEHAVIOR PARENT-CHILD PE-FIT ADJUSTMENT
            @R-23 FAMILY INTERACTION 1946M
                 (APPLICATIONS: 60)

R-24   REECE, M. M.
                 MASCULINITY AND FEMININITY: A FACTOR ANALYTIC STUDY.
                 PSYCHOLOGICAL REPORTS, 1964, 14, 123-139.
                 (CONCEPT MEANING MEASURE)
            @R-24 SEM-DIFFERENTIAL MASCULINITY FEMININITY SELF-IDENTITY ROLE SUB-IDENTITY
            @R-24 PERCEPTION SEX 1964M CONCEPTUAL THINKING
                 (APPLICATIONS: 85)

R-25   REHFISCH, J. M.
                 A SCALE FOR PERSONALITY RIGIDITY.
                 JOURNAL OF CONSULTING PSYCHOLOGY, 1958, 22, 11-15.
                 (REHFISCH RIGIDITY SCALE)*
            @R-25 RIGIDITY COPING-DEFENSE FLEXIBILITY DOGMATISM TOLERANCE AMBIGUITY 1958M
                 (APPLICATIONS: 111   678 1307)

R-26   RETTIG, S., & RAWSON, H. E.
                 THE RISK HYPOTHESIS IN PREDICTIVE JUDGMENTS OF UNETHICAL BEHAVIOR.
                 JOURNAL OF ABNORMAL AND SOCIAL PSYCHOLOGY, 1963, 66, 243-248.
                 (BEHAVIOR PREDICTION SCALE)
            @R-26 BEHAVIOR PREDICTION MORAL CONFLICT VALUES RISK-TAKING COPING-DEFENSE
            @R-26 APPROACH AVOIDANCE 1963M PREFERENCE
                 (APPLICATIONS: 94   198   440   917   2690   2817)

R-27   ROSANOFF, A. J.
                 FREE ASSOCIATION TEST.
                 IN A. J. ROSANOFF (ED.), MANUAL OF PSYCHIATRY. (7TH ED., REV.) NEW YORK:
                 WILEY, 1944.
                 (WORD ASSOCIATION TEST)*
            @R-27 ORIGINALITY CREATIVITY AUTONOMY INTELLIGENCE COGNITIVE FUNCTIONING
            @R-27 PSYCHIATRIC THINKING 1944M DIAGNOSIS
                 (APPLICATIONS: 332   626   631   632   663   688   699   772   905   946
                                   966   971   979   1037   1040   1057   1098   1107   2231   2314
                                  2392   2407   2583   2734)

R-28   REMMERS, H. H. & SHIMBERG, B.
                 MANUAL: SRA YOUTH INVENTORY, FORM S.
                 CHICAGO: SCIENCE RESEARCH ASSOCIATES, 1960.
                 (SRA YOUTH INVENTORY)*
            @R-28 ADJUSTMENT GLOBAL AFFECTIVE-STATES PROBLEM HEALTH FUTURE ADOLESCENT SCHOOL
            @R-28 SELF SOCIAL COMPETENCE
                 (APPLICATIONS: 1330   1398)

R-29   ROTHBART, M. K., & MACCOBY, E. E.
                 PARENTS' DIFFERENTIAL REACTIONS TO SONS AND DAUGHTERS.
                 JOURNAL OF PERSONALITY AND SOCIAL PSYCHOLOGY, 1966, 4, 237-243.
                 (QUESTIONNAIRE OF PARENTAL ATTITUDES ABOUT SEX DIFFERENCES IN CHILDREN)
            @R-29 PARENT-CHILD PARENTAL ATTITUDE SEX DIFFERENCES FAMILY INTERACTION
            @R-29 ADJUSTMENT 1966M

R-30   RORSCHACH, H.
               (TRANSL. BY P. LEMKAU & B. KRONENBURG.)
               PSYCHODIAGNOSTICS: A DIAGNOSTIC TEST BASED ON PERCEPTION. BERNE: HUBER,
               1942 (1ST GERMAN ED., 1921; U. S. DISTRIBUTOR, GRUNE & STRATTON.)
               (RORSCHACH TEST)*
           @R-30 1921M RORSCHACH PROJECTIVE MULTITRAIT ADJUSTMENT PSYCHOPATHY DIAGNOSIS
           @R-30 MENTAL-ILLNESS
               (APPLICATIONS: 65   103   109   150   181   183   253   295   318   322
                                  345   354   404   515   573   592   609   610   655   756
                                  804   805   826   857   881   909   919   929   937   945
                                  969   994   1007   1016   1061   1085   1105   1123   1130   1136
                                 1141   1168   1249   1250   1253   1408   1415   1457   1476   1560
                                 1561   1563   1583   1592   1597   1602   1607   1618   1625   1627
                                 1635   1652   1653   1664   1676   1686   1699   1705   1722   1723
                                 1724   1761   1764   1798   1804   1828   1830   1834   1848   1862
                                 1864   1867   1871   1880   1885   1898   1903   1915   1917   1927
                                 1928   1929   1939   1944   1974   1982   1992   1994   2004   2017
                                 2035   2062   2087   2098   2114   2117   2151   2159   2176   2177
                                 2178   2233   2251   2292   2298   2309   2320   2361   2374   2406
                                 2407   2409   2431   2671   2674   2733   2893   2912   2914   2959)

R-31   ROTTER, J. B., & RAFFERTY, J. C.
               MANUAL: THE ROTTER INCOMPLETE SENTENCES BLANK.
               NEW YORK: PSYCHOLOGICAL CORPORATION, 1950.
               (ROTTER INCOMPLETE SENTENCES BLANK)*
           @R-31 ADJUSTMENT DEFENSIVENESS PROJECTIVE NEED APPROVAL MULTITRAIT GLOBAL
           @R-31 COPING-DEFENSE AUTONOMY SELF-IDENTITY 1950M
               (APPLICATIONS: 77   281   787   919   945   1093   1168   1206   1321   1324
                                 1450   1800   1804   1958   2053   2069   2085   2099   2134   2374
                                 2378   2483   2867)

R-32   REHM, L. P., & MARSTON, A. R.
               REDUCTION OF SOCIAL ANXIETY THROUGH MODIFICATION OF SELF-REINFORCEMENT: AN
               INSTIGATION THERAPY TECHNIQUE.
               JOURNAL OF CONSULTING AND CLINICAL PSYCHOLOGY, 1968, 32, 565-574.
               (POSTTHERAPY QUESTIONNAIRE)*
           @R-32 ADJUSTMENT GLOBAL SOCIAL COMPETENCE INTERACTION INTERPERSONAL PROGNOSIS
           @R-32 RELATIONSHIPS DEVELOPMENT THERAPY MENTAL-HEALTH MENTAL-ILLNESS 1968M

R-33   REMPEL, A. M., & BENTLEY, R. R.
               THE MEASUREMENT OF TEACHER MORALE: A FACTOR ANALYSIS APPROACH.
               EDUCATIONAL AND PSYCHOLOGICAL MEASUREMENT, 1964, 24, 631-642.
               (PURDUE TEACHER MORALE INVENTORY)*
           @R-33 AFFECTIVE-STATES TEACHER MORALE INTERPERSONAL SOCIAL INTERACTION PE-FIT
           @SATISFACTION ADJUSTMENT ENVIRONMENT 1964M
               (APPLICATIONS: 1452)

R-34   ROSENKRANTZ, P. S., & CROCKETT, W. H.
               SOME FACTORS INFLUENCING THE ASSIMILATION OF DISPARATE INFORMATION IN
               IMPRESSION FORMATION.
               JOURNAL OF PERSONALITY AND SOCIAL PSYCHOLOGY, 1965, 2, 397-402.
               (MEASURE OF COGNITIVE COMPLEXITY)
           @R-34 COGNITIVE COMPLEXITY STRUCTURE FUNCTIONING IMPRESSION FORMATION
           @R-34 INTERPERSONAL PERCEPTION 1965M
               (APPLICATIONS: 96)

R-35   ROBERTSON, L. S., & DOTSON, L. E.
               PERCEIVED PARENTAL EXPRESSIVITY, REACTION TO STRESS, AND AFFILIATION.
               JOURNAL OF PERSONALITY AND SOCIAL PSYCHOLOGY, 1969, 12, 229-234.
               (MEASURE OF PARENTAL EXPRESSIVITY)
           @R-35 PARENT-CHILD PERCEIVED EXPRESSIVENESS PARENTAL FAMILY INTERACTION
           @R-35 ADJUSTMENT NEED AFFILIATION AFFECTION INTERPERSONAL 1969M

R-36   ROGERS, C. R., & RABLEN, R. A.
               A SCALE OF PROCESS IN PSYCHOTHERAPY.
               UNPUBLISHED MIMEO MANUAL. UNIVERSITY OF WISCONSIN, 1958.
               ROGERS, C. R.
               A TENTATIVE SCALE FOR THE MEASUREMENT OF PROCESS IN PSYCHOTHERAPY.
               IN E. A. RUBINSTEIN & M. B. PARLOFF (EDS.), RESEARCH IN PSYCHOTHERAPY.
               WASHINGTON, D. C.: AMERICAN PSYCHOLOGICAL ASSOCIATION, 1959, 96-107.
               (PROCESS SCALE FOR RATING CLIENT FUNCTIONING)
           @R-36 ADJUSTMENT MENTAL-ILLNESS PSYCHIATRIC THERAPY RATING 1958M COUNSELING
           @CHANGE MENTAL-HEALTH PROGNOSIS DIAGNOSIS PERSONAL SELF ACTUALIZATION
           @FUNCTIONING PATIENT
               (APPLICATIONS: 1550   1693   1782)

R-37   RACKOW, L., NAPOLI, P., KLEBANOFF, S., & SCHILLINGER, A.
        A GROUP METHOD FOR THE RAPID SCREENING OF CHRONIC PSYCHIATRIC PATIENTS.
        AMERICAN JOURNAL OF PSYCHIATRY, 1953, 109, 561-566.
        (MONTROSE RATING SCALE)*
        aR-37 1953M PSYCHIATRIC RATING PATIENT MENTAL-HEALTH MENTAL-ILLNESS DIAGNOSIS
        (APPLICATIONS: 781   962   992   1036   1145   1581   2402)

R-38   ROSENBERG, M. J.
        COGNITIVE STRUCTURE AND ATTITUDINAL AFFECT.
        JOURNAL OF ABNORMAL AND SOCIAL PSYCHOLOGY, 1956, 53, 367-372.
        (MEASURE OF VALUE IMPORTANCE AND PERCEIVED INSTRUMENTALITY)
        aR-38 COGNITIVE STRUCTURE PERCEPTION SATISFACTION AFFECTIVE-STATES VALUES
        aR-38 1956M PERCEIVED EFFECTIVENESS

R-39   ROBBINS, P. R.
        AN APPLICATION OF THE METHOD OF SUCCESSIVE INTERVALS TO THE STUDY OF FEAR-
        AROUSING INFORMATION.
        PSYCHOLOGICAL REPORTS, 1962, 11, 757-760.
        (CHECK LIST MEASURE OF LEVEL OF ANXIETY)
        aR-39 FEAR CHECKLIST ANXIETY AFFECTIVE-STATES SUBJECTIVE STRESS NEGATIVE 1962M

R-40   REDLICH, F., LEVINE, J., & SOHLER, T.
        A MIRTH RESPONSE TEST: PRELIMINARY REPORT ON A PSYCHODIAGNOSTIC TECHNIQUE
        UTILIZING DYNAMICS OF HUMOR.
        AMERICAN JOURNAL OF ORTHOPSYCHIATRY, 1951, 21, 717-734.
        (MIRTH RESPONSE TEST)*
        aR-40 HUMOR RESPONSE AFFECTIVE-STATES DIAGNOSIS MENTAL-ILLNESS PSYCHIATRIC
        aR-40 1951M
        (APPLICATIONS: 248   403   2325)

R-41   ROE, A., & SIEGELMAN, M.
        A PARENT-CHILD RELATIONS QUESTIONNAIRE.
        CHILD DEVELOPMENT, 1963, 34, 355-369.
        (PARENT-CHILD RELATIONS QUESTIONNAIRE)*
        aR-41 ADJUSTMENT FAMILY PARENTAL PARENT-CHILD INTERACTION BEHAVIOR RELATIONSHIPS
        aR-41 1963M
        (APPLICATIONS: 1027   1326   1907   1935   1966   2106   2843)

R-42   RICHARDSON, BELLOWS, & HENRY, INC.
        MANUAL OF TEST OF SUPERVISORY JUDGMENT, 1953.
        (R, B AND H TEST OF SUPERVISORY JUDGMENT)*
        aR-42 LEADERSHIP MANAGEMENT SUPERVISOR JUDGMENT JOB ADJUSTMENT SATISFACTION
        aR-42 1953M

R-43   ROZYNKO, V.
        MMPI INTERNALIZATION-EXTERNALIZATION SCALE NUMBER 3.
        AMERICAN LAKE, WASHINGTON: VETERANS ADMINISTRATION HOSPITAL, RESEARCH
        SERVICE, 1959.
        (MEASURE OF INTERNALISED REACTION TO STRESS)
        aR-43 STRESS COPING-DEFENSE GLOBAL AFFECTIVE-STATES ANXIETY SUBJECTIVE AUTONOMY
        aR-43 MMPI RESPONSE 1959M
        (APPLICATIONS: 792)

R-44   ROSENBERG, M.
        OCCUPATIONS AND VALUES.
        GLENCOE, ILLINOIS: FREE PRESS, 1957.
        (OCCUPATIONAL VALUES QUESTIONNAIRE)*
        aR-44 VOCATIONAL JOB VALUES INTEREST ORIENTATION INTRINSIC EXTRINSIC 1957M
        aR-44 PREFERENCE

R-45   REYNOLDS, J. H., & BRAEN, B. B.
        RELIABILITY OF A SOCIOMETRIC TECHNIQUE ADAPTED FOR USE WITH DISTURBED
        CHILDREN.
        PSYCHOLOGICAL REPORTS, 1961, 9, 591-597.
        (INDIVIDUALLY ADMINISTERED FORM OF SYRACUSE SCALES OF SOCIAL RELATIONS)
        aR-45 SOCIOMETRIC WARD GROUP TRUST STRUCTURE AFFILIATION ADJUSTMENT SOCIAL
        aR-45 CHILD COMPETENCE PATIENT MENTAL-HEALTH MENTAL-ILLNESS 1961M INTERPERSONAL
        aR-45 RELATIONSHIPS

R-46   RYDELL, S. T., & ROSEN, E.
              MEASUREMENT AND SOME CORRELATES OF NEED-COGNITION.
              PSYCHOLOGICAL REPORTS, 1966, 19, MONOGRAPH SUPPLEMENT 1-V19, 139-165.
              (SELF-OTHER TEST, FORM C)*
         @R-46 INTELLECTUAL ACADEMIC DEPENDENCE AUTONOMY ORIENTATION COGNITIVE NEED
         @R-46 TOLERANCE AMBIGUITY COPING-DEFENSE FLEXIBILITY RIGIDITY DOGMATISM 1966M
         @R-46 SELF OTHERS

R-47   ROOS, P., & ALBERS, R.
              PERFORMANCE OF ALCOHOLICS AND NORMALS ON A MEASURE OF TEMPORAL
              ORIENTATION.
              JOURNAL OF CLINICAL PSYCHOLOGY, 1965, 21, 34-36.
              (TIME REFERENCE INVENTORY)*
         @R-47 TIME ORIENTATION FUTURE PERSPECTIVE 1965M
              (APPLICATIONS: 277I)

R-48   REMMERS, H. H., & BAUERNFIEND, R. H.
              MANUAL FOR THE SRA JUNIOR AND SENIOR INVENTORY, FORM S.
              CHICAGO: SCIENCE RESEARCH ASSOCIATES, 1957.
              (SRA JUNIOR INVENTORY: ABOUT ME AND MY SCHOOL)*
         @R-48 AFFECTIVE-STATES GLOBAL SATISFACTION PE-FIT ADJUSTMENT STUDENT ATTITUDE
         @R-48 SCHOOL ACTIVITIES 1957M

R-49   RUST, R. M.
              EPIDEMIOLOGY OF MENTAL HEALTH IN COLLEGE.
              JOURNAL OF PSYCHOLOGY, 1960, 49, 235-248.
              ("TWELVE-PROBLEMS" SCALE)*
         @R-49 MENTAL-HEALTH MENTAL-ILLNESS GLOBAL ADJUSTMENT COLLEGE STUDENT PROBLEM
         @R-49 SOCIAL COMPETENCE INTERPERSONAL RELATIONSHIPS 1960M

R-50   ROKEACH, M.
              THE OPEN AND CLOSED MIND.
              NEW YORK: BASIC BOOKS, 1960.
              (OPINIONATION SCALE)*
         @R-50 DOGMATISM RIGIDITY FLEXIBILITY OPINION COPING-DEFENSE CONSERVATISM
         @R-50 LIBERALISM TOLERANCE 1960M
              (APPLICATIONS: 148   201   841)

R-51   RASMUSSEN, J. E.
              RELATIONSHIP OF EGO IDENTITY TO PSYCHOLOGICAL EFFECTIVENESS.
              PSYCHOLOGICAL REPORTS, 1964, 15, 815-825.
              (EGO IDENTITY SCALE)*
         @R-51 EGO IDENTITY COPING DEFENSE EGO-STRENGTH EGO-RESILIENCY SELF-IDENTITY
         @R-51 SELF PERCEPTION EVALUATION ESTEEM 1964M

R-52   RICHARDS, J. M., JR.
              A FACTOR ANALYTIC STUDY OF THE SELF-RATINGS OF COLLEGE FRESHMEN.
              EDUCATIONAL AND PSYCHOLOGICAL MEASUREMENT, 1966, 26, 861-870.
              (SELF-RATINGS OF 31 PERSONALITY TRAITS)
         @R-52 SELF-IDENTITY SELF RATING CONCEPT IDEAL IMAGE MULTITRAIT ESTEEM EVALUATION
         @R-52 PERCEPTION 1966M
              (APPLICATIONS: 1515)

R-53   ROBERTSON, L. S., & DOTSON, L. E.
              PERCEIVED PARENTAL EXPRESSIVITY, REACTION TO STRESS, AND AFFILIATION.
              JOURNAL OF PERSONALITY AND SOCIAL PSYCHOLOGY, 1969, 12, 229-234.
              (MEASURE OF ANXIETY)
         @R-53 ANXIETY AFFECTIVE-STATES NEGATIVE SUBJECTIVE STRESS 1969M

R-54   ROBERTSON, L. S., & DOTSON, L. E.
              PERCEIVED PARENTAL EXPRESSIVITY, REACTION TO STRESS, AND AFFILIATION.
              JOURNAL OF PERSONALITY AND SOCIAL PSYCHOLOGY, 1969, 12, 229-234.
              (AFFILIATION MEASURE)
         @R-54 AFFILIATION ACTIVITIES SOCIAL NEED AUTONOMY SCHOOL 1969M

R-55   RONNING, R. R., STELLWAGEN, W. R., & STEWART, L. H.
              APPLICATION OF MULTIDIMENSIONAL AND SCALE ANALYSIS TO INTEREST MEASUREMENT.
              UNITED STATES OFFICE OF EDUCATION, COOPERATIVE RESEARCH PROJECT NO. 1493,
              1963.
         RONNING, R. R., STEWART, L. H., & STELLWAGEN, W. R.
              AN EQUISECTION SCALE OF INTERESTS: A PRELIMINARY REPORT.
              JOURNAL OF COUNSELING PSYCHOLOGY, 1965, 12, 176-181.
              (EQUISECTION SCALE OF INTEREST)
         @R-55 1963M INTEREST PREFERENCE ACTIVITIES
              (APPLICATIONS: 1322   1336)

R-56   ROSANOFF, A. J.
              FREE ASSOCIATION TEST.
              IN A. J. ROSANOFF (ED.), MANUAL OF PSYCHIATRY. (7TH ED., REV.) NEW YORK:
              WILEY, 1944.
              (OBJECT SORTING TEST)*
         @R-56 ORIGINALITY CREATIVITY AUTONOMY INTELLIGENCE COGNITIVE FUNCTIONING
         @R-56 PSYCHIATRIC THINKING 1944M DIAGNOSIS

R-58   RAPAPORT, D., GILL. M., & SCHAFFER, R.
              DIAGNOSTIC PSYCHOLOGICAL TESTING, VOL. 1.
              CHICAGO: YEARBOOK PUBLISHERS, 1945.
              (MODIFIED OBJECT SORTING TEST)
         @R-58 CONCEPTUAL DEVELOPMENT COGNITIVE FUNCTIONING STRUCTURE 1945M
              (APPLICATIONS: 731   868   925   927   1008   1106   1618   2394   2454)

R-59   RONAN, W. W.
              RELATIVE IMPORTANCE OF JOB CHARACTERISTICS.
              JOURNAL OF APPLIED PSYCHOLOGY, 1970, 54, 192-200.
              (MEASURE OF IMPORTANCE OF JOB CHARACTERISTICS)
         @R-59 JOB PE-FIT ENVIRONMENT 1970M

R-60   REHBERG, R. A., SCHAFER, W. E., & SINCLAIR, J.
              TOWARD A TEMPORAL SEQUENCE OF ADOLESCENT ACHIEVEMENT VARIABLES.
              AMERICAN SOCIOLOGICAL REVIEW, 1970, 35, 34-48.
              (MEASURE OF MOBILITY ATTITUDES)
         @R-60 1970M ATTITUDE ACHIEVEMENT ORIENTATION AUTONOMY IE-CONTROL LOCUS CONTROL
         @R-60 ADOLESCENT

R-61   ROGERS, R. W., & THISTLETHWAITE, D. L.
              EFFECTS OF FEAR AROUSAL AND REASSURANCE ON ATTITUDE CHANGE.
              JOURNAL OF PERSONALITY AND SOCIAL PSYCHOLOGY, 1970, 15, 227-233.
              (MEASURE OF FEAR AROUSAL)
         @R-61 1970M FEAR AROUSAL AFFECTIVE-STATES MOOD

R-62   REYNOLDS, D. D.
              THE TEMPLE FEAR SURVEY INVENTORY.
              UNPUBLISHED MANUSCRIPT, TEMPLE UNIVERSITY, 1967.
              (FEAR SURVEY SCALE)*
         @R-62 1967M FEAR ANXIETY
              (APPLICATIONS: 2932)

R-63   ROBBINS, P. R.
              AN APPROACH TO MEASURING PSYCHOLOGICAL TENSIONS BY MEANS OF
              DREAM ASSOCIATIONS.
              PSYCHOLOGICAL REPORTS, 1966, 18, 959-971.
              (DREAM INCIDENT TECHNIQUE)
         @R-63 1966M FANTASY IMAGERY TENSION

R-64   ROE, A., & SIEGELMAN, M.
              THE ORIGIN OF INTEREST.
              WASHINGTON, D. C.: AMERICAN PERSONNEL AND GUIDANCE ASSOCIATION, 1964.
              (BIOGRAPHICAL QUESTIONNAIRE)*
         @R-64 1964M PARENTAL DOMINANCE ACCEPTANCE INTERACTION
              (APPLICATIONS: 1528   2853)

R-65   REITMAN, F., & ROBERTSON, J. P.
              REITMAN'S PIN MAN TEST: A MEANS OF DISCLOSING IMPAIRED CONCEPTUAL THINKING.
              JOURNAL OF NERVOUS AND MENTAL DISEASES, 1950, 112, 498-510.
              (REITMAN PIN MAN OR STICK FIGURE TEST)*
         @R-65 1950M PROJECTIVE AFFECTIVE-STATES BODY IMAGE CONCEPTUAL FUNCTIONING
         @R-65 DEVELOPMENT COGNITIVE THINKING
              (APPLICATIONS: 2963)

R-66   ROUTH, D. K., & SCHNEIDER, J. M.
              WORD ASSOCIATION AND INK BLOT RESPONSES AS A FUNCTION OF INSTRUCTIONAL SETS
              AND PSYCHOPATHOLOGY.
              JOURNAL OF PROJECTIVE TECHNIQUES AND PERSONALITY ASSESSMENT, 1970, 34,
              113-120.
              (WORD ASSOCIATION TEST)
         @R-66 1970M WORD ASSOCIATION COGNITIVE THINKING FUNCTIONING STRUCTURE

R-67   RINGNESS, T. A.
            NON-INTELLECTIVE VARIABLES RELATED TO ACADEMIC ACHIEVEMENT OF BRIGHT
            JUNIOR HIGH SCHOOL BOYS.
            (FINAL REPORT, U.S. OFFICE OF EDUCATION PROJECT, S-036) MADISON:
            UNIVERSITY OF WISCONSIN, 1965, (MIMEO).
            (MEASURE OF BEHAVIOR ORIENTATION)
        ƏR-67 1965M BEHAVIOR ORIENTATION Q-SORT ACHIEVEMENT INDEPENDENCE PEER
        ƏR-67 AFFILIATION ADOLESCENT
            (APPLICATIONS: 2796)

R-68   RINGNESS, T. A.
            IDENTIFYING FIGURES, THEIR ACHIEVEMENT VALUES, AND CHILDREN'S VALUES
            AS RELATED TO ACTUAL AND PREDICTED ACHIEVEMENT.
            JOURNAL OF EDUCATIONAL PSYCHOLOGY, 1970, 61, 174-185.
            (SCHOOL ATTITUDE RESEARCH INSTRUMENT)*
        ƏR-68 1970M ATTITUDE FAMILY INTERACTION PEER TEACHER ACHIEVEMENT VALUES
        ƏR-68 SCHOOL

R-70   RUTHERFORD, E., & MUSSEN, P.
            GENEROSITY IN NURSERY SCHOOL BOYS.
            CHILD DEVELOPMENT, 1968, 39, 755-765.
            (BEHAVIORAL MEASURE OF ALTRUISM)
        ƏR-70 1968M ALTRUISM CHILD SOCIAL DEVELOPMENT MORAL
            (APPLICATIONS: 2903)

R-71   ROBERTS, K. H., MILES, R. E., & BLANKENSHIP, L. V.
            ORGANIZATIONAL LEADERSHIP, SATISFACTION AND PRODUCTIVITY: A COMPARATIVE
            ANALYSIS.
            ACADEMY OF MANAGEMENT JOURNAL, 1968, 11, 401-414.
            (MEASURE OF SATISFACTION WITH IMMEDIATE SUPERVISION)
        ƏR-71 1968M LEADERSHIP SUPERVISOR SATISFACTION AFFECTIVE-STATES EMPLOYEE
        ƏR-71 RELATIONSHIPS MANAGEMENT JOB
            (APPLICATIONS: 2469)

R-72   ROSENCRANTZ, P., VOGEL, S., BEE, H., BROVERMAN, I., & BROVERMAN, D. M.
            SEX-ROLE STEREOTYPES AND SELF-CONCEPTS IN COLLEGE STUDENTS.
            JOURNAL OF CONSULTING AND CLINICAL PSYCHOLOGY, 1968, 32, 287-295.
            (SEX-ROLE STEREOTYPE QUESTIONNAIRE)
        ƏR-72 1968M SEX ROLE STEREOTYPE CONCEPT STUDENT MASCULINITY FEMININITY
        ƏR-72 SELF RATING
            (APPLICATIONS: 2455 2539)

R-73   RICHARDS, J. M., JR., SELIGMAN, R., & JONES, P. K.
            FACULTY AND CURRICULUM AS MEASURES OF COLLEGE ENVIRONMENT.
            JOURNAL OF EDUCATIONAL PSYCHOLOGY, 1970, 61, 324-332.
            (MEASURE OF COLLEGE ENVIRONMENT)
        ƏR-73 1970M COLLEGE ENVIRONMENT PE-FIT
        ƏR-73 ESTHETIC SOCIAL INTELLECTUAL EVALUATION

R-74   ROTTER, G. S., & TINKLEMAN, V.
            ANCHOR EFFECTS IN THE DEVELOPMENT OF BEHAVIOR RATING SCALES.
            EDUCATIONAL AND PSYCHOLOGICAL MEASUREMENT, 1970, 30, 311-318.
            (BEHAVIOR RATING SCALES)
        ƏR-74 1970M BEHAVIOR RATING ADJUSTMENT
        ƏR-74 SOCIAL INTERPERSONAL

R-75   ROGERS, C. R., & DYMOND, R. (EDS).
            PSYCHOTHERAPY AND PERSONALITY CHANGE.
            CHICAGO: UNIVERSITY OF CHICAGO PRESS, 1954.
            (MEASURE OF CHANGE IN SELF-CONCEPT DURING PSYCHOTHERAPY)
        ƏR-75 1954M SELF CONCEPT THERAPY COUNSELING IDEAL ADJUSTMENT CHANGE
        ƏPERSONALITY ACCEPTANCE ESTEEM
            (APPLICATIONS: 950 1490 2223)

R-77   ROSENBAUM, M. E., & DECHARMS, R.
            DIRECT AND VICARIOUS REDUCTION OF HOSTILITY.
            JOURNAL OF ABNORMAL AND SOCIAL PSYCHOLOGY, 1960, 60, 105-111.
            (SELF-ESTEEM SCALE)
        ƏR-77 1960M SELF ESTEEM NEED APPROVAL CONCEPT EGO-STRENGTH
        ƏR-77 AGGRESSION HOSTILITY SITUATIONAL
            (APPLICATIONS: 352 708)

R-78   ROBBINS, P. R.
                SOME EXPLORATIONS INTO THE NATURE OF ANXIETIES RELATING TO ILLNESS.
                GENETIC PSYCHOLOGY MONOGRAPHS, 1962, 66, 91-141.
                (MEDICAL ATTITUDE INVENTORY)
         aR-78 1962M ATTITUDE ANXIETY PHYSICAL ILLNESS FEAR
                (APPLICATIONS: 370)

R-79   RUEBUSH, B. K., & STEVENSON, H. W.
                THE EFFECTS OF MOTHERS AND STRANGERS ON THE PERFORMANCE OF ANXIOUS AND
                DEFENSIVE CHILDREN.
                JOURNAL OF PERSONALITY, 1964, 32, 587-600.
                (EMBEDDED FIGURES GAME)*
         aR-79 1964M FIGURE AGGRESSION DEPENDENCE
         aR-79 CHILD GRAPHIC FIELD DEPENDENCE

R-80   ROSENFELD, H. M.
                SOCIAL CHOICE CONCEIVED AS A LEVEL OF ASPIRATION.
                JOURNAL OF ABNORMAL AND SOCIAL PSYCHOLOGY, 1964, 68, 491-499.
                (MEASURE OF FEAR OF REJECTION)
         aR-80 1964M FEAR AFFILIATION SUPPORT NEED SECURITY SOCIAL COMPETENCE ANXIETY
         aR-80 INTERPERSONAL
                (APPLICATIONS: 146   514)

R-81   ROSENBERG, A. L.
                THE DEVELOPMENT OF AN INSTRUMENT FOR ASSESSING THE MODES OF RECONCILING
                CONTRADICTIONS.
                UNPUBLISHED MASTER'S THESIS, PURDUE UNIVERSITY, 1957.
                (SENTENCE COMPLETION MEASURE OF CONFLICT RESOLUTION)
         R-81 RELATIONSHIPS STYLE INTERACTION AGGRESSIVENESS EXPRESSION AVOIDANCE
         aR-81 1957M CONFLICT ORIENTATION BEHAVIOR SENTENCE-COMP SOCIAL INTERPERSONAL
                (APPLICATIONS: 1599)

R-82   RUNKEL, P. J.
                COGNITIVE SIMILARITY IN FACILITATING COMMUNICATION.
                SOCIOMETRY, 1956, 19, 178-191.
                (COGNITIVE STRUCTURE QUESTIONNAIRE)
         aR-82 1956M COGNITIVE STRUCTURE PREFERENCE CONSISTENCY RESPONSE
         aR-82 STYLE
                (APPLICATIONS: 524)

R-83   ROSENFELD, H. M., & NAUMAN, D. J.
                EFFECTS OF DOGMATISM ON THE DEVELOPMENT OF INFORMAL RELATIONSHIPS AMONG
                WOMEN.
                JOURNAL OF PERSONALITY, 1969, 37, 497-511.
                (MEASURE OF INTERPERSONAL RESPONSES)
         aR-83 1969M DOGMATISM INTERPERSONAL RELATIONSHIPS PEER COMPATABILITY
         aR-83 MOTIVE EVALUATION BEHAVIOR INTERACTION SOCIAL

R-84   ROGERS, C. R.
                MEASURING PERSONALITY ADJUSTMENT IN CHILDREN NINE TO THIRTEEN YEARS OF AGE.
                TEACHERS COLLEGE CONTR. EDUC., 1931, NO. 458.
                (ROGERS' RATING SCALE OF ADJUSTMENT)
         aR-84 1931M ADJUSTMENT TEACHER CHILD FANTASY AFFECTION DEPENDENCE AUTONOMY SEX
         aR-84 CONFLICT EMOTION AFFECTIVE-STATES AGGRESSION INFERIORITY FEELING SOCIAL
         aR-84 RELATIONSHIPS EXPRESSION ACCEPTANCE AUTHORITY
                (APPLICATIONS: 1590)

R-85   ROGERS, C. R.
                MANUAL OF DIRECTIONS: A TEST OF PERSONALITY ADJUSTMENT.
                NEW YORK: ASSOCIATION, 1931.
         ROGERS, C. R.
                MEASURING PERSONALITY ADJUSTMENT IN CHILDREN NINE TO THIRTEEN YEARS OF AGE.
                TEACHERS COLLEGE CONTRIBUTIONS TO EDUCATION, 1931, NO. 458.
                (ROGERS' TEST OF PERSONALITY ADJUSTMENT)*
         aR-85 1931M PERSONALITY ADJUSTMENT CHILD MALADJUSTMENT INFERIORITY FANTASY
         aR-85 FAMILY SOCIAL GLOBAL PARENT RELATIONSHIPS FEELING SELF
         aR-85 ESTEEM SECURITY
                (APPLICATIONS: 1590)

R-87   ROSENTHAL, I.
                RELIABILITY OF RETROSPECTIVE REPORTS OF ADOLESCENCE.
                JOURNAL OF CONSULTING PSYCHOLOGY, 1963, 27, 189-198.
                (WISHES-PARENTS TEST)*
         aR-87 1963M ADOLESCENT PARENT-CHILD HOME FAMILY AFFECTION ATTITUDE RELATIONSHIPS
         aR-87 PROBLEM CONFLICT IDEAL GLOBAL

R-88   ROKEACH, M.
               GENERALIZED MENTAL RIGIDITY AS A FACTOR IN ETHNOCENTRISM.
               JOURNAL OF ABNORMAL AND SOCIAL PSYCHOLOGY, 1948, 43, 259-278.
               (ROKEACH MAP TEST)
          aR-88 1948M RIGIDITY FLEXIBILITY COGNITIVE FUNCTIONING THINKING
               (APPLICATIONS: 1836)

R-89   RICHARDS, T. W., & SIMONS, M. P.
               THE FELS CHILD BEHAVIOR SCALES.
               GENETIC PSYCHOLOGY MONOGRAPHS, 1941, 24, 259-309.
               (FELS CHILD BEHAVIOR SCALES)
          aR-89 1941M CHILD BEHAVIOR AGGRESSIVENESS CONFORMITY COMPETITION EMOTION
          aR-89 CONTROL EXHIBITION AFFILIATION NEED ORIGINALITY HUMOR SENSITIVITY
               (APPLICATIONS: 1985 2843 2964)

R-92   RASKIN, A., SCHULTERBRANDT, J., REATIG, N., & RICE, C. E.
               FACTORS OF PSYCHOPATHOLOGY IN INTERVIEW, WARD BEHAVIOR, AND SELF REPORT
               RATINGS OF HOSPITALIZED DEPRESSIVES.
               JOURNAL OF CONSULTING PSYCHOLOGY, 1967, 31, 270-278.
               (MEASURE OF PSYCHIC AND SOMATIC COMPLAINTS)
          aR-92 1967M SYMPTOM PSYCHIATRIC DEPRESSION PARTICIPATION INTEREST HOSTILITY
          aR-92 ACTIVITIES TENSION GUILT MOOD AFFECTIVE-STATES PSYCHOSOMATIC

R-93   RASKIN, A., SCHULTERBRANDT, J., REATIG, N., & RICE, C. E.
               FACTORS OF PSYCHOPATHOLOGY IN INTERVIEW, WARD BEHAVIOR, AND SELF REPORT
               RATINGS OF HOSPITALIZED DEPRESSIVES.
               JOURNAL OF CONSULTING PSYCHOLOGY, 1967, 31, 270-278.
               (MOOD SCALES)
          aR-93 1967M MOOD AFFECTIVE-STATES CHECKLIST DEPRESSION INTEREST PARTICIPATION
          aR-93 ACTIVITIES HOSTILITY GUILT ANXIETY TENSION.

R-94   ROGERS, C. R. (ED.)
               THE THERAPEUTIC RELATIONSHIP AND ITS IMPACT: A STUDY OF PSYCHOTHERAPY
               WITH SCHIZOPHRENICS.
               MADISON: UNIVERSITY OF WISCONSIN, 1967, IN PRESS.
               (ANXIETY SCALE)
          aR-94 1967M ANXIETY TENSION MENTAL-HEALTH MENTAL-ILLNESS

R-95   ROGERS, C. R., GENDLIN, E. T., KIESLER, D. J., & TRUAX, C. B.
               THE THERAPEUTIC RELATIONSHIP AND ITS IMPACT: A STUDY OF PSYCHOTHERAPY WITH
               SCHIZOPHRENICS.
               MADISON: UNIVERSITY OF WISCONSIN PRESS, 1967.
               (EXPERIENCING SCALE)
          aR-95 1967M THERAPY RELATIONSHIPS INTERACTION PATIENT EXPERIENCE ADJUSTMENT
          aR-95 SELF AWARENESS
               (APPLICATIONS: 2090 2204)

R-96   ROTHSTEIN, R.
               AUTHORITARIANISM AND MEN'S REACTIONS TO SEXUALITY AND AFFECTION IN WOMEN.
               JOURNAL OF ABNORMAL AND SOCIAL PSYCHOLOGY, 1960, 61, 329-334.
               (HETEROSEXUAL QUESTIONNAIRE)*
          aR-96 1960M SEX AFFECTION ROLE SUB-IDENTITY SELF IDENTITY MASCULINITY FEMININITY

R-97   ROSENHAN, D., & LONDON, P.
               GROUP HYPNOTIC SUSCEPTIBILITY SCALE.
               PRINCETON, N. J.: AUTHOR, 1961 (MIMEO).
               (GROUP HYPNOTIC SUSCEPTIBILITY SCALE)
          aR-97 1961M HYPNOTIC SUGGESTIBILITY GROUP
               (APPLICATIONS: 775)

R-100   RUEBUSH, B. K.
               CHILDREN'S BEHAVIOR AS A FUNCTION OF ANXIETY AND DEFENSIVENESS.
               UNPUBLISHED DOCTORAL DISSERTATION, YALE UNIVERSITY, 1960.
               (DEFENSIVENESS SCALE FOR CHILDREN)
          aR-100 1960M CHILD DEFENSIVENESS RESPONSE SET NEGATIVE AFFECTIVE-STATES
          aR-100 ANXIETY GUILT HOSTILITY RESPONSE-BIAS
               (APPLICATIONS: 849)

R-101   RITCHEY, R. F.
               PREDICTING SUCCESS OF SCHIZOPHRENICS IN INDUSTRIAL THERAPY.
               JOURNAL OF COUNSELING PSYCHOLOGY, 1965, 12, 68-73.
               (WORK CONDITIONS PREFERENCE INVENTORY)
          aR-101 1965M JOB PREFERENCE INVENTORY SOCIAL INTERPERSONAL RELATIONSHIPS

R-103   RENZAGLIA, G. A.
               SOME CORRELATES OF THE SELF-STRUCTURES AS MEASURED BY AN INDEX OF
               ADJUSTMENT AND VALUES.
               UNPUBLISHED DOCTORAL DISSERTATION, UNIVERSITY OF MINNESOTA, 1952.
               (INDEX OF ADJUSTMENT AND VALUES)
           @R-103 1952M ADJUSTMENT VALUES SELF CONCEPT IDEAL SATISFACTION

R-104   RUNDQUIST, E. A., & SLETTO, R. F.
               SCORING INSTRUCTIONS FOR THE MINNESOTA SCALE FOR THE SURVEY OF OPINIONS.
               UNIVERSITY OF MINNESOTA PRESS, 1936.
               (MINNESOTA SCALE FOR THE SURVEY OF OPINIONS)*
           @R-104 1936M OPINION ATTITUDE ADJUSTMENT MORALE FAMILY CONSERVATISM
           @INFERIORITY

R-105   ROKEACH, M.
               ROKEACH INTERRELATION TASK AND SUSCEPTIBILITY TO CONFORMITY.
               UNPUBLISHED, 1968.
               (INTERRELATIONS TASK: IT)
           @R-105 1968M

R-106   REIMANIS, G.
               CHILDHOOD EXPERIENCE MEMORIES AND ANOMIE IN ADULTS AND COLLEGE STUDENTS.
               JOURNAL OF INDIVIDUAL PSYCHOLOGY, 1966, 22, 56-64.
               (CHILDHOOD EXPERIENCE QUESTIONNAIRE)
           @R-106 1966M CHILD EXPERIENCE SUBJECTIVE FAMILY RELATIONSHIPS ENVIRONMENTAL

R-111   RUDIE, R. R., & MCGAUGHRAN, L. S.
               DIFFERENCES IN DEVELOPMENTAL EXPERIENCE, DEFENSIVENESS, AND PERSONALITY
               ORGANIZATION BETWEEN TWO CLASSES OF PROBLEM DRINKERS.
               JOURNAL OF ABNORMAL AND SOCIAL PSYCHOLOGY, 1961, 62, 659-665.
               (QUESTIONNAIRE TO DISTINGUISH ESSENTIAL AND REACTIVE ALCOHOLICS)
           @R-111 1961M ALCOHOLISM DIAGNOSIS DEPENDENCE
           @R-111 ILLNESS

R-112   ROSENWALD, G. C.
               THE ASSESSMENT OF ANXIETY IN PSYCHOLOGICAL EXPERIMENTATION: A THEORETICAL
               REFORMULATION AND TEST.
               JOURNAL OF ABNORMAL AND SOCIAL PSYCHOLOGY, 1961, 62, 666-673.
               (ANAGRAMS TEST OF DEFENSIVENESS)
           @R-112 1961M DEFENSIVENESS ANXIETY EGO DEFENSE AGGRESSION COPING-DEFENSE

R-113   ROSENWALD, G. C.
               THE ASSESSMENT OF ANXIETY IN PSYCHOLOGICAL EXPERIMENTATION: A THEORETICAL
               REFORMULATION AND TEST.
               JOURNAL OF ABNORMAL AND SOCIAL PSYCHOLOGY, 1961, 62, 666-673.
               (STORY COMPLETION TEST FOR ANXIETY AND DEFENSIVENESS)
           @R-113 1961M PROJECTIVE ANXIETY DEFENSIVENESS EGO DEFENSE COPING-DEFENSE
           @R-113 STORY-COMPLETION

R-114   ROSENBERG, M.
               SOCIETY AND THE ADOLESCENT SELF-IMAGE.
               PRINCETON, N.J.: PRINCETON UNIVERSITY PRESS, 1965.
               (SELF-ESTEEM SCALE)
           @R-114 1965M SELF ESTEEM SELF IMAGE EVALUATION CONFIDENCE
           @R-114 PERCEPTION
               (APPLICATIONS: 1031 2789)

R-115   RUMA, E. H., & MOSHER, D. L.
               RELATIONSHIP BETWEEN MORAL JUDGMENT AND GUILT IN DELINQUENT BOYS.
               JOURNAL OF ABNORMAL PSYCHOLOGY, 1967, 72, 122-127.
               (INTERVIEW MEASURE OF MORAL STANDARDS)
           @R-115 1967M MORAL VALUES BELIEF DELINQUENCY ADOLESCENT INTERVIEW JUDGMENT

R-116   RUMA, E. H., & MOSHER, D. L.
               RELATIONSHIP BETWEEN MORAL JUDGMENT AND GUILT IN DELINQUENT BOYS.
               JOURNAL OF ABNORMAL PSYCHOLOGY, 1967, 72, 122-127.
               (GLOBAL CLINICAL RATING OF GUILT)
           @R-116 1967M GUILT RATING DELINQUENCY ADOLESCENT CONSCIENCE

R-118   RIMLAND, B.
               INFANTILE AUTISM.
               NEW YORK: APPLETON-CENTURY-CROFTS, 1964.
               (EXPERIMENTAL CHECKLIST FOR DIAGNOSIS OF AUTISM)*
          @R-118 1964M PSYCHIATRIC DIAGNOSIS CHECKLIST SCHIZOPHRENIA
               (APPLICATIONS: 1075)

R-119   ROKEACH, M.
               BELIEFS, ATTITUDES AND VALUES.
               SAN FRANCISCO: JOSSEY BASS, 1968.
          ROKEACH, M.
               THE ROLE OF VALUES IN PUBLIC OPINION RESEARCH.
               PUBLIC OPINION QUARTERLY, 1968-69, 32, 547-559.
               (ROKEACH VALUE SURVEY)*
          @R-119 1968M VALUES IDEALS LOCUS CONTROL SELF ESTEEM CONCEPT SELF-IDENTITY
          @R-119 SUB-IDENTITY MORAL RELIGION
               (APPLICATIONS: 2351)

R-120   ROSEN, H., & KOMORITA, S. S.
               A DECISION PARADIGM FOR ACTION RESEARCH: PROBLEMS OF EMPLOYING THE
               PHYSICALLY HANDICAPPED.
               JOURNAL OF APPLIED BEHAVIORAL SCIENCE, 1969, 5, 509-518.
               (CONSEQUENCES MODEL QUESTIONNAIRE)
          @R-120 1969M ATTITUDE BELIEF CHANGE TECHNIQUE
               (APPLICATIONS: 2359)

R-121   ROSENWALD, G. C., MENDELSOHN, G. A., FONTANA, A., & PORTZ, A. T.
               AN ACTION TEST OF HYPOTHESES CONCERNING THE ANAL PERSONALITY.
               JOURNAL OF ABNORMAL PSYCHOLOGY, 1966, 71, 304-309.
               (MEASURE OF ANAL PERSONALITY CHARACTERISTICS)
          @R-121 1966M ANXIETY ORALITY RIGIDITY COMPULSIVENESS NEUROTICISM ANALITY

R-122   ROSENBERG, M.
               SOCIETY AND THE ADOLESCENT SELF-IMAGE.
               PRINCETON, N.J.: PRINCETON UNIVERSITY PRESS, 1965.
               (MEASURE OF STABILITY OF SELF)
          @R-122 1965M SELF PERSONALITY IMAGE STABILITY
          @R-122 CONCEPT PERCEPTION

R-123   RUBIN, Z.
               THE SOCIAL PSYCHOLOGY OF ROMANTIC LOVE.
               ANN ARBOR, MICHIGAN: UNIVERSITY MICROFILMS, 1969.
          RUBIN, Z.
               MEASUREMENT OF ROMANTIC LOVE.
               JOURNAL OF PERSONALITY AND SOCIAL PSYCHOLOGY, 1970, 16, 265-273.
               (LIKING SCALE)
          @R-123 1969M SOCIAL INTERPERSONAL ATTRACTION

R-124   RUBIN, Z.
               THE SOCIAL PSYCHOLOGY OF ROMANTIC LOVE.
               ANN ARBOR, MICHIGAN: UNIVERSITY MICROFILMS, 1969.
          RUBIN, Z.
               MEASUREMENT OF ROMANTIC LOVE.
               JOURNAL OF PERSONALITY AND SOCIAL PSYCHOLOGY, 1970, 16, 265-273.
               (LOVE SCALE)
          @R-124 1969M ATTRACTION INTERPERSONAL LOVE AFFECTION FEELING NEED AFFILIATION
          @RESPONSIBILITY

R-126   RONAN, W. W.
               INDIVIDUAL AND SITUATIONAL VARIABLES RELATING TO JOB SATISFACTION.
               JOURNAL OF APPLIED PSYCHOLOGY MONOGRAPH, 1970, 54, (1, PT. 2).
               (JOB SATISFACTION QUESTIONNAIRES)
          @R-126 1970M JOB SATISFACTION PE-FIT ENVIRONMENT EVALUATION EMPLOYEE MANAGEMENT
          @RELATIONSHIPS FEELING

R-127   RIEDEL, W. W.
               AN INVESTIGATION OF PERSONAL CONSTRUCTS THROUGH NONVERBAL TASKS.
               JOURNAL OF ABNORMAL PSYCHOLOGY, 1970, 76, 173-179.
               (PERSONAL CONSTRUCT INVENTORY)*
          @R-127 1970M ROLE RELATIONSHIPS INTERPERSONAL PERCEPTION SELF OTHERS IDEAL

R-128   RYDELL, S. T., & ROSEN, E.
         MEASUREMENT AND SOME CORRELATES OF NEED-COGNITION.
         PSYCHOLOGICAL REPORTS, 1966, 19, 139-165 (MONOGRAPH SUPPLEMENT 1-V19).
         (RYDELL-ROSEN AMBIGUITY TOLERANCE SCALE)*
      @R-128 1966M TOLERANCE AMBIGUITY OPENNESS RIGIDITY FLEXIBILITY COMPLEXITY
         (APPLICATIONS: 2647)

R-129   REIMANIS, G.
         ADJECTIVE CHECK LIST TO ASSESS FEELING OR MOOD IN DOMICILIARY MEMBERS.
         UNPUBLISHED RESEARCH REPORT, VETERANS ADMINISTRATION CENTER, BATH, NEW YORK
         1960.
         (PRESENT LIFE GOAL MOOD DIFFERENCE)
      @R-129 1960M GOALS LIFE PURPOSE MOOD AFFECTIVE-STATES CHECKLIST
         (APPLICATIONS: 922)

R-130   ROSENBERG, M., & GLUECK, B.
         FURTHER DEVELOPMENTS IN AUTOMATION OF BEHAVIORAL OBSERVATION ON
         HOSPITALIZED PSYCHIATRIC PATIENTS.
         COMPARATIVE PSYCHIATRY, 1967, 8, 468-475.
         (AUTOMATED NURSING NOTES)
      @R-130 1967M PSYCHIATRIC PATIENT BEHAVIOR THERAPY RATING STAFF
         (APPLICATIONS: 2634)

R-131   RENNER, K. E., MAHER, B. A., & CAMPBELL, D. T.
         THE VALIDITY OF A METHOD FOR SCORING SENTENCE-COMPLETION RESPONSES FOR
         ANXIETY, DEPENDENCY, AND HOSTILITY.
         JOURNAL OF APPLIED PSYCHOLOGY, 1962, 46, 285-290.
         (SENTENCE COMPLETION MEASURE OF ANXIETY, DEPENDENCY AND HOSTILITY)
      @R-131 1962M SENTENCE-COMP ANXIETY HOSTILITY DEPENDENCE

R-132   ROTHENBERG, B. B.
         CHILDREN'S SOCIAL SENSITIVITY AND THE RELATIONSHIP TO INTERPERSONAL
         COMPETENCE, INTRAPERSONAL COMFORT, AND INTELLECTUAL LEVEL.
         DEVELOPMENTAL PSYCHOLOGY, 1970, 2, 335-350.
         (SOCIAL SENSITIVITY SCALE FOR CHILDREN)
      @R-132 1970M SOCIAL SENSITIVITY CHILD FEELING EMOTION PERCEPTION AWARENESS

R-133   RUNNER, K., & RUNNER, H.
         THE RUNNER STUDIES OF ATTITUDES PATTERNS, INTERVIEW FORM III.
         GOLDEN, COLORADO: AUTHORS, 1964.
         (RUNNER STUDIES OF ATTITUDES PATTERNS)*
      @R-133 1964M ATTITUDE BELIEF OPINION INVENTORY

R-134   RYBACK, D.
         OPTIMISM-PESSIMISM AS A CONSEQUENCE OF SUCCESS OR FAILURE IN CHILDREN.
         PSYCHOLOGICAL REPORTS, 1970, 26, 385.
         (MEASURE OF OPTIMISM-PESSIMISM)
      @R-134 1970M PREDICTION SUCCESS FAILURE OPTIMISM PESSIMISM PROJECTIVE

R-135   ROTHAUS, P., JOHNSON, D. L., HANSON, P. G., LYLE, F. A., & MOYER, R.
         PARTICIPATION AND SOCIOMETRY IN AUTONOMOUS AND TRAINER-LED PATIENT GROUPS.
         JOURNAL OF COUNSELING PSYCHOLOGY, 1966, 13, 68-76.
         (GROUP BEHAVIOR QUESTIONNAIRE)*
      @R-135 1966M GROUP BEHAVIOR INTERPERSONAL RELATIONSHIPS INTERACTION
      @SOCIOMETRIC PSYCHIATRIC PATIENT
         (APPLICATIONS: 1377)

R-136   ROTHAUS, P., JOHNSON, D. L., HANSON, P. G., BROWN, J. B., & LYLE, F. A.
         SENTENCE-COMPLETION TEST PREDICTION OF AUTONOMOUS AND THERAPIST-LED GROUP
         BEHAVIOR.
         JOURNAL OF COUNSELING PSYCHOLOGY, 1967, 14, 28-34.
         (MEASURE OF GROUP ATMOSHPERE)
      @R-136 1967M GROUP ENVIRONMENT BEHAVIOR INTERPERSONAL RELATIONSHIPS
      @CHECKLIST INTERACTION
         (APPLICATIONS: 1377)

R-137   ROTHAUS, P., JOHNSON, D. L., HANSON, P. G., BROWN, J. B., & LYLE, F. A.
         SENTENCE-COMPLETION TEST PREDICTION OF AUTONOMOUS AND THERAPIST-LED GROUP
         BEHAVIOR.
         JOURNAL OF COUNSELING PSYCHOLOGY, 1967, 14, 28-34.
         (MEASURE OF FEELINGS ABOUT GROUP/INTERPERSONAL RELATIONS)
      @R-137 1967M SENTENCE-COMP GROUP ORIENTATION INTERPERSONAL RELATIONSHIPS
      @PROJECTIVE INTERACTION EVALUATION SATISFACTION

R-138   ROE, A.
             THE PSYCHOLOGY OF OCCUPATIONS.
             NEW YORK: WILEY, 1956.
             (CLASSIFICATION OF OCCUPATIONS)
         aR-138 1956M JOB VOCATIONAL DESCRIPTION PREFERENCE ATTITUDE PERCEPTION
             (APPLICATIONS: 1369 1428 1444 1505)

R-139   ROEBER, E. C., SMITH, G. E., & ERICKSON, C. E.
             ORGANIZATION AND ADMINISTRATION OF GUIDANCE SERVICES.
             NEW YORK: MCGRAW-HILL, 1955.
             (PROBLEM AREA QUESTIONNAIRE)*
         aR-139 1955M PROBLEM INVENTORY ADJUSTMENT PERSONAL DIAGNOSIS COUNSELING

R-140   ROTHAUS, P., JOHNSON, D. L., & BLANK, G.
             CHANGING THE CONNOTATIONS OF MENTAL ILLNESS IN PSYCHIATRIC PATIENTS.
             JOURNAL OF COUNSELING PSYCHOLOGY, 1967, 14, 258-263.
             (TEST OF INSIGHT INTO HUMAN MOTIVES FOR MENTAL PATIENTS)
         aR-140 1967M SELF PERCEPTION MOTIVE MENTAL-ILLNESS PATIENT AWARENESS SENSITIVITY
         aPSYCHIATRIC

R-141   RAIMY, V. C.
             SELF REFERENCE IN COUNSELING INTERVIEWS.
             JOURNAL OF CONSULTING PSYCHOLOGY, 1948, 12, 153-163.
             (CONTENT ANALYSIS MEASURE OF SELF REFERENCE IN COUNSELING)
         aR-141 1948M CONTENT-ANALYSIS COUNSELING SELF DISCLOSURE THERAPY PATIENT
         aOPENNESS INTERVIEW
             (APPLICATIONS: 1199 1303)

R-142   ROBINSON, F. P.
             GUIDANCE FOR ALL: IN PRINCIPLE AND IN PRACTICE.
             PERSONNEL AND GUIDANCE JOURNAL, 1953, 31, 500-504.
         HEILFRON, M.
             THE FUNCTION OF COUNSELING AS PERCEIVED BY HIGH SCHOOL STUDENTS.
             PERSONNEL AND GUIDANCE JOURNAL, 1960, 39, 133-136.
             (MEASURE OF PERCEPTION OF COUNSELING FUNCTION)
         aR-142 1953M COUNSELING PERCEPTION RATING STUDENT BELIEF ATTITUDE
             (APPLICATIONS: 1167 1319)

R-143   RICHARDS, J. M., JR.
             LIFE GOALS OF AMERICAN COLLEGE FRESHMEN.
             JOURNAL OF COUNSELING PSYCHOLOGY, 1966, 13, 12-20.
             (GOALS-ASPIRATIONS INVENTORY)
         aR-143 1966M VOCATIONAL ASPIRATION LIFE GOALS PERSONAL SOCIAL COLLEGE STUDENT
             (APPLICATIONS: 1515)

R-144   RENZAGLIA, G. A., HENRY, D. R., & RYBOLT, G. A., JR.
             ESTIMATION AND MEASUREMENT OF PERSONALITY CHARACTERISTICS AND
             CORRELATES OF THEIR CONGRUENCE.
             JOURNAL OF COUNSELING PSYCHOLOGY, 1962, 9, 71-78.
             (SELF-ESTIMATION SCALE)*
         aR-144 1962M SELF DESCRIPTION PERSONALITY PERCEPTION REALITY DISCREPANCY
         aCONSISTENCY
             (APPLICATIONS: 1222)

R-145   RYAN, T. A., & KRUMBOLTZ, J. D.
             EFFECT OF PLANNED REINFORCEMENT COUNSELING ON CLIENT DECISION-MAKING
             BEHAVIOR.
             JOURNAL OF COUNSELING PSYCHOLOGY, 1964, 11, 315-323.
             (STORY COMPLETION TEST)
         aR-145 1964M STORY-COMPLETION PROJECTIVE CONFLICT DECISION IMPULSE CONTROL

R-146   ROLEDER, G. T.
             COLLEGE ATTITUDE MEASUREMENT BY DIRECTION OF PERCEPTION TECHNIQUE.
             UNPUBLISHED MASTERS THESIS, CLAREMONT GRADUATE SCHOOL, CLAREMONT, CALIF.
             1962.
             (COLLEGE ATTITUDE SCALE)
         aR-146 1962M COLLEGE ATTITUDE PROGNOSIS PREDICTION FAILURE OPINION STUDENT
             (APPLICATIONS: 1281)

R-147   RUSHING, W. A.
             CLASS, CULTURE, AND "SOCIAL STRUCTURE AND ANOMIE."
             AMERICAN JOURNAL OF SOCIOLOGY, 1971, 76, 857-872.
             (MEASURE OF NORMLESSNESS)
         aR-147 1971M ANOMIE ALIENATION POWERLESSNESS NORMS CULTURE GROUP
         aSOCIAL VALUES

R-148   RYCHLAK, J. F.
                 PERSONALITY DIMENSIONS IN RECALLED DREAM CONTENT.
                 JOURNAL OF ABNORMAL AND SOCIAL PSYCHOLOGY, 1960, 60, 140-143.
                 (DREAM THEME SCORING SYSTEM)
           @R-148 1960M PRIMARY-PROCESS THINKING FANTASY DEATH
           @DREAM CONTENT-ANALYSIS

R-149   ROSEN, B. C.
                 THE ACHIEVEMENT SYNDROME: A PSYCHOCULTURAL DIMENSION OF SOCIAL
                 STRATIFICATION.
                 AMERICAN SOCIOLOGICAL REVIEW, 1956, 21, 203-211.
                 (MEASURE OF VALUE ORIENTATIONS)
           @R-149 1956M ORIENTATION VALUES TIME FAMILY ACTIVE PASSIVE

R-151   ROSENZWEIG, S.
                 THE EXPERIMENTAL STUDY OF REPRESSION.
                 IN H. MURRAY, EXPLORATIONS IN PERSONALITY.
                 NEW YORK: OXFORD UNIVERSITY PRESS, 1938, PP. 585-599.
                 ROSENZWEIG, S., & SARASON, S.
                 AN EXPERIMENTAL STUDY OF THE TRIADIC HYPOTHESIS: REACTION TO
                 FRUSTRATION, EGO-DEFENSE AND HYPNOTIZABILITY: I. CORRELATIONAL APPROACH.
                 CHARACTER AND PERSONALITY, 1942, 11, 1-19.
                 (PUZZLES 'REPRESSION' TEST)
           @R-151 1938M REPRESSION EGO DEFENSE FRUSTRATION
                 (APPLICATIONS: 95)

R-152   ROSENTHAL, R., FODE, K. L., FRIEDMAN, C. J., & VIKAN, L. L.
                 SUBJECTS' PERCEPTION OF THEIR EXPERIMENTER UNDER CONDITIONS OF EXPERIMENTER
                 BIAS.
                 PERCEPTUAL AND MOTOR SKILLS, 1960, 11, 325-331.
                 (EXPERIMENTER RATING SCALES)
           @R-152 1960M PERCEPTION FIGURE GRAPHIC RATING FAILURE SUCCESS PERSON
           @INTERPERSONAL ATTRACTION TESTER BIAS
                 (APPLICATIONS: 98)

R-154   ROTTER, J. B., LIVERANT, S., & CROWNE, D. P.
                 THE GROWTH AND EXTINCTION OF EXPECTANCIES IN CHANCE AND SKILLED TASKS.
                 JOURNAL OF PSYCHOLOGY, 1961, 52, 161-177.
                 (VERTICAL ASPIRATION BOARD)
           @R-154 1961M LOCUS CONTROL SELF R-17R IE-CONTROL ABILITY PERFORMANCE ASPIRATION
                 (APPLICATIONS: 281)

R-155   RUBIN, Z., & MOORE, J. C., JR.
                 ASSESSMENT OF SUBJECTS' SUSPICIONS.
                 JOURNAL OF PERSONALITY AND SOCIAL PSYCHOLOGY, 1971, 17(2), 163-170.
                 (SUSPICION QUESTIONNAIRE)
           @R-155 1971M IMPRESSION TRUST EXPERIMENTER INFLUENCE SUBJECT AWARENESS
           @INTERPERSONAL

R-156   ROTENBERG, M., & SARBIN, T. R.
                 IMPACT OF DIFFERENTIALLY SIGNIFICANT OTHERS ON ROLE INVOLVEMENT: AN
                 EXPERIMENT WITH PRISON SOCIAL TYPES.
                 JOURNAL OF ABNORMAL PSYCHOLOGY, 1971, 77, 97-107.
                 (MEASURE OF DIFFERENTIAL ROLE PLAY INVOLVEMENT)
           @R-156 1971M ROLE ENACTMENT CONFLICT INVOLVEMENT DELINQUENCY RATING

R-157   REITAN, R.
                 TRAIL MAKING TEST: MANUAL FOR ADMINISTRATION, SCORING, AND INTERPRETATION.
                 DEPARTMENT OF NEUROLOGY, SECTION OF NEUROPSYCHOLOGY, INDIANA MEDICAL
                 CENTER, 1958.
                 (TRAIL MAKING TEST)*
           @R-157 1958M COGNITIVE FLEXIBILITY FUNCTIONING THINKING PERFORMANCE
                 (APPLICATIONS: 1047   1754   1787)

R-158   RAVEN, J. C.
                 GUIDE TO USING PROGRESSIVE MATRICES (1938) (5TH ED.).
                 LONDON: H. K. LEWIS, 1954.
                 (PROGRESSIVE MATRICES TEST)*
           @R-158 1954M CONSCIENCE EGO FUNCTIONING INTELLIGENCE
           @THINKING COGNITIVE ABILITY DELINQUENCY SOCIAL DEVIANCE ADJUSTMENT
                 (APPLICATIONS: 1826)

R-159   REYHER, J., & SHOEMAKER, D.
        A COMPARISON BETWEEN HYPNOTICALLY INDUCED AGE REGRESSIONS AND WAKING
        STORIES TO TAT CARDS: A PRELIMINARY REPORT.
        JOURNAL OF CONSULTING PSYCHOLOGY, 1961, 25, 409-413.
        (TAT MEASURE OF INDUCED AGE REGRESSION)
        @R-159 1961M PROJECTIVE CONFLICT ROLE ADJUSTMENT MENTAL-HEALTH MENTAL-ILLNESS
        @EXPRESSION IMPULSE HOSTILITY SELF ACTUALIZATION COPING DEFENSE THERAPY
        @SUCCESS CONTROL HYPNOTIC

R-160   RITCHEY, R. E.
        PREDICTING SUCCESS OF SCHIZOPHRENICS IN INDUSTRIAL THERAPY.
        JOURNAL OF COUNSELING PSYCHOLOGY, 1965, 12, 68-73.
        (INDUSTRIAL THERAPY RATING SCALE)
        @R-160 1965M JOB HISTORY EMPLOYEE BEHAVIOR PATIENT PSYCHIATRIC SCHIZOPHRENIA
        @SUCCESS SUPERVISOR

S-1   SANDLER, J.
        STUDIES IN PSYCHOPATHOLOGY USING A SELF-ASSESSMENT INVENTORY. I. THE
        DEVELOPMENT AND CONSTRUCTION OF THE INVENTORY.
        BRITISH JOURNAL OF MEDICAL PSYCHOLOGY, 1954, 27, 142.
        (TAVISTOCK SELF-ASSESSMENT INVENTORY)*
        @S-1 SOCIAL ANXIETY ADJUSTMENT PHOBIA AFFECTIVE-STATES SUBJECTIVE STRESS
        @S-1 MENTAL-ILLNESS SELF DESCRIPTION 1954M EVALUATION

S-2   SANFORD, R. N., CONRAD, H. S., & FRANCK, K.
        PSYCHOLOGICAL DETERMINANTS OF OPTIMISM REGARDING CONSEQUENCES OF THE WAR.
        JOURNAL OF PSYCHOLOGY, 1946, 22, 207-235.
        (MEASURE OF OPTIMISM-PESSIMISM)
        @S-2 OPTIMISM PESSIMISM AFFECTIVE-STATES GLOBAL NEGATIVE POSITIVE 1946M LIFE
        @S-2 ORIENTATION ATTITUDE

S-3   SAPPENFIELD, B. R., KAPLAN, B. B., & BALOGH, B.
        PERCEPTUAL CORRELATES OF STEREOTYPICAL MASCULINITY-FEMININITY.
        JOURNAL OF PERSONALITY AND SOCIAL PSYCHOLOGY, 1966, 4, 585-590.
        (REVISED CONCEPT MEANING MEASURE)*
        @S-3 SEM-DIFFERENTIAL SELF CONCEPT IDEAL MASCULINITY FEMININITY PERCEPTION
        @S-3 STEREOTYPE 1966M

S-4   SARASON, I. G.
        INTERRELATIONSHIPS AMONG INDIVIDUAL DIFFERENCE VARIABLES, BEHAVIOR IN
        PSYCHOTHERAPY, AND VERBAL CONDITIONING.
        JOURNAL OF ABNORMAL AND SOCIAL PSYCHOLOGY, 1958, 56, 339-344.
        (AUTOBIOGRAPHICAL SURVEY)*
        @S-4 ANXIETY HOSTILITY DEFENSIVENESS MULTITRAIT SUBJECTIVE STRESS TEST NEED
        @S-4 ACHIEVEMENT AUTONOMY AFFECTIVE-STATES NEGATIVE 1958M
        (APPLICATIONS: 33   204   226   633   764   773   835   1714)

S-5   SARASON, I. G., & GANZER, V. S.
        ANXIETY, REINFORCEMENT, AND EXPERIMENTAL INSTRUCTIONS IN A FREE
        VERBALIZATION SITUATION.
        JOURNAL OF ABNORMAL SOCIAL PSYCHOLOGY, 1962, 65, 300-307.
        (TEST ANXIETY SCALE)*
        @S-5 ANXIETY SUBJECTIVE AFFECTIVE-STATES STRESS TEST 1962M
        (APPLICATIONS: 22   74   75   79   93   174   204   265   465   483
                         492   511   526   564   631   633   720   758   773   838
                         898   1017   1658   1853   1865   1970   2029   2140   2217   2931)

S-6   SATTLER, J. M.
        THE RELATIVE MEANING OF EMBARRASSMENT.
        PSYCHOLOGICAL REPORTS, 1963, 12, 263-269.
        (SEMANTIC DIFFERENTIAL MEASURE OF EMBARRASSMENT)
        @S-6 EMBARRASSMENT AFFECTIVE-STATES GLOBAL NEGATIVE 1963M

S-7   SAWYER, J.
        THE ALTRUISM SCALE: A MEASURE OF COOPERATIVE, INDIVIDUALISTIC, AND
        COMPETITIVE INTERPERSONAL ORIENTATION.
        AMERICAN JOURNAL OF SOCIOLOGY, 1966, 71, 407-416.
        (ALTRUISM SCALE)*
        @S-7 ALTRUISM POSITIVE AFFECTIVE-STATES OTHERS ORIENTATION COOPERATION 1966M
        @S-7 INTERPERSONAL

S-8   SCHAEFFER, E. S.
               CHILDREN'S REPORTS OF PARENTAL BEHAVIOR: AN INVENTORY.
               CHILD DEVELOPMENT, 1965, 36, 413-424.
               (CHILDREN'S REPORTS OF PARENTAL BEHAVIOR INVENTORY)
           @S-8 PARENT-CHILD CHILD PARENTAL BEHAVIOR FAMILY INTERACTION ADJUSTMENT 1965M
               (APPLICATIONS: 343 1849 1960 2273 2377 2467 2892)

S-9   SCHAEFER, E. S., & BELL, R. Q.
               DEVELOPMENT OF A PARENTAL ATTITUDE RESEARCH INSTRUMENT.
               CHILD DEVELOPMENT, 1958, 29, 339-361.
               (PARENTAL ATTITUDE RESEARCH INSTRUMENT)*
           @S-9 HOSTILITY MATERNAL PATERNAL CONTROL PARENT-CHILD PARENTAL ATTITUDE FAMILY
           @S-9 INTERACTION ADJUSTMENT AUTHORITY 1958M
               (APPLICATIONS: 55   60   428   445   531   574   647   690   695   786
                                1065   1569   1725   1984   2055   2078   2178   2200   2263   2465
                                2498   2828   2843   2884   2890   2895   2965)

S-10   SCHEIER, I. H., & CATTELL, R. B.
               HANDBOOK FOR THE NEUROTICISM SCALE QUESTIONNAIRE.
               CHAMPAIGN, ILLINOIS: INSTITUTE FOR PERSONALITY AND ABILITY TESTING, 1961.
               (NEUROTICISM SCALE QUESTIONNAIRE)*
           @S-10 ADJUSTMENT NEUROTICISM GLOBAL MENTAL-ILLNESS COPING-DEFENSE DEFENSE 1961M
               (APPLICATIONS: 1177   1210   2920)

S-11   SCHUTZ, W.
               FIRO: A THREE-DIMENSIONAL THEORY OF INTERPERSONAL BEHAVIOR.
               NEW YORK: RHINEHART, 1958.
               (FUNDAMENTAL INTERPERSONAL RELATIONS ORIENTATION BEHAVIOR QUESTIONNAIRE)*
           @S-11 NEED AFFECTION AFFILIATION ORIENTATION CONTROL INTERPERSONAL RELATIONSHIPS
           @S-11 SOCIAL COMPETENCE ADJUSTMENT INTERACTION 1958M BEHAVIOR
               (APPLICATIONS: 15   145   154   382   549   563   627   743   935   956
                                1115   1604   1870   2189   2392   2449   2513   2864   2935   2961)

S-12   SCOTT, W. E., JR.
               THE DEVELOPMENT OF SEMANTIC DIFFERENTIAL SCALES AS MEASURES OF "MORALE".
               PERSONNEL PSYCHOLOGY, 1967, 20, 179-198.
               (MORALE SCALE)
           @S-12 JOB-HYGIENE ENVIRONMENT PE-FIT SUPERVISOR MANAGEMENT JOB SATISFACTION
           @S-12 ADJUSTMENT SEM-DIFFERENTIAL MORALE AFFECTIVE-STATES GLOBAL EMPLOYEE MOOD
           @S-12 STATE POSITIVE NEGATIVE 1967M

S-13   SEARS, R. R., MACCOBY, E. E., & LEVIN, H.
               PATTERNS OF CHILD-REARING.
               EVANSTON, ILLINOIS: ROW-PETERSON, 1957.
               (MEASURE OF MATERNAL CHILD-REARING ATTITUDES AND PRACTICES)
           @S-13 MATERNAL PARENTAL BEHAVIOR PARENT-CHILD ATTITUDE FAMILY INTERACTION 1957M
           @S-13 ADJUSTMENT
               (APPLICATIONS: 506   2843)

S-14   SEARS, R. R., RAU, L., & ALPERT, R.
               IDENTIFICATION AND CHILD-REARING.
               STANFORD, CALIFORNIA: STANFORD UNIVERSITY PRESS, 1965.
               (MEASURE OF SEX-ROLE IDENTITY)
           @S-14 BEHAVIOR SEX ROLE IDENTITY SELF-IDENTITY SUB-IDENTITY MASCULINITY CHILD
           @S-14 FEMININITY IDENTIFICATION 1965M

S-15   SECORD, P. F., & JOURARD, S. M.
               THE APPRAISAL OF BODY-CATHEXIS: BODY-CATHEXIS AND THE SELF.
               JOURNAL OF CONSULTING PSYCHOLOGY, 1953, 17, 343-347.
               (SELF-EVALUATION MEASURE OF BODY CATHEXIS)
           @S-15 AFFECTIVE-STATES SATISFACTION BODY CATHEXIS EVALUATION SELF SELF-IDENTITY
           @S-15 IMAGE PERCEPTION 1953M
               (APPLICATIONS: 1796   2324   2601)

S-16   SHAFFER, J. P.
               SOCIAL AND PERSONALITY CORRELATES OF CHILDREN'S ESTIMATES OF HEIGHT.
               GENETIC PSYCHOLOGY MONOGRAPHS, 1964, 70, 97-134.
               (HEIGHT TEST)*
           @S-16 INTERPERSONAL RELATIONSHIPS SOCIAL COMPETENCE TEACHER POWER ORIENTATION
           @S-16 SCHOOL BODY IMAGE CHILD PARENT-CHILD NEED ADJUSTMENT SELF-IDENTITY SELF
           @S-16 PERCEPTION 1964M

S-17   SCHLIEN, J. M.
              TOWARD WHAT LEVEL OF ABSTRACTION IN CRITERIA?
              RESEARCH IN PSYCHOTHERAPY, 1961, 2.
              (UNSTRUCTURED Q-SORT)
          ðS-17 Q-SORT SELF-IDENTITY SELF IDEAL IMAGE CONCEPT ESTEEM PERCEPTION 1961M
          ðS-17 EVALUATION ADJUSTMENT

S-18   SHERWOOD, J. J.
              SELF-REPORT AND PROJECTIVE MEASURES OF ACHIEVEMENT AND AFFILIATION.
              JOURNAL OF CONSULTING PSYCHOLOGY, 1966, 30, 329-337.
              (MEASURE OF NEED ACHIEVEMENT)
          ðS-18 SELF DESCRIPTION MOTIVE ORIENTATION NEED ACHIEVEMENT AUTONOMY BEHAVIOR
          ðS-18 1966M
              (APPLICATIONS: 285)

S-19   SHIPLEY, T. E., JR., & VEROFF, J.
              A PROJECTIVE MEASURE OF NEED FOR AFFILIATION.
              JOURNAL OF EXPERIMENTAL PSYCHOLOGY, 1952, 43, 349-356.
              (TAT SCORED FOR NEED AFFILIATION)
          ðS-19 PROJECTIVE AFFILIATION NEED TAT AUTONOMY SOCIAL APPROVAL INTERPERSONAL
          ðS-19 RELATIONSHIPS 1952M IMAGERY
              (APPLICATIONS: 99   382   679   2016)

S-20   SHIPMAN, W. G.
              A ONE-PAGE SCALE OF ANXIETY AND DEPRESSION.
              PSYCHOLOGICAL REPORTS, 1963, 13, 289-290.
              (ANXIETY-DEPRESSION SCALE)*
          ðS-20 DEPRESSION AFFECTIVE-STATES ANXIETY SUBJECTIVE STRESS GLOBAL NEGATIVE
          ðS-20 1963M

S-21   SHOSTROM, E. L.
              "PERSONAL ORIENTATION INVENTORY".
              SAN DIEGO, CALIFORNIA: EDUCATIONAL AND INDUSTRIAL TESTING SERVICE, 1963.
          SHOSTROM, E. L.
              AN INVENTORY FOR THE MEASUREMENT OF SELF-ACTUALIZATION.
              EDUCATIONAL AND PSYCHOLOGICAL MEASUREMENT, 1964, 24, 207-218.
              (PERSONAL ORIENTATION INVENTORY)*
          ðS-21 SELF ESTEEM TIME PERSONAL ORIENTATION VALUES SELF ACTUALIZATION 1963M
          ðS-21 EXISTENTIAL PERSONALITY SELF-IDENTITY ACCEPTANCE SPONTANEITY PERCEPTION
              (APPLICATIONS: 1413   1438   1442   1477   1504   1545   1937   2564   2687   2715
                               2753   2756   2829   2848   2881)

S-22   SIDLE, A., MOOS, R., ADAMS, J., & CADY, P.
              DEVELOPMENT OF A COPING SCALE.
              ARCHIVES OF GENERAL PSYCHIATRY, 1969, 20, 226-232.
              (COPING SCALE)
          ðS-22 COPING-DEFENSE GLOBAL COPING 1969M BEHAVIOR STYLE

S-23   SIEGEL, L.
              A BIOGRAPHICAL INVENTORY FOR STUDENTS: II. VALIDATION OF THE INSTRUMENT.
              JOURNAL OF APPLIED PSYCHOLOGY, 1956, 40, 122-126.
              (BIOGRAPHICAL INVENTORY)
          ðS-23 STUDENT LIFE DESCRIPTION BEHAVIOR ADJUSTMENT SOCIAL DEVELOPMENT GROWTH
          ðS-23 SELF SELF-IDENTITY 1956M ACTIVITIES

S-24   SIEGEL, S. M.
              THE RELATIONSHIP OF HOSTILITY TO AUTHORITARIANISM.
              JOURNAL OF ABNORMAL AND SOCIAL PSYCHOLOGY, 1956, 52, 368-372.
              (MANIFEST HOSTILITY SCALE)*
          ðS-24 HOSTILITY MANIFEST AFFECTIVE-STATES RESENTMENT MMPI AUTHORITARIANISM 1956M
              (APPLICATIONS: 12   331   454   635   708   770   792   1640   1753   2124
                               2140)

S-25   SILVERMAN, I.
              SELF-ESTEEM AND DIFFERENTIAL RESPONSIVENESS TO SUCCESS AND FAILURE.
              JOURNAL OF ABNORMAL AND SOCIAL PSYCHOLOGY, 1964, 69, 115-119.
              (MEASURE OF SELF-ESTEEM)
          ðS-25 SELF ESTEEM IMAGE CONCEPT SELF-IDENTITY PERCEPTION EVALUATION SUCCESS
          ðS-25 FAILURE 1964M

S-27   STEIN, M. I.
               THE THEMATIC APPERCEPTION TEST: AN INTRODUCTORY MANUAL FOR ITS CLINICAL
               USE WITH ADULT MALES.
               CAMBRIDGE: ADDISON-WESLEY, 1948.
               (TAT SCORED FOR COVERT NEED STRENGTH/DEPENDENCY)
          @S-27 TAT AUTONOMY IMAGERY DEPENDENCE PROJECTIVE NEED 1948M INTENSITY
               (APPLICATIONS: 1791)

S-28   SROLE, L.
               SOCIAL INTEGRATION AND CERTAIN COROLLARIES: AN EXPLORATORY STUDY.
               AMERICAN SOCIOLOGICAL REVIEW. 1956, 21, 709-716.
               (ANOMIE SCALE)*
          @S-28 ANOMIE ALIENATION SOCIAL AFFECTIVE-STATES INTEGRATION COMPETENCE 1956M
          @S-28 INTERPERSONAL RELATIONSHIPS MENTAL-HEALTH MENTAL-ILLNESS
               (APPLICATIONS: 613   647   747   800   1493   2588   2789   2963)

S-29   STEFFLRE, B.
               CONCURRENT VALIDITY OF THE VOCATIONAL VALUES INVENTORY.
               JOURNAL OF EDUCATIONAL RESEARCH, 1959, 52, 339-341.
               (VOCATIONAL VALUES INVENTORY)*
          @S-29 VOCATIONAL VALUES INTEREST JOB ALTRUISM AFFECTIVE-STATES PREFERENCE 1959M
               (APPLICATIONS: 1216)

S-30   STEPHENSON, W.
               THE STUDY OF BEHAVIOR: Q-TECHNIQUE AND ITS METHODOLOGY.
               CHICAGO: UNIVERSITY OF CHICAGO PRESS, 1953.
               (STEPHENSON'S Q-SORT)*
          @S-30 SELF CONCEPT Q-SORT SELF-IDENTITY EVALUATION PERCEPTION ESTEEM 1953M
          @S-30 SUB-IDENTITY ROLE IMAGE IDEAL
               (APPLICATIONS: 355   1176   1206   1256   1374   1482   1490   1585   1962)

S-31   STOTSKY, B. A., & WEINBERG, H.
               THE PREDICTION OF THE PSYCHIATRIC PATIENT'S WORK ADJUSTMENT.
               JOURNAL OF COUNSELING PSYCHOLOGY, 1956, 3, 3-7.
               (MEASURE OF WORK ADJUSTMENT FOR PSYCHIATRIC PATIENT)
          @S-31 SOCIAL COMPETENCE PSYCHIATRIC PATIENT JOB GLOBAL PREDICTION PROGNOSIS
          @S-31 MENTAL-HEALTH ADJUSTMENT AUTONOMY NEED ACHIEVEMENT MENTAL-ILLNESS 1956M
               (APPLICATIONS: 1161   1496   2663)

S-33   STRONG, E. K., JR.
               MANUAL, STRONG VOCATIONAL INTEREST BLANK SVIB.
               STANFORD, CALIF.: STANFORD UNIVERSITY PRESS, 1951.
               MANUAL FOR STRONG VOCATIONAL INTEREST BLANKS FOR MEN AND WOMEN, REVISED
               BLANKS (FORMS M AND W). PALO ALTO, CALIFORNIA: CONSULTING PSYCHOLOGISTS
               PRESS, 1959.
               (STRONG VOCATIONAL INTEREST BLANK)*
          @S-33 VOCATIONAL INTEREST MASCULINITY JOB FEMININITY PREFERENCE ROLE DEMANDS
          @S-33 1959M
               (APPLICATIONS: 142   430   481   538   1118   1154   1156   1158   1163   1170
                                1172   1182   1183   1185   1193   1204   1211   1216   1219   1225
                                1229   1230   1231   1234   1235   1246   1251   1259   1264   1265
                                1274   1282   1286   1298   1299   1300   1302   1308   1313   1315
                                1320   1335   1337   1341   1343   1344   1347   1352   1364   1365
                                1370   1392   1396   1421   1422   1424   1426   1427   1438   1441
                                1443   1445   1449   1451   1462   1465   1470   1474   1479   1480
                                1482   1483   1495   1508   1509   1523   1532   1540   1551   1553
                                1595   1766   1800   2043   2056   2118   2210   2247   2292   2336
                                2349   2363   2470   2552   2657   2701   2717   2749   2754   2762
                                2769   2773   2774   2778   2779   2850   2857   2863   2864   2924)

S-34   SANFORD, N., WEBSTER, H., & FREEDMAN, M.
               VC ATTITUDE INVENTORY
               POUGHKEEPSIE, NEW YORK: VASSAR COLLEGE, MARY CONOVER MELLON FOUNDATION,
               1957.
               (VASSAR COLLEGE ATTITUDE INVENTORY)*
          @S-34 ATTITUDE FEMININITY MASCULINITY INTEREST SEX IDENTITY SELF-IDENTITY
          @S-34 SENSITIVITY SUB-IDENTITY ROLE 1957M
               (APPLICATIONS: 110   1541)

S-35   SARASON, S. B., DAVIDSON, K. S., LIGHTHALL, F. F., WAITE, R. R., & RUEBUSH, B. K
          ANXIETY IN ELEMENTARY SCHOOL CHILDREN.
          NEW YORK: WILEY, 1960.
          (TEST ANXIETY SCALE FOR CHILDREN)*
        aS-35 TEST ANXIETY AFFECTIVE-STATES SUBJECTIVE STRESS NEGATIVE CHILD 1960M
          (APPLICATIONS: 368   762   822   849   1731   1838   1941   2115   2330   2461
                           2794)

S-36   SARASON, I. G., & WINKLE, G. H.
          INDIVIDUAL DIFFERENCES AMONG SUBJECTS AND EXPERIMENTERS AND SUBJECTS'
          SELF-DESCRIPTIONS.
          JOURNAL OF PERSONALITY AND SOCIAL PSYCHOLOGY, 1966, 3, 448-457.
          (BEHAVIORAL HOSTILITY SCALE)*
        aS-36 HOSTILITY AFFECTIVE-STATES RESENTMENT BEHAVIOR NEGATIVE 1966M
          (APPLICATIONS: 516   1017   2211)

S-37   SARBIN, T. R., & HARDYCK, C. D.
          CONFORMANCE IN ROLE PERCEPTION AS A PERSONALITY VARIABLE.
          JOURNAL OF CONSULTING PSYCHOLOGY, 1955, 19, 109-111.
          (STICK FIGURE TEST)*
        aS-37 EMPATHY ENACTMENT CONFORMITY PERCEPTION EMPATHY ROLE AFFECTIVE-STATES
        aS-37 OTHERS ORIENTATION AUTONOMY 1955M
          (APPLICATIONS: 81   1168   1660   1790)

S-38   SARBIN, T. R., & JONES, D. S.
          AN EXPERIMENTAL ANALYSIS OF ROLE BEHAVIOR.
          JOURNAL OF ABNORMAL AND SOCIAL PSYCHOLOGY, 1955, 51, 236-241.
          (AS-IF SCALE)*
        aS-38 INTERACTION SELF-IDENTITY SUB-IDENTITY PERCEPTION BEHAVIOR ENACTMENT SELF
        aS-38 ROLE FANTASY INTERPERSONAL RELATIONSHIPS 1955M
          (APPLICATIONS: 150)

S-40   SWEETLAND, A., & FRANK, G. H.
          A STUDY OF IDEAL PSYCHOLOGICAL ADJUSTMENT.
          JOURNAL OF CLINICAL PSYCHOLOGY, 1955, 11, 391-394.
          (IDEAL PERSONALITY ADJUSTMENT Q-SORT)
        aS-40 IDEAL CONCEPT SELF IMAGE SELF-IDENTITY PERCEPTION EVALUATION 1955M Q-SORT
        aS-40 ADJUSTMENT
          (APPLICATIONS: 1420)

S-41   SCHRODER, H. M., & STREUFERT, S.
          THE MEASUREMENT OF FOUR SYSTEMS OF PERSONALITY STRUCTURE VARYING IN LEVEL
          OF ABSTRACTNESS: SENTENCE COMPLETION METHOD.
          TECHNICAL REPORT NO. 11, PROJECT NR 171-055, 1963, PRINCETON UNIVERSITY,
          CONTRACT NONR 1858 (12), OFFICE OF NAVAL RESEARCH.
          (PARAGRAPH COMPLETION INVENTORY)*
        aS-41 COMPLEXITY CREATIVITY STRUCTURE COGNITIVE INTEGRATION COPING-DEFENSE
        aS-41 AUTONOMY ABSTRACTNESS CONCRETENESS PROJECTIVE CONCEPTUAL PERCEPTION 1963M
          (APPLICATIONS: 86   106   153   192   212   216   217   277   401   445
                            518   856   2271   2800   2917   2918)

S-42   SCHWARTZ, S. H.
          WORDS, DEEDS, AND THE PERCEPTION OF CONSEQUENCES AND RESPONSIBILITY IN
          ACTION SITUATIONS.
          JOURNAL OF PERSONALITY AND SOCIAL PSYCHOLOGY, 1968, 10, 232-242.
          (ASCRIPTION OF RESPONSIBILITY SCALE)*
        aS-42 ATTRIBUTION RESPONSIBILITY ADJUSTMENT OTHER-CATEGORY AUTONOMY LOCUS
        aS-42 CONTROL IE-CONTROL 1968M
          (APPLICATIONS: 2522)

S-43   SCHUMAN, H., & HARDING, J.
          PREJUDICE AND THE NORM OF RATIONALITY.
          SOCIOMETRY, 1964, 27, 353-371.
        SCHRODER, H. M., DRIVER, M. J., & STREUFERT, S.
          HUMAN INFORMATION PROCESSING: INDIVIDUALS AND GROUPS IN COMPLEX SOCIAL
          SITUATIONS.
          NEW YORK: HOLT, RINEHART & WINSTON, 1966.
          (SOCIAL PROBLEMS QUESTIONNAIRE)*
        aS-43 SOCIAL PREJUDICE AFFECTIVE-STATES OTHER-CATEGORY RACIAL CROSS-CULTURAL
        aS-43 NEGRO ETHNIC SOCIAL DISTANCE 1964M

S-44   SCHUMAN, H., & HARDING, I.
          SYMPATHETIC IDENTIFICATION WITH THE UNDERDOG.
          PUBLIC OPINION QUARTERLY, 1963, 27, 230-241.
          (MEASURE OF PREJUDICE/ACCEPTANCE OF OTHERS)
        aS-44 ACCEPTANCE OTHERS PREJUDICE AFFECTIVE-STATES OTHER-CATEGORY SOCIAL
        aS-44 DISTANCE 1963M

S-45   SEARS, R. R.
                  COMPARISON OF INTERVIEWS WITH QUESTIONNAIRES FOR MEASURING MOTHERS'
                  ATTITUDES TOWARD SEX AND AGGRESSION.
                  JOURNAL OF PERSONALITY AND SOCIAL PSYCHOLOGY, 1965, 2, 37-44.
                  (MOTHER ATTITUDE SCALES)
            aS-45 MATERNAL ATTITUDE SEX FAMILY INTERACTION ADJUSTMENT AGGRESSION 1965M
            aS-45 PARENT-CHILD CHILD BEHAVIOR

S-46   STALLING, R. B.
                  PERSONALITY SIMILARITY AND EVALUATIVE MEANING AS CONDITIONERS OF
                  ATTRACTION.
                  JOURNAL OF PERSONALITY AND SOCIAL PSYCHOLOGY, 1970, 14, 77-82.
                  (TRAIT TERMS RATED FOR EVALUATIVE MEANING AND SIMILARITY TO SELF)
            aS-46 TRAIT-TERMS SELF EVALUATION SIMILARITY 1970M

S-47   SEARS, R. R., WHITING, J. W. M., NOWLIS, H., & SEARS, P. S.
                  SOME CHILDREARING ANTECEDENTS OF DEPENDENCY AND AGGRESSION IN YOUNG
                  CHILDREN.
                  GENETIC PSYCHOLOGY MONOGRAPHS, 1953, 47, 135-234.
                  (AGGRESSION SCALE)*
            aS-47 NEGATIVE AGGRESSION AFFECTIVE-STATES RESENTMENT HOSTILITY CHILD 1953M
                  (APPLICATIONS: 117)

S-48   SHANNON, D. T., & SHOEMAKER, D. J.
                  A PICTORIAL IDENTIFICATION TECHNIQUE OF SELF-EVALUATION IN CHILDREN.
                  UNPUBLISHED RESEARCH, UNIVERSITY OF ILLINOIS, 1960.
                  (PICTURE IDENTIFICATION TEST)
            aS-48 SELF DESCRIPTION SELF-IDENTITY EVALUATION PERCEPTION ESTEEM IDEAL IMAGE
            aS-48 OTHERS CHILD 1960M
                  (APPLICATIONS: 83)

S-49   SHARAF, M. R.
                  AN APPROACH TO THE THEORY AND MEASUREMENT OF INTRACEPTION.
                  UNPUBLISHED DOCTORAL DISSERTATION, HARVARD UNIVERSITY, 1960.
                  (ANTIPSYCHOLOGICAL MINDEDNESS SCALE)*
            aS-49 ATTITUDE INTRACEPTION 1960M
                  (APPLICATIONS: 214)

S-50   SHAW, M.
                  ATTITUDES OF CHILD REARING PRACTICES OF THE PARENTS OF BRIGHT ACADEMIC
                  UNDERACHIEVERS: A PILOT STUDY.
                  (REPORT ON USPHS RESEARCH PROJECT NO. M-2843) WASHINGTON, D. C.: U. S.
                  GOVERNMENT PRINTING OFFICE, 1960.(MIMEO)
                  (PARENTAL CHILDREARING ATTITUDE MEASURE)
            aS-50 ATTITUDE PARENT-CHILD PARENTAL FAMILY ADJUSTMENT ACADEMIC INTERACTION
            aS-50 ACHIEVEMENT CHECKLIST STUDENT SCHOOL SECONDARY 1960M BEHAVIOR
                  (APPLICATIONS: 61)

S-51   SHOR, R. E.
                  THE FREQUENCY OF NATURALLY OCCURRING "HYPNOTIC-LIKE" EXPERIENCES IN THE
                  NORMAL COLLEGE POPULATION.
                  INTERNATIONAL JOURNAL OF CLINICAL AND EXPERIMENTAL HYPNOSIS, 1960, 8,
                  151-163.
                  (PERSONAL EXPERIENCES QUESTIONNAIRE)*
            aS-51 HYPNOTIC EXPERIENCE SUBJECTIVE FANTASY SUGGESTIBILITY PERSONAL 1960M

S-52   STEIN, D. D., HARDYCK, J. A., & SMITH, M. B.
                  RACE AND BELIEF: AN OPEN AND SHUT CASE.
                  JOURNAL OF PERSONAL AND SOCIAL PSYCHOLOGY, 1965, 1, 281-288.
                  (VALUE SCALE)
            aS-52 VALUES IDEALS LIFE GOALS ADOLESCENT BELIEF SELF-IDENTITY 1965M

S-53   STACHOWIAK, J. G., & MOSS, C. S.
                  HYPNOTIC ALTERATION OF SOCIAL ATTITUDES.
                  JOURNAL OF PERSONALITY AND SOCIAL PSYCHOLOGY, 1965, 2, 77-83.
                  (SEMANTIC DIFFERENTIAL FOR SOCIAL CONCEPTS)
            aS-53 ETHNOCENTRISM RACIAL PREJUDICE DISTANCE SOCIAL ATTITUDE AFFECTIVE-STATES
            aS-53 OTHER-CATEGORY SEM-DIFFERENTIAL 1965M

S-54   STECKLER, G. A.
                  AUTHORITARIAN IDEOLOGY IN NEGRO COLLEGE STUDENTS.
                  JOURNAL OF ABNORMAL AND SOCIAL PSYCHOLOGY, 1957, 54, 396-399.
                  (MEASURE OF ANTI-NEGRO BIAS)
            @S-54 ATTITUDE RACIAL PREJUDICE NEGRO AFFECTIVE-STATES OTHER-CATEGORY GROUP
            @S-54 AUTHORITARIANISM MINORITY NEGATIVE 1957M

S-55   STEIN, D. D., HARDYCK, J. A., & SMITH, M. B.
                  RACE AND BELIEF: AN OPEN AND SHUT CASE.
                  JOURNAL OF PERSONAL AND SOCIAL PSYCHOLOGY, 1965, 1, 281-288.
                  (SOCIAL DISTANCE SCALE)
            @S-55 SOCIAL DISTANCE ADOLESCENT PREJUDICE 1965M OTHERS RELATIONSHIPS
            @S-55 ORIENTATION
                  (APPLICATIONS: 2337)

S-56   STERN, G. G.
                  PRELIMINARY MANUAL: ACTIVITIES INDEX.
                  SYRACUSE, NEW YORK: PSYCHOLOGICAL RESEARCH CENTER, 1958.
            STERN, G. G.
                  SCORING INSTRUCTIONS AND COLLEGE NORMS: ACTIVITIES INDEX, COLLEGE
                  CHARACTERISTICS INDEX.
                  SYRACUSE, NEW YORK: PSYCHOLOGICAL RESEARCH CENTER, 1963.
                  (ACTIVITIES INDEX)*
            @S-56 NEED STRUCTURE AUTONOMY OTHER-CATEGORY MULTITRAIT PERSONALITY PE-FIT 1958M
                  (APPLICATIONS: 414   451   818   823   1083   1254   1328   1416   1485   2015
                                   2535   2952)
S-57   STERN, G. G., STEIN, M. I., & BLOOM, B. S.
                  METHODS IN PERSONALITY ASSESSMENT.
                  GLENCOE: FREE PRESS, 1956.
                  (PHYSIOGNOMIC CUE TEST)*
            @S-57 FIGURE PREFERENCE CREATIVITY AUTONOMY PERCEPTION AFFECTIVE-STATES
            @S-57 PROJECTIVE 1956M

S-58   STREUFERT, S., & SCHRODER, H. M.
                  THE MEASUREMENT OF FOUR SYSTEMS OF PERSONALITY STRUCTURE VARYING IN LEVEL
                  OF ABSTRACTNESS: IMPRESSION FORMATION METHOD.
                  TECHNICAL REPORT NO. 12, PROJECT NR171-055, 1963. PRINCETON UNIVERSITY,
                  CONTRACT NONR 1858(12), OFFICE OF NAVAL RESEARCH.
                  (IMPRESSION FORMATION TEST)*
            @S-58 CONCEPTUAL CONCRETENESS ABSTRACTNESS IMPRESSION FORMATION COGNITIVE
            @S-58 STRUCTURE FUNCTIONING PERSONALITY DIFFERENTIATION INTEGRATION 1963M
                  (APPLICATIONS: 106   856)

S-59   SUPER, D. E.
                  THE PSYCHOLOGY OF CAREERS. NEW YORK: HARPER, 1957.
                  (WORK VALUES INVENTORY)*
            @S-59 ADJUSTMENT JOB SATISFACTION INTRINSIC EXTRINSIC VALUES AFFECTIVE-STATES
            @S-59 GLOBAL 1957M
                  (APPLICATIONS: 1179   1213   1230   1244   2776)

S-60   STRICKLAND, L. H., & JANICKI, W. P.
                  AN ALTERNATIVE FORM OF A FORCED-CHOICE F SCALE.
                  PSYCHOLOGICAL REPORTS, 1965, 16, 933-940.
                  (FORCED-CHOICE F-SCALE)*
            @S-60 AUTHORITARIANISM COPING-DEFENSE OTHER-CATEGORY F-SCALE DOGMATISM RIGIDITY
            @S-60 FLEXIBILITY 1965M

S-61   STROOP, J. R.
                  STUDIES OF INTERFERENCE IN SERIAL VERBAL REACTIONS.
                  JOURNAL OF EXPERIMENTAL PSYCHOLOGY, 1935, 18, 643-661.
                  (COLOR-WORD INTERFERENCE TEST)*
            @S-61 COGNITIVE STYLE FUNCTIONING STRUCTURE PERCEPTION 1935M
                  (APPLICATIONS: 14   176   269   290   313   316   377   386   1003   1121
                                   1850   2074   2200   2238   2239   2493   2561   2734   2886)

S-62   SANFORD, N., WEBSTER, H., & FREEDMAN, M.
                  IMPULSE EXPRESSION AS A VARIABLE OF PERSONALITY.
                  PSYCHOLOGICAL MONOGRAPHS, 1957, 71, (WHOLE NO. 440).
                  (IMPULSE EXPRESSION SCALE)*
            @S-62 EXPRESSIVENESS EMOTION IMPULSE EXPRESSION SELF AFFECTIVE-STATES 1957M
            @S-62 OTHER-CATEGORY
                  (APPLICATIONS: 178   1282)

S-63   SCHLIEN, J. M.
        TOWARD WHAT LEVEL OF ABSTRACTION IN CRITERIA?
        RESEARCH IN PSYCHOTHERAPY, 1961, 2.
        (ABSTRACT APPARATUS)*
     aS-63 SELF CONCEPT GLOBAL ADJUSTMENT SELF-IDENTITY EVALUATION PERCEPTION ESTEEM
     aS-63 GRAPHIC IDEAL IMAGE 1961M ACCEPTANCE

S-64   SELLTIZ, C., EDRICH, H. & COOK, S.W.
        RATINGS OF FAVORABLENESS OF STATEMENTS ABOUT A SOCIAL GROUP AS AN INDICATOR
        OF ATTITUDE TOWARD THE GROUP.
        JOURNAL OF PERSONALITY AND SOCIAL PSYCHOLOGY, 1965, 2, 408-415.
        (MEASURE OF ATTITUDES TOWARD NEGROES)
     aS-64 SOCIAL DISTANCE RACIAL PREJUDICE RATING ATTITUDE NEGRO AFFECTIVE-STATES
     aS-64 OTHER-CATEGORY 1965M
        (APPLICATIONS: 179   1473)

S-65   SAUNDERS, D. R.
        SOME PRELIMINARY INTERPRETIVE MATERIAL FOR THE PRI.
        RESEARCH MEMORANDUM 55-15. PRINCETON, N. J.: EDUCATIONAL TESTING SERVICE,
        1955.
        (PERSONALITY RESEARCH INVENTORY)*
     aS-65 INVENTORY MULTITRAIT PERSONALITY RESPONSE STYLE RESPONSE-BIAS 1955M

S-66   STRICKER, L. J.
        ACQUIESCENCE AND SOCIAL DESIRABILITY RESPONSES STYLES, ITEM CHARACTERSITICS
        AND CONFORMITY.
        PSYCHOLOGICAL REPORTS, 1963, 12, 319-341.
        (SOCIAL DESIRABILITY RESPONSE STYLE SCALE)*
     aS-66 SOCIAL DESIRABILITY RESPONSE STYLE RESPONSE-BIAS ACQUIESCENCE 1963M
        (APPLICATIONS: 190   282   386)

S-67   SCHAEFER, J. B., & NORMAN, N.
        PUNISHMENT AND AGGRESSION IN FANTASY RESPONSES OF BOYS WITH ANTISOCIAL
        CHARACTER TRAITS.
        JOURNAL OF PERSONALITY AND SOCIAL PSYCHOLOGY, 1967, 6, 237-240.
        (PROJECTIVE MEASURE OF AGGRESSION)
     aS-67 PROJECTIVE IMAGERY FANTASY HOSTILITY AGGRESSION TAT AFFECTIVE-STATES
     aS-67 RESENTMENT PUNITIVENESS MATERNAL SOCIAL 1967M

S-68   SCHEIER, I. H., & CATTELL, R. B.
        HANDBOOK FOR THE IPAT 8 PARALLEL FORM ANXIETY BATTERY.
        CHAMPAIGN, ILLINOIS: INSTITUTE FOR PERSONALITY AND ABILITY TESTING, 1960.
        (IPAT 8 PARALLEL FORM ANXIETY BATTERY)*
     aS-68 ANXIETY AFFECTIVE-STATES SUBJECTIVE STRESS 1960M
        (APPLICATIONS: 1735   2829   2875   2919)

S-69   SHAW, M. E., & WRIGHT, J. M.
        SCALES FOR THE MEASUREMENT OF ATTITUDES.
        NEW YORK: MCGRAW HILL, 1967.
        (SOCIAL ATTITUDES BATTERY)
     aS-69 FAMILY IDEOLOGY AUTHORITARIANISM SOCIAL ETHNOCENTRISM ATTITUDE RELIGION
     aS-69 POLITICAL CONSERVATISM COPING-DEFENSE FLEXIBILITY RIGIDITY DOGMATISM
     aS-69 OTHER-CATEGORY 1967M ORIENTATION

S-70   SIMS, V. M.
        SIMS SCI OCCUPATIONAL RATING SCALE.
        YONKERS-ON-HUDSON: WORLD BOOK, 1952.
        (SIMS SCI OCCUPATIONAL RATING SCALE)*
     aS-70 VOCATIONAL RATING JOB STEREOTYPE STATUS SOCIAL 1952M PREFERENCE

S-71   SCHWARTZ, S. H.
        WORDS, DEEDS, AND THE PERCEPTION OF CONSEQUENCES AND RESPONSIBILITY IN
        ACTION SITUATIONS.
        JOURNAL OF PERSONALITY AND SOCIAL PSYCHOLOGY, 1968, 10, 232-242.
        (RATING SCALE OF INTERPERSONAL BEHAVIOR)
     aS-71 INTERPERSONAL BEHAVIOR RATING PEER INTERACTION SOCIAL COMPETENCE 1968M

S-72   STRUENING, E. L., & EFRAN, H.
          FACTORS UNDERLYING OPINIONS ABOUT SELF, WORK, AND THE SOCIAL CONTEXT IN
          FORMER MENTAL PATIENTS.
          PAPER PRESENTED AT THE MEETING OF THE AMERICAN PSYCHOLOGICAL ASSOCIATION,
          PHILADELPHIA, AUGUST, 1963.
          (WORK VALUES INVENTORY)*
        @S-72 JOB VALUES PROGNOSIS VOCATIONAL SUCCESS PSYCHIATRIC PATIENT PREDICTION
        @S-72 SELF MENTAL-ILLNESS MENTAL-HEALTH 1963M
          (APPLICATIONS: 1471 2096)

S-73   SCHWARTZ, S. H.
          WORDS, DEEDS, AND THE PERCEPTION OF CONSEQUENCES AND RESPONSIBILITY IN
          ACTION SITUATIONS.
          JOURNAL OF PERSONALITY AND SOCIAL PSYCHOLOGY, 1968, 10, 232-242.
          (AWARENESS OF CONSEQUENCES TEST)*
        @S-73 INTERPERSONAL BEHAVIOR ACTIVITIES DECISION SOCIAL COMPETENCE PROJECTIVE
        @S-73 RESPONSIBILITY AWARENESS 1968M

S-74   SCHWARTZ, S. H.
          WORDS, DEEDS, AND THE PERCEPTION OF CONSEQUENCES AND RESPONSIBILITY IN
          ACTION SITUATIONS.
          JOURNAL OF PERSONALITY AND SOCIAL PSYCHOLOGY, 1968, 10, 232-242.
          (TEST OF PERSONAL NORMS)
        @S-74 PERSONAL NORMS VALUES IDEALS ALTRUISM MORAL RESPONSIBILITY DECISION
        @S-74 BEHAVIOR 1968M

S-75   SHERWOOD, J. J.
          SELF-REPORT AND PROJECTIVE MEASURES OF ACHIEVEMENT AND AFFILIATION.
          JOURNAL OF CONSULTING PSYCHOLOGY, 1966, 30, 329-337.
          (MEASURE OF NEED AFFILIATION)
        @S-75 NEED AFFILIATION AUTONOMY SELF DESCRIPTION BEHAVIOR 1966M OTHERS

S-76   SCHRODER, H. M., & HUNT, D. F.
          FAILURE-AVOIDANCE IN SITUATIONAL INTERPRETATION AND PROBLEM SOLVING.
          PSYCHOLOGICAL MONOGRAPHS, 1957, 71 (3, WHOLE NO. 432).
          (CRITICISM-FAILURE SUBSCALE)
        @S-76 1957M ADOLESCENT AVOIDANCE FAILURE DECISION
          (APPLICATIONS: 2502)

S-77   SORENSON, A. G., HUSEK, T. R., & YU, C.
          DIVERGENT CONCEPTS OF TEACHER ROLE: AN APPROACH TO THE MEASUREMENT OF
          TEACHER EFFECTIVENESS.
          JOURNAL OF EDUCATIONAL PSYCHOLOGY, 1963, 54, 287-294.
          (TEACHER PRACTICES QUESTIONNAIRE)*
        @S-77 BEHAVIOR ATTITUDE TEACHER ROLE SELF SELF-IDENTITY SUB-IDENTITY PERCEPTION
        @S-77 1963M

S-78   SCHAEFER, E. S., AARONSON, M., & BURGCON, B.
          CLASSROOM BEHAVIOR INVENTORY (FORM FOR GRADES 3 THROUGH 12).
          NATIONAL INSTITUTE OF MENTAL HEALTH, 1966.(MIMEO)
          (CLASSROOM BEHAVIOR INVENTORY)*
        @S-78 SCHOOL TEACHER RATING ADJUSTMENT BEHAVIOR OTHER-CATEGORY ACTIVITIES CHILD
        @S-78 STUDENT ELEMENTARY 1966M

S-79   SARASON, S. B., DAVIDSON, K. S., LIGHTHALL, F. F., WAITE, R. R., & RUEBUSH,
          B. K.
          ANXIETY IN ELEMENTARY SCHOOL CHILDREN.
          NEW YORK: WILEY, 1960.
          (DEFENSIVENESS SCALE FOR CHILDREN)*
        @S-79 RESPONSE-BIAS COPING-DEFENSE GLOBAL BEHAVIOR DEFENSIVENESS CHILD 1960M
        @S-79 ADJUSTMENT
          (APPLICATIONS: 368   489   1017 2461 2964)

S-80   SINGER, D.
          (UNPUBLISHED) SEE CHILD, I. L. , DEVELOPMENT OF SENSITIVITY TO ESTHETIC
          VALUES. COOPERATIVE RESEARCH PROJECT NO. 1748, 1964, UNITED STATES OFFICE
          OF EDUCATION COOPERATIVE RESEARCH PROGRAM.(MIMEO)
          (REGRESSION IN SERVICE OF EGO SCALE)
        @S-80 SENSITIVITY ESTHETIC REGRESSION EGO COGNITIVE STYLE EGO-STRENGTH
        @S-80 AFFECTIVE-STATES ADJUSTMENT AUTONOMY
          (APPLICATIONS: 423   480   531 2323)

S-81   SALTZ, E., & WICKEY, J.
        RESOLUTIONS OF THE LIBERAL DILEMMA IN THE ASSASSINATION OF PRESIDENT
        KENNEDY.
        JOURNAL OF PERSONALITY, 1965, 33, 636-648.
        (LIBERAL-CONSERVATIVE SCALES)
        @S-81 LIBERALISM CONSERVATISM POLITICAL ORIENTATION ATTITUDE 1965M

S-82   SINGER, J. L., & MCCRAVEN, V. G.
        SOME CHARACTERISTICS OF ADULT DAYDREAMING.
        JOURNAL OF PSYCHOLOGY, 1961, 51, 151-164.
        SINGER, J. L., & SCHONBAR, R. A.
        CORRELATES OF DAYDREAMING: A DIMENSION OF SELF-AWARENESS.
        JOURNAL OF CONSULTING PSYCHOLOGY, 1961, 25, 1-6.
        (DAYDREAM QUESTIONNAIRE)
        @S-82 FANTASY BEHAVIOR 1961M SUBJECTIVE EXPERIENCE IMAGINATION
              (APPLICATIONS: 189   1436   1744   1946)

S-83   SINGER, J. L., & SCHONBAR, R. A.
        CORRELATES OF DAYDREAMING: A DIMENSION OF SELF-AWARENESS.
        JOURNAL OF CONSULTING PSYCHOLOGY, 1961, 25, 1-6.
        (MEASURE OF CREATIVITY IN DAYDREAMS)
        @S-83 PROJECTIVE SELF-IDENTITY SELF ESTEEM MOTIVE CREATIVITY NEED AFFILIATION
        @S-83 ACHIEVEMENT AUTONOMY 1961M FANTASY SUBJECTIVE EXPERIENCE
              (APPLICATIONS: 2267)

S-84   STERN, E. J., & RIEGEL, K. F.
        COMPARISONS OF THE RESTRICTED ASSOCIATION OF CHRONIC SCHIZOPHRENICS
        AND NORMAL CONTROL SUBJECTS.
        JOURNAL OF ABNORMAL PSYCHOLOGY, 1970, 75, 164-171.
        (WORD ASSOCIATION TECHNIQUE FOR DIFFERENTIATING BETWEEN NORMALS
        AND SCHIZOPHRENICS)
        @S-84 DIAGNOSIS SCHIZOPHRENIA MENTAL-HEALTH MENTAL-ILLNESS PSYCHIATRIC 1970M

S-85   SECHREST, L. B.
        THE DEVELOPMENT OF A PERSON PREFERENCE TEST.
        UNPUBLISHED MASTER'S THESIS, OHIO STATE UNIVERSITY, 1954.
        (PERSON PREFERENCE TEST)*
        @S-85 MULTITRAIT PERSONALITY PREFERENCE PERSON 1954M INTERPERSONAL ORIENTATION
        @S-85 OTHERS
              (APPLICATIONS: 1737)

S-86   SILLER, J.
        PERSONALITY DETERMINANTS OF REACTION TO THE PHYSICALLY HANDICAPPED.
        AMERICAN PSYCHOLOGIST, 1962, 17, 338.(ABSTRACT)
        (SOCIAL DISTANCE SCALE)*
        @S-86 ADJUSTMENT SOCIAL DISTANCE COMPETENCE INTERPERSONAL RELATIONSHIPS
        @S-86 AFFECTIVE-STATES DISABILITY ALIENATION 1962M
              (APPLICATIONS: 1807)

S-87   SILLER, J.
        PERSONALITY DETERMINANTS OF REACTION TO THE PHYSICALLY HANDICAPPED.
        AMERICAN PSYCHOLOGIST, 1962, 17, 338.(ABSTRACT)
        (FEELING CHECK LIST)*
        @S-87 INTERPERSONAL RELATIONSHIPS MOOD ORIENTATION DISABILITY AFFECTIVE-STATES
        @S-87 OTHERS ADJUSTMENT SOCIAL INTERACTION DISTANCE COMPETENCE 1962M EMOTION
              (APPLICATIONS: 1807)

S-88   SIEGEL, S.
        CERTAIN DETERMINANTS AND CORRELATES OF AUTHORITARIANISM.
        GENETIC PSYCHOLOGY MONOGRAPHS, 1954, 49, 187-229.
        (TOLERANCE-INTOLERANCE OF COGNITIVE AMBIGUITY)*
        @S-88 COGNITIVE AUTHORITARIANISM TOLERANCE AMBIGUITY COPING-DEFENSE FLEXIBILITY
        @S-88 RIGIDITY DOGMATISM PROJECTIVE 1954M
              (APPLICATIONS: 769 1959)

S-89   SPIVACK, G., & LEVINE, M.
        SELF-REGULATION IN ACTING OUT AND NORMAL ADOLESCENTS.
        REPORT, PUBLIC HEALTH SERVICE, NATIONAL INSTITUTE OF MENTAL HEALTH, GRANT
        M-4531, 1962.
        (MEASURE OF FUTURE ORIENTATION)
        @S-89 TIME PERSPECTIVE FUTURE ORIENTATION AFFECTIVE-STATES ADOLESCENT 1962M
        @S-89 DELINQUENCY
              (APPLICATIONS: 1959   2803)

S-90   SHOR, R. E., & ORNE, E. C.
          HARVARD GROUP SCALE OF HYPNOTIC SUSCEPTIBILITY.
          PALO ALTO, CALIFORNIA: CONSULTING PSYCHOLOGISTS PRESS, 1962.
          (HARVARD GROUP SCALE OF HYPNOTIC SUSCEPTIBILITY)*
    aS-90 HYPNOTIC SUGGESTIBILITY GROUP 1962M
        (APPLICATIONS: 469   955   985 1037 1088 1093 1144 1975 2124 2222
                      2378 2388 2419 2485 2550 2683)

S-91   STRODTBECK, F. L.
          HUSBAND-WIFE INTERACTION OVER REVEALED DIFFERENCES.
          AMERICAN SOCIOLOGICAL REVIEW, 1951, 16, 468-473.
          (STUDY OF HUSBAND-WIFE INTERACTION)
    aS-91 INTERPERSONAL RELATIONSHIPS MARITAL BEHAVIOR FAMILY INTERACTION ADJUSTMENT
    aS-91 CROSS-CULTURAL 1951M

S-92   SHALIT, B.
          ENVIRONMENTAL HOSTILITY AND HOSTILITY IN FANTASY.
          JOURNAL OF PERSONALITY AND SOCIAL PSYCHOLOGY, 1970, 15, 171-174.
          (TAT SCORED FOR HOSTILITY)
    aS-92 HOSTILITY AFFECTIVE-STATES NEGATIVE TAT PROJECTIVE 1970M
    aS-92 IMAGERY

S-93   SECORD, P. F.
          OBJECTIFICATION OF WORD-ASSOCIATION PROCEDURES BY USE OF HOMONYMS: A
          MEASURE OF BODY CATHEXIS.
          JOURNAL OF PERSONALITY, 1953, 21, 479-495.
          (HOMONYM TEST)*
    aS-93 BODY AWARENESS IMAGE 1953M
        (APPLICATIONS: 2298   2324)

S-94   STOTLAND, E., & PATCHEN, M.
          IDENTIFICATION AND CHANGES IN PREJUDICE AND IN AUTHORITARIANISM.
          JOURNAL OF ABNORMAL AND SOCIAL PSYCHOLOGY, 1961, 62, 265-274.
          (MEASURE OF RATIONALITY)
    aS-94 COGNITIVE STYLE LIFE RATIONALISM JUDGMENT 1961M

S-95   STOTLAND, E., & PATCHEN, M.
          IDENTIFICATION AND CHANGES IN PREJUDICE AND IN AUTHORITARIANISM.
          JOURNAL OF ABNORMAL AND SOCIAL PSYCHOLOGY, 1961, 62, 265-274.
          (NEGRO ATTITUDE SCALE)*
    aS-95 OTHER-CATEGORY AFFECTIVE-STATES SOCIAL DISTANCE NEGATIVE ATTITUDE NEGRO
    aS-95 STEREOTYPE RACIAL PREJUDICE IDENTIFICATION 1961M

S-96   SEARS, R. R.
          RELATION OF EARLY SOCIALIZATION EXPERIENCES TO AGGRESSION IN MIDDLE
          CHILDHOOD.
          JOURNAL OF ABNORMAL AND SOCIAL PSYCHOLOGY, 1961, 63, 466-492.
          (MEASURE OF AGGRESSION)
    aS-96 NEGATIVE CHILD HOSTILITY BEHAVIOR AGGRESSION AFFECTIVE-STATES RESENTMENT
    aS-96 SOCIAL COMPETENCE ADJUSTMENT 1961M

S-97   SHNEIDMAN, E. S.
          MANUAL FOR THE MAKE-A-PICTURE-STORY METHOD.
          PROJECTIVE TECHNIQUES MONOGRAPHS, 1952, NO. 2, 1-92.
          (MAKE-A-PICTURE STORY TEST)*
    aS-97 CONCEPTUAL BEHAVIOR COGNITIVE STYLE PROJECTIVE PERCEPTION 1952M
        (APPLICATIONS: 321   366   545   705   985 1168 2207 2214 2553)

S-98   STOTLAND, E., THORLEY, S., THOMAS, E., COHEN, A. R., & ZANDER, A.
          THE EFFECTS OF GROUP EXPECTATIONS AND SELF-ESTEEM UPON SELF-EVALUATION.
          JOURNAL OF ABNORMAL AND SOCIAL PSYCHOLOGY, 1957, 54, 55-63.
          (MEASURE OF SELF-ESTEEM)
    aS-98 AUTONOMY FRUSTRATION GROUP SOCIAL APPROVAL INTERACTION NEED BEHAVIOR SELF
    aS-98 ESTEEM SELF-IDENTITY PERCEPTION EVALUATION 1957M
        (APPLICATIONS: 717)

S-99   STRICKER, G.
          THE CONSTRUCTION AND PARTIAL VALIDATION OF AN OBJECTIVELY SCORABLE
          APPERCEPTION TEST.
          JOURNAL OF PERSONALITY, 1962, 30, 51-62.
          (OBJECTIVELY SCORABLE APPERCEPTION TEST)*
    aS-99 AGGRESSION SECURITY DEPENDENCE TAT PROJECTIVE AFFECTIVE-STATES IMAGERY
    aS-99 OTHER-CATEGORY 1962M PERCEPTION
        (APPLICATIONS: 821)

S-100   SHAW, M. E., & SULZER, J. L.
             AN EMPIRICAL TEST OF HEIDER'S LEVELS IN ATTRIBUTION OF RESPONSIBILITY.
             JOURNAL OF ABNORMAL AND SOCIAL PSYCHOLOGY, 1964, 69, 39-46.
             (TEST OF ATTRIBUTION-OF-RESPONSIBILITY)
         @S-100 PERCEPTION CHILD SOCIAL INTERPERSONAL RELATIONSHIPS ATTRIBUTION AUTONOMY
         @S-100 RESPONSIBILITY LOCUS CONTROL IE-CONTROL MORAL VALUES 1964M

S-101   SEEMAN, J.
             PERSONALITY INTEGRATION IN COLLEGE WOMEN.
             JOURNAL OF PERSONALITY AND SOCIAL PSYCHOLOGY, 1966, 4, 91-93.
             (MEASURE OF LOCUS OF CONTROL/EVALUATION)
         @S-101 LOCUS CONTROL EVALUATION PERSONALITY INTEGRATION AUTONOMY IE-CONTROL
         @S-101 1966M

S-102   SMITH, M. B.
             EXPLORATIONS IN COMPETENCE: A STUDY OF PEACE CORPS TEACHERS IN GHANA.
             AMERICAN PSYCHOLOGIST, 1966, 21, 555-566.
             (OVERSEAS Q-SORT)
         @S-102 COPING-DEFENSE Q-SORT ROLE PERCEPTION PERFORMANCE 1966M
             (APPLICATIONS: 2326)

S-103   SACKS, J. M., & LEVY, S.
             THE SENTENCE COMPLETION TEST.
             IN L. E. ABT AND L. BELLACK (EDS.), PROJECTIVE PSYCHOLOGY. NEW YORK:
             KNOPF, 1952.
             (SACKS SENTENCE COMPLETION TEST)*
         @S-103 OTHER DESCRIPTION SELF MULTITRAIT PROJECTIVE 1952M
             (APPLICATIONS: 1403 1618)

S-104   START, K. B.
             OVERESTIMATION OF PERSONAL ABILITIES AND SUCCESS AT FIRST-YEAR UNIVERSITY
             EXAMINATIONS.
             JOURNAL OF SOCIAL PSYCHOLOGY, 1963, 59, 337-345.
             (METHOD OF RATING SELF AND GROUP MEMBERS ON VARIOUS TRAITS)
         @S-104 RATING PEER DESCRIPTION EVALUATION ADJUSTMENT MULTITRAIT SELF GROUP
         @S-104 INTELLIGENCE SOCIAL COMPETENCE SUCCESS 1963M TRAIT

S-105   SHEARD, J. L.
             INTRASUBJECT PREDICTION OF PREFERENCES FOR ORGANIZATION TYPES.
             JOURNAL OF APPLIED PSYCHOLOGY, 1970, 54, 248-252.
             (ATTAINABILITY OF WORK GOALS SCALE)
         @S-105 1970M ORGANIZATION GOALS JOB

S-106   SMITH, R. J.
             EXPLORATIONS IN NONCONFORMITY.
             JOURNAL OF SOCIAL PSYCHOLOGY, 1967, 71, 133-150.
             (NONCONFORMITY SCALE)*
         @S-106 CONFORMITY AUTONOMY ATTITUDE SOCIAL DEPENDENCE ROLE NORMS 1967M

S-107.   SMITH, R. J.
             EXPLORATIONS IN NONCONFORMITY.
             JOURNAL OF SOCIAL PSYCHOLOGY, 1967, 71, 133-150.
             (FIGURE PREFERENCE TEST)*
         @S-107 SOCIAL INFLUENCE CONFORMITY-FIGURE PREFERENCE AUTONOMY DESIRABILITY
         @S-107 RESPONSE-BIAS CORRECTIVE-USE STUDENT RESPONSE STYLE 1967M PERCEPTION

S-108   SROLE, L.
             SOCIAL INTEGRATION AND CERTAIN COROLLARIES: AN EXPLORATORY STUDY.
             AMERICAN SOCIOLOGICAL REVIEW, 1956, 21, 709-716.
             (FIVE-ITEM VERSION OF F-SCALE)
         @S-108 AUTHORITARIANISM COPING-DEFENSE OTHER-CATGORY DOGMATISM FLEXIBILITY
         @S-108 RIGIDITY F-SCALE SOCIAL INTEGRATION 1956M

S-109   SHEIKH, A. A.
             STEREOTYPY IN INTERPERSONAL PERCEPTION AND INTERCORRELATION BETWEEN SOME
             ATTITUDE MEASURES.
             JOURNAL OF SOCIAL PSYCHOLOGY, 1968, 76, 175-179.
             (INTERPERSONAL PERCEPTION RATING SCALE)*
         @S-109 STEREOTYPE OTHERS PERCEPTION OTHER-CATEGORY INTERPERSONAL DOGMATISM
         @S-109 ETHNOCENTRISM ETHNIC MINORITY PREJUDICE ADJUSTMENT COPING-DEFENSE
         @S-109 RIGIDITY FLEXIBILITY 1968M RATING

S-110   STONE, J. B.
               STRUCTURED-OBJECTIVE RORSCHACH TEST, PRELIMINARY EDITION.
               LOS ANGELES: CALIFORNIA TEST BUREAU, 1958.
               (STRUCTURED-OBJECTIVE RORSCHACH TEST)*
           aS-110 RORSCHACH TRAIT DIAGNOSIS MULTITRAIT PROJECTIVE AFFECTIVE-STATES ANXIETY
           aS-110 SUBJECTIVE STRESS MENTAL-ILLNESS 1958M
               (APPLICATIONS: 1226   1989)

S-111   SPIEGEL, D. E.
               THE SPIEGEL PERSONALITY INVENTORY MANUAL.
               LOS ANGELES: AUTHOR, 1965.
               (SPIEGEL PERSONALITY INVENTORY)*
           aS-111 SELF-IDENTITY MULTITRAIT PERSONALITY AFFECTIVE-STATES GLOBAL ADJUSTMENT
           aS-111 AUTONOMY 1965M
               (APPLICATIONS: 2283)

S-112   SHRAUGER, S.
               COGNITIVE DIFFERENTIATION AND THE IMPRESSION-FORMATION PROCESS.
               JOURNAL OF PERSONALITY, 1967, 35, 402-414.
               (DIFFERENTIATION AMONG UNFAMILIAR PEOPLE)*
           aS-112 COGNITIVE DIFFERENTIATION RATING DESCRIPTION IMPRESSION FORMATION TRAIT
           aS-112 OTHERS 1967M

S-113   SHRAUGER, S.
               COGNITIVE DIFFERENTIATION AND THE IMPRESSION-FORMATION PROCESS.
               JOURNAL OF PERSONALITY, 1967, 35, 402-414.
               (DIFFERENTIATION AMONG FAMILIAR PEOPLE)*
           aS-113 IMPRESSION FORMATION COGNITIVE DIFFERENTIATION ROLE DESCRIPTION TRAIT
           aS-113 PERCEPTION OTHERS EVALUATION 1967M

S-114   SHRAUGHER, S.
               COGNITIVE DIFFERENTIATION AND THE IMPRESSION-FORMATION PROCESS.
               JOURNAL OF PERSONALITY, 1967, 35, 402-414.
               (INTERPRETIVE INFERENCE QUESTIONNAIRE)*
           aS-114 COGNITIVE DIFFERENTIATION IMPRESSION FORMATION OTHERS BEHAVIOR
           aS-114 DESCRIPTION 1967M FUNCTIONING

S-115   SHRAUGER, S.
               COGNITIVE DIFFERNTIATION AND THE IMPRESSION-FORMATION PROCESS.
               JOURNAL OF PERSONALITY, 1967, 35, 402-414.
               (EXTENDED INFERENCE QUESTIONNAIRE)*
           aS-115 IMPRESSION FORMATION COGNITIVE DIFFERENTIATION PERCEPTION FUNCTIONING
           aS-115 1967M

S-116   SMITH, W. J., ALBRIGHT, L. E., GLENNON, J. R., & OWENS, W. A.
               THE PREDICTION OF RESEARCH COMPETENCE AND CREATIVITY FROM PERSONAL HISTORY.
               JOURNAL OF APPLIED PSYCHOLOGY, 1961, 45, 59-62.
               (PERSONAL HISTORY MEASURE FOR PREDICTING RESEARCH CREATIVITY)
           aS-116 AUTONOMY CREATIVITY ORIGINALITY JOB PERSONAL HISTORY LIFE STYLE 1961M
           aS-116 PREDICTION

S-118   SCHAEFER, C. E., & ANASTASI, A.
               A BIOGRAPHICAL INVENTORY FOR IDENTIFYING CREATIVITY IN ADOLESCENT BOYS.
               JOURNAL OF APPLIED PSYCHOLOGY, 1968, 52, 42-48.
               (BIOGRAPHICAL INVENTORY)*
           aS-118 ENVIRONMENT ACTIVITIES AUTONOMY CREATIVITY MULTITRAIT ADOLESCENT 1968M

S-119   SHEARD, J. L.
               INTRASUBJECT PREDICTION OF PREFERENCES FOR ORGANIZATION TYPES.
               JOURNAL OF APPLIED PSYCHOLOGY, 1970, 54, 248-252.
               (PREFERENCE FOR TYPES OF ORGANIZATIONS SCALE)
           aS-119 1970M PREFERENCE ORGANIZATION JOB VOCATIONAL

S-120   SHEARD, J. L.
               INTRASUBJECT PREDICTION OF PREFERENCES FOR ORGANIZATION TYPES.
               JOURNAL OF APPLIED PSYCHOLOGY, 1970, 54, 248-252.
               (RATING OF WORK GOALS)
           aS-120 1970M RATING GOALS JOB

S-121   SOLOMON, L., & SPOHN, H. E.
          A METHOD FOR THE SYSTEMATIC ANALYSIS OF SOCIAL INTERACTION ON A WARD OF
          CHRONIC SCHIZOPHRENICS.
          PAPER PRESENTED AT THE MEETING OF THE AMERICAN PSYCHOLOGICAL ASSOCIATION,
          WASHINGTON, D. C., 1958.
          (INTERACTION PROTOCOL)*
          aS-121 SOCIAL INTERACTION ADJUSTMENT SCHIZOPHRENIA WARD BEHAVIOR COMMUNICATION
          aS-121 MOTIVE COMPETENCE INTERPERSONAL OTHER-CATEGORY RELATIONSHIPS PATIENT
          aS-121 1958M

S-122   SCHNEIDER, F. W., & SHAW, M. E.
          SANCTIONING BEHAVIOR IN NEGRO AND IN WHITE POPULATIONS.
          JOURNAL OF SOCIAL PSYCHOLOGY. 1970, 81, 63-72.
          (ASSIGNMENT OF SANCTIONS QUESTIONNAIRE)
          aS-122 1970M MORAL DEVELOPMENT CHILD RESPONSIBILITY ATTRIBUTION

S-123   SOLOMON, L., & KLEIN, E.
          THE RELATIONSHIP BETWEEN AGREEING RESPONSE SET AND SOCIAL DESIRABILITY.
          JOURNAL OF ABNORMAL AND SOCIAL PSYCHOLOGY, 1963, 66, 176-179.
          (MEASURE OF SOCIAL DESIRABILITY)
          aS-123 SOCIAL DESIRABILITY RESPONSE-BIAS 1963M
              (APPLICATIONS: 531   2162   2174)

S-124   SHIPLEY, W. C.
          A SELF-ADMINISTERING SCALE FOR MEASURING INTELLECTUAL IMPAIRMENT AND
          DETERIORATION.
          JOURNAL OF PSYCHOLOGY, 1940, 9, 371-377.
          (SHIPLEY-HARTFORD VOCABULARY AND ABSTRACTION SCALE)*
          aS-124 COGNITIVE INTELLECTUAL FUNCTIONING STRUCTURE MENTAL-ILLNESS ILLNESS
          aS-124 INTELLIGENCE 1940M

S-125   SHOSTROM, E. L.
          MANUAL FOR THE CARING RELATIONSHIP INVENTORY.
          SAN DIEGO: EDUCATIONAL AND INDUSTRIAL TESTING SERVICE, 1966.
          (CARING RELATIONSHIP INVENTORY)*
          aS-125 AFFECTION INTERACTION AFFECTIVE-STATES ALTRUISM EMPATHY MARITAL ATTITUDE
          aS-125 NEED EMOTION OTHERS ADJUSTMENT SATISFACTION INTERPERSONAL SELF
          aS-125 RELATIONSHIPS 1966M

S-126   SILLER, J., FERGUSON, L., HOLLAND, B., & VANN, D.
          MANUAL ON THE DISABILITY FACTOR SCALES.
          NEW YORK: AUTHORS, 1968.
          (OPINIONS ABOUT COSMETIC CONDITIONS SCALE)*
          aS-126 INTERPERSONAL RELATIONSHIPS SOCIAL DISTANCE DISABILITY ORIENTATION 1968M
          aS-126 OPINION ATTITUDE

S-128   SUEDFELD, P., GRISSOM, R. J., & VERNON, J.
          THE EFFECTS OF SENSORY DEPRIVATION AND SOCIAL ISOLATION ON THE PERFORMANCE
          OF AN UNSTRUCTURED COGNITIVE TASK.
          AMERICAN JOURNAL OF PSYCHOLOGY, 1964, 77, 111-115.
          (MEASURE OF COGNITIVE EFFICIENCY)
          aS-128 PROJECTIVE COGNITIVE EFFECTIVENESS FUNCTIONING STYLE STRUCTURE 1964M

S-129   SCHUTZ, R. E., & FOSTER, R. J.
          A FACTOR ANALYTIC STUDY OF ACQUIESCENT AND EXTREME RESPONSE SET.
          EDUCATIONAL AND PSYCHOLOGICAL MEASUREMENT, 1963, 23, 435-447.
          (APHORISMS QUESTIONNAIRE)*
          aS-129 ACQUIESCENCE RESPONSE SET RESPONSE-BIAS CORRECTIVE-USE 1963M

S-130   STERN, G., CHRISTIE, R., LANE, H., SANFORD, N., & WEBSTER, H.
          AUTHORITARIANISM WORKSHOP, RAQUETTE LAKE, N. Y., DITTOED MANUSCRIPT,
          SYRACUSE UNIVERSITY, SYRACUSE, N. Y., 1959.
          STERN, G., CHRISTIE, R., LANE, H., SANFORD, N., & WEBSTER, H.
          STEREOPATHY-ACQUIESCENCE WORKSHOP, STANFORD, CALIFORNIA. MIMEOGRAPHED
          TRANSCRIPT, SYRACUSE UNIVERSITY, SYRACUSE, N. Y., 1960.
          (STEREOPATHY-ACQUIESCENCE SCALES)*
          aS-130 1959M AUTHORITARIANISM ACQUIESCENCE STEREOTYPE
              (APPLICATIONS: 2271   2593   2828)

S-131   STRODTBECK, F. L.
              FAMILY INTERACTION, VALUES AND ACHIEVEMENT.
              IN D. C. MCCLELLAND AND ASSOCIATES (EDS.), TALENT AND SOCIETY. PRINCETON:
              VAN NOSTRAND, 1958.
              (ACHIEVEMENT VALUE INVENTORY)
         aS-131 AUTONOMY NEED ACHIEVEMENT VALUES MOTIVE ROLE ORIENTATION FAMILY IDENTITY
         aS-131 INTERACTION SELF-IDENTITY 1958M

S-132   STRODTBECK, F. L.
              FAMILY INTERACTION, VALUES AND ACHIEVEMENT.
              IN D. C. MCCLELLAND AND ASSOCIATES (EDS.), TALENT AND SOCIETY. PRINCETON:
              VAN NOSTRAND, 1958.
              (PERSONAL CONTROL SCALE)
         aS-132 AUTONOMY PERSONAL ENVIRONMENT LOCUS CONTROL IE-CONTROL COMPETENCE
         aS-132 ADJUSTMENT 1958M

S-133   SARASON, S. B., DAVIDSON, K. S., LIGHTHALL, F. F., WAITE, R. R., & RUEBUSH, B. K
              ANXIETY IN ELEMENTARY SCHOOL CHILDREN.
              NEW YORK: WILEY, 1960.
              (GENERAL ANXIETY SCALE FOR CHILDREN)*
         aS-133 ANXIETY CHILD AFFECTIVE-STATES SUBJECTIVE STRESS 1960M

S-134   SMITH, C. E.
              THE EFFECT OF ANXIETY ON THE PERFORMANCE AND ATTITUDES OF AUTHORITARIANS IN
              A SMALL GROUP SITUATION.
              JOURNAL OF PSYCHOLOGY, 1964, 58, 191-203.
              (PERSONAL SOCIAL DISTANCE SCALE)*
         aS-134 PERSONAL SOCIAL DISTANCE AFFECTIVE-STATES OTHER-CATEGORY COLLEGE STUDENT
         aS-134 INTERPERSONAL RELATIONSHIPS ALIENATION GROUP 1964M

S-135   SMITH, C. E.
              THE EFFECT OF ANXIETY ON THE PERFORMANCE AND ATTITUDES OF AUTHORITARIANS IN
              A SMALL GROUP SITUATION.
              JOURNAL OF PSYCHOLOGY, 1964, 58, 191-203.
              (STUDENT SOCIAL DISTANCE SCALE)*
         aS-135 SOCIAL DISTANCE STUDENT AFFECTIVE-STATES OTHER-CATEGORY ALIENATION
         aS-135 INTERPERSONAL RELATIONSHIPS GROUP 1964M

S-136   STEINMANN, A., & FOX, D. J.
              MALE-FEMALE PERCEPTIONS OF THE FEMALE ROLE IN THE UNITED STATES.
              JOURNAL OF PSYCHOLOGY, 1966, 64, 265-276.
              (INVENTORY OF FEMININE VALUES)*
         aS-136 FEMININITY VALUES SELF-IDENTITY SELF IDEAL SUB-IDENTITY SEX ROLE 1966M
         aS-136 ORIENTATION

S-137   SHAVER, P. R., & SCHEIBE, K. E.
              TRANSFORMATION OF SOCIAL IDENTITY: A STUDY OF CHRONIC MENTAL PATIENTS AND
              COLLEGE VOLUNTEERS IN A SUMMER CAMP SETTING.
              JOURNAL OF PSYCHOLOGY, 1967, 66, 19-37.
              (OPINIONS ABOUT MENTAL ILLNESS QUESTIONNAIRE)*
         aS-137 OPINION MENTAL-ILLNESS ATTITUDE 1967M DISABILITY

S-138   SCIORTINO, R.
              PERSONALITY AND CREATIVE ABILITIES.
              UNPUBLISHED DOCTORAL DISSERTATION, OHIO STATE UNIVERSITY, 1963. COLUMBUS,
              OHIO: UNIVERSITY MICROFILMS (NO. 64-6958).
              (MOTIVATIONAL ADJECTIVE CHECKLIST)*
         aS-138 MOTIVE CHECKLIST AUTONOMY MULTITRAIT SECURITY DEPENDENCE 1963M

S-139   SAMPSON, D. L., & SMITH, H. P.
              A SCALE TO MEASURE WORLD-MINDED ATTITUDES.
              JOURNAL OF SOCIAL PSYCHOLOGY, 1957, 45, 99-106.
              (WOLRDMINDEDNESS SCALE)*
         aS-139 INTERNATIONALISM ATTITUDE VALUES ORIENTATION 1957M
              (APPLICATIONS: 2885)

S-140   SCIORTINO, R.
          PERSONALITY AND CREATIVE ABILITIES.
          UNPUBLISHED DOCTORAL DISSERTATION, OHIO STATE UNIVERSITY, 1963.   COLUMBUS,
          OHIO: UNIVERSITY MICROFILMS (NO. 64-6958).
          (GENERAL ADAPTABILITY ADJECTIVE LIST)*
          @S-140 ADAPTABILITY SELF RATING AUTONOMY CREATIVITY TRAIT ABILITY MULTITRAIT
          @S-140 CHECKLIST 1963M ADJUSTMENT

S-141   SEARS, P. S.
          THE PURSUIT OF SELF-ESTEEM: THE MIDDLE CHILDHOOD YEARS.
          PAPER PRESENTED AT THE MEETING OF THE AMERICAN PSYCHOLOGICAL ASSOCIATION,
          CHICAGO, SEPTEMBER, 1960.
          (MEASURE OF SELF-CONCEPT)
          @S-141 CHILD SELF ESTEEM SELF-IDENTITY EVALUATION PERCEPTION CONCEPT IMAGE
          @S-141 SOCIAL COMPETENCE 1960M

S-142   SHAPIRO, J. G.
          THE PERSONALITY DESCRIPTION FORM.
          MIMEOGRAPHED TEST, ARKANSAS REHABILITATION RESEARCH AND TRAINING CENTER,
          1967.
          (PERSONALITY DESCRIPTION FORM)*
          @S-142 MULTITRAIT PERSONALITY GLOBAL DESCRIPTION EVALUATION 1967M SELF
              (APPLICATIONS: 1458   1537)

S-143   STRUPP, H. H.
          A MULTIDIMENSIONAL SYSTEM FOR ANALYZING PSYCHOTHERAPEUTIC TECHNIQUES.
          PSYCHIATRY, 1957, 20, 293-306.
          STRUPP, H. H.
          A MULTIDIMENSIONAL SYSTEM FOR ANALYZING PSYCHOTHERAPEUTIC RESPONSES:
          MANUAL (2ND ED.).
          CHAPEL HILL: UNIVERSITY OF NORTH CAROLINA, 1966.
          (THERAPEUTIC CLIMATE SCALE)*
          @S-143 1957M THERAPY BEHAVIOR RELATIONSHIPS INTERACTION PATIENT
          @S-143 ENVIRONMENT
              (APPLICATIONS: 1405   2923)

S-144   SHRAUGER, J. S., & ROSENBERG, S. E.
          SELF ESTEEM AND THE EFFECTS OF SUCCESS AND FAILURE FEEDBACK ON
          PERFORMANCE.
          JOURNAL OF PERSONALITY, 1970, 38, 404-417.
          (ADJECTIVE CHECKLIST FOR SELF DESCRIPTION)
          @S-144 1970M CHECKLIST TRAIT SELF ESTEEM SOCIAL SENSITIVITY CONCEPT

S-146   SANFORD, F. H., & OLDER, H. J.
          A SHORT AUTHORITARIAN-EQUALITARIAN SCALE.
          PHILADELPHIA: INSTITUTE FOR RESEARCH IN HUMAN RELATIONS, 1950.
          (AUTHORITARIANISM-EQUALITARIANISM SCALE)
          @S-146 1950M AUTHORITARIANISM TOLERANCE PUNITIVENESS PERSUASIBILITY ATTITUDE
          @S-146 CHANGE INFLUENCE OPINION
              (APPLICATIONS: 2342)

S-147   SPIELBERGER, C. D., & GORSUCH, R. L.
          THE DEVELOPMENT OF THE STATE-TRAIT ANXIETY INVENTORY.
          IN SPIELBERGER, C. D., & GORSUCH, R. L. (ED.)
          MEDIATING PROCESSES IN VERBAL CONDITIONING.
          FINAL REPORT TO NATIONAL INSTITUTE OF MENTAL HEALTH, WASHINGTON, D. C.:
          GOVERNMENT PRINTING OFFICE, 1966.
          SPIELBERGER, C. D., LUSHENE, R. E., & MCADOO, W. G.
          THEORY AND MEASUREMENT OF ANXIETY STATES.
          IN R. B. CATTELL (ED.)
          HANDBOOK OF MODERN PERSONALITY THEORY. CHICAGO: ADLINE, IN PRESS.
          (STATE-TRAIT ANXIETY INVENTORY)*
          @S-147 1967M ANXIETY FEAR STRESS
              (APPLICATIONS: 2721   2927   2931   2948)

S-148   SHARMA, S.
          RELATIONSHIP OF SELF-CONCEPT WITH ANXIETY AND SCHOOL ACHIEVEMENT OF
          ADOLESCENTS.
          UNPUBLISHED DOCTORAL DISSERTATION, PANJAB UNIVERSITY, 1967.
          (ANXIETY SCALE)
          @S-148 1967M ANXIETY PE-FIT FEAR FAILURE STRESS

S-149   STEIN, K. B., SARBIN, T. R., & KULIK, J. A.
              FUTURE TIME PERSPECTIVE: ITS RELATION TO THE SOCIALIZATION PROCESS
              AND THE DELINQUENT ROLE.
              JOURNAL OF CONSULTING AND CLINICAL PSYCHOLOGY, 1968, 32, 257-264.
              (FUTURE EVENTS TEST)*
          @S-149 1968M FUTURE TIME PERSPECTIVE ORIENTATION

S-151   SADLER, P. J.
              LEADERSHIP STYLE, CONFIDENCE IN MANAGEMENT, AND JOB SATISFACTION.
              JOURNAL OF APPLIED BEHAVIORAL SCIENCE, 1970, 6, 3-19.
              (MEASURE OF JOB SATISFACTION, CONFIDENCE, AND PERCEIVED LEADERSHIP STYLE)
          @S-151 1970M JOB SATISFACTION PERCEIVED LEADERSHIP PE-FIT STYLE

S-152   SMITH, K. H.
              CONFORMITY AS RELATED TO MASCULINITY, SELF, AND OTHER DESCRIPTIONS,
              SUSPICION, AND ARTISTIC PREFERENCE BY SEX GROUPS.
              JOURNAL OF SOCIAL PSYCHOLOGY, 1970, 80, 79-88.
              (GROUP-PRESSURE ITEMS)
          @S-152 1970M CONFORMITY GROUP SOCIAL PRESSURE

S-153   SMITH, K. H.
              CONFORMITY AS RELATED TO MASCULINITY, SELF, AND OTHER DESCRIPTIONS,
              SUSPICION, AND ARTISTIC PREFERENCE BY SEX GROUPS.
              JOURNAL OF SOCIAL PSYCHOLOGY, 1970, 80, 79-88.
              (SEMANTIC DIFFERENTIAL SCALES)
          @S-153 1970M SEM-DIFFERENTIAL
              (APPLICATIONS: 1094)

S-154   SHAFFER, W. F.
              TESTS OF HYPOTHESES RELATING PSYCHOPATHOLOGY TO EXTREME UPWARD MOBILITY.
              UNPUBLISHED DOCTORAL DISSERTATION, TEACHERS COLLEGE, COLUMBIA UNIVERSITY,
              1968.
              (MEASURE OF LOW SELF-ESTEEM)
          @S-154 1968M SELF-IDENTITY SELF ESTEEM CONCEPT IMAGE
              (APPLICATIONS: 2760)

S-155   SUPER, D. E., CRITES, J. O., HUMMEL, R. C., & WARNATH, C. P.
              VOCATIONAL DEVELOPMENT: A FRAMEWORK FOR RESEARCH.
              NEW YORK: BUREAU OF PUBLICATIONS, TEACHERS COLLEGE, COLUMBIA UNIVERSITY,
              1957.
              (BIOGRAPHICAL INVENTORY)*
          @S-155 1957M NEUROTICISM ADJUSTMENT
              (APPLICATIONS: 1213 1350 1461 2760)

S-156   SPITZER, R. L., & ENDICOTT, J. E.
              DIAGNO: A COMPUTER PROGRAM FOR PSYCHIATRIC DIAGNOSIS UTILIZING THE
              DIFFERENTIAL DIAGNOSTIC PROCEDURE.
              ARCHIVES OF GENERAL PSYCHIATRY, 1968, 18, 746-756.
              (PSYCHIATRIC STATUS SCHEDULE)*
          @S-156 1968M PSYCHIATRIC DIAGNOSIS MENTAL-ILLNESS SCHIZOPHRENIA NEUROTICISM
          @INVENTORY ADJUSTMENT SYMPTOM GUILT ANXIETY DEPRESSION
              (APPLICATIONS: 2847)

S-158   SIMMONS, D. D.
              DEVELOPMENT OF AN OBJECTIVE MEASURE OF IDENTITY ACHIEVEMENT STATUS.
              JOURNAL OF PROJECTIVE TECHNIQUES AND PERSONALITY ASSESSMENT, 1970, 34,
              241-244.
              (IDENTITY ACHIEVEMENT STATUS SCALE)*
          @S-158 1970M IDENTITY ACHIEVEMENT STATUS SELF ACTUALIZATION
          @S-158 CONCEPT IDEAL

S-159   SCHNEIDER, J. M.
              SKILL VERSUS CHANCE ACTIVITY PREFERENCE AND LOCUS OF CONTROL.
              JOURNAL OF CONSULTING AND CLINICAL PSYCHOLOGY, 1968, 32, 333-337.
              (SKILL-CHANCE INVENTORY)
          @S-159 1968M PREFERENCE IE-CONTROL LOCUS CONTROL
              (APPLICATIONS: 2563)

S-160   SCHNEIDER, L. & LYSGAARD, S.
              THE DEFERRED GRATIFICATION PATTERN: A PRELIMINARY STUDY.
              AMERICAN SOCIOLOGICAL REVIEW, 1953, 18, 142-149.
          STRAUS, M.
              DEFERRED GRATIFICATION, SOCIAL CLASS, AND THE ACHIEVEMENT SYNDROME.
              AMERICAN SOCIOLOGICAL REVIEW, 1962, 27, 326-335.
              (MEASURE OF DEFERRED GRATIFICATION)
          @S-160 1953M AUTONOMY NEED AFFILIATION AGGRESSION
              (APPLICATIONS: 35 2798)

S-162   SAGE, E. H.
              DEVELOPMENTAL SCALES FOR COLLEGE FRESHMEN.
              JOURNAL OF COUNSELING PSYCHOLOGY, 1968, 15, 381-385.
              (DEVELOPMENTAL SCALES)
          @S-162 1968M DEVELOPMENT STUDENT SOCIAL ADJUSTMENT COMPETENCE COLLEGE
              (APPLICATIONS: 2864)

S-163   SMITH, D. H., & INKELES, A.
              THE OM SCALE: A COMPARATIVE SOCIO-PSYCHOLOGICAL MEASURE OF INDIVIDUAL
              MODERNITY.
              SOCIOMETRY, 1966, 29, 353-377.
              (OVERALL MODERNITY SCALE)*
          @S-163 1966M ATTITUDE ADJUSTMENT VALUES ORIENTATION PERSONAL ASPIRATION
          @S-163 OPENNESS EXPERIENCE POLITICAL RELIGION EFFICACY

S-164   SCHWARTZ, M. M., STACK, H. F., & SCHIFFMAN, H. R.
              RESPONSES OF UNION AND MANAGEMENT LEADERS TO EMOTIONALLY-TONED INDUSTRIAL
              RELATIONS.
              PERSONNEL PSYCHOLOGY, 1970, 23, 361-367.
              (SEMANTIC DIFFERENTIAL MEASURE OF INDUSTRIAL RELATIONS CONCEPTS)
          @S-164 1970M SEM-DIFFERENTIAL CONCEPT EMPLOYEE JOB MANAGEMENT BEHAVIOR
          @S-164 RELATIONSHIPS

S-165   SINGER, M. I.
              COMPARISON OF INDICATORS OF HOMOSEXUALITY ON THE MMPI.
              JOURNAL OF CONSULTING AND CLINICAL PSYCHOLOGY, 1970, 34, 15-18.
              (MMPI SCORED FOR HOMOSEXUALITY)
          @S-165 1970M MMPI SEX IDENTIFICATION ROLE
          @S-165 HOMOSEXUALITY PSYCHIATRIC SUB-IDENTITY FEMININITY MASCULINITY

S-166   SMITH, P. A.
              A FACTOR ANALYTIC STUDY OF THE SELF-CONCEPT.
              JOURNAL OF CONSULTING PSYCHOLOGY, 1960, 24, 191.
              (SELF-RATING SCALE)
          @S-166 1960M SELF CONCEPT ESTEEM ANXIETY BODY IMAGE AUTONOMY
          @SOCIAL INTERPERSONAL RELATIONSHIPS

S-167   SHEERER, E. T.
              AN ANALYSIS OF THE RELATIONSHIP BETWEEN ACCEPTANCE OF AND RESPECT FOR
              SELF, AND ACCEPTANCE OF AND RESPECT FOR OTHERS IN 10 COUNSELING CASES.
              JOURNAL OF CONSULTING PSYCHOLOGY, 1949, 13, 169-175.
              (MEASURE OF ATTITUDE TOWARDS SELF AND OTHERS)
          @S-167 1949M ATTITUDE SELF OTHERS RESPECT EVALUATION ESTEEM ACCEPTANCE
              (APPLICATIONS: 1206)

S-168   SHACK, J. R.
              THE DEVELOPMENT OF AN OBJECTIVE FACTORIAL LEARNING MOTIVATIONAL
              ORIENTATION INVENTORY.
              UNPUBLISHED DOCTORAL DISSERTATION, CASE-WESTERN RESERVE UNIVERSITY,
              CLEVELAND, 1968.
              (EPISTEMIC ORIENTATION INVENTORY)
          @S-168 1968M MOTIVE ORIENTATION INTRINSIC EXTRINSIC SELF EXPLORATION STRUCTURE
          @S-168 RESISTANCE ACADEMIC NEED ACHIEVEMENT FUTURE
              (APPLICATIONS: 2881)

S-169   SARNOFF, I.
              REACTION FORMATION AND CYNICISM.
              JOURNAL OF PERSONALITY, 1960, 28, 129-143.
              (CYNICISM SCALE)*
          @S-169 1960M EMOTION ADJUSTMENT ATTITUDE BELIEF COPING-DEFENSE CYNICISM
          @S-169 INTERPERSONAL RELATIONSHIP PE-FIT PERSONALITY STRUCTURE

S-170   SCHACHTER, S.
            THE PSYCHOLOGY OF AFFILIATION.
            STANFORD: STANFORD UNIVERSITY PRESS, 1959.
            (ANXIETY SCALES)
        aS-170 1959M ANXIETY TEST DEPRESSION NEED AFFILIATION
            (APPLICATIONS: 324   519)

S-171   SCHAIE, K. W.
            MEASURING BEHAVIORAL RIGIDITY: A FACTORIAL INVESTIGATION OF SOME TESTS
            OF RIGID BEHAVIOR.
            UNPUBLISHED MASTERS THESIS, UNIVERSITY OF WASHINGTON, 1953.
            SCHAIE, K. W.
            A TEST OF BEHAVIORAL RIGIDITY.
            JOURNAL OF ABNORMAL AND SOCIAL PSYCHOLOGY, 1955, 51, 604-610.
            (TESTS OF BEHAVIORAL RIGIDITY)*
        aS-171 1953M BEHAVIOR RIGIDITY PERSONALITY PERCEPTION COGNITIVE RIGIDITY
            (APPLICATIONS: 2239   2886)

S-172   SCHOOLER, C., & SCARR, S.
            AFFILIATION AMONG CHRONIC SCHIZOPHRENICS: RELATION TO INTERPERSONAL
            AND BIRTH ORDER FACTORS.
            JOURNAL OF PERSONALITY, 1962, 30, 178-192.
            (INTERPERSONAL ATTITUDE SCALE)
        aS-172 1962M SOCIAL ATTITUDE INTERPERSONAL COGNITIVE STRUCTURE CONSISTENCY
        aS-172 COPING-DEFENSE DISCREPANCY PEOPLE BELIEF

S-173   SPOHN, H. E., & WOLK, W.
            THE EFFECT OF CHANGES IN THE SOCIAL STIMULUS SITUATION UPON SOCIAL
            PARTICIPATION IN CHRONIC SCHIZOPHRENICS.
            PAPER READ AT EASTERN PSYCHOLOGICAL ASSOCIATION, NEW YORK, APRIL, 1957.
            (SPOHN WARD BEHAVIOR SCALE)
        aS-173 1957M BEHAVIOR WARD PSYCHIATRIC SOCIAL INTERACTION INTERPERSONAL
            (APPLICATIONS: 354   1145)

S-174   STICE.
            NO REFERENCE; CITED IN:
            MESSICK, S., & FRITZKY, F. J.
            DIMENSIONS OF ANALYTIC ATTITUDE IN COGNITION AND PERSONALITY.
            JOURNAL OF PERSONALITY, 1963, 31, 346-370.
            (UNCONVENTIONALITY SCALE)
        aS-174 AUTONOMY BEHAVIOR CONFORMITY DEVIANCE SOCIAL DEPENDENCE ATTITUDE
            (APPLICATIONS: 386)

S-175   STICE.
            NO REFERENCE; CITED IN:
            MESSICK, S., & FRITZKY, F. J.
            DIMENSIONS OF ANALYTIC ATTITUDE IN COGNITION AND PERSONALITY.
            JOURNAL OF PERSONALITY, 1963, 31, 346-370.
            (AFFECTIVE-EFFECTIVE SCALE)
        aS-175 INTEREST ORIENTATION PERSONAL ACTIVITIES ESTHETIC
            (APPLICATIONS: 386)

S-176   SAPPENFIELD, B. R.
            TEST OF A SZONDI ASSUMPTION BY MEANS OF M-F PHOTOGRAPHS.
            JOURNAL OF PERSONALITY, 1965, 33, 409-417.
            (MEASURE OF PERCEIVED MASCULINITY-FEMININITY FROM PHOTOGRAPHS)
        aS-176 1965M MASCULINITY FEMINITY SELF-IDENTITY PERCEIVED SUB-IDENTITY
        aS-176 ROLE SEX IDENTITY INTERPERSONAL SOCIAL PERCEPTION

S-177   SCHRODER, H. M., & HUNT, D. E.
            THE ROLE OF THREE PROCESSES IN DETERMINING RESPONSES TO INTERPERSONAL
            DISAGREEMENT.
            JOINT ONR AND NIMH PROGRESS REPORT, 1959.
            (MEASURE OF SITUATIONAL INTERPRETATION)
        aS-177 1959M SITUATIONAL INTERPERSONAL IMAGINATION
        aS-177 PERCEPTION SOCIAL INTERACTION CONFLICT TENSION
            (APPLICATIONS: 366)

S-178   SECORD, P. F.
            STEREOTYPING AND FAVORABLENESS IN THE PERCEPTION OF NEGRO FACES.
            JOURNAL OF ABNORMAL AND SOCIAL PSYCHOLOGY, 1959, 59, 309-314.
            (PREJUDICE SCALE)
        aS-178 1969M PREJUDICE NEGRO ATTITUDE RACIAL STEREOTYPE
        aS-178 ETHNOCENTRISM
            (APPLICATIONS: 365)

S-179   SMITH, C. P., & FELD, S.
               HOW TO LEARN THE METHOD OF CONTENT ANALYSIS FOR N ACHIEVEMENT, N
               AFFILIATION AND N POWER.
               IN J.W. ATKINSON (ED.), MOTIVES IN FANTASY, ACTION, AND SOCIETY. PRINCETON,
               N.J.: VAN NOSTRAND, 1958.
               (TAT SCORING METHODS FOR NEED ACHIEVEMENT, AFFILIATION, AND POWER)
           @S-179 1958M TAT PROJECTIVE IMAGERY NEED AUTONOMY ACHIEVEMENT AFFILIATION POWER
               (APPLICATIONS: 455)

S-180   STEVENSON, H. W., & ALLEN, S. A.
               VARIABLES ASSOCIATED WITH ADULTS' EFFECTIVENESS AS REINFORCING AGENTS.
               JOURNAL OF PERSONALITY, 1967, 35, 246-264.
               (PERSON-PERCEPTION SCALE)
           @S-180 1967M SEM-DIFFERENTIAL OTHERS PERCEPTION DESCRIPTION IMPRESSION FORMATION

S-181   SULZER, J. L., & BURGLASS, R. K.
               RESPONSIBILITY ATTRIBUTION, EMPATHY, AND PUNITIVENESS.
               JOURNAL OF PERSONALITY, 1968, 36, 272-282.
               (ATTRIBUTION OF RESPONSIBILITY TEST)
           @S-181 1968M ATTRIBUTION RESPONSIBILITY GUILT PUNITIVENESS PROJECTIVE DIRECTION
           @S-181 AGGRESSION
               (APPLICATIONS: 485)

S-182   SECORD, P. F., & BERSCHEID, E. S.
               STEREOTYPING AND THE GENERALITY OF IMPLICIT PERSONALITY THEORY.
               JOURNAL OF PERSONALITY, 1963, 31, 65-78.
               (MEASURE OF STEREOTYPE SCORES FROM STIMULUS PERSON)
           @S-182 1963M STEREOTYPE STIMULUS PERSON TRAIT NEGRO PREJUDICE
           @S-182 PERCEPTION RIGIDITY ETHNOCENTRICITY

S-183   SCHILL, T.
               THE EFFECTS OF TYPE AND STRENGTH OF INDUCED CONFLICT ON CONFLICT
               GENERALIZATION AND LATER PREFERENCE FOR CONFLICT STIMULI.
               JOURNAL OF PERSONALITY, 1966, 34, 35-54.
               (TRAIT RATING QUESTIONNAIRE)
           @S-183 1966M TRAIT RATING APPROVAL SELF OTHERS PERSONALITY
           @S-183 SOCIAL DESIRABILITY IDEAL

S-184   STEINER, I. D., & SPAULDING, J.
               PREFERENCE FOR BALANCED SITUATIONS.
               TECHNICAL REPORT, NATIONAL INSTITUTES OF HEALTH, NO.M-4460 REPORT 1, 1966.
               (PREFERENCE FOR BALANCED SITUATIONS TEST)
           @S-184 1966M COGNITIVE STYLE COMPLEXITY
           @S-184 CONSISTENCY STRUCTURE PREFERENCE NEED
               (APPLICATIONS: 496   851)

S-186   STRUENING, E. L., & RICHARDSON, A. H.
               THE DIMENSIONAL STRUCTURE OF THE ALIENATION, ANOMIA, AND AUTHORITARIANISM
               DOMAIN.
               PAPER PRESENTED AT AMERICAN PSYCHOLOGICAL ASSOCIATION, LOS ANGELES, 1964.
           KLEIN, E. B., & STRUENING, E.
               ATTITUDES TOWARDS THE UNITED NATIONS.
               UNPUBLISHED STUDY, 1961.
               (MANIFEST ALIENATION MEASURE)*
           @S-186 1964M MANIFEST ALIENATION ANOMIE NEGATIVE AFFECTIVE-STATES CYNICISM
           @S-186 POLITICAL

S-187   SEEMAN, J.
               COUNSELOR JUDGMENTS OF THERAPUETIC PROCESS AND OUTCOME.
               IN C. R. ROGERS AND R. F. DYMOND (ED.), PSYCHOTHERAPY AND PERSONALITY
               CHANGE.
               CHICAGO: UNIVERSITY OF CHICAGO PRESS, 1954.
               (CASE RATING SCALE)*
           @S-187 1954M RATING COUNSELING THERAPY PROGNOSIS
               (APPLICATIONS: 57   1190   1632   1633   1769)

S-188   STERN, M.
               A STUDY OF THE RELATIONSHIP BETWEEN ATTITUDE TOWARD CERTAIN AUTHORITY
               FIGURES AND JOB STABILITY IN A GROUP OF PSYCHONEUROTIC VETERANS.
               UNPUBLISHED DOCTORAL DISSERTATION, NEW YORK UNIVERSITY, 1952.
               (TAT SCORED FOR ATTITUDES TOWARDS AUTHORITY FIGURES)
           @S-188 1952M TAT PROJECTIVE ATTITUDE AUTHORITY AGGRESSION DEPENDENCE JOB
           @S-188 SECURITY AUTONOMY AUTHORITARIANISM
               (APPLICATIONS: 1586)

S-190   SCHAFER, R.
              THE CLINICAL APPLICATION OF PSYCHOLOGICAL TESTS.
              NEW YORK: INTERNATIONAL UNIVERSITY PRESS, 1948
              (RORSCHACH SCORED FOR INDICES OF SCHIZOPHRENIC DISORGANIZATION)
         ƏS-190 1948M RORSCHACH SCHIZOPHRENIA MENTAL-ILLNESS SYMPTOM DIAGNOSTIC
         ƏS-190 PROJECTIVE PSYCHIATRIC
              (APPLICATIONS: 1627)

S-191   SHELDON, W. H.
              THE VARIETIES OF TEMPERAMENT.
              NEW-YORK: HARPER, 1942.
              (MEASURE OF TEMPERAMENT)
         ƏS-191 1942M TEMPERAMENT SOMATOTYPE BODY

S-192   SUTTON-SMITH, B., & ROSENBERG, B. G.
              A SCALE TO IDENTIFY IMPULSIVE BEHAVIOR IN CHILDREN.
              JOURNAL OF GENETIC PSYCHOLOGY, 1959, 95, 211-216.
              (MEASURE OF IMPULSIVE BEHAVIOR)
         ƏS-192 1959M CHILD IMPULSE EXPRESSION BEHAVIOR
         ƏS-192 CONTROL INHIBITION
              (APPLICATIONS: 1641 1837)

S-193   SHLEIN, J. M.
              AN EXPERIMENTAL EVALUATION OF TIME LIMITED, BRIEF, CLIENT-CENTERED
              PSYCHOTHERAPY.
              UNPUBLISHED DOCTORAL DISSERTATION, UNIVERSITY OF CHICAGO, 1957.
              (LEVEL OF ADJUSTMENT Q-SORT)
         ƏS-193 1957M ADJUSTMENT Q-SORT SELF IMAGE IDEAL SELF
              (APPLICATIONS: 1918)

S-194   SHEPPARD, E., & SAUL, L. J.
              A SYSTEMATIC STUDY OF EGO FUNCTION.
              PSYCHOANALYTIC QUARTERLY, 1958, 27, 237-245.
              (EGO RATING SYSTEM)
         ƏS-194 1958M EGO CONTROL PRIMARY-PROCESS THINKING BODY IMAGE
              (APPLICATIONS: 1951)

S-195   STEIN, K. B., & CRAIK, K. H.
              RELATIONSHIP BETWEEN MOTORIC AND IDEATIONAL ACTIVITY PREFERENCE AND TIME
              PERSPECTIVE IN NEUROTICS AND SCHIZOPHRENICS.
              JOURNAL OF CONSULTING PSYCHOLOGY, 1965, 29, 460-467.
              (MOTORIC-IDEATIONAL ACTIVITY PREFERENCE SCALE)*
         ƏS-195 1965M ACTIVITIES ACTIVE PASSIVE THINKING

S-196   STEIN, K. B., & CRAIK, K. H.
              RELATIONSHIP BETWEEN MOTORIC AND IDEATIONAL ACTIVITY PREFERENCE AND TIME
              PERSPECTIVE IN NEUROTICS AND SCHIZOPHRENICS.
              JOURNAL OF CONSULTING PSYCHOLOGY, 1965, 29, 460-467.
              (PAST EVENTS TEST)
         ƏS-196 1965M TIME PERSPECTIVE AFFECTIVE-STATES POSITIVE NEGATIVE

S-197   SPEISMAN, J. C., LAZARUS, R. S., DAVISON, L., & MORDKOFF, A. M.
              EXPERIMENTAL ANALYSIS OF A FILM USED AS A THREATENING STIMULUS
              JOURNAL OF CONSULTING PSYCHOLOGY, 1964, 28, 23-33.
              (SCALES FOR PRIMARY NARCISSISM AND SADO-MASOCHISM)
         ƏS-197 1964M AFFECTIVE-STATES PAIN TOLERANCE BODY SELF
         ƏS-197 AGGRESSION

S-198   SURBER, C. P.
              PREDICTING IMPROVEMENT OF PSYCHIATRIC PATIENTS FROM EARLY WARD SOCIALIZING
              RATINGS.
              JOURNAL OF CONSULTING PSYCHOLOGY, 1961, 25, 461.
              (MEASURE OF WARD ISOLATION AND SOCIALIZING BEHAVIOR)
         ƏS-198 1961M PSYCHIATRIC PATIENT WARD BEHAVIOR ACCULTURATION

S-199   SLATER, P. E.
              PSYCHOLOGICAL FACTORS IN ROLE SPECIALIZATION.
              UNPUBLISHED DOCTORAL DISSERTATION, HARVARD UNIVERSITY, 1955.
              SLATER, P. E.
              PSYCHOLOGICAL FACTORS IN ROLE SPECIALIZATION.
              (PARENT ROLE PATTERNS QUESTIONNAIRE)*
         ƏS-199 1955M PARENTAL PARENT-CHILD FAMILY INTERACTION BEHAVIOR PATERNAL MATERNAL
         ƏS-199 ROLE SUPPORT EMOTION INHIBITION DEMANDS
              (APPLICATIONS: 1986)

S-200   SIGAL, J. J.
              THE VERDUN ASSOCIATION LIST: A STANDARDIZED FOUR MEASURE SCREENING TEST.
              UNPUBLISHED DOCTORAL DISSERTATION, UNIVERSITY OF MONTREAL, 1956.
          SIGAL, J. J., & DORKEN, H.
              WORD ASSOCIATION COMMONALITY: A STANDARDIZED TEST AND A THEORY.
              JOURNAL OF CONSULTING PSYCHOLOGY, 1966, 30, 402-407.
              (VERDUN ASSOCIATION LIST)
          @S-200 1956M STIMULUS PATIENT DIFFERENTIATION

S-201   SHIPE, D.
              DISCREPANCIES BETWEEN THE PEABODY PICTURE VOCABULARY TEST AND THE WISC AS
              RELATED TO EMOTIONAL DISTURBANCE IN CHILDREN OF RETARDED AND NORMAL
              INTELLIGENCE.
              ANN ARBOR, MICHIGAN: UNIVERSITY MICROFILMS, 1962, NO. 63-1894.
              (BEHAVIOR RATING SCALE)
          @S-201 1962M BEHAVIOR RATING NORMALITY WITHDRAWAL INTELLIGENCE MENTAL-ILLNESS
              (APPLICATIONS: 1050 2007)

S-202   SUNDLAND, D. M., & BARKER, E. N.
              THE ORIENTATIONS OF PSYCHOTHERAPISTS.
              JOURNAL OF CONSULTING PSYCHOLOGY, 1962, 26, 201-212.
              (THERAPIST ORIENTATION QUESTIONNAIRE)*
          @S-202 1962M THERAPY COUNSELING ORIENTATION PATIENT RELATIONSHIPS
              (APPLICATIONS: 1874)

S-204   STEIN, M. I.
              EXPLORATIONS IN CREATIVITY.
              UNPUBLISHED MANUSCRIPT, 1960.
              (EGO-STRENGTH SCALE)
          @S-204 1960M EGO-STRENGTH EGO-RESILIENCY CONTROL
              (APPLICATIONS: 1856)

S-205   SHANAN, J.
              PERSONALITY CORRELATES OF CREATIVITY IN SCIENTISTS.
              UNPUBLISHED DOCTORAL DISSERTATION, UNIVERSITY OF CHICAGO, 1956.
              (MEASURE OF AUTONOMY)
          @S-205 1956M AUTONOMY CREATIVITY IMAGINATION ORIGINALITY
              (APPLICATIONS: 1856)

S-206   STEIN, M. I.
              EXPLORATIONS IN CREATIVITY.
              UNPUBLISHED MANUSCRIPT, 1960.
              (MEASURE OF OPTIMAL PERSONALITY INTEGRATION)
          @S-206 1960M PERSONALITY INTEGRATION NEED MANIFEST SELF DESCRIPTION IDEAL
          @S-206 1960M ABASEMENT ACHIEVEMENT DOMINANCE
              (APPLICATIONS: 1856)

S-208   SCHULTZ, S. D.
              A DIFFERENTIATION OF SEVERAL FORMS OF HOSTILITY BY SCALES EMPIRICALLY
              CONSTRUCTED FROM SIGNIFICANT ITEMS ON THE MMPI.
              DISSERTATION ABSTRACTS, 1955, 17, 717-720.
              (HOSTILITY CONTROL SCALE)
          @S-208 1955M MMPI HOSTILITY CONTROL AFFECTIVE-STATES
          @S-208 EXPRESSION INHIBITION
              (APPLICATIONS: 2019 2124)

S-209   STEIN, M. I.
              EXPLORATIONS IN CREATIVITY.
              UNPUBLISHED MANUSCRIPT, 1960.
              (MEASURES OF CREATIVITY)
          @S-209 1960M CREATIVITY PEER SUPERVISOR RATING ORIGINALITY NOVELTY
              (APPLICATIONS: 1856 2167)

S-210   SPILKEN, A. Z., JACOBS, M. A., MULLER, J. J., & KNITZER, J.
              PERSONALITY CHARACTERISTICS OF THERAPISTS: DESCRIPTION OF RELEVANT
              VARIABLES AND EXAMINATION OF CONSCIOUS PREFERENCES.
              JOURNAL OF CONSULTING AND CLINICAL PSYCHOLOGY, 1969, 33, 317-326.
              (PSYCHOTHERAPISTS PREFERENCE SCALE)
          @S-210 1969M COUNSELING ROLE PREFERENCE VALUES IDEALS PSYCHIATRIC RATING
          @S-210 THERAPY

S-211   SINES, J. O., PAUKER, J. D., SINES, L. K., & OWEN, D. R.
              IDENTIFICATION OF CLINICALLY RELEVANT DIMENSIONS IN CHILDREN'S BEHAVIOR.
              JOURNAL OF CONSULTING AND CLINICAL PSYCHOLOGY, 1969, 33, 728-734.
              (MISSOURI CHILDREN'S BEHAVIOR CHECKLIST)*
          @S-211 1969M CHILD BEHAVIOR CHECKLIST PARENTAL AGGRESSION ACTIVE PASSIVE
          @S-211 1969M INHIBITION SOCIABILITY

S-212   SMITH, G. M.
          USEFULNESS OF PEER RATINGS OF PERSONALITY IN EDUCATIONAL RESEARCH.
          EDUCATIONAL AND PSYCHOLOGICAL MEASUREMENT, 1967, 27, 967-984.
          (MEASURE OF PERSONALITY BY PEER RATINGS.)
     @S-212 1967 PEER RATING PERSONALITY TRAIT GLOBAL
          (APPLICATIONS: 2284)

S-213   SANTOSTEFANO, S.
          FORCED-CHOICE ACTS AS MEASURES OF PERSONALITY.
          UNPUBLISHED DOCTORAL DISSERTATION, PENNSYLVANIA STATE UNIVERSITY, 1957.
          (MEASURE OF PERSONALITY FROM FORCED-CHOICE ACTS)
     @S-213 1957M DECISION SITUATIONAL ACTIVITIES PERSONALITY
          (APPLICATIONS: 2291)

S-214   SHYBUT, J.
          DELAY OF GRATIFICATION AND SEVERITY OF PSYCHOLOGICAL DISTURBANCE AMONG
          HOSPITALIZED PSYCHIATRIC PATIENTS.
          JOURNAL OF CONSULTING AND CLINICAL PSYCHOLOGY, 1968, 32, 462-468.
          (SEVERITY OF DISTURBANCE RATING SCALE)
     @S-214 1968M MENTAL-ILLNESS RATING PSYCHIATRIC PATIENT ADJUSTMENT

S-215   SHYBUT, J.
          DELAY OF GRATIFICATION AND SEVERITY OF PSYCHOLOGICAL DISTURBANCE AMONG
          HOSPITALIZED PSYCHIATRIC PATIENTS.
          JOURNAL OF CONSULTING AND CLINICAL PSYCHOLOGY, 1968, 32, 462-468.
          (DELAY OF GRATIFICATION MEASURES)
     @S-215 1968M MENTAL-ILLNESS PATIENT PSYCHOANALYTIC FUTURE
     @S-215 PRESENT ORIENTATION TIME

S-216   SHOSTROM, E. L., & RILEY, C. M. D.
          PARAMETRIC ANALYSIS OF PSYCHOTHERAPY.
          JOURNAL OF CONSULTING AND CLINICAL PSYCHOLOGY, 1968, 32, 628-632.
          (THERAPEUTIC RATING FORM)
     @S-216 1968M THERAPY COUNSELING RATING EGO-STRENGTH FEELING EXPERIENCE
     @S-216 INTERPERSONAL CLIENT THERAPIST RELATIONSHIPS COUNSELOR PATIENT

S-217   SARASON, I. G.
          THE ANXIETY ABOUT HOSTILITY SCALE.
          UNPUBLISHED RESEARCH, UNIVERSITY OF WASHINGTON, 1961.
          (ANXIETY ABOUT HOSTILITY SCALE)
     @S-217 1961M ANXIETY HOSTILITY EXPRESSION INHIBITION CONTROL
          (APPLICATIONS: 2211)

S-218   SCHNEIDER, B., & BARTLETT, C. J.
          INDIVIDUAL DIFFERENCES AND ORGANIZATIONAL CLIMATE II: MEASUREMENT OF
          ORGANIZATIONAL CLIMATE BY THE MULTI-TRAIT, MULTI-RATER MATRIX.
          PERSONNEL PSYCHOLOGY, 1970, 23, 493-512.
          (AGENCY CLIMATE QUESTIONNAIRE)*
     @S-218 ORGANIZATION ENVIRONMENT EFFECTIVENESS JOB ADJUSTMENT ATTITUDE JOB
     @S-218 1970M SATISFACTION

S-219   SMITH, E. E.
          EFFECTS OF THREAT INDUCED BY AMBIGUOUS ROLE EXPECTATIONS ON DEFENSIVENESS
          AND PRODUCTIVITY IN SMALL GROUPS.
          TECHNICAL REPORT NO. 1, AUG. 1956, CONTRACT NONR-1147 (03) NR 170-226.
          (MEASURE OF DEFENSIVENESS TOWARD A GROUP)
     @S-219 1956M DEFENSIVENESS GROUP SECURITY SOCIAL COMPETENCE INTERPERSONAL
          (APPLICATIONS: 599)

S-221   SYMONDS, P. M.
          ADOLESCENT FANTASY.
          NEW YORK:COLUMBIA UNIVERSITY PRESS, 1949.
          (PICTURE STORY TEST)
     @S-221 1949M GRAPHIC FANTASY ADOLESCENT IMAGINATION
     @S-221 PROJECTIVE STORY-COMPLETION
          (APPLICATIONS: 727)

S-222   SPOHN, H. E., & WOLK, W.
          EFFECT OF GROUP PROBLEM SOLVING EXPERIENCE UPON SOCIAL WITHDRAWAL IN
          CHRONIC SCHIZOPHRENICS.
          JOURNAL OF ABNORMAL AND SOCIAL PSYCHOLOGY, 1963, 66, 187-190.
          (MEASURE OF LEVEL OF SOCIAL PARTICIPATION IN TASKS)
     @S-222 1963M SOCIAL PARTICIPATION ACTIVITIES GROUP SCHIZOPHRENIC PSYCHIATRIC
     @S-222 PATIENT WITHDRAWAL INTERACTION
          (APPLICATIONS: 992)

S-223   SARASON, I. G.
             INTERRELATIONSHIPS AMONG INDIVIDUAL DIFFERENCE VARIABLES, BEHAVIOR IN
             PSYCHOTHERAPY, AND VERBAL CONDITIONING.
             JOURNAL OF ABNORMAL AND SOCIAL PSYCHOLOGY, 1958, 56, 339-344.
             (LACK OF PROTECTION SCALE)*
         @S-223 1958M ANXIETY SITUATIONAL NEED DEPENDENCE FEELING POWERLESSNESS
             (APPLICATIONS: 631   633)

S-224   SASLOW, G., COUNTS, R. N., & DUBOIS, P. H.
             EVALUATION OF A NEW PSYCHIATRIC SCREENING TEST.
             PSYCHOSOMATIC MEDICINE, 1951, 13, 242-253.
             (SASLOW PSYCHOSOMATIC SCREENING INVENTORY)*
         @S-224 1951M EVALUATION DIAGNOSIS PSYCHOSOMATIC SYMPTOM PSYCHIATRIC
         @S-224 MENTAL-ILLNESS MENTAL-HEALTH
             (APPLICATIONS: 614)

S-225   SROLE, L.
             SOCIAL INTEGRATION AND CERTAIN COROLLARIES: AN EXPLORATORY STUDY.
             AMERICAN SOCIOLOGICAL REVIEW, 1956, 21, 709-716.
             (ANTIMINORITY SCALE)
         @S-225 1956M ATTITUDE MINORITY PREJUDICE ETHNOCENTRICISM ETHNIC RACIAL
             (APPLICATIONS: 613)

S-226   SCHULBERG, H. C.
             AUTHORITARIANISM, TENDENCY TO AGREE, AND INTERPERSONAL PERCEPTION.
             JOURNAL OF ABNORMAL AND SOCIAL PSYCHOLOGY, 1961, 63, 101-108.
             (ADJECTIVE RATING SCALE)*
         @S-226 1961M SELF RATING PERSONALITY ADJECTIVE SEM-DIFFERENTIAL
         @S-226 AUTHORITARIANISM DOGMATISM RIGIDITY FLEXIBILITY

S-227   SINNETT, E. R., & HANFORD, D. B.
             THE EFFECTS OF PATIENTS' RELATIONSHIPS WITH PEERS AND STAFF ON THEIR
             PSYCHIATRIC TREATMENT PROGRAMS.
             JOURNAL OF ABNORMAL AND SOCIAL PSYCHOLOGY, 1962, 64, 151-154.
             (MEASURE OF PATIENT'S RELATIONSHIPS)
         @S-227 1962M PATIENT THERAPY RELATIONSHIPS INTERPERSONAL SOCIOMETRIC
         @S-227 PEER

S-228   SNOEK, J. D.
             SOME EFFECTS OF REJECTION UPON ATTRACTION TO A GROUP.
             JOURNAL OF ABNORMAL AND SOCIAL PSYCHOLOGY, 1962, 64, 175-182.
             (MEASURE OF SUBJECTIVE PROBABILITY OF ACCEPTANCE)
         @S-228 1962M GROUP ACCEPTANCE SOCIAL
         @S-228 ATTRACTION INTERPERSONAL SECURITY

S-229   SZONDI, L.
             EXPERIMENTELLE TRIEBDIAGNOSTIK. BERN: HANS HUBER, 1947.
         GOLDMAN, G. D.
             THE VALIDATION OF THE PAROXYSMAL VECTOR OF THE SZONDI TEST.
             JOURNAL OF ABNORMAL AND SOCIAL PSYCHOLOGY, 1952, 47, 475-477.
             (SZONDI TEST)*
         @S-229 1947M LOCUS CONTROL EMOTION PSYCHOPATHOLOGY
             (APPLICATIONS: 421)

S-230   SCHAEFFER, E. S.
             MULTIVARIATE MEASUREMENT AND FACTORIAL STRUCTURE OF CHILDREN'S PERCEPTIONS
             OF MATERNAL AND PATERNAL BEHAVIOR.
             AMERICAN PSYCHOLOGIST, 1961, 16, 345-346. (ABSTRACT)
             (PARENT BEHAVIOR INVENTORY)
         @S-230 1961M PARENTAL BEHAVIOR PARENT-CHILD RELATIONSHIPS FAMILY INTERACTION
             (APPLICATIONS: 839)

S-231   SCOTT, W. A.
             INTERNATIONAL IDEOLOGY AND INTERPERSONAL IDEOLOGY.
             PUBLIC OPINION QUARTERLY, 1960, 24, 419-435.
             (SCALES OF PERSONAL VALUES)
         @S-231 1960M PERSONAL VALUES INTERPERSONAL RELATIONSHIPS SOCIAL NEED AUTONOMY
         @S-231 BEHAVIOR SELF DESCRIPTION EVALUATION INTERNATIONALISM POLITICAL
             (APPLICATIONS: 843)

S-232   SALTZ, G., & EPSTEIN, E.
             THEMATIC HOSTILITY AND GUILT RESPONSES AS RELATED TO SELF-REPORTED
             HOSTILITY, GUILT, AND CONFLICT.
             JOURNAL OF ABNORMAL AND SOCIAL PSYCHOLOGY, 1963, 67, 469-479.
             (THEMATIC HOSTILITY TEST)
         @S-232 1963M PROJECTIVE TAT HOSTILITY DIRECTION NEED GUILT AGGRESSION INTENSITY
         @S-232 EMOTION
             (APPLICATIONS: 1730)

S-233   SALTZ, G., & EPSTEIN, E.
             THEMATIC HOSTILITY AND GUILT RESPONSES AS RELATED TO SELF-REPORTED
             HOSTILITY, GUILT, AND CONFLICT.
             JOURNAL OF ABNORMAL AND SOCIAL PSYCHOLOGY, 1963, 67, 469-479.
             (QUESTIONNAIRE HOSTILITY, GUILT, AND CONFLICT)
         aS-233 1963M HOSTILITY GUILT CONFLICT MMPI DIRECTION AGGRESSION PE-FIT COPING
         aS-233 DEFENSE

S-234   SARASON, I. G.
             INTERRELATIONSHIPS AMONG INDIVIDUAL DIFFERENCE VARIABLES, BEHAVIOR IN
             PSYCHOTHERAPY, AND VERBAL CONDITIONING.
             JOURNAL OF ABNORMAL AND SOCIAL PSYCHOLOGY, 1958, 56, 339-344.
             (HOSTILITY SCALE)
         aS-234 1958M HOSTILITY NEGATIVE AFFECTIVE-STATES AGGRESSION
             (APPLICATIONS: 204   854)

S-235   SOUEIF, M. I.
             EXTREME RESPONSE SETS AS A MEASURE OF INTOLERANCE OF AMBIGUITY.
             BRITISH JOURNAL OF PSYCHOLOGY, 1958, 49, 329-334.
             (PERSONAL FRIENDS QUESTIONNAIRE)
         aS-235 1958M RESPONSE SET RIGIDITY FLEXIBILITY TOLERANCE AMBIGUITY PROJECTIVE
         aS-235 AUTHORITARIANISM

S-237   SCHLOSBERG, H.
             A SCALE FOR THE JUDGMENT OF FACIAL EXPRESSIONS.
             JOURNAL OF EXPERIMENTAL PSYCHOLOGY, 1941, 29, 497-510.
             (SCALE OF FACIAL EXPRESSIONS)
         aS-237 1941M GRAPHIC EXPRESSION FIGURE NEGATIVE POSITIVE AFFECTIVE-STATES
         aS-237 JUDGMENT EVALUATION SOCIAL INTERPERSONAL PERCEPTION
             (APPLICATIONS: 863)

S-239   SHORT, J. F., JR., & NYE, F. I.
             CRITERION OF DEVIANT BEHAVIOR.
             SOCIAL PROBLEMS, 1958, 5, 207-214.
             (MEASURE OF JUVENILE DELINQUENCY)
         aS-239 1958M DELINQUENCY CHILD BEHAVIOR ALIENATION SOCIAL ROLE
         aS-239 DEVIANCE ADJUSTMENT
             (APPLICATIONS: 986)

S-242   SPIVACK, G., & SWIFT, M. S.
             THE DEVEREUX ELEMENTARY SCHOOL RATING SCALE: A STUDY OF THE NATURE AND
             ORGANIZATION OF ACHIEVEMENT RELATED DISTURBED CLASSROM BEHAVIOR.
             JOURNAL OF SPECIAL EDUCATION, 1966, 1, 71-90.
             (DEVEREUX ELEMENTARY SCHOOL RATING SCALE)*
         aS-242 1966M CHILD BEHAVIOR TEACHER RATING SCHOOL
         aS-242 RELATIONSHIPS DEVIANCE
         aS-242 ADJUSTMENT INTERPERSONAL INTERACTION SOCIAL MATURITY
             (APPLICATIONS: 1094)

S-243   SPIVACK, G., & LEVINE, M.
             THE DEVEREUX CHILD BEHAVIOR RATING SCALES: A STUDY OF SYMPTOM BEHAVIORS
             IN LATENCY AGE ATYPICAL CHILDREN.
             AMERICAN JOURNAL OF MENTAL DEFICIENCY, 1964, 68, 700-717.
             (DEVEREUX CHILD BEHAVIOR RATING SCALES)*
         aS-243 1964M CHILD BEHAVIOR RATING TEACHER HOSTILITY DEPRESSION
         aS-243 MENTAL-ILLNESS PSYCHIATRIC DIAGNOSIS SOCIAL SENSITIVITY COOPERATIVENESS
             (APPLICATIONS: 1094)

S-244   STROOP, J. R.
             STUDIES IN INTERFERENCE IN SERIAL VERBAL REACTIONS.
             JOURNAL OF EXPERIMENTAL PSYCHOLOGY, 1935, 18, 643-661.
             (STROOP COLOR-WORD TEST)
         aS-244 1935M COGNITIVE FUNCTIONING PERCEPTION STIMULUS AMBIGUITY JUDGMENT

S-245   STEIN, K. B., & LENROW, P.
             EXPRESSIVE STYLES AND THEIR MEASUREMENT.
             JOURNAL OF PERSONALITY AND SOCIAL PSYCHOLOGY, 1970, 16, 656-664.
             (MOTORIC IDEATIONAL SENSORY TEST (MIST))*
         aS-245 1970M SENSORY ORIENTATION IMAGINATION ORIGINALITY PERCEPTION INTEREST
         aS-245 PERSONALITY SELF EXPRESSION COGNITIVE STYLE

S-246   STEIN, K. B., SARBIN, T. R., CHU, C. L., & KULIK, J. A.
         ADOLESCENT MORALITY: ITS DIFFERENTED STRUCTURE AND RELATICN TO DELINQUENT
         CONDUCT.
         MULTIVARIATE BEHAVIORAL RESEARCH, 1967, 2, 199-210.
         (MEASURES OF MORAL JUDGMENT)
         aS-246 1967M MORAL JUDGMENT ADOLESCENT DELINQUENT
         aS-246 VALUES

S-247   SARBIN, T. R., & STEIN, K. B.
         SELF-ROLE THEORY AND ANTISOCIAL CONDUCT, A PROGRESS REPORT.
         BETHESDA: NATIONAL INSTITUTE OF MENTAL HEALTH, 1967.
         (BODY CATHEXIS TEST)
         aS-247 1967M BODY CATHEXIS IMPULSE EXPRESION DIRECTION EMOTICN

S-248   SANTROCK, J. W.
         PATERNAL ABSENCE, SEX TYPING, AND IDENTIFICATION.
         DEVELOPMENTAL PSYCHOLOGY, 1970, 2, 264-272.
         (DOLL-PLAY INTERVIEW)
         aS-248 1970M DEPENDENCE AUTONOMY FEMININITY MASCULINITY SEX ROLE AGGRESSION
         aAGGRESSIVENESS HOSTILITY CONFRCNTATION DIRECTION EXPRESSION DOMINANCE

S-249   STORY, R. I.
         EFFECTS ON THINKING OF RELATIONSHIPS BETWEEN CONFLICT AROUSAL AND ORAL
         FIXATION.
         JOURNAL OF ABNORMAL PSYCHOLOGY, 1968, 73, 440-448.
         (PROVERBS TEST OF ORALITY)
         aS-249 1968M ORALITY ADJUSTMENT NEUROTICISM

S-251   STRODTBECK, F. L.
         FAMILY INTERACTION, VALUES, AND ACHIEVEMENT.
         IN D. C. MCCLELLAND, A. L. BALDWIN, U. BRONFENBRENNEC, & F. L. STRODTBECK
         (EDS.), TALENT AND SOCIETY.
         NEW YORK: VAN NOSTRAND, 1958.
         (FUTURE ORIENTATION SCALE)
         aS-251 1958M TIME PERSPECTIVE FUTURE ORIENTATION
         (APPLICATIONS: 2789)

S-252   SAVITSKY, J. C., & IZARD, C. E.
         DEVELOPMENTAL CHANGES IN THE USE OF EMOTION CUES IN A CCNCEPT-FORMATION
         TASK.
         DEVELOPMENTAL PSYCHOLOGY, 1970, 3, 350-357.
         (MEASURE OF CONCEPT-FORMATICN FROM PHCTOGRAPHS)
         aS-252 1970M CONCEPT IMAGE FIGURE GRAPHIC FORMATION IMPRESSICN EMOTION OTHERS

S-253   SMITH, T. E.
         FOUNDATIONS OF PARENTAL INFLUENCE UPON ADOLESCENTS: AN APPLICATION OF
         SOCIAL POWER THEORY.
         AMERICAN SOCIOLOGICAL REVIEW, 1970, 35, 860-873.
         (MEASURE OF POWER AND PARENTAL INFLUENCE)
         aS-253 1970M PARENTAL POWER ADOLESCENT INFLUENCE MATERNAL PATERNAL ACADEMIC SEX
         aDEPENDENCE AUTONCMY

S-254   SIGEL, I. E.
         SIGEL COGNITIVE STYLE TEST.
         DETROIT:MERRILL PALMER INSTITUTE, 1967.
         (COGNITIVE STYLE TEST)*
         aS-254 1967M COGNITIVE STYLE THINKING ANALYTIC
         (APPLICATIONS: 2787)

S-255   SHEEHAN, P. W.
         A SHORTENED FORM OF BETTS QUESTIONNAIRE UPON MENTAL IMAGERY.
         JOURNAL OF CLINICAL PSYCHOLOGY, 1967, 23, 386-389.
         (SHORT FORM OF QUESTIONNAIRE ON MENTAL IMAGERY)
         aS-255 1967M IMAGERY PRIMARY-PROCESS SENSORY B-226R

S-256   SCHWARTZ, B. J.
         THE MEASUREMENT OF CASTRATION ANXIETY AND ANXIETY CVER LOSS OF LOVE.
         JOURNAL OF PERSONALITY, 1955, 24, 204-219.
         (TAT SCORED FOR CASTRATION ANXIETY)
         aS-256 1956M TAT SEX ANXIETY FEAR BODY CASTRATION
         (APPLICATIONS: 2406)

S-257   SUTCLIFFE, J. P., PERRY, C. W., SHEEHAN, P. W., JONES, J. A., & BRISTOW, R. A.
             THE RELATION OF IMAGERY AND FANTASY TO HYPNOSIS.
             (NIMH PROJECT REPORT, UNITED STATES PUBLIC HEALTH SERVICE), WASHINGTON D.C.
             UNITED STATES GOVERNMENT PRINTING OFFICE, 1963.
         SUTCLIFFE, J. P., PERRY, C. W., & SHEEHAN, P. W.
             RELATION OF SOME ASPECTS OF IMAGERY AND FANTASY TO HYPNOTIC SUSCEPTIBILITY.
             JOURNAL OF ABNORMAL PSYCHOLOGY, 1970, 76, 279-287.
             (QUESTIONNAIRE MEASURE OF DREAM CONTENT)
         @S-257 1963M PRIMARY-PROCESS THINKING CONTENT-ANALYSIS DREAM

S-258   SUTCLIFFE, J. P., PERRY, C. W., SHEEHAN, P. W., JONES, J. A., & BRISTOW, R. A.
             THE RELATION OF IMAGERY AND FANTASY TO HYPNOSIS.
             (NIMH PROJECT REPORT, UNITED STATES PUBLIC HEALTH SERVICE), WASHINGTON D.C.
             UNITED STATES GOVERNMENT PRINTING OFFICE, 1963.
         SUTCLIFFE, J. P., PERRY, C. W., & SHEEHAN, P. W.
             RELATION OF SOME ASPECTS OF IMAGERY AND FANTASY TO HYPNOTIC SUSCEPTIBILITY.
             JOURNAL OF ABNORMAL PSYCHOLOGY, 1970, 76, 279-287.
             (TEST OF HYPNOTIZABILITY)
         @S-258 1963M HYPNOTIC SUGGESTIBILITY SENSORY ORIENTATION EXPERIENCE INTENSITY

S-259   SPIEGLER, M. D., & LIEBERT, R. M.
             SOME CORRELATES OF SELF-REPORTED FEAR.
             PSYCHOLOGICAL REPORTS, 1970, 26, 691-695.
             (SELF-REPORT FEAR INVENTORY)
         @S-259 1970M FEAR ANXIETY SOCIAL DESIRABILITY RATIONAL IRRATIONAL ORIENTATION
         @SELF CONCEPT

S-262   SINHA, D.
             SINHA'S ANXIETY SCALE.
             VARANASI: RUPA PSYCHOLOGICAL CORPORATION, 1966.
             (SINHA'S ANXIETY SCALE)
         @S-262 1966M ANXIETY TENSION
             (APPLICATIONS: 2656)

S-263   SARASON, S. B., DAVIDSON, K. S., LIGHTHALL, F. F., WAITE, R. R., &
         RUEBUSH, B. K.
             ANXIETY IN ELEMENTARY SCHOOL CHILDREN.
             NEW YORK: WILEY, 1960.
             (LIE SCALE FOR CHILDREN)
         @S-263 1960M RESPONSE-BIAS ACQUIESCENCE FAKING CHILD
             (APPLICATIONS: 2461)

S-266   SHUMAN, H., & HARDING, J.
             SYMPATHETIC IDENTIFICATION WITH THE UNDERDOG.
             PUBLIC OPINION QUARTERLY, 1963, 27, 230-241.
             (SYMPATHETIC IDENTIFICATION QUESTIONNAIRE)
         @S-266 1963M IDENTIFICATION PREJUDICE CONCERN PEOPLE OTHERS EMPATHY ATTITUDE
         @SENSITIVITY SOCIAL CONSCIENCE
             (APPLICATIONS: 2677)

S-267   SMITH, D. H., & OLSON, J. T.
             SOCIOMETRIC STATUS IN A PSYCHIATRICALLY DEVIANT ADOLESCENT COLLECTIVITY.
             PSYCHOLOGICAL REPORTS, 1970, 27, 483-497.
             (SOCIOMETRIC QUESTIONNAIRE FOR HOSPITALIZED PSYCHIATRIC PATIENTS)
         @S-267 SOCIOMETRIC 1970M PEER RELATIONSHIPS POWER STRUCTURE PERCEPTION
         @PSYCHIATRIC PATIENT

S-268   SMITH, D. H., & OLSON, J. T.
             SOCIOMETRIC STATUS IN A PSYCHIATRICALLY DEVIANT ADOLESCENT COLLECTIVITY.
             PSYCHOLOGICAL REPORTS, 1970, 27, 483-497.
             (PSYCHIATRIC RATINGS OF GENERAL PSYCHIATRIC HEALTH)
         @S-268 1970M PSYCHIATRIC RATING THERAPIST RESILIENCY EGO STRENGTH CONTROL
         @COPING MENTAL-HEALTH MENTAL-ILLNESS ADJUSTMENT IMPULSE

S-269   SMITH, D. H., & OLSON, J. T.
             SOCIOMETRIC STATUS IN A PSYCHIATRICALLY DEVIANT ADOLESCENT COLLECTIVITY.
             PSYCHOLOGICAL REPORTS, 1970, 27, 483-497.
             (NURSE RATINGS OF PERSONAL CHARACTERISTICS OF PSYCHIATRIC PATIENTS)
         @S-269 1970M PSYCHIATRIC RATING STAFF PATIENT MENTAL-HEALTH MENTAL-ILLNESS
         @ADJUSTMENT BEHAVIOR WARD

S-270   SCHUMER, H., & STANFIELD, R. E.
               ASSESSMENT OF STUDENT ROLE ORIENTATIONS IN COLLEGE.
               PROCEEDINGS OF THE AMERICAN PSYCHOLOGICAL ASSOCIATION, 1966, 285-286.
               (STUDENT PREFERENCE SCHEDULE)*
           aS-270 1966M STUDENT ROLE ORIENTATION COLLEGE ENVIRONMENT PREFERENCE BEHAVIOR
           aINTEREST ACADEMIC SOCIAL ACTIVITIES
               (APPLICATIONS: 2747)

S-271   SCHIFFER, D.
               RELATION OF INHIBITION OF CURIOSITY TO HOMOSEXUALITY.
               PSYCHOLOGICAL REPORTS, 1970, 27, 771-776.
               (MEASURE OF CURIOSITY)
           aS-271 1970M INTEREST ENVIRONMENT NEED NOVELTY VARIETY PERCEPTION PERSONALITY
           aSTYLE

S-272   SCIORTINO, R.
               PERSONALITY AND CREATIVE ABILITIES.
               UNPUBLISHED DOCTORAL DISSERTATION, OHIO STATE UNIVERSITY, 1963.
               (PERSONALITY ADJECTIVE LIST (PAL-1))*
           aS-272 1963M PERSONALITY CHECKLIST INTEREST ENVIRONMENT INTELLIGENCE IMAGINATION
           aTHINKING AFFECTIVE-STATES AFFILIATION CONFIDENCE

S-273   SCIORTINO, R.
               PERSONALITY AND CREATIVE ABILITIES.
               DOCTORAL DISSERTATION, OHIO STATE UNIVERSITY, COLUMBUS, OHIO, 1963.
               NO. 64-6958.
           SCIORTINO, R.
               FACTORIAL STUDY AND ANALYSIS OF FACTOR VARIANCE OF INTELLECTIVE SELF-RATING
               FROM A COMBINED SAMPLE OF MALE AND FEMALE SUBJECTS.
               JOURNAL OF PSYCHOLOGY, 1969, 71, 261-269.
               (INTELLECTIVE ADJECTIVE LIST)*
           aS-273 1963M INTELLECTUAL ABILITY CHECKLIST

S-274   STENFORS, B. D., & WOODMANSEE, J. J.
               A SCALE OF BLACK POWER SENTIMENT.
               PSYCHOLOGICAL REPORTS, 1968, 22, 802.
               (BLACK POWER SENTIMENT SCALE)*
           aS-274 1968M ETHNIC RACIAL PREJUDICE NEGRO MINORITY ATTITUDE FEELING
           aIDENTITY GROUP SOCIAL AWARENESS SELF CONCEPT

S-275   SCHILL, T., & SCHNEIDER, L.
               RELATIONSHIPS BETWEEN HOSTILITY GUILT AND SEVERAL MEASURES OF HOSTILITY.
               PSYCHOLOGICAL REPORTS, 1970, 27, 967-970.
               (SENTENCE AND CONSTRUCTION TASK)
           aS-275 1970M PROJECTIVE HOSTILITY AGGRESSION EXPRESSION INHIBITION GUILT SELF
           aCONCEPT

S-276   SEDLACEK, W. E., & BROOKS, G. C., JR.
               MEASURING RACIAL ATTITUDES IN A SITUATIONAL CONTEXT.
               PSYCHOLOGICAL REPORTS, 1970, 27, 971-980.
               (SITUATIONAL ATTITUDE SCALE)*
           aS-276 1970M NEGRO ATTITUDE RACIAL PREJUDICE ETHNIC SITUATIONAL MINORITY
           aSEM-DIFFERENTIAL ETHNOCENTRISM

S-277   SCIORTINO, R.
               PERSONALITY CHARACTERISTICS INVENTORY: I. FACTOR STRUCTURE FOR A COMBINED
               SAMPLE OF MALE AND FEMALE COLLEGE STUDENTS.
               PSYCHOLOGICAL REPORTS, 1970, 27, 619-622.
               (PERSONALITY CHARACTERISTICS INVENTORY, PCI-1)*
           aS-277 1970M EVALUATION AWARENESS SENSITIVITY STUDENT COLLEGE PERSONALITY
           aSTRUCTURE AUTONOMY DEPENDENCE PURPOSE IMAGINATION CREATIVITY FANTASY
           aORIGINALITY SELF-CONCEPT ESTEEM INVENTORY MULTITRAIT

S-279   SACHSON, A. D., RAPPOPORT, L., & SINNETT, E. R.
               THE ACTIVITY RECORD: A MEASURE OF SOCIAL ISOLATION-INVOLVEMENT.
               PSYCHOLOGICAL REPORTS, 1970, 26, 413-414.
               (THE ACTIVITY RECORD)
           aS-279 1970M COLLEGE RELATIONSHIPS INTERACTION INTERPERSONAL ADJUSTMENT NEED
           aINTROVERSION EXTRAVERSION AFFILIATION ACTIVITIES SOCIAL SCHOOL

S-280   STEININGER, M. P.
              ON MEASURING A COMPLEX ATTITUDE: THE CONSTRUCT VALIDITY OF AN
              ATTITUDE-TOWARD-PSYCHOLOGY SCALE.
              PSYCHOLOGICAL REPORTS, 1970, 26, 501-502.
              (ATTITUDE-TOWARD-PSYCHOLOGY SCALE)
           aS-280 1970M ATTITUDE COLLEGE ACADEMIC SCHOOL STUDENT OPINION

S-281   SANTOSTEFANO, S.
              ASSESSMENT OF MOTIVES IN CHILDREN.
              PSYCHOLOGICAL REPORTS, 1970, 26, 639-649.
              (CONTINUOUS WORD ASSOCIATION TEST)
           aS-281 1970M AGGRESSION SUCCORANCE INHIBITION IMPULSE PROJECTIVE MOTIVE NEED
           aBEHAVIOR EXPRESSION ACTIVITIES PREFERENCE WORD ASSOCIATION

S-282   SECORD, P. F., & JOURARD, S. M.
              THE APPRAISAL OF BODY-CATHEXIS: BODY-CATHEXIS AND THE SELF.
              JOURNAL OF CONSULTING PSYCHOLOGY, 1953, 17, 343-347.
              (BODY CATHEXIS-SELF CATHEXIS SCALE)
           aS-282 1953M SELF IMAGE PERCEPTION SATISFACTION ATTITUDE ACCEPTANCE
           aBODY CATHEXIS
              (APPLICATIONS: 2601)

S-283   SANTOSTEFANO, S.
              AN EXPLORATION OF PERFORMANCE MEASURES OF PERSONALITY.
              JOURNAL OF CLINICAL PSYCHOLOGY, 1960, 16, 373-377.
              (MINIATURE SITUATIONS TEST)*
           aS-283 1968M SUCCORANCE AGGRESSIVENESS MOTIVE EXPRESSION DELAY AGGRESSION
           aPROJECTIVE ACTIVITIES PREFERENCE BEHAVIOR

S-284   SCOTT, W. A.
              COGNITIVE COMPLEXITY AND COGNITIVE FLEXIBILITY.
              SOCIOMETRY, 1962, 25, 405-414.
              (SORTING TASK)
           aS-284 1962M COGNITIVE COMPLEXITY FLEXIBILITY FUNCTIONING

S-285   SPRINTHALL, N. A.
              SUPERVISOR RATING SCALE.
              CAMBRIDGE, MASS.: HARVARD UNIVERSITY, 1965 (MIMEO).
              (SUPERVISOR RATING SCALE)
           aS-285 1965M SUPERVISOR RATING LEADERSHIP BEHAVIOR
              (APPLICATIONS: 1378)

S-286   SARGENT, H. D.
              AN EXPERIMENTAL APPLICATION OF PROJECTIVE PRINCIPLES TO A PAPER AND PENCIL
              PERSONALITY TEST.
              PSYCHOLOGICAL MONOGRAPHS, 1944, 57 (5, WHOLE NO. 265).
              (TEST OF INSIGHT INTO HUMAN MOTIVES -- A PERSONALITY MEASURE)*
           aS-286 1944M SELF PERCEPTION MOTIVE SENSITIVITY PERSONALITY PROJECTIVE CONFLICT
           aDEPRESSION INVENTORY ANXIETY DEPENDENCE
              (APPLICATIONS: 1409)

S-287   SCIENCE RESEARCH ASSOCIATES
              MANUAL FOR THE RATING SCALE FOR PUPIL ADJUSTMENT.
              CHICAGO: AUTHOR, 1953.
              (RATING SCALE FOR PUPIL ADJUSTMENT)*
           aS-287 1953M RATING STUDENT COLLEGE ADJUSTMENT EMOTION SOCIAL MATURITY SECURITY
           aIMPULSIVENESS
              (APPLICATIONS: 1391)

S-288   SCHISSEL, R. F.
              DEVELOPMENT OF A CAREER ORIENTATION SCALE FOR WOMEN.
              JOURNAL OF COUNSELING PSYCHOLOGY, 1968, 16, 257-262.
              (CAREER ORIENTATION SCALE FOR WOMEN)
           aS-288 1968M JOB VOCATIONAL ORIENTATION ROLE ATTITUDE PREFERENCE
           aSEX ACCEPTANCE

S-289   SHAPIRO, J. G., KRAUSS, H. H., & TRUAX, C. B.
              THERAPEUTIC CONDITIONS AND DISCLOSURE BEYOND THE THERAPEUTIC ENCOUNTER.
              JOURNAL OF COUNSELING PSYCHOLOGY, 1969, 16, 290-294.
              (MODIFIED BARRETT-LENNARD RELATIONSHIPS QUESTIONNAIRE)
           aS-289 1969M THERAPY COUNSELING RELATIONSHIPS PSYCHIATRIC INVENTORY
           aEMPATHY PATIENT THERAPIST B-SOR

S-290   SHAPIRO, J. G., KRAUSS, H. H., & TRUAX, C. B.
               THERAPEUTIC CONDITIONS AND DISCLOSURE BEYOND THE THERAPEUTIC ENCOUNTER.
               JOURNAL OF COUNSELING PSYCHOLOGY, 1969, 16, 290-294.
               (SELF-DISCLOSURE INVENTORY)
           aS-290 1969M SELF CONCEPT DESCRIPTION DISCLOSURE IMAGE IDENTITY POSITIVE
           aNEGATIVE INVENTORY EMOTION BEHAVIOR OPENNESS

S-292   SHAPIRO, J. G.
               THE INTERPERSONAL PERCEPTION QUESTIONNAIRE.
               ARKANSAS REHABILITATION RESEARCH AND TRAINING CENTER, 1967 (MIMEO).
               (INTERPERSONAL PERCEPTION QUESTIONNAIRE)*
           aS-292 1967M INTERPERSONAL PERCEPTION SENSITIVITY AWARENESS SOCIAL OTHERS
           aPEOPLE
               (APPLICATIONS: 1458)

S-293   STEWART, C. C.
               ATTITUDE CHANGE FOLLOWING COUNSELING SEMINAR.
               PERSONNEL AND GUIDANCE JOURNAL, 1963, 41, 415-419.
               (COUNSELING ATTITUDE SCALE)
           aS-293 1963M COUNSELING ATTITUDE CHANGE

S-294   SACKS, J. M.
               SOCIAL ADJUSTMENT AND VERBAL EXPRESSION OF ACTIVITY-PASSIVITY AND FEELING
               TONE.
               JOURNAL OF COUNSELING PSYCHOLOGY, 1969, 16, 486-490.
               (VERB RESPONSE TEST)*
           aS-294 1969M RESPONSE SPECIFICITY PROJECTIVE WORD ASSOCIATION
           aACTIVE PASSIVE

S-295   SPITZER, S. P., & SOBEL, R.
               SELECTIVE PERCEPTION AND STAFF CONSENSUS IN THE VIEWING OF PSYCHIATRIC
               PATIENTS.
               JOURNAL OF COUNSELING PSYCHOLOGY, 1965, 12, 100.
               (ADJECTIVE RATING SCALE)
           aS-295 1965M CHECKLIST SEM-DIFFERENTIAL MULTITRAIT

S-296   STERN, G. G., STEIN, M. I., & BLOOM, B. S.
               METHODS IN PERSONALITY ASSESSMENT.
               GLENCOE, ILL.: FREE PRESS, 1956.
               (WORKER ATTITUDE INVENTORY)
           aS-296 1956M ATTITUDE JOB INVOLVEMENT INTEREST SATISFACTION
           aEMPLOYEE
               (APPLICATIONS: 1267)

S-297   SHOBEN, E. J., JR.
               THE ASSESSMENT OF PARENT ATTITUDES IN RELATION TO CHILD ADJUSTMENT.
               GENETIC PSYCHOLOGY MONOGRAPHS, 1949, 39, 103-147.
               (U.S.C. PARENT ATTITUDE SURVEY)*
           aS-297 1949M PARENTAL ATTITUDE CHILD FAMILY INTERACTION RELATIONSHIPS
           aSELF INVENTORY
               (APPLICATIONS: 676 1225)

S-298   SWITZER, D. K., GRIGG, A. E., MILLER, J. S., & YOUNG, R. K.
               EARLY EXPERIENCES AND OCCUPATIONAL CHOICE: A TEST OF ROE'S HYPOTHESIS.
               JOURNAL OF COUNSELING PSYCHOLOGY, 1962, 9, 45-48.
               (MEASURE OF PERCEIVED PARENTAL ATTITUDES)
           aS-298 1962M PARENTAL ATTITUDE ORIENTATION CHILD REJECTION DEMANDS FAMILY
           aINTERACTION PERCEIVED RELATIONSHIPS

S-299   SEVERINSEN, K. N.
               CLIENT EXPECTATION AND PERCEPTION OF THE COUNSELOR'S ROLE AND THEIR
               RELATIONSHIP TO CLIENT SATISFACTION.
               JOURNAL OF COUNSELING PSYCHOLOGY, 1966, 13, 109-112.
               (COUNSELING QUESTIONNAIRE)*
           aS-299 1966M COUNSELING THERAPY PSYCHIATRIC PATIENT RELATIONSHIPS ROLE
           aPERCEPTION THERAPIST

S-300   SCHUTZ, R. E., & MAZER, G. E.
               A FACTOR ANALYSIS OF THE OCCUPATIONAL CHOICE MOTIVES OF COUNSELORS.
               JOURNAL OF COUNSELING PSYCHOLOGY, 1964, 11, 267-271.
               (OCCUPATIONAL CHOICE INVENTORY)
           aS-300 1964M COUNSELING THERAPY PREFERENCE VOCATIONAL THERAPIST MOTIVE

S-301   STEFFLRE, B., KING, P., & LEAFGREN, F.
              CHARACTERISTICS OF COUNSELORS JUDGED EFFECTIVE BY THEIR PEERS.
              JOURNAL OF COUNSELING PSYCHOLOGY, 1962, 9, 335-340.
              (Q-SORT MEASURE OF PERCEIVED EFFECTIVENESS OF FELLOW COUNSELOR)
         @S-301 1962M Q-SORT PERCEIVED EFFECTIVENESS COUNSELING
         @PEER THERAPIST PERCEPTION COMPETENCE ABILITY

S-302   SYMONDS, P. M.
              A MANUAL OF INSTRUCTIONS FOR EDUCATIONAL INTEREST INVENTORY.
              NEW YORK: TEACHERS COLLEGE, COLUMBIA UNIVERSITY, BUREAU OF PUBLICATIONS,
              1958.
              (EDUCATIONAL INTEREST INVENTORY)*
         @S-302 1958M ACADEMIC INTEREST INVENTORY SCHOOL ORIENTATION TEACHER
              (APPLICATIONS: 1216)

S-303   SHELLEY, E. L. V., & JOHNSON, W. F., JR.
              EVALUATING AN ORGANIZED COUNSELING SERVICE FOR YOUTHFUL OFFENDERS.
              JOURNAL OF COUNSELING PSYCHOLOGY, 1961, 8, 351-354.
              (TAT SCORED FOR ANTISOCIAL THEMES)
         @S-303 1961M TAT SOCIAL ATTITUDES AGGRESSION HOSTILITY PROJECTIVE FANTASY
         @DEVIANCE DELINQUENCY

S-304   STOGDILL, R. M.
              THE STRUCTURE OF ORGANIZATION BEHAVIOR.
              MULTIVARIATE BEHAVIORAL RESEARCH, 1967, 2, 47-62.
              (LEADER BEHAVIOR DESCRIPTION QUESTIONNAIRE)
         @S-304 1967M LEADERSHIP SUPERVISOR JOB EMPLOYEE RELATIONSHIPS DOMINANCE CONCERN
         @ATTITUDE

S-305   STAR, S. A.
              THE PUBLIC'S IDEAS ABOUT MENTAL ILLNESS.
              NATIONAL OPINION RESEARCH CENTER, UNIVERSITY OF CHICAGO, 1955,
              MIMEOGRAPHED.
              (MEASURE OF PUBLIC TOLERANCE FOR PATHOLOGICAL BEHAVIOR)
         @S-305 1955M PUBLIC ATTITUDE BEHAVIOR MENTAL-ILLNESS TOLERANCE
         @PSYCHIATRIC DEVIANCE SOCIAL
              (APPLICATIONS: 1410   2559)

S-306   SONG, R. H., & SONG, A. Y.
              DEVELOPMENT OF A VOCATIONAL ADJUSTMENT RATING SCALE FOR THE RETARDED.
              JOURNAL OF COUNSELING PSYCHOLOGY, 1971, 18, 173-176.
              (VOCATIONAL ADJUSTMENT RATING SCALE FOR THE RETARDED)
         @S-306 1971M VOCATIONAL ADJUSTMENT MENTAL-ILLNESS BEHAVIOR AGGRESSION
         @WITHDRAWAL JOB ABILITY HABITS RETARDATION

S-307   SMITH, D. P.
              LEARNING TO LEARN.
              NEW YORK: HARCOURT, BRACE AND WORLD, 1961.
              (IMPULSIVITY-CONSTRICTED SCALE)
         @S-307 1961M IMPULSIVENESS COGNITIVE STYLE IMPULSE CONTROL EXPRESSION
         @INHIBITION

S-308   STOVER, L., GUERNEY, B. G., JR., & O'CONNELL, M.
              MEASUREMENTS OF ACCEPTANCE, ALLOWING SELF-DIRECTION, INVOLVEMENT AND
              EMPATHY IN ADULT-CHILD INTERACTION.
              JOURNAL OF PSYCHOLOGY, 1971, 77, 261-269.
              (MEASURE OF EMPATHY)
         @S-308 1971M RELATIONSHIPS INTERACTION PARENTAL ACCEPTANCE SELF
         @CHILD DIRECTION AUTONOMY AFFECTION INVOLVEMENT

S-309   SEGALL, M. H.
              THE EFFECT OF ATTITUDE AND EXPERIENCE ON JUDGMENTS OF CONTROVERSIAL
              STATEMENTS.
              JOURNAL OF ABNORMAL AND SOCIAL PSYCHOLOGY, 1959, 58, 61-68.
              (ATTITUDE SCALES)
         @S-309 1959M ATTITUDE OPINION SOCIAL STUDENT ORGANIZATION
              (APPLICATIONS: 147)

S-310   SMITH, L. M.
              THE CONCURRENT VALIDITY OF SIX PERSONALITY AND ADJUSTMENT TESTS FOR
              CHILDREN.
              PSYCHOLOGICAL MONOGRAPHS, 1958, 72 (4, WHOLE NO. 457).
              (TEACHER NOMINATION FORM)*
          @S-310 1952M ADJUSTMENT CHILD BEHAVIOR RATING MENTAL-HEALTH MENTAL-ILLNESS
          @SCHOOL TEACHER SOCIAL
              (APPLICATIONS: 1629)

S-312   STANFORD, P., DEMBER, W., & STANFORD, F.
              A CHILDREN'S FORM OF THE ALPERT-HABER ACHIEVEMENT ANXIETY SCALE.
              CHILD DEVELOPMENT, 1963, 34, 1027-1032.
              (CHILDREN'S FORM OF ALPERT-HABER ACHIEVEMENT ANXIETY SCALE)
          @S-312 1963M ANXIETY PERFORMANCE ACHIEVEMENT CHILD A-8R
              (APPLICATIONS: 246)

S-313   SPERBER, Z.
              TEST ANXIETY AND PERFORMANCE UNDER STRESS.
              JOURNAL OF CONSULTING PSYCHOLOGY, 1961, 25, 226-233.
              (TEST REACTION QUESTIONNAIRE--TRQ)*
          @S-313 1961M ANXIETY TEST SITUATIONAL STRESS

S-314   SILVERMAN, L. H., & SILVERMAN, D. K.
              A CLINICAL-EXPERIMENTAL APPROACH TO THE STUDY OF SUBLIMINAL STIMULATION:
              THE EFFECTS OF A DRIVE-RELATED STIMULUS UPON RORSCHACH RESPONSES.
              JOURNAL OF ABNORMAL AND SOCIAL PSYCHOLOGY, 1964, 69, 158-172.
              (RORSCHACH SCORING KEYS)
          @S-314 1964M RORSCHACH PROJECTIVE SEX DRIVE AROUSAL DENIAL DEFENSIVENESS

S-315   SAMPSON, E. E.
              AN EXPERIMENT ON ACTIVE AND PASSIVE RESISTANCE TO SOCIAL POWER.
              UNPUBLISHED DOCTORAL DISSERTATION, UNIVERSITY OF MICHIGAN, 1960.
              (SOCIAL INDEPENDENCE AND TASK INDEPENDENCE SCALES)
          @S-315 1960M AUTONOMY DEPENDENCE SOCIAL

S-316   SISTRUNK, F., & MCDAVID, J. W.
              SEX VARIABLE IN CONFORMING BEHAVIOR.
              JOURNAL OF PERSONALITY AND SOCIAL PSYCHOLOGY, 1971, 17(2), 200-207.
              (CONFORMITY SCALE)
          @S-316 1971M CONFORMITY SEX DIFFERENCES INFLUENCE OTHERS SOCIAL

S-317   SCHAFER, R.
              PSYCHOANALYTIC INTERPRETATION IN RORSCHACH TESTING.
              NEW YORK: GRUNE AND STRATTON, 1954.
              (RORSCHACH CONTENT CATEGORIES FOR CASTRATION ANXIETY)
          @S-317 1954M PROJECTIVE RORSCHACH ANXIETY NEUROTICISM CASTRATION
              (APPLICATIONS: 2406)

S-320   STOTSKY, B. A., & WEINBERG, H.
              THE PREDICTION OF THE PSYCHIATRIC PATIENT'S WORK ADJUSTMENT.
              JOURNAL OF COUNSELING PSYCHOLOGY, 1956, 3, 3-7.
              (SENTENCE-COMPLETION MEASURE OF MOTIVATION FOR VOCATIONAL OBJECTIVES)
          @S-320 1956M DEPENDENCE SELF CONFIDENCE ADJUSTMENT EGO-STRENGTH

S-321   SUCHOTLIFF, L. C.
              RELATION OF FORMAL THOUGHT DISORDER TO THE COMMUNICATION DEFICIT IN
              SCHIZOPHRENICS.
              JOURNAL OF ABNORMAL PSYCHOLOGY, 1970, 76, 250-257.
              (PROVERB MATCH TEST)
          @S-321 1970M THINKING COGNITIVE SCHIZOPHRENIA COMPLEXITY FUNCTIONING STRUCTURE
          @FLEXIBILITY

S-322   SPITZER, R. L., ENDICOTT, J., & FLEISS, J. L.
              INSTRUMENTS AND RECORDING FORMS FOR EVALUATING PSYCHIATRIC STATUS AND
              HISTORY: RATIONALE, METHOD OF DEVELOPMENT AND DESCRIPTION.
              COMPREHENSIVE PSYCHIATRY, 1967, 8, 321-343.
              (PSYCHIATRIC EVALUATION FORM)
          @S-322 1967M

S-323   SECORD, P. F., & JOURARD, S. M.
              MOTHER-CONCEPTS AND JUDGMENTS OF YOUNG WOMEN'S FACES.
              JOURNAL OF ABNORMAL AND SOCIAL PSYCHOLOGY, 1956, 52, 246-250.
              (RATING SCALE FOR MOTHER AND FEMALE IMAGES)
         @S-323 1956M MATERNAL CONCEPT STEREOTYPE MORAL TRAIT ATTRIBUTION
              (APPLICATIONS: 943)

S-324   STAR, S. A.
              THE SCREENING OF PSYCHONEUROTICS IN THE ARMY: TECHNICAL DEVELOPMENT OF
              TESTS.
              IN S. A. STOUFFER, L. GUTTMAN, E. A. SUCHMAN, P. F. LAZARSFELD, S. A.
              STAR, & J. A. CLAUSEN (EDS.). MEASUREMENT AND PREDICTION.
              PRINCETON, N. J.: PRINCETON UNIVERSITY PRESS, 1950.
              (ARMY NEUROPSYCHIATRIC SCREENING ADJUNCT)*
         @S-324 1950M PSYCHIATRIC RATING NEUROTICISM MENTAL-ILLNESS ANXIETY DEPRESSION
         @ADEQUACY PERSONAL ADJUSTMENT
              (APPLICATIONS: 949)

S-326   SAPOLSKY, A.
              RELATIONSHIP BETWEEN PATIENT-DOCTOR COMPATIBILITY, MUTUAL PERCEPTION AND
              OUTCOME OF TREATMENT.
              JOURNAL OF ABNORMAL PSYCHOLOGY, 1965, 70, 70-76.
              (A SEMANTIC DIFFERENTIAL SCALE OF PATIENT PERCEPTIONS)
         @S-326 1965M SEM-DIFFERENTIAL INTERPERSONAL PERCEPTION
         @SELF PATIENT THERAPY SIMILARITY THERAPIST RELATIONSHIPS

S-327   SIEVEKING, N. A.
              EFFECTS OF AGE ON PREFERENCE FOR INCONGRUITY.
              UNPUBLISHED MASTER'S THESIS, UNIVERSITY OF ILLINOIS, 1965.
              (MEASURE OF PICTURE PREFERENCE)
         @S-327 1965M PREFERENCE FIGURE GRAPHIC NOVELTY CONSISTENCY AMBIGUITY TOLERANCE

S-329   STRUMPTER, D. J. W.
              A STUDY OF SOME COMMUNICABLE MEASURES FOR THE EVALUATION OF HUMAN FIGURE
              DRAWINGS.
              UNPUBLISHED PH.D. DISSERTATION, PURDUE UNIVERSITY, 1959.
              (SCORING OF DRAW-A-PERSON TEST FOR AGGRESSION)
         @S-329 1959M GRAPHIC FIGURE PROJECTIVE AGGRESSION
         @EXPRESSION HOSTILITY AGGRESSIVENESS
              (APPLICATIONS: 1701)

S-330   SWENSEN, C. H.
              SEXUAL DIFFERENTIATION ON THE DRAW-A-PERSON TEST.
              JOURNAL OF CLINICAL PSYCHOLOGY, 1955, 11, 37-40.
              (SCORING OF DRAW-A-PERSON TEST FOR SEXUAL DIFFERENTIATION)
         @S-330 1955M FIGURE GRAPHIC SEX PROJECTIVE DIFFERENTIATION DIFFERENCES
              (APPLICATIONS: 1701)

S-333   STERN, G. G., STEIN, M. I., & BLOOM, B. S.
              METHODS IN PERSONALITY ASSESSMENT.
              GLENCOE, ILLINOIS: FREE PRESS, 1956.
              (INVENTORY OF BELIEFS)*
         @S-333 1956M INVENTORY BELIEF CONVICTION ATTITUDE
              (APPLICATIONS: 1231 1299)

S-334   STEWART, L. H.
              CHANGE IN PERSONALITY TEST SCORES DURING COLLEGE.
              JOURNAL OF COUNSELING PSYCHOLOGY, 1964, 11, 211-219.
              (DEVELOPMENT STATUS SCALE)
         @S-334 1964M STATUS SOCIAL DEVELOPMENT GROWTH PERSONAL TOLERANCE AMBIGUITY
         @OTHERS FLEXIBILITY

S-335   STRUPP, H. H.
              A MULTIDIMENSIONAL SYSTEM FOR ANALYSING PSYCHOTHERAPEUTIC TECHNIQUES.
              PSYCHIATRY, 1957, 20, 293-306.
              (STRUPP SCALE OF THERAPEUTIC ACTIVITY)*
         @S-335 1957M THERAPY RELATIONSHIPS ACTIVITIES BEHAVIOR COUNSELING THERAPIST
              (APPLICATIONS: 1303)

S-336   STEIMEL, R. J.
              CHILDHOOD EXPERIENCES AND MASCULINITY-FEMININITY SCORES.
              JOURNAL OF COUNSELING PSYCHOLOGY, 1960, 3, 212-217.
              (MEASURE OF CHILDHOOD IDENTIFICATION)
         @S-336 1960M MASCULINITY FEMININITY CHILD IDENTIFICATION EXPERIENCE
         @INTEREST SIMILARITY PERCEIVED PARENTAL SEX ROLE IDENTITY
              (APPLICATIONS: 1265)

S-337   STOLER, N.
             CLIENT LIKABILITY: A VARIABLE IN THE STUDY OF PSYCHOTHERAPY.
             JOURNAL OF CONSULTING PSYCHOLOGY, 1963, 27, 175-178.
             (MEASURE OF CLIENT LIKABILITY)
             aS-337 1963M THERAPY COUNSELING INTERPERSONAL ATTRACTION DESIRABILITY
             aPERSON PERCEPTION PATIENT

S-338   SECHREST, J. B., & JACKSON, D. N.
             SOCIAL INTELLIGENCE AND ACCURACY OF INTERPERSONAL PREDICTIONS.
             JOURNAL OF PERSONALITY, 1961, 29, 167-182.
             (REVISED FIGURE PREFERENCE TEST)
             aS-338 1961M FIGURE GRAPHIC PREFERENCE
             (APPLICATIONS: 1737)

S-339   SNYDER, W. U.
             AN INVESTIGATION OF THE NATURE OF NON-DIRECTIVE PSYCHOTHERAPY.
             JOURNAL OF GENERAL PSYCHOLOGY, 1945, 33, 193-223.
             (MEASURE OF DIRECTIVE-NONDIRECTIVE COUNSELOR RESPONSE)
             aS-339 1945M COUNSELING THERAPY RESPONSE BEHAVIOR
             (APPLICATIONS: 1334)

S-340   SCHIMEK, J. G.
             COGNITIVE STYLE AND DEFENSES: A LONGITUDINAL STUDY OF INTELLECTUALIZATION
             AND FIELD INDEPENDENCE.
             JOURNAL OF ABNORMAL AND SOCIAL PSYCHOLOGY, 1968, 73, 575-580.
             (RORSCHACH RATING OF DEFENSE STYLE OF INTELLECTUALIZATION)
             aS-340 1968M RORSCHACH DEFENSE COGNITIVE STYLE INTELLECTUAL

S-341   SNYDER, W. U.
             AN INVESTIGATION OF THE NATURE OF NON-DIRECTIVE THERAPY.
             JOURNAL OF GENERAL PSYCHOLOGY, 1945, 33, 193-223.
             (CATEGORIZATION OF CLIENT-THERAPIST VERBAL INTERACTION)
             aS-341 1945M PATIENT THERAPY STYLE RELATIONSHIPS INTERACTION ACCEPTANCE
             aAPPROVAL
             (APPLICATIONS: 2091)

S-342   SNYDER, W. U.
             THE PSYCHOTHERAPY RELATIONSHIP.
             NEW YORK: MACMILLAN, 1961.
             (PAC-NAC AND PAT-NAT SCALES OF CLIENT-THERAPIST ATTITUDES)*
             aS-342 1961M AFFECTIVE-STATES THERAPY RELATIONSHIPS ATTITUDE PATIENT
             (APPLICATIONS: 1549)

S-343   SPITZER, R. L., FLEISS, J. L., BURDOCK, E. I., & HARDESBY, A. S.
             THE MENTAL STATUS SCHEDULE: RATIONALE, RELIABILITY & VALIDITY.
             COMPREHENSIVE PSYCHIATRY, 1964, 5, 384-395.
             (MENTAL STATUS SCHEDULE)
             aS-343 MENTAL ILLNESS PSYCHIATRIC

S-344   SHEEHAN, P. W.
             ARTIFICIAL INDUCTION OF POSTHYPNOTIC CONFLICT.
             JOURNAL OF ABNORMAL PSYCHOLOGY, 1969, 74, 16-25.
             (WORD ASSOCIATION TEST)
             aS-344 1964M COGNITIVE FUNCTIONING WORD ASSOCIATION STIMULUS RESPONSE HYPNOSIS

S-345   SCHRODER, H. M., & HUNT, D. E.
             FAILURE-AVOIDANCE IN SITUATIONAL INTERPRETATION AND PROBLEM SOLVING.
             PSYCHOLOGICAL MONOGRAPHS, 1957, 71 (WHOLE NO. 432), 1-22.
             (SITUATIONAL INTERPRETATION TEST)*
             aS-345 1957M SITUATIONAL INTERPRETATION SELF EVALUATION SOCIAL APPROVAL
             aESTEEM AUTONOMY ADJUSTMENT

T-1   TAYLOR, D. A., & ALTMAN, I.
             INTIMACY-SCALED STIMULI FOR USE IN STUDIES OF INTERPERSONAL RELATIONS.
             PSYCHOLOGICAL REPORTS, 1966, 19, 729-730.
             (RATINGS OF INTERPERSONAL INTIMACY)
             aT-1 INTERPERSONAL RELATIONSHIPS COMMUNICATION INTERACTION ACCESSIBILITY
             aT-1 SELF DISCLOSURE 1966M

T-2   TAYLOR, J. A.
             A PERSONALITY SCALE OF MANIFEST ANXIETY.
             JOURNAL OF ABNORMAL AND SOCIAL PSYCHOLOGY, 1953, 48, 285-290.
             (TAYLOR MANIFEST ANXIETY SCALE)*
         @T-2 ANXIETY SUBJECTIVE AFFECTIVE-STATES STRESS MANIFEST TAYLOR-MA NEGATIVE
         @T-2 1953M
             (APPLICATIONS: 3   4   7   19   21   22   40   43   45   64
                               78   98   116   121   123   124   126   143   150   185
                              187   207   232   240   241   271   279   330   348   371
                              378   385   398   400   402   410   414   426   441   444
                              451   452   465   480   533   558   568   584   586   591
                              602   604   605   607   614   636   642   645   664   666
                              715   726   749   757   788   790   792   793   809   825
                              864   866   870   886   890   895   923   926   953   960
                              980   994   998   1080   1086   1102   1124   1165   1187   1191
                             1208   1216   1270   1307   1351   1372   1475   1489   1531   1554
                             1560   1568   1571   1587   1596   1601   1605   1614   1622   1656
                             1661   1672   1677   1699   1710   1726   1727   1734   1738   1753
                             1765   1766   1771   1775   1797   1832   1833   1853   1856   1865
                             1873   1895   1899   1909   1924   1926   1970   1979   1989   2019
                             2039   2042   2059   2093   2097   2123   2124   2136   2140   2143
                             2206   2240   2264   2275   2296   2301   2315   2345   2361   2414
                             2418   2443   2504   2530   2538   2552   2557   2560   2580   2629
                             2656   2661   2662   2726   2760   2790   2828   2862   2868   2875
                             2880   2897 2951)

T-3   TERMAN, L. M., & MILES, C. C.
             MANUAL OF INFORMATION AND DIRECTIONS FOR USE OF ATTITUDE-INTEREST ANALYSIS
             (MF) TEST. NEW YORK: MCGRAW-HILL, 1938.
             (ATTITUDE-INTEREST ANALYSIS (MF) TEST)*
         @T-3 MASCULINITY FEMININITY SELF-IDENTITY SUB-IDENTITY ATTITUDE INTEREST
         @T-3 THINKING INTROVERSION SEX NORMS 1938M
             (APPLICATIONS: 421   565   2043   2128)

T-4   TERMAN, L. M.
             PSYCHOLOGICAL FACTORS IN MARITAL HAPPINESS. NEW YORK: MCGRAW-HILL, 1938.
             (SELF-RATING HAPPINESS IN MARRIAGE SCALE)*
         @T-4 MARITAL HAPPINESS POSITIVE ADJUSTMENT AFFECTIVE-STATES GLOBAL FAMILY
         @T-4 SATISFACTION 1938M
             (APPLICATIONS: 1577   2052)

T-5   THAYER, R. E.
             MEASUREMENT OF ACTIVATION THROUGH SELF-REPORT.
             PSYCHOLOGICAL REPORTS, 1967, 20, 663-678.
             (ACTIVATION-DEACTIVATION ADJECTIVE CHECK LIST)*
         @T-5 REACTIVITY DRIVE ANXIETY STRESS ACTIVATION CHECKLIST AFFECTIVE-STATES
         @T-5 OTHER-CATEGORY 1967M

T-6   THORNE, E. C.
             SCALES FOR RATING SEXUAL EXPERIENCE.
             JOURNAL OF CLINICAL PSYCHOLOGY MONOGRAPH SUPPLEMENT, 1966, NO. 21, 40-43.
             (RATING SCALES OF SEXUAL EXPERIENCE)
         @T-6 SEX EXPERIENCE ACTIVITIES AFFECTIVE-STATES GLOBAL SATISFACTION BEHAVIOR
         @T-6 SUBJECTIVE NEED 1966M

T-7   THORNDIKE, R. L.
             MANUAL, THORNDIKE DIMENSIONS OF TEMPERAMENT. NEW YORK: PSYCHOLOGICAL
             CORPORATION, 1966.
             (THORNDIKE DIMENSIONS OF TEMPERAMENT)*
         @T-7 TEMPERAMENT MULTITRAIT AFFECTIVE-STATES GLOBAL MOOD 1966M

T-8   TRIANDIS, H. C., & TRIANDIS, L. M.
             RACE, SOCIAL CLASS, RELIGION, AND NATIONALITY AS DETERMINANTS OF SOCIAL
             DISTANCE.
             JOURNAL OF ABNORMAL AND SOCIAL PSYCHOLOGY, 1960, 61, 110-118.
             (SOCIAL DISTANCE SCALE)
         @T-8 ETHNIC RACIAL ATTITUDE NATIONALISM RELIGION ACCEPTANCE OTHERS SOCIAL
         @T-8 DISTANCE AFFECTIVE-STATES OTHER-CATEGORY 1960M
             (APPLICATIONS: 26   579   630   821)

T-9   TANAKA, Y., & OSGOOD, C. E.
             CROSS-CULTURE, CROSS-CONCEPT, AND CROSS-SUBJECT GENERALITY OF AFFECTIVE
             MEANING SYSTEMS.
             JOURNAL OF PERSONALITY AND SOCIAL PSYCHOLOGY, 1965, 2, 143-153.
             (SEMANTIC DIFFERENTIAL FOR RATING OF PERCEPTUAL MATERIAL)
         @T-9 SEM-DIFFERENTIAL PERCEPTION AFFECTIVE-STATES CONCEPT CONCEPTUAL RATING
         @T-9 CROSS-CULTURAL 1965M

T-10   TANNENBAUM, P. H., & GAER, E. P.
                MOOD CHANGE AS A FUNCTION OF STRESS OF PROTAGONIST AND DEGREE OF
                IDENTIFICATION IN A FILM VIEWING SITUATION.
                JOURNAL OF PERSONALITY AND SOCIAL PSYCHOLOGY, 1965, 2, 612-616.
                (MEASURE OF DEGREE OF IDENTIFICATION)
            @T-10 SEM-DIFFERENTIAL PERCEPTION RATING SELF OTHERS IMAGE CONCEPT
            @T-10 SELF-IDENTITY OTHER-CATEGORY IDENTIFICATION 1965M

T-11   TORRANCE, E. P., & ZILLER, R. C.
                RISK AND LIFE EXPERIENCE: DEVELOPMENT OF A SCALE FOR MEASURING RISK-TAKING
                TENDENCIES.
                TECHNICAL REPORT NUMBER 57-23, 1957, UNITED STATES AIR FORCE, WASHINGTON
                AIR DEFENSE CENTER.
                (RISK SCALE)*
            @T-11 IMPULSE AFFECTIVE-STATES OTHER-CATEGORY RISK-TAKING BEHAVIOR AUTONOMY
            @T-11 1957M PREFERENCE
                (APPLICATIONS: 741   1299)

T-12   TRIANDIS, H. C.
                EXPLORATORY FACTOR ANALYSES OF THE BEHAVIORAL COMPONENT OF SOCIAL
                ATTITUDES.
                JOURNAL OF ABNORMAL AND SOCIAL PSYCHOLOGY, 1964, 68, 420-430.
                (BEHAVIORAL DIFFERENTIAL)*
            @T-12 BEHAVIOR RATING SOCIAL ATTITUDE ACCEPTANCE MARITAL INTERPERSONAL
            @T-12 RELATIONSHIPS COMPETENCE 1964M ADJUSTMENT
                (APPLICATIONS: 10   108   133   2337   2827)

T-13   TRIPODI, T., & BIERI, J.
                COGNITIVE COMPLEXITY AS A FUNCTION OF OWN AND PROVIDED CONSTRUCTS.
                PSYCHOLOGICAL REPORTS, 1963, 13, 26.
                (MODIFICATION OF KELLY'S ROLE CONSTRUCT REPERTORY TEST)
            @T-13 COGNITIVE COMPLEXITY ROLE STRUCTURE FUNCTIONING PERCEPTION SOCIAL
            @T-13 RELATIONSHIPS INTERPERSONAL INTERACTION 1963M
                (APPLICATIONS: 219   260   391   1461   2180   2499)

T-14   TRUMBO, D. A.
                INDIVIDUAL AND GROUP CORRELATES OF ATTITUDES TOWARD WORK-RELATED CHANGE.
                JOURNAL OF APPLIED PSYCHOLOGY, 1961, 45, 338-344.
                (MEASURE OF ATTITUDES TOWARD CHANGE)
            @T-14 CHANGE JOB SATISFACTION AFFECTIVE-STATES PE-FIT ADJUSTMENT ATTITUDE 1961M

T-15   TSUSHIMA, W. T.
                A COMPARATIVE STUDY OF THE ATTITUDES OF IRISH AND ITALIAN PATIENTS OF TWO
                SOCIAL LEVELS UNDER PRE-OPERATIVE STRESS.
                UNPUBLISHED DOCTORAL DISSERTATION, FORDHAM UNIVERSITY, 1967.
            TSUSHIMA, W. T.
                RESPONSES OF IRISH AND ITALIAN PATIENTS OF TWO SOCIAL CLASSES UNDER
                PRE-OPERATIVE STRESS.
                JOURNAL OF PERSONALITY AND SOCIAL PSYCHOLOGY, 1968, 8, 43-48.
                (TENSION-HOSTILITY QUESTIONNAIRE)*
            @T-15 TENSION HOSTILITY AFFECTIVE-STATES RESENTMENT CROSS-CULTURAL
            @T-15 HOSPITALIZATION ANXIETY EMOTION NEGATIVE SITUATIONAL STRESS 1967M

T-16   TUCKMAN, B. W.
                INTEGRATIVE COMPLEXITY: ITS MEASUREMENT AND RELATION TO CREATIVITY.
                EDUCATIONAL AND PSYCHOLOGICAL MEASUREMENT, 1966, 26, 369-382.
                (INTERPERSONAL TOPICAL INVENTORY)*
            @T-16 FUNCTIONING CONCRETENESS ABSTRACTNESS CONTROL ORIENTATION CREATIVITY
            @T-16 AUTONOMY ORIGINALITY STRUCTURE INTERPERSONAL RELATIONSHIPS INTERACTION
            @T-16 AFFECTIVE-STATES PERSONALITY COGNITIVE INTEGRATION COMPLEXITY 1966M
                (APPLICATIONS: 91   535   2532)

T-17   TRIANDIS, H. C., & VASSILIOU, V.
                FREQUENCY OF CONTACT AND STEREOTYPING.
                JOURNAL OF PERSONALITY AND SOCIAL PSYCHOLOGY, 1967, 7, 316-328.
                (SEMANTIC-DIFFERENTIAL MEASURE OF STEREOTYPING)
            @T-17 STEREOTYPE SOCIAL DISTANCE CROSS-CULTURAL NATIONAL TRAIT MULTITRAIT
            @T-17 SEM-DIFFERENTIAL 1967M

T-18   TROLDAHL, V. C., & POWELL, F. A.
                A SHORT-FORM DOGMATISM SCALE FOR USE IN FIELD STUDIES.
                SOCIAL FORCES, 1965, 44, 211-214.
                (SHORT FORM OF DOGMATISM SCALE)
            @T-18 DOGMATISM COPING-DEFENSE FLEXIBILITY RIGIDITY AUTHORITARIANISM 1965M
                (APPLICATIONS: 104   242   2527   2887)

T-19   TULKIN, S. R.
        RACE, CLASS, FAMILY AND SCHOOL ACHIEVEMENT.
        JOURNAL OF PERSONALITY AND SOCIAL PSYCHOLOGY, 1968, 9, 31-37.
        (CULTURAL PARTICIPATION SCALE)*
        aT-19 ACCULTURATION CHILD PARENT-CHILD CULTURE PARTICIPATION FAMILY INTERACTION
        aT-19 ADJUSTMENT SOCIAL COMPETENCE 1968M

T-20   THURSTONE, L. L., & JEFFERY, T. E.
        CLOSURE FLEXIBILITY: CONCEALED FIGURES: TEST ADMINISTRATION MANUAL.
        CHICAGO: EDUCATIONAL INDUSTRY SERVICE, 1959.
        (CONCEALED FIGURES TEST)*
        aT-20 PERCEPTION FIGURE COGNITIVE COMPLEXITY AUTONOMY FIELD FLEXIBILITY
        aT-20 COPING-DEFENSE RIGIDITY DOGMATISM DEPENDENCE 1959M
        (APPLICATIONS: 70   349   371   528   1047   1916   2249)

T-21   THORPE, M. D.
        THE FACTORED DIMENSIONS OF AN OBJECTIVE INVENTORY OF ACADEMIC MOTIVATION
        BASED ON ELEVENTH GRADE MALE OVER- AND UNDERACHIEVERS.
        UNPUBLISHED DOCTORAL DISSERTATION, MICHIGAN STATE UNIVERSITY, 1961.
        (GENERALIZED SITUATIONAL CHOICE INVENTORY)*
        aT-21 AUTONOMY MOTIVE NEED STUDENT PREFERENCE ACHIEVEMENT SITUATIONAL 1961M
        (APPLICATIONS: 1217)

T-22   TAYLOR, R. G.
        PERSONALITY FACTORS ASSOCIATED WITH ELEVENTH GRADE MALE AND FEMALE DISCREP-
        ANT ACHIEVEMENT.
        UNPUBLISHED DOCTORAL DISSERTATION, MICHIGAN STATE UNIVERSITY, 1962.
        (HUMAN TRAIT INVENTORY)*
        aT-22 MULTITRAIT SELF RATING SECONDARY SCHOOL STUDENT DESCRIPTION 1962M
        (APPLICATIONS: 1217 1316)

T-23   THURSTONE, L. L.; & CHAVE, E. J.
        ATTITUDES TOWARD THE CHURCH. CHICAGO: UNIVERSITY OF CHICAGO PRESS, 1929.
        (THURSTONE AND CHAVE SCALE FOR MEASURING ATTITUDES TOWARD THE CHURCH)*
        aT-23 ATTITUDE ORIENTATION RELIGION 1929M
        (APPLICATIONS: 930   1434   2331   2594   2708)

T-24   TRUAX, C. B.
        A SCALE FOR THE MEASUREMENT OF ACCURATE EMPATHY.
        PSYCHIATRIC INSTITUTE BULLETIN, WISCONSIN PSYCHIATRIC INSTITUTE, UNIVERSITY
        OF WISCONSIN, 1961, 1, NO. 10.
        (ACCURATE EMPATHY SCALE)*
        aT-24 AFFECTIVE-STATES EMPATHY OTHERS ORIENTATION THERAPY COUNSELING EMOTION
        aT-24 1961M AWARENESS
        (APPLICATIONS: 1002   1006   1153   1249   1376   1486   1497   1925   1943   2012
                         2285   2417)

T-25   THORPE, L.P., CLARK, W. W., & TIEGS, E. W.
        MANUAL: CALIFORNIA TEST OF PERSONALITY. MONTEREY, CALIFORNIA: CALIFORNIA
        TEST BUREAU, 1953.
        (CALIFORNIA TEST OF PERSONALITY)*
        aT-25 MULTITRAIT PERSONALITY CHILD 1953M
        (APPLICATIONS: 474   487   591   868   1188   1327   1391   1498   1575   2316
                         2654   2970)

T-26   TRIPODI, T., & BIERI, J.
        COGNITIVE COMPLEXITY, PERCEIVED CONFLICT, AND CERTAINTY.
        JOURNAL OF PERSONALITY, 1966, 34, 144-153.
        (COGNITIVE COMPLEXITY MEASURE)
        aT-26 PROJECTIVE PERCEIVED CONFLICT PERCEPTION OTHERS RATING COGNITIVE SOCIAL
        aT-26 COMPLEXITY STRUCTURE FUNCTIONING RELATIONSHIPS INTERACTION INTERPERSONAL
        aT-26 1966M

T-27   THURSTONE, L. L.
        EXAMINER'S MANUAL FOR THE THURSTONE TEMPERAMENT SCHEDULE.
        SCIENCE RESEARCH ASSOCIATES, INC. CHICAGO, 1949-53.
        (THURSTONE TEMPERAMENT SCHEDULE)*
        aT-27 SOCIAL COMPETENCE STABILITY PERSONAL TEMPERAMENT MULTITRAIT AUTONOMY
        aT-27 ADJUSTMENT AFFECTIVE-STATES IMPULSE DOMINANCE 1949M
        (APPLICATIONS: 521   1604)

T-28   TORRANCE, E. P.
        GUIDING CREATIVE TALENT.
        ENGLEWOOD CLIFFS, NEW JERSEY: PRENTICE-HALL, 1962.
        (TEST OF IMAGINATION)*
        aT-28 AUTONOMY CREATIVITY ORIGINALITY FLEXIBILITY IMAGINATION 1962M
        (APPLICATIONS: 2486   2912)

T-29   TURNURE, J., & ZIGLER, E.
                OUTER-DIRECTEDNESS IN THE PROBLEM SOLVING OF NORMAL AND RETARDED CHILDREN.
                JOURNAL OF ABNORMAL AND SOCIAL PSYCHOLOGY, 1964, 69, 427-436.
                (STICKER GAME)*
            @T-29 LOCUS CONTROL IMITATION OTHERS ORIENTATION AUTONOMY CHILD IE-CONTROL
            @T-29 INTELLIGENCE COGNITIVE FUNCTIONING SOCIAL INFLUENCE 1964M

T-30   TURNURE, J., & ZIGLER, E.
                OUTER-DIRECTEDNESS IN THE PROBLEM SOLVING OF NORMAL AND RETARDED CHILDREN.
                JOURNAL OF ABNORMAL AND SOCIAL PSYCHOLOGY, 1964, 69, 427-436.
                (BOX GAME)*
            @T-30 AUTONOMY LOCUS CONTROL IMITATION OTHERS ORIENTATION INTELLIGENCE COGNITIVE
            @T-30 FUNCTIONING IE-CONTROL 1964M

T-31   TULKIN, S. R.
                RACE, CLASS, FAMILY AND SCHOOL ACHIEVEMENT.
                JOURNAL OF PERSONALITY AND SOCIAL PSYCHOLOGY, 1968, 9, 31-37.
                (FAMILY PARTICIPATION SCALE)*
            @T-31 PARENT-CHILD FAMILY INTERACTION ADJUSTMENT CHILD RELATIONSHIPS
            @T-31 PARTICIPATION 1968M INTERPERSONAL

T-32   TRENT, R. D., FERNANDEZ-MARINA, R., & MALDONADO-SIERRA, E. D.
                THE CROSS-CULTURAL APPLICATION OF THE ADJECTIVAL CHECK LIST
                ADJUSTMENT INDEX: A PRELIMINARY REPORT.
                JOURNAL OF SOCIAL PSYCHOLOGY, 1960, 51, 265-276.
                (ADJECTIVE CHECK LIST MEASURE OF ADJUSTMENT)
            @T-32 CHECKLIST ACCEPTANCE PERCEPTION ESTEEM CONCEPT IDEAL SELF-IDENTITY SELF
            @T-32 ADJUSTMENT IMAGE CROSS-CULTURAL 1960M

T-33   TOBAN, E.
                SUPERVISORY FEEDBACK, PERCEPTION OF JOB CHARACTERISTICS, AND JOB
                SATISFACTION AMONG COMMUNITY HEALTH TRAINEES.
                JOURNAL OF SOCIAL PSYCHOLOGY, 1969, 79, 279-280.
                (MEASURE OF JOB SATISFACTION)
            @T-33 INTRINSIC EXTRINSIC PE-FIT SUPERVISOR EMPLOYEE JOB SATISFACTION GLOBAL
            @T-33 AFFECTIVE-STATES PERCEPTION ADJUSTMENT 1969M

T-34   TUPES, E. C., & CHRISTAL, R. E.
                STABILITY OF PERSONALITY TRAIT RATING FACTORS OBTAINED UNDER DIVERSE
                CONDITIONS.
                USAF WADC TECHNICAL NOTE, 1958, NO. 58-61.
                (PERSONALITY TRAIT RATING SCALE)
            @T-34 PEER RATING EXTRAVERSION MULTITRAIT CULTURE EMOTION STABILITY
            @T-34 CONSCIENTIOUSNESS 1958M TRAIT
                (APPLICATIONS: 807)

T-36   TRUAX, C. B.
                ANXIETY REACTION SCALE.
                UNPUBLISHED MANUSCRIPT, UNIVERSITY OF WISCONSIN, 1960.
                (ANXIETY REACTION SCALE)*
            @T-36 AFFECTIVE-STATES ANXIETY SUBJECTIVE STRESS SELF CONFIDENCE SOCIAL
            @T-36 COMPETENCE MENTAL-HEALTH MENTAL-ILLNESS NEGATIVE 1960M
                (APPLICATIONS: 1002 2147 2417 2906)

T-37   TRUAX, C. B.
                A TENTATIVE SCALE FOR THE MEASUREMENT OF DEPTH OF INTRAPERSONAL EXPLORATION
                (DX).
                IN DISCUSSION PAPERS, WISCONSIN PSYCHIATRIC INSTITUTE. MADISON: UNIVERSITY
                OF WISCONSIN PRESS, 1962.
                (DEPTH OF INTRAPERSONAL EXPLORATION SCALE)*
            @T-37 OTHER-CATEGORY PERSONAL SUBJECTIVE PATIENT ADJUSTMENT THERAPY SELF
            @T-37 PERCEPTION SELF-IDENTITY EVALUATION COUNSELING 1962M AWARENESS
                (APPLICATIONS: 1362 1376 1469 1925 2297)

T-38   TRUAX, C. B., & CARKHUFF, R. R.
                FOR BETTER OR FOR WORSE: THE PROCESS OF PSYCHOTHERAPEUTIC PERSONALITY
                CHANGE.
                IN, RECENT ADVANCES IN THE STUDY OF BEHAVIOR CHANGE. MONTREAL, CANADA:
                MCGILL UNIVERSITY PRESS, 1963.
                (CONSTRUCTIVE PERSONALITY CHANGE INDEX)*
            @T-38 GLOBAL PERSONALITY CHANGE PATIENT THERAPY ADJUSTMENT OTHER-CATEGORY MMPI
            @T-38 COUNSELING MENTAL-HEALTH MENTAL-ILLNESS 1963M
                (APPLICATIONS: 1249 1454 2117 2297 2417)

T-39   TORRANCE, E. P., YAMAMOTO, K., SCHENETZKI, D., PALAMUTLU, N., & LUTHER, B.
                ASSESSING THE CREATIVE THINKING ABILITIES OF CHILDREN.
                MINNEAPOLIS: BUREAU OF EDUCATIONAL RESEARCH, 1960.
        YAMAMOTO, K.
                REVISED SCORING MANUAL FOR TESTS OF CREATIVE THINKING (FORMS VA AND NVA).
                MINNEAPOLIS: UNIVERSITY OF MINNESOTA, 1962.
        TORRANCE, E. P.
                TORRANCE TESTS OF CREATIVE THINKING: DIRECTIONS MANUAL AND SCORING GUIDE.
                FIGURAL TEST BOOKLET A. PRINCETON, N. J.: PERSONNEL PRESS, 1966.
        TORRANCE, E. P.
                TORRANCE TESTS OF CREATIVE THINKING: NORMS-TECHNICAL MANUAL. (RESEARCH ED.)
                PRINCETON, N.J.: PERSONNEL PRESS, 1966.
                (TESTS OF CREATIVE THINKING)*
        @T-39 CREATIVITY AUTONOMY ORIGINALITY THINKING COGNITIVE STRUCTURE FUNCTIONING
        @T-39 CHILD 1960M
                (APPLICATIONS: 127 1478 2608 2678 2767 2792 2912 2976)

T-40   TREFFINGER, D. J., & O'REILLY, R. P.
                TEACHER RANKING OF PUPIL ANXIETY.
                ITHACA, NEW YORK: CORNELL UNIVERSITY, 1965, UNPUBLISHED MIMEO.
                (TEACHER RANKING OF PUPIL ANXIETY)*
        @T-40 AFFECTIVE-STATES SUBJECTIVE STRESS ANXIETY STUDENT RATING TEACHER SCHOOL
        @T-40 NEGATIVE 1965M

T-41   THORPE, L. P., & CLARK, W. W.
                MENTAL HEALTH ANALYSIS. LOS ANGELES: CALIFORNIA TEST BUREAU, 1959.
                (MENTAL HEALTH ANALYSIS)*
        @T-41 GROWTH ACTUALIZATION ADJUSTMENT GLOBAL MENTAL-HEALTH STUDENT DESCRIPTION
        @T-41 SELF 1959M DIAGNOSIS

T-42   THARP, R. G.
                DIMENSIONS OF MARRIAGE ROLES.
                MARRIAGE AND FAMILY LIVING, 1963, 25, 389-404.
                (MARRIAGE ROLE QUESTIONNAIRE)*
        @T-42 ROLE MARITAL ADJUSTMENT INTERPERSONAL BEHAVIOR RELATIONSHIPS SEX
        @T-42 SATISFACTION RESPONSIBILITY FAMILY 1963M
                (APPLICATIONS: 2202)

T-43   TIFFIN, J., & LAWSHE, C. H.
                MANUAL FOR ADAPTABILITY TEST.
                CHICAGO: SCIENCE RESEARCH ASSOCIATES, 1954.
                (ADAPTABILITY TEST)*
        @T-43 1954M JOB LEARNING ADJUSTMENT PREDICTION BEHAVIOR
                (APPLICATIONS: 2367)

T-44   TOLOR, A., BRANNIGAN, G. G., & MURPHY, V. M.
                PSYCHOLOGICAL DISTANCE, FUTURE TIME PERSPECTIVE, AND INTERNAL-EXTERNAL
                EXPECTANCY.
                JOURNAL OF PROJECTIVE TECHNIQUES AND PERSONALITY ASSESSMENT, 1970, 34, 283-
                294.
                (PSYCHOLOGICAL DISTANCE SCALE)
        @T-44 1970M FAMILY INTERACTION SOCIAL DISTANCE AFFECTIVE-STATES INTERPERSONAL
        @T-44 RELATIONSHIPS

T-46   TEDESCHI, J. T., CHRISTIANSEN, P., HORAI, J., & GAHAGAN, J. P.
                MYTHOLOGICAL ETHNOCENTRISM AS A DETERMINANT OF INTERNATIONAL ATTITUDES.
                JOURNAL OF SOCIAL PSYCHOLOGY, 1970, 80, 113-114.
                (INTERNATIONAL ATTITUDES TEST)*
        @T-46 1970M NATIONAL ATTITUDE INTERNATIONALISM ETHNOCENTRISM

T-47   TOBAN, E. V.
                RELATIONSHIP OF SOCIOECONOMIC STATUS AND PREFERENCE FOR SYMPTOMS IN A
                ROLE-PLAYING SITUATION.
                JOURNAL OF SOCIAL PSYCHOLOGY, 1970, 80, 59-62.
                (MEASURE OF CHARACTERISTIC MENTAL SYMPTOMS OF SOCIO-ECONOMIC STATUS)
        @T-47 1970M SOCIAL STATUS SYMPTOM PREFERENCE ATTITUDE MENTAL-ILLNESS PSYCHIATRIC

T-48   TRUAX, C. B.
                RELATIONSHIP QUESTIONNAIRE. (TEST AND MANUAL)
                UNIVERSITY OF WISCONSIN, 1962, (MIMEO.).
                (RELATIONSHIP QUESTIONNAIRE)*
        @T-48 1962M THERAPY PATIENT RELATIONSHIPS EMPATHY
                (APPLICATIONS: 1376 2443 2847)

T-49   THURSTONE, L. L.
                NO REFERENCE -- CITED IN:
                BARRY, W. A.
                MARRIAGE RESEARCH AND CONFLICT: AN INTEGRATIVE REVIEW.
                PSYCHOLOGICAL BULLETIN, 1970, 73, 41-54.
                (THURSTONE NEUROTIC INVENTORY)
            aT-49 NEUROTICISM MENTAL-HEALTH MENTAL-ILLNESS ADJUSTMENT
                (APPLICATIONS: 2911)

T-51   THOMAS, W.
                (NO REFERENCE AVAILABLE: GEORGIA SOUTHWESTERN COLLEGE, AMERICUS, GEORGIA)
            LIEBERMAN, LEWIS R.
                LIFE SATISFACTION IN THE YOUNG AND.THE OLD.
                PSYCHOLOGICAL REPORTS, 1970, 27, 75-79.
                (MORALE SCALE)*
            aT-51 AFFECTIVE-STATES MORALE GLOBAL
                (APPLICATIONS: 2698)

T-52   TSENG, M. S., & CARTER, A. R.
                ACHIEVEMENT MOTIVATION AND FEAR OF FAILURE AS DETERMINANTS OF VOCATIONAL
                CHOICE, VOCATIONAL ASPIRATION, AND PERCEPTION OF VOCATIONAL PRESTIGE.
                JOURNAL OF COUNSELING PSYCHOLOGY, 1970, 17, 150-156.
                (OCCUPATIONAL PRESTIGE SCALE)
            aT-52 1970M JOB ASPIRATION EVALUATION PRESTIGE ACHIEVEMENT MOTIVE PREFERENCE
            aPERCEPTION

T-53   TIFFANY, D. W., COWAN, J. R., & BLINN, E.
                SAMPLE AND PERSONALITY BIASES OF VOLUNTEER SUBJECTS.
                JOURNAL OF CONSULTING AND CLINICAL PSYCHOLOGY, 1970, 35, 38-43.
                (LIFE AND WORK INTEREST QUESTIONNAIRE)*
            aT-53 1970M LIFE JOB VOCATIONAL INTEREST
            aT-53 PREFERENCE ACTIVITIES

T-54   TAFT, R.
                PEAK EXPERIENCES AND EGO PERMISSIVENESS: AN EXPLORATORY FACTOR STUDY
                OF THEIR DIMENSIONS IN NORMAL PERSONS.
                ACTA PSYCHOLOGICA, 1969, 29, 35-64.
                (EXPERIENCE QUESTIONNAIRE)
            aT-54 1969M AROUSAL EXPERIENCE FANTASY INTELLECTUAL COMPETENCE
            aT-54 EMOTIONAL MENTAL-HEALTH PRIMARY-PROCESS BELIEF RELIGION
                (APPLICATIONS: 2804)

T-55   TURNER, W. D.
                ALTRUISM AND ITS MEASUREMENT IN CHILDREN.
                JOURNAL OF ABNORMAL AND SOCIAL PSYCHOLOGY, 1948, 43, 502-516.
                (ALTRUISM SCALE)
            aT-55 1948M ALTRUISM SOCIAL OTHERS ORIENTATION CHILD BEHAVIOR MORAL DEVELOPMENT
                (APPLICATIONS: 2903)

T-56   TRYON, R. C.
                UNRESTRICTED CLUSTER AND FACTOR ANALYSIS, WITH APPLICATION TO THE MMPI
                AND HOLZINGER-HARMAN PROBLEMS.
                MULTIVARIATE BEHAVIORAL RESEARCH, 1966, 1, 229-244.
                (TSC SCALES OF MMPI)
            aT-56 1966M MMPI INTROVERSION BODY SYMPTOM DEPRESSION RESENTMENT TENSION
            aT-56 1966M NEGATIVE AFFECTIVE-STATES

T-57   TREADWELL, Y.
                HUMOR AND CREATIVITY.
                PSYCHOLOGICAL REPORTS, 1970, 26, 55-58.
                (CARTOONS TEST OF HUMOR CREATION)
            aT-57 1970M CREATIVITY HUMOR ORIGINALITY IMAGINATION

T-58   TREADWELL, Y.
                HUMOR AND CREATIVITY.
                PSYCHOLOGICAL REPORTS, 1970, 26, 55-58.
                (SELF-REPORT OF HUMOR USE AND APPRECIATION)
            aT-58 1970M HUMOR SELF DESCRIPTION BEHAVIOR PREFERENCE

T-59   TREICHEL, B., & NANCE, D.
                ATTITUDE OF EDUCATED YOUNG ADULTS TOWARD CHILD REARING.
                PSYCHOLOGICAL REPORTS, 1970, 26, 53-54.
                (Q-SORT MEASURE OF CONCERN ABOUT DIFFERENT BEHAVIORS OF CHILDREN)
            aT-59 1970M PARENT-CHILD RELATIONSHIPS ATTITUDE CHILD BEHAVIOR ADJUSTMENT
            aT-59 Q-SORT

T-60   TAYLOR, J. B., HAEFELE, E., THOMPSON, P., & O'DONOGHUE, C.
         RATING SCALES AS MEASURES OF CLINICAL JUDGMENT II: THE RELIABILITY OF
         EXAMPLE-ANCHORED SCALES UNDER CONDITIONS OF RATER HETEROGENEITY AND
         DIVERGENT BEHAVIOR SAMPLING.
         EDUCATIONAL AND PSYCHOLOGICAL MEASUREMENT, 1970, 30, 301-310.
         (EXAMPLE-ANCHORED DESCRIPTIVE RATING SCALES)
         aT-60 1970M RATING DESCRIPTION ADJUSTMENT GLOBAL
         aT-60 GERIATRIC COPING PHYSICAL HEALTH SOCIAL SUPPORT

T-61   TRENT, R. D., FERNANDEZ-MARINA, R., & MALDONADO-SIERRA, E. D.
         THE CROSS-CULTURAL APPLICATION OF THE ADJECTIVAL CHECKLIST ADJUSTMENT
         INDEX: A PRELIMINARY REPORT.
         JOURNAL OF SOCIAL PSYCHOLOGY, 1960, 51, 265-276.
         (ADJECTIVE CHECK LIST FOR LATIN AMERICAN SUBJECTS)
         aT-61 1960M CROSS-CULTURAL DIAGNOSIS NEUROTICISM SELF IDEAL ACCEPTANCE
         aADJUSTMENT CHECKLIST

T-62   TRIPODI, T., & BIERI, J.
         INFORMATION TRANSMISSION IN CLINICAL JUDGEMENTS AS A FUNCTION OF STIMULUS
         DIMENSIONALITY AND COGNITIVE COMPLEXITY.
         JOURNAL OF PERSONALITY, 1964, 32, 119-137.
         (MEASURE OF PATHOLOGICAL SOCIAL BEHAVIOR)
         aT-62 1964M PSYCHOPATHY AGGRESSION AGGRESSIVENESS BODY AWARENESS
         aT-62 SOCIAL WITHDRAWAL ADJUSTMENT DEVIANCE ANXIETY

T-63   TRIPODI, T., & BIERI, J.
         COGNITIVE COMPLEXITY, PERCEIVED CONFLICT, AND CERTAINTY.
         JOURNAL OF PERSONALITY, 1966, 34, 144-153.
         (TEST OF JUDGMENTAL CERTAINTY)
         aT-63 1966M JUDGMENT AGGRESSIVE BEHAVIOR ADJUSTMENT STIMULUS CONFLICT TOLERANCE
         aT-63 COMPLEXITY AMBIGUITY COGNITIVE

T-64   TORGOFF, I., & TESI, G.
         EFFECT OF DIFFERENCES IN ACHIEVEMENT MOTIVATION AND SOCIAL RESPONSIBILITY
         ON RESPONSES TO MORAL CONFLICT.
         JOURNAL OF PERSONALITY, 1968, 36, 513-527.
         (CONCERN FOR OTHERS SCALE)*
         aT-64 1968M INTERPERSONAL CONSCIENCE DIFFERENTIATION DISCREPANCY MORAL VALUES
         aT-64 ATTITUDE OTHERS ORIENTATION FAMILY IDEOLOGY INTERACTION
         aT-64 SENSITIVITY SOCIAL RESPONSIBILITY ALTRUISM

T-65   TRYON, C. M.
         A STUDY OF SOCIAL AND EMOTIONAL ADJUSTMENTS: THE INTERNAL CONSISTENCY AND
         INTER-RELATIONSHIPS OF MEASUREMENTS BY DIFFERENT TECHNIQUES.
         UNPUBLISHED DOCTORAL DISSERTATION, UNIVERSITY OF CALIFORNIA, 1933.
         (ADJUSTMENT INVENTORY)
         aT-65 1933M ADJUSTMENT MALADJUSTMENT GLOBAL TENSION BEHAVIOR RATING SELF
         aT-65 ADOLESCENT
         (APPLICATIONS: 944   1775)

T-67   TYLER, F. B.
         A CONCEPTUAL MODEL FOR ASSESSING PARENT-CHILD MOTIVATIONS.
         CHILD DEVELOPMENT, 1960, 31, 807-815.
         (MEASURE OF MOTIVATION OF PARENTS AND CHILDREN)
         aT-67 1960M PARENT-CHILD MOTIVE STATUS AFFECTION DOMINANCE DEPENDENCE
         aT-67 PROTECTIVENESS AFFECTIVE-STATES CHILD ACTIVITIES

T-68   TIFFANY, D. W., & SHONTZ, F. C.
         THE MEASUREMENT OF EXPERIENCED CONTROL IN PREADOLESCENTS.
         JOURNAL OF CONSULTING PSYCHOLOGY, 1962, 26, 491-497.
         (PICTURE Q TECHNIQUE)*
         aT-68 1962M Q-SORT PROJECTIVE SELF CONCEPT ADULT CONTROL INTERPERSONAL
         aT-68 PARENT-CHILD INTERACTION FAMILY AUTONOMY DEPENDENCE PARENTAL CHILD
         (APPLICATIONS: 1793)

T-69   TRUAX, C. B.
         EFFECTIVE INGREDIENTS IN PSYCHOTHERAPY: AN APPROACH TO UNRAVELING THE
         PATIENT-THERAPIST INTERACTION.
         JOURNAL OF COUNSELING PSYCHOLOGY, 1963, 10, 256-263.
         (UNCONDITIONAL POSITIVE REGARD SCALE)*
         aT-69 1963M AFFECTIVE-STATES POSITIVE THERAPIST RELATIONSHIPS ACCEPTANCE PATIENT
         (APPLICATIONS: 1002   1249   1362   1925   1943   2012   2417   2763)

T-70   TOMKINS, S. S., & MINER, J. B.
            THE TOMKINS-HORN PICTURE ARRANGEMENT TEST.
            NEW YORK: SPRINGER, 1957.
            (TOMKINS-HORN PICTURE-ARRANGEMENT TEST)*
        @T-70 1957M GRAPHIC CONSCIENCE INTENSITY JOB FANTASY PROJECTIVE
            (APPLICATIONS: 1826 2525)

T-72   TEMPONE, V. J., & LAMB, W.
            REPRESSION-SENSITIZATION AND ITS RELATION TO MEASURES OF ADJUSTMENT AND
            CONFLICT.
            JOURNAL OF CONSULTING PSYCHOLOGY, 1967, 31, 131-136.
            (QUESTIONNAIRE MEASURE OF CONFLICT)
        @T-72 1967M CONFLICT ADJUSTMENT COGNITIVE STRUCTURE ATTITUDE

T-73   TANNENBAUM, A. S., & ALLPORT, F. H.
            PERSONALITY STRUCTURE AND GROUP STRUCTURE: AN INTERPRETIVE STUDY OF
            THEIR RELATIONSHIP THROUGH AN EVENT-STRUCTURE HYPOTHESIS.
            JOURNAL OF ABNORMAL AND SOCIAL PSYCHOLOGY, 1956, 53, 272-280.
            (MEASURE OF PERSONALITY TREND-STRUCTURE)
        @T-73 1956M AUTONOMY CONTROL MOTIVE JOB GROUP
            (APPLICATIONS: 578)

T-74   TRUAX, C. B., & CARKHUFF, R. R.
            TOWARD EFFECTIVE COUNSELING AND PSYCHOTHERAPY: TRAINING AND PRACTICE.
            CHICAGO: ALDINE, 1967.
            (TRUAX EMPATHY SCALE)
        @T-74 1967M THERAPY PATIENT EMPATHY SENSITIVITY COUNSELING AFFECTIVE-STATES
        @T-74 POSITIVE
            (APPLICATIONS: 1362 2156 2763)

T-75   TRUAX, C. B., & CARKHUFF, R. R.
            TOWARD EFFECTIVE COUNSELING AND PSYCHOTHERAPY: TRAINING AND PRACTICE.
            CHICAGO: ALDINE, 1967.
            (THERAPIST WARMTH SCALE)
        @T-75 1967M THERAPY PATIENT RELATIONSHIPS COUNSELING SENSITIVITY AFFECTIVE-
        @T-75 STATES POSITIVE
            (APPLICATIONS: 1006 2156)

T-76   TOMKINS, S.
            THE PSYCHOLOGY OF KNOWLEDGE.
            PAPER PRESENTED AT THE MEETING OF THE AMERICAN PSYCHOLOGICAL ASSOCIATION,
            LOS ANGELES, SEPTEMBER 1964.
            (POLARITY SCALE)
        @T-76 1964M ATTITUDES PERSONAL ORIENTATION
            (APPLICATIONS: 2271 2525)

T-77   TAYLOR, J. B.
            WHAT DO ATTITUDE SCALES MEASURE: THE PROBLEM OF SOCIAL DESIRABILITY.
            JOURNAL OF ABNORMAL AND SOCIAL PSYCHOLOGY, 1961, 62, 386-390.
            (REVERSED SOCIAL DESIRABILITY SCALE)
        @T-77 1961M RESPONSE-BIAS MMPI SOCIAL DESIRABILITY

T-78   TAYLOR, J. B.
            WHAT DO ATTITUDE SCALES MEASURE: THE PROBLEM OF SOCIAL DESIRABILITY.
            JOURNAL OF ABNORMAL AND SOCIAL PSYCHOLOGY, 1961, 62, 386-390.
            (PERSONAL SOCIAL DESIRABILITY SCALE)
        @T-78 1961M MMPI SOCIAL DESIRABILITY RESPONSE-BIAS

T-79   TAYLOR, J. B.
            WHAT DO ATTITUDE SCALES MEASURE: THE PROBLEM OF SOCIAL DESIRABILITY.
            JOURNAL OF ABNORMAL AND SOCIAL PSYCHOLOGY, 1961, 62, 386-390.
            (ATTITUDE SOCIAL DESIRABILITY SCALE)
        @T-79 1961M SOCIAL DESIRABILITY RESPONSE-BIAS

T-80   TALBOT, E., MILLER, S. C., & WHITE, R. B.
            SOME ASPECTS OF SELF-CONCEPTIONS AND ROLE DEMANDS IN A THERAPEUTIC
            COMMUNITY.
            JOURNAL OF ABNORMAL AND SOCIAL PSYCHOLOGY, 1961, 63, 338-345.
            (SEMANTIC DIFFERENTIAL MEASURE OF ROLE DEMAND AND SELF CONCEPT)
        @T-80 1961M SEM-DIFFERENTIAL ROLE DEMANDS SELF CONCEPT PSYCHIATRIC PATIENT

T-81   THELEN, H. A., STOCK, D., BEN-ZEEV, S., GRADOLPH, I., GRADOLPH, P., &
          HILL, W. F.
               METHODS FOR STUDYING WORK AND EMOTIONALITY IN GROUPS.
               CHICAGO: UNIVERSITY OF CHICAGO, HUMAN DYNAMICS LABORATORY, 1954.
               (SENTENCE COMPLETION TEST FOR PSYCHIATRIC DIAGNOSIS)
          @T-81 1954M PSYCHIATRIC DIAGNOSIS FANTASY IMAGINATION
          @T-81 SENTENCE-COMP PROJECTIVE
               (APPLICATIONS: 779   950)

T-82   TENNESSEE DEPARTMENT OF MENTAL HEALTH.
               MANUAL FOR THE TDMH SELF-CONCEPT SCALE.
               NASHVILLE: TDMH, 1956 (MIMEC.).
               (TENNESSEE MENTAL HEALTH INVENTORY)
          @T-82 1956M MENTAL-HEALTH MENTAL-ILLNESS PSYCHIATRIC PATIENT
          @T-82 SELF CONCEPT ESTEEM DIAGNOSIS
               (APPLICATIONS: 789)

T-83   THURSTONE, L. L.
               A FACTORIAL STUDY OF PERCEPTION.
               CHICAGO: UNIVERSITY OF CHICAGO PRESS, 1944.
               (GOTTSCHALDT FIGURES TEST)
          @T-83 1944M PERCEPTION AUTONOMY FIELD DEPENDENCE
               (APPLICATIONS: 878   1612)

T-84   THURSTONE, L. L.
               A FACTORIAL STUDY OF PERCEPTION.
               CHICAGO: UNIVERSITY OF CHICAGO PRESS, 1944.
               (HIDDEN PICTURES TEST)
          @T-84 1944 GRAPHIC PERCEPTION FIGURE
               (APPLICATIONS: 673)

T-85   TUDDENHAM, R. D.
               STUDIES IN REPUTATION: I. SEX AND GRADE DIFFERENCES IN SCHOOL CHILDREN'S
               EVALUATIONS OF THEIR PEERS. II. THE DIAGNOSIS OF SOCIAL ADJUSTMENT.
               PSYCHOLOGICAL MONOGRAPHS, 1952, 66, (1, WHOLE NO. 333)
               (CALIFORNIA REPUTATION TEST)
          @T-85 1952M PEER ACCEPTANCE SOCIAL RELATIONSHIPS INTERACTION
               (APPLICATIONS: 848)

T-86   TRIANDIS, L. M., & LAMBERT, W. W.
               PANCULTURAL FACTOR ANALYSIS OF REPORTED SOCIALIZATION PRACTICES.
               JOURNAL OF ABNORMAL AND SOCIAL PSYCHOLOGY, 1961, 62, 631-639.
               (INTERVIEW INVENTORY OF CHILD-TRAINING PRACTICES)
          @T-86 1961M CHILD PARENTAL PARENT-CHILD BEHAVIOR MATERNAL RELATIONSHIPS
          @T-86 FAMILY INTERVIEW

T-88   TOLOR, A., & REZNIKOFF, M.
               A NEW APPROACH TO INSIGHT: A PRELIMINARY REPORT.
               JOURNAL OF NERVOUS AND MENTAL DISEASE, 1960, 130, 286-296.
               (TEST OF INSIGHT)
          @T-88 1960M SELF AWARENESS SENSITIVITY JUDGMENT COPING-DEFENSE
          @T-88 INTROCEPTIVE PERCEPTION

T-89   TRUAX, C. B.
               A TENTATIVE SCALE FOR THE MEASUREMENT OF THERAPIST GENUINENESS OR SELF-
               CONGRUENCE.
               DISCUSSION PAPERS, WISCONSIN PSYCHIATRIC INSTITUTE, UNIVERSITY OF
               WISCONSIN, 1962, 35.
               (THERAPIST GENUINENESS SCALE)
          @T-89 1962M THERAPY COUNSELING SELF CONSISTENCY
               (APPLICATIONS: 1249   1362   1925   2012   2156   2417   2763)

T-90   TYLER, L. E., & SUNDBERG, N. D.
               FACTORS AFFECTING CAREER CHOICES OF ADOLESCENTS.
               (U.S. OFFICE OF EDUCATION, REPORT FOR COOPERATIVE RESEARCH PROJECT NO.
               2455), EUGENE: UNIVERSITY OF OREGON, 1964.
          SUNDBERG, N. D., ROHILA, P. K., & TYLER, L. E.
               VALUES OF INDIAN AND AMERICAN ADOLESCENTS.
               JOURNAL OF PERSONALITY AND SOCIAL PSYCHOLOGY, 1970, 16, 374-397.
               (PERSONAL DIRECTIONS Q-SORT)
          @T-90 1964M Q-SORT VALUES PERSONAL ORIENTATION POWER NEED ACHIEVEMENT INVENTORY
          @CONCERN OTHERS PEOPLE ATTITUDE PRESTIGE DOMINANCE RELIGION ACADEMIC
               (APPLICATIONS: 1487   2516)

T-91   TYLER, L. E., & SUNDBERG, N. D.
                 FACTORS AFFECTING CAREER CHOICES OF ADOLESCENTS.
                 (U.S. OFFICE OF EDUCATION, REPORT FOR COOPERATIVE RESEARCH PROJECT NO.
                 2455), EUGENE: UNIVERSITY OF OREGON, 1964.
            SUNDBERG, N. D., ROHILA, P. K., & TYLER, L. E.
                 VALUES OF INDIAN AND AMERICAN ADOLESCENTS.
                 JOURNAL OF PERSONALITY AND SOCIAL PSYCHOLOGY, 1970, 16, 374-397.
                 (PERSONAL ASSUMPTIONS Q-SORT)
            aT-91 1964M Q-SORT VALUES PERSONAL ORIENTATION NEED PLANNING INVENTORY BELIEF
            aCONSERVATISM PEOPLE CONFORMITY AUTONOMY IE-CONTROL ATTITUDE ALTRUISM SOCIAL
            aRESPONSIBILITY MORAL JUDGMENT RELIGION AUTHORITARIANISM
                 (APPLICATIONS: 2516)

T-92   TART, C. T., & DICK, L.
                 CONSCIOUS CONTROL OF DREAMING: I. THE POSTHYPNOTIC DREAM.
                 JOURNAL OF ABNORMAL PSYCHOLOGY, 1970, 76, 304-315.
                 (METHOD OF SCORING POSTHYPNOTIC COMPLIANCE)
            aT-92 1970M HYPNOTIC PRIMARY-PROCESS STIMULUS BEHAVIOR INFLUENCE

T-94   TART, C. T.
                 A COMPARISON OF SUGGESTED DREAMS OCCURING IN HYPNOSIS AND SLEEP.
                 UNPUBLISHED MASTERS THESIS, UNIVERSITY OF NORTH CAROLINA, 1962.
            TART, C. T.
                 SELF-REPORT SCALES OF HYPNOTIC DEPTH.
                 INTERNATIONAL JOURNAL OF CLINICAL AND EXPERIMENTAL HYPNOSIS, 1970, 18, 105-
                 125.
                 (NORTH CAROLINA SELF-REPORT SCALE OF HYPNOTIC DEPTH)*
            aT-94 1962M HYPNOTIC SUGGESTIBILITY PRIMARY-PROCESS INTENSITY EXPERIENCE SYMPTOM
                 (APPLICATIONS: 2415)

T-96   TEMPLER, D. I.
                 DEATH ANXIETY SCALE.
                 PROCEEDINGS OF THE 77TH ANNUAL CONVENTION OF THE AMERICAN PSYCHOLOGICAL
                 ASSOCIATION, 1969, 4, 737-738.
            TEMPLER, D. I.
                 THE CONSTRUCTION AND VALIDATION OF A DEATH ANXIETY SCALE.
                 JOURNAL OF GENERAL PSYCHOLOGY, 1970, 82, 165-177.
                 (DEATH ANXIETY SCALE)*
            aT-96 1969M DEATH ANXIETY ATTITUDE MORTALITY FEAR
                 (APPLICATIONS: 2659)

T-98   THOMPSON, A., & ZIMMERMAN, R.
                 GOALS OF COUNSELING: WHOSE? WHEN?
                 JOURNAL OF COUNSELING PSYCHOLOGY, 1969, 16, 121-125.
                 (GOALS CHECKLIST)
            aT-98 1969M GOALS COUNSELING THERAPY CHECKLIST VOCATIONAL SELF DEVELOPMENT
            aFAMILY SOCIAL ADJUSTMENT THERAPIST PATIENT

T-99   THORESON, C. E., & KRUMBOLTZ, J. D.
                 RELATIONSHIP OF COUNSELOR REINFORCEMENT OF SELECTED RESPONSES TO EXTERNAL
                 BEHAVIOR.
                 JOURNAL OF COUNSELING PSYCHOLOGY, 1967, 14, 140-144.
                 (METHOD FOR CATEGORIZING VERBAL RESPONSES IN COUNSELING INTERVIEW)
            aT-99 1967M COUNSELING CONTENT-ANALYSIS INTERVIEW BEHAVIOR RESPONSE VERBAL

T-100   TROW, W. C.
                 PHANTASY AND VOCATIONAL CHOICE.
                 OCCUPATIONS, 1941, 20, 89-93.
                 (VOCATIONAL CHOICE INVENTORY)*
            aT-100 VOCATIONAL 1941M PREFERENCE JOB INTEREST INVENTORY
                 (APPLICATIONS: 1301 1364)

T-101   THOMPSON, A.
                 CONDITIONING OF WORK ORIENTED AND WORK AVERSIVE STATEMENTS OF
                 NEUROPSYCHIATRIC PATIENTS.
                 UNPUBLISHED DOCTORAL DISSERTATION, UNIVERSITY OF MINNESOTA, 1963.
                 (SENTENCE COMPLETION TEST)
            aT-101 1963M SENTENCE-COMP VOCATIONAL ATTITUDES
                 (APPLICATIONS: 1311 1317)

T-102   TREHUB, A.
                 EGO DISJUNCTION AND PSYCHOPATHOLOGY.
                 JOURNAL OF ABNORMAL AND SOCIAL PSYCHOLOGY, 1959, 58, 191-194.
                 (EGO DISJUNCTION SCALE)
            aT-102 1959M CONFLICT EGO FUNCTIONING INTEGRATION EGO-STRENGTH
                 (APPLICATIONS: 1284)

T-104   TIPTON, R. M.
          VOCATIONAL IDENTIFICATION AND ACADEMIC ACHIEVEMENT.
          JOURNAL OF COUNSELING PSYCHOLOGY, 1966, 13, 425-430.
          (MEASURE OF VOCATIONAL IDENTIFICATION)
          @T-104 1966M VOCATIONAL INTEREST IDENTIFICATION INTERPERSONAL RELATIONSHIPS
          @DISTANCE PREFERENCE

T-105   TRUAX, C. B., & CARKHUFF, R. R.
          TOWARD EFFECTIVE COUNSELING AND PSYCHOTHERAPY: TEACHING AND PRACTICE.
          CHICAGO: ALDINE, 1967.
          (DEPTH OF SELF EXPLORATION)
          @T-105 1967M SELF EXPLORATION INTRACEPTIVE THERAPY DISCLOSURE OPENNESS PATIENT
          @PSYCHIATRIC COUNSELING

T-107   TEAHAN, J. E.
          FUTURE TIME PERSPECTIVE, OPTIMISM, AND ACADEMIC ACHIEVEMENT.
          JOURNAL OF ABNORMAL AND SOCIAL PSYCHOLOGY, 1958, 57, 379-380.
          (TAT MEASURE OF FUTURE PERSPECTIVE)
          @T-107 1956M FUTURE TIME PROJECTIVE TAT ORIENTATION PERSPECTIVE
              (APPLICATIONS: 247)

T-109   THAYS, R. G.
          DIMENSIONS OF MARRIAGE ROLES.
          MARRIAGE AND FAMILY LIVING, 1963, 25, 389-404.
          (MARRIAGE ROLE QUESTIONNAIRE)* (MRQ)
          @T-109 1963M MARITAL ROLE RELATIONSHIPS ADJUSTMENT

T-110   TAYLOR, D. W.
          VARIABLES RELATED TO CREATIVITY AND PRODUCTIVITY OF ARMY MEN IN TWO
          RESEARCH LABORATORIES.
          IN C. W. TAYLOR (ED.), RESEARCH CONFERENCE ON THE IDENTIFICATION OF
          CREATIVE SCIENTIFIC TALENT.
          SALT LAKE CITY: UNIVERSITY OF UTAH PRESS, 1957, PP. 20-54.
          (CREATIVITY RATING SCALE)*
          @T-110 1957M CREATIVITY RATING
              (APPLICATIONS: 1799)

T-111   TATZ, S. J.
          SYMBOLIC MEDIATION IN "LEARNING WITHOUT AWARENESS."
          UNPUBLISHED DOCTORAL DISSERTATION, YALE UNIVERSITY, 1956.
          (MEASURE OF CONDITIONING AWARENESS)
          @T-111 1956M AWARENESS

T-113   TAYLOR, C., & COMBS, A. W.
          SELF-ACCEPTANCE AND ADJUSTMENT.
          JOURNAL OF CONSULTING PSYCHOLOGY, 1952, 16, 89-91.
          (MEASURE OF ABILITY TO ACCEPT DAMAGING STATEMENTS ABOUT SELF)
          @T-113 1952M SELF ACCEPTANCE ADJUSTMENT
              (APPLICATIONS: 2654)

T-114   TYLER, L. E.
          RESEARCH EXPLORATIONS IN THE REALM OF CHOICE.
          JOURNAL OF COUNSELING PSYCHOLOGY, 1961, 8, 195-201.
          (CHOICE-PATTERN TECHNIQUE)
          @T-114 1961M JOB VOCATIONAL PREFERENCE ACTIVITIES NEED POWER PRESTIGE STATUS
          @SOCIAL RESPONSIBILITY EXTRAVERSION SECURITY

U-1   ULLMANN, L. P., & GIOVANNONI, J. M.
          THE DEVELOPMENT OF A SELF-REPORT MEASURE OF THE PROCESS-REACTIVE CONTINUUM.
          JOURNAL OF NERVOUS AND MENTAL DISEASE, 1964, 138, 38-42.
          (PALO ALTO SOCIAL BACKGROUND INVENTORY)*
          @U-1 1964M SOCIAL FUNCTIONING LIFE HISTORY PSYCHIATRIC DIAGNOSIS
              (APPLICATIONS: 2096)

U-2   ULMER, R. A., & LIEBERMAN, M.
          THE CHILDREN'S MINIMAL SOCIAL BEHAVIOR SCALE: A SHORT OBJECTIVE MEASURE OF
          PERSONALITY FUNCTIONING (10 YEAR LEVEL).
          PSYCHOLOGICAL REPORTS, 1968, 22, 283-286.
          (CHILDREN'S MINIMAL SOCIAL BEHAVIOR SCALE)*
          @U-2 FUNCTIONING CHILD BEHAVIOR MENTAL-HEALTH PERSONALITY SOCIAL ADJUSTMENT
          @U-2 COMPETENCE GLOBAL MENTAL-ILLNESS 1968M

U-3   UHLMANN, F. W.
                TEST OF COLOR RECOGNITION: FORM DE X-27-61. DETROIT: THE DETROIT EDUCATION
                COMPANY, 1962.
                (GROUP ADAPTATION OF STROOP'S COLOR-WORD INTERFERENCE TEST)*
           @U-3 FLEXIBILITY PERCEPTION GROUP COGNITIVE STRUCTURE FUNCTIONING 1962M
                (APPLICATIONS: 70)

U-4   ULLMANN, L. P.
                CLINICAL CORRELATES OF FACILITATION AND INHIBITION OF RESPONSE TO
                EMOTIONAL STIMULI.
                JOURNAL OF PROJECTIVE TECHNIQUES, 1958, 22, 341-347.
                (FACILITATION-INHIBITION SCALE)
           @U-4 1958M DEFENSE INHIBITION FACILITATION PROJECTIVE TAT EMOTION LIFE HISTORY
           @U-4 RATING
                (APPLICATIONS: 1054 1713 1899)

U-5   ULLMANN, L. P., & GIOVANNONI, J. M.
                THE DEVELOPMENT OF A SELF-REPORT MEASURE OF THE PROCESS-REACTIVE CONTINUUM.
                JOURNAL OF NERVOUS AND MENTAL DISEASE, 1964, 138, 38-42.
                (SELF REPORT MEASURE OF PROCESS-REACTIVE SCHIZOPHRENIA)
           @U-5 1964M SELF DESCRIPTION SCHIZOPHRENIA MENTAL-ILLNESS PRIMARY-PROCESS
           @U-5 REACTIVITY
                (APPLICATIONS: 476   1010   1033   2092   2193   2243   2268   2439   2583   2725)

U-6   UHRBROCK, R. S.
                2000 SCALED ITEMS.
                PERSONNEL PSYCHOLOGY, 1961, 14, 375-420.
                (MEASURE OF EMPLOYEE ATTITUDES)
           @U-6 1961M ABILITY LEADERSHIP SUPERVISOR INTERPERSONAL RELATIONSHIPS
           @U-6 EFFECTIVENESS JOB
                (APPLICATIONS: 2705)

U-7   UZGIRIS, I., & HUNT, J. MCV.
                AN INSTRUMENT FOR ASSESSING PSYCHOLOGICAL DEVELOPMENT.
                URBANA: UNIVERSITY OF ILLINOIS, PSYCHOLOGICAL DEVELOPMENT LABORATORY,
                1966 (MIMEO).
                (INFANT PSYCHOLOGICAL DEVELOPMENT SCALE)*
           @U-7 1966M CHILD DEVELOPMENT GROWTH MATURITY PERSONALITY
                (APPLICATIONS: 2972)

U-8   ULLMANN, L. P., & MCFARLAND, R. L.
                PRODUCTIVITY AS A VARIABLE IN TAT PROTOCOLS: A METHODOLOGICAL STUDY.
                JOURNAL OF PROJECTIVE TECHNIQUES, 1957, 21, 80-88.
                (INDEX OF PROJECTIVE PRODUCTIVITY)
           @U-8 1957M PROJECTIVE EMOTION FANTASY TAT RESPONSE

U-9   ULLMANN, L. P., & MCFARLAND, R. L.
                PRODUCTIVITY AS A VARIABLE IN TAT PROTOCOLS--A METHODOLOGICAL STUDY.
                JOURNAL OF PROJECTIVE TECHNIQUES, 1957, 21, 80-87.
                (INDEX OF EMOTIONAL RESPONSES TO TAT)
           @U-9 1957M EMOTION MOOD TAT EXPRESSION PROJECTIVE RESPONSE

U-10   UTTON, A. C.
                RECALLED PARENT-CHILD RELATIONS AS DETERMINANTS OF VOCATIONAL CHOICE.
                JOURNAL OF COUNSELING PSYCHOLOGY, 1962, 9, 49-53.
                (CHILDHOOD EXPERIENCE RATING SCALES)*
           @U-10 1962M CHILD RATING SELF EXPERIENCE ACTIVITIES BEHAVIOR LIFE HISTORY
           @FAMILY ENVIRONMENT ACCEPTANCE AFFECTION RELATIONSHIPS PARENTAL
                (APPLICATIONS: 1546)

V-1   VAN DE CASTLE, R. L.
                DEVELOPMENT AND VALIDATION OF A PERCEPTUAL MATURITY SCALE USING FIGURE
                PREFERENCES.
                JOURNAL OF CONSULTING PSYCHOLOGY, 1965, 29, 314-319.
                (PERCEPTUAL MATURITY SCALE)*
           @V-1 PERCEPTION MATURITY ADJUSTMENT OTHER-CATEGORY FIGURE PREFERENCE 1965M

V-2   VERNON, D. T. A., FOLEY, J. M., & SCHULMAN, J. L.
                EFFECT OF MOTHER-CHILD SEPARATION AND BIRTH ORDER ON YOUNG CHILDREN'S
                RESPONSES TO TWO POTENTIALLY STRESSFUL EXPERIENCES.
                JOURNAL OF PERSONALITY AND SOCIAL PSYCHOLOGY, 1967, 5, 162-174.
                (PARENT ACTIVITY QUESTIONNAIRE)
           @V-2 PARENTAL BEHAVIOR PARENT-CHILD PROTECTIVENESS AFFECTION DEPENDENCE FAMILY
           @V-2 INTERACTION ADJUSTMENT 1967M

V-3   VAUGHAN, J. A., & KNAPP, R. H.
               A STUDY IN PESSIMISM.
               JOURNAL OF SOCIAL PSYCHOLOGY, 1963, 59, 77-92.
               (MEASURE OF PESSIMISM)
           aV-3 MORAL ORIENTATION PESSIMISM AFFECTIVE-STATES NEGATIVE 1963M PERSONAL

V-4   VEROFF, J.
               DEVELOPMENT AND VALIDATION OF A PROJECTIVE MEASURE OF POWER MOTIVATION.
               JOURNAL OF ABNORMAL AND SOCIAL PSYCHOLOGY, 1957, 54, 1-8.
           VEROFF, J.
               DEVELOPMENT AND VALIDATION OF A PROJECTIVE MEASURE OF POWER MOTIVATION.
               IN J. W. ATKINSON (ED.), MOTIVES IN FANTASY, ACTION, AND SOCIETY.
               PRINCETON: VAN NOSTRAND, 1958.
               (TAT SCORED FOR NEED POWER)
           aV-4 NEED POWER TAT ADJUSTMENT PROJECTIVE IMAGERY MOTIVE 1958M AUTONOMY
               (APPLICATIONS: 342 1168 2014)

V-5   VALINS, S.
               PSYCHOPATHY AND PHYSIOLOGICAL REACTIVITY UNDER STRESS.
               UNPUBLISHED MASTER'S THESIS, COLUMBIA UNIVERSITY, 1963.
               (QUESTIONNAIRE OF "EMOTIONALITY" OR "NERVOUSNESS")
           aV-5 ADJUSTMENT PSYCHOPATHY MENTAL-ILLNESS EMOTION NERVOUSNESS AFFECTIVE-STATES
           aV-5 REACTIVITY 1963M ANXIETY

V-6   VERNON, D. T. A., FOLEY, J. M., & SCHULMAN, J. L.
               EFFECT OF MOTHER-CHILD SEPARATION AND BIRTH ORDER ON YOUNG CHILDREN'S
               RESPONSES TO TWO POTENTIALLY STRESSFUL EXPERIENCES.
               JOURNAL OF PERSONALITY AND SOCIAL PSYCHOLOGY, 1967, 5, 162-174.
               (DEPENDENCY SCALES)
           aV-6 PARENT-CHILD DEPENDENCE PROTECTIVENESS ORIENTATION BEHAVIOR RATING FAMILY
           aV-6 INTERACTION ADJUSTMENT AUTONOMY 1967M

V-7   VELDMAN, D. J., & WORCHEL, P.
               DEFENSIVENESS AND SELF-ACCEPTANCE IN THE MANAGEMENT OF HOSTILITY.
               JOURNAL OF ABNORMAL AND SOCIAL PSYCHOLOGY, 1961, 63, 319-325.
               (HOSTILE ATTITUDES INDEX)*
           aV-7 1961M HOSTILITY ANGER ATTITUDE AGGRESSION

V-8   VOGEL, J. L.
               AUTHORITARIANISM IN THE THERAPEUTIC RELATIONSHIP.
               JOURNAL OF CONSULTING PSYCHOLOGY, 1961, 25, 102-108.
               (AUTHORITARIAN-EQUALITARIAN THERAPY SORT)*
           aV-8 Q-SORT ADJUSTMENT OTHER-CATEGORY COPING-DEFENSE AUTHORITARIANISM THERAPY
           aV-8 COUNSELING INTERPERSONAL RELATIONSHIPS STYLE INTERACTION PATIENT 1961M
           aV-8 MENTAL-ILLNESS MENTAL-HEALTH

V-9   VELDMAN, D. J., & PECK, R. F.
               STUDENT TEACHER CHARACTERISTICS FROM THE PUPILS' VIEWPOINT.
               JOURNAL OF EDUCATIONAL PSYCHOLOGY, 1963, 54, 346-355.
               (PUPIL OBSERVATION SURVEY)*
           aV-9 STUDENT TEACHER EVALUATION ELEMENTARY SCHOOL SECONDARY TRAIT 1963M BEHAVIOR

V-10   VONDRACEK, F. W.
               THE MANIPULATION OF SELF-DISCLOSURE IN AN EXPERIMENTAL INTERVIEW SITUATION.
               UNPUBLISHED DOCTORAL DISSERTATION, PENNSYLVANIA STATE UNIVERSITY, 1968.
               (BEHAVIORAL MEASURE OF SELF-DISCLOSURE)
           aV-10 SELF-IDENTITY SELF DISCLOSURE RATING COMMUNICATION BEHAVIOR ACCESSIBILITY
           aV-10 PERSONAL INTERPERSONAL RELATIONSHIPS INTERACTION 1968M

V-11   VAN DER VEEN, F.
               THE FAMILY CONCEPT Q SORT.
               DANE COUNTY GUIDANCE CENTER, MADISON, WISCONSIN, 1960, UNPUBLISHED PAPER.
           VAN DER VEEN, F.
               RELATIONSHIPS BETWEEN THE PARENTS' CONCEPT OF THE FAMILY AND FAMILY
               ADJUSTMENT.
               AMERICAN JOURNAL OF ORTHOPSYCHIATRY, 1964, 34, 45-55.
               (FAMILY-CONCEPT Q SORT)*
           aV-11 1960M CHILD MARITAL Q-SORT DESCRIPTION FAMILY CONCEPT IDEAL INTERACTION
           aEVALUATION PERCEPTION ROLE ATTITUDE PARENTAL ADJUSTMENT

V-12   VAN DER VEEN, F., HUEBNER, B., JORGENS, B., & NEJA, P., JR.
        RELATIONSHIPS BETWEEN THE PARENT'S CONCEPT OF THE FAMILY AND FAMILY
        ADJUSTMENT.
        AMERICAN JOURNAL OF ORTHOPSYCHIATRY, 1964, 34, 45-55.
        (FAMILY SEMANTIC TEST)*
     @V-12 RELATIONSHIPS STABILITY SEM-DIFFERENTIAL EVALUATION CONCEPT FAMILY
     @V-12 ADJUSTMENT INTERACTION DESCRIPTION MARITAL INTERACTION PARENT-CHILD 1964M
        (APPLICATIONS: 2316)

V-13   VAN DER WERFF, J. J.
        CONTRADICTIONS AND INCOMPATIBILITIES IN THE SELF AND THE IDEAL-SELF
        CONCEPT.
        ACTA PSYCHOLOGICA, 1967, 26, 249-256.
        (MEASURE OF THE DIVERGENCY OF SELF AND IDEAL-SELF CONCEPTS)
     @V-13 DISCREPANCY CONCEPT SELF IDEAL GLOBAL ADJUSTMENT SELF-IDENTITY PERCEPTION
     @V-13 EVALUATION ESTEEM IMAGE 1967M

V-14   VELDMAN, D. J., & WORCHEL, P.
        DEFENSIVENESS AND SELF-ACCEPTANCE IN THE MANAGEMENT OF HOSTILITY.
        JOURNAL OF ABNORMAL AND SOCIAL PSYCHOLOGY, 1961, 63, 319-325.
        (PROJECTED ANGER INDEX)*
     @V-14 1961M HOSTILITY ANGER PROJECTIVE EMOTION

V-15   VELDMAN, D. J., & WORCHEL, P.
        DEFENSIVENESS AND SELF-ACCEPTANCE IN THE MANAGEMENT OF HOSTILITY.
        JOURNAL OF ABNORMAL AND SOCIAL PSYCHOLOGY, 1961, 63, 319-325.
        (DIRECT ANGER INDEX)*
     @V-15 1961M HOSTILITY ANGER EMOTION

V-16   VROOM, V.
        SOME PERSONALITY DETERMINANTS OF THE EFFECTS OF PARTICIPATION. ENGLEWOOD
        CLIFFS, NEW JERSEY: PRENTICE-HALL, 1960.
        (AUTHORITARIAN SCALE)
     @V-16 AUTHORITARIANISM COPING-DEFENSE 1960M
        (APPLICATIONS: 2471)

V-17   VROOM, V.
        SOME PERSONALITY DETERMINANTS OF THE EFFECTS OF PARTICIPATION. ENGLEWOOD
        CLIFFS, NEW JERSEY: PRENTICE-HALL, 1960.
        (NEED FOR INDEPENDENCE)
     @V-17 NEED DEPENDENCE AUTONOMY 1960M
        (APPLICATIONS: 2471)

V-18   VROOM, V.
        SOME PERSONALITY DETERMINANTS OF THE EFFECTS OF PARTICIPATION. ENGLEWOOD
        CLIFFS, NEW JERSEY: PRENTICE-HALL, 1960.
        (EFFECTIVENESS MEASURE)
     @V-18 JOB EFFFCTIVENESS COMPETENCE RATING EMPLOYEE 1960M
        (APPLICATIONS: 2471)

V-19   VROOM, V.
        SOME PERSONALITY DETERMINANTS OF THE EFFECTS OF PARTICIPATION. ENGLEWOOD
        CLIFFS, NEW JERSEY: PRENTICE-HALL, 1960.
        (ATTITUDE TOWARD THE JOB SCALE)
     @V-19 JOB SATISFACTION SUPERVISOR ATTITUDE AFFECTIVE-STATES 1960M
        (APPLICATIONS: 2471)

V-20   VROOM, V.
        SOME PERSONALITY DETERMINANTS OF THE EFFECTS OF PARTICIPATION. ENGLEWOOD
        CLIFFS, NEW JERSEY: PRENTICE-HALL, 1960.
        (PSYCHOLOGICAL INFLUENCE SCALE)
     @V-20 PARTICIPATION JOB INFLUENCE MANAGEMENT 1960M
        (APPLICATIONS: 2471)

V-21   VROOM, V. H.
        ORGANIZATIONAL CHOICE: A STUDY OF PRE- AND POST-DECISION PROCESSES.
        ORGANIZATIONAL BEHAVIOR AND HUMAN PERFORMANCE, 1966, 1, 212-225.
        (INSTRUMENTALITY-GOAL INDEX)*
     @V-21 1970M GOALS JOB VOCATIONAL PREFERENCE
        (APPLICATIONS: 2347)

V-22   VERINIS, J. S.
        THERAPEUTIC EFFECTIVENESS OF UNTRAINED VOLUNTEERS WITH CHRONIC PATIENTS.
        JOURNAL OF CONSULTING AND CLINICAL PSYCHOLOGY, 1970, 34, 152-155.
        (RATING SCALE FOR BEHAVIOR OF MENTAL PATIENTS)
     @V-22 1970M RATING MENTAL-ILLNESS BEHAVIOR WARD PSYCHIATRIC PATIENT DIAGNOSIS
     @V-22 PROGNOSIS

V-23   VEROFF, J., ATKINSON, J. W., FELD, S. C., & GURIN, G.
         THE USE OF THEMATIC APPERCEPTION TO ASSESS MOTIVATION IN A NATIONWIDE
         INTERVIEW STUDY.
         PSYCHOLOGICAL MONOGRAPHS, 1960, 74 (12,-WHOLE NO. 499).
         (SURVEY MEASURE OF NEED ACHIEVEMENT)
      aV-23 1960M TAT IMAGERY PROJECTIVE ACHIEVEMENT MOTIVE DRIVE
      aV-23 NEED AUTONOMY
            (APPLICATIONS: 92   2165   2761   2839)

V-24   VIGOTSKY, L. S.
         NO REFERENCE--CITED IN:
         MYDEN, W.
         INTERPRETATION AND EVALUATION OF CERTAIN PERSONALITY CHARACTERISTICS
         INVOLVED IN CREATIVE PRODUCTION.
         PERCEPTUAL AND MOTOR SKILLS, 1959, 9, 139-158.
         (VIGOTSKY CONCEPT FORMATION TEST)
      aV-24 1959M CREATIVITY COGNITIVE STYLE FUNCTIONING THINKING CONCEPT FORMATION
            (APPLICATIONS: 2912)

V-25   VELDMAN, D. J., & PARKER, G. V. C.
         ADJECTIVE RATING SCALES FOR SELF DESCRIPTION.
         MULTIVARIATE BEHAVIORAL RESEARCH, 1970, 5, 295-302.
         (ADJECTIVE RATING SCALES FOR SELF DESCRIPTION)
      aV-25 1970M SELF DESCRIPTION RATING SOCIAL ADJUSTMENT COMPETENCE
            (APPLICATIONS: 2978)

V-26   VOGEL, J. L.
         AUTHORITARIANISM IN THE THERAPEUTIC RELATIONSHIP.
         JOURNAL OF CONSULTING PSYCHOLOGY, 1961, 25, 102-108.
         (OBSERVER RATING SCALE)
      aV-26 1961M THERAPY PATIENT COUNSELING RELATIONSHIPS SATISFACTION BEHAVIOR
      aV-26 AGGRESSION ANXIETY DOMINANCE RIGIDITY FLEXIBILITY

V-27   VINGOE, F. J.
         ROGERS' SELF THEORY AND EYSENCK'S EXTRAVERSION AND NEUROTICISM.
         JOURNAL OF CONSULTING AND CLINICAL PSYCHOLOGY, 1968, 32, 618-620.
         (SELF AND PEER RATING SCALES)
      aV-27 1968M SELF PEER RATING DOMINANCE EXTRAVERSION SELF-ACCEPTANCE SOCIABILITY
      aV-27 RESPONSIBILITY SOCIAL DESIRABILITY

V-28   VELDMAN, D. J.
         FORTRAN PROGRAMMING FOR THE BEHAVIORAL SCIENCES.
         NEW YORK: HOLT, RINEHART, & WINSTON, 1967.
         VELDMAN, D. J., & BROWN, O. H.
         PERSONALITY AND PERFORMANCE CHARACTERISTICS ASSOCIATED WITH CIGARETTE
         SMOKING AMONG COLLEGE FRESHMEN.
         JOURNAL OF CONSULTING AND CLINICAL PSYCHOLOGY, 1969, 33, 109-119.
         (ONE-WORD SENTENCE COMPLETION TEST)*
      aV-28 1967M ATTITUDE SELF-IDENTITY ADJUSTMENT PERSONAL ORIENTATION
      aV-28 AFFECTIVE-STATES MULTITRAIT
            (APPLICATIONS: 1382   2242)

V-29   VAN BUSKIRK, C.
         PERFORMANCE ON COMPLEX REASONING TASKS AS A FUNCTION OF ANXIETY.
         JOURNAL OF ABNORMAL AND SOCIAL PSYCHOLOGY, 1961, 62, 201-209.
         (PICTURE INTERPRETATION TEST)
      aV-29 1961M PROJECTIVE MANIFEST ANXIETY AFFECTIVE-STATES
      aV-29 FRUSTRATION

V-30   VAN BUSKIRK, C.
         PERFORMANCE ON COMPLEX REASONING TASKS AS A FUNCTION OF ANXIETY.
         JOURNAL OF ABNORMAL AND SOCIAL PSYCHOLOGY, 1961, 62, 201-209.
         (SELF-DESCRIPTION INVENTORY MEASURE OF ANXIETY)
      aV-30 1961M AFFECTIVE-STATES MANIFEST ANXIETY FEAR FAILURE AUTONOMY ACHIEVEMENT
      aV-30 NEED FRUSTRATION

V-31   VEROFF, J., ATKINSON, J. W., FELD, S. C., & GURIN, G.
         THE USE OF THEMATIC APPERCEPTION TO ASSESS MOTIVATION IN A NATIONWIDE
         INTERVIEW STUDY.
         PSYCHOLOGICAL MONOGRAPHS, 1960, 74, (12, WHOLE NO. 499).
         (SURVEY MEASURE OF NEED AFFILIATION)
      aV-31 1960M TAT IMAGERY NEED AFFILIATION AUTONOMY
      aV-31 INTERPERSONAL RELATIONSHIPS PROJECTIVE
            (APPLICATIONS: 129)

V-32   VAUGHAN, G. M., & THOMPSON, R. H. T.
              NEW ZEALAND CHILDREN'S ATTITUDES TOWARD MAORIS.
              JOURNAL OF ABNORMAL AND SOCIAL PSYCHOLOGY, 1961, 62, 701-704.
              (TAT PICTURES INVOLVING MAORI AND WHITE INDIVIDUALS)
          aV-32 1961M PROJECTIVE ATTITUDE MINORITY RACIAL ETHNIC ETHNOCENTRISM
          aV-32 PREJUDICE TOLERANCE STEREOTYPE

V-33   VOGEL, W., KUN, K. J., & MESHORER, E.
              CHANGES IN ADAPTIVE BEHAVIOR IN INSTITUTIONALIZED RETARDATES IN RESPONSE
              TO ENVIRONMENTAL ENRICHMENT OR DEPRIVATION.
              JOURNAL OF CONSULTING AND CLINICAL PSYCHOLOGY, 1968, 32, 76-82.
              (SOCIAL AND EMOTIONAL BEHAVIOR INVENTORY)
          aV-33 1968M SOCIAL EMOTION BEHAVIOR
              (APPLICATIONS: 1128)

V-34   VENABLES, P. H.
              A SHORT SCALE FOR RATING "ACTIVITY-WITHDRAWAL" IN SCHIZOPHRENICS.
              JOURNAL OF MENTAL SCIENCE, 1957, 103, 197-199.
              (MEASURE OF BEHAVIOR WITHDRAWAL)
          aV-34 1957M BEHAVIOR SCHIZOPHRENIA WITHDRAWAL MENTAL-ILLNESS PATIENT
          aV-34 SYMPTOM
              (APPLICATIONS: 1001)

V-35   VENABLES, P. J., & O'CONNOR, N.
              A SHORT SCALE FOR RATING PARANOID SCHIZOPHRENIA.
              JOURNAL OF MENTAL SCIENCE, 1959, 105, 815-818.
              (RATING SCALE FOR PARANOID SCHIZOPHRENIA)
          aV-35 1959M SCHIZOPHRENIA RATING MENTAL-ILLNESS PSYCHIATRIC DIAGNOSIS PARANOID
          aBEHAVIOR

V-36   VON SINGER, R., & PEDERSON, M. G.
              BEHAVIORAL CORRELATES OF THE ACL HETEROSEXUAL SCALE.
              PSYCHOLOGICAL REPORTS, 1970, 26, 719-722.
              (HETEROSEXUAL BEHAVIOR SURVEY QUESTIONNAIRE)
          aV-36 1970M SEX ROLE MASCULINITY IDENTIFICATION AWARENESS BEHAVIOR

V-38   VIDMAR, N., & MCGRATH, J. E.
              ROLE STRUCTURE, LEADERSHIP AND NEGOTIATION EFFECTIVENESS.
              (TECH. REP. NO. 6).
              URBANA: UNIVERSITY OF ILLINOIS, DEPARTMENT OF PSYCHOLOGY, 1967.
          VIDMAR, N.
              EFFECTS OF REPRESENTATIONAL ROLES AND MEDIATORS ON NEGOTIATION
              EFFECTIVENESS.
              JOURNAL OF PERSONALITY AND SOCIAL PSYCHOLOGY, 1971, 17(1), 48-58.
              (MEASURE OF PREFERENCE FOR BROAD OR CAREER ORIENTED EDUCATION)
          aV-38 1971M PREFERENCE COLLEGE ACADEMIC SEM-DIFFERENTIAL INTEREST
          aATTITUDE ORIENTATION

V-39   VIDMAR, N., & MCGRATH, J. E.
              ROLE STRUCTURE, LEADERSHIP AND NEGOTIATION EFFECTIVENESS.
              (TECH. REP. NO. 6).
              URBANA: UNIVERSITY OF ILLINOIS, DEPARTMENT OF PSYCHOLOGY, 1967.
          VIDMAR, N.
              EFFECTS OF REPRESENTATIONAL ROLES AND MEDIATORS ON NEGOTIATION
              EFFECTIVENESS.
              JOURNAL OF PERSONALITY AND SOCIAL PSYCHOLOGY, 1971, 17, 48-58.
              (OTHER-ESTEEM QUESTIONNAIRE)
          aV-39 1971M SEM-DIFFERENTIAL OTHERS ESTEEM EVALUATION ATTITUDE

V-40   VIDMAR, N., & MCGRATH, J. E.
              ROLE STRUCTURE, LEADERSHIP AND NEGOTIATION EFFECTIVENESS.
              (TECH. REP. NO. 6).
              URBANA: UNIVERSITY OF ILLINOIS, DEPARTMENT OF PSYCHOLOGY, 1967.
          VIDMAR, N.
              EFFECTS OF REPRESENTATIONAL ROLES AND MEDIATORS ON NEGOTIATION
              EFFECTIVENESS.
              JOURNAL OF PERSONALITY AND SOCIAL PSYCHOLOGY, 1971, 17, 48-58.
              (POSTMEETING QUESTIONNAIRE)
          aV-40 1971M GROUP SATISFACTION FEELING ACHIEVEMENT

V-41   VIDMAR, N., & MCGRATH, J. E.
                ROLE STRUCTURE, LEADERSHIP AND NEGOTIATION EFFECTIVENESS.
                (TECH. REP. NO. 6).
                URBANA: UNIVERSITY OF ILLINOIS, DEPARTMENT OF PSYCHOLOGY, 1967.
           VIDMAR, N.
                EFFECTS OF REPRESENTATIONAL ROLES AND MEDIATORS ON NEGOTIATION
                EFFECTIVENESS.
                JOURNAL OF PERSONALITY AND SOCIAL PSYCHOLOGY, 1971, 17, 48-58.
                (BEHAVIOR DESCRIPTION QUESTIONNAIRE)
           aV-41 1971M BEHAVIOR GROUP SATISFACTION DESCRIPTION

V-43   VAN DE CASTLE, R. L.
                PERCEPTUAL IMMATURITY AND ACQUIESCENCE AMONG VARIOUS DEVELOPMENTAL LEVELS.
                JOURNAL OF CONSULTING PSYCHOLOGY, 1962, 26, 167-171.
                (PERCEPTUAL MATURITY SCALE)
           aV-43 1962M MATURITY PERCEPTION

V-44   VOIGT, J.
                DIE AKTUALGENESE IN DER PSYCHOLOGISCHENS DIAGNOSTIK.
                PSYCHOL. BEIT., 1956, 2, 586-636.
           DRAGUNS, J. G., & MULTARI, G.
                RECOGNITION OF PERCEPTUALLY AMBIGUOUS STIMULI IN GRADE SCHOOL CHILDREN.
                CHILD DEVELOPMENT, 1961, 32, 541-550.
                (PERCEPTUAL AMBIGUITY TASK)
           aV-44 1956M PERCEPTION AMBIGUITY STIMULUS GRAPHIC

V-45   VAVRA, C. E., & RAINBOTH, E. D.
                A STUDY OF PATIENTS' ATTITUDES TOWARD CARE AT FIRLAND SANITORIUM.
                UNPUBLISHED MANUSCRIPT. SEATTLE: DEPT. OF PUBLIC HEALTH, SCHOOL OF
                MEDICINE, UNIVERSITY OF WASHINGTON, 1955.
                (PATIENT'S OPINION FORM)
           aV-45 1955M OPINION ATTITUDE PATIENT HOSPITALIZATION ENVIRONMENT
                (APPLICATIONS: 1981)

V-46   VIELHAUER, J.
                THE DEVELOPMENT OF A SEMANTIC SCALE FOR THE DESCRIPTION OF THE PHYSICAL
                ENVIRONMENT.
                DISSERTATION ABSTRACTS, 1965, NO. 66-759.
                (ENVIRONMENTAL DESCRIPTION SCALE)
           aV-46 1965M ENVIRONMENT PHYSICAL DESCRIPTION
                (APPLICATIONS: 2145)

W-1   WAHLER, H. J.
                THE SELF-DESCRIPTION INVENTORY MEASURING LEVELS OF SELF-EVALUATIVE BEHAVIOR
                IN TERMS OF FAVORABLE OR UNFAVORABLE PERSONALITY ATTRIBUTES.
                JOURNAL OF CLINICAL PSYCHOLOGY, 1968, 24, 40-45.
                (SELF-DESCRIPTION INVENTORY)*
           aW-1 W-108R 1968M SELF-IDENTITY PERCEPTION ESTEEM DESCRIPTION IMAGE SOCIAL
           aRESPONSE-BIAS DESIRABILITY SELF EVALUATION

W-2   WALLACH, M. A., & KOGAN, N.
                SEX DIFFERENCES AND JUDGMENT PROCESSES.
                JOURNAL OF PERSONALITY, 1959, 27, 555-564.
                (CHOICE DILEMMAS QUESTIONNAIRE)*
           aW-2 RISK-TAKING BEHAVIOR COPING-DEFENSE APPROACH AVOIDANCE JUDGMENT AUTONOMY
           aW-2 1959M
                (APPLICATIONS: 190   212   461   537   2345   2492   2496   2497   2529)

W-3   WASHBURN, W. C.
                PATTERNS OF SELF-CONCEPTUALIZATION IN HIGH SCHOOL AND COLLEGE STUDENTS.
                JOURNAL OF EDUCATIONAL PSYCHOLOGY, 1961, 52, 123-131.
                (CALIFORNIA SELF-STRUCTURE SCALE)*
           aW-3 LOCUS CONTROL IE-CONTROL AUTONOMY SELF STRUCTURE COPING-DEFENSE INTEGRATION
           aW-3 SELF-IDENTITY ACTUALIZATION DEVELOPMENT DOMINANCE SUBMISSION 1961M
                (APPLICATIONS: 1745)

W-4   WEBSTER, H.
                ATTITUDE INVENTORY.
                BERKELEY: CENTER FOR THE STUDY OF HIGHER EDUCATION, 1959.
                (RESPONSE SET SCALE)
           aW-4 ACQUIESCENCE RESPONSE-BIAS RESPONSE SET 1959M

W-5   WECHSLER, D.
              THE MEASUREMENT AND APPRAISAL OF ADULT INTELLIGENCE.
              BALTIMORE: WILLIAMS AND WILKINS, 1958.
              (MASCULINITY-FEMININITY MEASURE FROM WAIS)
          aW-5 MASCULINITY FEMININITY SELF-IDENTITY SEX SUB-IDENTITY INTELLIGENCE ROLE
          aW-5 IMAGE CONCEPT SELF ADULT IDENTITY 1958M
              (APPLICATIONS: 2572)

W-6   WECHSLER, H., GROSSER, G. H., & BUSFIELD, B. L., JR.
              THE DEPRESSION RATING SCALE: A QUANTITATIVE APPROACH TO THE ASSESSMENT OF
              DEPRESSIVE SYMPTOMATOLOGY.
              ARCHIVES OF GENERAL PSYCHIATRY, 1963, 9, 334-343.
              (DEPRESSION RATING SCALE)*
          aW-6 DEPRESSION AFFECTIVE-STATES NEGATIVE RATING SYMPTOM MENTAL-ILLNESS
          aW-6 DIAGNOSIS. PSYCHIATRIC 1963M

W-7   WEINER, B.
              ROLE OF SUCCESS AND FAILURE IN THE LEARNING OF EASY AND COMPLEX TASKS.
              JOURNAL OF PERSONALITY AND SOCIAL PSYCHOLOGY, 1966, 3, 339-344.
              (INDEX OF RESULTANT ACHIEVEMENT MOTIVATION)
          aW-7 APPROACH AVOIDANCE MOTIVE AFFECTIVE-STATES TAT ACHIEVEMENT ANXIETY TEST
          aW-7 SUBJECTIVE STRESS AUTONOMY IMAGERY 1966M

W-8   WELSH, G. S.
              FACTOR DIMENSIONS A AND R.
              IN WELSH AND DALSTROM (EDS.). BASIC READINGS ON THE MMPI IN PSYCHOLOGY AND
              MEDICINE. MINNEAPOLIS: UNIVERSITY OF MINNESOTA PRESS, 1956.
              (WELSH ANXIETY SCALE)*
          aW-8 NEUROTICISM MMPI GLOBAL ADJUSTMENT AFFECTIVE-STATES ANXIETY SUBJECTIVE
          aW-8 STRESS NEGATIVE 1956M
              (APPLICATIONS: 21   82   128   202   271   322   378   464   507   577
                              584   657   675   710   757   859   967   970   975   1060
                             1067   1131   1208   1248   1288   1307   1418   1432   1475   1489
                             1570   1587   1622   1624   1643   1739   1746   1807   1854   1899
                             1924   1932   1946   1948   1962   1988   2000   2011   2042   2073
                             2107   2108   2147   2239   2297   2302   2307   2309   2332   2418
                             2420   2517   2528   2581   2677   2725   2910)

W-9   WELSH, G. S.
              MANUAL FOR THE WELSH FIGURE PREFERENCE TEST.
              PALO ALTO: CONSULTING PSYCHOLOGISTS PRESS, 1959.
              (WELSH FIGURE PREFERENCE TEST)*
          aW-9 ESTHETIC PREFERENCE FIGURE PERCEPTION COGNITIVE STRUCTURE FUNCTIONING 1959M
              (APPLICATIONS: 286   358   456   1165   1703   1754   1999   2118   2210   2552
                             2912)

W-10   WEIDER, A., BRODMAN, K., MITTELMANN, B., WECHSLER, D., & WOLFF, H. G.
              THE CORNELL INDEX: A METHOD FOR QUICKLY ASSAYING PERSONALITY AND
              PSYCHOSOMATIC DISTURBANCES, TO BE USED AS AN ADJUNCT TO INTERVIEW.
              PSYCHOSOMATIC MEDICINE, 1946, 8, 411-413.
              (CORNELL INDEX)*
          aW-10 ADJUSTMENT MENTAL-ILLNESS GLOBAL PSYCHIATRIC PATIENT SYMPTOM DIAGNOSIS.
          aW-10 PSYCHOSOMATIC 1946M
              (APPLICATIONS: 1112 2039 2100 2420)

W-11   WESLEY, E.
              PERSEVERATIVE BEHAVIOR IN A CONCEPT-FORMATION TASK AS A FUNCTION OF
              MANIFEST ANXIETY AND RIGIDITY.
              JOURNAL OF ABNORMAL AND SOCIAL PSYCHOLOGY, 1953, 48, 129-134.
              (RIGIDITY SCALE)*
          aW-11 AUTHORITARIANISM COPING-DEFENSE OTHER-CATEGORY RIGIDITY FLEXIBILITY
          aW-11 DOGMATISM THINKING COGNITIVE STRUCTURE FUNCTIONING 1953M
              (APPLICATIONS: 598   678 1704 2140)

W-12   WESSMAN, A. E., & RICKS, D. F.
              MOOD AND PERSONALITY.
              NEW YORK: HOLT, RINEHART, AND WINSTON, 1966.
              (PERSONAL FEELING SCALES)*
          aW-12 PERSONALITY MOOD EMOTION GLOBAL AFFECTIVE-STATES SELF RATING CHANGE 1966M
              (APPLICATIONS: 155 2494 2522)

W-13   WALTHER, R. H.
              SELF-DESCRIPTION AS A PREDICTOR OF SUCCESS OR FAILURE IN FOREIGN SERVICE
              CLERICAL JOBS.
              JOURNAL OF APPLIED PSYCHOLOGY, 1961, 45, 16-21.
              (SELF-DESCRIPTIVE QUESTIONNAIRE)
          aW-13 FAMILY RELATIONSHIPS INTEREST SCHOOL SUCCESS FAILURE JOB PERFORMANCE
          aW-13 VOCATIONAL ADJUSTMENT SELF DESCRIPTION PREDICTION 1961M

W-14   WIGGINS, J. S.
            INTERRELATIONSHIPS AMONG MMPI MEASURES OF DISSIMULATION UNDER STANDARD AND
            SOCIAL DESIRABILITY INSTRUCTIONS.
            JOURNAL OF CONSULTING PSYCHOLOGY, 1959, 23, 419-427.
            (WIGGINS SOCIAL DESIRABILITY SCALE)*
        aW-14 SOCIAL DESIRABILITY RESPONSE-BIAS MMPI 1959M
            (APPLICATIONS: 26   190   859   1414   1626   1702   1816   1854   1872   1899
                            2085   2910)

W-15   WIGGINS, J. S., & WINDER, C. L.
            THE PEER NOMINATION INVENTORY: AN EMPIRICALLY DERIVED SOCIOMETRIC MEASURE
            OF ADJUSTMENT IN PREADOLESCENT BOYS.
            PSYCHOLOGICAL REPORTS, 1961, 9(MONOGRAPH SUPPLEMENT NO. 5), 643-677.
            (PEER NOMINATION INVENTORY)*
        aW-15 SOCIAL ADJUSTMENT AGGRESSION WITHDRAWAL DEPENDENCE DEPRESSION COMPETENCE
        aW-15 PEER SOCIOMETRIC ADOLESCENT STATUS 1961M
            (APPLICATIONS: 903)

W-16   WILLIAMSON, E. G., & DARLEY, J. G.
            THE MINNESOTA INVENTORY OF SOCIAL BEHAVIOR.
            NEW YORK: THE PSYCHOLOGICAL CORPORATION, 1937.
            (MINNESOTA INVENTORY OF SOCIAL BEHAVIOR)*
        aW-16 SOCIAL ADJUSTMENT INVENTORY COMPETENCE INTERPERSONAL RELATIONSHIPS
        aW-16 INTERACTION BEHAVIOR 1937M
            (APPLICATIONS: 2244)

W-17   WILSON, R. S.
            PERSONALITY PATTERNS, SOURCE ATTRACTIVENESS, AND CONFORMITY.
            JOURNAL OF PERSONALITY, 1960, 28, 186-199.
            (MEASURES OF CONFORMITY)
        aW-17 CONFORMITY AUTONOMY 1960M

W-18   WINDER, C. L., & RAU, L. R.
            PARENTAL ATTITUDES ASSOCIATED WITH SOCIAL DEVIANCE IN PREADOLESCENT BOYS.
            JOURNAL OF ABNORMAL AND SOCIAL PSYCHOLOGY, 1962, 64, 418-424.
            (STANFORD PARENT ATTITUDE QUESTIONNAIRE)*
        aW-18 PARENT-CHILD CHILD PARENTAL ATTITUDE FAMILY INTERACTION ADJUSTMENT SOCIAL
        aW-18 COMPETENCE 1962M

W-19   WITKIN, H. A.
            INDIVIDUAL DIFFERENCES IN EASE OF PERCEPTION OF EMBEDDED FIGURES.
            JOURNAL OF PERSONALITY, 1950, 19, 1-15.
            WITKIN, H. A., LEWIS, H. B., HERTZMAN, M., MACHOVER, K., MEISSNER, P. B.,
            & WARNER, S.
            PERSONALITY THROUGH PERCEPTION.
            NEW YORK: HARPER AND BROTHERS, 1954.
            (EMBEDDED FIGURES TEST)*
        aW-19 FIELD DEPENDENCE FIGURE PERCEPTION STRUCTURE FUNCTIONING AUTONOMY 1950M
            (APPLICATIONS: 191   381   387   412   416   488   528   546   564   616
                             672   673   963   1119   1121   1126   1495   1638   1768   1786
                            1850   1959   2017   2120   2131   2188   2281   2348   2385   2387
                            2405   2410   2507   2967)

W-20   WITKIN, H. A., DYK, R. B., FATERSON, H. F., GOODENOUGH, D. R., & KARP, S. A.
            PSYCHOLOGICAL DIFFERENTIATION.
            NEW YORK: WILEY, 1962.
            (SOPHISTICATION OF BODY ARTICULATION SCALE FOR THE DRAW-A-PERSON TEST)
        aW-20 COGNITIVE STYLE STRUCTURE SELF-IDENTITY SUB-IDENTITY FIELD DEPENDENCE
        aW-20 AUTONOMY IDENTITY DIFFERENTIATION FUNCTIONING 1962M
            (APPLICATIONS: 67   381   416   869   1119   1495   2967)

W-21   WORCHEL, P.
            ADAPTABILITY SCREENING OF FLYING PERSONNEL: DEVELOPMENT OF A SELF-CONCEPT
            INVENTORY FOR PREDICTING MALADJUSTMENT.
            USAF SCHOOL OF AVIATION MEDICINE REPORT, 1957, NO. 56-62.
            (SELF-ACTIVITY INVENTORY)*
        aW-21 DISCREPANCY PREDICTION SELF CONCEPT HOSTILITY DEPENDENCE ACHIEVEMENT
        aW-21 GLOBAL ADJUSTMENT SELF-IDENTITY IDEAL EVALUATION PERCEPTION ESTEEM 1957M
            (APPLICATIONS: 132   327   342   373   580   688   696   1206   1221   1461
                            1566   2834   2874   2909)

W-22   WRIGHT, L., BOND, D., & DENISON, J. W.
            AN EXPANDED SOCIOMETRIC DEVICE FOR MEASURING PERSONAL EFFECTIVENESS.
            PSYCHOLOGICAL REPORTS, 1968, 23, 263-269.
            (MEASURE OF PERSONAL EFFECTIVENESS)
        aW-22 SOCIOMETRIC EGO-STRENGTH PERSONAL EFFECTIVENESS SOCIAL COMPETENCE
        aW-22 ADJUSTMENT EGO FUNCTIONING EGO-RESILIENCY 1968M
            (APPLICATIONS: 2710)

W-23   WRIGHT, J. H., & HICKS, J. M.
                 CONSTRUCTION AND VALIDATION OF A THURSTONE SCALE OF LIBERALISM-CONSERVATISM
                 JOURNAL OF APPLIED PSYCHOLOGY, 1966, 50, 9-12.
                 (SCALE OF LIBERALISM-CONSERVATISM)
            @W-23 LIBERALISM CONSERVATISM POLITICAL ORIENTATION ATTITUDE 1966M
                 (APPLICATIONS: 2489)

W-24   WRIGHTSMAN, L. S., JR.
                 MEASUREMENT OF PHILOSOPHIES OF HUMAN NATURE.
                 PSYCHOLOGICAL REPORTS, 1964, 14, 743-751.
                 (PHILOSOPHIES OF HUMAN NATURE SCALE)*
            @W-24 ORIENTATION OTHERS ALTRUISM DEPENDENCE TRUST SOCIAL RATIONALITY COMPLEXITY
            @W-24 AUTONOMY ADJUSTMENT AFFECTIVE-STATES ATTITUDE 1964M
                 (APPLICATIONS: 111 1513 2832 2835)

W-25   WIGGINS, J. S.
                 STRATEGIC, METHOD, AND STYLISTIC VARIANCE IN THE MMPI.
                 PSYCHOLOGICAL BULLETIN, 1962, 59, 224-242.
                 (WIGGINS ACQUIESCENCE SCALE)*
            @W-25 ACQUIESCENCE RESPONSE-BIAS MMPI 1962M
                 (APPLICATIONS: 26 1854)

W-26   WALLACH, M. A., & KOGAN, N.
                 MODES OF THINKING IN YOUNG CHILDREN: A STUDY OF THE CREATIVITY-INTELLIGENCE
                 DISTINCTION.
                 NEW YORK: HOLT, RINEHART AND WINSTON, 1965.
                 (MEASURE OF CREATIVITY/THINKING)
            @W-26 CREATIVITY AUTONOMY THINKING COGNITIVE STRUCTURE FUNCTIONING STYLE
            @W-26 INTELLIGENCE CHILD 1965M
                 (APPLICATIONS: 489 2912)

W-27   WALY, P. & COOK, S. W.
                 EFFECT OF ATTITUDE ON JUDGMENTS OF PLAUSIBILITY.
                 JOURNAL OF PERSONALITY AND SOCIAL PSYCHOLOGY, 1965, 2, 745-749.
                 (MEASURE OF ATTITUDES TOWARD NEGROES)
            @W-27 RACIAL PREJUDICE ATTITUDE NEGRO AFFECTIVE-STATES OTHER-CATEGORY
            @W-27 DESEGREGATION 1965M

W-28   WEBSTER, H.
                 VC FIGURE PREFERENCE TEST.
                 POUGHKEEPSIE, NEW YORK: VASSAR COLLEGE, MARY CONOVER MELLON FOUNDATION,
                 1957.
                 (VASSAR COLLEGE FIGURE PREFERENCE TEST)*
            @W-28 MASCULINITY FEMININITY FIGURE PREFERENCE SEX ROLE SELF-IDENTITY ESTHETIC
            @W-28 SUB-IDENTITY HOMOSEXUALITY IDENTITY 1957M
                 (APPLICATIONS: 110   430)

W-29   WEINSTEIN, L.
                 SOCIAL EXPERIENCE AND SOCIAL SCHEMATA.
                 JOURNAL OF PERSONALITY AND SOCIAL PSYCHOLOGY, 1967, 6, 429-434.
                 (PARENTAL ACCEPTANCE MEASURE)
            @W-29 RELATIONSHIPS PARENT-CHILD CHILD PARENTAL ACCEPTANCE PEER SOCIAL
            @W-29 COMPETENCE ADJUSTMENT FAMILY INTERACTION BEHAVIOR 1967M

W-30   WEISSKOPF, E. A.
                 A TRANSCENDENCE INDEX AS A PROPOSED MEASURE IN THE TAT.
                 JOURNAL OF PSYCHOLOGY, 1950, 29, 379-390.
                 (TAT SCORED FOR TRANSCENDENCE/FANTASY ABILITY)
            @W-30 PROJECTIVE TRANSCENDENCE FANTASY ABILITY TAT IMAGERY EXPERIENCE SUBJECTIVE
            @W-30 1950M
                 (APPLICATIONS: 363)

W-31   WEITZENHOFFER, A. M., & HILGARD, E. R.
                 STANFORD HYPNOTIC SUSCEPTIBILTIY SCALE.
                 PALO ALTO, CALIFORNIA: CONSULTING PSYCHOLOGISTS PRESS, 1959.
                 (STANFORD HYPNOTIC SUSCEPTIBILITY SCALE)*
            @W-31 HYPNOTIC SUGGESTIBILITY 1959M
                 (APPLICATIONS: 2   29   95   336   340   406   432   497   759   777
                                    809   850   859   905   938   945   948   955   958   972
                                    976   985   997   1013   1055   1093   1099   1110   1143   1144
                                   1728   1740   1779   1806   1961   2196   2378   2379   2384   2385
                                   2388   2400   2413   2415   2419   2424   2428   2485   2785)

W-32   WILKINSON, H. J. F.
            IMPULSIVITY-DELIBERATIVENESS AND TIME ESTIMATION.
            UNPUBLISHED DOCTORAL DISSERTATION, UNIVERSITY OF PITTSBURGH, 1962.
            (IMPULSIVITY SCALE)
        aW-32 JUDGMENT 1962M TIME REACTIVITY IMPULSE EXPRESSION AFFECTIVE-STATES
        aW-32 OTHER-CATEGORY

W-33   WILSON, W. C.
            EXTRINSIC RELIGIOUS VALUES AND PREJUDICE.
            JOURNAL OF ABNORMAL AND SOCIAL PSYCHOLOGY, 1960, 60, 286-288.
            (EXTRINSIC RELIGIOUS VALUES SCALE)*
        aW-33 RELIGION VALUES IDEALS EXTRINSIC ORIENTATION INTRINSIC MOTIVE AUTONOMY
        aW-33 LIFE STYLE GLOBAL 1960M
            (APPLICATIONS: 169)

W-34   WOHLFORD, P.
            EXTENSION OF PERSONAL TIME, AFFECTIVE STATES, AND EXPECTATION OF PERSONAL
            DEATH.
            JOURNAL OF PERSONALITY AND SOCIAL PSYCHOLOGY, 1966, 3, 559-566.
            (MEASURE OF PROTENSION AND RETROTENSION BY TEMPORAL ASSOCIATIONS)
        aW-34 PERSONAL TIME AFFECTIVE FUTURE ORIENTATION PERSPECTIVE 1966M

W-35   WYER, R. S., JR.
            EFFECT OF CHILD-REARING ATTITUDES AND BEHAVIOR ON CHILDREN'S RESPONSES TO
            HYPOTHETICAL SOCIAL SITUATIONS.
            JOURNAL OF PERSONALITY AND SOCIAL PSYCHOLOGY, 1965, 2, 480-486.
            (INDEX OF SOCIAL UNCERTAINTY)
        aW-35 TIME DECISION 1965M SOCIAL INHIBITION COMPETENCE ADJUSTMENT CHILD
        aW-35 BEHAVIOR SELF EXPRESSION

W-36   WINTERBOTTOM, M. R.
            THE RELATION OF CHILDHOOD TRAINING IN INDEPENDENCE TO ACHIEVEMENT
            MOTIVATION.
            UNPUBLISHED DOCTORAL DISSERTATION, UNIVERSITY OF MICHIGAN, 1953.
            (CHILDHOOD MATERNAL PRACTICES CHECK LIST)*
        aW-36 CHECKLIST PARENT-CHILD RELATIONSHIPS NEED ACHIEVEMENT MATERNAL FAMILY
        aW-36 DEPENDENCE INTERACTION ADJUSTMENT AUTONOMY 1953M

W-37   WOLPE, J., & LANG, P. J.
            A FEAR SURVEY SCHEDULE FOR USE IN BEHAVIOUR THERAPY.
            BEHAVIOR RESEARCH AND THERAPY, 1964, 2, 27-30.
            (FEAR SURVEY SCHEDULE)*
        aW-37 NEGATIVE FEAR PHOBIA AFFECTIVE-STATES ANXIETY SUBJECTIVE BEHAVIOR THERAPY
        aW-37 1964M
            (APPLICATIONS: 229   300   1134   2206   2293   2406   2414   2429   2640   2725)

W-38   WILLIAMS, L. K.
            SOME CORRELATES OF RISK-TAKING.
            PERSONNEL PSYCHOLOGY, 1965, 18, 297-310.
            (JOB PREFERENCE INVENTORY)*
        aW-38 JOB PREFERENCE VOCATIONAL SATISFACTION ENVIROMENT PE-FIT RISK-TAKING
        aW-38 1965M
            (APPLICATIONS: 285   741)

W-39   WORTHY, M., GARY, A. L., & KAHN, G. M.
            SELF-DISCLOSURE AS AN EXCHANGE PROCESS.
            JOURNAL OF PERSONALITY AND SOCIAL PSYCHOLOGY, 1969, 13, 59-63.
            (INTIMACY RATINGS FOR SELF-DISCLOSURE)
        aW-39 SELF DISCLOSURE RESPONSE-BIAS COMMUNICATION DISTANCE ACCESSIBILITY
        aW-39 PERSONAL 1969M

W-40   WRIGHT, F. H., & SHRADER, R. R.
            INFLUENCE OF OPEN AND CLOSED MENTAL HOSPITALS ON ATTITUDES IN THE UNITED
            STATES AND BRITAIN.
            JOURNAL OF COUNSELING PSYCHOLOGY, 1965, 12, 372-378.
            (WRIGHT MENTAL ILLNESS QUESTIONNAIRE)*
        aW-40 ATTITUDE MENTAL-ILLNESS HOSPITALIZATION PERCEPTION VALUES ADJUSTMENT
        aW-40 DISABILITY 1965M
            (APPLICATIONS: 1346)

W-41   WELSH, G. S.
        FACTOR DIMENSIONS A AND R.
        IN WELSH AND DALSTROM (EDS.), BASIC READINGS ON THE MMPI IN PSYCHOLOGY AND
        MEDICINE. MINNEAPOLIS: UNIVERSITY OF MINNESOTA PRESS, 1956.
        (WELSH REPRESSION SCALE)*
        @W-41 COPING-DEFENSE REALITY PERCEPTION DENIAL REPRESSION RESPONSE-BIAS
        @W-41 OTHER-CATEGORY MMPI NEUROTICISM 1956M
        (APPLICATIONS: 34 82 128 202 322 657 667 710 757 792
  859 910 970 1060 1067 1307 1570 1587 1622 1624
  1643 1746 1807 1854 1899 1924 1932 1946 2011 2073
  2107 2108 2239 2302 2309 2420 2528 2581 2677 2725
  2910 2975 2979)

W-42   WENDT, G. R., & CAMERON, J. S.
        CHEMICAL STUDIES OF BEHAVIOR: V. PROCEDURES IN DRUG EXPERIMENTATION WITH
        COLLEGE STUDENTS.
        JOURNAL OF PSYCHOLOGY, 1961, 51, 173-211.
        (SELF DESCRIPTION FOR REACTIONS TO DRUG-TAKING)
        @W-42 1961M CHECKLIST DRUG INFLUENCE SELF DESCRIPTION BEHAVIOR MOOD CHANGE
        @W-42 AFFECTIVE-STATES

W-43   WIENER, M., CARPENTER, B., & CARPENTER, J. T.
        DETERMINATION OF DEFENSE MECHANISMS FOR CONFLICT AREAS FROM VERBAL MATERIAL
        JOURNAL OF COUNSULTING PSYCHOLOGY, 1956, 20, 215-219.
        (MEASURE OF REPRESSIVE AND SENSITIZING DEFENSE MECHANISMS)
        @W-43 DEFENSIVENESS STYLE 1956M REPRESSION SENSITIZATION DEFENSE COPING-DEFENSE
        @W-43 RESPONSE-BIAS

W-44   WITTMAN, P.
        SCALE FOR MEASURING PROGNOSIS IN SCHIZOPHRENIC PATIENTS.
        ELGIN STATE HOSPITAL PAPERS, 1941, 4, 20-33.
        (ELGIN PROGNOSTIC SCALE)*
        @W-44 SCHIZOPHRENIA 1941M GLOBAL OTHER-CATEGORY ADJUSTMENT MENTAL-HEALTH
        @W-44 MENTAL-ILLNESS DIAGNOSIS PROGNOSIS PATIENT THERAPY RATING

W-45   WHITING, J. W. M., ANTONOVSKY, H., CHASDI, E., & AYRES, B.
        THE LEARNING OF VALUES.
        IN E. Z. VOGT AND E. M. ALBERT (EDS.), THE PEOPLE OF RIMROCK. CAMBRIDGE,
        MASSACHUSETTS: HARVARD UNIVERSITY PRESS, 1966.
        (MAGIC MAN TEST)*
        @W-45 MOTIVE CONFLICT 1966M ROLE PREFERENCE VALUES CHILD PROJECTIVE
        @W-45 SELF-IDENTITY CROSS-CULTURAL CULTURE DIFFERENCES
        (APPLICATIONS: 1079)

W-46   WHITING, J. W. M.
        FIGURE PREFERENCE TEST.
        CAMBRIDGE, MASSACHUSETTS: HARVARD UNIVERSITY, DEPARTMENT OF SOCIAL
        RELATIONS, 1965, (MIMEO).
        (WHITING FIGURE PREFERENCE TEST)*
        @W-46 PERCEPTION 1965M MASCULINITY FEMININITY FIGURE PREFERENCE SEX ROLE
        @W-46 DIFFERENCES IDENTITY SELF-IDENTITY SUB-IDENTITY
        (APPLICATIONS: 1079)

W-47   WINTERS, S., BARTLETT, C. J. & LEVE, R.
        INSTRUCTIONAL AND RESPONSE-STYLE FACTORS WITH FORCED-CHOICE RESPONSE.
        AMERICAN PSYCHOLOGIST, 1965, 20, 498. (ABS.)
        (FORCED-CHOICE SOCIAL DESIRABILITY SCALE)
        @W-47 SOCIAL DESIRABILITY RESPONSE-BIAS MMPI 1965M

W-48   WATERHOUSE, I.K., & CHILD, I. L.
        FRUSTRATION AND THE QUALITY OF PERFORMANCE. III. AN EXPERIMENTAL STUDY.
        JOURNAL OF PERSONALITY, 1953, 21, 298-311.
        (MEASURE OF HABITUAL RESPONSE TO FRUSTRATIONS)
        @W-48 PERSONAL RESPONSE STYLE PERFORMANCE AGGRESSION PESSIMISM DEFENSIVENESS
        @W-48 FRUSTRATION AFFECTIVE-STATES ANXIETY SUBJECTIVE STRESS 1953M

W-49   WEGROCKI, H.
        GENERALIZING ABILITY IN SCHIZOPHRENIA: AN INQUIRY INTO THE DISORDERS OF
        PROBLEM THINKING IN SCHIZOPHRENIA.
        ARCHIVES OF PSYCHOLOGY, NEW YORK: 1940, NO. 254.
        (PROVERB INTERPRETATION TEST OF CONCEPTUAL THINKING)
        @W-49 CONCEPTUAL THINKING COGNITIVE FUNCTIONING PROBLEM SCHIZOPHRENIA
        @W-49 MENTAL-ILLNESS DIAGNOSIS 1940M
        (APPLICATIONS: 703)

W-50   WEGROCKI, H.
        GENERALIZING ABILITY IN SCHIZOPHRENIA: AN INQUIRY INTO THE DISORDERS OF
        PROBLEM THINKING IN SCHIZOPHRENIA.
        ARCHIVES OF PSYCHOLOGY, NEW YORK, 1940, NO. 254.
        (ESSENTIAL DIFFERENCES TEST OF CONCEPTUAL THINKING)
        @W-50 CONCEPTUAL THINKING COGNITIVE FUNCTIONING PROBLEM SCHIZOPHRENIA
        @W-50 MENTAL-ILLNESS DIAGNOSIS 1940M
        (APPLICATIONS: 703)

W-51   WINTER, D. G.
        PERSONALITY EFFECTS OF A SUMMER ADVANCED STUDIES PROGRAM.
        UNPUBLISHED BACHELOR'S THESIS, HARVARD UNIVERSITY, 1960.
        (MEASURE OF IDEALS, ATTITUDES, INTERESTS)
        @W-51 STUDY HABITS INTEREST MULTITRAIT IDEALS LIFE GOALS ORIENTATION STYLE
        @W-51 FAMILY RELIGION ATTITUDE 1960M
        (APPLICATIONS: 823)

W-52   WESSMAN, A. E., RICKS, D. F., & TYL, M. M.
        CHARACTERISTICS AND CONCOMITANTS OF MOOD FLUCTUATION IN COLLEGE WOMEN.
        JOURNAL OF ABNORMAL AND SOCIAL PSYCHOLOGY, 1960, 60, 117-126.
        (WRT MOOD SCALE)*
        @W-52 ELATION DEPRESSION NEGATIVE GLOBAL POSITIVE MOOD AFFECTIVE-STATES 1960M
        @W-52 ADJUSTMENT
        (APPLICATIONS: 934 1894 2335)

W-54   WINTERBOTTOM, M. R.
        THE RELATION OF NEED FOR ACHIEVEMENT TO LEARNING EXPERIENCES IN
        INDEPENDENCE AND MASTERY.
        IN J. W. ATKINSON (ED.), MOTIVES IN FANTASY, ACTION, AND SOCIETY.
        PRINCETON, NEW JERSEY: VAN NOSTRAND, 1958.
        (SCALE OF INDEPENDENCE TRAINING)
        @W-54 ADJUSTMENT FAMILY INTERACTION AUTONOMY DEPENDENCE PARENT-CHILD
        @W-54 RELATIONSHIPS 1958M
        (APPLICATIONS: 195 1655)

W-55   WEBSTER, H., SANFORD, N., & FREEDMAN, M.
        A NEW INSTRUMENT FOR STUDYING AUTHORITARIANISM IN PERSONALITY.
        JOURNAL OF PSYCHOLOGY, 1955, 40, 73-84.
        (MEASURE OF AUTHORITARIANISM)
        @W-55 1955M PERSONALITY TRAIT AUTHORITARIANISM COPING-DEFENSE OTHER-CATEGORY
        @F-SCALE ETHNOCENTRISM RIGIDITY COMPULSIVENESS TOLERANCE AMBIGUITY
        (APPLICATIONS: 379   681   1282   1307)

W-56   WHITING, J. W. M.
        (NO REFERENCE AVAILABLE) (1962) SEE ALSO W-45, W-46
        LLOYD, B. B.
        CHOICE BEHAVIOR AND SOCIAL STRUCTURE: A COMPARISON OF TWO AFRICAN
        SOCIETIES.
        JOURNAL OF SOCIAL PSYCHOLOGY, 1968, 74, 3-12.
        (PRETEND GAME TEST)*
        @W-56 TAT PROJECTIVE ROLE PREFERENCE SELF-IDENTITY SEX CHILD CROSS-CULTURAL
        @W-56 DIFFERENCES CULTURE 1962M

W-57   WELSH, G. S.
        AN ANXIETY INDEX AND AN INTERNALIZATION RATIO FOR THE MMPI.
        JOURNAL OF CONSULTING PSYCHOLOGY, 1952, 16, 65-72.
        (INTERNALIZATION OF ANXIETY RATIO)*
        @W-57 AFFECTIVE-STATES ANXIETY SUBJECTIVE STRESS MMPI 1952M
        (APPLICATIONS: 650   1739   2297)

W-58   WORELL, L.
        PREFERENCE AND BEHAVIOR INVENTORY.
        UNPUBLISHED REVISION OF THE EDWARDS PERSONAL PREFERENCE SCHEDULE.
        OKLAHOMA STATE UNIVERSITY, 1965.
        (PREFERENCE AND BEHAVIOR INVENTORY)*
        @W-58 NEED ACHIEVEMENT AFFILIATION AUTONOMY NURTURANCE AGGRESSION ABASEMENT
        @W-58 PREFERENCE BEHAVIOR 1965M
        (APPLICATIONS: 465)

W-59   WALLACH, M. A., & BRANTLEY, H. T.
        RELATIVE GRAPHIC EXPANSIVENESS AS A FUNCTION OF GROSS BODILY ACTIVITY AND
        LEVEL OF PSYCHOLOGICAL DISTURBANCE.
        JOURNAL OF PERSONALITY, 1968, 36, 246-258.
        (GRAPHIC EXPANSIVENESS MEASURE)
        @W-59 INTERACTION ADJUSTMENT COMPETENCE ALIENATION AFFECTIVE-STATES SOCIAL
        @W-59 GRAPHIC EXPANSIVENESS PROJECTIVE MENTAL-ILLNESS DIAGNOSIS 1968M

W-60   WRIGLEY, C., CHERRY, C. N., LEE, M. C., & MCQUITTY, L. L.
            USE OF THE SQUARE ROOT METHOD TO IDENTIFY FACTORS IN THE JOB PERFORMANCE OF
            AIRCRAFT MECHANICS.
            PSYCHOLOGICAL MONOGRAPHS, 1957, 71, (1, WHOLE NO. 430).
            (SUPERVISORY RATING SCALE)
            aW-60 VOCATIONAL LEADERSHIP PERFORMANCE SUPERVISOR BEHAVIOR JOB ADJUSTMENT
            aW-60 RATING MANAGEMENT SATISFACTION 1957M

W-61   WINNE, J. F.
            A SCALE OF NEUROTICISM: AN ADAPTATION OF THE MMPI.
            JOURNAL OF CLINICAL PSYCHOLOGY, 1951, 7, 117-122.
            (NEUROTICISM SCALE)
            aW-61 NEUROTICISM MMPI COPING-DEFENSE STYLE HISTORY ADJUSTMENT 1951M
            (APPLICATIONS: 14   1568)

W-62   WESTIE, F. R.
            A TECHNIQUE FOR THE MEASUREMENT OF RACE ATTITUDES.
            AMERICAN SOCIOLOGICAL REVIEW, 1953, 18, 73-78.
            (MEASURE OF RACIAL ATTITUDES)
            aW-62 1953M RACIAL PREJUDICE AFFECTIVE-STATES OTHER-CATERGORY NEGRO ATTITUDE
            aW-62 SOCIAL DISTANCE

W-63   WEISS, R. L., ULLMANN, L. P., & KRASNER, L.
            ON THE RELATIONSHIP BETWEEN HYPNOTIZABILITY AND RESPONSE TO VERBAL OPERANT
            CONDITIONING.
            PSYCHOLOGICAL REPORTS, 1960, 6, 59-60.
            (MEASURE OF LIKELIHOOD OF HYPOTIZABILITY)
            aW-63 HYPNOTIC SUGGESTIBILITY 1960M

W-64   WELSH, G. S.
            FACTOR DIMENSIONS OF THE MMPI.
            IN G. S. WELSH & W. G. DAHLSTROM (EDS.), BASIC READINGS ON THE MMPI IN
            PSYCHOLOGY AND MEDICINE. MINNEAPOLIS: UNIVESITY OF MINNESOTA PRESS, 1960.
            (CONTROL (C) SCALE)
            aW-64 CONTROL EGO MMPI 1960M
            (APPLICATIONS: 2910)

W-65   WALKER, R. E., & NICOLAY, R. C.
            A RE-EXAMINATION OF ANXIETY: THE NICOLAY-WALKER PERSONAL REACTION SCHEDULE.
            CHICAGO: LOYOLA UNIVERSITY, 1963.
            (NICOLAY-WALKER PERSONAL REACTION SCHEDULE)*
            aW-65 TENSION PRESS SELF CONCEPT ACHIEVEMENT ANXIETY DEMANDS COMPETENCE GUILT
            aW-65 HELPLESSNESS AFFECTIVE-STATES AUTONOMY NEED SUBJECTIVE STRESS MULTITRAIT
            aW-65 1963M
            (APPLICATIONS: 452)

W-66   WEIGEL, V. M., & WEIGEL, R. G.
            EFFECT OF ITEM MEANINGFULNESS ON A SELF-IDEAL-SELF MEASURE.
            PSYCHOLOGICAL REPORTS, 1965, 25, 412-414.
            (SELF/IDEAL-SELF MEASURE)
            aW-66 IDEAL SELF CONCEPT IMAGE SELF-IDENTITY EVALUATION PERCEPTION ESTEEM 1965M

W-67   WEBB, A. P., & EIKENBERY, J.
            A GROUP COUNSELING APPROACH TO THE ACTING-OUT PREADOLESCENT.
            PSYCHOLOGY IN THE SCHOOLS, 1964, 1, 395-400.
            (BEHAVIOR RATING SCALE)
            aW-67 IMPULSE ACHIEVEMENT HAPPINESS HOSTILITY SECURITY CONTROL BEHAVIOR RATING
            aW-67 MULTITRAIT STUDENT TEACHER ADOLESCENT EMOTION SOCIAL MATURITY
            aW-67 AFFECTIVE-STATES 1964M

W-68   WALDER, L. O., ABELSON, R. P., ERON, L. D., BANTA, T. J., & LAULICHT, J. H.
            DEVELOPMENT OF A PEER-RATING MEASURE OF AGGRESSION.
            PSYCHOLOGICAL REPORTS, 1961, 9, 497-556.
            (PEER-RATING MEASURE OF AGGRESSION)
            aW-68 NEGATIVE HOSTILITY BEHAVIOR PEER AGGRESSION AFFECTIVE-STATES 1961M RATING
            aW-68 RESENTMENT ELEMENTARY SCHOOL CHILD
            (APPLICATIONS: 837)

W-69   WENDT, G. R., & CAMERON, J. S.
            CHEMICAL STUDIES OF BEHAVIOR: V. PROCEDURES IN DRUG EXPERIMENTATION WITH
            COLLEGE STUDENTS.
            JOURNAL OF PSYCHOLOGY, 1961, 51, 173-211.
            (MOOD CHECKLIST)
            aW-69 1961M DESCRIPTION CHECKLIST SELF CONCEPT SELF-IDENTITY EVALUATION ESTEEM
            aW-69 PERCEPTION IMAGE MOOD EMOTION

W-70   WEISGERBER, C. A.
        CONSCIOUS PERSEVERATION AND THE PERSISTENCE OF AUTONOMIC ACTIVITY AS
        MEASURED BY RECOVERY FROM THE PSYCHOGALVANIC RESPONSE.
        JOURNAL OF GENERAL PSYCHOLOGY, 1951, 45, 83-93.
        (MEASURE OF CONSCIOUS PERSEVERATION)
     aW-70 COGNITIVE STRUCTURE RIGIDITY FLEXIBILITY FUNCTIONING EXPERIENCE PERCEPTION
     aW-70 1951M

W-71   WEINBERGER, B.
        ACHIEVEMENT MOTIVATION AND THE SELF-CONCEPT.
        UNPUBLISHED HONORS THESIS, UNIVERSITY OF MICHIGAN, 1951.
        (MEASURE OF SELF-ESTEEM)
     aW-71 SELF ESTEEM IMAGE Q-SORT CONCEPT SELF-IDENTITY MULTITRAIT TRAIT EVALUATION
     aW-71 IDEAL DESCRIPTION PERCEPTION 1951M
        (APPLICATIONS: 338   729   810)

W-72   WELSH, G. S.
        WELSH FIGURE PREFERENCE TEST: PRELIMINARY MANUAL. (RESEARCH ED.) PALO ALTO,
        CALIF.: CONSULTING PSYCHOLOGISTS PRESS, 1959.
        (REVISED ART (RA) SCALE)*
     aW-72 FIGURE PREFERENCE ESTHETIC STIMULUS 1959M
        (APPLICATIONS: 181   381   616   672   673   1888   2017   2049   2120   2131
                         2188   2213   2410   2411   2486   2912)

W-73   WITKIN, H. A.
        THE EFFECT OF TRAINING AND OF STRUCTURAL AIDS ON PERFORMANCE IN THREE TESTS
        OF SPACE ORIENTATION.
        CIVIL AERONAUTICS ADMINISTRATION, DIVISION OF RESEARCH, REPORT NO. 80,
        WASHINGTON, D.C.
        WITKIN, H. A., LEWIS, H. B., HERTZMAN, M., MACHOVER, K., MEISSNER, P. B.,
        & WARNER, S.
        PERSONALITY THROUGH PERCEPTION.
        NEW YORK: HARPER AND BROTHERS, 1954.
        (TILTING ROOM TEST)*
     aW-73 FUNCTIONING AUTONOMY FIELD DEPENDENCE PERCEPTION COGNITIVE STYLE STRUCTURE
     aW-73 1948M
        (APPLICATIONS: 181   673   963   1119   1786   2017   2131   2967)

W-74   WEINER, B., & KUKLA, A.
        AN ATTRIBUTIONAL ANALYSIS OF ACHIEVEMENT MOTIVATION.
        JOURNAL OF PERSONALITY AND SOCIAL PSYCHOLOGY, 1970, 15, 1-20.
        (CHILDREN'S ACHIEVEMENT SCALE)*
     aW-74 CHILD ACHIEVEMENT MOTIVE NEED AUTONOMY 1970M
        (APPLICATIONS: 2929)

W-75   WILSON, W.
        RANK ORDER OF DISCRIMINATION AND ITS RELEVANCE TO CIVIL RIGHTS PRIORITIES.
        JOURNAL OF PERSONALITY AND SOCIAL PSYCHOLOGY, 1970, 15, 118-124.
        (RACIAL ATTITUDE MEASURE)
     aW-75 RACIAL ATTITUDE NEGRO PREJUDICE DESEGREGATION 1970M MINORITY GROUP

W-76   WERNER, M., STABENAU, J. R., & POLLIN, W.
        THEMATIC APPERCEPTION TEST METHOD FOR THE DIFFERENTIATION OF FAMILIES OF
        SCHIZOPHRENICS, DELINQUENTS, AND "NORMALS."
        JOURNAL OF ABNORMAL PSYCHOLOGY, 1970, 75, 139-145.
        (TAT METHOD FOR DIFFERENTIATING FAMILIES OF SCHIZOPHRENICS. DELINQUENTS,
        AND NORMALS)
     aW-76 FAMILY SCHIZOPHRENIA TAT PROJECTIVE PARENT-CHILD INTERACTION
     aW-76 DELINQUENCY IMAGERY 1970M

W-78   WIENS, A. N., MATARAZZO, J. D., & SASLOW, G.
        THE INTERACTION RECORDER: AN ELECTRIC PUNCHED PAPER TAPE UNIT FOR RECORDING
        SPEECH BEHAVIOR DURING INTERVIEWS.
        JOURNAL OF CLINICAL PSYCHOLOGY, 1965, 21, 142-145.
        (INTERACTION RECORDER)*
     aW-78 1965M INTERACTION INTERPERSONAL BEHAVIOR RELATIONSHIPS
        (APPLICATIONS: 2361)

W-79   WATSON, G., & GLASER, E. M.
        THE WATSON-GLASER CRITICAL THINKING APPRAISAL: MANUAL.
        NEW YORK: HARCOURT, 1952 (REVISED 1964).
        (WATSON-GLASER CRITICAL THINKING APPRAISAL)*
     aW-79 1952M THINKING COGNITIVE FUNCTIONING STRUCTURE
        (APPLICATIONS: 1333   2362   2887   2902)

W-80   WATERS, L. K., & WATERS, C. W.
         PEER NOMINATIONS AS PREDICTORS OF SHORT-TERM SALES PERFORMANCE.
         JOURNAL OF APPLIED PSYCHOLOGY, 1970, 54, 42-44.
         (PEER NOMINATION FORM)
         @W-80 PEER RATING MULTITRAIT PERFORMANCE JOB PREDICTION 1970M

W-81   WERNIMONT, P. F., TOREN, P., & KAPELL, H.
         COMPARISON OF SOURCES OF PERSONAL SATISFACTION AND OF WORK MOTIVATION.
         JOURNAL OF APPLIED PSYCHOLOGY, 1970, 54, 95-102.
         (MEASURE OF FACTORS CONTRIBUTING TO JOB SATISFACTION AND MOTIVATION)
         @W-81·1970M JOB SATISFACTION PE-FIT ENVIRONMENT MOTIVE
             (APPLICATIONS: 2350)

W-83   WOFFORD, J. C.
         FACTOR ANALYSIS OF MANAGERIAL BEHAVIOR VARIABLES.
         JOURNAL OF APPLIED PSYCHOLOGY, 1970, 54, 169-173.
         (MEASURE OF MANAGERIAL BEHAVIOR)
         @W-83 1970M MANAGEMENT SUPERVISOR BEHAVIOR PERFORMANCE STYLE LEADERSHIP

W-84   WOLLACK, S., WIJTING, J. P., GOODALE, J. G., & SMITH, P. C.
         WEIGHTING AGREEMENT RESPONSES BY ITEM SCALE VALUES.
         JOURNAL OF APPLIED PSYCHOLOGY, 1970, 54, 174-175.
         (SURVEY OF WORK VALUES)*
         @W-84 1970M VALUES JOB EMPLOYEE ORIENTATION

W-85   WYER, R. S., JR.
         THE PREDICTION OF EVALUATIONS OF SOCIAL ROLE OCCUPANTS AS A FUNCTION OF
         THE FAVORABLENESS, RELEVANCE AND PROBABILITY ASSOCIATED WITH ATTRIBUTES OF
         THESE OCCUPANTS.
         SOCIOMETRY, 1970, 33, 79-96.
         (PROCEDURE FOR DETERMINING BASES OF EVALUATIONS OF SOCIAL ROLE OCCUPANTS)
         @W-85 1970M ROLE ATTITUDE SOCIAL DESCRIPTION EVALUATION

W-86   WILLOUGHBY, R. R.
         SOME PROPERTIES OF THE THURSTONE PERSONALITY SCHEDULE AND A SUGGESTED
         REVISION.
         JOURNAL OF SOCIAL PSYCHOLOGY, 1932, 3, 401-424.
         (WILLOUGHBY PERSONALITY INVENTORY)*
         @W-86 1932M MULTITRAIT PERSONALITY SOCIAL ADJUSTMENT EXTRAVERSION SEX
             (APPLICATIONS: 2855)

W-87   WILSON, G. D., & PATTERSON, J. R.
         A NEW MEASURE OF CONSERVATISM.
         BRITISH JOURNAL OF SOCIAL AND CLINICAL PSYCHOLOGY, 1968, 7, 264-269.
         (CONSERVATISM SCALE)
         @W-87 1968M CONSERVATISM DOGMATISM AUTHORITARIANISM
             (APPLICATIONS: 2276   2448   2833)

W-89   WILSON, W., CHUN, N., & KAYATANI, M.
         PROJECTION, ATTRACTION, AND STRATEGY CHOICES IN INTERGROUP COMPETITION.
         JOURNAL OF PERSONALITY AND SOCIAL PSYCHOLOGY, 1965, 2, 432-435.
         (SUBJECT EVALUATION OF WORK-PARTNER)
         @W-89 1965M INTERPERSONAL EVALUATION EMPLOYEE JOB ATTRACTIVENESS
             (APPLICATIONS: 2809)

W-90   WEISSKOPF-JOELSON, E., ZIMMERMAN, J., & MCDANIEL, M.
         SIMILARITY BETWEEN SUBJECT AND STIMULUS AS AN INFLUENCE ON PROJECTION.
         JOURNAL OF PROJECTIVE TECHNIQUES AND PERSONALITY ASSESSMENT, 1970, 34,
         328-331.
         (SEMANTIC DIFFERENTIAL MEASURE OF SELF-CONCEPT)
         @W-90 1970M SEM-DIFFERENTIAL STIMULUS SELF CONCEPT SELF-IDENTITY

W-91   WHITEHORN, J. C., & BETZ, B. J.
         A STUDY OF PSYCHOTHERAPEUTIC RELATIONSHIPS BETWEEN PHYSICIANS AND
         SCHIZOPHRENIC PATIENTS.
         AMERICAN JOURNAL OF PSYCHIATRY, 1954, 111, 321-331.
         (WHITEHORN-BETZ AB SCALE)
         @W-91 1954M THERAPY INTERACTION STYLE RELATIONSHIPS
             (APPLICATIONS: 1738   1904   2037   2190   2223   2286   2847   2943)

W-92   WILE, D. B., BRON, G. D., & POLLACK, H. B.
        THE GROUP THERAPY QUESTIONNAIRE: AN INSTRUMENT FOR STUDY OF LEADERSHIP
        IN SMALL GROUPS.
        PSYCHOLOGICAL REPORTS, 1970, 27, 263-273.
        (GROUP THERAPY QUESTIONNAIRE)*
    @W-92 1970M GROUP THERAPY LEADERSHIP STYLE INTERACTION INTERPERSONAL
    @W-92 RELATIONSHIPS

W-93   WILBURN, W. V.
        TESTING TALCOTT PARSONS' THEORY OF MOTIVATION.
        JOURNAL OF SOCIAL PSYCHOLOGY, 1970, 80, 239-240.
        (MEASURE OF GRATIFICATION/DEPRIVATION IN THE HOME)
    @W-93 1970M FAMILY INTERACTION PARENT-CHILD PARENTAL BEHAVIOR

W-94   WALLACH, M. A., & KOGAN, N.
        MODES OF THINKING IN YOUNG CHILDREN.
        NEW YORK: HOLT, RINEHART AND WINSTON, 1965.
        (TEST ANXIETY SCALE FOR CHILDREN)
    @W-94 1965M TEST ANXIETY DEFENSIVENESS NEED SECURITY
        (APPLICATIONS: 489 2806)

W-95   WEINBERG, J. A.
        RELATIONSHIPS BETWEEN THE ORGANIZATION OF REPORTED EMOTIONAL EXPERIENCE
        AND THE ORGANIZATION OF PERCEPTUAL-COGNITIVE PROCESSES.
        UNPUBLISHED DOCTORAL DISSERTATION, TEACHERS COLLEGE, COLUMBIA UNIVERSITY,
        1968.
        (SCORING OF EMOTIONAL EXPERIENCES)
    @W-95 1968M EMOTION AFFECTIVE-STATES COMPLEXITY DIFFERENTIATION
    @W-95 EXPERIENCE ANXIETY ELATION
        (APPLICATIONS: 2950)

W-96   WALLACH, M. A., & KOGAN, N.
        SEX DIFFERENCES AND JUDGMENT PROCESSES.
        JOURNAL OF PERSONALITY, 1959, 27, 555-564.
        (JUDGEMENT OF PROBABILITY OF EVENTS)
    @W-96 1959M JUDGMENT RESPONSE BEHAVIOR INTENSITY STYLE PROBABILITY EXTREMITY
    @CONSERVATISM CERTAINTY

W-97   WEISS, D. J., DAWIS, R. V., ENGLAND, G. W., & LOFQUIST, L. H.
        INSTRUMENT FOR THE THEORY OF WORK ADJUSTMENT.
        MINNESOTA STUDIES IN VOCATIONAL REHABILITATION, 1966, 21, 11-26.
        (MINNESOTA IMPORTANCE QUESTIONNAIRE)
    @W-97 1966M JOB ADJUSTMENT VOCATIONAL NEED
    @W-97 PREFERENCE ENVIRONMENT RELATIONSHIPS
        (APPLICATIONS: 1427 2707)

W-98   WERNER, H., & KAPLAN, B.
        PAST AND PROJECTED RESEARCH ON LANGUAGE ABILITY IN THE CLARK UNIVERSITY
        DEPARTMENT OF PSYCHOLOGY.
        MIMEOGRAPHED REPORT, CLARK UNIVERSOTY, 1955.
        (METHOD OF RESPONSE EQUIVALENCE)
    @W-98 1955M EMOTION AFFECTIVE-STATES PERCEPTION

W-99   WATTENBERG, W., & CLIFFORD, C.
        RELATIONSHIPS OF THE SELF-CONCEPT TO BEGINNING ACHIEVEMENTS IN READING.
        DETROIT, MICHIGAN: WAYNE STATE UNIVERSITY, 1962.
        (QUANTIFIED SELF-CONCEPT INVENTORY)
    @W-99 1962M SELF CONCEPT PERCEPTION GLOBAL
    @W-99 SENTENCE-COMP ESTEEM
        (APPLICATIONS: 2889)

W-100   WILKINS, E. J., & DECHARMS, R.
        AUTHORITARIANISM AND RESPONSE TO POWER CUES.
        JOURNAL OF PERSONALITY, 1962, 30, 439-457.
        (ACCEPTANCE SCALE)
    @W-100 1962M ACCEPTANCE POSITIVE TRAIT TERMS STIMULUS PERSON ATTITUDE OTHERS

W-101   WEITMAN, M.
        MORE THAN ONE KIND OF AUTHORITARIANISM.
        JOURNAL OF PERSONALITY, 1962, 30, 193-208.
        (ACQUIESCENCE TEST)*
    @W-101 1962M ACQUIESCENCE TOLERANCE AMBIGUITY COGNITIVE STYLE
    @W-101 RESPONSE-BIAS

W-102   WEINER, M., CARPENTER, J. T., & CARPENTER, B.
                EXTERNAL VALIDATION OF A MEASURE OF CONFORMITY BEHAVIOR.
                JOURNAL OF ABNORMAL AND SOCIAL PSYCHOLOGY, 1956, 52, 421-422.
                (SOCIAL CONFORMITY MEASURE)
            aW-102 1956M SOCIAL CONFORMITY NEED APPROVAL
            aW-102 JUDGMENT ATTITUDE CHANGE FIGURE
                (APPLICATIONS: 398)

W-103   WEITZENHOFFER, A. M., & HILGARD, E. R.
                STANFORD PROFILE SCALES OF HYPNOTIC SUSCEPTIBILITY, FORMS 1 AND 2.
                PALO ALTO CALIFORNIA: CONSULTING PSYCHOLOGISTS PRESS, 1963.
                (STANFORD PROFILE SCALES OF HYPNOTIC SUSCEPTIBILITY)*
            aW-103 1963M HYPNOTIC SUGGESTIBILITY POSITIVE NEGATIVE HALLUCINATION
                (APPLICATIONS: 406 2415)

W-104   WANG, C. K. A., & THURSTONE, L. L.
                THE MEASUREMENT OF SOCIAL ATTITUDES.
                CHICAGO: UNIVERSITY OF CHICAGO PRESS, 1931.
                (ATTITUDE TOWARD THE PUNISHMENT OF CRIMINALS SCALE - COLLEGE FORM)*
            aW-104 PUNITIVENESS PROJECTIVE COLLEGE HOSTILITY EXPRESSION
                (APPLICATIONS: 485)

W-105   WUNDT, W.
                QUOTED IN R. S. WOODWORTH & H. SCHLOSENBERG, EXPERIMENTAL PSYCHOLOGY.
                NEW YORK: HOLT, 1958.
                (SELF-RATING SCALE OF FEELING)
            aW-105 1958M SELF RATING AFFECTIVE-STATES
                (APPLICATIONS: 441)

W-106   WINTER, S. K.
                CHARACTERISTICS OF FANTASY WHILE NURSING.
                JOURNAL OF PERSONALITY, 1969, 37, 58-72.
                (TAT SCORED FOR AROUSED FANTASY RESPONSES WHILE NURSING)
            aW-106 1969M TAT PROJECTIVE MATERNAL AFFECTIVE-STATES EMOTION FANTASY
            aW-106 SEX

W-107   WILENSKY, H., & SOLOMON, L.
                CHARACTERISTICS OF UNTESTABLE CHRONIC SCHIZOPHRENICS.
                JOURNAL OF ABNORMAL AND SOCIAL PSYCHOLOGY, 1960, 61, 155-158.
                (TEST OF INDEPENDENCE OF FUNCTION)
            aW-107 1960M AUTONOMY DEPENDENCE PHYSICAL NEED FUNCTIONING EGO COGNITIVE
            aW-107 ACCEPTANCE RESPONSIBILITY SCHIZOPHRENIA
                (APPLICATIONS: 1767)

W-108   WAHLER, H. J.
                RESPONSE STYLES IN CLINICAL AND NONCLINICAL GROUPS.
                JOURNAL OF CONSULTING PSYCHOLOGY, 1961, 25, 533-539.
                (SELF-DESCRIPTION INVENTORY, 1961 VERSION)
            aW-108 1961M SELF DESCRIPTION RATING ADJUSTMENT RESPONSE-BIAS SOCIAL
            aW-108 DESIRABILITY

W-109   WALLACE, M.
                FUTURE TIME PERSPECTIVE IN SCHIZOPHRENIA.
                JOURNAL OF ABNORMAL AND SOCIAL PSYCHOLOGY, 1956, 52, 240-245.
                (MEASURE OF FUTURE TIME PERSPECTIVE)
            aW-109 1956M TIME PERSPECTIVE ORIENTATION FUTURE
                (APPLICATIONS: 247   487 1670 1977 2133)

W-110   WHITE, A. M., FICHTENBAUM, L., & DOLLARD, J.
                MEASURE FOR PREDICTING DROPPING OUT OF PSYCHOTHERAPY.
                JOURNAL OF CONSULTING PSYCHOLOGY, 1964, 28, 326-332.
                (MEASURE FOR PREDICTING DROPPING OUT OF PSYCHOTHERAPY)
            aW-110 1964M THERAPY PATIENT SUCCESS MENTAL-ILLNESS ADJUSTMENT

W-111   WEINER, I. B.
                THREE RORSCHACH SCORES INDICATIVE OF SCHIZOPHRENIA.
                JOURNAL OF CONSULTING PSYCHOLOGY, 1961, 25, 436-439.
                (RORSCHACH SCORED FOR SCHIZOPHRENIC SYMPTOMS)
            aW-111 1961M RORSCHACH SCHIZOPHRENIA MENTAL-ILLNESS SYMPTOM CHECKLIST DIAGNOSIS

W-112   WINSLOW, C. N., & RAPERSAND, I.
                POSTDICTION OF THE OUTCOME OF SOMATIC THERAPY FROM THE RORSCHACH RECORDS
                OF SCHIZOPHRENIC PATIENTS.
                JOURNAL OF CONSULTING PSYCHOLOGY, 1964, 28, 243-247.
                (CONTENT ANALYSIS OF RORSCHACH)
            aW-112 1964M RORSCHACH CONTENT-ANALYSIS CONFLICT CONTROL DRIVE FLEXIBILITY

W-113   WHEELER, W. M.
               AN ANALYSIS OF RORSCHACH INDICES OF MALE HOMOSEXUALITY.
               RORSCHACH RESEARCH EXCHANGE AND JOURNAL OF PROJECTIVE TECHNIQUES, 1949,
               13, 97-126.
               (RORSCHACH SCORED FOR HOMOSEXUALITY)
           aW-113 1949M RORSCHACH PROJECTIVE HOMOSEXUALITY
               (APPLICATIONS: 110   756   2025)

W-114   WALLACH, M. S., & STRUPP, H. H.
               DIMENSIONS OF PSYCHOTHERAPISTS' ACTIVITY.
               JOURNAL OF CONSULTING PSYCHOLOGY, 1964, 28, 120-125.
               (SCALE OF THERAPISTS USUAL THERAPEUTIC PRACTICES)
           aW-114 1964M THERAPY ACTIVITIES PERSONAL DISTANCE VERBAL CREATIVITY ABILITY
           aW-114 PSYCHIATRIC MENTAL-ILLNESS
               (APPLICATIONS: 2170)

W-115   WATSON, D., & FRIEND, R.
               MEASUREMENT OF SOCIAL-EVALUATIVE ANXIETY.
               JOURNAL OF CONSULTING AND CLINICAL PSYCHOLOGY, 1969, 33, 448-457.
               (SOCIAL AVOIDANCE AND DISTRESS SCALE)*
           aW-115 1969M AVOIDANCE SOCIAL INTERPERSONAL NEGATIVE AFFECTIVE-STATES

W-116   WATSON, D., & FRIEND, R.
               MEASUREMENT OF SOCIAL-EVALUATIVE ANXIETY.
               JOURNAL OF CONSULTING AND CLINICAL PSYCHOLOGY, 1969, 33, 448-457.
               (FEAR OF NEGATIVE EVALUATION SCALE)*
           aW-116 1969M EVALUATION FEAR FAILURE NEGATIVE

W-118   WILSON, R. C., CHRISTENSEN, P. R., MERRIFIELD, P. R., & GUILFORD, J. P.
               ALTERNATE USES: MANUAL.
               BEVERLY HILLS, CALIF.: SHERIDAN SUPPLY, 1960.
               (ALTERNATE USES)*
           aW-118 1960M CREATIVITY ORIGINALITY COGNITIVE STRUCTURE FUNCTIONING
               (APPLICATIONS: 933   1461   2253)

W-119   WURSTER, C. R., BASS, B. M., & ALCOCK, W.
               A TEST OF THE PROPOSITION: WE WANT TO BE ESTEEMED MOST BY THOSE WE ESTEEM
               MOST HIGHLY.
               JOURNAL OF ABNORMAL AND SOCIAL PSYCHOLOGY, 1961, 63, 650-653.
               (MEASURE OF SCHOLASTIC AND SOCIAL ESTEEM)
           aW-119 1961M SOCIAL ACADEMIC ESTEEM PEER RELATIONSHIPS INTERPERSONAL

W-120   WEATHERLEY, D.
               ANTI-SEMITISM AND THE EXPRESSION OF FANTASY AGGRESSION.
               JOURNAL OF ABNORMAL AND SOCIAL PSYCHOLOGY, 1961, 62, 454-457.
               (MEASURE OF FANTASY AGGRESSION)
           aW-120 1961M IMAGERY PROJECTIVE PREJUDICE RACIAL AGGRESSION FANTASY AFFECTIVE-
           aW-120 STATES

W-121   WOLINS, L. A.
               A PROCEDURE FOR ESTIMATING THE AMOUNT TRAIT, METHOD AND ERROR VARIANCE
               ATTRIBUTABLE TO A MEASURE.
               PROJECT C-998 CONTRACT 0-2C-001, OFFICE OF EDUCATION, U.S. DEPARTMENT OF
               HEALTH, EDUCATION AND WELFARE: (DONALD T. CAMPBELL, PRINCIPLE INVESTIGATOR)
               1964.
               (RATING QUESTIONNAIRE OF SUPERVISOR)
           aW-121 1964M RATING SUPERVISOR BEHAVIOR JOB ENVIRONMENT
               (APPLICATIONS: 2705)

W-122   WINDER, C. L., & WIGGINS, J. S.
               MEASUREMENT OF SOCIAL ADJUSTMENT IN PREADOLESCENT BOYS.
               PROGRESS REPORT, NOV. 7, 1960, USPHS GRANT M-2745 (C1).
               (PEER NOMINATION INVENTORY)
           aW-122 1960M PEER RATING CHILD AGGRESSION DEPENDENCY DEPRESSION WITHDRAWAL
           aW-122 SOCIOMETRIC

W-123   WIENER, D. N.
               SUBTLE AND OBVIOUS KEYS FOR THE MMPI.
               JOURNAL OF CONSULTING PSYCHOLOGY, 1948, 12, 164-170.
               ("SUBTLE" AND "OBVIOUS" SCALES FROM MMPI)
           aW-123 1948M MMPI RESPONSE-BIAS

W-124   WEITZENHOFFER, A. M.
               CONSOLIDATED SCALE OF HYPNOTIC RESPONSIVENESS.
               (UNPUBLISHED)
               STANFORD LABORATORY OF HUMAN DEVELOPMENT.
               (CONSOLIDATED SCALE OF HYPNOTIC RESPONSIVENESS)
           @W-124 HYPNOTIC SUGGESTIBILITY HALLUCINATION FANTASY COGNITIVE EXPERIENCE
           @INTENSITY

W-125   WEATHERLEY, D.
               MATERNAL RESPONSE TO CHILDHOOD AGGRESSION AND SUBSEQUENT ANTI-SEMITISM.
               JOURNAL OF ABNORMAL AND SOCIAL PSYCHOLOGY, 1963, 66, 183-185.
               (SEMANTIC DIFFERENTIAL MEASURE OF ANTI-SEMITISM)
           @W-125 1963M SEM-DIFFERENTIAL RACIAL ETHNIC PREJUDICE ETHNOCENTRISM EVALUATION

W-126   WEATHERLEY, D.
               MATERNAL RESPONSE TO CHILDHOOD AGGRESSION AND SUBSEQUENT ANTI-SEMITISM.
               JOURNAL OF ABNORMAL AND SOCIAL PSYCHOLOGY, 1963, 66, 183-185.
               (MEASURE OF MOTHER'S RESPONSES TO CHILDHOOD AGGRESSION)
           @W-126 1963M CHILD MATERNAL AGGRESSION PARENTAL PUNITIVENESS DIRECTION HOSTILITY

W-127   WINTER, D. G.
               PERSONALITY EFFECTS OF A SUMMER ADVANCED STUDIES PROGRAM.
               UNPUBLISHED BACHELOR'S THESIS, HARVARD UNIVERSITY, 1960.
               (TAT MEASURE OF ASSOCIATIVE PROCESSES AND IMAGINATION)
           @W-127 1960M TAT PROJECTIVE SCHOOL ACADEMIC INFLUENCE

W-128   WINTER, D. G.
               PERSONALITY EFFECTS OF A SUMMER ADVANCED STUDIES PROGRAM.
               UNPUBLISHED BACHELOR'S THESIS, HARVARD UNIVERSITY, 1960.
               (SEMANTIC DIFFERENTIAL MEASURE OF EDUCATIONAL VALUES)
           @W-128 1960M SEM-DIFFERENTIAL VALUES SCHOOL ACADEMIC

W-129   WILSON, W., & MILLER, N.
               SHIFTS IN EVALUATIONS OF PARTICIPANTS FOLLOWING INTERGROUP COMPETITION.
               JOURNAL OF ABNORMAL AND SOCIAL PSYCHOLOGY, 1961, 63, 428-431.
               (INTERPERSONAL RATING SCALE)
           @W-129 1961M INTERPERSONAL TRAIT RATING SELF OTHERS GROUP

W-130   WORCHEL, P.
               STATUS RESTORATION AND THE REDUCTION OF HOSTILITY.
               JOURNAL OF ABNORMAL AND SOCIAL PSYCHOLOGY, 1961, 63, 443-445.
               (TEST OF SOCIAL SENSITIVITY AND INSIGHT)
           @W-130 1961M SOCIAL SENSITIVITY SELF AGGRESSION EXPERIMENTER HOSTILITY
           @W-130 PERCEPTION

W-131   WORCHEL, P.
               STATUS RESTORATION AND THE REDUCTION OF HOSTILITY.
               JOURNAL OF ABNORMAL AND SOCIAL PSYCHOLOGY, 1961, 63, 443-445.
               (MEASURE OF AGGRESSION ANXIETY)
           @W-131 1961M AGGRESSION ANXIETY TAT PROJECTIVE SELF

W-132   WEINGARTEN K. P.
               PICTURE INTEREST INVENTORY.
               LOS ANGELES: CALIFORNIA TEST BUREAU, 1958.
               (CALIFORNIA PICTURE INTEREST INVENTORY)*
           @W-132 1958M INTEREST VOCATIONAL JOB PREFERENCE

W-133   WILLIAMS, W. C.
               THE PALS TEST: A TECHNIQUE FOR CHILDREN TO EVALUATE BOTH PARENTS.
               JOURNAL OF CONSULTING PSYCHOLOGY, 1958, 22, 487-495.
               PARENTAL AUTHORITY-LOVE STATEMENTS (PALS) TEST)*
           @W-133 1958M CHILD PARENTAL EVALUATION
           @W-133 PARENT-CHILD
               (APPLICATIONS: 884)

W-135   WALK, R. D.
               SELF RATINGS OF FEAR IN A FEAR-INVOKING SITUATION.
               JOURNAL OF ABNORMAL AND SOCIAL PSYCHOLOGY, 1956, 52, 171-178.
               (FEAR THERMOMETER)
           @W-135 1956M FEAR ANXIETY SITUATIONAL TENSION BEHAVIOR AVOIDANCE
               (APPLICATIONS: 809   972   1134   2416   2855)

W-136   WOLOWITZ, H. M.
         ATTRACTION AND AVERSION TO POWER: A PSYCHOANALYTIC CONFLICT THEORY OF
         HOMOSEXUALITY IN MALE PARANOIDS.
         JOURNAL OF ABNORMAL PSYCHOLOGY, 1965, 70, 360-370.
         (SEMANTIC DIFFERENTIAL MEASURE OF PERCEIVED POWER IN PHOTOGRAPHS)
         aW-136 1965M SEM-DIFFERENTIAL POWER PERCEIVED GRAPHIC FIGURE

W-138   WINTER, W. D., FERREIRA, A. J., & OLSON, J. L.
         STORY SEQUENCE ANALYSIS OF FAMILY TAT'S.
         JOURNAL OF PROJECTIVE TECHNIQUES, 1965, 29, 392-397.
         (STORY SEQUENCE ANALYSIS OF FAMILY TAT'S)
         aW-138 1965M TAT PROJECTIVE FAMILY INTERACTION
            (APPLICATIONS: 1133)

W-140   WRIGHT, N. A., & ABBEY, D. S.
         PERCEPTUAL DEPRIVATION TOLERANCE AND ADEQUACY OF DEFENSES.
         PERCEPTUAL AND MOTOR SKILLS, 1965, 20, 35-38.
         (RORSCHACH INDEX OF CONTROL)
         aW-140 1965M CONTROL AUTONOMY RORSCHACH PROJECTIVE
         aDEFENSE INHIBITION IMPULSE EMOTION
            (APPLICATIONS: 1130)

W-141   WOOD, J. R.
         AUTHORITY AND CONTROVERSIAL POLICY: THE CHURCHES AND CIVIL RIGHTS.
         AMERICAN SOCIOLOGICAL REVIEW, 1970, 35, 1057-1069.
         (INTEGRATION POLICY STRENGTH SCALE)
         aW-141 1970M INTEGRATION ATTITUDE RELIGION CONFORMITY ORIENTATION GROUP NORMS
         aW-141 FLEXIBILITY BELIEFS RIGIDITY

W-142   WEISSENBERG, P.
         PSYCHOLOGICAL DIFFERENTIATION AND JOB SATISFACTION.
         DOCTORAL DISSERTATION, CORNELL UNIVERSITY.
         ANN ARBOR, MICH.: UNIVERSITY MICROFILMS, 1967, NO. 67-13, 934.
         WEISSENBERG, P., & GRUENFELD, L. W.
         RELATIONSHIP BETWEEN JOB SATISFACTION AND JOB INVOLVEMENT.
         JOURNAL OF APPLIED PSYCHOLOGY, 1968, 52, 469-473.
         (GROUP EMBEDDED FIGURES TEST)*
         aW-142 FIGURE GROUP PROJECTIVE 1967M COGNITIVE ABILITY FUNCTIONING
         aPERCEPTION FIELD DEPENDENCE
            (APPLICATIONS: 2350)

W-143   WING, J. K.
         A SIMPLE AND RELIABLE SUBCLASSIFICATION OF CHRONIC SCHIZOPHRENIA.
         JOURNAL OF MENTAL SCIENCE, 1961, 107, 862-875.
         (SCALE OF PARANOID BEHAVIOR)
         aW-143 1961M SCHIZOPHRENIA MENTAL-ILLNESS PSYCHIATRIC
         aW-143 DIAGNOSIS
            (APPLICATIONS: 1145)

W-144   WAGNER, A. W.
         ANALYSIS OF PERSONAL BEHAVIOR IN GROUPS.
         QUESTIONNAIRE FROM UNPUBLISHED DOCTORAL DISSERTATION.
         CLEVELAND, OHIO: CASE INSTITUTE OF TECHNOLOGY, 1965.
         (ANALYSIS OF PERSONAL BEHAVIOR IN GROUPS QUESTIONNAIRE)
         aW-144 1965M GROUP INTERPERSONAL BEHAVIOR RELATIONSHIPS INTERACTION
            (APPLICATIONS: 2961)

W-145   WINTERBOTTOM, M. R.
         THE RELATION OF NEED FOR ACHIEVEMENT TO LEARNING EXPERIENCES IN
         INDEPENDENCE AND MASTERY.
         IN J. W. ATKINSON (ED.), MOTIVES IN FANTASY ACTION AND SOCIETY.
         PRINCETON, N. J.: VAN NOSTRAND, 1958
         (MEASURE OF ACHIEVEMENT MOTIVATION IN CHILDREN)
         aW-145 1958M NEED ACHIEVEMENT
            (APPLICATIONS: 344)

W-146   WOLPE, J., & LAZARUS, A. A.
         BEHAVIOR THERAPY TECHNIQUES.
         OXFORD: PERGAMON PRESS, 1966.
         (ASSERTIVE SCALE)
         aW-146 1966M ASSERTIVENESS AGGRESSIVENESS DOMINANCE SELF CONFIDENCE
            (APPLICATIONS: 2414)

W-147   WEISS, B. A.
                 THE RELATIONSHIP BETWEEN DEVELOPMENTAL EXPERIENCES AND CHOICE OF
                 DEFENSIVE BEHAVIOR: STUDY II. FEMALES.
                 UNPUBLISHED DOCTORAL DISSERTATION, UNIVERSITY OF HOUSTON, 1956.
                 (RORSCHACH SCORED FOR DEFENSIVE BEHAVIOR)
             @W-147 1954M REPRESSION EGO DEFENSE INTELLECTUALIZE OPENNESS RORSCHACH
             @W-147 PROJECTIVE DEFENSIVENESS BEHAVIOR

W-148   WEST, L. W., & ZINGLE, H. W.
                 A SELF-DISCLOSURE INVENTORY FOR ADOLESCENTS.
                 PSYCHOLOGICAL REPORTS, 1969, 24, 439-445.
                 (SELF-DISCLOSURE INVENTORY FOR ADOLESCENTS)*
             @W-148 1969M SELF DISCLOSURE NEED PRIVACY OPENNESS EXPRESSION ADOLESCENT
                 (APPLICATIONS: 2626)

W-149   WORTHY, M., & CRADDICK, R. A.
                 SEMANTIC DIFFERENTIAL INVESTIGATION OF SEXUALLY SYMBOLIC CONCEPTS.
                 JOURNAL OF PROJECTIVE TECHNIQUES AND PERSONALITY ASSESSMENT, 1969, 33,
                 78-80.
                 (SEMANTIC DIFFERENTIAL RATING OF MASCULINITY-FEMININITY)
             @W-149 1969M SEM-DIFFERENTIAL SEX MASCULINITY FEMININITY IDENTITY ROLE

W-150   WOODMANSEE, J. J., & TUCKER, R. D.
                 A SCALE OF BLACK SEPARATISM.
                 PSYCHOLOGICAL REPORTS, 1970, 27, 855-858.
                 (REVISED BLACK POWER SENTIMENT SCALE)
             @W-150 1970M ETHNIC RACIAL PREJUDICE NEGRO MINORITY ATTITUDE POWER
             @AFFILIATION DISTANCE POLITICAL IDEOLOGY IDENTITY GROUP SELF CONCEPT AWARENESS

W-151   WILLERMAN, B., LEWIT, D., & TELLEGEN, A.
                 SEEKING AND AVOIDING SELF-EVALUATION BY WORKING INDIVIDUALLY OR IN GROUPS.
                 IN D. WILLNER (ED.), DECISIONS, VALUES AND GROUPS: I.
                 LONDON: PERGAMON, 1960.
                 (FORCED-CHOICE VERSION OF THE FRENCH TEST OF INSIGHT)
             @W-151 1960M NEED MOTIVE ACHIEVEMENT SELF PERCEPTION F-20R

W-152   WATSON, C. G., KLETT, W. G., & LOREI, T. W.
                 TOWARD AN OPERATIONAL DEFINITION OF ANHEDONIA.
                 PSYCHOLOGICAL REPORTS, 1970, 26, 371-376.
                 (FUN-SEEKING SCALE)
             @W-152 1970M ACTIVITIES PREFERENCE MENTAL-HEALTH MENTAL-ILLNESS HAPPINESS
             @SEEKING GRATIFICATION
                 (APPLICATIONS: 2604)

W-153   WATSON, C. G., KLETT, W. G., & LOREI, T. W.
                 TOWARD AN OPERATIONAL DEFINITION OF ANHEDONIA.
                 PSYCHOLOGICAL REPORTS, 1970, 26, 371-376.
                 (MMPI ANHEDONIA SCALE)
             @W-153 1970M ACTIVITIES PREFERENCE MENTAL-HEALTH MENTAL-ILLNESS SCHIZOPHRENIA
             @GRATIFICATION SEEKING HAPPINESS
                 (APPLICATIONS: 2604)

W-154   WATSON, C. G., KLETT, W. G., & LOREI, T. W.
                 TOWARD AN OPERATIONAL DEFINITION OF ANHEDONIA.
                 PSYCHOLOGICAL REPORTS, 1970, 26, 371-376.
                 (PSYCHOTIC INPATIENT PROFILE ANHEDONIA SCALE)
             @W-154 1970M HAPPINESS INTEREST MENTAL-HEALTH MENTAL-ILLNESS SCHIZOPHRENIA
             @EXPRESSION EMOTION GRATIFICATION SEEKING HAPPINESS
                 (APPLICATIONS: 2604)

W-155   WATSON, C. G., KLETT, W. G., & LOREI, T. W.
                 TOWARD AN OPERATIONAL DEFINITION OF ANHEDONIA.
                 PSYCHOLOGICAL REPORTS, 1970, 26, 371-376.
                 (NURSES' OBSERVATION SCALE FOR INPATIENT EVALUATION ANHEDONIA SCALE)
             @W-155 1970M ACTIVITIES PREFERENCE MENTAL-HEALTH MENTAL-ILLNESS SCHIZOPHRENIA
             @RATING BEHAVIOR EXPRESSION EMOTION HAPPINESS STAFF PSYCHIATRIC PATIENT
                 (APPLICATIONS: 2604)

W-156   WATSON, C. G., KLETT, W. G., & LOREI, T. W.
                 TOWARD AN OPERATIONAL DEFINITION OF ANHEDONIA.
                 PSYCHOLOGICAL REPORTS, 1970, 26, 371-376.
                 (INTEREST INVENTORY)
             @W-156 1970M ACTIVITIES PREFERENCE MENTAL-HEALTH MENTAL-ILLNESS SCHIZOPHRENIA
             @LIFE SATISFACTION GLOBAL INTEREST
                 (APPLICATIONS: 2604)

W-157   WARR, P. B., FAUST, J., & HARRISON, G. J.
          A BRITISH ETHNOCENTRISM SCALE.
          BRITISH JOURNAL OF SOCIAL AND CLINICAL PSYCHOLOGY, 1967, 6, 267-277.
          (BRITISH ETHNOCENTRISM SCALE)
          @W-157 1967M ETHNOCENTRISM PREJUDICE RACIAL ETHNIC ATTITUDE NATIONALISM
          (APPLICATIONS: 2596)

W-158   WEISS, D. J., DAWIS, R. V., LOFQUIST, L. H., & ENGLAND, G. W.
          INSTRUMENTATION FOR THE THEORY OF WORK ADJUSTMENT.
          MINNEAPOLIS: INDUSTRIAL RELATIONS CENTER, 1966.
          (MINNESOTA STUDIES IN VOCATIONAL REHABILITATION, XXI.)
          (MINNESOTA SATISFACTION QUESTIONNAIRE)*
          @W-158 1966M JOB EMPLOYEE MANAGEMENT SATISFACTION ADJUSTMENT PERCEPTION
          (APPLICATIONS: 2585)

W-159   WEISS, D. J., DAWIS, R. V., LOFQUIST, L. H., & ENGLAND, G. W.
          INSTRUMENTATION FOR THE THEORY OF WORK ADJUSTMENT.
          MINNEAPOLIS: INDUSTRIAL RELATIONS CENTER, 1966.
          (MINNESOTA STUDIES IN VOCATIONAL REHABILITATION, XXI.)
          (MINNESOTA SATISFACTORINESS SCALES)*
          @W-159 1966M JOB EMPLOYEE MANAGEMENT SATISFACTION ADJUSTMENT PERCEPTION PE-FIT
          (APPLICATIONS: 2585)

W-160   WARNER, W. L., MEEKER, M., & EELLS, K.
          SOCIAL CLASS IN AMERICA.
          CHICAGO: SCIENCE RESEARCH ASSOCIATES, 1949.
          (MEASURE OF SOCIO-ECONOMIC STATUS)
          @W-160 1949M SOCIAL STATUS WELL-BEING
          (APPLICATIONS: 1444)

W-161   WHITELEY, J. M., SPRINTHALL, N. A., MOSHER, R. L., & DONAGHY, R. T.
          SELECTION AND EVALUATION OF COUNSELOR EFFECTIVENESS.
          JOURNAL OF COUNSELING PSYCHOLOGY, 1967, 14, 226-234.
          (PERSONAL DIFFERENTIATION TEST)*
          @W-161 1967M COGNITIVE FLEXIBILITY DIFFERENTIATION RIGIDITY

W-162   WHITELEY, J. M., SPRINTHALL, N. A., MOSHER, R. L., & DONAGHY, R. T.
          SELECTION AND EVALUATION OF COUNSELOR EFFECTIVENESS.
          JOURNAL OF COUNSELING PSYCHOLOGY, 1967, 14, 226-234.
          (MEASURE OF RESPONSE TO CRITICAL CASE STUDIES)
          @W-162 1967M FLEXIBILITY RIGIDITY COUNSELING THERAPY RESPONSE BEHAVIOR
          @ABILITY

W-163   WHITELEY, J. M., SPRINTHALL, N. A., MOSHER, R. L., & DONAGHY, R. T.
          SELECTION AND EVALUATION OF COUNSELOR EFFECTIVENESS.
          JOURNAL OF COUNSELING PSYCHOLOGY, 1967, 14, 226-234.
          (COUNSELOR RATING SCALE)
          @W-163 1967M COUNSELING THERAPY RATING BEHAVIOR RESPONSE COGNITIVE ATTITUDE
          @EFFECTIVENESS ABILITY THERAPIST

W-164   WIGGINS, J. S., & RUMRILL, C.
          SOCIAL DESIRABILITY IN THE MMPI AND WELSH'S FACTOR SCALES A AND R.
          JOURNAL OF CONSULTING PSYCHOLOGY, 1959, 23, 100-106.
          (MEASURE OF SOCIAL DESIRABILITY IN WELSH A AND R SCALES)
          @W-164 1959M SOCIAL DESIRABILITY RESPONSE-BIAS MMPI
          (APPLICATIONS: 1414)

W-165   WHITE, A. M., FICHTENBAUM, L., & DOLLARD, J.
          MEASURED RELATIONSHIPS BETWEEN SEXUAL MOTIVATION AND ANXIETY.
          JOURNAL OF COUNSELING PSYCHOLOGY, 1967, 14, 544-549.
          (CONTENT ANALYSIS MEASURE OF SEXUAL CONTENT AT THERAPY INTERVIEWS)
          @W-165 1967M CONTENT-ANALYSIS THERAPY COUNSELING SEX MOTIVE ANXIETY SELF SYMPTOM
          @INTERVIEW

W-166   WRIGHT, J. J.
          THE IMPACT OF PERCEIVED STRESS ON ACADEMIC ACHIEVEMENT WHEN FAMILY INCOME
          LEVEL AND SELF-CONCEPT ARE TAKEN INTO ACCOUNT.
          JOURNAL OF COLLEGE STUDENT PERSONNEL, 1966, 7, 113-117.
          (PERSONAL STRESS SCALE)
          @W-166 1966M PERSONAL RATING STRESS SUBJECTIVE LIFE SATISFACTION PRESS
          @ADJUSTMENT PERCEIVED TENSION ENVIRONMENT
          (APPLICATIONS: 1417)

W-167   WALSH, W. B., & LACEY, D. W.
              PERCEIVED CHANGE AND HOLLAND'S THEORY.
              JOURNAL OF COUNSELING PSYCHOLOGY, 1969, 16, 348-352.
              (PERSONAL SURVEY)*
         @W-167 1969M PERSONAL ORIENTATION TRAIT PERCEPTION INTELLECTUAL SOCIAL
         @INVENTORY

W-168   WARMAN, R. E.
              DIFFERENTIAL PERCEPTIONS OF COUNSELING ROLE.
              JOURNAL OF COUNSELING PSYCHOLOGY, 1960, 7, 269-274.
              (COUNSELING APPROPRIATENESS CHECKLIST)*
         @W-168 1960M COUNSELING THERAPY PERCEPTION ROLE EVALUATION ATTITUDE
         @THERAPIST CHECKLIST
              (APPLICATIONS: 1178 1525)

W-169   WHEELER, C. L., & CARNES, E. F.
              RELATIONSHIPS AMONG SELF-CONCEPTS, IDEAL-SELF-CONCEPTS, AND STEREOTYPES
              OF PROBABLE AND IDEAL VOCATIONAL CHOICES.
              JOURNAL OF COUNSELING PSYCHOLOGY, 1968, 15, 530-535.
              (MODIFIED DESCRIPTIVE CHECK LIST)
         @W-169 1968M CHECKLIST SELF IDEAL VOCATIONAL IDENTITY RATING DESCRIPTION
         @DISCREPANCY CONSISTENCY

W-170   WRENN, R. L.
              COUNSELOR ORIENTATION: THEORETICAL OR SITUATIONAL?
              JOURNAL OF COUNSELING PSYCHOLOGY, 1960, 7, 40-45.
              (MEASURE OF EFFECT OF SITUATIONAL AND THEORETICAL VARIABLES ON COUNSELOR
              RESPONSE)
         @W-170 1960M COUNSELING SITUATIONAL THERAPY RESPONSE STORY-COMPLETION
         @THERAPIST VERBAL INTERACTION

W-172   WESSMAN, A. E., RICKS, D. F., & TYL, M. M.
              CHARACTERISTICS AND CONCOMITANTS OF MOOD FLUCTUATION IN COLLEGE WOMEN.
              JOURNAL OF ABNORMAL AND SOCIAL PSYCHOLOGY, 1960, 60, 117-126.
              (Q-SORT MEASURE OF SELF AND IDEAL CONCEPT IN ELATION AND DEPRESSION)
         @W-172 1960M SELF IDEAL CONCEPT DEPRESSION Q-SORT ELATION ESTEEM MOOD
         @DISCREPANCY CONSISTENCY

W-173   WALZ, G. R., & JOHNSTON, J. A.
              COUNSELORS LOOK AT THEMSELVES ON VIDEO TAPE.
              JOURNAL OF COUNSELING PSYCHOLOGY, 1963, 10, 232-236.
              (INTERVIEW CHECK LIST)
         @W-173 1963M CHECKLIST INTERVIEW SELF PERCEPTION COUNSELING RATING EVALUATION

W-174   WHITLOCK, G. E.
              PASSIVITY OF PERSONALITY AND ROLE CONCEPTS IN VOCATIONAL CHOICE.
              JOURNAL OF COUNSELING PSYCHOLOGY, 1962, 9, 88-90.
              (SENTENCE COMPLETION MEASURE OF PASSIVITY)
         @W-174 1962M SENTENCE-COMP PASSIVE ACTIVE PERSONAL ORIENTATION
         @IE-CONTROL DOMINANCE AGGRESSIVENESS AUTONOMY INITIATIVE ROLE NEED

W-176   WALK, R. D.   .
              PERCEPTION AND PERSONALITY: A PRETEST.
              UNPUBLISHED, SOCIAL RELATIONS LIBRARY, HARVARD UNIVERSITY, 1950.
              (MEASURE OF INTOLERANCE FOR AMBIGUITY)
         @W-176 1950M INTOLERANCE AMBIGUITY RIGIDITY COGNITIVE STRUCTURE
         @STYLE

W-177   WASHBURNE, J. N.
              MANUAL, WASHBURNE SOCIAL ADJUSTMENT INVENTORY.
              CHICAGO: WORLD BOOK, 1940.
         KORZI, J. R.
              THE VALIDITY OF THE WASHBURNE SOCIAL ADJUSTMENT INVENTORY IN MEASURING
              COLLEGE FRESHMAN ADJUSTMENT.
              PERSONNEL AND GUIDANCE JOURNAL, 1962, 40, 462-466.
              (WASHBURNE SOCIAL ADJUSTMENT INVENTORY)*
         @W-177 1940M SOCIAL ADJUSTMENT INVENTORY COLLEGE STUDENT

W-180   WATERHOUSE, I. K. & CHILD I. L.
         FRUSTRATION AND THE QUALITY OF PERFORMANCE: III . AN EXPERIMENTAL STUDY.
         JOURNAL OF PERSONALITY, 1953. 21, 298-311.
         (FRUSTRATION REACTION INVENTORY)
         @W-180 1953M FRUSTRATION AGGRESSION COPING DEFENSE RESPONSE PE-FIT PUNITIVENESS
             (APPLICATIONS: 399)

W-183   WATSON, R. E., PRITZKER, L., & MADISON, P.
         HOSTILITY IN NEUROTICS AND NORMALS.
         JOURNAL OF ABNORMAL AND SOCIAL PSYCHOLOGY, 1955, 50, 36-40.
         (SENTENCE CONSTRUCTION MEASURE OF HOSTILITY)
         @W-183 1955M HOSTILITY REPRESSION PROJECTIVE AMBIGUITY STIMULUS IMPULSE
         @EXPRESSION INHIBITION
             (APPLICATIONS: 33 1567)

W-187   WHITING, J. F., MURRAY, M. A., WHITING, L., SACHS, E. J., & HULL, V.
         THE NURSE-PATIENT RELATIONSHIP AND THE HEALING PROCESS.
         NEW YORK: AMERICAN NURSES' FOUNDATION, RESEARCH REPORTS, 1958.
         (Q-SORT OF NURSE-PATIENT RELATIONSHIPS)
         @W-187 1958M Q-SORT PATIENT RELATIONSHIPS STAFF HOSPITALIZATION

W-188   WITKIN, H. A.
         THE EFFECT OF TRAINING AND OF STRUCTURAL AIDS ON PERFORMANCE IN THREE TESTS
         OF SPACE ORIENTATION.
         CIVIL AERONAUTICS ADMINISTRATION, DIVISION OF RESEARCH, REPORT NO. 80,
         WASHINGTON, D.C.
         WITKIN, H. A., LEWIS, H. B., HERTZMAN, M., MACHOVER, K., MEISSNER, P. B.,
         & WARNER, S.
         PERSONALITY THROUGH PERCEPTION.
         NEW YORK: HARPER AND BROTHERS, 1954.
         (ROD AND FRAME TEST)*
         @W-188 1948M PERCEPTION COGNITIVE AUTONOMY STYLE STRUCTURE FIELD DEPENDENCE
         @FUNCTIONING
             (APPLICATIONS: 412   413   673   963   1085   1089 1145   1151   1768   1786
                              2281   2348   2397   2547   2746   2967)

W-190   WOLLERSHEIM, J. P.
         EFFFCTIVENESS OF GROUP THERAPY BASED UPON LEARNING PRINCIPLES IN THE
         TREATMENT OF OVERWEIGHT WOMEN.
         JOURNAL OF ABNORMAL PSYCHOLOGY, 1970, 76, 462-474.
         (EATING PATTERNS QUESTIONNAIRE)
         @W-190 1970M BEHAVIOR EMOTION RESPONSE EVALUATION SITUATIONAL INTERPERSONAL

W-191   WEBB, W. W.
         PREMORBID ADJUSTMENT AND THE PERCEPTION OF MEANING.
         PERCEPTUAL AND MOTOR SKILLS, 1963, 17, 762.
         (MEASURE OF WORD PERCEPTION FOR DISTINGUISHING GOOD AND POOR PREMORBID
         SCHIZOPHRENIA)
         @W-191 1964M SCHIZOPHRENIA PERCEPTION DIFFERENTIATION SENSITIVITY STIMULUS
         @AMBIGUITY WORD EVALUATION ACTIVE POWER

W-193   WAGNER, M. E., & SCHUBERT, H. J. P.
         DAP QUALITY SCALE FOR LATE ADOLESCENTS AND YOUNG ADULTS.
         BUFFALO, N.Y.: AUTHORS, 1955.
         (ARTISTIC QUALITY MEASURE FOR DRAW-A-PERSON TEST)
         @W-193 1955M FIGURE GRAPHIC PROJECTIVE ESTHETIC

W-194   WEBSTER, H.
         VC ATTITUDE INVENTORY AND VC PREFERENCE TEST RESEARCH MANUAL.
         POUGHKEPSIE: MARY CONOVER MELLON FOUNDATION, 1957.
         (DOMINANCE AND CONFIDENCE SCALE)
         @W-194 1957M DOMINANCE CONFIDENCE SOCIAL COMPETENCE BEHAVIOR INTERPERSONAL NEED
         @GROUP LEADERSHIP SELF
             (APPLICATIONS: 1282)

W-195   WOODMANSEE, J. J., & COOK, S. W.
         DIMENSIONS OF VERBAL RACIAL ATTITUDES: THEIR IDENTIFICATION AND
         MEASUREMENT.
         JOURNAL OF PERSONALITY AND SOCIAL PSYCHOLOGY, 1967, 7, 240-250.
         (INVENTORY OF VERBAL RACIAL ATTITUDES)
         @W-195 1967M ATTITUDE BELIEF RACIAL NEGRO PREDJUDICE INFERIORITY ETHNIC
             (APPLICATIONS: 1701)

W-196   WILLIAMSON, E. G., & DARLEY, J. G.
                MANUAL FOR THE MINNESOTA INVENTORIES OF SOCIAL ATTITUDES.
                NEW YORK: THE PSYCHOLOGICAL CORPORATION, 1937.
                (MINNESOTA INVENTORIES OF SOCIAL ATTITUDES)
          @W-196 1937M SOCIAL ATTITUDE COMPETENCE BEHAVIOR PREFERENCE
          @SELF ESTEEM ACTIVITIES PREFERENCE EVALUATION INVENTORY

W-197   WIGGINS, J. S.
                SUBSTANTIVE DIMENSIONS OF SELF-REPORT IN THE MMPI ITEM POOL.
                PSYCHOLOGICAL MONOGRAPHS, 1966, 80 (22, WHOLE NO. 630).
                (MMPI CONTENT SCALES)
          @W-197 1966M MMPI
                (APPLICATIONS: 228)

W-199   WHITMAN, T. L.
                EFFECTS OF VERBAL TRAINING ON CONCEPT SORTING BEHAVIOR ON THREE
                SCHIZOPHRENIC GROUPS.
                UNPUBLISHED DOCTORAL DISSERTATION, UNIVERSITY OF ILLINOIS, 1967.
                (BEHAVIOR CHECKLIST)
          @W-199 1967M BEHAVIOR CHECKLIST
                (APPLICATIONS: 2439)

W-200   WRIGHT, J. J.
                THE IMPACT OF PERCEIVED STRESS ON ACADEMIC ACHIEVEMENT WHEN FAMILY INCOME
                LEVEL AND SELF-CONCEPT ARE TAKEN INTO ACCOUNT.
                JOURNAL OF COLLEGE STUDENT PERSONNEL, 1966, 7, 113-117.
                (ACTIVITY STRESS SCALE)
          @W-200 1966M ENVIRONMENT PRESS STRESS SITUATIONAL PRESSURE SOCIAL
          @ACTIVITIES PHYSICAL ACADEMIC ADJUSTMENT

W-201   WILCOX, P. H.
                THE GARDNER BEHAVIOR CHART.
                AMERICAN JOURNAL OF PSYCHIATRY, 1942, 98, 874-880.
                (GARDNER BEHAVIOR CHART)*
          @W-201 1942M SOCIAL ADAPTATION BEHAVIOR WARD HOSPITAL PATIENT

W-202   WALLEN, R.
                SEX DIFFERENCES IN FOOD AVERSIONS.
                JOURNAL OF APPLIED PSYCHOLOGY, 1943, 27, 288-298.
                (FOOD PREFERENCE AND AVERSION SCALE)
          @W-202 1943M PREFERENCE AVOIDANCE

Y-1   YUKER, H. E., BLOCK, J. R., & CAMPBELL, W. J.
                A SCALE TO MEASURE ATTITUDES TOWARD DISABLED PERSONS.
                HUMAN RESOURCES STUDY NO. 5. ALBERTSON, NEW YORK: HUMAN RESOURCES
                FOUNDATION, 1960.
                (ATTITUDES TOWARDS DISABLIED PERSONS SCALE)*
          @Y-1 ATTITUDE DISABILITY PERCEPTION ORIENTATION PHYSICAL NORMS HEALTH ILLNESS
          @Y-1 SOCIAL DISTANCE 1960M
                (APPLICATIONS: 53 1543 1807 2324)

Y-2   YUZUK, R. P.
                THE ASSESSMENT OF EMPLOYEE MORALE.
                COLUMBUS, OHIO: OHIO STATE UNIVERSITY PRESS, 1961.
                (MEASURE OF JOB SATISFACTION)
          @Y-2 PE-FIT MORALE ENVIRONMENT EMPLOYEE MANAGEMENT SUPERVISOR LEADERSHIP JOB
          @Y-2 SATISFACTION AFFECTIVE-STATES GLOBAL ADJUSTMENT 1961M

Y-3   YUKL, G.
                LEADER LPC SCORES: ATTITUDE DIMENSIONS AND BEHAVIORAL CORRELATES.
                JOURNAL OF SOCIAL PSYCHOLOGY, 1970, 80, 207-212.
                (SCALE FOR DESCRIPTION OF LEAST PREFFERED COWORKER)
          @Y-3 1970M ATTITUDE EVALUATION OTHERS EMPLOYEE JOB LEADERSHIP PERCEPTION

Y-4   YULIS, S. & KIESLER, D. J.
                COUNTERTRANSFERENCE RESPONSE AS A FUNCTION OF THERAPIST ANXIETY AND
                CONTENT OF PATIENT TALK.
                JOURNAL OF CONSULTING AND CLINICAL PSYCHOLOGY, 1968, 32, 413-419.
                (MEASURE OF PERSONAL INVOLVEMENT OF THERAPIST)
          @Y-4 1968M THERAPY COUNSELING RESPONSE BEHAVIOR PERSONAL INVOLVEMENT SEX
          @Y-4 AGGRESSION PATIENT RELATIONSHIPS COUNSELOR THERAPIST

Y-5   YACORZYNSKI, G. K.
            CONCEPT FORMATION AS A FUNCTION OF PERSONALITY STRUCTURE.
            AMERICAN PSYCHOLOGIST, 1950, 5, 322. (ABSTRACT).
            (CONCEPT FORMATION TEST)
        aY-5 1950M CONCEPT FORMATION
            (APPLICATIONS: 939)

Y-6   YARROW, M. R., CAMPBELL, J. D., & BURTON, R. V.
            RECOLLECTIONS OF CHILDHOOD: A STUDY OF THE RETROSPECTIVE METHOD.
            MONOGRAPHS OF THE SOCIETY FOR RESEARCH IN CHILD DEVELOPMENT, 1970, 35 (5,
            SERIAL NO. 138).
            (CHILD QUESTIONNAIRE FOR EARLY CHILDHOOD BEHAVIOR AND RELATIONSHIPS)
        aY-6 1970M CHILD BEHAVIOR FAMILY INTERACTION RELATIONSHIPS PARENTAL

Y-7   YARROW, M. R., CAMPBELL, J. D., & BURTON, R. V.
            RECOLLECTIONS OF CHILDHOOD: A STUDY OF THE RETROSPECTIVE METHOD.
            MONOGRAPHS OF THE SOCIETY FOR RESEARCH IN CHILD DEVELOPMENT, 1970, 35 (5,
            SERIAL NO. 138).
            (MOTHER INTERVIEW OF CHILD'S BEHAVIOR AND RELATIONSHIPS)
        aY-7 1970M CHILD BEHAVIOR MATERNAL FAMILY INTERACTION RELATIONSHIPS INTERVIEW
        aPARENTAL

Y-8   YAMAMOTO, K., & DIZNEY, H. F.
            REJECTION OF THE MENTALLY ILL: A STUDY OF ATTITUDES OF STUDENT TEACHERS.
            JOURNAL OF COUNSELING PSYCHOLOGY, 1967, 14, 264-268.
            (TOLERANCE SCALE)
        aY-8 1967M SOCIAL TOLERANCE AFFILIATION PREFERENCE RELATIONSHIPS
        aATTITUDE PSYCHIATRIC DISABILITY

Y-9   YAMAMOTO, K., & DIZNEY, H. F.
            REJECTION OF THE MENTALLY ILL: A STUDY OF ATTITUDES OF STUDENT TEACHERS.
            JOURNAL OF COUNSELING PSYCHOLOGY, 1967, 14, 264-268.
            (HELP SOURCE SCALE)
        aY-9 1967M MENTAL-ILLNESS ATTITUDE HOSPITALIZATION DISABILITY

Z-1   ZINGLE, H. W.
            A RATIONAL THERAPY APPROACH TO COUNSELING THE LAGGARD.
            UNPUBLISHED DOCTORAL DISSERTATION, UNIVERSITY OF ALBERTA, 1965.
            (IRRATIONAL IDEAS INVENTORY)*
        aZ-1 INTERPERSONAL RELATIONSHIPS NEUROTICISM IRRATIONAL COMPLEXITY ACHIEVEMENT
        aZ-1 RIGIDITY FLEXIBILITY IMPULSE GLOBAL ADJUSTMENT THINKING COGNITIVE STRUCTURE
        aZ-1 FUNCTIONING 1965M

Z-2   ZUCKER, R. A.
            SEX-ROLE IDENTITY PATTERNS AND DRINKING BEHAVIOR OF ADOLESCENTS.
            QUARTERLY JOURNAL OF STUDIES ON ALCOHOL, 1968, 29, 868-884.
            (ASSESSMENT OF UNCONSCIOUS SEX-ROLE IDENTITY)
        aZ-2 SEX ROLE IDENTITY SELF-IDENTITY SUB-IDENTITY ADOLESCENT FANTASY MASCULINITY
        aZ-2 FEMININITY 1968M

Z-3   ZUCKERMAN, M., KOLIN, E. A., PRICE, L., & ZOOB, I.
            DEVELOPMENT OF A SENSATION-SEEKING SCALE.
            JOURNAL OF CONSULTING PSYCHOLOGY, 1964, 28, 477-482.
            (SENSATION SEEKING SCALE)*
        aZ-3 NEED VARIETY STIMULUS SENSATION SEEKING EXPERIENCE AUTONOMY PREFERENCE
        aZ-3 1964M
            (APPLICATIONS: 240   285   1064   1541   2079   2097   2188   2218   2277   2302
                            2535   2642   2667   2868)
Z-4   ZUCKERMAN, M., LUBIN, B., VOGEL, L., & VALERIUS, E.
            MEASUREMENT OF EXPERIMENTALLY INDUCED AFFECTS.
            JOURNAL OF CONSULTING PSYCHOLOGY, 1964, 28, 418-425.
            ZUCKERMAN, M., & LUBIN, B.
            MANUAL FOR THE MULTIPLE AFFECT ADJECTIVE CHECKLIST.
            SAN DIEGO, CALIFORNIA: EDUCATIONAL AND INDUSTRIAL TESTING SERVICE, 1965.
            (MULTIPLE AFFECT ADJECTIVE CHECK LIST)*
        aZ-4 AFFECTIVE-STATES ANXIETY HOSTILITY DEPRESSION OTHER-CATEGORY CHECKLIST
        aZ-4 NEGATIVE 1964M MOOD EMOTION
            (APPLICATIONS: 468   1064   1967   2124   2188   2430   2549)

Z-5   ZUNG, W. W. K.
          A SELF-RATING DEPRESSION SCALE.
          ARCHIVES OF GENERAL PSYCHIATRY, 1965, 12, 63-70.
          (SELF-RATING DEPRESSION SCALE)*
       aZ-5 MENTAL-ILLNESS DIAGNOSIS PATIENT SELF RATING DEPRESSION AFFECTIVE-STATES
       aZ-5 NEGATIVE 1965M
          (APPLICATIONS: 1077 2697)

Z-6   ZILLER, R. C., LONG, B. H., RAMANA, K. V., & REDDY, V. E.
          SELF-OTHER ORIENTATIONS OF INDIAN AND AMERICAN ADOLESCENTS.
          JOURNAL OF PERSONALITY, 1968, 36, 315-330.
          (MEASURE OF SELF ESTEEM)
       aZ-6 CROSS-CULTURAL ADOLESCENT GRAPHIC SOCIAL ORIENTATION SELF-IDENTITY IMAGE
       aZ-6 EVALUATION SELF PERCEPTION ESTEEM OTHERS 1968M
          (APPLICATIONS: 2620)

Z-7   ZAKS, M. S., & WALTERS, R. H.
          FIRST STEPS IN THE CONSTRUCTION OF A SCALE FOR THE MEASUREMENT OF
          AGGRESSION.
          JOURNAL OF PSYCHOLOGY, 1959, 47, 199-208.
          (AGGRESSION SCALE)
       aZ-7 NEGATIVE AFFECTIVE-STATES HOSTILITY RESENTMENT AGGRESSION 1959M
          (APPLICATIONS: 1807 2072)

Z-8   ZIMMER, H.
          (NO REFERENCE AVAILABLE), 1957. SEE GUNDERSON, E. K. E., & NELSON, P. D.
          MEASUREMENT OF GROUP EFFECTIVENESS IN NATURAL ISOLATED GROUPS. JOURNAL OF
          SOCIAL PSYCHOLOGY, 1965, 66, 241-249.
          (ATTITUDE STUDY AND GROUP BEHAVIOR DESCRIPTION QUESTIONNAIRES)*
       aZ-8 PE-FIT EFFECTIVENESS ATTITUDE BEHAVIOR ENVIRONMENT MOTIVE INTERPERSONAL
       aZ-8 RELATIONSHIPS GROUP SOCIAL INTERACTION ADJUSTMENT 1957M

Z-9   ZILLER, R. C., LONG, B. H., RAMANA, K. V., & REDDY, V. E.
          SELF-OTHER ORIENTATIONS OF INDIAN AND AMERICAN ADOLESCENTS.
          JOURNAL OF PERSONALITY, 1968, 36, 315-330.
          (SOCIAL INTEREST MEASURE)
       aZ-9 INTERPERSONAL RELATIONSHIPS ORIENTATION SELF OTHERS SOCIAL INTEREST
       aZ-9 PERSONAL CROSS-CULTURAL GRAPHIC 1968M

Z-10   ZILLER, R. C., LONG, B. H., RAMANA, K. V., & REDDY, V. E.
          SELF-OTHER ORIENTATIONS OF INDIAN AND AMERICAN ADOLESCENTS.
          JOURNAL OF PERSONALITY, 1968, 36, 315-330.
          (MEASURE OF IDENTIFICATION)
       aZ-10 CROSS-CULTURAL PERSONAL SOCIAL DISTANCE IDENTIFICATION INTENSITY
       aZ-10 INTERPERSONAL ORIENTATION RELATIONSHIPS ADOLESCENT 1968M

Z-11   ZILLER, R. C., LONG, B. H., RAMANA, K. V., & REDDY, V. E.
          SELF-OTHER ORIENTATIONS OF INDIAN AND AMERICAN ADOLESCENTS.
          JOURNAL OF PERSONALITY, 1968, 36, 315-330.
          (MEASURE OF SPAN OF IDENTIFICATION OR SOCIAL INCLUSION)
       aZ-11 ORIENTATION PERSONAL SOCIAL INTERPERSONAL RELATIONSHIPS ADOLESCENT
       aZ-11 IDENTIFICATION CROSS-CULTURAL 1968M DISTANCE

Z-12   ZUCKERMAN, M.
          THE VALIDITY OF THE EDWARDS PERSONAL PREFERENCE SCHEDULE IN THE MEASUREMENT
          OF DEPENDENCY-REBELLIOUSNESS.
          JOURNAL OF CLINICAL PSYCHOLOGY, 1958, 14, 379-382.
          (INDEX OF DEPENDENCY-REBELLIOUSNESS)
       aZ-12 AUTONOMY DEPENDENCE DOMINANCE ABASEMENT AGGRESSION 1958M

Z-13   ZUCKERMAN, M.
          THE DEVELOPMENT OF AN AFFECT ADJECTIVE CHECK LIST FOR THE MEASUREMENT OF
          ANXIETY.
          JOURNAL OF CONSULTING PSYCHOLOGY, 1960, 24, 457-462.
          (AFFECT ADJECTIVE CHECK LIST)*
       aZ-13 AFFECTIVE-STATES NEGATIVE CHECKLIST ANXIETY GLOBAL ADJUSTMENT SUBJECTIVE
       aZ-13 STRESS 1960M MOOD EMOTION
          (APPLICATIONS: 88   172   241   824   901   968   991 1071 1080 1726
                          1797 1807 1833 2240 2296 2494 2530)

Z-14   ZIMMER, H.
                SCORING MANUAL FOR A SENTENCE COMPLETION TEST OF HOSTILITY, AGGRESSION
                ANXIETY, AND PROJECTION.
                AIR FORCE OFFICE OF SCIENTIFIC RESEARCH, SEPT., 1959.
                (SENTENCE COMPLETION TEST OF HOSTILITY, AGGRESSION ANXIETY, AND PROJECTION)
            aZ-14 1959M PROJECTIVE AGGRESSION HOSTILITY ANXIETY
                (APPLICATIONS: 688 1956)

Z-15   ZELLNER, M.
                SELF-ESTEEM, RECEPTION, AND INFLUENCEABILITY.
                JOURNAL OF PERSONALITY AND SOCIAL PSYCHOLOGY, 1970, 15, 87-93.
                (PERCENTILE SELF-ESTEEM SCALE)
            aZ-15 SELF ESTEEM CONCEPT IMAGE SECONDARY SCHOOL STUDENT 1970M
            aZ-15 SELF-IDENTITY

Z-16   ZELLNER, M.
                SELF-ESTEEM, RECEPTION, AND INFLUENCEABILITY.
                JOURNAL OF PERSONALITY AND SOCIAL PSYCHOLOGY, 1970, 15, 87-93.
                (GENERAL SELF-ESTEEM SCALE)
            aZ-16 1970 SELF ESTEEM IMAGE CONCEPT EVALUATION SELF-IDENTITY

Z-17   ZELLNER, M.
                SELF-ESTEEM, RECEPTION, AND INFLUENCEABILITY.
                JOURNAL OF PERSONALITY AND SOCIAL PSYCHOLOGY, 1970, 15, 87-93.
                (SEMANTIC DIFFERENTIAL SELF-ESTEEM SCALE)
            aZ-17 SELF ESTEEM SEM-DIFFERENTIAL IMAGE CONCEPT EVALUATION IDEAL SATISFACTION
            aZ-17 1970M SELF-IDENTITY

Z-18   ZIGLER, E., BUTTERFIELD, E. C., & GOFF, G.
                A MEASURE OF PREINSTITUTIONAL SOCIAL DEPRIVATION FOR INSTITUTIONALIZED
                RETARDATES.
                AMERICAN JOURNAL OF MENTAL DEFICIENCY, 1966, 70, 873-885.
                (PREINSTITUTIONAL SOCIAL DEPRIVATION SCALE)
            aZ-18 SOCIAL DEPRIVATION CHILD HOSPITALIZATION PSYCHIATRIC MENTAL-HEALTH RATING
            aZ-18 HISTORY FAMILY PARENT-CHILD 1966M
                (APPLICATIONS: 2375)

Z-19   ZELEN, S. L., & ZELEN, G. J.
                LIFE-SPAN EXPECTATIONS AND ACHIEVEMENT EXPECTANCIES OF UNDERPRIVILEGED
                AND MIDDLE-CLASS ADOLESCENTS.
                JOURNAL OF SOCIAL PSYCHOLOGY, 1970, 80, 111-112.
                (MEASURE OF LIFE-SPAN EXPECTATIONS AND ACHIEVEMENT EXPECTANCIES)
            aZ-19 1970M ACHIEVEMENT FUTURE HOPE PREDICTION SUCCESS MOTIVE

Z-20   ZILLER, R. C., MEGAS, J., & DE CENCIO, D.
                SELF-SOCIAL CONSTRUCTS OF NORMALS AND ACUTE NEUROPSYCHIATRIC PATIENTS.
                JOURNAL OF CONSULTING PSYCHOLOGY, 1964, 28, 59-63.
                (NONVERBAL MEASURE OF SELF-SOCIAL CONSTRUCTS)
            aZ-20 1964M SELF SELF-IDENTITY SUB-IDENTITY DIAGNOSIS SOCIAL ADJUSTMENT
            aZ-20 MENTAL-ILLNESS PATIENT PROJECTIVE

Z-21   ZIMMERMAN, W. S., & GUILFORD, J. P.
                THE ZIMMERMAN-GUILFORD INTEREST INVENTORY.
                BEVERLY HILLS, CALIFORNIA: SHERIDAN SUPPLY, 1963.
                (CREATIVE INTERESTS SCALE)
            aZ-21 1963M INTEREST ACHIEVEMENT CREATIVITY
            aZ-21 PREFERENCE NOVELTY ESTHETIC ACTIVITIES
                (APPLICATIONS: 2804)

Z-22   ZIMBARDO, P. G.
                INVOLVEMENT AND COMMUNICATION DISCREPANCY AS DETERMINANTS OF
                OPINION CONFORMITY.
                JOURNAL OF ABNORMAL AND SOCIAL PSYCHOLOGY, 1960, 60, 86-94.
                (COMPOSITE CHANGE INDEX)
            aZ-22 1960M ATTITUDE CHANGE RATING
            aZ-22 CONFORMITY GROUP DISSONANCE
                (APPLICATIONS: 369)

Z-24   ZANDER, A., & WULFF, D.
                MEMBERS' TEST ANXIETY AND COMPETENCE: DETERMINANTS OF A GROUP'S
                ASPIRATIONS.
                JOURNAL OF PERSONALITY, 1966, 34, 55-70.
                (MEASURE OF PERCEIVED SKILL IN GROUP TASKS)
            aZ-24 1966M PERCEIVED COMPETENCE ASPIRATION GROUP ABILITY

Z-25   ZARLOCK, S. P.
                MAGICAL THINKING AND ASSOCIATED PSYCHOLOGICAL REACTIONS TO BLINDNESS.
                JOURNAL OF CONSULTING PSYCHOLOGY, 1961, 25, 155-159.
                (MEASURE OF SOCIAL ADJUSTMENT TO BLINDNESS)
           aZ-25 1961M DISABILITY SOCIAL ADJUSTMENT MATURITY
           aZ-25 PHYSICAL ILLNESS CHECKLIST COMPETENCE

Z-26   ZARLOCK, S. P.
                MAGICAL THINKING AND ASSOCIATED PSYCHOLOGICAL REACTIONS TO BLINDNESS.
                JOURNAL OF CONSULTING PSYCHOLOGY, 1961, 25, 155-159.
                (MEASURE OF CONFIDENCE IN MEDICINE OR RELIGION TO EFFECT CURE)
           aZ-26 1961M DISABILITY RELIGION CONFIDENCE IRRATIONAL
           aZ-26 PHYSICAL ILLNESS CHECKLIST COMPETENCE

Z-27   ZUCKERMAN, M., LEVITT, E. E., & LUBIN, B.
                CONCURRENT AND CONSTRUCT VALIDITY OF DIRECT AND INDIRECT MEASURES OF
                DEPENDENCY.
                JOURNAL OF CONSULTING PSYCHOLOGY, 1961, 25, 316-323.
                (PEER RATING INSTRUMENT)
           aZ-27 1961M PEER RATING SOCIOMETRIC DEPENDENCE DOMINANCE SUBMISSION SHAME
           aZ-27 SELF ESTEEM

Z-28   ZIGLER, E., & PHILLIPS, L.
                SOCIAL EFFECTIVENESS AND SYMPTOMATIC BEHAVIORS.
                JOURNAL OF ABNORMAL AND SOCIAL PSYCHOLOGY, 1960, 61, 231-238.
                (SOCIAL COMPETENCE SCALE)
           aZ-28 1960M COMPETENCE SOCIAL ACADEMIC SCHOOL COLLEGE JOB MARITAL SUCCESS
                (APPLICATIONS: 877   1047   1079   1108   2299   2426   2742)

Z-29   ZILLER, R. C., HAGEY, J., SMITH, M. D. C., & LONG, B. H.
                SELF-ESTEEM: A SELF-SOCIAL CONSTRUCT.
                JOURNAL OF CONSULTING AND CLINICAL PSYCHOLOGY, 1969, 33, 84-95.
                (MEASURE OF SOCIAL SELF-ESTEEM)
           aZ-29 1969M SELF-IDENTITY SELF IDENTITY ESTEEM SOCIAL INTERPERSONAL IMAGE
           aZ-29 RELATIONSHIPS CONCEPT PROJECTIVE

Z-30   ZUCKERMAN, M., ALBRIGHT, R. J., MARKS, C. S., & MILLER, G. L.
                STRESS AND HALLUCINATORY EFFECTS OF PERCEPTUAL ISOLATION AND CONFINEMENT.
                PSYCHOLOGICAL MONOGRAPHS, 1962, 76 (30, WHOLE NO. 549).
                (SOMATIC SYMPTOM CHECK LIST)
           aZ-30 1962M SYMPTOM CHECKLIST HALLUCINATION BODY PSYCHOSOMATIC
                (APPLICATIONS: 968)

Z-32   ZUCKERMAN, M., PERSKY, H., LINK, K. E., & BASU, G. K.
                EXPERIMENTAL AND SUBJECT FACTORS DETERMINING RESPONSES TO SENSORY
                DEPRIVATION, SOCIAL ISOLATION, AND CONFINEMENT.
                JOURNAL OF ABNORMAL PSYCHOLOGY, 1968, 73, 183-194.
                (ISOLATION RESPONSE INVENTORY)
           aZ-32 1968M SENSORY DEPRIVATION ORIENTATION

Z-33   ZEISSET, R. M.
                DESENSITIZATION AND RELAXATION IN THE MODIFICATION OF PSYCHIATRIC PATIENTS'
                INTERVIEW BEHAVIOR.
                UNPUBLISHED DOCTORAL DISSERTATION, UNIVERSITY OF ILLINOIS, 1966.
                (CHECKLIST FOR ANXIETY-BEHAVIOR OBSERVATION)
           aZ-33 1966M ANXIETY TENSION BEHAVIOR CHECKLIST MANIFEST SYMPTOM
                (APPLICATIONS: 2725)

Z-34   ZIMMER, H.
                THE ROLES OF CONFLICT AND INTERNALIZED DEMANDS IN PROJECTION.
                JOURNAL OF ABNORMAL AND SOCIAL PSYCHOLOGY, 1955, 50, 188-192.
                (MEASURE OF DEFENSIVE PROJECTION)
           aZ-34 1955M PROJECTIVE DEFENSE
                (APPLICATIONS: 1054)

Z-37   ZAJONC, R. B.
                COGNITIVE STRUCTURE AND COGNITIVE TUNING.
                UNPUBLISHED DOCTORAL DISSERTATION, UNIVERSITY OF MICHIGAN, 1954.
                (COGNITIVE ORGANIZATION MEASURE)
           aZ-37 1954M COGNITIVE INTEGRATION DIFFERENTIATION CONSISTENCY STRUCTURE
           aORGANIZATION OPINION
                (APPLICATIONS: 194   396)

Z-38   ZELEN, S. L., & LEVITT, E. E.
            NOTES ON THE WESLEY RIGIDITY SCALE: THE DEVELOPMENT OF A SHORT FORM.
            JOURNAL OF ABNORMAL AND SOCIAL PSYCHOLOGY, 1954, 49, 472-473.
            (REVISED RIGIDITY SCALE)
        aZ-38 1954M W-11R RIGIDITY FLEXIBILITY COGNITIVE FUNCTIONING COPING DEFENSE
            (APPLICATIONS: 2239)

Z-39   ZAX, M., & LOISELLE, R. H.
            STIMULUS VALUE OF RORSCHACH INKBLOTS AS MEASURED BY THE SEMANTIC
            DIFFERENTIAL.
            JOURNAL OF CLINICAL PSYCHOLOGY, 1960, 16, 160-163.
            (SEMANTIC DIFFERENTIAL FOR THE RORSCHACH)
        aZ-39 1960M RORSCHACH SEM-DIFFERENTIAL RATING
            (APPLICATIONS: 937)

Z-40   ZIGLER, E., LEVINE, J., & GOULD, L.
            COGNITIVE PROCESSES IN THE DEVELOPMENT OF CHILDREN'S APPRECIATION OF
            HUMOR.
            CHILD DEVELOPMENT, 1966, 37, 507-518.
            (CHILDREN'S MIRTH RESPONSE TEST)*
        aZ-40 1966M HUMOR CHILD RESPONSE EXPRESSION
            (APPLICATIONS: 2325)

Z-42   ZILLER, R. C.
            VOCATIONAL CHOICE AND UTILITY FOR RISK.
            JOURNAL OF COUNSELING PSYCHOLOGY, 1957, 48, 61-64.
            (MEASURE OF UTILITY FOR RISK)
        aZ-42 1957M RISK-TAKING ACHIEVEMENT DECISION
            (APPLICATIONS: 1218)

A-5   (CALIFORNIA F-SCALE)* (See page 56)
            (APPLICATIONS: 10   26   40   56   62   66   111   115   137   144
                             162   163   175   200   206   234   342   349   351   357
                             379   386   389   427   436   463   464   543   547   548
                             549   560   579   583   589   596   600   637   640   647
                             668   670   671   678   706   709   724   726   729   747
                             761   770   789   800   844   851   872   934   1014   1063
                            1087   1249   1656   1766   1836   2010   2074   2324   2332   2334
                            2470   2489   2555   2595   2605   2631   2653   2684   2827   2830
                            2842   2883   2911   2960)

5

APPLICATIONS

2   STACHOWIAK, J. G., & MOSS, C.
              HYPNOTIC ALTERATION OF SOCIAL ATTITUDES.
              JOURNAL OF PERSONALITY AND SOCIAL PSYCHOLOGY, 1965, 2, 77-83.
                   (CORRELATES:PSYCHOLOGICAL, ENVIRONMENTAL; N=40 MALE UNDERGRADUATES)
         @APPLICATION 1965 W-31 B-58 O-16

3   RYCHLAK, J. F., & LERNER, J. J.
              AN EXPECTANCY INTERPRETATION OF MANIFEST ANXIETY.
              JOURNAL OF PERSONALITY AND SOCIAL PSYCHOLOGY, 1965, 2, 677-684.
                   (CORRELATES:BEHAVIORAL, PSYCHOLOGICAL, ENVIRONMENTAL; USED AS
                   CRITERION; NORMATIVE DATA; N=273 UNDERGRADUATES, 80 SELECTED)
         @APPLICATION 1965 T-2

4   LATZ, A., & HONIGFELD, G.
              SOME EFFECTS OF ANXIETY ON THE INTELLIGIBILITY OF VERBAL COMMUNICATION
              IN PSYCHOTHERAPY.
              JOURNAL OF PERSONALITY AND SOCIAL PSYCHOLOGY, 1965, 2, 122-125.
                   (MODIFICATION; RELIABILITY:INTERRATER; CORRELATES:BEHAVIORAL,
                   PSYCHOLOGICAL; USED AS CRITERION; N=30 UNDERGRADUATES)
         @APPLICATION 1965 T-2 D-56

5   PHARES, E. J.
              INTERNAL-EXTERNAL CONTROL AS A DETERMINANT OF AMOUNT OF SOCIAL
              INFLUENCE EXERTED.
              JOURNAL OF PERSONALITY AND SOCIAL PSYCHOLOGY, 1965, 2, 642-647.
                   (CORRELATES:BEHAVIORAL, PSYCHOLOGICAL, INTELLIGENCE; USED AS
                   CRITERION; N=179 MALES AND 256 FEMALES)
         @APPLICATION 1965 R-18 C-27

6   BAXTER, J. C., LERNER, M. J., & MILLER, J. S.
              IDENTIFICATION AS A FUNCTION OF THE REINFORCING QUALITY OF THE MODEL AND
              THE SOCIALIZATION BACKGROUND OF THE SUBJECT.
              JOURNAL OF PERSONALITY AND SOCIAL PSYCHOLOGY, 1965, 2, 692-697.
                   (MODIFICATION; CORRELATES:ENVIRONMENTAL; N=54 MALE UNDERGRADUATES)
         @APPLICATION 1965 L-10

7   WALKER, R. E., HUNT, W. A., & SCHWARTZ, M. L.
              MANIFEST ANXIETY AND CLINICAL JUDGMENT IN A GROUP SETTING.
              JOURNAL OF PERSONALITY AND SOCIAL PSYCHOLOGY, 1965, 2, 762-765.
                   (CORRELATES:PSYCHOLOGICAL; USED AS CRITERION; NORMATIVE DATA;
                   3 STUDIES: N=103 UNDERGRADUATES, 40 SELECTED, N=78, 24 SELECTED,
                   N=100, 40 SELECTED)
         @APPLICATION 1965 T-2 H-205

8   MCDAVID, J. W.
              APPROVAL SEEKING MOTIVATION AND THE VOLUNTEER SUBJECT.
              JOURNAL OF PERSONALITY AND SOCIAL PSYCHOLOGY, 1965, 2, 115-117.
                   (CORRELATES:PSYCHOLOGICAL, ENVIRONMENTAL; NORMATIVE DATA; N=136 MALE
                   UNDERGRADUATES)
         @APPLICATION 1965 M-8

9   WYER, R. S., & TERRELL, G.
              SOCIAL ROLE AND ACADEMIC ACHIEVEMENT.
              JOURNAL OF PERSONALITY AND SOCIAL PSYCHOLOGY, 1965, 2, 117-121.
                   (MODIFICATION; CORRELATES:PSYCHOLOGICAL, DEMOGRAPHIC, INTELLIGENCE;
                   USED AS CRITERION; N=225 MALE AND 351 FEMALE UNDERGRADUATES)
         @APPLICATION 1965 L-29 C-10

10   TRIANDIS, H. C., & DAVIS, E. E.
              RACE AND BELIEF AS DETERMINANTS OF BEHAVIORAL INTENTIONS.
              JOURNAL OF PERSONALITY AND SOCIAL PSYCHOLOGY, 1965, 2, 715-725.
                   (CORRELATES:BEHAVIORAL, PSYCHOLOGICAL, DEMOGRAPHIC; FACTOR ANALYSIS;
                   N=300 WHITE MALE UNDERGRADUATES)
         @APPLICATION 1965 O-16 T-12 A-5 D-12

11   KRASNER, L., KNOWLES, J. B., & ULLMAN, L. P.
         EFFECT OF VERBAL CONDITIONING OF ATTITUDES ON SUBSEQUENT MOTOR
         PERFORMANCE.
         JOURNAL OF PERSONALITY AND SOCIAL PSYCHOLOGY, 1965, 1, 407-412.
             (CORRELATES:BEHAVIORAL, PSYCHOLOGICAL, ENVIRONMENTAL; USED AS
             CRITERION; NORMATIVE DATA; N=80 MOTHERS)
      @APPLICATION 1965 C-27 E-5 K-121 K-159

12   WYER, R. S., JR., WEATHERLEY, D. A., & TERRELL, G.
         SOCIAL ROLE, AGGRESSION, AND ACADEMIC ACHIEVEMENT.
         JOURNAL OF PERSONALITY AND SOCIAL PSYCHOLOGY, 1965, 1, 645-649.
             (CORRELATES:PSYCHOLOGICAL, DEMOGRAPHIC, INTELLIGENCE; USED AS
             CRITERION; NORMATIVE DATA; N=45 MALES AND 48 FEMALES HIGH AND LOW
             HOSTILITY OUT OF 576 UNDERGRADUATES)
      @APPLICATION 1965 S-24

13   COMREY, A. L., MESCHIERI, L., MISITI, R., & NENCINI, R.
         A COMPARISON OF PERSONALITY FACTOR STRUCTURE IN AMERICAN AND ITALIAN
         SUBJECTS.
         JOURNAL OF PERSONALITY AND SOCIAL PSYCHOLOGY, 1965, 1, 257-261.
             (CORRELATES:PSYCHOLOGICAL, DEMOGRAPHIC; FACTOR ANALYSIS; N=284 MALE
             AND 223 FEMALE STUDENTS)
      @APPLICATION 1965 C-19

14   AMSTER, H.
         THE RELATION BETWEEN INTENTIONAL AND INCIDENTAL CONCEPT FORMATION AS A
         FUNCTION OF TYPE OF MULTIPLE STIMULATION AND COGNITIVE STYLE.
         JOURNAL OF PERSONALITY AND SOCIAL PSYCHOLOGY, 1965, 1, 217-223.
             (CORRELATES:BEHAVIORAL, PSYCHOLOGICAL, ENVIRONMENTAL; USED AS
             CRITERION; N=57 MALE UNDERGRADUATES)
      @APPLICATION 1965 S-61 W-61

15   EXLINE, R., GRAY, D., & SCHUETTE, D.
         VISUAL BEHAVIOR IN A DYAD AS AFFECTED BY INTERVIEW CONTENT AND SEX OF
         RESPONDENT.
         JOURNAL OF PERSONALITY AND SOCIAL PSYCHOLOGY, 1965, 1, 201-209.
             (CORRELATES:BEHAVIORAL, PSYCHOLOGICAL; N=40 MALE AND 40 FEMALE
             UNDERGRADUATES)
      @APPLICATION 1965 S-11 O-16

16   BAYTON, J. A., AUSTIN, L. J., & BURKE, K. R.
         NEGRO PERCEPTION OF NEGRO AND WHITE PERSONALITY TRAITS.
         JOURNAL OF PERSONALITY AND SOCIAL PSYCHOLOGY, 1965, 1, 250-253.
             (CORRELATES:PSYCHOLOGICAL, DEMOGRAPHIC; N=120 MALE, 120 FEMALE
             NEGRO UNDERGRADUATES)
      @APPLICATION 1965 G-26

17   HARVEY, O. J.
         SOME SITUATIONAL AND COGNITIVE DETERMINANTS OF DISSONANCE RESOLUTION.
         JOURNAL OF PERSONALITY AND SOCIAL PSYCHOLOGY, 1965, 1, 349-355.
             (RELIABILITY:INTERRATER; CORRELATES:BEHAVIORAL, PSYCHOLOGICAL,
             ENVIRONMENTAL; USED AS CRITERION; N=220 MALE UNDERGRADUATES)
      @APPLICATION 1965 H-32

18   HETHERINGTON, E. M.
         A DEVELOPMENTAL STUDY OF THE EFFECTS OF SEX OF THE DOMINANT PARENT ON
         SEX-ROLE PREFERENCE, IDENTIFICATION AND IMITATION IN CHILDREN.
         JOURNAL OF PERSONALITY AND SOCIAL PSYCHOLOGY, 1965, 2, 188-194.
             (CORRELATES:PSYCHOLOGICAL, DEMOGRAPHIC; USED AS CRITERION;
             NORMATIVE DATA; 3 SAMPLES: N=36 BOYS AND 36 GIRLS AGES 4-5, 6-8,
             9-11)
      @APPLICATION 1965 F-15 B-35

19   KASL, S. V., & MAHL, G. F.
         THE RELATIONSHIP OF DISTURBANCES AND HESITATIONS IN SPONTANEOUS SPEECH TO
         ANXIETY.
         JOURNAL OF PERSONALITY AND SOCIAL PSYCHOLOGY, 1965, 1, 425-433.
             (CORRELATES:PSYCHOLOGICAL, PHYSIOLOGICAL; N=45 MALE UNDERGRADUATES)
      @APPLICATION 1965 D-45 T-2

20   KISSEL, S.
         STRESS REDUCING PROPERTIES OF SOCIAL STIMULI.
         JOURNAL OF PERSONALITY AND SOCIAL PSYCHOLOGY, 1965, 2, 378-384.
             (RELIABILITY:INTERRATER; CORRELATES:PSYCHOLOGICAL, PHYSIOLOGICAL,
             ENVIRONMENTAL; USED AS CRITERION; N=284 UNDERGRADUATES)
      @APPLICATION 1965 M-47 H-150 M-4 F-126

21   KATKIN, E. S.
              RELATIONSHIP BETWEEN MANIFEST ANXIETY AND TWO INDICES OF AUTONOMIC
              RESPONSE TO STRESS.
              JOURNAL OF PERSONALITY AND SOCIAL PSYCHOLOGY, 1965, 2, 324-333.
                    (MODIFICATION; CORRELATES:PHYSIOLOGICAL, ENVIRONMENTAL; USED AS
                    CRITERION; BIAS:RESPONSE; N=26 HIGH AND 26 LOW ANXIETY MALE
                    UNDERGRADUATES)
              @APPLICATION 1965 D-45 W-8 C-27 T-2

22   KOLB, D. A.
              ACHIEVEMENT MOTIVATION TRAINING FOR UNDERACHIEVING HIGH-SCHOOL BOYS.
              JOURNAL OF PERSONALITY AND SOCIAL PSYCHOLOGY, 1965, 2, 783-792.
                    (MODIFICATION; RELIABILITY:INTERRATER; CORRELATES:BEHAVIORAL,
                    PSYCHOLOGICAL, DEMOGRAPHIC, INTELLIGENCE; N=57 UNDERACHIEVING HIGH
                    SCHOOL BOYS)
              @APPLICATION 1965 F-20 T-2 S-5 L-28

23   KONSTADT, N., & FORMAN, E.
              FIELD DEPENDENCE AND EXTERNAL DIRECTEDNESS.
              JOURNAL OF PERSONALITY AND SOCIAL PSYCHOLOGY, 1965, 1, 490-493.
                    (MODIFICATION; CORRELATES:BEHAVIORAL, ENVIRONMENTAL; USED AS
                    CRITERION; N=20 MALE AND 18 FEMALE 4TH GRADERS)
              @APPLICATION 1965 G-33

24   LEFCOURT, H. M., & LADWIG, G. W.
              THE AMERICAN NEGRO: A PROBLEM IN EXPECTANCIES.
              JOURNAL OF PERSONALITY AND SOCIAL PSYCHOLOGY, 1965, 1, 377-380.
                    (DESCRIPTION; CORRELATES:BEHAVIORAL, PSYCHOLOGICAL, DEMOGRAPHIC;
                    NORMATIVE DATA; N=60 NEGRO AND 60 WHITE INMATES)
              @APPLICATION 1965 R-17 R-18 D-13

25   LEFCOURT, H. M., & LADWIG, G. W.
              THE EFFECT OF PREFERENCE GROUP UPON NEGROES TASK PERSISTENCE IN A
              BIRACIAL COMPETITIVE GAME.
              JOURNAL OF PERSONALITY AND SOCIAL PSYCHOLOGY, 1965, 1, 668-671.
                    (CORRELATES:PSYCHOLOGICAL, ENVIRONMENTAL; NORMATIVE DATA; N=60 NEGRO
                    INMATES)
              @APPLICATION 1965 R-18 R-17

26   TRIANDIS, H. C., DAVIS, E. E., & TAKEZAWA, S.
              SOME DETERMINANTS OF SOCIAL DISTANCE AMONG AMERICAN, GERMAN, AND
              JAPANESE STUDENTS.
              JOURNAL OF PERSONALITY AND SOCIAL PSYCHOLOGY, 1965, 2, 540-551.
                    (DESCRIPTION; RELIABILITY:RETEST, INTERNAL CONSISTENCY;
                    VALIDITY:CROSS-VALIDATION (TOTAL N=208); CORRELATES:PSYCHOLOGICAL,
                    DEMOGRAPHIC; CROSS-CULTURAL APPLICATION; FACTOR ANALYSIS;
                    BIAS:RESPONSE; 2 STUDIES: N=88 MALE GERMAN HIGH SCHOOL STUDENTS AND
                    100 JAPANESE UNIVERSITY STUDENTS, N=93, 90 AMERICAN MALE
                    UNDERGRADUATES)
              @APPLICATION 1965 T-8 W-14 E-1 A-16 C-27 W-25 J-4 C-23 A-5 B-4 D-12 B-37

27   LITTIG, L. W., & YERACARIS, C. A.
              ACHIEVEMENT MOTIVATION AND INTERGENERATIONAL OCCUPATIONAL MOBILITY.
              JOURNAL OF PERSONALITY AND SOCIAL PSYCHOLOGY, 1965, 1, 386-389.
                    (CORRELATES:BEHAVIORAL, DEMOGRAPHIC; USED AS CRITERION; N=177 MEN
                    AND 179 WOMEN)
              @APPLICATION 1965 M-47

28   MCGINN, N. F., HARBURG, E., & JULIUS, S.
              BLOOD PRESSURE REACTIVITY AND RECALL OF TREATMENT BY PARENTS.
              JOURNAL OF PERSONALITY AND SOCIAL PSYCHOLOGY, 1965, 1, 147-153.
                    (DESCRIPTION; RELIABILITY:RETEST; VALIDITY:CRITERION;
                    CORRELATES:PSYCHOLOGICAL, PHYSIOLOGICAL; FACTOR ANALYSIS; N=107 WHITE
                    MALE UNDERGRADUATES)
              @APPLICATION 1965 H-27 H-199

29   MARKWELL, E. D., JR.
              ALTERATIONS IN SELF-CONCEPT UNDER HYPNOSIS.
              JOURNAL OF PERSONALITY AND SOCIAL PSYCHOLOGY, 1965, 1, 154-161.
                    (DESCRIPTION; RELIABILITY:RETEST; CORRELATES:PSYCHOLOGICAL,
                    DEMOGRAPHIC, ENVIRONMENTAL; USED AS CRITERION; N=44 UNDERGRADUATES)
              @APPLICATION 1965 G-21 F-81 D-45 D-77 W-31

30   MARSTON, A. R.
          IMITATION, SELF-REINFORCEMENT, AND REINFORCEMENT OF ANOTHER PERSON.
          JOURNAL OF PERSONALITY AND SOCIAL PSYCHOLOGY, 1965, 2, 255-261.
                    (CORRELATES:BEHAVIORAL, PSYCHOLOGICAL; 2 STUDIES: N=135 MALE
                    UNDERGRADUATES, 90 MALE UNDERGRADUATES)
          aAPPLICATION 1965 C-29

31   MCCLELLAND, D. C.
          N ACHIEVEMENT AND ENTREPRENEURSHIP: A LONGITUDINAL STUDY.
          JOURNAL OF PERSONALITY AND SOCIAL PSYCHOLOGY, 1965, 1, 389-392.
                    (VALIDITY:CONSTRUCT, CRITERION, CROSS-VALIDATION;
                    CORRELATES:BEHAVIORAL, INTELLIGENCE; N=55 COLLEGE ALUMNI)
          aAPPLICATION 1965 M-7

32   MCCLINTOCK, C. G., GALLO, P., & HARRISON, A. A.
          SOME EFFECTS OF VARIATION IN OTHER STRATEGY UPON GAME BEHAVIOR.
          JOURNAL OF PERSONALITY AND SOCIAL PSYCHOLOGY, 1965, 1, 319-325.
                    (CORRELATES:BEHAVIORAL, PSYCHOLOGICAL, ENVIRONMENTAL; USED AS
                    CRITERION; N=18 MALE AND 18 FEMALE UNDERGRADUATES)
          aAPPLICATION 1965 L-31

33   SARASON, I. G., GANZER, V. J., & GRANGER, J. W.
          SELF-DESCRIPTION OF HOSTILITY AND ITS CORRELATES.
          JOURNAL OF PERSONALITY AND SOCIAL PSYCHOLOGY, 1965, 1, 361-365.
                    (CORRELATES:BEHAVIORAL, PSYCHOLOGICAL; USED AS CRITERION;
                    3 STUDIES: N=112 UNDERGRADUATES, 324 HIGH SCHOOL STUDENTS, 59
                    FEMALE, 60 MALE UNDERGRADUATES)
          aAPPLICATION 1965 S-4 W-183

34   MCDONALD, R.
          EGO-CONTROL PATTERNS AND ATTRIBUTION OF HOSTILITY TO SELF AND OTHERS.
          JOURNAL OF PERSONALITY AND SOCIAL PSYCHOLOGY, 1965, 2, 273-277.
                    (MODIFICATION; CORRELATES:PSYCHOLOGICAL; USED AS CRITERION;
                    NORMATIVE DATA; N=177 SINGLE WHITE PREGNANT FEMALES)
          aAPPLICATION 1965 B-46 W-41 L-93

35   MCDONALD, R. L., & GYNTHER, M. D.
          RELATIONSHIPS OF SELF AND IDEAL-SELF DESCRIPTIONS WITH SEX, RACE, AND CLASS
          IN SOUTHERN ADOLESCENTS.
          JOURNAL OF PERSONALITY AND SOCIAL PSYCHOLOGY, 1965, 1, 85-88.
                    (RELIABILITY:INTERRATER; CORRELATES:PSYCHOLOGICAL, DEMOGRAPHIC;
                    NORMATIVE DATA; N=151 FEMALE AND 110 MALE NEGRO AND 114 FEMALE AND
                    97 MALE WHITE HIGH SCHOOL SENIORS)
          aAPPLICATION 1965 L-35 S-160

36   GUNDERSON, E. K. E.
          BODY SIZE, SELF-EVALUATION, AND MILITARY EFFECTIVENESS.
          JOURNAL OF PERSONALITY AND SOCIAL PSYCHOLOGY, 1965, 2, 902-906.
                    (CORRELATES:BEHAVIORAL, PSYCHOLOGICAL, INTELLIGENCE, PHYSICAL;
                    NORMATIVE DATA; N=485 NAVY ENLISTED MEN)
          aAPPLICATION 1965 J-12

37   HAERTZEN, C. A., & MINER, E. J.
          EFFECT OF ALCOHOL ON THE GUILFORD-ZIMMERMAN SCALES OF EXTRAVERSION.
          JOURNAL OF PERSONALITY AND SOCIAL PSYCHOLOGY, 1965, 1, 333-336.
                    (CORRELATES:PSYCHOLOGICAL, ENVIRONMENTAL; NORMATIVE DATA; N=80 MALE
                    NARCOTIC POSTADDICTS)
          aAPPLICATION 1965 G-26 C-10

38   BATTLE, E. S.
          MOTIVATIONAL DETERMINANTS OF ACADEMIC TASK PERSISTENCE.
          JOURNAL OF PERSONALITY AND SOCIAL PSYCHOLOGY, 1965, 2, 209-218.
                    (MODIFICATION; CORRELATES:PSYCHOLOGICAL, DEMOGRAPHIC; USED AS
                    CRITERION; N= OVER 500 JUNIOR HIGH SCHOOL STUDENTS)
          aAPPLICATION 1965 C-42

39   BECKWITH, J., IVERSON, M. A., & REUDER, M. E.
          TEST ANXIETY, TASK RELEVANCE OF GROUP EXPERIENCE, AND CHANGE IN LEVEL OF
          ASPIRATION.
          JOURNAL OF PERSONALITY AND SOCIAL PSYCHOLOGY, 1965, 1, 579-588.
                    (CORRELATES:BEHAVIORAL, PSYCHOLOGICAL; USED AS CRITERION; N=104 HIGH
                    AND LOW TEST ANXIOUS FEMALE UNDERGRADUATES)
          aAPPLICATION 1965 M-4

40   MISCHEL, W.
            PREDICTING THE SUCCESS OF PEACE CORPS VOLUNTEERS IN NIGERIA.
            JOURNAL OF PERSONALITY AND SOCIAL PSYCHOLOGY, 1965, 1, 510-517.
                (MODIFICATION; VALIDITY:CRITERION; CORRELATES:BEHAVIORAL,
                INTELLIGENCE; USED AS CRITERION; N=28 MALE AND 13 FEMALE PEACE CORPS
                VOLUNTEERS)
        @APPLICATION 1965 A-5 L-1C B-5 T-2

41   MOULTON, R. W.
            EFFECTS OF SUCCESS AND FAILURE ON LEVEL OF ASPIRATION AS RELATED TO
            ACHIEVEMENT MOTIVE.
            JOURNAL OF PERSONALITY AND SOCIAL PSYCHOLOGY, 1965, 1, 399-406.
                (RELIABILITY:INTERRATER; CORRELATES:BEHAVIORAL, PSYCHOLOGICAL,
                INTELLIGENCE, ENVIRONMENTAL; USED AS CRITERION; N=93 MALE HIGH
                SCHOOL STUDENTS)
        @APPLICATION 1965 M-7 M-25

42   FISHBEIN, M.
            PREDICTION OF INTERPERSONAL PREFERENCES AND GROUP MEMBER SATISFACTION FROM
            ESTIMATED ATTITUDES.
            JOURNAL OF PERSONALITY AND SOCIAL PSYCHOLOGY, 1965, 1, 663-667.
                (DESCRIPTION; CORRELATES:BEHAVIORAL, PSYCHOLOGICAL; N=200 STUDENTS)
        @APPLICATION 1965 M-28 F-50

43   PATTERSON, G. R.
            PARENTS AS DISPENSERS OF AVERSIVE STIMULI.
            JOURNAL OF PERSONALITY AND SOCIAL PSYCHOLOGY, 1965, 2, 844-851.
                (RELIABILITY:INTERRATER; CORRELATES:BEHAVIORAL, PSYCHOLOGICAL,
                DEMOGRAPHIC; N=30 BOYS AND 30 GIRLS AND 60 PARENTS)
        @APPLICATION 1965 P-27 D-45 T-2 K-147 B-167

44   DECHARMS, R., & DAVE, P. N.
            HOPE OF SUCCESS, FEAR OF FAILURE, SUBJECTIVE PROBABILITY, AND
            RISK-TAKING BEHAVIOR.
            JOURNAL OF PERSONALITY AND SOCIAL PSYCHOLOGY, 1965, 1, 558-568.
                (DESCRIPTION; RELIABILITY:INTERRATER; VALIDITY:CRITERION;
                CORRELATES:BEHAVIORAL, PSYCHOLOGICAL; USED AS CRITERION; N=71
                ELEMENTARY SCHOOL BOYS)
        @APPLICATION 1965 M-20 M-25

45   EBNER, E.
            VERBAL CONDITIONING IN SCHIZOPHRENIA AS A FUNCTION OF DEGREE OF SOCIAL
            INTERACTION.
            JOURNAL OF PERSONALITY AND SOCIAL PSYCHOLOGY, 1965, 1, 528-532.
                (DESCRIPTION; VALIDITY:CRITERION; CORRELATES:PSYCHOLOGICAL,
                ENVIRONMENTAL; USED AS CRITERION; N=36 SCHIZOPHRENICS, 36 VA
                PATIENTS)
        @APPLICATION 1965 T-2

46   FEATHER, N. T.
            THE RELATIONSHIP OF EXPECTATION OF SUCCESS TO NEED ACHIEVEMENT AND TEST
            ANXIETY.
            JOURNAL OF PERSONALITY AND SOCIAL PSYCHOLOGY, 1965, 1, 118-126.
                (DESCRIPTION; RELIABILITY:INTERRATER; VALIDITY:CRITERION;
                CORRELATES:ENVIRONMENTAL; USED AS CRITERION; N=168 MALE
                UNDERGRADUATES)
        @APPLICATION 1965 M-4 M-7

47   HARLESTON, B. W., SMITH, M. G., & AREY, D.
            TEST-ANXIETY LEVEL, HEART RATE, AND ANAGRAM PROBLEM SOLVING.
            JOURNAL OF PERSONALITY AND SOCIAL PSYCHOLOGY, 1965, 1, 551-557.
                (CORRELATES:BEHAVIORAL, PHYSIOLOGICAL; USED AS CRITERION;
                NORMATIVE DATA; N=42 FEMALE UNDERGRADUATES)
        @APPLICATION 1965 H-28

48   FOULKES, D., & FOULKES, S. H.
            SELF-CONCEPT, DOGMATISM, AND TOLERANCE OF TRAIT INCONSISTENCY.
            JOURNAL OF PERSONALITY AND SOCIAL PSYCHOLOGY, 1965, 2, 104-110.
                (CORRELATES:PSYCHOLOGICAL, INTELLIGENCE; USED AS CRITERION; NORMATIVE
                DATA; N=62 FRESHMAN WOMEN)
        @APPLICATION 1965 K-151 C-39 R-8

49   HERRON, E. W.
          PERSONALITY FACTORS ASSOCIATED WITH THE ACQUISITION OF THE
          CONDITIONED EYELID RESPONSE.
          JOURNAL OF PERSONALITY AND SOCIAL PSYCHOLOGY, 1965, 2, 775-777.
                  (CORRELATES:BEHAVIORAL, PSYCHOLOGICAL, DEMOGRAPHIC; NORMATIVE DATA;
                  N=32 UNDERGRADUATES)
      @APPLICATION 1965 H-37

50   STONE, L. A.
          SOCIAL DESIRABILITY CORRELATES OF SOCIAL RESPONSIBILITY.
          JOURNAL OF PERSONALITY AND SOCIAL PSYCHOLOGY, 1965, 2, 756-757.
                  (CORRELATES:PSYCHOLOGICAL; N=49 PATIENTS)
      @APPLICATION 1965 B-54 C-27 D-45 F-1

51   FISHER, S.
          BODY-BOUNDARY SENSATIONS AND ACQUIESCENCE.
          JOURNAL OF PERSONALITY AND SOCIAL PSYCHOLOGY, 1965, 1, 381-383.
                  (DESCRIPTION; CORRELATES:BEHAVIORAL, PSYCHOLOGICAL, PHYSIOLOGICAL;
                  BIAS:RESPONSE; 2 SAMPLES: N=51 MALE AND N=54 FEMALE UNDERGRADUATES)
      @APPLICATION 1965 B-7

52   FISHMAN, CLAIRE, G.
          NEED FOR APPROVAL AND THE EXPRESSION OF AGGRESSION UNDER VARYING
          CONDITIONS OF FRUSTRATION.
          JOURNAL OF PERSONALITY AND SOCIAL PSYCHOLOGY, 1965, 2, 809-816.
                  (DESCRIPTION; MODIFICATION; CORRELATES:PSYCHOLOGICAL,
                  PHYSIOLOGICAL; USED AS CRITERION; N=60 FEMALE UNDERGRADUATES)
      @APPLICATION 1965 C-27 M-20 G-63

53   CHESLER, M. A.
          ETHNOCENTRISM AND ATTITUDES TOWARD THE PHYSICALLY DISABLED.
          JOURNAL OF PERSONALITY AND SOCIAL PSYCHOLOGY, 1965, 2, 877-882.
                  (REVISION; DESCRIPTION; RELIABILITY:INTERNAL CONSISTENCY;
                  VALIDITY:CRITERION; CORRELATES:PSYCHOLOGICAL, DEMOGRAPHIC; NORMATIVE
                  DATA; 2 SAMPLES: N=77 COLLEGE STUDENTS, 243 HIGH SCHOOL STUDENTS)
      @APPLICATION 1965 L-32 A-17 Y-1

54   BYRNE, D.
          PARENTAL ANTECEDENTS OF AUTHORITARIANISM.
          JOURNAL OF PERSONALITY AND SOCIAL PSYCHOLOGY, 1965, 1, 369-373.
                  (MODIFICATION; RELIABILITY:INTERNAL CONSISTENCY; VALIDITY:CRITERION;
                  CORRELATES:PSYCHOLOGICAL; N=108 COLLEGE STUDENTS, 216 THEIR PARENTS)
      @APPLICATION 1965 A-5 L-10

55   BRODY, GRACE F.
          RELATIONSHIP BETWEEN MATERNAL ATTITUDES AND BEHAVIOR.
          JOURNAL OF PERSONALITY AND SOCIAL PSYCHOLOGY, 1965, 2, 317-323.
                  (MODIFICATION; RELIABILITY:INTERRATER; VALIDITY:CRITERION;
                  CORRELATES:BEHAVIORAL, PSYCHOLOGICAL; USED AS CRITERION; N=50
                  MOTHERS, 22 MALE AND 28 FEMALE CHILDREN)
      @APPLICATION 1965 S-9 P-50

56   FRY, C.
          PERSONALITY AND ACQUISITION FACTORS IN THE DEVELOPMENT OF COORDINATION
          STRATEGY.
          JOURNAL OF PERSONALITY AND SOCIAL PSYCHOLOGY, 1965, 2, 403-407.
                  (DESCRIPTION; CORRELATES:BEHAVIORAL, INTELLIGENCE; N=16 FEMALE AND
                  20 MALE UNDERGRADUATES)
      @APPLICATION 1965 A-6 A-5

57   GLIXMAN, A. F.
          CATEGORIZING BEHAVIOR AS A FUNCTION OF MEANING DOMAIN.
          JOURNAL OF PERSONALITY AND SOCIAL PSYCHOLOGY, 1965, 2, 370-377.
                  (CORRELATES:BEHAVIORAL, PSYCHOLOGICAL; N=19 MALE, 17 FEMALE
                  UNDERGRADUATES)
      @APPLICATION 1965

58   GOLDSTEIN, M. J., JONES, R. B., CLEMENS, T. L., FLAGG, G. W., & ALEXANDER, F. G.
          COPING STYLE AS A FACTOR IN PSYCHOPHYSIOLOGICAL RESPONSE TO A
          TENSION-AROUSING FILM.
          JOURNAL OF PERSONALITY AND SOCIAL PSYCHOLOGY, 1965, 1, 290-302.
                  (CORRELATES:PSYCHOLOGICAL, PHYSIOLOGICAL, INTELLIGENCE; USED AS
                  CRITERION; NORMATIVE DATA; N=32 FEMALE AND 8 MALE NONPSYCHIATRIC
                  AND PATIENT VOLUNTEERS)
      @APPLICATION 1965 G-32

59   ZAVALLONI, M., & COOK, S. W.
            INFLUENCE OF JUDGES' ATTITUDES ON RATINGS OF FAVORABLENESS OF STATEMENTS
            ABOUT A SOCIAL GROUP.
            JOURNAL OF PERSONALITY AND SOCIAL PSYCHOLOGY, 1965, 1, 43-54.
                (CORRELATES:BEHAVIORAL, PSYCHOLOGICAL; USED AS CRITERION;
                    2 SAMPLES: N=336 COLLEGE STUDENTS, N=93 COLLEGE STUDENTS)
        @APPLICATION 1965 H-36

60   WYER, R. S., JR.
            EFFECT OF CHILD-REARING ATTITUDES AND BEHAVIOR ON CHILDREN'S RESPONSES TO
            HYPOTHETICAL SOCIAL SITUATIONS.
            JOURNAL OF PERSONALITY AND SOCIAL PSYCHOLOGY, 1965, 2, 480-486.
                (MODIFICATION; CORRELATES:BEHAVIORAL, PSYCHOLOGICAL; FACTOR
                    ANALYSIS; N=18 FEMALE AND 17 MALE CHILDREN)
        @APPLICATION 1965 S-9 R-23

61   WYER, R. S., JR.
            SELF ACCEPTANCE, DISCREPANCY BETWEEN PARENTS' PERCEPTIONS OF THEIR
            CHILDREN, AND GOAL SEEKING EFFECTIVENESS.
            JOURNAL OF PERSONALITY AND SOCIAL PSYCHOLOGY, 1965, 2, 311-316.
                (MODIFICATION; DESCRIPTION; CORRELATES:PSYCHOLOGICAL, DEMOGRAPHIC,
                    INTELLIGENCE; N=393 MALE AND 496 FEMALE COLLEGE STUDENTS, 350 FATHERS
                    AND 383 MOTHERS OF MALE SUBJECTS, 399 FATHERS AND 444 MOTHERS OF
                    FEMALE SUBJECTS)
        @APPLICATION 1965 S-50

62   WRIGHT, J. M., & HARVEY, O. J.
            ATTITUDE CHANGE AS A FUNCTION OF AUTHORITARIANISM AND PUNITIVENESS.
            JOURNAL OF PERSONALITY AND SOCIAL PSYCHOLOGY, 1965, 1, 177-181.
                (RELIABILITY:RETEST, INTERNAL CONSISTENCY; CORRELATES:BEHAVIORAL,
                    PSYCHOLOGICAL, ENVIRONMENTAL; N=55 COLLEGE STUDENTS)
        @APPLICATION 1965 A-5 R-12 H-112

63   WRENCH, D., & ENDICOTT, K.
            DENIAL OF AFFECT AND CONFORMITY.
            JOURNAL OF PERSONALITY AND SOCIAL PSYCHOLOGY, 1965, 1, 484-486.
                (VALIDITY:CRITERION; CORRELATES:BEHAVIORAL, PSYCHOLOGICAL;
                    2 SAMPLES: N=22 UNDERGRADUATES, N=22 UNDERGRADUATES)
        @APPLICATION 1965 B-2 C-110

64   WOLFF, C.
            MANIFEST ANXIETY, REACTION POTENTIAL CEILING, AND WORD ASSOCIATION.
            JOURNAL OF PERSONALITY AND SOCIAL PSYCHOLOGY, 1965, 2, 570-573.
                (CORRELATES:BEHAVIORAL, ENVIRONMENTAL; USED AS CRITERION; NORMATIVE
                    DATA; N=57 MALE UNDERGRADUATES)
        @APPLICATION 1965 T-2

65   WILD, C.
            CREATIVITY AND ADAPTIVE REGRESSION.
            JOURNAL OF PERSONALITY AND SOCIAL PSYCHOLOGY, 1965, 2, 161-169.
                (CORRELATES:BEHAVIORAL, ENVIRONMENTAL; N=18 MALE AND 12 FEMALE
                    ART STUDENTS, 26 TEACHERS, 26 SCHIZOPHRENICS)
        @APPLICATION 1965 R-30

66   WHITE, B. J., ALTER, R. D., & RARDIN, M.
            AUTHORITARIANISM, DOGMATISM, AND USAGE OF CONCEPTUAL CATEGORIES.
            JOURNAL OF PERSONALITY AND SOCIAL PSYCHOLOGY, 1965, 2, 293-295.
                (CORRELATES:BEHAVIORAL, PSYCHOLOGICAL; USED AS CRITERION; NORMATIVE
                    DATA; N=24 OUT OF 410 UNDERGRADUATES)
        @APPLICATION 1965 R-8 A-5

67   WEINER, I. B., & ADER, R.
            DIRECTION OF AGGRESSION AND ADAPTATION TO FREE OPERANT AVOIDANCE
            CONDITIONING.
            JOURNAL OF PERSONALITY AND SOCIAL PSYCHOLOGY, 1965, 2, 426-429.
                (VALIDITY:CRITERION; CORRELATES:BEHAVIORAL, ENVIRONMENTAL; N=26 MALE
                    MEDICAL AND GRADUATE STUDENTS)
        @APPLICATION 1965 N-17 R-12 W-20

68   WEINER, B.
            NEED ACHIEVEMENT AND THE RESUMPTION OF INCOMPLETED TASKS.
            JOURNAL OF PERSONALITY AND SOCIAL PSYCHOLOGY, 1965, 1, 165-168.
                (RELIABILITY:INTERRATER; CORRELATES:BEHAVIORAL, ENVIRONMENTAL; N=30
                    MALE UNDERGRADUATES)
        @APPLICATION 1965 M-47

69   WARD, C. D.
            EGO INVOLVEMENT AND THE ABSOLUTE JUDGMENT OF ATTITUDE STATEMENTS.
            JOURNAL OF PERSONALITY AND SOCIAL PSYCHOLOGY, 1965, 2, 202-208.
                (DESCRIPTION; VALIDITY:CRITERION; CORRELATES:BEHAVIORAL,
                PSYCHOLOGICAL; N=60 WHITE COLLEGE STUDENTS)
        @APPLICATION 1965 D-18 H-36

70   UHLMANN, F. W., & SALTZ, E.
            RETENTION OF ANXIETY MATERIAL AS A FUNCTION OF COGNITIVE DIFFERENTIATION.
            JOURNAL OF PERSONALITY AND SOCIAL PSYCHOLOGY, 1965, 1, 55-62.
                (DESCRIPTION; CORRELATES:BEHAVIORAL, INTELLIGENCE; USED AS
                CRITERION; N=56 HIGH AND 50 LOW DIFFERENTIATORS SELECTED FROM
                164 MEN)
        @APPLICATION 1965 T-20 U-3

71   TANNENBAUM, P. H., & GAER, E. P.
            MOOD CHANGE AS A FUNCTION OF STRESS OF PROTAGONIST AND DEGREE OF
            IDENTIFICATION IN A FILM-VIEWING SITUATION.
            JOURNAL OF PERSONALITY AND SOCIAL PSYCHOLOGY, 1965, 2, 612-616.
                (CORRELATES:PSYCHOLOGICAL, ENVIRONMENTAL; USED AS CRITERION;
                N=123 UNDERGRADUATES)
        @APPLICATION 1965 G-24 O-16

72   STOLLAK, G. E.
            EPPS PERFORMANCE UNDER SOCIAL DESIRABILITY INSTRUCTIONS.
            JOURNAL OF PERSONALITY AND SOCIAL PSYCHOLOGY, 1965, 2, 430-432.
                (CORRELATES:BEHAVIORAL, ENVIRONMENTAL; NORMATIVE DATA; BIAS:RESPONSE;
                N=384 MALE UNDERGRADUATES)
        @APPLICATION 1965 E-2

73   STEINER, I. D., & JOHNSON, H. H.
            CATEGORY WIDTH AND RESPONSES TO INTERPERSONAL DISAGREEMENTS.
            JOURNAL OF PERSONALITY AND SOCIAL PSYCHOLOGY, 1965, 2, 290-292.
                (CORRELATES:BEHAVIORAL, ENVIRONMENTAL; USED AS CRITERION; NORMATIVE
                DATA; N=64 MALE UNDERGRADUATES)
        @APPLICATION 1965 P-7

74   SARASON, I. G., & HARMATZ, M. G.
            TEST ANXIETY AND EXPERIMENTAL CONDITIONS.
            JOURNAL OF PERSONALITY AND SOCIAL PSYCHOLOGY, 1965, 1, 499-505.
                (CORRELATES:BEHAVIORAL, PSYCHOLOGICAL, ENVIRONMENTAL; USED AS
                CRITERION; NORMATIVE DATA; BIAS:TESTER; N=72 MALE AND 72 FEMALE
                HIGH SCHOOL SOPHOMORES)
        @APPLICATION 1965 S-5

75   SARASON, I. G., & HARMATZ, M. G.
            SEX DIFFERENCES AND EXPERIMENTAL CONDITIONS IN SERIAL LEARNING.
            JOURNAL OF PERSONALITY AND SOCIAL PSYCHOLOGY, 1965, 1, 521-524.
                (CORRELATES:BEHAVIORAL, ENVIRONMENTAL; USED AS CRITERION;
                N=60 MALE, 60 FEMALE UNDERGRADUATES)
        @APPLICATION 1965 S-5

76   SAMPLE, J. A., & WILSON, T. R.
            LEADER BEHAVIOR, GROUP PRODUCTIVITY, AND RATING OF LEAST PREFERRED
            CO-WORKER.
            JOURNAL OF PERSONALITY AND SOCIAL PSYCHOLOGY, 1965, 1, 266-270.
                (CORRELATES:BEHAVIORAL, PSYCHOLOGICAL, ENVIRONMENTAL; USED AS
                CRITERION; N=32 UNDERGRADUATES)
        @APPLICATION 1965 B-2

77   RYCHLAK, J. F.
            THE SIMILARITY, COMPATIBILITY OR INCOMPATIBILITY OR NEEDS IN
            INTERPERSONAL SELECTION.
            JOURNAL OF PERSONALITY AND SOCIAL PSYCHOLOGY, 1965, 2, 334-340.
                (DESCRIPTION; CORRELATES:PSYCHOLOGICAL, INTELLIGENCE; USED AS
                CRITERION; NORMATIVE DATA; N=96 MALES)
        @APPLICATION 1965 B-192 E-2 G-40 R-31

78   RYAN, E. D., & LAKIE, W. L.
            COMPETITIVE AND NONCOMPETITIVE PERFORMANCE IN RELATION TO ACHIEVEMENT
            MOTIVE AND MANIFEST ANXIETY.
            JOURNAL OF PERSONALITY AND SOCIAL PSYCHOLOGY, 1965, 1, 342-345.
                (CORRELATES:BEHAVIORAL, PSYCHOLOGICAL; USED AS CRITERION; NORMATIVE
                DATA; N=20 HIGH, 20 LOW ANXIETY MALE UNDERGRADUATES FROM 300 TESTED)
        @APPLICATION 1965 T-2 F-20

79   RUSSELL, D. G., & SARASON, I. G.
            TEST ANXIETY, SEX, AND EXPERIMENTAL CONDITIONS IN RELATION TO ANAGRAM
            SOLUTION.
            JOURNAL OF PERSONALITY AND SOCIAL PSYCHOLOGY, 1965, 1, 493-496.
                (CORRELATES:BEHAVIORAL, PSYCHOLOGICAL, DEMOGRAPHIC,
                ENVIRONMENTAL; USED AS CRITERION; NORMATIVE DATA; N=48 MALE AND 48
                FEMALE HIGH AND LOW ANXIETY UNDERGRADUATES)
        @APPLICATION 1965 S-5

80   ROTTER, J. B., & MULRY, R. C.
            INTERNAL VERSUS EXTERNAL CONTROL OF REINFORCEMENT AND DECISION TIME.
            JOURNAL OF PERSONALITY AND SOCIAL PSYCHOLOGY, 1965, 2, 598-604.
                (CORRELATES:BEHAVIORAL, ENVIRONMENTAL; USED AS CRITERION; NORMATIVE
                DATA; N=61 FEMALE AND 59 MALE UNDERGRADUATES)
        @APPLICATION 1965 R-18

81   ROSENBERG, B. G., & LANGER, J.
            A STUDY OF POSTURAL-GESTURAL COMMUNICATION.
            JOURNAL OF PERSONALITY AND SOCIAL PSYCHOLOGY, 1965, 2, 593-597.
                (CORRELATES:BEHAVIORAL, PSYCHOLOGICAL; N=57 FEMALE AND 30 MALE
                UNDERGRADUATES)
        @APPLICATION 1965 S-37

82   RINGUETTE, E. L.
            SELECTED PERSONALITY CORRELATES OF MODE OF CONFLICT RESOLUTION.
            JOURNAL OF PERSONALITY AND SOCIAL PSYCHOLOGY, 1965, 2, 506-512.
                (VALIDITY:CRITERION; CORRELATES:BEHAVIORAL, PSYCHOLOGICAL; NORMATIVE
                DATA; N=79 HOSPITALIZED MALES AND 30 NONHOSPITALIZED MALES)
        @APPLICATION 1965 B-5 W-8 W-41 D-45

83   PERKINS, C. W., & SHANNON, D. T.
            THREE TECHNIQUES FOR OBTAINING SELF-PERCEPTIONS IN PREADOLESCENT BOYS.
            JOURNAL OF PERSONALITY AND SOCIAL PSYCHOLOGY, 1965, 2, 443-447.
                (DESCRIPTION; MODIFICATION; RELIABILITY:RETEST, INTERNAL
                CONSISTENCY; VALIDITY:CRITERION; CORRELATES:BEHAVIORAL,
                INTELLIGENCE; USED AS CRITERION; N=64 6TH GRADE BOYS)
        @APPLICATION 1965 M-58 S-48 P-18

84   MEADE, R. D.
            ACHIEVEMENT MOTIVATION, ACHIEVEMENT, AND PSYCHOLOGICAL TIME.
            JOURNAL OF PERSONALITY AND SOCIAL PSYCHOLOGY, 1966, 4, 577-580.
                (RELIABILITY:INTERRATER; CORRELATES:BEHAVIORAL, PSYCHOLOGICAL; USED
                AS CRITERION; NORMATIVE DATA; N=295 MALE UNDERGRADUATES, 80 SELECTED)
        @APPLICATION 1966 M-47

85   SAPPENFIELD, B. R., KAPLAN, B. B., & BALOGH, B.
            PERCEPTUAL CORRELATES OF STEREOTYPICAL MASCULINITY-FEMININITY.
            JOURNAL OF PERSONALITY AND SOCIAL PSYCHOLOGY, 1966, 4, 585-590.
                (CORRELATES:PSYCHOLOGICAL, DEMOGRAPHIC; NORMATIVE DATA; 4 STUDIES:
                N=20, 192, 80, 60 UNDERGRADUATES)
        @APPLICATION 1966 R-24

86   SIEBER, J. E., & LANZETTA, J. T.
            SOME DETERMINANTS OF INDIVIDUAL DIFFERENCES IN PREDECISION
            INFORMATION-PROCESSING BEHAVIOR.
            JOURNAL OF PERSONALITY AND SOCIAL PSYCHOLOGY, 1966, 4, 561-571.
                (CORRELATES:BEHAVIORAL, DEMOGRAPHIC, ENVIRONMENTAL; USED AS
                CRITERION; N=489 UNDERGRADUATES, 60 SELECTED)
        @APPLICATION 1966 S-41

87   CROWNE, D. P.
            FAMILY ORIENTATION, LEVEL OF ASPIRATION, AND INTERPERSONAL BARGAINING.
            JOURNAL OF PERSONALITY AND SOCIAL PSYCHOLOGY, 1966, 3, 641-645.
                (CORRELATES:BEHAVIORAL, DEMOGRAPHIC; N=28 MALE AND 48 FEMALE
                UNDERGRADUATES)
        @APPLICATION 1966 R-17

88   WILLIAMS, A. F.
            SOCIAL DRINKING, ANXIETY, AND DEPRESSION.
            JOURNAL OF PERSONALITY AND SOCIAL PSYCHOLOGY, 1966, 3, 689-693.
                (CORRELATES:BEHAVIORAL; N=91 MALE UNDERGRADUATES)
        @APPLICATION 1966 P-128 Z-13

89   WEINER, B.
            ACHIEVEMENT MOTIVATION AND TASK RECALL IN COMPETITIVE SITUATIONS.
            JOURNAL OF PERSONALITY AND SOCIAL PSYCHOLOGY, 1966, 3, 693-696.
                (CORRELATES:PSYCHOLOGICAL, DEMOGRAPHIC; N=33 MALE AND 37 FEMALE)
        @APPLICATION 1966 O-3

90   TURIEL, E.
            AN EXPERIMENTAL TEST OF THE SEQUENTIALITY OF DEVELOPMENTAL STAGES IN THE
            CHILD'S MORAL JUDGMENTS.
            JOURNAL OF PERSONALITY AND SOCIAL PSYCHOLOGY, 1966, 3, 611-618.
                (RELIABILITY:INTERRATER; CORRELATES:PSYCHOLOGICAL, ENVIRONMENTAL;
                N=44 7TH GRADE BOYS)
        @APPLICATION 1966 K-27

91   TUCKMAN, B. W.
            INTERPERSONAL PROBING AND REVEALING AND SYSTEMS OF INTEGRATIVE COMPLEXITY.
            JOURNAL OF PERSONALITY AND SOCIAL PSYCHOLOGY, 1966, 3, 655-664.
                (DESCRIPTION; CORRELATES:BEHAVIORAL, PSYCHOLOGICAL; N=299 NAVAL
                RECRUITS)
        @APPLICATION 1966 T-16 J-14 F-142

92   VEROFF, J., FIELD, S., & CROCKETT, H.
            EXPLORATIONS INTO THE EFFECTS OF PICTURE CUES ON THEMATIC APPERCEPTIVE
            EXPRESSION OF ACHIEVEMENT MOTIVATION.
            JOURNAL OF PERSONALITY AND SOCIAL PSYCHOLOGY, 1966, 3, 171-181.
                (RELIABILITY:INTERRATER; CORRELATES:PSYCHOLOGICAL, DEMOGRAPHIC;
                N=SUBSETS OF 2,460 ADULTS)
        @APPLICATION 1966 V-23 V-42

93   KOENIG, K. P.
            VERBAL BEHAVIOR AND PERSONALITY CHANGE.
            JOURNAL OF PERSONALITY AND SOCIAL PSYCHOLOGY, 1966, 3, 223-237.
                (CORRELATES:BEHAVIORAL, PSYCHOLOGICAL; USED AS CRITERION; N=20 MALE
                AND 20 FEMALE UNDERGRADUATES)
        @APPLICATION 1966 S-5

94   RETTIG, S.
            GROUP DISCUSSION AND PREDICTED ETHICAL RISK TAKING.
            JOURNAL OF PERSONALITY AND SOCIAL PSYCHOLOGY, 1966, 3, 629-633.
                (CORRELATES:BEHAVIORAL, ENVIRONMENTAL; NORMATIVE DATA; N=160
                UNDERGRADUATES)
        '@APPLICATION 1966 R-26

95   SHOR, R. E., ORNE, M. E., & O'CONNELL, D. N.
            PSYCHOLOGICAL CORRELATES OF PLATEAU HYPNOTIZABILITY IN A SPECIAL
            VOLUNTEER SAMPLE.
            JOURNAL OF PERSONALITY AND SOCIAL PSYCHOLOGY, 1966, 3, 80-95.
                (CORRELATES:PSYCHOLOGICAL, INTELLIGENCE; N=25 UNDERGRADUATES)
        @APPLICATION 1966 D-77 M-20 D-45 D-88 R-12 C-23 R-151 W-31

96   MELTZER, B., CROCKETT, W. H., & ROSENKRANTZ, P. S.
            COGNITIVE COMPLEXITY, VALUE CONGRUITY, AND THE INTEGRATION OF POTENTIALLY
            INCOMPATIBLE INFORMATION IN IMPRESSIONS OF OTHERS.
            JOURNAL OF PERSONALITY AND SOCIAL PSYCHOLOGY, 1966, 4, 338-343.
                (CORRELATES:PSYCHOLOGICAL, ENVIRONMENTAL; USED AS CRITERION; N=80
                MALE UNDERGRADUATES)
        @APPLICATION 1966 R-34 A-7

97   MOULTON, R. W., BURNSTEIN, E., LIBERTY, P. G., & ALTUCHER, N.
            PATTERNING OF PARENTAL AFFECTION AND DISCIPLINARY DOMINANCE AS A
            DETERMINANT OF GUILT AND SEX TYPING.
            JOURNAL OF PERSONALITY AND SOCIAL PSYCHOLOGY, 1966, 4, 356-363.
                (CORRELATES:BEHAVIORAL, PSYCHOLOGICAL; USED AS CRITERION; N=176
                MALE UNDERGRADUATES)
        @APPLICATION 1966 G-20 A-90

98   ROSENTHAL, R., KOHN, P., GREENFIELD, P. M., & CAROTE, N.
            DATA DESIRABILITY, EXPERIMENTER EXPECTANCY, AND THE RESULTS OF
            PSYCHOLOGICAL RESEARCH.
            JOURNAL OF PERSONALITY AND SOCIAL PSYCHOLOGY, 1966, 3, 20-27.
                (CORRELATES:BEHAVIORAL, PSYCHOLOGICAL, DEMOGRAPHIC, ENVIRONMENTAL;
                BIAS:TESTER; N=60 FEMALE STUDENTS)
        @APPLICATION 1966 C-27 T-2 R-152

99   MCKEACHIE, W. J., LIN, Y., MILHOLLAND, J., & ISAACSON, R.
          STUDENT AFFILIATION MOTIVES, TEACHER WARMTH, AND ACADEMIC ACHIEVEMENT.
          JOURNAL OF PERSONALITY AND SOCIAL PSYCHOLOGY, 1966, 4, 457-461.
               (RELIABILITY:INTERRATER; 3 STUDIES: N=533, N=406 FEMALE AND 348 MALE,
               N=481 FEMALE AND 466 MALE UNDERGRADUATES)
      @APPLICATION 1966 S-19 M-221

100   MORRIS, J. L.
          PROPENSITY FOR RISK TAKING AS A DETERMINANT OF VOCATIONAL CHOICE: AN
          EXTENSION OF THE THEORY OF ACHIEVEMENT MOTIVE.
          JOURNAL OF PERSONALITY AND SOCIAL PSYCHOLOGY, 1966, 3, 328-335.
               (CORRELATES:BEHAVIORAL, PSYCHOLOGICAL, INTELLIGENCE; USED AS
               CRITERION; N=94 MALE HIGH SCHOOL SENIORS)
      @APPLICATION 1966 M-7 M-25 K-34

101   MURPHY, D. F.
          SENSORY DEPRIVATION, SUGGESTION, FIELD DEPENDENCE, AND PERCEPTUAL
          REGRESSION.
          JOURNAL OF PERSONALITY AND SOCIAL PSYCHOLOGY, 1966, 4, 289-294.
               (CORRELATES:BEHAVIORAL, PSYCHOLOGICAL, ENVIRONMENTAL; USED AS
               CRITERION; N=8 FIELD-DEPENDENT AND 8 FIELD-INDEPENDENT)
      @APPLICATION 1966 J-17 L-27

102   PARK, J. N., & SMITH, A. J.
          RECOGNITION THRESHOLDS FOR VALUE-RELATED WORDS: DIFFERENCES BETWEEN
          INNER-DIRECTED AND OTHER-DIRECTED SUBJECTS.
          JOURNAL OF PERSONALITY AND SOCIAL PSYCHOLOGY, 1966, 3, 248-252.
               (MODIFICATION; CORRELATES:BEHAVIORAL, PSYCHOLOGICAL; USED AS
               CRITERION; N=12 INNER-DIRECTED AND 12 OTHER-DIRECTED UNDERGRADUATES)
      @APPLICATION 1966 B-267 A-7

103   PHARES, E. J., & DAVIS, W. L.
          BREADTH OF CATEGORIZATION AND THE GENERALIZATION OF EXPECTANCIES.
          JOURNAL OF PERSONALITY AND SOCIAL PSYCHOLOGY, 1966, 4, 461-464.
               (CORRELATES:BEHAVIORAL, PSYCHOLOGICAL; USED AS CRITERION;
               NORMATIVE DATA; N=450 FEMALE UNDERGRADUATES)
      @APPLICATION 1966 P-7 R-30

104   POWELL, F. A.
          LATTITUDES OF ACCEPTANCE AND REJECTION AND THE BELIEF-DISBELIEF
          DIMENSION: A CORRELATIONAL COMPARISON.
          JOURNAL OF PERSONALITY AND SOCIAL PSYCHOLOGY, 1966, 4, 453-457.
               (CORRELATES:PSYCHOLOGICAL; USED AS CRITERION; 3 STUDIES: N=84, 84, 80
               UNDERGRADUATES)
      @APPLICATION 1966 T-18

105   RAMSAY, R. W.
          PERSONALITY AND SPEECH.
          JOURNAL OF PERSONALITY AND SOCIAL PSYCHOLOGY, 1966, 4, 116-118.
               (CORRELATES:BEHAVIORAL, PSYCHOLOGICAL, INTELLIGENCE; USED AS
               CRITERION; N=23 FEMALE UNDERGRADUATES)
      @APPLICATION 1966 E-6 M-20

106   STREUFERT, S.
          CONCEPTUAL STRUCTURE, COMMUNICATOR IMPORTANCE, AND INTERPERSONAL
          ATTITUDES TOWARD CONFORMING AND DEVIANT GROUP MEMBERS.
          JOURNAL OF PERSONALITY AND SOCIAL PSYCHOLOGY, 1966, 4, 100-103.
               (CORRELATES:BEHAVIORAL, PSYCHOLOGICAL; USED AS CRITERION:
               N=384 HIGH SCHOOL SENIORS)
      @APPLICATION 1966 O-16 S-41 S-58

107   TAFT, R.
          ACCURACY OF EMPATHIC JUDGMENTS OF ACQUAINTANCES AND STRANGERS.
          JOURNAL OF PERSONALITY AND SOCIAL PSYCHOLOGY, 1966, 3, 600-604.
               (CORRELATES:PSYCHOLOGICAL; NORMATIVE DATA; N=30 MALE AND 32 FEMALE
               UNDERGRADUATES)
      @APPLICATION 1966 C-41

108   TRIANDIS, H. C., LOH, W. D., & LEVIN, L. A.
          RACE, STATUS, QUALITY OF SPOKEN ENGLISH, AND OPINIONS ABOUT CIVIL RIGHTS
          AS DETERMINANTS OF INTERPERSONAL ATTITUDES.
          JOURNAL OF PERSONALITY AND SOCIAL PSYCHOLOGY, 1966, 3, 468-472.
               (RELIABILITY:RETEST; CORRELATES:PSYCHOLOGICAL, DEMOGRAPHIC,
               ENVIRONMENTAL; N=56 MALE AND 38 FEMALE UNDERGRADUATES)
      @APPLICATION 1966 T-12

109   HARDYCK, C. D.
            PERSONALITY CHARACTERISTICS AND MOTOR ACTIVITY.
            JOURNAL OF PERSONALITY AND SOCIAL PSYCHOLOGY, 1966, 4, 181-188.
                    (CORRELATES:BEHAVIORAL, PSYCHOLOGICAL, PHYSIOLOGICAL; N=40 MALE
                    UNDERGRADUATES)
        @APPLICATION 1965 R-30 G-80 B-57 G-22

110   GREENSTEIN, J. M.
            FATHER CHARACTERISTICS AND SEX TYPING.
            JOURNAL OF PERSONALITY AND SOCIAL PSYCHOLOGY, 1966, 3, 271-277.
                    (MODIFICATION; RELIABILITY:INTERRATER; CORRELATES:BEHAVIORAL,
                    PSYCHOLOGICAL; N=75 DELINQUENT BOYS)
        @APPLICATION 1966 W-113 W-28 M-20 S-34

111   WRIGHTSMAN, L. S.
            PERSONALITY AND ATTITUDINAL CORRELATES OF TRUSTING AND TRUSTWORTHY
            BEHAVIORS IN A TWO-PERSON GAME.
            JOURNAL OF PERSONALITY AND SOCIAL PSYCHOLOGY, 1966, 4, 328-332.
                    (CORRELATES:BEHAVIORAL, PSYCHOLOGICAL, ENVIRONMENTAL; 2 STUDIES:
                    N=15 MALES AND 69 FEMALES, N=56 FEMALES)
        @APPLICATION 1966 B-44 R-25 B-54 A-5 A-22 W-24 C-14 C-27 E-1

112   WOHLFORD, P.
            EXTENSION OF PERSONAL TIME, AFFECTIVE STATES, AND EXPECTATION OF
            PERSONAL DEATH.
            JOURNAL OF PERSONALITY AND SOCIAL PSYCHOLOGY, 1966, 3, 559-566.
                    (CORRELATES:PSYCHOLOGICAL, DEMOGRAPHIC, ENVIRONMENTAL; NORMATIVE
                    DATA: N=70 MALE AND 77 FEMALE UNDERGRADUATES)
        @APPLICATION 1966 M-20 E-13

113   WEINER, B.
            ROLE OF SUCCESS AND FAILURE IN THE LEARNING OF EASY AND COMPLEX TASKS.
            JOURNAL OF PERSONALITY AND SOCIAL PSYCHOLOGY, 1966, 3, 339-344.
                    (CORRELATES:BEHAVIORAL, PSYCHOLOGICAL, ENVIRONMENTAL; USED AS
                    CRITERION; NORMATIVE DATA; N=62 HIGH AND LOW ACHIEVERS OUT OF 195
                    MALE UNDERGRADUATES)
        @APPLICATION 1966 M-47 M-4

114   WALSTER, E., ARONSON, V., ABRAHAMS, D., & ROTTMANN, L.
            IMPORTANCE OF PHYSICAL ATTRACTIVENESS IN DATING BEHAVIOR.
            JOURNAL OF PERSONALITY AND SOCIAL PSYCHOLOGY, 1966, 4, 508-516.
                    (CORRELATES:PSYCHOLOGICAL, INTELLIGENCE, PHYSICAL; N=376 MALE AND
                    376 FEMALE UNDERGRADUATES)
        @APPLICATION 1966 B-13 B-11 D-45

115   RULE, B. G.
            ANTI-SEMITISM, STRESS, AND JUDGMENTS OF STRANGERS.
            JOURNAL OF PERSONALITY AND SOCIAL PSYCHOLOGY, 1966, 3, 132-134.
                    (CORRELATES:BEHAVIORAL, PSYCHOLOGICAL; USED AS CRITERION; N=27
                    HIGH, MEDIUM AND LOW-PREJUDICED OUT OF 950 UNDERGRADUATES)
        @APPLICATION 1966 A-15 A-5

116   HAYWOOD, H. C., & SPIELBERGER, C. D.
            PALMAR SWEATING AS A FUNCTION OF INDIVIDUAL DIFFERENCES IN MANIFEST
            ANXIETY.
            JOURNAL OF PERSONALITY AND SOCIAL PSYCHOLOGY, 1966, 3, 103-105.
                    (CORRELATES:PHYSIOLOGICAL; USED AS CRITERION; N=61 MALE
                    UNDERGRADUATES)
        @APPLICATION 1966 T-2

117   HETHERINGTON, E. M.
            EFFECTS OF PATERNAL ABSENCE ON SEX-TYPED BEHAVIORS IN NEGRO AND WHITE
            PREADOLESCENT MALES.
            JOURNAL OF PERSONALITY AND SOCIAL PSYCHOLOGY, 1966, 4, 87-91.
                    (DESCRIPTION; CORRELATES:DEMOGRAPHIC, PSYCHOLOGICAL; N=32 NEGRO AND
                    32 WHITE BOYS AGED 9-12)
        @APPLICATION 1966 B-35 B-52 S-47

118   HETHERINGTON, E. M., & WRAY, N. P.
            EFFECTS OF NEED AGGRESSION, STRESS, AND AGGRESSIVE BEHAVIOR ON HUMOR
            PREFERENCES.
            JOURNAL OF PERSONALITY AND SOCIAL PSYCHOLOGY, 1966, 4, 229-233.
                    (CORRELATES:PSYCHOLOGICAL, ENVIRONMENTAL; USED AS CRITERION; N=80
                    FEMALE UNDERGRADUATES)
        @APPLICATION 1966 E-2

119   HIMMELFARB, S.
            STUDIES IN THE PERCEPTION OF ETHNIC GROUP MEMBERS: I. ACCURACY, RESPONSE
            BIAS, AND ANTI-SEMITISM.
            JOURNAL OF PERSONALITY AND SOCIAL PSYCHOLOGY, 1966, 4, 347-355.
                (CORRELATES:BEHAVIORAL. DEMOGRAPHIC; BIAS:RESPONSE; 2 STUDIES:
                N=29 MALE, 29 FEMALE AND N=53 MALE, 46 FEMALE NON-JEWISH
                UNDERGRADUATES)
        @APPLICATION 1966 A-23 A-15

120   HOFFMAN, L. R., & MAIER, N. R. F.
            AN EXPERIMENTAL REEXAMINATION OF THE SIMILARITY-ATTRACTION HYPOTHESIS.
            JOURNAL OF PERSONALITY AND SOCIAL PSYCHOLOGY, 1966, 3, 145-152.
                (CORRELATES:BEHAVIORAL. PSYCHOLOGICAL; USED AS CRITERION;
                NORMATIVE DATA; N=132 UNDERGRADUATES)
        @APPLICATION 1966 G-26

121   JULIAN, J. W., BISHOP, D. W., & FIEDLER, F. A.
            QUASI-THERAPEUTIC EFFECTS OF INTERGROUP COMPETITION.
            JOURNAL OF PERSONALITY AND SOCIAL PSYCHOLOGY, 1966, 3, 321-327.
                (CORRELATES:BEHAVIORAL. PSYCHOLOGICAL, ENVIRONMENTAL; FACTOR
                ANALYSIS; N=178 ARMY MEN)
        @APPLICATION 1966 T-2 O-16 H-200

122   LAZARUS, R. S., TOMITA, M., OPTON, E., & KODAMA, M.
            A CROSS-CULTURAL STUDY OF STRESS-REACTION PATTERNS IN JAPAN.
            JOURNAL OF PERSONALITY AND SOCIAL PSYCHOLOGY, 1966, 4, 622-633.
                (MODIFICATION: CORRELATES:PSYCHOLOGICAL, PHYSIOLOGICAL,
                ENVIRONMENTAL; CROSS-CULTURAL APPLICATION; 2 SAMPLES: N=80
                JAPANESE MALE UNDERGRADUATES, N=48 JAPANESE MALES 36-58 YEARS OLD)
        @APPLICATION 1966 L-103 W-185 H-92 H-71 N-5

123   KATAHN, M.
            INTERACTION OF ANXIETY AND ABILITY IN COMPLEX LEARNING SITUATIONS.
            JOURNAL OF PERSONALITY AND SOCIAL PSYCHOLOGY, 1966, 3, 475-479.
                (CORRELATES:BEHAVIORAL. INTELLIGENCE; USED AS CRITERION; 2 STUDIES:
                N=46, 64 UNDERGRADUATES)
        @APPLICATION 1966 T-2

124   LEVY, P., & LANG, P. J.
            ACTIVATION, CONTROL, AND THE SPIRAL AFTERMOVEMENT.
            JOURNAL OF PERSONALITY AND SOCIAL PSYCHOLOGY, 1966, 3, 105-112.
                (RELIABILITY:INTERNAL CONSISTENCY; CORRELATES:PSYCHOLOGICAL,
                PHYSIOLOGICAL; USED AS CRITERION; N=60 MALE UNDERGRADUATES)
        @APPLICATION 1966 T-2 W-32

125   BUCKHOUT, R.
            CHANGES IN HEART RATE ACCOMPANYING ATTITUDE CHANGE.
            JOURNAL OF PERSONALITY AND SOCIAL PSYCHOLOGY, 1966, 4, 695-699.
                (CORRELATES:PSYCHOLOGICAL, PHYSIOLOGICAL; USED AS CRITERION;
                N=20 MALE, 20 FEMALE UNDERGRADUATES)
        @APPLICATION 1966 C-27

126   CARBS, J. M., JR., & LEVENTHAL, H.
            EFFECTS OF VARYING THE RECOMMENDATIONS IN A FEAR-AROUSING COMMUNICATION.
            JOURNAL OF PERSONALITY AND SOCIAL PSYCHOLOGY, 1966, 4, 525-531.
                (MODIFICATION; RELIABILITY:RETEST; CORRELATES:BEHAVIORAL,
                ENVIRONMENTAL; USED AS CRITERION; N=182 COLLEGE SENIORS)
        @APPLICATION 1966 T-2

127   DUNCAN, C. B.
            A REPUTATION TEST OF PERSONALITY INTEGRATION.
            JOURNAL OF PERSONALITY AND SOCIAL PSYCHOLOGY, 1966, 3, 516-524.
                (DESCRIPTION; RELIABILITY:RETEST; CORRELATES:PSYCHOLOGICAL,
                INTELLIGENCE; USED AS CRITERION; 2 STUDIES: N=454, 663 ACTIVE
                FRATERNITY MEMBERS)
        @APPLICATION 1966 F-7 L-30 T-39

128   FITZGERALD, E. T.
            MEASUREMENT OF OPENNESS TO EXPERIENCE: A STUDY OF REGRESSION IN THE SERVICE
            OF THE EGO.
            JOURNAL OF PERSONALITY AND SOCIAL PSYCHOLOGY, 1966, 4, 655-663.
                (VALIDITY:CRITERION; CORRELATES:BEHAVIORAL, PSYCHOLOGICAL,
                DEMOGRAPHIC; N=62 COLLEGE MALES, 81 COLLEGE FEMALES)
        @APPLICATION 1966 G-21 B-5 W-8 W-41

129   FISHMAN, D. B.
            NEED AND EXPECTANCY AS DETERMINANTS OF AFFILIATIVE BEHAVIOR IN SMALL
            GROUPS.
            JOURNAL OF PERSONALITY AND SOCIAL PSYCHOLOGY, 1966, 4, 155-164.
                (MODIFICATION; DESCRIPTION; VALIDITY:CRITERION;
                CORRELATES:BEHAVIORAL, PSYCHOLOGICAL; USED AS CRITERION; NORMATIVE
                DATA; N=80 FEMALE UNDERGRADUATES)
        @APPLICATION 1966 M-20 V-31 L-29 M-24 F-8 M-217 B-2 D-30

130   GHEI, S. N.
            A CROSS-CULTURAL STUDY OF NEED PROFILES.
            JOURNAL OF PERSONALITY AND SOCIAL PSYCHOLOGY, 1966, 3, 580-585.
                (RELIABILITY:INTERNAL CONSISTENCY (N=108); VALIDITY:CRITERION,
                CROSS-VALIDATION; CORRELATES:DEMOGRAPHIC; CROSS-CULTURAL
                APPLICATION; NORMATIVE DATA; N=110 MALES, 102 FEMALES FROM U.S. AND
                106 MALES, 110 FEMALES FROM INDIA)
        @APPLICATION 1966 E-2

131   GREENBAUM, C. W.
            EFFECT OF SITUATIONAL AND PERSONALITY VARIABLES ON IMPROVISATION AND
            ATTITUDE CHANGE.
            JOURNAL OF PERSONALITY AND SOCIAL PSYCHOLOGY, 1966, 4, 260-269.
                (MODIFICATION; CORRELATES:BEHAVIORAL, PSYCHOLOGICAL, ENVIRONMENTAL;
                USED AS CRITERION; BIAS:TESTER; N=68 MALE AND 32 FEMALE
                UNDERGRADUATES)
        @APPLICATION 1966 J-7 C-27

132   GRIFFITT, W. B.
            INTERPERSONAL ATTRACTION AS A FUNCTION OF SELF-CONCEPT AND PERSONALITY
            SIMILARITY-DISSIMILARITY.
            JOURNAL OF PERSONALITY AND SOCIAL PSYCHOLOGY, 1966, 4, 581-584.
                (RELIABILITY:INTERNAL CONSISTENCY; CORRELATES:PSYCHOLOGICAL; USED
                AS CRITERION; NORMATIVE DATA; N=25 HIGH AND 23 LOW-DISCREPANCY
                UNDERGRADUATES)
        @APPLICATION 1966 W-21 B-65

133   FOA, U. G., TRIANDIS, H. C., & KATZ, E. W.
            CROSS-CULTURAL INVARIANCE IN THE DIFFERENTIATION AND ORGANIZATION OF
            FAMILY ROLES.
            JOURNAL OF PERSONALITY AND SOCIAL PSYCHOLOGY, 1966, 4, 316-327.
                (MODIFICATION; CORRELATES:PSYCHOLOGICAL; CROSS-CULTURAL
                APPLICATION; 2 STUDIES: UNKNOWN N OF MALE UNDERGRADUATES AND GREEK
                MALE STUDENTS, UNKNOWN N OF HAWAIIAN STUDENTS AND JAPANESE STUDENTS)
        @APPLICATION 1966 T-12

134   FEATHER, N. T.
            EFFECTS OF PRIOR SUCCESS AND FAILURE ON EXPECTATIONS OF SUCCESS AND
            SUBSEQUENT PERFORMANCE.
            JOURNAL OF PERSONALITY AND SOCIAL PSYCHOLOGY, 1966, 3, 287-298.
                (DESCRIPTION; VALIDITY:CRITERION; CORRELATES:BEHAVIORAL,
                ENVIRONMENTAL; USED AS CRITERION; N=96 FEMALE UNDERGRADUATES)
        @APPLICATION 1966 M-7 M-4

135   EPSTEIN, R., & KOMORITA, S. S.
            PREJUDICE AMONG NEGRO CHILDREN AS RELATED TO PARENTAL ETHNOCENTRISM AND
            PUNITIVENESS.
            JOURNAL OF PERSONALITY AND SOCIAL PSYCHOLOGY, 1966, 1, 643-647.
                (DESCRIPTION; RELIABILITY:INTERNAL CONSISTENCY;
                CORRELATES:PSYCHOLOGICAL, DEMOGRAPHIC; N=120 NEGRO 5TH GRADERS)
        @APPLICATION 1966 E-15

136   EPSTEIN, R., & KOMORITA, S. S.
            CHILDHOOD PREJUDICE AS A FUNCTION OF PARENTAL ETHNOCENTRISM, PUNITIVENESS,
            AND OUTGROUP CHARACTERISTICS.
            JOURNAL OF PERSONALITY AND SOCIAL PSYCHOLOGY, 1966, 3, 259-264.
                (DESCRIPTION; RELIABILITY:INTERNAL CONSISTENCY;
                CORRELATES:PSYCHOLOGICAL; USED AS CRITERION; N=180 3RD, 4TH, 5TH
                GRADERS IN CATHOLIC SCHOOL)
        @APPLICATION 1966 E-15

137   EPSTEIN, R.
            AGGRESSION TOWARD OUTGROUPS AS A FUNCTION OF AUTHORITARIANISM AND
            IMITATION OF AGGRESSIVE MODELS.
            JOURNAL OF PERSONALITY AND SOCIAL PSYCHOLOGY, 1966, 3, 574-579.
                    (DESCRIPTION; CORRELATES:PSYCHOLOGICAL, ENVIRONMENTAL; USED AS
                    CRITERION; NORMATIVE DATA; N=144 WHITE MALE UNDERGRADUATES)
        @APPLICATION 1966 A-5

138   CRUSE, D. B.
            SOME RELATIONS BETWEEN MINIMAL CONTENT, ACQUIESCENT-DISSENTIENT, AND SOCIAL
            DESIRABILITY SCALES.
            JOURNAL OF PERSONALITY AND SOCIAL PSYCHOLOGY, 1966, 3, 112-119.
                    (MODIFICATION; DESCRIPTION; RELIABILITY:INTERNAL CONSISTENCY;
                    VALIDITY:CRITERION; CORRELATES:PSYCHOLOGICAL, ENVIRONMENTAL;
                    BIAS:RESPONSE; 2 STUDIES: N=68 UNDERGRADUATES, 150 UNDERGRADUATES)
        @APPLICATION 1966 D-45 C-43 E-1

139   CRANDALL, V. C.
            PERSONALITY CHARACTERISTICS AND SOCIAL AND ACHIEVEMENT BEHAVIORS
            ASSOCIATED WITH CHILDREN'S SOCIAL DESIRABILITY RESPONSE TENDENCIES.
            JOURNAL OF PERSONALITY AND SOCIAL PSYCHOLOGY, 1966, 4, 477-486.
                    (MODIFICATION; DESCRIPTION; VALIDITY:CRITERION;
                    CORRELATES:BEHAVIORAL, PSYCHOLOGICAL, DEMOGRAPHIC, INTELLIGENCE;
                    2 STUDIES: N=33 MALE, 43 FEMALE 10TH GRADERS)
        @APPLICATION 1966 C-42 G-22

140   CARRIGAN, W. C., & JULIAN, J. W.
            SEX AND BIRTH-ORDER DIFFERENCES IN CONFORMITY AS A FUNCTION OF NEED
            AFFILIATION AROUSAL.
            JOURNAL OF PERSONALITY AND SOCIAL PSYCHOLOGY, 1966, 3, 479-483.
                    (MODIFICATION; VALIDITY:CRITERION; CORRELATES:PSYCHOLOGICAL,
                    DEMOGRAPHIC, ENVIRONMENTAL; NORMATIVE DATA; N=96 6TH GRADERS)
        @APPLICATION 1966 M-20 E-2

141   BROWN, D. R., & YARDELL, R. J.
            INDIVIDUAL PERCEPTUAL STYLES FOLLOWING INDUCED FAILURE.
            JOURNAL OF PERSONALITY AND SOCIAL PSYCHOLOGY, 1966, 3, 359-362.
                    (DESCRIPTION; VALIDITY:CRITERION; CORRELATES:PSYCHOLOGICAL; N=67
                    MALE UNDERGRADUATES)
        @APPLICATION 1966 G-21 D-45 G-22

142   BLANCHARD, W. A.
            ASSIMILATION AND CONTRAST IN INTERPERSONAL PREDICTION WITH CONTROL FOR
            THE INTERACTION OF REAL SIMILARITY AND DIFFERENTIAL ACCURACY.
            JOURNAL OF PERSONALITY AND SOCIAL PSYCHOLOGY, 1966, 3, 567-573.
                    (MODIFICATION; VALIDITY:CRITERION; CORRELATES:PSYCHOLOGICAL; USED AS
                    CRITERION; N=75 FEMALE, 77 MALE COLLEGE STUDENTS)
        @APPLICATION 1966 S-33

143   BANDURA, A., & ROSENTHAL, T. L.
            VICARIOUS CLASSICAL CONDITIONING AS A FUNCTION OF AROUSAL LEVEL.
            JOURNAL OF PERSONALITY AND SOCIAL PSYCHOLOGY, 1966, 3, 54-62.
                    (DESCRIPTION; CORRELATES:PSYCHOLOGICAL, PHYSIOLOGICAL; N=100
                    COLLEGE STUDENTS)
        @APPLICATION 1966 T-2

144   BERG, K. R.
            ETHNIC ATTITUDES AND AGREEMENT WITH A NEGRO PERSON.
            JOURNAL OF PERSONALITY AND SOCIAL PSYCHOLOGY, 1966, 4, 215-220.
                    (DESCRIPTION; MODIFICATION; CORRELATES:PSYCHOLOGICAL, DEMOGRAPHIC;
                    N=135 UNDERGRADUATES)
        @APPLICATION 1966 A-17 A-5 B-58

145   BECKER, L. A., & BROCK, T. C.
            PROSPECTIVE RECIPIENTS' ESTIMATES OF WITHHELD EVALUATION.
            JOURNAL OF PERSONALITY AND SOCIAL PSYCHOLOGY, 1966, 4, 147-154.
                    (DESCRIPTION; VALIDITY:CRITERION; CORRELATES:PSYCHOLOGICAL;
                    BIAS:TESTER; N=80 COLLEGE MALES)
        @APPLICATION 1966 S-11 H-34

146   BECHTEL, R. B., & ROSENFELD, H. M.
           EXPECTATIONS OF SOCIAL ACCEPTANCE AND COMPATIBILITY AS RELATED TO STATUS
           DISCREPANCY AND SOCIAL MOTIVES.
           JOURNAL OF PERSONALITY AND SOCIAL PSYCHOLOGY, 1966, 3, 344-349.
               (DESCRIPTION; MODIFICATION; RELIABILITY:INTERRATER;
               VALIDITY:CRITERION; CORRELATES:PSYCHOLOGICAL, ENVIRONMENTAL; N=159
               FEMALE UNDERGRADUATES)
       @APPLICATION 1966 M-20 M-4 R-80

147   ATKINS, A. L.
           OWN ATTITUDE AND DISCRIMINABILITY IN RELATION TO ANCHORING EFFECTS IN
           JUDGMENT.
           JOURNAL OF PERSONALITY AND SOCIAL PSYCHOLOGY, 1966, 4, 497-507.
               (DESCRIPTION; VALIDITY:CRITERION; CORRELATES:PSYCHOLOGICAL;
               BIAS:RESPONSE; N=96 MALE UNDERGRADUATES)
       @APPLICATION 1966 S-309

148   ANDERSON, C. C., & COTE, A. D. J.
           BELIEF DISSONANCE AS A SOURCE OF DISAFFECTION BETWEEN ETHNIC GROUPS.
           JOURNAL OF PERSONALITY AND SOCIAL PSYCHOLOGY, 1966, 4, 447-453.
               (DESCRIPTION; MODIFICATION; VALIDITY:CRITERION, CROSS-VALIDATION;
               CORRELATES:PSYCHOLOGICAL, DEMOGRAPHIC; CROSS-CULTURAL APPLICATION;
               N=116, 67, 130 FRENCH-CANADIANS, 113 ENGLISH-CANADIANS)
       @APPLICATION 1966 R-50 R-150 G-22

149   BATTLE, E. S.
           MOTIVATIONAL DETERMINANTS OF ACADEMIC COMPETENCE.
           JOURNAL OF PERSONALITY AND SOCIAL PSYCHOLOGY, 1966, 4, 634-642.
               (MODIFICATION; CORRELATES:PSYCHOLOGICAL, INTELLIGENCE; BIAS:RESPONSE;
               N=OVER 500 JUNIOR HIGH STUDENTS)
       @APPLICATION 1966 C-42

150   ELMS, A. C.
           INFLUENCE OF FANTASY ABILITY ON ATTITUDE CHANGE THROUGH ROLE PLAYING.
           JOURNAL OF PERSONALITY AND SOCIAL PSYCHOLOGY, 1966, 4, 36-43.
               (CORRELATES:BEHAVIORAL, PSYCHOLOGICAL, INTELLIGENCE, ENVIRONMENTAL;
               N=68 MALE, 12 FEMALE SMOKERS)
       @APPLICATION 1966 T-2 S-38 R-30 M-20

151   BYRNE, D., GRIFFITT, W., & STEFANIAK, D.
           ATTRACTION AND SIMILARITY OF PERSONALITY CHARACTERISTICS.
           JOURNAL OF PERSONALITY AND SOCIAL PSYCHOLOGY, 1967, 5, 82-90.
               (MODIFICATION; RELIABILITY:INTERNAL CONSISTENCY;
               VALIDITY:CRITERION; CORRELATES:PSYCHOLOGICAL; USED AS CRITERION;
               NORMATIVE DATA; 2 STUDIES: N=151 COLLEGE STUDENTS, 149 COLLEGE
               STUDENTS)
       @APPLICATION 1967 B-46 B-65

152   ABATE, M., & BERRIEN, F. K.
           VALIDATION OF STEREOTYPES: JAPANESE VERSUS AMERICAN STUDENTS.
           JOURNAL OF PERSONALITY AND SOCIAL PSYCHOLOGY, 1967, 7, 435-438.
               (MODIFICATION; VALIDITY:CRITERION; CORRELATES:PSYCHOLOGICAL,
               DEMOGRAPHIC; USED AS CRITERION; CROSS-CULTURAL APPLICATION; N=225
               MALES, 118 FEMALES IN U.S., 240 MALES, 240 FEMALES IN JAPAN)
       @APPLICATION 1967 E-2

153   CRANO, W. D., & SCHRODER, H. M.
           COMPLEXITY OF ATTITUDE STRUCTURE AND PROCESS OF CONFLICT RESOLUTION.
           JOURNAL OF PERSONALITY AND SOCIAL PSYCHOLOGY, 1967, 5, 110-114.
               (DESCRIPTION; CORRELATES:PSYCHOLOGICAL; USED AS CRITERION; N=31 HIGH
               AND LOW COMPLEXITY MALE UNDERGRADUATES)
       @APPLICATION 1967 S-41 O-16

154   BIXENSTINE, V. E., & DOUGLAS, J.
           EFFECTS OF PSYCHOPATHOLOGY ON GROUP CONSENSUS AND COOPERATIVE CHOICE
           IN A SIX-PERSON GAME.
           JOURNAL OF PERSONALITY AND SOCIAL PSYCHOLOGY, 1967, 5, 32-37.
               (VALIDITY:CRITERION; CORRELATES:BEHAVIORAL, PSYCHOLOGICAL; USED AS
               CRITERION; N=96 MALE COLLEGE STUDENTS)
       @APPLICATION 1967 D-45 S-11

155   CONSTANTINOPLE, A.
            PERCEIVED INSTRUMENTALITY OF THE COLLEGE AS A MEASURE OF ATTITUDES TOWARD
            COLLEGE.
            JOURNAL OF PERSONALITY AND SOCIAL PSYCHOLOGY, 1967, 5, 196-201.
                (RELIABILITY:RETEST; CORRELATES:PSYCHOLOGICAL, DEMOGRAPHIC; USED AS
                CRITERION; N=99 MALE, 89 FEMALE COLLEGE FRESHMEN, 90 MALE, 75 FEMALE
                COLLEGE JUNIORS)
        @APPLICATION 1967 W-12

156   FEATHER, N. T.
            LEVEL OF ASPIRATION AND PERFORMANCE VARIABILITY.
            JOURNAL OF PERSONALITY AND SOCIAL PSYCHOLOGY, 1967, 6, 37-46.
                (VALIDITY:CRITERION; CORRELATES:BEHAVIORAL, PSYCHOLOGICAL; USED AS
                CRITERION; N=26 MALE AND 80 FEMALE UNDERGRADUATES)
        @APPLICATION 1967 M-7 A-8 B-37 P-7

157   ALPER, T. G., & GREENBERGER, E.
            RELATIONSHIP OF PICTURE STRUCTURE TO ACHIEVEMENT MOTIVATION IN COLLEGE
            WOMEN.
            JOURNAL OF PERSONALITY AND SOCIAL PSYCHOLOGY, 1967, 7, 362-371.
                (MODIFICATION; VALIDITY:CRITERION; CORRELATES:PSYCHOLOGICAL; N=223
                UNDERGRADUATE WOMEN)
        @APPLICATION 1967 M-36 M-20 M-7

158   FORD, L. H., & HERSEN, M.
            NEED APPROVAL, DEFENSIVE DENIAL, AND DIRECTION OF AGGRESSION IN A
            FAILURE-FRUSTRATION SITUATION.
            JOURNAL OF PERSONALITY AND SOCIAL PSYCHOLOGY, 1967, 6, 228-232.
                (DESCRIPTION; CORRELATES:PSYCHOLOGICAL; USED AS CRITERION;
                NORMATIVE DATA; BIAS:RESPONSE; N=80 MALE UNDERGRADUATES)
        @APPLICATION 1967 F-9 E-1

159   FEATHER, N. T., & SAVILLE, M. R.
            EFFECTS OF AMOUNT OF PRIOR SUCCESS AND FAILURE ON EXPECTATIONS OF SUCCESS
            AND SUBSEQUENT TASK PERFORMANCE.
            JOURNAL OF PERSONALITY AND SOCIAL PSYCHOLOGY, 1967, 5, 226-232.
                (RELIABILITY:INTERRATER; CORRELATES:BEHAVIORAL, PSYCHOLOGICAL,
                ENVIRONMENTAL; NORMATIVE DATA; N=52 MALE, 82 FEMALE UNDERGRADUATES)
        @APPLICATION 1967 M-7 M-4

160   FEATHER, N. T.
            VALENCE OF OUTCOME AND EXPECTATION OF SUCCESS IN RELATION TO TASK
            DIFFICULTY AND PERCEIVED LOCUS OF CONTROL.
            JOURNAL OF PERSONALITY AND SOCIAL PSYCHOLOGY, 1967, 7, 372-386.
                (DESCRIPTION; MODIFICATION; RELIABILITY:INTERRATER;
                VALIDITY:CRITERION; CORRELATES:BEHAVIORAL, ENVIRONMENTAL; N=30 MALE,
                46 FEMALE UNDERGRADUATES)
        @APPLICATION 1967 M-7 A-8 R-18

161   DWORKIN, E. S., & EFRAN, J. S.
            THE ANGERED: THEIR SUSCEPTIBILITY TO VARIETIES OF HUMOR.
            JOURNAL OF PERSONALITY AND SOCIAL PSYCHOLOGY, 1967, 6, 233-236.
                (MODIFICATION; VALIDITY:CRITERION; CORRELATES:PSYCHOLOGICAL;
                CLUSTER ANALYSIS; N=50 MALE UNDERGRADUATES)
        @APPLICATION 1967 N-17

162   DUSTIN, D. S., & DAVIS, H. P.
            AUTHORITARIANISM AND SANCTIONING BEHAVIOR.
            JOURNAL OF PERSONALITY AND SOCIAL PSYCHOLOGY, 1967, 6, 222-224.
                (MODIFICATION; VALIDITY:CRITERION; CORRELATES:BEHAVIORAL,
                PSYCHOLOGICAL, ENVIRONMENTAL; USED AS CRITERION; N=40 MALE
                UNDERGRADUATES)
        @APPLICATION 1967 A-5

163   COWEN, E. L., BOBROVE, P. H., ROCHWAY, A. M., & STEVENSON, J.
            DEVELOPMENT AND EVALUATION OF AN ATTITUDES TO DEAFNESS SCALE.
            JOURNAL OF PERSONALITY AND SOCIAL PSYCHOLOGY, 1967, 6, 183-191.
                (MODIFICATION; DESCRIPTION; VALIDITY:CRITERION;
                CORRELATES:PSYCHOLOGICAL; BIAS:RESPONSE; N=160 MALE WHITE
                UNDERGRADUATES)
        @APPLICATION 1967 A-5 A-15 C-27 B-44 R-18

164   CATTELL, R. B., & NESSELROADE, J. R.
            LIKENESS AND COMPLETENESS THEORIES EXAMINED BY SIXTEEN PERSONALITY
            FACTOR MEASURES ON STABLY AND UNSTABLY MARRIED COUPLES.
            JOURNAL OF PERSONALITY AND SOCIAL PSYCHOLOGY, 1967, 7, 351-361.
                    (MODIFICATION; CORRELATES:BEHAVIORAL, PSYCHOLOGICAL; NORMATIVE DATA;
                    N=102 STABLY MARRIED COUPLES, 37 UNSTABLY MARRIED COUPLES)
        @APPLICATION 1967 C-10

165   BISHOP, F. V.
            THE ANAL CHARACTER: A REBEL IN THE DISSONANCE FAMILY.
            JOURNAL OF PERSONALITY AND SOCIAL PSYCHOLOGY, 1967, 6, 23-26.
                    (MODIFICATION; CORRELATES:PSYCHOLOGICAL; USED AS CRITERION;
                    N=67 MALE UNDERGRADUATES)
        @APPLICATION 1967 G-43

166   BARUCH, R.
            THE ACHIEVEMENT MOTIVE IN WOMEN: IMPLICATIONS FOR CAREER DEVELOPMENT.
            JOURNAL OF PERSONALITY AND SOCIAL PSYCHOLOGY, 1967, 5, 260-267.
                    (MODIFICATION; VALIDITY:CROSS-VALIDATION; CORRELATES:BEHAVIORAL;
                    N=137 FEMALE "ACHIEVERS," 763 FEMALES)
        @APPLICATION 1967 M-20

167   BARATZ, S. S.
            EFFECT OF RACE OF EXPERIMENTER, INSTRUCTIONS, AND COMPARISON POPULATION
            UPON LEVEL OF REPORTED ANXIETY IN NEGRO SUBJECTS.
            JOURNAL OF PERSONALITY AND SOCIAL PSYCHOLOGY, 1967, 7, 194-196.
                    (DESCRIPTION; CORRELATES:PSYCHOLOGICAL, ENVIRONMENTAL; BIAS:TESTER;
                    N=53 MALES, 67 FEMALE NEGRO UNDERGRADUATES)
        @APPLICATION 1967 M-4

168   ANDREWS, J. D. W.
            THE ACHIEVEMENT MOTIVE AND ADVANCEMENT IN TWO TYPES OF ORGANIZATIONS.
            JOURNAL OF PERSONALITY AND SOCIAL PSYCHOLOGY, 1967, 6, 163-168.
                    (MODIFICATION; RELIABILITY:RETEST; VALIDITY:CONSTRUCT;
                    CORRELATES:ENVIRONMENTAL; N=SOME MEXICAN EXECUTIVES IN ONE HIGH AND
                    ONE LOW ACHIEVEMENT-ORIENTED BUSINESS FIRMS)
        @APPLICATION 1967 M-20

169   ALLPORT, G. W., & ROSS, J. M.
            PERSONAL RELIGIOUS ORIENTATION AND PREJUDICE.
            JOURNAL OF PERSONALITY AND SOCIAL PSYCHOLOGY, 1967, 5, 432-443.
                    (MODIFICATION; CORRELATES:PSYCHOLOGICAL; USED AS CRITERION; N=309
                    MEMBERS OF DIFFERENT RELIGIOUS GROUPS)
        @APPLICATION 1967 H-196 G-31 W-33

170   FRY, C. L.
            A DEVELOPMENTAL EXAMINATION OF PERFORMANCE IN A TACIT COORDINATION GAME
            SITUATION.
            JOURNAL OF PERSONALITY AND SOCIAL PSYCHOLOGY, 1967, 5, 277-281.
                    (DESCRIPTION; RELIABILITY:INTERRATER; CORRELATES:BEHAVIORAL,
                    PSYCHOLOGICAL; USED AS CRITERION; N=24 4TH AND 24 8TH GRADERS AND
                    36 COLLEGE UNDERGRADUATES)
        @APPLICATION 1967 A-6

171   GALL, M., & MENDELSOHN, G. A.
            EFFECTS OF FACILITATING TECHNIQUES AND SUBJECT-EXPERIMENTER INTERACTION
            ON CREATIVE PROBLEM SOLVING.
            JOURNAL OF PERSONALITY AND SOCIAL PSYCHOLOGY, 1967, 5, 211-216.
                    (DESCRIPTION; CORRELATES:BEHAVIORAL, PSYCHOLOGICAL, INTELLIGENCE;
                    N=30 MALE AND 30 FEMALE UNDERGRADUATES)
        @APPLICATION 1967 M-29

172   GEER, J. H., & TURTELTAUB, A.
            FEAR REDUCTION FOLLOWING OBSERVATION OF A MODEL.
            JOURNAL OF PERSONALITY AND SOCIAL PSYCHOLOGY, 1967, 6, 327-331.
                    (VALIDITY:CRITERION; CORRELATES:BEHAVIORAL, PSYCHOLOGICAL; USED AS
                    CRITERION; N=60 FEMALE UNDERGRADUATES)
        @APPLICATION 1967 G-41 Z-13

173   GERGEN, K. J., & BAUER, R. A.
            INTERACTIVE EFFECTS OF SELF-ESTEEM AND TASK DIFFICULTY ON SOCIAL
            CONFORMITY.
            JOURNAL OF PERSONALITY AND SOCIAL PSYCHOLOGY, 1967, 6, 16-22.
                    (VALIDITY:CRITERION; CORRELATES:BEHAVIORAL, PSYCHOLOGICAL; USED AS
                    CRITERION; NORMATIVE DATA; N=67 FEMALE UNDERGRADUATES)
        @APPLICATION 1967 J-7

174   FELD, S. C.
            LONGITUDINAL STUDY OF THE ORIGINS OF ACHIEVEMENT STRIVINGS.
            JOURNAL OF PERSONALITY AND SOCIAL PSYCHOLOGY, 1967, 7, 408-414.
                (MODIFICATION; RELIABILITY:RETEST; VALIDITY:CRITERION;
                CORRELATES:PSYCHOLOGICAL; USED AS CRITERION; N=29 BOYS AND 29
                MOTHERS)
            @APPLICATION 1967 M-7 S-5

175   FISCHER, D., & RULE, B. G.
            ANTI-SEMITISM, STRESS, AND ANCHOR EFFECTS ON INTERPERSONAL JUDGMENTS.
            JOURNAL OF PERSONALITY AND SOCIAL PSYCHOLOGY, 1967, 6, 447-450.
                (CORRELATES:PSYCHOLOGICAL, ENVIRONMENTAL; USED AS CRITERION;
                BIAS:RESPONSE; N=96 UNDERGRADUATES)
            @APPLICATION 1967 A-5

176   WOLITZKY, D. L.
            COGNITIVE CONTROL AND COGNITIVE DISSONANCE.
            JOURNAL OF PERSONALITY AND SOCIAL PSYCHOLOGY, 1967, 5, 486-490.
                (DESCRIPTION; CORRELATES:BEHAVIORAL, PSYCHOLOGICAL; USED AS
                CRITERION; NORMATIVE DATA; N=78 MALE UNDERGRADUATE SMOKERS AND
                NONSMOKERS)
            @APPLICATION 1967 S-61

177   WRIGHT, L.
            FACTOR STRUCTURE OF DUNCAN'S PERSONALITY INTEGRATION SCALE.
            JOURNAL OF PERSONALITY AND SOCIAL PSYCHOLOGY, 1967, 5, 348-350.
                (VALIDITY:CONSTRUCT; CORRELATES:PSYCHOLOGICAL, DEMOGRAPHIC;
                FACTOR ANALYSIS; 3 STUDIES: N=43 FEMALE UNDERGRADUATES, 92 MALE
                UNDERGRADUATES, 129 FEMALE UNDERGRADUATES)
            @APPLICATION 1967 D-9

178   OPTON, E. M., & LAZARUS, R. S.
            PERSONALITY DETERMINANTS OF PSYCHOPHYSIOLOGICAL RESPONSE TO STRESS: A
            THEORETICAL ANALYSIS AND AN EXPERIMENT.
            JOURNAL OF PERSONALITY AND SOCIAL PSYCHOLOGY, 1967, 6, 291-303.
                (VALIDITY; CORRELATES:PSYCHOLOGICAL, PHYSIOLOGICAL, ENVIRONMENTAL;
                USED AS CRITERION; N=48 MALE UNDERGRADUATES)
            @APPLICATION 1967 N-5 B-63 D-45 S-62 M-3 A-21

179   WOODMANSEE, J. J., & COOK, S. W.
            DIMENSIONS OF VERBAL RACIAL ATTITUDES: THEIR IDENTIFICATION AND
            MEASUREMENT.
            JOURNAL OF PERSONALITY AND SOCIAL PSYCHOLOGY, 1967, 7, 240-250.
                (DESCRIPTION; MODIFICATION; VALIDITY:CONSTRUCT;
                CORRELATES:DEMOGRAPHIC; USED AS CRITERION; FACTOR ANALYSIS; CLUSTER
                ANALYSIS; NORMATIVE DATA; 3 STUDIES: 593 WHITE COLLEGE STUDENTS,
                609 WHITE COLLEGE STUDENTS, 630 WHITE COLLEGE STUDENTS)
            @APPLICATION 1967 C-50 S-64 H-196

180   NISBETT, R. E., & GORDON, A.
            SELF-ESTEEM AND SUSCEPTIBILITY TO SOCIAL INFLUENCE.
            JOURNAL OF PERSONALITY AND SOCIAL PSYCHOLOGY, 1967, 5, 268-276.
                (MODIFICATION; CORRELATES:PSYCHOLOGICAL, INTELLIGENCE, ENVIRONMENTAL;
                USED AS CRITERION; N=152 UNDERGRADUATES)
            @APPLICATION 1967 D-45 F-50 M-219 J-7

181   WITKIN, H. A., GOODENOUGH, D. R., & KARP, S. A.
            STABILITY OF COGNITIVE STYLE FROM CHILDHOOD TO YOUNG ADULTHOOD.
            JOURNAL OF PERSONALITY AND SOCIAL PSYCHOLOGY, 1967, 7, 291-300.
                (DESCRIPTION; RELIABILITY:RETEST; VALIDITY:CROSS-VALIDATION;
                CORRELATES:PSYCHOLOGICAL, DEMOGRAPHIC, INTELLIGENCE; NORMATIVE DATA;
                2 STUDIES: CROSS-SECTIONAL, 8-17 AND COLLEGE WITH APPROXIMATELY 25
                MALES AND 25 FEMALES IN 8 AGE GROUPS, AND LONGITUDINAL 10-24 YEARS,
                N=51 BOYS AND GIRLS, AND 8-13 YEARS, N=47 BOYS AND GIRLS)
            @APPLICATION 1967 G-33 W-72 W-73 R-30 M-20

182   WHEELER, L., & SMITH, S.
            CENSURE OF THE MODEL IN THE CONTAGION OF AGGRESSION.
            JOURNAL OF PERSONALITY AND SOCIAL PSYCHOLOGY, 1967, 6, 93-98.
                (DESCRIPTION; CORRELATES:ENVIRONMENTAL; NORMATIVE DATA; N=119 MALE
                NAVY TRAINEES)
            @APPLICATION 1967 B-66 M-37

183   WEINSTOCK, A. R.
           FAMILY ENVIRONMENT AND THE DEVELOPMENT OF DEFENSE AND COPING MECHANISMS.
           JOURNAL OF PERSONALITY AND SOCIAL PSYCHOLOGY, 1967, 5, 67-75.
                (RELIABILITY:INTERRATER; VALIDITY:CONSTRUCT;
                CORRELATES:PSYCHOLOGICAL, ENVIRONMENTAL; N=39 MALES AND THEIR PARENTS
                IN A LONGITUDINAL STUDY)
        @APPLICATION 1967 R-30 D-45 W-184

184   WATSON, D., AND BAUMAL, E.
           EFFECTS OF LOCUS OF CONTROL AND EXPECTATION OF FUTURE CONTROL UPON PRESENT
           PERFORMANCE.
           JOURNAL OF PERSONALITY AND SOCIAL PSYCNOLOGY, 1967, 6, 212-215.
                (CORRELATES:BEHAVIORAL, PSYCHOLOGICAL; USED AS CRITERION; N=60 FEMALE
                UNDERGRADUATES)
        @APPLICATION 1967 R-18

185   WATSON, D.
           RELATIONSHIP BETWEEN LOCUS OF CONTROL AND ANXIETY.
           JOURNAL OF PERSONALITY AND SOCIAL PSYCHOLOGY, 1967, 6, 91-92.
                (RELIABILITY; CORRELATES:PSYCHOLOGICAL, DEMOGRAPHIC; N=648 MALE AND
                FEMALE UNDERGRADUATES)
        @APPLICATION 1967 R-18 A-8 T-2

186   WARE, R., & HARVEY, O. J.
           A COGNITIVE DETERMINANT OF IMPRESSION FORMATION.
           JOURNAL OF PERSONALITY AND SOCIAL PSYCHOLOGY, 1967, 5, 38-44.
                (DESCRIPTION; CORRELATES:BEHAVIORAL, PSYCHOLOGICAL; USED AS
                CRITERION; N=36 COLLEGE UNDERGRADUATES)
        @APPLICATION 1967 H-32

187   VASSILIOU, V., GEORGAS, J. G., & VASSILIOU, G.
           VARIATIONS IN MANIFEST ANXIETY DUE TO SEX, AGE, AND EDUCATION.
           JOURNAL OF PERSONALITY AND SOCIAL PSYCHOLOGY, 1967, 6, 194-197.
                (MODIFICATION; CORRELATES:DEMOGRAPHIC; CROSS-CULTURAL APPLICATION;
                NORMATIVE DATA; N=REPRESENTATIVE SAMPLE (SEX, AGE, EDUCATION, INCOME)
                OF 400 ATHENIAN ADULTS)
        @APPLICATION 1967 T-2

188   VALINS, S.
           EMOTIONALITY AND INFORMATION CONCERNING INTERNAL REACTIONS.
           JOURNAL OF PERSONALITY AND SOCIAL PSYCHOLOGY, 1967, 6, 458-463.
                (DESCRIPTION; VALIDITY:CONSTRUCT; CORRELATES:BEHAVIORAL,
                PSYCHOLOGICAL; USED AS CRITERION; N=81 MALE UNDERGRADUATES, INCLUDING
                18 CONTROLS)
        @APPLICATION 1967 L-22 V-37 D-45

189   WAGMAN, H.
           SEX DIFFERENCES IN TYPES OF DAYDREAMS.
           JOURNAL OF PERSONALITY AND SOCIAL PSYCHOLOGY, 1967, 7, 329-332.
                (MODIFICATION; DESCRIPTION; CORRELATES:PSYCHOLOGICAL, DEMOGRAPHIC;
                NORMATIVE DATA; N=206 MALE AND FEMALE UNDERGRADUATES)
        @APPLICATION 1967 S-82

190   STRICKER, L. J., MESSICK, S., & JACKSON, D. N.
           SUSPICION OF DECEPTION: IMPLICATIONS FOR CONFORMITY RESEARCH.
           JOURNAL OF PERSONALITY AND SOCIAL PSYCHOLOGY, 1967, 5, 379-389.
                (MODFFICATION; RELIABILITY; VALIDITY:CONSTRUCT;
                CORRELATES:BEHAVIORAL, PSYCHOLOGICAL, DEMOGRAPHIC, INTELLIGENCE,
                ENVIRONMENTAL; N=190 11TH AND 12TH GRADE BOYS AND GIRLS)
        @APPLICATION 1967 F-34 S-65 B-7 C-23 C-32 S-66 E-1 W-14 C-27 G-40 G-39 B-4 C-110
        @G-1 W-2 B-116 H-190 J-2

191   STEWART, R. H.
           BIRTH ORDER AND DEPENDENCY.
           JOURNAL OF PERSONALITY AND SOCIAL PSYCHOLOGY, 1967, 6, 192-194.
                (REVISION; CORRELATES:PSYCHOLOGICAL, DEMOGRAPHIC; BIAS:RESPONSE;
                N=100 MALE UNDERGRADUATES)
        @APPLICATION 1967 L-35 B-4 J-54 W-19

192   STAGER, P.
           CONCEPTUAL LEVEL AS A COMPOSITION VARIABLE IN SMALL-GROUP DECISION MAKING.
           JOURNAL OF PERSONALITY AND SOCIAL PSYCHOLOGY, 1967, 5, 152-161.
                (CORRELATES:BEHAVIORAL: USED AS CRITERION; N=80 MALE COLLEGE
                STUDENTS)
        @APPLICATION 1967 S-41 E-2

193   SMITH, K. H., & RICHARDS, B.
              EFFECTS OF A RATIONAL APPEAL AND OF ANXIETY ON CONFORMITY BEHAVIOR.
              JOURNAL OF PERSONALITY AND SOCIAL PSYCHOLOGY, 1967, 5, 122-126.
                   (VALIDITY:CONSTRUCT; CORRELATES:BEHAVIORAL, PSYCHOLOGICAL; USED AS
                   CRITERION; N=80 UNDERGRADUATES)
        @APPLICATION 1967 B-184 C-23

194   SEARS, D. O.
              SOCIAL ANXIETY, OPINION STRUCTURE, AND OPINION CHANGE.
              JOURNAL OF PERSONALITY AND SOCIAL PSYCHOLOGY, 1967, 7, 142-151.
                   (MODIFICATION; CORRELATES:BEHAVIORAL, ENVIRONMENTAL; N=112
                   UNDERGRADUATES)
        @APPLICATION 1967 M-4 Z-37

195   SAMPSON, E. E., & HANCOCK, F. T.
              AN EXAMINATION OF THE RELATIONSHIP BETWEEN ORDINAL POSITION, PERSONALITY,
              AND CONFORMITY: AN EXTENSION, REPLICATION, AND PARTIAL VERIFICATION.
              JOURNAL OF PERSONALITY AND SOCIAL PSYCHOLOGY, 1967, 5, 398-407.
                   (MODIFICATION; CORRELATES:BEHAVIORAL, DEMOGRAPHIC; NORMATIVE DATA;
                   N=251 MALE AND FEMALE 10TH, 11TH, AND 12TH GRADE STUDENTS FROM ONE-
                   AND TWO-CHILD FAMILIES)
        @APPLICATION 1967 E-2 W-54 M-25 F-20

196   RUBIN, I. M.
              INCREASED SELF-ACCEPTANCE: A MEANS OF REDUCING PREJUDICE.
              JOURNAL OF PERSONALITY AND SOCIAL PSYCHOLOGY, 1967, 5, 233-238.
                   (DESCRIPTION; MODIFICATION; RELIABILITY:RETEST - 2 WEEKS;
                   CORRELATES:PSYCHOLOGICAL, ENVIRONMENTAL; N=41 MALE AND FEMALE
                   PARTICIPANTS IN A SENSITIVITY TRAINING LABORATORY, INCLUDING 11
                   CONTROLS)
        @APPLICATION 1967 D-17 S-44

197   RHINE, R. J.
              THE 1964 PRESIDENTIAL ELECTION AND CURVES OF INFORMATION SEEKING AND
              AVOIDING.
              JOURNAL OF PERSONALITY AND SOCIAL PSYCHOLOGY, 1967, 5, 416-423.
                   (MODIFICATION; CORRELATES:BEHAVIORAL, NORMATIVE DATA;
                   N=58 STRONGLY POLITICALLY COMMITTED UNDERGRADUATES (24 CONTROLS)
                   SELECTED FROM 161 UNDERGRADUATES WITH 36 CONTROLS)
        @APPLICATION 1967 A-15 A-29

198   RETTIG, S., & TUROFF, S. J.
              EXPOSURE TO GROUP DISCUSSION AND PREDICTED ETHICAL RISK TAKING.
              JOURNAL OF PERSONALITY AND SOCIAL PSYCHOLOGY, 1967, 7, 177-180.
                   (CORRELATES:ENVIRONMENTAL; N=160 MALE AND FEMALE UNDERGRADUATES)
        @APPLICATION 1967 R-26

199   REIMANIS, G.
              INCREASE IN PSYCHOLOGICAL ANOMIE AS A RESULT OF RADICAL AND UNDESIRABLE
              CHANGE EXPECTANCY.
              JOURNAL OF PERSONALITY AND SOCIAL PSYCHOLOGY, 1967, 6, 454-457.
                   (DESCRIPTION; VALIDITY:CONSTRUCT; CORRELATES:DEMOGRAPHIC,
                   ENVIRONMENTAL; 2 STUDIES: N=130 IN FIRST AND 92 IN SECOND STUDY MALE
                   VA DOMICILIARY MEMBERS, 32 MALE AND 37 FEMALE VA EMPLOYEES, 99 MALE
                   AND 104 FEMALE AND 44 MALE AND 94 FEMALE TOWN RESIDENTS IN FIRST AND
                   SECOND STUDY RESPECTIVELY, 72 MALE AND 63 FEMALE RESIDENTS IN A
                   CONTROL TOWN)
        @APPLICATION 1967 R-153

200   PYRON, B., & KAFER, J., JR.
              RECALL OF NONSENSE AND ATTITUDINAL RIGIDITY.
              JOURNAL OF PERSONALITY AND SOCIAL PSYCHOLOGY, 1967, 5, 463-466.
                   (CORRELATES:BEHAVIORAL; N=38 MALE AND 22 FEMALE COLLEGE
                   SOPHOMORES)
        @APPLICATION 1967 R-8 P-24 A-5

201   PORIER, G. W., & LOTT, A. J.
              GALVANIC SKIN RESPONSES AND PREJUDICE.
              JOURNAL OF PERSONALITY AND SOCIAL PSYCHOLOGY, 1967, 5, 253-259.
                   (MODIFICATION; VALIDITY:CRITERION;
                   CORRELATES:PHYSIOLOGICAL; N=60 WHITE MALE UNDERGRADUATES)
        @APPLICATION 1967 C-30 R-50

202   MENDELSOHN, G. A., & GRISWOLD, B. B.
              ANXIETY AND REPRESSION AS PREDICTORS OF THE USE OF INCIDENTAL CUES
              IN PROBLEM SOLVING.
              JOURNAL OF PERSONALITY AND SOCIAL PSYCHOLOGY, 1967, 6, 353-359.
                     (DESCRIPTION; CORRELATES:BEHAVIORAL, DEMOGRAPHIC; NORMATIVE
                     DATA; 2 SAMPLES OF UNDERGRADUATES:N=33 MALES ,46 FEMALES; 42 MALES,
                     60 FEMALES)
              @APPLICATION 1967 W-8 W-41 B-46

203   MCBRIDE, L., & MORAN, G.
              DOUBLE AGREEMENT AS A FUNCTION OF ITEM AMBIGUITY AND SUSCEPTIBILITY TO
              DEMAND IMPLICATIONS OF THE PSYCHOLOGICAL SITUATION.
              JOURNAL OF PERSONALITY AND SOCIAL PSYCHOLOGY, 1967, 6, 115-118.
                     (DESCRIPTION; CORRELATES:BEHAVIORAL, PSYCHOLOGICAL, ENVIRONMENTAL;
                     N=108 MALE AND 72 FEMALE COLLEGE FRESHMEN)
              @APPLICATION 1967 P-16 C-27

204   PYTKOWICZ, A. R., WAGNER, N. N., & SARASON, I. G.
              AN EXPERIMENTAL STUDY OF THE REDUCTION OF HOSTILITY THROUGH FANTASY.
              JOURNAL OF PERSONALITY AND SOCIAL PSYCHOLOGY, 1967, 5, 295-303.
                     (MODIFICATION; CORRELATES:PSYCHOLOGICAL, DEMOGRAPHIC, ENVIRONMENTAL;
                     USED AS CRITERION; NORMATIVE DATA; N=60 MALE AND 60 FEMALE
                     UNDERGRADUATES (EXPERIMENTAL AND CONTROL) SELECTED FROM 331 STUDENTS
                     AS BEING HIGH OR LOW FREQUENCY DAYDREAMERS)
              @APPLICATION 1967 F-83 G-63 S-4 S-5 A-91 E-1 M-20 S-234

205   LIPSITT, P. D., & STRODTBECK, F. L.
              DEFENSIVENESS IN DECISION MAKING AS A FUNCTION OF SEX-ROLE IDENTIFICATION.
              JOURNAL OF PERSONALITY AND SOCIAL PSYCHOLOGY, 1967, 6, 10-15.
                     (MODIFICATION; RELIABILITY:INTERRATER; CORRELATES:BEHAVIORAL; N=380
                     MALE NAVAL ENLISTED PERSONNEL AGES 18 TO 29)
              @APPLICATION 1967 F-11 G-20

206   LIPETZ, M. E., & OSSORIO, P. G.
              AUTHORITARIANISM, AGGRESSION, AND STATUS.
              JOURNAL OF PERSONALITY AND SOCIAL PSYCHOLOGY, 1967, 5, 468-472.
                     (VALIDITY:CONSTRUCT; CORRELATES:BEHAVIORAL, PSYCHOLOGICAL;
                     NORMATIVE DATA; N=94 HIGH AND LOW AUTHORITARIAN MALE COLLEGE
                     STUDENTS)
              @APPLICATION 1967 A-5 B-44

207   KIMBLE, G. A., & POSNICK, G. M.
              ANXIETY?
              JOURNAL OF PERSONALITY AND SOCIAL PSYCHOLOGY, 1967, 7, 108-110.
                     (CORRELATES:PSYCHOLOGICAL, DEMOGRAPHIC; BIAS:RESPONSE; N=74 MALE AND
                     40 FEMALE UNDERGRADUATES)
              @APPLICATION 1967 T-2

208   LAUGHLIN, P. R.
              INCIDENTAL CONCEPT FORMATION AS A FUNCTION OF CREATIVITY AND INTELLIGENCE.
              JOURNAL OF PERSONALITY AND SOCIAL PSYCHOLOGY, 1967, 5, 115-119.
                     (CORRELATES:BEHAVIORAL, INTELLIGENCE; USED AS CRITERION;
                     NORMATIVE DATA; N=148 UNDERGRADUATES)
              @APPLICATION 1967 M-29

209   LEVENTHAL, H., WATTS, J. C., & PAGANO, F.
              EFFECTS OF FEAR AND INSTRUCTIONS ON HOW TO COPE WITH DANGER.
              JOURNAL OF PERSONALITY AND SOCIAL PSYCHOLOGY, 1967, 6, 313-321.
                     (MODIFICATION; CORRELATES:ENVIRONMENTAL; N=129 YALE UNDERGRADUATE
                     (2/3 FRESHMEN, 1/3 UPPERCLASSMEN) CIGARETTE SMOKERS)
              @APPLICATION 1967 N-17

210   LERNER, M. J., DILLEHAY, R. C., & SHERER, W. C.
              SIMILARITY AND ATTRACTION IN SOCIAL CONTEXTS.
              JOURNAL OF PERSONALITY AND SOCIAL PSYCHOLOGY, 1967, 5, 481-486.
                     (MODIFICATION; CORRELATES:PSYCHOLOGICAL, ENVIRONMENTAL; N=39 MALE
                     UNDERGRADUATES AND 20 CONTROLS)
              @APPLICATION 1967 M-32

211   LEFCOURT, H. M.
              EFFECTS OF CUE EXPLICATION UPON PERSONS MAINTAINING EXTERNAL CONTROL
              EXPECTANCIES.
              JOURNAL OF PERSONALITY AND SOCIAL PSYCHOLOGY, 1967, 5, 372-378.
                     (CORRELATES:BEHAVIORAL, PSYCHOLOGICAL, ENVIRONMENTAL; USED AS
                     CRITERION; NORMATIVE DATA; N=132 UNDERGRADUATES)
              @APPLICATION 1967 R-18 R-17

212 LAMM, H.
WILL AN OBSERVER ADVISE HIGHER RISK TAKING AFTER HEARING A DISCUSSION
OF THE DECISION PROBLEM?
JOURNAL OF PERSONALITY AND SOCIAL PSYCHOLOGY, 1967, 6, 467-471.
(CORRELATES:BEHAVIORAL, PSYCHOLOGICAL, ENVIRONMENTAL; USED AS
CRITERION; NORMATIVE DATA; N=78 MALE COLLEGE STUDENTS SCORING EITHER
HIGH OR LOW IN CONCEPTUAL COMPLEXITY)
@APPLICATION 1967 S-41 W-2

213 KLINGER, E.
MODELING EFFECTS ON ACHIEVEMENT IMAGERY.
JOURNAL OF PERSONALITY AND SOCIAL PSYCHOLOGY, 1967, 7, 49-62.
(MODIFICATION; RELIABILITY:INTERRATER; VALIDITY:CONSTRUCT;
CORRELATES:BEHAVIORAL, PSYCHOLOGICAL, ENVIRONMENTAL; NORMATIVE DATA;
2 EXPERIMENTS: N=104 MALE COLLEGE STUDENTS, N=221 MALE COLLEGE
STUDENTS)
@APPLICATION 1967 G-21 M-7 H-150 B-98 K-149

214 KLEIN, M. H.
COMPLIANCE, CONSISTENT CONFORMITY, AND PERSONALITY.
JOURNAL OF PERSONALITY AND SOCIAL PSYCHOLOGY, 1967, 5, 239-245.
(MODIFICATION; CORRELATES:BEHAVIORAL, PSYCHOLOGICAL, DEMOGRAPHIC;
N=210 UNDERGRADUATES)
@APPLICATION 1967 C-23 S-49 C-27 K-23 H-150 C-34

215 KLECK, R. E., & WHEATON, J.
DOGMATISM AND RESPONSES TO OPINION-CONSISTENT AND OPINION-INCONSISTENT
INFORMATION.
JOURNAL OF PERSONALITY AND SOCIAL PSYCHOLOGY, 1967, 5, 249-252.
(VALIDITY:CRITERION; CORRELATES:BEHAVIORAL; USED AS CRITERION;
NORMATIVE DATA; N=72 MALE AND FEMALE HIGH SCHOOL JUNIORS)
@APPLICATION 1967 R-8

216 KARLINS, M., & LAMM, H.
INFORMATION SEARCH AS A FUNCTION OF CONCEPTUAL STRUCTURE IN A COMPLEX
PROBLEM-SOLVING TASK.
JOURNAL OF PERSONALITY AND SOCIAL PSYCHOLOGY, 1967, 5, 456-459.
(CORRELATES:BEHAVIORAL; USED AS CRITERION; NORMATIVE DATA; N=60
PEACE CORPS VOLUNTEERS MATCHED ON INTELLIGENCE AND VARYING IN
CONCEPTUAL LEVEL)
@APPLICATION 1967 S-41

217 KARLINS, M.
CONCEPTUAL COMPLEXITY AND REMOTE-ASSOCIATIVE PROFICIENCY AS CREATIVITY
VARIABLES IN A COMPLEX PROBLEM-SOLVING TASK.
JOURNAL OF PERSONALITY AND SOCIAL PSYCHOLOGY, 1967, 6, 264-278.
(VALIDITY:CRITERION; CORRELATES:BEHAVIORAL, PSYCHOLOGICAL; USED AS
CRITERION; NORMATIVE DATA; N=60 MALE UNDERGRADUATES SELECTED FROM
AN INITIAL SAMPLE OF 300 MATCHED IN INTELLIGENCE, AND VARYING
CONCOMITANTLY IN CONCEPTUAL LEVEL AND ASSOCIATIVE PROFICIENCY)
@APPLICATION 1967 M-29 S-41

218 IVERSON, M. A., & SCHWAB, H. G.
ETHNOCENTRIC DOGMATISM AND BINOCULAR FUSION OF SEXUALLY AND RACIALLY
DISCREPANT STIMULI.
JOURNAL OF PERSONALITY AND SOCIAL PSYCHOLOGY, 1967, 7, 73-81.
(CORRELATES:BEHAVIORAL, PSYCHOLOGICAL, PHYSIOLOGICAL, DEMOGRAPHIC;
USED AS CRITERION; NORMATIVE DATA; N=32 HIGH ETHNOCENTRIC AND
DOGMATIC AND 32 OPEN-MINDED MALE AND FEMALE COLLEGE STUDENTS)
@APPLICATION 1967 R-8 A-17

219 IRWIN, M., TRIPODI, T., & BIERI, J.
AFFECTIVE STIMULUS VALUE AND COGNITIVE COMPLEXITY.
JOURNAL OF PERSONALITY AND SOCIAL PSYCHOLOGY, 1967, 5, 444-448.
(MODIFICATION; CORRELATES:BEHAVIORAL, DEMOGRAPHIC; NORMATIVE DATA;
2 STUDIES: 64 MALE AND 51 FEMALE UNDERGRADUATES, 40 MALE AND 40
FEMALE UNDERGRADUATES)
@APPLICATION 1967 T-13 B-97 C-27

220 HUNT, R. G., & LIN, T. K.
ACCURACY OF JUDGMENTS OF PERSONAL ATTRIBUTES FROM SPEECH.
JOURNAL OF PERSONALITY AND SOCIAL PSYCHOLOGY, 1967, 6, 450-453.
(CORRELATES:BEHAVIORAL, PSYCHOLOGICAL, DEMOGRAPHIC, ENVIRONMENTAL;
USED AS CRITERION; N=24 FEMALE AND 54 MALE UNDERGRADUATES--28 HIGH
DOGMATIC AND 24 LOW DOGMATIC AND 26 INTERMEDIATES)
@APPLICATION 1967 R-8 M-226

221   HOLZMAN, P. S., BERGER, A., & ROUSEY, C.
            VOICE CONFRONTATION: A BILINGUAL STUDY.
            JOURNAL OF PERSONALITY AND SOCIAL PSYCHOLOGY, 1967, 7, 423-428.
                (MODIFICATION; CORRELATES:PSYCHOLOGICAL, ENVIRONMENTAL; N=12 (10 MEN
                AND 2 WOMEN) SPANISH-SPEAKING LATIN AMERICANS WHO LEARNED ENGLISH
                AFTER AGE OF 16)
            @APPLICATION 1967 H-43 M-35

222   HOLMES, D. S.
            PUPILLARY RESPONSE, CONDITIONING, AND PERSONALITY.
            JOURNAL OF PERSONALITY AND SOCIAL PSYCHOLOGY, 1967, 5, 98-103.
                (CORRELATES:PSYCHOLOGICAL, PHYSIOLOGICAL; N=49 UNDERGRADUATE WOMEN)
            @APPLICATION 1967 D-45 E-5

223   HELMREICH, R. L., & COLLINS, B. E.
            SITUATIONAL DETERMINANTS OF AFFILIATIVE PREFERENCE UNDER STRESS.
            JOURNAL OF PERSONALITY AND SOCIAL PSYCHOLOGY, 1967, 6, 79-85.
                (MODIFICATION; CORRELATES:BEHAVIORAL, PSYCHOLOGICAL, DEMOGRAPHIC,
                ENVIRONMENTAL; USED AS CRITERION; 2 STUDIES: N=60 MALE HIGH SCHOOL
                STUDENTS (30 FIRSTBORNS AND 30 LATERBORNS), N=108 MALE HIGH SCHOOL
                STUDENTS (54 FIRSTBORNS AND 54 LATERBORNS) SELECTED FROM SAMPLE OF
                120)
            @APPLICATION 1967 C-10 J-7 N-17

224   HATTON, J. M.
            REACTIONS OF NEGROES IN A BIRACIAL BARGAINING SITUATION.
            JOURNAL OF PERSONALITY AND SOCIAL PSYCHOLOGY, 1967, 7, 301-306.
                (MODIFICATION; CORRELATES:BEHAVIORAL, DEMOGRAPHIC; USED AS
                CRITERION; NORMATIVE DATA; N=40 NEGRO HIGH SCHOOL GIRLS SELECTED
                FROM 83 ON BASIS OF RESPONSES TO A MEASURE OF PERCEIVED PREJUDICE)
            @APPLICATION 1967 K-29

225   HARVEY, O. J., & WARE, R.
            PERSONALITY DIFFERENCES IN DISSONANCE RESOLUTION.
            JOURNAL OF PERSONALITY AND SOCIAL PSYCHOLOGY, 1967, 7, 227-230.
                (CORRELATES:BEHAVIORAL, PSYCHOLOGICAL; USED AS CRITERION; N=17
                CONCRETE AND 17 ABSTRACT UNDERGRADUATES SELECTED FROM LARGER SAMPLE)
            @APPLICATION 1967 H-32

226   HARMATZ, M. G.
            VERBAL CONDITIONING AND CHANGE ON PERSONALITY MEASURES.
            JOURNAL OF PERSONALITY AND SOCIAL PSYCHOLOGY, 1967, 5, 175-185.
                (DESCRIPTION; MODIFICATION; CORRELATES:BEHAVIORAL, PSYCHOLOGICAL,
                DEMOGRAPHIC, ENVIRONMENTAL; USED AS CRITERION; N=25 MALE AND 25
                FEMALE UNDERGRADUATES SELECTED FROM MIDDLE 20% OF SOCIAL
                DESIRABILITY SCALE)
            @APPLICATION 1967 E-1 S-4 O-16 B-60

227   PILISUK, M., SKOLNICK, P., & OVERSTREET, E.
            PREDICTING COOPERATION FROM THE TWO SEXES IN A CONFLICT SIMULATION.
            JOURNAL OF PERSONALITY AND SOCIAL PSYCHOLOGY, 1968, 10, 35-43.
                (CORRELATES:BEHAVIORAL, PSYCHOLOGICAL, DEMOGRAPHIC, ENVIRONMENTAL;
                N=120 MALE AND 56 FEMALE UNDERGRADUATES)
            @APPLICATION 1968 G-26

228   WIGGINS, J. S., WIGGINS, N., & CONGER, J. C.
            CORRELATES OF HETEROSEXUAL SOMATIC PREFERENCE.
            JOURNAL OF PERSONALITY AND SOCIAL PSYCHOLOGY, 1968, 10, 82-90.
                (CORRELATES:BEHAVIORAL, PSYCHOLOGICAL, DEMOGRAPHIC, ENVIRONMENTAL;
                NORMATIVE DATA; N=95 MALE UNDERGRADUATES)
            @APPLICATION 1968 E-2 D-45 O-16 W-197

229   GROSSBERG, J. M., & WILSON, H. K.
            PHYSIOLOGICAL CHANGES ACCOMPANYING THE VISUALIZATION OF FEARFUL AND
            NEUTRAL SITUATIONS.
            JOURNAL OF PERSONALITY AND SOCIAL PSYCHOLOGY, 1968, 10, 124-133.
                (CORRELATES:PSYCHOLOGICAL, PHYSIOLOGICAL; USED AS CRITERION; N=302
                FEMALE UNDERGRADUATES, 36 SELECTED)
            @APPLICATION 1968 W-37

230   GALBRAITH, G. G., & MOSHER, D. L.
              ASSOCIATIVE SEXUAL RESPONSES IN RELATION TO SEXUAL AROUSAL, GUILT, AND
              EXTERNAL APPROVAL CONTINGENCIES.
              JOURNAL OF PERSONALITY AND SOCIAL PSYCHOLOGY, 1968, 10, 142-147.
                     (RELIABILITY:INTERNAL CONSISTENCY, INTERRATER; CORRELATES:BEHAVIORAL,
                     PSYCHOLOGICAL; USED AS CRITERION; NORMATIVE DATA; N=168
                     UNDERGRADUATES)
              @APPLICATION 1968 M-16 M-64

231   LONDON, P., & MADSEN, C. H., JR.
              EFFECT OF ROLE PLAYING ON HYPNOTIC SUSCEPTIBILITY IN CHILDREN.
              JOURNAL OF PERSONALITY AND SOCIAL PSYCHOLOGY, 1968, 10, 66-68.
                     (CORRELATES:BEHAVIORAL, PSYCHOLOGICAL; USED AS CRITERION; NORMATIVE
                     DATA; N=19 BOYS AND 15 GIRLS)
              @APPLICATION 1968 L-33 L-34

232   HARRISON, R. H., & KASS, E. H.
              MMPI CORRELATES OF NEGRO ACCULTURATION.
              JOURNAL OF PERSONALITY AND SOCIAL PSYCHOLOGY, 1968, 10, 262-270.
                     (CORRELATES:BEHAVIORAL, PSYCHOLOGICAL, DEMOGRAPHIC; NORMATIVE DATA;
                     N=326 LOWER-CLASS PREGNANT WOMEN)
              @APPLICATION 1968 D-45 B-5 T-2 H-202

233   JOHNSON, H. H., & TORCIVIA, J. M.
              ACQUIESCENCE RESPONSE STYLE AND ATTITUDE CHANGE.
              JOURNAL OF PERSONALITY AND SOCIAL PSYCHOLOGY, 1968, 8, 349-350.
                     (CORRELATES:BEHAVIORAL, PSYCHOLOGICAL; BIAS:RESPONSE; N=247
                     UNDERGRADUATES)
              @APPLICATION 1968 N-10 M-219

234   JOHNSON, H. H., TORCIVIA, J. M., & POPRICK, M. A.
              EFFECTS OF SOURCE CREDIBILITY ON THE RELATIONSHIP BETWEEN AUTHORITARIANISM
              AND ATTITUDE CHANGE.
              JOURNAL OF PERSONALITY AND SOCIAL PSYCHOLOGY, 1968, 9, 179-183.
                     (CORRELATES:PSYCHOLOGICAL, ENVIRONMENTAL; N=152 UNDERGRADUATES)
              @APPLICATION 1968 M-223 A-5

235   KARABENICK, S. A., & YOUSSEF, Z. I.
              PERFORMANCE AS A FUNCTION OF ACHIEVEMENT MOTIVE LEVEL AND PERCEIVED
              DIFFICULTY.
              JOURNAL OF PERSONALITY AND SOCIAL PSYCHOLOGY, 1968, 10, 414-419.
                     (CORRELATES:BEHAVIORAL, PSYCHOLOGICAL, ENVIRONMENTAL; USED AS
                     CRITERION; NORMATIVE DATA; N=76 MALE UNDERGRADUATES)
              @APPLICATION 1968 M-47 M-4

236   KATZ, I., HENCHY, T., & ALLEN, H.
              EFFECTS OF RACE OF TESTER, APPROVAL-DISAPPROVAL, AND NEED ON NEGRO
              CHILDREN'S LEARNING.
              JOURNAL OF PERSONALITY AND SOCIAL PSYCHOLOGY, 1968, 8, 38-42.
                     (MODIFICATION; CORRELATES:PSYCHOLOGICAL, ENVIRONMENTAL; USED AS
                     CRITERION; BIAS:TESTER; N=148 NEGRO BOYS AGES 7-10)
              @APPLICATION 1968 C-27

237   KANUNGA, R. N.
              RETENTION OF AFFECTIVE MATERIAL: ROLE OF EXTRAVERSION AND INTENSITY OF
              AFFECT.
              JOURNAL OF PERSONALITY AND SOCIAL PSYCHOLOGY, 1968, 8, 63-68.
                     (CORRELATES:BEHAVIORAL, PSYCHOLOGICAL, ENVIRONMENTAL; USED AS
                     CRITERION; NORMATIVE DATA; N=68 UNDERGRADUATES)
              @APPLICATION 1968 E-5

238   JULIAN, J. W., & KATZ, S. B.
              INTERNAL CONTROL AND SELF-DETERMINATION OF REWARDS.
              JOURNAL OF PERSONALITY AND SOCIAL PSYCHOLOGY, 1968, 8, 89-98.
                     (CORRELATES:BEHAVIORAL, PSYCHOLOGICAL; USED AS CRITERION; NORMATIVE
                     DATA; 2 STUDIES: N=42 UNDERGRADUATES, 56 UNDERGRADUATES)
              @APPLICATION 1968 R-18

239   JACOBSON, L. I., ELENEWSKI, J. J., LORDAHL, D. S., & LIROFF, J. H.
              ROLE OF CREATIVITY AND INTELLIGENCE IN CONCEPTUALIZATION.
              JOURNAL OF PERSONALITY AND SOCIAL PSYCHOLOGY, 1968, 10, 431-436.
                     (CORRELATES:PSYCHOLOGICAL, INTELLIGENCE; USED AS CRITERION;
                     NORMATIVE DATA; N=115 UNDERGRADUATES)
              @APPLICATION 1968 M-29

240   KIPNIS, D.
             STUDIES IN CHARACTER STRUCTURE.
             JOURNAL OF PERSONALITY AND SOCIAL PSYCHOLOGY, 1968, 8, 217-227.
                  (MODIFICATION; CORRELATES:PSYCHOLOGICAL, INTELLIGENCE; USED AS
                   CRITERION: 2 STUDIES: N=161 NAVY ENLISTED MEN, 63168 NAVY MEN)
        @APPLICATION 1968 Z-3 L-22 L-24 T-2

241   HODGES, W. F.
             EFFECTS OF EGO THREAT AND THREAT OF PAIN ON STATE ANXIETY.
             JOURNAL OF PERSONALITY AND SOCIAL PSYCHOLOGY, 1968, 8, 364-372.
                  (CORRELATES:PSYCHOLOGICAL, PHYSIOLOGICAL, ENVIRONMENTAL; USED AS
                   CRITERION; N=108 MALE UNDERGRADUATES)
        @APPLICATION 1968 T-2 D-45 Z-13

242   HUNT, M. F., JR., & MILLER, G. R.
             OPEN- AND CLOSED-MINDEDNESS, BELIEF-DISCREPANT COMMUNICATION BEHAVIOR, AND
             TOLERANCE FOR COGNITIVE INCONSISTENCY.
             JOURNAL OF PERSONALITY AND SOCIAL PSYCHOLOGY, 1968, 8, 35-37.
                  (CORRELATES:PSYCHOLOGICAL, ENVIRONMENTAL; USED AS CRITERION;
                   N=77 UNDERGRADUATES)
        @APPLICATION 1968 T-18 O-16

243   NOMIKOS, M. S., OPTON, E., AVERILL, J. R., & LAZARUS, R. S.
             SURPRISE VERSUS SUSPENSE IN THE PRODUCTION OF STRESS REACTION.
             JOURNAL OF PERSONALITY AND SOCIAL PSYCHOLOGY, 1968, 8, 204-208.
                  (CORRELATES:PSYCHOLOGICAL, PHYSIOLOGICAL, ENVIRONMENTAL; N=25 MALE
                   AND 27 FEMALE UNDERGRADUATES)
        @APPLICATION 1968 M-222 C-16 K-24

244   SLOBIN, D. I., MILLER, S. H., & PORTER, L. W.
             FORMS OF ADDRESS AND SOCIAL RELATIONS IN A BUSINESS ORGANIZATION.
             JOURNAL OF PERSONALITY AND SOCIAL PSYCHOLOGY, 1968, 8, 289-293.
                  (CORRELATES:BEHAVIORAL, DEMOGRAPHIC; N=57 MALE AND 30 FEMALE
                   EMPLOYEES)
        @APPLICATION 1968 G-59

245.   TAYLOR, D. A., WHEELER, L., & ALTMAN, I.
             STRESS RELATIONS IN SOCIALLY ISOLATED GROUPS.
             JOURNAL OF PERSONALITY AND SOCIAL PSYCHOLOGY, 1968, 9, 369-376.
                  (CORRELATES:BEHAVIORAL, PSYCHOLOGICAL, ENVIRONMENTAL; N=168 NAVY MEN)
        @APPLICATION 1968 S-311 K-24

246   MARLETT, N. J., & WATSON, D.
             TEST ANXIETY AND IMMEDIATE OR DELAYED FEEDBACK IN A TEST-LIKE AVOIDANCE
             TASK.
             JOURNAL OF PERSONALITY AND SOCIAL PSYCHOLOGY, 1968, 8, 200-203.
                  (CORRELATES:BEHAVIORAL, PHYSIOLOGICAL, ENVIRONMENTAL; USED AS
                   CRITERION; N=220 9TH GRADE MALES, 56 SELECTED)
        @APPLICATION 1968 S-312

247   KLINEBERG, S. L.
             FUTURE TIME PERSPECTIVE AND DELAYED REWARD.
             JOURNAL OF PERSONALITY AND SOCIAL PSYCHOLOGY, 1968, 8, 253-257.
                  (CORRELATES:BEHAVIORAL, PSYCHOLOGICAL; CROSS-CULTURAL APPLICATION;
                   N=47 FRENCH MALADJUSTED AND NORMAL BOYS)
        @APPLICATION 1968 M-20 T-107 W-109 M-159

248   LAMB, C. W.
             PERSONALITY CORRELATES OF HUMOR ENJOYMENT FOLLOWING MOTIVATIONAL AROUSAL.
             JOURNAL OF PERSONALITY AND SOCIAL PSYCHOLOGY, 1968, 9, 237-241.
                  (RELIABILITY:INTERRATER; CORRELATES:PSYCHOLOGICAL, DEMOGRAPHIC,
                   ENVIRONMENTAL; NORMATIVE DATA; N=80 MALE UNDERGRADUATES)
        @APPLICATION 1968 M-16 C-27 R-40

249   LAUGHLIN, P. R., DOHERTY, M. A., & DUNN, R. F.
             INTENTIONAL AND INCIDENTAL CONCEPT FORMATION AS A FUNCTION OF
             MOTIVATION, CREATIVITY, INTELLIGENCE AND SEX.
             JOURNAL OF PERSONALITY AND SOCIAL PSYCHOLOGY, 1968, 8, 401-409.
                  (CORRELATES:PSYCHOLOGICAL, DEMOGRAPHIC, INTELLIGENCE, ENVIRONMENTAL;
                   NORMATIVE DATA; N=348 MALE AND 348 FEMALE HIGH SCHOOL STUDENTS)
        @APPLICATION 1968 M-29

250   LEVANTHAL, D. B., SHEMBERG, K. M., & VAN SCHOELANDT, S. K.
            EFFECTS OF SEX-ROLE ADJUSTMENT UPON THE EXPRESSION OF AGGRESSION.
            JOURNAL OF PERSONALITY AND SOCIAL PSYCHOLOGY, 1968, 8, 393-396.
                (CORRELATES:PSYCHOLOGICAL, DEMOGRAPHIC, ENVIRONMENTAL; USED AS
                CRITERION; BIAS:RESPONSE; 2 STUDIES: N=400 UNDERGRADUATES, 20 MEN
                AND 20 WOMEN SELECTED, N=184 UNDERGRADUATES)
        @APPLICATION 1968 G-26 C-27

251   LEVONIAN, E.
            SELF-ESTEEM AND OPINION CHANGE.
            JOURNAL OF PERSONALITY AND SOCIAL PSYCHOLOGY, 1968, 9, 257-259.
                (RELIABILITY:RETEST; CORRELATES:PSYCHOLOGICAL, ENVIRONMENTAL;
                N=540 UNDERGRADUATES)
        @APPLICATION 1968 L-36

252   MILLMAN, S.
            ANXIETY, COMPREHENSION, AND SUSCEPTIBILITY TO SOCIAL INFLUENCE.
            JOURNAL OF PERSONALITY AND SOCIAL PSYCHOLOGY, 1968, 9, 251-256.
                (CORRELATES:PSYCHOLOGICAL, ENVIRONMENTAL; USED AS CRITERION;
                N=48 UNDERGRADUATES)
        @APPLICATION 1968 B-184 C-27 A-26

253   PHARES, E. J., RICHIE, D. E., & DAVIS, W. L.
            INTERNAL-EXTERNAL CONTROL AND REACTION TO THREAT.
            JOURNAL OF PERSONALITY AND SOCIAL PSYCHOLOGY, 1968, 10, 402-405.
                (MODIFICATION; CORRELATES:PSYCHOLOGICAL, INTELLIGENCE; NORMATIVE
                DATA; N=225 UNDERGRADUATES, 40 SELECTED)
        @APPLICATION 1968 R-18 R-30 M-20 B-46

254   TORCIVIA, J. M., & LAUGHLIN, P. R.
            DOGMATISM AND CONCEPT-ATTAINMENT STRATEGIES.
            JOURNAL OF PERSONALITY AND SOCIAL PSYCHOLOGY, 1968, 8, 397-400.
                (CORRELATES:BEHAVIORAL, PSYCHOLOGICAL, INTELLIGENCE, ENVIRONMENTAL;
                USED AS CRITERION; NORMATIVE DATA; N=42 FEMALE HIGH SCHOOL JUNIORS
                AND SENIORS, 28 SELECTED)
        @APPLICATION 1968 R-8

255   TSUSHIMA, W. T.
            RESPONSES OF IRISH AND ITALIAN PATIENTS OF TWO SOCIAL CLASSES UNDER
            PREOPERATIVE STRESS.
            JOURNAL OF PERSONALITY AND SOCIAL PSYCHOLOGY, 1968, 8, 43-48.
                (DESCRIPTION; RELIABILITY:INTERRATER; CORRELATES:PSYCHOLOGICAL,
                DEMOGRAPHIC; NORMATIVE DATA; BIAS:RESPONSE; N=100 MALE PATIENTS)
        @APPLICATION 1968 H-22 M-20 C-27

256   WALLACH, M. A., & WING, C. W., JR.
            IS RISK A VALUE?
            JOURNAL OF PERSONALITY AND SOCIAL PSYCHOLOGY, 1968, 9, 101-106.
                (CORRELATES:PSYCHOLOGICAL, ENVIRONMENTAL; N=292 MALE AND 195 FEMALE
                UNDERGRADUATES)
        @APPLICATION 1968 K-94

257   ZANDER, A., & FORWARD, J.
            POSITION IN GROUP, ACHIEVEMENT MOTIVATION, AND GROUP ASPIRATIONS.
            JOURNAL OF PERSONALITY AND SOCIAL PSYCHOLOGY, 1968, 8, 282-288.
                (CORRELATES:BEHAVIORAL, PSYCHOLOGICAL, ENVIRONMENTAL; USED AS
                CRITERION; N=120 11TH GRADE BOYS)
        @APPLICATION 1968 M-47 C-40

258   HAMSHER, J. H., GELLER, J. D., & ROTTER, J. B.
            INTERPERSONAL TRUST, INTERNAL-EXTERNAL CONTROL, AND THE WARREN COMMISSION
            REPORT.
            JOURNAL OF PERSONALITY AND SOCIAL PSYCHOLOGY, 1968, 9, 210-215.
                (VALIDITY:CONSTRUCT; CORRELATES:PSYCHOLOGICAL, DEMOGRAPHIC; NORMATIVE
                DATA; N=288 MALE AND 369 FEMALE UNDERGRADUATES AND SMALLER SUBSETS)
        @APPLICATION 1968 R-16 R-18

259   COHEN, A. M., & FOERST, J. R., JR.
            ORGANIZATIONAL BEHAVIORS AND ADAPTATIONS TO ORGANIZATIONAL CHANGE OF
            SENSITIZER AND REPRESSER PROBLEM-SOLVING GROUPS.
            JOURNAL OF PERSONALITY AND SOCIAL PSYCHOLOGY, 1968, 8, 209-216.
                (VALIDITY:CRITERION; CORRELATES:BEHAVIORAL, PSYCHOLOGICAL; USED AS
                CRITERION; N=120 MALE UNDERGRADUATES)
        @APPLICATION 1968 B-46

260   BAXTER, J. C., WINTERS, E. P., & HAMMER, R. E.
          GESTURAL BEHAVIOR DURING A BRIEF INTERVIEW AS A FUNCTION OF COGNITIVE
          VARIABLES.
          JOURNAL OF PERSONALITY AND SOCIAL PSYCHOLOGY, 1968, 8, 303-307.
                (CORRELATES:BEHAVIORAL; USED AS CRITERION; N=20 MALE, 20 FEMALE
                UNDERGRADUATES)
        @APPLICATION 1968 K-23 T-13

261   FEATHER, N. T.
          CHANGE IN CONFIDENCE FOLLOWING SUCCESS OR FAILURE AS A PREDICTOR OF
          SUBSEQUENT PERFORMANCE.
          JOURNAL OF PERSONALITY AND SOCIAL PSYCHOLOGY, 1968, 9, 38-46.
                (DESCRIPTION; VALIDITY:CRITERION; CORRELATES:BEHAVIORAL,
                PSYCHOLOGICAL; USED AS CRITERION; NORMATIVE DATA; N=24 MALE, 36
                FEMALE UNDERGRADUATES)
        @APPLICATION 1968 R-18

262   DARLEY, J. M., & LATANE, B.
          BYSTANDER INTERVENTION IN EMERGENCIES: DIFFUSION OF RESPONSIBILITY.
          JOURNAL OF PERSONALITY AND SOCIAL PSYCHOLOGY, 1968, 8, 377-383.
                (VALIDITY:CRITERION; CORRELATES:BEHAVIORAL, PSYCHOLOGICAL; N=59
                FEMALE AND 13 MALE UNDERGRADUATES)
        @APPLICATION 1968 C-14 C-27 D-95

263   GRIM, P. F., KOHLBERG, L., & WHITE, S. H.
          SOME RELATIONSHIPS BETWEEN CONSCIENCE AND ATTENTIONAL PROCESSES.
          JOURNAL OF PERSONALITY AND SOCIAL PSYCHOLOGY, 1968, 8, 239-252.
                (DESCRIPTION; CORRELATES:PSYCHOLOGICAL, PHYSIOLOGICAL; FACTOR
                ANALYSIS; NORMATIVE DATA; BIAS:RESPONSE; N=22 1ST GRADERS, 22 6TH
                GRADERS, 22 ADULTS)
        @APPLICATION 1968 H-30 H-197 H-198

264   GREENWALD, A. G., & ALBERT, R. D.
          ACCEPTANCE AND RECALL OF IMPROVISED ARGUMENTS.
          JOURNAL OF PERSONALITY AND SOCIAL PSYCHOLOGY, 1968, 8, 31-34.
                (CORRELATES:PSYCHOLOGICAL, ENVIRONMENTAL; 3 SAMPLES: N=47, 47, 104
                MALE AND FEMALE UNDERGRADUATES)
        @APPLICATION 1968 B-18

265   GANZER, V. J.
          EFFECTS OF AUDIENCE PRESENCE AND TEST ANXIETY ON LEARNING AND RETENTION IN
          A SERIAL LEARNING SITUATION.
          JOURNAL OF PERSONALITY AND SOCIAL PSYCHOLOGY, 1968, 8, 194-199.
                (CORRELATES:BEHAVIORAL, PSYCHOLOGICAL; USED AS CRITERION; N=72 FEMALE
                UNDERGRADUATES)
        @APPLICATION 1968 S-5

266   CROWNE, D. P., HOLLAND, C. H., & CONN, L. K.
          PERSONALITY FACTORS IN DISCRIMINATION LEARNING IN CHILDREN.
          JOURNAL OF PERSONALITY AND SOCIAL PSYCHOLOGY, 1968, 10, 420-430.
                (DESCRIPTION; CORRELATES:BEHAVIORAL, PHYSIOLOGICAL, INTELLIGENCE;
                USED AS CRITERION; N=64 MALE, 54 FEMALE 5TH AND 6TH GRADERS)
        @APPLICATION 1968 C-42

267   CLORE, G. L., & BALDRIDGE, B.
          INTERPERSONAL ATTRACTION: THE ROLE OF AGREEMENT AND TOPIC INTEREST.
          JOURNAL OF PERSONALITY AND SOCIAL PSYCHOLOGY, 1968, 9, 340-346.
                (DESCRIPTION; RELIABILITY:INTERNAL CONSISTENCY;
                CORRELATES:PSYCHOLOGICAL, ENVIRONMENTAL; 2 STUDIES: N=84
                UNDERGRADUATES, 84 UNDERGRADUATES)
        @APPLICATION 1968 B-65

268   COWAN, G., & GOLDBERG, F. J.
          NEED ACHIEVEMENT AS A FUNCTION OF THE RACE AND SEX OF FIGURES OF
          SELECTED TAT CARDS.
          JOURNAL OF PERSONALITY AND SOCIAL PSYCHOLOGY, 1967, 5, 245-249.
                (MODIFICATION; RELIABILITY:INTERRATER; CORRELATES:PSYCHOLOGICAL,
                DEMOGRAPHIC; N=67 NEGRO FEMALE UNDERGRADUATES)
        @APPLICATION 1967 M-7 M-20

269   GAMBLE, K. R., & KELLNER, H.
          CREATIVE FUNCTIONING AND COGNITIVE REGRESSION.
          JOURNAL OF PERSONALITY AND SOCIAL PSYCHOLOGY, 1968, 9, 266-271.
                (VALIDITY:CRITERION; CORRELATES:PSYCHOLOGICAL, INTELLIGENCE; USED AS
                CRITERION; N=52 MALE UNDERGRADUATES)
        @APPLICATION 1968 M-29 S-61

270   EPSTEIN, R.
              EFFECTS OF COMMITMENT TO SOCIAL ISOLATION ON CHILDREN'S IMITATIVE BEHAVIOR.
              JOURNAL OF PERSONALITY AND SOCIAL PSYCHOLOGY, 1968, 9, 90-95.
                    (DESCRIPTION; RELIABILITY:RETEST, INTERNAL CONSISTENCY;
                    CORRELATES:PSYCHOLOGICAL, ENVIRONMENTAL; USED AS CRITERION; N=40
                    3RD AND 4TH GRADE GIRLS)
         @APPLICATION 1968 C-42

271   WEINSTEIN, J., AVERILL, J. R., OPTON, E. M., JR., & LAZARUS, R. S.
              DEFENSIVE STYLE AND DISCREPANCY BETWEEN SELF-REPORT AND PHYSIOLOGICAL
              INDEXES OF STRESS.
              JOURNAL OF PERSONALITY AND SOCIAL PSYCHOLOGY, 1968, 10, 406-413.
                    (CORRELATES:PSYCHOLOGICAL, PHYSIOLOGICAL, ENVIRONMENTAL; USED AS
                    CRITERION; 6 STUDIES: N=69, 46, 55, 63, 88 MALE UNDERGRADUATES, 80
                    STUDENTS AND 48 MALE JAPANESE ADULTS)
         @APPLICATION 1968 D-45 B-46 G-22 N-5 B-62 M-222 T-2 W-8

272   HARVEY, O. J., REICH, J. W., & WYER, R. S.
              EFFECTS OF ATTITUDE DIRECTION, ATTITUDE INTENSITY, AND STRUCTURE OF
              BELIEFS UPON DIFFERENTIATION.
              JOURNAL OF PERSONALITY AND SOCIAL PSYCHOLOGY, 1968, 10, 472-478.
                    (CORRELATES:PSYCHOLOGICAL; USED AS CRITERION; NORMATIVE DATA; N=150
                    UNDERGRADUATES, 40 SELECTED)
         @APPLICATION 1968 H-32

273   WYER, R. S., JR., & DERMER, M.
              EFFECT OF CONTEXT AND INSTRUCTIONAL SET UPON EVALUATIONS OF
              PERSONALITY-TRAIT ADJECTIVES.
              JOURNAL OF PERSONALITY AND SOCIAL PSYCHOLOGY, 1968, 9, 7-14.
                    (CORRELATES:PSYCHOLOGICAL, ENVIRONMENTAL; 3 STUDIES: N=33, N=APPROX.
                    68, N=98)
         @APPLICATION 1968 A-92

274   MAEHR, M. L., & VIDEBECK, R.
              PREDISPOSITION TO RISK AND PERSISTENCE UNDER VARYING
              REINFORCEMENT-SUCCESS SCHEDULES.
              JOURNAL OF PERSONALITY AND SOCIAL PSYCHOLOGY, 1968, 9, 96-100.
                    (VALIDITY:CONSTRUCT; CORRELATES:BEHAVIORAL, PSYCHOLOGICAL,
                    ENVIRONMENTAL; FACTOR ANALYSIS; NORMATIVE DATA; N=107 MALE
                    UNDERGRADUATES)
         @APPLICATION 1968 K-87 K-94

275   LEVY, L. H.
              ORIGINALITY AS ROLE-DEFINED BEHAVIOR.
              JOURNAL OF PERSONALITY AND SOCIAL PSYCHOLOGY, 1968, 9, 72-78.
                    (CORRELATES:BEHAVIORAL, PSYCHOLOGICAL, ENVIRONMENTAL; NORMATIVE DATA;
                    N=50 MALE AND 15 FEMALE UNDERGRADUATES)
         @APPLICATION 1968 H-37

276   MARKOWITZ, A.
              INFLUENCE OF THE REPRESSION-SENSITIZATION DIMENSION, AFFECT VALUE, AND
              EGO THREAT ON INCIDENTAL LEARNING.
              JOURNAL OF PERSONALITY AND SOCIAL PSYCHOLOGY, 1969, 11, 374-380.
                    (CORRELATES:BEHAVIORAL, PSYCHOLOGICAL, ENVIRONMENTAL; USED AS
                    CRITERION; NORMATIVE DATA; N=209 FEMALE UNDERGRADUATES)
         @APPLICATION 1969 B-46

277   STREUFERT, S., & STREUFERT, S. C.
              EFFECTS OF CONCEPTUAL STRUCTURE, FAILURE, AND SUCCESS ON ATTRIBUTION OF
              CAUSALITY AND INTERPERSONAL ATTITUDES.
              JOURNAL OF PERSONALITY AND SOCIAL PSYCHOLOGY, 1969, 11, 138-147.
                    (CORRELATES:BEHAVIORAL, PSYCHOLOGICAL, ENVIRONMENTAL; USED AS
                    CRITERION; N=596 UNDERGRADUATES)
         @APPLICATION 1969 S-41

278   STAPERT, J. C., & CLORE, G. L.
              ATTRACTION AND DISAGREEMENT-PRODUCED AROUSAL.
              JOURNAL OF PERSONALITY AND SOCIAL PSYCHOLOGY, 1969, 13, 64-69.
                    (CORRELATES:PSYCHOLOGICAL, ENVIRONMENTAL; NORMATIVE DATA; N=110
                    UNDERGRADUATES)
         @APPLICATION 1969 B-65 B-48 B-195

279   MARTENS, R.
            EFFECT OF AN AUDIENCE ON LEARNING AND PERFORMANCE OF A COMPLEX MOTOR
            SKILL.
            JOURNAL OF PERSONALITY AND SOCIAL PSYCHOLOGY, 1969, 12, 252-260.
                  (CORRELATES:BEHAVIORAL, PSYCHOLOGICAL, PHYSIOLOGICAL; USED AS
                  CRITERION; N=519 MALE UNDERGRADUATES, 96 SELECTED)
       @APPLICATION 1969 T-2

280   PARSONS, O. A., FULGENZI, L. B., & EDELBERG, R.
            AGGRESSIVENESS AND PSYCHOPHYSIOLOGICAL RESPONSIVITY IN GROUPS OF
            REPRESSORS ANS SENSITIZERS.
            JOURNAL OF PERSONALITY AND SOCIAL PSYCHOLOGY, 1969, 12, 235-244.
                  (RELIABILITY:INTERRATER; CORRELATES:BEHAVIORAL, PSYCHOLOGICAL,
                  PHYSIOLOGICAL; USED AS CRITERION; NORMATIVE DATA; 2 STUDIES: N=510
                  MALE UNDERGRADUATES, 120 SELECTED, 30 SELECTED)
       @APPLICATION 1969 B-46 B-2

281   SCHWARZ, J. C.
            CONTRIBUTION OF GENERALIZED EXPECTANCY TO STATED EXPECTANCY UNDER
            CONDITIONS OF SUCCESS AND FAILURE.
            JOURNAL OF PERSONALITY AND SOCIAL PSYCHOLOGY, 1969, 11, 157-164.
                  (CORRELATES:PSYCHOLOGICAL, ENVIRONMENTAL; NORMATIVE DATA; N=136
                  MALE UNDERGRADUATES)
       @APPLICATION 1969 R-154 B-4 C-27 R-18 R-31

282   SUEDFELD, P.
            SENSORY DEPRIVATION STRESS: BIRTH ORDER AND INSTRUCTIONAL SET AS
            INTERACTING VARIABLES.
            JOURNAL OF PERSONALITY AND SOCIAL PSYCHOLOGY, 1969, 11, 70-74.
                  (CORRELATES:PSYCHOLOGICAL, DEMOGRAPHIC, ENVIRONMENTAL; NORMATIVE
                  DATA; N=78 MALE UNDERGRADUATES)
       @APPLICATION 1969 S-66 B-62

283   VINOKUR, A.
            DISTRIBUTION OF INITIAL RISK LEVELS AND GROUP DECISIONS INVOLVING RISK.
            JOURNAL OF PERSONALITY AND SOCIAL PSYCHOLOGY, 1969, 13, 207-214.
                  (CORRELATES:BEHAVIORAL, PSYCHOLOGICAL; USED AS CRITERION; N=78 MALE
                  UNDERGRADUATES)
       @APPLICATION 1969 K-94

284   WAGNER, C., & WHEELER, L.
            MODEL, NEED, AND COST EFFECTS IN HELPING BEHAVIOR.
            JOURNAL OF PERSONALITY AND SOCIAL PSYCHOLOGY, 1969, 12, 111-116.
                  (CORRELATES:BEHAVIORAL, PSYCHOLOGICAL, ENVIRONMENTAL; N=144 NAVY
                  ENLISTED MEN)
       @APPLICATION 1969 F-48 K-66

285   WEINSTEIN, M. S.
            ACHIEVEMENT MOTIVATION AND RISK PREFERENCE.
            JOURNAL OF PERSONALITY AND SOCIAL PSYCHOLOGY, 1969, 13, 153-172.
                  (DESCRIPTION; CORRELATES:BEHAVIORAL, PSYCHOLOGICAL; USED AS
                  CRITERION; FACTOR ANALYSIS; NORMATIVE DATA; N=198 MALE
                  UNDERGRADUATES)
       @APPLICATION 1969 M-47 F-20 A-28 E-2 G-22 S-18 O-3 M-4 M-224 R-18 C-27 A-8 Z-3
       @W-38

286   WIGGINS, N., HOFFMAN, P. J., & TABER, T.
            TYPES OF JUDGES AND CUE UTILIZATION IN JUDGMENTS OF INTELLIGENCE.
            JOURNAL OF PERSONALITY AND SOCIAL PSYCHOLOGY, 1969, 12, 52-59.
                  (RELIABILITY:RETEST; CORRELATES:BEHAVIORAL, PSYCHOLOGICAL,
                  INTELLIGENCE; FACTOR ANALYSIS; N=145 SUBJECTS)
       @APPLICATION 1969 W-9 M-43 S-69 G-186

287   WORTHY, M., GARY, A. L., & KAHN, G. M.
            SELF-DISCLOSURE AS AN EXCHANGE PROCESS.
            JOURNAL OF PERSONALITY AND SOCIAL PSYCHOLOGY, 1969, 13, 59-63.
                  (CORRELATES:BEHAVIORAL, PSYCHOLOGICAL; USED AS CRITERION; N=48
                  UNMARRIED FEMALE UNDERGRADUATES)
       @APPLICATION 1968 R-8

288   WYER, R. S., JR., & SCHWARTZ, S.
            SOME CONTINGENCIES IN THE EFFECTS OF THE SOURCE OF A COMMUNICATION ON THE
            EVALUATION OF THAT COMMUNICATION.
            JOURNAL OF PERSONALITY AND SOCIAL PSYCHOLOGY, 1969, 11, 1-9.
                  (MODIFICATION; CORRELATES:PSYCHOLOGICAL, DEMOGRAPHIC, ENVIRONMENTAL;
                  N=384 UNDERGRADUATES)
       @APPLICATION 1969 H-36

289   HAMILTON, D. L.
        RESPONSES TO COGNITIVE INCONSISTENCIES: PERSONALITY, DISCREPANCY LEVEL, AND
        RESPONSE STABILITY.
        JOURNAL OF PERSONALITY AND SOCIAL PSYCHOLOGY, 1969, 11, 351-362.
            (CORRELATES:BEHAVIORAL, PSYCHOLOGICAL; USED AS CRITERION; NORMATIVE
            DATA: N=229 MALE UNDERGRADUATES)
        aAPPLICATION 1969 B-46 C-27 R-8 L-35

290   ELLIOTT, R.
        TONIC HEART RATE: EXPERIMENTS ON THE EFFECTS OF COLLATIVE VARIABLES LEAD TO
        A HYPOTHESIS ABOUT ITS MOTIVATIONAL SIGNIFICANCE.
        JOURNAL OF PERSONALITY AND SOCIAL PSYCHOLOGY, 1969, 12, 211-228.
            (CORRELATES:PSYCHOLOGICAL, PHYSIOLOGICAL, ENVIRONMENTAL; 2 STUDIES:
            N=64 MALE UNDERGRADUATES, N=24 MALE UNDERGRADUATES)
        aAPPLICATION 1969 S-61

291   FEATHER, N. T.
        ATTRIBUTION OF RESPONSIBILITY AND VALENCE OF SUCCESS AND FAILURE IN
        RELATION TO INITIAL CONFIDENCE AND TASK PERFORMANCE.
        JOURNAL OF PERSONALITY AND SOCIAL PSYCHOLOGY, 1969, 13, 129-144.
            (CORRELATES:PSYCHOLOGICAL; USED AS CRITERION; N=89 MALE, 78 FEMALE
            UNDERGRADUATES)
        aAPPLICATION 1969 J-7

292   GAMBARO, S., & RABIN, A. I.
        DIASTOLIC BLOOD PRESSURE RESPONSES FOLLOWING DIRECT AND DISPLACED
        AGGRESSION AFTER ANGER AROUSAL IN HIGH- AND LOW-GUILT SUBJECTS.
        JOURNAL OF PERSONALITY AND SOCIAL PSYCHOLOGY, 1969, 12, 87-94.
            (RELIABILITY:INTERRATER; CORRELATES:PSYCHOLOGICAL, PHYSIOLOGICAL;
            USED AS CRITERION; N=80 MALE UNDERGRADUATES)
        aAPPLICATION 1969 M-16

293   FEATHER, N. T.
        ATTITUDE AND SELECTIVE RECALL.
        JOURNAL OF PERSONALITY AND SOCIAL PSYCHOLOGY, 1969, 12, 310-319.
            (DESCRIPTION; VALIDITY:CRITERION; CORRELATES:BEHAVIORAL,
            PSYCHOLOGICAL; N=94 MALE AND 83 FEMALE UNDERGRADUATES, 87 MALE AND
            76 FEMALE UNDERGRADUATES)
        aAPPLICATION 1969 R-8 B-37

294   EPSTEIN, G. F.
        MACHIAVELLI AND THE DEVIL'S ADVOCATE.
        JOURNAL OF PERSONALITY AND SOCIAL PSYCHOLOGY, 1969, 11, 38-41.
            (DESCRIPTION; CORRELATES:PSYCHOLOGICAL, ENVIRONMENTAL; USED AS
            CRITERION; N=80 MALE UNDERGRADUATES)
        aAPPLICATION 1969 C-14

295   DOSEY, M. A., & MEISELS, M.
        PERSONAL SPACE AND SELF-PROTECTION.
        JOURNAL OF PERSONALITY AND SOCIAL PSYCHOLOGY, 1969, 11, 93-97.
            (MODIFICATION; RELIABILITY:INTERRATER; VALIDITY:CRITERION;
            CORRELATES:BEHAVIORAL, ENVIRONMENTAL; NORMATIVE DATA; N=91 MALE AND
            95 FEMALE UNDERGRADUATES)
        aAPPLICATION 1969 R-30 J-22

296   CLARK, R. D., III, & WILLEMS, E. P.
        WHERE IS THE RISKY SHIFT? DEPENDENCE ON INSTRUCTIONS.
        JOURNAL OF PERSONALITY AND SOCIAL PSYCHOLOGY, 1969, 13, 215-221.
            (MODIFICATION; CORRELATES:PSYCHOLOGICAL, ENVIRONMENTAL;
            NORMATIVE DATA; N=200 MALE UNDERGRADUATES)
        aAPPLICATION 1969 K-87

297   CLAEYS, W.
        ZEIGARNIK EFFECT, "REVERSED ZEIGARNIK EFFECT," AND PERSONALITY.
        JOURNAL OF PERSONALITY AND SOCIAL PSYCHOLOGY, 1969, 12, 320-327.
            (DESCRIPTION; VALIDITY:CRITERION; CORRELATES:PSYCHOLOGICAL,
            ENVIRONMENTAL; USED AS CRITERION; CROSS-CULTURAL APPLICATION;
            N=40 MALE CONGOLESE STUDENTS)
        aAPPLICATION 1969 E-5

298   CHILD, I. L., COOPERMAN, M., & WOLOWITZ, H. M.
         ESTHETIC PREFERENCE AND OTHER CORRELATES OF ACTIVE VERSUS PASSIVE FOOD
         PREFERENCE.
         JOURNAL OF PERSONALITY AND SOCIAL PSYCHOLOGY, 1969, 11, 75-84.
            (MODIFICATION; DESCRIPTION; RELIABILITY:INTERNAL CONSISTENCY;
            CORRELATES:PSYCHOLOGICAL; FACTOR ANALYSIS; N=105 COLLEGE MEN)
      @APPLICATION 1969 W-182 C-45

299   BERKOWITZ, L. LEPINSKI, J. P., & ANGULO, E. J.
         AWARENESS OF OWN ANGER LEVEL AND SUBSEQUENT AGGRESSION.
         JOURNAL OF PERSONALITY AND SOCIAL PSYCHOLOGY, 1969, 11, 293-300.
            (DESCRIPTION; VALIDITY:CRITERION; CORRELATES:ENVIRONMENTAL; N=48
            COLLEGE MEN)
      @APPLICATION 1969 N-17

300   BANDURA, A., BLANCHARD, E. B., & RITTER, B.
         RELATIVE EFFICACY OF DESENSITIZATION AND MODELING APPROACHES FOR INDUCING
         BEHAVIORAL, AFFECTIVE, AND ATTITUDINAL CHANGES.
         JOURNAL OF PERSONALITY AND SOCIAL PSYCHOLOGY, 1969, 13, 173-199.
            (MODIFICATION; CORRELATES:BEHAVIORAL, PSYCHOLOGICAL; N=23 MALE
            PHOBIC INDIVIDUALS)
      @APPLICATION 1969 W-37

301   BAKER, J. W., II, & SCHAIE, K. W.
         EFFECTS OF AGGRESSING "ALONE" OR "WITH ANOTHER" ON PHYSIOLOGICAL AND
         PSYCHOLOGICAL AROUSAL.
         JOURNAL OF PERSONALITY AND SOCIAL PSYCHOLOGY, 1969, 12, 80-86.
            (DESCRIPTION; CORRELATES:PSYCHOLOGICAL, PHYSIOLOGICAL, ENVIRONMENTAL;
            N=64 UNDERGRADUATE MALES)
      @APPLICATION 1969 C-136

302   AMOROSO, D. M., & WALTERS, R. H.
         EFFECTS OF ANXIETY AND SOCIALLY MEDIATED ANXIETY REDUCTION ON
         PAIRED-ASSOCIATE LEARNING.
         JOURNAL OF PERSONALITY AND SOCIAL PSYCHOLOGY, 1969, 11, 388-396.
            (DESCRIPTION; CORRELATES:BEHAVIORAL, PSYCHOLOGICAL, PHYSIOLOGICAL,
            ENVIRONMENTAL; N=60 FIRSTBORN FEMALE UNDERGRADUATES)
      @APPLICATION 1969 W-181

303   MEHRABIAN, A., & WILLIAMS, M.
         NONVERBAL CONCOMITANTS OF PERCEIVED AND INTENDED PERSUASIVENESS.
         JOURNAL OF PERSONALITY AND SOCIAL PSYCHOLOGY, 1969, 13, 37-58.
            (CORRELATES:BEHAVIORAL, PSYCHOLOGICAL, DEMOGRAPHIC, INTELLIGENCE;
            FACTOR ANALYSIS; 2 STUDIES: N=36 MALE AND 36 FEMALE UNDERGRADUATES,
            N=72)
      @APPLICATION 1969 E-6 J-57 M-4

304   SCHNEIDER, D. J.
         TACTICAL SELF-PRESENTATION AFTER SUCCESS AND FAILURE.
         JOURNAL OF PERSONALITY AND SOCIAL PSYCHOLOGY, 1969, 13, 262-268.
            (CORRELATES:PSYCHOLOGICAL, ENVIRONMENTAL; N=117 MALE UNDERGRADUATES)
      @APPLICATION 1969 C-27 D-5

305   JOHNSON, H. H., & IZZETT, R. R.
         RELATIONSHIP BETWEEN AUTHORITARIANISM AND ATTITUDE CHANGE AS A FUNCTION OF
         SOURCE CREDIBILITY AND TYPE OF COMMUNICATION.
         JOURNAL OF PERSONALITY AND SOCIAL PSYCHOLOGY, 1969, 13, 317-321.
            (CORRELATES:PSYCHOLOGICAL; USED AS CRITERION; NORMATIVE DATA;
            N=468 UNDERGRADUATES)
      @APPLICATION 1969 M-219 J-58 A-5

306   ROGERS, R. W., & THISTLETHWAITE, D. L.
         AN ANALYSIS OF ACTIVE AND PASSIVE DEFENSES IN INDUCING RESISTANCE TO
         PERSUASION.
         JOURNAL OF PERSONALITY AND SOCIAL PSYCHOLOGY, 1969, 11, 301-308.
            (CORRELATES:PSYCHOLOGICAL, ENVIRONMENTAL; N=108 UNDERGRADUATES)
      @APPLICATION 1969 G-12 M-225

307   TEGER, A. I., KATKIN, E. S., & PRUITT, D. G.
         EFFECTS OF ALCOHOLIC BEVERAGES AND THEIR CONGENER CONTENT ON LEVEL AND
         STYLE OF RISK TAKING.
         JOURNAL OF PERSONALITY AND SOCIAL PSYCHOLOGY, 1969, 11, 170-176.
            (CORRELATES:BEHAVIORAL, PSYCHOLOGICAL, DEMOGRAPHIC; N=36 MALE
            GRADUATE STUDENTS)
      @APPLICATION 1969 K-87 K-94

308   LEVINGER, G., & SCHNEIDER, D. J.
               TEST OF THE "RISK IS A VALUE" HYPOTHESIS.
               JOURNAL OF PERSONALITY AND SOCIAL PSYCHOLOGY, 1969, 11, 165-169.
                    (CORRELATES:BEHAVIORAL, PSYCHOLOGICAL; N=250 UNDERGRADUATES)
           @APPLICATION 1969 K-87

309   KARLINS, M., COFFMAN, T. L., & WALTERS, G.
               ON THE FADING OF SOCIAL STEREOTYPES: STUDIES IN THREE GENERATIONS OF
               COLLEGE STUDENTS.
               JOURNAL OF PERSONALITY AND SOCIAL PSYCHOLOGY, 1969, 13, 1-16.
                    (MODIFICATION; CORRELATES:PSYCHOLOGICAL, DEMOGRAPHIC; NORMATIVE
                    DATA; N=150 UNDERGRADUATES)
           @APPLICATION 1969 K-30

310   LAY, C. H., & JACKSON, D. N.
               ANALYSIS OF THE GENERALITY OF TRAIT-INFERENTIAL RELATIONSHIPS.
               JOURNAL OF PERSONALITY AND SOCIAL PSYCHOLOGY, 1969, 12, 12-21.
                    (MODIFICATION; CORRELATES:PSYCHOLOGICAL, DEMOGRAPHIC; FACTOR
                    ANALYSIS; N=235 UNDERGRADUATES)
           @APPLICATION 1969 J-1

311   ROSENBERG, M. J.
               COGNITIVE REORGANIZATION IN RESPONSE TO THE HYPNOTIC REVERSAL OF
               ATTITUDINAL AFFECT.
               JOURNAL OF PERSONALITY, 1960, 28, 39-63.
                    (DESCRIPTION; CORRELATES:BEHAVIORAL; N=22)
           @APPLICATION 1960 R-38

312   WALLACH, M. A., & GAHM, R. C.
               PERSONALITY FUNCTIONS OF GRAPHIC CONSTRICTION AND EXPANSIVENESS.
               JOURNAL OF PERSONALITY, 1960, 28, 73-88.
                    (CORRELATES:BEHAVIORAL, PSYCHOLOGICAL; N=76 FEMALE COLLEGE STUDENTS)
           @APPLICATION 1960 E-40 E-5

313   BROVERMAN, D. M.
               DIMENSIONS OF COGNITIVE STYLE.
               JOURNAL OF PERSONALITY, 1960, 28, 167-185.
                    (DESCRIPTION; CORRELATES:PSYCHOLOGICAL, INTELLIGENCE;
                    USED AS CRITERION; NORMATIVE DATA; N=46 MALE STUDENTS)
           @APPLICATION 1960 S-61

314   SARNOFF, I.
               REACTION FORMATION AND CYNICISM.
               JOURNAL OF PERSONALITY, 1960, 28, 129-143.
                    (CORRELATES:PSYCHOLOGICAL; N=124 MALE UNDERGRADUATES)
           @APPLICATION 1960 B-176 M-20

315   CHANCE, J. E., & MEADERS, W.
               NEEDS AND INTERPERSONAL PERCEPTION.
               JOURNAL OF PERSONALITY, 1960, 28, 200-209.
                    (CORRELATES:BEHAVIORAL; USED AS CRITERION; N=96 MALE UNDERGRADUATES)
           @APPLICATION 1960 E-2

316   BROVERMAN, D. M.
               COGNITIVE STYLE AND INTRA-INDIVIDUAL VARIATION IN ABILITIES.
               JOURNAL OF PERSONALITY, 1960, 28, 240-255.
                    (CORRELATES:INTELLIGENCE; USED AS CRITERION; N=35 MALES)
           @APPLICATION 1960 S-61

317   GOLDMAN, A. E.
               SYMBOLIC REPRESENTATION IN SCHIZOPHRENIA.
               JOURNAL OF PERSONALITY, 1960, 28, 293-316.
                    (CORRELATES:PSYCHOLOGICAL; N=15 NORMAL AND 15 SCHIZOPHRENIC FEMALES)
           @APPLICATION 1960 O-16

318   ROSEN, E.
               CONNOTATIVE MEANINGS OF RORSCHACH INKBLOTS, RESPONSES, AND DETERMINANTS.
               JOURNAL OF PERSONALITY, 1960, 28, 413-426.
                    (VALIDITY:CONSTRUCT; CORRELATES:PSYCHOLOGICAL; N=28 MALE, 29
                    FEMALE STUDENTS, 29 MALE AND 7 FEMALE CLINICIANS)
           @APPLICATION 1960 R-30

319   ROSENSTEIN, A. J.
          PSYCHOMETRIC VERSUS PHYSIOLOGICAL ANXIETY AND SERIAL LEARNING.
          JOURNAL OF PERSONALITY, 1960, 28, 279-292.
               (VALIDITY:CONSTRUCT; CORRELATES:PSYCHOLOGICAL, PHYSIOLOGICAL,
               INTELLIGENCE; USED AS CRITERION; N=104 STUDENTS)
       @APPLICATION 1960 M-4

320   SNYDER, A. F., MISCHEL, W., & LOTT, B. E.
          VALUE, INFORMATION, AND CONFORMITY BEHAVIOR.
          JOURNAL OF PERSONALITY, 1960, 28, 333-341.
               (USED AS CRITERION; N=106 STUDENTS)
       @APPLICATION 1960 A-7

321   FEFFER, M. H., & GOUREVITCH, V.
          COGNITIVE ASPECTS OF ROLE-TAKING IN CHILDREN.
          JOURNAL OF PERSONALITY, 1960, 28, 383-396.
               (MODIFICATION; RELIABILITY:INTERNAL CONSISTENCY;
               CORRELATES:PSYCHOLOGICAL, INTELLIGENCE; N=68 BOYS)
       @APPLICATION 1960 S-97

322   VAN DE CASTLE, R. L.
          PERCEPTUAL DEFENSE IN A BINOCULAR-RIVALRY SITUATION.
          JOURNAL OF PERSONALITY, 1960, 28, 448-462.
               (CORRELATES PSYCHOLOGICAL; USED AS CRITERION; N=225 STUDENTS)
       @APPLICATION 1960 R-30 W-8 W-41 E-2

323   MUUSS, R. E.
          THE EFFECTS OF A ONE- AND TWO-YEAR CAUSAL-LEARNING PROGRAM.
          JOURNAL OF PERSONALITY, 1960, 28, 479-491.
               (DESCRIPTION; RELIABILITY:INTERNAL CONSISTENCY; CORRELATES:
               PSYCHOLOGICAL, ENVIRONMENTAL; N=280 SIXTH-GRADERS)
       @APPLICATION 1960 G-111 C-55 K-38 L-116 L-117 O-9 C-249

324   WALTERS, R. H., MARSHALL, W. E., & SHOOTER, J. R.
          ANXIETY, ISOLATION, AND SUSCEPTIBILITY TO SOCIAL INFLUENCE.
          JOURNAL OF PERSONALITY, 1960, 28, 518-529
               (MODIFICATION; CORRELATES:BEHAVIORAL; N=36 BOYS)
       @APPLICATION 1960 S-170

325   ZANDER, A., STOTLAND, E., & WOLFE, D.
          UNIT OF GROUP, IDENTIFICATION WITH GROUP, AND SELF-ESTEEM OF MEMBERS.
          JOURNAL OF PERSONALITY, 1960, 28, 463-478.
               (CORRELATES:BEHAVIORAL, PSYCHOLOGICAL, ENVIRONMENTAL;
               N=162 FEMALE STUDENTS)
       @APPLICATION 1960 J-32

326   DECHARMS, R., & ROSENBAUM, M. E.
          STATUS VARIABLES AND MATCHING BEHAVIOR.
          JOURNAL OF PERSONALITY, 1960, 28, 492-502.
               (CORRELATES:BEHAVIORAL; N=72 NAVEL CADETS)
       @APPLICATION 1960 D-14

327   ROTHAUS, P., & WORCHEL, P.
          THE INHIBITION OF AGGRESSION UNDER NON-ARBITRARY FRUSTRATION.
          JOURNAL OF PERSONALITY, 1960, 28, 108-117.
               (MODIFICATION; CORRELATES:PSYCHOLOGICAL; N=120 MALE AND 98 FEMALE
               COLLEGE STUDENTS)
       @APPLICATION 1960 W-21 P-72

328   WAGNER, R. F., & WILLIAMS, J. E.
          AN ANALYSIS OF SPEECH BEHAVIOR ON GROUPS DIFFERING IN ACHIEVEMENT IMAGERY
          AND DEFENSIVENESS.
          JOURNAL OF PERSONALITY, 1961, 29, 1-9.
               (MODIFICATION; CORRELATES:PSYCHOLOGICAL; USED AS CRITERION; N=170
               MALE COLLEGE STUDENTS)
       @APPLICATION 1961 H-74 D-45

329   SIMKINS, L.
          GENERALIZATION EFFECTS OF HOSTILE VERB REINFORCEMENT AS A FUNCTION OF
          STIMULUS SIMILARITY AND TYPE OF REINFORCER.
          JOURNAL OF PERSONALITY, 1961, 29, 64-72.
               (CORRELATES:PSYCHOLOGICAL, ENVIRONMENTAL; USED AS CRITERION;
               N=40 COLLEGE STUDENTS)
       @APPLICATION 1961 R-12

330   WORELL, L., & CASTENADA, A.
            RESPONSE TO CONFLICT AS A FUNCTION OF RESPONSE-DEFINED ANXIETY.
            JOURNAL OF PERSONALITY, 1961, 29, 10-29.
                (CORRELATES:PSCYHOLOGICAL, ENVIRONMENTAL; USED AS CRITERION;
                N=64 COLLEGE MALES)
         @APPLICATION 1961 T-2

331   HOKANSON, J. E.
            VASCULAR AND PSYCHOGALVANIC EFFECTS OF EXPERIMENTALLY AROUSED ANGER.
            JOURNAL OF PERSONALITY, 1961, 29, 30-39.
                (CORRELATES:PHYSIOLOGICAL; USED AS CRITERION; N=80 COLLEGE MALES)
         @APPLICATION 1961 S-24 M-20

332   HOWARD, K. I., & FISKE, D. W.
            CHANGES IN RELATIVE STRENGTH OF NATURALLY ACQUIRED RESPONSES AS A FUNCTION
            OF INTERVENING EXPERIENCE.
            JOURNAL OF PERSONALITY, 1961, 29, 73-80.
                (CORRELATES:ENVIRONMENTAL; USED AS CRITERION; N=48 MALE
                VETERAN PATIENTS)
         @APPLICATION 1961 R-27

333   MILGRAM, N., & GOODGLASS, H.
            ROLE STYLE VERSUS COGNITIVE MATURATION IN WORD ASSOCIATIONS OF ADULTS AND
            CHILDREN.
            JOURNAL OF PERSONALITY, 1961, 29, 81-93.
                (CORRELATES: PSYCHOLOGICAL, DEMOGRAPHIC, ENVIRONMENTAL;
                USED AS CRITERION: NORMATIVE DATA; N=300 ELEMENTARY SCHOOL CHILDREN)
         @APPLICATION 1961 M-247

334   BIRNEY, R. C., & HOUSTON, J. P.
            THE EFFECTS OF CREATIVITY, NORM DISTANCE, AND INSTRUCTIONS ON SOCIAL
            INFLUENCE.
            JOURNAL OF PERSONALITY, 1961, 29, 294-302.
                (CORRELATES:BEHAVIORAL: 60 COLLEGE FRESHMEN MALES)
         @APPLICATION 1961 B-156 B-157 B-158

335   BIALER, I.
            CONCEPTUALIZATION OF SUCCESS AND FAILURE IN MENTALLY RETARDED AND NORMAL
            CHILDREN.
            JOURNAL OF PERSONALITY, 1961, 29, 303-320.
                (CORRELATES:BEHAVIORAL, PSYCHOLOGICAL, INTELLIGENCE; N=44 NORMAL
                AND 45 RETARDED CHILDREN)
         @APPLICATION 1961 J-6

336   LONDON, P., & FUHRER, M.
            HYPNOSIS, MOTIVATION AND PERFORMANCE.
            JOURNAL OF PERSONALITY, 1961, 29, 321-333.
                (CORRELATES:PHYSIOLOGICAL; USED AS CRITERION; N=55 FEMALES)
         @APPLICATION 1961 W-31

337   LOSEN, S. M.
            THE DIFFERENTIAL EFFECTS OF CENSURE ON THE PROBLEM-SOLVING BEHAVIOR OF
            SCHIZOPHRENIC AND NORMAL SUBJECTS.
            JOURNAL OF PERSONALITY, 1961, 29, 259-272.
                (CORRELATES:INTELLIGENCE; USED AS CRITERION; N=60 SCHIZOPHRENIC
                AND 45 NORMAL ADULTS)
         @APPLICATION 1961 P-32

338   STOTLAND, E., & COLTRELL, N. B.
            SELF-ESTEEM, GROUP INTERACTION, AND GROUP INFLUENCE ON PERFORMANCE.
            JOURNAL OF PERSONALITY, 1961, 29, 273-284.
                (CORRELATES:BEHAVIORAL: N=147 STUDENTS)
         @APPLICATION 1961 W-71

339   SECHREST, L., & JACKSON, D. N.
            SOCIAL INTELLIGENCE AND ACCURACY OF INTERPERSONAL PREDICTIONS.
            JOURNAL OF PERSONALITY, 1961, 29, 167-182.
                (RELIABILITY:INTERNAL CONSISTENCY; VALIDITY:CONSTRUCT, CRITERION;
                CORRELATES:PSYCHOLOGICAL; BIAS:RESPONSE; N=60 FIRST YEAR FEMALE
                NURSING TRAINEES)
         @APPLICATION 1961 B-76 B-154 B-153 D-45

340   HILGARD, E. R., & HOMMEL, L. S.
              SELECTIVE AMNESIA FOR EVENTS WITHIN HYPNOSIS IN RELATION TO REPRESSION.
              JOURNAL OF PERSONALITY, 1961, 29, 205-216.
                    (MODIFICATION; RELIABILITY:RETEST; CORRELATES:BEHAVIORAL;
                    USED AS CRITERION; N=124 COLLEGE STUDENTS)
        @APPLICATION 1961 W-31

341   CARLSON, E. R.
              MOTIVATION AND SET IN ACQUIRING INFORMATION ABOUT PERSONS.
              JOURNAL OF PERSONALITY, 1961, 29, 285-293.
                    (CORRELATES:PSYCHOLOGICAL; N=63 MALE AND 69 FEMALE UNDERGRADUATES)
        @APPLICATION 1961 E-2

342   BYRNE, D.
              THE REPRESSION-SENSITIZATION SCALE: RATIONALE, RELIABILITY AND VALIDITY.
              JOURNAL OF PERSONALITY, 1961, 29, 334-349.
                    (RELIABILITY:RETEST, INTERNAL CONSISTENCY; VALIDITY:CONSTRUCT;
                    CORRELATES:PSYCHOLOGICAL, INTELLIGENCE; N=90 COLLEGE STUDENTS
                    IN SEVEN STUDIES)
        @APPLICATION 1961 D-45 V-4 W-21 A-5 M-20 G-21

343   CROMWELL, R. L., ROSENTHAL, D., SHAKOW, D., & ZAHN, T. P.
              REACTION TIME, LOCUS OF CONTROL, CHOICE BEHAVIOR, AND DESCRIPTIONS OF
              PARENTAL BEHAVIOR IN SCHIZOPHRENIC AND NORMAL SUBJECTS.
              JOURNAL OF PERSONALITY, 1961, 29, 363-379.
                    (DESCRIPTION; CORRELATES:PSYCHOLOGICAL, ENVIRONMENTAL;
                    NORMATIVE DATA; N=15 MALE SCHIZOPHRENICS AND 15 NORMALS)
        @APPLICATION 1961 J-6 B-115 S-8 L-159

344   SINGER, J. L.
              IMAGINATION AND WAITING ABILITY IN YOUNG CHILDREN.
              JOURNAL OF PERSONALITY, 1961, 29, 396-413.
                    (CORRELATES:BEHAVIORAL, PSYCHOLOGICAL, INTELLIGENCE; N=40 CHILDREN
                    AGES 6-9)
        @APPLICATION W-145 M-7

345   KAGAN, J., & MOSS, H. A.
              AVAILABILITY OF CONFLICTFUL IDEAS: A NEGLECTED PARAMETER IN ASSESSING
              PROJECTIVE TEST RESPONSES.
              JOURNAL OF PERSONALITY, 1961, 29, 217-234.
                    (MODIFICATION; DESCRIPTION; RELIABILITY:INTERNAL CONSISTENCY,
                    INTER-RATER; CORRELATES:PSYCHOLOGICAL; N=69 MALE AND FEMALE
                    YOUNG ADULTS AND 30 COLLEGE FEMALES)
        @APPLICATION 1961 M-20 K-86 H-37 R-30

346   BUDNER, S.
              INTOLERANCE OF AMBIGUITY AS A PERSONALITY VARIABLE.
              JOURNAL OF PERSONALITY, 1962, 30, 29-50.
                    (CORRELATES:PSYCHOLOGICAL; 17 SAMPLES OF STUDENTS MEDIAN N=57)
        @APPLICATION 1962 C-31 C-14 E-1 S-65 E-41 O-14

347   STRICKER, G.
              THE CONSTRUCTION AND PARTIAL VALIDATION OF AN OBJECTIVELY SCORABLE
              APPERCEPTION TEST.
              JOURNAL OF PERSONALITY, 1962, 30, 51-62.
                    (CORRELATES:PSYCHOLOGICAL; USED AS CRITERION; N=47 COLLEGE FRESHMEN)
        @APPLICATION 1962 C-27 N-17

348   RYCHLAK, J. F., & EACKER, J. N.
              THE EFFECTS OF ANXIETY, DELAY, AND REINFORCEMENT ON GENERALIZED
              EXPECTANCIES.
              JOURNAL OF PERSONALITY, 1962, 30, 123-134.
                    (CORRELATES:BEHAVIORAL, PSYCHOLOGICAL; USED AS CRITERION;
                    N=58 UNDERGRADUATES)
        @APPLICATION 1962 T-2

349   WEITMAN, M.
              MORE THAN ONE KIND OF AUTHORITARIANISM.
              JOURNAL OF PERSONALITY, 1962, 30, 193-208.
                    (RELIABILITY:INTER-RATER; VALIDITY:CONSTRUCT; CORRELATES:
                    PSYCHOLOGICAL, DEMOGRAPHIC; USED AS CRITERION; N=121 COLLEGE
                    STUDENTS)
        @APPLICATION T-20 A-29 H-113 A-5

350   MADDI, S. R., CHARLENS, A. M., MADDI, D., & SMITH, A. J.
            EFFECTS OF MONOTONY AND NOVELTY ON IMAGINATIVE PRODUCTIONS.
            JOURNAL OF PERSONALITY, 1962, 30, 513-527.
                (RELIABILITY:INTER-RATER;; CORRELATES:PSYCHOLOGICAL; N=204
                MALE UNDERGRADUATES)
        @APPLICATION 1962 M-20

351   WILKINS, E. J., & DECHARMS, R.
            AUTHORITARIANISM AND RESPONSE TO POWER CUES.
            JOURNAL OF PERSONALITY, 1962, 30, 439-457.
                (CORRELATES:PSYCHOLOGICAL, DEMOGRAPHIC; USED AS CRITERION; N=80
                MALE STUDENTS)
        @APPLICATION 1962 A-5

352   ROSENBAUM, M. E., HORNE, W. C., & CHALMERS, D. K.
            LEVEL OF SELF-ESTEEM AND THE LEARNING OF IMITATION AND NONIMITATION.
            JOURNAL OF PERSONALITY, 1962, 30, 147-156.
                (CORRELATES:PSYCHOLOGICAL, INTELLIGENCE; USED AS CRITERION;
                N=84 COLLEGE STUDENTS)
        @APPLICATION 1962 R-77

353   BYRNE, D.
            RESPONSE TO ATTITUDE SIMILARITY-DISSIMILARITY AS A FUNCTION OF AFFILIATION
            NEED.
            JOURNAL OF PERSONALITY, 1962, 30, 164-177.
                (MODIFICATION; RELIABILITY:INTER-RATER; CORRELATES: PSYCHOLOGICAL;
                USED AS CRITERION: NORMATIVE DATA; N=112 COLLEGE STUDENTS)
        @APPLICATION 1962 B-65 B-195 H-150

354   SCHOOLER, C., & SCARR, S.
            AFFILIATION AMONG CHRONIC SCHIZOPHRENICS: RELATION TO INTERPERSONAL AND
            BIRTH ORDER FACTORS.
            JOURNAL OF PERSONALITY, 1962, 30, 178-192.
                (RELIABILITY:INTER-RATER; CORRELATES: BEHAVIORAL, PSYCHOLOGICAL,
                INTELLIGENCE, ENVIRONMENTAL; FACTOR ANALYSIS; N=45 CAUCASIAN
                FEMALES AGES 21-65 HOSPITALIZED AS SCHIZOPHRENICS AT LEAST 21
                MONTHS)
        @APPLICATION 1962 R-30 K-89 S-173

355   ALLPORT, G. W.
            THE GENERAL AND THE UNIQUE IN PSYCHOLOGICAL SCIENCE.
            JOURNAL OF PERSONALITY, 1962, 30, 405-422.
                (DESCRIPTION; REVIEW ARTICLE; NO SAMPLE)
        @APPLICATION 1962 C-2 K-23 A-7 S-30

356   HARLESTON, B. W.
            TEST ANXIETY AND PERFORMANCE IN PROBLEM-SOLVING SITUATIONS.
            JOURNAL OF PERSONALITY, 1962, 30, 557-573.
                (MODIFICATION; CORRELATES:BEHAVIORAL, INTELLIGENCE; USED AS
                CRITERION; N=60 MALE AND 60 FEMALE UNDERGRADUATES; 21 MALE
                AND 21 FEMALE UNDERGRADUATES)
        @APPLICATION 1962 M-4

357   CHILD, I. L.
            PERSONAL PREFERENCES AS AN EXPRESSION OF AESTHETIC SENSITIVITY.
            JOURNAL OF PERSONALITY, 1962, 30, 496-512.
                (MENTION; CORRELATES:PSYCHOLOGICAL; N=44 MALE STUDENTS)
        @APPLICATION 1962 B-77 B-76 M-22 C-61 A-5

358   GOLANN, S. E.
            THE CREATIVITY MOTIVE.
            JOURNAL OF PERSONALITY, 1962, 30, 588-600.
                (CORRELATES:PSYCHOLOGICAL; N=150 UNDERGRADUATES, 24 EIGHTH GRADERS
                AND 29 SIXTH GRADERS)
        @APPLICATION 1962 W-9

359   EXLINE, R. V.
            EFFECTS OF NEED FOR AFFILIATION, SEX, AND THE SIGHT OF OTHERS UPON INITIAL
            COMMUNICATIONS IN PROBLEM-SOLVING GROUPS.
            JOURNAL OF PERSONALITY, 1962, 30, 541-556.
                (VALIDITY:CRITERION; CORRELATES:BEHAVIORAL, PSYCHOLOGICAL,
                ENVIRONMENTAL; USED AS CRITERION; N=48 MALE, 48 FEMALE
                UNDERGRADUATES)
        @APPLICATION 1962 F-20

360   BYRNE, D., MCDONALD, R. D., & MIKAWA, J.
             APPROACH AND AVOIDANCE AFFILIATION MOTIVES.
             JOURNAL OF PERSONALITY, 1963, 31, 21-37.
                  (RELIABILITY:INTERNAL CONSISTENCY; INTERRATER; VALIDITY:CONSTRUCT;
                  CORRELATES:PSYCHOLOGICAL; USED AS CRITERION; N=105 STUDENT
                  EXPERIMENT 1 AND 89 STUDENT EXPERIMENT 2)
        @APPLICATION 1963 M-47 M-123 M-20

361   EXLINE, R. V.
             EXPLORATIONS IN THE PROCESS OF PERSON PERCEPTION: VISUAL INTERACTION IN
             RELATION TO COMPETITION, SEX, AND NEED FOR AFFILIATION.
             JOURNAL OF PERSONALITY, 1963, 31, 1-20.
                  (CORRELATES:BEHAVIORAL; USED AS CRITERION; N=16 GROUPS OF 3 MEN AND
                  16 GROUPS OF 3 WOMEN)
        @APPLICATION 1963 F-20

362   KLEIN, E. B.
             STYLISTIC COMPONENTS OF RESPONSE AS RELATED TO ATTITUDE CHANGE.
             JOURNAL OF PERSONALITY, 1963, 31, 38-51.
                  (CORRELATES:PSYCHOLOGICAL; USED AS CRITERION; CROSS-CULTURAL
                  APPLICATION; N=300 STUDENTS FROM EACH OF 3 COLLEGES)
        @APPLICATION 1963 C-31 K-92

363   LEVITT, E. E., BRADY, J. P., & LUBIN, B.
             CORRELATES OF HYPNOTIZABILITY IN YOUNG WOMEN: ANXIETY AND DEPENDENCY.
             JOURNAL OF PERSONALITY, 1963, 31, 52-57.
                  (CORRELATES:PSYCHOLOGICAL; N=31 STUDENT NURSES)
        @APPLICATION 1963 E-2 G-26 L-82 C-136 W-30

364   GORE, P. M., & ROTTER, J. B.
             A PERSONALITY CORRELATE OF SOCIAL ACTION.
             JOURNAL OF PERSONALITY, 1963, 31, 58-64.
                  (CORRELATES:BEHAVIORAL; N=62 MALE STUDENTS AND 54 FEMALE STUDENTS)
        @APPLICATION 1963 R-18 C-27

365   SECORD, P. F., & BERSCHEID, E. S.
             STEREOTYPING AND THE GENERALITY OF IMPLICIT PERSONALITY THEORY.
             JOURNAL OF PERSONALITY, 1963, 31, 65-78.
                  (RELIABILITY:RETEST; USED AS CRITERION; N=79 UPPER DIVISION
                  EDUCATION STUDENTS)
        @APPLICATION 1963 S-178

366   WOLFE, R.
             THE ROLE OF CONCEPTUAL SYSTEMS IN COGNITIVE FUNCTIONING AT VARYING LEVELS
             OF AGE AND INTELLIGENCE.
             JOURNAL OF PERSONALITY, 1963, 31, 108-123.
                  (MODIFICATION; CORRELATES:PSYCHOLOGICAL, DEMOGRAPHIC, INTELLIGENCE;
                  USED AS CRITERION; N=910 BOYS)
        @APPLICATION 1963 S-177 S-97 G-122

367   HOOD, A. B.
             A STUDY OF THE RELATIONSHIP BETWEEN PHYSIQUE AND PERSONALITY VARIABLES
             MEASURED BY THE MMPI.
             JOURNAL OF PERSONALITY, 1963, 31, 97-107.
                  (CORRELATES:PHYSIOLOGICAL; N= STUDENTS IN EXTREMES OF HEIGHT AND
                  WEIGHT)
        @APPLICATION 1963 D-45

368   ZIMBARDO, P. G., BARNARD, J. W., & BERKOWITZ, L.
             THE ROLE OF ANXIETY AND DEFENSIVENESS IN CHILDREN'S VERBAL BEHAVIOR.
             JOURNAL OF PERSONALITY, 1963, 31, 79-96.
                  (CORRELATES:BEHAVIORAL, PSYCHOLOGICAL, INTELLIGENCE; USED AS
                  CRITERION; N=40 THIRD GRADERS)
        @APPLICATION 1963 S-35 S-79

369   ZIMBARDO, P.
             EMOTIONAL COMPARISON AND SELF ESTEEM AS DETERMINANTS OF AFFILIATION.
             JOURNAL OF PERSONALITY, 1963, 31, 142-162.
                  (CORRELATES:BEHAVIORAL, DEMOGRAPHIC; N=99 MALE UNDERGRADUATES)
        @APPLICATION 1963 J-34 Z-22

370   ROBBINS, P. R.
             LEVEL OF ANXIETY, INTERFERENCE PRONENESS, AND DEFENSIVE REACTIONS TO FEAR-
             AROUSING INFORMATION.
             JOURNAL OF PERSONALITY, 1963, 31, 163-178.
                    (MODIFICATION; RELIABILITY:INTERNAL CONSISTENCY;
                    CORRELATES:PSYCHOLOGICAL; N=83 MALE AND FEMALE STUDENTS)
             @APPLICATION 1963 N-17 L-80 R-78

371   NUNNALLY, J. C., & MAUGHER, R. L.
             CORRELATES OF SEMANTIC HABITS.
             JOURNAL OF PERSONALITY, 1963, 31, 192-202.
                    (MENTION; CORRELATES:PSYCHOLOGICAL, INTELLIGENCE; BIAS:RESPONSE; N=83
                    MALE AND FEMALE STUDENTS)
             @APPLICATION 1963 N-6 T-20 E-5 E-2 T-2 C-123 D-45

372   BREGER, L.
             CONFORMITY AS A FUNCTION OF THE ABILITY TO EXPRESS HOSTILITY.
             JOURNAL OF PERSONALITY, 1963, 31, 247-257.
                    (RELIABILITY:INTERRATER; CORRELATES:BEHAVIORAL, PSYCHOLOGICAL; N=104
                    FEMALE UNDERGRADUATES)
             @APPLICATION 1963 B-32

373   WORCHEL, P., & MCCORMICK, B. L.
             SELF-CONCEPT AND DISSONANCE REDUCTION.
             JOURNAL OF PERSONALITY, 1963, 31, 588-599.
                    (USED AS CRITERION: N=60 COLLEGE MALES)
             @APPLICATION 1963 W-21

374   SMITH, C. P.
             ACHIEVEMENT-RELATED MOTIVES AND GOAL SETTING UNDER DIFFERENT CONDITIONS.
             JOURNAL OF PERSONALITY, 1963, 31, 124-140.
                    (RELIABILITY:INTERRATER; CORRELATES:PSYCHOLOGICAL, INTELLIGENCE; USED
                    AS CRITERION; N=125 STUDENTS)
             @APPLICATION 1963 M-4 M-7

375   WALLACH, M. A., & THOMAS, H. L.
             GRAPHIC CONSTRICTION AND EXPANSIVENESS AS A FUNCTION OF INDUCED SOCIAL
             ISOLATION AND SOCIAL INTERACTION: EXPERIMENTAL MANIPULATIONS AND
             PERSONALITY EFFECTS.
             JOURNAL OF PERSONALITY, 1963, 31, 491-509.
                    (USED AS CRITERION; N=80 COLLEGE FEMALES)
             @APPLICATION 1963 E-5

376   SAMPSON, E. E.
             ACHIEVEMENT IN CONFLICT.
             JOURNAL OF PERSONALITY, 1963, 31, 510-516.
                    (USED AS CRITERION; N=48 COLLEGE FEMALES)
             @APPLICATION 1963 F-20

377   RAND, G., WAPNER, S., WERNER, H., & MCFARLAND, J. H.
             AGE DIFFERENCES IN PERFORMANCE ON THE STROOP COLOR-WORD TEST.
             JOURNAL OF PERSONALITY, 1963, 31, 534-558.
                    (DESCRIPTION; CORRELATES:DEMOGRAPHIC; NORMATIVE DATA; N=40 CHILDREN
                    AGES 6-17)
             @APPLICATION 1963 S-61

378   PALMER, R. D.
             HAND DIFFERENTIATION AND PSYCHOLOGICAL FUNCTIONING.
             JOURNAL OF PERSONALITY, 1963, 31, 445-461.
                    (MODIFICATION; MENTION; CORRELATES:PSYCHOLOGICAL, INTELLIGENCE; USED
                    AS CRITERION; N=35 COLLEGE MALES AND 55 COLLEGE MALES)
             @APPLICATION 1963 G-21 T-2 W-185 D-45 G-22 W-8 B-5 G-118K-17

379   HARVEY, O. J.
             AUTHORITARIANISM AND CONCEPTUAL FUNCTIONING IN VARIED CONDITIONS.
             JOURNAL OF PERSONALITY, 1963, 31, 462-470.
                    (MENTION; REVIEW; CORRELATES:BEHAVIORAL, PSYCHOLOGICAL; MEDIAN
                    N=105)
             @APPLICATION 1963 A-5 W-55 H-112

380   BATTLE, E. S., & ROTTER, J. B.
            CHILDREN'S FEELINGS OF PERSONAL CONTROL AS RELATED TO SOCIAL CLASS AND
            ETHNIC GROUP.
            JOURNAL OF PERSONALITY, 1963, 31, 482-490.
                (CORRELATES:DEMOGRAPHIC; N=80 ELEMENTARY SCHOOL CHILDREN)
        @APPLICATION 1963 B-115

381   KARP, S. A., POSTER, D. C., & GOODMAN, A.
            DIFFERENTIATION IN ALCOHOLIC WOMEN.
            JOURNAL OF PERSONALITY, 1963, 31, 386-393.
                (CORRELATES:BEHAVIORAL, PSYCHOLOGICAL, DEMOGRAPHIC; N=24 ALCOHOLIC
                WOMEN, 24 CONTROLS)
        @APPLICATION 1963 W-19 W-72 W-20 M-58

382   CONNERS, C. K.
            BIRTH ORDER AND NEEDS FOR AFFILIATION.
            JOURNAL OF PERSONALITY, 1963, 31, 408-416.
                (MODIFICATION; CORRELATES:PSYCHOLOGICAL, DEMOGRAPHIC; N=172 COLLEGE
                FRATERNITY MALES)
        @APPLICATION 1963 S-11 S-19

383   LITTIG, L. W.
            EFFECTS OF MOTIVATION ON PROBABILITY PREFERENCES.
            JOURNAL OF PERSONALITY, 1963, 31, 417-427.
                (RELIABILITY:INTERRATER; CORRELATES:BEHAVIORAL; USED AS CRITERION;
                N=50 COLLEGE MALES)
        @APPLICATION 1963 M-7 M-4

384   FEATHER, N. T.
            THE EFFECT OF DIFFERENTIAL FAILURE ON EXPECTATION OF SUCCESS, REPORTED
            ANXIETY, AND RESPONSE UNCERTAINTY.
            JOURNAL OF PERSONALITY, 1963, 31, 289-312.
                (CORRELATES:PSYCHOLOGICAL, INTELLIGENCE; N=60 COLLEGE FEMALES)
        @APPLICATION 1963 A-8 F-20

385   ROSENTHAL, R., PERSINGER, G. W., KLINE, L. V., & MULRY, R. C.
            THE ROLE OF THE RESEARCH ASSISTANT IN THE MEDIATION OF EXPERIMENTER BIAS.
            JOURNAL OF PERSONALITY, 1963, 31, 313-335.
                (CORRELATES:PSYCHOLOGICAL; BIAS:TESTER; N=270 COLLEGE STUDENTS)
        @APPLICATION 1963 T-2 C-27

386   MESSICK, S., & FRITZKY, F. J.
            DIMENSIONS OF ANALYTIC ATTITUDE IN COGNITION AND PERSONALITY.
            JOURNAL OF PERSONALITY, 1963, 31, 346-370.
                (CORRELATES:PSYCHOLOGICAL, INTELLIGENCE; FACTOR ANALYSIS; N=88
                COLLEGE MALES)
        @APPLICATION 1963 S-66 S-65 B-4 C-63 B-79 F-34 C-23 A-5 R-8 K-1 B-160 B-37 S-174
        @S-175 G-76 J-17 S-61 C-116 C-117 C-118 C-119 C-121 C-120 C-122

387   CRANDALL, V. J., & SINKELDAM, C.
            CHILDREN'S DEPENDENT AND ACHIEVEMENT BEHAVIORS IN SOCIAL SITUATIONS AND
            THEIR PERCEPTUAL FIELD DEPENDENCE.
            JOURNAL OF PERSONALITY, 1964, 32, 1-22.
                (CORRELATES:BEHAVIORAL, DEMOGRAPHIC; N=50 GRADE SCHOOL CHILDREN)
        @APPLICATION 1964 W-19

388   KUETHE, J. L., & WEINGARTNER, H.
            MALE-FEMALE SCHEMATA OF HOMOSEXUAL AND NON-HOMOSEXUAL PENITENTIARY INMATES.
            JOURNAL OF PERSONALITY, 1964, 32, 23-31.
                (CORRELATES:BEHAVIORAL, PSYCHOLOGICAL; N=100 PRISON INMATES)
        @APPLICATION 1964 K-46

389   BECKER, G.
            THE COMPLEMENTARY-NEEDS HYPOTHESIS, AUTHORITARIANISM, DOMINANCE, AND
            OTHER EDWARDS PERSONAL PREFERENCE SCHEDULE SCORES.
            JOURNAL OF PERSONALITY, 1964, 32, 45-56.
                (CORRELATES:PSYCHOLOGICAL, DEMOGRAPHIC; N=39 COUPLES)
        @APPLICATION 1964 E-2 A-5 O-23

390   WEITMAN, M.
            FORMS OF FAILURE TO RESPOND AND VARIETIES OF AUTHORITARIANISM.
            JOURNAL OF PERSONALITY, 1964, 32, 109-118.
                (USED AS CRITERION; N=85 PRISON INMATES)
        @APPLICATION 1964 H-113

391   TRIPODI, T.
            INFORMATION TRANSMISSION IN CLINICAL JUDGMENTS AS A FUNCTION OF STIMULUS
            DIMENSIONALITY AND COGNITIVE COMPLEXITY.
            JOURNAL OF PERSONALITY, 1964, 32, 119-137.
                (MODIFICATION; CORRELATES:PSYCHOLOGICAL; N=64 GRADUATE STUDENTS)
        aAPPLICATION 1964 T-13 K-23

392   DAVISON, G. C.
            THE NEGATIVE EFFECTS OF EARLY EXPOSURE TO SUBOPTICAL STIMULI.
            JOURNAL OF PERSONALITY, 1964, 32, 278-295.
                (CORRELATES:BEHAVIORAL; N=20 UNDERGRADUATES)
        aAPPLICATION 1964 G-76

393   ALPER, T. G., LEVIN, V. S., & KLEIN, M. H.
            AUTHORITARIAN VS. HUMANISTIC CONSCIENCE.
            JOURNAL OF PERSONALITY, 1964, 32, 313-333.
                (CORRELATES:PSYCHOLOGICAL, DEMOGRAPHIC; USED AS CRITERION;
                N=107 MEN AND 186 WOMEN)
        aAPPLICATION 1964 O-23

394   CONN, L. K., & CROWNE, D. P.
            INSTIGATION TO AGGRESSION, EMOTIONAL AROUSAL AND DEFENSIVE EMULATION.
            JOURNAL OF PERSONALITY, 1964, 32, 163-179.
                (CORRELATES:BEHAVIORAL, PSYCHOLOGICAL; USED AS CRITERION; N=74 MALE
                UNDERGRADUATES)
        aAPPLICATION 1964 C-27

395   HANCOCK, J. G., & TEEVAN, R. C.
            FEAR OF FAILURE AND RISK TAKING BEHAVIOR.
            JOURNAL OF PERSONALITY, 1964, 32, 200-209.
                (CORRELATES:BEHAVIORAL, PSYCHOLOGICAL; N=60 MALE HIGH SCHOOL
                SOPHOMORES)
        aAPPLICATION 1964 B-98 M-20

396   LEVENTHAL, H., & SINGER, D. L.
            COGNITIVE COMPLEXITY, IMPRESSION FORMATION AND IMPRESSION CHANGE.
            JOURNAL OF PERSONALITY, 1964, 32, 210-226.
                (MODIFICATION; CORRELATES:BEHAVIORAL, PSYCHOLOGICAL; N=101 MALE
                COLLEGE STUDENTS)
        aAPPLICATION 1964 K-23 Z-37

397   ROTHAUS, P.
            EGO-SUPPORT COMMUNICATION, CATHARSIS, AND HOSTILITY.
            JOURNAL OF PERSONALITY, 1964, 32, 296-319.
                (RELIABILITY:INTERRATER; CORRELATES:DEMOGRAPHIC, ENVIRONMENTAL;
                USED AS CRITERION; N=171 MEN AND 150 WOMEN)
        aAPPLICATION 1964 B-44 M-20 P-74

398   VAUGHAN, G. M.
            THE TRANS-SITUATIONAL ASPECT OF CONFORMING BEHAVIOR.
            JOURNAL OF PERSONALITY, 1964, 32, 335-354.
                (CORRELATES:BEHAVIORAL, PSYCHOLOGICAL; USED AS CRITERION; N=64
                FEMALE COLLEGE STUDENTS)
        aAPPLICATION 1964 B-7 W-102 T-2 A-6 A-7 R-8 C-125 C-10

399   BUTTERFIELD, E. C.
            LOCUS OF CONTROL, TEST ANXIETY, REACTIONS TO FRUSTRATION, AND ACHIEVEMENT
            ATTITUDES.
            JOURNAL OF PERSONALITY, 1964, 32, 355-370.
                (MODIFICATION; CORRELATES:BEHAVIORAL, PSYCHOLOGICAL; N=22 FEMALE,
                25 MALE COLLEGE STUDENTS)
        aAPPLICATION 1964 L-30 A-8 C-126 W-180

400   HAYWOOD, H. C., & DOBBS, V.
            MOTIVATION AND ANXIETY IN HIGH SCHOOL BOYS.
            JOURNAL OF PERSONALITY, 1964, 32, 371-379.
                (MODIFICATION; VALIDITY:CRITERION; CORRELATES:PSYCHOLOGICAL,
                INTELLIGENCE; N=100 BOYS)
        aAPPLICATION 1964 T-2 E-17 H-48

401   SIEBER, J. E., & LANZETTA, J. T.
            CONFLICT AND CONCEPTUAL STRUCTURE AS DETERMINANTS OF DECISION-MAKING
            BEHAVIOR.
            JOURNAL OF PERSONALITY, 1964, 32, 622-641.
                (RELIABILITY:INTERNAL CONSISTENCY; USED AS CRITERION; N=30 STUDENTS)
        aAPPLICATION 1964 S-41

402   KATAHN, M.
              EFFECT OF ANXIETY (DRIVE) ON THE ACQUISITION AND AVOIDANCE OF A DOMINANT
              INTRATASK RESPONSE.
              JOURNAL OF PERSONALITY, 1964, 32, 642-650.
                    (CORRELATES:BEHAVIORAL, PSYCHOLOGICAL; USED AS CRITERION; N=24 MALE,
                    16 FEMALE UNDERGRADUATES)
        @APPLICATION 1964 T-2

403   ROSENWALD, G. C.
              THE RELATION OF DRIVE DISCHARGE TO THE ENJOYMENT OF HUMOR.
              JOURNAL OF PERSONALITY, 1964, 32, 682-698.
                    (RELIABILITY:INTERRATER; CORRELATES:PSYCHOLOGICAL;
                    USED AS CRITERION: NORMATIVE DATA; N=29 MALE HIGH SCHOOL STUDENTS)
        @APPLICATION 1964 M-20 R-40 P-28

404   GLASS, D. C.
              CHANGES IN LIKING AS A MEANS OF REDUCING COGNITIVE DISCREPANCIES BETWEEN
              SELF-ESTEEM AND AGGRESSION.
              JOURNAL OF PERSONALITY, 1964, 32, 531-549.
                    (MENTION; N=60 STUDENTS)
        @APPLICATION 1964 C-27 R-30

405   KASL, S. V., SAMPSON, E. E., & FRENCH, J. R. P.
              THE DEVELOPMENT OF A PROJECTIVE MEASURE OF THE NEED FOR INDEPENDENCE: A
              THEORETICAL STATEMENT AND SOME PRELIMINARY EVIDENCE.
              JOURNAL OF PERSONALITY, 1964, 32, 566-586.
                    (DESCRIPTION; CORRELATES:PSYCHOLOGICAL; N=51 FEMALE STUDENTS)
        @APPLICATION 1964 F-20

406   SLOTNICK, R. S., LIEBERT, R. M., & HILGARD, E. R.
              THE ENHANCEMENT OF MUSCULAR PERFORMANCE IN HYPNOSIS THROUGH EXHORTATION
              AND INVOLVING INSTRUCTIONS.
              JOURNAL OF PERSONALITY, 1965, 33, 37-45.
                    (CORRELATES:BEHAVIORAL; USED AS CRITERION; N=12 FEMALE STUDENTS)
        @APPLICATION 1965 W-31 W-103

407   GREENBAUM, C. W., COHN, A., & KRAUSS, R. M.
              CHOICE, NEGATIVE INFORMATION, AND ATTRACTIVENESS OF TASKS.
              JOURNAL OF PERSONALITY, 1965, 33, 46-59.
                    (MENTION)
        @APPLICATION 1965 B-5 C-27

408   BURKE, W. W.
              LEADERSHIP BEHAVIOR AS A FUNCTION OF THE LEADER, THE FOLLOWER, AND THE
              SITUATION.
              JOURNAL OF PERSONALITY, 1965, 33, 60-81.
                    (USED AS CRITERION; N=600 FRATERNITY PLEDGES)
        @APPLICATION 1965 E-2 F-50

409   MADDI, S. R., PROPST, B. S., & FELDINGER, T.
              THREE EXPRESSIONS OF NEED FOR VARIETY.
              JOURNAL OF PERSONALITY, 1965, 33, 82-98.
                    (VALIDITY:CONSTRUCT; N=62 STUDENTS)
        @APPLICATION 1965 B-78 G-113 M-244 M-261

410   CRANDALL, J. E.
              SOME RELATIONSHIPS AMONG SEX, ANXIETY, AND CONSERVATISM OF JUDGMENT.
              JOURNAL OF PERSONALITY, 1965, 33, 99-107.
                    (MODIFICATION; CORRELATES:PSYCHOLOGICAL, DEMOGRAPHIC: USED AS
                    CRITERION; N=96 STUDENTS)
        @APPLICATION 1965 T-2 P-7 O-16

411   ANDREWS, F. M.
              FACTORS AFFECTING THE MANIFESTATION OF CREATIVE ABILITY BY SCIENTISTS.
              JOURNAL OF PERSONALITY, 1965, 33, 140-152.
                    (CORRELATES:INTELLIGENCE; N=214 SCIENTISTS)
        @APPLICATION 1965 M-29

412   KASWAN, J., HARALSON, S., & CLINE, R.
              VARIABLES IN PERCEPTUAL AND COGNITIVE ORGANIZATION AND DIFFERENTIATION.
              JOURNAL OF PERSONALITY, 1965, 33, 164-177.
                    (CORRELATES:BEHAVIORAL, PSYCHOLOGICAL, INTELLIGENCE; N=39 MALE
                    STUDENTS)
        @APPLICATION 1965 W-19 W-188

413   VAUGHT, G. M.
            THE RELATIONSHIP OF ROLE IDENTIFICATION AND EGO STRENGTH TO SEX DIFFERENCES
            IN THE ROD-AND-FRAME TEST.
            JOURNAL OF PERSONALITY, 1965, 33, 271-283.
                    (CORRELATES:PSYCHOLOGICAL, DEMOGRAPHIC; USED AS CRITERION;
                    NORMATIVE DATA; N=90 MALE AND 90 FEMALE STUDENTS)
        @APPLICATION 1965 G-20 B-5 W-188

414   MADDI, S. R.
            MOTIVATIONAL ASPECTS OF CREATIVITY.
            JOURNAL OF PERSONALITY, 1965, 33, 330-347.
                    (MENTION; CORRELATES:PSYCHOLOGICAL; NO SAMPLE INFORMATION)
        @APPLICATION 1965 C-10 S-56 T-2 M-101 M-244 M-261

415   WEINER, B.
            THE EFFECTS OF UNSATISFIED ACHIEVEMENT MOTIVATION ON PERSISTENCE AND
            SUBSEQUENT PERFORMANCE.
            JOURNAL OF PERSONALITY, 1965, 33, 428-442.
                    (RELIABILITY:RETEST; CORRELATES:BEHAVIORAL; USED AS CRITERION; N=128
                    COLLEGE MALES)
        @APPLICATION 1965 M-7 M-4

416   CORAH, N. L.
            DIFFERENTIATION IN CHILDREN AND THEIR PARENTS.
            JOURNAL OF PERSONALITY, 1965, 33, 301-308.
                    (MODIFICATION; RELIABILITY:INTERRATER; CORRELATES:INTELLIGENCE; N=
                    FAMILIES OF 30 BOYS, 30 GIRLS)
        @APPLICATION 1965 W-19 M-58 W-20 K-90

417   FEATHER, N. T.
            PERFORMANCE AT A DIFFICULT TASK IN RELATION TO INITIAL EXPECTATION OF
            SUCCESS, TEST ANXIETY, AND NEED ACHIEVEMENT.
            JOURNAL OF PERSONALITY, 1965, 33, 200-217.
                    (USED AS CRITERION; N=168 MALE STUDENTS)
        @APPLICATION 1965 M-4 M-7

418   RESNICK, J. H.
            REVERSALS IN THE SUPERIORITY OF PERFORMANCE OF HIGH AND LOW-ANXIOUS SAMPLES
            IN VERBAL CONDITIONING.
            JOURNAL OF PERSONALITY, 1965, 33, 218-232.
                    (USED AS CRITERION; N=72 MALE, 96 FEMALE UNDERGRADUATES)
        @APPLICATION 1965 M-4

419   ZIMBARDO, P. G.
            COMMUNICATOR EFFECTIVENESS IN PRODUCING PUBLIC CONFORMITY AND PRIVATE
            ATTITUDE CHANGE.
            JOURNAL OF PERSONALITY, 1965, 33, 233-256.
                    (USED AS CRITERION; N=243 STUDENTS AND ARMY RESERVISTS)
        @APPLICATION 1965 G-21

420   BARBER, T. B., & CALVERLEY, D. S.
            EMPIRICAL EVIDENCE FOR A THEORY OF HYPNOTIC BEHAVIOR: THE SUGGESTIBILITY
            ENHANCING EFFECTS OF MOTIVATIONAL SUGGESTIONS, RELAXATION AND SLEEP
            SUGGESTIONS, AND SUGGESTIONS THAT SUBJECT WILL BE EFFECTIVELY HYPNOTIZED.
            JOURNAL OF PERSONALITY, 1965, 33, 257-270.
                    (CORRELATES:BEHAVIORAL, ENVIRONMENTAL; N=56 FEMALE STUDENT NURSES
                    (EXP. 1) AND 84 NURSES (EXP. 2))
        @APPLICATION 1965 B-3

421   SAPPENFIELD, B. R.
            TEST OF A SZONDI ASSUMPTION BY MEANS OF M-F PHOTOGRAPHS.
            JOURNAL OF PERSONALITY, 1965, 33, 409-417.
                    (USED AS CRITERION; N=185 MALE COLLEGE STUDENTS)
        @APPLICATION 1965 T-3 S-229

422   SCHLACHET, P. J.
            THE EFFECT OF DISSONANCE AROUSAL ON THE RECALL OF FAILURE STIMULI.
            JOURNAL OF PERSONALITY, 1965, 33, 443-461.
                    (CORRELATES:ENVIRONMENTAL; USED AS CRITERION; N=101 COLLEGE MALES)
        @APPLICATION 1965 E-2

423   CHILD, I. L.
          PERSONALITY CORRELATES OF ESTHETIC JUDGMENT IN COLLEGE STUDENTS.
          JOURNAL OF PERSONALITY, 1965, 33, 476-511.
                 (RELIABILITY:INTERNAL CONSISTENCY; CORRELATES:PSYCHOLOGICAL,
                 INTELLIGENCE; N=137 UNDERGRADUATES AND 1 GRADUATE STUDENT)
       @APPLICATION 1965 B-162 B-4 M-22 S-80 C-128 G-20 F-11 B-76 C-61 C-27

424   SMITH, M. B.
          AN ANALYSIS OF TWO MEASURES OF "AUTHORITARIANISM" AMONG PEACE CORPS
          TEACHERS.
          JOURNAL OF PERSONALITY, 1965, 33, 513-535.
                 (VALIDITY:CONSTRUCT; CORRELATES:PSYCHOLOGICAL; N=58 PEACE CORPS
                 TEACHERS)
       @APPLICATION 1965 C-81 O-23 B-126

425   FISHER, S.
          THE BODY IMAGE AS A SOURCE OF SELECTIVE COGNITIVE SETS.
          JOURNAL OF PERSONALITY, 1965, 33, 536-552.
                 (CORRELATES:PSYCHOLOGICAL; SEVEN STUDIES--MEDIAN N=59 COLLEGE
                 STUDENTS)
       @APPLICATION 1965 F-75

426   OGAWA, J., & OAKES, W. F.
          SEX OF EXPERIMENTER AND MANIFEST ANXIETY AS RELATED TO VERBAL CONDITIONING.
          JOURNAL OF PERSONALITY, 1965, 33, 553-569.
                 (USED AS CRITERION; N=96 COLLEGE STUDENTS)
       @APPLICATION 1965 T-2

427   WARR, P. B., & SIMS, A.
          A STUDY OF COJUDGMENT PROCESSES.
          JOURNAL OF PERSONALITY, 1965, 33, 598-604.
                 (CORRELATES:PSYCHOLOGICAL; N=56 HIGH SCHOOL STUDENTS)
       @APPLICATION 1965 A-5

428   HALL, C. L., JR.
          MATERNAL CONTROL AS RELATED TO SCHIZOID BEHAVIORS IN GROSSLY NORMAL MALES.
          JOURNAL OF PERSONALITY, 1965, 33, 613-621.
                 (MODIFICATION; CORRELATES:PSYCHOLOGICAL, INTELLIGENCE; USED AS
                 CRITERION; N=127 COLLEGE MALES)
       @APPLICATION 1965 S-9 D-45

429   ROSENFELD, H. M., & JACKSON, J.
          TEMPORAL MEDIATION OF THE SIMILARITY-ATTRACTION HYPOTHESIS.
          JOURNAL OF PERSONALITY, 1965, 33, 649-655.
                 (MODIFICATION; USED AS CRITERION; N=72 FEMALE WHITE COLLAR WORKERS)
       @APPLICATION 1965 G-26

430   HELSON, R.
          PERSONALITY OF WOMEN WITH IMAGINATIVE AND ARTISTIC INTERESTS: THE ROLE
          OF MASCULINITY, ORIGINALITY AND THE CHARACTERISTICS IN THEIR CREATIVITY.
          JOURNAL OF PERSONALITY, 1966, 34, 1-25.
                 (VALIDITY:CONSTRUCT, CRITERION; CORRELATES:BEHAVIORAL, PSYCHOLOGICAL,
                 DEMOGRAPHIC; USED AS CRITERION; N=51 FEMALE ART STUDENTS (EXP. 1) AND
                 139 STUDENTS (EXP. 2))
       @APPLICATION 1966 B-4 B-78 B-79 G-52 G-53 M-22 C-62 G-22 H-45 G-21 S-33 M-20
       C-63 G-50 B-76 A-7 G-20 W-28 D-45

431   ZANDER, A., & WULFF, D.
          MEMBERS' TEST ANXIETY AND COMPETENCE: DETERMINANTS OF A GROUP'S
          ASPIRATIONS.
          JOURNAL OF PERSONALITY, 1966, 34, 55-70.
                 (USED AS CRITERION; N=144 ELEVENTH GRADE BOYS)
       @APPLICATION 1966 M-4

432   LONDON, P., CONART, M., & DAVISON, G. C.
          MORE HYPNOSIS IN THE UNHYPNOTIZABLE: EFFECTS OF HYPNOSIS AND EXHORTATION
          ON ROTE LEARNING.
          JOURNAL OF PERSONALITY, 1966, 34, 71-79.
                 (USED AS CRITERION; N=40 MALE UNDERGRADUATES)
       @APPLICATION 1966 W-31

433   LIBERTY, P. G., JR., BUNSTEIN, E., & MOULTON, R. W.
            CONCERN WITH MASTERY AND OCCUPATIONAL ATTRACTION.
            JOURNAL OF PERSONALITY, 1966, 34, 105-117.
                (VALIDITY:CONSTRUCT; CORRELATES:PSYCHOLOGICAL; USED AS CRITERION;
                N=160 MALE STUDENTS)
         @APPLICATION 1966 S-132 D-28 R-18 M-4 M-7

434   KAGAN, J.
            BODY BUILD AND CONCEPTUAL IMPULSIVITY IN CHILDREN.
            JOURNAL OF PERSONALITY, 1966, 34, 118-128.
                (CORRELATES:PHYSIOLOGICAL; USED AS CRITERION; N=198 THIRD GRADERS)
         @APPLICATION 1966 K-60

435   PUROHIT, A. P.
            LEVELS OF INTROVERSION AND COMPETITIONAL PAIRED-ASSOCIATE LEARNING.
            JOURNAL OF PERSONALITY, 1966, 34, 129-143.
                (CORRELATES:PSYCHOLOGICAL, PHYSIOLOGICAL, INTELLIGENCE; N=64 MALE, 64
                FEMALE UNDERGRADUATES)
         @APPLICATION 1966 E-5

436   RAYNOR, J. O., & SMITH, C. P.
            ACHIEVEMENT-RELATED MOTIVES AND RISK-TAKING IN GAMES OF SKILL AND CHANCE.
            JOURNAL OF PERSONALITY, 1966, 34, 176-198.
                (CORRELATES:BEHAVIORAL, PSYCHOLOGICAL; N=62 COLLEGE MALES)
         @APPLICATION 1966 M-7 M-4 D-28 A-5

437   LOMONT, J. F.
            REPRESSORS AND SENSITIZERS AS DESCRIBED BY THEMSELVES AND THEIR PAIRS.
            JOURNAL OF PERSONALITY, 1966, 34, 224-240.
                (CORRELATES:PSYCHOLOGICAL; N=136 FRATERNITY AND SORORITY MEMBERS)
         @APPLICATION 1966 B-46 L-35

438   TRIPODI, T., & BIERI, J.
            COGNITIVE COMPLEXITY, PERCEIVED CONFLICT, AND CERTAINTY.
            JOURNAL OF PERSONALITY, 1966, 34, 144-153.
                (MODIFICATION; RELIABILITY:RETEST; CORRELATES:PSYCHOLOGICAL;
                TWO STUDIES: N=64 AND 72 GRADUATE STUDENTS)
         @APPLICATION 1966 K-23 F-77

439   FANCHER, R. E.
            EXPLICIT PERSONALITY THEORIES AND ACCURACY IN PERSON PERCEPTION.
            JOURNAL OF PERSONALITY, 1966, 34, 252-261.
                (CORRELATES:PSYCHOLOGICAL; NORMATIVE DATA; N=24 MALE STUDENTS)
         @APPLICATION 1966 K-23

440   RETTIG, S.
            BAD FAITH AND ETHICAL RISK SENSITIVITY.
            JOURNAL OF PERSONALITY, 1966, 34, 275-286.
                (CORRELATES:BEHAVIORAL; N=210 MALE UNDERGRADUATES)
         @APPLICATION 1966 R-26

441   KATAHN, M., & LYDA, L. L.
            ANXIETY AND THE LEARNING OF RESPONSES VARYING IN INITIAL RANK IN THE
            RESPONSE HIERARCHY.
            JOURNAL OF PERSONALITY, 1966, 34, 287-299.
                (USED AS CRITERION; N=24 MALE, 16 FEMALE COLLEGE STUDENTS)
         @APPLICATION 1966 T-2 W-105

442   JOHNSON, M. H., & MEADOW, A.
            PARENTAL IDENTIFICATION AMONG MALE SCHIZOPHRENICS.
            JOURNAL OF PERSONALITY, 1966, 34, 300-309.
                (USED AS CRITERION; NORMATIVE DATA; N=3 GROUPS OF 40 SCHIZOPHRENIC
                PATIENTS AND CONTROLS)
         @APPLICATION 1966 P-32

443   STEIN, K. S., & LANGER, J.
            THE RELATION OF COVERT COGNITIVE INTERFERENCE IN THE COLOR-PHONETIC
            SYMBOL TEST TO PERSONALITY CHARACTERISTICS AND ADJUSTMENT.
            JOURNAL OF PERSONALITY, 1966, 34, 241-251.
                (CORRELATES:PSYCHOLOGICAL, INTELLIGENCE; USED AS CRITERION;
                NORMATIVE DATA; N=81 FEMALE UNDERGRADUATES)
         @APPLICATION 1966 G-21 L-87

444   GORSUCH, R. L., & SPIELBERGER, C. D.
            ANXIETY, THREAT, AND AWARENESS IN VERBAL CONDITIONING.
            JOURNAL OF PERSONALITY, 1966, 34, 336-347.
                (CORRELATES:PHYSIOLOGICAL; USED AS CRITERION; N=103 COLLEGE MALES)
        @APPLICATION 1966 T-2 D-45

445   CROSS, H. J.
            THE RELATION OF PARENTAL TRAINING CONDITIONS TO CONCEPTUAL LEVEL IN
            ADOLESCENT BOYS.
            JOURNAL OF PERSONALITY, 1966, 34, 348-365.
                (CORRELATES:PSYCHOLOGICAL; USED AS CRITERION; N=182 MOTHER-FATHER
                PAIRS)
        @APPLICATION 1966 S-9 S-41

446   LEFCOURT, H. M., & STEFFY, R. A.
            SEX-LINKED CENSURE EXPECTANCIES IN PROCESS AND REACTIVE SCHIZOPHRENICS.
            JOURNAL OF PERSONALITY, 1966, 34, 366-380.
                (CORRELATES:BEHAVIORAL: USED AS CRITERION; N=32 PSYCHIATRIC PATIENTS)
        @APPLICATION 1966 H-37 W-44

447   BARBER, T. X., & CALVERLEY, D. S.
            TOWARD A THEORY OF HYPNOTIC BEHAVIOR: EXPERIMENTAL EVALUATION OF HULL'S
            POSTULATE THAT HYPNOTIC SUSCEPTIBILITY IS A HABIT PHENOMENON.
            JOURNAL OF PERSONALITY, 1966, 34, 416-433.
                (RELIABILITY:RETEST; CORRELATES:PSYCHOLOGICAL; N=15 FEMALE STUDENT
                NURSES)
        @APPLICATION 1966 B-3

448   SILVERMAN, I., FORD, L. H., JR., & MORGANTI, J. B.
            INTER-RELATED EFFECTS OF SOCIAL DESIRABLILITY, SEX, SELF-ESTEEM, AND
            COMPLEXITY OF ARGUMENT ON PERSUASIBILITY.
            JOURNAL OF PERSONALITY, 1966, 34, 555-568.
                (MODIFICATION; CORRELATES:PSYCHOLOGICAL; N=100 MALE AND 100 FEMALE
                COLLEGE STUDENTS)
        @APPLICATION 1966 C-27 F-9 J-7 J-8

449   BYRNE, D., GRIFFITT, W., & GOLIGHTLY, C.
            PRESTIGE AS A FACTOR IN DETERMINING THE EFFECT OF ATTITUDE SIMILARITY-
            DISSIMILARITY ON ATTRACTION.
                (RELIABILITY:INTERNAL CONSISTENCY; USED AS CRITERION; N=85 COLLEGE
                MALES)
        @APPLICATION 1966 B-65

450   JACOBSON, L. I., & FORD, L. H., JR.
            NEED FOR APPROVAL, DEFENSIVE DENIAL, AND SENSITIVITY TO CULTURAL
            STEREOTYPES.
            JOURNAL OF PERSONALITY, 1966, 34, 596-609.
                (CORRELATES:PSYCHOLOGICAL; BIAS:RESPONSE; N=112 COLLEGE MALES)
        @APPLICATION 1966 F-9 E-1

451   MADDI, S. R., & ANDREWS, S. L.
            THE NEED FOR VARIETY IN FANTASY AND SELF-DESCRIPTION.
            JOURNAL OF PERSONALITY, 1966, 34, 610-625.
                (CORRELATES:PSYCHOLOGICAL, INTELLIGENCE; N=87 COLLEGE MALES AND 56
                NAVY MEDICAL CORPSMEN)
        @APPLICATION 1966 C-10 T-2 E-5 B-5 C-27 S-56 M-261

452   DOHERTY, M. A., & WALKER, R. E.
            THE RELATIONAHIP OF PERSONALITY CHARACTERISTICS, AWARENESS, AND ATTITUDE
            IN A VERBAL CONDITIONING SITUATION.
            JOURNAL OF PERSONALITY, 1966, 34 504-516.
                (MODIFICATION; CORRELATES:BEHAVIORAL, PSYCHOLOGICAL; USED AS
                CRITERION; N=120 FEMALE RELIGIOUS NOVICES)
        @APPLICATION 1966 T-2 C-10 W-65 D-45

453   SIGNELL, K. A.
            COGNITIVE COMPLEXITY IN PERSON PERCEPTION AND NATION PERCEPTION: A
            DEVELOPMENTAL APPROACH.
            JOURNAL OF PERSONALITY, 1966, 34, 517-537.
                (MODIFICATION; CORRELATES:DEMOGRAPHIC, INTELLIGENCE; USED AS
                CRITERION; N=36 ELEMENTARY AND HIGH SCHOOL STUDENTS)
        @APPLICATION 1966 K-23

454   KAUFMANN, H.
            HOSTILITY, PERCEIVED SIMILARITY, AND PUNITIVITY UNDER AROUSED CONDITION.
            JOURNAL OF PERSONALITY, 1966, 34, 538-545
                 (CORRELATES:BEHAVIORAL: USED AS CRITERION; N=174 COLLEGE STUDENTS)
        @APPLICATION 1966 S-24

455   ROSENFELD, H. M.
            RELATIONSHIPS OF ORDINAL POSITION TO AFFILIATION AND ACHIEVEMENT MOTIVES:
            DIRECTION AND GENERALITY.
            JOURNAL OF PERSONALITY, 1966, 34, 467-480.
                 (RELIABILITY:INTERRATER; CORRELATES:PSYCHOLOGICAL, DEMOGRAPHIC;
                 5 STUDIES--MEDIAN N=87 COLLEGE STUDENTS)
        @APPLICATION 1966 M-4 S-179

456   CASHDAN, S., & WELSH, G. S.
            PERSONALITY CORRELATES OF CREATIVE POTENTIAL IN TALENTED HIGH SCHOOL
            STUDENTS.
            JOURNAL OF PERSONALITY, 1966, 34, 445-455.
                 (CORRELATES:BEHAVIORAL, PSYCHOLOGICAL; USED AS CRITERION; N=311
                 ADOLESCENTS)
        @APPLICATION 1966 G-21 W-9

457   MILLER, N., & ZIMBARDO, P. G.
            MOTIVES FOR FEAR-INDUCED AFFILIATION: EMOTIONAL COMPARISON OR INTERPERSONAL
            SIMILARITY.
            JOURNAL OF PERSONALITY, 1966, 34, 481-503.
                 (CORRELATES:BEHAVIORAL, PSYCHOLOGICAL; N=132 HIGH SCHOOL STUDENTS)
        @APPLICATION 1966 R-8 C-27 J-7

458   GETTER, H.
            A PERSONALITY DETERMINANT OF VERBAL CONDITIONING.
            JOURNAL OF PERSONALITY, 1966, 34, 397-405.
                 (CORRELATES:BEHAVIORAL; N=130 MALE AND FEMALE COLLEGE STUDENTS)
        @APPLICATION 1966 R-18

459   GIDDAN, N. S.
            RECOVERY THROUGH IMAGES OF BRIEFLY FLASHED STIMULI.
            JOURNAL OF PERSONALITY, 1967, 35, 1-19.
                 (MENTION; CORRELATES:BEHAVIORAL; N=245 COLLEGE STUDENTS)
        @APPLICATION 1967 B-91

460   RYCHLAK, J. F., & LEGERSKI, A. T.
            A SOCIOCULTURAL THEORY OF APPROPRIATE SEXUAL ROLE IDENTIFICATION AND LEVEL
            OF PERSONAL ADJUSTMENT.
            JOURNAL OF PERSONALITY, 1967, 35, 31-49.
                 (CORRELATES:PSYCHOLOGICAL, INTELLIGENCE; N=30 HIGH SCHOOL BOYS, 61
                 DELINQUENT AND NONDELINQUENT GIRLS)
        @APPLICATION 1967 C-89 D-45 L-71

461   KOGAN, N., & WALLACH, M. A.
            GROUP RISK TAKING AS A FUNCTION OF MEMBERS' ANXIETY AND DEFENSIVENESS
            LEVELS.
            JOURNAL OF PERSONALITY, 1967, 35, 50-63.
                 (CORRELATES:BEHAVIORAL, PSYCHOLOGICAL; USED AS CRITERION; N=180
                 COLLEGE FEMALES)
        @APPLICATION 1967 C-27 A-8 W-2 K-94

462   PALMER, J., & ALTROCCHI, J.
            ATTRIBUTION OF HOSTILE INTENT AS UNCONSCIOUS.
            JOURNAL OF PERSONALITY, 1967, 35, 164-177.
                 (CORRELATES:BEHAVIORAL; USED AS CRITERION; N=99 AND 65 COLLEGE MALES
                 IN TWO STUDIES)
        @APPLICATION 1967 C-27 B-46 A-54

463   SMITH, W. P.
            POWER STRUCTURE AND AUTHORITARIANISM IN THE USE OF POWER IN THE TRIAD.
            JOURNAL OF PERSONALITY, 1967, 35, 64-90.
                 (MODIFICATION; CORRELATES:BEHAVIORAL; NORMATIVE DATA; N=72 COLLEGE
                 MALES)
        @APPLICATION 1967 A-5 C-31

464   MARCIA, J. E.
            EGO IDENTITY STATUS: RELATIONSHIP TO CHANGE IN SELF—ESTEEM, GENERAL
            MALADJUSTMENT, AND AUTHORITARIANISM.
            JOURNAL OF PERSONALITY, 1967, 35, 118-133.
                (CORRELATES:PSYCHOLOGICAL; USED AS CRITERION; N=72 COLLEGE MALES)
        @APPLICATION 1967 D-14 W-8 M-125 A-5

465   HAYS, L. W., & WORELL, L.
            ANXIETY DRIVE, ANXIETY HABIT, AND ACHIEVEMENT: A THEORETICAL REFORMULATION
            IN TERMS OF OPTIMAL MOTIVATION.
            JOURNAL OF PERSONALITY, 1967, 35, 145-163.
                (CORRELATES:BEHAVIORAL, PSYCHOLOGICAL, INTELLIGENCE; USED AS
                CRITERION; N=80 COLLEGE STUDENTS)
        @APPLICATION 1967 T-2 S-5 W-58

466   LEVY, L. H.
            THE EFFECTS OF VARIANCE ON PERSONALITY IMPRESSION FORMATION.
            JOURNAL OF PERSONALITY, 1967, 35, 179-193.
                (CORRELATES:PSYCHOLOGICAL, DEMOGRAPHIC; N=100 COLLEGE STUDENTS)
        @APPLICATION 1967 P-7

467   MCDONALD, R. L.
            THE EFFECTS OF STRESS ON SELF-ATTRIBUTION OF HOSTILITY AMONG EGO CONTROL
            PATTERNS.
            JOURNAL OF PERSONALITY, 1967, 35, 234-245.
                (CORRELATES:BEHAVIORAL, PSYCHOLOGICAL; N=182 PREGNANT FEMALES)
        @APPLICATION 1967 L-35 B-46 A-54 D-45

468   EPSTEIN, S., & TAYLOR, S. P.
            INSTIGATION TO AGGRESSION AS A FUNCTION OF DEGREE OF DEFEAT AND PERCEIVED
            AGGRESSIVE INTENT OF THE OPPONENT.
            JOURNAL OF PERSONALITY, 1967, 35, 265-289.
                (CORRELATES:BEHAVIORAL, PHYSIOLOGICAL; N=27 COLLEGE MALES)
        @APPLICATION 1967 N-17 Z-4

469   BOWERS, P. G.
            EFFECT OF HYPNOSIS AND SUGGESTIONS OF REDUCED DEFENSIVENESS ON CREATIVITY
            TEST PERFORMANCE.
            JOURNAL OF PERSONALITY, 1967, 35, 311-322.
                (CORRELATES:PSYCHOLOGICAL; USED AS CRITERION; N=80 COLLEGE FEMALES)
        @APPLICATION 1967 S-90 G-50

470   BRAGINSKY, B. M., HOLZBERG, J. D., FINISON, L., & RING, K.
            CORRELATES OF THE MENTAL PATIENT'S ACQUISITION OF HOSPITAL INFORMATION.
            JOURNAL OF PERSONALITY, 1967, 35, 323-342.
                (CORRELATES:PSYCHOLOGICAL, DEMOGRAPHIC; N=206 MALE AND FEMALE
                HOSPITAL PATIENTS)
        @APPLICATION 1967 C-69

471   TAYLOR, S. P.
            AGGRESSIVE BEHAVIOR AND PHYSIOLOGICAL AROUSAL AS A FUNCTION OF PROVOCATION
            AND THE TENDENCY TO INHIBIT AGGRESSION.
            JOURNAL OF PERSONALITY, 1967, 35, 297-310.
                (CORRELATES:BEHAVIORAL, PHYSIOLOGICAL; N=183 COLLEGE MALES)
        @APPLICATION 1967 E-35

472   HELSON, R.
            SEX DIFFERENCES IN CREATIVE STYLE.
            JOURNAL OF PERSONALITY, 1967, 35, 214-233.
                (CORRELATES:PSYCHOLOGICAL, DEMOGRAPHIC; CLUSTER ANALYSIS; N=34
                CREATIVE MEN AND 47 CREATIVE WOMEN)
        @APPLICATION 1967 G-22

473   BACK, K. W., WILSON, S. R., BOGDONOFF, M. D., & TROYER, W. G.
            IN-BETWEEN TIMES AND EXPERIMENTAL STRESS.
            JOURNAL OF PERSONALITY, 1967, 35, 456-473.
                (CORRELATES:BEHAVIORAL, PHYSIOLOGICAL; USED AS CRITERION; N=80
                COLLEGE MALES)
        @APPLICATION 1967 C-27

474   LESSING, E. E., & OBERLANDER, M.
                DEVELOPMENTAL STUDY OF ORDINAL POSITION AND PERSONALITY ADJUSTMENT AS
                EVALUATED BY THE CALIFORNIA TEST OF PERSONALITY.
                JOURNAL OF PERSONALITY, 1967, 35, 487-497.
                    (CORRELATES:DEMOGRAPHIC, INTELLIGENCE; N=855 ELEMENTARY SCHOOL
                    CHILDREN)
        @APPLICATION 1967 T-25

475   MEUNIER, C., & RULE, B. G.
                ANXIETY, CONFIDENCE, AND CONFORMITY.
                JOURNAL OF PERSONALITY, 1967, 35, 498-504.
                    (CORRELATES:BEHAVIORAL: USED AS CRITERION; N=60 CANADIAN COLLEGE
                    FEMALES)
        @APPLICATION 1967 M-4

476   LEFCOURT, H. M., ROTENBERG, F., BUCKSPAN, B., & STEFFY, R. A.
                VISUAL INTERACTION AND PERFORMANCE OF PROCESS AND REACTIVE SCHIZOPHRENICS
                AS A FUNCTION OF EXAMINER'S SEX.
                JOURNAL OF PERSONALITY, 1967, 35, 535-546.
                    (RELIABILITY:INTERRATER; CORRELATES:PSYCHOLOGICAL; USED AS CRITERION;
                    N=30 MALE, 30 FEMALE SCHIZOPHRENICS)
        @APPLICATION 1967 W-44 U-5

477   DAVIS, W. L., & PHARES, E. J.
                INTERNAL-EXTERNAL CONTROL AS A DETERMINANT OF INFORMATION-SEEKING IN A
                SOCIAL INFLUENCE SITUATION.
                JOURNAL OF PERSONALITY, 1967, 35, 547-561.
                    (CORRELATES:BEHAVIORAL, PSYCHOLOGICAL; USED AS CRITERION; N=84
                    COLLEGE MALES)
        @APPLICATION 1967 R-18

478   TAFT, R.
                EXTRAVERSION, NEUROTICISM, AND EXPRESSIVE BEHAVIOR: AN APPLICATION OF
                WALLACH'S MODERATOR EFFECT TO HANDWRITING ANALYSIS.
                JOURNAL OF PERSONALITY, 1967, 35, 570-584.
                    (CORRELATES:BEHAVIORAL: USED AS CRITERION; N=32 MALE, 54 FEMALE
                    COLLEGE STUDENTS)
        @APPLICATION 1967 E-5

479   PERVIN, L. A.
                SATISFACTION AND PERCEIVED SELF-ENVIRONMENT SIMILARITY: A SEMANTIC
                DIFFERENTIAL STUDY OF STUDENT-COLLEGE INTERACTION.
                JOURNAL OF PERSONALITY, 1967, 35, 623-634.
                    (CORRELATES:PSYCHOLOGICAL, ENVIRONMENTAL; N=365 COLLEGE STUDENTS)
        @APPLICATION 1967 P-76

480   MACHOTKA, P.
                DEFENSIVE STYLE AND ESTHETIC DISTORTION.
                JOURNAL OF PERSONALITY, 1967, 35, 600-622.
                    (CORRELATES:PSYCHOLOGICAL; N=16 MALE, 20 FEMALE COLLEGE STUDENTS)
        @APPLICATION 1967 B-46 B-5 T-2 B-4 C-74 S-80 C-35 C-57 C-75 C-73 C-61 M-182 C-59
        @D-45

481   HELSON, R.
                GENERALITY OF SEX DIFFERENCES IN CREATIVE STYLE.
                JOURNAL OF PERSONALITY, 1968, 36, 33-48.
                    (VALIDITY:CONSTRUCT, CROSS-VALIDATION; CORRELATES:DEMOGRAPHIC; N=97
                    MATHEMATICIANS, 83 ARCHITECTS, AND 51 COLLEGE SENIORS)
        @APPLICATION 1968 S-33 G-21

482   KAPLAN, M. F.
                ELICITATION OF INFORMATION AND RESPONSE BIASES OF REPRESSORS, SENSITIZERS,
                AND NEUTRALS IN BEHAVIOR PREDICTION.
                JOURNAL OF PERSONALITY, 1968, 36, 84-91.
                    (CORRELATES:PSYCHOLOGICAL; USED AS CRITERION; N=600 COLLEGE
                    STUDENTS; N=461 COLLEGE STUDENTS)
        @APPLICATION 1968 G-21 B-46

483   NEALE, J. M., & KATAHN, M.
                ANXIETY, CHOICE, AND STIMULUS UNCERTAINTY.
                JOURNAL OF PERSONALITY, 1968, 36, 235-245.
                    (CORRELATES:PSYCHOLOGICAL, INTELLIGENCE: USED AS CRITERION; N=48
                    COLLEGE STUDENTS)
        @APPLICATION 1968 S-5 M-248

484   BYRNE, D., LONDON, O., & REEVES, K.
            THE EFFECTS OF PHYSICAL ATTRACTIVENESS, SEX, AND ATTITUDE SIMILARITY ON
            INTERPERSONAL ATTRACTION.
            JOURNAL OF PERSONALITY, 1968, 36, 259-271.
                    (CORRELATES:BEHAVIORAL, PSYCHOLOGICAL; N=47 MALE, 42 FEMALE COLLEGE
                    STUDENTS)
        @APPLICATION 1968 B-65

485   SULZER, J. L., & BURGLASS, R. K.
            RESPONSIBILITY ATTRIBUTION, EMPATHY, AND PUNITIVENESS.
            JOURNAL OF PERSONALITY, 1968, 36, 272-282.
                    (MENTION; RELIABILITY:INTERNAL CONSISTENCY; VALIDITY:CONSTRUCT;
                    CORRELATES:PSYCHOLOGICAL; N=112 FEMALE COLLEGE STUDENTS, AND 68
                    AIR MEN)
        @APPLICATION 1968 W-104 S-181 K-9

486   LEVENTHAL, H., & TREMBLY, G.
            NEGATIVE EMOTIONS AND PERSUASION.
            JOURNAL OF PERSONALITY, 1968, 36, 154-168.
                    (CORRELATES:PSYCHOLOGICAL; N=203 MALE HIGH SCHOOL STUDENTS)
        @APPLICATION 1968 N-17

487   LESSING, E. E.
            DEMOGRAPHIC, DEVELOPMENTAL, AND PERSONALITY CORRELATES OF LENGTH OF
            FUTURE TYPE PERSPECTIVE (FTP).
            JOURNAL OF PERSONALITY, 1968, 36, 183-201.
                    (RELIABILITY:INTERNAL CONSISTENCY; VALIDITY:CONSTRUCT;
                    CORRELATES:PSYCHOLOGICAL, INTELLIGENCE; N=746 SCHOOL CHILDREN)
        @APPLICATION 1968 S-132 T-25 B-186 W-109

488   WACHTEL, P. L.
            STYLE AND CAPACITY IN ANALYTIC FUNCTIONING.
            JOURNAL OF PERSONALITY, 1968, 36, 202-212.
                    (CORRELATES:BEHAVIORAL, PSYCHOLOGICAL; USED AS CRITERION; N=44 MALE
                    COLLEGE STUDENTS)
        @APPLICATION 1968 W-19 K-114

489   PARKOVE, E., & KOGAN, N.
            CREATIVE ABILITY AND RISK-TAKING IN ELEMENTARY SCHOOL CHILDREN.
            JOURNAL OF PERSONALITY, 1968, 36, 420-439.
                    (RELIABILITY:INTERNAL CONSISTENCY; CORRELATES:PSYCHOLOGICAL,
                    INTELLIGENCE; N=84 BOYS AND 78 GIRLS)
        @APPLICATION 1968 W-26 S-79 W-94

490   MURDOCH, P.
            EXPLOITATION-ACCOMMODATION AND SOCIAL RESPONSIBILITY IN A BARGAINING
            GAME.
            JOURNAL OF PERSONALITY, 1968, 36, 440-453.
                    (CORRELATES:BEHAVIORAL, PSYCHOLOGICAL; N=192 COLLEGE STUDENTS)
        @APPLICATION 1968 B-54

491   GLASS, D. C., CANAVAN, D., & SCHIAVO, S.
            ACHIEVEMENT MOTIVATION, DISSONANCE, AND DEFENSIVENESS.
            JOURNAL OF PERSONALITY, 1968, 36, 474-492.
                    (MODIFICATION; CORRELATES:PSYCHOLOGICAL, ENVIRONMENTAL; USED AS
                    CRITERION; N=76 FEMALE COLLEGE STUDENTS)
        @APPLICATION 1968 E-2 B-46

492   SARASON, I. G., PEDERSON, A. M., & NYMAN, B.
            TEST ANXIETY AND THE OBSERVATION OF MODELS.
            JOURNAL OF PERSONALITY, 1968, 36, 493-511.
                    (MODIFICATION; CORRELATES:PSYCHOLOGICAL, INTELLIGENCE; USED AS
                    CRITERION; N=252 FEMALE COLLEGE STUDENTS)
        @APPLICATION 1968 S-5

493   TORGOFF, I., & TESI, G.
            EFFECT OF DIFFERENCES IN ACHIEVEMENT MOTIVATION AND SOCIAL
            RESPONSIBILITY ON RESPONSES TO MORAL CONFLICT.
            JOURNAL OF PERSONALITY, 1968, 36, 513-527.
                    (MODIFICATION; CORRELATES:PSYCHOLOGICAL; USED AS CRITERION;
                    CROSS-CULTURAL APPLICATION; N=167 ITALIAN WORKING-CLASS
                    APPRENTICE ADOLESCENTS)
        @APPLICATION 1968 S-131 M-20 G-188

494   HELMREICH, R., & KUIKEN, D.
            EFFECTS OF STRESS AND BIRTH ORDER ON ATTITUDE CHANGE.
            JOURNAL OF PERSONALITY, 1968, 36, 466-473.
                (USED AS CRITERION; N=258 NAVAL RECRUITS)
        @APPLICATION 1968 H-111

495   PARLOFF, M. B., DALTA, L., KLEMAN, M., & HANDLON, J. H.
            PERSONALITY CHARACTERISTICS WHICH DIFFERENTIATE CREATIVE MALE ADOLESCENTS
            AND ADULTS.
            JOURNAL OF PERSONALITY, 1968, 36, 528-552.
                (VALIDITY:CONSTRUCT; FACTOR ANALYSIS; N=938 ADOLESCENTS AND 200
                ADULTS)
        @APPLICATION 1968 G-22

496   STEINER, I. D.
            REACTIONS TO ADVERSE AND FAVORABLE EVALUATIONS OF ONE'S SELF.
            JOURNAL OF PERSONALITY, 1968, 36, 553-563.
                (MENTION; CORRELATES:BEHAVIORAL, PSYCHOLOGICAL; N=52 MALE COLLEGE
                STUDENTS)
        @APPLICATION 1968 B-37 C-14 S-184

497   BRIGHTBILL, R., & ZAMANSKY, H. S.
            THE EFFECT OF EXPECTANCY AND FREQUENCY ON THE WORD-RECOGNITION THRESHOLD.
            JOURNAL OF PERSONALITY, 1968, 36, 564-573.
                (CORRELATES:PSYCHOLOGICAL, PHYSIOLOGICAL, INTELLIGENCE; N=11 MALE,
                4 FEMALE COLLEGE STUDENTS)
        @APPLICATION 1968 W-31

498   HELSON, R.
            EFFECTS OF SIBLING CHARACTERISTICS AND PARENTAL VALUES ON CREATIVE INTEREST
            AND ACHIEVEMENT.
            JOURNAL OF PERSONALITY, 1968, 36, 589-607.
                (CORRELATES:BEHAVIORAL, DEMOGRAPHIC, ENVIRONMENTAL; N=152)
        @APPLICATION 1968 B-4 G-22 M-22 B-76 B-6 B-78 G-118

499   WEINSTEIN, E. A., BECKHOUSE, L. S., BLUMSTEIN, P. W., & STEIN, R. B.
            INTERPERSONAL STRATEGIES UNDER CONDITIONS OF GAIN AND LOSS.
            JOURNAL OF PERSONALITY, 1968, 36, 616-634.
                (VALIDITY:CONSTRUCT; CORRELATES:BEHAVIORAL; N=48 COLLEGE STUDENTS)
        @APPLICATION 1968 C-14 C-27 J-15 K-94

500   PHARES, E. J.
            DIFFERENTIAL UTILIZATION OF INFORMATION AS A FUNCTION OF INTERNAL-EXTERNAL
            CONTROL.
            JOURNAL OF PERSONALITY, 1968, 36, 649-662.
                (USED AS CRITERION; N=214 MALE COLLEGE STUDENTS)
        @APPLICATION 1968 R-18

501   LEFCOURT, H. M., LEWIS, L., & SILVERMAN, I. W.
            INTERNAL VS. EXTERNAL CONTROL OF REINFORCEMENT AND ATTENTION IN A
            DECISION-MAKING TASK.
            JOURNAL OF PERSONALITY, 1968, 36, 663-682.
                (CORRELATES:BEHAVIORAL; N=80 COLLEGE STUDENTS)
        @APPLICATION 1968 R-18

502   CRANDALL, J. E.
            EFFECTS OF NEED FOR APPROVAL AND INTOLERANCE OF AMBIGUITY UPON STIMULUS
            PREFERENCE.
            JOURNAL OF PERSONALITY, 1968, 36, 67-83.
                (CORRELATES:PSYCHOLOGICAL; USED AS CRITERION; N=29 COLLEGE STUDENTS
                (EXP. 1), 20 COLLEGE STUDENTS (EXP. 2), 32 COLLEGE STUDENTS (EXP. 3))
        @APPLICATION 1968 C-27 B-37 E-1

503   ENDLER, N. S., & HUNT, J. M. V.
            GENERALIZABILITY OF CONTRIBUTIONS FROM SOURCES OF VARIANCE IN THE S-R
            INVENTORIES OF ANXIOUSNESS.
            JOURNAL OF PERSONALITY, 1969, 37, 1-24.
                (REVISION; VALIDITY:CONSTRUCT, CRITERION; CORRELATES:DEMOGRAPHIC;
                NORMATIVE DATA; FORTY-THREE SAMPLES: MEDIAN N= APPROXIMATELY
                100 COLLEGE STUDENTS)
        @APPLICATION 1969 E-16

504   SCHWARTZ, S. H., FELDMAN, K. A., BROWN, M. E., & HEINGARTNER, A.
            SOME PERSONALITY CORRELATES OF CONDUCT IN TWO SITUATIONS OF MORAL CONFLICT.
            JOURNAL OF PERSONALITY, 1969, 37, 41-57.
                .(CORRELATES:BEHAVIORAL: N=35 STUDENTS)
        aAPPLICATION 1969 P-75 A-55 K-27

505   WINTER, S. K.
            CHARACTERISTICS OF FANTASY WHILE NURSING.
            JOURNAL OF PERSONALITY, 1969, 37, 58-72.
                (RELIABILITY:INTERRATER; VALIDITY:CROSS-VALIDATION; N=29 MIDDLE-CLASS
                MOTHERS OF FIRST BABIES)
        aAPPLICATION 1969 M-20

506   CROWNE, D. P., CONN, L. K., MARLOWE, D., & EDWARDS, C. N.
            SOME DEVELOPMENTAL ANTECEDENTS OF LEVEL OF ASPIRATION.
            JOURNAL OF PERSONALITY, 1969, 37, 73-92.
                (CORRELATES:PSYCHOLOGICAL, DEMOGRAPHIC, ENVIRONMENTAL; N=46 MALE,
                37 FEMALE YOUNG ADULTS)
        aAPPLICATION 1969 S-13 G-20 R-17

507   SINGER, S.
            FACTORS RELATED TO PARTICIPANTS' MEMORY OF A CONVERSATION.
            JOURNAL OF PERSONALITY, 1969, 37, 93-110.
                (MODIFICATION; CORRELATES:PSYCHOLOGICAL; N=64 FEMALE UNDERGRADUATES)
        aAPPLICATION 1969 G-22 W-8 C-27 G-21

508   FEATHER, N. T.
            COGNITIVE DEFFERENTIATION, ATTITUDE STRENGTH AND DOGMATISM.
            JOURNAL OF PERSONALITY, 1969, 37, 111-126.
                (CORRELATES:PSYCHOLOGICAL; N=167 MALE UNDERGRADUATES)
        aAPPLICATION 1969 R-8

509   CRANDALL, J. E.
            SELF-PERCEPTION AND INTERPERSONAL ATTRACTION AS RELATED TO TOLERANCE-
            INTOLERANCE OF AMBIGUITY.
            JOURNAL OF PERSONALITY, 1969, 37, 127-140.
                (CORRELATES:PSYCHOLOGICAL; USED AS CRITERION; N=69 UNDERGRADUATES)
        aAPPLICATION 1969 B-37 L-35 C-27

510   MILLER, A. G.
            AMOUNT OF INFORMATION AND STIMULUS VALENCE AS DETERMINANTS OF COGNITIVE
            COMPLEXITY.
            JOURNAL OF PERSONALITY, 1969, 37, 141-157.
                (CORRELATES:PSYCHOLOGICAL, DEMOGRAPHIC; USED AS CRITERION;
                N=179 MALE AND 167 FEMALE STUDENTS)
        aAPPLICATION 1969 C-76 B-97

511   SARASON, I. G.
            BIRTH ORDER, TEST ANXIETY AND LEARNING.
            JOURNAL OF PERSONALITY, 1969, 37, 171-177.
                (CORRELATES:PSYCHOLOGICAL, DEMOGRAPHIC, INTELLIGENCE; USED AS
                CRITERION; N=80 MALE STUDENTS)
        aAPPLICATION 1969 S-5

512   ALKER, H. A.
            RATIONALITY AND ACHIEVEMENT: A COMPARISON OF THE ATKINSON-MCCLELLAND
            AND KOGAN-WALLACH FORMULATIONS.
            JOURNAL OF PERSONALITY, 1969, 37, 207-224.
                (RELIABILITY:INTERRATER; VALIDITY:CONSTRUCT;
                CORRELATES:PSYCHOLOGICAL; N=96 HIGH SCHOOL MALES)
        aAPPLICATION 1969 A-8 M-7 H-22 C-27

513   REST, J., TURIEL, E., & KOHLBERG, L.
            LEVEL OF MORAL DEVELOPMENT AS A DETERMINANT OF PREFERENCE AND
            COMPREHENSION OF MORAL JUDGMENTS MADE BY OTHERS.
            JOURNAL OF PERSONALITY, 1969, 37, 225-252.
                (RELIABILITY:INTERRATER; VALIDITY:CONSTRUCT; CORRELATES:DEMOGRAPHIC;
                N=23 MALE, 22 FEMALE GRADE SCHOOL CHILDREN)
        aAPPLICATION 1969 K-27

514   GOLDSTEIN, J. W., & ROSENFELD, H. M.
            INSECURITY AND PREFERENCE FOR PERSONS SIMILAR TO ONESELF.
            JOURNAL OF PERSONALITY, 1969, 37, 253-268.
                (CORRELATES:PSYCHOLOGICAL; N=16 FEMALE STUDENTS (EXP. 1) AND 63 MALE
                AND FEMALE STUDENTS EACH (EXP. 2))
        @APPLICATION 1969 M-50 C-27 R-80 G-115 G-116

515   BLATT, S. J., ALLISON, J., & FEIRSTEIN, A.
            THE CAPACITY TO COPE WITH COGNITIVE COMPLEXITY.
            JOURNAL OF PERSONALITY, 1969, 37, 269-288.
                (RELIABILITY:INTERRATER; CORRELATES:PSYCHOLOGICAL, INTELLIGENCE; N=50
                MALE GRADUATE STUDENTS)
        @APPLICATION 1969 R-30 H-117

516   KAPLAN, M. F.
            EXPRESSION OF TAT HOSTILITY AS A FUNCTION OF SELF-REPORTED HOSTILITY,
            AROUSAL, AND CUE CHARACTERISTICS.
            JOURNAL OF PERSONALITY, 1969, 37, 289-296.
                (RELIABILITY:INTERRATER; USED AS CRITERION; N=149 FEMALE STUDENTS AND
                N=40 FEMALES)
        @APPLICATION 1969 S-36 E-36

517   FORWARD, J. R.
            GROUP ACHIEVEMENT MOTIVATION AND INDIVIDUAL MOTIVES TO ACHIEVE SUCCESS
            AND TO AVOID FAILURE.
            JOURNAL OF PERSONALITY, 1969, 37, 297-309.
                (CORRELATES:PSYCHOLOGICAL; USED AS CRITERION; N=64 SENIOR HIGH SCHOOL
                BOYS)
        @APPLICATION 1969 M-7 M-4

518   CARR, J. E.
            DIFFERENTIATION AS A FUNCTION OF SOURCE CHARACTERISTICS AND JUDGES
            CONCEPTUAL STRUCTURE.
            JOURNAL OF PERSONALITY, 1969, 37, 378-386.
                (USED AS CRITERION; N=20 MALE STUDENTS (EXP. 1), AND 27 MALE
                MEDICAL STUDENTS (EXP. 2))
        @APPLICATION 1969 C-77 S-41

519   SHAPIRO, K. J., & ALEXANDER, I. E.
            EXTRAVERSION-INTROVERSION, AFFILIATION, AND ANXIETY.
            JOURNAL OF PERSONALITY, 1969, 37, 387-406.
                (MODIFICATION; USED AS CRITERION; N=171 UNDERGRADUATES)
        @APPLICATION 1969 M-22 S-170 M-20

520   GLASS, D. C., LAVIN, D. E., HENCHY, T., GORDON, A., MAHEW, P., & DONOHOE, P.
            OBESITY AND PERSUASIBILITY.
            JOURNAL OF PERSONALITY, 1969, 37, 407-414.
                (MENTION; CORRELATES:PHYSIOLOGICAL; N=65 MALES, 51 FEMALES)
        @APPLICATION 1969 J-8 F-56 F-72 J-7

521   BUTT, D. S., & FISKE, D. W.
            DIFFERENTIAL CORRELATES OF DOMINANCE SCALES.
            JOURNAL OF PERSONALITY, 1969, 37, 415-428.
                (VALIDITY:CONSTRUCT; CORRELATES:PSYCHOLOGICAL; N=118 STUDENTS AND 248
                AIRMEN)
        @APPLICATION 1969 G-19 A-6 C-10 E-2 J-1 T-27 B-99

522   RITCHIE, E., & PHARES, E. J.
            ATTITUDE CHANGE AS A FUNCTION OF INTERNAL-EXTERNAL CONTROL AND
            COMMUNICATOR STATUS.
            JOURNAL OF PERSONALITY, 1969, 37, 429-443.
                (USED AS CRITERION; N=152 FEMALE STUDENTS)
        @APPLICATION 1969 R-18

523   RULE, B. G., & SANDILANDS, M. L.
            TEST ANXIETY, CONFIDENCE, COMMITMENT, AND CONFORMITY.
            JOURNAL OF PERSONALITY, 1969, 37, 460-467.
                (CORRELATES:BEHAVIORAL; USED AS CRITERION; N=96 FEMALE STUDENTS)
        @APPLICATION 1969 M-4

524   MENGES, R. J.
            STUDENT-INSTRUCTOR COGNITIVE COMPATIBILITY IN THE LARGE LECTURE CLASS.
            JOURNAL OF PERSONALITY, 1969, 37, 444-459.
                (CORRELATES:PSYCHOLOGICAL; N=280 STUDENTS)
        @APPLICATION 1969 M-129 R-82

525   ROSENFELD, H. M., & NAUMAN, D. J.
            EFFECTS OF DOGMATISM ON THE DEVELOPMENT OF INFORMAL RELATIONSHIPS AMONG
            WOMEN.
            JOURNAL OF PERSONALITY, 1969, 37, 497-511.
                (CORRELATES:PSYCHOLOGICAL, ENVIRONMENTAL; N=68 FRESHMEN WOMEN)
        @APPLICATION 1969 R-8

526   RESNICK, J. H.
            EFFECTS OF SWITCHING CONDITIONS OF THREAT ON HIGH- AND LOW-ANXIOUS SUBJECTS
            MIDWAY THROUGH VERBAL CONDITIONING.
            JOURNAL OF PERSONALITY, 1969, 37, 567-580.
                (VALIDITY:CONSTRUCT; CORRELATES:BEHAVIORAL, PSYCHOLOGICAL,
                ENVIRONMENTAL; USED AS CRITERION; N=64 COLLEGE MALES)
        @APPLICATION 1969 S-5

527   EAGLEY, A. H.
            SEX DIFFERENCES IN THE RELATIONSHIP BETWEEN SELF-ESTEEM AND SUSCEPTIBILITY
            TO SOCIAL INFLUENCE.
            JOURNAL OF PERSONALITY, 1969, 37, 581-591.
                (DESCRIPTION; MENTION; RELIABILITY:INTERNAL CONSISTENCY; CORRELATES:
                PSYCHOLOGICAL; USED AS CRITERION; N=217 NINTH-GRADERS)
        @APPLICATION 1969 G-20 J-7 E-47 H-190

528   PALMER, R. D., & BROVERMAN, D. M.
            AUTOMATIZATION AND HYPOCHONDRIASIS.
            JOURNAL OF PERSONALITY, 1969, 37, 592-600.
                (CORRELATES:PSYCHOLOGICAL; FACTOR ANALYSIS; N=60 COLLEGE MALES AND
                30 HOSPITALIZED MALES)
        @APPLICATION 1969 D-45 C-153 P-22 W-19 G-78 T-20

529   EAGLY, A. H.
            RESPONSES TO ATTITUDE-DISCREPANT INFORMATION AS A FUNCTION OF INTOLERANCE
            OF INCONSISTENCY AND CATEGORY WIDTH.
            JOURNAL OF PERSONALITY, 1969, 37, 601-617.
                (RELIABILITY:INTERNAL CONSISTENCY; CORRELATES:PSYCHOLOGICAL; N=189
                MALE AND FEMALE COLLEGE STUDENTS)
        @APPLICATION 1969 B-37 R-8 P-7

530   COTTLE, T. J., HOWARD, P., & PLECK, J.
            ADOLESCENT PERCEPTIONS OF TIME: THE EFFECT OF AGE, SEX, AND SOCIAL CLASS.
            JOURNAL OF PERSONALITY, 1969, 37, 636-650.
                (DESCRIPTION; CORRELATES:PSYCHOLOGICAL, DEMOGRAPHIC; USED AS
                CRITERION; N=180 AUSTRIAN BOYS AND GIRLS)
        @APPLICATION 1969 C-154 C-155 C-156 C-166

531   KLEIN, E. B., & GOULD, L. J.
            ALIENATION AND IDENTIFICATION IN COLLEGE WOMEN.
            JOURNAL OF PERSONALITY, 1969, 37, 468-480.
                (RELIABILITY:INTERNAL CONSISTENCY; VALIDITY:CONSTRUCT;
                CORRELATES:PSYCHOLOGICAL; USED AS CRITERION; N=150 FEMALE STUDENTS)
        @APPLICATION 1969 S-9 S-123 C-31 S-80 D-45 C-23 C-27 H-22 S-186 C-137

532   PEARSON, P. H.
            OPENNESS TO EXPERIENCE AS RELATED TO ORGANISMIC VALUEING.
            JOURNAL OF PERSONALITY, 1969, 37, 481-496.
                (MENTION; RELIABILITY:INTERNAL CONSISTENCY; VALIDITY:CONSTRUCT;
                CORRELATES:PSYCHOLOGICAL; 3 STUDENT SAMPLES: N=52, 29, AND 20)
        @APPLICATION 1969, M-20 C-27 P-78 P-79 P-80 P-81 P-83 M-101
        @M-261

533   BIERI, J.
            CATEGORY WIDTH AS A MEASURE OF DISCRIMINATION.
            JOURNAL OF PERSONALITY, 1969, 37, 513-521.
                (CORRELATES:PSYCHOLOGICAL, DEMOGRAPHIC, ENVIRONMENTAL;
                USED AS CRITERION; NORMATIVE DATA; N=151 FEMALE, 167 MALE COLLEGE
                STUDENTS)
        @APPLICATION 1969 P-7 T-2

534   PRESS, A. N., CROCKETT, W. H., & ROSENKRANTZ, P. S.
            COGNITIVE COMPLEXITY AND THE LEARNING OF BALANCED AND UNBALANCED SOCIAL
            STRUCTURES.
            JOURNAL OF PERSONALITY, 1969, 37, 541-553.
                (CORRELATES:PSYCHOLOGICAL; USED AS CRITERION; N=108 HIGH SCHOOL
                STUDENTS)
        @APPLICATION 1969 C-76

535   CORFIELD, V. K.
            THE ROLE OF AROUSAL AND COGNITIVE COMPLEXITY IN SUSCEPTIBILITY TO SOCIAL
            INFLUENCE.
            JOURNAL OF PERSONALITY, 1969, 37, 554-566.
                (CORRELATES:PSYCHOLOGICAL, PHYSIOLOGICAL; USED AS CRITERION;
                N=120 MALE COLLEGE STUDENTS)
        @APPLICATION 1969 T-16 B-18

536   BARCLAY, A. M.
            THE EFFECTS OF HOSTILITY ON PHYSIOLOGICAL AND FANTASY RESPONSES.
            JOURNAL OF PERSONALITY, 1969, 37, 651-667.
                (VALIDITY:CONSTRUCT, CRITERION; CORRELATES:PSYCHOLOGICAL,
                PHYSIOLOGICAL; USED AS CRITERION; N=64 MEMBERS OF SORORITIES AND A
                FRATERNITY)
        @APPLICATION 1969 M-20 B-184 F-83

537   WHITELEY, R. H., JR., & WATTS, W. A.
            INFORMATION COST, DECISION CONSEQUENCE, AND SELECTED PERSONALITY VARIABLES
            AS FACTORS IN PREDECISION INFORMATION SEEKING.
            JOURNAL OF PERSONALITY, 1969, 37, 325-341.
                (CORRELATES:BEHAVIORAL; N=72 FEMALE STUDENTS)
        @APPLICATION 1969 H-12 G-76 P-7 G-21 W-2 K-94

538   CLINE, V. B., & RICHARDS, J. M., JR.
            ACCURACY OF INTERPERSONAL PERCEPTION--A GENERAL TRAIT?
            JOURNAL OF ABNORMAL AND SOCIAL PSYCHOLOGY, 1960, 60, 1-7.
                (CORRELATES:BEHAVIORAL, PSYCHOLOGICAL; USED AS CRITERION; N=50
                COLLEGE STUDENTS)
        @APPLICATION 1960 D-45 S-33 G-22 G-21

539   REITMAN, W. R.
            MOTIVATIONAL INDUCTION AND THE BEHAVIORAL CORRELATES OF THE ACHIEVEMENT
            AND AFFILIATION MOTIVES.
            JOURNAL OF ABNORMAL AND SOCIAL PSYCHOLOGY, 1960, 60, 8-13.
                (CORRELATES:BEHAVIORAL, INTELLIGENCE; N=258 COLLEGE MALES)
        @APPLICATION 1960 M-7

540   BERKOWITZ, L.
            SOME FACTORS AFFECTING THE REDUCTION OF OVERT HOSTILITY.
            JOURNAL OF ABNORMAL AND SOCIAL PSYCHOLOGY, 1960, 60, 14-21.
                (MENTION; N=40 COLLEGE STUDENTS)
        @APPLICATION 1960 M-20

541   GOLDSTEIN, M. J., & BARTHOL, R. P.
            FANTASY RESPONSES TO SUBLIMINAL STIMULI.
            JOURNAL OF ABNORMAL AND SOCIAL PSYCHOLOGY, 1960, 60, 22-26.
                (CORRELATES:PSYCHOLOGICAL; N=36 COLLEGE STUDENTS)
        @APPLICATION 1960 M-20

542   ATKINSON, J. W., BASTIAN, J. R., EARL, R. W., & LITWIN, G. H.
            THE ACHIEVEMENT MOTIVE, GOAL SETTING, AND PROBABILITY PREFERENCES.
            JOURNAL OF ABNORMAL AND SOCIAL PSYCHOLOGY, 1960, 60, 27-36.
                (CORRELATES:BEHAVIORAL, PSYCHOLOGICAL; N=66 COLLEGE MALES)
        @APPLICATION 1960 F-20

543   LAMBERT, W. E., HODGSON, R. C., GARDNER, R. C., & FILLENBAUM, S.
            EVALUATIONAL REACTIONS TO SPOKEN LANGUAGES.
            JOURNAL OF ABNORMAL AND SOCIAL PSYCHOLOGY, 1960, 60, 44-51.
                (CORRELATES:PSYCHOLOGICAL, ENVIRONMENTAL; CROSS-CULTURAL
                APPLICATION; N=64 ENGLISH SPEAKING AND 66 FRENCH SPEAKING COLLEGE
                STUDENTS)
        @APPLICATION 1960 A-5

544   ATKINSON, J. W., & LITWIN, G. H.
            ACHIEVEMENT MOTIVE AND TEST ANXIETY CONCEIVED AS MOTIVE TO APPROACH SUCCESS
            AND MOTIVE TO AVOID FAILURE.
            JOURNAL OF ABNORMAL AND SOCIAL PSYCHOLOGY, 1960, 60, 52-63.
                (CORRELATES:BEHAVIORAL, PSYCHOLOGICAL; N=49 COLLEGE MALES)
        @APPLICATION 1960 F-20 E-2 M-4

545   PINE, F.
            INCIDENTAL STIMULATION; A STUDY OF PRECONSCIOUS TRANSFORMATIONS.
            JOURNAL OF ABNORMAL AND SOCIAL PSYCHOLOGY, 1960, 60, 68-75.
                (USED AS CRITERION; N=24 COLLEGE MALES)
        @APPLICATION 1960 S-97 M-20

546   BIERI, J.
            PARENTAL IDENTIFICATION, ACCEPTANCE OF AUTHORITY AND WITHIN-SEX
                (CORRELATES:PSYCHOLOGICAL, DEMOGRAPHIC, INTELLIGENCE; N=25 GIRLS AND
                17 BOYS)
        @APPLICATION 1960 W-19 B-190 O-16

547   LIPETZ, M. E.
            THE EFFECTS OF INFORMATION ON THE ASSESSMENT OF ATTITUDES BY AUTHORITARIANS
            AND NONAUTHORITARIANS.
            JOURNAL OF ABNORMAL AND SOCIAL PSYCHOLOGY, 1960, 60, 95-99.
                (CORRELATES:PSYCHOLOGICAL; USED AS CRITERION; N=96 COLLEGE MALES)
        @APPLICATION 1960 A-5

548   ROSENBAUM, M. E., & DE CHARMS, R.
            DIRECT AND VICARIOUS REDUCTION OF HOSTILITY.
            JOURNAL OF ABNORMAL AND SOCIAL PSYCHOLOGY, 1960, 60, 105-111.
                (MENTION; CORRELATES:BEHAVIORAL, PSYCHOLOGICAL; N=56 COLLEGE MALES)
        @APPLICATION 1960 J-7 A-5

549   BORG, W. R.
            PREDICTION OF SMALL GROUP ROLE BEHAVIOR FROM PERSONALITY VARIABLES.
            JOURNAL OF ABNORMAL AND SOCIAL PSYCHOLOGY, 1960, 60, 112-116.
                (CORRELATES:BEHAVIORAL; VALIDITY:CRITERION; FACTOR ANALYSIS;
                N=819 AIR FORCE PERSONNEL)
        @APPLICATION 1960 S-11 A-5 C-125 G-39 G-61

550   WESSMAN, A. E., RICKS, D. F., & TYL, M. M.
            CHARACTERISTICS AND CONCOMITANTS OF MOOD FLUCTUATION IN COLLEGE WOMEN.
            JOURNAL OF ABNORMAL AND SOCIAL PSYCHOLOGY, 1960, 60, 117-126.
                (CORRELATES:PSYCHOLOGICAL, PHYSIOLOGICAL, ENVIRONMENTAL; N=25
                COLLEGE FEMALES)
        @APPLICATION 1960 R-12

551   FULKERSON, S. C.
            INDIVIDUAL DIFFERENCES IN REACTION TO FAILURE-INDUCED STRESS.
            JOURNAL OF ABNORMAL AND SOCIAL PSYCHOLOGY, 1960, 60, 136-139.
                (CORRELATES:BEHAVIORAL, ENVIRONMENTAL; N=287 LOW AND 294 HIGH
                ADJUSTMENT AIR FORCE CADETS)
        @APPLICATION 1960 D-45

552   WILSON, W. C.
            EXTRINSIC RELIGIOUS VALUES AND PREJUDICE.
            JOURNAL OF ABNORMAL AND SOCIAL PSYCHOLOGY, 1960, 60, 286-288.
                (VALIDITY:CONSTRUCT; N=207 SUBJECTS COVERING WIDE SCOPE OF RELIGIOUS,
                ETHNIC, AND GEOGRAPHIC VARIATIONS)
        @APPLICATION 1960 O-17 L-32

553   COOPERSMITH, S.
            SELF-ESTEEM AND NEED ACHIEVEMENT AS DETERMINANTS OF SELECTIVE RECALL AND
            REPETITION.
            JOURNAL OF ABNORMAL AND SOCIAL PSYCHOLOGY, 1960, 60, 310-317.
                (RELIABILITY:INTERRATER; CORRELATES:BEHAVIORAL, PSYCHOLOGICAL;
                USED AS CRITERION; N=48 SCHOOL CHILDREN)
        @APPLICATION 1960 C-38 M-7 C-190

554   RYCHLAK, J. F.
            RECALLED DREAM THEMES AND PERSONALITY.
            JOURNAL OF ABNORMAL AND SOCIAL PSYCHOLOGY, 1960, 60, 140-143.
            DEFFERENCES IN COGNITIVE BEHAVIOR.
            JOURNAL OF ABNORMAL AND SOCIAL PSYCHOLOGY, 1960, 60, 76-79.
                  (CORRELATES:PSYCHOLOGICAL, DEMOGRAPHIC; USED AS CRITERION; N=30 MALE,
                  30 FEMALE COLLEGE STUDENTS)
       @APPLICATION 1960 E-2

555   WORRELL, I.
            EPPS N ACHIEVEMENT AND VERBAL PAIRED-ASSOCIATES LEARNING.
            JOURNAL OF ABNORMAL AND SOCIAL PSYCHOLOGY, 1960, 60, 147-150.
                  (CORRELATES:BEHAVIORAL, PSYCHOLOGICAL; N=38 COLLEGE STUDENTS)
       @APPLICATION 1960 E-2

556   CHANEY, M. V., & VINACKE, W. E.
            ACHIEVEMENT AND NURTURANCE IN TRIADS VARYING IN POWER DISTRIBUTION.
            JOURNAL OF ABNORMAL AND SOCIAL PSYCHOLOGY, 1960, 60, 175-181.
                  (CORRELATES:BEHAVIORAL; N=60 COLLEGE MALES)
       @APPLICATION 1960 C-89

557   BORGATTA, E. F.
            THE STABILITY OF INTERPERSONAL JUDGMENTS IN INDEPENDENT SITUATIONS.
            JOURNAL OF ABNORMAL AND SOCIAL PSYCHOLOGY, 1960, 60, 188-194.
                  (MODIFICATION; VALIDITY:CONSTRUCT; N=99 COLLEGE MALES)
       @APPLICATION 1960 B-26

558   ROGERS, J. M.
            OPERANT CONDITIONING IN A QUASI-THERAPY SETTING.
            JOURNAL OF ABNORMAL AND SOCIAL PSYCHOLOGY, 1960, 60, 247-252.
                  (RELIABILITY:INTERRATER; USED AS CRITERION; N=36 COLLEGE MALES)
       @APPLICATION 1960 T-2
       @B-60

559   MAHONE, C. H.
            FEAR OF FAILURE AND UNREALISTIC VOCATIONAL ASPRIATION.
            JOURNAL OF ABNORMAL AND SOCIAL PSYCHOLOGY, 1960, 60, 253-261.
                  (VALIDITY:CONSTRUCT; CORRELATES:PSYCHOLOGICAL; N=135 COLLEGE MALES)
       @APPLICATION 1960 M-7 A-8

560   MOGAR, R. E.
            THREE VERSIONS OF THE F SCALE AND PERFORMANCE ON THE SEMANTIC DIFFERENTIAL.
            JOURNAL OF ABNORMAL AND SOCIAL PSYCHOLOGY, 1960, 60, 262-265.
                  (RELIABILITY:RETEST; VALIDITY:CONSTRUCT; CORRELATES:PSYCHOLOGICAL,
                  ENVIRONMENTAL; N=315 COLLEGE STUDENTS)
       @APPLICATION 1960 A-5 J-4 B-192 O-16

561   BENEDETTI, D. T., & HILL, J. G.
            A DETERMINER OF THE CENTRALITY OF A TRAIT IN IMPRESSION FORMATION.
            JOURNAL OF ABNORMAL AND SOCIAL PSYCHOLOGY, 1960, 60, 278-280.
                  (CORRELATES:BEHAVIORAL, ENVIRONMENTAL; USED AS CRITERION; N=204
                  COLLEGE STUDENTS)
       @APPLICATION 1960 G-70

562   GAGE, N. L., & CHATTERJEE, B. B.
            THE PSYCHOLOGICAL MEANING OF ACQUIESCENCE SET: FURTHER EVIDENCE.
            JOURNAL OF ABNORMAL AND SOCIAL PSYCHOLOGY, 1960. 60, 280-283.
                  (REVIEW ARTICLE; VALIDITY:CONTENT)
       @APPLICATION 1960 C-57

563   SAPOLSKY, A.
            EFFECT OF INTERPERSONAL RELATIONSHIPS UPON VERBAL CONDITIONING.
            JOURNAL OF ABNORMAL AND SOCIAL PSYCHOLOGY, 1960, 60, 241-246.
                  (CORRELATES:ENVIRONMENTAL; USED AS CRITERION; N=30 COLLEGE FEMALES)
       @APPLICATION 1960 S-11 G-81

564   RUEBUSH, B. K.
            INTERFERING AND FACILITATING EFFECTS OF TEST ANXIETY.
            JOURNAL OF ABNORMAL AND SOCIAL PSYCHOLOGY, 1960, 60, 205-212.
                  (CORRELATES:PSYCHOLOGICAL; USED AS CRITERION; N=280 SCHOOLBOYS)
       @APPLICATION 1960 S-5 W-15

565   MILGRAM, N. A.
             COGNITIVE AND EMPATHIC FACTORS IN ROLE-TAKING BY SCHIZOPHRENIC AND BRAIN-
             DAMAGED PATIENTS.
             JOURNAL OF ABNORMAL AND SOCIAL PSYCHOLOGY, 1960, 60, 219-224.
                    (CORRELATES:PSYCHOLOGICAL; N=32 SCHIZOPHRENIC, 30 BRAIN DAMAGED
                    PATIENTS AND 20 NORMAL SS)
        @APPLICATION 1960 T-3 A-60

566   MARTIN, B., LUNDY, R. M., & LEWIN, M. H.
             VERBAL AND GSR RESPONSES IN EXPERIMENTAL INTERVIEWS AS A FUNCTION OF
             THREE DEGREES OF "THERAPIST" COMMUNICATION.
             JOURNAL OF ABNORMAL AND SOCIAL PSYCHOLOGY, 1960, 60, 234-240.
                    (CORRELATES:BEHAVIORAL. PHYSIOLOGICAL; USED AS CRITERION;
                    N=240 COLLEGE STUDENTS)
        @APPLICATION 1960 H-51 M-154

567   MCDONNELL, G. J., & CARPENTER, J. A.
             MANIFEST ANXIETY AND PRESTIMULUS CONDUCTANCE LEVELS.
             JOURNAL OF ABNORMAL AND SOCIAL PSYCHOLOGY, 1960, 60, 437-438.
                    (CORRELATES:PHYSIOLOGICAL; N=32 MEN AND 8 WOMEN)
        @APPLICATION 1960 M-4

568   GILBERSTADT, H., & DAVENPORT, G.
             SOME RELATIONS BETWEEN GSR CONDITIONING AND JUDGMENT OF ANXIETY.
             JOURNAL OF ABNORMAL AND SOCIAL PSYCHOLOGY, 1960, 60, 441-443.
                    (CORRELATES:PHYSIOLOGICAL; N=19 PSYCHIATRIC PATIENTS)
        @APPLICATION 1960 D-45 T-2

569   FORDYCE, W. E., & CROW, W. R.
             EGO DISJUNCTION: A FAILURE TO REPLICATE TREHULIS' RESULTS.
             JOURNAL OF ABNORMAL AND SOCIAL PSYCHOLOGY, 1960, 60, 446-448.
                    (VALIDITY:CONSTRUCT; N=104 PSYCHIATRIC PATIENTS)
        @APPLICATION 1960 D-45 E-2

570   BROVERMAN, D. M., JORDON, E. J., JR., & PHILLIPS, L.
             ACHIEVEMENT MOTIVATION IN FANTASY AND BEHAVIOR.
             JOURNAL OF ABNORMAL AND SOCIAL PSYCHOLOGY, 1960, 60, 374-378.
                    (CORRELATES:BEHAVIORAL. PSYCHOLOGICAL, N=37 CHURCH MEMBERS)
        @APPLICATION 1960 P-84 F-76

571   ALTMAN, I., & MCGINNIES, E.
             INTERPERSONAL PERCEPTION AND COMMUNICATION IN DISCUSSION GROUPS OF VARIED
             ATTITUDINAL COMPOSITION.
             JOURNAL OF ABNORMAL AND SOCIAL PSYCHOLOGY, 1960, 60, 390-395.
                    (USED AS CRITERION; N=500 BOYS)
        @APPLICATION 1960 A-17

572   ZUCKERMAN, M.
             THE EFFECTS OF SUBLIMINAL AND SUPRALIMINAL SUGGESTION ON VERBAL
             PRODUCTIVITY.
             JOURNAL OF ABNORMAL AND SOCIAL PSYCHOLOGY, 1960, 60, 404-411.
                    (CORRELATES:ENVIRONMENTAL; N=33 STUDENT NURSES AND 3 SECRETARIES)
        @APPLICATION 1960 M-20

573   EIGENBRODE, C. R., & SHIPMAN, W. Q.
             THE BODY IMAGE BARRIER CONCEPT.
             JOURNAL OF ABNORMAL AND SOCIAL PSYCHOLOGY, 1960, 60, 450-452.
                    (RELIABILITY:INTERRATER; VALIDITY:CONSTRUCT; N=83 PSYCHOSOMATIC
                    PATIENTS)
        @APPLICATION 1960 R-30 F-135

574   FARINA, A.
             PATTERNS OF ROLE DOMINANCE AND CONFLICT IN PARENTS OF SCHIZOPHRENIC
             PATIENTS.
             JOURNAL OF ABNORMAL AND SOCIAL PSYCHOLOGY, 1960, 61, 31-38.
                    (DESCRIPTION; RELIABILITY:INTERRATER; CORRELATES:BEHAVIORAL,
                    PSYCHOLOGICAL, DEMOGRAPHIC; N=36 PARENTS OF WHITE MALE
                    SCHIZOPHRENICS)
        @APPLICATION 1960 S-9 F-15

575   IZARD, C. E.
            PERSONALITY SIMILARITY AND FRIENDSHIP.
            JOURNAL OF ABNORMAL AND SOCIAL PSYCHOLOGY, 1960, 61, 47-51.
                    (CORRELATES:BEHAVIORAL, PSYCHOLOGICAL; N=200 HIGH SCHOOL AND
                    COLLEGE STUDENTS)
        @APPLICATION 1960 E-2 M-145

576   BECKER, W. C.
            CORTICAL INHIBITION AND EXTRAVERSION-INTROVERSION.
            JOURNAL OF ABNORMAL AND SOCIAL PSYCHOLOGY, 1960, 61, 52-66.
                    (MENTION; RELIABILITY:INTERNAL CONSISTENCY; CORRELATES:PSYCHOLOGICAL,
                    PHYSIOLOGICAL; N=62 COLLEGE STUDENTS)
        @APPLICATION 1960 G-26 E-5 C-10

577   ALTROCCHI, J., PARSONS, O. A., & DICKOFF, H.
            CHANGES IN SELF-IDEAL DISCREPANCY IN REPRESSORS AND SENSITIZERS.
            JOURNAL OF ABNORMAL AND SOCIAL PSYCHOLOGY, 1960, 61, 67-72.
                    (CORRELATES:PSYCHOLOGICAL; USED AS CRITERION; N=88 STUDENT NURSES)
        @APPLICATION 1960 D-45 W-8 L-35

578   ZIPF, S. G.
            RESISTANCE AND CONFORMITY UNDER REWARD AND PUNISHMENT.
            JOURNAL OF ABNORMAL AND SOCIAL PSYCHOLOGY, 1960, 61, 102-109.
                    (MODIFICATION; CORRELATES:BEHAVIORAL, PSYCHOLOGICAL; N=102 COLLEGE
                    FEMALES)
        @APPLICATION 1960 T-73

579   TRIANDIS, H. C., & TRIANDIS, L. M.
            RACE, SOCIAL CLASS, RELIGION, AND NATIONALITY AS DETERMINANTS OF SOCIAL
            DISTANCE.
            JOURNAL OF ABNORMAL AND SOCIAL PSYCHOLOGY, 1960, 61, 110-118.
                    (DESCRIPTION; RELIABILITY:INTERNAL CONSISTENCY; CORRELATES:
                    PSYCHOLOGICAL, DEMOGRAPHIC; N=86 COLLEGE STUDENTS)
        @APPLICATION 1960 T-8 A-5

580   O'CONNELL, W. E.
            THE ADAPTIVE FUNCTIONS OF WIT AND HUMOR.
            JOURNAL OF ABNORMAL AND SOCIAL PSYCHOLOGY, 1960, 61, 263-270.
                    (RELIABILITY:RETEST; CORRELATES:PSYCHOLOGICAL; N=332 COLLEGE
                    STUDENTS)
        @APPLICATION 1960 W-21

581   KING, G. F., ARMITAGE, S. G., & TILTON, J. R.
            A THERAPEUTIC APPROACH TO SCHIZOPHRENICS OF EXTREME PATHOLOGY: AN OPERANT-
            INTERPERSONAL METHOD.
            JOURNAL OF ABNORMAL AND SOCIAL PSYCHOLOGY, 1960, 61, 276-286.
                    (DESCRIPTION; RELIABILITY:RETEST, INTERRATER; VALIDITY:CRITERION;
                    CORRELATES: BEHAVIORAL, PSYCHOLOGICAL; N=300 MALE PSYCHOTICS)
        @APPLICATION 1960 F-1 L-39 K-112

582   DAVIDS, A., & SILVERMAN, M.
            CASE REPORT: A PSYCHOLOGICAL CASE STUDY OF DEATH DURING PREGNANCY.
            JOURNAL OF ABNORMAL AND SOCIAL PSYCHOLOGY, 1960, 61, 287-291.
                    (CORRELATES:PSYCHOLOGICAL, INTELLIGENCE; N=1 FEMALE PSYCHIATRIC
                    PATIENT)
        @APPLICATION 1960 M-20

583   ROTHSTEIN, R.
            AUTHORITARIANISM AND MEN'S REACTIONS TO SEXUALITY.
            JOURNAL OF ABNORMAL AND SOCIAL PSYCHOLOGY, 1960, 61, 329-334.
                    (MODIFICATION; RELIABILITY:INTERRATER; CORRELATES:PSYCHOLOGICAL;
                    USED AS CRITERION; N=64 STUDENTS)
        @APPLICATION 1960 A-5 M-20

584   ALPERT, R., & HABER, R. N.
            ANXIETY IN ACADEMIC ACHIEVEMENT SITUATIONS.
            JOURNAL OF ABNORMAL AND SOCIAL PSYCHOLOGY, 1960, 61, 207-215.
                    (DESCRIPTION; RELIABILITY:RETEST, INTERNAL CONSISTENCY;
                    CORRELATES:INTELLIGENCE; N=APPROX. 300 COLLEGE MALES)
        @APPLICATION 1960 T-2 W-8 F-35 M-4 A-8

585   MORAN, L. J., GORHAM, D. R., HOLTZMAN, W. H.
           VOCABULARY KNOWLEDGE AND USAGE OF SCHIZOPHRENIC SUBJECTS: A SIX-YEAR
           FOLLOW UP.
           JOURNAL OF ABNORMAL AND SOCIAL PSYCHOLOGY, 1960, 61, 246-254.
                 (RELIABILITY:RETEST, INTER-RATER; CORRELATES: PSYCHOLOGICAL,
                 INTELLIGENCE; N=55 CHRONIC PARANOID SCHIZOPHRENICS)
       @APPLICATION 1960 P-80

586   MATARAZZO, J. D., SASLOW, G., & PAREIS, E. N.
           VERBAL CONDITIONING OF TWO RESPONSE CLASSES: SOME METHODOLOGICAL
           CONSIDERATIONS.
           JOURNAL OF ABNORMAL AND SOCIAL PSYCHOLOGY, 1960, 61, 190-206.
                 (CORRELATES:PSYCHOLOGICAL; N=80 COLLEGE STUDENTS)
       @APPLICATION 1960 T-2

587   REILLY, M. A., COMMINS, W. D., & STEFIC, F. C.
           THE COMPLEMENTARITY OF PERSONALITY NEEDS IN FRIENDSHIP CHOICE.
           JOURNAL OF ABNORMAL AND SOCIAL PSYCHOLOGY, 1960, 61, 292-294.
                 (CORRELATES:BEHAVIORAL, PSYCHOLOGICAL; N=100 COLLEGE STUDENTS)
       @APPLICATION 1960 A-7 E-2

588   GETZELS, J. W., & JACKSON, P. W.
           OCCUPATIONAL CHOICE AND COGNITIVE FUNCTIONING: CAREER ASPIRATIONS OF HIGHLY
           CREATIVE ADOLESCENTS.
           JOURNAL OF ABNORMAL AND SOCIAL PSYCHOLOGY, 1960, 61, 119-123.
                 (DESCRIPTION; RELIABILITY; CORRELATES:PSYCHOLOGICAL, DEMOGRAPHIC,
                 INTELLIGENCE; N=449 ADOLESCENTS)
       @APPLICATION 1960 G-50 G-62

589   DEUTSCH, M.
           TRUST, TRUSTWORTHINESS, AND THE F-SCALE.
           JOURNAL OF ABNORMAL AND SOCIAL PSYCHOLOGY, 1960, 61, 138-190.
                 (MENTION; CORRELATES:BEHAVIORAL, PSYCHOLOGICAL; N=55 COLLEGE
                 STUDENTS)
       @APPLICATION 1960 A-5

590   SECORD, P. F., & SAUMER, E.
           IDENTIFYING JEWISH NAMES: DOES PREJUDICE INCREASE ACCURACY?
           JOURNAL OF ABNORMAL AND SOCIAL PSYCHOLOGY, 1960, 61, 144-145.
                 (CORRELATES:PSYCHOLOGICAL; USED AS CRITERION; N=67 STUDENTS AND
                 197 SOLDIERS)
       @APPLICATION 1960 A-15

591   ROEN, S. R.
           PERSONALITY AND NEGRO-WHITE INTELLIGENCE.
           JOURNAL OF ABNORMAL AND SOCIAL PSYCHOLOGY, 1960, 61, 148-150.
                 (CORRELATES:PSYCHOLOGICAL, DEMOGRAPHIC, INTELLIGENCE; N=50 NEGRO AND
                 50 WHITE MALE SOLDIERS)
       @APPLICATION 1960 T-2 T-25 B-99

592   WILENSKY, H., & SOLOMON, L.
           CHARACTERISTICS OF UNTESTABLE CHRONIC SCHIZOPHRENICS.
           JOURNAL OF ABNORMAL AND SOCIAL PSYCHOLOGY, 1960, 61, 155-158.
                 (CORRELATES:PSYCHOLOGICAL, DEMOGRAPHIC, INTELLIGENCE; N=101 CHRONIC
                 MALE SCHIZOPHRENICS)
       @APPLICATION 1960 R-30

593   RECHTSCHAFFEN, A., & BOOKBINDER, L. J.
           INTROVERSION-EXTRAVERSION AND KINESTHETIC AFTEREFFECTS.
           JOURNAL OF ABNORMAL AND SOCIAL PSYCHOLOGY, 1960, 61, 495-496.
                 (VALIDITY:CONSTRUCT; CORRELATES:BEHAVIORAL, PSYCHOLOGICAL;
                 N=74 UNDERGRADUATES)
       @APPLICATION 1960 G-39

594   LEVIN, H., BALDWIN, A. L., GALLWEY, M., & PAIVIO, A.
           AUDIENCE STRESS, PERSONALITY, AND SPEECH.
           JOURNAL OF ABNORMAL AND SOCIAL PSYCHOLOGY, 1960, 61, 469-473.
                 (DESCRIPTION; CORRELATES:BEHAVIORAL, PSYCHOLOGICAL; USED AS
                 CRITERION; N=48 CHILDREN)
       @APPLICATION 1960 P-87 P-86

595   WAGNER, R. A.
            DIFFERENCES IN RESPONSE LATENCY AND RESPONSE VARIABILITY BETWEEN HIGH
            AND LOW ANXIETY SUBJECTS IN A FLICKER-FUSION TASK.
            JOURNAL OF ABNORMAL AND SOCIAL PSYCHOLOGY, 1960, 61, 355-359.
                    (MENTION; CORRELATES:PSYCHOLOGICAL; USED AS CRITERION; N=20 HIGH
                    ANXIETY PSYCHIATRIC OUTPATIENTS, 20 LOW ANXIETY RELATIVES)
        @APPLICATION 1960 L-160

596   BECKER, J.
            ACHIEVEMENT RELATED CHARACTERISTICS OF MANIC-DEPRESSIVES.
            JOURNAL OF ABNORMAL AND SOCIAL PSYCHOLOGY, 1960, 60, 334-339.
                    (CORRELATES: BEHAVIORAL, ENVIRONMENTAL; N=24 REMITTED
                    MANIC-DEPRESSIVES AND 30 NONPSYCHOTIC PATIENTS)
        @APPLICATION 1960 H-54 D-28 A-5 O-23

597   IZARD, C. E.
            PERSONALITY SIMILARITY, POSITIVE AFFECT, AND INTERPERSONAL ATTRACTION.
            JOURNAL OF ABNORMAL AND SOCIAL PSYCHOLOGY, 1960, 61, 484-485.
                    (CORRELATES:BEHAVIORAL, PSYCHOLOGICAL; N=47 FEMALE UNDERGRADUATES)
        @APPLICATION 1960 E-2

598   CHOWN, S. M.
            A FACTOR ANALYSIS OF THE WESLEY RIGIDITY INVENTORY: ITS RELATIONSHIP TO
            AGE AND NONVERBAL INTELLIGENCE.
            JOURNAL OF ABNORMAL AND SOCIAL PSYCHOLOGY, 1960, 61, 491-494.
                    (CORRELATES:PSYCHOLOGICAL, INTELLIGENCE; FACTOR ANALYSIS; N=200
                    MALES)
        @APPLICATION 1960 W-11

599   KATZ, I., & BENJAMIN, L.
            EFFECTS OF WHITE AUTHORITARIANISM IN BIRACIAL WORK GROUPS.
            JOURNAL OF ABNORMAL AND SOCIAL PSYCHOLOGY, 1960, 61, 448-456.
                    (CORRELATES:BEHAVIORAL, PSYCHOLOGICAL, DEMOGRAPHIC, INTELLIGENCE;
                    N=64 UNDERGRADUATES)
        @APPLICATION 1960 G-145 S-219

600   PEAK, H.
            THE EFFECT OF AROUSED MOTIVATION ON ATTITUDES.
            JOURNAL OF ABNORMAL AND SOCIAL PSYCHOLOGY, 1960, 61, 463-468.
                    (MODIFICATION; CORRELATES:PSYCHOLOGICAL, ENVIRONMENTAL; N=115
                    FEMALE AND 85 MALE UNDERGRADUATES)
        @APPLICATION 1960 M-7 A-5

601   PERVIN, L. A.
            RIGIDITY IN NEUROSIS AND GENERAL PERSONALITY FUNCTIONING.
            JOURNAL OF ABNORMAL AND SOCIAL PSYCHOLOGY, 1960, 61, 389-395.
                    (CORRELATES:BEHAVIORAL, PSYCHOLOGICAL, INTELLIGENCE; N=15 NORMAL AND
                    15 NEUROTIC HOSPITALIZED PATIENTS)
        @APPLICATION 1960 L-45

602   WALLACH, M. A.
            TWO CORRELATES OF SYMBOLIC SEXUAL AROUSAL: LEVEL OF ANXIETY AND LIKING FOR
            ESTHETIC MATERIAL.
            JOURNAL OF ABNORMAL AND SOCIAL PSYCHOLOGY, 1960, 61, 396-401.
                    (CORRELATES:BEHAVIORAL, PSYCHOLOGICAL; N=73 COLLEGE FEMALES)
        @APPLICATION 1960 E-5 T-2

603   SMITH, A. J.
            THE ATTRIBUTION OF SIMILARITY: THE INFLUENCE OF SUCCESS AND FAILURE.
            JOURNAL OF ABNORMAL AND SOCIAL PSYCHOLOGY, 1960, 61, 419-423.
                    (CORRELATES:PSYCHOLOGICAL, ENVIRONMENTAL; N=128 UNDERGRADUATES)
        @APPLICATION 1960 A-7

604   MANGAN, G. L., QUARTERMAIN, D., & VAUGHAN, G. M.
            TAYLOR MAS AND GROUP CONFORMITY PRESSURE.
            JOURNAL OF ABNORMAL AND SOCIAL PSYCHOLOGY, 1960, 61, 146-147.
                    (CORRELATES:PSYCHOLOGICAL, ENVIRONMENTAL; USED AS CRITERION; N=24
                    COLLEGE STUDENTS)
        @APPLICATION 1960 T-2

605   ZAHN, T. P.
            SIZE ESTIMATION OF PICTURES ASSOCIATED WITH SUCCESS AND FAILURE AS A
            FUNCTION OF MANIFEST ANXIETY.
            JOURNAL OF ABNORMAL AND SOCIAL PSYCHOLOGY, 1960, 61, 457-462.
                (MODIFICATION; CORRELATES:PSYCHOLOGICAL, PHYSIOLOGICAL; USED AS
                CRITERION; N=48 UNDERGRADUATES)
       @APPLICATION 1960 T-2 D-45

606   KUETHE, J. L.
            ACQUIESCENT RESPONSE SET AND THE PSYCHASTHENIA SCALE: AN ANALYSIS VIA THE
            AUSSAGE EXPERIMENT.
            JOURNAL OF ABNORMAL AND SOCIAL PSYCHOLOGY, 1960, 61, 319-322.
                (MODIFICATION; CORRELATES:BEHAVIORAL; BIAS:RESPONSE; N=230
                COLLEGE STUDENTS)
       @APPLICATION 1960 D-45 K-43

607   KANFER, F. H.
            VERBAL RATE, EYEBLINK, AND CONTENT IN STRUCTURED PSYCHIATRIC INTERVIEWS.
            JOURNAL OF ABNORMAL AND SOCIAL PSYCHOLOGY, 1960, 61, 341-347.
                (CORRELATES:BEHAVIORAL, PSYCHOLOGICAL; N=36 FEMALE PSYCHIATRIC
                INPATIENTS)
       @APPLICATION 1960 D-45 T-2

608   RAO, K. V., & RUSSELL, R. W.
            EFFECTS OF STRESS ON GOAL SETTING BEHAVIOR.
            JOURNAL OF ABNORMAL AND SOCIAL PSYCHOLOGY, 1960, 61, 380-388.
                (CORRELATES:BEHAVIORAL, PSYCHOLOGICAL, ENVIRONMENTAL; N=160
                ADOLESCENT BOYS)
       @APPLICATION 1960 R-17

609   PINE, F., & HOLT, R. R.
            CREATIVITY AND PRIMARY PROCESS: A STUDY OF ADAPTIVE REGRESSION.
            JOURNAL OF ABNORMAL AND SOCIAL PSYCHOLOGY, 1960, 61, 370-379.
                (RELIABILITY:INTERRATER; CORRELATES:PSYCHOLOGICAL, DEMOGRAPHIC,
                INTELLIGENCE; N=13 MALE AND 14 FEMALE UNDERGRADUATES)
       @APPLICATION 1960 D-45 M-20 R-30 H-117 G-142 G-143 G-194 G-80

610   MISCHEL, W.
            PREFERENCE FOR DELAYED REINFORCEMENT AND SOCIAL RESPONSIBILITY.
            JOURNAL OF ABNORMAL AND SOCIAL PSYCHOLOGY, 1961, 62, 1-7.
                (MENTION; MODIFICATION; CORRELATES:BEHAVIORAL, PSYCHOLOGICAL; CROSS
                CULTURAL APPLICATION; NORMATIVE DATA; N=206 TRINIDADIAN NEGRO
                CHILDREN AGE 12-14: 78 NORMAL BOYS, 58 NORMAL GIRLS, 70 REFORM
                SCHOOL BOYS)
       @APPLICATION 1961 R-30 H-29

611   LOEHLIN, J. C.
            WORD MEANINGS AND SELF-DESCRIPTIONS.
            JOURNAL OF ABNORMAL AND SOCIAL PSYCHOLOGY, 1961, 62, 28-34.
                (CORRELATES:PSYCHOLOGICAL; USED AS CRITERION; N=71 INTRODUCTORY
                PERSONALITY STUDENTS GENERALLY IN THEIR 2ND SEMESTER OF PSYCHOLOGY)
       @APPLICATION 1961 O-16 K-23

612   BABLADELIS, G.
            PERSONALITY AND VERBAL CONDITIONING EFFECTS.
            JOURNAL OF ABNORMAL AND SOCIAL PSYCHOLOGY, 1961, 62, 41-43.
                (CORRELATES:PSYCHOLOGICAL, ENVIRONMENTAL; USED AS CRITERION; N=102
                UNDERGRADUATES)
       @APPLICATION 1961 E-2

613   KOGAN, N.
            ATTITUDES TOWARD OLD PEOPLE: THE DEVELOPMENT OF A SCALE AND AN EXAMINATION
            OF CORRELATES.
            JOURNAL OF ABNORMAL AND SOCIAL PSYCHOLOGY, 1961, 62, 44-54.
                (RELIABILITY:INTERNAL CONSISTENCY; CORRELATES:PSYCHOLOGICAL; FACTOR
                ANALYSIS; 3 SAMPLES: N=128 MALE COLLEGE STUDENTS, N=186 MALE COLLEGE
                STUDENTS, AND N=168 COLLEGE STUDENTS)
       @APPLICATION 1961 A-5 G-31 C-173 S-28 S-225 J-4 C-174 B-276

614   MATARAZZO, R. G., MATARAZZO, J. D., & SASLOW, G.
            THE RELATIONSHIP BETWEEN MEDICAL AND PSYCHIATRIC SYMPTOMS.
            JOURNAL OF ABNORMAL AND SOCIAL PSYCHOLOGY, 1961, 62, 55-61.
                (CORRELATES:PSYCHOLOGICAL, PHYSIOLOGICAL, DEMOGRAPHIC; USED AS
                CRITERION; N=40 MEDICAL INPATIENTS, 42 MEDICAL OUTPATIENTS, 40
                PSYCHIATRIC INPATIENTS, 40 PSYCHIATRIC OUTPATIENTS, ALL WHITE MALES
                AND FEMALES, AGES 14-78)
        @APPLICATION 1961 B-127 T-2 S-224 D-45

615   BIERI, J., & LOBECK, R.
            SELF-CONCEPT DIFFERENCES IN RELATION TO IDENTIFICATION, RELIGION, AND
            SOCIAL CLASS.
            JOURNAL OF ABNORMAL AND SOCIAL PSYCHOLOGY, 1961, 62, 94-98.
                (CORRELATES:PSYCHOLOGICAL, DEMOGRAPHIC; N=89 ARMY RESERVISTS, AGES
                19-40)
        @APPLICATION 1961 L-35 B-204 H-22

616   GARDNER, R. W.
            COGNITIVE CONTROLS OF ATTENTION DEPLOYMENT AS DETERMINANTS OF VISUAL
            ILLUSIONS.
            JOURNAL OF ABNORMAL AND SOCIAL PSYCHOLOGY, 1961, 62, 120-127.
                (MENTION; DESCRIPTION; RELIABILITY:INTERNAL CONSISTENCY; CORRELATES:
                PSYCHOLOGICAL; FACTOR ANALYSIS; 2 STUDIES: N=80 SORORITY MEMBERS,
                68 FEMALE BUSINESS COLLEGE STUDENTS, NURSING STUDENTS AND SECRETARIES
                AGES 17-30)
        @APPLICATION 1961 K-120 W-19 W-72

617   ULLMAN, L. P., KRASNER, L., & COLLINS, B. J.
            MODIFICATIONS OF BEHAVIOR THROUGH VERBAL CONDITIONING: EFFECTS IN GROUP
            THERAPY.
            JOURNAL OF ABNORMAL AND SOCIAL PSYCHOLOGY, 1961, 62, 128-132.
                (DESCRIPTION; RELIABILITY:INTERRATER; CORRELATES:PSYCHOLOGICAL,
                ENVIRONMENTAL; N=30 MALE VA NEUROPSYCHIATRIC HOSPITAL PATIENTS)
        @APPLICATION 1961 M-20 F-45

618   STAYTON, S. E., & WIENER, M.
            VALUE, MAGNITUDE, AND ACCENTUATION.
            JOURNAL OF ABNORMAL AND SOCIAL PSYCHOLOGY, 1961, 62, 145-147.
                (CORRELATES:PSYCHOLOGICAL; N=25 ADULT EVENING COLLEGE STUDENTS)
        @APPLICATION 1961 O-16

619   EDWARDS, A. L., & WALKER, J. N.
            A NOTE ON THE COUCH AND KENISTON MEASURE OF AGREEMENT RESPONSE SET.
            JOURNAL OF ABNORMAL AND SOCIAL PSYCHOLOGY, 1961, 62, 173-174.
                (VALIDITY:CONSTRUCT; CORRELATES:PSYCHOLOGICAL; NO SAMPLE INFORMATION)
        @APPLICATION 1961 E-1 D-45 C-23

620   COUCH, A., & KENISTON, K.
            AGREEING RESPONSE SET AND SOCIAL DESIRABILITY.
            JOURNAL OF ABNORMAL AND SOCIAL PSYCHOLOGY, 1961, 62, 175-179.
                (VALIDITY:CONSTRUCT; CORRELATES:PSYCHOLOGICAL; FACTOR ANALYSIS;
                NORMATIVE DATA; N=61 COLLEGE STUDENTS)
        @APPLICATION 1961 E-1 C-23 C-188 D-45

621   OSGOOD, C. E., WARE, E. E., & MORRIS, C.
            ANALYSIS OF THE CONNOTATIVE MEANINGS OF A VARIETY OF HUMAN VALUES AS
            EXPRESSED BY AMERICAN COLLEGE STUDENTS.
            JOURNAL OF ABNORMAL AND SOCIAL PSYCHOLOGY, 1961, 62, 62-73.
                (REVIEW ARTICLE; VALIDITY:CONSTRUCT; CORRELATES:PSYCHOLOGICAL;
                FACTOR ANALYSIS; N=55 MALE UNDERGRADUATES)
        @APPLICATION 1961 O-16

622   EHRLICH, H. J.
            DOGMATISM AND LEARNING.
            JOURNAL OF ABNORMAL AND SOCIAL PSYCHOLOGY, 1961, 62, 148-149.
                (RELIABILITY:RETEST, INTERNAL CONSISTENCY; VALIDITY:CONSTRUCT;
                CORRELATES:PSYCHOLOGICAL, INTELLIGENCE; N=100 COLLEGE STUDENTS)
        @APPLICATION 1961 R-8

623   TAYLOR, J. B.
            THE "YEASAYER" AND SOCIAL DESIRABILITY: A COMMENT ON THE COUCH AND KENISTON
            PAPER.
            JOURNAL OF ABNORMAL AND SOCIAL PSYCHOLOGY, 1961, 62, 172.
                (FACTOR ANALYSIS; N=55 MALE COLLEGE STUDENTS).
        @APPLICATION 1961 E-1 C-23

624   WEISS, W.
            THE EFFECTS OF A COMMUNICATION ATTITUDE CHANGE AND SCALE JUDGMENTS.
            JOURNAL OF ABNORMAL AND SOCIAL PSYCHOLOGY, 1961, 62, 133-140.
                (CORRELATES:PSYCHOLOGICAL, ENVIRONMENTAL; N=141 COLLEGE STUDENTS)
        @APPLICATION 1961 O-16

625   SARNOFF, I., & ZIMBARDO, P. G.
            ANXIETY, FEAR, AND SOCIAL AFFILIATION.
            JOURNAL OF ABNORMAL AND SOCIAL PSYCHOLOGY, 1961, 62, 356-363.
                (CORRELATES:BEHAVIORAL. PSYCHOLOGICAL, ENVIRONMENTAL; USED AS
                CRITERION; N=72 MALE UNDERGRADUATES)
        @APPLICATION 1961 B-176 G-198

626   MILGRAM, N. A.
            MICROGENETIC ANALYSIS OF WORD ASSOCIATIONS IN SCHIZOPHRENIC AND BRAIN-
            DAMAGED PATIENTS.
            JOURNAL OF ABNORMAL AND SOCIAL PSYCHOLOGY, 1961, 62, 364-366.
                (CORRELATES:PSYCHOLOGICAL; USED AS CRITERION; NORMATIVE DATA; N=32
                SCHIZOPHRENICS, 30 BRAIN DAMAGED PATIENTS)
        @APPLICATION 1961 R-27

627   SCHUTZ, W. C.
            ON GROUP COMPOSITION.
            JOURNAL OF ABNORMAL AND SOCIAL PSYCHOLOGY, 1961, 62, 275-281.
                (VALIDITY:CRITERION; USED AS CRITERION; N=70 ADULTS UNDERGOING
                LABORATORY TRAINING)
        @APPLICATION 1961 S-11

628   REITMAN, W. R.
            NEED ACHIEVEMENT, FEAR OF FAILURE, AND SELECTIVE RECALL.
            JOURNAL OF ABNORMAL AND SOCIAL PSYCHOLOGY, 1961, 62, 142-144.
                (CORRELATES:PSYCHOLOGICAL, ENVIRONMENTAL; NORMATIVE DATA; 2 STUDIES:
                N=108 MALE COLLEGE STUDENTS AND 68 MALE COLLEGE STUDENTS)
        @APPLICATION 1961 M-20 M-7

629   EDWARDS, A. L., & WALKER, J. N.
            SOCIAL DESIRABILITY AND AGREEMENT RESPONSE SET.
            JOURNAL OF ABNORMAL AND SOCIAL PSYCHOLOGY, 1961, 62, 180-183.
                (VALIDITY:CONSTRUCT; CORRELATES:PSYCHOLOGICAL; FACTOR ANALYSIS;
                NORMATIVE DATA; N=46 COLLEGE STUDENTS)
        @APPLICATION 1961 E-1 C-23 D-45 C-172

630   TRIANDIS, H. C.
            A NOTE ON ROKEACH'S THEORY OF PREJUDICE.
            JOURNAL OF ABNORMAL AND SOCIAL PSYCHOLOGY, 1961, 62, 184-186.
                (CORRELATES:PSYCHOLOGICAL, DEMOGRAPHIC; USED AS CRITERION; N=112
                WHITE MALE AND FEMALE COLLEGE STUDNETS)
        @APPLICATION 1961 T-8

631   SARASON, I. G.
            A NOTE ON ANXIETY, INSTRUCTIONS, AND WORD ASSOCIATION PERFORMANCE.
            JOURNAL OF ABNORMAL AND SOCIAL PSYCHOLOGY, 1961, 62, 153-154.
                (CORRELATES:PSYCHOLOGICAL, ENVIRONMENTAL; USED AS CRITERION; N=80
                COLLEGE STUDENTS)
        @APPLICATION 1961 S-5 S-223 R-27 B-184

632   SALTZ, E.
            THE EFFECT OF INDUCED STRESS ON FREE ASSOCIATIONS.
            JOURNAL OF ABNORMAL AND SOCIAL PSYCHOLOGY, 1961, 62, 161-164.
                (CORRELATES:PSYCHOLOGICAL, ENVIRONMENTAL; USED AS CRITERION;
                N=57 COLLEGE STUDENTS)
        @APPLICATION 1961 R-27

633   SARASON, I. G.
              THE EFFECTS OF ANXIETY AND THREAT ON THE SOLUTION OF A DIFFICULT TASK.
              JOURNAL OF ABNORMAL AND SOCIAL PSYCHOLOGY, 1961, 62, 165-168.
                     (VALIDITY:CONSTRUCT; CORRELATES:PSYCHOLOGICAL, ENVIRONMENTAL; USED AS
                     CRITERION; NORMATIVE DATA; N=191 COLLEGE STUDENTS)
              @APPLICATION 1961 S-4 S-5 S-223 B-184

634   SMITH, K. H.
              EGO STRENGTH AND PERCEIVED COMPETENCE AS CONFORMITY VARIABLES.
              JOURNAL OF ABNORMAL AND SOCIAL PSYCHOLOGY, 1961, 62, 169-171.
                     (VALIDITY:CONSTRUCT; CORRELATES:BEHAVIORAL; NORMATIVE DATA; N=48
                     COLLEGE STUDENTS)
              @APPLICATION 1961 B-5

635   HOKANSON, J. E.
              THE EFFECTS OF FRUSTRATION AND ANXIETY ON OVERT AGGRESSION.
              JOURNAL OF ABNORMAL AND SOCIAL PSYCHOLOGY, 1961, 62, 346-351.
                     (CORRELATES:PSYCHOLOGICAL, PHYSIOLOGICAL, ENVIRONMENTAL; USED AS
                     CRITERION; N=80 WHITE MALE UNDERGRADUATES)
              @APPLICATION 1961 S-24 M-20

636   VAN BUSKIRK, C.
              PERFORMANCE ON COMPLEX REASONING TASKS AS A FUNCTION OF ANXIETY.
              JOURNAL OF ABNORMAL AND SOCIAL PSYCHOLOGY, 1961, 62, 201-209.
                     (DESCRIPTION; RELIABILITY:INTERRATER; CORRELATES:BEHAVIORAL,
                     PSYCHOLOGICAL; USED AS CRITERION; FIVE SAMPLES, MEDIAN N=24)
              @APPLICATION 1961 K-117 T-2 M-7

637   BERKOWITZ, L.
              ANTI-SEMITISM, JUDGMENTAL PROCESSES, AND DISPLACEMENT OF HOSTILITY.
              JOURNAL OF ABNORMAL AND SOCIAL PSYCHOLOGY, 1961, 62, 210-215.
                     (CORRELATES:PSYCHOLOGICAL, ENVIRONMENTAL; USED AS CRITERION;
                     NORMATIVE DATA; N=65 FEMALE AND 33 MALE COLLEGE STUDENTS)
              @APPLICATION 1961 A-5 A-15

638   REESE, H. W.
              RELATIONSHIPS BETWEEN SELF-ACCEPTANCE AND SOCIOMETRIC CHOICES.
              JOURNAL OF ABNORMAL AND SOCIAL PSYCHOLOGY, 1961, 62, 472-474.
                     (CORRELATES:PSYCHOLOGICAL; USED AS CRITERION; N=507 CHILDREN)
              @APPLICATION 1961 L-109

639   DAVIDS, A., & LAWTON, M. J.
              SELF-CONCEPT, MOTHER CONCEPT, AND FOOD AVERSIONS IN EMOTIONALLY DISTURBED
              AND NORMAL CHILDREN.
              JOURNAL OF ABNORMAL AND SOCIAL PSYCHOLOGY, 1961, 62, 309-314.
                     (RELIABILITY:INTERRATER; CORRELATES:BEHAVIORAL, PSYCHOLOGICAL;
                     NORMATIVE DATA; N=30 NORMAL, 25 DISTURBED BOYS AGES 10-12)
              @APPLICATION 1961 B-176 B-186

640   STOTLAND, E., & PATCHEN, M.
              IDENTIFICATION AND CHANGES IN PREJUDICE AND IN AUTHORITARIANISM.
              JOURNAL OF ABNORMAL AND SOCIAL PSYCHOLOGY, 1961, 62, 265-274.
                     (DESCRIPTION; CORRELATES:PSYCHOLOGICAL, ENVIRONMENTAL; USED AS
                     CRITERION; NORMATIVE DATA; N=85 COLLEGE FEMALES)
              @APPLICATION 1961 K-44 A-5 M-241

641   GOCKA, E. F., & ROZYNKO, V.
              SOME COMMENTS ON THE EPPS EGO DISJUNCTION SCORE.
              JOURNAL OF ABNORMAL AND SOCIAL PSYCHOLOGY, 1961, 62, 458-460.
                     (VALIDITY:CRITERION; NORMATIVE DATA; N=4922 FEMALES)
              @APPLICATION 1961 E-2

642   REITMAN, E. E., & WILLIAMS, C. D.
              RELATIONSHIPS BETWEEN HOPE OF SUCCESS AND FEAR OF FAILURE, ANXIETY, AND
              NEED FOR ACHIEVEMENT.
              JOURNAL OF ABNORMAL AND SOCIAL PSYCHOLOGY, 1961, 62, 465-467.
                     (RELIABILITY:INTERRATER; CORRELATES:PSYCHOLOGICAL; NORMATIVE DATA;
                     N=113 COLLEGE MALES)
              @APPLICATION 1961 T-2 M-7 C-126

643 GOLDSTEIN, M. J.
THE RELATIONSHIP BETWEEN ANXIETY AND ORAL WORD ASSOCIATION PERFORMANCE.
JOURNAL OF ABNORMAL AND SOCIAL PSYCHOLOGY, 1961, 62, 468-471.
(CORRELATES:PSYCHOLOGICAL, DEMOGRAPHIC; USED AS CRITERION; N=40
COLLEGE MALES AND FEMALES)
@APPLICATION 1961 H-51

644 BYRNE, D., TERRILL, J., & MCREYNOLDS, P.
INCONGRUENCY AS A PREDICTOR OF RESPONSE TO HUMOR.
JOURNAL OF ABNORMAL AND SOCIAL PSYCHOLOGY, 1961, 62, 435-438.
(CORRELATES:PSYCHOLOGICAL; USED AS CRITERION; N=33 MALE PSYCHIATRIC
PATIENTS)
@APPLICATION 1961 D-45 M-130 B-169

645 BASS, A. R., & FIEDLER, F. E.
INTERPERSONAL PERCEPTION SCORES AND THEIR COMPONENTS AS PREDICTORS OF
PERSONAL ADJUSTMENT.
JOURNAL OF ABNORMAL AND SOCIAL PSYCHOLOGY, 1961, 62, 442-445.
(DESCRIPTION; CORRELATES:PSYCHOLOGICAL; N=200 ANTIAIRCRAFT ARTILLERY
PERSONNEL)
@APPLICATION 1961 T-2

646 WEATHERLEY, D.
ANTI-SEMITISM AND THE EXPRESSION OF FANTASY AGGRESSION.
JOURNAL OF ABNORMAL AND SOCIAL PSYCHOLOGY, 1961, 62, 454-457.
(CORRELATES:PSYCHOLOGICAL, DEMOGRAPHIC; USED AS CRITERION; N=100
COLLEGE MALES)
@APPLICATION 1961 L-32

647 TAYLOR, J. B.
WHAT DO ATTITUDE SCALES MEASURE: THE PROBLEM OF SOCIAL DESIRABILITY.
JOURNAL OF ABNORMAL AND SOCIAL PSYCHOLOGY, 1961, 62, 386-390.
(RELIABILITY:INTERNAL CONSISTENCY; CORRELATES:PSYCHOLOGICAL;
BIAS:RESPONSE; 3 STUDIES: N=53 COLLEGE STUDENTS, N=53 COLLEGE
SUTDENTS, N=50 COLLEGE STUDENTS)
@APPLICATION 1961 A-5 S-9 A-17 S-28
@E-41

648 HOFFMAN, L. R., & MAIER, N. R. F.
QUALITY AND ACCEPTANCE OF PROBLEM SOLUTIONS BY MEMBERS OF HOMOGENEOUS AND
HETEROGENEOUS GROUPS.
JOURNAL OF ABNORMAL AND SOCIAL PSYCHOLOGY, 1961, 62, 401-407.
(CORRELATES:PSYCHOLOGICAL, DEMOGRAPHIC; USED AS CRITERION; N=164
COLLEGE STUDENTS)
@APPLICATION 1961 G-26

649 BECKER, W. C., & MATTESON, H. H.
GSR CONDITIONING, ANXIETY, AND EXTRAVERSION.
JOURNAL OF ABNORMAL AND SOCIAL PSYCHOLOGY, 1961, 62, 427-430.
(RELIABILITY:INTERNAL CONSISTENCY; CORRELATES:PHYSIOLOGICAL; USED AS
CRITERION; N=273 COLLEGE MALES, 40 SELECTED)
@APPLICATION 1961 G-39 C-97

650 PAINTING, D. H.
THE PERFORMANCE OF PSYCHOPATHIC INDIVIDUALS UNDER CONDITIONS OF POSITIVE
AND NEGATIVE PARTIAL REINFORCEMENT.
JOURNAL OF ABNORMAL AND SOCIAL PSYCHOLOGY, 1961, 62, 352-355.
(CORRELATES:BEHAVIORAL, PSYCHOLOGICAL, ENVIRONMENTAL; USED AS
CRITERION; NORMATIVE DATA; N=72 NEGRO MALE POSTNARCOTIC ADDICTS,
36 NEGRO MALE UNDERGRADUATES)
@APPLICATION 1961 D-45 W-57

651 MOSS, H. A., & KAGAN, J.
STABILITY OF ACHIEVEMENT AND RECOGNITION SEEKING BEHAVIORS FROM EARLY
CHILDHOOD THROUGH ADULTHOOD.
JOURNAL OF ABNORMAL AND SOCIAL PSYCHOLOGY, 1961, 62, 504-513.
(RELIABILITY:RETEST, INTERRATER; CORRELATES:PSYCHOLOGICAL,
DEMOGRAPHIC, INTELLIGENCE, ENVIRONMENTAL; N=36 MALES, 35 FEMALES
FROM FELS RESEARCH INSTITUTE'S LONGITUDINAL POPULATION)
@APPLICATION 1961 M-20 M-7

652   ALTROCCHI, J.
            INTERPERSONAL PERCEPTIONS OF REPRESSORS AND SENSITIZERS AND COMPONENT
            ANALYSIS OF ASSUMED DISSIMILARITY SCORES.
            JOURNAL OF ABNORMAL AND SOCIAL PSYCHOLOGY, 1961, 62, 528-534.
                    (CORRELATES:PSYCHOLOGICAL; USED AS CRITERION; NORMATIVE DATA; N=227
                    SENIOR NURSING STUDENTS)
        aAPPLICATION 1961 D-45 L-35

653   SMELSER, W. T.
            DOMINANCE AS A FACTOR IN ACHIEVEMENT AND PERCEPTION IN COOPERATIVE PROBLEM
            SOLVING INTERACTIONS.
            JOURNAL OF ABNORMAL AND SOCIAL PSYCHOLOGY, 1961, 62, 535-542.
                    (CORRELATES:BEHAVIORAL, PSYCHOLOGICAL, ENVIRONMENTAL; NORMATIVE DATA;
                    N=748 COLLEGE MALES IN UNIVERSITY ARMED FORCES TRAINING)
        aAPPLICATION 1961 G-22 G-19 G-36 L-35

654   MISCHEL, W.
            DELAY OF GRATIFICATION, NEED FOR ACHIEVEMENT, AND ACQUIESCENCE IN ANOTHER
            CULTURE.
            JOURNAL OF ABNORMAL AND SOCIAL PSYCHOLOGY, 1961, 62, 543-552.
                    (CORRELATES:BEHAVIORAL, PSYCHOLOGICAL; CROSS CULTURAL APPLICATION;
                    N=68 MALE, 44 FEMALE TRINIDADIAN NEGRO SCHOOL CHILDREN, 11-14 YEARS
                    OLD)
        aAPPLICATION 1961 M-20 M-7 H-29

655   RUDIE, R. R., & MCGAUGHRAN, L. S.
            DIFFERENCES IN DEVELOPMENTAL EXPERIENCE, DEFENSIVENESS, AND PERSONALITY
            ORGANIZATION BETWEEN TWO CLASSES OF PROBLEM DRINKERS.
            JOURNAL OF ABNORMAL AND SOCIAL PSYCHOLOGY, 1961, 62, 659-665.
                    (MODIFICATION; CORRELATES:PSYCHOLOGICAL; NORMATIVE DATA; N=188
                    MALE ALCOHOLIC PATIENTS)
        aAPPLICATION 1961 B-85 W-134 R-30 W-147

656   MANN, R. D.
            DIMENSIONS OF INDIVIDUAL PERFORMANCE IN SMALL GROUPS UNDER TASK AND SOCIAL-
            EMOTIONAL CONDITIONS.
            JOURNAL OF ABNORMAL AND SOCIAL PSYCHOLOGY, 1961, 62, 674-682.
                    (MODIFICATION; CORRELATES:BEHAVIORAL, PSYCHOLOGICAL,
                    ENVIRONMENTAL; USED AS CRITERION; N=100 MALE UNDERGRADUATES)
        aAPPLICATION 1961 B-2

657   FORSYTH, R. P., & FAIRWEATHER, G. W.
            PSYCHOTHERAPEUTIC AND OTHER HOSPITAL TREATMENT CRITERION: THE DILEMMA.
            JOURNAL OF ABNORMAL AND SOCIAL PSYCHOLOGY, 1961, 62, 598-604.
                    (VALIDITY:CRITERION; CORRELATES:BEHAVIORAL, PSYCHOLOGICAL; FACTOR
                    ANALYSIS; N=96 VA PSYCHIATRIC PATIENTS)
        aAPPLICATION 1961 M-20 D-45 H-21 F-45 W-41 W-8

658   GROSS, C. F.
            INTRAJUDGE CONSISTENCY IN RATINGS OF HETEROGENEOUS PERSONS.
            JOURNAL OF ABNORMAL AND SOCIAL PSYCHOLOGY, 1961, 62, 605-610.
                    (MENTION; N=35 FEMALE, AND 27 MALE UNDERGRADUATES)
        aAPPLICATION 1961 G-26

659   SPENCE, D. P.
            AN EXPERIMENTAL TEST OF SCHEMA INTERACTION.
            JOURNAL OF ABNORMAL AND SOCIAL PSYCHOLOGY, 1961, 62, 611-615.
                    (USED AS CRITERION; N=13 MALE, 10 FEMALE UNDERGRADUATES)
        aAPPLICATION 1961 D-16

660   KOGAN, N.
            ATTITUDES TOWARD OLD PEOPLE IN AN OLDER SAMPLE.
            JOURNAL OF ABNORMAL AND SOCIAL PSYCHOLOGY, 1961, 62, 616-622.
                    (RELIABILITY:INTERNAL CONSISTENCY; CORRELATES:PSYCHOLOGICAL,
                    DEMOGRAPHIC; NORMATIVE DATA; BIAS:RESPONSE; N=89 MALES, 115 FEMALES,
                    APPROX. MEAN AGE 70; AND 87 MALE AND 81 FEMALE UNDERGRADUATES)
        aAPPLICATION 1961 K-16 D-17

661   MIRON, M. S.
            A CROSS-LINGUISTIC INVESTIGATION OF PHONETIC SYMBOLISM.
            JOURNAL OF ABNORMAL AND SOCIAL PSYCHOLOGY, 1961, 62, 623-630.
                    (CORRELATES:PSYCHOLOGICAL, DEMOGRAPHIC; USED AS CRITERION;
                    CROSS-CULTURAL APPLICATION; FACTOR ANALYSIS; N=79 AMERICAN COLLEGE
                    STUDENTS, 41 JAPANESE STUDENTS IN U.S. SCHOOLS)
        aAPPLICATION 1961 D-16

662   PULOS, L., & SPILKA, B.
            PERCEPTUAL SELECTIVITY, MEMORY, AND ANTI-SEMITISM.
            JOURNAL OF ABNORMAL AND SOCIAL PSYCHOLOGY, 1961, 62, 690-692.
                    (CORRELATES:PSYCHOLOGICAL; USED AS CRITERION; N=220 MALE
                    UNDERGRADUATES)
        @APPLICATION 1961 L-32

663   KUETHE, J. L.
            THE INTERACTION OF PERSONALITY AND MUSCLE TENSION IN PRODUCING AGREEMENT ON
            COMMONALITY OF VERBAL ASSOCIATION.
            JOURNAL OF ABNORMAL AND SOCIAL PSYCHOLOGY, 1961, 62, 696-697.
                    (CORRELATES:PSYCHOLOGICAL, PHYSIOLOGICAL; N=40 MALE UNDERGRADUATES)
        @APPLICATION 1961 D-45 R-27

664   BENDIG, A. W., & EIGENBRODE, C. R.
            A FACTOR ANALYTIC INVESTIGATION OF PERSONALITY VARIABLES AND REMINISCENCE
            IN MOTOR LEARNING.
            JOURNAL OF ABNORMAL AND SOCIAL PSYCHOLOGY, 1961, 62, 698-700.
                    (MENTION; CORRELATES:PSYCHOLOGICAL; FACTOR ANALYSIS; N=160 MALE
                    UNDERGRADUATES)
        @APPLICATION 1961 G-26 G-39 T-2 E-5 E-29

665   STAPLES, F. R., & WALTERS, R. H.
            ANXIETY, BIRTH ORDER, AND SUSCEPTIBILITY TO SOCIAL INFLUENCE.
            JOURNAL OF ABNORMAL AND SOCIAL PSYCHOLOGY, 1961, 62, 716-719.
                    (CORRELATES:PSYCHOLOGICAL, DEMOGRAPHIC; N=26 FIRST-BORN,
                    26 LATER-BORN FEMALES)
        @APPLICATION 1961 M-20 H-150

666   GELFAND, D. M., & WINDER, C. L.
            OPERANT CONDITIONING OF VERBAL BEHAVIOR OF DYSTHYMICS AND HYSTERICS.
            JOURNAL OF ABNORMAL AND SOCIAL PSYCHOLOGY, 1961, 62, 688-689.
                    (CORRELATES:PSYCHOLOGICAL; N=26 FEMALE MENTAL INPATIENTS--10
                    DYSTHYMICS, 16 HYSTERICS)
        @APPLICATION 1961 D-45 G-39 T-2 E-1

667   MEIER, M. J.
            INTERRELATIONSHIPS AMONG PERSONALITY VARIABLES, KINESTHETIC FIGURAL
            AFTEREFFECT, AND REMINISCENCE IN MOTOR LEARNING.
            JOURNAL OF ABNORMAL AND SOCIAL PSYCHOLOGY, 1961, 63, 87-94.
                    (RELIABILITY:INTERNAL CONSISTENCY; CORRELATES:BEHAVIORAL; USED AS
                    CRITERION; NORMATIVE DATA; N=128 MALE VETERANS)
        @APPLICATION 1961 D-45 W-41

668   SCHULBERG, H. C.
            AUTHORITARIANISM, TENDENCY TO AGREE, AND INTERPERSONAL PERCEPTION.
            JOURNAL OF ABNORMAL AND SOCIAL PSYCHOLOGY, 1961, 63, 101-108.
                    (CORRELATES:PSYCHOLOGICAL, ENVIRONMENTAL; NORMATIVE DATA; N=237
                    COLLEGE STUDENTS)
        @APPLICATION 1961 C-31 A-5

669   SUINN, R. M.
            THE RELATIONSHIP BETWEEN SELF-ACCEPTANCE AND ACCEPTANCE OF OTHERS: A
            LEARNING THEORY ANALYSIS.
            JOURNAL OF ABNORMAL AND SOCIAL PSYCHOLOGY, 1961, 63, 37-42.
                    (MODIFICATION; CORRELATES:PSYCHOLOGICAL; N=82 HIGH SCHOOL MALES)
        @APPLICATION 1961 G-21

670   SINGER, R. D.
            VERBAL CONDITIONING AND GENERALIZATION OF PRODEMOCRATIC RESPONSES.
            JOURNAL OF ABNORMAL AND SOCIAL PSYCHOLOGY, 1961, 63, 43-46.
                    (CORRELATES:BEHAVIORAL; USED AS CRITERION; NORMATIVE DATA; N=250
                    COLLEGE FEMALES, 48 SELECTED)
        @APPLICATION 1961 A-5 A-17 C-31

671   PEABODY, D.
            ATTITUDE CONTENT AND AGREEMENT SET IN SCALES OF AUTHORITARIANISM,
            DOGMATISM, ANTI-SEMITISM, AND ECONOMIC CONSERVATISM.
            JOURNAL OF ABNORMAL AND SOCIAL PSYCHOLOGY, 1961, 63, 1-11.
                    (RELIABILITY:INTERNAL CONSISTENCY; CORRELATES:PSYCHOLOGICAL,
                    DEMOGRAPHIC; CROSS-CULTURAL APPLICATION; NORMATIVE DATA;
                    BIAS:RESPONSE; N=88 U.S. AND 75 BRITISH COLLEGE STUDENTS)
        @APPLICATION 1961 A-5 R-8 A-15

672   ELLIOTT, R.
            INTERRELATIONSHIPS AMONG MEASURES OF FIELD DEPENDENCE, ABILITY, AND
            PERSONALITY TRAITS.
            JOURNAL OF ABNORMAL AND SOCIAL PSYCHOLOGY, 1961, 63, 27-36.
                (RELIABILITY:INTERRATER; CORRELATES:BEHAVIORAL, PSYCHOLOGICAL;
                NORMATIVE DATA; N=128 MALE UNDERGRADUATES)
        @APPLICATION 1961 W-19 W-72 B-4 K-23

673   GOODENOUGH, D. R., & KARP, S. A.
            FIELD DEPENDENCE AND INTELLECTUAL FUNCTIONING.
            JOURNAL OF ABNORMAL AND SOCIAL PSYCHOLOGY, 1961, 63, 241-246.
                (CORRELATES:PSYCHOLOGICAL, INTELLIGENCE; FACTOR ANALYSIS;
                2 SAMPLES: N=25 BOYS AND 25 GIRLS, AND 30 BOYS)
        @APPLICATION 1961 W-19 W-72 W-73 G-33 T-84 W-188

674   NORCROSS, K. J., LIPMAN, R. S., & SPITZ, H. H.
            THE RELATIONSHIP OF EXTRAVERSION-INTROVERSION TO VISUAL AND KINESTHETIC
            AFTEREFFECTS.
            JOURNAL OF ABNORMAL AND SOCIAL PSYCHOLOGY, 1961, 63, 210-211.
                (CORRELATES:BEHAVIORAL: N=127 COLLEGE STUDENTS)
        @APPLICATION 1961 E-5

675   FILLENBAUM, S., & JACKMAN, A.
            DOGMATISM AND ANXIETY IN RELATION TO PROBLEM SOLVING: AN EXTENSION OF
            ROKEACH'S RESULTS.
            JOURNAL OF ABNORMAL AND SOCIAL PSYCHOLOGY, 1961, 63, 212-214.
                (CORRELATES:BEHAVIORAL, PSYCHOLOGICAL; USED AS CRITERION;
                NORMATIVE DATA; N=73 COLLEGE STUDENTS)
        @APPLICATION 1961 R-8 W-8

676   GARMEZY, N., CLARKE, A. R., & STOCKNER, C.
            CHILD REARING ATTITUDES OF MOTHERS AND FATHERS AS REPORTED BY
            SCHIZOPHRENIC AND NORMAL PATIENTS.
            JOURNAL OF ABNORMAL AND SOCIAL PSYCHOLOGY, 1961, 63, 176-182.
                (MODIFICATION; CORRELATES:BEHAVIORAL, PSYCHOLOGICAL; USED AS
                CRITERION; NORMATIVE DATA; N=30 SCHIZOPHRENICS AND 15 NORMALS)
        @APPLICATION 1961 P-32 S-297

677   ROSEN, S.
            POSTDECISION AFFINITY FOR INCOMPATIBLE INFORMATION.
            JOURNAL OF ABNORMAL AND SOCIAL PSYCHOLOGY, 1961, 63, 188-190.
                (MODIFICATION; CORRELATES:BEHAVIORAL; N=77 MALE AND 43 FEMALE
                UNDERGRADUATES)
        @APPLICATION 1961 P-7

678   WRIGHTSMAN, L. S., JR., & BAUMEISTER, A. A.
            A COMPARISON OF ACTUAL AND PAPER-AND-PENCIL VERSIONS OF THE WATER JAR TEST
            OF RIGIDITY.
            JOURNAL OF ABNORMAL AND SOCIAL PSYCHOLOGY, 1961, 63, 191-193.
                (RELIABILITY:INTERNAL CONSISTENCY; CORRELATES:BEHAVIORAL,
                PSYCHOLOGICAL, INTELLIGENCE; N=76 UNDERGRADUATES)
        @APPLICATION 1961 L-45 A-5 W-11 R-25

679   BYRNE, D.
            ANXIETY AND THE EXPERIMENTAL AROUSAL OF AFFILIATION NEED.
            JOURNAL OF ABNORMAL AND SOCIAL PSYCHOLOGY, 1961, 63, 660-662.
                (RELIABILITY:INTERRATER; CORRELATES:PSYCHOLOGICAL, ENVIRONMENTAL;
                USED AS CRITERION: NORMATIVE DATA; N=84 COLLEGE STUDENTS)
        @APPLICATION 1961 S-19

680   MONROE, J. J., & ASTIN, A. W.
            IDENTIFICATION PROCESSES IN HOSPITALIZED NARCOTIC DRUG ADDICTS.
            JOURNAL OF ABNORMAL AND SOCIAL PSYCHOLOGY, 1961, 63, 215-218.
                (RELIABILITY:INTERNAL CONSISTENCY; CORRELATES:PSYCHOLOGICAL; N=100
                MALE DRUG ADDICTS AND 60 HOSPITAL PERSONNEL)
        @APPLICATION 1961 D-45 A-70

681   HARVEY, O. J., & BEVERLY, G. D.
            SOME PERSONALITY CORRELATES OF CONCEPT CHANGE THROUGH ROLE PLAYING.
            JOURNAL OF ABNORMAL AND SOCIAL PSYCHOLOGY, 1961, 63, 125-130.
                (CORRELATES:PSYCHOLOGICAL; USED AS CRITERION; N=137 COLLEGE STUDENTS)
        @APPLICATION 1961 W-55

682   FOSTER, R. J.
           ACQUIESCENT RESPONSE SET AS A MEASURE OF ACQUIESCENCE.
           JOURNAL OF ABNORMAL AND SOCIAL PSYCHOLOGY, 1961, 63, 155-160.
                (MODIFICATION; RELIABILITY:INTERNAL CONSISTENCY;
                CORRELATES:DEMOGRAPHIC; BIAS:RESPONSE; N=75 MALE AND 75 FEMALE
                COLLEGE STUDENTS)
        aAPPLICATION 1961 G-1 B-279

683   LEIMAN, A. H., & EPSTEIN, S.
           THEMATIC SEXUAL RESPONSES AS RELATED TO SEXUAL DRIVE AND GUILT.
           JOURNAL OF ABNORMAL AND SOCIAL PSYCHOLOGY, 1961, 63, 169-175.
                (RELIABILITY:INTERRATER; CORRELATES:BEHAVIORAL, PSYCHOLOGICAL;
                NORMATIVE DATA; N=66 COLLEGE MALES)
        aAPPLICATION 1961 E-60 M-20

684   FISHER, S.
           ACHIEVEMENT THEMES AND DIRECTIONALITY OF AUTOKINETIC MOVEMENT.
           JOURNAL OF ABNORMAL AND SOCIAL PSYCHOLOGY, 1961, 63, 64-68.
                (VALIDITY:CROSS-VALIDATION; CORRELATES:BEHAVIORAL; USED AS CRITERION;
                THREE SAMPLES: N=91 COLLEGE MALES AND FEMALES, 51 FEMALES, AND 46
                MALES)
        aAPPLICATION 1961 M-7

685   GURMAN, E. B., & BASS, B. M.
           OBJECTIVE COMPARED WITH SUBJECTIVE MEASURES OF THE SAME BEHAVIOR IN GROUPS.
           JOURNAL OF ABNORMAL AND SOCIAL PSYCHOLOGY, 1961, 63, 368-374.
                (RELIABILITY:INTERRATER; VALIDITY:CONSTRUCT, CRITERION;
                CORRELATES:PSYCHOLOGICAL, ENVIRONMENTAL; N=42 MALE AND 18 FEMALE
                UNDERGRADUATES)
        aAPPLICATION 1961 B-201 B-287

686   CROWNE, D. P., & STRICKLAND, B. R.
           THE CONDITIONING OF VERBAL BEHAVIOR AS A FUNCTION OF THE NEED FOR SOCIAL
           APPROVAL.
           JOURNAL OF ABNORMAL AND SOCIAL PSYCHOLOGY, 1961, 63, 395-401.
                (CORRELATES:PSYCHOLOGICAL, INTELLIGENCE, ENVIRONMENTAL; USED AS
                CRITERION; NORMATIVE DATA; N=74 MALE AND 71 FEMALE UNDERGRADUATES)
        aAPPLICATION 1961 C-27

687   JONES, E. E., DAVIS, K. E., & GERGEN, K. J.
           ROLE PLAYING-VARIATIONS AND THEIR INFORMATIONAL VALUE FOR PERSON
           PERCEPTION.
           JOURNAL OF ABNORMAL AND SOCIAL PSYCHOLOGY, 1961, 63, 302-310.
                (CORRELATES:BEHAVIORAL, PSYCHOLOGICAL; USED AS CRITERION; N=134 MALE
                UNDERGRADUATES)
        aAPPLICATION 1961 C-48

688   VELDMAN, D. J., & WORCHEL, P.
           DEFENSIVENESS AND SELF-ACCEPTANCE IN THE MANAGEMENT OF HOSTILITY.
           JOURNAL OF ABNORMAL AND SOCIAL PSYCHOLOGY, 1961, 63, 319-325.
                (CORRELATES:PSYCHOLOGICAL, INTELLIGENCE, ENVIRONMENTAL; USED AS
                CRITERION; NORMATIVE DATA; N=80 MALE UNDERGRADUATES)
        aAPPLICATION 1961 D-45 W-21 R-27 7-14

689   EDWARDS, A. L.
           SOCIAL DESIRABILITY OR ACQUIESCENCE IN THE MMPI? A CASE STUDY WITH THE SD
           SCALE.
           JOURNAL OF ABNORMAL AND SOCIAL PSYCHOLOGY, 1961, 63, 351-359.
                (DESCRIPTION; REVIEW ARTICLE; VALIDITY:CONSTRUCT; NO SAMPLE
                DESCRIPTION)
        aAPPLICATION 1961 E-1 D-45

690   MARGOLIS, M.
           THE MOTHER-CHILD RELATIONSHIP IN BRONCHIAL ASTHMA.
           JOURNAL OF ABNORMAL AND SOCIAL PSYCHOLOGY, 1961, 63, 360-367.
                (CORRELATES:PSYCHOLOGICAL, DEMOGRAPHIC, ENVIRONMENTAL; BIAS:RESPONSE;
                N= MOTHERS OF 50 ASTHMATIC CHILDREN, 50 CHRONICALLY ILL NONASTHMATIC
                CHILDREN, AND 50 HEALTHY CHILDREN)
        aAPPLICATION 1961 B-176 S-9 J-4

691   SEARS, R. R.
            RELATION OF EARLY SOCIALIZATION EXPERIENCES TO AGGRESSION IN MIDDLE
            CHILDHOOD.
            JOURNAL OF ABNORMAL AND SOCIAL PSYCHOLOGY, 1961, 63, 466-492.
                 (VALIDITY:CRITERION; CORRELATES:BEHAVIORAL, PSYCHOLOGICAL; N=537
                 SIXTH GRADERS)
        @APPLICATION 1961 G-141 G-22 H-22

692   FEATHER, N. T.
            THE RELATIONSHIP OF PERSISTENCE AT A TASK TO EXPECTATION OF SUCCESS AND
            ACHIEVEMENT RELATED MOTIVES.
            JOURNAL OF ABNORMAL AND SOCIAL PSYCHOLOGY, 1961, 63, 552-561.
                 (RELIABILITY:INTERRATER; CORRELATES:BEHAVIORAL, ENVIRONMENTAL; USED
                 AS CRITERION; N=89 COLLEGE MALES)
        @APPLICATION 1961 M-20 M-4 M-7

693   FESHBACH, S.
            THE STIMULATING VERSUS CATHARTIC EFFECTS OF A VICARIOUS AGGRESSIVE
            ACTIVITY.
            JOURNAL OF ABNORMAL AND SOCIAL PSYCHOLOGY, 1961, 63, 381-385.
                 (CORRELATES:PSYCHOLOGICAL, ENVIRONMENTAL; USED AS CRITERION;
                 NORMATIVE DATA; N=101 COLLEGE MALES)
        @APPLICATION 1961 F-83 G-63

694   RAVEN, B. H., & FISHBEIN, M.
            ACCEPTANCE OF PUNISHMENT AND CHANGE IN BELIEF.
            JOURNAL OF ABNORMAL AND SOCIAL PSYCHOLOGY, 1961, 63, 411-416.
                 (CORRELATES:DEMOGRAPHIC, ENVIRONMENTAL; N=26 MALE AND 26 FEMALE
                 UNDERGRADUATES)
        @APPLICATION 1961 F-96 O-16

695   GUERTIN, W. H.
            ARE DIFFERENCES IN SCHIZOPHRENIC SYMPTOMS RELATED TO THE MOTHERS' AVOWED
            ATTITUDES TOWARD CHILD REARING?
            JOURNAL OF ABNORMAL AND SOCIAL PSYCHOLOGY, 1961, 63, 440-442.
                 (CORRELATES:PSYCHOLOGICAL, ENVIRONMENTAL; N=28 HOSPITALIZED MALE
                 SCHIZOPHRENICS, 31 PARENTS AND RELATIVES)
        @APPLICATION 1961 S-9 B-85

696   WORCHEL, P.
            STATUS RESTORATION AND THE REDUCTION OF HOSTILITY.
            JOURNAL OF ABNORMAL AND SOCIAL PSYCHOLOGY, 1961, 63, 443-445.
                 (CORRELATES:PSYCHOLOGICAL, DEMOGRAPHIC, ENVIRONMENTAL; USED AS
                 CRITERION; NORMATIVE DATA; N=48 MALE AND 48 FEMALE UNDERGRADUATES)
        @APPLICATION 1961 W-21

697   LYNN, R.
            INTROVERSION-EXTRAVERSION DIFFERENCES IN JUDGMENTS OF TIME.
            JOURNAL OF ABNORMAL AND SOCIAL PSYCHOLOGY, 1961, 63, 457-458.
                 (CORRELATES:PSYCHOLOGICAL; USED AS CRITERION; N=MALE STUDENTS OF
                 WHOM 20 EXTRAVERTED, 20 INTROVERTED WERE SELECTED)
        @APPLICATION 1961 E-5

698   VOGEL, M. D.
            G.S.R. CONDITIONING AND PERSONALITY FACTORS IN ALCOHOLICS AND NORMALS.
            JOURNAL OF ABNORMAL AND SOCIAL PSYCHOLOGY, 1961, 63, 417-421.
                 (CORRELATES:PHYSIOLOGICAL, ENVIRONMENTAL; USED AS CRITERION;
                 NORMATIVE DATA; N=48 MALE ALCOHOLICS, 41 NORMAL MALE CONTROLS)
        @APPLICATION 1961 E-5

699   VESTRE, N. D.
            THE EFFECTS OF THORAZINE ON LEARNING AND RETENTION IN SCHIZOPHRENIC
            PATIENTS.
            JOURNAL OF ABNORMAL AND SOCIAL PSYCHOLOGY, 1961, 63, 432-435.
                 (CORRELATES:PSYCHOLOGICAL, PHYSIOLOGICAL, ENVIRONMENTAL; N=40
                 SCHIZOPHRENIC PATIENTS)
        @APPLICATION 1961 R-27

700   HEILIZER, F.
            A NOTE ON THE SCORING OF EGO DISJUNCTION.
            JOURNAL OF ABNORMAL AND SOCIAL PSYCHOLOGY, 1961, 63, 438-439.
                 (MENTION; NO SAMPLE DESCRIPTION)
        @APPLICATION 1961 E-2

701   MURSTEIN, B. I.
            THE COMPLEMENTARY NEED HYPOTHESIS IN NEWLYWEDS AND MIDDLE-AGED MARRIED
            COUPLES.
            JOURNAL OF ABNORMAL AND SOCIAL PSYCHOLOGY, 1961, 63, 194-197.
                (VALIDITY:CONSTRUCT, CRITERION; CORRELATES:PSYCHOLOGICAL; N=68
                MARRIED COUPLES)
        @APPLICATION 1961 E-2 B-81 L-15

702   MEYER, H. H., WALKER, W. B., & LITWIN, G. H.
            MOTIVE PATTERNS AND RISK PREFERENCES ASSOCIATED WITH ENTREPRENEURSHIP.
            JOURNAL OF ABNORMAL AND SOCIAL PSYCHOLOGY, 1961, 63, 570-574.
                (CORRELATES:BEHAVIORAL, PSYCHOLOGICAL; N=31 MANAGERS, 31 SPECIALISTS)
        @APPLICATION 1961 M-7

703   FEFFER, M. H.
            THE INFLUENCE OF AFFECTIVE FACTORS ON CONCEPTUALIZATION IN SCHIZOPHRENICS.
            JOURNAL OF ABNORMAL AND SOCIAL PSYCHOLOGY, 1961, 63, 588-596.
                (RELIABILITY:INTERNAL CONSISTENCY; CORRELATES:PSYCHOLOGICAL,
                ENVIRONMENTAL; N=25 SCHIZOPHRENICS, AND 16 NORMALS)
        @APPLICATION 1961 W-49 W-50

704   OVERALL, J. E., GORHAM, D. R., & SHAWYER, J. R.
            BASIC DIMENSIONS OF CHANGE IN THE SYMPTOMATOLOGY OF CHRONIC SCHIZOPHRENICS.
            JOURNAL OF ABNORMAL AND SOCIAL PSYCHOLOGY, 1961, 63, 597-602.
                (FACTOR ANALYSIS; N=120 CHRONIC SCHIZOPHRENICS)
        @APPLICATION 1961 L-39

705   MOSS, H. A.
            THE INFLUENCES OF PERSONALITY AND SITUATIONAL CAUTIOUSNESS ON CONCEPTUAL
            BEHAVIOR.
            JOURNAL OF ABNORMAL AND SOCIAL PSYCHOLOGY, 1961, 63, 629-635.
                (CORRELATES:BEHAVIORAL, PSYCHOLOGICAL, INTELLIGENCE, ENVIRONMENTAL;
                USED AS CRITERION; NORMATIVE DATA; N=109 UNIVERSITY STUDENTS)
        @APPLICATION 1961 R-17 M-20 S-97

706   LICHTENSTEIN, E., QUINN, R. P., & HOVER, G. L.
            DOGMATISM AND ACQUIESCENCE TO RESPONSE SET.
            JOURNAL OF ABNORMAL AND SOCIAL PSYCHOLOGY, 1961, 63, 636-638.
                (RELIABILITY:INTERNAL CONSISTENCY; CORRELATES:PSYCHOLOGICAL,
                INTELLIGENCE; NORMATIVE DATA; N=40 MALE PSYCHIATRIC PATIENTS)
        @APPLICATION 1961 A-5 R-8 D-45

707   VIDULICH, R. N., & KAIMAN, I. P.
            THE EFFECTS OF INFORMATION SOURCE STATUS AND DOGMATISM UPON CONFORMITY
            BEHAVIOR.
            JOURNAL OF ABNORMAL AND SOCIAL PSYCHOLOGY, 1961, 63, 639-642.
                (CORRELATES:BEHAVIORAL, ENVIRONMENTAL; USED AS CRITERION;
                NORMATIVE DATA; N=307 COLLEGE STUDENTS, 60 SELECTED)
        @APPLICATION 1961 R-8

708   ROSENBAUM, M. E., & STANNERS, R. F.
            SELF-ESTEEM, MANIFEST HOSTILITY, AND EXPRESSION OF HOSTILITY.
            JOURNAL OF ABNORMAL AND SOCIAL PSYCHOLOGY, 1961, 63, 646-649.
                (VALIDITY:CRITERION; CORRELATES:PSYCHOLOGICAL; USED AS CRITERION;
                N=40 COLLEGE MALES)
        @APPLICATION 1961 S-24 R-77 H-140

709   SIEGMAN, A. W.
            A CROSS-CULTURAL INVESTIGATION OF THE RELATIONSHIP BETWEEN ETHNIC
            PREJUDICE, AUTHORITARIAN IDEOLOGY, AND PERSONALITY.
            JOURNAL OF ABNORMAL AND SOCIAL PSYCHOLOGY, 1961, 63, 654-655.
                (CORRELATES:PSYCHOLOGICAL; CROSS-CULTURAL APPLICATION;
                NORMATIVE DATA; N=38 FEMALE AND 16 MALE COLLEGE STUDENTS)
        @APPLICATION 1961 G-18 A-5

710   GUMPERT, P., THIBAUT, J. W., & SHUFORD, E. H.
            EFFECT OF PERSONALITY AND STATUS EXPERIENCE UPON THE VALUATION OF
            UNOBTAINED STATUSES.
            JOURNAL OF ABNORMAL AND SOCIAL PSYCHOLOGY, 1961, 63, 47-52.
                (USED AS CRITERION; N=62 JUNIOR HIGH SCHOOL GIRLS)
        @APPLICATION 1961 W-8 W-41

711   FIELD, J. G., & BRENGLEMANN, J. C.
            EYELID CONDITIONING AND THREE PERSONALITY PARAMETERS.
            JOURNAL OF ABNORMAL AND SOCIAL PSYCHOLOGY, 1961, 63, 517-523.
                (VALIDITY:CONSTRUCT; CORRELATES:BEHAVIORAL, PSYCHOLOGICAL,
                PHYSIOLOGICAL, INTELLIGENCE; NORMATIVE DATA; N=75 PRISONERS, MEAN
                AGE 25.81)
        @APPLICATION 1961 B-93 D-45 E-5 L-22 C-168 G-22 R-8

712   ZANDER, A., & CURTIS, T.
            EFFECTS OF SOCIAL POWER ON ASPIRATION SETTING AND STRIVING.
            JOURNAL OF ABNORMAL AND SOCIAL PSYCHOLOGY, 1962, 64, 63-74.
                (DESCRIPTION; CORRELATES:PSYCHOLOGICAL, ENVIRONMENTAL; N=60 HIGH
                SCHOOL BOYS)
        @APPLICATION 1962 R-17

713   SAXTON, G. H.
            SPONTANEOUS FANTASY AS A RESOURCE OF HIGH GRADE RETARDATES FOR COPING WITH
            A FAILURE-STRESS FRUSTRATION.
            JOURNAL OF ABNORMAL AND SOCIAL PSYCHOLOGY, 1962, 64, 81-84.
                (RELIABILITY:INTERNAL CONSISTENCY; CORRELATES:PSYCHOLOGICAL,
                INTELLIGENCE; N=86 INSTITUTIONALIZED RETARDATES)
        @APPLICATION 1962 P-14 C-55

714   UPSHAW, H. S.
            OWN ATTITUDE AS AN ANCHOR IN EQUAL-APPEASING INTERVALS.
            JOURNAL OF ABNORMAL AND SOCIAL PSYCHOLOGY, 1962, 64, 85-96.
                (USED AS CRITERION; N=500 UNDERGRADUATES, 321 SELECTED)
        @APPLICATION 1962 L-112

715   BRAMEL, D.
            A DISSONANCE THEORY APPROACH TO DEFENSIVE PROJECTION.
            JOURNAL OF ABNORMAL AND SOCIAL PSYCHOLOGY, 1962, 64, 121-129.
                (MENTION; CORRELATES:PSYCHOLOGICAL; USED AS CRITERION; N=98
                UNDERGRADUATES)
        @APPLICATION 1962 T-2 D-45

716   SNOEK, J. D.
            SOME EFFECTS OF REJECTION UPON ATTRACTION TO A GROUP.
            JOURNAL OF ABNORMAL AND SOCIAL PSYCHOLOGY, 1962, 64, 175-182.
                (CORRELATES:PSYCHOLOGICAL, ENVIRONMENTAL; N=57 COLLEGE STUDENTS)
        @APPLICATION 1962 L-115

717   STOTLAND, E., & COTTRELL, N.
            SIMILARITY OF PERFORMANCE AS INFLUENCED BY INTERACTION, SELF-ESTEEM, AND
            BIRTH ORDER.
            JOURNAL OF ABNORMAL AND SOCIAL PSYCHOLOGY, 1962, 64, 183-191.
                (CORRELATES:BEHAVIORAL, PSYCHOLOGICAL; N=95 COLLEGE STUDENTS)
        @APPLICATION 1962 S-98

718   EYSENCK, H. J., & CLARIDGE, G.
            THE POSITION OF HYSTERICS AND DYSTHYMICS IN A TWO-DIMENSIONAL FREMEWORK
            OF PERSONALITY DESCRIPTION.
            JOURNAL OF ABNORMAL AND SOCIAL PSYCHOLOGY, 1962, 64, 46-55.
                (CORRELATES:BEHAVIORAL, PSYCHOLOGICAL; FACTOR ANALYSIS; NORMATIVE
                DATA; N=48 OF 16 NORMALS, 16 HYSTERICS, 16 DYSTHYMICS)
        @APPLICATION 1962 E-5

719   CERBUS, G., & NICHOLS, R. C.
            PERSONALITY CORRELATES OF PICTURE PREFERENCES.
            JOURNAL OF ABNORMAL AND SOCIAL PSYCHOLOGY, 1962, 64, 75-78.
                (VALIDITY:CRITERION; CORRELATES:PSYCHOLOGICAL; N=106
                NEUROPSYCHIATRIC PATIENTS)
        @APPLICATION 1962 G-22 D-45 L-39

720   LONGENECKER, E. D.
            PERCEPTUAL RECOGNITION AS A FUNCTION OF ANXIETY, MOTIVATION, AND THE
            TESTING SITUATION.
            JOURNAL OF ABNORMAL AND SOCIAL PSYCHOLOGY, 1962, 64, 215-221.
                (CORRELATES:PSYCHOLOGICAL, INTELLIGENCE, ENVIRONMENTAL; USED AS
                CRITERION; N=292 MALE SUBJECTS, 72 SELECTED)
        @APPLICATION 1962 M-4 E-2 H-124 S-5

721   BERKOWITZ, L., & GREEN, J. A.
            THE STIMULUS QUALITIES OF THE SCAPEGOAT.
            JOURNAL OF ABNORMAL AND SOCIAL PSYCHOLOGY, 1962, 64, 293-301.
                (CORRELATES:ENVIRONMENTAL; N=72 MALE UNDERGRADUATES)
        ƏAPPLICATION 1962 B-196

722   SAMPSON, E. E.
            BIRTH ORDER, NEED ACHIEVEMENT, AND CONFORMITY.
            JOURNAL OF ABNORMAL AND SOCIAL PSYCHOLOGY, 1962, 64, 155-159.
                (CORRELATES:PSYCHOLOGICAL, DEMOGRAPHIC; THREE SAMPLES: N=88
                FEMALE STUDENTS, 116 MALE RECRUITS, 31 MALE AND 30 FEMALE STUDENTS)
        ƏAPPLICATION 1962 F-20 M-4

723   LACHMANN, F. M., LAPKIN, B., & HANDELMAN, N. S.
            THE RECALL OF DREAMS: ITS RELATION TO REPRESSION AND COGNITIVE CONTROL.
            JOURNAL OF ABNORMAL AND SOCIAL PSYCHOLOGY, 1962, 64, 160-162.
                (CORRELATES:BEHAVIORAL, PSYCHOLOGICAL; USED AS CRITERION; N=30
                FEMALE UNDERGRADUATES)
        ƏAPPLICATION 1962 H-147

724   MCGEE, R. K.
            THE RELATIONSHIP BETWEEN RESPONSE STYLE AND PERSONALITY VARIABLES: I. THE
            MEASUREMENT OF RESPONSE ACQUIESCENCE.
            JOURNAL OF ABNORMAL AND SOCIAL PSYCHOLOGY, 1962, 64, 229-233.
                (DESCRIPTION; RELIABILITY:INTERNAL CONSISTENCY;
                CORRELATES:PSYCHOLOGICAL; BIAS:RESPONSE; N=218 UNDERGRADUATES)
        ƏAPPLICATION 1962 B-7 A-5 C-23 N-10 B-118 B-81

725   BURNSTEIN, E., & MCRAE, A. V.
            SOME EFFECTS OF SHARED THREAT AND PREJUDICE IN RACIALLY MIXED GROUPS.
            JOURNAL OF ABNORMAL AND SOCIAL PSYCHOLOGY, 1962, 64, 257-263.
                (CORRELATES:PSYCHOLOGICAL, ENVIRONMENTAL; USED AS CRITERION; N=48
                MALE UNDERGRADUATES)
        ƏAPPLICATION 1962 K-29

726   LORR, M., MCNAIR, D. M., MICHAUX, W. W., & RASKIN, A.
            FREQUENCY OF TREATMENT AND CHANGE IN PSYCHOTHERAPY.
            JOURNAL OF ABNORMAL AND SOCIAL PSYCHOLOGY, 1962, 64, 281-292.
                (RELIABILITY:INTERNAL CONSISTENCY; CORRELATES:PSYCHOLOGICAL,
                ENVIRONMENTAL; USED AS CRITERION; N=133 MALE VETERANS WITH
                SERVICE-CONNECTED PSYCHIATRIC DISABILITIES)
        ƏAPPLICATION 1962 T-2 B-5 G-26 L-35 A-5 L-88 A-63 M-156

727   SANDLER, T.
            THE EFFECT OF NEGATIVE VERBAL CLUES UPON VERBAL BEHAVIOR.
            JOURNAL OF ABNORMAL AND SOCIAL PSYCHOLOGY, 1962, 64, 312-316.
                (CORRELATES:PSYCHOLOGICAL, INTELLIGENCE, ENVIRONMENTAL; N=60 MALE
                NEUROPSYCHIATRIC VETERAN PATIENTS)
        ƏAPPLICATION 1962 M-20 S-221

728   MAHLER, I.
            YEASAYERS AND NAYSAYERS: A VALIDATING STUDY.
            JOURNAL OF ABNORMAL AND SOCIAL PSYCHOLOGY, 1962, 64, 317-318.
                (VALIDITY:CONSTRUCT; CORRELATES:BEHAVIORAL, DEMOGRAPHIC;
                NORMATIVE DATA; N=219 MALE AND 163 FEMALE UNDERGRADUATES)
        ƏAPPLICATION 1962 C-23

729   STOTLAND, E., & HILLMER, M. L., JR.
            IDENTIFICATION, AUTHORITARIAN DEFENSIVENESS, AND SELF-ESTEEM.
            JOURNAL OF ABNORMAL AND SOCIAL PSYCHOLOGY, 1962, 64, 334-342.
                (CORRELATES:PSYCHOLOGICAL, ENVIRONMENTAL; N=37 FEMALE AND 55 MALE
                UNDERGRADUATES)
        ƏAPPLICATION 1962 W-71 A-5

730   GYNTHER, M. D.
            CRIME AND PSYCHOPATHOLOGY.
            JOURNAL OF ABNORMAL AND SOCIAL PSYCHOLOGY, 1962, 64, 378-380.
                (CORRELATES:BEHAVIORAL, PSYCHOLOGICAL, INTELLIGENCE; NORMATIVE DATA;
                N=251 WHITE MALE COURT REFERRALS)
        ƏAPPLICATION 1962 D-45

731   SILVERMAN, L. H., & SILVERMAN, D. K.
            EGO IMPAIRMENT IN SCHIZOPHRENIA AS REFLECTED IN THE OBJECT SORTING TEST.
            JOURNAL OF ABNORMAL AND SOCIAL PSYCHOLOGY, 1962, 64, 381-385.
                    (VALIDITY:CRITERION; CORRELATES:PSYCHOLOGICAL; NORMATIVE DATA; N=40
                    ADOLESCENT PSYCHIATRIC PATIENTS)
            @APPLICATION 1962 R-58 M-242

732   DEWOLFE, A.
            THE EFFECT OF AFFECTIVE TONE ON THE VERBAL BEHAVIOR OF PROCESS AND REACTIVE
            SCHIZOPHRENICS.
            JOURNAL OF ABNORMAL AND SOCIAL PSYCHOLOGY, 1962, 64, 450-455.
                    (CORRELATES:BEHAVIORAL. USED AS CRITERION; N=30 SCHIZOPHRENICS, 15
                    NORMAL CONTROL PATIENTS)
            @APPLICATION 1962 P-32

733   EDWARDS, A. L., & WALKER, J. N.
            RELATIONSHIP BETWEEN PROBABILITY OF ITEM ENDORSEMENT AND SOCIAL
            DESIRABILITY SCALE VALUE FOR HIGH AND LOW GROUPS ON EDWARDS SD SCALE.
            JOURNAL OF ABNORMAL AND SOCIAL PSYCHOLOGY, 1962, 64, 458-460.
                    (USED AS CRITERION; NORMATIVE DATA; BIAS:RESPONSE; N=237
                    UNDERGRADUATES)
            @APPLICATION 1962 E-1 E-2

734   BAXTER, J. C., & BECKER, J.
            ANXIETY AND AVOIDANCE BEHAVIOR IN SCHIZOPHRENICS IN RESPONSE TO PARENTAL
            JOURNAL OF ABNORMAL AND SOCIAL PSYCHOLOGY, 1962, 64, 432-437.
                    (RELIABILITY:INTERRATER; CORRELATES:PSYCHOLOGICAL; USED AS
                    CRITERION; N=66 MALE PATIENTS)
            @APPLICATION 1962 P-32 M-47

735   HOKANSON, J. E., & BURGESS, M.
            THE EFFECTS OF THREE TYPES OF AGGRESSION ON VASCULAR PROCESSES.
            JOURNAL OF ABNORMAL AND SOCIAL PSYCHOLOGY, 1962, 64, 446-449.
                    (MODIFICATION; CORRELATES:PSYCHOLOGICAL, PHYSIOLOGICAL,
                    ENVIRONMENTAL; N=56 FEMALE AND 24 MALE WHITE COLLEGE STUDENTS)
            @APPLICATION 1962 H-140 M-47

736   WINDER, C. L., & RAU, L.
            PARENTAL ATTITUDES ASSOCIATED WITH SOCIAL DEVIANCE IN PREADOLESCENT BOYS.
            JOURNAL OF ABNORMAL AND SOCIAL PSYCHOLOGY, 1962, 64, 418-424.
                    (CORRELATES:PSYCHOLOGICAL; USED AS CRITERION; N=710 FOURTH, FIFTH,
                    AND SIXTH GRADE BOYS)
            @APPLICATION 1962 W-122

737   WEATHERLEY, D.
            MATERNAL PERMISSIVENESS TOWARD AGGRESSION AND SUBSEQUENT TAT AGGRESSION.
            JOURNAL OF ABNORMAL AND SOCIAL PSYCHOLOGY, 1962, 65, 1-5.
                    (MODIFICATION; CORRELATES:PSYCHOLOGICAL; N=100 FEMALE UNDERGRADUATES)
            @APPLICATION 1962 M-20

738   LEWIT, D. W., BRAYER, A. R., & LEIMAN, A. H.
            EXTERNALIZATION IN PERCEPTUAL DEFENSE.
            JOURNAL OF ABNORMAL AND SOCIAL PSYCHOLOGY, 1962. 65, 6-13.
                    (RELIABILITY:RETEST; VALIDITY:CONSTRUCT; CORRELATES:PSYCHOLOGICAL,
                    ENVIRONMENTAL; BIAS:RESPONSE; N=134 MALE UNDERGRADUATES)
            @APPLICATION 1962 D-45 G-36

739   ROWLEY, V., & KELLER, E. D.
            CHANGES IN CHILDREN'S VERBAL BEHAVIOR AS A FUNCTION OF SOCIAL APPROVAL
            AND MANIFEST ANXIETY.
            JOURNAL OF ABNORMAL AND SOCIAL PSYCHOLOGY, 1962, 65, 53-57.
                    (CORRELATES:BEHAVIORAL. PSYCHOLOGICAL; USED AS CRITERION;
                    N=60 BOYS AND 30 GIRLS)
            @APPLICATION 1962 C-55

740   POWELL, F. A.
            OPEN- AND CLOSED-MINDEDNESS AND THE ABILITY TO DIFFERENTIATE SOURCE AND
            MESSAGE.
            JOURNAL OF ABNORMAL AND SOCIAL PSYCHOLOGY, 1962, 65, 61-64.
                    (CORRELATES:PSYCHOLOGICAL, ENVIRONMENTAL; N=76 PEOPLE)
            @APPLICATION 1962 R-8 O-16

741   SLOVIC, P.
           CONVERGENT VALIDATION OF RISK TAKING MEASURES.
           JOURNAL OF ABNORMAL AND SOCIAL PSYCHOLOGY, 1962, 65, 68-71.
                (VALIDITY:CONSTRUCT; CORRELATES:BEHAVIORAL; N=82 FRATERNITY SENIORS)
       @APPLICATION 1962 T-11 W-38 C-248

742   ANDERSON, C. C.
           A DEVELOPMENTAL STUDY OF DOGMATISM DURING ADOLESCENCE WITH REFERENCE TO
           SEX DIFFERENCES.
           JOURNAL OF ABNORMAL AND SOCIAL PSYCHOLOGY, 1962, 65, 132-135.
                (CORRELATES:INTELLIGENCE, DEMOGRAPHIC; NORMATIVE DATA; N=290 SCHOOL
                CHILDREN)
       @APPLICATION 1962 R-8

743   MOOS, R. H., & SPEISMAN, J. C.
           GROUP COMPATABILITY AND PRODUCTIVITY.
           JOURNAL OF ABNORMAL AND SOCIAL PSYCHOLOGY, 1962, 65, 190-196.
                (CORRELATES:BEHAVIORAL, PSYCHOLOGICAL, DEMOGRAPHIC, INTELLIGENCE;
                USED AS CRITERION; N=60 MALE AND 60 FEMALE UNDERGRADUATES)
       @APPLICATION 1962 S-11 G-19 L-35

744   LEWINSOHN, P. M., & RIGGS, A.
           THE EFFECT OF CONTENT UPON THE THINKING OF ACUTE AND CHRONIC
           SCHIZOPHRENICS.
           JOURNAL OF ABNORMAL AND SOCIAL PSYCHOLOGY, 1962, 65, 206-207.
                (RELIABILITY:INTERNAL CONSISTENCY; CORRELATES:PSYCHOLOGICAL;
                NORMATIVE DATA; N=30 ACUTE AND 30 CHRONIC SCHIZOPHRENICS, 30
                NONSCHIZOPHRENIC PATIENTS AND 30 NORMALS)
       @APPLICATION 1962 L-39 S-124 L-158

745   COLE, D., JACOBS, S., ZUBOK, B., FAGOT, B., & HUNTER, I.
           THE RELATION OF ACHIEVEMENT IMAGERY SCORES TO ACADEMIC PERFORMANCE.
           JOURNAL OF ABNORMAL AND SOCIAL PSYCHOLOGY, 1962, 65, 208-211.
                (RELIABILITY:INTERRATER; VALIDITY:CRITERION; CORRELATES:DEMOGRAPHIC,
                INTELLIGENCE; 2 STUDIES: N=46 UNDERGRADUATES, N=130 FRESHMEN)
       @APPLICATION 1962 M-7

746   HOROWITZ, F. D.
           THE RELATIONSHIP OF ANXIETY, SELF-CONCEPT, AND SOCIOMETRIC STATUS AMONG
           FOURTH, FIFTH, AND SIXTH GRADE CHILDREN.
           JOURNAL OF ABNORMAL AND SOCIAL PSYCHOLOGY, 1962, 65, 212-214.
                (RELIABILITY:RETEST; VALIDITY:CONSTRUCT; CORRELATES:PSYCHOLOGICAL,
                DEMOGRAPHIC; N=40 FOURTH, 51 FIFTH, AND 20 SIXTH GRADERS)
       @APPLICATION 1962 C-55 L-109

747   ANSFELD, M., BOGO, N., & LAMBERT, W. E.
           EVALUATIONAL REACTIONS TO ACCENTED ENGLISH SPEECH.
           JOURNAL OF ABNORMAL AND SOCIAL PSYCHOLOGY, 1962, 65, 223-231.
                (CORRELATES:PSYCHOLOGICAL, DEMOGRAPHIC, ENVIRONMENTAL; N=64 JEWS &
                114 GENTILES)
       @APPLICATION 1962 A-5 S-28 A-15

748   TERWILLIGER, R. F.
           SOCIAL DESIRABILITY OF SELF-REFERENCE STATEMENTS AS A FUNCTION OF FREE
           ASSOCIATION PATTERNS.
           JOURNAL OF ABNORMAL AND SOCIAL PSYCHOLOGY, 1962, 65, 162-169.
                (MODIFICATION; BIAS:RESPONSE; N=100 FEMALE UNDERGRADUATES)
       @APPLICATION 1962 B-99

749   WISHNER, J.
           STUDIES IN EFFICIENCY: GSR CONDITIONING AS A FUNCTION OF DEGREE OF TASK
           CENTERING.
           JOURNAL OF ABNORMAL AND SOCIAL PSYCHOLOGY, 1962, 65, 170-177.
                (CORRELATES:BEHAVIORAL, PHYSIOLOGICAL, DEMOGRAPHIC, ENVIRONMENTAL;
                N=20 MALE AND 20 FEMALE UNDERGRADUATES)
       @APPLICATION 1962 T-2 P-22

750   FILLENBAUM, S., & JONES, L. V.
           AN APPLICATION OF "CLOZE" TECHNIQUE TO THE STUDY OF APHASIC SPEECH.
           JOURNAL OF ABNORMAL AND SOCIAL PSYCHOLOGY, 1962, 65, 183-189.
                (CORRELATES:BEHAVIORAL, PSYCHOLOGICAL; N=38 STUDENTS)
       @APPLICATION 1962 M-20

751   BYRNE, D., & WONG, T. J.
            RACIAL PREJUDICE, INTERPERSONAL ATTRACTION, AND ASSUMED DISSIMILARITY OF
            ATTITUDES.
            JOURNAL OF ABNORMAL AND SOCIAL PSYCHOLOGY, 1962, 65, 246-253.
                (MODIFICATION; CORRELATES:PSYCHOLOGICAL; USED AS CRITERION;
                NORMATIVE DATA; 2 STUDIES: N=34 COLLEGE MALES AND 20 COLLEGE
                FEMALES, N=59 COLLEGE MALES AND 61 COLLEGE FEMALES)
        @APPLICATION 1962 K-29 B-195 B-65

752   MALOF, M., & LOTT, A. J.
            ETHNOCENTRISM AND THE ACCEPTANCE OF NEGRO SUPPORT IN A GROUP PRESSURE
            SITUATION.
            JOURNAL OF ABNORMAL AND SOCIAL PSYCHOLOGY, 1962, 65, 254-258.
                (CORRELATES:PSYCHOLOGICAL, ENVIRONMENTAL; USED AS CRITERION; N=60
                WHITE COLLEGE MALES)
        @APPLICATION 1962 A-17

753   GELFAND, D. M.
            THE INFLUENCE OF SELF-ESTEEM ON RATE OF VERBAL CONDITIONING AND SOCIAL
            MATCHING BEHAVIOR.
            JOURNAL OF ABNORMAL AND SOCIAL PSYCHOLOGY, 1962, 65, 259-265.
                (CORRELATES:BEHAVIORAL, PSYCHOLOGICAL, ENVIRONMENTAL; USED AS
                CRITERION; N=30 BOYS AND 30 GIRLS)
        @APPLICATION 1962 S-141

754   ZIGLER, E., & DE LABRY, J.
            CONCEPT-SWITCHING IN MIDDLE-CLASS, LOWER-CLASS, AND RETARDED CHILDREN.
            JOURNAL OF ABNORMAL AND SOCIAL PSYCHOLOGY, 1962, 65, 267-273.
                (CORRELATES:INTELLIGENCE; USED AS CRITERION; N=3 GROUPS OF 22
                CHILDREN: ONE RETARDED, ONE MIDDLE CLASS, AND ONE LOWER CLASS)
        @APPLICATION 1962 G-78

755   KISSEL, S., & LITTIG, L. W.
            TEST ANXIETY AND SKIN CONDUCTANCE.
            JOURNAL OF ABNORMAL AND SOCIAL PSYCHOLOGY, 1962, 65, 276-278.
                (CORRELATES:PHYSIOLOGICAL; USED AS CRITERION; N=284 COLLEGE
                STUDENTS, 96 SELECTED)
        @APPLICATION 1962 M-4

756   MEKETON, B. W., GRIFFITH, R. M., TAYLOR, V. H., & WEIDEMAN, J. S.
            RORSCHACH HOMOSEXUAL SIGNS IN PARANOID SCHIZOPHRENICS.
            JOURNAL OF ABNORMAL AND SOCIAL PSYCHOLOGY, 1962, 65, 280-284.
                (VALIDITY:CONSTRUCT; N=189 PSYCHIATRIC PATIENTS)
        @APPLICATION 1962 R-30 W-113

757   JACKSON, D. N., & MESSICK, S.
            RESPONSE STYLES ON THE MMPI: COMPARISON OF CLINICAL AND NORMAL SAMPLES.
            JOURNAL OF ABNORMAL AND SOCIAL PSYCHOLOGY, 1962, 65, 285-299.
                (VALIDITY:CONSTRUCT; CORRELATES:PSYCHOLOGICAL; FACTOR ANALYSIS;
                BIAS:RESPONSE; N=119 MALE AND 75 FEMALE PSYCHIATRIC PATIENTS, 160
                MALE AND 174 FEMALE COLLEGE STUDENTS)
        @APPLICATION 1962 D-45 T-2 B-5 E-1 H-122 C-58 F-34 W-8 W-41

758   SARASON, I. G., & GANZER, V. J.
            ANXIETY REINFORCEMENT, AND EXPERIMENTAL INSTRUCTIONS IN A FREE
            VERBALIZATION SITUATION.
            JOURNAL OF ABNORMAL AND SOCIAL PSYCHOLOGY, 1962, 65, 300-307.
                (CORRELATES:BEHAVIORAL, ENVIRONMENTAL; N=48 MALE & 48 FEMALE COLLEGE
                STUDENTS)
        @APPLICATION 1962 S-5

759   FIEDLER, F. E.
            LEADER ATTITUDES, GROUP CLIMATE, AND GROUP CREATIVITY.
            JOURNAL OF ABNORMAL AND SOCIAL PSYCHOLOGY, 1962, 65, 308-318.
                (MODIFICATION; RELIABILITY:INTERRATER; CORRELATES:PSYCHOLOGICAL,
                ENVIRONMENTAL; USED AS CRITERION; 3 STUDIES: N=64 COLLEGE
                STUDENTS, 24 FEMALES, 71 WOMEN AND 37 MEN)
        @APPLICATION 1962 M-20 W-31 B-2

760   LOCKWOOD, D. H., & GUERNEY, B., JR.
           IDENTIFICATION AND EMPATHY IN RELATION TO SELF-DISSATISFACTION AND
           ADJUSTMENT.
           JOURNAL OF ABNORMAL AND SOCIAL PSYCHOLOGY, 1962, 65, 343-347.
                   (CORRELATES:PSYCHOLOGICAL, DEMOGRAPHIC, INTELLIGENCE; NORMATIVE DATA;
                   N=20 MALE AND 20 FEMALE HIGH SCHOOL STUDENTS)
           @APPLICATION 1962 L-35 B-128

761   MCGEE, R. K.
           THE RELATIONSHIP BETWEEN RESPONSE STYLE AND PERSONALITY VARIABLES: II. THE
           PREDICTION OF INDEPENDENT CONFORMITY BEHAVIOR.
           JOURNAL OF ABNORMAL AND SOCIAL PSYCHOLOGY, 1962, 65, 347-351.
                   (CORRELATES:BEHAVIORAL, PSYCHOLOGICAL; NORMATIVE DATA; N=60 MALE AND
                   44 FEMALE COLLEGE STUDENTS)
           @APPLICATION 1962 C-31 A-5 C-27 B-4

762   PENNEY, R. K., & MCCANN, B.
           THE INSTRUMENTAL ESCAPE CONDITIONING OF ANXIOUS AND NONANXIOUS CHILDREN.
           JOURNAL OF ABNORMAL AND SOCIAL PSYCHOLOGY, 1962, 65, 351-354.
                   (CORRELATES:BEHAVIORAL; USED AS CRITERION; N=101 CHILDREN)
           @APPLICATION 1962 S-35 S-133

763   MORIARTY, D., & KATES, S. L.
           CONCEPT ATTAINMENT OF SCHIZOPHRENICS ON MATERIAL INVOLVING SOCIAL
           APPROVAL AND DISAPPROVAL.
           JOURNAL OF ABNORMAL AND SOCIAL PSYCHOLOGY, 1962, 65, 355-364.
                   (RELIABILITY:INTERRATER; CORRELATES:BEHAVIORAL, PSYCHOLOGICAL,
                   INTELLIGENCE; N=32 MALE SCHIZOPHRENICS)
           @APPLICATION 1962 P-32

764   SARASON, I. W.
           INDIVIDUAL DIFFERENCES, SITUATIONAL VARIABLES, AND PERSONALITY RESEARCH.
           JOURNAL OF ABNORMAL AND SOCIAL PSYCHOLOGY, 1962, 65, 376-380.
                   (CORRELATES:BEHAVIORAL, ENVIRONMENTAL; USED AS CRITERION; NORMATIVE
                   DATA; N=160 COLLEGE STUDENTS)
           @APPLICATION 1962 S-4

765   TUTKO, T. A., & SPENCE, J. T.
           THE PERFORMANCE OF PROCESS AND REACTIVE SCHIZOPHRENICS AND BRAIN INJURED
           SUBJECTS ON A CONCEPTUAL TASK.
           JOURNAL OF ABNORMAL AND SOCIAL PSYCHOLOGY, 1962, 65, 387-394.
                   (CORRELATES:PSYCHOLOGICAL, INTELLIGENCE; NORMATIVE DATA; N=15
                   NORMAL SS, 15 BRAIN INJURED, AND 30 PSYCHIATRIC PATIENTS)
           @APPLICATION 1962 P-32

766   DEMBER, W. N., NAIRNE, F., & MILLER, F. J.
           FURTHER VALIDATION OF THE ALPERT-HABER ACHIEVEMENT ANXIETY TEST.
           JOURNAL OF ABNORMAL AND SOCIAL PSYCHOLOGY, 1962, 65, 427-428.
                   (VALIDITY:CONSTRUCT; CORRELATES:DEMOGRAPHIC, INTELLIGENCE; 2 STUDIES;
                   N=39 COLLEGE MALES, N=25 MALE & 39 FEMALE COLLEGE STUDENTS)
           @APPLICATION 1962 A-8

767   MEGARGEE, E. I., & MENDELSOHN, G. A.
           A CROSS-VALIDATION OF TWELVE MMPI INDICES OF HOSTILITY AND CONTROL.
           JOURNAL OF ABNORMAL AND SOCIAL PSYCHOLOGY, 1962, 65, 431-438.
                   (VALIDITY:CROSS-VALIDATION; N=14 EXTREMELY ASSAULTIVE MEN, 25
                   MODERATELY ASSAULTIVE MEN, & 25 MEN AS CONTROLS)
           @APPLICATION 1962 D-45

768   WILLIAMS, J. E.
           ACCEPTANCE BY OTHERS AND ITS RELATIONSHIP TO ACCEPTANCE OF SELF AND
           OTHERS: A REPEAT OF FEY'S STUDY.
           JOURNAL OF ABNORMAL AND SOCIAL PSYCHOLOGY, 1962, 65, 438-442.
                   (VALIDITY:CROSS-VALIDATION; NORMATIVE DATA; N=74 MEMBERS OF 2 SOCIAL
                   FRATERNITIES)
           @APPLICATION 1962 F-91

769   DRAGUNS, J. G.
           RESPONSES TO COGNITIVE AND PERCEPTUAL AMBIGUITY IN CHRONIC AND ACUTE
           SCHIZOPHRENICS.
           JOURNAL OF ABNORMAL AND SOCIAL PSYCHOLOGY, 1963, 66, 24-30.
                   (CORRELATES:PSYCHOLOGICAL, ENVIRONMENTAL, INTELLIGENCE; N=34 CHRONIC
                   SCHIZOPHRENICS, 25 ACUTE, 36 HOSPITAL STAFF CONTROLS)
           @APPLICATION 1963 D-45 V-44 S-88

770   ANISFELD, M., MUNOZ, S. R., & LAMBERT, W. E.
            THE STRUCTURE AND DYNAMICS OF THE ETHNIC ATTITUDES OF JEWISH ADOLESCENTS.
            JOURNAL OF ABNORMAL AND SOCIAL PSYCHOLOGY, 1963, 66, 31-36.
                (MODIFICATION; CORRELATES:PSYCHOLOGICAL, INTELLIGENCE; FACTOR
                ANALYSIS; N=63 MALE, 37 FEMALE 10TH GRADE JEWISH STUDENTS)
        @APPLICATION 1963 A-5 A-35 S-24 H-144 A-15 O-16

771   LESSER, G. S., KRAWITZ, R. N., & PACKARD, R.
            EXPERIMENTAL AROUSAL OF ACHIEVEMENT MOTIVATION IN ADOLESCENT GIRLS.
            JOURNAL OF ABNORMAL AND SOCIAL PSYCHOLOGY, 1963, 66, 59-66.
                (RELIABILITY:INTERRATER; CORRELATES:INTELLIGENCE, ENVIRONMENTAL;
                NORMATIVE DATA; N=80 JUNIOR AND SENIOR HIGH SCHOOL GIRLS)
        @APPLICATION 1963 M-7

772   HORTON, D. L., MARLOWE, D., & CROWNE, D. P.
            THE EFFECT OF INSTRUCTIONAL SET AND NEED FOR SOCIAL APPROVAL ON
            COMMONALITY OF WORD ASSOCIATION RESPONSES.
            JOURNAL OF ABNORMAL AND SOCIAL PSYCHOLOGY, 1963, 66, 67-72.
                (CORRELATES:PSYCHOLOGICAL, ENVIRONMENTAL; NORMATIVE DATA; N=177
                FEMALE, 118 MALE UNDERGRADUATES)
        @APPLICATION 1963 C-27 R-27

773   SARASON, I. G.
            TEST ANXIETY AND INTELLECTUAL PERFORMANCE.
            JOURNAL OF ABNORMAL AND SOCIAL PSYCHOLOGY, 1963, 66, 73-75.
                (CORRELATES:PSYCHOLOGICAL, DEMOGRAPHIC, INTELLIGENCE; NORMATIVE DATA;
                N=232 MALE, 228 FEMALE 11TH AND 12TH GRADERS)
        @APPLICATION 1963 S-5 S-4

774   CHRISTENSEN, C. M.
            A NOTE ON "DOGMATISM AND LEARNING."
            JOURNAL OF ABNORMAL AND SOCIAL PSYCHOLOGY, 1963, 66, 75-76.
                (CORRELATES:PSYCHOLOGICAL, INTELLIGENCE; N=117 FEMALE, 49 MALE
                UNDERGRADUATES)
        @APPLICATION 1963 R-8

775   ROSENHAN, D., & LONDON, P.
            HYPNOSIS: EXPECTATION, SUSCEPTIBILITY, AND PERFORMANCE.
            JOURNAL OF ABNORMAL AND SOCIAL PSYCHOLOGY, 1963, 66, 77-81.
                (CORRELATES:BEHAVIORAL, ENVIRONMENTAL; USED AS CRITERION; N=68 MALE
                STUDENTS)
        @APPLICATION 1963 R-97

776   CARRIER, N. A.
            NEED CORRELATES OF "GULLIBILITY."
            JOURNAL OF ABNORMAL AND SOCIAL PSYCHOLOGY, 1963, 66, 84-86.
                (CORRELATES:PSYCHOLOGICAL, DEMOGRAPHIC; USED AS CRITERION; N=87
                MALE, 41 FEMALE UNDERGRADUATES)
        @APPLICATION 1963 E-2 F-96 S-331

777   AS, A.
            HYPNOTIZABILITY AS A FUNCTION OF NONHYPNOTIC EXPERIENCES.
            JOURNAL OF ABNORMAL AND SOCIAL PSYCHOLOGY, 1963, 66, 142-150.
                (DESCRIPTION; RELIABILITY:INTERNAL CONSISTENCY; VALIDITY:CRITERION;
                CORRELATES:PSYCHOLOGICAL; N=102 COLLEGE FEMALES)
        @APPLICATION 1963 W-31 A-69 W-124

778   FEATHER, N. T.
            COGNITIVE DISSONANCE, SENSITIVITY, AND EVALUATION.
            JOURNAL OF ABNORMAL AND SOCIAL PSYCHOLOGY, 1963, 66, 157-163.
                (CORRELATES:BEHAVIORAL; N=152 MALE STUDENTS, SMOKERS AND NONSMOKERS)
        @APPLICATION 1963 F-5

779   CARTWRIGHT, D. S., KIRTNER, W. L., & FISKE, D. W.
            METHOD FACTOR IN CHANGES ASSOCIATED WITH PSYCHOTHERAPY.
            JOURNAL OF ABNORMAL AND SOCIAL PSYCHOLOGY, 1963, 66, 164-175.
                (RELIABILITY:RETEST; VALIDITY:CRITERION; FACTOR ANALYSIS; N=93
                THERAPY PATIENTS)
        @APPLICATION 1963 D-45 B-60 O-17 O-18 M-20 C-143 O-23 T-81

780   ZLOTOWSKI, M., & BAKAN, P.
            BEHAVIORAL VARIABILITY OF PROCESS AND REACTIVE SCHIZOPHRENICS IN A BINARY
            GUESSING TASK.
            JOURNAL OF ABNORMAL AND SOCIAL PSYCHOLOGY, 1963, 66, 185-187.
                    (CORRELATES:BEHAVIORAL, PSYCHOLOGICAL; USED AS CRITERION; N=16
                    PROCESS AND 13 REACTIVE SCHIZOPHRENICS)
        aAPPLICATION 1963 B-82

781   SPOHN, H. E., & WOLK, W.
            EFFECT OF GROUP PROBLEM SOLVING EXPERIENCE UPON SOCIAL WITHDRAWAL IN
            CHRONIC SCHIZOPHRENICS.
            JOURNAL OF ABNORMAL AND SOCIAL PSYCHOLOGY, 1963, 66, 187-190.
                    (CORRELATES:BEHAVIORAL; USED AS CRITERION; N=32 HOSPITALIZED MALE
                    CHRONIC SCHIZOPHRENICS)
        aAPPLICATION 1963 R-37

782   KNIGHT, K. E.
            EFFECT OF EFFORT ON BEHAVIORAL RIGIDITY IN A LUCHINS WATER JAR TASK.
            JOURNAL OF ABNORMAL AND SOCIAL PSYCHOLOGY, 1963, 66, 190-192.
                    (MODIFICATION; CORRELATES:PSYCHOLOGICAL, ENVIRONMENTAL; N=46 MALE
                    UNDERGRADUATES)
        aAPPLICATION 1963 L-45

783   FEATHER, N. T.
            THE RELATIONSHIP OF EXPECTATION OF SUCCESS TO REPORTED PROBABILITY, TASK
            STRUCTURE, AND ACHIEVEMENT RELATED MOTIVATION.
            JOURNAL OF ABNORMAL AND SOCIAL PSYCHOLOGY, 1963, 66, 231-238.
                    (RELIABILITY:INTERRATER; CORRELATES:PSYCHOLOGICAL, ENVIRONMENTAL;
                    NORMATIVE DATA; BIAS:RESPONSE; N=126 COLLEGE MALES)
        aAPPLICATION 1963 A-8 M-7

784   MCCORD, J., MCCORD, W., & HOWARD, A.
            FAMILY INTERACTION AS ANTECEDENT TO THE DIRECTION OF MALE AGGRESSIVENESS.
            JOURNAL OF ABNORMAL AND SOCIAL PSYCHOLOGY, 1963, 66, 239-242.
                    (RELIABILITY:INTERRATER; CORRELATES:BEHAVIORAL, ENVIRONMENTAL;
                    N= FOLLOW-UP OF 255 BOYS)
        /aAPPLICATION 1963 M-162 M-231

785   SWEETBAUM, H. A.
            COMPARISON OF THE EFFECTS OF INTROVERSION-EXTRAVERSION AND ANXIETY ON
            CONDITIONING.
            JOURNAL OF ABNORMAL AND SOCIAL PSYCHOLOGY, 1963, 66, 249-254.
                    (CORRELATES:PSYCHOLOGICAL, ENVIRONMENTAL; USED AS CRITERION; N=56
                    MALE SURGICAL PATIENTS)
        aAPPLICATION 1963 G-39

786   ROBBINS, L. C.
            THE ACCURACY OF PARENTAL RECALL OF ASPECTS OF CHILD DEVELOPMENT AND OF
            CHILD REARING PRACTICES.
            JOURNAL OF ABNORMAL AND SOCIAL PSYCHOLOGY, 1963, 66, 261-270.
                    (RELIABILITY:INTERRATER; CORRELATES:PSYCHOLOGICAL; BIAS:RESPONSE;
                    N=47 FAMILIES WITH 3 YEAR OLD CHILD)
        aAPPLICATION 1963 S-9

787   JESSOR, R., LIVERANT, S., & OPOCHINSKY, S.
            INBALANCE IN NEED STRUCTURE AND MALADJUSTMENT.
            JOURNAL OF ABNORMAL AND SOCIAL PSYCHOLOGY, 1963, 66, 271-275.
                    (RELIABILITY:INTERRATER; VALIDITY:CONSTRUCT;
                    CORRELATES:PSYCHOLOGICAL; USED AS CRITERION; 4 STUDIES: TOTAL N=1367
                    COLLEGE AND 68 HIGH SCHOOL STUDENTS)
        aAPPLICATION 1963 R-31 L-29

788   KAMARO, D. K.
            RELATIONSHIP OF EGO DISJUNCTION AND MANIFEST ANXIETY TO CONFLICT
            RESOLUTION.
            JOURNAL OF ABNORMAL AND SOCIAL PSYCHOLOGY, 1963, 66, 281-284.
                    (VALIDITY:CRITERION; CORRELATES:BEHAVIORAL, PSYCHOLOGICAL; USED AS
                    CRITERION; N=76 MALE UNDERGRADUATES)
        aAPPLICATION 1963 E-2 T-2

789   SOLOMON, L., & KLEIN, E.
            THE RELATIONSHIP BETWEEN AGREEING RESPONSE SET AND SOCIAL DESIRABILITY.
            JOURNAL OF ABNORMAL AND SOCIAL PSYCHOLOGY, 1963, 66, 176-179.
                (MODIFICATION; CORRELATES:PSYCHOLOGICAL; FACTOR ANALYSIS;
                BIAS:RESPONSE; N=125 SCHIZOPHRENICS, 135 NORMAL CONTROLS)
        aAPPLICATION 1963 C-31 A-5 C-23 E-1 T-82 D-45

790   VAUGHAN, G. M., & MANGAN, G. L.
            CONFORMITY TO GROUP PRESSURE IN RELATION TO THE VALUE OF THE TASK MATERIAL.
            JOURNAL OF ABNORMAL AND SOCIAL PSYCHOLOGY, 1963, 66, 179-183.
                (MODIFICATION; CORRELATES:PSYCHOLOGICAL; USED AS CRITERION;
                NORMATIVE DATA; N=20 MALE UNDERGRADUATES)
        aAPPLICATION 1963 A-7 T-2

791   WEATHERLEY, D.
            MATERNAL RESPONSE TO CHILDHOOD AGGRESSION AND SUBSEQUEN. ANTI-SEMITISM.
            JOURNAL OF ABNORMAL AND SOCIAL PSYCHOLOGY, 1963, 66, 183-185.
                (CORRELATES:PSYCHOLOGICAL; N=39 NON-JEWISH FEMALE UNDERGRADUATES AND
                THEIR MOTHERS)
        aAPPLICATION 1963 L-32 O-16

792   MARKS, J., STAUFFACHER, J. C., & LYLE, C.
            PREDICTING OUTCOME IN SCHIZOPHRENIA.
            JOURNAL OF ABNORMAL AND SOCIAL PSYCHOLOGY, 1963, 66, 117-127.
                (VALIDITY:CRITERION; CORRELATES:PSYCHOLOGICAL, DEMOGRAPHIC; USED AS
                CRITERION; N=115 SCHIZOPHRENIC MALE VETERANS)
        aAPPLICATION 1963 R-17 M-2 C-150 C-10 W-41 T-2 S-24 N-14 R-43 E-1 B-5 E-20 J-39
        aH-145 W-123 M-160 D-45

793   STEINER, I. D., & ROGERS, E. D.
            ALTERNATIVE RESPONSES TO DISSONANCE.
            JOURNAL OF ABNORMAL AND SOCIAL PSYCHOLOGY, 1963, 66, 128-136.
                (CORRELATES:BEHAVIORAL, PSYCHOLOGICAL, ENVIRONMENTAL; N=50 MALE, 50
                FEMALE STUDENTS AND 23 MALE, 24 FEMALE CONTROLS)
        aAPPLICATION 1963 D-45 T-2

794   HOUSTON, J. P., & MEDNICK, S. A.
            CREATIVITY AND THE NEED FOR NOVELTY.
            JOURNAL OF ABNORMAL AND SOCIAL PSYCHOLOGY, 1963, 66, 137-141.
                (CORRELATES:PSYCHOLOGICAL, ENVIRONMENTAL; USED AS CRITERION;
                NORMATIVE DATA; N=60 UNDERGRADUATES)
        aAPPLICATION 1963 M-29

795   BRODY, N.
            N ACHIEVEMENT, TEST ANXIETY, AND SUBJECTIVE PROBABILITY OF SUCCESS IN
            RISK TAKING BEHAVIOR.
            JOURNAL OF ABNORMAL AND SOCIAL PSYCHOLOGY, 1963, 66, 413-418.
                (RELIABILITY:RETEST; CORRELATES:BEHAVIORAL, PSYCHOLOGICAL; N=115 MALE
                UNDERGRADUATES)
        aAPPLICATION 1963 M-7 M-4

796   ROLAND, A.
            PERSUASIBILITY IN YOUNG CHILDREN AS A FUNCTION OF AGGRESSIVE MOTIVATION AND
            AND AGGRESSION CONFLICT.
            JOURNAL OF ABNORMAL AND SOCIAL PSYCHOLOGY, 1963, 66, 454-461.
                (MODIFICATION; RELIABILITY:RETEST, INTERRATER; VALIDITY:CRITERION;
                CORRELATES:BEHAVIORAL, PSYCHOLOGICAL; NORMATIVE DATA; N=169 FIRST
                GRADE BOYS)
        aAPPLICATION 1963 A-67 A-68 L-113

797   DECHARMS, R., & WILKINS, E. J.
            SOME EFFECTS OF VERBAL EXPRESSION OF HOSTILITY.
            JOURNAL OF ABNORMAL AND SOCIAL PSYCHOLOGY, 1963, 66, 462-470.
                (CORRELATES:BEHAVIORAL, PSYCHOLOGICAL; N=113 MALE UNDERGRADUATES)
        aAPPLICATION 1963 D-14

798   BRAMEL, D.
            SELECTION OF A TARGET FOR DEFENSIVE PROJECTION.
            JOURNAL OF ABNORMAL AND SOCIAL PSYCHOLOGY, 1963, 66, 318-324.
                (CORRELATES:BEHAVIORAL, PSYCHOLOGICAL, ENVIRONMENTAL; N=109 COLLEGE
                MALES)
        aAPPLICATION 1963 M-20

799   PEARL, D., & BERG, P. S. D.
            TIME PERCEPTION AND CONFLICT AROUSAL IN SCHIZOPHRENIA.
            JOURNAL OF ABNORMAL AND SOCIAL PSYCHOLOGY, 1963, 66, 332-338.
                (MODIFICATION; CORRELATES:PSYCHOLOGICAL; N=48 SCHIZOPHRENICS)
        @APPLICATION 1963 M-20

800   LAMBERT, W. E., GARDNER, R. C., BARIK, H. C., & TUNSTALL, K.
            ATTITUDINAL AND COGNITIVE ASPECTS OF INTENSIVE STUDY OF A SECOND
            LANGUAGE.
            JOURNAL OF ABNORMAL AND SOCIAL PSYCHOLOGY, 1963, 66, 358-368.
                (MODIFICATION; CORRELATES:BEHAVIORAL, PSYCHOLOGICAL; FACTOR
                ANALYSIS; N=192 STUDENTS)
        @APPLICATION 1963 A-5 S-28

801   BROXTON, J. A.
            A TEST OF INTERPERSONAL ATTRACTION PREDICTIONS DERIVED FROM BALANCE THEORY.
            JOURNAL OF ABNORMAL AND SOCIAL PSYCHOLOGY, 1963, 66, 394-397.
                (MODIFICATION; CORRELATES:PSYCHOLOGICAL, ENVIRONMENTAL; USED AS
                CRITERION; N=121 COLLEGE FEMALES)
        @APPLICATION 1963 G-21

802   BANTA, T. J., & HETHERINGTON, M.
            RELATIONS BETWEEN NEEDS OF FRIENDS AND FIANCES.
            JOURNAL OF ABNORMAL AND SOCIAL PSYCHOLOGY, 1963, 66, 401-404.
                (CORRELATES:BEHAVIORAL, PSYCHOLOGICAL; N=174)
        @APPLICATION 1963 E-2

803   KATZ, I., & GREENBAUM, C.
            EFFECTS OF ANXIETY, THREAT, AND RACIAL ENVIRONMENT ON TASK PERFORMANCE OF
            NEGRO COLLEGE STUDENTS.
            JOURNAL OF ABNORMAL AND SOCIAL PSYCHOLOGY, 1963, 66, 562-567.
                (CORRELATES:BEHAVIORAL, PSYCHOLOGICAL, ENVIRONMENTAL; USED AS
                CRITERION; N=115 MALE NEGRO STUDENTS)
        @APPLICATION 1963 H-51

804   BAXTER, J. C., BECKER, J., & HOOKS, W.
            DEFENSIVE STYLE IN THE FAMILIES OF SCHIZOPHRENICS AND CONTROLS.
            JOURNAL OF ABNORMAL AND SOCIAL PSYCHOLOGY, 1963, 66, 512-518.
                (CORRELATES:PSYCHOLOGICAL, DEMOGRAPHIC, INTELLIGENCE, ENVIRONMENTAL;
                USED AS CRITERION; N=20 SCHIZOPHRENICS, 10 NEUROTIC CONTROLS, 30
                PAIRS OF PARENTS)
        @APPLICATION 1963 P-32 R-30

805   ZAX, M., COWEN, E. L., & PETER, M.
            A COMPARATIVE STUDY OF NOVICE NUNS AND COLLEGE FEMALES USING THE RESPONSE
            SET APPROACH.
            JOURNAL OF ABNORMAL AND SOCIAL PSYCHOLOGY, 1963, 66, 369-375.
                (MODIFICATION; CORRELATES:PSYCHOLOGICAL; NORMATIVE DATA; N=40 COLLEGE
                FEMALES, 40 NOVICE NUNS)
        @APPLICATION 1963 R-30 O-16

806   GRINDER, R. E., & MCMICHAEL, R. E.
            CULTURAL INFLUENCE ON CONSCIENCE DEVELOPMENT: RESISTANCE TO TEMPTATION
            AND GUILT AMONG SAMOANS AND AMERICAN CAUCASIANS.
            JOURNAL OF ABNORMAL AND SOCIAL PSYCHOLOGY, 1963, 66, 503-507.
                (CORRELATES:BEHAVIORAL, DEMOGRAPHIC; CROSS-CULTURAL APPLICATION;
                N=15 AMERICAN CAUCASIANS (4 BOYS, 11 GIRLS) AND 19 SAMOANS (12 BOYS,
                7 GIRLS) IN 6TH AND 7TH GRADE)
        @APPLICATION 1963 A-71

807   NORMAN, W. T.
            TOWARD AN ADEQUATE TAXONOMY OF PERSONALITY ATTRIBUTES: REPLICATED FACTOR
            STRUCTURE IN PEER NOMINATION PERSONALITY RATINGS.
            JOURNAL OF ABNORMAL AND SOCIAL PSYCHOLOGY, 1963, 66, 574-583.
                (CORRELATES:BEHAVIORAL, PSYCHOLOGICAL; FACTOR ANALYSIS; N=622
                COLLEGE STUDENTS)
        @APPLICATION 1963 T-34

808   BARBER, T. X., & CALVERLEY, D. S.
            "HYPNOTIC-LIKE" SUGGESTIBILITY IN CHILDREN AND ADULTS.
            JOURNAL OF ABNORMAL AND SOCIAL PSYCHOLOGY, 1963, 66, 589-597.
                (DESCRIPTION; RELIABILITY:RETEST; CORRELATES:BEHAVIORAL, DEMOGRAPHIC;
                NORMATIVE DATA; N=724 SUBJECTS AGES 6-22)
        @APPLICATION 1963 B-3

809   LANG, P. J. & LAZOVIK, A. D.
            EXPERIMENTAL DESENSITIZATION OF A PHOBIA.
            JOURNAL OF ABNORMAL AND SOCIAL PSYCHOLOGY, 1963, 66, 519-525.
                    (CORRELATES:PSYCHOLOGICAL, ENVIRONMENTAL; USED AS CRITERION; N=24
                    STUDENTS WITH STATIC PHOBIA)
        @APPLICATION 1963 W-31 L-24 D-45 W-135 T-2

810   STOTLAND, E., & DUNN, R. E.
            EMPATHY, SELF-ESTEEM, AND BIRTH ORDER.
            JOURNAL OF ABNORMAL AND SOCIAL PSYCHOLOGY, 1963, 66, 532-540.
                    (CORRELATES:PSYCHOLOGICAL, PHYSIOLOGICAL, ENVIRONMENTAL;
                    N=132 UNDERGRADUATES)
        @APPLICATION 1963 W-71

811   CROWNE, D. P., & LIVERANT, S.
            CONFORMITY UNDER VARYING CONDITIONS OF PERSONAL COMMITMENT.
            JOURNAL OF ABNORMAL AND SOCIAL PSYCHOLOGY, 1963, 66, 547-555.
                    (CORRELATES:PSYCHOLOGICAL, ENVIRONMENTAL; N=40 MALE AND 70 FEMALE
                    COLLEGE STUDENTS)
        @APPLICATION 1963 R-18 R-17 C-27 L-159

812   IZARD, C. E.
            PERSONALITY SIMILARITY AND FRIENDSHIP.
            JOURNAL OF ABNORMAL AND SOCIAL PSYCHOLOGY, 1963, 66, 598-600.
                    (CORRELATES:PSYCHOLOGICAL; N=323 STUDENTS)
        @APPLICATION 1963 E-2

813   FEATHER, N. T.
            PERSISTANCE AT A DIFFICULT TASK WITH ALTERNATIVE TASK OF INTERMEDIATE
            DIFFICULTY.
            JOURNAL OF ABNORMAL AND SOCIAL PSYCHOLOGY, 1963, 66, 604-609.
                    (RELIABILITY:INTERRATER; CORRELATES:PSYCHOLOGICAL; USED AS CRITERION;
                    N=60 MALE STUDENTS)
        @APPLICATION 1963 M-4 M-7 M-2C

814   CRUMPTON, E.
            PERSISTENCE OF MALADAPTIVE RESPONSES IN SCHIZOPHRENIA.
            JOURNAL OF ABNORMAL AND SOCIAL PSYCHOLOGY, 1963, 66, 615-618.
                    (RELIABILITY:INTERRATER; CORRELATES:BEHAVIORAL, PSYCHOLOGICAL,
                    INTELLIGENCE; N=30 SCHIZOPHRENIC PATIENTS, 30 PSYCHIATRIC AIDES)
        @APPLICATION 1963 G-83

815   O'CONNOR, W. F.
            A METHODOLOGICAL NOTE ON THE CLINE AND RICHARDS' STUDIES ON ACCURACY IN
            INTERPERSONAL PERCEPTION.
            JOURNAL OF ABNORMAL AND SOCIAL PSYCHOLOGY, 1963, 66, 194-195.
                    (VALIDITY:CONTENT; NO SAMPLE DESCRIPTION)
        @APPLICATION 1963 C-169

816   KATZ, I., COHEN, M., & CASTIGLIONE, L.
            EFFECT OF ONE TYPE OF NEED COMPLEMENTARITY ON MARRIAGE PARTNERS' CONFORMITY
            TO ONE ANOTHER'S JUDGMENTS.
            JOURNAL OF ABNORMAL AND SOCIAL PSYCHOLOGY, 1963, 67, 8-14.
                    (CORRELATES:PSYCHOLOGICAL; N=55 MARRIED COUPLES)
        @APPLICATION 1963 K-97

817   RUTTIGER, K. F.
            INDIVIDUAL DIFFERENCES IN REACTION TO MEPROBROMATE: A STUDY IN VISUAL
            PERCEPTION.
            JOURNAL OF ABNORMAL AND SOCIAL PSYCHOLOGY, 1963, 67, 37-43.
                    (CORRELATES:BEHAVIORAL, PHYSIOLOGICAL, INTELLIGENCE; N=68 COLLEGE
                    MALES)
        @APPLICATION 1963 E-5

818   LORR, M., & MCNAIR, D. M.
            AN INTERPERSONAL BEHAVIOR CIRCLE.
            JOURNAL OF ABNORMAL AND SOCIAL PSYCHOLOGY, 1963, 67, 68-75.
                    (VALIDITY:CONSTRUCT; CORRELATES:PSYCHOLOGICAL; N=211 MALE AND 135
                    FEMALE OUTPATIENTS)
        @APPLICATION 1963 L-35 C-177 S-56

819   IZARD, C. E.
        PERSONALITY PROFILE SIMILARITY AS A FUNCTION OF GROUP MEMBERSHIP.
        JOURNAL OF ABNORMAL AND SOCIAL PSYCHOLOGY, 1963, 67, 404-408.
            (CORRELATES:DEMOGRAPHIC, ENVIRONMENTAL; N=OVER 600 COLLEGE STUDENTS)
    @APPLICATION 1963 E-2

820   JOHNSON, H. J.
        DECISION MAKING, CONFLICT, AND PHYSIOLOGICAL AROUSAL.
        JOURNAL OF ABNORMAL AND SOCIAL PSYCHOLOGY, 1963, 67, 114-124.
            (CORRELATES:PSYCHOLOGICAL, PHYSIOLOGICAL, ENVIRONMENTAL; N=60
            FEMALES)
    @APPLICATION 1963 A-26

821   STRICKER, G.
        SCAPEGOATING: AN EXPERIMENTAL INVESTIGATION.
        JOURNAL OF ABNORMAL AND SOCIAL PSYCHOLOGY, 1963, 67, 125-131.
            (MODIFICATION; CORRELATES:PSYCHOLOGICAL, ENVIRONMENTAL; USED AS
            CRITERION; N=425 WHITE COLLEGE MALES)
    @APPLICATION 1963 A-37 G-18 S-99 T-8 D-45 N-5 M-20

822   PAIVIO, A.
        AUDIENCE INFLUENCE, SOCIAL ISOLATION, AND SPEECH.
        JOURNAL OF ABNORMAL AND SOCIAL PSYCHOLOGY, 1963, 67, 247-253.
            (CORRELATES:BEHAVIORAL, PSYCHOLOGICAL, DEMOGRAPHIC, ENVIRONMENTAL;
            USED AS CRITERION; N=80 4TH AND 5TH GRADERS)
    @APPLICATION 1963 C-55 S-35 P-90

823   WINTER, D. G., ALPERT, R., & MCCLELLAND, D. C.
        THE CLASSIC PERSONAL STYLE.
        JOURNAL OF ABNORMAL AND SOCIAL PSYCHOLOGY, 1963, 67, 254-265.
            (MODIFICATION; CORRELATES:PSYCHOLOGICAL, INTELLIGENCE, ENVIRONMENTAL;
            N=268 BOYS)
    @APPLICATION 1963 W-51 S-56 A-7 O-16

824   BROEN, W. E., JR., STORMS, L. H., & GOLDBERG, D. H.
        DECREASED DISCRIMINATION AS A FUNCTION OF INCREASED DIRVE.
        JOURNAL OF ABNORMAL AND SOCIAL PSYCHOLOGY, 1963, 67, 266-273.
            (CORRELATES:BEHAVIORAL, PSYCHOLOGICAL; USED AS CRITERION;
            2 STUDIES: N=17 MALE COLLEGE PSYCHIATRIC OUTPATIENTS, 22
            SCHIZOPHRENIC INPATIENTS)
    @APPLICATION 1963 D-45 Z-13

825   WEISS, R. F., RAWSON, H. E., & PASANARICK, B.
        ARGUMENT STRENGTH, DELAY OF ARGUMENT, AND ANXIETY IN THE 'CONDITIONING'
        AND 'SELECTIVE LEARNING' OF ATTITUDES.
        JOURNAL OF ABNORMAL AND SOCIAL PSYCHOLOGY, 1963, 67, 157-165.
            (CORRELATES:PSYCHOLOGICAL; USED AS CRITERION; 2 STUDIES: N=48 UNDER-
            GRADUATES; 363 UNDERGRADUATES)
    @APPLICATION 1963 T-2

826   HARROW, M., & SCHULBERG, H. C.
        IMPLICATIONS FROM PSYCHOLOGICAL TESTING FOR THEORETICAL FORMULATIONS OF
        FOLIE A DEUX.
        JOURNAL OF ABNORMAL AND SOCIAL PSYCHOLOGY, 1963, 67, 166-172.
            (CORRELATES:PSYCHOLOGICAL, INTELLIGENCE; N=2 SCHIZOPHRENIC BROTHERS)
    @APPLICATION 1963 R-30 M-20 E-2 H-57 K-34 D-45

827   MANIS, M., HOUTS, P. S., & BLAKE, J. B.
        BELIEFS ABOUT MENTAL ILLNESS AS A FUNCTION OF PSYCHIATRIC STATUS AND
        PSYCHIATRIC HOSPITALIZATION.
        JOURNAL OF ABNORMAL AND SOCIAL PSYCHOLOGY, 1963, 67, 226-233.
            (VALIDITY:CROSS-VALIDATION; CORRELATES:PSYCHOLOGICAL, INTELLIGENCE;
            4 SAMPLES: TOTAL N=112 MALE PSYCHIATRIC PATIENTS, 69 NONPSYCHIATRIC
            CONTROLS)
    @APPLICATION 1963 D-45 B-119 N-32

828   BRADBURN, N. M.
        N ACHIEVEMENT AND FATHER DOMINANCE IN TURKEY.
        JOURNAL OF ABNORMAL AND SOCIAL PSYCHOLOGY, 1963, 67, 464-468.
            (CORRELATES:PSYCHOLOGICAL; CROSS-CULTURAL APPLICATION; 2 STUDIES:
            N=49 TURKISH AND 46 AMERICAN JUNIOR EXECUTIVES, N=47 TEACHERS, 47
            GRADUATE STUDENTS AND 24 SENIOR EXECUTIVES, ALL TURKISH)
    @APPLICATION 1963 M-7

829   SALTZ, G., & EPSTEIN, S.
            THEMATIC HOSTILITY AND GUILT RESPONSES AS RELATED TO SELF-REPORTED
            HOSTILITY, GUILT AND CONFLICT.
            JOURNAL OF ABNORMAL AND SOCIAL PSYCHOLOGY, 1963, 67, 469-479.
                (MODIFICATION; CORRELATES:PSYCHOLOGICAL; USED AS CRITERION;
                NORMATIVE DATA; N=181 MALE UNDERGRADUATES)
        @APPLICATION 1963 M-20 D-45 E-2

830   GILL, W. S.
            INTERPERSONAL AFFECT AND CONFORMITY BEHAVIOR IN SCHIZOPHRENICS.
            JOURNAL OF ABNORMAL AND SOCIAL PSYCHOLOGY, 1963, 67, 502-505.
                (MODIFICATION; CORRELATES:BEHAVIORAL, PSYCHOLOGICAL; N=28
                SCHIZOPHRENIC AND 28 NORMAL MALES)
        @APPLICATION 1963 M-20

831   HAYWOOD, H. C., & HUNT, J. M. V.
            EFFECTS OF EPINEPHRENE UPON NOVELTY PREFERENCE AND AROUSAL.
            JOURNAL OF ABNORMAL AND SOCIAL PSYCHOLOGY, 1963, 67, 206-213.
                (CORRELATES:PHYSIOLOGICAL; N=45 CIVIL SERVICE EMPLOYEES)
        @APPLICATION 1963 H-148

832   SPIELBERGER, C. D., BERGER, A., & HOWARD, K.
            CONDITIONING OF VERBAL BEHAVIOR AS A FUNCTION OF AWARENESS, NEED FOR
            SOCIAL APPROVAL, AND MOTIVATION TO RECEIVE REINFORCEMENT.
            JOURNAL OF ABNORMAL AND SOCIAL PSYCHOLOGY, 1963, 67, 241-246.
                (CORRELATES:PSYCHOLOGICAL; USED AS CRITERION; N=61 COLLEGE MALES)
        @APPLICATION 1963 C-27

833   HINCKLEY, E. D.
            A FOLLOW-UP STUDY OF THE INFLUENCE OF INDIVIDUAL OPINION ON THE
            CONSTRUCTION OF AN ATTITUDE SCALE.
            JOURNAL OF ABNORMAL AND SOCIAL PSYCHOLOGY, 1963, 67, 290-292.
                (VALIDITY:CONTENT; BIAS:TESTER; N=298 WHITE COLLEGE STUDENTS)
        @APPLICATION 1963 H-36

834   FOSTER, R. J., & GRIGG, A. E.
            ACQUIESCENT RESPONSE SET AS A MEASURE OF ACQUIESCENCE: FURTHER EVIDENCE.
            JOURNAL OF ABNORMAL AND SOCIAL PSYCHOLOGY, 1963, 67, 304-306.
                (RELIABILITY:INTERNAL CONSISTENCY; VALIDITY:CONSTRUCT;
                CORRELATES:BEHAVIORAL, PSYCHOLOGICAL; NORMATIVE DATA; N=75 MALE AND
                75 FEMALE UNDERGRADUATES)
        @APPLICATION 1963 C-31 B-118

835   SARASON, I. G., & MINARD, J.
            INTERRELATIONSHIPS AMONG SUBJECT, EXPERIMENTER, AND SITUATIONAL VARIABLES.
            JOURNAL OF ABNORMAL AND SOCIAL PSYCHOLOGY, 1963, 67, 87-91.
                (CORRELATES:BEHAVIORAL, ENVIRONMENTAL; N=64 MALE AND 64 FEMALE
                UNDERGRADUATES)
        @APPLICATION 1963 S-4

836   BURNSTEIN, E.
            FEAR OF FAILURE, ACHIEVEMENT MOTIVATION, AND ASPIRING TO PRESTIGEFUL
            OCCUPATIONS.
            JOURNAL OF ABNORMAL AND SOCIAL PSYCHOLOGY, 1963, 67, 189-193.
                (CORRELATES:PSYCHOLOGICAL, DEMOGRAPHIC; USED AS CRITERION; N=67 MALE
                UNDERGRADUATES)
        @APPLICATION 1963 M-4 M-7

837   ERON, L. D.
            RELATIONSHIP OF TV VIEWING HABITS AND AGGRESSIVE BEHAVIOR IN CHILDREN.
            JOURNAL OF ABNORMAL AND SOCIAL PSYCHOLOGY, 1963, 67, 193-196.
                (CORRELATES:BEHAVIORAL. N=644 BOYS AND 567 GIRLS)
        @APPLICATION 1963 W-68

838   SARASON, I. G., & GANZER, V. J.
            EFFECTS OF TEST ANXIETY AND REINFORCEMENT HISTORY ON VERBAL BEHAVIOR.
            JOURNAL OF ABNORMAL AND SOCIAL PSYCHOLOGY, 1963, 67, 513-519.
                (CORRELATES:BEHAVIORAL, PSYCHOLOGICAL, ENVIRONMENTAL; USED AS
                CRITERION; N=24 MALE AND 24 FEMALE UNDERGRADUATES)
        @APPLICATION 1963 D-45 G-22 S-5

839   DROPPLEMAN, L. F., & SCHAEFER, E. S.
          BOYS' AND GIRLS' REPORTS OF MATERNAL AND PATERNAL BEHAVIOR.
          JOURNAL OF ABNORMAL AND SOCIAL PSYCHOLOGY, 1963, 67, 648-654.
               (RELIABILITY:INTERNAL CONSISTENCY; CORRELATES:PSYCHOLOGICAL;
               2 STUDIES: N=165 7TH GRADE BOYS AND GIRLS, N=70 11TH GRADE BOYS AND
               GIRLS)
          @APPLICATION 1963 S-230

840   MCCLINTOCK, C. G., HARRISON, A. A., STRAND, S., & GALLO, P.
          INTERNATIONALISM-ISOLATIONISM, STRATEGY OF THE OTHER PLAYER, AND TWO-
          PERSON GAME BEHAVIOR.
          JOURNAL OF ABNORMAL AND SOCIAL PSYCHOLOGY, 1963, 67, 631-636.
               (CORRELATES:BEHAVIORAL: USED AS CRITERION; N=168 UNDERGRADUATES)
          @APPLICATION 1963 L-31 K-87

841   BYRNE, D., & BLAYLOCK, B.
          SIMILARITY AND ASSUMED SIMILARITY OF ATTITUDES BETWEEN HUSBANDS AND WIVES.
          JOURNAL OF ABNORMAL AND SOCIAL PSYCHOLOGY, 1963, 67, 636-640.
               (CORRELATES:PSYCHOLOGICAL, DEMOGRAPHIC; USED AS CRITERION;
               NORMATIVE DATA; N=36 MARRIED COUPLES)
          @APPLICATION 1963 R-8 R-50

842   EHRLICH, M. P.
          SELECTIVE ROLE OF AGGRESSION IN CONCEPT FORMATION.
          JOURNAL OF ABNORMAL AND SOCIAL PSYCHOLOGY, 1963, 67, 640-643.
               (MODIFICATION; CORRELATES:PSYCHOLOGICAL; USED AS CRITERION; N=75
               ADOLESCENT BOYS)
          @APPLICATION 1963 L-113 M-20

843   SCOTT, W. A.
          SOCIAL DESIRABILITY AND INDIVIDUAL CONCEPTIONS OF THE DESIRABLE.
          JOURNAL OF ABNORMAL AND SOCIAL PSYCHOLOGY, 1963, 67, 574-585.
               (RELIABILITY:INTERNAL CONSISTENCY; CORRELATES:BEHAVIORAL,
               PSYCHOLOGICAL; BIAS:RESPONSE; SEVERAL SAMPLES, MEDIAN N=APPROX. 200).
          @APPLICATION 1963 E-2 S-231

844   KELMAN, H. C., & BARCLAY, J.
          THE F SCALE AS A MEASURE OF BREADTH OF PERSPECTIVE.
          JOURNAL OF ABNORMAL AND SOCIAL PSYCHOLOGY, 1963, 67, 608-615.
               (VALIDITY:CONSTRUCT; CORRELATES:PSYCHOLOGICAL, DEMOGRAPHIC,
               ENVIRONMENTAL; NORMATIVE DATA; N=282 NEGRO UNDERGRADUATES)
          @APPLICATION 1963 A-5 W-176

845   FARINA, A., GARMEZY, N., & BARRY, H., III.
          RELATIONSHIP OF MARITAL STATUS TO INCIDENCE AND PROGNOSIS OF
          SCHIZOPHRENIA.
          JOURNAL OF ABNORMAL AND SOCIAL PSYCHOLOGY, 1963, 67, 624-630.
               (DESCRIPTION; RELIABILITY:INTERRATER; VALIDITY:CRITERION; CORRELATES:
               DEMOGRAPHIC; N=83 MALE AND 85 FEMALE SCHIZOPHRENICS)
          @APPLICATION 1963 P-32

846   CARON, A. J.
          CURIOSITY, ACHIEVEMENT, AND AVOIDANT MOTIVATION AS DETERMINANTS OF
          EPISTEMIC BEHAVIOR.
          JOURNAL OF ABNORMAL AND SOCIAL PSYCHOLOGY, 1963, 67, 535-549.
               (CORRELATES:BEHAVIORAL, PSYCHOLOGICAL; USED AS CRITERION; NORMATIVE
               DATA; N=241 COLLEGE MALES)
          @APPLICATION 1963 M-4 M-7

847   BARBER, T. X., & CALVERLEY, D. S.
          TOWARD A THEORY OF HYPNOTIC BEHAVIOR: EFFECTS OF SUGGESTIBILITY OF TASK
          MOTIVATING INSTRUCTIONS AND ATTITUDES TOWARD HYPNOSIS.
          JOURNAL OF ABNORMAL AND SOCIAL PSYCHOLOGY, 1963, 67, 557-565.
               (DESCRIPTION; VALIDITY:CRITERION; CORRELATES:PSYCHOLOGICAL,
               ENVIRONMENTAL; NORMATIVE DATA; N=59 MALE AND 16 FEMALE
               UNDERGRADUATES)
          @APPLICATION 1963 B-3

848   CARLSON, R.
          IDENTIFICATION AND PERSONALITY STRUCTURE IN PREADOLESCENTS.
          JOURNAL OF ABNORMAL AND SOCIAL PSYCHOLOGY, 1963, 67, 566-573.
               (MODIFICATION; CORRELATES:PSYCHOLOGICAL; N=43 6TH GRADERS AND
               PARENTS)
          @APPLICATION 1963 T-85

849   RUEBUSH, B. K., BYRUM, M., & FARNHAM, L. J.
            PROBLEM SOLVING AS A FUNCTION OF CHILDREN'S DEFENSIVENESS AND PARENTAL
            BEHAVIOR.
            JOURNAL OF ABNORMAL AND SOCIAL PSYCHOLOGY, 1963, 67, 355-362.
                    (CORRELATES:BEHAVIORAL, PSYCHOLOGICAL; USED AS CRITERION; N=32
                    FIFTH GRADE BOYS SELECTED FROM N OF 299)
        @APPLICATION 1963 S-35 R-100

850   SCHULMAN, R. E., & LONDON, P.
            HYPNOSIS AND VERBAL LEARNING.
            JOURNAL OF ABNORMAL AND SOCIAL PSYCHOLOGY, 1963, 67, 363-370.
                    (RELIABILITY:RETEST; CORRELATES:BEHAVIORAL, PSYCHOLOGICAL,
                    ENVIRONMENTAL; USED AS CRITERION; NORMATIVE DATA; N=20 VERY
                    TRANCEABLE, 20 TRANCEABLE AND 20 UNTRANCEABLE FEMALE UNDERGRADUATES
                    SELECTED FROM N OF 400)
        @APPLICATION 1963 L-90 W-31 H-149

851   STEINER, I. D., & JOHNSON, H. H.
            AUTHORITARIANISM AND 'TOLERANCE OF TRAIT INCONSISTENCY.'
            JOURNAL OF ABNORMAL AND SOCIAL PSYCHOLOGY, 1963, 67, 388-391.
                    (REVISION; CORRELATES:BEHAVIORAL, PSYCHOLOGICAL; 2 STUDIES: N=75
                    MALE UNDERGRADUATES; 24 MALE UNDERGRADUATES)
        @APPLICATION 1963 A-5 S-184

852   STRICKER, L. J., & ROSS, J.
            AN ASSESSMENT OF SOME STRUCTURAL PROPERTIES OF THE JUNGIAN PERSONALITY
            TYPOLOGY.
            JOURNAL OF ABNORMAL AND SOCIAL PSYCHOLOGY, 1964, 68, 62-71.
                    (RELIABILITY:RETEST; VALIDITY:CRITERION, CONSTRUCT; CORRELATES:
                    PSYCHOLOGICAL, INTELLIGENCE; 5 STUDIES: TOTAL N INDETERMINATE,
                    RANGE 41 TO 2,389)
        @APPLICATION 1964 M-22 D-45

853   DAS, J. P.
            HYPNOSIS, VERBAL SATIATION, VIGILANCE, AND PERSONALITY FACTORS.
            JOURNAL OF ABNORMAL AND SOCIAL PSYCHOLOGY, 1964, 68, 72-78.
                    (CORRELATES:PSYCHOLOGICAL; N=62 POSTGRADUATE STUDENTS)
        .@APPLICATION 1964 E-5 S-332

854   GANZER, V. J., & SARASON, I. G.
            INTERRELATIONSHIPS AMONG HOSTILITY, EXPERIMENTAL CONDITIONS, AND VERBAL
            BEHAVIOR.
            JOURNAL OF ABNORMAL AND SOCIAL PSYCHOLOGY, 1964, 68, 79-84.
                    (CORRELATES:BEHAVIORAL, ENVIRONMENTAL; USED AS CRITERION;
                    NORMATIVE DATA; N=40 MALE COLLEGE STUDENTS)
        @APPLICATION 1964 S-234

855   LEAGUE, B. J., & JACKSON, D. N.
            CONFORMITY, VERIDICALITY, AND SELF-ESTEEM.
            JOURNAL OF ABNORMAL AND SOCIAL PSYCHOLOGY, 1964, 68, 113-115.
                    (CORRELATES:BEHAVIORAL; USED AS CRITERION; N=62 MALE & 56 FEMALE
                    UNDERGRADUATES)
        @APPLICATION 1964 D-14

856   SUEDFELD, P.
            ATTITUDE MANIPULATION IN RESTRICTED ENVIRONMENTS: CONCEPTUAL STRUCTURE AND
            RESPONSE TO PROPAGANDA.
            JOURNAL OF ABNORMAL AND SOCIAL PSYCHOLOGY, 1964, 68, 242-247.
                    (CORRELATES:ENVIRONMENTAL; USED AS CRITERION; N=334 MALE
                    UNDERGRADUATES)
        @APPLICATION 1964 S-58 S-41 O-16 M-232

857   FISHER, S., & FISHER, R. L.
            BODY IMAGE BOUNDARIES AND PATTERNS OF BODY PERCEPTIONS.
            JOURNAL OF ABNORMAL AND SOCIAL PSYCHOLOGY, 1964, 68, 255-262.
                    (CORRELATES:PSYCHOLOGICAL, PHYSIOLOGICAL; 4 STUDIES: TOTAL N=108 MALE
                    AND 134 FEMALE COLLEGE STUDENTS)
        @APPLICATION 1964 R-30 F-75

858   BERKOWITZ, L., & DANIELS, L. R.
          AFFECTING THE SALIENCE OF THE SOCIAL RESPONSIBILITY NORM: EFFECTS OF PAST
          HELP ON THE RESPONSE TO DEPENDENCY RELATIONSHIPS.
          JOURNAL OF ABNORMAL AND SOCIAL PSYCHOLOGY, 1964, 68, 275-281.
                 (MODIFICATION; CORRELATES:BEHAVIORAL; N=80 FEMALE UNDERGRADUATES)
          @APPLICATION 1964 H-29

859   MOORE, R. K.
          SUSCEPTIBILITY TO HYPNOSIS AND SUSCEPTIBILITY TO SOCIAL INFLUENCE.
          JOURNAL OF ABNORMAL AND SOCIAL PSYCHOLOGY, 1964, 68, 282-294.
                 (MODIFICATION; RELIABILITY:RETEST, INTERNAL CONSISTENCY;
                 CORRELATES:PSYCHOLOGICAL, DEMOGRAPHIC; FACTOR ANALYSIS; N=80 MALE
                 UNDERGRADUATES)
          @APPLICATION 1964 W-31 G-22 W-8 W-41 W-14 F-34 J-8 D-45 B-4

860   BURDICK, H. A.
          NEED FOR ACHIEVEMENT, AND SCHEDULES OF VARIABLE REINFORCEMENT.
          JOURNAL OF ABNORMAL AND SOCIAL PSYCHOLOGY, 1964, 68, 302-306.
                 (CORRELATES:PSYCHOLOGICAL, ENVIRONMENTAL; USED AS CRITERION; N=59
                 MALE UNDERGRADUATES)
          @APPLICATION 1964 M-7

861   BROEN, W. E., JR., & STORMS, L. H.
          THE DIFFERENTIAL EFFECT OF INDUCED MUSCULAR TENSION (DRIVE) ON
          DISCRIMINATION IN SCHIZOPHRENICS AND NORMALS.
          JOURNAL OF ABNORMAL AND SOCIAL PSYCHOLOGY, 1964, 68, 349-353.
                 (CORRELATES:PHYSIOLOGICAL, ENVIRONMENTAL; N=62 ADULT MALE VETERAN
                 PATIENTS AND 35 SCHIZOPHRENICS)
          @APPLICATION 1964 D-45

862   FRENCH, E. G., & LESSER, G. S.
          SOME CHARACTERISTICS OF THE ACHIEVEMENT MOTIVE IN WOMEN.
          JOURNAL OF ABNORMAL AND SOCIAL PSYCHOLOGY, 1964, 68, 119-128.
                 (CORRELATES:BEHAVIORAL, PSYCHOLOGICAL, ENVIRONMENTAL;
                 NORMATIVE DATA; N=432 FEMALE COLLEGE STUDENTS)
          @APPLICATION 1964 F-20

863   THOMPSON, D. F., & MELTZER, L.
          COMMUNICATION OF EMOTIONAL INTENT BY FACIAL EXPRESSION.
          JOURNAL OF ABNORMAL AND SOCIAL PSYCHOLOGY, 1964, 68, 129-135.
                 (VALIDITY:CONSTRUCT; CORRELATES:PSYCHOLOGICAL; N=50 GRADUATE
                 AND UNDERGRADUATE STUDENTS)
          @APPLICATION 1964 G-22 S-237

864   DAVIDSON, P. O., PAYNE, R. W., & SLOANE, R. B.
          INTROVERSION, NEUROTICISM, AND CONDITIONING.
          JOURNAL OF ABNORMAL AND SOCIAL PSYCHOLOGY, 1964, 68, 136-143.
                 (CORRELATES:PSYCHOLOGICAL, PHYSIOLOGICAL, DEMOGRAPHIC, INTELLIGENCE;
                 NORMATIVE DATA; N=35 MALE, 38 FEMALE UNDERGRADUATES)
          @APPLICATION 1964 T-2 E-5

866   SPENCE, K. W., & SPENCE, J. T.
          RELATION OF EYELID CONDITIONING TO MANIFEST ANXIETY, EXTRAVERSION, AND
          RIGIDITY.
          JOURNAL OF ABNORMAL AND SOCIAL PSYCHOLOGY, 1964, 68, 144-149.
                 (CORRELATES:PSYCHOLOGICAL; N=100 MALE, 60 FEMALE COLLEGE STUDENTS)
          @APPLICATION 1964 D-45 E-5 B-93 T-2 G-22 R-8

867   BERLEW, D. E., & WILLIAMS, A. F.
          INTERPERSONAL SENSITIVITY UNDER MOTIVE AROUSING CONDITIONS.
          JOURNAL OF ABNORMAL AND SOCIAL PSYCHOLOGY, 1964, 68, 150-159.
                 (MODIFICATION; CORRELATES:PSYCHOLOGICAL, ENVIRONMENTAL;
                 NORMATIVE DATA; N=25 MALE UNDERGRADUATES)
          @APPLICATION 1964 M-20 M-7 B-120

868   KENNEDY, K., & KATES, S. L.
          CONCEPTUAL SORTING AND PERSONALITY ADJUSTMENT IN CHILDREN.
          JOURNAL OF ABNORMAL AND SOCIAL PSYCHOLOGY, 1964, 68, 211-214.
                 (CORRELATES:PSYCHOLOGICAL, INTELLIGENCE; USED AS CRITERION;
                 NORMATIVE DATA; N=150 6TH GRADERS, 48 SELECTED)
          @APPLICATION 1964 T-25 R-58

869   REITMAN, E. E., & CLEVELAND, S. E.
              CHANGES IN BODY IMAGE FOLLOWING SENSORY DEPRIVATION IN SCHIZOPHRENIC AND
              CONTROL GROUPS.
              JOURNAL OF ABNORMAL AND SOCIAL PSYCHOLOGY, 1964, 68, 168-176.
                     (VALIDITY:CRITERION; CORRELATES:PHYSIOLOGICAL, ENVIRONMENTAL;
                     N=40 SCHIZOPHRENIC, 20 NONPSYCHOTIC PATIENTS)
       @APPLICATION 1964 M-58 H-37 W-20

870   BRODY, N.
              ANXIETY AND THE VARIABILITY OF WORD ASSOCIATES.
              JOURNAL OF ABNORMAL AND SOCIAL PSYCHOLOGY, 1964, 68, 331-334.
                     (CORRELATES:PSYCHOLOGICAL; USED AS CRITERION; 2 STUDIES, TOTAL N=60
                     MALE HIGH SCHOOL STUDENTS)
       @APPLICATION 1964 T-2

871   LYERLY, S. B., ROSS, S., KRUGMAN, A. D., & CLYDE, D. J.
              DRUGS AND PLACEBOS: THE EFFECT OF INSTRUCTIONS UPON PERFORMANCE AND MOOD
              UNDER AMPHETAMINE SULPHATE AND CHLORAL HYDRATE.
              JOURNAL OF ABNORMAL AND SOCIAL PSYCHOLOGY, 1964, 68, 321-327.
                     (CORRELATES:BEHAVIORAL, PHYSIOLOGICAL, ENVIRONMENTAL; N=90 OLDER MEN)
       @APPLICATION 1964 C-16

872   SAMELSON, F.
              AGREEMENT SET AND ANTICONTENT ATTITUDES IN THE F SCALE.
              JOURNAL OF ABNORMAL AND SOCIAL PSYCHOLOGY, 1964, 68, 338-342.
                     (MENTION; BIAS:RESPONSE; NO SAMPLE DESCRIPTION)
       @APPLICATION 1964 R-8 A-5 A-15 A-29

873   MENDELSOHN, G. A., & GRISWOLD, B. B.
              DIFFERENTIAL USE OF INCIDENTAL STIMULI IN PROBLEM SOLVING AS A FUNCTION
              OF CREATIVITY.
              JOURNAL OF ABNORMAL AND SOCIAL PSYCHOLOGY, 1964, 68, 431-436.
                     (CORRELATES:BEHAVIORAL; USED AS CRITERION; NORMATIVE DATA; N=108
                     UNDERGRADUATE MALES AND FEMALES)
       @APPLICATION 1964 M-29

874   FRIEDMAN, A. S.
              MINIMAL EFFECTS OF SEVERE DEPRESSION ON COGNITIVE FUNCTIONING.
              JOURNAL OF ABNORMAL AND SOCIAL PSYCHOLOGY, 1964, 69, 237-243.
                     (CORRELATES:BEHAVIORAL, PSYCHOLOGICAL, INTELLIGENCE; NORMATIVE DATA;
                     N=55 DEPRESSIVES AND 65 NORMALS)
       @APPLICATION 1964 M-20 C-16

875   SECORD, P. F., BACKMAN, C. W., & EACHUS, H. T.
              EFFECTS OF IMBALANCE IN THE SELF-CONCEPT ON THE PERCEPTION OF PERSONS.
              JOURNAL OF ABNORMAL AND SOCIAL PSYCHOLOGY, 1964, 68, 442-446.
                     (CORRELATES:ENVIRONMENTAL; USED AS CRITERION; N=29 UNDERGRADUATES)
       @APPLICATION 1964 E-2 G-70

876   SPEISMAN, J. C., LAZARUS, R. S., MORDKOFF, A., & DAVISON, L.
              EXPERIMENTAL REDUCTION OF STRESS BASED ON EGO-DEFENSE THEORY.
              JOURNAL OF ABNORMAL AND SOCIAL PSYCHOLOGY, 1964, 68, 367-380.
                     (CORRELATES:PSYCHOLOGICAL, PHYSIOLOGICAL, ENVIRONMENTAL;
                     2 SAMPLES: N=42 AIRLINE EXECUTIVES AND 56 UNDERGRADUATES)
       @APPLICATION 1964 D-45 L-93 B-91 N-5 B-199

877   PHILLIPS, L., & ZIGLER, E.
              ROLE ORIENTATION, THE ACTION-THOUGHT DIMENSION, AND OUTCOME IN PSYCHIATRIC
              DISORDER.
              JOURNAL OF ABNORMAL AND SOCIAL PSYCHOLOGY, 1964, 68, 381-389.
                     (VALIDITY:CRITERION; CORRELATES:BEHAVIORAL, PSYCHOLOGICAL,
                     DEMOGRAPHIC; USED AS CRITERION; NORMATIVE DATA; N=129 MALE AND 122
                     FEMALE PSYCHIATRIC PATIENTS)
       @APPLICATION 1964 P-45 P-51 Z-28

878   BLANTON, R. L., & NUNNALLY, J. C.
              SEMANTIC HABITS AND COGNITIVE STYLE PROCESSES IN THE DEAF.
              JOURNAL OF ABNORMAL AND SOCIAL PSYCHOLOGY, 1964, 68, 397-402.
                     (CORRELATES:PSYCHOLOGICAL, PHYSIOLOGICAL, DEMOGRAPHIC; NORMATIVE
                     DATA; N=81 MALE AND 92 FEMALE DEAF CHILDREN AND ADOLESCENTS AND 83
                     MALE AND 95 FEMALE NORMAL CONTROLS)
       @APPLICATION 1964 P-7 B-115 T-83 N-6 N-25

879   ISAACSON, R. L.
        RELATION BETWEEN N ACHIEVEMENT, TEST ANXIETY, AND CURRICULAR CHOICES.
        JOURNAL OF ABNORMAL AND SOCIAL PSYCHOLOGY, 1964, 68, 447-452.
                (CORRELATES:BEHAVIORAL, PSYCHOLOGICAL, DEMOGRAPHIC, INTELLIGENCE;
                USED AS CRITERION; N=108 MALE AND 109 FEMALE UNDERGRADUATES)
      @APPLICATION 1964 M-4 M-7 F-20

880   HUSTMYER, F. E., JR., & KARNES, E.
        BACKGROUND AUTONOMIC ACTIVITY AND "ANALYTIC PERCEPTION."
        JOURNAL OF ABNORMAL AND SOCIAL PSYCHOLOGY, 1964, 68, 467-468.
                (CORRELATES:PHYSIOLOGICAL; NORMATIVE DATA; N=22 COLLEGE MALES)
      @APPLICATION 1964 J-54

881   KLEIN, E. B., & SPOHN, H. E.
        FURTHER COMMENTS ON CHARACTERISTICS OF UNTESTABLE CHRONIC SCHIZOPHRENICS.
        JOURNAL OF ABNORMAL AND SOCIAL PSYCHOLOGY, 1964, 68, 355-358.
                (VALIDITY:CRITERION; CORRELATES:BEHAVIORAL; USED AS CRITERION;
                N=95 MALE CHRONIC SCHIZOPHRENICS)
      @APPLICATION 1964 R-30 S-121 H-68

882   MAYO, C. W., & CROCKETT, W. H.
        COGNITIVE COMPLEXITY AND PRIMARY-RECENCY EFFECTS IN IMPRESSION FORMATION.
        JOURNAL OF ABNORMAL AND SOCIAL PSYCHOLOGY, 1964, 68, 335-338.
                (MODIFICATION; CORRELATES:PSYCHOLOGICAL; USED AS CRITERION; N=36
                MALES AND FEMALES SELECTED FROM 44 MALE AND 36 FEMALE UNDERGRADUATES)
      @APPLICATION 1964 K-23 A-93

883   HEILIZER, F.
        CONJUNCTIVE AND DISJUNCTIVE CONFLICT: A THEORY OF NEED CONFLICT.
        JOURNAL OF ABNORMAL AND SOCIAL PSYCHOLOGY, 1964, 68, 21-37.
                (VALIDITY:CRITERION; CORRELATES:PSYCHOLOGICAL; FACTOR ANALYSIS; N=80
                MALES, 20 EACH OF COLLEGE STUDENTS, SCHIZOPHRENICS, PERSONALITY
                DISORDER PATIENTS AND NEUROTICS)
      @APPLICATION 1964 E-2

884   CLARKE, A. R.
        CONFORMITY BEHAVIOR OF SCHIZOPHRENIC SUBJECTS WITH MATERNAL FIGURES.
        JOURNAL OF ABNORMAL AND SOCIAL PSYCHOLOGY, 1964, 68, 45-53.
                (CORRELATES:BEHAVIORAL, PSYCHOLOGICAL; USED AS CRITERION;
                NORMATIVE DATA; N=40 MALES, 10 EACH OF NONDRUG POOR PREMORBID
                SCHIZOPHRENICS, DRUG POOR PREMORBID SCHIZOPHRENICS, ALCOHOLICS, AND
                NORMALS)
      @APPLICATION 1964 P-32 W-132 W-133

885   LUOTO, K.
        PERSONALITY AND PLACEBO EFFECTS UPON TIMING BEHAVIOR.
        JOURNAL OF ABNORMAL AND SOCIAL PSYCHOLOGY, 1964, 68, 54-61.
                (CORRELATES:BEHAVIORAL, PSYCHOLOGICAL, ENVIRONMENTAL; USED AS
                CRITERION; N=40 MALE AND FEMALE UNDERGRADUATES SELECTED FROM ORIGINAL
                SAMPLE OF OVER 600)
      @APPLICATION 1964 B-84

886   ARMILLA, J.
        ANXIETY IN TAKING THE ROLE OF THE LEADER.
        JOURNAL OF ABNORMAL AND SOCIAL PSYCHOLOGY, 1964, 68, 550-552.
                (MENTION; VALIDITY:CONSTRUCT; CORRELATES:BEHAVIORAL, PSYCHOLOGICAL;
                NORMATIVE DATA; N=36 MALE AND 14 FEMALE PEACE CORPS TRAINEES)
      @APPLICATION 1964 M-4 T-2 D-45

887   DEMBER, W. N.
        BIRTH ORDER AND NEED AFFILIATION.
        JOURNAL OF ABNORMAL AND SOCIAL PSYCHOLOGY, 1964, 68, 555-557.
                (CORRELATES:DEMOGRAPHIC; USED AS CRITERION; N=16 MALES AND 28
                FEMALES, AGE 11-62)
      @APPLICATION 1964 H-150

888   PAYNE, R. W., CAIRD, W. K., & LAVERTY, S. G.
        OVERINCLUSIVE THINKING AND DELUSIONS IN SCHIZOPHRENIC PATIENTS.
        JOURNAL OF ABNORMAL AND SOCIAL PSYCHOLOGY, 1964, 68, 562-566.
                (MODIFICATION; CORRELATES:BEHAVIORAL, PSYCHOLOGICAL; NORMATIVE DATA;
                N=10 MALE AND 5 FEMALE NONDELUDED SCHIZOPHRENICS, 6 MALE AND 9
                FEMALE DELUDED SCHIZOPHRENICS, 8 MALE AND 7 FEMALE NONSCHIZOPHRENIC
                HOSPITALIZED CONTROLS)
      @APPLICATION 1964 B-94

889   SMITH, C. P.
            RELATIONSHIP BETWEEN ACHIEVEMENT-RELATED MOTIVES AND INTELLIGENCE,
            PERFORMANCE LEVEL, AND PERSISTENCE.
            JOURNAL OF ABNORMAL AND SOCIAL PSYCHOLOGY, 1964, 68, 523-532.
                    (CORRELATES:BEHAVIORAL, PSYCHOLOGICAL, INTELLIGENCE; NORMATIVE DATA;
                    N=146 UNDERGRADUATES)
        @APPLICATION 1964 M-4 M-7 F-20

890   BRODY, N.
            ANXIETY, INDUCED MUSCULAR TENSION, AND THE STATISTICAL STRUCTURE OF
            BINARY RESPONSE SEQUENCES.
            JOURNAL OF ABNORMAL AND SOCIAL PSYCHOLOGY, 1964, 68, 540-543.
                    (CORRELATES:BEHAVIORAL, PHYSIOLOGICAL; USED AS CRITERION; N=60 HIGH
                    SCHOOL MALES)
        @APPLICATION 1964 T-2

891   GOUGH, H. G., & SANDHU, H. S.
            VALIDATION OF THE CPI SOCIALIZATION SCALE IN INDIA.
            JOURNAL OF ABNORMAL AND SOCIAL PSYCHOLOGY, 1964, 68, 544-547.
                    (DESCRIPTION; MODIFICATION; VALIDITY:CRITERION;
                    CORRELATES:BEHAVIORAL; CROSS-CULTURAL APPLICATION; NORMATIVE DATA;
                    N=203 INDIAN PRISONERS AND 48 INDIAN MALE AND FEMALE COLLEGE
                    STUDENTS)
        @APPLICATION 1964 G-22

892   TODD, F. J., & RAPPOPORT, L.
            A COGNITIVE STRUCTURE APPROACH TO PERSON PERCEPTION: A COMPARISON OF TWO
            MODELS.
            JOURNAL OF ABNORMAL AND SOCIAL PSYCHOLOGY, 1964, 68, 469-478.
                    (MODIFICATION; CORRELATES:PSYCHOLOGICAL; FACTOR ANALYSIS;
                    N=8 MALE AND 6 FEMALE UNDERGRADUATES)
        @APPLICATION 1964 K-23

893   ROSENFELD, H. M.
            SOCIAL CHOICE CONCEIVED AS A LEVEL OF ASPIRATION.
            JOURNAL OF ABNORMAL AND SOCIAL PSYCHOLOGY, 1964, 68, 491-499.
                    (CORRELATES:PSYCHOLOGICAL; N=110 HIGH SCHOOL MALES)
        @APPLICATION 1964 M-4 M-7 H-150

894   ERVIN, S. M.
            LANGUAGE AND TAT CONTENT IN BILINGUALS.
            JOURNAL OF ABNORMAL AND SOCIAL PSYCHOLOGY, 1964, 68, 500-507.
                    (MODIFICATION; RELIABILITY:INTERRATER; CORRELATES:DEMOGRAPHIC,
                    ENVIRONMENTAL; CROSS-CULTURAL APPLICATION; NORMATIVE DATA; N=64 MALE
                    AND FEMALE FRENCH ADULT BILINGUALS)
        @APPLICATION 1964 M-7 M-20 A-94

895   BROD, D., KERNOFF, P., & TERWILLIGER, R. F.
            ANXIETY AND SEMANTIC DIFFERENTIAL RESPONSES.
            JOURNAL OF ABNORMAL AND SOCIAL PSYCHOLOGY, 1964, 68, 570-574.
                    (CORRELATES:PSYCHOLOGICAL, INTELLIGENCE; BIAS:RESPONSE; N=50 FEMALE
                    UNDERGRADUATES)
        @APPLICATION 1964 T-2 D-45 O-16

896   BARBER, T. X., & CALVERLEY, D. S.
            TOWARD A THEORY OF HYPNOTIC BEHAVIOR: EFFECTS ON SUGGESTIBILITY OF
            DEFINING THE SITUATION AS HYPNOSIS AND DEFINING RESPONSE TO SUGGESTIONS
            AS EASY.
            JOURNAL OF ABNORMAL AND SOCIAL PSYCHOLOGY, 1964, 68, 585-592.
                    (CORRELATES:BEHAVIORAL, PSYCHOLOGICAL, ENVIRONMENTAL; N=79 MALE AND
                    17 FEMALE COLLEGE STUDENTS)
        @APPLICATION 1964 B-3

897   NUTTALL, R. L.
            SOME CORRELATES OF HIGH NEED FOR ACHIEVEMENT AMONG URBAN NORTHERN
            NEGROES.
            JOURNAL OF ABNORMAL AND SOCIAL PSYCHOLOGY, 1964, 68, 593-600.
                    (MODIFICATION; RELIABILITY:INTERRATER; CORRELATES:
                    PSYCHOLOGICAL, PHYSIOLOGICAL, DEMOGRAPHIC, ENVIRONMENTAL; N=200
                    NEGRO HOUSEHOLD UNITS)
        @APPLICATION 1964 R-12 M-7 C-179 C-180 C-181 C-182 C-183 C-184

898   WINKEL, G. H., & SARASON, I. G.
          SUBJECT, EXPERIMENTER, AND SITUATIONAL VARIABLES IN RESEARCH ON ANXIETY.
          JOURNAL OF ABNORMAL AND SOCIAL PSYCHOLOGY, 1964, 68, 601-608.
                  (CORRELATES:BEHAVIORAL, DEMOGRAPHIC, ENVIRONMENTAL; USED AS
                  CRITERION; NORMATIVE DATA; N=72 COLLEGE MALES AND 72 COLLEGE
                  FEMALES)
      @APPLICATION 1964 S-5

899   LOEB, A., BECK, A. T., FESHBACH, S., & WOLF, A.
          SOME EFFECTS OF REWARD UPON THE SOCIAL PERCEPTION AND MOTIVATION OF
          PSYCHIATRIC PATIENTS VARYING IN DEPRESSION.
          JOURNAL OF ABNORMAL AND SOCIAL PSYCHOLOGY, 1964, 68, 609-616.
                  (CORRELATES:ENVIRONMENTAL; USED AS CRITERION; N=42 MALE PSYCHIATRIC
                  PATIENTS)
      @APPLICATION 1964 B-8

900   RESTLE, F., ANDREWS, M., & ROKEACH, M.
          DIFFERENCES BETWEEN OPEN- AND CLOSED-MINDED SUBJECTS ON LEARNING-SET AND
          ODDITY PROBLEMS.
          JOURNAL OF ABNORMAL AND SOCIAL PSYCHOLOGY, 1964, 68, 648-654.
                  (VALIDITY:CONSTRUCT; CORRELATES:BEHAVIORAL, ENVIRONMENTAL;
                  USED AS CRITERION; NORMATIVE DATA; N=640 MALE AND FEMALE COLLEGE
                  STUDENTS, 80 SELECTED)
      @APPLICATION 1964 R-8

901   ZUCKERMAN, M., & COHEN, N.
          IS SUGGESTION THE SOURCE OF REPORTED VISUAL SENSATIONS IN PERCEPTUAL
          ISOLATION?
          JOURNAL OF ABNORMAL AND SOCIAL PSYCHOLOGY, 1964, 68, 655-660.
                  (CORRELATES:ENVIRONMENTAL; N=58 MALE UNDERGRADUATES)
      @APPLICATION 1964 Z-13

902   LEVY, L. H.
          GROUP VARIANCE AND GROUP ATTRACTIVENESS.
          JOURNAL OF ABNORMAL AND SOCIAL PSYCHOLOGY, 1964, 68, 661-664.
                  (CORRELATES:PSYCHOLOGICAL; N=31 MALE & 39 FEMALE UNDERGRADUATES)
      @APPLICATION 1964 E-2

903   WINDER, C. L., & WIGGINS, J. S.
          SOCIAL REPUTATION AND SOCIAL BEHAVIOR: A FURTHER VALIDATION OF THE PEER
          NOMINATION INVENTORY.
          JOURNAL OF ABNORMAL AND SOCIAL PSYCHOLOGY, 1964, 68, 681-684.
                  (VALIDITY:CONSTRUCT; CORRELATES:BEHAVIORAL; USED AS CRITERION;
                  N=255 BOYS)
      @APPLICATION 1964 W-15

904   HETHERINGTON, E. M., & WRAY, N. P.
          AGGRESSION, NEED FOR SOCIAL APPROVAL, AND HUMOR PREFERENCES.
          JOURNAL OF ABNORMAL AND SOCIAL PSYCHOLOGY, 1964, 68, 685-689.
                  (CORRELATES:BEHAVIORAL, PSYCHOLOGICAL, ENVIRONMENTAL; USED AS
                  CRITERION; N=192 MALE UNDERGRADUATES)
      @APPLICATION 1964 C-27 E-2

905   CLEMES, S.
          REPRESSION AND HYPNOTIC AMNESIA.
          JOURNAL OF ABNORMAL AND SOCIAL PSYCHOLOGY, 1964, 69, 62-69.
                  (CORRELATES:BEHAVIORAL, PSYCHOLOGICAL; USED AS CRITERION;
                  NORMATIVE DATA; N=14 FEMALES AND 12 MALES IN EXPERIMENTAL GROUP
                  SELECTED FROM LARGER N, 10 FEMALE AND 6 MALE UNDERGRADUATE CONTROLS,
                  4 MALE AND 4 FEMALE HYPNOTIC UNSUSCEPTIBLE CONTROLS)
      @APPLICATION 1964 W-31 R-27

906   INDIK, B., SEASHORE, S. E., & SLESINGER, J.
          DEMOGRAPHIC CORRELATES OF PSYCHOLOGICAL STRAIN.
          JOURNAL OF ABNORMAL AND SOCIAL PSYCHOLOGY, 1964, 69, 26-38.
                  (MODIFICATION; DESCRIPTION; RELIABILITY:INTERNAL CONSISTENCY,
                  INTERRATER; CORRELATES:PSYCHOLOGICAL, DEMOGRAPHIC; FACTOR ANALYSIS;
                  CLUSTER ANALYSIS; N=8234 MALE AND FEMALE RESPONDENTS OF A COMPANY)
      @APPLICATION 1964 G-151

907   MEDNICK, M. T., MEDNICK, S. A., & MEDNICK, E. V.
            INCUBATION OF CREATIVE PERFORMANCE AND SPECIFIC ASSOCIATIVE PRIMING.
            JOURNAL OF ABNORMAL AND SOCIAL PSYCHOLOGY, 1964, 69, 84-88.
                (CORRELATES:PSYCHOLOGICAL, ENVIRONMENTAL; USED AS CRITERION;
                2 STUDIES: N=17 MALE AND 13 FEMALE SUMMER SCHOOL STUDENTS, 48
                UNDERGRADUATES)
        @APPLICATION 1964 M-29

908   MILHOLLAND, J. E.
            NOTE ON THE FURTHER VALIDATION OF THE ALPERT-HABER ACHIEVEMENT ANXIETY
            TEST.
            JOURNAL OF ABNORMAL AND SOCIAL PSYCHOLOGY, 1964, 69, 236.
                (VALIDITY:CRITERION; CORRELATES:DEMOGRAPHIC; N=241 MALE AND 302
                FEMALE UNDERGRADUATES)
        @APPLICATION 1964 A-8

909   SILVERMAN, L. H., & SILVERMAN, D. K.
            A CLINICAL-EXPERIMENTAL APPROACH TO THE STUDY OF SUBLIMINAL STIMULATION:
            THE EFFECTS OF A DRIVE-RELATED STIMULUS UPON RORSCHACH RESPONSES.
            JOURNAL OF ABNORMAL AND SOCIAL PSYCHOLOGY, 1964, 69, 158-172.
                (CORRELATES:PSYCHOLOGICAL, ENVIRONMENTAL; USED AS CRITERION; N=60
                MALES)
        @APPLICATION 1964 R-30

910   LAZARUS, R. S., & ALFERT, E.
            SHORT-CIRCUITING OF THREAT BY EXPERIMENTALLY ALTERING COGNITIVE APPRAISAL.
            JOURNAL OF ABNORMAL AND SOCIAL PSYCHOLOGY, 1964, 69, 195-205.
                (VALIDITY:CRITERION; CORRELATES:PSYCHOLOGICAL, PHYSIOLOGICAL,
                ENVIRONMENTAL; N=69 MALE COLLEGE STUDENTS)
        @APPLICATION 1964 N-5 D-45 L-93 W-41 B-46

911   KELLY, F. J., & VELDMAN, D. J.
            DELINQUENCY AND SCHOOL DROPOUT BEHAVIOR AS A FUNCTION OF IMPULSIVITY
            AND NONDOMINANT VALUES.
            JOURNAL OF ABNORMAL AND SOCIAL PSYCHOLOGY, 1964, 69, 190-194.
                (CORRELATES:BEHAVIORAL, PSYCHOLOGICAL, DEMOGRAPHIC, INTELLIGENCE;
                N=340 MALE ADOLESCENTS ATTENDING SCHOOL, 52 MALE DROPOUTS, 32 MALE
                DELINQUENTS)
        @APPLICATION 1964 C-89 M-42

912   RICKS, D., UMBARGER, C., & MACK, R.
            A MEASURE OF INCREASED TEMPORAL PERSPECTIVE IN SUCCESSFULLY TREATED
            ADOLESCENT DELINQUENT BOYS.
            JOURNAL OF ABNORMAL AND SOCIAL PSYCHOLOGY, 1964, 69, 685-689.
                (RELIABILITY:INTERRATER; VALIDITY:CONSTRUCT;
                CORRELATES:PSYCHOLOGICAL, ENVIRONMENTAL; N=20 DELINQUENT BOYS)
        @APPLICATION 1964 M-164 E-13

913   HERRON, E. W.
            RELATIONSHIP OF EXPERIMENTALLY AROUSED ACHIEVEMENT MOTIVATION TO ACADEMIC
            ACHIEVEMENT ANXIETY.
            JOURNAL OF ABNORMAL AND SOCIAL PSYCHOLOGY, 1964, 69, 690-694.
                (VALIDITY:CONSTRUCT, CRITERION; CORRELATES:PSYCHOLOGICAL,
                DEMOGRAPHIC, INTELLIGENCE, ENVIRONMENTAL; NORMATIVE DATA; N=90 MEN
                AND 90 WOMEN UNDERGRADUATES)
        @APPLICATION 1964 H-37 F-20 A-8

914   SILVERMAN, I.
            SELF-ESTEEM AND DIFFERENTIAL RESPONSIVENESS TO SUCCESS AND FAILURE.
            JOURNAL OF ABNORMAL AND SOCIAL PSYCHOLOGY, 1964, 69, 115-119.
                (MODIFICATION; VALIDITY:CRITERION; CORRELATES:PSYCHOLOGICAL,
                ENVIRONMENTAL; USED AS CRITERION; N=103 COLLEGE MALES AND FEMALES)
        @APPLICATION 1964 J-7

915   DEWOLFE, A. S., & GOVERNALE, C. N.
            FEAR AND ATTITUDE CHANGE.
            JOURNAL OF ABNORMAL AND SOCIAL PSYCHOLOGY, 1964, 69, 119-123.
                (CORRELATES:PSYCHOLOGICAL; N=70 STUDENT NURSES IN EXPERIMENTAL
                GROUPS AND 50 STUDENT NURSE CONTROLS)
        @APPLICATION 1964 C-136 W-187

916   EPSTEIN, R.
             NEED FOR APPROVAL AND THE CONDITIONING OF VERBAL HOSTILITY IN ASTHMATIC
             CHILDREN.
             JOURNAL OF ABNORMAL AND SOCIAL PSYCHOLOGY, 1964, 69, 105-109.
                  (CORRELATES:BEHAVIORAL, INTELLIGENCE; USED AS CRITERION; NORMATIVE
                  DATA; N=100 MALE ASTHMATICS, 7 TO 12 YEARS OLD)
        @APPLICATION 1964 E-21

917   RETTIG, S., & PASAMANICK, B.
             DIFFERENTIAL JUDGMENT OF ETHICAL RISK BY CHEATERS AND NONCHEATERS.
             JOURNAL OF ABNORMAL AND SOCIAL PSYCHOLOGY, 1964, 69, 109-113.
                  (RELIABILITY:INTERNAL CONSISTENCY; CORRELATES:BEHAVIORAL,
                  PSYCHOLOGICAL; N=MALE COLLEGE STUDENTS, 27 CHEATERS AND
                  22 NONCHEATERS)
        @APPLICATION 1964 R-26

918   HETHERINGTON, E. M., & KLINGER, E.
             PSYCHOPATHY AND PUNISHMENT.
             JOURNAL OF ABNORMAL AND SOCIAL PSYCHOLOGY, 1964, 69, 113-115.
                  (CORRELATES:BEHAVIORAL; USED AS CRITERION; N=150 SELECTED
                  FEMALE UNDERGRADUATES)
        @APPLICATION 1964 D-45

919   MACDORMAN, C. F., RIVOIRE, J. L., GALLAGHER, P. J., & MACDORMAN, C. F.
             SIZE CONSTANCY OF ADOLESCENT SCHIZOPHRENICS.
             JOURNAL OF ABNORMAL AND SOCIAL PSYCHOLOGY, 1964, 69, 258-263.
                  (CORRELATES:BEHAVIORAL, PSYCHOLOGICAL; N= 10 SCHIZOPHRENICS AND
                  10 NORMAL ADOLESCENTS, SELECTED FROM N OF 46)
        @APPLICATION 1964 D-45 C-89 R-30 M-20 R-31

920   LEWIS, M., & RICHMAN, S.
             SOCIAL ENCOUNTERS AND THEIR EFFECT ON SUBSEQUENT SOCIAL REINFORCEMENT.
             JOURNAL OF ABNORMAL AND SOCIAL PSYCHOLOGY, 1964, 69, 253-257.
                  (CORRELATES:BEHAVIORAL; USED AS CRITERION; N=33 3RD GRADE GIRLS)
        @APPLICATION 1964 E-2

921   MESSICK, S., & DAMARIN, F.
             COGNITIVE STYLES AND MEMORY FOR FACES.
             JOURNAL OF ABNORMAL AND SOCIAL PSYCHOLOGY, 1964, 69, 313-318.
                  (CORRELATES:PSYCHOLOGICAL; N=40 MALE AND 10 FEMALE COLLEGE STUDENTS)
        @APPLICATION 1964 J-17 P-7

922   REIMANIS, G.
             DISPARITY THEORY AND ACHIEVEMENT MOTIVATION.
             JOURNAL OF ABNORMAL AND SOCIAL PSYCHOLOGY, 1964, 69, 206-210.
                  (DESCRIPTION; MODIFICATION; CORRELATES:PSYCHOLOGICAL; N=40
                  VETERANS ADMINISTRATION DOMICILIARY MEMBERS)
        @APPLICATION 1964 M-163 F-20 M-7 H-74 R-129

923   MCREYNOLDS, P., COLLINS, B., & ACKER, M.
             DELUSIONAL THINKING AND COGNITIVE ORGANIZATION IN SCHIZOPHRENIA.
             JOURNAL OF ABNORMAL AND SOCIAL PSYCHOLOGY, 1964, 69, 210-212.
                  (MODIFICATION; MENTION; CORRELATES:PSYCHOLOGICAL; NORMATIVE DATA;
                  N=24 DELUSIONAL AND 25 NONDELUSIONAL SCHIZOPHRENICS)
        @OPPLICATION 1964 T-2 M-229

924   REITZ, W. E., & JACKSON, D. N.
             AFFECT AND STEREOSCOPIC RESOLUTION.
             JOURNAL OF ABNORMAL AND SOCIAL PSYCHOLOGY, 1964, 69, 212-215.
                  (DESCRIPTION; CORRELATES:PSYCHOLOGICAL; N=12 MALE, 4 FEMALE
                  UNDERGRADUATES)
        @APPLICATION 1964 J-42

925   STURM, I. E.
             "CONCEPTUAL AREA" AMONG PATHOLOGICAL GROUPS: A FAILURE TO REPLICATE.
             JOURNAL OF ABNORMAL AND SOCIAL PSYCHOLOGY, 1964, 69, 216-223.
                  (MODIFICATION; RELIABILITY:INTERRATER, INTERNAL CONSISTENCY;
                  CORRELATES:PSYCHOLOGICAL, PHYSIOLOGICAL; N=125 HOSPITALIZED MALES: 40
                  TUBERCULOUS, 40 BRAIN-DAMAGED, AND 45 SCHIZOPHRENIC)
        @APPLICATION 1964 R-58

926   DU PREEZ, P. D.
              JUDGMENT OF TIME AND ASPECTS OF PERSONALITY.
              JOURNAL OF ABNORMAL AND SOCIAL PSYCHOLOGY, 1964, 69, 228-233.
                     (CORRELATES:BEHAVIORAL, PSYCHOLOGICAL; N=62 MALE AND FEMALE
                     UNDERGRADUATES)
         @APPLICATION 1964 T-2 M-7 K-14 E-75

927   HOLTZMAN, W. H., GORHAM, D. R., & MORAN, L. J.
              A FACTOR-ANALYTIC STUDY OF SCHIZOPHRENIC THOUGHT PROCESSES.
              JOURNAL OF ABNORMAL AND SOCIAL PSYCHOLOGY, 1964, 69, 355-364.
                     (VALIDITY:CONSTRUCT; CORRELATES:PSYCHOLOGICAL, INTELLIGENCE;
                     FACTOR ANALYSIS; CLUSTER ANALYSIS; NORMATIVE DATA; N=99 CHRONIC
                     PARANOID SCHIZOPHRENICS)
         @APPLICATION 1964 H-37 G-83 R-58

928   MISCHEL, W., & GILLIGAN, C.
              DELAY OF GRATIFICATION, MOTIVATION FOR THE PROHIBITED GRATIFICATION, AND
              RESPONSES TO TEMPTATION.
              JOURNAL OF ABNORMAL AND SOCIAL PSYCHOLOGY, 1964, 69, 411-417.
                     (MODIFICATION; DESCRIPTION; CORRELATES:BEHAVIORAL; USED AS CRITERION;
                     N=49 6TH GRADE BOYS)
         @APPLICATION 1964 G-141 M-7 M-165

929   FISKE, D. W., CARTWRIGHT, D. S., & KIRTNER, W. I.
              ARE PSYCHOTHERAPEUTIC CHANGES PREDICTABLE?
              JOURNAL OF ABNORMAL AND SOCIAL PSYCHOLOGY, 1964, 69, 418-426.
                     (VALIDITY:CONSTRUCT; CORRELATES:PSYCHOLOGICAL, INTELLIGENCE; N=93
                     PSYCHIATRIC CLIENTS)
         @APPLICATION 1964 D-45 M-20 R-30 B-5 K-13 K-152

930   MCGINNIES, E., DONELSON, E., & HAAF, R.
              LEVEL OF INITIAL ATTITUDE, ACTIVE REHEARSAL, AND INSTRUCTIONAL SET AS
              FACTORS IN ATTITUDE CHANGE.
              JOURNAL OF ABNORMAL AND SOCIAL PSYCHOLOGY, 1964, 69, 437-440.
                     (MODIFICATION; CORRELATES:BEHAVIORAL, PSYCHOLOGICAL, ENVIRONMENTAL;
                     USED AS CRITERION; 2 STUDIES: N=30 PROCHURCH AND 30 NEUTRAL
                     UNDERGRADUATES, N=24 PROCHURCH CATHOLICS AND 24 PROCHURCH
                     NONCATHOLICS)
         @APPLICATION 1964 T-23

931   MCNAIR, D. M., & LORR, M.
              AN ANALYSIS OF MOOD IN NEUROTICS.
              JOURNAL OF ABNORMAL AND SOCIAL PSYCHOLOGY, 1964, 69, 620-627.
                     (MODIFICATION; DESCRIPTION; MENTION; VALIDITY:CONSTRUCT, CRITERION;
                     CORRELATES:PSYCHOLOGICAL, PHYSIOLOGICAL; USED AS CRITERION; CLUSTER
                     ANALYSIS; 3 STUDIES: TOTAL N=873 MALE PSYCHOTHERAPY OUTPATIENTS)
         @APPLICATION 1964 L-17 L-150 C-27

932   FARNHAM-DIGGORY, S.
              SELF-EVALUATION AND SUBJECTIVE LIFE EXPECTANCY AMONG SUICIDAL AND
              NONSUICIDAL PSYCHOTIC MALES.
              JOURNAL OF ABNORMAL AND SOCIAL PSYCHOLOGY, 1964, 69, 628-634.
                     (DESCRIPTION; CORRELATES:BEHAVIORAL, PSYCHOLOGICAL; N=96 ACUTELY
                     PSYCHOTIC MALES)
         @APPLICATION 1964 C-96

933   GARWOOD, D. S.
              PERSONALITY FACTORS RELATED TO CREATIVITY IN YOUNG SCIENTISTS.
              JOURNAL OF ABNORMAL AND SOCIAL PSYCHOLOGY, 1964, 68, 413-419.
                     (MODIFICATION; VALIDITY:CRITERION; CORRELATES:PSYCHOLOGICAL; USED AS
                     CRITERION; NORMATIVE DATA; N=18 HIGH CREATIVE AND 18 LOW CREATIVE
                     COLLEGE STUDENTS)
         @APPLICATION 1964 G-22 L-35 M-20 G-50 W-118 C-226 G-192 G-53

934   BECKER, J., & NICHOLS, C. H.
              COMMUNALITY OF MANIC-DEPRESSIVE AND "MILD" CYCLOTHYMIC CHARACTERISTICS.
              JOURNAL OF ABNORMAL AND SOCIAL PSYCHOLOGY, 1964, 69, 531-538.
                     (CORRELATES:PSYCHOLOGICAL, PHYSIOLOGICAL, DEMOGRAPHIC, ENVIRONMENTAL;
                     N=53 MALE AND 135 FEMALE UNDERGRADUATES IN ORIGINAL SAMPLE, 45
                     FEMALES COMPLETED STUDY)
         @APPLICATION 1964 D-45 W-52 H-54 A-5 D-28 M-7 H-150 D-30 O-23

935   GARD, J. G.
                INTERPERSONAL ORIENTATIONS IN CLINICAL GROUPS.
                JOURNAL OF ABNORMAL AND SOCIAL PSYCHOLOGY, 1964, 69, 516-521.
                        (VALIDITY:CONSTRUCT; CORRELATES:PSYCHOLOGICAL; N=32 HOSPITALIZED
                NEUROTICS, 28 OUTPATIENT NEUROTICS, 60 HOSPITALIZED SCHIZOPHRENICS
                AND 20 HOSPITALIZED NORMALS, ALL MALES)
        ə APPLICATION 1964 S-11

936   KALIN, R.
                EFFECTS OF ALCOHOL ON MEMORY.
                JOURNAL OF ABNORMAL AND SOCIAL PSYCHOLOGY, 1964, 69, 635-641.
                        (CORRELATES:PHYSIOLOGICAL, ENVIRONMENTAL; N=35 COLLEGE MALES)
        ə APPLICATION 1964 M-20

937   ZAX, M., GARDINER, D. H., & LOWY, D. G.
                EXTREME RESPONSE TENDENCY AS A FUNCTION OF EMOTIONAL ADJUSTMENT.
                JOURNAL OF ABNORMAL AND SOCIAL PSYCHOLOGY, 1964, 69, 654-657.
                        (CORRELATES:PSYCHOLOGICAL; BIAS:RESPONSE; N=15 ADJUSTED AND 15
                MALADJUSTED FEMALE UNDERGRADUATES, 30 MALE HOSPITAL ATTENDANTS,
                30 MALE CHRONIC SCHIZOPHRENICS, 38 MENTALLY DISTURBED AND 42 NORMAL
                CHILDREN)
        ə APPLICATION 1964 R-30 B-176 Z-39

938   KRAMER, E., & BRENNAN, E. P.
                HYPNOTIC SUSCEPTIBILITY OF SCHIZOPHRENIC PATIENTS.
                JOURNAL OF ABNORMAL AND SOCIAL PSYCHOLOGY, 1964, 69, 657-659.
                        (CORRELATES:BEHAVIORAL, PSYCHOLOGICAL; N=25 FEMALE SCHIZOPHRENICS)
        ə APPLICATION 1964 W-31

939   FROMM, E., SAWYER, J., & ROSENTHAL, V.
                HYPNOTIC SIMULATION OF ORGANIC BRAIN DAMAGE.
                JOURNAL OF ABNORMAL AND SOCIAL PSYCHOLOGY, 1964, 69, 482-492.
                        (CORRELATES:BEHAVIORAL, ENVIRONMENTAL; N=3 MALE MEDICAL STUDENTS &
                6 FEMALES)
        ə APPLICATION 1964 D-77 M-58 G-150 Y-5 A-74

940   FISHBEIN, M., & HUNTER, R.
                SUMMATION VERSUS BALANCE IN ATTITUDE ORGANIZATION AND CHANGE.
                JOURNAL OF ABNORMAL AND SOCIAL PSYCHOLOGY, 1964, 69, 505-510.
                        (CORRELATES:PSYCHOLOGICAL, ENVIRONMENTAL; N=80 MALES & 80 FEMALES)
        ə APPLICATION 1964 F-96

941   GOODMAN, D.
                PERFORMANCE OF GOOD AND POOR PREMORBID MALE SCHIZOPHRENICS AS A FUNCTION
                OF PATERNAL VERSUS MATERNAL CENSURE.
                JOURNAL OF ABNORMAL AND SOCIAL PSYCHOLOGY, 1964, 69, 550-555.
                        (MENTION; CORRELATES:PSYCHOLOGICAL, DEMOGRAPHIC, INTELLIGENCE;
                N=80 GOOD AND 80 BAD PREMORBID ADJUSTMENT PATIENTS, 80 MEDICAL AND
                SURGICAL PATIENTS, ALL MALES)
        ə APPLICATION 1964 P-32 N-5

942   SILVERMAN, I.
                DIFFERENTIAL EFFECTS OF EGO THREAT UPON PERSUASIBILITY FOR HIGH AND LOW
                SELF-ESTEEM SUBJECTS.
                JOURNAL OF ABNORMAL AND SOCIAL PSYCHOLOGY, 1964, 69, 567-572.
                        (MODIFICATION; CORRELATES:BEHAVIORAL, PSYCHOLOGICAL; USED AS
                CRITERION; NORMATIVE DATA; N=66 MALE VA DOMICILIARY RESIDENTS)
        ə APPLICATION 1964 J-7 J-8

943   DIEN, D. S., & VINACKE, W. E.
                SELF-CONCEPT AND PARENTAL IDENTIFICATION OF YOUNG ADULTS WITH MIXED
                CAUCASIAN-JAPANESE PARENTAGE.
                JOURNAL OF ABNORMAL AND SOCIAL PSYCHOLOGY, 1964, 69, 463-466.
                        (MODIFICATION; MENTION; CORRELATES:PSYCHOLOGICAL, DEMOGRAPHIC;
                N=8 MALE AND 7 FEMALE COLLEGE STUDENTS OF CAUCASIAN-JAPANESE
                PARENTAGE)
        ə APPLICATION A-7 O-16 S-323

944   HAAN, N.
          THE RELATIONSHIP OF EGO FUNCTIONING AND INTELLIGENCE TO SOCIAL STATUS
          AND SOCIAL MOBILITY.
          JOURNAL OF ABNORMAL AND SOCIAL PSYCHOLOGY, 1964, 69, 594-605.
                 (CORRELATES:PSYCHOLOGICAL, DEMOGRAPHIC; N=49 MEN AND 50 WOMEN)
       @APPLICATION 1964 G-22 T-65

945   GEER, J. H.
          PHOBIA TREATED BY RECIPROCAL INHIBITION.
          JOURNAL OF ABNORMAL AND SOCIAL PSYCHOLOGY, 1964, 69, 642-645.
                 (MENTION; CORRELATES:PSYCHOLOGICAL, ENVIRONMENTAL; USED AS CRITERION;
                 N=1 SEVENTEEN YEAR OLD WHITE GIRL)
       @APPLICATION 1964 R-31 M-20 R-30 D-45 W-31

946   MEDNICK, M. T., MEDNICK, S. A., & JUNG, C. C.
          CONTINUAL ASSOCIATION AS A FUNCTION OF LEVEL OF CREATIVITY AND TYPE OF
          VERBAL STIMULUS.
          JOURNAL OF ABNORMAL AND SOCIAL PSYCHOLOGY, 1964, 69, 511-515.
                 (CORRELATES:BEHAVIORAL, PSYCHOLOGICAL; USED AS CRITERION;
                 N=289 MALE UNDERGRADUATES, 48 SELECTED)
       @APPLICATION 1964 M-29 R-27

947   BUSS, A. H., & LANG, P. J.
          PSYCHOLOGICAL DEFICIT IN SCHIZOPHRENIA: I. AFFECT, REINFORCEMENT, AND
          CONCEPT ATTAINMENT.
          JOURNAL OF ABNORMAL PSYCHOLOGY, 1965, 70, 2-24.
                 (REVIEW ARTICLE; MODIFICATION; CORRELATES:PSYCHOLOGICAL; USED AS
                 CRITERION)
       @APPLICATION 1965 M-20 E-38 P-32

948   SLOTNICK, R., & LONDON, P.
          INFLUENCE OF INSTRUCTIONS ON HYPNOTIC AND NONHYPNOTIC PERFORMANCE.
          JOURNAL OF ABNORMAL PSYCHOLOGY, 1965, 70, 38-46.
                 (CORRELATES:BEHAVIORAL, ENVIRONMENTAL; USED AS CRITERION; N=50
                 FEMALES SELECTED FROM A LARGER N)
       @APPLICATION 1965 W-31

949   DOHRENWEND, B. P., & DOHRENWEND, B. S.
          THE PROBLEM OF VALIDITY IN FIELD STUDIES OF PSYCHOLOGICAL DISORDER.
          JOURNAL OF ABNORMAL PSYCHOLOGY, 1965, 70, 52-69.
                 (MODIFICATION; MENTION; REVIEW ARTICLE; CORRELATES:DEMOGRAPHIC;
                 USED AS CRITERION)
       @APPLICATION 1965 D-45 L-1 S-324

950   FISKE, D. W., & GOODMAN, G.
          THE POSTTHERAPY PERIOD.
          JOURNAL OF ABNORMAL PSYCHOLOGY, 1965, 70, 169-179.
                 (MENTION; DESCRIPTION; REVISION; RELIABILITY:RETEST, INTERNAL
                 CONSISTENCY; CORRELATES:BEHAVIORAL, PSYCHOLOGICAL, ENVIRONMENTAL; N=
                 69 FORMER PATIENTS)
       @APPLICATION 1965 D-45 M-20 C-12 T-81 R-75 E-1 G-19 N-14

951   ELLSWORTH, R. B.
          A BEHAVIORAL STUDY OF STAFF ATTITUDES TOWARD MENTAL ILLNESS.
          JOURNAL OF ABNORMAL PSYCHOLOGY, 1965, 70, 194-200.
                 (CORRELATES:BEHAVIORAL, PSYCHOLOGICAL; FACTOR ANALYSIS; N=65 NURSES
                 AND AIDES; 188 HOSPITALIZED PSYCHIATRIC PATIENTS)
       @APPLICATION 1965 C-69 S-375

952   MANASSE, G.
          SELF-REGARD AS A FUNCTION OF ENVIRONMENTAL DEMANDS IN CHRONIC
          SCHIZOPHRENICS.
          JOURNAL OF ABNORMAL PSYCHOLOGY, 1965, 70, 210-213.
                 (CORRELATES:ENVIRONMENTAL; 2 GROUPS: N=51 HOSPITALIZED CHRONIC
                 SCHIZOPHRENICS, N=51 OUTPATIENT CHRONIC SCHIZOPHRENICS)
       @APPLICATION 1965 H-57

953   LANG, P. J., & BUSS, A. H.
          PSYCHOLOGICAL DEFICIT IN SCHIZOPHRENIA: II. INTERFERENCE AND ACTIVATION.
          JOURNAL OF ABNORMAL PSYCHOLOGY, 1965, 70, 77-106.
                 (REVIEW ARTICLE; MENTION; CORRELATES:BEHAVIORAL, PSYCHOLOGICAL)
       @APPLICATION 1965 T-2

954   BYRNE, D., & SHEFFIELD, J.
         RESPONSE TO SEXUALLY AROUSING STIMULI AS A FUNCTION OF REPRESSING AND
         SENSITIZING DEFENSES.
         JOURNAL OF ABNORMAL PSYCHOLOGY, 1965, 70, 114-118.
                (VALIDITY:CRITERION; CORRELATES:PSYCHOLOGICAL; USED AS CRITERION;
                NORMATIVE DATA; N=44 REPRESSOR MALE UNDERGRADUATES AND 44 SENSITIZER
                MALE UNDERGRADUATES)
      @APPLICATION 1965 B-46

955   WILLIAMSEN, J. A., JOHNSON, H. J., & ERIKSEN, C. W.
         SOME CHARACTERISTICS OF POSTHYPNOTIC AMNESIA.
         JOURNAL OF ABNORMAL PSYCHOLOGY, 1965, 70, 123-131.
                (MENTION; CORRELATES:BEHAVIORAL, PSYCHOLOGICAL; USED AS CRITERION;
                NORMATIVE DATA; 2 STUDIES: N=30 HIGH SUSCEPTIBLE AND 30 LOW
                SUSCEPTIBLE FEMALE UNDERGRADUATES; N=21 HIGH SUSCEPTIBLE FEMALE
                UNDERGRADUATES)
      @APPLICATION 1965 W-31 S-90

956   SAPOLSKY, A.
         RELATIONSHIP BETWEEN PATIENT-DOCTOR COMPATIBILITY, MUTUAL PERCEPTION, AND
         OUTCOME OF TREATMENT.
         JOURNAL OF ABNORMAL PSYCHOLOGY, 1965, 70, 70-76.
                (VALIDITY:CRITERION; CORRELATES:PSYCHOLOGICAL; N=25 FEMALE
                PSYCHIATRIC PATIENTS AND 3 PSYCHIATRIC RESIDENTS)
      @APPLICATION 1965 S-11 D-16

957   HARGREAVES, W. A., STARKWEATHER, J. A., & BLACKER, K. H.
         VOICE QUALITY IN DEPRESSION.
         JOURNAL OF ABNORMAL PSYCHOLOGY, 1965, 70, 218-220.
                (MODIFICATION; VALIDITY:CROSS-VALIDATION; CORRELATES:PSYCHOLOGICAL;
                FACTOR ANALYSIS; N=32 DEPRESSED PATIENTS: 23 WOMEN AND 9 MEN)
      @APPLICATION 1965 O-20 O-22

958   BARBER, T. X.
         EXPERIMENTAL ANALYSES OF "HYPNOTIC" BEHAVIOR: A REVIEW OF RECENT
         EMPIRICAL FINDINGS.
         JOURNAL OF ABNORMAL PSYCHOLOGY, 1965, 70, 132-154.
                (MENTION; REVIEW ARTICLE; CORRELATES:PSYCHOLOGICAL, ENVIRONMENTAL;
                BIAS:RESPONSE)
      @APPLICATION 1965 B-3 W-31 O-45 G-26 E-5 E-2 L-35

959   JOHNSTON, R., & MCNEAL, B. F.
         RESIDUAL PSYCHOPATHOLOGY IN RELEASED PSYCHIATRIC PATIENTS AND ITS RELATION
         TO READMISSION.
         JOURNAL OF ABNORMAL PSYCHOLOGY, 1965, 70, 337-342.
                (VALIDITY:CRITERION; CORRELATES:ENVIRONMENTAL; USED AS CRITERION;
                NORMATIVE DATA; N=147 HOSPITALIZED PSYCHIATRIC PATIENTS)
      @APPLICATION 1965 D-45 F-99

960   HUSE, M. H., & PARSONS, O. A.
         PURSUIT-ROTOR PERFORMANCE IN THE BRAIN DAMAGED.
         JOURNAL OF ABNORMAL PSYCHOLOGY, 1965, 70, 350-359.
                (MENTION; NORMATIVE DATA; N=40 BRAIN DAMAGED, 40 CONTROL MALE
                PATIENTS)
      @APPLICATION 1965 T-2

961   GOLDSTEIN, R. H., & SALZMAN, L. F.
         PROVERB WORD COUNTS AS A MEASURE OF OVERINCLUSIVENESS IN DELUSIONAL
         SCHIZOPHRENICS.
         JOURNAL OF ABNORMAL PSYCHOLOGY, 1965, 70, 244-245.
                (CORRELATES:PSYCHOLOGICAL; NORMATIVE DATA; N=132 DIFFERING DIAGNOSIS
                PSYCHIATRIC PATIENTS)
      @APPLICATION 1965 G-83

962   BLUMENTHAL, R., MELTZOFF, J., & ROSENBERG, S.
         SOME DETERMINANTS OF PERSISTENCE IN CHRONIC SCHIZOPHRENIC SUBJECTS.
         JOURNAL OF ABNORMAL PSYCHOLOGY, 1965, 70, 246-250.
                (CORRELATES:BEHAVIORAL, PSYCHOLOGICAL, ENVIRONMENTAL; USED AS
                CRITERION; NORMATIVE DATA; N=90 MALE SCHIZOPHRENIC PATIENTS)
      @APPLICATION 1965 B-205 R-37

963   KARP, S. A., WITKIN, H. A., & GOODENOUGH, D. R.
           ALCOHOLISM AND PSYCHOLOGICAL DIFFERENTIATION: EFFECT OF ALCOHOL ON FIELD
           DEPENDENCE.
           JOURNAL OF ABNORMAL PSYCHOLOGY, 1965, 70, 262-265.
                   (CORRELATES:PSYCHOLOGICAL, PHYSIOLOGICAL; N=24 MALE ALCOHOLICS)
       @APPLICATION 1965 W-19 W-73 W-188

964   LICHTENSTEIN, E., & BRYAN, J. H.
           ACQUIESCENCE AND THE MMPI: AN ITEM REVERSAL APPROACH.
           JOURNAL OF ABNORMAL PSYCHOLOGY, 1965, 70, 290-293.
                   (MODIFICATION; RELIABILITY:RETEST; VALIDITY:CONTENT; BIAS:RESPONSE;
                   N=35 MALE AND FEMALE NORMALS, 54 NEWLY ADMITTED MALE AND FEMALE
                   PSYCHIATRIC PATIENTS)
       @APPLICATION 1965 D-45

965   MEGARGEE, E. I.
           RELATION BETWEEN BARRIER SCORES AND AGGRESSIVE BEHAVIOR.
           JOURNAL OF ABNORMAL PSYCHOLOGY, 1965, 70, 307-311.
                   (RELIABILITY:INTERRATER; CORRELATES:BEHAVIORAL, PSYCHOLOGICAL; USED
                   AS CRITERION; NORMATIVE DATA; N=75 MALE JUVENILE DELINQUENTS)
       @APPLICATION 1965 N-34 H-37

966   DOKECKI, P. R., POLIDORO, L. G., & CROMWELL, R. L.
           COMMONALITY AND STABILITY OF WORD ASSOCIATION RESPONSES IN GOOD AND POOR
           PREMORBID SCHIZOPHRENICS.
           JOURNAL OF ABNORMAL PSYCHOLOGY, 1965, 70, 312-316.
                   (CORRELATES:PSYCHOLOGICAL; USED AS CRITERION; NORMATIVE DATA;
                   N=18 GOOD PREMORBID AND 18 POOR PREMORBID MALE
                   SCHIZOPHRENIC PATIENTS, 18 TUBERCULOSIS CONTROLS)
       @APPLICATION 1965 P-32 R-27

967   GOUGH, H. G.
           CONCEPTUAL ANALYSIS OF PSYCHOLOGICAL TEST SCORES AND OTHER DIAGNOSTIC
           VARIABLES.
           JOURNAL OF ABNORMAL PSYCHOLOGY, 1965, 70, 294-302.
                   (MENTION; VALIDITY:CONTENT, CONSTRUCT, CRITERION;
                   CORRELATES:PSYCHOLOGICAL, DEMOGRAPHIC, INTELLIGENCE; CROSS-CULTURAL
                   APPLICATION; NO SAMPLE IN ARTICLE; SEVERAL STUDIES MENTIONED)
       @APPLICATION 1965 G-22 G-21 E-1 B-5 W-8 D-45

968   ZUCKERMAN, M., & HABER, M. M.
           NEED FOR STIMULATION AS A SOURCE OF STRESS RESPONSE TO PERCEPTUAL
           ISOLATION.
           JOURNAL OF ABNORMAL PSYCHOLOGY, 1965, 70, 371-377.
                   (MODIFICATION; CORRELATES:PSYCHOLOGICAL, PHYSIOLOGICAL,
                   ENVIRONMENTAL; N=24 FEMALE UNDERGRADUATES FROM PREVIOUS STUDY)
       @APPLICATION 1965 Z-13 Z-30 O-16

969   LUBORSKY, L., BLINDER, B., & SCHIMEK, J.
           LOOKING, RECALLING, AND GSR AS A FUNCTION OF DEFENSE.
           JOURNAL OF ABNORMAL PSYCHOLOGY, 1965, 70, 270-280.
                   (CORRELATES:BEHAVIORAL, PSYCHOLOGICAL, PHYSIOLOGICAL; N=5 MALES,
                   11 FEMALES INCLUDING STUDENTS, HOUSEWIVES AND SECRETARIES)
       @APPLICATION 1965 R-30 L-26 G-153 L-119 M-20

970   GOUGH, H. G., WENK, E. A., & ROZYNKO, V. V.
           PAROLE OUTCOME AS PREDICTED FROM THE CPI, THE MMPI, AND A BASE EXPECTANCY
           TABLE.
           JOURNAL OF ABNORMAL PSYCHOLOGY, 1965, 70, 432-441.
                   (MENTION; VALIDITY:CRITERION, CROSS-VALIDATION;
                   CORRELATES:BEHAVIORAL; FACTOR ANALYSIS; NORMATIVE DATA; N=737 YOUTH
                   AUTHORITY WARDS)
       @APPLICATION 1965 G-22 D-45 W-8 W-41 B-5 P-139 C-246 G-21

971   HIGGINS, J., MEDNICK, S. A., & PHILIP, F. J.
           ASSOCIATIVE DISTURBANCE AS A FUNCTION OF CHRONICITY IN SCHIZOPHRENIA.
           JOURNAL OF ABNORMAL PSYCHOLOGY, 1965, 70, 451-452.
                   (VALIDITY:CRITERION; CORRELATES:PSYCHOLOGICAL; NORMATIVE DATA;
                   N=47 MALE SCHIZOPHRENICS)
       @APPLICATION 1965 R-27

972   LANG, P. J., LAZOVIK, A. D., & REYNOLDS, D. J.
          DESENSITIZATION, SUGGESTIBILITY, AND PSEUDOTHERAPY.
          JOURNAL OF ABNORMAL PSYCHOLOGY, 1965, 70, 395-402.
              (CORRELATES:BEHAVIORAL, PSYCHOLOGICAL, ENVIRONMENTAL; USED AS
              CRITERION; N=44 SNAKE PHOBIC UNDERGRADUATES)
      @APPLICATION 1965 L-46 W-31 W-135 L-135 D-45

973   DONOVAN, M. J., & WEBB, W. W.
          MEANING DIMENSIONS AND MALE-FEMALE VOICE PERCEPTION IN SCHIZOPHRENICS
          WITH GOOD AND POOR PREMORBID ADJUSTMENT.
          JOURNAL OF ABNORMAL PSYCHOLOGY, 1965, 70, 426-431.
              (MODIFICATION; CORRELATES:PSYCHOLOGICAL; USED AS CRITERION; N=40
              MALE SCHIZOPHRENIC PATIENTS, 20 MALE NORMAL CONTROLS)
      @APPLICATION 1965 P-32 O-16 J-20 W-191

974   WEINSTEIN, L.
          SOCIAL SCHEMATA OF EMOTIONALLY DISTURBED BOYS.
          JOURNAL OF ABNORMAL PSYCHOLOGY, 1965, 70, 457-461.
              (MODIFICATION; VALIDITY:CRITERION; CORRELATES:PSYCHOLOGICAL,
              DEMOGRAPHIC, INTELLIGENCE; 2 STUDIES: 40 MALE EMOTIONALLY
              DISTURBED CHILDREN, 20 MALE CONTROLS; 25 MALE EMOTIONALLY DISTURBED
              CHILDREN, 37 NORMAL MALE CONTROLS)
      @APPLICATION 1965 K-46

975   RIEDEL, W. W.
          ANXIETY LEVEL AND THE "DOUBTFUL" JUDGMENT IN A PSYCHOPHYSICAL EXPERIMENT.
          JOURNAL OF ABNORMAL PSYCHOLOGY, 1965, 70, 462-464.
              (VALIDITY:CRITERION; CORRELATES:PSYCHOLOGICAL; USED AS CRITERION;
              N=46 MALE, 43 FEMALE UNDERGRADUATES: 12 ANXIOUS AND 12 NON-ANXIOUS
              SUBJECTS SELECTED)
      @APPLICATION 1965 D-45 W-8

976   PLAPP, J. M., & EDMONSTON, W. E., JR.
          EXTINCTION OF A CONDITIONED MOTOR RESPONSE FOLLOWING HYPNOSIS.
          JOURNAL OF ABNORMAL PSYCHOLOGY, 1965, 70, 378-382.
              (CORRELATES:PSYCHOLOGICAL, ENVIRONMENTAL; N=8 FEMALE AND 4 MALE
              COLLEGE STUDENTS)
      @APPLICATION 1965 W-31

977   HAMLIN, R. M., HAYWOOD, H. C., & FOLSOM, A. T.
          EFFECT OF ENRICHED INPUT ON SCHIZOPHRENIC ABSTRACTION.
          JOURNAL OF ABNORMAL PSYCHOLOGY, 1965, 70, 390-394.
              (VALIDITY:CRITERION; CORRELATES:PSYCHOLOGICAL, INTELLIGENCE;
              NORMATIVE DATA; N=42 SCHIZOPHRENIC AND 14 NON-PSYCHOTIC MALE
              PATIENTS)
      @APPLICATION 1965 B-274 L-70

978   HARE, R. D.
          TEMPORAL GRADIENT OF FEAR AROUSAL IN PSYCHOPATHS.
          JOURNAL OF ABNORMAL PSYCHOLOGY, 1965, 70, 442-445.
              (CORRELATES:PHYSIOLOGICAL; USED AS CRITERION; N=11 PSYCHOPATHIC MALE
              CRIMINALS, 11 NON-PSYCHOPATHIC MALE CRIMINALS AND 11 MALE CONTROLS)
      @APPLICATION 1965 C-189

979   SHAKOW, D., & JELLINEK, E. M.
          COMPOSITE INDEX OF THE KENT-ROSANOFF FREE ASSOCIATION TEST.
          JOURNAL OF ABNORMAL PSYCHOLOGY, 1965, 70, 403-404.
              (VALIDITY:CRITERION; CORRELATES:PSYCHOLOGICAL; NORMATIVE DATA; N=200
              NORMAL, 100 SCHIZOPHRENIC SUBJECTS)
      @APPLICATION 1965 R-27

980   TECCE, J. J.
          RELATIONSHIP OF ANXIETY (DRIVE) AND RESPONSE COMPETITION IN PROBLEM
          SOLVING.
          JOURNAL OF ABNORMAL PSYCHOLOGY, 1965, 70, 465-467.
              (CORRELATES:PSYCHOLOGICAL; USED AS CRITERION; N=68 MALES, 122
              FEMALES)
      @APPLICATION 1965 T-2

981   LORR, M., BISHOP, P. F., & MCNAIR, D. M.
            INTERPERSONAL TYPES AMONG PSYCHIATRIC PATIENTS.
            JOURNAL OF ABNORMAL PSYCHOLOGY, 1965, 70, 468-472.
                (CORRELATES:PSYCHOLOGICAL, DEMOGRAPHIC; CLUSTER ANALYSIS; N=212
                MALES, 313 FEMALES IN PSYCHOTHERAPY)
        @APPLICATION 1965 L-49

982   WARD, W. D., & CARLSON, W. A.
            AUTONOMIC RESPONSIVITY TO VARIABLE INPUT RATES AMONG SCHIZOPHRENICS
            CLASSIFIED ON THE PROCESS-REACTIVE DIMENSION.
            JOURNAL OF ABNORMAL PSYCHOLOGY, 1966, 71, 10-16.
                (REVISION; RELIABILITY:INTERRATER; CORRELATES:BEHAVIORAL,
                PSYCHOLOGICAL, ENVIRONMENTAL; USED AS CRITERION; N=36 MALE
                HOSPITALIZED SCHIZOPHRENICS, 12 NORMAL MALES)
        @APPLICATION 1966 W-44 B-275

983   KAGAN, J.
            REFLECTION-IMPULSIVITY: THE GENERALITY AND DYNAMICS OF CONCEPTUAL TEMPO.
            JOURNAL OF ABNORMAL PSYCHOLOGY, 1966, 71, 17-24.
                (CORRELATES:PSYCHOLOGICAL, DEMOGRAPHIC, ENVIRONMENTAL; USED AS
                CRITERION; N=53 REFLECTIVE BOYS AND 65 IMPULSIVE BOYS, 43 REFLECTIVE
                GIRLS AND 40 IMPULSIVE GIRLS, SELECTED FROM 243 THIRD GRADERS)
        @APPLICATION 1966 K-60

984   MINKOWICH, A., WEINGARTEN, L. L., & BLUM, G. S.
            EMPIRICAL CONTRIBUTIONS TO A THEORY OF AMBIVALENCE.
            JOURNAL OF ABNORMAL PSYCHOLOGY, 1966, 71, 30-41.
                (MODIFICATION; VALIDITY:CONSTRUCT; CORRELATES:PSYCHOLOGICAL,
                DEMOGRAPHIC; FACTOR ANALYSIS; 3 STUDIES: N=29 MALE AND 37 FEMALE
                COLLEGE STUDENTS, 28 HOSPITALIZED MALE CHRONIC SCHIZOPHRENICS, 29
                MALE 6TH, 7TH, AND 8TH GRADERS)
        @APPLICATION 1966 M-167 B-176 B-209 O-16

985   BOWERS, K.
            HYPNOTIC BEHAVIOR: THE DIFFERENTIATION OF TRANCE AND DEMAND CHARACTERISTIC
            VARIABLES.
            JOURNAL OF ABNORMAL PSYCHOLOGY, 1966, 71, 42-51.
                (MODIFICATION; CORRELATES:BEHAVIORAL, PSYCHOLOGICAL; USED AS
                CRITERION; N=450 FEMALE UNDERGRADUATES, 37 SELECTED)
        @APPLICATION 1966 W-31 S-90 S-97

986   SIEGMAN, A. W.
            FATHER ABSENCE DURING EARLY CHILDHOOD AND ANTISOCIAL BEHAVIOR.
            JOURNAL OF ABNORMAL PSYCHOLOGY, 1966, 71, 71-74.
                (MODIFICATION; RELIABILITY:RETEST; CORRELATES:PSYCHOLOGICAL,
                ENVIRONMENTAL; FACTOR ANALYSIS; N=51 "FATHER-ABSENT" MALE MEDICAL
                STUDENTS AND 89 "FATHER-PRESENT" STUDENTS)
        @APPLICATION 1966 S-239 E-1

987   LERNER, B.
            RORSCHACH MOVEMENT AND DREAMS: A VALIDATION STUDY USING DRUG-INDUCED DREAM
            DEPRIVATION.
            JOURNAL OF ABNORMAL PSYCHOLOGY, 1966, 71, 75-86.
                (RELIABILITY:RETEST, INTERRATER; VALIDITY:CONSTRUCT;
                CORRELATES:BEHAVIORAL, PSYCHOLOGICAL, ENVIRONMENTAL; NORMATIVE DATA;
                N=50 MALE AND FEMALE GRADUATES AND UNDERGRADUATES, AGE 17-28)
        @APPLICATION 1966 H-37

988   BARBER, T. X., & CALVERLEY, D. S.
            TOWARD A THEORY OF "HYPNOTIC" BEHAVIOR: EXPERIMENTAL ANALYSES OF
            SUGGESTED AMNESIA.
            JOURNAL OF ABNORMAL PSYCHOLOGY, 1966, 71, 95-107.
                (MODIFICATION; CORRELATES:PSYCHOLOGICAL, ENVIRONMENTAL; N=144 STUDENT
                NURSES, AGES 17-25)
        @APPLICATION 1966 B-3 W-192

989   GEER, J. H.
            EFFECT OF FEAR AROUSAL UPON TASK PERFORMANCE AND VERBAL BEHAVIOR.
            JOURNAL OF ABNORMAL PSYCHOLOGY, 1966, 71, 119-123.
                (CORRELATES:BEHAVIORAL, PSYCHOLOGICAL; USED AS CRITERION; N=80
                UNDERGRADUATE FEMALES)
        @APPLICATION 1966 G-41

990   PAUL, G. L., & SHANNON, D. T.
          TREATMENT OF ANXIETY THROUGH SYSTEMATIC DESENSITIZATION IN THERAPY GROUPS.
          JOURNAL OF ABNORMAL PSYCHOLOGY, 1966, 71, 124-135.
                  (MENTION; CORRELATES:BEHAVIORAL, PSYCHOLOGICAL, ENVIRONMENTAL;
                  USED AS CRITERION; NORMATIVE DATA; N=50 HIGHLY ANXIOUS MALE
                  UNDERGRADUATES)
       @APPLICATION 1966 D-45 C-136 B-84 E-16 P-82 A-26

991   KATKIN, E. S.
          THE RELATIONSHIP BETWEEN A MEASURE OF TRANSITORY ANXIETY AND SPONTANEOUS
          AUTONOMIC ACTIVITY.
          JOURNAL OF ABNORMAL PSYCHOLOGY, 1966, 71, 142-146.
                  (CORRELATES:PSYCHOLOGICAL, PHYSIOLOGICAL; USED AS CRITERION;
                  NORMATIVE DATA; N=52 MALE UNDERGRADUATES)
       @APPLICATION 1966 7-13

992   SPOHN, H. E., & WOLK, W. P.
          SOCIAL PARTICIPATION IN HOMOGENEOUS AND HETEROGENEOUS GROUPS OF CHRONIC
          SCHIZOPHRENICS.
          JOURNAL OF ABNORMAL PSYCHOLOGY, 1966, 71, 147-150.
                  (RELIABILITY:INTERRATER; CORRELATES:BEHAVIORAL, PSYCHOLOGICAL; USED
                  AS CRITERION; N=32 HOSPITALIZED CHRONIC SCHIZOPHRENICS)
       @APPLICATION 1966 R-37 S-222

993   GEER, J. H., & KATKIN, E. S.
          TREATMENT OF INSOMNIA USING A VARIANT OF SYSTEMATIC DESENSITIZATION: A
          CASE REPORT.
          JOURNAL OF ABNORMAL PSYCHOLOGY, 1966, 71, 161-164.
                  (MENTION; CORRELATES:PSYCHOLOGICAL; N=1 29 YEAR OLD WHITE FEMALE)
       @APPLICATION 1966 D-45

994   PERSONS, R. W., & BRUNING, J. L.
          INSTRUMENTAL LEARNING WITH SOCIOPATHS: A TEST OF CLINICAL THEORY.
          JOURNAL OF ABNORMAL PSYCHOLOGY, 1966, 71, 165-168.
                  (CORRELATES:BEHAVIORAL, PSYCHOLOGICAL; USED AS CRITERION; N=27
                  INCARCERATED SOCIOPATHS, 27 INCARCERATED NONSOCIOPATHS, 27 NORMAL
                  COLLEGE FRESHMEN, AND 14 CONTROL INCARCERATED S'S, ALL MALE)
       @APPLICATION 1966 D-45 R-30 P-31 T-2

995   BARBER, T. X., & CALVERLEY, D. S.
          EFFECTS ON RECALL OF HYPNOTIC INDUCTION, MOTIVATIONAL SUGGESTIONS, AND
          SUGGESTED REGRESSION: A METHODOLOGICAL AND EXPERIMENTAL ANALYSIS.
          JOURNAL OF ABNORMAL PSYCHOLOGY, 1966, 71, 169-180.
                  (MENTION; CORRELATES:PSYCHOLOGICAL; USED AS CRITERION; N=30 MALE
                  AND FEMALE UNDERGRADUATES OUT OF STUDY INVOLVING 90)
       @APPLICATION 1966 B-3

996   GOUGH, H. G.
          APPRAISAL OF SOCIAL MATURITY BY MEANS OF THE CPI.
          JOURNAL OF ABNORMAL PSYCHOLOGY, 1966, 71, 189-195.
                  (VALIDITY:CONTENT, CRITERION, CROSS-VALIDATION;
                  CORRELATES:BEHAVIORAL, PSYCHOLOGICAL; CROSS-CULTURAL APPLICATION;
                  NORMATIVE DATA; 4 STUDIES: N=4628 NONDELINQUENT MALES, 1290
                  INSTITUTIONALIZED DELINQUENTS, AND ADULT PRISON MALES; 659
                  NONDELINQUENT ITALIAN MEN AND 38 ITALIAN MALE PRISONERS; 78 COLLEGE
                  CHEATERS & NONCHEATERS, AND 659 HIGH SCHOOL MALES; 100 MILITARY
                  OFFICERS, A FRATERNITY (41 MALES) AND 45 FEMALES FROM A SORORITY)
       @APPLICATION 1966 G-22 G-21

997   HILGARD, E. R., & TART, C. T.
          RESPONSIVENESS TO SUGGESTIONS FOLLOWING WAKING AND IMAGINATION INSTRUCTIONS
          AND FOLLOWING INDUCTION OF HYPNOSIS.
          JOURNAL OF ABNORMAL PSYCHOLOGY, 1966, 71, 196-208.
                  (CORRELATES:BEHAVIORAL, PSYCHOLOGICAL; NORMATIVE DATA; 2 STUDIES:
                  N=60 UNDERGRADUATES; 90 UNDERGRADUATES)
       @APPLICATION 1966 W-31

998   DAVIDSON, P. O., PAYNE, R. W., & SLOANE, R. B.
          CORTICAL INHIBITION, DRIVE LEVEL, AND CONDITIONING.
          JOURNAL OF ABNORMAL PSYCHOLOGY, 1966, 71, 310-314.
                  (CORRELATES:PSYCHOLOGICAL, PHYSIOLOGICAL; N=40 FEMALE NEUROTIC
                  PATIENTS)
       @APPLICATION 1966 T-2 E-5

999   GEER, J. H.
            FEAR AND AUTONOMIC AROUSAL.
            JOURNAL OF ABNORMAL PSYCHOLOGY, 1966, 71, 253-255.
                (CORRELATES:PHYSIOLOGICAL; USED AS CRITERION: N=32 FEMALE
                UNDERGRADUATES)
        @APPLICATION 1966 G-41

1000   EISENMAN, R.
            PSYCHOPATHOLOGY AND SOCIOMETRIC CHOICE.
            JOURNAL OF ABNORMAL PSYCHOLOGY, 1966, 71, 256-259.
                (CORRELATES:PSYCHOLOGICAL; N=84 HOSPITALIZED MALE AND FEMALE
                PSYCHIATRIC PATIENTS)
        @APPLICATION 1966 D-45 M-178

1001   SPAIN, B.
            EYELID CONDITIONING AND AROUSAL IN SCHIZOPHRENIC AND NORMAL SUBJECTS.
            JOURNAL OF ABNORMAL PSYCHOLOGY, 1966, 71, 260-266.
                (CORRELATES:PHYSIOLOGICAL; N=32 MALE SCHIZOPHRENIC PATIENTS,
                22 CHRONIC FEMALE PATIENTS, 12 NORMAL MALES AND 12 NORMAL FEMALES)
        @APPLICATION 1966 V-34

1002   TRUAX, C. B., WARGO, D. G., & SILBER, L. D.
            EFFECTS OF GROUP PSYCHOTHERAPY WITH HIGH ACCURATE EMPATHY AND
            NONPOSSESSIVE WARMTH UPON FEMALE INSTITUTIONALIZED DELINQUENTS.
            JOURNAL OF ABNORMAL PSYCHOLOGY, 1966, 71, 267-274.
                (MODIFICATION; CORRELATES:BEHAVIORAL, ENVIRONMENTAL; USED AS
                CRITERION; N=70 FEMALE DELINQUENTS AND 16 THERAPISTS)
        @APPLICATION 1966 B-60 T-24 T-69 T-36 B-11

1003   GULLER, I. B.
            STABILITY OF SELF-CONCEPT IN SCHIZOPHRENIA.
            JOURNAL OF ABNORMAL PSYCHOLOGY, 1966, 71, 275-279.
                (CORRELATES:PSYCHOLOGICAL, ENVIRONMENTAL; NORMATIVE DATA; N=42 MALE
                SCHIZOPHRENICS, 42 MALE CONTROLS)
        @APPLICATION 1966 D-45 S-61

1004   FOULKES, D., SPEAR, P. S., & SYMONDS, J. D.
            INDIVIDUAL DIFFERENCES IN MENTAL ACTIVITY AT SLEEP ONSET.
            JOURNAL OF ABNORMAL PSYCHOLOGY, 1966, 71, 280-286.
                (RELIABILITY:INTERRATER; CORRELATES:PSYCHOLOGICAL, PHYSIOLOGICAL;
                N=16 MALE, 16 FEMALE COLLEGE STUDENTS)
        @APPLICATION 1966 G-22 M-20

1005   ROSENWALD, G. C., MENDELSOHN, G. A., FONTANA, A., & PORTZ, A. T.
            AN ACTION TEST OF HYPOTHESES CONCERNING THE ANAL PERSONALITY.
            JOURNAL OF ABNORMAL PSYCHOLOGY, 1966, 71, 304-309.
                (MODIFICATION; CORRELATES:BEHAVIORAL, PSYCHOLOGICAL; N=48 MALE
                UNDERGRADUATES)
        @APPLICATION 1966 M-29

1006   BERGIN, A. E.
            SOME IMPLICATIONS OF PSYCHOTHERAPY RESEARCH FOR THERAPEUTIC PRACTICE.
            JOURNAL OF ABNORMAL PSYCHOLOGY, 1966, 71, 235-246.
                (REVIEW ARTICLE; MENTION; CORRELATES:PSYCHOLOGICAL, ENVIRONMENTAL)
        @APPLICATION 1966 B-60 B-148 T-24 M-20 T-75 B-50

1007   SARETSKY, T.
            EFFECTS OF CHLORPROMAZINE ON PRIMARY-PROCESS THOUGHT MANIFESTATIONS.
            JOURNAL OF ABNORMAL PSYCHOLOGY, 1966, 71, 247-252.
                (RELIABILITY:INTERRATER; VALIDITY:CRITERION; CORRELATES:
                PHYSIOLOGICAL; N=40 MALE SCHIZOPHRENIC PATIENTS)
        @APPLICATION 1966 R-30 L-39 H-117 H-156

1008   WILLNER, A. E., & REITZ, W. E.
            ASSOCIATION, ABSTRACTION, AND THE CONCEPTUAL ORGANIZATION OF RECALL:
            IMPLICATIONS FOR CLINICAL TESTS.
            JOURNAL OF ABNORMAL PSYCHOLOGY, 1966, 71, 315-327.
                (MODIFICATION; CORRELATES:BEHAVIORAL, INTELLIGENCE; 5 STUDIES:
                MEDIAN N=APPROX. 46 UNDERGRADUATES)
        @APPLICATION 1966 M-168 R-58

1009   ZUBEK, J. P., & SCHUTTE, W.
            URINARY EXCRETION OF ADRENALINE AND NORADRENALINE DURING PROLONGED
            PERCEPTUAL DEPRIVATION.
            JOURNAL OF ABNORMAL PSYCHOLOGY, 1966, 71, 328-334.
                    (CORRELATES:PSYCHOLOGICAL, PHYSIOLOGICAL; N=31 MALE UNIVERSITY
                    STUDENTS)
        aAPPLICATION 1966 B-62 M-53

1010   MEICHENBAUM, D. H.
            EFFECTS OF SOCIAL REINFORCEMENT ON THE LEVEL OF ABSTRACTION IN
            SCHIZOPHRENICS.
            JOURNAL OF ABNORMAL PSYCHOLOGY, 1966, 71, 354-362.
                    (VALIDITY:CONSTRUCT, CRITERION; CORRELATES:PSYCHOLOGICAL,
                    INTELLIGENCE; USED AS CRITERION; NORMATIVE DATA; N=64 MALE
                    SCHIZOPHRENICS)
        aAPPLICATION 1966 U-5 K-123

1011   NOVICK, J.
            SYMPTOMATIC TREATMENT OF ACQUIRED AND PERSISTENT ENURESIS.
            JOURNAL OF ABNORMAL PSYCHOLOGY, 1966, 71, 363-368.
                    (MODIFICATION; CORRELATES:BEHAVIORAL, PSYCHOLOGICAL; N=45 MALE
                    ENURETICS, 6 TO 13 YEARS OF AGE)
        aAPPLICATION 1966 C-102 L-122

1012   D'ZURILLA, T. J.
            PERSUASION AND PRAISE AS TECHNIQUES FOR MODIFYING VERBAL BEHAVIOR IN A
            "REAL-LIFE" GROUP SETTING.
            JOURNAL OF ABNORMAL PSYCHOLOGY, 1966, 71, 369-376.
                    (MODIFICATION; MENTION: N=96 MALE UNDERGRADUATES)
        aAPPLICATION 1966 A-26 P-82 B-84 C-136 E-16

1013   TART, C. T.
            TYPES OF HYPNOTIC DREAMS AND THEIR RELATION TO HYPNOTIC DEPTH.
            JOURNAL OF ABNORMAL PSYCHOLOGY, 1966, 71, 377-382.
                    (MODIFICATION; CORRELATES:BEHAVIORAL, PSYCHOLOGICAL; 2 STUDIES: N=58
                    MALE AND FEMALE UNDERGRADUATES, AND 92 MALE AND FEMALE
                    UNDERGRADUATES)
        aAPPLICATION 1966 W-31

1014   KATKIN, E. S., SASMOR, D. B., & LAN, R.
            CONFORMITY AND ACHIEVEMENT-RELATED CHARACTERISTICS OF DEPRESSED PATIENTS.
            JOURNAL OF ABNORMAL PSYCHOLOGY, 1966, 71, 407-412.
                    (DESCRIPTION; MODIFICATION; CORRELATES:BEHAVIORAL, PSYCHOLOGICAL;
                    USED AS CRITERION; NORMATIVE DATA; N=10 DEPRESSIVE PATIENTS AND 11
                    SCHIZOPHRENIC FEMALES)
        aAPPLICATION 1966 D-45 A-5 D-28 E-1 O-23

1015   POLLACK, D.
            COPING AND AVOIDANCE IN INEBRIATED ALCOHOLICS AND NORMALS.
            JOURNAL OF ABNORMAL PSYCHOLOGY, 1966, 71, 417-419.
                    (RELIABILITY:RETEST, INTERRATER; CORRELATES:PHYSIOLOGICAL; N=20
                    ALCOHOLICS & 20 NORMALS)
        aAPPLICATION 1966 G-10

1016   FISHER, R. L.
            FAILURE OF THE CONCEPTUAL STYLES TEST TO DISCRIMINATE NORMAL AND HIGHLY
            IMPULSIVE CHILDREN.
            JOURNAL OF ABNORMAL PSYCHOLOGY, 1966, 71, 429-431.
                    (VALIDITY:CONSTRUCT; CORRELATES:BEHAVIORAL, PSYCHOLOGICAL; N=92
                    SCHOOLBOYS)
        aAPPLICATION 1966 K-122 R-30 F-75

1017   KAPLAN, F.
            EFFECTS OF ANXIETY AND DEFENSE IN A THERAPY-LIKE SITUATION.
            JOURNAL OF ABNORMAL PSYCHOLOGY, 1966, 71, 449-458.
                    (DESCRIPTION; RELIABILITY:INTERRATER; VALIDITY:CONSTRUCT; CORRELATES:
                    PSYCHOLOGICAL; USED AS CRITERION; N=52 FEMALE COLLEGE STUDENTS)
        aAPPLICATION 1966 S-5 S-36 S-79 B-180 M-35 D-35

1018   PESKIN, H.
            PUBERTAL ONSET AND EGO FUNCTIONING.
            JOURNAL OF ABNORMAL PSYCHOLOGY, 1967, 72, 1-15.
                    (VALIDITY:CRITERION; CORRELATES:BEHAVIORAL, PSYCHOLOGICAL,
                    PHYSIOLOGICAL; N=18 LATE, 22 EARLY MATURING BOYS)
        aAPPLICATION 1967 M-20 B-208 B-207

1019   MENAKER, T.
           ANXIETY ABOUT DRINKING IN ALCOHOLICS.
           JOURNAL OF ABNORMAL PSYCHOLOGY, 1967, 72, 43-49.
               (VALIDITY:CRITERION; CORRELATES:PSYCHOLOGICAL, ENVIRONMENTAL;
               N=30 ALCOHOLICS, 30 NORMALS, AND 30 SCHIZOPHRENICS)
       @APPLICATION 1967 N-17

1020   BUSS, A. H., & DANIELL, E. F.
           STIMULUS GENERALIZATION AND SCHIZOPHRENIA.
           JOURNAL OF ABNORMAL PSYCHOLOGY, 1967, 72, 50-53.
               (CORRELATES:PSYCHOLOGICAL, PHYSIOLOGICAL; USED AS CRITERION; N=30
               CHRONIC SCHIZOPHRENIC MALE PATIENTS, 15 NORMAL MALE PATIENTS)
       @APPLICATION 1967 O-20

1021   GILDSTON, P.
           STUTTERERS' SELF-ACCEPTANCE AND PERCEIVED PARENTAL ACCEPTANCE.
           JOURNAL OF ABNORMAL PSYCHOLOGY, 1967, 72, 59-64.
               (RELIABILITY:INTERNAL CONSISTENCY; VALIDITY:CRITERION;
               CORRELATES:PSYCHOLOGICAL; N=110 WHITE HIGH SCHOOL STUDENTS)
       @APPLICATION 1967 H-52

1022   BRYAN, J. H., & KAPCHE, R.
           PSYCHOPATHY AND VERBAL CONDITIONING.
           JOURNAL OF ABNORMAL PSYCHOLOGY, 1967, 72, 71-73.
               (CORRELATES:PSYCHOLOGICAL; USED AS CRITERION; N=423 NAVAL PRISONERS,
               46 PSYCHOPATHS AND 54 NORMALS SELECTED)
       @APPLICATION 1967 Q-7

1023   LORR, M., KLETT, C. J., & CAVE, R.
           HIGHER-LEVEL PSYCHOTIC SYNDROMES.
           JOURNAL OF ABNORMAL PSYCHOLOGY, 1967, 72, 74-77.
               (FACTOR ANALYSIS; N=2303 FUNCTIONAL MALE AND FEMALE PSYCHOTIC
               PATIENTS)
       @APPLICATION 1967 L-39

1024   ROBACK, H. B.
           FOLLOW-UP STUDY OF THE HOSPITAL ADJUSTMENT SCALE.
           JOURNAL OF ABNORMAL PSYCHOLOGY, 1967, 72, 110-111.
               (VALIDITY:CRITERION; NORMATIVE DATA; N=113 PSYCHIATRIC PATIENTS)
       @APPLICATION 1967 M-66

1025   MERBAUM, M., & KAZAOKA, K.
           REPORTS OF EMOTIONAL EXPERIENCE BY SENSITIZERS AND REPRESSORS DURING AN
           INTERVIEW TRANSACTION.
           JOURNAL OF ABNORMAL PSYCHOLOGY, 1967, 72, 101-105.
               (CORRELATES:PSYCHOLOGICAL, DEMOGRAPHIC; USED AS CRITERION;
               NORMATIVE DATA; N=200 MALE AND FEMALE COLLEGE STUDENTS:
               10 SENSITIZERS AND 10 REPRESSORS SELECTED)
       @APPLICATION 1967 B-46

1026   PAYNE, R. W., & CAIRD, W. K.
           REACTION TIME, DISTRACTIBILITY AND OVER-INCLUSIVE THINKING IN PSYCHOTICS.
           JOURNAL OF ABNORMAL PSYCHOLOGY, 1967, 72, 112-121.
               (CORRELATES:BEHAVIORAL, PSYCHOLOGICAL; NORMATIVE DATA; N=45 MALE AND
               FEMALE PSYCHIATRIC PATIENTS)
       @APPLICATION 1967 B-94

1027   KLEIN, E. B., CICCHETTI, D., & SPOHN, H.
           A TEST OF THE CENSURE-DEFICIT MODEL AND ITS RELATION TO PREMORBIDITY IN THE
           PERFORMANCE OF SCHIZOPHRENICS.
           JOURNAL OF ABNORMAL PSYCHOLOGY, 1967, 72, 174-181.
               (CORRELATES:PSYCHOLOGICAL, DEMOGRAPHIC; USED AS CRITERION; N=72
               WHITE MALE SCHIZOPHRENICS AND 36 WHITE MALE AIDES)
       @APPLICATION 1967 R-41 P-32 L-124

1028   RUMA, E. H., & MOSHER, D. L.
           RELATIONSHIP BETWEEN MORAL JUDGMENT AND GUILT IN DELINQUENT BOYS.
           JOURNAL OF ABNORMAL PSYCHOLOGY, 1967, 72, 122-127.
               (MODIFICATION; RELIABILITY:INTERRATER; VALIDITY:CRITERION;
               CORRELATES:PSYCHOLOGICAL; N=36 MALE ADOLESCENT DELINQUENTS)
       @APPLICATION 1967 K-27 M-64

1029   SHIMKUNAS, A. M., GYNTHER, M. D., & SMITH, K.
         SCHIZOPHRENIC RESPONSES TO THE PROVERBS TEST: ABSTRACT, CONCRETE OR
         AUTISTIC.
         JOURNAL OF ABNORMAL PSYCHOLOGY, 1967, 72, 128-133.
              (RELIABILITY:INTERRATER; VALIDITY:CRITERION;
              CORRELATES:PSYCHOLOGICAL, INTELLIGENCE, ENVIRONMENTAL; N=36 MALE,
              44 FEMALE SCHIZOPHRENIC PATIENTS, BLACK AND WHITE)
         @APPLICATION 1967 L-39 G-83 N-35

1030   ZUBEK, J. P., & MACNEILL, M.
         PERCEPTUAL DEPRIVATION PHENOMENA: ROLE OF THE RECUMBENT POSITION.
         JOURNAL OF ABNORMAL PSYCHOLOGY, 1967, 72, 147-150.
              (CORRELATES:ENVIRONMENTAL; N=54 COLLEGE MALES)
         @APPLICATION 1967 M-94

1031   SCHOOLER, C., & TECCE, J. J.
         VERBAL PAIRED-ASSOCIATES LEARNING IN CHRONIC SCHIZOPHRENICS AS A FUNCTION
         OF POSITIVE AND NEGATIVE EVALUATION.
         JOURNAL OF ABNORMAL PSYCHOLOGY, 1967, 72, 151-156.
              (DESCRIPTION; CORRELATES:PSYCHOLOGICAL; N=72 CHRONIC SCHIZOPHRENICS
              AND 36 NORMALS, MALES AND FEMALES)
         @APPLICATION 1967 R-114

1032   KLEINMUNTZ, B.
         SIGN AND SEER: ANOTHER EXAMPLE.
         JOURNAL OF ABNORMAL PSYCHOLOGY, 1967, 72, 163-165.
              (COMPARISON OF CLINICIANS AND COMPUTER INTERPRETATIONS; N=8 MMPI
              INTERPRETERS & 5 SAMPLES OF PROFILES)
         @APPLICATION 1967 D-45 B-5

1033   MCINNIS, T. L., & ULLMANN, L. P.
         POSITIVE AND NEGATIVE REINFORCEMENT WITH SHORT- AND LONG-TERM HOSPITALIZED
         SCHIZOPHRENICS IN A PROBABILITY LEARNING SITUATION.
         JOURNAL OF ABNORMAL PSYCHOLOGY, 1967, 72, 157-162.
              (CORRELATES:PSYCHOLOGICAL, ENVIRONMENTAL; N=80 MALE SCHIZOPHRENICS)
         @APPLICATION 1967 E-62 U-5 M-166

1034   KAPLAN, M. F.
         REPRESSION-SENSITIZATION AND PREDICTION OF SELF-DESCRIPTIVE BEHAVIOR:
         RESPONSE VERSUS SITUATIONAL CUE VARIABLES.
         JOURNAL OF ABNORMAL PSYCHOLOGY, 1967, 72, 354-361.
              (VALIDITY:CRITERION; CORRELATES:PSYCHOLOGICAL; USED AS CRITERION;
              N=308 MALE UNDERGRADUATES: 30 REPRESSORS, 30 SENSITIZERS, AND 31
              NEUTRALS SELECTED)
         @APPLICATION 1967 B-46 G-21 C-66 K-42

1035   CHAPMAN, L. J., & CHAPMAN, J. P.
         GENESIS OF POPULAR BUT ERRONEOUS PSYCHODIAGNOSTIC OBSERVATIONS.
         JOURNAL OF ABNORMAL PSYCHOLOGY, 1967, 72, 193-204.
              (CORRELATES:PSYCHOLOGICAL, ENVIRONMENTAL; BIAS:TESTER;
              6 STUDIES: N=44 CLINICIANS AND MEDIAN NUMBER OF S'S = 44)
         @APPLICATION 1967 M-58

1036   BERNSTEIN, A. S.
         ELECTRODERMAL BASE LEVEL, TONIC AROUSAL, AND ADAPTATION IN CHRONIC
         SCHIZOPHRENICS.
         JOURNAL OF ABNORMAL PSYCHOLOGY, 1967, 72, 221-232.
              (CORRELATES:PHYSIOLOGICAL; USED AS CRITERION; N=80 SCHIZOPHRENIC
              PATIENTS, 28 NORMAL MALE HOSPITAL EMPLOYEES)
         @APPLICATION 1967 R-37

1037   THORNE, D. E.
         IS THE HYPNOTIC TRANCE NECESSARY FOR PERFORMANCE OF HYPNOTIC PHENOMENA?
         JOURNAL OF ABNORMAL PSYCHOLOGY, 1967, 72, 233-239.
              (MODIFICATION; CORRELATES:PSYCHOLOGICAL; USED AS CRITERION; N=148
              COLLEGE STUDENTS, 40 HIGHLY SUSCEPTIBLE SELECTED)
         @APPLICATION 1967 S-90 R-27

1038   VESTRE, N. D., & LOREI, T. W.
         RELATIONSHIPS BETWEEN SOCIAL HISTORY FACTORS AND PSYCHIATRIC SYMPTOMS.
         JOURNAL OF ABNORMAL PSYCHOLOGY, 1967, 72, 247-250.
              (CORRELATES:PSYCHOLOGICAL; N=120 CONSECUTIVELY ADMITTED NON-GERIATRIC
              FUNCTIONAL PSYCHIATRIC PATIENTS)
         @APPLICATION 1967 D-45 B-85

1039   MONROE, L. J.
           PSYCHOLOGICAL AND PHYSIOLOGICAL DIFFERENCES BETWEEN GOOD AND POOR SLEEPERS.
           JOURNAL OF ABNORMAL PSYCHOLOGY, 1967, 72, 255-264.
                  (VALIDITY:CRITERION; CORRELATES:PSYCHOLOGICAL, PHYSIOLOGICAL; N=16
                  "GOOD SLEEPERS", & 16 "BAD SLEEPERS.")
        @APPLICATION 1967 D-45 B-127

1040   BRENNER, A. R.
           EFFECTS OF PRIOR EXPERIMENTER-SUBJECT RELATIONSHIPS ON RESPONSES TO THE
           KENT-ROSANOFF WORD-ASSOCIATION LIST IN SCHIZOPHRENICS.
           JOURNAL OF ABNORMAL PSYCHOLOGY, 1967, 72, 273-276.
                  (MODIFICATION; CORRELATES:PSYCHOLOGICAL, ENVIRONMENTAL; N=22 FEMALE
                  CHRONIC SCHIZOPHRENICS)
        @APPLICATION 1967 R-27

1041   NATHANSON, I. A.
           A SEMANTIC DIFFERENTIAL ANALYSIS OF PARENT-SON RELATIONSHIPS IN
           SCHIZOPHRENIA.
           JOURNAL OF ABNORMAL PSYCHOLOGY, 1967, 72, 277-281.
                  (VALIDITY:CRITERION; CORRELATES:PSYCHOLOGICAL; USED AS CRITERION;
                  N=36 WHITE GOOD PREMORBID AND POOR PREMORBID MALE SCHIZOPHRENIC
                  PATIENTS AND 18 NONPSYCHIATRIC PATIENT CONTROLS)
        @APPLICATION 1967 P-32 O-16

1042   CICCHETTI, D. V.
           REPORTED FAMILY DYNAMICS AND PSYCHOPATHOLOGY: I. THE REACTIONS OF
           SCHIZOPHRENICS AND NORMALS TO PARENTAL DIALOGUES.
           JOURNAL OF ABNORMAL PSYCHOLOGY, 1967, 72, 282-289.
                  (MODIFICATION; REVISION; CORRELATES:PSYCHOLOGICAL; USED AS
                  CRITERION; N=36 WHITE MALE SCHIZOPHRENICS AND 18 CONTROLS)
        @APPLICATION 1967 P-32 G-55 F-136 O-16

1043   MCREYNOLDS, P., & GUEVARA, C.
           ATTITUDES OF SCHIZOPHRENICS AND NORMALS TOWARD SUCCESS AND FAILURE.
           JOURNAL OF ABNORMAL PSYCHOLOGY, 1967, 72, 303-310.
                  (MODIFICATION; DESCRIPTION; RELIABILITY:INTERNAL CONSISTENCY;
                  VALIDITY:CRITERION; CORRELATES:PSYCHOLOGICAL, DEMOGRAPHIC,
                  INTELLIGENCE; NORMATIVE DATA; N=136 HOSPITALIZED MALE
                  SCHIZOPHRENICS, 103 NORMALS, AND 52 NEUROTICS)
        @APPLICATION 1967 G-28

1044   FONTANA, A. F., KLEIN, E. B., & CICCHETTI, D. V.
           CENSURE SENSITIVITY IN SCHIZOPHRENIA.
           JOURNAL OF ABNORMAL PSYCHOLOGY, 1967, 72, 294-302.
                  (MODIFICATION; RELIABILITY:INTERNAL CONSISTENCY;
                  CORRELATES:BEHAVIORAL, PSYCHOLOGICAL; USED AS CRITERION; N=24
                  WHITE MALE SCHIZOPHRENICS & 12 NORMAL CONTROLS)
        @APPLICATION 1967 P-32 G-55 C-23

1045   CICCHETTI, D. V., KLEIN, E. B., FONTANA, A. F., & SPOHN, H. E.
           A TEST OF THE CENSURE-DEFICIT MODEL IN SCHIZOPHRENIA, EMPLOYING THE
           RODNICK-GARMEZY VISUAL-DISCRIMINATION TASK.
           JOURNAL OF ABNORMAL PSYCHOLOGY, 1967, 72, 326-334.
                  (CORRELATES:BEHAVIORAL, PSYCHOLOGICAL; USED AS CRITERION;
                  N=60 WHITE MALE PSYCHIATRIC PATIENTS, 30 WHITE MALE CONTROLS)
        @APPLICATION 1967 F-136

1046   MERBAUM, M., & BADIA, P.
           TOLERANCE OF REPRESSORS AND SENSITIZERS TO NOXIOUS STIMULATION.
           JOURNAL OF ABNORMAL PSYCHOLOGY, 1967, 72, 349-353.
                  (CORRELATES:PSYCHOLOGICAL, DEMOGRAPHIC; USED AS CRITERION;
                  NORMATIVE DATA; N=84 MALE, 116 FEMALE COLLEGE STUDENTS IN
                  INTRODUCTORY PSYCHOLOGY CLASSES)
        @APPLICATION 1967 B-46

1047   SCHWARTZ, S.
           DIAGNOSIS, LEVEL OF SOCIAL ADJUSTMENT, AND COGNITIVE DEFICITS.
           JOURNAL OF ABNORMAL PSYCHOLOGY, 1967, 72, 446-450.
                  (MODIFICATION; VALIDITY:CRITERION; CORRELATES:PSYCHOLOGICAL;
                  NORMATIVE DATA; N=24 SCHIZOPHRENICS, 24 NONSCHIZOPHRENIC
                  PSYCHIATRIC PATIENTS AND 24 CONTROLS)
        @APPLICATION 1967 G-83 T-20 Z-28 E-38 R-157 B-277

1048   LLOYD, D. N.
            OVERINCLUSIVE THINKING AND DELUSIONS IN SCHIZOPHRENIC PATIENTS: A CRITIQUE.
            JOURNAL OF ABNORMAL PSYCHOLOGY, 1967, 72, 451-453.
                (VALIDITY:CRITERION; CORRELATES:PSYCHOLOGICAL; NORMATIVE DATA; N=42
                LONG-TERM HOSPITALIZED MALE SCHIZOPHRENICS)
        @APPLICATION 1967 B-94

1049   FARINA, A., & HOLZBERG, J. D.
            ATTITUDES AND BEHAVIORS OF FATHERS AND MOTHERS OF MALE SCHIZOPHRENIC
            PATIENTS.
            JOURNAL OF ABNORMAL PSYCHOLOGY, 1967, 72, 381-387.
                (DESCRIPTION; RELIABILITY:INTERRATER; CORRELATES:BEHAVIORAL,
                PSYCHOLOGICAL; USED AS CRITERION; N=74 SETS OF PARENTS AND THEIR
                PSYCHIATRIC PATIENT SONS)
        @APPLICATION 1967 P-32 G-55 F-15

1050   DAVIS, D., CROMWELL, R. L., & HELD, J. M.
            SIZE ESTIMATION IN EMOTIONALLY DISTURBED CHILDREN AND SCHIZOPHRENIC ADULTS.
            JOURNAL OF ABNORMAL PSYCHOLOGY, 1967, 72, 395-401.
                (CORRELATES:BEHAVIORAL, PSYCHOLOGICAL; USED AS CRITERION; 2 STUDIES:
                N=93 EMOTIONALLY DISTURBED CHILDREN AND 20 NONDISTURBED CHILDREN,
                N=44 SCHIZOPHRENIC MALES)
        @APPLICATION 1967 S-201 P-32

1051   BECKER, J., & MCARDLE, J.
            NONLEXICAL SPEECH SIMILARITIES AS AN INDEX OF INTRAFAMILIAL
            IDENTIFICATIONS.
            JOURNAL OF ABNORMAL PSYCHOLOGY, 1967, 72, 408-414.
                (CORRELATES:PSYCHOLOGICAL; N=PARENTS & SONS OF 18 PSYCHIATRIC CLINIC
                & 19 NONCLINIC FAMILIES)
        @APPLICATION 1967 B-217

1052   MAGARO, P. A.
            PERCEPTUAL DISCRIMINATION PERFORMANCE OF SCHIZOPHRENICS AS A FUNCTION OF
            CENSURE, SOCIAL CLASS, AND PREMORBID ADJUSTMENT.
            JOURNAL OF ABNORMAL PSYCHOLOGY, 1967, 72, 415-420.
                (CORRELATES:PSYCHOLOGICAL, DEMOGRAPHIC; USED AS CRITERION; N=40
                WHITE MALE HOSPITALIZED SCHIZOPHRENICS AND NORMAL CONTROLS)
        @APPLICATION 1967 P-32

1053   TOLOR, A., & REZNIKOFF, M.
            RELATION BETWEEN INSIGHT, REPRESSION-SENSITIZATION, INTERNAL-EXTERNAL
            CONTROL, AND DEATH ANXIETY.
            JOURNAL OF ABNORMAL PSYCHOLOGY, 1967, 72, 426-430.
                (DESCRIPTION; MODIFICATION; CORRELATES:PSYCHOLOGICAL, INTELLIGENCE;
                N=79 MALE COLLEGE STUDENTS)
        @APPLICATION 1967 R-18 B-46 T-88 L-130

1054   ALKER, H. A.
            COGNITIVE CONTROLS AND THE HAAN-KROEBER MODEL OF EGO FUNCTIONING.
            JOURNAL OF ABNORMAL PSYCHOLOGY, 1967, 72, 434-440.
                (MODIFICATION; CORRELATES:PSYCHOLOGICAL, DEMOGRAPHIC; USED AS
                CRITERION; N=100 MALE, 100 FEMALE UNDERGRADUATES, 48 MALES AND 48
                FEMALES SELECTED)
        @APPLICATION 1967 H-1 U-4 M-177 P-7 Z-34 H-39 B-46 E-10

1055   VINGOE, F. J.
            SELF-AWARENESS, SELF-ACCEPTANCE, AND HYPNOTIZABILITY.
            JOURNAL OF ABNORMAL PSYCHOLOGY, 1967, 72, 454-456.
                (MODIFICATION; CORRELATES:PSYCHOLOGICAL; NORMATIVE DATA; N=32 FEMALE
                COLLEGE STUDENTS)
        @APPLICATION 1967 G-22 E-6 W-31 G-161

1056   FELDMAN, M. M., & HERSEN, M.
            ATTITUDES TOWARD DEATH IN NIGHTMARE SUBJECTS.
            JOURNAL OF ABNORMAL PSYCHOLOGY, 1967, 72, 421-425.
                (REVISION; CORRELATES:BEHAVIORAL, PSYCHOLOGICAL, DEMOGRAPHIC,
                ENVIRONMENTAL; N=168 MALE AND FEMALE UNDERGRADUATES)
        @APPLICATION 1967 M-99

1057   RIES, H. A., & JOHNSON, M. H.
            COMMONALITY OF WORD ASSOCIATIONS AND GOOD AND POOR PREMORBID SCHIZOPHRENIA.
            JOURNAL OF ABNORMAL PSYCHOLOGY, 1967, 72, 487-488.
                    (VALIDITY:CONSTRUCT; CORRELATES:INTELLIGENCE, ENVIRONMENTAL; USED AS
                    CRITERION; NORMATIVE DATA; N=40 POOR PREMORBID AND 32 GOOD PREMORBID
                    MALE SCHIZOPHRENICS)
            @APPLICATION 1967 S-124 P-32 R-27

1058   LIVSON, N., & PESKIN, H.
            PREDICTION OF ADULT PSYCHOLOGICAL HEALTH IN A LONGITUDINAL STUDY.
            JOURNAL OF ABNORMAL PSYCHOLOGY, 1967, 72, 509-518.
                    (RELIABILITY:INTERRATER; CORRELATES:PSYCHOLOGICAL, DEMOGRAPHIC;
                    CLUSTER ANALYSIS; NORMATIVE DATA; N=31 MEN, 33 WOMEN)
            @APPLICATION 1967 B-126 M-238

1059   FOULKES, D., PIVIK, T., STEADMAN, H. S., SPEAR, P. S., & SYMONDS, J. D.
            DREAMS OF THE MALE CHILD: AN EEG STUDY.
            JOURNAL OF ABNORMAL PSYCHOLOGY, 1967, 72, 457-467.
                    (RELIABILITY:INTERRATER; CORRELATES:PSYCHOLOGICAL, PHYSIOLOGICAL;
                    N=32 BOYS, AGES 6-12)
            @APPLICATION 1967 B-210

1060   LEVIS, D. J., & CARRERA, R.
            EFFECTS OF TEN HOURS OF IMPLOSIVE THERAPY IN THE TREATMENT OF OUTPATIENTS:
            A PRELIMINARY REPORT.
            JOURNAL OF ABNORMAL PSYCHOLOGY, 1967, 72, 504-508.
                    (VALIDITY:CONSTRUCT; CORRELATES:BEHAVIORAL, PSYCHOLOGICAL,
                    ENVIRONMENTAL; USED AS CRITERION; NORMATIVE DATA; N=40 PSYCHOTHERAPY
                    PATIENTS)
            @APPLICATION 1967 D-45 W-8 W-41 B-5

1061   FREEDMAN, N., ROSEN, B., ENGELHARDT, D. M., & MARGOLIS, R.
            PREDICTION OF PSYCHIATRIC HOSPITALIZATION: I. THE MEASUREMENT OF
            HOSPITALIZATION PRONENESS.
            JOURNAL OF ABNORMAL PSYCHOLOGY, 1967, 72, 468-477.
                    (CORRELATES:BEHAVIORAL, PSYCHOLOGICAL; N=543 CHRONIC SCHIZOPHRENIC
                    OUTPATIENTS)
            @APPLICATION 1967 R-30 M-20 R-12 B-184 P-22

1062   ALPERN, G. D.
            MEASUREMENT OF "UNTESTABLE" AUTISTIC CHILDREN.
            JOURNAL OF ABNORMAL PSYCHOLOGY, 1967, 72, 478-486.
                    (MODIFICATION; DESCRIPTION; RELIABILITY:RETEST;
                    VALIDITY:CONSTRUCT; CORRELATES:PSYCHOLOGICAL, DEMOGRAPHIC,
                    INTELLIGENCE; N=14 SCHIZOPHRENIC INPATIENTS: 6 GIRLS, 8 BOYS, AGES
                    3-7 YEARS)
            @APPLICATION 1967 C-197 D-7

1063   MEGARGEE, E. I., COOK, P. E., & MENDELSOHN, G. A.
            DEVELOPMENT AND VALIDATION OF AN MMPI SCALE OF ASSAULTIVENESS IN
            OVERCONTROLLED INDIVIDUALS.
            JOURNAL OF ABNORMAL PSYCHOLOGY, 1967, 72, 519-528.
                    (VALIDITY:CONSTRUCT, CROSS-VALIDATION; 4 STUDIES: N=136 CRIMINAL AND
                    NORMAL S'S, 45 CRIMINALS, 100 MALE & 126 FEMALE UNDERGRADUATES, 22
                    MALE & 30 FEMALE STUDENTS)
            @APPLICATION 1967 D-45 B-46 A-5 G-22 E-1

1064   ZUCKERMAN, M., PERSKY, H., LINK, K. E., & BASU, G. K.
            EXPERIMENTAL AND SUBJECT FACTORS DETERMINING RESPONSES TO SENSORY
            DEPRIVATION, SOCIAL ISOLATION, AND CONFINEMENT.
            JOURNAL OF ABNORMAL PSYCHOLOGY, 1968, 73, 183-194.
                    (CORRELATES:PSYCHOLOGICAL, PHYSIOLOGICAL, DEMOGRAPHIC, ENVIRONMENTAL;
                    N=36 MALE, 36 FEMALE COLLEGE STUDENTS)
            @APPLICATION 1968 Z-4 M-94 Z-3

1065   CICCHETTI, D. V., & ORNSTON, P. S.
            REPORTED FAMILY DYNAMICS AND PSYCHOPATHOLOGY: II. THE REACTIONS OF MENTAL
            PATIENTS TO A DISTURBED FAMILY IN PSYCHOTHERAPY.
            JOURNAL OF ABNORMAL PSYCHOLOGY, 1968, 73, 156-161.
                    (CORRELATES:PSYCHOLOGICAL, INTELLIGENCE; USED AS CRITERION; N=18
                    INADEQUATELY ADJUSTED AND 16 ADEQUATELY ADJUSTED PSYCHIATRIC
                    PATIENTS)
            @APPLICATION 1968 L-124 S-9 C-23 G-55

1066   EISENTHAL, S.
             DEATH IDEATION IN SUICIDAL PATIENTS.
             JOURNAL OF ABNORMAL PSYCHOLOGY, 1968, 73, 162-167.
                      (CORRELATES:PSYCHOLOGICAL; N=90 MALE NEUROPSYCHIATRIC PATIENTS)
         aAPPLICATION 1968 N-17

1067   MILLER, C., KNAPP, S. C., & DANIELS, C. W.
             MMPI STUDY OF NEGRO MENTAL HYGIENE CLINIC PATIENTS.
             JOURNAL OF ABNORMAL PSYCHOLOGY, 1968, 73, 168-173.
                      (CORRELATES:PSYCHOLOGICAL, DEMOGRAPHIC; CLUSTER ANALYSIS; NORMATIVE
                      DATA; N=100 BLACK AND 100 WHITE PSYCHIATRIC PATIENTS)
         aAPPLICATION 1968 D-45 W-8 W-41

1068   WACHTEL, P. L.
             ANXIETY, ATTENTION, AND COPING WITH THREAT.
             JOURNAL OF ABNORMAL PSYCHOLOGY, 1968, 73, 137-143.
                      (CORRELATES:BEHAVIORAL, PSYCHOLOGICAL, ENVIRONMENTAL; N=70 MALE
                      UNDERGRADUATES)
         aAPPLICATION 1968 R-12 M-4

1069   SCHWARTZ, M. L.
             DIAGNOSTIC JUDGMENTAL CONFUSION AND PROCESS-REACTIVE SCHIZOPHRENIA.
             JOURNAL OF ABNORMAL PSYCHOLOGY, 1968, 73, 150-153.
                      (USED AS CRITERION; N=10 MALE NORMALS, 10 MALE ORGANIC, 10 MALE
                      MENTAL RETARDATE, 10 MALE PROCESS SCHIZOPHRENICS, AND 10 MALE
                      REACTIVE SCHIZOPHRENICS)
         aAPPLICATION 1968 P-32

1070   BYRNE, D., STEINBERG, M. A., & SCHWARTZ, M. S.
             RELATIONSHIP BETWEEN REPRESSION-SENSITIZATION AND PHYSICAL ILLNESS.
             JOURNAL OF ABNORMAL PSYCHOLOGY, 1968, 73, 154-155.
                      (CORRELATES:PHYSIOLOGICAL, DEMOGRAPHIC; USED AS CRITERION;
                      2 STUDIES: N=492 UNDERGRADUATES, N=85 EXTREME SENSITIZER
                      UNDERGRADUATES)
         aAPPLICATION 1968 B-46

1071   FOLKINS, C. H., LAWSON, K. D., OPTON, E. M., JR., & LAZARUS, R. S.
             DESENSITIZATION AND THE EXPERIMENTAL REDUCTION OF THREAT.
             JOURNAL OF ABNORMAL PSYCHOLOGY, 1968, 73, 100-113.
                      (CORRELATES:BEHAVIORAL, PSYCHOLOGICAL, PHYSIOLOGICAL, DEMOGRAPHIC,
                      ENVIRONMENTAL; N=58 MALE AND 51 FEMALE STUDENTS)
         aAPPLICATION 1968 K-24 Z-13 G-21

1072   PAUL, G. L.
             TWO-YEAR FOLLOW-UP OF SYSTEMATIC DESENSITIZATION IN THERAPY GROUPS.
             JOURNAL OF ABNORMAL PSYCHOLOGY, 1968, 73, 119-130.
                      (MENTION; CORRELATES:PSYCHOLOGICAL, ENVIRONMENTAL; USED AS CRITERION;
                      N=50 MALES)
         aAPPLICATION 1968 B-84 C-136 E-16 P-82
         aA-026
         aA-26

1073   HEILBRUN, A. B., JR.
             SEX ROLE, INSTRUMENTAL-EXPRESSIVE BEHAVIOR, AND PSYCHOPATHOLOGY IN FEMALES.
             JOURNAL OF ABNORMAL PSYCHOLOGY, 1968, 73, 131-136.
                      (CORRELATES:BEHAVIORAL, PSYCHOLOGICAL; USED AS CRITERION;
                      NORMATIVE DATA; 2 STUDIES: TOTAL N=55 FEMALE UNDERGRADUATES)
         aAPPLICATION 1968 G-21 H-34

1074   GROSZ, H. J., & GROSSMAN, K. G.
             CLINICIAN'S RESPONSE STYLE: A SOURCE OF VARIATION AND BIAS IN CLINICAL
             JUDGMENTS.
             JOURNAL OF ABNORMAL PSYCHOLOGY, 1968, 73, 207-214.
                      (BIAS:RESPONSE, TESTER; N=5 PSYCHIATRIC REGISTRARS)
         aAPPLICATION 1968 G-156

1075   LEVINE, M., & OLSON, R. P.
             INTELLIGENCE OF PARENTS OF AUTISTIC CHILDREN.
             JOURNAL OF ABNORMAL PSYCHOLOGY, 1968, 73, 215-217.
                      (VALIDITY:CONSTRUCT; CORRELATES:INTELLIGENCE; USED AS CRITERION;
                      N=PARENTS OF 3 AUTISTIC CHILDREN)
         aAPPLICATION 1968 R-118

1076   ZUBEK, J. P.
            URINARY EXCRETION OF ADRENALINE AND NORADRENALINE DURING PROLONGED
            IMMOBILIZATION.
            JOURNAL OF ABNORMAL PSYCHOLOGY, 1968, 73, 223-225.
                (CORRELATES:BEHAVIORAL, PHYSIOLOGICAL, ENVIRONMENTAL; N=26 MALE
                COLLEGE STUDENTS)
        ∂APPLICATION 1968 B-62 M-53

1077   WEINGOLD, H. P., LACHIN, J. M., BELL, A. H., & COXE, R. C.
            DEPRESSION AS A SYMPTOM OF ALCOHOLISM: SEARCH FOR A PHENOMENON.
            JOURNAL OF ABNORMAL PSYCHOLOGY, 1968, 73, 195-197.
                (VALIDITY:CIRTERION; CORRELATES:PSYCHOLOGICAL, PHYSIOLOGICAL,
                ENVIRONMENTAL; NORMATIVE DATA; N=73 MALE CONSECUTIVE ADMISSIONS TO
                ALCOHOLIC TREATMENT CENTER)
        ∂APPLICATION 1968 Z-5

1078   APPERSON, L. B., & MCADOO, W. G., JR.
            PARENTAL FACTORS IN THE CHILDHOOD OF HOMOSEXUALS.
            JOURNAL OF ABNORMAL PSYCHOLOGY, 1968, 73, 201-206.
                (REVISION; DESCRIPTION; RELIABILITY:RETEST; VALIDITY:CRITERION;
                CORRELATES:PSYCHOLOGICAL, ENVIRONMENTAL; FACTOR ANALYSIS; N=22 MALE
                HOMOSEXUALS, 22 CONTROLS MALES, 35 MALE SCHIZOPHRENICS)
        ∂APPLICATION 1968 A-33

1079   MCCLELLAND, D. C., & WATT, N. F.
            SEX-ROLE ALIENATION IN SCHIZOPHRENIA.
            JOURNAL OF ABNORMAL PSYCHOLOGY, 1968, 73, 226-239.
                (MODIFICATION; CORRELATES:PSYCHOLOGICAL, DEMOGRAPHIC; USED AS
                CRITERION; N=23 MALE, 22 FEMALE SCHIZOPHRENICS, 20 MALE AND 20
                FEMALE HOSPITAL EMPLOYEES)
        ∂APPLICATION 1968 M-20 W-46 H-53 Z-28 W-45 D-45 M-55

1080   JOHNSON, D. T.
            EFFECTS OF INTERVIEW STRESS ON MEASURES OF STATE AND TRAIT ANXIETY.
            JOURNAL OF ABNORMAL PSYCHOLOGY, 1968, 73, 245-251.
                (MODIFICATION; CORRELATES:PHYSIOLOGICAL, ENVIRONMENTAL; N=48 MALE
                NEUROPSYCHIATRIC INPATIENTS)
        ∂APPLICATION 1968 Z-13 T-2 D-45

1081   GOODMAN, I. Z.
            INFLUENCE OF PARENTAL FIGURES ON SCHIZOPHRENIC PATIENTS.
            JOURNAL OF ABNORMAL PSYCHOLOGY, 1968, 73, 503-512.
                (RELIABILITY:INTERRATER; USED AS CRITERION; N=32 MALE SCHIZOPHRENIC
                PATIENTS, 32 MALE NORMAL COLLEGE STUDENTS)
        ∂APPLICATION 1968 P-32

1082   COSTELLO, C. G.
            ANXIETY, INTELLIGENCE, AND DISCRIMINATION.
            JOURNAL OF ABNORMAL PSYCHOLOGY, 1968, 73, 594.
                (CORRELATES:PSYCHOLOGICAL, INTELLIGENCE; N=60 FEMALE NURSES)
        ∂APPLICATION 1968 C-198 O-16

1083   MOOS, R. H., & HOUTS, P. S.
            ASSESSMENT OF THE SOCIAL ATMOSPHERES OF PSYCHIATRIC WARDS.
            JOURNAL OF ABNORMAL PSYCHOLOGY, 1968, 73, 595-604.
                (MODIFICATION; REVISION; N=365 PSYCHIATRIC PATIENTS, 131 STAFF)
        ∂APPLICATION 1968 S-56 K-6

1084   RALPH, D. E.
            STIMULUS GENERALIZATION AMONG SCHIZOPHRENICS AND NORMAL SUBJECTS.
            JOURNAL OF ABNORMAL PSYCHOLOGY, 1968, 73, 605-609.
                (CORRELATES:PSYCHOLOGICAL; USED AS CRITERION; N=48 MALE CHRONIC
                POOR PREMORBID SCHIZOPHRENIC PATIENTS, 48 NORMAL CONTROLS)
        ∂APPLICATION 1968 P-32 L-39

1085   SHIMEK, J. G.
            COGNITIVE STYLE AND DEFENSES: A LONGITUDINAL STUDY OF INTELLECTUALIZATION
            AND FIELD INDEPENDENCE.
            JOURNAL OF ABNORMAL PSYCHOLOGY, 1968, 73, 575-580.
                (RELIABILITY:RETEST, INTERRATER; CORRELATES:PSYCHOLOGICAL,
                INTELLIGENCE; N=28 MALES PARTICIPATING IN LONGITUDINAL STUDY)
        ∂APPLICATION 1968 R-30 W-188

1086   BRILLIANT, P. J.
        DIFFERENCES IN STIMULUS GENERALIZATION AMONG PSYCHIATRIC PATIENTS AS A
        FUNCTION OF ANXIETY LEVEL-EGO STRENGTH, SEX, AND TIME OF TESTING.
        JOURNAL OF ABNORMAL PSYCHOLOGY, 1968, 73, 581-584.
              (MENTION; CORRELATES:PSYCHOLOGICAL; USED AS CRITERION; N=40 MALE, 40
              FEMALE NONORGANIC PSYCHIATRIC PATIENTS)
        @APPLICATION 1968 T-2 B-5 D-45

1087   BECKER, J., & ALTROCCHI, J.
        PEER CONFORMITY AND ACHIEVEMENT IN FEMALE MANIC-DEPRESSIVES.
        JOURNAL OF ABNORMAL PSYCHOLOGY, 1968, 73, 585-589.
              (CORRELATES:PSYCHOLOGICAL, ENVIRONMENTAL; N=16 MANIC-DEPRESSIVE
              FEMALE PATIENTS, 16 NONPSYCHIATRIC FEMALE CONTROLS)
        @APPLICATION 1968 A-5 C-3C D-23 H-54 D-28

1088   LONDON, P., OGLE, M. E., & UNIKEL, I. P.
        EFFECTS OF HYPNOSIS AND MOTIVATION ON RESISTANCE TO HEAT STRESS.
        JOURNAL OF ABNORMAL PSYCHOLOGY, 1968, 73, 532-541.
              (CORRELATES:BEHAVIORAL, ENVIRONMENTAL; USED AS CRITERION; N=40 MALE
              COLLEGE STUDENTS SELECTED FROM 80)
        @APPLICATION 1968 S-90

1089   JACOBSON, G. R.
        REDUCTION OF FIELD DEPENDENCE IN CHRONIC ALCOHOLIC PATIENTS.
        JOURNAL OF ABNORMAL PSYCHOLOGY, 1968, 73, 547-549.
              (CORRELATES:PSYCHOLOGICAL, ENVIRONMENTAL; N=30 CHRONIC MALE
              ALCOHOLICS)
        @APPLICATION 1968 W-188

1090   MITCHELL, K. M.
        AN ANALYSIS OF THE SCHIZOPHRENOGENIC MOTHER CONCEPT BY MEANS OF THE
        THEMATIC APPERCEPTION TEST.
        JOURNAL OF ABNORMAL PSYCHOLOGY, 1968, 73, 571-574.
              (RELIABILITY:INTERNAL CONSISTENCY; VALIDITY:CRITERION;
              CORRELATES:PSYCHOLOGICAL; N=20 MOTHERS OF SCHIZOPHRENIC CHILDREN, 20
              MOTHERS OF NORMAL CHILDREN)
        @APPLICATION 1968 M-20

1091   MAGARO, P. A.
        SIZE ESTIMATION IN SCHIZOPHRENIA AS A FUNCTION OF CENSURE, DIAGNOSIS,
        PREMORBID ADJUSTMENT, AND CHRONICITY.
        JOURNAL OF ABNORMAL PSYCHOLOGY, 1969, 74, 306-313.
              (CORRELATES:BEHAVIORAL; USED AS CRITERION; NORMATIVE DATA; N=72 MALE
              SCHIZOPHRENICS, 12 CONTROLS)
        @APPLICATION 1969 P-32

1092   HIRT, M., & KURTZ, R.
        A REEXAMINATION OF THE RELATIONSHIP BETWEEN BODY BOUNDARY AND SITE OF
        DISEASE.
        JOURNAL OF ABNORMAL PSYCHOLOGY, 1969, 74, 67-70.
              (CORRELATES:PSYCHOLOGICAL, PHYSIOLOGICAL; 2 STUDIES: N=40 MEDICAL
              PATIENTS, N=24 MEDICAL PATIENTS)
        @APPLICATION 1969 D-45 H-37

1093   SHEEHAN, P. W.
        ARTIFICIAL INDUCTION OF POSTHYPNOTIC CONFLICT.
        JOURNAL OF ABNORMAL PSYCHOLOGY, 1969, 74, 16-25.
              (MODIFICATION; VALIDITY:CONSTRUCT; CORRELATES:BEHAVIORAL,
              PSYCHOLOGICAL, ENVIRONMENTAL; USED AS CRITERION; N=14 MALE AND 3
              FEMALE SUSCEPTIBLE S'S AND 14 UNSUSCEPTIBLE MALE S'S)
        @APPLICATION 1969 W-31 S-90 M-20 R-31 O-16 P-141

1094   BAKER, B. L.
        SYMPTOM TREATMENT AND SYMPTOM SUBSTITUTION IN ENURESIS.
        JOURNAL OF ABNORMAL PSYCHOLOGY, 1969, 74, 42-49.
              (MODIFICATION; RELIABILITY:RETEST, INTERNAL CONSISTENCY, INTERRATER;
              CORRELATES:BEHAVIORAL, PSYCHOLOGICAL, INTELLIGENCE, ENVIRONMENTAL;
              N=90 ELEMENTARY MALE AND FEMALE SCHOOL CHILDREN, 30 ENURETICS AND 60
              CONTROLS)
        @APPLICATION 1969 S-153 L-125 S-242 S-243 M-20 M-58

1095   ORRIS, J. B.
            VISUAL MONITORING PERFORMANCE IN THREE SUBGROUPS OF MALE DELINQUENTS.
            JOURNAL OF ABNORMAL PSYCHOLOGY, 1969, 74, 227-229.
                    (CORRELATES:BEHAVIORAL, PSYCHOLOGICAL; USED AS CRITERION;
                    N=268 INSTITUTIONALIZED MALE DELINQUENTS, 45 SELECTED)
        ƏAPPLICATION 1969 Q-7

1096   ZUBEK, J. P., BAYER, L., MILSTEIN, S., & SHEPHARD, J. M.
            BEHAVIORAL AND PHYSIOLOGICAL CHANGES DURING PROLONGED IMMOBILIZATION PLUS
            PERCEPTUAL DEPRIVATION.
            JOURNAL OF ABNORMAL PSYCHOLOGY, 1969, 74, 230-236.
                    (CORRELATES:BEHAVIORAL, PSYCHOLOGICAL, PHYSIOLOGICAL, INTELLIGENCE,
                    ENVIRONMENTAL; N=44 MALE UNIVERSITY STUDENTS)
        ƏAPPLICATION 1969 M-53 B-62

1097   DECKNER, C. W., & BLANTON, R. L.
            EFFECT OF CONTEXT AND STRENGTH OF ASSOCIATION ON SCHIZOPHRENIC VERBAL
            BEHAVIOR.
            JOURNAL OF ABNORMAL PSYCHOLOGY, 1969, 74, 348-351.
                    (CORRELATES:BEHAVIORAL; USED AS CRITERION; 2 STUDIES: N=36 MALE
                    SCHIZOPHRENICS, 18 MALE GENERAL MEDICAL PATIENTS; N= SAME S'S AS IN
                    STUDY 1)
        ƏAPPLICATION 1969 P-32 P-141

1098   FRANKEL, A. S., & BUCHWALD, A. M.
            VERBAL CONDITIONING OF COMMON ASSOCIATIONS IN LONG-TERM SCHIZOPHRENICS: A
            FAILURE.
            JOURNAL OF ABNORMAL PSYCHOLOGY, 1969, 74, 372-374.
                    (CORRELATES:ENVIRONMENTAL; USED AS CRITERION; NORMATIVE DATA; N=60
                    MALE SCHIZOPHRENICS)
        ƏAPPLICATION 1969 R-27 P-141

1099   SANDERS, R. S., JR., & REYHER, J.
            SENSORY DEPRIVATION AND THE ENHANCEMENT OF HYPNOTIC SUSCEPTIBILITY.
            JOURNAL OF ABNORMAL PSYCHOLOGY, 1969, 74, 375-381.
                    (RELIABILITY:INTERRATER; CORRELATES:PSYCHOLOGICAL, PHYSIOLOGICAL,
                    ENVIRONMENTAL; USED AS CRITERION; N=20 COLLEGE FEMALES)
        ƏAPPLICATION 1969 W-31

1100   SKRZYPEK, G. J.
            EFFECT OF PERCEPTUAL ISOLATION AND AROUSAL ON ANXIETY, COMPLEXITY
            PREFERENCE, AND NOVELTY PREFERENCE IN PSYCHOPATHIC AND NEUROTIC
            DELINQUENTS.
            JOURNAL OF ABNORMAL PSYCHOLOGY, 1969, 74, 321-329.
                    (CORRELATES:BEHAVIORAL, PSYCHOLOGICAL, ENVIRONMENTAL; USED AS
                    CRITERION; NORMATIVE DATA; N=33 PSYCHOPATHIC, 33 NEUROTIC
                    DELINQUENTS)
        ƏAPPLICATION 1969 P-31 S-327 M-240 A-26

1101   BECKER, J., & IWAKAMI, E.
            CONFLICT AND DOMINANCE WITHIN FAMILIES OF DISTURBED CHILDREN.
            JOURNAL OF ABNORMAL PSYCHOLOGY, 1969, 74, 330-335.
                    (RELIABILITY:INTERRATER, RETEST; VALIDITY:CRITERION; CORRELATES:
                    BEHAVIORAL, PSYCHOLOGICAL; N=26 DISTURBED CHILDREN AND PARENTS,
                    42 NONCLINIC CONTROL CHILDREN AND PARENTS)
        ƏAPPLICATION 1969 G-22 B-217 F-11 J-44

1102   PIERS, E. V., & KIRCHNER, E. P.
            EYELID CONDITIONING AND PERSONALITY: POSITIVE RESULTS FROM NONPARTISANS.
            JOURNAL OF ABNORMAL PSYCHOLOGY, 1969, 74, 336-339.
                    (CORRELATES:BEHAVIORAL; USED AS CRITERION; NORMATIVE DATA; N=55
                    COLLEGE MALES AND 24 COLLEGE FEMALES)
        ƏAPPLICATION 1969 E-5 T-2

1103   HIGGINS, J., PETERSON, J. C., & DOLBY, L. L.
            SOCIAL ADJUSTMENT AND FAMILIAL SCHEMA.
            JOURNAL OF ABNORMAL PSYCHOLOGY, 1969, 74, 296-299.
                    (MENTION; CORRELATES:BEHAVIORAL, PSYCHOLOGICAL; USED AS CRITERION;
                    NORMATIVE DATA; N=100 MALE UNDERGRADUATES)
        ƏAPPLICATION 1969 K-46 G-100 C-27

1104   O'NEILL, M., & KEMPLER, B.
         APPROACH AND AVOIDANCE RESPONSES OF THE HYSTERICAL PERSONALITY TO SEXUAL
         STIMULI.
         JOURNAL OF ABNORMAL PSYCHOLOGY, 1969, 74, 300-305.
             (CORRELATES:BEHAVIORAL, PSYCHOLOGICAL; USED AS CRITERION; N=32
             FEMALE HYSTERICS, 32 NONHYSTERICS SELECTED FROM 150)
         ƏAPPLICATION 1969 G-26 E-2 O-7

1105   CHAPMAN, L. J., & CHAPMAN, J. P.
         ILLUSORY CORRELATION AS AN OBSTACLE TO THE USE OF VALID PSYCHODIAGNOSTIC
         SIGNS.
         JOURNAL OF ABNORMAL PSYCHOLOGY, 1969, 74, 271-280.
             (VALIDITY:CONTENT; BIAS:TESTER; 3 STUDIES: N=32 PRACTICING
             PSYCHODIAGNOSTICIANS; N=693 UNDERGRADUATES AS DIAGNOSERS)
         ƏAPPLICATION 1969 R-30

1106   SCHOPLER, E., & LOFTIN, J.
         THINKING DISORDERS IN PARENTS OF YOUNG PSYCHOTIC CHILDREN.
         JOURNAL OF ABNORMAL PSYCHOLOGY, 1969, 74, 281-287.
             (RELIABILITY:INTERRATER; VALIDITY:CRITERION;
             CORRELATES:PSYCHOLOGICAL, DEMOGRAPHIC, INTELLIGENCE; USED AS
             CRITERION; NORMATIVE DATA; N= PARENTS OF 17 AUSTIC, 11 RETARDED, AND
             21 NORMAL CHILDREN)
         ƏAPPLICATION R-58 L-157

1107   MINTZ, S.
         EFFECT OF ACTUAL STRESS ON WORD ASSOCIATIONS.
         JOURNAL OF ABNORMAL PSYCHOLOGY, 1969, 74, 293-295.
             (CORRELATES:PSYCHOLOGICAL, ENVIRONMENTAL; N=15 NURSES UNDER STRESS,
             15 NOT UNDER STRESS)
         ƏAPPLICATION 1969 R-27

1108   ROSEN, B., KLEIN, D. F., LEVENSTEIN, S., & SHAHINIAN, S. P.
         SOCIAL COMPETENCE AND POSTHOSPITAL OUTCOME AMONG SCHIZOPHRENIC AND
         NONSCHIZOPHRENIC PSYCHIATRIC PATIENTS.
         JOURNAL OF ABNORMAL PSYCHOLOGY, 1969, 74, 401-404.
             (VALIDITY:CRITERION; CORRELATES:BEHAVIORAL, PSYCHOLOGICAL; USED AS
             CRITERION; NORMATIVE DATA; N=81 SCHIZOPHRENIC AND 85
             NONSCHIZOPHRENIC PATIENTS)
         ƏAPPLICATION 1969 Z-28

1109   SCHWARTZ, M. L., DENNERLL, R. D., & LIN, Y.
         SIMILARITY OF PERSONALITY TRAIT INTERRELATIONSHIPS IN PERSONS WITH AND
         WITHOUT EPILEPTOGENIC CEREBRAL DYSFUNCTION.
         JOURNAL OF ABNORMAL PSYCHOLOGY, 1969, 74, 205-208.
             (VALIDITY:CONSTRUCT; CORRELATES:PSYCHOLOGICAL, PHYSIOLOGICAL,
             DEMOGRAPHIC; N=125 MALE AND 74 FEMALE EPILEPTICS)
         ƏAPPLICATION 1969 G-22 E-2

1110   BARBER, T. X., & CALVERLEY, D. S.
         MULTIDIMENSIONAL ANALYSIS OF "HYPNOTIC" BEHAVIOR.
         JOURNAL OF ABNORMAL PSYCHOLOGY, 1969, 74, 209-220.
             (CORRELATES:BEHAVIORAL, PSYCHOLOGICAL, ENVIRONMENTAL; N=110 FEMALE
             STUDENT NURSES AND 50 CONTROLS)
         ƏAPPLICATION 1969 W-31

1111   IRWIN, L., & RENNER, K. E.
         EFFECT OF PRAISE AND CENSURE ON THE PERFORMANCE OF SCHIZOPHRENICS.
         JOURNAL OF ABNORMAL PSYCHOLOGY, 1969, 74, 221-226.
             (CORRELATES:BEHAVIORAL, PSYCHOLOGICAL; USED AS CRITERION; N=36
             NORMALS, 36 GOOD AND 36 POOR PREMORBID MALE SCHIZOPHRENICS)
         ƏAPPLICATION 1969 P-32

1112   MEADOW, A., & BRONSON, L.
         RELIGIOUS AFFILIATION AND PSYCHOPATHOLOGY IN A MEXICAN-AMERICAN
         POPULATION.
         JOURNAL OF ABNORMAL PSYCHOLOGY, 1969, 74, 177-180.
             (MODIFICATION; CORRELATES:DEMOGRAPHIC; CROSS-CULTURAL APPLICATION;
             N=54 PROTESTANT MEXICAN-AMERICAN MALES AND MATCHED CATHOLIC GROUP)
         ƏAPPLICATION 1969 W-10

1113   BECKER, J., & SIEFKES, H.
        PARENTAL DOMINANCE, CONFLICT, AND DISCIPLINARY COERCIVENESS IN FAMILIES OF
        FEMALE SCHIZOPHRENICS.
        JOURNAL OF ABNORMAL PSYCHOLOGY, 1969, 74, 193-198.
                (RELIABILITY:INTERRATER; CORRELATES:PSYCHOLOGICAL, INTELLIGENCE;
                USED AS CRITERION; N=15 GOOD PREMORBID, 15 POOR PREMORBID & 15
                NONPSYCHIATRIC CONTROL DAUGHTERS & PARENTS)
        @APPLICATION 1969 G-22 F-11 J-44 G-55 F-136 R-45

1114   KLORMAN, R., & CHAPMAN, L. J.
        REGRESSION IN SCHIZOPHRENIC THOUGHT DISORDER.
        JOURNAL OF ABNORMAL PSYCHOLOGY, 1969, 74, 199-204.
                (VALIDITY:CONSTRUCT; CORRELATES:PSYCHOLOGICAL, DEMOGRAPHIC; NORMATIVE
                DATA; N=32 THIRD, 33 FOURTH AND 32 EIGHTH GRADERS)
        @APPLICATION 1969 C-20

1115   MENDELSOHN, G. A., & RANKIN, N. O.
        CLIENT-COUNSELOR COMPATIBILITY AND THE OUTCOME OF COUNSELING.
        JOURNAL OF ABNORMAL PSYCHOLOGY, 1969, 74, 157-163.
                (DESCRIPTION; VALIDITY:CRITERION; CORRELATES:BEHAVIORAL,
                PSYCHOLOGICAL, DEMOGRAPHIC; N=73 MALE AND 42 FEMALE COUNSELING
                CLIENTS, 6 MALE AND 5 FEMALE COUNSELORS)
        @APPLICATION 1969 S-11 M-174

1116   GOLDMAN, R. K., & MENDELSOHN, G. A.
        PSYCHOTHERAPEUTIC CHANGE AND SOCIAL ADJUSTMENT: A REPORT OF A NATIONAL
        SURVEY OF PSYCHOTHERAPISTS.
        JOURNAL OF ABNORMAL PSYCHOLOGY, 1969, 74, 164-172.
                (USED AS CRITERION; N=421 PSYCHOTHERAPISTS)
        @APPLICATION 1969 G-21

1117   MARTIN, D. G.
        CONSISTENCY OF SELF-DESCRIPTIONS UNDER DIFFERENT ROLE SETS IN NEUROTIC
        AND NORMAL ADOLESCENTS AND ADULTS.
        JOURNAL OF ABNORMAL PSYCHOLOGY, 1969, 74, 173-176.
                (MODIFICATION; CORRELATES:PSYCHOLOGICAL, DEMOGRAPHIC; USED AS
                CRITERION; N=15 NEUROTIC AND 15 NORMAL BOYS, 15 NEUROTIC AND 15
                NORMAL ADULT MALES)
        @APPLICATION 1969 B-60

1118   BERZINS, J. I., FRIEDMAN, W. H., & SEIDMAN, E.
        RELATIONSHIP OF THE A-B VARIABLE TO PATIENT SYMPTOMATOLOGY AND
        PSYCHOTHERAPY EXPECTANCIES.
        JOURNAL OF ABNORMAL PSYCHOLOGY, 1969, 74, 119-125.
                (VALIDITY:CONSTRUCT, CRITERION; CORRELATES:BEHAVIORAL,
                PSYCHOLOGICAL; USED AS CRITERION; N=68 MALE PSYCHIATRIC PATIENTS)
        @APPLICATION 1969 D-45 S-33 L-3 M-172 B-214 K-157 L-17

1119   MINARD, J. G., & MOONEY, W.
        PSYCHOLOGICAL DIFFERENTIATION AND PERCEPTUAL DEFENSE: STUDIES OF THE
        SEPARATION OF PERCEPTION FROM EMOTION.
        JOURNAL OF ABNORMAL PSYCHOLOGY, 1969, 74, 131-139.
                (VALIDITY:CONSTRUCT; CORRELATES:BEHAVIORAL, PSYCHOLOGICAL,
                INTELLIGENCE; 2 STUDIES: N=30 COLLEGE MALES, N=33 COLLEGE MALES)
        @APPLICATION 1969 W-19 W-20 W-73

1120   BENTLER, P. M., & PRINCE, C.
        PERSONALITY CHARACTERISTICS OF MALE TRANSVESTITES: III.
        JOURNAL OF ABNORMAL PSYCHOLOGY, 1969, 74, 140-143.
                (CORRELATES:BEHAVIORAL, PSYCHOLOGICAL; N=181 TRANSVESTITES AND 62
                CONTROLS)
        @APPLICATION 1969 J-1

1121   STEELE, J.
        THE HYSTERIA AND PSYCHASTHENIA CONSTRUCTS AS AN ALTERNATIVE TO MANIFEST
        ANXIETY AND CONFLICT-FREE EGO FUNCTIONS.
        JOURNAL OF ABNORMAL PSYCHOLOGY, 1969, 74, 79-85.
                (CORRELATES:PSYCHOLOGICAL, INTELLIGENCE, ENVIRONMENTAL; USED AS
                CRITERION; N=128 UNDERGRADUATES)
        @APPLICATION 1969 D-45 W-19 S-61

1122   GUNDERSON, E. K. E., & ARTHUR, R. J.
            A BRIEF MENTAL HEALTH INDEX.
            JOURNAL OF ABNORMAL PSYCHOLOGY, 1969, 74, 100-104.
                    (VALIDITY:CONTENT, CRITERION, CROSS-VALIDATION; N=630 PSYCHIATRIC
                    PATIENTS AND 454 CONTROLS)
        @APPLICATION 1969 B-127

1123   BERTRAND, S., & MASLING, J.
            ORAL IMAGERY AND ALCOHOLISM.
            JOURNAL OF ABNORMAL PSYCHOLOGY, 1969, 74, 50-53.
                    (RELIABILITY:INTERRATER; CORRELATES:BEHAVIORAL, PSYCHOLOGICAL;
                    N=40 MALE VETERAN PSYCHIATRIC PATIENTS)
        @APPLICATION 1969 R-30

1124   KATKIN, E. S., & MCCUBBIN, R. J.
            HABITUATION OF THE ORIENTING RESPONSE AS A FUNCTION OF INDIVIDUAL
            DIFFERENCES IN ANXIETY AND AUTONOMIC LABILITY.
            JOURNAL OF ABNORMAL PSYCHOLOGY, 1969, 74, 54-60.
                    (CORRELATES:PHYSIOLOGICAL; USED AS CRITERION; N=59 MALE
                    UNDERGRADUATES)
        @APPLICATION 1969 D-45 T-2

1125   MARKEL, N. N.
            RELATIONSHIP BETWEEN VOICE-QUALITY PROFILES AND MMPI PROFILES IN
            PSYCHIATRIC PATIENTS.
            JOURNAL OF ABNORMAL PSYCHOLOGY, 1969, 74, 61-66.
                    (CORRELATES:BEHAVIORAL. PSYCHOLOGICAL; N=78 MALE
                    NEUROPSYCHIATRIC PATIENTS)
        @APPLICATION 1969 D-45

1126   ENDICOTT, N. A., JORTNER, S., & ABRAMOFF, E.
            OBJECTIVE MEASURES OF SUSPICIOUSNESS.
            JOURNAL OF ABNORMAL PSYCHOLOGY, 1969, 74, 26-32.
                    (MODIFICATION; VALIDITY:CONSTRUCT, CROSS-VALIDATION;
                    CORRELATES:BEHAVIORAL, PSYCHOLOGICAL, INTELLIGENCE; N=90 HOSPITALIZED
                    PATIENTS, 40 OUTPATIENTS, 84 MIXED HOSPITALIZED PATIENTS AND
                    OUTPATIENTS)
        @APPLICATION 1969 D-45 H-37 M-58 G-78 W-19 C-125

1127   GOSS, A., & MOROSKO, T. E.
            ALCOHOLISM AND CLINICAL SYMPTOMS.
            JOURNAL OF ABNORMAL PSYCHOLOGY, 1969, 74, 682-684.
                    (MENTION; CORRELATES:BEHAVIORAL, INTELLIGENCE; N=200 MALE
                    ALCOHOLICS)
        @APPLICATION 1969 D-45 E-2 R-18

1128   VOGEL, W., KUN, K. J., & MESHORER, E.
            DETERMINANTS OF INSTITUTIONAL RELEASE AND PROGNOSIS IN MENTAL RETARDATES.
            JOURNAL OF ABNORMAL PSYCHOLOGY, 1969, 74, 685-692.
                    (DESCRIPTION; RELIABILITY:INTERRATER; CORRELATES:BEHAVIORAL,
                    PSYCHOLOGICAL, ENVIRONMENTAL; NORMATIVE DATA; N=240 FAMILIAL
                    RETARDATES)
        @APPLICATION 1969 V-33 D-78

1129   BENJAMIN, T. B., & WATT, N. F.
            PSYCHOPATHOLOGY AND SEMANTIC INTERPRETATION OF AMBIGUOUS WORDS.
            JOURNAL OF ABNORMAL PSYCHOLOGY, 1969, 74, 706-714.
                    (DESCRIPTION; CORRELATES:PSYCHOLOGICAL; NORMATIVE DATA;
                    N=44 CHRONIC SCHIZOPHRENIC VETERANS ADMINISTRATION PATIENTS, 11 BRAIN
                    DAMAGED PATIENTS, 20 NORMALS AND 22 ALCOHOLICS)
        @APPLICATION 1969 S-124

1130   WRIGHT, N. A., & ZUBEK, J. P.
            RELATIONSHIP BETWEEN PERCEPTUAL DEPRIVATION TOLERANCE AND ADEQUACY OF
            DEFENSES AS MEASURED BY THE RORSCHACH.
            JOURNAL OF ABNORMAL PSYCHOLOGY, 1969, 74, 615-617.
                    (DESCRIPTION; CORRELATES:BEHAVIORAL, PSYCHOLOGICAL; USED AS
                    CRITERION; N=31 COLLEGE MALES)
        @APPLICATION 1969 R-30 H-117 W-140

1131   STRAUGHAN, J. H., & DUFORT, W. H.
            TASK DIFFICULTY, RELAXATION, AND ANXIETY LEVEL DURING VERBAL LEARNING AND
            RECALL.
            JOURNAL OF ABNORMAL PSYCHOLOGY, 1969, 74, 621-624.
                (CORRELATES:BEHAVIORAL, ENVIRONMENTAL; USED AS CRITERION; N=121
                COLLEGE STUDENTS)
        aAPPLICATION 1969 D-45 W-8

1132   ZUBEK, J. P., BAYER, L., & SHEPHARD, J. M.
            RELATIVE EFFECTS OF PROLONGED SOCIAL ISOLATION AND CONFINEMENT: BEHAVIORAL
            AND EEG CHANGES.
            JOURNAL OF ABNORMAL PSYCHOLOGY, 1969, 74, 625-631.
                (DESCRIPTION; VALIDITY:CRITERION; CORRELATES:PSYCHOLOGICAL,
                PHYSIOLOGICAL, INTELLIGENCE, ENVIRONMENTAL; N=66 COLLEGE MALES)
        aAPPLICATION 1969 M-53 M-94 B-62

1133   WINTER, W. D., & FERREIRA, A. J.
            TALKING TIME AS AN INDEX OF INTRAFAMILIAL SIMILARITY IN NORMAL AND
            ABNORMAL FAMILIES.
            JOURNAL OF ABNORMAL PSYCHOLOGY, 1969, 74, 574-575.
                (DESCRIPTION; CORRELATES:PSYCHOLOGICAL; N=127 FAMILY TRIADS--NORMALS,
                EMOTIONALLY MALADJUSTED SCHIZOPHRENICS AND DELINQUENTS)
        aAPPLICATION 1969 W-138 M-20

1134   BARRETT, C. L.
            SYSTEMATIC DESENSITIZATION VERSUS IMPLOSIVE THERAPY.
            JOURNAL OF ABNORMAL PSYCHOLOGY, 1969, 74, 587-592.
                (DESCRIPTION; USED AS CRITERION; N=8 MALES & 28 FEMALES)
        aAPPLICATION 1969 W-37 E-16 L-135 W-135 D-45

1135   MACK, J. L.
            THE MMPI AND RECIDIVISM.
            JOURNAL OF ABNORMAL PSYCHOLOGY, 1969, 74, 612-619.
                (CORRELATES:BEHAVIORAL: NORMATIVE DATA; N=80 RECIDIVISTS AND 68
                NONRECIDIVISTS PAROLED)
        aAPPLICATION 1969 D-45

1136   HEINICKE, C. M.
            FREQUENCY OF PSYCHOTHERAPEUTIC SESSION AS A FACTOR AFFECTING OUTCOME:
            ANALYSES OF CLINICAL RATINGS AND TEST RESULTS.
            JOURNAL OF ABNORMAL PSYCHOLOGY, 1969, 74, 553-560.
                (MENTION; DESCRIPTION; RELIABILITY:INTERRATER;
                CORRELATES:PSYCHOLOGICAL, INTELLIGENCE, ENVIRONMENTAL; USED AS
                CRITERION; N=8 BOYS)
        aAPPLICATION 1969 R-30 M-20 G-78 H-154

1137   FONG, S. L. M., & PESKIN, H.
            SEX-ROLE STRAIN AND PERSONALITY ADJUSTMENT OF CHINA-BORN STUDENTS IN
            AMERICA: A PILOT STUDY.
            JOURNAL OF ABNORMAL PSYCHOLOGY, 1969, 74, 563-567.
                (MENTION; CORRELATES:DEMOGRAPHIC; CROSS-CULTURAL APPLICATION;
                NORMATIVE DATA; N=43 MALE AND 43 FEMALE CHINA-BORN COLLEGE STUDENTS)
        aAPPLICATION 1969 F-102 G-22

1138   NASH, M. M., & ZIMRING, F. M.
            PREDICTION OF REACTION TO PLACEBO.
            JOURNAL OF ABNORMAL PSYCHOLOGY, 1969, 74, 568-573.
                (DESCRIPTION; RELIABILITY:RETEST; CORRELATES:PSYCHOLOGICAL; USED AS
                CRITERION; N=22 MALES AND 77 FEMALES BETWEEN 62 AND 94 YEARS OF AGE)
        aAPPLICATION 1969 M-20 R-117 N-36

1139   COLE, C. W., OETTING, E. R., & MISKIMINS, R. W.
            SELF-CONCEPT THERAPY FOR ADOLESCENT FEMALES.
            JOURNAL OF ABNORMAL PSYCHOLOGY, 1969, 74, 642-645.
                (DESCRIPTION; CORRELATES:ENVIRONMENTAL; N=22 DELINQUENT AND
                NONDELINQUENT ADOLESCENT FEMALES)
        aAPPLICATION 1969 C-91 A-26 O-16

1140   GOLDSTEIN, S. G., & LINDEN, J. D.
            MULTIVARIATE CLASSIFICATION OF ALCOHOLICS BY MEANS OF THE MMPI.
            JOURNAL OF ABNORMAL PSYCHOLOGY, 1969, 74, 661-669.
                (CORRELATES:BEHAVIORAL: CLUSTER ANALYSIS; N=513 BEHAVIORALLY
                IDENTIFIED ALCOHOLIC MALES)
        aAPPLICATION 1969 D-45 B-5 C-150

1141   ROBERTS, A. H., & ERIKSCN, R. V.
               MEASURING IMPULSE CONTROL IN INSTITUTIONALIZED DELINQUENTS USING RORSCHACH
               CONTENT AND THOUGHT PROCESS SCALES.
               JOURNAL OF ABNORMAL PSYCHOLOGY, 1969, 74, 632-634.
                    (RELIABILITY:INTERRATER; VALIDITY:CRITERION; CORRELATES:BEHAVIORAL,
                    PSYCHOLOGICAL, INTELLIGENCE; N=47 INSTITUTIONALIZED DELINQUENT MALES)
           @APPLICATION 1969 R-30

1142   MITCHELL, K. M.
               CONCEPT OF "PATHOGENESIS" IN PARENTS OF SCHIZOPHRENIC AND NORMAL CHILDREN.
               JOURNAL OF ABNORMAL PSYCHOLOGY, 1969, 74, 423-424.
                    (RELIABILITY:INTERRATER; VALIDITY:CROSS-VALIDATION;
                    CORRELATES:PSYCHOLOGICAL; N=5 SETS OF PARENTS OF NCRMAL AND
                    SCHIZOPHRENIC CHILDREN)
           @APPLICATION 1969 M-20

1143   PAUL, G. L.
               PHYSIOLOGICAL EFFECTS OF RELAXATION TRAINING AND HYPNOTIC SUGGESTION.
               JOURNAL OF ABNORMAL PSYCHOLOGY, 1969, 74, 425-437.
                    (CORRELATES:PSYCHOLOGICAL, PHYSIOLOGICAL, ENVIRONMENTAL; NORMATIVE
                    DATA; N=60 FEMALE COLLEGE STUDENTS)
           @APPLICATION 1969 W-31

1144   BOWERS, K. S., & GILMORE, J. B.
               SUBJECTIVE REPORT AND CREDIBILITY: AN INQUIRY INVOLVING HYPNOTIC
               HALLUCINATIONS.
               JOURNAL OF ABNORMAL PSYCHOLOGY, 1969, 74, 443-451.
                    (CORRELATES:ENVIRONMENTAL; USED AS CRITERION; BIAS:RESPONSE; N=23
               SUSCEPTIBLE SS, 14 UNSUSCEPTIBLE)
           @APPLICATION 1969 W-31 S-90

1145   SCHOOLER, C., & SILVERMAN, J.
               PERCEPTUAL STYLES AND THEIR CORRELATES AMONG SCHIZOPHRENIC PATIENTS.
               JOURNAL OF ABNORMAL PSYCHOLOGY, 1969, 74, 459-470.
                    (RELIABILITY:INTERRATER; CORRELATES:PSYCHOLOGICAL; FACTOR ANALYSIS;
                    CLUSTER ANALYSIS; N=20 PARANOID, 15 NCNPARANOID CHRONIC
                    SCHIZOPHRENICS, 9 NONPARANOID AND 6 PARANOID ACUTE SCHIZOPHRENICS)
           @APPLICATION 1969 L-39 R-37 W-143 P-7 P-32 S-173 W-188

1146   HIRT, M., ROSS, W. D., KURTZ, R., & GLESER, G. L.
               ATTITUDES TO BODY PRODUCTS AMONG NORMAL SUBJECTS.
               JOURNAL OF ABNORMAL PSYCHOLOGY, 1969, 74, 486-489.
                    (DESCRIPTION; CORRELATES:DEMOGRAPHIC; N=160 CAUCASIAN MALES, 39
                    FEMALES, 11 NEGROES)
           @APPLICATION 1969 O-16

1147   ARONSON, H., & WEINTRAUB, W.
               CERTAIN INITIAL VARIABLES AS PREDICTORS OF CHANGE WITH CLASSICAL
               PSYCHOANALYSIS.
               JOURNAL OF ABNORMAL PSYCHOLCGY, 1969, 74, 490-497.
                    (VALIDITY:CRITERION; CORRELATES:BEHAVIORAL, PSYCHOLOGICAL; N=127
                    PSYCHOANALYTIC CASES REPORTED ON BY 28 ANALYSTS)
           @APPLICATION 1969 A-72

1148   HARFORD, T., & SOLOMON, L.
               EFFECTS OF A "REFORMED SINNER" AND A "LAPSED SAINT" STRATEGY UPON TRUST
               FORMATION IN PARANOID AND NONPARANOID SCHIZOPHRENIC PATIENTS.
               JOURNAL OF ABNORMAL PSYCHOLOGY, 1969, 74, 498-504.
                    (CORRELATES:BEHAVIORAL, PSYCHOLOGICAL; N=48 MALE HOSPITALIZED
                    SCHIZOPHRENIC PATIENTS & 24 MALE COLLEGE STUDENTS)
           @APPLICATION 1969 P-32 B-242

1149   BECKER, J., & FINKEL, P.
               PREDICTABILITY AND ANXIETY IN SPEECH BY PARENTS OF FEMALE SCHIZOPHRENICS.
               JOURNAL OF ABNORMAL PSYCHOLCGY, 1969, 74, 517-523.
                    (CORRELATES:PSYCHOLOGICAL; USED AS CRITERION; N=30 PAIRS OF PARENTS
                    OF SCHIZOPHRENICS, 15 PAIRS OF PARENTS OF CONTRCLS)
           @APPLICATION 1969 P-45 F-136

1150   LORR, M., & KLETT, C. J.
            CROSS-CULTURAL COMPARISON OF PSYCHOTIC SYNDROMES.
            JOURNAL OF ABNORMAL PSYCHOLOGY, 1969, 74, 531-543.
                    (CROSS-CULTURAL APPLICATION; FACTOR ANALYSIS; N=1107 DRUG FREE MALE
                    AND FEMALE NEWLY HOSPITALIZED PSYCHIATRIC PATIENTS IN ENGLAND,
                    GERMANY, FRANCE, ITALY, JAPAN, AND SWEDEN)
            @APPLICATION 1969 L-39 L-134

1151   CANCRO, R., & SUGERMAN, A. A.
            PSYCHOLOGICAL DIFFERENTIATION AND PROCESS REACTIVE SCHIZOPHRENIA.
            JOURNAL OF ABNORMAL PSYCHOLOGY, 1969, 74, 415-419.
                    (VALIDITY:CRITERION; CORRELATES:PSYCHOLOGICAL; N=51 CONSECUTIVE MALE
                    ADMISSIONS TO PSYCHIATRIC HOSPITAL)
            @APPLICATION 1969 P-32 B-94 C-201 W-188 C-233 M-239

1152   BEHAR, L., & SPENCER, R. F.
            RELATIONSHIP BETWEEN PSYCHOSOCIAL ADJUSTMENT AND PERCEPTION OF MATERNAL
            ATTITUDES.
            JOURNAL OF ABNORMAL PSYCHOLOGY, 1969, 74, 471-473.
                    (VALIDITY:CRITERION; USED AS CRITERION; N=26 ADULT MALE HEMOPHILIACS)
            @APPLICATION 1969 G-22 H-159

1153   BERGIN, A. E., & JASPER, L. G.
            CORRELATES OF EMPATHY IN PSYCHOTHERAPY: A REPLICATION.
            JOURNAL OF ABNORMAL PSYCHOLOGY, 1969, 74, 477-481.
                    (REVISION; VALIDITY:CROSS-VALIDATION; CORRELATES:PSYCHOLOGICAL,
                    DEMOGRAPHIC, INTELLIGENCE; NORMATIVE DATA; 2 STUDIES: N=18
                    THERAPISTS AND 26 CLIENTS, N=36 THERAPISTS AND 48 CLIENTS)
            @APPLICATION 1969 D-45 E-2 T-24 B-148

1154   APOSTAL, R. A.
            TWO METHODS OF EVALUATING VOCATIONAL COUNSELING.
            JOURNAL OF COUNSELING PSYCHOLOGY, 1960, 7, 171-175.
                    (MENTION; MODIFICATION; CORRELATES:BEHAVIORAL; USED AS CRITERION;
                    N=109 COUNSELING CASES)
            @APPLICATION 1960 S-33 A-88 B-266

1155   MOORE, M. R., AND POPHAM, W. J.
            EFFECTS OF TWO INTERVIEW TECHNIQUES ON ACADEMIC ACHIEVEMENT.
            JOURNAL OF COUNSELING PSYCHOLOGY, 1960, 7, 176-179.
                    (DESCRIPTION; CORRELATES:PSYCHOLOGICAL,INTELLIGENCE,ENVIRONMENTAL;
                    USED AS CRITERION; N=75 UNDERGRADUATES)
            @APPLICATION 1960 B-247

1156   EDDY, R. T.
            INTEREST PATTERNS OF REHABILITATION COUNSELORS.
            JOURNAL OF COUNSELING PSYCHOLOGY, 1960, 7, 202-208.
                    (VALIDITY:CRITERION; CORRELATES:PSYCHOLOGICAL,DEMOGRAPHIC; NORMATIVE
                    DATA; N=252 EXPERIENCED MALE AND FEMALE REHABILITATION COUNSELORS,
                    75 TRAINEES)
            @APPLICATION 1960 S-33

1157   KLEINMUNTZ, B.
            IDENTIFICATION OF MALADJUSTED COLLEGE STUDENTS.
            JOURNAL OF COUNSELING PSYCHOLOGY, 1960, 7, 209-211.
                    VALIDITY:CRITERION; CORRELATES:PSYCHOLOGICAL; NORMATIVE DATA; N=40
                    MALE AND FEMALE MALADJUSTED STUDENTS, 40 NORMAL ADJUSTED CONTROLS,
                    50 FEMALE ADJUSTED STUDENTS, 21 MALADJUSTED STUDENTS)
            @APPLICATION 1960 D-45

1158   STEIMEL, R. J.
            CHILDHOOD EXPERIENCES AND MASCULINITY-FEMININITY SCORES.
            JOURNAL OF COUNSELING PSYCHOLOGY, 1960, 7, 212-217.
                    (CORRELATES:PSYCHOLOGICAL,ENVIRONMENTAL; NORMATIVE DATA; N=201 HIGH
                    SCHOOL SENIOR BOYS)
            @APPLICATION 1960 D-45 S-33

1159   BERDIE, R. F., AND LAYTON, W. L.
            RESEARCH ON THE MINNESOTA COUNSELING INVENTORY.
            JOURNAL OF COUNSELING PSYCHOLOGY, 1960, 7, 218-224.
                    (RELIABILITY:RETEST, INTERNAL CONSISTENCY; VALIDITY:CRITERION,
                    CROSS-VALIDATION; CORRELATES:PSYCHOLOGICAL,DEMOGRAPHIC; NORMATIVE
                    DATA; 4 VALIDITY GROUPS: MALE AND FEMALE, 9TH AND 10TH GRADERS, 11TH
                    AND 12TH GRADERS, 4 SIMILAR CROSS-VALIDATING GROUPS)
            @APPLICATION 1960 B-11

1160   GUSTAV, A.
           USE OF TWO TESTS IN BRIEF COUNSELING.
           JOURNAL OF COUNSELING PSYCHOLOGY, 1960, 7, 228-229.
               (CORRELATES:PSYCHOLOGICAL; N=DENTISTS AT POSTGRADUATE WORKSHOP)
        @APPLICATION 1960 E-2 G-185

1161   CONNERS, J. E., WOLKON, G. H., HAEFNER, D. P., AND STOTSKY, B. A.
           OUTCOME OF POST-HOSPITAL REHABILITATIVE TREATMENT OF MENTAL PATIENTS AS A
           FUNCTION OF EGO STRENGTH.
           JOURNAL OF COUNSELING PSYCHOLOGY, 1960, 7, 278-282.
               (RELIABILITY:RETEST,INTERRATER; VALIDITY:CRITERION; CORRELATES:
               BEHAVIORAL,PSYCHOLOGICAL; N=40 MALE SCHIZOPHRENICS APPROVED FOR
               REHABILITATION PROGRAM, 23 MALE SCHIZOPHRENICS WHO HAD COMPLETED
               PROGRAM)
        @APPLICATION 1960 S-31

1162   KLUGMAN, S. F.
           COMPARISON OF TOTAL INTEREST PROFILES OF A PSYCHOTIC AND A NORMAL GROUP.
           JOURNAL OF COUNSELING PSYCHOLOGY, 1960, 7, 283-288.
               (CORRELATES:PSYCHOLOGICAL; N=60 MALE MENTAL PATIENTS, 60 APPLICANTS
               FOR COUNSELING)
        @APPLICATION 1960 K-34

1163   NORRELL, G., & GRATER, H.
           INTEREST AWARENESS AS AN ASPECT OF SELF-AWARENESS.
           JOURNAL OF COUNSELING PSYCHOLOGY, 1960, 7, 289-292.
               (CORRELATES:PSYCHOLOGICAL; USED AS CRITERION; N=53 MALE SOPHOMORE
               STUDENTS UNDECIDED ABOUT MAJOR FIELD)
        @APPLICATION 1960 E-2 S-33

1164   MILES, M. B.
           HUMAN RELATIONS TRAINING: PROCESSES AND OUTCOMES.
           JOURNAL OF COUNSELING PSYCHOLOGY, 1960, 7, 301-306.
               (CORRELATES:BEHAVIORAL, ENVIRONMENTAL; USED AS CRITERION; N=34
               ELEMENTARY SCHOOL PRINCIPALS IN HUMAN RELATIONS TRAINING LABORATORY,
               34 MATCHED CONTROLS, AND 148 RANDOMLY CHOSEN PRINCIPALS)
        @APPLICATION 1960 S-117 P-123 F-20

1165   ANDERSON, G. V.
           TEST REVIEW: TWO EXPERIMENTAL APPROACHES.
           JOURNAL OF COUNSELING PSYCHOLOGY, 1960, 7, 310-311.
               (MENTION,DESCRIPTION; RELIABILITY:RETEST,INTERNAL CONSISTENCY;
               VALIDITY:CRITERION,CONSTRUCT; CORRELATES:PSYCHOLOGICAL; REVIEW
               ARTICLE -- NO SAMPLE USED)
        @APPLICATION 1960 W-9 C-224 D-45 G-21 G-22 E-2 C-136 T-2

1166   DICKEN, C. F.
           SIMULATED PATTERNS ON THE CALIFORNIA PSYCHOLOGICAL INVENTORY.
           JOURNAL OF COUNSELING PSYCHOLOGY, 1960, 7, 24-31.
               (MENTION; BIAS:RESPONSE; N=100 MALE & FEMALE UNDERGRADUATE STUDENTS,
               10 COUNSELORS)
        @APPLICATION 1960 G-22 E-2 D-45

1167   WRENN, R. L.
           COUNSELOR ORIENTATION: THEORETICAL OR SITUATIONAL?
           JOURNAL OF COUNSELING PSYCHOLOGY, 1960, 7, 40-45.
               (RELIABILITY:INTER-RATER; VALIDITY:CRITERION; CORRELATES:BEHAVIORAL;
               N=54 COUNSELORS)
        @APPLICATION 1960 B-2 R-142

1168   LANGLAND, L.
           PROJECTIVE TECHNIQUES AND COUNSELING PSYCHOLOGY.
           JOURNAL OF COUNSELING PSYCHOLOGY, 1960, 7, 102-107.
               (MENTION -- REVIEW ARTICLE)
        @APPLICATION 1960 R-30 M-20 S-97 R-12 B-176 R-31 R-17 G-78 K-23 B-58 O-16 V-4
        @M-7 S-37 D-45 G-26

1169   NAKAMURA, C. Y.
           VALIDITY OF K SCALE (MMPI) IN COLLEGE COUNSELING.
           JOURNAL OF COUNSELING PSYCHOLOGY, 1960, 7, 108-115.
               (VALIDITY:CRITERION,CONSTRUCT; BIAS:RESPONSE; N=110 MALE, 93 FEMALE
               COLLEGE STUDENTS AND STUDENT OFFENDERS)
        @APPLICATION 1960 D-45

1170   STEWART, L. H.
            MODES OF RESPONSE ON THE STRONG BLANK AND SELECTED PERSONALITY VARIABLES.
            JOURNAL OF COUNSELING PSYCHOLOGY, 1960, 7, 127-131.
                (DESCRIPTION; CORRELATES:PSYCHOLOGICAL,DEMOGRAPHIC; BIAS:RESPONSE;
                N=593 MEN, 238 WOMEN)
        @APPLICATION 1960 S-33 A-7 H-12

1171   GHEI, S.
            VOCATIONAL INTERESTS, ACHIEVEMENT AND SATISFACTION.
            JOURNAL OF COUNSELING PSYCHOLOGY, 1960, 7, 132-136.
                (REVISION; VALIDITY:CRITERION; N=453 IBM WORKERS, 575 TRADESMEN IN
                GENERAL)
        @APPLICATION 1960 C-52

1172   CRITES, J. O.
            EGO-STRENGTH IN RELATION TO VOCATIONAL INTEREST DEVELOPMENT.
            JOURNAL OF COUNSELING PSYCHOLOGY, 1960, 7, 137-143.
                DESCRIPTION; CORRELATES:PSYCHOLOGICAL,DEMOGRAPHIC,INTELLIGENCE;
                NORMATIVE DATA; N=100 MALE STUDENTS IN 2 AGE GROUPS)
        @APPLICATION 1960 S-33 B-5

1173   GRIFFITH, A. V., AND FOWLER, R. D.
            PSYCHASTHENIC AND HYPOMANIC SCALES OF THE MMPI AND REACTION TO AUTHORITY.
            JOURNAL OF COUNSELING PSYCHOLOGY, 1960, 7, 146-147.
                (VALIDITY:CRITERION; USED AS CRITERION; N=1200 MALE STUDENTS)
        @APPLICATION 1960 D-45

1174   MCARTHUR, C. C.
            COMMENT.
            JOURNAL OF COUNSELING PSYCHOLOGY, 1961, 8, 312-313.
                (MENTION -- REVIEW ARTICLE)
        @APPLICATION 1961 G-72 D-22

1175   IKENBERRY, S. O.
            FACTORS IN COLLEGE PERSISTENCE.
            JOURNAL OF COUNSELING PSYCHOLOGY, 1961, 8, 322-329.
                (VALIDITY:CRITERION; CORRELATES:BEHAVIORAL, PSYCHOLOGICAL,
                DEMOGRAPHIC, INTELLIGENCE; N=RANDOM SAMPLE OF 250 UNDERGRADUATES AND
                303 STUDENTS WITHDRAWN FROM COLLEGE)
        @APPLICATION 1961 R-8

1176   LESSER, W. M.
            THE RELATIONSHIP BETWEEN COUNSELING PROGRESS AND EMPATHIC UNDERSTANDING.
            JOURNAL OF COUNSELING PSYCHOLOGY, 1961, 8, 330-336.
                (VALIDITY:CONSTRUCT; CORRELATES:PSYCHOLOGICAL; N=11 COUNSELORS, 22
                MALE AND FEMALE STUDENT CLIENTS)
        @APPLICATION 1961 B-60 B-9 S-30

1177   SIEGEL, L. E., AND CRITES, J. O.
            TEST REVIEWS: THE NEUROTICISM SCALE QUESTIONNAIRE.
            JOURNAL OF COUNSELING PSYCHOLOGY, 1961, 8, 373-374.
                (DESCRIPTION; RELIABILITY:INTERNAL CONSISTENCY; VALIDITY:CRITERION;
                FACTOR ANALYSIS; REVIEW ARTICLE -- NO SAMPLE USED)
        @APPLICATION 1961
        @S-10

1178   WARMAN, R. E.
            THE COUNSELING ROLE OF COLLEGE AND UNIVERSITY COUNSELING CENTERS.
            JOURNAL OF COUNSELING PSYCHOLOGY, 1961, 8, 231-238.
                (MODIFICATION; CORRELATES:ENVIRONMENTAL; USED AS CRITERION; NORMATIVE
                DATA; N=21 COUNSELING CENTER DIRECTORS)
        @APPLICATION 1961 W-168

1179   O'CONNOR, J. P., AND KINNANE, J. F.
            A FACTOR ANALYSIS OF WORK VALUES.
            JOURNAL OF COUNSELING PSYCHOLOGY, 1961, 8, 263-267.
                (MODIFICATION; VALIDITY:CONTENT; FACTOR ANALYSIS; N=191 MALE UNDER-
                GRADUATES)
        @APPLICATION 1961 S-59

1180   KLEINMUNTZ, B.
            COMMENTS AND LETTERS: SCREENING: IDENTIFICATION OR PREDICTION?
            JOURNAL OF COUNSELING PSYCHOLOGY, 1961, 8, 279-280.
                (MENTION; VALIDITY:CRITERION; REVIEW ARTICLE -- NO SAMPLE USED)
        @APPLICATION 1961 K-138

1181   HOLLAND, J. L.
        SOME EXPLORATIONS WITH OCCUPATIONAL TITLES.
        JOURNAL OF COUNSELING PSYCHOLOGY, 1961, 8, 82-85.
             (DESCRIPTION; VALIDITY:CRITERION; CORRELATES:PSYCHOLOGICAL,
             DEMOGRAPHIC. INTELLIGENCE; N=1177 NATIONAL MERIT FINALISTS)
        @APPLICATION 1961 H-21

1182   SEGAL, S. J.
        A PSYCHOANALYTIC ANALYSIS OF PERSONALITY FACTORS IN VOCATIONAL CHOICE.
        JOURNAL OF COUNSELING PSYCHOLOGY, 1961, 8, 202-210.
             (MODIFICATION; VALIDITY:CONSTRUCT; CORRELATES:BEHAVIORAL,
             PSYCHOLOGICAL, DEMOGRAPHIC, INTELLIGENCE; USED AS CRITERION; N=30
             COLLEGE UNDERGRADUATES)
        @APPLICATION 1961 S-33 K-13 D-111

1183   LEWIS, E. C., AND MACKINNEY, A. C.
        COUNSELOR VS. STATISTICAL PREDICTIONS OF JOB SATISFACTION IN
        ENGINEERING.
        JOURNAL OF COUNSELING PSYCHOLOGY, 1961, 8, 224-229.
             (RELIABILITY:INTERNAL CONSISTENCY; VALIDITY:CRITERION;
             CORRELATES:BEHAVIORAL, PSYCHOLOGICAL, DEMOGRAPHIC, INTELLIGENCE;
             N=70 ENGINEERING GRADUATES AND 6 COLLEGE COUNSELORS)
        @APPLICATION 1961 S-33 K-34 F-118

1184   KIBRICK, A. K., AND TIEDEMAN, D. V.
        CONCEPTIONS OF SELF AND PERCEPTION OF ROLE IN SCHOOLS OF NURSING.
        JOURNAL OF COUNSELING PSYCHOLOGY, 1961, 8, 62-69.
             (CORRELATES:BEHAVIORAL. PSYCHOLOGICAL, ENVIRONMENTAL; N=460 FEMALE
             NURSING STUDENTS FROM 7 SCHOOLS)
        @APPLICATION 1961 K-33

1185   DUNKLEBERGER, C. J., & TYLER, L. E.
        INTEREST STABILITY AND PERSONALITY TRAITS.
        JOURNAL OF COUNSELING PSYCHOLOGY, 1961, 8, 70-74.
             (CORRELATES:BEHAVIORAL. PSYCHOLOGICAL, DEMOGRAPHIC, INTELLIGENCE;
             USED AS CRITERION; N=136 HIGH SCHOOL MALES AND FEMALES)
        @APPLICATION 1961 E-2 G-22 S-33

1186   PIERCE-JONES, J.
        SOCIAL MOBILITY ORIENTATIONS AND INTERESTS OF ADOLESCENTS.
        JOURNAL OF COUNSELING PSYCHOLOGY, 1961, 8, 75-78.
             (RELIABILITY:INTERNAL CONSISTENCY; CORRELATES:PSYCHOLOGICAL,
             DEMOGRAPHIC; USED AS CRITERION; NORMATIVE DATA; N=136 HIGH SCHOOL
             MALES AND FEMALES, 196 SELECTED)
        @APPLICATION 1961 K-34 P-118 G-121

1187   BARRINGTON, B. L.
        PREDICTION FROM COUNSELOR BEHAVIOR OF CLIENT PERCEPTION AND OF CASE
        OUTCOME.
        JOURNAL OF COUNSELING PSYCHOLOGY, 1961, 8, 37-42.
             (VALIDITY:CRITERION; CORRELATES:BEHAVIORAL, PSYCHOLOGICAL;
             ENVIRONMENTAL; USED AS CRITERION; N=10 THERAPISTS, 2 CLIENTS EACH)
        @APPLICATION 1961 B-50 D-45 T-2

1188   HILLS, J. R.
        THE INFLUENCE OF INSTRUCTIONS ON PERSONALITY INVENTORY SCORES.
        JOURNAL OF COUNSELING PSYCHOLOGY, 1961, 8, 43-48.
             (RELIABILITY:RETEST; CORRELATES:ENVIRONMENTAL; USED AS CRITERION;
             FACTOR ANALYSIS; NORMATIVE DATA; BIAS:RESPONSE, TESTER; N=605 NAVAL
             ACADEMY MIDSHIPMEN)
        @APPLICATION 1961 T-25

1189   PUMROY, D. K.
        SOME COUNSELING BEHAVIOR CORRELATES OF THE SOCIAL DESIRABILITY SCALE.
        JOURNAL OF COUNSELING PSYCHOLOGY, 1961, 8, 49-53.
             (VALIDITY:CONSTRUCT; CORRELATES:BEHAVIORAL, PSYCHOLOGICAL; USED AS
             CRITERION; NORMATIVE DATA; N=40 COLLEGE MALES IN COUNSELING)
        @APPLICATION 1961 E-1 D-45

1190   BRAATEN, L. J.
        THE MOVEMENT FROM NON-SELF TO SELF IN CLIENT-CENTERED PSYCHOTHERAPY.
        JOURNAL OF COUNSELING PSYCHOLOGY, 1961, 8, 20-24.
             (VALIDITY:CRITERION; CORRELATES:PSYCHOLOGICAL; USED AS CRITERION;
             N=14 MALE AND FEMALE COLLEGE STUDENTS IN COUNSELING)
        @APPLICATION 1961 B-60 D-25
        @S-187

1191   BRAMS, J. M.
           COUNSELOR CHARACTERISTICS AND EFFECTIVE COMMUNICATION IN COUNSELING.
           JOURNAL OF COUNSELING PSYCHOLOGY, 1961, 8, 25-30.
               (MODIFICATION; VALIDITY:CRITERION; CORRELATES:BEHAVIORAL,
               PSYCHOLOGICAL, DEMOGRAPHIC; NORMATIVE DATA; N=27 MALE AND FEMALE
               GRADUATE STUDENTS COUNSELING TRAINEES)
       @APPLICATION 1961 D-45 T-2 B-18 G-18 A-81 A-82 G-19 G-36 G-121

1192   HEILBRUN, A. B., JR.
           MALE AND FEMALE PERSONALITY CORRELATES OF EARLY TERMINATION IN COUNSELING.
           JOURNAL OF COUNSELING PSYCHOLOGY, 1961, 8, 31-36.
               (MENTION; CORRELATES:BEHAVIORAL, PSYCHOLOGICAL, DEMOGRAPHIC;
               NORMATIVE DATA; N=73 COLLEGE MALES AND FEMALES IN COUNSELING)
       @APPLICATION 1961 G-21 E-2 G-22

1193   STEPHENSON, R. R.
           A NEW PATTERN ANALYSIS TECHNIQUE FOR THE SVIB.
           JOURNAL OF COUNSELING PSYCHOLOGY, 1961, 8, 355-362.
               (RELIABILITY:INTERRATER; N=100 PROFILES, 24 JUDGES AT VARIOUS
               EXPERIENCE LEVELS)
       @APPLICATION 1961 S-33

1194   BOROW, H.
           REPORT ON A UNIQUE RESEARCH PLANNING WORKSHOP AT CORNELL.
           JOURNAL OF COUNSELING PSYCHOLOGY, 1961, 8, 363-367.
               (MENTION; REVIEW ARTICLE)
       @APPLICATION 1961 G-188 G-190 G-141

1195   NASS, G. D.
           LITERATURE ON MEASUREMENT OF THE SELF CONCEPT: A SOCIOLOGIST'S ADDENDUM.
           JOURNAL OF COUNSELING PSYCHOLOGY, 1961, 8, 368.
               (MENTION; NO SAMPLE SIZE GIVEN)
       @APPLICATION 1961 K-21

1196   FARSON, R. E.
           INTROJECTION IN THE PSYCHOTHERAPEUTIC RELATIONSHIP.
           JOURNAL OF COUNSELING PSYCHOLOGY, 1961, 8, 337-342.
               (CORRELATES:PSYCHOLOGICAL, ENVIRONMENTAL; N=18 CLIENTS, 6 THERAPISTS)
       @APPLICATION 1961 B-60

1197   TIEDEMAN, D. V.
           COMMENT.
           JOURNAL OF COUNSELING PSYCHOLOGY, 1961, 8, 342-343.
               (MENTION; NO SAMPLE SIZE GIVEN)
       @APPLICATION 1961 B-60

1198   ENDLER, N. S.
           CHANGES IN MEANING DURING PSYCHOTHERAPY AS MEASURED BY THE SEMANTIC
           DIFFERENTIAL.
           JOURNAL OF COUNSELING PSYCHOLOGY, 1961, 8, 105-111.
               (MODIFICATION; VALIDITY:CRITERION; CORRELATES:PSYCHOLOGICAL,
               DEMOGRAPHIC, ENVIRONMENTAL; N=5 FEMALE, 17 MALE STUDENTS IN
               PSYCHOTHERAPY & 8 COUNSELORS)
       @APPLICATION 1961 O-16 H-185

1199   TODD, W. B., & EWING, T. N.
           CHANGES IN SELF-REFERENCE DURING COUNSELING.
           JOURNAL OF COUNSELING PSYCHOLOGY, 1961, 8, 112-115.
               (MODIFICATION; RELIABILITY:INTERRATER; VALIDITY:CRITERION;
               CORRELATES:PSYCHOLOGICAL, ENVIRONMENTAL; N=34 COUNSELING CLIENTS)
       @APPLICATION 1961 R-141 H-185

1200   WIENER, D. M.
           EVALUATION OF SELECTION PROCEDURES FOR A MANAGEMENT DEVELOPMENT PROGRAM.
           JOURNAL OF COUNSELING PSYCHOLOGY, 1961, 8, 121-128.
               (CORRELATES:BEHAVIORAL, PSYCHOLOGICAL, DEMOGRAPHIC, INTELLIGENCE;
               USED AS CRITERION; N=117 MALE MANAGEMENT TRAINEE VOLUNTEERS)
       @APPLICATION 1961 D-45

1201   PATTERSON, C. H.
            COMMENT.
            JOURNAL OF COUNSELING PSYCHOLOGY, 1961, 8, 145.
                (MENTION)
        aAPPLICATION 1961 B-69

1202   GOODSTEIN, L. D., CRITES, J. O., HEILBRUN, A. B., JR., & REMPEL, P. P.
            JOURNAL OF COUNSELING PSYCHOLOGY, 1961, 8, 147-153.
                (DESCRIPTION; VALIDITY:CRITERION; CORRELATES:BEHAVIORAL,
                PSYCHOLOGICAL, DEMOGRAPHIC; NORMATIVE DATA; N=30 MALE, 30 FEMALE
                PERSONAL ADJUSTMENT PROBLEM CLIENTS, 30 MALE, 30 FEMALE NONCLIENT
                CONTROLS)
        aAPPLICATION 1961 G-22

1203   PARKER, C. A.
            THE PREDICTIVE USE OF THE MMPI IN A COLLEGE COUNSELING CENTER.
            JOURNAL OF COUNSELING PSYCHOLOGY, 1961, 8, 154-158.
                (MODIFICATION; VALIDITY:CRITERION; CORRELATES:PSYCHOLOGICAL;
                N=279 COLLEGE STUDENTS EVALUATED FOR COUNSELING, 182 CONTROLS)
        aAPPLICATION 1961 D-45

1204   PALUBINSKAS, A. L., & EYDE, L. D.
            SVIB PATTERNS OF MEDICAL SCHOOL APPLICANTS.
            JOURNAL OF COUNSELING PSYCHOLOGY, 1961, 8, 159-163.
                (VALIDITY:CRITERION; N=265 MALE APPLICANTS FOR MEDICAL SCHOOL)
        aAPPLICATION 1961 S-33

1205   WARREN, J. R.
            SELF CONCEPT, OCCUPATIONAL ROLE EXPECTATION, AND CHANGE IN COLLEGE MAJOR.
            JOURNAL OF COUNSELING PSYCHOLOGY, 1961, 8, 164-169.
                (CORRELATES:BEHAVIORAL, PSYCHOLOGICAL, INTELLIGENCE; N=525 MALE
                COLLEGE FRESHMEN OF HIGH ABILITY)
        aAPPLICATION 1961 H-12

1206   STRONG, D. J., & FEDER, D. D.
            MEASUREMENT OF THE SELF CONCEPT: A CRITIQUE OF THE LITERATURE.
            JOURNAL OF COUNSELING PSYCHOLOGY, 1961, 8, 170-178.
                (DESCRIPTION; REVIEW)
        aAPPLICATION 1961 S-30 B-60 B-18 B-36 B-13 P-19 W-21 J-37 F-91 S-167 E-39
        aB-39 R-31 L-35 M-120 M-215

1207   DICKEN, C. F.
            NOTE ON THE BISERIAL CORRELATION AND THE VALIDITY OF THE
            CALIFORNIA PSYCHOLOGICAL INVENTORY.
            JOURNAL OF COUNSELING PSYCHOLOGY, 1961, 8, 185-186.
                (VALIDITY:CONSTRUCT, CRITERION; NO SAMPLE USED -- REVIEW ARTICLE)
        aAPPLICATION 1961 C-22

1208   SPIELBERGER, C. D., WEITZ, H., AND DENNY, J. P.
            GROUP COUNSELING AND THE ACADEMIC PERFORMANCE OF ANXIOUS COLLEGE
            FRESHMEN.
            JOURNAL OF COUNSELING PSYCHOLOGY, 1962, 9, 195-204.
                (MODIFICATION; CORRELATES:BEHAVIORAL, INTELLIGENCE; USED AS
                CRITERION; NORMATIVE DATA; N=565 MALE FRESHMEN, 56 IN CRITERION
                GROUPS)
        aAPPLICATION 1962 D-45 W-8 T-2 B-74 K-34

1209   BORISLOW, B.
            SELF-EVALUATION AND ACADEMIC ACHIEVEMENT.
            JOURNAL OF COUNSELING PSYCHOLOGY, 1962, 9, 246-254.
                (MODIFICATION; VALIDITY:CRITERION; CORRELATES:INTELLIGENCE; N=197
                FRESHMEN COLLEGE STUDENTS)
        aAPPLICATION 1962 F-5 F-119

1210   SCHEIER, I. H.
            A REPLY TO CRITES REVIEW OF THE NEUROTICISM SCALE QUESTIONNAIRE.
            JOURNAL OF COUNSELING PSYCHOLOGY, 1962, 9, 280-281.
                (DESCRIPTION; RELIABILITY:INTERNAL CONSISTENCY; VALIDITY:CONSTRUCT;
                NO SAMPLE USED --- REVIEW ARTICLE)
        aAPPLICATION 1962
        aS-10

1211   KORN, H. A.
           DIFFERENCES BETWEEN MAJORS IN ENGINEERING AND PHYSICAL SCIENCES ON CPI AND
           SVIB SCORES.
           JOURNAL OF COUNSELING PSYCHOLOGY, 1962, 9, 306-312.
               (MODIFICATION; VALIDITY:CRITERION; CORRELATES:PSYCHOLOGICAL;
               N=846 MALE COLLEGE FRESHMEN)
       ∂APPLICATION 1962 G-22 S-33

1212   SPANGLER, D. P., AND THOMAS, C. W.
           THE EFFECTS OF AGE, SEX, AND PHYSICAL DISABILITY UPON MANIFEST NEEDS.
           JOURNAL OF COUNSELING PSYCHOLOGY, 1962, 9, 313-319.
               (CORRELATES:PHYSIOLOGICAL, DEMOGRAPHIC; N=80 DISABLED PATIENTS,
               80 UNDISABLED CONTROLS AT 4 AGE LEVELS)
       ∂APPLICATION 1962 E-2

1213   KINNANE, J. F., AND PABLE, M. W.
           FAMILY BACKGROUND AND WORK VALUE ORIENTATION.
           JOURNAL OF COUNSELING PSYCHOLOGY, 1962, 9, 320-325.
               (MODIFICATION; VALIDITY:CONSTRUCT; CORRELATES:PSYCHOLOGICAL,
               INTELLIGENCE; N=121 11TH GRADE WHITE HIGH SCHOOL BOYS)
       ∂APPLICATION 1962 S-155 S-59

1214   KEMP, C. G.
           COUNSELING RESPONSES AND NEED STRUCTURES OF HIGH SCHOOL PRINCIPALS AND OF
           COUNSELORS.
           JOURNAL OF COUNSELING PSYCHOLOGY, 1962, 9, 326-328.
               (VALIDITY:CRITERION; CORRELATES:PSYCHOLOGICAL; N=45 SECONDARY SCHOOL
               PRINCIPALS, 45 COUNSELORS)
       ∂APPLICATION 1962 E-2 P-116

1215   CAMPBELL, R. E.
           COUNSELOR PERSONALITY AND BACKGROUND AND HIS INTERVIEW SUBROLE BEHAVIOR.
           JOURNAL OF COUNSELING PSYCHOLOGY, 1962, 9, 329-334.
               (CORRELATES:BEHAVIORAL, PSYCHOLOGICAL; N=14 MALE, 10 FEMALE COUNSELOR
               TRAINEES, 144 TAPED CLIENT RECORDS)
       ∂APPLICATION 1962 G-26 K-34

1216   STEFFLRE, B., KING, P., & LEAFGREN, F.
           CHARACTERISTICS OF COUNSELORS JUDGED EFFECTIVE BY THEIR PEERS.
           JOURNAL OF COUNSELING PSYCHOLOGY, 1962, 9, 335-340.
               (CORRELATES:PSYCHOLOGICAL; N=40 COUNSELING PARTICIPANTS IN GUIDANCE
               INSTITUTE)
       ∂APPLICATION 1962 S-29 S-33 S-302 T-2 R-8 B-18 E-2

1217   FARQUHAR, W. W.
           RESEARCH FRONTIER: AN INTEGRATED RESEARCH ATTACK ON ACADEMIC MOTIVATION.
           JOURNAL OF COUNSELING PSYCHOLOGY, 1962, 9, 84-86.
               (REVISION; VALIDITY:CRITERION, CONTENT, CROSS VALIDATION; CORRELATES:
               DEMOGRAPHIC, INTELLIGENCE; USED AS CRITERION; FACTOR ANALYSIS; N=4200
               UNDERGRADUATES)
       ∂APPLICATION 1962 T-22 T-21 F-25

1218   STONE, L. A.
           THE RELATIONSHIP OF UTILITY FOR RISK TO COLLEGE YEAR, SEX, AND VOCATIONAL
           CHOICE.
           JOURNAL OF COUNSELING PSYCHOLOGY, 1962, 9, 87.
               (MODIFICATION; CORRELATES:BEHAVIORAL, DEMOGRAPHIC; USED AS CRITERION;
               N=116 MALE, 163 FEMALE UNDERGRADUATES)
       ∂APPLICATION 1962 Z-42

1219   WHITLOCK, G. E.
           PASSIVITY OF PERSONALITY AND ROLE CONCEPTS IN VOCATIONAL CHOICE.
           JOURNAL OF COUNSELING PSYCHOLOGY, 1962, 9, 88-90.
               (CORRELATES:BEHAVIORAL, PSYCHOLOGICAL; N=25 COLLEGE MALE CANDIDATES
               FOR MINISTRY)
       ∂APPLICATION 1962 S-33 G-22

1220   HEILBRUN, A. B., JR.
           PREDICTION OF FIRST YEAR COLLEGE DROP-OUT, USING ACL NEED SCORES.
           JOURNAL OF COUNSELING PSYCHOLOGY, 1962, 9, 58-63.
               (VALIDITY:CRITERION; CORRELATES:BEHAVIORAL; NORMATIVE DATA; N=169
               COLLEGE FEMALES)
       ∂APPLICATION 1962 G-21 H-216

1221   STRONG, D. J.
            A FACTOR-ANALYTIC STUDY OF SEVERAL MEASURES OF SELF CONCEPT.
            JOURNAL OF COUNSELING PSYCHOLOGY, 1962, 9, 64-70.
                    (DESCRIPTION; VALIDITY:CONSTRUCT; CORRELATES:PSYCHOLOGICAL; FACTOR
                    ANALYSIS; N=105 MALE UNDERGRADUATES)
            @APPLICATION 1962 B-60 B-18 W-21 B-27

1222   RENZAGLIA, G. A., HENRY, D. R., & RYBOLT, G. A., JR.
            ESTIMATION AND MEASUREMENT OF PERSONALITY CHARACTERISTICS AND CORRELATES OF
            THEIR CONGRUENCE.
            JOURNAL OF COUNSELING PSYCHOLOGY, 1962, 9, 71-78.
                    (REVISION; CORRELATES:PSYCHOLOGICAL, INTELLIGENCE; NORMATIVE DATA;
                    N=89 MALE, 63 FEMALE UNDERGRADUATES)
            @APPLICATION 1962 E-2 B-18 R-144

1223   WILLIAMS, J. E.
            CHANGES IN SELF AND OTHER PERCEPTIONS FOLLOWING BRIEF
            EDUCATIONAL-VOCATIONAL COUNSELING.
            JOURNAL OF COUNSELING PSYCHOLOGY, 1962, 9, 18-28.
                    (MODIFICATION; CORRELATES:ENVIRONMENTAL; USED AS CRITERION; NORMATIVE
                    DATA; N=121 COUNSELED AND NON-COUNSELED UNDERGRADUATES)
            @APPLICATION 1962 B-60

1224   SHLIEN, J. M., MOSAK, H. H., & DREIKURS, R.
            EFFECT OF TIME LIMITS: A COMPARISON OF TWO PSYCHOTHERAPIES.
            JOURNAL OF COUNSELING PSYCHOLOGY, 1962, 9, 31-34.
                    (MODIFICATION; CORRELATES:PSYCHOLOGICAL, ENVIRONMENTAL; USED AS
                    CRITERION; N=23 THERAPISTS, AND 3 SAMPLES OF 30, 20, AND 20
                    ADULTS IN THERAPY)
            @APPLICATION 1962 B-60

1225   UTTON, A. C.
            RECALLED PARENT-CHILD RELATIONS AS DETERMINANTS OF VOCATIONAL CHOICE.
            JOURNAL OF COUNSELING PSYCHOLOGY, 1962, 9, 49-53.
                    (MODIFICATION; RELIABILITY:RETEST; VALIDITY:CRITERION; USED AS
                    CRITERION; NORMATIVE DATA; N=127 ADULT WOMEN IN 4 PROFESSIONAL
                    OCCUPATIONS)
            @APPLICATION 1962 A-7 B-1 S-33 S-297

1226   LAW, D. H., & NORTON, J. L.
            THE SORT AS A DIFFERENTIATOR BETWEEN HIGH AND LOW ACHIEVERS.
            JOURNAL OF COUNSELING PSYCHOLOGY, 1962, 9, 184.
                    (VALIDITY:CRITERION; CORRELATES:INTELLIGENCE; N=21 FEMALE, 41 MALE
                    UNDERGRADUATES)
            @APPLICATION 1962 S-110

1227   DRAKE, L. E.
            MMPI PATTERNS PREDICTIVE OF UNDERACHIEVEMENT.
            JOURNAL OF COUNSELING PSYCHOLOGY, 1962, 9, 164-167.
                    (VALIDITY:CRITERION, CROSS-VALIDATION; CORRELATES:INTELLIGENCE;
                    2 SAMPLES: N=1004 MALE UNDERGRADUATES; N=1834 MALE UNDERGRADUATES)
            @APPLICATION 1962 D-45

1228   MOGAR, R. E.
            COMPETITION, ACHIEVEMENT, AND PERSONALITY.
            JOURNAL OF COUNSELING PSYCHOLOGY, 1962, 9, 168-172.
                    (CORRELATES:BEHAVIORAL, DEMOGRAPHIC, INTELLIGENCE; USED AS CRITERION;
                    2 STUDIES: N=58 MALE, 58 FEMALE UNDERGRADUATES; N=41 MALE, 43 FEMALE
                    UNDERGRADUATES)
            @APPLICATION 1962 E-2

1229   KLEIN, F. L., MCNAIR, D. M., & LORR, M.
            SVIB SCORES OF CLINICAL PSYCHOLOGISTS, PSYCHIATRISTS, AND SOCIAL WORKERS.
            JOURNAL OF COUNSELING PSYCHOLOGY, 1962, 9, 176-179.
                    (VALIDITY:CRITERION; CORRELATES:PSYCHOLOGICAL; N=27 PSYCHIATRISTS, 46
                    CLINICAL PSYCHOLOGISTS, 26 SOCIAL WORKERS)
            @APPLICATION 1962 S-33

1230   KINNANE, J. F., & SUZIEDELIS, A.
            WORK VALUE ORIENTATION AND INVENTORIED INTERESTS.
            JOURNAL OF COUNSELING PSYCHOLOGY, 1962, 9, 144-148.
                    (MODIFICATION; CORRELATES:PSYCHOLOGICAL; USED AS CRITERION; N=191
                    MALE UNDERGRADUATES)
            @APPLICATION 1962 S-33 S-59

1231   ARMATAS, J. P., & COLLISTER, E. G.
             PERSONALITY CORRELATES OF SVIB PATTERNS.
             JOURNAL OF COUNSELING PSYCHOLOGY, 1962, 9, 149-154.
                  (CORRELATES:PSYCHOLOGICAL, INTELLIGENCE; USED AS CRITERION;
                  NORMATIVE DATA; BIAS:RESPONSE; N=513 MALE UNDERGRADUATES)
        @APPLICATION 1962 S-33 E-2 C-10 S-333

1232   KEMP, C. G.
             INFLUENCE OF DOGMATISM ON THE TRAINING OF COUNSELORS.
             JOURNAL OF COUNSELING PSYCHOLOGY, 1962, 9, 155-157. .
                  (RELIABILITY:INTERRATER; CORRELATES:PSYCHOLOGICAL, ENVIRONMENTAL;
                  USED AS CRITERION; N=50 GRADUATE COUNSELOR TRAINEES)
        @APPLICATION 1962 R-8 P-116

1233   SIEGEL, L.
             TEST REVIEWS.
             JOURNAL OF COUNSELING PSYCHOLOGY, 1962, 9, 92-93.
                  (DESCRIPTION; REVIEW ARTICLE -- NO SAMPLE USED)
        @APPLICATION 1962 G-13

1234   TYLER, L. E.
             RESEARCH ON INSTRUMENTS USED BY COUNSELORS IN VOCATIONAL GUIDANCE.
             JOURNAL OF COUNSELING PSYCHOLOGY, 1962, 9, 99-105.
                  (MENTION; REVIEW ARTICLE)
        @APPLICATION 1962 S-33 K-148

1235   MILLER, S., JR.
             RELATIONSHIP OF PERSONALITY TO OCCUPATION, SETTING, AND FUNCTION.
             JOURNAL OF COUNSELING PSYCHOLOGY, 1962, 9, 115-121.
                  (CORRELATES:PSYCHOLOGICAL, DEMOGRAPHIC, ENVIRONMENTAL; USED AS
                  CRITERION; N=150 MEN AND WOMEN IN 3 OCCUPATIONS)
        @APPLICATION 1962 S-33 E-2 D-45

1236   MENDELSOHN, G. A., & KIRK, B. A.
             PERSONALITY DIFFERENCES BETWEEN STUDENTS WHO DO AND DO NOT USE A
             COUNSELING FACILITY.
             JOURNAL OF COUNSELING PSYCHOLOGY, 1962, 9, 341-346.
                  (DESCRIPTION; CORRELATES:DEMOGRAPHIC, INTELLIGENCE, ENVIRONMENTAL;
                  NORMATIVE DATA; N=31 MALE, 41 FEMALE UNDERGRADUATES IN CLIENT SAMPLE,
                  97 MALES, 103 FEMALES IN NONCLIENT SAMPLE)
        @APPLICATION 1962 M-22

1237   HEILBRUN, A. B., JR.
             PSYCHOLOGICAL FACTORS RELATED TO COUNSELING READINESS AND IMPLICATIONS FOR
             COUNSELOR BEHAVIOR.
             JOURNAL OF COUNSELING PSYCHOLOGY, 1962, 9, 353-358.
                  (CORRELATES:PSYCHOLOGICAL, DEMOGRAPHIC; N=261 MALE, 126 FEMALE
                  COLLEGE STUDENT COUNSELING CLIENTS)
        @APPLICATION 1962 G-22 H-200 G-21

1238   WILLIAMS, J. E., & HILLS, D. A.
             MORE ON BRIEF EDUCATIONAL-VOCATIONAL COUNSELING.
             JOURNAL OF COUNSELING PSYCHOLOGY, 1962, 9, 366-368.
                  (CORRELATES:ENVIRONMENTAL; N=54 EDUCATIONAL-VOCATIONAL CLIENTS AT
                  COLLEGE COUNSELING CENTER)
        @APPLICATION 1962 W-175

1239   CRITES, J. O.
             TEST REVIEW.
             JOURNAL OF COUNSELING PSYCHOLOGY, 1962, 9, 369-372.
                  (REVIEW; DESCRIPTION)
        @APPLICATION 1962 D-90

1240   KLEINMUNTZ, B.
             ANNOTATED BIBLIOGRAPHY OF MMPI RESEARCH AMONG COLLEGE POPULATIONS.
             JOURNAL OF COUNSELING PSYCHOLOGY, 1962, 9, 373-396.
                  (REVIEW; VALIDITY:CONSTRUCT, CRITERION; CROSS-CULTURAL APPLICATION;
                  NORMATIVE DATA; BIAS:RESPONSE; NO SAMPLE SIZE USED)
        @APPLICATION 1962 D-45

1241   PATTERSON, C. H.
            COMMENT TO THE EDITOR.
            JOURNAL OF COUNSELING PSYCHOLOGY, 1962, 9, 281-282.
                (REVIEW)
        @APPLICATION 1962 L-38

1242   SIEGEL, L.
            TEST REVIEW: SUPERVISOR'S EVALUATION OF RESEARCH PERSONNEL.
            JOURNAL OF COUNSELING PSYCHOLOGY, 1963, 10, 101-102.
                (REVIEW ARTICLE; DESCRIPTION; RELIABILITY:RETEST, INTERNAL
                CONSISTENCY: VALIDITY:CROSS-VALIDATION; NORMATIVE DATA; MEDIAN N=84)
        @APPLICATION 1963 B-252

1243   KLEINMUNTZ, B.
            PROFILE ANALYSIS REVISITED: A HEURISTIC APPROACH.
            JOURNAL OF COUNSELING PSYCHOLOGY, 1963, 10, 315-324.
                (REVIEW)
        @APPLICATION 1963 D-45

1244   KINNANE, J. F., & GAUBINGER, J. R.
            LIFE VALUES AND WORK VALUES.
            JOURNAL OF COUNSELING PSYCHOLOGY, 1963, 10, 362-367.
                (MODIFICATION; VALIDITY:CONSTRUCT; CORRELATES:PSYCHOLOGICAL; N=143
                COLLEGE FRESHMEN)
        @APPLICATION 1963 S-59 A-7

1245   KEMP, C. G.
            BEHAVIORS IN GROUP GUIDANCE (SOCIO-PROCESS) AND GROUP COUNSELING
            (PSYCHO-PROCESS).
            JOURNAL OF COUNSELING PSYCHOLOGY, 1963, 10, 373-377.
                (CORRELATES:BEHAVIORAL, ENVIRONMENTAL; USED AS CRITERION; N=90
                GRADUATE STUDENTS)
        @APPLICATION 1963 R-8

1246   KING, P., NORRELL, G., & POWERS, G. P.
            RELATIONSHIPS BETWEEN TWIN SCALES ON THE SVIB AND THE KUDER.
            JOURNAL OF COUNSELING PSYCHOLOGY, 1963, 10, 395-401.
                (VALIDITY:CONSTRUCT; CORRELATES:PSYCHOLOGICAL; N=464 MALE COLLEGE
                STUDENTS)
        @APPLICATION 1963 S-33 K-34

1247   WINKLER, R. C., MUNGER, P. F., GUST, C. T., & TEIGLAND, J. J.
            CHANGES IN THE CONCEPTS OF SELF AND OTHERS OF NDEA GUIDANCE INSTITUTE
            MEMBERS.
            JOURNAL OF COUNSELING PSYCHOLOGY, 1963, 10, 227-231.
                (CORRELATES:ENVIRONMENTAL; USED AS CRITERION; N=28 MALE, 1 FEMALE
                MEMBERS OF NDEA GUIDANCE INSTITUTE, 39 MALE MEMBERS OF SCIENCE
                INSTITUTE)
        @APPLICATION 1963 B-60

1248   WALZ, G. R., & JOHNSTON, J. A.
            COUNSELORS LOOK AT THEMSELVES ON VIDEO TAPE.
            JOURNAL OF COUNSELING PSYCHOLOGY, 1963, 10, 232-236.
                (CORRELATES:BEHAVIORAL, PSYCHOLOGICAL; USED AS CRITERION; N=30 NDEA
                COUNSELORS)
        @APPLICATION 1963 B-18 W-8

1249   TRUAX, C. B.
            EFFECTIVE INGREDIENTS IN PSYCHOTHERAPY: AN APPROACH TO UNRAVELING THE
            PATIENT-THERAPIST INTERACTION.
            JOURNAL OF COUNSELING PSYCHOLOGY, 1963, 10, 256-263.
                (MENTION, DESCRIPTION; CORRELATES:PSYCHOLOGICAL, ENVIRONMENTAL;
                REVIEW ARTICLE -- NO SAMPLE USED)
        @APPLICATION 1963 T-38 R-30 D-45 M-20 A-5 T-69 T-24 T-89

1250   SCHULMAN, R. E.
            USE OF RORSCHACH PROGNOSTIC RATING SCALE IN PREDICTING MOVEMENT IN
            COUNSELING.
            JOURNAL OF COUNSELING PSYCHOLOGY, 1963, 10, 198-199.
                (VALIDITY:CRITERION; CORRELATES:PSYCHOLOGICAL; N=20 MALE STUDENT
                COUNSELING CLIENTS)
        @APPLICATION 1963 K-13 R-30 C-4 H-185

1251   BROWN, F. G.
        FURTHER EVIDENCE ON STRONG V.I.B. RESPONSE TENDENCIES AND PERSONALITY
        CHARACTERISTICS.
        JOURNAL OF COUNSELING PSYCHOLOGY, 1963, 10, 199-200.
            (CORRELATES:PSYCHOLOGICAL; BIAS:RESPONSE; N=220 FEMALE NURSING
            STUDENTS
        @APPLICATION 1963 S-33 D-45 K-34 G-26

1252   DOLE, A. A.
        PREDICTION OF ACADEMIC SUCCESS UPON READMISSION TO COLLEGE.
        JOURNAL OF COUNSELING PSYCHOLOGY, 1963, 10, 169-175.
            (REVISION; VALIDITY:CRITERION; CORRELATES:PSYCHOLOGICAL,INTELLIGENCE;
            3 SAMPLES: N=60, 186, 115 COLLEGE STUDENTS APPLYING FOR READMISSION)
        @APPLICATION 1963 B-74 M-20 D-93

1253   WHARTON, W. P.
        THE CASE OF HARRY AND THERAPIST FLEXIBILITY.
        JOURNAL OF COUNSELING PSYCHOLOGY, 1963, 10, 179-184.
            (MENTION; USED AS CRITERION; N=1 MENTAL PATIENT)
        @APPLICATION 1963 D-45 R-30

1254   MUELLER, W. J.
        THE INFLUENCE OF SELF-INSIGHT ON SOCIAL PERCEPTION SCORES.
        JOURNAL OF COUNSELING PSYCHOLOGY, 1963, 10, 185-191.
            (DESCRIPTION; REVISION; CORRELATES:PSYCHOLOGICAL; N=31 GRADUATE
            STUDENTS IN GUIDANCE TRAINING)
        @APPLICATION 1963 S-56

1255   WRIGHT, E. W.
        A COMPARISON OF INDIVIDUAL AND MULTIPLE COUNSELING FOR TEST INTERPRÉTATION
        INTERVIEWS.
        JOURNAL OF COUNSELING PSYCHOLOGY, 1963, 10, 126-135.
            (CORRELATES:PSYCHOLOGICAL; USED AS CRITERION; NORMATIVE DATA; N=300
            COLLEGE FRESHMEN)
        @APPLICATION 1963 K-34

1256   NEFF, W. S., & HELFAND, A.
        A Q-SORT INSTRUMENT TO ASSESS THE MEANING OF WORK.
        JOURNAL OF COUNSELING PSYCHOLOGY, 1963, 10, 139-145.
            (REVISION; 2 STUDIES: N=5 PROFESSIONALLY TRAINED VOCATIONAL
            COUNSELORS, N=16 HANDICAPPED CLIENTS)
        @APPLICATION 1963 S-30

1257   SEEGARS, J. E., JR., & MCDONALD, R. L.
        THE ROLE OF INTERACTION GROUPS IN COUNSELOR EDUCATION.
        JOURNAL OF COUNSELING PSYCHOLOGY, 1963, 10, 156-162.
            (DESCRIPTION; CORRELATES:PSYCHOLOGICAL, ENVIRONMENTAL; USED AS
            CRITERION; N=4 FEMALE, 5 MALE GRADUATE STUDENTS IN COUNSELING)
        @APPLICATION 1963 L-35

1258   GONYEA, G. G.
        JOB PERCEPTIONS IN RELATION TO VOCATIONAL PREFERENCE.
        JOURNAL OF COUNSELING PSYCHOLOGY, 1963, 10, 20-26.
            (DESCRIPTION; VALIDITY:CONSTRUCT; CORRELATES:PSYCHOLOGICAL; N=118
            MALE FRESHMEN)
        @APPLICATION 1963 G-72 G-183

1259   FULLER, F. F.
        INFLUENCE OF SEX OF COUNSELOR AND OF CLIENT ON CLIENT EXPRESSIONS OF
        FEELING.
        JOURNAL OF COUNSELING PSYCHOLOGY, 1963, 10, 34-40.
            (CORRELATES:PSYCHOLOGICAL, DEMOGRAPHIC; NORMATIVE DATA; N=32
            UNIVERSITY COUNSELING CENTER CLIENTS, 8 COUNSELORS)
        @APPLICATION 1963 K-158 S-33

1260   CARTWRIGHT, R. D.
        SELF-CONCEPTION PATTERNS OF COLLEGE STUDENTS, AND ADJUSTMENT TO
        COLLEGE LIFE.
        JOURNAL OF COUNSELING PSYCHOLOGY, 1963, 10, 47-52.
            (DESCRIPTION; CORRELATES:PSYCHOLOGICAL; USED AS CRITERION; N=30
            COLLEGE STUDENT APPLICANTS FOR PERSONAL COUNSELING AND 22 COLLEGE
            CONTROLS)
        @APPLICATION 1963 B-60

1261   SIEGEL, L.
             TEST REVIEW: MYERS-BRIGGS TYPE INDICATOR.
             JOURNAL OF COUNSELING PSYCHOLOGY, 1963, 10, 307-308.
                   (REVIEW ARTICLE; DESCRIPTION)
        @APPLICATION 1963 M-22

1262   GONYEA, G. G.
             APPROPRIATENESS OF VOCATIONAL CHOICES OF COUNSELED AND UNCOUNSELED
             COLLEGE STUDENTS.
             JOURNAL OF COUNSELING PSYCHOLOGY, 1963, 10, 269-275.
                   (CORRELATES:BEHAVIORAL, PSYCHOLOGICAL; USED AS CRITERION; N=74
                   COLLEGE STUDENTS RECEIVING VOCATIONAL COUNSELING, 74 COLLEGE
                   STUDENT CONTROLS)
        @APPLICATION 1963 G-40

1263   POWELL, W. J., & JOURARD, S. M.
             SOME OBJECTIVE EVIDENCE OF IMMATURITY IN UNDERACHIEVING COLLEGE STUDENTS.
             JOURNAL OF COUNSELING PSYCHOLOGY, 1963, 10, 276-282.
                   (DESCRIPTION; MODIFICATION; CORRELATES:PSYCHOLOGICAL, DEMOGRAPHIC,
                   INTELLIGENCE; USED AS CRITERION; NORMATIVE DATA; N=20 MALE AND 20
                   FEMALE COLLEGE UNDERACHIEVERS)
        @APPLICATION 1963 A-85
        @J-15

1264   CARKHUFF, R. R., & DRASGOW, J.
             THE CONFUSING LITERATURE ON THE OL SCALE OF THE SVIB.
             JOURNAL OF COUNSELING PSYCHOLOGY, 1963, 10, 283-288.
                   (DESCRIPTION; REVIEW ARTICLE; VALIDITY:CONSTRUCT, CRITERION;
                   CORRELATES:PSYCHOLOGICAL, DEMOGRAPHIC)
        @APPLICATION 1963 S-33

1265   STEIMEL, R. J., & SUZIEDELIS, A.
             PERCEIVED PARENTAL INFLUENCE AND INVENTORIED INTERESTS.
             JOURNAL OF COUNSELING PSYCHOLOGY, 1963, 10, 289-295.
                   (MODIFICATION; DESCRIPTION; CORRELATES:PSYCHOLOGICAL, DEMOGRAPHIC;
                   NORMATIVE DATA; N=198 COLLEGE MALES)
        @APPLICATION 1963 S-33 S-336

1266   SCHULDT, W. J.
             EVALUATION MODALITIES OF THERAPISTS.
             JOURNAL OF COUNSELING PSYCHOLOGY, 1963, 10, 296.
                   (CORRELATES:PSYCHOLOGICAL, ENVIRONMENTAL; USED AS CRITERION; N=16
                   MALE GRADUATE STUDENTS IN EACH: THERAPY, EXPERIMENTAL PSYCHOLOGY,
                   OTHER THAN PSYCHOLOGY)
        @APPLICATION 1963 E-18

1267   ARMATAS, J. P.
             THE CONFORMING ROLE OF THE SUCCESSFUL FOOD SERVICE WORKERS.
             JOURNAL OF COUNSELING PSYCHOLOGY, 1963, 10, 304-305.
                   (DESCRIPTION; RELIABILITY:RETEST; VALIDITY:CRITERION; CORRELATES:
                   BEHAVIORAL, PSYCHOLOGICAL, DEMOGRAPHIC; N=30 FEMALE AND 24 MALE FOOD
                   SERVICE WORKERS)
        @APPLICATION 1963 S-296

1268   COLE, M., FLETCHER, F. M., & PRESSEY, S. L.
             FORTY-YEAR CHANGES IN COLLEGE STUDENT ATTITUDES.
             JOURNAL OF COUNSELING PSYCHOLOGY, 1963, 10, 53-55.
                   (DESCRIPTION; CORRELATES:ENVIRONMENTAL; USED AS CRITERION; 6 SAMPLES:
                   MEDIAN N=192 COLLEGE MALES AND 184 COLLEGE FEMALES)
        @APPLICATION 1963 P-121

1269   MENDELSOHN, G. A., & GELLER, M. H.
             EFFECTS OF COUNSELOR-CLIENT SIMILARITY ON THE OUTCOME OF COUNSELING.
             JOURNAL OF COUNSELING PSYCHOLOGY, 1963, 10, 71-77.
                   (CORRELATES:BEHAVIORAL, PSYCHOLOGICAL; N=41 FEMALE, 31 MALE STUDENT
                   COUNSELING CLIENTS, 10 COUNSELORS)
        @APPLICATION 1963 M-22

1270   WINKLER, R. C., & MYERS, R. A.
             SOME CONCOMITANTS OF SELF-IDEAL DISCREPANCY MEASURES OF SELF-ACCEPTANCE.
             JOURNAL OF COUNSELING PSYCHOLOGY, 1963, 10, 83-86.
                   VALIDITY:CONSTRUCT; CORRELATES:PSYCHOLOGICAL; BIAS:RESPONSE; N=24
                   COLLEGE MALES, 62 COLLEGE FEMALES)
        @APPLICATION 1963 B-60 T-2 C-23 C-27 B-7 B-18

1271   KLUGMAN, S. F.
            INTRA-INDIVIDUAL VARIABILITY FINDINGS FOR A PSYCHOTIC POPULATION ON
            VOCATIONAL INTEREST INVENTORIES.
            JOURNAL OF COUNSELING PSYCHOLOGY, 1964, 11, 191-193.
                (VALIDITY:CONSTRUCT, CRITERION; N=100 MALE PSYCHOTIC PATIENTS
                COMPARED WITH RESULTS OF EARLIER STUDIES WITH NORMALS)
        @APPLICATION 1964 K-34 L-40

1272   CRITES, J. O.
            TEST REVIEW: THE CALIFORNIA PSYCHOLOGICAL INVENTORY: I. AS A MEASURE OF
            THE NORMAL PERSONALITY.
            JOURNAL OF COUNSELING PSYCHOLOGY, 1964, 11, 197-202.
                (DESCRIPTION; VALIDITY:CONSTRUCT; FACTOR ANALYSIS; REVIEW ARTICLE --
                NO SAMPLE USED)
        @APPLICATION 1964 G-22

1273   HANSEN, J. C., & BARKER, E. N.
            EXPERIENCING AND THE SUPERVISORY RELATIONSHIP.
            JOURNAL OF COUNSELING PSYCHOLOGY, 1964, 11, 107-111.
                (CORRELATES:PSYCHOLOGICAL; NORMATIVE DATA; N=8 FEMALE, 20 MALE
                COUNSELING TRAINEES, 3 SUPERVISORS)
        @APPLICATION 1964 B-50 G-189

1274   DOLE, A. A.
            THE PREDICTION OF EFFECTIVENESS IN SCHOOL COUNSELING.
            JOURNAL OF COUNSELING PSYCHOLOGY, 1964, 11, 112-121.
                (RELIABILITY:RETEST, INTERNAL CONSISTENCY, INTERRATER; VALIDITY:
                CRITERION; CORRELATES:PSYCHOLOGICAL; 3 GROUPS OF SUBJECTS: N=92
                TEACHERS ENROLLED IN SCHOOL COUNSELING WORKSHOP, 29 ENROLLEES IN
                NDEA INSTITUTE NOT ELIGIBLE FOR CERTIFICATION, 30 ENROLLEES ELIGIBLE
                FOR CERTIFICATION)
        @APPLICATION 1964 S-33 G-70 C-228 D-93 D-92 C-57 R-8

1275   MUTHARD, J. E., & MILLER, L. A.
            CRITERIA FOR REHABILITATION COUNSELOR PERFORMANCE IN STATE VOCATIONAL
            REHABILITATION AGENCIES.
            JOURNAL OF COUNSELING PSYCHOLOGY, 1964, 11, 123-128.
                (MODIFICATION; RELIABILITY:INTERNAL CONSISTENCY; CORRELATES:
                PSYCHOLOGICAL; CLUSTER ANALYSIS; N=143 REHABILITATION COUNSELORS)
        @APPLICATION 1964 J-53

1276   GOODMAN, M.
            EXPRESSED SELF-ACCEPTANCE AND INTERSPOUSAL NEEDS: A BASIS FOR MATE
            SELECTION.
            JOURNAL OF COUNSELING PSYCHOLOGY, 1964, 11, 129-135.
                (CORRELATES:PSYCHOLOGICAL; USED AS CRITERION; NORMATIVE DATA; N=75
                RECENTLY MARRIED COUPLES)
        @APPLICATION 1964 B-18 E-2

1277   LUCKEY, E. B.
            MARITAL SATISFACTION AND ITS CONCOMITANT PERCEPTIONS OF SELF AND SPOUSE.
            JOURNAL OF COUNSELING PSYCHOLOGY, 1964, 11, 136-145.
                (CORRELATES:PSYCHOLOGICAL; N=80 MARRIED COUPLES)
        @APPLICATION 1964 L-35 L-144

1278   EWING, T. N.
            CHANGES DURING COUNSELING APPROPRIATE TO THE CLIENT'S INITIAL PROBLEM.
            JOURNAL OF COUNSELING PSYCHOLOGY, 1964, 11, 146-151.
                (MENTION; RELIABILITY:RETEST; VALIDITY:CRITERION; FACTOR ANALYSIS;
                N=90 COLLEGE STUDENTS IN COUNSELING AND NORMAL GROUP OF STUDENTS NOT
                IN COUNSELING -- UNSPECIFIED NUMBER)
        @APPLICATION 1964 E-39 H-185

1279   SPRINGOB, H. K., & STRUENING, E. L.
            A FACTOR ANALYSIS OF THE CALIFORNIA PSYCHOLOGICAL INVENTORY ON A HIGH
            SCHOOL POPULATION.
            JOURNAL OF COUNSELING PSYCHOLOGY, 1964, 11, 173-179.
                (FACTOR ANALYSIS; N=226 JUNIOR AND SENIOR HIGH SCHOOL BOYS)
        @APPLICATION 1964 G-22

1280   GLOYE, E. E.
         A NOTE ON THE DISTINCTION BETWEEN SOCIAL DESIRABILITY AND ACQUIESCENT
         RESPONSE STYLES AS SOURCES OF VARIANCE IN THE MMPI.
         JOURNAL OF COUNSELING PSYCHOLOGY, 1964, 11, 180-184.
                 (VALIDITY:CONSTRUCT; BIAS:RESPONSE; N=108 COLLEGE STUDENTS)
         @APPLICATION 1964 D-45

1281   KUNHART, W. E., & ROLEDER, G.
         COUNSELING TECHNIQUES WITH POTENTIAL DROP-OUT STUDENTS IN JUNIOR COLLEGE.
         JOURNAL OF COUNSELING PSYCHOLOGY, 1964, 11, 190-191.
                 (USED AS CRITERION; N=450 COLLEGE STUDENTS)
         @APPLICATION 1964 R-146

1282   STEWART, L. H.
         CHANGE IN PERSONALITY TEST SCORES DURING COLLEGE.
         JOURNAL OF COUNSELING PSYCHOLOGY, 1964, 11, 211-219.
                 (MODIFICATION; RELIABILITY:RETEST; CORRELATES:PSYCHOLOGICAL; USED AS
                 CRITERION; N=287 UNDERGRADUATES)
         @APPLICATION 1964 S-33 A-7 H-12 C-45 D-99 G-36 B-6 B-78 A-5 S-62 E-78 B-5 W-194
         @E-72
         @W-55

1283   LOWE, C. M.
         A MULTI-DIMENSIONAL APPROACH TO SELF-CONCEPT IN THREE PATIENT GROUPS.
         JOURNAL OF COUNSELING PSYCHOLOGY, 1964, 11, 251-255.
                 (CORRELATES:PSYCHOLOGICAL; USED AS CRITERION; NORMATIVE DATA; N=30
                 PSYCHIATRIC PSYCHOTIC, 30 PSYCHIATRIC NONPSYCHOTIC PATIENTS, 30
                 TUBERCULAR PATIENTS)
         @APPLICATION 1964 J-52

1284   STERN, L. S.
         EGO STRENGTH AND BELIEFS ABOUT THE CAUSE OF ILLNESS.
         JOURNAL OF COUNSELING PSYCHOLOGY, 1964, 11, 257-261.
                 (CORRELATES:PSYCHOLOGICAL, DEMOGRAPHIC, INTELLIGENCE; USED AS
                 CRITERION; N=47 WHITE MEN AFFLICTED WITH PARKINSON'S DISEASE)
         @APPLICATION 1964 T-102 B-5 P-84

1285   OLIVE, L. E.
         RELATIONSHIP OF VALUES TO THE PERCEPTION OF ACTIVITIES INVOLVED IN AN
         OCCUPATION.
         JOURNAL OF COUNSELING PSYCHOLOGY, 1964, 11, 262-266.
                 (DESCRIPTION; CORRELATES:PSYCHOLOGICAL; USED AS CRITERION; 2 STUDIES;
                 N=321 FRESHMEN ENGINEERS; N=49 FRESHMEN TEACHERS)
         @APPLICATION 1964 P-112 O-25

1286   CARNES, G. D.
         VOCATIONAL INTEREST CHARACTERISTICS OF ABNORMAL PERSONALITIES.
         JOURNAL OF COUNSELING PSYCHOLOGY, 1964, 11, 272-279.
                 (CORRELATES:PSYCHOLOGICAL, DEMOGRAPHIC; USED AS CRITERION; NORMATIVE
                 DATA; N=40 MALE PSYCHIATRIC PATIENTS)
         @APPLICATION 1964 S-33 L-39

1287   STONE, L. A.
         A FACTOR ANALYSIS OF THE BERGER WILLINGNESS TO ACCEPT LIMITATIONS SCALE --
         A BRIEF.
         JOURNAL OF COUNSELING PSYCHOLOGY, 1964, 11, 285.
                 (FACTOR ANALYSIS; N=84 UNDERGRADUATES)
         @APPLICATION 1964 B-69

1288   EHRLE, R. A., & AUVENSHINE, C. D.
         ANXIETY LEVEL, NEED FOR COUNSELING, AND CLIENT IMPROVEMENT IN AN
         OPERATIONAL SETTING.
         JOURNAL OF COUNSELING PSYCHOLOGY, 1964, 11, 286-287.
                 (CORRELATES:PSYCHOLOGICAL; USED AS CRITERION; N=164 COUNSELING
                 CLIENTS)
         @APPLICATION 1964 W-8

1289   FISHBURN, W. R., & KING, P. T.
         THE RELATIONSHIP BETWEEN VALUES AND PERCEIVED PROBLEMS.
         JOURNAL OF COUNSELING PSYCHOLOGY, 1964, 11, 288-290.
                 (CORRELATES:PSYCHOLOGICAL; N=24 MALE, 64 FEMALE UNDERGRADUATES)
         @APPLICATION 1964 A-7 M-172

1290   HEILBRUN, A. B., JR.
          FURTHER VALIDATION OF THE COUNSELING READINESS SCALE.
          JOURNAL OF COUNSELING PSYCHOLOGY, 1964, 11, 290-292.
               (VALIDITY:CRITERION; NORMATIVE DATA; N=50 COUNSELING CLIENTS)
        @APPLICATION 1964 G-21 H-200

1291   CRITES, J. O.
          TEST REVIEWS: THE CALIFORNIA PSYCHOLOGICAL INVENTORY: II. AS A MEASURE OF
          CLIENT PERSONALITIES.
          JOURNAL OF COUNSELING PSYCHOLOGY, 1964, 11, 299-306.
               (REVIEW ARTICLE)
        @APPLICATION 1964 G-22

1292   LANDFIELD, A. W., & NAWAS, M. M.
          PSYCHOTHERAPEUTIC IMPROVEMENT AS A FUNCTION OF COMMUNICATION AND ADOPTION
          OF THERAPIST'S VALUES.
          JOURNAL OF COUNSELING PSYCHOLOGY, 1964, 11, 336-341.
               (MODIFICATION; CORRELATES:PSYCHOLOGICAL; USED AS CRITERION; N=36
               COUNSELING CLIENTS, 6 PSYCHOLOGISTS)
        @APPLICATION 1964 K-23

1293   MATULEF, N. J., WARMAN, R. E., & BROCK, T. C.
          EFFECTS OF BRIEF VOCATIONAL COUNSELING ON TEMPORAL ORIENTATION.
          JOURNAL OF COUNSELING PSYCHOLOGY, 1964, 11, 352-356.
               (CORRELATES:PSYCHOLOGICAL, ENVIRONMENTAL; NORMATIVE DATA; N=103
               COLLEGE STUDENTS REQUESTING COUNSELING)
        @APPLICATION 1964 L-57 M-207 B-259

1294   SATTLER, J. M.
          COUNSELOR COMPETENCE, INTEREST AND TIME PERSPECTIVE.
          JOURNAL OF COUNSELING PSYCHOLOGY, 1964, 11, 357-360.
               (CORRELATES:PSYCHOLOGICAL; N=28 NATIONAL DEFENSE EDUCATION ACT
               GUIDANCE INSTITUTE PARTICIPANTS)
        @APPLICATION 1964 K-34

1295   STEINMANN, A., LEVI, J., & FOX, D. J.
          SELF-CONCEPT OF COLLEGE WOMEN COMPARED WITH THEIR CONCEPT OF IDEAL WOMAN
          AND MEN'S IDEAL WOMAN.
          JOURNAL OF COUNSELING PSYCHOLOGY, 1964, 11, 370-374.
               (MODIFICATION; CORRELATES:PSYCHOLOGICAL; USED AS CRITERION; NORMATIVE
               DATA; N=75 FEMALE UNDERGRADUATES)
        @APPLICATION 1964 B-258

1296   MATTHEWS, E., & TIEDEMAN, D. V.
          ATTITUDES TOWARD CAREER AND MARRIAGE AND THE DEVELOPMENT OF LIFE STYLE IN
          YOUNG WOMEN.
          JOURNAL OF COUNSELING PSYCHOLOGY, 1964, 11, 375-384.
               (CORRELATES:PSYCHOLOGICAL, DEMOGRAPHIC; N=1237 FEMALES, AGES 11-26)
        @APPLICATION 1964 M-208

1297   DE SENA, P. A.
          THE EFFECTIVENESS OF TWO STUDY-HABITS INVENTORIES IN PREDICTING CONSISTENT
          OVER-, UNDER- AND NORMAL ACHIEVEMENT IN COLLEGE.
          JOURNAL OF COUNSELING PSYCHOLOGY, 1964, 11, 388-393.
               (RELIABILITY:INTERNAL CONSISTENCY; VALIDITY:CRITERION; N=126 MALE
               UNDERGRADUATES)
        @APPLICATION 1964 B-74 B-247

1298   CAMPBELL, D. P.
          RESEARCH FRONTIER: THE CENTER FOR INTEREST MEASUREMENT RESEARCH.
          JOURNAL OF COUNSELING PSYCHOLOGY, 1964, 11, 395-399.
               (MENTION; REVIEW ARTICLE)
        @APPLICATION 1964 S-33 C-52

1299   ASTIN, A. W.
          THE USE OF TESTS IN RESEARCH ON STUDENTS OF HIGH ABILITY.
          JOURNAL OF COUNSELING PSYCHOLOGY, 1964, 11, 400-404.
               (REVIEW ARTICLE)
        @APPLICATION 1964 S-33 C-10 G-22 H-21 H-12 M-22 G-53 B-37 B-4 B-79 B-5 B-6 N-42
        @R-8 T-11 B-282 S-333

1300   MCARTHUR, C.
            THE VALIDITY OF THE YALE STRONG SCALES AT HARVARD.
            JOURNAL OF COUNSELING PSYCHOLOGY, 1965, 12, 35-38.
                    (REVIEW ARTICLE; VALIDITY:CROSS-VALIDATION; N=246 UNDERGRADUATES)
        @APPLICATION 1965 S-33 R-21

1301   BRUNKEN, R. J.
            PERCEIVED PARENTAL ATTITUDES AND PARENTAL IDENTIFICATION IN RELATION TO
            FIELD OF VOCATIONAL CHOICE.
            JOURNAL OF COUNSELING PSYCHOLOGY, 1965, 12, 39-47.
                    (CORRELATES:PSYCHOLOGICAL; NORMATIVE DATA; N=298 MALE UNDERGRADUATES)
        @APPLICATION 1965 B-135 T-100 D-16

1302   KASSARJIAN, H. H., & KASSARJIAN, W. M.
            OCCUPATIONAL INTERESTS, SOCIAL VALUES AND SOCIAL CHARACTER.
            JOURNAL OF COUNSELING PSYCHOLOGY, 1965, 12, 48-54.
                    (CORRELATES:PSYCHOLOGICAL; USED AS CRITERION; NORMATIVE DATA; N=233
                    UNDERGRADUATES)
        @APPLICATION 1965 K-35 A-7 S-33

1303   ROBERTS, R. R., JR., & RENZAGLIA, G. A.
            THE INFLUENCE OF TAPE RECORDING ON COUNSELING.
            JOURNAL OF COUNSELING PSYCHOLOGY, 1965, 12, 10-16.
                    (CORRELATES:BEHAVIORAL, PSYCHOLOGICAL, ENVIRONMENTAL; USED AS
                    CRITERION; N=48 UNDERGRADUATES)
        @APPLICATION 1965 M-172 R-141 S-335

1304   POOL, D. A.
            THE RELATIONSHIP OF PERSONALITY NEEDS TO VOCATIONAL COUNSELING OUTCOME.
            JOURNAL OF COUNSELING PSYCHOLOGY, 1965, 12, 23-27.
                    (MODIFICATION; RELIABILITY:RETEST, INTERRATER;
                    CORRELATES:PSYCHOLOGICAL; USED AS CRITERION; NORMATIVE DATA; N=50
                    WHITE MALE HOSPITALIZED PATIENTS)
        @APPLICATION 1965 C-223 E-2

1305   ASTIN, A. W.
            EFFECTS OF DIFFERENT COLLEGE ENVIRONMENTS ON THE VOCATIONAL CHOICES OF HIGH
            APTITUDE STUDENTS.
            JOURNAL OF COUNSELING PSYCHOLOGY, 1965, 12, 28-34.
                    (CORRELATES:BEHAVIORAL, PSYCHOLOGICAL, INTELLIGENCE; N=3538 MALE
                    UNDERGRADUATES)
        @APPLICATION 1965 A-31

1306   RITCHEY, R. E.
            PREDICTING SUCCESS OF SCHIZOPHRENICS IN INDUSTRIAL THERAPY.
            JOURNAL OF COUNSELING PSYCHOLOGY, 1965, 12, 68-73.
                    (MENTION; CORRELATES:BEHAVIORAL, PSYCHOLOGICAL; N=192 MALE
                    SCHIZOPHRENIC VETERAN PATIENTS)
        @APPLICATION 1965 G-26 J-60 P-144

1307   CAUGHREN, H. J., JR.
            THE RELATIONSHIP OF STIMULUS-STRUCTURE AND SELECTED PERSONALITY
            VARIABLES TO THE DISCOMFORT-RELIEF QUOTIENT IN AUTOBIOGRAPHIES.
            JOURNAL OF COUNSELING PSYCHOLOGY, 1965, 12, 74-80.
                    (RELIABILITY:INTER-RATER; CORRELATES:BEHAVIORAL, PSYCHOLOGICAL,
                    ENVIRONMENTAL; N=85 MALE, 91 FEMALE UNDERGRADUATES)
        @APPLICATION 1965 W-41 D-45 L-93 L-103 G-22 R-25 T-2 W-8 C-136 D-56
        @W-55

1308   CRITES, J. O.
            RESEARCH FRONTIER: THE VOCATIONAL DEVELOPMENT PROJECT AT THE UNIVERSITY
            OF IOWA.
            JOURNAL OF COUNSELING PSYCHOLOGY, 1965, 12, 81-86.
                    (MENTION)
        @APPLICATION 1965 C-217 B-118 E-2 S-33

1309   HEILBRUN, A. B., JR.
            COUNSELING READINESS: A TREATMENT-SPECIFIC OR GENERAL FACTOR?
            JOURNAL OF COUNSELING PSYCHOLOGY, 1965, 12, 87-90.
                    (MENTION; CORRELATES:BEHAVIORAL, PSYCHOLOGICAL; USED AS CRITERION;
                    NORMATIVE DATA; N=72 MALE COLLEGE STUDENTS)
        @APPLICATION 1965 G-21 C-221 H-200

1310   WATLEY, D. J.
            THE MINNESOTA COUNSELING INVENTORY AND PERSISTENCE IN AN INSTITUTE OF
            TECHNOLOGY.
            JOURNAL OF COUNSELING PSYCHOLOGY, 1965, 12, 94-97.
                (CORRELATES:BEHAVIORAL, INTELLIGENCE; USED AS CRITERION; NORMATIVE
                DATA; N=6C8 FRESHMAN MALES)
        aAPPLICATION 1965 B-11

1311   THOMPSON, A.
            CONDITIONING OF WORK ORIENTED AND WORK AVERSIVE STATEMENTS OF
            NEUROPSYCHIATRIC PATIENTS.
            JOURNAL OF COUNSELING PSYCHOLOGY, 1965, 12, 115-120.
                (RELIABILITY:INTER-RATER; CORRELATES:PSYCHOLOGICAL, ENVIRONMENTAL;
                NORMATIVE DATA; N=45 MALE PSYCHIATRIC PATIENTS)
        aAPPLICATION 1965 T-101

1312   HERSHENSON, D. B.
            SOME PERSONAL AND SOCIAL DETERMINANTS OF OCCUPATIONAL ROLE-TAKING IN
            COLLEGE STUDENTS.
            JOURNAL OF COUNSELING PSYCHOLOGY, 1965, 12, 206-208.
                (DESCRIPTION; CORRELATES:PSYCHOLOGICAL, DEMOGRAPHIC; USED AS
                CRITERION; N=162 MALE UNDERGRADUATES)
        aAPPLICATION 1965 H-186 P-111

1313   HILLS, D. A., & WILLIAMS, J. E.
            EFFECTS OF TEST INFORMATION UPON SELF-EVALUATION IN BRIEF
            EDUCATIONAL-VOCATIONAL COUNSELING.
            JOURNAL OF COUNSELING PSYCHOLOGY, 1965, 12, 275-281.
                (MENTION; CORRELATES:PSYCHOLOGICAL, ENVIRONMENTAL; 5 SAMPLES: TOTAL
                N=250 COUNSELING CLIENTS)
        aAPPLICATION 1965 S-33 K-34 B-6C

1314   CLELAND, R. S., & CARNES, G. D.
            EMOTIONAL VS. IDEATIONAL EMPHASIS DURING GROUP COUNSELING WITH STUDENT
            NURSES.
            JOURNAL OF COUNSELING PSYCHOLOGY, 1965, 12, 282-286.
                (CORRELATES:PSYCHOLOGICAL, ENVIRONMENTAL; USED AS CRITERION; N=143
                PSYCHIATRIC STUDENT NURSES)
        aAPPLICATION 1965 G-31 J-14

1315   ZYTOWSKI, D. G.
            CHARACTERISTICS OF MALE UNIVERSITY STUDENTS WITH WEAK OCCUPATIONAL
            SIMILARITY ON THE STRONG VOCATIONAL INTEREST BLANK.
            JOURNAL OF COUNSELING PSYCHOLOGY, 1965, 12, 182-185.
                (VALIDITY:CONSTRUCT; USED AS CRITERION; NORMATIVE DATA; N=70 MALE
                STUDENTS)
        aAPPLICATION 1965 S-33 K-34

1316   TAYLOR, R. G., & FARQUHAR, W.
            PERSONALITY, MOTIVATION AND ACHIEVEMENT: THEORETICAL CONSTRUCTS AND
            EMPIRICAL FACTORS.
            JOURNAL OF COUNSELING PSYCHOLOGY, 1965, 12, 186-191.
                (DESCRIPTION; VALIDITY:CONSTRUCT; FACTOR ANALYSIS; N=75 MALE, 75
                FEMALE OVERACHIEVING, 75 MALE, 75 FEMALE UNDERACHIEVING STUDENTS)
        aAPPLICATION 1965 T-22

1317   CAHOON, D. D.
            A COMPARISON OF THE EFFECTIVENESS OF VERBAL REINFORCEMENT APPLIED IN GROUP
            AND INDIVIDUAL INTERVIEWS.
            JOURNAL OF COUNSELING PSYCHOLOGY, 1965, 12, 121-126.
                (DESCRIPTION, MODIFICATION; CORRELATES:PSYCHOLOGICAL, ENVIRONMENTAL;
                USED AS CRITERION; N=48 MALE NEUROPSYCHIATRIC PATIENTS)
        aAPPLICATION 1965 T-101

1318   STRONG, D. J., & INSEL, S. A.
            PERCEPTIONS OF THE COUNSELOR ROLE AMONG A VARIETY OF REHABILITATION
            COUNSELING SUPERVISORS.
            JOURNAL OF COUNSELING PSYCHOLOGY, 1965, 12, 141-147.
                (FACTOR ANALYSIS; N=25 COUNSELING SUPERVISORS INVOLVED IN
                REHABILITATION COUNSELING)
        aAPPLICATION 1965 A-83

1319   PERRONE, P. A., WEIKING, M. L., & NAGEL, E. H.
        THE COUNSELING FUNCTION AS SEEN BY STUDENTS, PARENTS AND TEACHERS.
        JOURNAL OF COUNSELING PSYCHOLOGY, 1965, 12, 148-152.
                (MODIFICATION; RELIABILITY:INTERRATER; CORRELATES:BEHAVIORAL,
                PSYCHOLOGICAL; USED AS CRITERION; NORMATIVE DATA; N=371 7TH AND 8TH
                GRADERS, 250 PAIRS OF PARENTS, 9 CLASSROOM TEACHERS)
        @APPLICATION 1965 R-142 M-172

1320   CAMPBELL, D. P.
        ACHIEVEMENTS OF COUNSELED AND NON-COUNSELED STUDENTS TWENTY-FIVE YEARS
        AFTER COUNSELING.
        JOURNAL OF COUNSELING PSYCHOLOGY, 1965, 12, 287-293.
                (CORRELATES:PSYCHOLOGICAL, INTELLIGENCE; N=427 COUNSELED, 297
                NON-COUNSELED SUBJECTS IN FOLLOW-UP STUDY)
        @APPLICATION 1965 S-33

1321   MUENCH, G. P.
        AN INVESTIGATION OF THE EFFICACY OF TIME-LIMITED PSYCHOTHERAPY.
        JOURNAL OF COUNSELING PSYCHOLOGY, 1965, 12, 294-299.
                (CORRELATES:PSYCHOLOGICAL, ENVIRONMENTAL; N=105 COUNSELING CLIENTS)
        @APPLICATION 1965 R-31 M-50

1322   STEWART, L. H., RONNING, R. R., & STELLWAGEN, W. R.
        FACTOR STRUCTURE UNDERLYING ITEM DOMAINS ON AN EQUISECTION MEASURE OF
        INTERESTS.
        JOURNAL OF COUNSELING PSYCHOLOGY, 1965, 12, 300-305.
                (FACTOR ANALYSIS; N=188 JUNIOR COLLEGE MALES)
        @APPLICATION 1965 R-55

1323   SCHROEDER, P.
        RELATIONSHIP OF KUDER'S CONFLICT AVOIDANCE AND DOMINANCE TO ACADEMIC
        ACHIEVEMENT.
        JOURNAL OF COUNSELING PSYCHOLOGY, 1965, 12, 395-399.
                (CORRELATES:INTELLIGENCE; USED AS CRITERION; NORMATIVE DATA;
                2 STUDIES: N=192 UNDERGRADUATES, 468 UNDERGRADUATES)
        @APPLICATION 1965 K-34

1324   ROSE, H. A.
        PREDICTION AND PREVENTION OF FRESHMAN ATTRITION.
        JOURNAL OF COUNSELING PSYCHOLOGY, 1965, 12, 399-403.
                (VALIDITY:CONSTRUCT, CRITERION; CORRELATES:BEHAVIORAL, PSYCHOLOGICAL;
                N=60 DEFAULTING, 46 PERSISTING COLLEGE MALES)
        @APPLICATION 1965 R-31 H-12

1325   MARR, E.
        SOME BEHAVIORS AND ATTITUDES RELATING TO VOCATIONAL CHOICE.
        JOURNAL OF COUNSELING PSYCHOLOGY, 1965, 12, 404-408.
                (MODIFICATION; CORRELATES:PSYCHOLOGICAL, INTELLIGENCE; USED AS
                CRITERION; NORMATIVE DATA; N=129 9TH GRADE BOYS)
        @APPLICATION 1965 B-18

1326   GREEN, L. B., & PARKER, H. J.
        PARENTAL INFLUENCE UPON ADOLESCENTS' OCCUPATIONAL CHOICE: A TEST OF AN
        ASPECT OF ROE'S THEORY.
        JOURNAL OF COUNSELING PSYCHOLOGY, 1965, 12, 379-383.
                (RELIABILITY:INTERNAL CONSISTENCY; CORRELATES:PSYCHOLOGICAL,
                DEMOGRAPHIC; NORMATIVE DATA; N=205 MALE, 150 FEMALE 7TH GRADERS)
        @APPLICATION 1965 R-41

1327   WINKLER, R. C., TEIGLAND, J. J., MUNGER, P. F., & KRANZLER, G. D.
        THE EFFECTS OF SELECTED COUNSELING AND REMEDIAL TECHNIQUES ON
        UNDERACHIEVING ELEMENTARY SCHOOL STUDENTS.
        JOURNAL OF COUNSELING PSYCHOLOGY, 1965, 12, 384-387.
                (CORRELATES:PSYCHOLOGICAL, INTELLIGENCE, ENVIRONMENTAL; USED AS
                CRITERION; N=79 MALE, 29 FEMALE ELEMENTARY SCHOOL UNDERACHIEVERS)
        @APPLICATION 1965 T-25

1328   CHESTNUT, W. J.
        THE EFFECTS OF STRUCTURED AND UNSTRUCTURED GROUP COUNSELING ON MALE
        COLLEGE STUDENTS' UNDERACHIEVEMENT.
        JOURNAL OF COUNSELING PSYCHOLOGY, 1965, 12, 388-394.
                (CORRELATES:BEHAVIORAL, PSYCHOLOGICAL, INTELLIGENCE, ENVIRONMENTAL;
                N=683 MALE UNDERGRADUATES)
        @APPLICATION 1965 S-56 B-74

1329   MILLS, D. H., & ABELES, N.
        COUNSELOR NEEDS FOR AFFILIATION AND NURTURANCE AS RELATED TO LIKING FOR
        CLIENTS AND COUNSELING PROCESS.
        JOURNAL OF COUNSELING PSYCHOLOGY, 1965, 12, 353-358.
            (CORRELATES:PSYCHOLOGICAL, ENVIRONMENTAL: USED AS CRITERION: N=37
            COUNSELORS WITH VARYING DEGREES OF EXPERIENCE)
        @APPLICATION 1965 E-2 O-16

1330   PALLONE, N. J., & GRANDE, P. P.
        COUNSELOR VERBAL MODE, PROBLEM RELEVANT COMMUNICATION, AND CLIENT RAPPORT.
        JOURNAL OF COUNSELING PSYCHOLOGY, 1965, 12, 359-365.
            (CORRELATES:BEHAVIORAL, PSYCHOLOGICAL; USED AS CRITERION; N=80
            SECONDARY SCHOOL STUDENTS)
        @APPLICATION 1965 R-28 A-84

1331   OURTH, L., & LANDFIELD, A. W.
        INTERPERSONAL MEANINGFULNESS AND NATURE OF TERMINATION IN PSYCHOTHERAPY.
        JOURNAL OF COUNSELING PSYCHOLOGY, 1965, 12, 366-371.
            (MODIFICATION; CORRELATES:BEHAVIORAL; NORMATIVE DATA; N=17 MALE,
            22 FEMALE CLIENTS, 1 FEMALE, 5 MALE THERAPISTS)
        @APPLICATION 1965 K-23

1332   WHITELEY, J. M., & HUMMEL, R.
        ADAPTIVE EGO FUNCTIONING IN RELATION TO ACADEMIC ACHIEVEMENT.
        JOURNAL OF COUNSELING PSYCHOLOGY, 1965, 12, 306-310.
            (CORRELATES:PSYCHOLOGICAL, INTELLIGENCE; N=20 SUPERIOR ACHIEVING,
            20 UNDERACHIEVING HIGH SCHOOL BOYS)
        @APPLICATION 1965 M-20

1333   CRITES, J. O.
        TEST REVIEWS.
        JOURNAL OF COUNSELING PSYCHOLOGY, 1965, 12, 328-331.
            (DESCRIPTION; REVIEW ARTICLE)
        @APPLICATION 1965 W-79 F-7

1334   BOHN, M. J., JR.
        COUNSELOR BEHAVIOR AS A FUNCTION OF COUNSELOR DOMINANCE, COUNSELOR
        EXPERIENCE AND CLIENT TYPE.
        JOURNAL OF COUNSELING PSYCHOLOGY, 1965, 12, 346-352.
            (CORRELATES:BEHAVIORAL, PSYCHOLOGICAL; USED AS CRITERION;
            NORMATIVE DATA; N=30 MALE EXPERIENCED COUNSELOR GRADUATE STUDENTS, 30
            MALE INEXPERIENCED COUNSELOR UNDERGRADUATES)
        @APPLICATION 1965 G-22 G-19 S-339

1335   FOREMAN, M. E.
        SOME EMPIRICAL CORRELATES OF PSYCHOLOGICAL HEALTH.
        JOURNAL OF COUNSELING PSYCHOLOGY, 1966, 13, 3-11.
            (CORRELATES:BEHAVIORAL, PSYCHOLOGICAL; NORMATIVE DATA; N=29 NORMAL,
            29 ZESTFUL COLLEGE STUDENTS)
        @APPLICATION 1966 S-33 M-172

1336   STEWART, L. H.
        CHARACTERISTICS OF JUNIOR COLLEGE STUDENTS IN OCCUPATIONALLY ORIENTED
        CURRICULA.
        JOURNAL OF COUNSELING PSYCHOLOGY, 1966, 13, 46-52.
            (DESCRIPTION; CORRELATES:PSYCHOLOGICAL, DEMOGRAPHIC; USED AS
            CRITERION; NORMATIVE DATA; N=285 MALE, 115 FEMALE STUDENTS IN
            VOCATIONAL CURRICULA, 282 JUNIOR COLLEGE STUDENTS)
        @APPLICATION 1966 R-55 H-12

1337   WATLEY, D. J.
        COUNSELOR VARIABILITY IN MAKING ACCURATE PREDICTIONS.
        JOURNAL OF COUNSELING PSYCHOLOGY, 1966, 13, 53-62.
            (RELIABILITY:INTER-RATER; VALIDITY:CRITERION; CORRELATES:
            PSYCHOLOGICAL, INTELLIGENCE; USED AS CRITERION; N=66 COUNSELORS,
            45 STUDENT JUDGES, 200 COLLEGE MALES)
        @APPLICATION 1966 D-45 S-33 E-2

1338   WATLEY, D. J.
        COUNSELOR CONFIDENCE IN ACCURACY OF PREDICTIONS.
        JOURNAL OF COUNSELING PSYCHOLOGY, 1966, 13, 62-67.
            (VALIDITY:CONSTRUCT; CORRELATES:PSYCHOLOGICAL, INTELLIGENCE;
            N=66 COUNSELORS, 200 COLLEGE MALES)
        @APPLICATION 1966 E-2 D-45

1339   COOK, T. E.
        THE INFLUENCE OF CLIENT-COUNSELOR VALUE SIMILARITY ON CHANGE IN MEANING
        DURING BRIEF COUNSELING.
        JOURNAL OF COUNSELING PSYCHOLOGY, 1966, 13, 77-81.
            (RELIABILITY:RETEST; CORRELATES:PSYCHOLOGICAL; USED AS CRITERION;
            N=54 MALE, 38 FEMALE COLLEGE STUDENTS, 45 ADVANCED COUNSELING
            TRAINEES)
    @APPLICATION 1966 A-7 O-16

1340   MILLS, D. H., CHESTNUT, W. J., & HARTZELL, J. P.
        THE NEEDS OF COUNSELORS: A COMPONENT ANALYSIS.
        JOURNAL OF COUNSELING PSYCHOLOGY, 1966, 13, 82-84.
            (VALIDITY:CONSTRUCT; CORRELATES:PSYCHOLOGICAL; USED AS CRITERION;
            CLUSTER ANALYSIS; N=37 COUNSELING CENTER STAFF MEMBERS)
    @APPLICATION 1966 E-2

1341   HEWER, V. H.
        EVALUATION OF A CRITERION: REALISM OF VOCATIONAL CHOICE.
        JOURNAL OF COUNSELING PSYCHOLOGY, 1966, 13, 289-294.
            (CORRELATES:PSYCHOLOGICAL, DEMOGRAPHIC, INTELLIGENCE; USED AS
            CRITERION; N=78 MEN AND 15 WOMEN)
    @APPLICATION 1966 S-33 D-45

1342   HARMON, L. W.
        OCCUPATIONAL SATISFACTION: A BETTER CRITERION?
        JOURNAL OF COUNSELING PSYCHOLOGY, 1966, 13, 295-299.
            (REVISION; RELIABILITY:INTERNAL CONSISTENCY; VALIDITY:CONSTRUCT,
            CRITERION; NORMATIVE DATA; N=128 STUDENTS SEEKING JOBS)
    @APPLICATION 1966 H-188

1343   BOHN, M, J., JR.
        PSYCHOLOGICAL NEEDS RELATED TO VOCATIONAL PERSONALITY TYPES.
        JOURNAL OF COUNSELING PSYCHOLOGY, 1966, 13, 306-309.
            (CORRELATES:PSYCHOLOGICAL; N=75 MALE CLIENTS OF UNIVERSITY
            COUNSELING)
    @APPLICATION 1966 S-33 G-21

1344   BROWN, R. A., & POOL, D. A.
        PSYCHOLOGICAL NEEDS AND SELF-AWARENESS.
        JOURNAL OF COUNSELING PSYCHOLOGY, 1966, 13, 85-88.
            (VALIDITY:CONSTRUCT; CORRELATES:PSYCHOLOGICAL; USED AS CRITERION;
            N=50 WHITE MALE PATIENTS)
    @APPLICATION 1966 E-2 S-33

1345   GROSS, W. F., & DERIDDER, L. M.
        SIGNIFICANT MOVEMENT IN COMPARATIVELY SHORT-TERM COUNSELING.
        JOURNAL OF COUNSELING PSYCHOLOGY, 1966, 13, 98-99.
            (CORRELATES:BEHAVIORAL, PSYCHOLOGICAL; N=8 COUNSELING CENTER CLIENTS)
    @APPLICATION 1966 B-50

1346   WRIGHT, F. H., & KLEIN, R. A.
        ATTITUDES OF HOSPITAL PERSONNEL AND THE COMMUNITY REGARDING MENTAL
        ILLNESS.
        JOURNAL OF COUNSELING PSYCHOLOGY, 1966, 13, 106-107.
            (CORRELATES:BEHAVIORAL, PSYCHOLOGICAL; N=100 PEOPLE)
    @APPLICATION 1966 W-40

1347   WILLIAMS, V.
        DIFFICULTIES IN IDENTIFYING RELATIVELY PERMANENT CHARACTERISTICS RELATED
        TO PERSISTENCE IN COLLEGE.
        JOURNAL OF COUNSELING PSYCHOLOGY, 1966, 13, 108.
            (VALIDITY:CROSS-VALIDATION; CORRELATES:BEHAVIORAL, PSYCHOLOGICAL,
            INTELLIGENCE; 2 STUDIES: N=17 DROP-OUTS, 17 PERSISTER MALE
            UNDERGRADUATES; 18 DROP-OUTS, 18 PERSISTER MALE UNDERGRADUATES)
    @APPLICATION 1966 S-33 B-128 G-26

1348   HARTLAGE, L. C.
        RECEPTIVITY OF EMPLOYERS TO HIRING MENTALLY RETARDED AND EX-MENTAL
        PATIENTS.
        JOURNAL OF COUNSELING PSYCHOLOGY, 1966, 13, 112-114.
            (CORRELATES:BEHAVIORAL, PSYCHOLOGICAL; USED AS CRITERION; N=120
            EMPLOYERS)
    @APPLICATION 1966 H-189

1349   CRITES, J. O.
            TEST REVIEWS.
            JOURNAL OF COUNSELING PSYCHOLOGY, 1966, 13, 120-122.
                (REVIEW ARTICLE)
        @APPLICATION 1966 H-188 K-139 B-215

1350   RABINOWITZ, M.
            THE RELATIONSHIP OF SELF REGARD TO THE EFFECTIVENESS OF LIFE
            EXPERIENCES.
            JOURNAL OF COUNSELING PSYCHOLOGY, 1966, 13, 139-143.
                (CORRELATES:PSYCHOLOGICAL; USED AS CRITERION; N=70 WHITE MALES)
        @APPLICATION 1966 B-18 S-155

1351   MUELLER, W. J.
            ANXIETY LEVEL, INFERRED IDENTIFICATION AND RESPONSE TENDENCIES ON A
            SEMANTIC DIFFERENTIAL.
            JOURNAL OF COUNSELING PSYCHOLOGY, 1966, 13, 144-152.
                (CORRELATES:PSYCHOLOGICAL; USED AS CRITERION; N=346 MALE, 300 FEMALE
                UNDERGRADUATES)
        @APPLICATION 1966 D-45 T-2

1352   OPPENHEIMER, E. A.
            THE RELATIONSHIP BETWEEN CERTAIN SELF CONSTRUCTS AND OCCUPATIONAL
            PREFERENCES.
            JOURNAL OF COUNSELING PSYCHOLOGY, 1966, 13, 191-197.
                (MODIFICATION; RELIABILITY:RETEST; VALIDITY: CONSTRUCT;
                CORRELATES:BEHAVIORAL, PSYCHOLOGICAL; N=81 MALE UNDERGRADUATES)
        @APPLICATION 1966 S-33 K-23

1353   CATRON, D. W.
            EDUCATIONAL-VOCATIONAL GROUP COUNSELING: THE EFFECTS ON PERCEPTION OF
            SELF AND OTHERS.
            JOURNAL OF COUNSELING PSYCHOLOGY, 1966, 13, 202-207.
                (MODIFICATION; CORRELATES:BEHAVIORAL, PSYCHOLOGICAL; USED AS
                CRITERION; N=110 HIGH SCHOOL STUDENTS)
        @APPLICATION 1966 B-60

1354   NEURINGER, C., MYERS, R., & NORDMARK, T., JR.
            THE TRANSFER OF A VERBALLY CONDITIONED RESPONSE CLASS.
            JOURNAL OF COUNSELING PSYCHOLOGY, 1966, 13, 208-213.
                (VALIDITY:CONSTRUCT; CORRELATES:BEHAVIORAL; USED AS CRITERION;
                N=26 PAIRS OF UNDERGRADUATES)
        @APPLICATION 1966 A-7

1355   WHITTEMORE, R. G., JR., & HEIMANN, R. A.
            MODIFICATION OF ORIGINALITY RESPONSES.
            JOURNAL OF COUNSELING PSYCHOLOGY, 1966, 13, 213-218.
                (MODIFICATION; VALIDITY:CONSTRUCT, CRITERION; CORRELATES:BEHAVIORAL,
                PSYCHOLOGICAL; USED AS CRITERION; N=80 MALE STUDENTS)
        @APPLICATION 1966 F-39 B-257 C-226 M-72 H-187 M-29

1356   ARKOFF, A., THAVER, F., & ELKIND, L.
            MENTAL HEALTH AND COUNSELING IDEAS OF ASIAN AND AMERICAN STUDENTS.
            JOURNAL OF COUNSELING PSYCHOLOGY, 1966, 13, 219-223.
                (CORRELATES:BEHAVIORAL, PSYCHOLOGICAL; CROSS-CULTURAL APPLICATION;
                N=24 AMERICAN, 19 CHINESE, 19 FILIPINOS, 21 JAPANESE, 15 THAI
                GRADUATE STUDENTS)
        @APPLICATION 1966 N-25

1357   OETTING, E. R.
            EXAMINATION ANXIETY: PREDICTION, PHYSIOLOGICAL RESPONSE AND RELATION TO
            SCHOLASTIC PERFORMANCE.
            JOURNAL OF COUNSELING PSYCHOLOGY, 1966, 13, 224-227.
                (VALIDITY:CONSTRUCT, CRITERION; CORRELATES:PSYCHOLOGICAL,
                PHYSIOLOGICAL, INTELLIGENCE, ENVIRONMENTAL; USED AS CRITERION;
                N=50 UNDERGRADUATES)
        @APPLICATION 1966 D-45

1358   MENDELSOHN, G. A.
            EFFECTS OF CLIENT PERSONALITY AND CLIENT-COUNSELOR SIMILARITY ON THE
            DURATION OF COUNSELING: A REPLICATION AND EXTENSION.
            JOURNAL OF COUNSELING PSYCHOLOGY, 1966, 13, 228-234.
                (CORRELATES:BEHAVIORAL, PSYCHOLOGICAL; USED AS CRITERION; N=111 MALE,
                90 FEMALE CLIENTS, 5 MALE, 6 FEMALE COUNSELORS)
        @APPLICATION 1966 M-22

1359   LUNNEBORG, P. W., & LUNNEBORG, C. E.
            THE UTILITY OF EPPS SCORES FOR PREDICTION OF ACADEMIC ACHIEVEMENT AMONG
            COUNSELING CLIENTS.
            JOURNAL OF COUNSELING PSYCHOLOGY, 1966, 13, 241-245.
                (VALIDITY:CONSTRUCT; CORRELATES:PSYCHOLOGICAL, DEMOGRAPHIC,
                INTELLIGENCE; N=300 COUNSELING CLIENTS)
        @APPLICATION 1966 E-2

1360   BERZON, B., & SOLOMON, L. N.
            THE SELF-DIRECTED THERAPEUTIC GROUP: THREE STUDIES.
            JOURNAL OF COUNSELING PSYCHOLOGY, 1966, 13, 491-497.
                (CORRELATES:ENVIRONMENTAL; USED AS CRITERION; N=96 ADULT MEN AND
                WOMEN IN 12 THERAPEUTIC GROUPS)
        @APPLICATION 1966 B-50 D-45

1361   DELANEY, D. J., & HEIMANN, R. A.
            EFFECTIVENESS OF SENSITIVITY TRAINING ON THE PERCEPTION OF NON-VERBAL
            COMMUNICATIONS.
            JOURNAL OF COUNSELING PSYCHOLOGY, 1966, 13, 436-440.
                (MODIFICATION; CORRELATES:ENVIRONMENTAL; NORMATIVE DATA; N=16 MALE
                AND FEMALE COUNSELING STUDENTS)
        @APPLICATION 1966 O-16

1362   BERENSON, B. G., CARKHUFF, R. R., & MYRUS, P.
            THE INTERPERSONAL FUNCTIONING AND TRAINING OF COLLEGE STUDENTS.
            JOURNAL OF COUNSELING PSYCHOLOGY, 1966, 13, 441-446.
                (MODIFICATION; RELIABILITY:RETEST; VALIDITY:CRITERION; NORMATIVE
                DATA; N=36 MALE AND FEMALE UNDERGRADUATES)
        @APPLICATION 1966 T-37 T-89 T-69 T-74

1363   OSEAS, L.
            "GIVE US THE FIRST NATURAL ANSWER."
            JOURNAL OF COUNSELING PSYCHOLOGY, 1966, 13, 454-458.
                (USED AS CRITERION; NORMATIVE DATA; BIAS:RESPONSE, TESTER; N=1
                PSYCHOLOGIST)
        @APPLICATION 1966 C-10

1364   BRUNKAN, R. J.
            PERCEIVED PARENTAL ATTITUDES AND PARENTAL IDENTIFICATION IN RELATION TO
            PROBLEMS IN VOCATIONAL CHOICE.
            JOURNAL OF COUNSELING PSYCHOLOGY, 1966, 13, 394-402.
                (MODIFICATION; CORRELATES:PSYCHOLOGICAL, INTELLIGENCE; USED AS
                CRITERION; NORMATIVE DATA; N=289 MALE UNDERGRADUATES)
        @APPLICATION 1966 S-33 B-135 T-100 O-16

1365   CAMPBELL, D. P., & JOHANSSON, C. B.
            ACADEMIC INTERESTS, SCHOLASTIC ACHIEVEMENTS AND EVENTUAL OCCUPATIONS.
            JOURNAL OF COUNSELING PSYCHOLOGY, 1966, 13, 416-424.
                (REVISION; RELIABILITY:RETEST; VALIDITY:CRITERION, CROSS-VALIDATION;
                NORMATIVE DATA; N=712 MALE UNDERGRADUATES, 283 ADULTS)
        @APPLICATION 1966 S-33

1366   ELTON, C. F., & ROSE, H. A.
            PERSONALITY CHARACTERISTICS: THEIR RELEVANCE IN DISCIPLINARY CASES.
            JOURNAL OF COUNSELING PSYCHOLOGY, 1966, 13, 431-435.
                (CORRELATES:BEHAVIORAL, INTELLIGENCE; USED AS CRITERION; NORMATIVE
                DATA; N=520 MALE UNDERGRADUATES WITH DISCIPLINARY RECORDS)
        @APPLICATION 1966 H-12

1367   FRETZ, B. R.
            POSTURAL MOVEMENTS IN A COUNSELING DYAD.
            JOURNAL OF COUNSELING PSYCHOLOGY, 1966, 13, 335-343.
                (DESCRIPTION; RELIABILITY:INTERNAL CONSISTENCY;
                CORRELATES:BEHAVIORAL, PSYCHOLOGICAL; USED AS CRITERION; NORMATIVE
                DATA; N=4 GRADUATE MALE AND 8 GRADUATE FEMALE COUNSELORS, 17 CLIENTS,
                AND 13 OBSERVERS)
        @APPLICATION 1966 B-50 C-230

1368   FRETZ, B. R.
            PERSONALITY CORRELATES OF POSTURAL MOVEMENTS.
            JOURNAL OF COUNSELING PSYCHOLOGY, 1966, 13, 344-347.
                (DESCRIPTION; CORRELATES:BEHAVIORAL, PSYCHOLOGICAL; USED AS
                CRITERION; NORMATIVE DATA; N=17 PATIENT-CLIENT DYADS)
        @APPLICATION 1966 M-22 R-8 C-27 J-6 A-28

1369   WHITE, W. F., & PORTER, T. L.
        SELF CONCEPT REPORTS AMONG HOSPITALIZED ALCOHOLICS DURING EARLY PERIODS
        OF SOBRIETY.
        JOURNAL OF COUNSELING PSYCHOLOGY, 1966, 13, 352-355.
              (MENTION; CORRELATES:BEHAVIORAL, PSYCHOLOGICAL; USED AS CRITERION;
              N=35 HOSPITALIZED MALE ALCOHOLICS)
        @APPLICATION 1966 R-138 M-9

1370   BERDIE, R. F., & STEIN, J.
        A COMPARISON OF NEW UNIVERSITY STUDENTS WHO DO AND DO NOT SEEK COUNSELING.
        JOURNAL OF COUNSELING PSYCHOLOGY, 1966, 13, 310-317.
              (CORRELATES:BEHAVIORAL, PSYCHOLOGICAL, DEMOGRAPHIC, INTELLIGENCE,
              ENVIRONMENTAL; USED AS CRITERION; N=3937 COLLEGE STUDENTS)
        @APPLICATION 1966 S-33

1371   FOLDS, J. H., & GAZDA, G. M.
        A COMPARISON OF THE EFFECTIVENESS AND EFFICIENCY OF THREE METHODS OF TEST
        INTERPRETATION.
        JOURNAL OF COUNSELING PSYCHOLOGY, 1966, 13, 318-324.
              (DESCRIPTION; USED AS CRITERION; BIAS:RESPONSE; N=108 FEMALE COLLEGE
              STUDENTS)
        @APPLICATION 1966 B-18 E-2

1372   PERSONS, R. W., & PEPINSKY, H. B.
        CONVERGENCE IN PSYCHOTHERAPY WITH DELINQUENT BOYS.
        JOURNAL OF COUNSELING PSYCHOLOGY, 1966, 13, 329-334.
              (CORRELATES:BEHAVIORAL, PSYCHOLOGICAL; N=41 INCARCERATED
              DELINQUENTS)
        @APPLICATION 1966 T-2 G-82 D-45 K-34

1373   VAN ATTA, R. E.
        A METHOD FOR THE STUDY OF CLINICAL THINKING.
        JOURNAL OF COUNSELING PSYCHOLOGY, 1966, 13, 259-266.
              (RELIABILITY:INTERRATER; USED AS CRITERION; FACTOR ANALYSIS; N=8
              PSYCHOLOGISTS)
        @APPLICATION 1966 B-126

1374   HARREN, V. A.
        THE VOCATIONAL DECISION-MAKING PROCESS AMONG COLLEGE MALES.
        JOURNAL OF COUNSELING PSYCHOLOGY, 1966, 13, 271-277.
              (MENTION; CORRELATES:PSYCHOLOGICAL, DEMOGRAPHIC; N=86 LIBERAL ARTS
              UNDERGRADUATE MALES--STRATIFIED SAMPLE)
        @APPLICATION 1966 S-30 E-1

1375   HOLLAND, J. L.
        A PSYCHOLOGICAL CLASSIFICATION SCHEME FOR VOCATIONS AND MAJOR FIELDS.
        JOURNAL OF COUNSELING PSYCHOLOGY, 1966, 13, 278-288.
              (DESCRIPTION; CORRELATES:PSYCHOLOGICAL, DEMOGRAPHIC; USED AS
              CRITERION; NORMATIVE DATA; N=5600 MALES AND 5560 FEMALES)
        @APPLICATION 1966 H-21 N-12 R-8 F-26

1376   MARTIN, J. C., CARKHUFF, R. R., & BERENSON, B. G.
        PROCESS VARIABLES IN COUNSELING AND PSYCHOTHERAPY: A STUDY OF COUNSELING
        AND FRIENDSHIP.
        JOURNAL OF COUNSELING PSYCHOLOGY, 1966, 13, 356-359.
              (MODIFICATION)
        @APPLICATION 1966 T-24 T-37 T-48

1377   ROTHAUS, P., JOHNSON, D. L., HANSON, P. G., BROWN, J. B., & LYLE, F. A.
        SENTENCE-COMPLETION TEST PREDICTION OF AUTONOMOUS AND THERAPIST-LED
        GROUP BEHAVIOR.
        JOURNAL OF COUNSELING PSYCHOLOGY, 1967, 14, 28-34.
              (VALIDITY:CRITERION; CORRELATES:BEHAVIORAL, PSYCHOLOGICAL,
              ENVIRONMENTAL; N=63 PSYCHIATRIC PATIENTS)
        @APPLICATION 1967 R-135 R-136

1378   ALLEN, T. W.
        EFFECTIVENESS OF COUNSELOR TRAINEES AS A FUNCTION OF PSYCHOLOGICAL
        OPENNESS.
        JOURNAL OF COUNSELING PSYCHOLOGY, 1967, 14, 35-40.
              (DESCRIPTION; RELIABILITY:INTERRATER; VALIDITY:CRITERION;
              CORRELATES:BEHAVIORAL, PSYCHOLOGICAL; N=26 GRADUATE STUDENTS IN
              COUNSELING)
        @APPLICATION 1967 L-26 S-285

1379   MCGREEVY, C. P.
              FACTOR ANALYSIS OF MEASURES USED IN THE SELECTION AND EVALUATION OF
              COUNSELOR EDUCATION CANDIDATES.
              JOURNAL OF COUNSELING PSYCHOLOGY, 1967, 14, 51-56.
                    (CORRELATES:PSYCHOLOGICAL, DEMOGRAPHIC, INTELLIGENCE; FACTOR
                    ANALYSIS; N=86 COUNSELING-GUIDANCE STUDENTS)
        @APPLICATION 1967 D-45 E-2

1380   ASTIN, A. S.
              ASSESSMENT OF EMPATHIC ABILITY BY MEANS OF A SITUATIONAL TEST.
              JOURNAL OF COUNSELING PSYCHOLOGY, 1967, 14, 57-60.
                    (VALIDITY:CRITERION; CORRELATES:BEHAVIORAL, PSYCHOLOGICAL; N=16
                    GRADUATE STUDENTS)
        @APPLICATION 1967 A-7

1381   CUMMINS, E. J., & LINDBLADE, Z. G.
              SEX-BASED DIFFERENCES AMONG STUDENT DISCIPLINARY OFFENDERS.
              JOURNAL OF COUNSELING PSYCHOLOGY, 1967, 14, 81-85.
                    (DESCRIPTION; VALIDITY:CRITERION; CORRELATES:BEHAVIORAL,
                    PSYCHOLOGICAL; N=95 MALE, 49 FEMALE COLLEGE STUDENTS)
        @APPLICATION 1967 R-8 P-111

1382   VELDMAN, D. J.
              COMPUTER-BASED SENTENCE-COMPLETION INTERVIEWS.
              JOURNAL OF COUNSELING PSYCHOLOGY, 1967, 14, 153-157.
                    (MODIFICATION; VALIDITY:CONTENT; N=6 MALE, 6 FEMALE UNDERGRADUATES)
        @APPLICATION 1967 V-28

1383   ASHBROOK, J. B., & POWELL, R. K.
              COMPARISON OF GRADUATING AND NONGRADUATING THEOLOGICAL STUDENTS ON THE
              MINNESOTA MULTIPHASIC PERSONALITY INVENTORY.
              JOURNAL OF COUNSELING PSYCHOLOGY, 1967, 14, 171-174.
                    (VALIDITY:CRITERION; USED AS CRITERION; N=162 THEOLOGICAL STUDENTS)
        @APPLICATION 1967 D-45

1384   FRETZ, B. R., & SCHMIDT, L. D.
              COMPARISON OF IMPROVERS AND NONIMPROVERS IN AN EDUCATIONAL SKILLS COURSE.
              JOURNAL OF COUNSELING PSYCHOLOGY, 1967, 14, 175-176.
                    (VALIDITY:CRITERION; CORRELATES:BEHAVIORAL, INTELLIGENCE;
                    NORMATIVE DATA; N=144 UNDERGRADUATES)
        @APPLICATION 1967 M-22 C-27 R-8 J-6

1385   GABBERT, K. H., IVEY, A. E., & MILLER, C. D.
              COUNSELOR ASSIGNMENT AND CLIENT ATTITUDE.
              JOURNAL OF COUNSELING PSYCHOLOGY, 1967, 14, 131-136.
                    (CORRELATES:PSYCHOLOGICAL; USED AS CRITERION; N=405 UNDERGRADUATES)
        @APPLICATION 1967 L-76

1386   MINGE, M. R., & BOWMAN, T. F.
              PERSONALITY DIFFERENCES AMONG NONCLIENTS AND VOCATIONAL-EDUCATIONAL AND
              PERSONAL COUNSELING CLIENTS.
              JOURNAL OF COUNSELING PSYCHOLOGY, 1967, 14, 137-139.
                    (VALIDITY:CRITERION; CORRELATES:PSYCHOLOGICAL; N=71 UNDERGRADUATES IN
                    COUNSELING, 54 CONTROLS)
        @APPLICATION 1967 E-2

1387   DICKEN, C., & FORDHAM, M.
              EFFECTS OF REINFORCEMENT OF SELF-REFERENCES IN QUASI-THERAPEUTIC
              INTERVIEWS.
              JOURNAL OF COUNSELING PSYCHOLOGY, 1967, 14, 145-152.
                    (CORRELATES:BEHAVIORAL, PSYCHOLOGICAL, ENVIRONMENTAL;
                    USED AS CRITERION; N=100 FEMALE UNDERGRADUATES, 50 SELECTED)
        @APPLICATION 1967 G-22

1388   ELTON, C. F.
              MALE CAREER ROLE AND VOCATIONAL CHOICE: THEIR PREDICTION WITH PERSONALITY
              AND APTITUDE VARIABLES.
              JOURNAL OF COUNSELING PSYCHOLOGY, 1967, 14, 99-105.
                    (CORRELATES:BEHAVIORAL, DEMOGRAPHIC; USED AS CRITERION; N=875 MALE
                    UNDERGRADUATES)
        @APPLICATION 1967 H-12

1389   MADAUS, G. F., & O'HARA, R. P.
            VOCATIONAL INTEREST PATTERNS OF HIGH SCHOOL BOYS: A MULTIVARIATE
            APPROACH.
            JOURNAL OF COUNSELING PSYCHOLOGY, 1967, 14, 106-112.
                    (VALIDITY:CRITERION; USED AS CRITERION; N=979 HIGH SCHOOL MALES)
        @APPLICATION 1967 K-34

1390   CATTELL, R. B., & KRUG, S.
            PERSONALITY FACTOR PROFILE PECULIAR TO THE STUDENT SMOKER.
            JOURNAL OF COUNSELING PSYCHOLOGY, 1967, 14, 116-121.
                    (CORRELATES:BEHAVIORAL: USED AS CRITERION; N=256 MALE AND FEMALE
                    UNDERGRADUATES)
        @APPLICATION 1967 C-10

1391   CRITES, J. O., & SENTER, I. J.
            ADJUSTMENT, EDUCATIONAL ACHIEVEMENT, AND VOCATIONAL MATURITY AS
            DIMENSIONS OF DEVELOPMENT IN ADOLESCENCE.
            JOURNAL OF COUNSELING PSYCHOLOGY, 1967, 14, 489-496.
                    (RELIABILITY:RETEST, INTERRATER; VALIDITY:CRITERION;
                    CORRELATES:PSYCHOLOGICAL, INTELLIGENCE; N=483 5TH GRADE SCHOOL
                    CHILDREN FOLLOWED UP AS 12TH GRADERS)
        @APPLICATION 1967 S-287 T-25

1392   ROSSMANN, J. E., & LIPS, O.
            VOCATIONAL INTERESTS OF SOCIOLOGISTS.
            JOURNAL OF COUNSELING PSYCHOLOGY, 1967, 14, 497-502.
                    (CORRELATES:BEHAVIORAL, PSYCHOLOGICAL; N=179 MALE MEMBERS OF MIDWEST
                    SOCIOLOGICAL SOCIETY)
        @APPLICATION 1967 S-33

1393   WINBORN, B. B., & JANSEN, D. G.
            PERSONALITY CHARACTERISTICS OF CAMPUS SOCIAL-POLITICAL ACTION LEADERS.
            JOURNAL OF COUNSELING PSYCHOLOGY, 1967, 14, 509-513.
                    (CORRELATES:BEHAVIORAL, DEMOGRAPHIC; N=257 ELECTED LEADERS OF
                    STUDENT ORGANIZATIONS)
        @APPLICATION 1967 C-10

1394   LUNNEBORG, C. E., & LUNNEBORG, P. W.
            EPPS PATTERNS IN THE PREDICTION OF ACADEMIC ACHIEVEMENT.
            JOURNAL OF COUNSELING PSYCHOLOGY, 1967, 14, 389-390.
                    (VALIDITY:CRITERION; CORRELATES:BEHAVIORAL, INTELLIGENCE; USED AS
                    CRITERION; N=62 MALE, 59 FEMALE UNDERGRADUATES)
        @APPLICATION 1967 E-2

1395   HIGGINS, M. J.
            TEST REVIEWS.
            JOURNAL OF COUNSELING PSYCHOLOGY, 1967, 14, 392-393.
                    (REVIEW ARTICLE)
        @APPLICATION 1967 B-74

1396   ROTHNEY, J. W. M.
            TEST REVIEWS.
            JOURNAL OF COUNSELING PSYCHOLOGY, 1967, 14, 187-191.
                    (REVIEW ARTICLE; RELIABILITY:RETEST; VALIDITY:CRITERION; NO SAMPLE
                    DESCRIPTION)
        @APPLICATION 1967 S-33 C-52

1397   GRIFFITH, A. V.
            SELF-EXPRESSIVE STYLES AMONG ADULTS ENROLLED IN NON-CREDIT CONTINUING
            EDUCATION COURSES.
            JOURNAL OF COUNSELING PSYCHOLOGY, 1967, 14, 514-522.
                    (VALIDITY:CONSTRUCT, CRITERION; N=132 ADULTS ENROLLED IN ADULT
                    EDUCATION CLASSES)
        @APPLICATION 1967 D-40

1398   PALLONE, N. J., & DIBENNARDO, F. R.
            INTERVIEW SEQUENCE IN RELATION TO COUNSELOR VERBAL MODE, CLIENT
            PROBLEM-RELATED CONTENT, AND RAPPORT.
            JOURNAL OF COUNSELING PSYCHOLOGY, 1967, 14, 523-525.
                    (CORRELATES:BEHAVIORAL, PSYCHOLOGICAL; N=42 SECONDARY SCHOOL
                    COUNSELING CLIENTS)
        @APPLICATION 1967 R-28 A-84 P-114 P-115

1399   MCGREEVY, C. P., & DAANE, C. J.
        CHANGES IN SEMANTIC DIFFERENTIAL MEANING THAT ACCOMPANY COUNSELING.
        JOURNAL OF COUNSELING PSYCHOLOGY, 1967, 14, 526-534.
                (VALIDITY:CRITERION; N=28 CLIENTS, 14 DOCTORAL COUNSELING MAJORS)
        @APPLICATION 1967 O-16

1400   ROCHESTER, D. E.
        PERSISTENCE OF ATTITUDES AND VALUES OF NDEA COUNSELOR TRAINEES.
        JOURNAL OF COUNSELING PSYCHOLOGY, 1967, 14, 535-537.
                (VALIDITY:CRITERION; NORMATIVE DATA; N=126 COUNSELOR TRAINEES)
        @APPLICATION 1967 A-7 P-116

1401   ELTON, C. F., & ROSE, H. A.
        TRADITIONAL SEX ATTITUDES AND DISCREPANT ABILITY MEASURES IN COLLEGE
        WOMEN.
        JOURNAL OF COUNSELING PSYCHOLOGY, 1967, 14, 538-543.
                (VALIDITY:CROSS-VALIDATION; CORRELATES:INTELLIGENCE; FACTOR ANALYSIS;
                2 STUDIES: N=349 FRESHMEN WOMEN, N=148 FRESHMEN WOMEN)
        @APPLICATION 1967 H-12

1402   BARCLAY, J. R.
        APPROACH TO THE MEASUREMENT OF TEACHER "PRESS" IN THE SECONDARY
        CURRICULUM.
        JOURNAL OF COUNSELING PSYCHOLOGY, 1967, 14, 552-567.
                (CORRELATES:PSYCHOLOGICAL, DEMOGRAPHIC, INTELLIGENCE,
                ENVIRONMENTAL; NORMATIVE DATA; N=1562 MALE, 1602 FEMALE HIGH SCHOOL
                STUDENTS)
        @APPLICATION 1967 H-21 G-22 C-52 F-129 L-128

1403   FERNALD, P. S., & MAKAREWICZ, J. F.
        USE OF PERSONAL VALIDATION.
        JOURNAL OF COUNSELING PSYCHOLOGY, 1967, 14, 568-569.
                (VALIDITY:CRITERION; N=16 MALE, 6 FEMALE COLLEGE FRESHMEN)
        @APPLICATION 1967 F-96 S-103

1404   MILLS, D. H., & ZYROWSKI, D. G.
        HELPING RELATIONSHIP: A STRUCTURAL ANALYSIS.
        JOURNAL OF COUNSELING PSYCHOLOGY, 1967, 14, 193-197.
                (RELIABILITY:RETEST, INTERNAL CONSISTENCY; N=79 UNDERGRADUATE
                FEMALES)
        @APPLICATION 1967 B-50

1405   ZIMMER, J. M., & PARK, P.
        FACTOR ANALYSIS OF COUNSELOR COMMUNICATIONS.
        JOURNAL OF COUNSELING PSYCHOLOGY, 1967, 14, 198-203.
                (FACTOR ANALYSIS; N=75 HIGH SCHOOL GRADUATES)
        @APPLICATION 1967 S-143

1406   EMERY, J. R., & KRUMBOLTZ, J. D.
        STANDARD VERSUS INDIVIDUALIZED HIERARCHIES IN DESENSITIZATION TO REDUCE
        TEST ANXIETY.
        JOURNAL OF COUNSELING PSYCHOLOGY, 1967, 14, 204-209.
                (CORRELATES:BEHAVIORAL, PSYCHOLOGICAL; USED AS CRITERION; N=830 MALE,
                248 FEMALE COLLEGE STUDENTS)
        @APPLICATION 1967 E-70

1407   MENDELSOHN, G. A., & GELLER, M. H.
        SIMILARITY, MISSED SESSIONS, AND EARLY TERMINATION.
        JOURNAL OF COUNSELING PSYCHOLOGY, 1967, 14, 210-215.
                (CORRELATES:BEHAVIORAL: N=11 MALE, 90 FEMALE COUNSELING CLIENTS,
                11 COUNSELORS)
        @APPLICATION 1967 M-22

1408   WHITELEY, J. M., SPRINTHALL, N. A., MOSHER, R. L., & DONAGHY, R. T.
        SELECTION AND EVALUATION OF COUNSELOR EFFECTIVENESS.
        JOURNAL OF COUNSELING PSYCHOLOGY, 1967, 14, 226-234.
                (RELIABILITY:INTERRATER; VALIDITY:CRITERION;
                CORRELATES:PSYCHOLOGICAL, INTELLIGENCE; N=7 MALE, 12 FEMALE STUDENTS)
        @APPLICATION 1967 R-30 M-20 A-79

1409   ROTHAUS, P., JOHNSON, D. L., & BLANK, G.
            CHANGING THE CONNOTATIONS OF MENTAL ILLNESS IN PSYCHIATRIC PATIENTS.
            JOURNAL OF COUNSELING PSYCHOLOGY, 1967, 14, 258-263.
                (MODIFICATION; REVISION; RELIABILITY:INTERRATER;
                VALIDITY:CRITERION; N=70 PSYCHIATRIC PATIENTS IN HUMAN RELATIONS
                TRAINING).
        @APPLICATION 1967 S-286

1410   YAMAMOTO, K., & DIZNEY, H. F.
            REJECTION OF THE MENTALLY ILL: A STUDY OF ATTITUDES OF STUDENT TEACHERS.
            JOURNAL OF COUNSELING PSYCHOLOGY, 1967, 14, 264-268.
                (MODIFICATION; CORRELATES:PSYCHOLOGICAL, DEMOGRAPHIC; N=70 MALE, 110
                FEMALE STUDENT TEACHERS)
        @APPLICATION 1967 S-305 P-105

1411   IRVIN, F. S.
            SENTENCE-COMPLETION RESPONSES AND SCHOLASTIC SUCCESS OR FAILURE.
            JOURNAL OF COUNSELING PSYCHOLOGY, 1967, 14, 269-271.
                (REVISION; CORRELATES:PSYCHOLOGICAL, INTELLIGENCE; N=171 1ST YEAR
                COLLEGE STUDENTS)
        @APPLICATION 1967 P-113 Z-36

1412   ROTH, R. M., & PURI, P.
            DIRECTION OF AGGRESSION AND THE NONACHIEVEMENT SYNDROME.
            JOURNAL OF COUNSELING PSYCHOLOGY, 1967, 14, 277-281.
                (RELIABILITY:INTERRATER; VALIDITY:CRITERION; CORRELATES:DEMOGRAPHIC,
                INTELLIGENCE; N= UNKNOWN NUMBER OF SCHOOL CHILDREN FROM 3RD, 6TH,
                9TH, AND 12TH GRADES)
        @APPLICATION 1967 R-12

1413   LEIB, J. W., & SNYDER, W. V.
            EFFECTS OF GROUP DISCUSSIONS ON UNDERACHIEVEMENT AND SELF-ACTUALIZATION.
            JOURNAL OF COUNSELING PSYCHOLOGY, 1967, 14, 282-285.
                (CORRELATES:PSYCHOLOGICAL; ENVIRONMENTAL; USED AS CRITERION; N=28
                UNDERACHIEVING COLLEGE STUDENTS)
        @APPLICATION 1967 S-21

1414   BAKER, J. N.
            EFFECTIVENESS OF CERTAIN MMPI DISSIMULATION SCALES UNDER 'REAL LIFE'
            SITUATIONS.
            JOURNAL OF COUNSELING PSYCHOLOGY, 1967, 14, 286-292.
                (BIAS:RESPONSE; N=106 UNDERGRADUATE FEMALES)
        @APPLICATION 1967 D-45 E-1 W-14 F-13 C-58 H-122 G-127 W-164

1415   LADD, C. E.
            RECORD-KEEPING AND RESEARCH IN PSYCHIATRIC AND PSYCHOLOGICAL CLINICS.
            JOURNAL OF COUNSELING PSYCHOLOGY, 1967, 14, 361-367.
                (MENTION)
        @APPLICATION 1967 D-45 R-30 M-20 G-78

1416   STRICKER, G.
            INTERRELATIONSHIPS OF ACTIVITIES INDEX AND COLLEGE CHARACTERISTICS INDEX
            SCORES.
            JOURNAL OF COUNSELING PSYCHOLOGY, 1967, 14, 368-370.
                (CORRELATES:PSYCHOLOGICAL, ENVIRONMENTAL; USED AS CRITERION;
                N=821 MALE AND FEMALE UNDERGRADUATES)
        @APPLICATION 1967 P-30 S-56

1417   WRIGHT, J. J.
            REPORTED PERSONAL STRESS SOURCES AND ADJUSTMENT OF ENTERING FRESHMEN.
            JOURNAL OF COUNSELING PSYCHOLOGY, 1967, 14, 371-373.
                (VALIDITY:CRITERION; CORRELATES:PSYCHOLOGICAL; USED AS CRITERION;
                N=500 MALE AND FEMALE UNDERGRADUATES)
        @APPLICATION 1967 D-45 W-166 L-68

1418   COOKE, M. K., & KIESLER, C. J.
            PREDICTION OF COLLEGE STUDENTS WHO LATER REQUIRE PERSONAL COUNSELING.
            JOURNAL OF COUNSELING PSYCHOLOGY, 1967, 14, 346-349.
                (VALIDITY:CRITERION; CORRELATES:BEHAVIORAL, PSYCHOLOGICAL; NORMATIVE
                DATA; N=40 MALE, 40 FEMALE UNDERGRADUATES)
        @APPLICATION 1967 D-45 W-8

1419   CARKHUFF, R. R., & ALEXIK, M.
            EFFECT OF CLIENT DEPTH OF SELF-EXPLORATION UPON HIGH- AND LOW-FUNCTIONING
            COUNSELORS.
            JOURNAL OF COUNSELING PSYCHOLOGY, 1967, 14, 350-355.
                (DESCRIPTION; RELIABILITY:RETEST; CORRELATES:BEHAVIORAL; N=1 CLIENT,
                    8 COUNSELORS)
        @APPLICATION 1967 C-218

1420   FRANK, G. H., & HIESTER, D. S.
            RELIABILITY OF THE IDEAL-SELF-CONCEPT.
            JOURNAL OF COUNSELING PSYCHOLOGY, 1967, 14, 356-357.
                (RELIABILITY:RETEST; USED AS CRITERION; NORMATIVE DATA; N=40 MALE,
                    40 FEMALE UNDERGRADUATES)
        @APPLICATION 1967 S-40

1421   GOLDSCHMID, M. L.
            PREDICTION OF COLLEGE MAJORS BY PERSONALITY TESTS.
            JOURNAL OF COUNSELING PSYCHOLOGY, 1967, 14, 302-308.
                (VALIDITY:CRITERION, CROSS-VALIDATION; CORRELATES:BEHAVIORAL;
                    N = APPROX. 2400 MALE AND FEMALE COLLEGE STUDENTS)
        @APPLICATION 1967 G-22 D-45 M-22 H-12 S-33

1422   WATLEY, D. J.
            COUNSELOR PREDICTIVE SKILL AND DIFFERENTIAL JUDGMENTS OF OCCUPATIONAL
            STABILITY.
            JOURNAL OF COUNSELING PSYCHOLOGY, 1967, 14, 309-313.
                (CORRELATES:BEHAVIORAL; USED AS CRITERION; N=50 COLLEGE MALES)
        @APPLICATION 1967 D-45 S-33

1423   HERSHENSON, D. B.
            SENSE OF IDENTITY, OCCUPATIONAL FIT, AND ENCULTURATION IN ADOLESCENCE.
            JOURNAL OF COUNSELING PSYCHOLOGY, 1967, 14, 319-324.
                (DESCRIPTION; RELIABILITY:INTERNAL CONSISTENCY;
                    CORRELATES:PSYCHOLOGICAL; USED AS CRITERION; NORMATIVE DATA;
                    N=162 COLLEGE MALES)
        @APPLICATION 1967 B-36 C-152 P-111 H-186

1424   ZYTOWSKI, D. G.
            INTERNAL-EXTERNAL CONTROL OF REINFORCEMENT AND THE STRONG VOCATIONAL
            INTEREST BLANK.
            JOURNAL OF COUNSELING PSYCHOLOGY, 1967, 14, 177-179.
                (VALIDITY:CRITERION; CORRELATES:BEHAVIORAL, PSYCHOLOGICAL;
                    USED AS CRITERION; NORMATIVE DATA; N=62 MALE UNDERGRADUATES)
        @APPLICATION 1967 S-33 R-18

1425   ELTON, C. F., & ROSE, H. A.
            SIGNIFICANCE OF PERSONALITY IN THE VOCATIONAL CHOICE OF COLLEGE WOMEN.
            JOURNAL OF COUNSELING PSYCHOLOGY, 1967, 14, 293-298.
                (VALIDITY: CRITERION; CORRELATES:BEHAVIORAL; NORMATIVE DATA; N=510
                    FEMALE UNDERGRADUATES)
        @APPLICATION 1967 H-12

1426   HARMON, L. W.
            WOMEN'S WORKING PATTERNS RELATED TO THEIR SVIB HOUSEWIFE AND "OWN"
            OCCUPATIONAL SCORES.
            JOURNAL OF COUNSELING PSYCHOLOGY, 1967, 14, 299-301.
                (VALIDITY:CRITERION; CORRELATES:BEHAVIORAL, DEMOGRAPHIC; NORMATIVE
                    DATA; N=98 ADULT WOMEN)
        @APPLICATION 1967 S-33

1427   THORNDIKE, R. M., WEISS, D. J., & DAVIS, R. V.
            CANONICAL CORRELATION OF VOCATIONAL INTERESTS AND VOCATIONAL NEEDS.
            JOURNAL OF COUNSELING PSYCHOLOGY, 1968, 15, 101-106.
                (DESCRIPTION; CORRELATES:PSYCHOLOGICAL; N=269 MALE UNDERGRADUATES)
        @APPLICATION 1968 S-33 W-97

1428   HUTCHINSON, T., & ROE, A.
            STUDIES OF OCCUPATIONAL HISTORY: PART II. ATTRACTIVENESS OF OCCUPATIONAL
            GROUPS OF THE ROE SYSTEM.
            JOURNAL OF COUNSELING PSYCHOLOGY, 1968, 15, 107-110.
                (CORRELATES:BEHAVIORAL; N=804 MEN)
        @APPLICATION 1968 R-138

1429   JOHNSON, R. W., & FREDRICKSON, R. H.
            EFFECT OF FINANCIAL REMUNERATION AND CASE DESCRIPTION ON COUNSELOR
            PERFORMANCE.
            JOURNAL OF COUNSELING PSYCHOLOGY, 1968, 15, 130-135.
                (CORRELATES:ENVIRONMENTAL; N=48 UNDERGRADUATES)
        @APPLICATION 1968 K-134

1430   GILLILAND, B. E.
            SMALL GROUP COUNSELING WITH NEGRO ADOLESCENTS IN A PUBLIC HIGH SCHOOL.
            JOURNAL OF COUNSELING PSYCHOLOGY, 1968, 15, 147-152.
                (CORRELATES:INTELLIGENCE; USED AS CRITERION; N=15 BOYS AND 15 GIRLS)
        @APPLICATION 1968 H-26 C-26 B-18

1431   SCHULDT, W. J., & TRUAX, C. B.
            CLIENT AWARENESS OF ADJUSTMENT IN SELF- AND IDEAL-SELF-CONCEPTS.
            JOURNAL OF COUNSELING PSYCHOLOGY, 1968, 15, 158-159.
                (CORRELATES:PSYCHOLOGICAL; USED AS CRITERION; N=114 HOSPITALIZED
                MENTAL PATIENTS)
        @APPLICATION 1968 B-60

1432   PARSONS, O. A., YOURSHAW, S., & BORSTELMANN, L.
            SELF-IDEAL-SELF DISCREPANCIES ON THE MMPI: CONSISTENCIES OVER TIME AND
            GEOGRAPHIC REGION.
            JOURNAL OF COUNSELING PSYCHOLOGY, 1968, 15, 160-166.
                (USED AS CRITERION; N=33 MALE AND 25 FEMALE UNDERGRADUATES)
        @APPLICATION 1968 D-45 W-8 B-46

1433   BAIRD, L. L.
            THE INDECISION SCALE: A REINTERPRETATION.
            JOURNAL OF COUNSELING PSYCHOLOGY, 1968, 15, 174-179.
                (VALIDITY:CONSTRUCT, CROSS-VALIDATION; CORRELATES:PSYCHOLOGICAL,
                DEMOGRAPHIC, INTELLIGENCE; 2 SAMPLES: N=6,290 MALE AND 6,143 FEMALE
                COLLEGE FRESHMEN, 1576 MALE AND 1571 FEMALE COLLEGE FRESHMEN)
        @APPLICATION 1968 H-46 A-2 N-12

1434   TENNISON, J. C., & SNYDER, W. U.
            SOME RELATIONSHIPS BETWEEN ATTITUDES TOWARD THE CHURCH AND CERTAIN
            PERSONALITY CHARACTERISTICS.
            JOURNAL OF COUNSELING PSYCHOLOGY, 1968, 15, 187-189.
                (CORRELATES:PSYCHOLOGICAL; N=299 COLLEGE STUDENTS)
        @APPLICATION 1968 T-23 K-36 E-2

1435   IVEY, A. E., MILLER, C. D., & GABBERT, K. H.
            COUNSELOR ASSIGNMENT AND CLIENT ATTITUDE: A SYSTEMATIC REPLICATION.
            JOURNAL OF COUNSELING PSYCHOLOGY, 1968, 15, 194-195.
                (USED AS CRITERION; N=492 COLLEGE STUDENTS)
        @APPLICATION 1968 L-76

1436   WAZMAN, M.
            UNIVERSITY ACHIEVEMENT AND DAYDREAMING BEHAVIOR.
            JOURNAL OF COUNSELING PSYCHOLOGY, 1968, 15, 196-198.
                (DESCRIPTION; MODIFICATION; CORRELATES:PSYCHOLOGICAL, DEMOGRAPHIC,
                INTELLIGENCE; N=105 MALE AND 101 FEMALE UNDERGRADUATES)
        @APPLICATION 1968 S-82

1437   EYDE, L. D.
            WORK MOTIVATION OF WOMEN COLLEGE GRADUATES: FIVE-YEAR FOLLOW-UP.
            JOURNAL OF COUNSELING PSYCHOLOGY, 1968, 15, 199-202.
                (CORRELATES:PSYCHOLOGICAL, ENVIRONMENTAL; NORMATIVE DATA; N=106
                COLLEGE GRADUATES)
        @APPLICATION 1968 E-68 E-69

1438   LEMAY, M. L., & CHRISTENSEN, O. C., JR.
            THE UNCONTROLLABLE NATURE OF CONTROL GROUPS.
            JOURNAL OF COUNSELING PSYCHOLOGY, 1968, 15, 63-67.
                (USED AS CRITERION; N=144 UNDERACHIEVING COLLEGE FRESHMEN)
        @APPLICATION 1968 S-33 S-21

1439   PAYNE, P. A.
            PLACEBO EFFECTS IN TEST TAKING?
            JOURNAL OF COUNSELING PSYCHOLOGY, 1968, 15, 80-83.
                (USED AS CRITERION; N=80 COLLEGE STUDENTS)
        @APPLICATION 1968 E-2 M-172

1440   EBER, H. W.
              RELATION OF AGE, EDUCATION, AND PERSONALITY CHARACTERISTICS TO MILITARY
              RANK IN AN ARMY RESERVE UNIT.
              JOURNAL OF COUNSELING PSYCHOLOGY, 1968, 15, 89-90.
                     (CORRELATES:DEMOGRAPHIC, INTELLIGENCE; N=306 ARMY RESERVISTS)
       aAPPLICATION 1968 C-10

1441   FAUNCE, P. S.
              PERSONALITY CHARACTERISTICS AND VOCATIONAL INTERESTS RELATED TO THE
              COLLEGE PERSISTENCE OF ACADEMICALLY GIFTED WOMEN.
              JOURNAL OF COUNSELING PSYCHOLOGY, 1968, 15, 31-40.
                     (CORRELATES:PSYCHOLOGICAL, DEMOGRAPHIC; N=723 FEMALE COLLEGE
                     GRADUATES, 526 FEMALES WHO DID NOT GRADUATE)
       aAPPLICATION 1968 D-45 S-33

1442   CULBERT, S. A., CLARK, J. V., & BCHELE, H. K.
              MEASURES OF CHANGE TOWARD SELF-ACTUALIZATION IN TWO SENSITIVITY TRAINING
              GROUPS.
              JOURNAL OF COUNSELING PSYCHOLOGY, 1968, 15, 53-57.
                     (CORRELATES:BEHAVIORAL: USED AS CRITERION; N=20 COLLEGE STUDENTS)
       aAPPLICATION 1968 S-21

1443   ELDER, G. H.
              OCCUPATIONAL LEVEL, ACHIEVEMENT MOTIVATION, AND SOCIAL MOBILITY: A
              LONGITUDINAL ANALYSIS.
              JOURNAL OF COUNSELING PSYCHOLOGY, 1968, 15, 1-7.
                     (CORRELATES:PSYCHOLOGICAL; USED AS CRITERION; N=69 BOYS AND GRILS)
       aAPPLICATION 1968 S-33 H-22 G-22

1444   LUNNEBORG, P. W., & LUNNEBCRG, C. E.
              ROE'S CLASSIFICATION OF OCCUPATIONS IN PREDICTING ACADEMIC ACHIEVEMENT.
              JOURNAL OF COUNSELING PSYCHOLOGY, 1968, 15, 8-16.
                     (REVIEW ARTICLE: DESCRIPTION; RELIABILITY:INTERRATER;
                     VALIDITY:CONTENT, CRITERION; CORRELATES:PSYCHOLOGICAL, DEMOGRAPHIC,
                     INTELLIGENCE; SEVERAL STUDIES)
       aAPPLICATION 1968 W-160 R-138

1445   HARMON, L. W., & CAMPBELL, D. P.
              USE OF INTEREST INVENTORIES WITH NON-PROFESSIONAL WOMEN: STEWARDESSES
              VERSUS DENTAL ASSISTANTS.
              JOURNAL OF COUNSELING PSYCHOLOGY, 1968, 15, 17-22.
                     (REVISION; NORMATIVE DATA; N=440 AIRLINE STEWARDESSES, 417 DENTAL
                     ASSISTANTS)
       aAPPLICATION 1968 S-33

1446   VINGOE, F. J., & ANTONOFF, S. R.
              PERSONALITY CHARACTERISTICS CF GOOD JUDGES OF OTHERS.
              JOURNAL OF COUNSELING PSYCHOLOGY, 1968, 15, 91-93.
                     (CORRELATES:BEHAVIORAL, PSYCHOLOGICAL; N=66 18-YEAR OLD FEMALE
                     COLLEGE FRESHMEN)
       aAPPLICATION 1968 G-22 E-6

1447   DOLE, A. A.
              LOOKING BACKWARD: HOW CONSISTENT ARE RETROSPECTIVE REASONS FOR GOING TO
              COLLEGE?
              JOURNAL OF COUNSELING PSYCHOLOGY, 1968, 15, 263-268.
                     (DESCRIPTION; RELIABILITY:RETEST; NORMATIVE DATA; BIAS:RESPONSE;
                     N=63 MALE AND 59 FEMALE COLLEGE GRADUATES)
       aAPPLICATION 1968
       aD-87

1448   GOUGH, H. G.
              COLLEGE ATTENDANCE AMONG HIGH-APTITUDE STUDENTS AS PREDICTED FROM THE
              CALIFORNIA PSYCHOLOGICAL INVENTORY.
              JOURNAL OF COUNSELING PSYCHOLOGY, 1968, 15, 269-278.
                     (VALIDITY:CRITERION, CROSS-VALIDATION; CORRELATES:DEMOGRAPHIC,
                     INTELLIGENCE; N=220 HIGH-APTITUDE COLLEGE STUDENTS)
       aAPPLICATION 1968 G-22

1449   WILLIAMS, P. A., KIRK, B. A., & FRANK, A. C.
              NEW MEN'S SVIB: A COMPARISON WITH THE OLD.
              JOURNAL OF COUNSELING PSYCHOLOGY, 1968, 15, 287-294.
                     (REVISION; RELIABILITY:INTERRATER; NORMATIVE DATA; N=200 STUDENTS)
       aAPPLICATION 1968 S-33 S-291

1450   BARRY, J. R., DUNTEMAN, G. H., & WEBB, M. W.
            PERSONALITY AND MOTIVATION IN REHABILITATION.
            JOURNAL OF COUNSELING PSYCHOLOGY, 1968, 15, 237-244.
                (CORRELATES:BEHAVIORAL, PSYCHOLOGICAL; FACTOR ANALYSIS; N=110 WHITE
                AND 15 NEGRO MENTAL PATIENTS)
        aAPPLICATION 1968 G-78 S-124 C-27 B-83 B-18 M-32 R-31 M-58

1451   SCHISSEL, R. F.
            DEVELOPMENT OF A CAREER-ORIENTATION SCALE FOR WOMEN.
            JOURNAL OF COUNSELING PSYCHOLOGY, 1968, 15, 257-262.
                (REVISION; CLUSTER ANALYSIS; N=400 FEMALES)
        aAPPLICATION 1968 S-33

1452   POE, C. A.
            ASSESSMENT OF HEATH'S MODEL OF PERSONALITY.
            JOURNAL OF COUNSELING PSYCHOLOGY, 1968, 15, 203-207.
                (RELIABILITY:INTERRATER; VALIDITY:CONSTRUCT;
                CORRELATES:PSYCHOLOGICAL; N=74 MALE UNDERGRADUATES)
        aAPPLICATION 1968 M-20 R-33 M-22

1453   CHAMBERS, J. L., WILSON, W. T., & BARGER, B.
            NEED DIFFERENCES BETWEEN STUDENTS WITH AND WITHOUT RELIGIOUS
            AFFILIATION.
            JOURNAL OF COUNSELING PSYCHOLOGY, 1968, 15, 208-210.
                (DESCRIPTION; CORRELATES:PSYCHOLOGICAL; N=2844 COLLEGE STUDENTS)
        aAPPLICATION 1968 C-13

1454   TRUAX, C. B.
            THERAPIST INTERPERSONAL REINFORCEMENT OF CLIENT SELF-EXPLORATION AND
            THERAPEUTIC OUTCOME IN GROUP PSYCHOTHERAPY.
            JOURNAL OF COUNSELING PSYCHOLOGY, 1968, 15, 225-231.
                (RELIABILITY:INTERRATER; CORRELATES:BEHAVIORAL; USED AS CRITERION;
                N=30 MENTAL PATIENTS)
        aAPPLICATION 1968 D-45 T-38

1455   BUDIE, R. F.
            PERSONALITY CHANGES FROM HIGH SCHOOL ENTRANCE TO COLLEGE MATRICULATION.
            JOURNAL OF COUNSELING PSYCHOLOGY, 1968, 15, 376-380.
                (CORRELATES:DEMOGRAPHIC; NORMATIVE DATA; N=148 MALE AND 111 FEMALE
                COLLEGE STUDENTS)
        aAPPLICATION 1968 B-11

1456   SAGE, E. H.
            DEVELOPMENTAL SCALES FOR COLLEGE FRESHMEN.
            JOURNAL OF COUNSELING PSYCHOLOGY, 1968, 15, 381-385.
                (REVISION; VALIDITY:CROSS-VALIDATION; CORRELATES:DEMOGRAPHIC,
                INTELLIGENCE; N=148 MALE AND 111 FEMALE COLLEGE STUDENTS)
        aAPPLICATION 1968 B-11

1457   PIERCE, R. M.
            COMMENT ON THE PREDICTION OF POST-HOSPITAL WORK ADJUSTMENT WITH
            PSYCHOLOGICAL TESTS.
            JOURNAL OF COUNSELING PSYCHOLOGY, 1968, 15, 386-387.
                (REVIEW ARTICLE)
        aAPPLICATION 1968 D-45 R-30

1458   SHAPIRO, J. G.
            PERCEPTION OF THERAPEUTIC CONDITIONS FROM DIFFERENT VANTAGE POINTS.
            JOURNAL OF COUNSELING PSYCHOLOGY, 1968, 15, 346-350.
                (DESCRIPTION; VALIDITY:CONSTRUCT; CORRELATES:PSYCHOLOGICAL;
                N=16 MALE AND FEMALE SPEECH CLINICIANS)
        aAPPLICATION 1968 S-142 S-292

1459   HAASE, R. F., & MILLER, C. D.
            COMPARISON OF FACTOR ANALYTIC STUDIES OF THE COUNSELING EVALUATION
            INVENTORY.
            JOURNAL OF COUNSELING PSYCHOLOGY, 1968, 15, 363-367.
                (FACTOR ANALYSIS; N=1159 COLLEGE STUDENTS)
        aAPPLICATION 1968 L-76

1460   ELTON, C. F., & ROSE, H. A.
            THE FACE OF CHANGE.
            JOURNAL OF COUNSELING PSYCHOLOGY, 1968, 15, 372-375.
                (FACTOR ANALYSIS; N=76 COLLEGE STUDENTS)
        @APPLICATION 1968 H-12

1461   STIMSON, R. C., JR.
            FACTOR ANALYTIC APPROACH TO THE STRUCTURAL DIFFERENTIATION OF DESCRIPTION.
            JOURNAL OF COUNSELING PSYCHOLOGY, 1968, 15, 301-307.
                (DESCRIPTION; CORRELATES:INTELLIGENCE; FACTOR ANALYSIS; NORMATIVE
                DATA; N=106 SINGLE MALE COLLEGE STUDENTS)
        @APPLICATION 1968 B-18 B-60 D-25 W-21 W-118 G-22 B-34 S-155 T-13 K-23 M-20

1462   HEALY, C. C.
            RELATION OF OCCUPATIONAL CHOICE TO THE SIMILARITY BETWEEN SELF-RATINGS
            AND OCCUPATIONAL RATINGS.
            JOURNAL OF COUNSELING PSYCHOLOGY, 1968, 15, 317-323.
                (VALIDITY:CONSTRUCT; CORRELATES:PSYCHOLOGICAL, DEMOGRAPHIC,
                INTELLIGENCE; N=147 MALE COLLEGE STUDENTS)
        @APPLICATION 1968 K-23 S-33

1463   BYERS, A. P., FORREST, G. G., & ZACCARIA, J. S.
            RECALLED EARLY PARENT-CHILD RELATIONS, ADULT NEEDS, AND OCCUPATIONAL
            CHOICE: A TEST OF ROE'S THEORY.
            JOURNAL OF COUNSELING PSYCHOLOGY, 1968, 15, 324-328.
                (DESCRIPTION; VALIDITY:CONSTRUCT; CORRELATES:PSYCHOLOGICAL,
                DEMOGRAPHIC; N=79 JUNIOR AND 65 SENIOR THEOLOGICAL STUDENTS AND
                127 CLERGY)
        @APPLICATION 1968 E-2 B-135

1464   ROCHESTER, D. E.
            THE USE OF PORTER'S TEST OF COUNSELOR ATTITUDES TO DISCRIMINATE BETWEEN
            ADLERIAN- AND PHENOMENOLOGICALLY-ORIENTED STUDENTS.
            JOURNAL OF COUNSELING PSYCHOLOGY, 1968, 15, 427-429.
                (USED AS CRITERION; N=87 COUNSELOR TRAINEES)
        @APPLICATION 1968 P-116 H-181

1465   OSIPOW, S. H., & GOLD, J. A.
            PERSONAL ADJUSTMENT AND CAREER DEVELOPMENT.
            JOURNAL OF COUNSELING PSYCHOLOGY, 1968, 15, 439-443.
                (CORRELATES:PSYCHOLOGICAL, DEMOGRAPHIC; USED AS CRITERION; N=42
                MALE AND 23 FEMALE COLLEGE STUDENTS)
        @APPLICATION 1968 S-33

1466   RAND, L.
            MASCULINITY OR FEMININITY: DIFFERENTIATING CAREER-ORIENTED AND
            HOMEMAKING-ORIENTED COLLEGE FRESHMEN WOMEN.
            JOURNAL OF COUNSELING PSYCHOLOGY, 1968, 15, 444-450.
                (VALIDITY:CONSTRUCT; CORRELATES:PSYCHOLOGICAL; NORMATIVE DATA;
                N=300 CAREER-ORIENTED WOMEN AND 548 HOMEMAKING-ORIENTED FRESHMEN
                WOMEN)
        @APPLICATION 1968 A-2

1467   BROWN, O. B., & CALLIA, V. F.
            TWO METHODS OF INITIATING STUDENT INTERVIEWS: SELF-INITIATED VS. REQUIRED.
            JOURNAL OF COUNSELING PSYCHOLOGY, 1968, 15, 402-406.
                (CORRELATES:PSYCHOLOGICAL, ENVIRONMENTAL; N=392 COLLEGE FRESHMEN)
        @APPLICATION 1968 B-50

1468   APOSTAL, R. A.
            COMPARISON OF COUNSELEES AND NONCOUNSELEES WITH TYPE OF PROBLEM CONTROLLED.
            JOURNAL OF COUNSELING PSYCHOLOGY, 1968, 15, 407-410.
                (USED AS CRITERION; N=128 COLLEGE STUDENTS COUNSELLED, PLUS CONTROL
                GROUP)
        @APPLICATION 1968 P-68

1469   ZIMMER, J. M., & ANDERSON, S.
            DIMENSIONS OF POSITIVE REGARD AND EMPATHY.
            JOURNAL OF COUNSELING PSYCHOLOGY, 1968, 15, 417-426.
                (DESCRIPTION; FACTOR ANALYSIS; N=100 COUNSELOR RESPONSES)
        @APPLICATION 1968 T-37 C-218

1470   WILSON, R. N., & KAISER, H. E.
           A COMPARISON OF SIMILAR SCALES ON THE SVIB AND THE KUDER, FORM DD.
           JOURNAL OF COUNSELING PSYCHOLOGY, 1968, 15, 468-470.
               (VALIDITY:CONSTRUCT; N=100 MALE FRESHMEN STUDENTS)
       @APPLICATION 1968 S-33 K-34

1471   GASS, A. M.
           IMPORTANCE OF DIAGNOSTIC CATEGORIES IN EVALUATING PSYCHOLOGICAL DATA.
           JOURNAL OF COUNSELING PSYCHOLOGY, 1968, 15, 476-478.
               (USED AS CRITERION; N=98 NEUROPSYCHIATRIC PATIENTS)
       @APPLICATION 1968 S-72

1472   WHEELER, C. L., & CARNES, E. F.
           RELATIONSHIPS AMONG SELF-CONCEPTS, IDEAL-SELF-CONCEPTS, AND STEREOTYPES OF
           PROBABLE AND IDEAL VOCATIONAL CHOICES.
           JOURNAL OF COUNSELING PSYCHOLOGY, 1968, 15, 530-535.
               (DESCRIPTION; REVISION)
       @APPLICATION 1968 B-248

1473   ASTIN, H. S.
           CAREER DEVELOPMENT OF GIRLS DURING THE HIGH SCHOOL YEARS.
           JOURNAL OF COUNSELING PSYCHOLOGY, 1968, 15, 536-540.
               (VALIDITY:CRITERION; CORRELATES:PSYCHOLOGICAL, DEMOGRAPHIC,
               ENVIRONMENTAL; N=817 FEMALE HIGH SCHOOL SENIORS)
       @APPLICATION 1968 S-64

1474   GIPHERS, N. C., JOHNSTON, J. A., & GUST, T.
           CHARACTERISTICS OF HOMEMAKER- AND CAREER-ORIENTED WOMEN.
           JOURNAL OF COUNSELING PSYCHOLOGY, 1968, 15, 541-546.
               (CORRELATES:BEHAVIORAL, PSYCHOLOGICAL, DEMOGRAPHIC; USED AS
               CRITERION: NORMATIVE DATA; N=130 WOMEN)
       @APPLICATION 1968 S-33

1475   LEVENTHAL, A. M.
           ADDITIONAL TECHNICAL DATA ON THE CPI ANXIETY SCALE.
           JOURNAL OF COUNSELING PSYCHOLOGY, 1968, 15, 479-480.
               (RELIABILITY:RETEST; VALIDITY:CONSTRUCT; CORRELATES:PSYCHOLOGICAL;
               NORMATIVE DATA; 3 SAMPLES: N=1454 MALES AND 1291 FEMALES, N=20 MALES
               AND 54 FEMALES, N=2047 MALES AND 2032 FEMALES)
       @APPLICATION 1968 D-45 G-22 L-7 T-2 W-8 C-136

1476   MARTIN, D. G.
           TEST REVIEW: HOLTZMAN INKBLOT TECHNIQUE.
           JOURNAL OF COUNSELING PSYCHOLOGY, 1968, 15, 481-484.
               (MENTION; DESCRIPTION; REVIEW ARTICLE; RELIABILITY:RETEST,
               INTERRATER; VALIDITY:CONSTRUCT, CRITERION; FACTOR ANALYSIS; NORMATIVE
               DATA; NO SAMPLE SIZE IS GIVEN)
       @APPLICATION 1968 H-37 R-30

1477   LEIB, J. W., & SNYDER, W. V.
           ACHIEVEMENT AND POSITIVE MENTAL HEALTH: A SUPPLEMENTARY REPORT.
           JOURNAL OF COUNSELING PSYCHOLOGY, 1968, 15, 388-389.
               (CORRELATES:PSYCHOLOGICAL, INTELLIGENCE; N=354 INTRODUCTORY
               PSYCHOLOGY STUDENTS IN COLLEGE)
       @APPLICATION 1968 S-21

1478   HOLLAND, J. L.
           TEST REVIEWS: TORRANCE TESTS OF CREATIVE THINKING.
           JOURNAL OF COUNSELING PSYCHOLOGY, 1968, 15, 297-298.
               (DESCRIPTION; REVIEW ARTICLE; RELIABILITY:RETEST, INTERRATER;
               VALIDITY:CONSTRUCT, CRITERION; NO SAMPLE SIZE IS GIVEN)
       @APPLICATION 1968 T-39

1479   IRVIN, F. S.
           PERSONALITY CHARACTERISTICS AND VOCATIONAL IDENTIFICATION.
           JOURNAL OF COUNSELING PSYCHOLOGY, 1968, 15, 329-333.
               (DESCRIPTION; CORRELATES:PSYCHOLOGICAL, DEMOGRAPHIC; N=40 COLLEGE
               STUDENTS)
       @APPLICATION 1968 S-33 I-4

1480   MARSHALL, J. C., & MOWRER, G. E.
             VALIDITY OF PARENTS' PERCEPTIONS OF THEIR SON'S INTERESTS.
             JOURNAL OF COUNSELING PSYCHOLOGY, 1968, 15, 334-337.
                      (VALIDITY:CONSTRUCT; N=30 MALE HIGH SCHOOL SONS)
        @APPLICATION 1968 S-33

1481   VAN ATTA, R. E.
             CONCEPTS EMPLOYED BY ACCURATE AND INACCURATE CLINICIANS.
             JOURNAL OF COUNSELING PSYCHOLOGY, 1968, 15, 338-345.
                      (RELIABILITY:INTERRATER; USED AS CRITERION; N=18 CLINICIANS)
        @APPLICATION 1968 B-126

1482   BRANDT, J. E., & WOOD, A. B.
             EFFECT OF PERSONALITY ADJUSTMENT ON THE PREDICTIVE VALIDITY OF THE STRONG
             VOCATIONAL INTEREST BLANK.
             JOURNAL OF COUNSELING PSYCHOLOGY, 1968, 15, 547-551.
                      (VALIDITY:CRITERION; CORRELATES:PSYCHOLOGICAL; N=915 COLLEGE MALES)
        @APPLICATION 1968 S-33 D-45 H-188 H-183 S-30

1483   BAROCAS, R., & CHRISTENSEN, D.
             IMPRESSION MANAGEMENT, FAKEABILITY, AND ACADEMIC PERFORMANCE.
             JOURNAL OF COUNSELING PSYCHOLOGY, 1968, 15, 569-571.
                      (CORRELATES:INTELLIGENCE; USED AS CRITERION; N=74 MALE
                      UNDERGRADUATES)
        @APPLICATION 1968 S-33

1484   WALSH, R. P., ENGBRETSON, R. O., & O'BRIEN, B. A.
             ANXIETY AND TEST-TAKING BEHAVIOR.
             JOURNAL OF COUNSELING PSYCHOLOGY, 1968, 15, 572-575.
                      (CORRELATES:BEHAVIORAL, INTELLIGENCE; 2 SAMPLES: N=103 (46 MALE,
                      57 FEMALE) SOPHOMORE COLLEGE STUDENTS, N=94 (42 MALE, 52 FEMALE)
                      SOPHOMORE COLLEGE STUDENTS)
        @APPLICATION 1968 A-8

1485   GILBREATH, S. H.
             APPROPRIATE AND INAPPROPRIATE GROUP COUNSELING WITH ACADEMIC
             UNDERACHIEVERS.
             JOURNAL OF COUNSELING PSYCHOLOGY, 1968, 15, 506-511.
                      (CORRELATES:INTELLIGENCE, ENVIRONMENTAL; USED AS CRITERION; N=97
                      COLLEGE MALE UNDERACHIEVERS)
        @APPLICATION 1968 S-56

1486   PAYNE, P. A., & GRALINSKI, D. M.
             EFFECTS OF SUPERVISION STYLE AND EMPATHY UPON COUNSELOR LEARNING.
             JOURNAL OF COUNSELING PSYCHOLOGY, 1968, 15, 517-521.
                      (DESCRIPTION; REVISION: USED AS CRITERION; N=42 MALE UNDERGRADUATE
                      COUNSELORS AND 14 GRADUATE STUDENT SUPERVISORS)
        @APPLICATION 1968 T-24 B-21

1487   TYLER, L. E., SUNDBERG, N. D., ROHILA, P. K., & GREENE, M. M.
             PATTERN CHOICES IN DUTCH, AMERICAN, AND INDIAN ADOLESCENTS.
             JOURNAL OF COUNSELING PSYCHOLOGY, 1968, 15, 522-529.
                      (CROSS-CULTURAL APPLICATION; NORMATIVE DATA; 3 SAMPLES:
                      N=APPROX. 200 AMERICAN ADOLESCENTS, 200 DUTCH ADOLESCENTS, 200
                      INDIAN ADOLESCENTS)
        @APPLICATION 1968 T-90

1488   MCCLAIN, E. W.
             SIXTEEN PERSONALITY FACTOR QUESTIONNAIRE SCORES AND SUCCESS IN
             COUNSELING.
             JOURNAL OF COUNSELING PSYCHOLOGY, 1968, 15, 492-496.
                      (CORRELATES:BEHAVIORAL, DEMOGRAPHIC; N=137 HIGH SCHOOL COUNSELORS)
        @APPLICATION 1968 C-10

1489   SIMONS, R. B.
             ANXIETY AND INVOLVEMENT IN COUNSELING.
             JOURNAL OF COUNSELING PSYCHOLOGY, 1968, 15, 497-499.
                      (VALIDITY:CRITERION; CORRELATES:PSYCHOLOGICAL; N=679 MALE AND 326
                      FEMALE UNDERGRADUATES)
        @APPLICATION 1968 D-45 T-2 W-8

1490   MANDEL, H. P., ROTH, R. M., & BERENBAUM, H. L.
            RELATIONSHIP BETWEEN PERSONALITY CHANGE AND ACHIEVEMENT CHANGE AS A
            FUNCTION OF PSYCHODIAGNOSIS.
            JOURNAL OF COUNSELING PSYCHOLOGY, 1968, 15, 500-505.
                    (MODIFICATION; DESCRIPTION; CORRELATES:BEHAVIORAL, PSYCHOLOGICAL;
                    USED AS CRITERION; N=67 COLLEGE STUDENTS)
            @APPLICATION 1968 S-30 R-75

1491   ROSE, H. A., & ELTON, C. F.
            ACCEPTORS AND REJECTORS CF COUNSELING.
            JOURNAL OF COUNSELING PSYCHOLOGY, 1968, 15, 578-580.
                    (CORRELATES:BEHAVIORAL; N=60 MALE COLLEGE STUDENTS ON ACADEMIC
                    PROBATION)
            @APPLICATION 1968 H-12

1492   NAUSS, A. H.
            THE MINISTERIAL PERSONALITY: ON AVOIDING A STEREOTYPE TRAP.
            JOURNAL OF COUNSELING PSYCHOLOGY, 1968, 15, 581-582.
                    (REVIEW ARTICLE; CORRELATES:DEMOGRAPHIC; NORMATIVE DATA)
            @APPLICATION 1968 M-22 D-45 G-26 C-10 G-22

1493   WATTS, W. A., LYNCH, S., & WHITTAKER, D.
            ALIENATION AND ACTIVISM IN TODAY'S COLLEGE-AGE YOUTH: SOCIALIZATION
            PATTERNS AND CURRENT FAMILY RELATIONSHIPS.
            JOURNAL OF COUNSELING PSYCHOLOGY, 1969, 16, 1-7.
                    (CORRELATES:BEHAVIORAL, PSYCHOLOGICAL, DEMOGRAPHIC; N=151
                    NONSTUDENTS, 56 COLLEGE STUDENTS)
            @APPLICATION 1969 S-28

1494   KERPELMAN, L. C.
            STUDENT POLITICAL ACTIVISM AND IDEOLOGY: COMPARATIVE CHARACTERISTICS OF
            ACTIVISTS AND NONACTIVISTS.
            JOURNAL OF COUNSELING PSYCHOLOGY, 1969, 16, 8-13.
                    (VALIDITY:CONSTRUCT; CORRELATES:BEHAVIORAL, PSYCHOLOGICAL,
                    INTELLIGENCE; USED AS CRITERION; N=73 UNDERGRADUATES)
            @APPLICATION 1969 L-139 G-70 G-13

1495   ZYTOWSKI, D. G., MILLS, D. H., & PAEPE, C.
            PSYCHOLOGICAL DIFFERENTIATION AND THE STRONG VOCATIONAL INTEREST BLANK.
            JOURNAL OF COUNSELING PSYCHOLOGY, 1969, 16, 41-44.
                    (RELIABILITY:INTERRATER; VALIDITY:CONSTRUCT, CRITERION;
                    CORRELATES:PSYCHOLOGICAL, DEMOGRAPHIC, INTELLIGENCE; USED AS
                    CRITERION; NORMATIVE DATA; N=62 MALE COLLEGE STUDENTS)
            @APPLICATION 1969 S-33 W-19 W-20

1496   BIDWELL, G. P.
            EGO STRENGTH, SELF-KNOWLEDGE, AND VOCATIONAL PLANNING OF SCHIZOPHRENICS.
            JOURNAL OF COUNSELING PSYCHOLOGY, 1969, 16, 45-49.
                    (CORRELATES:BEHAVIORAL, PSYCHOLOGICAL, INTELLIGENCE; N=51 MALE
                    SCHIZOPHRENICS)
            @APPLICATION 1969 S-31

1497   REDDY, W. B.
            EFFECTS OF IMMEDIATE AND DELAYED FEEDBACK ON THE LEARNING OF EMPATHY.
            JOURNAL OF COUNSELING PSYCHOLOGY, 1969, 16, 59-62.
                    (DESCRIPTION; MODIFICATION; RELIABILITY:INTERRATER;
                    VALIDITY:CONSTRUCT; CORRELATES:BEHAVIORAL, PSYCHOLOGICAL,
                    ENVIRONMENTAL; N=36 MALE UNDERGRADUATES)
            @APPLICATION 1969 T-24

1498   HARTLEY, D. L.
            PERCEIVED COUNSELOR CREDIBILITY AS A FUNCTION OF THE EFFECTS OF
            COUNSELING INTERACTION.
            JOURNAL OF COUNSELING PSYCHOLOGY, 1969, 16, 63-68.
                    (CORRELATES:BEHAVIORAL, PSYCHOLOGICAL, INTELLIGENCE, ENVIRONMENTAL;
                    USED AS CRITERION; N=10 FIFTH GRADERS FROM EACH OF FOUR ELEMENTARY
                    SCHOOLS)
            @APPLICATION 1969 T-25 L-140

1499   THOMPSON, C. L.
            THE SECONDARY SCHOOL COUNSELOR'S IDEAL CLIENT.
            JOURNAL OF COUNSELING PSYCHOLOGY, 1969, 16, 69-74.
                    (CORRELATES:PSYCHOLOGICAL; N=5 MALE AND 5 FEMALE COUNSELORS)
            @APPLICATION 1969 M-22

1500   FINNEY, B. C., & VAN DALSEN, E.
            GROUP COUNSELING FOR GIFTED UNDERACHIEVING HIGH SCHOOL STUDENTS.
            JOURNAL OF COUNSELING PSYCHOLOGY, 1969, 16, 87-94.
                    (VALIDITY:CONSTRUCT; CORRELATES:BEHAVIORAL, PSYCHOLOGICAL,
                    INTELLIGENCE, ENVIRONMENTAL; N=98 FEMALE, 98 MALE UNDERGRADUATES)
        aAPPLICATION 1969 C-54 G-22

1501   ELTON. C. F.
            PATTERNS OF CHANGE IN PERSONALITY TEST SCORES.
            JOURNAL OF COUNSELING PSYCHOLOGY, 1969, 16, 95-99.
                    (RELIABILITY:RETEST; CORRELATES:PSYCHOLOGICAL; USED AS CRITERION;
                    FACTOR-ANALYSIS; N=438 UNDERGRADUATE FEMALES, 130 UNDERGRADUATE
                    FEMALES)
        aAPPLICATION 1969 H-12

1502   STAHMANN, R. F.
            PREDICTING GRADUATION MAJOR FIELD FROM FRESHMEN ENTRANCE DATE.
            JOURNAL OF COUNSELING PSYCHOLOGY, 1969, 16, 109-113.
                    (VALIDITY:CRITERION, CROSS-VALIDATION; USED AS CRITERION; N=439
                    MALE, 265 FEMALE UNDERGRADUATES)
        aAPPLICATION 1969 L-40

1503   OLIVE, L. E.
            RELATIONSHIPS OF VALUES AND OCCUPATIONAL ROLE PERCEPTIONS FOR FRESHMEN
            AND SENIOR STUDENTS IN A COLLEGE OF ENGINEERING.
            JOURNAL OF COUNSELING PSYCHOLOGY, 1969, 16, 114-120.
                    (DESCRIPTION; VALIDITY:CRITERION, CROSS-VALIDATION;
                    CORRELATES:BEHAVIORAL, PSYCHOLOGICAL; USED AS CRITERION; 2 STUDIES:
                    N=321 MALE UNDERGRADUATES, 213 GRADUATING ENGINEERS)
        aAPPLICATION 1969 P-112 C-25

1504   FOULDS, M. L.
            SELF-ACTUALIZATION AND THE COMMUNICATION OF FACILITATIVE CONDITIONS
            DURING COUNSELING.
            JOURNAL OF COUNSELING PSYCHOLOGY, 1969, 16, 132-136.
                    (RELIABILITY:INTERRATER; VALIDITY:CONSTRUCT;
                    CORRELATES:PSYCHOLOGICAL; N=30 GRADUATE STUDENTS)
        aAPPLICATION 1969 C-218 S-21

1505   ARMSTRONG, J. C.
            PERCEIVED INTIMATE FRIENDSHIP AS A QUASI-THERAPEUTIC AGENT.
            JOURNAL OF COUNSELING PSYCHOLOGY, 1969, 16, 137-141.
                    (MODIFICATION; DESCRIPTION; CORRELATES:BEHAVIORAL, PSYCHOLOGICAL,
                    DEMOGRAPHIC; USED AS CRITERION; N=50 MALE, 50 FEMALE HIGHLY ANXIOUS
                    COLLEGE STUDENTS)
        aAPPLICATION 1969 C-136 B-50 R-138

1506   MCGUFFIE, R. A., JANZEN, F. V., SAMUELSON, C. O., & MCPHEE, W. M.
            SELF-CONCEPT AND IDEAL-SELF IN ASSESSING THE REHABILITATION APPLICANT.
            JOURNAL OF COUNSELING PSYCHOLOGY, 1969, 16, 157-161.
                    (MODIFICATION; VALIDITY:CRITERION; CORRELATES:BEHAVIORAL,
                    PSYCHOLOGICAL; USED AS CRITERION; N=712 REHABILITATION APPLICANTS)
        aAPPLICATION 1969 J-49

1507   DESIDERATO, O., & KOSKINEN, P.
            ANXIETY, STUDY HABITS AND ACADEMIC ACHIEVEMENT.
            JOURNAL OF COUNSELING PSYCHOLOGY, 1969, 16, 162-165.
                    (CORRELATES:BEHAVIORAL, PSYCHOLOGICAL, INTELLIGENCE; N=94 FEMALE
                    UNDERGRADUATES)
        aAPPLICATION 1969 A-8 B-74 M-20

1508   DOLLIVER, R. H.
            "3.5 TO 1" ON THE STRONG VOCATIONAL INTEREST BLANK AS A PSEUDO-EVENT.
            JOURNAL OF COUNSELING PSYCHOLOGY, 1969, 16, 172-174.
                    (REVIEW ARTICLE)
        aAPPLICATION 1969 S-33

1509   CAMPBELL, D. P.
            COMMENT ON "3.5 TO 1" ON THE STRONG VOCATIONAL INTEREST BLANK.
            JOURNAL OF COUNSELING PSYCHOLOGY, 1969, 16, 175-176.
                    (REVIEW ARTICLE)
        aAPPLICATION 1969 S-33

1510   SHAPIRO, A., & SWENSÉN, C.
            PATTERNS OF SELF-DISCLOSURE AMONG MARRIED COUPLES.
            JOURNAL OF COUNSELING PSYCHOLOGY, 1969, 16, 179-180.
                (MODIFICATION; CORRELATES:PSYCHOLOGICAL; USED AS CRITERION; N=30
                MARRIED COUPLES)
        @APPLICATION 1969 J-15

1511   CRITES, J. O.
            TEST REVIEWS.
            JOURNAL OF COUNSELING PSYCHOLOGY, 1969, 16, 181-184.
                (REVIEW ARTICLE)
        @APPLICATION 1969 J-1 M-41

1512   ALEXANDER, J. F., & ABELES, H.
            PSYCHOTHERAPY PROCESS: SEX DIFFERENCES AND DEPENDENCY.
            JOURNAL OF COUNSELING PSYCHOLOGY, 1969, 16, 191-196.
                (USED AS CRITERION; N=10 MALE, 10 FEMALE PSYCHIATRIC CLIENTS)
        @APPLICATION 1969 D-45

1513   DOLE, A. A., NOTTINGHAM, J., & WRIGHTSMAN, L. S., JR.
            BRIEFS ABOUT HUMAN NATURE HELD BY COUNSELING, CLINICAL, AND
            REHABILITATION STUDENTS.
            JOURNAL OF COUNSELING PSYCHOLOGY, 1969, 16, 197-202.
                (DESCRIPTION; CORRELATES:PSYCHOLOGICAL; USED AS CRITERION; N=132
                MALE, 44 FEMALE GRADUATE STUDENTS)
        @APPLICATION 1969 W-24

1514   BROWN, R. D.
            EFFECTS OF STRUCTURED AND UNSTRUCTURED GROUP COUNSELING WITH HIGH- AND
            LOW-ANXIOUS COLLEGE UNDERACHIEVERS.
            JOURNAL OF COUNSELING PSYCHOLOGY, 1969, 16, 209-214.
                (VALIDITY:CONSTRUCT; CORRELATES:PSYCHOLOGICAL, ENVIRONMENTAL; USED
                AS CRITERION; N=21 HIGH-, 21 LOW-ANXIETY UNDERGRADUATES)
        @APPLICATION 1969 B-184 G-49 B-69 G-180

1515   BAIRD, L. L.
            PREDICTION OF ACCOMPLISHMENT IN COLLEGE: A STUDY OF ACHIEVEMENT.
            JOURNAL OF COUNSELING PSYCHOLOGY, 1969, 16, 246-253.
                (DESCRIPTION; VALIDITY:CONSTRUCT, CRITERION, CROSS-VALIDATION;
                CORRELATES:BEHAVIORAL, PSYCHOLOGICAL, INTELLIGENCE, ENVIRONMENTAL;
                USED AS CRITERION; 2 STUDIES: N=5129 UNDERGRADUATES, 1576 MALE,
                1571 FEMALE COLLEGE STUDENTS)
        @APPLICATION 1969 A-2 H-21 H-20 H-19 Q-8 H-46 R-52 N-42 H-206 R-8 H-44 R-143
        @N-12 H-218

1516   FOLSOM, C. H., JR.
            AN INVESTIGATION OF HOLLAND'S THEORY OF VOCATIONAL CHOICE.
            JOURNAL OF COUNSELING PSYCHOLOGY, 1969, 16, 260-266.
                (VALIDITY:CONSTRUCT; CORRELATES:PSYCHOLOGICAL; USED AS CRITERION;
                N=449 FEMALE, 554 MALE UNDERGRADUATES)
        @APPLICATION 1969 P-68

1517   HURLEY, J. R., & HURLEY, S. J.
            TOWARD AUTHENTICITY IN MEASURING SELF-DISCLOSURE.
            JOURNAL OF COUNSELING PSYCHOLOGY, 1969, 16, 271-274.
                (MODIFICATION; VALIDITY:CONTENT, CRITERION; N=50 COLLEGE STUDENTS)
        @APPLICATION 1969 J-15 H-107 H-106

1518   GRIFFITH, A. V., & TROGDON, K. P.
            SELF-EXPRESSIVE STYLES AMONG COLLEGE STUDENTS PREPARING FOR CAREERS IN
            NURSING AND MUSIC.
            JOURNAL OF COUNSELING PSYCHOLOGY, 1969, 16, 275-277.
                (VALIDITY:CONSTRUCT; N=26 SCHOOL OF NURSING, 22 SCHOOL OF MUSIC
                STUDENTS)
        @APPLICATION 1969 D-40

1519   GOUGH, H. G.
            A LEADERSHIP INDEX ON THE CALIFORNIA PSYCHOLOGICAL INVENTORY.
            JOURNAL OF COUNSELING PSYCHOLOGY, 1969, 16, 283-289.
                (REVIEW ARTICLE; VALIDITY:CONSTRUCT, CRITERION, CROSS-VALIDATION;
                NORMATIVE DATA; N=90 MALE, 90 FEMALE LEADERS, 2411 STUDENTS)
        @APPLICATION 1969 G-22

1520   SHAPIRO, J. G., KRAUSS, H. H., & TRUAX, C. B.
            THERAPEUTIC CONDITIONS AND DISCLOSURE BEYOND THE THERAPEUTIC ENCOUNTER.
            JOURNAL OF COUNSELING PSYCHOLOGY, 1969, 16, 290-294.
                (REVISION; N=36 UNDERGRADUATES, 39 POLICE APPLICANTS, 20 DAY
                HOSPITAL PATIENTS)
        @APPLICATION 1969 B-50

1521   ELTON, C. F., & ROSE, H. A.
            PERSONALITY ASSESSMENTS COMPARED WITH PERSONALITY INFERRED FROM
            OCCUPATIONAL CHOICES.
            JOURNAL OF COUNSELING PSYCHOLOGY, 1969, 16, 329-334.
                (VALIDITY:CONSTRUCT; CORRELATES:BEHAVIORAL; FACTOR ANALYSIS; N=980
                (CORRELATES:PSYCHOLOGICAL, INTELLIGENCE; N=205 MALE, 206 FEMALE
                FRESHMEN)
                MALE, 738 FEMALE UNDERGRADUATES)
        @APPLICATION 1969 H-12

1522   KIPNIS, D., LANE, G., & BERGER, L.
            CHARACTER STRUCTURE, VOCATIONAL INTEREST, AND ACHIEVEMENT.
            JOURNAL OF COUNSELING PSYCHOLOGY, 1969, 16, 335-341.
                (CORRELATES:BEHAVIORAL, PSYCHOLOGICAL, INTELLIGENCE; N=628 MALE
                UNDERGRADUATES)
        @APPLICATION 1969 K-135

1523   HEILBRUN, A. B., JR.
            PARENTAL IDENTIFICATION AND THE PATTERNING OF VOCATIONAL INTERESTS IN
            COLLEGE MALES AND FEMALES.
            JOURNAL OF COUNSELING PSYCHOLOGY, 1969, 16, 342-347.
                (CORRELATES:BEHAVIORAL, PSYCHOLOGICAL; N=47 MALE, 33 FEMALE
                UNDERGRADUATES)
        @APPLICATION 1969 G-21 H-66 S-33

1524   WALSH, W. B., & LACEY, D. W.
            PERCEIVED CHANGE AND HOLLAND'S THEORY.
            JOURNAL OF COUNSELING PSYCHOLOGY, 1969, 16, 348-352.
                (REVISION; N=151 MALE COLLEGE SENIORS)
        @APPLICATION 1969 H-47

1525   OGSTON, D. G., ALTMANN, H. A., & CONKLIN, R. C.
            PROBLEMS APPROPRIATE FOR DISCUSSION IN UNIVERSITY COUNSELING CENTERS: A
            REPLICATION.
            JOURNAL OF COUNSELING PSYCHOLOGY, 1969, 16, 361-364.
                (CORRELATES:ENVIRONMENTAL; FACTOR ANALYSIS; N=21 COLLEGE AND
                UNIVERSITY COUNSELING CENTERS)
        @APPLICATION 1969 W-168

1526   GREENFIELD, M.
            TYPOLOGIES OF PERSISTING AND NONPERSISTING JEWISH CLERGYMEN.
            JOURNAL OF COUNSELING PSYCHOLOGY, 1969, 16, 368-372.
                (CORRELATES:DEMOGRAPHIC; USED AS CRITERION; N=194 NONPERSISTING,
                125 PERSISTING JEWISH RABBIS)
        @APPLICATION 1969 M-22

1527   ELTON, C. F., & TERRY, T. R.
            FACTOR STABILITY OF THE OMNIBUS PERSONALITY INVENTORY.
            JOURNAL OF COUNSELING PSYCHOLOGY, 1969, 16, 373-374.
                (RELIABILITY:INTERNAL CONSISTENCY; FACTOR ANALYSIS; N=105 FEMALE
                EDUCATION MAJORS)
        @APPLICATION 1969 H-12

1528   MEDVENE, A. M.
            OCCUPATIONAL CHOICE OF GRADUATE STUDENTS IN PSYCHOLOGY AS A FUNCTION OF
            EARLY PARENT-CHILD INTERACTIONS.
            JOURNAL OF COUNSELING PSYCHOLOGY, 1969, 16, 385-389.
                (DESCRIPTION; CORRELATES:DEMOGRAPHIC; USED AS CRITERION; N=461 MALE
                GRADUATE STUDENTS)
        @APPLICATION 1969 R-64 B-135

1529   BEDNAR, R. L., & PARKER, C. A.
            CLIENT SUSCEPTIBILITY TO PERSUASION AND COUNSELING OUTCOME.
            JOURNAL OF COUNSELING PSYCHOLOGY, 1969, 16, 415-420.
                (CORRELATES:BEHAVIORAL; USED AS CRITERION; N=250 UNDERGRADUATES)
        @APPLICATION 1969 J-50

1530 PASSONS, W. R., & OLSEN, L. C.
          RELATIONSHIP OF COUNSELOR CHARACTERISTICS AND EMPATHIC SENSITIVITY.
          JOURNAL OF COUNSELING PSYCHOLOGY, 1969, 16, 440-445.
              (CORRELATES:BEHAVIORAL, PSYCHOLOGICAL; USED AS CRITERION; N=30
              NATIONAL DEFENSE EDUCATIONAL ACT COUNSELING AND GUIDANCE INSTITUTE
              ENROLLEES)
      @APPLICATION 1969 R-8 F-7

1531 LAXER, R. M., QUARTER, J., KOSMAN, A., & WALKER, K.
          SYSTEMATIC DESENSITIZATION AND RELAXATION OF HIGH TEST-ANXIOUS SECONDARY
          SCHOOL STUDENTS.
          JOURNAL OF COUNSELING PSYCHOLOGY, 1969, 16, 446-451.
              (CORRELATES:BEHAVIORAL, PSYCHOLOGICAL, ENVIRONMENTAL; N=129 9TH-13TH
              GRADERS)
      @APPLICATION 1969 T-2 A-8

1532 KATZ, M.
          INTERESTS AND VALUES: A COMMENT.
          JOURNAL OF COUNSELING PSYCHOLOGY, 1969, 16, 460-462.
              (REVIEW ARTICLE)
      @APPLICATION 1969 S-33

1533 PRICE, L. Z., & IVERSON, M. F.
          STUDENTS' PERCEPTION OF COUNSELORS WITH VARYING STATUSES AND ROLE
          BEHAVIORS IN THE INITIAL INTERVIEW.
          JOURNAL OF COUNSELING PSYCHOLOGY, 1969, 16, 469-475.
              (CORRELATES:BEHAVIORAL, PSYCHOLOGICAL; N=120 UNDERGRADUATES)
      @APPLICATION 1969 P-120

1534 DONNAN, H. H., HARLAN, G. E., & THOMPSON, S. A.
          COUNSELOR PERSONALITY AND LEVEL OF FUNCTIONING AS PERCEIVED BY
          COUNSELEES.
          JOURNAL OF COUNSELING PSYCHOLOGY, 1969, 16, 482-485.
              (REVISION; CORRELATES:BEHAVIORAL, PSYCHOLOGICAL; N=22 COUNSELORS,
              880 PROSPECTIVE COLLEGE FRESHMEN
      @APPLICATION 1969 C-10 B-50

1535 HOUNTRAS, P. T., & REDDING, A. J.
          EFFECTS OF TRAINING IN INTERACTION ANALYSIS UPON COUNSELING PRACTICUM
          STUDENTS.
          JOURNAL OF COUNSELING PSYCHOLOGY, 1969, 16, 491-494.
              (MODIFICATION; CORRELATES:BEHAVIORAL, PSYCHOLOGICAL, ENVIRONMENTAL;
              NORMATIVE DATA; N=30 BEGINNING COUNSELING PRACTICUM STUDENTS)
      @APPLICATION 1969 F-114

1536 WITTMER, J., & WEBSTER, Q. B.
          THE RELATIONSHIP BETWEEN TEACHING EXPERIENCE AND COUNSELOR TRAINEE
          DOGMATISM.
          JOURNAL OF COUNSELING PSYCHOLOGY, 1969, 16, 499-504.
              (CORRELATES:DEMOGRAPHIC; USED AS CRITERION; N=49 COUNSELORS IN
              PREPARATION)
      @APPLICATION 1969 R-8

1537 SHAPIRO, J. G., & VOOG, T.
          EFFECTS OF THE INHERENTLY HELPFUL PERSON ON STUDENT ACADEMIC ACHIEVEMENT.
          JOURNAL OF COUNSELING PSYCHOLOGY, 1969, 16, 505-509.
              (CORRELATES:BEHAVIORAL, PSYCHOLOGICAL, INTELLIGENCE; N=58 MALE
              FRESHMEN)
      @APPLICATION 1969 S-142

1538 WALKER, B. S., & LITTLE, D. F.
          FACTOR ANALYSIS OF THE BARRETT-LENNARD RELATIONSHIP INVENTORY.
          JOURNAL OF COUNSELING PSYCHOLOGY, 1969, 16, 516-521.
              (DESCRIPTION; FACTOR ANALYSIS; N=98 MALE, 52 FEMALE UNDERGRADUATES)
      @APPLICATION 1969 B-50

1539 OSIPOW, S. H.
          COGNITIVE STYLES AND EDUCATIONAL-VOCATIONAL PREFERENCES AND SELECTION.
          JOURNAL OF COUNSELING PSYCHOLOGY, 1969, 16, 534-546.
              (VALIDITY:CONSTRUCT; CORRELATES:BEHAVIORAL, PSYCHOLOGICAL; N=24
              FEMALE INTRODUCTORY PSYCHOLOGY STUDENTS, 223 NURSING STUDENTS, 20
              HOME ECONOMICS MAJORS, 22 DENTAL HYGIENE MAJORS, 39 SPECIAL
              EDUCATION MAJORS, 17 MALE PHARMACY, 20 MALE FISHERIES STUDENTS)
      @APPLICATION 1969 H-21 M-201

1540   FOREMAN, M. E., & JAMES, L. E.
            VOCATIONAL RELEVANCE AND ESTIMATED AND MEASURED TEST SCORES.
            JOURNAL OF COUNSELING PSYCHOLOGY, 1969, 16, 547-550.
                    (MODIFICATION; CORRELATES:BEHAVIORAL, PSYCHOLOGICAL; N=120 MALE
                    COLLEGE STUDENTS)
        aAPPLICATION 1969 E-2 S-33 K-34

1541   KISH, G. B., & DONNENWERTH, G. V.
            INTERESTS AND STIMULUS SEEKING.
            JOURNAL OF COUNSELING PSYCHOLOGY, 1969, 16, 551-556.
                    (VALIDITY:CONSTRUCT; CORRELATES:PSYCHOLOGICAL; 3 STUDIES: N=41
                    ALCOHOLIC PATIENTS, 32 MALE COLLEGE STUDENTS, 46 FEMALE COLLEGE
                    STUDENTS)
        aAPPLICATION 1969 Z-3 K-34 S-34

1542   NEAL, R., & KING, P.
            COMPARISON OF A MULTIVARIATE AND A CONFIGURAL ANALYSIS FOR CLASSIFYING
            ENGINEERING STUDENTS.
            JOURNAL OF COUNSELING PSYCHOLOGY, 1969, 16, 563-568.
                    (CORRELATES:BEHAVIORAL; USED AS CRITERION; N=301 UNDERGRADUATES)
        aAPPLICATION 1969 H-184

1543   CORDARO, L. L., & SHONTZ, F. C.
            PSYCHOLOGICAL SITUATIONS AS DETERMINANTS OF SELF-EVALUATIONS.
            JOURNAL OF COUNSELING PSYCHOLOGY, 1969, 16, 575-578.
                    (VALIDITY:CONSTRUCT; CORRELATES:PSYCHOLOGICAL; N=11 MALES, 14
                    FEMALES WITH EXPLICIT DIAGNOSES OF DISABILITIES)
        aAPPLICATION 1969 B-249 Y-1

1544   HJELLE, L. A.
            PERSONALITY CHARACTERISTICS ASSOCIATED WITH INTERPERSONAL PERCEPTION
            ACCURACY.
            JOURNAL OF COUNSELING PSYCHOLOGY, 1969, 16, 579-581.
                    (VALIDITY:CONSTRUCT; CORRELATES:PSYCHOLOGICAL; USED AS CRITERION;
                    N=72 MALE FRESHMAN ROOMMATES)
        aAPPLICATION 1969 G-22

1545   LE MAY, M. L.
            SELF-ACTUALIZATION AND COLLEGE ACHIEVEMENT AT THREE ABILITY LEVELS.
            JOURNAL OF COUNSELING PSYCHOLOGY, 1969, 16, 582-583.
                    (CORRELATES:PSYCHOLOGICAL, DEMOGRAPHIC, INTELLIGENCE; N=205 MALE,
                    206 FEMALE FRESHMEN)
        aAPPLICATION 1969 S-21

1546   BRUNKAN, R. J., & CRITES, J. O.
            AN INVENTORY TO MEASURE THE PARENTAL ATTITUDE VARIABLES IN ROE'S THEORY OF
            VOCATIONAL CHOICE.
            JOURNAL OF COUNSELING PSYCHOLOGY, 1964, 11, 3-12.
                    (CORRELATES:PSYCHOLOGICAL; N=142 COLLEGE STUDENTS)
        aAPPLICATION 1964 U-10 G-193

1547   GRIBBONS, W. D., & LOHNES, P. R.
            VALIDATION OF VOCATIONAL PLANNING INTERVIEW SCALES.
            JOURNAL OF COUNSELING PSYCHOLOGY, 1964, 11, 20-26.
                    (VALIDITY:CRITERION; N=110 8TH GRADE SCHOOL CHILDREN)
        aAPPLICATION 1964 G-46

1548   HOLLAND, J. L., & NICHOLS, R. C.
            THE DEVELOPMENT AND VALIDATION OF AN INDECISION SCALE: THE NATURAL HISTORY
            OF A PROBLEM IN BASIC RESEARCH.
            JOURNAL OF COUNSELING PSYCHOLOGY, 1964, 11, 27-34.
                    (CORRELATES:PSYCHOLOGICAL; 2 STUDIES: N=239 BOYS, 259 GIRLS;
                    N=307 BOYS, 314 GIRLS; ALL WERE HIGH SCHOOL STUDENTS)
        aAPPLICATION 1964 H-21 B-4

1549   CANON, H. J.
            PERSONALITY VARIABLES AND COUNSELOR-CLIENT AFFECT.
            JOURNAL OF COUNSELING PSYCHOLOGY, 1964, 11, 35-41.
                    (MODIFICATION; CORRELATES:PSYCHOLOGICAL; N=18 MALE COUNSELORS AND
                    36 FEMALE, 85 MALE COLLEGE STUDENT CLIENTS)
        aAPPLICATION 1964 H-12 S-342

1550   COOK, J. J.
            SILENCE IN PSYCHOTHERAPY.
            JOURNAL OF COUNSELING PSYCHOLOGY, 1964, 11, 42-46.
                (RELIABILITY:INTERRATER; CORRELATES:BEHAVIORAL, PSYCHOLOGICAL;
                N=40 COUNSELING CLIENTS)
        @APPLICATION 1964 R-36

1551   POOL, D. A., & BROWN, R. A.
            KUDER-STRONG DISCREPANCIES AND PERSONALITY ADJUSTMENT.
            JOURNAL OF COUNSELING PSYCHOLOGY, 1964, 11, 63-66.
                (CORRELATES:PSYCHOLOGICAL; N=27 PHYSICALLY HANDICAPPED HOSPITALIZED
                VETERANS)
        @APPLICATION 1964 K-34 S-33 D-45

1552   DRASGOW, J., & CARKHUFF, R. R.
            KUDER NEUROPSYCHIATRIC KEYS BEFORE AND AFTER PSYCHOTHERAPY.
            JOURNAL OF COUNSELING PSYCHOLOGY, 1964, 11, 67-69.
                (CORRELATES:PSYCHOLOGICAL, ENVIRONMENTAL; N=30 PSYCHIATRIC PATIENTS)
        @APPLICATION 1964 K-34

1553   WALDROP, R. S.
            COMMENT ON TWO ARTICLES.
            JOURNAL OF COUNSELING PSYCHOLOGY, 1964, 11, 70-71.
                (REVIEW ARTICLE; NO SAMPLE USED)
        @APPLICATION 1964 D-45 S-33 K-34

1554   MALNIG, L. R.
            ANXIETY AND ACADEMIC PREDICTION.
            JOURNAL OF COUNSELING PSYCHOLOGY, 1964, 11, 72-75.
                (CORRELATES:INTELLIGENCE; N=210 MALE COLLEGE FRESHMEN)
        @APPLICATION 1964 T-2

1555   BUTCHER, J., BALL, B., & RAY, E.
            EFFECTS OF SOCIO-ECONOMIC LEVEL ON MMPI DIFFERENCES IN NEGRO-WHITE COLLEGE
            STUDENTS.
            JOURNAL OF COUNSELING PSYCHOLOGY, 1964, 11, 83-87.
                (CORRELATES:DEMOGRAPHIC; N=66 NEGRO, 66 WHITE FEMALES, 76 NEGRO,
                76 WHITE MALES IN COLLEGE)
        @APPLICATION 1964 D-45

1556   COOLEY, W. W.
            CURRENT RESEARCH ON THE CAREER DEVELOPMENT OF SCIENTISTS.
            JOURNAL OF COUNSELING PSYCHOLOGY, 1964, 11, 88-93.
            (REVIEW AND DISCUSSION OF MEASUREMENT APPROACHES; NO SAMPLE DESCRIBED)
        @APPLICATION 1964 K-34

1557   WAGNER, E. E., & SOBER, K. A.
            EFFECTIVENESS OF THE GUILFORD-ZIMMERMAN TEMPERAMENT SURVEY AS A PREDICTOR
            OF SCHOLASTIC SUCCESS IN COLLEGE.
            JOURNAL OF COUNSELING PSYCHOLOGY, 1964, 11, 94-95.
                (CORRELATES:INTELLIGENCE; N=776 ENTERING COLLEGE FRESHMEN)
        @APPLICATION 1964 G-26

1558   SIEGEL, L.
            TEST REVIEWS: THE AESTHETIC PERCEPTION TEST; THE ADJUSTMENT INVENTORY:
            STUDENT FORM.
            JOURNAL OF COUNSELING PSYCHOLOGY, 1964, 11, 98-99.
                (MENTION; REVIEW ARTICLE; NO SAMPLE USED)
        @APPLICATION 1964 M-252 B-281 M-253

1559   GOUGH, H. G.
            THEORY AND MEASUREMENT OF SOCIALIZATION.
            JOURNAL OF CONSULTING PSYCHOLOGY, 1960, 24, 23-30.
                (VALIDITY:CRITERION; NORMATIVE DATA; 25 SAMPLES, MEDIAN N=132 MALES)
        @APPLICATION 1960 G-22

1560   LEVITT, E. E., & GROSZ, H. J.
            A COMPARISON OF QUANTIFIABLE RORSCHACH ANXIETY INDICATORS IN HYPNOTICALLY
            INDUCED ANXIETY AND NORMAL STATES.
            JOURNAL OF CONSULTING PSYCHOLOGY, 1960, 24, 31-34.
                (CORRELATES:PSYCHOLOGICAL; USED AS CRITERION; N=12 NORMAL MEDICAL
                AND NURSING STUDENTS)
        @APPLICATION 1960 T-2 B-5 R-30

1561   WALLER, P. F.
            A COMPARISON OF SHADING RESPONSES OBTAINED WITH TWO RORSCHACH METHODOLOGIES
            FROM PSYCHIATRIC AND NONPSYCHIATRIC SUBJECTS.
            JOURNAL OF CONSULTING PSYCHOLOGY, 1960, 24, 43-45.
                (RELIABILITY:INTERRATER; VALIDITY:CRITERION; N=60 PSYCHIATRIC AND 162
                NORMAL ADULTS)
        @APPLICATION 1960 R-30 P-126 P-64 B-285

1562   SEIDEL, C.
            THE RELATIONSHIP BETWEEN KLOPFER'S RORSCHACH PROGNOSTIC RATING SCALE AND
            PHILLIPS' CASE HISTORY PROGNOSTIC RATING SCALE.
            JOURNAL OF CONSULTING PSYCHOLOGY, 1960, 24, 46-49.
                (VALIDITY:CRITERION; CORRELATES:PSYCHOLOGICAL, DEMOGRAPHIC; N=100
                PSYCHIATRIC PATIENTS)
        @APPLICATION 1960 K-13 P-32

1563   GOTTLIEB, A. L., & PARSONS, O. A.
            A COACTION COMPASS EVALUATION OF RORSCHACH DETERMINANTS IN BRAIN DAMAGED
            INDIVIDUALS.
            JOURNAL OF CONSULTING PSYCHOLOGY, 1960, 24, 54-60.
                (RELIABILITY:RETEST, INTERRATER; VALIDITY:CRITERION;
                CORRELATES:PSYCHOLOGICAL, DEMOGRAPHIC; NORMATIVE DATA; N=20 BRAIN
                DAMAGED AND 20 NON-BRAIN DAMAGED PATIENTS)
        @APPLICATION 1960 R-30 P-126 P-64

1564   BRIGGS, P. F., & WIRT, R. D.
            INTRA-Q DECK RELATIONSHIPS AS INFLUENCES AND REALITIES IN PERSONALITY
            ASSESSMENT.
            JOURNAL OF CONSULTING PSYCHOLOGY, 1960, 24, 61-66.
                (VALIDITY:CONTENT; USED AS CRITERION; NORMATIVE DATA; 4 SAMPLES,
                MEDIAN N=70 DELINQUENTS AND NONDELINQUENTS)
        @APPLICATION 1960 D-45 B-126

1565   GRIGG, A. E., & THORPE, J. S.
            DEVIANT RESPONSES IN COLLEGE ADJUSTMENT CLIENTS: A TEST OF BERG'S DEVIATION
            HYPOTHESIS.
            JOURNAL OF CONSULTING PSYCHOLOGY, 1960, 24, 92-94.
                (REVISION; CORRELATES:BEHAVIORAL, DEMOGRAPHIC; USED AS CRITERION;
                NORMATIVE DATA; 2 SAMPLES: 181 COLLEGE MALES AND 92 COLLEGE
                FEMALES, 1400 FRESHMEN COLLEGE STUDENTS)
        @APPLICATION 1960 G-21 G-125

1566   DOIDGE, W. T., & HOLTZMAN, W. H.
            IMPLICATIONS OF HOMOSEXUALITY AMONG AIR FORCE TRAINEES.
            JOURNAL OF CONSULTING PSYCHOLOGY, 1960, 24, 9-13.
                (MODIFICATION; CORRELATES:BEHAVIORAL, PSYCHOLOGICAL; N=80
                HOMOSEXUAL AND HETEROSEXUAL AIR FORCE AIRMEN)
        @APPLICATION 1960 E-2 H-51 W-21 B-176 D-45

1567   CAINE, T. M.
            THE EXPRESSION OF HOSTILITY AND GUILT IN MELANCHOLIC AND PARANOID WOMEN.
            JOURNAL OF CONSULTING PSYCHOLOGY, 1960, 24, 18-22.
                (CORRELATES:PSYCHOLOGICAL; NORMATIVE DATA; N=31 PSYCHIATRIC FEMALE
                PATIENTS)
        @APPLICATION 1960 M-20 W-183

1568   BENDIG, A. W.
            FACTOR ANALYSES OF "ANXIETY" AND "NEUROTICISM" INVENTORIES.
            JOURNAL OF CONSULTING PSYCHOLOGY, 1960, 24, 161-168.
                (CORRELATES:PSYCHOLOGICAL; FACTOR ANALYSIS; 2 STUDIES: N=261 COLLEGE
                MALES AND 164 COLLEGE FEMALES, 197 COLLEGE MALES AND 66 COLLEGE
                FEMALES)
        @APPLICATION 1960 T-2 E-1 E-5 C-135 C-136 W-61 D-45

1569   HEILBRUN, A. B., JR.
            PERCEPTION OF MATERNAL CHILD REARING ATTITUDES IN SCHIZOPHRENICS.
            JOURNAL OF CONSULTING PSYCHOLOGY, 1960, 24, 169-173.
                (NORMATIVE DATA; N=26 SCHIZOPHRENIC AND 27 NORMAL FEMALES)
        @APPLICATION 1960 S-9

1570   CHANCE, J. E.
            PERSONALITY DIFFERENCES AND LEVEL OF ASPIRATION.
            JOURNAL OF CONSULTING PSYCHOLOGY, 1960, 24, 111-115.
                (CORRELATES:BEHAVIORAL; USED AS CRITERION; N=147 COLLEGE MALES AND
                FEMALES)
        @APPLICATION 1960 W-8 W-41 D-45

1571   BROEN, W. E., JR.
            AMBIGUITY AND DISCRIMINATING POWER IN PERSONALITY INVENTORIES.
            JOURNAL OF CONSULTING PSYCHOLOGY, 1960, 24, 174-179.
                (MENTION; VALIDITY:CONTENT)
        @APPLICATION 1960 T-2

1572   CARTWRIGHT, R. D., & VOGEL, J. L.
            A COMPARISON OF CHANGES IN PSYCHONEUROTIC PATIENTS DURING MATCHED PERIODS
            OF THERAPY AND NO THERAPY.
            JOURNAL OF CONSULTING PSYCHOLOGY, 1960, 24, 121-127.
                (CORRELATES:ENVIRONMENTAL; N=22 PSYCHONEUROTIC PATIENTS, 19
                THERAPISTS)
        @APPLICATION 1960 B-60 D-25

1573   BENDIG, A. W.
            AGE DIFFERENCES IN THE INTERSCALE FACTOR STRUCTURE OF THE
            GUILFORD-ZIMMERMAN TEMPERAMENT SURVEY.
            JOURNAL OF CONSULTING PSYCHOLOGY, 1960, 24, 134-138.
                (CORRELATES:DEMOGRAPHIC; FACTOR ANALYSIS; NORMATIVE DATA; N=400 MEN
                DRAWN FROM 4 AGE RANGES)
        @APPLICATION 1960 G-26

1574   MCDONOUGH, J. M.
            CRITICAL FLICKER FREQUENCY AND THE SPIRAL AFTEREFFECT WITH PROCESS AND
            REACTIVE SCHIZOPHRENICS.
            JOURNAL OF CONSULTING PSYCHOLOGY, 1960, 24, 150-155.
                (RELIABILITY:INTERRATER; USED AS CRITERION; N=80 MALE VETERANS,
                20 NORMALS, 20 BRAIN DAMAGED, 40 SCHIZOPHRENIC)
        @APPLICATION 1960 B-242

1575   ISCOE, I., & COCHRAN, I.
            SOME CORRELATES OF MANIFEST ANXIETY IN CHILDREN.
            JOURNAL OF CONSULTING PSYCHOLOGY, 1960, 24, 97.
                (VALIDITY:CONSTRUCT, CRITERION; CORRELATES:PSYCHOLOGICAL; 2 STUDIES:
                N=214 ELEMENTARY SCHOOL CHILDREN, 228 ELEMENTARY SCHOOL CHILDREN)
        @APPLICATION 1960 C-55 T-25

1576   KLABER, M. M.
            MANIFESTATIONS OF HOSTILITY IN NEURODERMATITIS.
            JOURNAL OF CONSULTING PSYCHOLOGY, 1960, 24, 116-120.
                (MODIFICATION; RELIABILITY:INTERNAL CONSISTENCY;
                CORRELATES:PSYCHOLOGICAL; N=40 NEURODERMATITIS PATIENTS)
        @APPLICATION 1960 A-56 M-20

1577   LUCKEY, E. B.
            MARITAL SATISFACTION AND PARENT CONCEPTS.
            JOURNAL OF CONSULTING PSYCHOLOGY, 1960, 24, 195-204.
                (CORRELATES:PSYCHOLOGICAL; USED AS CRITERION; N=454 FORMER STUDENTS,
                NOW MARRIED, 81 SELECTED)
        @APPLICATION 1960 T-4 L-15 L-35

1578   KATZ, I., GLUCKSBERG, S., & KRAUSS, R.
            NEED SATISFACTION AND EDWARDS PPS SCORE IN MARRIED COUPLES.
            JOURNAL OF CONSULTING PSYCHOLOGY, 1960, 24, 205-208.
                (MODIFICATION; CORRELATES>PSYCHOLOGICAL; USED AS CRITERION; N=56
                GRADUATE STUDENT COUPLES)
        @APPLICATION 1960 E-2

1579   CLEVELAND, S. E.
            BODY IMAGE CHANGES ASSOCIATED WITH PERSONALITY REORGANIZATION.
            JOURNAL OF CONSULTING PSYCHOLOGY, 1960, 24, 256-261.
                (VALIDITY:CROSS-VALIDATION; CORRELATES:BEHAVIORAL, PSYCHOLOGICAL;
                2 SAMPLES: 24 MALE PSYCHIATRIC PATIENTS, 45 SCHIZOPHRENIC PATIENTS)
        @APPLICATION 1960 L-39 H-37 F-75 F-135

1580   FAGER, R. E.
            RELATION OF RORSCHACH MOVEMENT AND COLOR RESPONSES TO COGNITIVE
            INHIBITION.
            JOURNAL OF CONSULTING PSYCHOLOGY, 1960, 24, 276.
                (CORRELATES:INTELLIGENCE; N=205 PSYCHIATRIC PATIENTS AND CONTROLS)
        @APPLICATION 1960 L-89

1581   COOPER, R.
            OBJECTIVE MEASURES OF PERCEPTION IN SCHIZOPHRENICS AND NORMALS.
            JOURNAL OF CONSULTING PSYCHOLOGY, 1960, 24, 209-214.
                (RELIABILITY:INTERNAL CONSISTENCY; CORRELATES:PSYCHOLOGICAL; N=66
                SCHIZOPHRENIC VETERANS, 36 MEDICAL VETERAN PATIENT CONTROLS)
        aAPPLICATION 1960 R-37

1582   KING, G. F., & SCHILLER, M.
            EGO STRENGTH AND TYPE OF DEFENSIVE BEHAVIOR.
            JOURNAL OF CONSULTING PSYCHOLOGY, 1960, 24, 215-217.
                (VALIDITY:CROSS-VALIDATION; CORRELATES:PSYCHOLOGICAL; 2 SAMPLES:
                N=60, N=50 PROBLEM DRIVERS)
        aAPPLICATION 1960 K-96 B-5

1583   NEEL, A. F.
            INHIBITION AND PERCEPTION OF MOVEMENT ON THE RORSCHACH.
            JOURNAL OF CONSULTING PSYCHOLOGY, 1960, 24, 224-230.
                (CORRELATES:ENVIRONMENTAL; N=93 STUDENTS)
        aAPPLICATION 1960 R-30

1584   MARSHALL, S.
            PERSONALITY CORRELATES OF PEPTIC ULCER PATIENTS.
            JOURNAL OF CONSULTING PSYCHOLOGY, 1960, 24, 218-223.
                (CORRELATES:PSYCHOLOGICAL; NORMATIVE DATA; N=40 ULCER PATIENTS, 20
                PSYCHOSOMATIC CASES AND 40 WITH OTHER PHYSICAL DISORDERS)
        aAPPLICATION 1960 E-2

1585   RUBIN, M., & SHONTZ, F. C.
            DIAGNOSTIC PROTOTYPES AND DIAGNOSTIC PROCESSES OF CLINICAL PSYCHOLOGISTS.
            JOURNAL OF CONSULTING PSYCHOLOGY, 1960, 24, 234-239.
                (MODIFICATION; RELIABILITY:INTERRATER, RETEST; N=25 RATERS, PARANOID
                SCHIZOPHRENICS)
        aAPPLICATION 1960 S-30

1586   SMITH, A. B., BASSIN, A., & FROEHLICH, A.
            CHANGE IN ATTITUDES AND DEGREE OF VERBAL PARTICIPATION IN GROUP THERAPY
            WITH ADULT OFFENDERS.
            JOURNAL OF CONSULTING PSYCHOLOGY, 1960, 24, 247-249.
                (RELIABILITY:INTERRATER; CORRELATES:PSYCHOLOGICAL; N=15 PROBATION
                PLACEMENTS)
        aAPPLICATION 1960 B-15 S-188 M-20

1587   CROWNE, D. P., & MARLOWE, D.
            A NEW SCALE OF SOCIAL DESIRABILITY INDEPENDENT OF PSYCHOPATHOLOGY.
            JOURNAL OF CONSULTING PSYCHOLOGY, 1960, 24, 349-354.
                (VALIDITY:CONSTRUCT; CORRELATES:PSYCHOLOGICAL; NORMATIVE DATA;
                BIAS:RESPONSE; N=39 COLLEGE STUDENTS)
        aAPPLICATION 1960 E-1 D-45 G-18 B-5 T-2 W-8 W-41 G-121

1588   GILBERSTADT, H., & DUKER, J.
            CASE HISTORY CORRELATES OF THREE MMPI PROFILE TYPES.
            JOURNAL OF CONSULTING PSYCHOLOGY, 1960, 24, 361-367.
                (NORMATIVE DATA; N=62 PSYCHIATRIC PATIENTS)
        aAPPLICATION 1960 D-45

1589   WEINBERG, J. R.
            A FURTHER INVESTIGATION OF BODY-CATHEXIS AND THE SELF.
            JOURNAL OF CONSULTING PSYCHOLOGY, 1960, 24, 277.
                (CORRELATES:PSYCHOLOGICAL, DEMOGRAPHIC; N=108 MALE AND 104 FEMALE
                STUDENTS)
        aAPPLICATION 1960 M-50

1590   L'ABATE, L.
            PERSONALITY CORRELATES OF MANIFEST ANXIETY IN CHILDREN.
            JOURNAL OF CONSULTING PSYCHOLOGY, 1960, 24, 342-348.
                (RELIABILITY:INTERRATER; VALIDITY:CONSTRUCT;
                CORRELATES:PSYCHOLOGICAL, DEMOGRAPHIC, INTELLIGENCE; NORMATIVE DATA;
                N=96 FOURTH-EIGHTH GRADERS)
        aAPPLICATION 1960 R-84 R-85 C-55

1591   KNOWLES, J. B.
        THE TEMPORAL STABILITY OF MPI SCORES IN NORMAL AND PSYCHIATRIC
        POPULATIONS.
        JOURNAL OF CONSULTING PSYCHOLOGY, 1960, 24, 278.
            (RELIABILITY:RETEST, INTERNAL CONSISTENCY; VALIDITY:CONSTRUCT; N=63
            PSYCHIATRIC PATIENTS AND 93 SURGICAL PATIENTS)
        @APPLICATION 1960 E-5

1592   KASWAN, J., WASMAN, M., & FREEDMAN, L. Z.
        AGGRESSION AND THE PICTURE-FRUSTRATION STUDY.
        JOURNAL OF CONSULTING PSYCHOLOGY, 1960, 24, 446-452.
            (RELIABILITY:INTERRATER; CORRELATES:BEHAVIORAL, PSYCHOLOGICAL;
            NORMATIVE DATA; N=121 MALE PRISONERS)
        @APPLICATION 1960 R-12 R-30 E-76

1593   MITCHELL, J. V., JR., & PIERCE-JONES, J.
        A FACTOR ANALYSIS OF GOUGH'S CALIFORNIA PSYCHOLOGICAL INVENTORY.
        JOURNAL OF CONSULTING PSYCHOLOGY, 1960, 24, 453-456.
            (FACTOR ANALYSIS; N=213 FEMALE, 45 MALE COLLEGE STUDENTS)
        @APPLICATION 1960 G-22

1594   HARTUP, W. W., & ZOOK, E. A.
        SEX-ROLE PREFERENCES IN THREE- AND FOUR-YEAR-OLD CHILDREN.
        JOURNAL OF CONSULTING PSYCHOLOGY, 1960, 24, 420-426.
            (RELIABILITY:RETEST; CORRELATES:DEMOGRAPHIC, ENVIRONMENTAL;
            NORMATIVE DATA; N=161 MALE AND FEMALE CHILDREN, AGES 3 TO 5)
        @APPLICATION 1960 B-35

1595   BARROWS, G. A., & ZUCKERMAN, M.
        CONSTRUCT VALIDITY OF THREE MASCULINITY-FEMININITY TESTS.
        JOURNAL OF CONSULTING PSYCHOLOGY, 1960, 24, 441-445.
            (VALIDITY:CONSTRUCT; CORRELATES:PSYCHOLOGICAL, DEMOGRAPHIC,
            INTELLIGENCE; NORMATIVE DATA; N=2296 CANADIAN WHITE-COLLAR MALES)
        @APPLICATION 1960 G-26 S-33 D-45 K-34

1596   HEILIZER, F.
        AN EXPLORATION OF THE RELATIONSHIP BETWEEN HYPNOTIZABILITY AND ANXIETY
        AND/OR NEUROTICISM.
        JOURNAL OF CONSULTING PSYCHOLOGY, 1960, 24, 432-436.
            (CORRELATES:BEHAVIORAL, PSYCHOLOGICAL; N=62 COLLEGE FEMALES)
        @APPLICATION 1960 B-18 T-2 M-20 D-56 D-45

1597   GOLDMAN, R.
        CHANGES IN RORSCHACH PERFORMANCE AND CLINICAL IMPROVEMENT IN SCHIZOPHRENIA.
        JOURNAL OF CONSULTING PSYCHOLOGY, 1960, 24, 403-407.
            (VALIDITY:CRITERION; CORRELATES:PSYCHOLOGICAL; USED AS CRITERION;
            N=45 SCHIZOPHRENIC PATIENTS)
        @APPLICATION 1960 R-30

1598   HARE, A. P., WAXLER, N., SASLOW, G., & MATARAZZO, J. D.
        SIMULTANEOUS RECORDING OF BALES AND CHAPPLE INTERACTION MEASURES DURING
        INITIAL PSYCHIATRIC INTERVIEWS.
        JOURNAL OF CONSULTING PSYCHOLOGY, 1960, 24, 193.
            (CORRELATES:PSYCHOLOGICAL; N=24 ADULT HOSPITAL OUTPATIENTS)
        @APPLICATION 1960 B-2 C-66

1599   NICHOLS, R. C., & BECK, K. W.
        FACTORS IN PSYCHOTHERAPY CHANGE.
        JOURNAL OF CONSULTING PSYCHOLOGY, 1960, 24, 388-399.
            (CORRELATES:ENVIRONMENTAL; USED AS CRITERION; FACTOR ANALYSIS;
            NORMATIVE DATA; N=75 COLLEGE STUDENTS AT PSYCHOLOGICAL CLINIC AND 42
            MATCHED CONTROL UNDERGRADUATES)
        @APPLICATION 1960 G-22 R-81

1600   FELDMAN, M. J., & CORAH, N. L.
        SOCIAL DESIRABILITY AND THE FORCED CHOICE METHOD.
        JOURNAL OF CONSULTING PSYCHOLOGY, 1960, 24, 480-482.
            (MODIFICATION; BIAS:RESPONSE; 2 SAMPLES: N=100 MALE UNDERGRADUATES,
            N=98 MALE UNDERGRADUATES)
        @APPLICATION 1960 E-2 B-44 D-45

1601   MATTSSON, P. O.
            COMMUNICATED ANXIETY IN A TWO-PERSON SITUATION.
            JOURNAL OF CONSULTING PSYCHOLOGY, 1960, 24, 488-495.
                (USED AS CRITERION; N=80 COLLEGE MALES)
        aAPPLICATION 1960 T-2

1602   SCHROEDER, P.
            CLIENT ACCEPTANCE OF RESPONSIBILITY AND DIFFICULTY OF THERAPY.
            JOURNAL OF CONSULTING PSYCHOLOGY, 1960, 24, 467-471.
                (MENTION; RELIABILITY:INTERRATER; CORRELATES:PSYCHOLOGICAL; N=48
                COLLEGE STUDENT COUNSELING CLIENTS)
        aAPPLICATION 1960 E-37 R-30 M-20

1603   COROTTO, L. V., & CURNUTT, R. H.
            THE EFFECTIVENESS OF THE BENDER-GESTALT IN DIFFERENTIATING A FLIGHT
            GROUP FROM AN AGGRESSIVE GROUP OF ADOLESCENTS.
            JOURNAL OF CONSULTING PSYCHOLOGY, 1960, 24, 368-369.
                (CORRELATES:BEHAVIORAL, DEMOGRAPHIC; N=92 MALE AND FEMALE
                ADOLESCENTS FROM PSYCHIATRIC UNIT)
        aAPPLICATION 1960 P-77

1604   FISKE, D. W., HOWARD, K., & RECHENBERG, W.
            THE EPPS PROFILE STABILITY COEFFICIENT.
            JOURNAL OF CONSULTING PSYCHOLOGY, 1960, 24, 370.
                (MENTION; CORRELATES:BEHAVIORAL, PSYCHOLOGICAL, INTELLIGENCE; N=135
                STUDENTS)
        aAPPLICATION 1960 E-2 T-27 S-11

1605   WILLIAMS, C. D., TALLARICO, R. B., & TEDESCHI, J. T.
            MANIFEST NEEDS AND MANIFEST ANXIETY.
            JOURNAL OF CONSULTING PSYCHOLOGY, 1960, 24, 371.
                (CORRELATES:PSYCHOLOGICAL, DEMOGRAPHIC; USED AS CRITERION; N=543
                STUDENTS, 38 HIGH AND 39 LOW ANXIETY S'S SELECTED)
        aAPPLICATION 1960 E-2 T-2

1606   KORMAN, M.
            EGO STRENGTH AND CONFLICT DISCRIMINATION: AN EXPERIMENTAL CONSTRUCT
            VALIDATION OF THE EGO STRENGTH SCALE.
            JOURNAL OF CONSULTING PSYCHOLOGY, 1960, 24, 294-298.
                (MENTION; VALIDITY:CONSTRUCT; CORRELATES:BEHAVIORAL, PSYCHOLOGICAL;
                USED AS CRITERION; N=47 PSYCHIATRIC PATIENTS)
        aAPPLICATION 1960 B-5 D-45

1607   ZAX, M., & STRICKER, G.
            THE EFFECT OF A STRUCTURED INQUIRY ON RORSCHACH SCORES.
            JOURNAL OF CONSULTING PSYCHOLOGY, 1960, 24, 328-332.
                (RELIABILITY:INTERRATER; CORRELATES:ENVIRONMENTAL; N=75 MALES AND
                FEMALES)
        aAPPLICATION 1960 R-30

1608   CATTELL, R. B., & MCMICHAEL, R. E.
            CLINICAL DIAGNOSIS BY THE IPAT MUSIC PREFERENCE TEST.
            JOURNAL OF CONSULTING PSYCHOLOGY, 1960, 24, 333-341.
                (VALIDITY; CORRELATES:PSYCHOLOGICAL, PHYSIOLOGICAL, DEMOGRAPHIC;
                N=104 MALE MENTAL PATIENTS, 86 FEMALE MENTAL PATIENTS, 26 CONTROL
                MALES AND 34 CONTROL FEMALES)
        aAPPLICATION 1960 C-141

1609   GARDNER, E. F., & THOMPSON, G. G.
            (REVIEW OF SYRACUSE SCALES OF SOCIAL RELATIONS)--REVIEWED BY BIRDIN, E. S.
            JOURNAL OF CONSULTING PSYCHOLOGY, 1960, 24, 466.
                (REVIEW ARTICLE; DESCRIPTION; RELIABILITY:RETEST)
        aAPPLICATION 1960 G-81

1610   KLEINMUNTZ, B.
            AN EXTENSION OF THE CONSTRUCT VALIDITY OF THE EGO STRENGTH SCALE.
            JOURNAL OF CONSULTING PSYCHOLOGY, 1960, 24, 463-464.
                (VALIDITY:CONSTRUCT; CORRELATES:PSYCHOLOGICAL; USED AS CRITERION;
                N=50 COLLEGE MALES AND FEMALES AND 33 STUDENTS UNDER PSYCHIATRIC
                TREATMENT)
        aAPPLICATION 1960 B-5 D-45

1611   IZARD, C. E.
            PERSONALITY CHARACTERISTICS ASSOCIATED WITH RESISTANCE TO CHANGE.
            JOURNAL OF CONSULTING PSYCHOLOGY, 1960, 24, 437-440.
                    (VALIDITY:CONSTRUCT; CORRELATES:BEHAVIORAL, DEMOGRAPHIC; N=39
                    COLLEGE MALES AND FEMALES)
        @APPLICATION 1960 E-2

1612   HONIGFELD, G., & SPIGEL, I. M.
            ACHIEVEMENT MOTIVATION AND FIELD INDEPENDENCE.
            JOURNAL OF CONSULTING PSYCHOLOGY, 1960, 24, 550-551.
                    (MODIFICATION; RELIABILITY:INTERRATER; CORRELATES:PSYCHOLOGICAL,
                    DEMOGRAPHIC; N=28 COLLEGE MALES AND FEMALES)
        @APPLICATION 1960 M-7 T-83

1613   DAVITZ, J. R., & MASON, D. J.
            MANIFEST ANXIETY AND SOCIAL PERCEPTION.
            JOURNAL OF CONSULTING PSYCHOLOGY, 1960, 24, 554.
                    (CORRELATES:PSYCHOLOGICAL; USED AS CRITERION; N=156 COLLEGE
                    FRATERNITY MALES)
        @APPLICATION 1960 B-184

1614   MCNAIR, D. M., & LORR, M.
            THERAPISTS' JUDGMENTS OF APPROPRIATENESS OF PSYCHOTHERAPY FREQUENCY
            SCHEDULES.
            JOURNAL OF CONSULTING PSYCHOLOGY, 1960, 24, 500-506.
                    (MODIFICATION; CORRELATES:PSYCHOLOGICAL, ENVIRONMENTAL; USED AS
                    CRITERION; NORMATIVE DATA; N=133 PSYCHIATRIC OUTPATIENTS)
        @APPLICATION 1960 T-2 B-5 G-26 A-42 L-35 L-88 D-45

1615   WAGNER, N. N.
            DEVELOPMENTAL ASPECTS OF IMPULSE CONTROL.
            JOURNAL OF CONSULTING PSYCHOLOGY, 1960, 24, 537-540.
                    (DESCRIPTION; RELIABILITY:INTERRATER; CORRELATES:BEHAVIORAL,
                    PSYCHOLOGICAL; N=36 EMOTIONALLY DISTURBED BOYS)
        @APPLICATION 1960 B-165

1616   SIMKINS, L.
            EXAMINER REINFORCEMENT AND SITUATIONAL VARIABLES IN A PROJECTIVE TESTING
            SITUATION.
            JOURNAL OF CONSULTING PSYCHOLOGY, 1960, 24, 541-547.
                    (CORRELATES:ENVIRONMENTAL; 2 STUDIES: N=36 MALE AND FEMALE
                    UNDERGRADUATES AND 25 CONTROLS, N=12 UNDERGRADUATES AND CONTROLS)
        @APPLICATION 1960 H-37

1617   DENNIS, W., & RASKIN, E.
            FURTHER EVIDENCE CONCERNING THE EFFECT OF HANDWRITING HABITS UPON THE
            LOCATION OF DRAWINGS.
            JOURNAL OF CONSULTING PSYCHOLOGY, 1960, 24, 548-549.
                    (CORRELATES:BEHAVIORAL, DEMOGRAPHIC; CROSS-CULTURAL APPLICATION;
                    MEDIAN N=307 FOR SAMPLES OF TURKISH, CAMBODIAN, JAPANESE,
                    IRANIAN, AND ISRAELI SUBJECTS)
        @APPLICATION 1960 G-78 M-58

1618   LOTHROP, W. W.
            PSYCHOLOGICAL TEST COVARIATES OF CONCEPTUAL DEFICIT IN SCHIZOPHRENIA.
            JOURNAL OF CONSULTING PSYCHOLOGY, 1960, 24, 496-499.
                    (CORRELATES:PSYCHOLOGICAL, DEMOGRAPHIC, INTELLIGENCE; N=36 MALE
                    VETERAN SCHIZOPHRENICS)
        @APPLICATION 1960 S-103 R-30 R-58

1619   QUAY, H. C., PETERSON, D. R., & CONSALVI, C.
            THE INTERPRETATION OF THREE PERSONALITY FACTORS IN JUVENILE DELINQUENCY.
            JOURNAL OF CONSULTING PSYCHOLOGY, 1960, 24, 555.
                    (VALIDITY:CRITERION; CORRELATES:BEHAVIORAL, PSYCHOLOGICAL,
                    DEMOGRAPHIC, INTELLIGENCE; N=263 MALE JUVENILE DELINQUENTS)
        @APPLICATION 1960 C-55 P-31

1620   BENDIG, A. W.
            THE FACTORIAL VALIDITY OF ITEMS ON THE IPAT ANXIETY SCALE.
            JOURNAL OF CONSULTING PSYCHOLOGY, 1960, 24, 374.
                    (RELIABILITY:INTERNAL CONSISTENCY; VALIDITY:CONSTRUCT; FACTOR
                    ANALYSIS; N=100 MALE AND 100 FEMALE UNDERGRADUATE AND GRADUATE
                    STUDENTS)
        @APPLICATION 1960 C-136

1621   MESSICK, S.
            DIMENSIONS OF SOCIAL DESIRABILITY.
            JOURNAL OF CONSULTING PSYCHOLOGY, 1960, 24, 279-287.
                 (FACTOR ANALYSIS; BIAS:RESPONSE; N=108 DISTURBED MENTAL HOSPITAL
                 PATIENTS)
            aAPPLICATION 1960 E-2

1622   EICHMAN, W. J.
            REPLICATED FACTORS ON THE MMPI WITH FEMALE NP PATIENTS.
            JOURNAL OF CONSULTING PSYCHOLOGY, 1961, 25, 55-60.
                 (FACTOR ANALYSIS; 2 SAMPLES: N=62 AND 85 FEMALE PSYCHIATRIC PATIENTS)
            aAPPLICATION 1961 D-45 T-2 W-41 W-8 B-5 N-14

1623   ARMSTRONG, R. G., & HAUCK, P. A.
            SEXUAL IDENTIFICATION AND THE FIRST FIGURE DRAWN.
            JOURNAL OF CONSULTING PSYCHOLOGY, 1961, 25, 51-54.
                 (CORRELATES:PSYCHOLOGICAL; NORMATIVE DATA; N=57 MALE, 57 FEMALE
                 COLLEGE STUDENTS)
            aAPPLICATION 1961 M-58 L-35

1624   SINGER, J. L., & SCHONBAR, R. A.
            CORRELATES OF DAYDREAMING: A DIMENSION OF SELF-AWARENESS.
            JOURNAL OF CONSULTING PSYCHOLOGY, 1961, 25, 1-6.
                 (CORRELATES:PSYCHOLOGICAL, INTELLIGENCE; N=44 NEGRO AND WHITE WOMEN
                 GRADUATE STUDENTS)
            aAPPLICATION 1961 W-41 W-8 D-57 C-5 M-7 D-45

1625   GOLDFARB, A.
            PERFORMANCE UNDER STRESS IN RELATION TO INTELLECTUAL CONTROL AND SELF-
            ACCEPTANCE.
            JOURNAL OF CONSULTING PSYCHOLOGY, 1961, 25, 7-12.
                 (CORRELATES:PSYCHOLOGICAL, INTELLIGENCE, ENVIRONMENTAL; NORMATIVE
                 DATA; N=30 COLLEGE STUDENTS)
            aAPPLICATION 1961 B-13 R-30

1626   HANLEY, C.
            SOCIAL DESIRABILITY AND RESPONSE BIAS IN THE MMPI.
            JOURNAL OF CONSULTING PSYCHOLOGY, 1961, 25, 13-20.
                 (DESCRIPTION; MENTION; REVIEW ARTICLE; BIAS:RESPONSE)
            aAPPLICATION 1961 E-1 F-13 W-14 C-58 H-122 D-45 G-127

1627   BLOOM, B. L., & ARKOFF, A.
            ROLE PLAYING IN ACUTE AND CHRONIC SCHIZOPHRENIA.
            JOURNAL OF CONSULTING PSYCHOLOGY, 1961, 25, 24-28.
                 (NORMATIVE DATA; BIAS:RESPONSE; N=56 FEMALE CAUCASIAN AND ORIENTAL
                 SCHIZOPHRENICS)
            aAPPLICATION 1961 R-30 S-190 D-45

1628   PARLOFF, M. B.
            THERAPIST-PATIENT RELATIONSHIPS AND OUTCOME OF PSYCHOTHERAPY.
            JOURNAL OF CONSULTING PSYCHOLOGY, 1961, 25, 29-38.
                 (MODIFICATION; VALIDITY:CRITERION; CORRELATES:PSYCHOLOGICAL; N=21
                 PSYCHIATRIC PATIENTS)
            aAPPLICATION 1961 K-32 F-81

1629   STOLTZ, R. E., & COLTHARP, F. C.
            CLINICAL JUDGMENTS AND THE DRAW-A-PERSON TEST.
            JOURNAL OF CONSULTING PSYCHOLOGY, 1961, 25, 43-45.
                 (VALIDITY:CRITERION; CORRELATES:PSYCHOLOGICAL, INTELLIGENCE; N=60
                 FOURTH GRADERS)
            aAPPLICATION 1961 M-58 G-78 S-310

1630   DAVIDS, A., DEVAULT, S., & TALMADGE, M.
            ANXIETY, PREGNANCY, AND CHILDBIRTH ABNORMALITIES.
            JOURNAL OF CONSULTING PSYCHOLOGY, 1961, 25, 74-77.
                 (VALIDITY:CONSTRUCT; CORRELATES:ENVIRONMENTAL; N=48 PREGNANT WOMEN)
            aAPPLICATION 1961 M-2

1631   HAWORTH, M. R.
        REPEAT STUDY WITH A PROJECTIVE FILM FOR CHILDREN.
        JOURNAL OF CONSULTING PSYCHOLOGY, 1961, 25, 78-83.
                (RELIABILITY:INTERRATER; VALIDITY:CROSS-VALIDATION;
                CORRELATES:BEHAVIORAL, DEMOGRAPHIC; N=257 KINDERGARTEN, FIRST AND
                SECOND GRADE CHILDREN)
        @APPLICATION 1961 H-121

1632   CARTWRIGHT, D. S., ROBERTSON, R. J., FISKE, D. W., & KIRTNER, W. L.
        LENGTH OF THERAPY IN RELATION TO OUTCOME AND CHANGE IN PERSONAL
        INTEGRATION.
        JOURNAL OF CONSULTING PSYCHOLOGY, 1961, 25, 84-88.
                (CORRELATES:PSYCHOLOGICAL; USED AS CRITERION; N=52 MALE, 35 FEMALE
                THERAPY CLIENTS)
        @APPLICATION 1961
        @S-187

1633   VOGEL, J. L.
        AUTHORITARIANISM IN THE THERAPEUTIC RELATIONSHIP.
        JOURNAL OF CONSULTING PSYCHOLOGY, 1961, 25, 102-108.
                (REVISION; CORRELATES:PSYCHOLOGICAL; N=32 PSYCHIATRIC OUTPATIENTS
                AND 49 THERAPISTS)
        @APPLICATION 1961 A-5
        @S-187

1634   MARLOWE, D., & CROWNE, D. P.
        SOCIAL DESIRABILITY AND RESPONSE TO PERCEIVED SITUATIONAL DEMANDS.
        JOURNAL OF CONSULTING PSYCHOLOGY, 1961, 25, 109-115.
                (VALIDITY:CONSTRUCT; CORRELATES:BEHAVIORAL, ENVIRONMENTAL; N=57 MALE
                UNDERGRADUATES)
        @APPLICATION 1961 E-1 C-27 B-4

1635   PIOTROWSKI, Z. A., & BRICKLIN, B.
        A SECOND VALIDATION OF A LONG-TERM RORSCHACH PROGNOSTIC INDEX FOR
        SCHIZOPHRENIC PATIENTS.
        JOURNAL OF CONSULTING PSYCHOLOGY, 1961, 25, 123-128.
                (VALIDITY:CRITERION, CROSS-VALIDATION; 2 STUDIES: N=29 MALE, 41
                FEMALE SCHIZOPHRENICS, N=97 MALE, 6 FEMALE PSYCHOTIC PATIENTS)
        @APPLICATION 1961 R-30 P-126

1636   MILGRAM, N. A., & HELPER, M. M.
        THE SOCIAL DESIRABILITY SET IN INDIVIDUAL AND GROUPED SELF-RATINGS.
        JOURNAL OF CONSULTING PSYCHOLOGY, 1961, 25, 91.
                (CORRELATES:ENVIRONMENTAL; BIAS:RESPONSE; N=80 FRESHMEN MALE
                MEDICAL STUDENTS)
        @APPLICATION 1961 E-2

1637   HAND, J., & REYNOLDS, H. H.
        SUPPRESSING DISTORTIONS IN TEMPERAMENT INVENTORIES.
        JOURNAL OF CONSULTING PSYCHOLOGY, 1961, 25, 180-181.
                (VALIDITY; CORRELATES:PSYCHOLOGICAL; NORMATIVE DATA; BIAS:RESPONSE;
                N=373 AIR FORCE TRAINEES)
        @APPLICATION 1961 G-26 H-72

1638   ISCOE, I., & CARDEN, J. A.
        FIELD DEPENDENCE, MANIFEST ANXIETY, AND SOCIOMETRIC STATUS IN CHILDREN.
        JOURNAL OF CONSULTING PSYCHOLOGY, 1961, 25, 184.
                (CORRELATES:PSYCHOLOGICAL, DEMOGRAPHIC, ENVIRONMENTAL; N=16 MALE, 15
                FEMALE 6TH GRADERS)
        @APPLICATION 1961 W-19 C-55

1639   SPANNER, M.
        ATTRIBUTION OF TRAITS AND EMOTIONAL HEALTH AS FACTORS ASSOCIATED WITH THE
        PREDICTION OF PERSONALITY CHARACTERISTICS OF OTHERS.
        JOURNAL OF CONSULTING PSYCHOLOGY, 1961, 25, 210-215.
                (CORRELATES:PSYCHOLOGICAL; N=100 AIR FORCE OFFICERS)
        @APPLICATION 1961 C-146 C-236

1640   SWICKARD, D. L., & SPILKA, B.
        HOSTILITY EXPRESSION AMONG DELINQUENTS OF MINORITY AND MAJORTY GROUPS.
        JOURNAL OF CONSULTING PSYCHOLOGY, 1961, 25, 216-220.
                (CORRELATES:PSYCHOLOGICAL, DEMOGRAPHIC; NORMATIVE DATA; N=81 MALE AND
                FEMALE DELINQUENTS FROM MINORITY AND MAJORITY GROUPS)
        @APPLICATION 1961 R-12 S-24 E-1 D-45

1641   ROSENBERG, B. G., SUTTON-SMITH, B., & MORGAN, E.
            THE USE OF OPPOSITE SEX SCALES AS A MEASURE OF PSYCHOSEXUAL DEVIANCY.
            JOURNAL OF CONSULTING PSYCHOLOGY, 1961, 25, 221-225.
                (CORRELATES:BEHAVIORAL, PSYCHOLOGICAL, DEMOGRAPHIC; NORMATIVE DATA;
                N=337 FOURTH, FIFTH AND SIXTH GRADERS)
        @APPLICATION 1961 C-55 R-11 S-192 B-174

1642   BOOMER, D. S., & GOODRICH, D. W.
            SPEECH DISTURBANCE AND JUDGED ANXIETY.
            JOURNAL OF CONSULTING PSYCHOLOGY, 1961, 25, 160-164.
                (RELIABILITY:INTERRATER; CORRELATES:PSYCHOLOGICAL; N=2 PSYCHOTHERAPY
                OUTPATIENTS)
        @APPLICATION 1961 M-35

1643   BRANCA, A. A., & PODOLNICK, E. E.
            NORMAL, HYPNOTICALLY INDUCED, AND FEIGNED ANXIETY AS REFLECTED IN AND
            DETECTED BY THE MMPI.
            JOURNAL OF CONSULTING PSYCHOLOGY, 1961, 25, 165-170.
                (CORRELATES:PSYCHOLOGICAL; NORMATIVE DATA; N=8 FEMALE, 2 MALE
                UNDERGRADUATES)
        @APPLICATION 1961 D-45 W-8 W-41

1644   OLSON, G. W.
            THE INFLUENCE OF CONTEXT ON THE DEPRESSION SCALE OF THE MMPI IN A PSYCHOTIC
            POPULATION.
            JOURNAL OF CONSULTING PSYCHOLOGY, 1961, 25, 178-179.
                (RELIABILITY:RETEST; VALIDITY; BIAS:RESPONSE; N=30 FEMALE, 20 MALE
                PSYCHIATRIC PATIENTS)
        @APPLICATION 1961 D-45

1645   GILBERSTADT, H., & FARKAS, E.
            ANOTHER LOOK AT MMPI PROFILES TYPES IN MULTIPLE SCLEROSIS.
            JOURNAL OF CONSULTING PSYCHOLOGY, 1961, 25, 440-444.
                (CORRELATES:PHYSIOLOGICAL, DEMOGRAPHIC; N=25 MULTIPLE SCLEROSIS
                PATIENTS AND 25 BRAIN-INJURED PATIENTS, ALL MALE)
        @APPLICATION 1961 D-45

1646   JONES, R. E.
            IDENTIFICATION IN TERMS OF PERSONAL CONSTRUCTS: RECONCILING A PARADOX
            IN THEORY.
            JOURNAL OF CONSULTING PSYCHOLOGY, 1961, 25, 276.
                (RELIABILITY:RETEST; VALIDITY:CONSTRUCT; CORRELATES:PSYCHOLOGICAL;
                USED AS CRITERION; N=36 MALE PSYCHIATRIC PATIENTS, 36 MALE NORMALS)
        @APPLICATION 1961 K-23

1647   HELLER, K., & GOLDSTEIN, A. P.
            CLIENT DEPENDENCY AND THERAPIST EXPECTANCY AS RELATIONSHIP MAINTAINING
            VARIABLES IN PSYCHOTHERAPY.
            JOURNAL OF CONSULTING PSYCHOLOGY, 1961, 25, 371-375.
                (MODIFICATION; CORRELATES:PSYCHOLOGICAL; N=30 CLIENTS, 10 MALE
                THERAPISTS)
        @APPLICATION 1961 E-2 L-95 B-138 G-126

1648   CARTWRIGHT, R. D.
            THE EFFECTS OF PSYCHOTHERAPY ON SELF CONSISTENCY: A REPLICATION AND
            EXTENSION.
            JOURNAL OF CONSULTING PSYCHOLOGY, 1961, 25, 376-382.
                (CORRELATES:PSYCHOLOGICAL, ENVIRONMENTAL; N=19 PSYCHOTHERAPY CLIENTS
                AND 30 CONTROLS)
        @APPLICATION 1961 B-60 M-20

1649   ESTES, B. W., CURTIN, M. E., DEBURGER, R. A., & DENNY, C.
            RELATIONSHIPS BETWEEN 1960 STANFORD-BINET, 1937 STANFORD-BINET, WISC,
            RAVEN, AND DRAW-A-MAN.
            JOURNAL OF CONSULTING PSYCHOLOGY, 1961, 25, 388-391.
                (CORRELATES:INTELLIGENCE; N=47 MALE, 35 FEMALE SCHOOL CHILDREN)
        @APPLICATION 1961 G-78

1650   KRAUSE, M. S., & PILISUK, M.
            ANXIETY IN VERBAL BEHAVIOR: A VALIDATION STUDY.
            JOURNAL OF CONSULTING PSYCHOLOGY, 1961, 25, 414-419.
                (MODIFICATION; RELIABILITY:INTERRATER; VALIDITY:CRITERION)
        @APPLICATION 1961 M-35 D-63

1651   ANKER, J. M.
            CHRONICITY OF NEUROPSYCHIATRIC HOSPITALIZATION: A PREDICTIVE SCALE.
            JOURNAL OF CONSULTING PSYCHOLOGY, 1961, 25, 425-432.
                (VALIDITY:CRITERION, CROSS-VALIDATION; NORMATIVE DATA; 2 STUDIES:
                N=358 PSYCHIATRIC PATIENTS, N=103 SHORT TERM PATIENTS AND 63 LONG
                TERM PATIENTS, ALL MALE)
        @APPLICATION 1961 D-45 M-137

1652   WEINER, I. B.
            THREE RORSCHACH SCORES INDICATIVE OF SCHIZOPHRENIA.
            JOURNAL OF CONSULTING PSYCHOLOGY, 1961, 25, 436-439.
                (VALIDITY:CROSS-VALIDATION; 3 SAMPLES: N=71, N=52, N=89 PSYCHIATRIC
                PATIENTS)
        @APPLICATION 1961 R-30

1653   ROOS, P.
            EVALUATION OF PSYCHOTHERAPY AS AN ADJUNCT TO INSULIN-COMA THERAPY.
            JOURNAL OF CONSULTING PSYCHOLOGY, 1961, 25, 450-455.
                (USED AS CRITERION; N=19 EXPERIMENTAL AND 18 CONTROL CASES, ALL
                RECEIVING INSULIN THERAPY)
        @APPLICATION 1961 L-39 R-30

1654   GOUWS, D. J.
            PREDICTION OF RELAPSE FOR PSYCHIATRIC PATIENTS.
            JOURNAL OF CONSULTING PSYCHOLOGY, 1961, 25, 142-145.
                (VALIDITY:CONSTRUCT, CRITERION, CROSS-VALIDATION;
                CORRELATES:PSYCHOLOGICAL; NORMATIVE DATA; BIAS:RESPONSE; N=94
                PSYCHIATRIC PATIENTS)
        @APPLICATION 1961 F-80 D-45 F-34 F-127

1655   CHANCE, J. E.
            INDEPENDENCE TRAINING AND FIRST GRADERS' ACHIEVEMENT.
            JOURNAL OF CONSULTING PSYCHOLOGY, 1961, 25, 149-154.
                (MODIFICATION; CORRELATES:INTELLIGENCE; N=32 FEMALE, 33 MALE FIRST
                GRADERS)
        @APPLICATION 1961 W-54

1656   ZARLOCK, S. P.
            MAGICAL THINKING AND ASSOCIATED PSYCHOLOGICAL REACTIONS TO BLINDNESS.
            JOURNAL OF CONSULTING PSYCHOLOGY, 1961, 25, 155-159.
                (CORRELATES:PSYCHOLOGICAL; USED AS CRITERION; N=52 MALE BLIND
                PERSONS, AGES 20-45 YEARS AND 25 NORMAL CONTROLS)
        @APPLICATION 1961 B-5 T-2 A-5 F-128

1657   HEILBRUN, A. B., JR., & GOODSTEIN, L. D.
            THE RELATIONSHIPS BETWEEN INDIVIDUALLY DEFINED AND GROUP DEFINED SOCIAL
            DESIRABILITY AND PERFORMANCE ON THE EDWARDS PERSONAL PREFERENCE SCHEDULE.
            JOURNAL OF CONSULTING PSYCHOLOGY, 1961, 25, 200-204.
                (VALIDITY:CONSTRUCT; NORMATIVE DATA; BIAS:RESPONSE; N=29 MALE, 29
                FEMALE COLLEGE STUDENTS)
        @APPLICATION 1961 E-2

1658   SPERBER, Z.
            TEST ANXIETY AND PERFORMANCE UNDER STRESS.
            JOURNAL OF CONSULTING PSYCHOLOGY, 1961, 25, 226-233.
                (REVISION; CORRELATES:PSYCHOLOGICAL, INTELLIGENCE, ENVIRONMENTAL;
                N=399 AIR FORCE RECRUITS)
        @APPLICATION 1961 S-5 D-45

1659   LUBIN, B.
            JUDGMENTS OF ADJUSTMENT FROM TAT STORIES AS A FUNCTION OF EXPERIMENTALLY
            ALTERED SETS.
            JOURNAL OF CONSULTING PSYCHOLOGY, 1961, 25, 249-252.
                (RELIABILITY:INTERRATER; CORRELATES:ENVIRONMENTAL; BIAS:RESPONSE,
                TESTER; N=60 COLLEGE FRESHMEN, 10 CLINICAL PSYCHOLOGISTS AS RATERS)
        @APPLICATION 1961 D-25 M-20

1660   LEVI, A.
            ORTHOPEDIC DISABILITY AS A FACTOR IN HUMAN-FIGURE PERCEPTION.
            JOURNAL OF CONSULTING PSYCHOLOGY, 1961, 25, 253-256.
                (CORRELATES:PSYCHOLOGICAL, PHYSIOLOGICAL; NORMATIVE DATA; N=36
                SUBJECTS WITH ORTHOPEDIC DISABILITIES)
        @APPLICATION 1961 S-37

1661   PHARES, E. J.
            TAT PERFORMANCE AS A FUNCTION OF ANXIETY AND COPING-AVOIDING BEHAVIOR.
            JOURNAL OF CONSULTING PSYCHOLOGY, 1961, 25, 257-259.
                (CORRELATES:PSYCHOLOGICAL; USED AS CRITERION; N=263 COLLEGE STUDENTS)
        @APPLICATION 1961 T-2 M-20 G-10

1662   PHILLIPS, J. S., MATARAZZO, R. G., MATARAZZO, J. D., SASLOW, G., & KANFER, F. H.
            RELATIONSHIPS BETWEEN DESCRIPTIVE CONTENT AND INTERACTION BEHAVIOR IN
            INTERVIEWS.
            JOURNAL OF CONSULTING PSYCHOLOGY, 1961, 25, 260-266.
                (DESCRIPTION; VALIDITY:CONSTRUCT, CRITERION; CORRELATES:BEHAVIORAL,
                PSYCHOLOGICAL; N=17 FEMALE, 13 MALE PSYCHIATRIC OUTPATIENTS)
        @APPLICATION 1961 C-66 P-79

1663   KRAUSE, M. S.
            ANXIETY IN VERBAL BEHAVIOR: AN INTERCORRELATIONAL STUDY.
            JOURNAL OF CONSULTING PSYCHOLOGY, 1961, 25, 272.
                (VALIDITY:CONSTRUCT; CORRELATES:PSYCHOLOGICAL; N=15 MALE MENTAL
                PATIENTS)
        @APPLICATION 1961 M-35 C-63

1664   BURSTEIN, A. G.
            A NOTE ON TIME OF FIRST RESPONSES IN RORSCHACH PROTOCOLS.
            JOURNAL OF CONSULTING PSYCHOLOGY, 1961, 25, 549-550.
                (DESCRIPTION; MENTION)
        @APPLICATION 1961 R-30

1665   STEFFY, R. A., & BECKER, W. C.
            MEASUREMENT OF THE SEVERITY OF DISORDER IN SCHIZOPHRENIA BY MEANS OF THE
            HOLTZMAN INKBLOT TEST.
            JOURNAL OF CONSULTING PSYCHOLOGY, 1961, 25, 555.
                (VALIDITY:CONSTRUCT, CRITERION; CORRELATES:PSYCHOLOGICAL; N=36 MALE
                SCHIZOPHRENICS)
        @APPLICATION 1961 H-37 B-82

1666   WHITAKER, L., JR.
            THE USE OF AN EXTENDED DRAW-A-PERSON TEST TO IDENTIFY HOMOSEXUAL AND
            EFFEMINATE MEN.
            JOURNAL OF CONSULTING PSYCHOLOGY, 1961, 25, 482-485.
                (VALIDITY:CRITERION; USED AS CRITERION; N=236 MEN, AGED 16-65)
        @APPLICATION 1961 M-58

1667   MURSTEIN, B. I., DAVID, C., FISHER, D., & FURTH, H. G.
            THE SCALING OF THE TAT FOR HOSTILITY BY A VARIETY OF SCALING METHODS.
            JOURNAL OF CONSULTING PSYCHOLOGY, 1961, 25, 497-504.
                (MODIFICATION; RELIABILITY:INTERNAL CONSISTENCY; USED AS CRITERION)
        @APPLICATION 1961 M-20

1668   CHAMBERS, J. L.
            TRAIT JUDGMENT OF PHOTOGRAPHS AND ADJUSTMENT OF COLLEGE STUDENTS.
            JOURNAL OF CONSULTING PSYCHOLOGY, 1961, 25, 433-435.
                (VALIDITY:CRITERION; CORRELATES:PSYCHOLOGICAL, DEMOGRAPHIC,
                INTELLIGENCE; N=441 COLLEGE STUDENTS)
        @APPLICATION 1961 C-13

1669   HEILBRUN, A. B., JR.
            THE PSYCHOLOGICAL SIGNIFICANCE OF THE MMPI K SCALE IN A NORMAL POPULATION.
            JOURNAL OF CONSULTING PSYCHOLOGY, 1961, 25, 486-491.
                (VALIDITY:CONSTRUCT; CORRELATES:PSYCHOLOGICAL; NORMATIVE DATA;
                N=299 MALE, 343 FEMALE COLLEGE STUDENTS)
        @APPLICATION 1961 D-45 G-21

1670   SIEGMAN, A. W.
            THE RELATIONSHIP BETWEEN FUTURE TIME PERSPECTIVE, TIME ESTIMATION, AND
            IMPULSE CONTROL IN A GROUP OF YOUNG OFFENDERS AND IN A CONTROL GROUP.
            JOURNAL OF CONSULTING PSYCHOLOGY, 1961, 25, 470-475.
                (MODIFICATION; CORRELATES:BEHAVIORAL, INTELLIGENCE; USED AS
                CRITERION; NORMATIVE DATA; CROSS-CULTURAL APPLICATION; N=30 ISRAELI
                JUVENILE DELINQUENTS, 22 CONTROLS)
        @APPLICATION 1961 W-109

1671   BLOCK, J.
            EGO IDENTITY, ROLE VARIABILITY, AND ADJUSTMENT.
            JOURNAL OF CONSULTING PSYCHOLOGY, 1961, 25, 392-397.
                (CORRELATES:PSYCHOLOGICAL: N=41 PSYCHOLOGY STUDENTS)
        @APPLICATION 1961 G-22 B-199

1672   KORCHIN, S. J., & HEATH, H. A.
            SOMATIC EXPERIENCE IN THE ANXIETY STATE: SOME SEX AND PERSONALITY
            CORRELATES OF "AUTONOMIC FEEDBACK."
            JOURNAL OF CONSULTING PSYCHOLOGY, 1961, 25, 398-404.
                (CORRELATES:PSYCHOLOGICAL, DEMOGRAPHIC; NORMATIVE DATA; N=139 MALE,
                37 FEMALE COLLEGE STUDENTS)
        @APPLICATION 1961 N-17 B-5 T-2 M-3

1673   REYHER, J., & SHOEMAKER, D.
            A COMPARISON BETWEEN HYPNOTICALLY INDUCED AGE REGRESSIONS AND WAKING
            STORIES TO TAT CARDS: A PRELIMINARY REPORT.
            JOURNAL OF CONSULTING PSYCHOLOGY, 1961, 25, 409-413.
                (CORRELATES:PSYCHOLOGICAL, ENVIRONMENTAL; USED AS CRITERION   N=5
                PSYCHOTHERAPY CLIENTS)
        @APPLICATION 1961 M-20

1674   BRIGGS, P. F., WIRT, R. D., & JOHNSON, R.
            AN APPLICATION OF PREDICTION TABLES TO THE STUDY OF DELINQUENCY.
            JOURNAL OF CONSULTING PSYCHOLOGY, 1961, 25, 46-50.
                (VALIDITY:CRITERION; CORRELATES:PSYCHOLOGICAL, ENVIRONMENTAL; N=573
                BOYS)
        @APPLICATION 1961 D-45

1675   ANKER, J. M., & WALSH, R. P.
            GROUP PSYCHOTHERAPY, A SPECIAL ACTIVITY PROGRAM, AND GROUP STRUCTURE IN THE
            TREATMENT OF CHRONIC SCHIZOPHRENICS.
            JOURNAL OF CONSULTING PSYCHOLOGY, 1961, 25, 476-481.
                (RELIABILITY:INTERRATER; CORRELATES: PSYCHOLOGICAL, ENVIRONMENTAL;
                USED AS CRITERION; N=134 MALE SCHIZOPHRENICS)
        @APPLICATION 1961 L-39 E-20

1676   EPSTEIN, S.
            FOOD-RELATED RESPONSES TO AMBIGUOUS STIMULI AS A FUNCTION OF HUNGER AND
            EGO STRENGTH.
            JOURNAL OF CONSULTING PSYCHOLOGY, 1961, 25, 463-469.
                (CORRELATES:PHYSIOLOGICAL; USED AS CRITERION; N=180 COLLEGE MALES AND
                FEMALES)
        @APPLICATION 1961 K-13 R-30

1677   BERGS, L. P., & MARTIN, B.
            THE EFFECT OF INSTRUCTIONAL TIME INTERVAL AND SOCIAL DESIRABILITY ON THE
            VALIDITY OF A FORCED-CHOICE ANXIETY SCALE.
            JOURNAL OF CONSULTING PSYCHOLOGY, 1961, 25, 528-532.
                (REVISION; RELIABILITY:RETEST; CORRELATES:PSYCHOLOGICAL, PHYSIO-
                LOGICAL, ENVIRONMENTAL; NORMATIVE DATA; BIAS:RESPONSE; N=110 COLLEGE
                STUDENTS)
        @APPLICATION 1961 T-2 B-184

1678   WAHLER, H. J.
            RESPONSE STYLES IN CLINICAL ADN NONCLINICAL GROUPS.
            JOURNAL OF CONSULTING PSYCHOLOGY, 1961, 25, 533-539.
                (CORRELATES:PSYCHOLOGICAL; N=44 FEMALE, 65 MALE NORMALS, 47 MALE OUT-
                PATIENTS, AND 75 MALE HOSPITALIZED PSYCHIATRIC PATIENTS)
        @APPLICATION 1961 D-45

1679   GYNTHER, M. D.
            THE CLINICAL UTILITY OF "INVALID" MMPI F SCORES.
            JOURNAL OF CONSULTING PSYCHOLOGY, 1961, 25, 540-542.
                (VALIDITY:CRITERION; CORRELATES:PSYCHOLOGICAL; NORMATIVE DATA; N=246
                WHITE MALE COURT REFERRALS)
        @APPLICATION 1961 D-45

1680   BLOCK, J.
            EGO STRENGTH AND CONFLICT DISCRIMINATION: A FAILURE OF REPLICATION.
            JOURNAL OF CONSULTING PSYCHOLOGY, 1961, 25, 551-552.
                (MENTION)
        @APPLICATION 1961 B-5

1681   LESSING, E. E.
              A NOTE ON THE SIGNIFICANCE OF DISCREPANCIES BETWEEN GOODENOUGH AND BINET
              IQ SCORES.
              JOURNAL OF CONSULTING PSYCHOLOGY, 1961, 25, 456-457.
                    (VALIDITY:CRITERION; CORRELATES:INTELLIGENCE; N=23 WELL ADJUSTED
                    CHILDREN)
        @APPLICATION 1961 G-78

1682   GOODSTEIN, L. D., & ROWLEY, V. N.
              A FURTHER STUDY OF MMPI DIFFERENCES BETWEEN PARENTS OF DISTURBED AND
              NONDISTURBED CHILDREN.
              JOURNAL OF CONSULTING PSYCHOLOGY, 1961, 25, 460.
                    (VALIDITY:CROSS-VALIDATION; N=50 PAIRS OF PARENTS)
        @APPLICATION 1961 D-45

1683   BENDIG, A. W.
              IMPROVING THE FACTORIAL PURITY OF GUILFORD'S RESTRAINT AND THOUGHTFULNESS
              SCALES.
              JOURNAL OF CONSULTING PSYCHOLOGY, 1961, 25, 462.
                    (FACTOR ANALYSIS; N=300, 130, 145 STUDENTS)
        @APPLICATION 1961 G-20

1684   CAIRNS, R. B., & LEWIS, M.
              DEPENDENCY AND THE REINFORCEMENT VALUE OF A VERBAL STIMULUS.
              JOURNAL OF CONSULTING PSYCHOLOGY, 1962, 26, 1-8.
                    (CORRELATES:BEHAVIORAL; USED AS CRITERION; N=60 MALE COLLEGE
                    STUDENTS)
        @APPLICATION 1962 E-2 L-35

1685   WASKOW, I. E.
              REINFORCEMENT IN A THERAPY-LIKE SITUATION THROUGH SELECTIVE RESPONDING
              TO FEELINGS OR CONTENT.
              JOURNAL OF CONSULTING PSYCHOLOGY, 1962, 26, 11-19.
                    (USED AS CRITERION; N=36 COLLEGE STUDENTS)
        @APPLICATION 1962 H-51

1686   GEERTSMA, R. H.
              FACTOR ANALYSIS OF RORSCHACH SCORING CATEGORIES FOR A POPULATION OF
              NORMAL SUBJECTS.
              JOURNAL OF CONSULTING PSYCHOLOGY, 1962, 26, 20-25.
                    (FACTOR ANALYSIS; N=71 MALES AND 86 FEMALES FROM VARYING
                    OCCUPATIONS)
        @APPLICATION 1962 R-30

1687   CARSON, R. C., & HEINE, R. W.
              SIMILARITY AND SUCCESS IN THERAPEUTIC DYADS.
              JOURNAL OF CONSULTING PSYCHOLOGY, 1962, 26, 38-43.
                    (CORRELATES:PSYCHOLOGICAL; USED AS CRITERION; NORMATIVE DATA; N=35
                    FEMALE AND 25 MALE PSYCHIATRIC PATIENTS AND 60 MEDICAL STUDENTS)
        @APPLICATION 1962 D-45

1688   DENTLER, R. A., & MACKLER, B.
              THE PORTEUS MAZE TEST AS A PREDICTOR OF FUNCTIONING ABILITIES OF RETARDED
              CHILDREN.
              JOURNAL OF CONSULTING PSYCHOLOGY, 1962, 26, 50-55.
                    (VALIDITY:CRITERION; CORRELATES:PSYCHOLOGICAL, INTELLIGENCE; N=29
                    RETARDED CHILDREN)
        @APPLICATION 1962 D-7 P-22

1689   WEISS, P., & EMMERICH, W.
              DEPENDENCY FANTASY AND GROUP CONFORMITY IN ULCER PATIENTS.
              JOURNAL OF CONSULTING PSYCHOLOGY, 1962, 26, 61-64.
                    (CORRELATES:BEHAVIORAL, PSYCHOLOGICAL; N=38 MALE MEDICAL PATIENTS)
        @APPLICATION 1962 M-20 K-68

1690   HAVENER, P. H., & IZARD, C. E.
              UNREALISTIC SELF-ENHANCEMENT IN PARANOID SCHIZOPHRENICS.
              JOURNAL OF CONSULTING PSYCHOLOGY, 1962, 26, 65-68.
                    (CORRELATES:PSYCHOLOGICAL; USED AS CRITERION; N=20 HOSPITALIZED
                    PARANOID SCHIZOPHRENICS, 20 PSYCHIATRIC PATIENTS WITH OTHER DIAG-
                    NOSES, 20 CONTROLS)
        @APPLICATION 1962 L-39 F-7 B-13

1691   FARINA, A., GARMEZY, N., ZALUSKY, M., & BECKER, J.
            PREMORBID BEHAVIOR AND PROGNOSIS IN FEMALE SCHIZOPHRENIC PATIENTS.
            JOURNAL OF CONSULTING PSYCHOLOGY, 1962, 26, 56-60.
                (RELIABILITY:INTERNAL CONSISTENCY; CORRELATES:PSYCHOLOGICAL,
                DEMOGRAPHIC; N=50 RECOVERED, 33 NONRECOVERED FEMALE SCHIZOPHRENICS)
        aAPPLICATION 1962 P-32

1692   KOGAN, W. S., & FORDYCE, W. E.
            THE CONTROL OF SOCIAL DESIRABILITY: A COMPARISON OF THREE DIFFERENT
            Q SORTS AND A CHECK LIST, ALL COMPOSED OF THE SAME ITEMS.
            JOURNAL OF CONSULTING PSYCHOLOGY, 1962, 26, 26-30.
                (VALIDITY:CONTENT; N=39 MALE VETERAN PSYCHIATRIC PATIENTS)
        aAPPLICATION 1962 E-1 L-35

1693   TOMLINSON, T. M., & HART, J. T., JR.
            A VALIDATION STUDY OF THE PROCESS SCALE.
            JOURNAL OF CONSULTING PSYCHOLOGY, 1962, 26, 74-78.
                (RELIABILITY:INTERRATER; VALIDITY:CONSTRUCT, CRITERION; N=10
                PATIENTS)
        aAPPLICATION 1962 R-36

1694   MARLOWE, D.
            NEED FOR SOCIAL APPROVAL AND THE OPERANT CONDITIONING OF MEANINGFUL VERBAL
            BEHAVIOR.
            JOURNAL OF CONSULTING PSYCHOLOGY, 1962, 26, 79-83.
                (VALIDITY:CONSTRUCT; CORRELATES:BEHAVIORAL; USED AS CRITERION; N=34
                MALE, 42 FEMALE COLLEGE STUDENTS)
        aAPPLICATION 1962 C-27

1695   EDWARDS, A.L., & FEATHERS, L. B.
            THE FIRST FACTOR OF THE MMPI: SOCIAL DESIRABILITY OR EGO STRENGTH?
            JOURNAL OF CONSULTING PSYCHOLOGY, 1962, 26, 99-100.
                (MENTION; VALIDITY:CONTENT, CONSTRUCT)
        aAPPLICATION 1962 E-1 D-45

1696   EKMAN, P., FRIESEN, W. V., & LUTZKER, D. R.
            PSYCHOLOGICAL REACTIONS TO INFANTRY BASIC TRAINING.
            JOURNAL OF CONSULTING PSYCHOLOGY, 1962, 26, 103-104.
                (CORRELATES:ENVIRONMENTAL; USED AS CRITERION; N=93 ACTIVE ARMY
                PERSONNEL)
        aAPPLICATION 1962 D-45

1697   DASTON, P. G., & MCCONNELL, O. L.
            STABILITY OF RORSCHACH PENETRATION AND BARRIER SCORES OVER TIME.
            JOURNAL OF CONSULTING PSYCHOLOGY, 1962, 26, 104.
                (RELIABILITY:RETEST, INTERRATER; N=20 HOSPITALIZED MEN)
        aAPPLICATION 1962 F-75 F-135

1698   GYNTHER, M. D.
            DEGREE OF AGREEMENT AMONG THREE "INTERPERSONAL SYSTEM" MEASURES.
            JOURNAL OF CONSULTING PSYCHOLOGY, 1962, 26, 107.
                (VALIDITY:CONTENT; N=67 MALE AND 33 FEMALE COLLEGE STUDENTS)
        .aAPPLICATION 1962 D-45 L-35

1699   MOGAR, R. E.
            ANXIETY INDICES IN HUMAN FIGURE DRAWINGS: A REPLICATION AND EXTENSION.
            JOURNAL OF CONSULTING PSYCHOLOGY, 1962, 26, 108.
                (VALIDITY:CONSTRUCT, CRITERION; CORRELATES:PSYCHOLOGICAL,
                INTELLIGENCE; N=123 SUBJECTS)
        aAPPLICATION 1962 T-2 R-3C E-76

1700   GOTTESMAN, L. E.
            THE RELATIONSHIP OF COGNITIVE VARIABLES TO THERAPEUTIC ABILITY AND TRAINING
            OF CLIENT CENTERED THERAPISTS.
            JOURNAL OF CONSULTING PSYCHOLOGY, 1962, 26, 119-125.
                (MODIFICATION; CORRELATES:PSYCHOLOGICAL; USED AS CRITERION; N=32
                CLINICAL PSYCHOLOGY STUDENTS)
        aAPPLICATION 1962 K-23

1701   NICHOLS, R. C., & STRUMPFER, D. J. W.
            A FACTOR ANALYSIS OF DRAW-A-PERSON TEST SCORES.
            JOURNAL OF CONSULTING PSYCHOLOGY, 1962, 26, 156-161.
                (RELIABILITY:INTERRATER; FACTOR ANALYSIS; N=107 MALE COLLEGE STUDENTS
                AND 90 MALE VETERAN PATIENTS)
        aAPPLICATION 1962 G-78 M-58 W-195 S-330 D-100 S-329 A-389 B-175 F-138

1702   WALKER, J. N.
           AN EXAMINATION OF THE ROLE OF THE EXPERIMENTALLY DETERMINED RESPONSE SET IN
           EVALUATING EDWARDS' SOCIAL DESIRABILITY SCALE.
           JOURNAL OF CONSULTING PSYCHOLOGY, 1962, 26, 162-166.
               (USED AS CRITERION; NORMATIVE DATA; BIAS:RESPONSE; N=120 MALE COLLEGE
               STUDENTS)
       @APPLICATION 1962 D-45 W-14

1703   VAN DE CASTLE, R. L.
           PERCEPTUAL IMMATURITY AND ACQUIESCENCE AMONG VARIOUS DEVELOPMENTAL LEVELS.
           JOURNAL OF CONSULTING PSYCHOLOGY, 1962, 26, 167-171.
               (CORRELATES:PSYCHOLOGICAL; USED AS CRITERION; BIAS:RESPONSE; N=200
               SCHOOL CHILDREN, 200 COLLEGE STUDENTS AND 78 SCHIZOPHRENICS)
       @APPLICATION 1962 W-9 D-45

1704   SPERBER, Z.
           RIGIDITY AND CONFORMITY TENDENCIES OF JUDGES AND THEIR UTILIZATION OF
           AUTOBIOGRAPHICAL MATERIAL IN MAKING PREDICTIONS.
           JOURNAL OF CONSULTING PSYCHOLOGY, 1962, 26, 144-148.
               (CORRELATES:PSYCHOLOGICAL; N=99 COLLEGE STUDENTS)
       @APPLICATION 1962 W-11 G-39 A-5 E-76

1705   BUSS, A. H., FISCHER, H., & SIMMONS, A. J.
           AGGRESSION AND HOSTILITY IN PSYCHIATRIC PATIENTS.
           JOURNAL OF CONSULTING PSYCHOLOGY, 1962, 26, 84-89.
               (CORRELATES:PSYCHOLOGICAL, DEMOGRAPHIC; FACTOR ANALYSIS; N=63 FEMALE
               AND 33 MALE PSYCHIATRIC PATIENTS)
       @APPLICATION 1962 B-44 R-30 H-74 E-76 D-112

1706   GOLDFRIED, M. R., & MCKENZIE, J. D., JR.
           SEX DIFFERENCES IN THE EFFECT OF ITEM STYLE ON SOCIAL DESIRABILITY AND
           FREQUENCY OF ENDORSEMENT.
           JOURNAL OF CONSULTING PSYCHOLOGY, 1962, 26, 126-128.
               (CORRELATES:PSYCHOLOGICAL, DEMOGRAPHIC; BIAS:RESPONSE; N=100 COLLEGE
               STUDENTS AND 420 COLLEGE STUDENTS)
       @APPLICATION 1962 B-280

1707   LUBIN, B., LEVITT, E. E., & ZUCKERMAN, M.
           SOME PERSONALITY DIFFERENCES BETWEEN RESPONDERS AND NONRESPONDERS TO A
           SURVEY QUESTIONNAIRE.
           JOURNAL OF CONSULTING PSYCHOLOGY, 1962, 26, 192.
               (CORRELATES:PSYCHOLOGICAL, BEHAVIORAL; N=72 NURSES)
       @APPLICATION 1962 E-2

1708   GETTER, H., & SUNDLAND, D. M.
           THE BARRON EGO STRENGTH SCALE AND PSYCHOTHERAPEUTIC OUTCOME.
           JOURNAL OF CONSULTING PSYCHOLOGY, 1962, 26, 195.
               (CORRELATES:PSYCHOLOGICAL, DEMOGRAPHIC; N=59 CANDIDATES FOR PSYCHO-
               THERAPY)
       @APPLICATION 1962 B-5

1709   MARKWELL, E. D., JR.
           AUTONOMIC NERVOUS SYSTEM MEASURES AND FACTOR CORRELATES WITH PERSONALITY
           INDICES IN A TUBERCULOUS POPULATION.
           JOURNAL OF CONSULTING PSYCHOLOGY, 1962, 26, 194.
               (CORRELATES:PHYSIOLOGICAL; N=75 TUBERCULOUS SUBJECTS)
       @APPLICATION 1962 D-45

1710   CRADDICK, R. A., LEIPOLD, W. D., & CACAVAS, P. D.
           THE RELATIONSHIP OF SHADING ON THE DRAW-A-PERSON TEST TO MANIFEST ANXIETY
           SCORES.
           JOURNAL OF CONSULTING PSYCHOLOGY, 1962, 26, 193.
               (RELIABILITY:INTERRATER; CORRELATES:PSYCHOLOGICAL; N=121 COLLEGE
               MALES, 151 COLLEGE FEMALES)
       @APPLICATION 1962 M-58 T-2

1711   CROVITZ, H. F.
           ON DIRECTION IN DRAWING A PERSON.
           JOURNAL OF CONSULTING PSYCHOLOGY, 1962, 26, 196.
               (CORRELATES:DEMOGRAPHIC; N=480 COLLEGE STUDENTS)
       @APPLICATION 1962 G-78 M-58

1712   BENDIG, A. W.
              FACTOR ANALYTIC SCALES OF COVERT AND OVERT HOSTILITY.
              JOURNAL OF CONSULTING PSYCHOLOGY, 1962, 26, 200.
                    (REVISION; FACTOR ANALYSIS; N=218 COLLEGE STUDENTS)
        @APPLICATION 1962 B-44

1713   ULLMAN, L. P., & LIM, D. T.
              CASE HISTORY MATERIAL AS A SOURCE OF THE IDENTIFICATION OF PATTERNS OF
              RESPONSE TO EMOTIONAL STIMULI IN A STUDY OF HUMOR.
              JOURNAL OF CONSULTING PSYCHOLOGY, 1962, 26, 221-225.
                    (VALIDITY:CONSTRUCT; CORRELATES:BEHAVIORAL, PSYCHOLOGICAL,
                    INTELLIGENCE; USED AS CRITERION; 3 STUDIES: N=33 MALE PSYCHIATRIC
                    PATIENTS, 64 MALE PSYCHIATRIC PATIENTS, 63 PSYCHIATRIC PATIENTS)
        @APPLICATION 1962 S-124 D-45 B-169 M-130 U-4

1714   SARASON, I. G., & CAMPBELL, J. M.
              ANXIETY AND THE VERBAL CONDITIONING OF MILDLY HOSTILE VERBS.
              JOURNAL OF CONSULTING PSYCHOLOGY, 1962, 26, 213-216.
                    (CORRELATES:PSYCHOLOGICAL; USED AS CRITERION; N=30 MALE
                    NEUROPSYCHIATRIC PATIENTS)
        @APPLICATION 1962 S-4

1715   SIEGMAN, A. W.
              PERSONALITY VARIABLES ASSOCIATED WITH ADMITTED CRIMINAL BEHAVIOR.
              JOURNAL OF CONSULTING PSYCHOLOGY, 1962, 26, 199.
                    (CORRELATES:PSYCHOLOGICAL; N=54 FEMALE AND 25 MALE ISRAELI
                    UNIVERSITY STUDENTS)
        @APPLICATION 1962 P-31 G-21

1716   JOHNS, J. H., & QUAY, H. C.
              THE EFFECT OF SOCIAL REWARD ON VERBAL CONDITIONING IN PSYCHOPATHIC AND
              NEUROTIC MILITARY OFFENDERS.
              JOURNAL OF CONSULTING PSYCHOLOGY, 1962, 26, 217-220.
                    (USED AS CRITERION; N=264 MALE PRISONERS)
        @APPLICATION 1962 P-31

1717   MCNEIL, E. B.
              AGGRESSION IN FANTASY AND BEHAVIOR.
              JOURNAL OF CONSULTING PSYCHOLOGY, 1962, 26, 232-240.
                    (CORRELATES:BEHAVIORAL, PSYCHOLOGICAL; N=95 AGGRESSIVE, ANTISOCIAL
                    BOYS)
        @APPLICATION 1962 M-20

1718   GUERTIN, W. H., & JOURARD, S. M.
              CHARACTERISTICS OF REAL-SELF-IDEAL-SELF DISCREPANCY SCORES REVEALED BY
              FACTOR ANALYSIS.
              JOURNAL OF CONSULTING PSYCHOLOGY, 1962, 26, 241-245.
                    (CORRELATES:DEMOGRAPHIC; FACTOR ANALYSIS; N=50 MALE AND 54 FEMALE
                    COLLEGE STUDENTS)
        @APPLICATION 1962 J-37

1719   LEVINE, D., & COHEN, J.
              SYMPTOMS AND EGO STRENGTH MEASURES AS PREDICTORS OF THE OUTCOME OF
              HOSPITALIZATION IN FUNCTIONAL PSYCHOSES.
              JOURNAL OF CONSULTING PSYCHOLOGY, 1962, 26, 246-250.
                    (RELIABILITY:INTERRATER; VALIDITY:CONSTRUCT, CRITERION;
                    CORRELATES:PSYCHOLOGICAL, DEMOGRAPHIC; FACTOR ANALYSIS; N=113
                    PSYCHIATRIC PATIENTS)
        @APPLICATION 1962 B-5 J-39 F-122

1720   SOUTHWELL, E. A.
              CONDITIONING OF HOSTILE AND NEUTRAL VERBS IN NEUROTICS AND NORMALS.
              JOURNAL OF CONSULTING PSYCHOLOGY, 1962, 26, 257-262.
                    (CORRELATES:PSYCHOLOGICAL; USED AS CRITERION; N=60 MALE NEUROTICS AND
                    60 MALE NORMALS)
        @APPLICATION 1962 B-44

1721   BECK, A. T., FESHBACH, S., & LEGG, D.
              THE CLINICAL UTILITY OF THE DIGIT SYMBOL TEST.
              JOURNAL OF CONSULTING PSYCHOLOGY, 1962, 26, 263-268.
                    (CORRELATES:INTELLIGENCE; N=178 PSYCHIATRIC PATIENTS)
        @APPLICATION 1962 B-8

1722   WOLFENSBERGER, W. P., MILLER, M. B., FOSHEE, J. G., & CROMWELL, R. L.
        RORSCHACH CORRELATES OF ACTIVITY LEVEL IN HIGH SCHOOL CHILDREN.
        JOURNAL OF CONSULTING PSYCHOLOGY, 1962, 26, 269-272.
            (CORRELATES:BEHAVIORAL: N=44 SCHOOL CHILDREN HIGH AND LOW IN
            ACTIVITY LEVEL)
        @APPLICATION 1962 R-30

1723   SMITH, T. E.
        THE RELATIONSHIP BETWEEN DEPRESSIVE PERSONALITY CHARACTERISTICS AND
        RORSCHACH CARD PREFERENCE.
        JOURNAL OF CONSULTING PSYCHOLOGY, 1962, 26, 286.
            (CORRELATES:PSYCHOLOGICAL; USED AS CRITERION; N=40 COLLEGE STUDENTS)
        @APPLICATION 1962 D-45 R-30

1724   LUCAS, C.
        FRUSTRATION AND THE PERCEPTION OF AGGRESSIVE ANIMALS.
        JOURNAL OF CONSULTING PSYCHOLOGY, 1962, 26, 287.
            (CORRELATES:PSYCHOLOGICAL; USED AS CRITERION; N=60 MALE COLLEGE
            STUDENTS)
        @APPLICATION 1962 R-30

1725   BELL, R. Q., HARTUP, W. W., & CROWELL, D. H.
        MAILED VERSUS SUPERVISED ADMINISTRATION OF A PROJECTIVE QUESTIONNAIRE.
        JOURNAL OF CONSULTING PSYCHOLOGY, 1962, 26, 290.
            (CORRELATES:ENVIRONMENTAL: N=48 MOTHERS)
        @APPLICATION 1962 S-9

1726   ZUCKERMAN, M., & BIASE, D. V.
        REPLICATION AND FURTHER DATA ON THE VALIDITY OF THE AFFECT ADJECTIVE CHECK
        LIST MEASURE OF ANXIETY.
        JOURNAL OF CONSULTING PSYCHOLOGY, 1962, 26, 291.
            (VALIDITY:CONSTRUCT; CORRELATES:PSYCHOLOGICAL, ENVIRONMENTAL;
            2 STUDIES: N=32 COLLEGE STUDENTS, 103 PSYCHIATRIC PATIENTS)
        @APPLICATION 1962 Z-13 T-2

1727   WORELL, L., & HILL, L. K.
        EGO STRENGTH AND ANXIETY IN DISCRIMINATION CONFLICT PERFORMANCE.
        JOURNAL OF CONSULTING PSYCHOLOGY, 1962, 26, 311-316.
            (CORRELATES:PSYCHOLOGICAL; USED AS CRITERION; N=354 UNDERGRADUATE
            STUDENTS)
        @APPLICATION 1962 T-2 B-5 D-45

1728   HILGARD, E. R., & LAUER, L. W.
        LACK OF CORRELATION BETWEEN THE CALIFORNIA PSYCHOLOGICAL INVENTORY AND
        HYPNOTIC SUSCEPTIBILITY.
        JOURNAL OF CONSULTING PSYCHOLOGY, 1962, 26, 331-335.
            (RELIABILITY:RETEST; CORRELATES:PSYCHOLOGICAL; N=110 COLLEGE MALES,
            106 COLLEGE FEMALES)
        @APPLICATION 1962 G-22 W-31

1729   DOLLIN, A., & SAKODA, J. M.
        THE EFFECT OF ORDER OF PRESENTATION ON PERCEPTION OF TAT PICTURES.
        JOURNAL OF CONSULTING PSYCHOLOGY, 1962, 26, 340-344.
            (CORRELATES:ENVIRONMENTAL; 2 STUDIES: N=25 MALE AND 26 FEMALE COLLEGE
            STUDENTS, 60 COLLEGE MALES AND 60 COLLEGE FEMALES)
        @APPLICATION 1962 M-20 E-48

1730   NELSON, J. T., & EPSTEIN, S.
        RELATIONSHIPS AMONG THREE MEASURES OF CONFLICT OVER HOSTILITY.
        JOURNAL OF CONSULTING PSYCHOLOGY, 1962, 26, 345-350.
            (CORRELATES:PSYCHOLOGICAL, PHYSIOLOGICAL; USED AS CRITERION; N=180
            COLLEGE STUDENTS)
        @APPLICATION 1962 S-232

1731   BRYAN, J. H., & LODER, E.
        ANXIETY AND THE SPIRAL AFTEREFFECT TEST.
        JOURNAL OF CONSULTING PSYCHOLOGY, 1962, 26, 351-354.
            (CORRELATES:PSYCHOLOGICAL, INTELLIGENCE; NORMATIVE DATA; N=96 FIFTH
            GRADE CHILDREN)
        @APPLICATION 1962 G-78 S-35 S-133

1732   ROSENHAN, D.
            NAYSAYING AND THE CALIFORNIA PSYCHOLOGICAL INVENTORY.
            JOURNAL OF CONSULTING PSYCHOLOGY, 1962, 26, 382-383.
                (VALIDITY:CONSTRUCT; CORRELATES:PSYCHOLOGICAL; BIAS:RESPONSE; N=49
                COLLEGE STUDENTS)
        @APPLICATION 1962 C-23 G-22

1733   HEILBRUN, A. B., JR.
            SOCIAL DESIRABILITY AND THE RELATIVE VALIDITIES OF ACHIEVEMENT SCALES.
            JOURNAL OF CONSULTING PSYCHOLOGY, 1962, 26, 383-386.
                (VALIDITY:CONSTRUCT, CRITERION; CORRELATES:PSYCHOLOGICAL,
                DEMOGRAPHIC; NORMATIVE DATA; N=76 COLLEGE FEMALES, 80 COLLEGE MALES)
        @APPLICATION 1962 G-21 E-2

1734   JOHNSTON, R. A., & CROSS, H. J.
            A FURTHER INVESTIGATION CF THE RELATION BETWEEN ANXIETY ANC DIGIT SYMBOL
            PERFORMANCE.
            JOURNAL OF CONSULTING PSYCHOLOGY, 1962, 26, 390.
                (CORRELATES:INTELLIGENCE; USED AS CRITERION; N=109 CCLLEGE STUDENTS)
        @APPLICATION 1962 T-2

1735   BENDIG, A. W., & BRUDER, G.
            THE EFFECT OF REPEATED TESTING ON ANXIETY SCALE SCORES.
            JOURNAL OF CONSULTING PSYCHOLOGY, 1962, 26, 392.
                (RELIABILITY:RETEST: N=48 COLLEGE STUDENTS)
        @APPLICATION 1962 S-68

1736   IZARD, C. E.
            PERSONALITY CHARACTERISTICS (EPPS), LEVEL CF EXPECTATICN, AND PERFORMANCE.
            JOURNAL OF CONSULTING PSYCHOLOGY, 1962, 26, 394.
                (VALIDITY:CRITERION; CORRELATES:BEHAVIORAL, PSYCHOLOGICAL; N=53
                FEMALE, 33 MALE CCLLEGE STUDENTS)
        @APPLICATION 1962 E-2

1737   SECHREST, L., & JACKSON, C. N.
            THE GENERALITY OF DEVIANT RESPONSE TENDENCIES.
            JOURNAL OF CONSULTING PSYCHOLOGY, 1962, 26, 395-401.
                (MODIFICATION; REVISION; RELIABILITY:INTERNAL CONSISTENCY;
                CORRELATES:PSYCHOLOGICAL; 2 SAMPLES: 64 COLLEGE FEMALES, 59 COLLEGE
                MALES, 60 FEMALE NURSING STUDENTS)
        @APPLICATION 1962 B-118 D-45 J-23 S-85 S-338

1738   MCNAIR, D. M., CALLAHAN, C. M., & LORR, M.
            THERAPIST "TYPE" AND PATIENT RESPONSE TO PSYCHOTHERAPY.
            JOURNAL OF CONSULTING PSYCHOLOGY, 1962, 26, 425-429.
                (RELIABILITY:INTERNAL CONSISTENCY; CORRELATES:PSYCHOLOGICAL,
                ENVIRONMENTAL; N=40 MALE PSYCHIATRIC OUTPATIENTS, 55 MALE THERAPISTS)
        @APPLICATION 1962 T-2 B-5 W-91 M-156 L-88

1739   L'ABATE, L.
            THE RELATIONSHIP BETWEEN WAIS-DERIVED INDICES OF MALADJUSTMENT AND MMPI
            IN DEVIANT GROUPS.
            JOURNAL OF CONSULTING PSYCHCLOGY, 1962, 26, 441-445.
                (CORRELATES:INTELLIGENCE; N=295 MALES AND 153 FEMALES)
        @APPLICATION 1962 D-45 W-57 W-8 L-68

1740   LANG, P. J., & LAZOVIK, A. D.
            PERSCNALITY AND HYPNCTIC SUSCEPTIBILITY.
            JOURNAL OF CONSULTING PSYCHCLOGY, 1962, 26, 317-322.
                (RELIABILITY:INTERNAL CONSISTENCY; CORRELATES:PSYCHOLOGICAL,
                DEMOGRAPHIC; N=22 COLLEGE MALES, 24 COLLEGE FEMALES)
        @APPLICATION 1962 W-31 B-84 D-45 E-2 E-75 E-29

1741   VOGEL, W.
            SOME EFFECTS OF BRAIN LESICNS CN MMPI PROFILES.
            JOURNAL OF CONSULTING PSYCHOLOGY, 1962, 26, 412-415.
                (CORRELATES:PHYSIOLOGICAL, INTELLIGENCE; N=37 BRAIN CAMAGED MALE
                SOLDIERS)
        @APPLICATION 1962 D-45

1742   KORMAN, M., & COLTHARP, F.
          TRANSPARENCY IN THE EDWARDS PERSONAL PREFERENCE SCHEDULE.
          JOURNAL OF CONSULTING PSYCHOLOGY, 1962, 26, 379-382.
                (VALIDITY:CONTENT; CORRELATES:PSYCHOLOGICAL; BIAS:RESPONSE; N=98
                FRESHMAN MEDICAL STUDENTS)
       @APPLICATION 1962 E-2

1743   LAFORGE, R.
          A CORRELATIONAL STUDY OF TWO PERSONALITY TESTS: THE MMPI AND CATTELL 16 PF.
          JOURNAL OF CONSULTING PSYCHOLOGY, 1962, 26, 402-411.
                (RELIABILITY:RETEST (N=44); CORRELATES:PAYCHOLOGICAL; FACTOR
                ANALYSIS; N=49 COLLEGE MALES, 128 COLLEGE FEMALES)
       @APPLICATION 1962 D-45 C-10

1744   SINGER, J. L., & ROWE, R.
          AN EXPERIMENTAL STUDY OF SOME RELATICNSHIPS BETWEEN DAYDREAMING AND
          ANXIETY.
          JOURNAL OF CONSULTING PSYCHOLOGY, 1962, 26, 446-454.
                (CORRELATES:BEHAVIORAL, PSYCHOLCGICAL; N=43 EXPERIMENTAL AND 43
                CONTROL GRADUATE STUDENTS)
       @APPLICATION 1962 S-82 A-8 C-136

1745   WASHBURN, W. C.
          THE EFFECTS OF PHYSIQUE AND INTRAFAMILY TENSION CN SELF-CCNCEPTS IN
          ADOLESCENT MALES.
          JOURNAL OF CONSULTING PSYCHOLOGY, 1962, 26, 460-466.
                (DESCRIPTION; CORRELATES:PHYSIOLOGICAL, ENVIRCNMENTAL; N=160 HIGH
                SCHOOL BOYS)
       @APPLICATION 1962 W-3

1746   TART, C. T.
          FREQUENCY OF DREAM RECALL AND SCME PERSONALITY MEASURES.
          JOURNAL OF CONSULTING PSYCHOLOGY, 1962, 26, 467-470.
                (CORRELATES:BEHAVIORAL; USED AS CRITERION; N=45 COLLEGE STUDENTS)
       @APPLICATION 1962 D-45 W-8 W-41 B-5

1747   CARKHUFF, R. R.
          THE GOODENOUGH DRAW-A-MAN TEST AS A MEASURE OF INTELLIGENCE IN
          NONINSTITUTIONALIZED SUBNORMAL ADULTS.
          JOURNAL OF CCNSULTING PSYCHOLOGY, 1962, 26, 476.
                (RELIABILITY:RETEST, INTERRATER; CORRELATES:INTELLIGENCE; NORMATIVE
                DATA; N=36 SUSPECTED MENTAL DEFECTIVES)
       @APPLICATION 1962 G-78

1748   PANEK, R. E., & HANNUM, T. E.
          RELATION BETWEEN AUTOKINESIS AND INTROVERSION-EXTRAVERSION.
          JOURNAL OF CONSULTING PSYCHOLOGY, 1962, 26, 477.
                (CORRELATES:PSYCHOLCGICAL, DEMOGRAPHIC; N=25 COLLEGE MALES AND
                25 COLLEGE FEMALES)
       @APPLICATION 1962 G-39

1749   HEILBRUN, A. B., JR.
          FURTHER VALIDATION OF THE NEED SCALES: THE ORDER SCALE.
          JOURNAL OF CONSULTING PSYCHOLOGY, 1962, 26, 478.
                (VALIDITY:CRITERION; N=384 COLLEGE STUDENTS)
        APPLICATION 1962 G-21 H-216

1750   TUTKO, T. A., & SECHREST, L.
          CONCEPTUAL PERFORMANCE AND PERSONALITY VARIABLES.
          JOURNAL OF CONSULTING PSYCHOLOGY, 1962, 26, 481.
                (CORRELATES:BEHAVIORAL, PSYCHOLCGICAL; N=100 MALE COLLEGE STUDENTS)
       @APPLICATION 1962 E-2

1751   IZARD, C. E.
          PERSONALITY CHANGE DURING COLLEGE YEARS.
          JOURNAL OF CONSULTING PSYCHOLOGY, 1962, 26, 482.
                (RELIABILITY:RETEST; CORRELATES:ENVIRONMENTAL; USED AS CRITERION;
                N=627 COLLEGE STUDENTS)
       @APPLICATION 1962 E-2

1752   MARKS, P. A., & SEEMAN, W.
           ADDENDUM TO "AN ASSESSMENT OF THE DIAGNOSTIC PROCESS IN A CHILD GUIDANCE
           SETTING."
           JOURNAL OF CONSULTING PSYCHOLOGY, 1962, 26, 485.
               (VALIDITY:CRITERION; CORRELATES:PSYCHOLOGICAL; N=13 CHILD GUIDANCE
               REFERRALS)
       @APPLICATION 1962 D-45 M-135

1753   FORD, L. H., JR., & SEMPERT, E. L.
           RELATIONS AMONG SOME OBJECTIVE MEASURES OF HOSTILITY, NEED AGGRESSION,
           AND ANXIETY.
           JOURNAL OF CONSULTING PSYCHOLOGY, 1962, 26, 486.
               (CORRELATES:PSYCHOLOGICAL; N=90 MALE AND 92 FEMALE SCHOOL
               CHILDREN)
       @APPLICATION 1962 B-44 S-24 E-2 T-2

1754   L'ABATE, L., BOELLING, G. M., HUTTON, R. D., & MATHEWS, D. L., JR.
           THE DIAGNOSTIC USEFULNESS OF FOUR POTENTIAL TESTS OF BRAIN DAMAGE.
           JOURNAL OF CONSULTING PSYCHOLOGY, 1962, 26, 479.
               (VALIDITY:CRITERION; CORRELATES:PSYCHOLOGICAL; N=60 BRAIN DAMAGED
               AND 60 SCHIZOPHRENICS)
       @APPLICATION 1962 W-9 K-81 R-157

1755   ROSENBERG, L. A.
           IDEALIZATION OF SELF AND SOCIAL ADJUSTMENT.
           JOURNAL OF CONSULTING PSYCHOLOGY, 1962, 26, 487.
               (CORRELATES:PSYCHOLOGICAL; N=144 STUDENTS IN MILITARY COURSES)
       @APPLICATION 1962 G-22

1756   GAURON, E., SEVERSON, R., & ENGELHART, R.
           MMPI F SCORES AND PSYCHIATRIC DIAGNOSIS.
           JOURNAL OF CONSULTING PSYCHOLOGY, 1962, 26, 488.
               (CORRELATES:PSYCHOLOGICAL; N=98 PSYCHIATRIC PATIENTS)
       @APPLICATION 1962 D-45

1757   MERCER, M., & KYRIAZIS, C.
           RESULTS OF THE ROSENZWEIG PICTURE-FRUSTRATION STUDY FOR PHYSICALLY
           ASSAULTIVE PRISONER MENTAL PATIENTS.
           JOURNAL OF CONSULTING PSYCHOLOGY, 1962, 26, 490.
               (CORRELATES:BEHAVIORAL:, N=32 MALE PRISONER PSYCHIATRIC PATIENTS, 35
               NORMAL MALES)
       @APPLICATION 1962 R-12

1758   FELDSTEIN, S., & JAFFE, J.
           THE RELATIONSHIP OF SPEECH DISRUPTION TO THE EXPERIENCE OF ANGER.
           JOURNAL OF CONSULTING PSYCHOLOGY, 1962, 26, 505-509.
               (RELIABILITY:INTERRATER; CORRELATES:BEHAVIORAL, ENVIRONMENTAL; N=18
               COLLEGE STUDENTS)
       @APPLICATION 1962 R-12
       @M-35

1759   CATTELL, R. B., & MORONY, J. H.
           THE USE OF THE 16 PF IN DISTINGUISHING HOMOSEXUALS, NORMALS, AND GENERAL
           CRIMINALS)
           JOURNAL OF CONSULTING PSYCHOLOGY, 1962, 26, 531-540.
               (CORRELATES:BEHAVIORAL: USED AS CRITERION; NORMATIVE DATA;, N=100
               MALE ADULT CRIMINALS)
       @APPLICATION 1962 C-10

1760   BARTHEL, C. E., & CROWNE, D. P.
           THE NEED FOR APPROVAL, TASK CATEGORIZATION, AND PERCEPTUAL DEFENSE.
           JOURNAL OF CONSULTING PSYCHOLOGY, 1962, 26, 547-555.
               (CORRELATES:BEHAVIORAL: N=96 FEMALE COLLEGE STUDENTS)
       @APPLICATION 1962 C-27

1761   PRUITT, W. A., & VAN DE CASTLE, R. L.
           DEPENDENCY MEASURES AND WELFARE CHRONICITY.
           JOURNAL OF CONSULTING PSYCHOLOGY, 1962, 26, 559-560.
               (VALIDITY:CRITERION; CORRELATES:BEHAVIORAL, PSYCHOLOGICAL; N=30
               UNEMPLOYED-EMPLOYABLE GENERAL ASSISTANCE CLIENTS)
       @APPLICATION 1962 N-14 R-30

1763   EXNER, J. E., JR., MCDOWELL, E., PABST, J., STACKMAN, W., & KIRK, L.
            ON THE DETECTION OF WILLFUL FALSIFICATIONS IN THE MMPI.
            JOURNAL OF CONSULTING PSYCHOLOGY, 1963, 27, 91-94.
                    (VALIDITY:CRITERION; BIAS:RESPONSE; N=25 COLLEGE MALES AND 25
                    COLLEGE FEMALES)
        @APPLICATION 1963 D-45

1764   FISHER, S.
            A FURTHER APPRAISAL OF THE BODY BOUNDARY CONCEPT.
            JOURNAL OF CONSULTING PSYCHOLOGY, 1963, 27, 62-74.
                    (REVIEW ARTICLE; DESCRIPTION; RELIABILITY:RETEST, INTERRATER;
                    CORRELATES:PSYCHOLOGICAL, PHYSIOLOGICAL; CROSS-CULTURAL APPLICATION)
        @APPLICATION 1963 F-75 K-30 H-37 D-45 L-39 R-30 O-16 B-6 G-139

1765   ADAMS, H. E. & KIRBY, A. C.
            MANIFEST ANXIETY, SOCIAL DESIRABILITY, OR RESPONSE SET.
            JOURNAL OF CONSULTING PSYCHOLOGY, 1963, 27, 59-61.
                    (VALIDITY:CONTENT; CORRELATES:PSYCHOLOGICAL; NORMATIVE DATA;
                    BIAS:RESPONSE; N=22 MALE AND 29 FEMALE COLLEGE STUDENTS)
        @APPLICATION 1963 E-1 T-2

1766   MCNAIR, D. M., LORR, M., & CALLAHAN, D. M.
            PATIENT AND THERAPIST INFLUENCES ON QUITTING PSYCHOTHERAPY.
            JOURNAL OF CONSULTING PSYCHOLOGY, 1963, 27, 10-17.
                    (MODIFICATION; VALIDITY:CRITERION; CORRELATES:BEHAVIORAL,
                    PSYCHOLOGICAL, DEMOGRAPHIC; USED AS CRITERION; N=282 PATIENTS)
        @APPLICATION 1963 T-2 A-5 G-26 A-42 S-33

1767   NORMAN, R. P.
            LEVEL OF ASPIRATION AND SOCIAL DESIRABILITY IN CHRONIC SCHIZOPHRENICS.
            JOURNAL OF CONSULTING PSYCHOLOGY, 1963, 27, 40-44.
                    (MODIFICATION; VALIDITY:CRITERION; CORRELATES:BEHAVIORAL,
                    PSYCHOLOGICAL; USED AS CRITERION; N=107 HOSPITALIZED SCHIZOPHRENIC
                    PATIENTS, 48 SELECTED)
        @APPLICATION 1963 E-1 W-107

1768   FISHBEIN, G. M.
            PERCEPTUAL MODES AND ASTHMATIC SYMPTOMS: AN APPLICATION OF WITKIN'S
            HYPOTHESIS
            JOURNAL OF CONSULTING PSYCHOLOGY, 1963, 27, 54-58.
                    (MODIFICATION; CORRELATES:PSYCHOLOGICAL, PHYSIOLOGICAL, ENVIRONMENTAL
                    N=85 CHRONIC ASTHMATIC MALE AND FEMALE CHILDREN)
        @APPLICATION 1963 W-19 W-188

1769   STRICKLAND, B. R., & CROWNE, D. P.
            NEED FOR APPROVAL AND THE PREMATURE TERMINATION OF PSYCHOTHERAPY.
            JOURNAL OF CONSULTING PSYCHOLOGY, 1963, 27, 95-101.
                    (MODIFICATION; RELIABILITY:RETEST; VALIDITY:CRITERION,
                    CROSS-VALIDATION; CORRELATES:BEHAVIORAL, PSYCHOLOGICAL, DEMOGRAPHIC;
                    N=85 PSYCHIATRIC OUTPATIENTS)
        @APPLICATION 1963 C-27 H-22 S-187

1770   MCDONALD, R. L., & GYNTHER, M. D.
            MMPI DIFFERENCES ASSOCIATED WITH SEX, RACE, AND CLASS IN TWO ADOLESCENT
            SAMPLES.
            JOURNAL OF CONSULTING PSYCHOLOGY, 1963, 27, 112-116.
                    (CORRELATES:DEMOGRAPHIC; NORMATIVE DATA; N=360 HIGH SCHOOL STUDENTS)
        @APPLICATION 1963 D-45

1771   WIGGINS, J. S.
            SOCIAL DESIRABILITY UNDER ROLE PLAYING INSTRUCTIONS: A REPLY TO WALKER.
            JOURNAL OF CONSULTING PSYCHOLOGY, 1963, 27, 107-111.
                    (REVIEW ARTICLE; MENTION; VALIDITY:CRITERION)
        @APPLICATION 1963 E-1 D-45 T-2

1772   HELLER, K., MYERS, R. A., & KLINE, L. V.
            INTERVIEWER BEHAVIOR AS A FUNCTION OF STANDARDIZED CLIENT ROLES.
            JOURNAL OF CONSULTING PSYCHOLOGY, 1963, 27, 117-122.
                    (MODIFICATION; RELIABILITY:INTERRATER; CORRELATES:PSYCHOLOGICAL;
                    USED AS CRITERION; N=34 INTERVIEWERS IN TRAINING)
        @APPLICATION 1963 L-35

1773   CARTWRIGHT, R. D., & LERNER, B.
            EMPATHY, NEED TO CHANGE, AND IMPROVEMENT WITH PSYCHOTHERAPY.
            JOURNAL OF CONSULTING PSYCHOLOGY, 1963, 27, 138-144.
                (MENTION; CORRELATES:BEHAVIORAL, DEMOGRAPHIC; N=14 MALE AND 14 FEMALE
                PATIENTS)
        @APPLICATION 1963 K-23

1774   WYLIE, R. C., SISSON, B. D., & TAULBEE, E.
            INTRAINDIVIDUAL CONSISTENCY IN "CREATIVE" AND "MEMORY" STORIES WRITTEN FOR
            TAT PICTURES.
            JOURNAL OF CONSULTING PSYCHOLOGY, 1963, 27, 145-151.
                (RELIABILITY:RETEST, INTERRATER; CORRELATES:ENVIRONMENTAL; N=108
                COLLEGE FEMALES)
        @APPLICATION 1963 M-20 A-94

1775   ROSENTHAL, I.
            RELIABILITY OF RETROSPECTIVE REPORTS OF ADOLESCENCE.
            JOURNAL OF CONSULTING PSYCHOLOGY, 1963, 27, 189-198.
                (MODIFICATION; DESCRIPTION; MENTION; RELIABILITY:RETEST;
                CORRELATES:PSYCHOLOGICAL, DEMOGRAPHIC; N=48 MALE AND 52 FEMALE
                SUBJECTS IN A LONGITUDINAL STUDY)
        @APPLICATION 1963 N-27 T-65 T-66 D-45 T-2

1776   CAINE, T. M., & HAWKINS, L. G.
            QUESTIONNAIRE MEASURE OF THE HYSTEROID/OBSESSOID COMPONENT OF PERSONALITY:
            THE HOQ.
            JOURNAL OF CONSULTING PSYCHOLOGY, 1963, 27, 206-209.
                (DESCRIPTION; MENTION; RELIABILITY:INTERNAL CONSISTENCY, INTERRATER;
                CORRELATES:PSYCHOLOGICAL; N=93 MALE AND FEMALE NEUROTIC PATIENTS)
        @APPLICATION 1963 D-45 F-82 E-5

1777   HESTERLY, S. O.
            DEVIANT RESPONSE PATTERNS AS A FUNCTION OF CHRONOLOGICAL AGE.
            JOURNAL OF CONSULTING PSYCHOLOGY, 1963, 27, 210-214.
                (MODIFICATION; VALIDITY:CROSS-VALIDATION; CORRELATES:PSYCHOLOGICAL,
                DEMOGRAPHIC; USED AS CRITERION; NORMATIVE DATA; N=2253 ADULTS AND
                CHILDREN)
        @APPLICATION 1963 B-118

1778   HEILBRUN, A. B., JR.
            EVIDENCE REGARDING THE EQUIVALENCE OF IPSATIVE AND NORMATIVE PERSONALITY
            SCALES.
            JOURNAL OF CONSULTING PSYCHOLOGY, 1963, 27, 152-156.
                (RELIABILITY:RETEST; VALIDITY:CRITERION; CORRELATES:BEHAVIORAL,
                PSYCHOLOGICAL; N=197 COLLEGE STUDENTS)
        @APPLICATION 1963 G-21

1779   SCHULMAN, R. E., & LONDON, P.
            HYPNOTIC SUSCEPTIBILITY AND MMPI PROFILES.
            JOURNAL OF CONSULTING PSYCHOLOGY, 1963, 27, 157-160.
                (CORRELATES:PSYCHOLOGICAL; USED AS CRITERION; N=87 COLLEGE FEMALES)
        @APPLICATION 1963 D-45 W-31

1780   HEILBRUN, A. B., JR.
            REVISION OF THE MMPI K CORRECTION PROCEDURE FOR IMPROVED DETECTION OF
            MALADJUSTMENT IN A NORMAL COLLEGE POPULATION.
            JOURNAL OF CONSULTING PSYCHOLOGY, 1963, 27, 161-165.
                (VALIDITY:CROSS-VALIDATION; CORRELATES:DEMOGRAPHIC; 3 STUDIES: 50
                MALE AND 50 FEMALE UNDERGRADUATE CLIENTS AND 450 MALE AND 450 FEMALE
                ADJUSTED UNDERGRADUATES; N=30 MALE AND 30 FEMALE UNDERGRADUATE
                CLIENTS AND 270 MALE AND 270 FEMALE ADJUSTED UNDERGRADUATES; N=50
                MALE AND 50 FEMALE PATIENTS AND 450 MALE AND 450 FEMALE ADJUSTED
                UNDERGRADUATES)
        @APPLICATION 1963 D-45

1781   NORMAN, W. T.
            RELATIVE IMPORTANCE OF TEST ITEM CONTENT.
            JOURNAL OF CONSULTING PSYCHOLOGY, 1963, 27, 166-174.
                (VALIDITY:CONTENT, CROSS-VALIDATION; N=538 COLLEGE MALES)

1782   STOLER, N.
            CLIENT LIKABILITY: A VARIABLE IN THE STUDY OF PSYCHOTHERAPY.
            JOURNAL OF CONSULTING PSYCHOLOGY, 1963, 27, 175-178.
                (CORRELATES:BEHAVIORAL, PSYCHOLOGICAL; USED AS CRITERION;
                BIAS:RESPONSE; N=10 RATERS, 10 RECORDED THERAPY CASES)
        @APPLICATION 1963 R-36

1783   THORNE, G. L.
            DISCRIMINATIONS WITHIN THE DELINQUENCY CONTINUUM ON GOUGH'S
            SOCIALIZATION SCALE.
            JOURNAL OF CONSULTING PSYCHOLOGY, 1963, 27, 183.
                (VALIDITY:CRITERION; CORRELATES:BEHAVIORAL, PSYCHOLOGICAL,
                INTELLIGENCE; N=58 DELINQUENT BOYS.)
        @APPLICATION 1963 G-22

1784   VOGEL, J. L.
            FAILURE TO VALIDATE AND CR AND SM SCALES OF THE MMPI.
            JOURNAL OF CONSULTING PSYCHOLOGY, 1963, 27, 367.
                (VALIDITY:CRITERION; NORMATIVE DATA; N=9 MALE AND 16 FEMALE
                PSYCHOSOMATIC PATIENTS AND 13 MALE AND 12 FEMALE SOMATIC PATIENTS)
        @APPLICATION 1963 D-45

1785   BOE, E. E., & KOGAN, W. S.
            SOCIAL DESIRABILITY RESPONSE SET IN THE INDIVIDUAL.
            JOURNAL OF CONSULTING PSYCHOLOGY, 1963, 27, 369.
                (MODIFICATION; CORRELATES:PSYCHOLOGICAL; N=186 COLLEGE STUDENTS)
        @APPLICATION 1963 D-45

1786   KARP, S. A.
            FIELD DEPENDENCE AND OVERCOMING EMBEDDEDNESS.
            JOURNAL OF CONSULTING PSYCHOLOGY, 1963, 27, 294-302.
                (CORRELATES:PSYCHOLOGICAL, INTELLIGENCE; FACTOR ANALYSIS; N=150
                MALE COLLEGE STUDENTS)
        @APPLICATION 1963 W-19 H-124 W-188 W-73

1787   KORMAN, M., & BLUMBERG, S.
            COMPARATIVE EFFICIENCY OF SOME TESTS OF CEREBRAL DAMAGE.
            JOURNAL OF CONSULTING PSYCHOLOGY, 1963, 27, 303-309.
                (CORRELATES:PSYCHOLOGICAL, PHYSIOLOGICAL, DEMOGRAPHIC; NORMATIVE
                DATA; N=40 NORMALS AND 40 PATIENTS WITH CEREBRAL DAMAGE)
        @APPLICATION 1963 D-45 R-157 G-150

1788   JORDAN, E. J., JR.
            MMPI PROFILES OF EPILEPTICS: A FURTHER EVALUATION.
            JOURNAL OF CONSULTING PSYCHOLOGY, 1963, 27, 267-269.
                (VALIDITY:CRITERION; CORRELATES:PSYCHOLOGICAL, PHYSIOLOGICAL,
                DEMOGRAPHIC, INTELLIGENCE; USED AS CRITERION; N=96 PATIENTS)
        @APPLICATION 1963 D-45

1789   LAGRONE, C. W.
            SEX AND PERSONALITY DIFFERENCES IN RELATION TO FANTASY.
            JOURNAL OF CONSULTING PSYCHOLOGY, 1963, 27, 270-272.
                (CORRELATES:PSYCHOLOGICAL, DEMOGRAPHIC; N=96 FEMALE AND 123 MALE
                UNDERGRADUATES)
        @APPLICATION 1963 D-45

1790   FESHBACK, S., SINGER, R. D., & FESHBACK, N.
            EFFECTS OF ANGER AROUSAL AND SIMILARITY UPON THE ATTRIBUTION OF HOSTILITY
            TO PICTORIAL STIMULI.
            JOURNAL OF CONSULTING PSYCHOLOGY, 1963, 27, 248-252.
                (CORRELATES:PSYCHOLOGICAL, DEMOGRAPHIC, ENVIRONMENTAL; 2 STUDIES:
                N=57 COLLEGE STUDENTS, N=65 COLLEGE STUDENTS)
        @APPLICATION 1963 R-12 S-37

1791   SILVER, A. W.
            TAT AND MMPI PSYCHOPATH DEVIANT SCALE DIFFERENCES BETWEEN DELINQUENT AND
            NON-DELINQUENT ADOLESCENTS.
            JOURNAL OF CONSULTING PSYCHOLOGY, 1963, 27, 370.
            JOURNAL OF CONSULTING PSYCHOLOGY, 1963, 27, 270-272.
                (VALIDITY:CRITERION; CORRELATES:BEHAVIORAL, PSYCHOLOGICAL,
                ENVIRONMENTAL; N=20 REFORM SCHOOL STUDENTS COMPARED TO MILD
                OFFENDERS, TO ORPHANS' HOME RESIDENTS AND TO HIGH SCHOOL STUDENTS)
        @APPLICATION 1963 D-45 M-20 S-27

1792   SCHAIE, K. W.
            SCALING THE SCALES: USE OF EXPERT JUDGMENT IN IMPROVING THE VALIDITY OF
            QUESTIONNAIRE SCALES.
            JOURNAL OF CONSULTING PSYCHOLOGY, 1963, 27, 350-357.
                    (MODIFICATION; VALIDITY:CRITERION; CORRELATES:PSYCHOLOGICAL; FACTOR
                    ANALYSIS; N=30 PSYCHOLOGISTS, 43 DELINQUENT GIRLS)
        @APPLICATION 1963 C-89

1793   TIFFANY, D. W., & SHONTZ, F. C.
            FANTASIZED DANGER AS A FUNCTION OF PARENT-CHILD CONTROLLING PRACTICES.
            JOURNAL OF CONSULTING PSYCHOLOGY, 1963, 27, 278.
                    (MODIFICATION; VALIDITY:CONSTRUCT; CORRELATES:PSYCHOLOGICAL; USED AS
                    CRITERION; N=22 PREADOLESCENT BOYS)
        @APPLICATION 1963 T-68 D-45

1794   STRAITS, B. C., & SECHREST, L.
            FURTHER SUPPORT OF SOME FINDINGS ABOUT THE CHARACTERISTICS OF SMOKERS AND
            NONSMOKERS.
            JOURNAL OF CONSULTING PSYCHOLOGY, 1963, 27, 282.
                    (CORRELATES:BEHAVIORAL, DEMOGRAPHIC; N=245 MALE COLLEGE STUDENTS)
        @APPLICATION 1963 D-45

1795   DAHLKE, A. E., & DANA, R. H.
            INTRAINDIVIDUAL VERBAL-NUMERICAL DISCREPANCIES AND PERSONALITY.
            JOURNAL OF CONSULTING PSYCHOLOGY, 1963, 27, 182.
                    (CORRELATES:INTELLIGENCE; N=425 COLLEGE STUDENTS)
        @APPLICATION 1963 D-45

1796   CENTERS, L., & CENTERS, R.
            BODY CATHEXES OF PARENTS OF NORMAL AND MALFORMED CHILDREN FOR PROGENY AND
            SELF.
            JOURNAL OF CONSULTING PSYCHOLOGY, 1963, 27, 319-323.
                    (CORRELATES:PSYCHOLOGICAL; N=26 PARENTS OF MALFORMED CHILDREN, 21
                    PARENTS OF NORMAL CHILDREN)
        @APPLICATION 1963 S-15

1797   ZUCKERMAN, M., NURNBERGER, J. I., GARDINER, S. H., VANDIVEER, J. M.,
        BARRETT, B. H., & BREEIJEN, A. D.
            PSYCHOLOGICAL CORRELATES OF SOMATIC COMPLAINTS IN PREGNANCY AND
            DIFFICULTY IN CHILDBIRTH.
            JOURNAL OF CONSULTING PSYCHOLOGY, 1963, 27, 324-329.
                    (CORRELATES:PSYCHOLOGICAL, PHYSIOLOGICAL; N=52 PRIMIPAROUS FEMALES IN
                    TWO STUDIES)
        @APPLICATION 1963 Z-13 D-45 T-2 O-16

1798   CANTER, F. M.
            SIMULATION ON THE CALIFORNIA PSYCHOLOGICAL INVENTORY AND THE ADJUSTMENT
            OF THE SIMULATOR.
            JOURNAL OF CONSULTING PSYCHOLOGY, 1963, 27, 253-256.
                    (CORRELATES:PSYCHOLOGICAL, ENVIRONMENTAL; NORMATIVE DATA;
                    BIAS:RESPONSE; N=50 ALCOHOLICS AND 50 JOB APPLICANTS)
        @APPLICATION 1963 G-22 R-30

1799   MEDNICK, M. T.
            RESEARCH CREATIVITY IN PSYCHOLOGY GRADUATE STUDENTS.
            JOURNAL OF CONSULTING PSYCHOLOGY, 1963, 27, 265-266.
                    (MODIFICATION; RELIABILITY:INTERNAL CONSISTENCY; VALIDITY:CRITERION;
                    CORRELATES:BEHAVIORAL, PSYCHOLOGICAL; NORMATIVE DATA; N=43 GRADUATE
                    STUDENTS)
        @APPLICATION 1963 M-29 T-110

1800   NICHOLS, R. C., & SCHNELL, R. R.
            FACTOR SCALES FOR THE CALIFORNIA PSYCHOLOGICAL INVENTORY.
            JOURNAL OF CONSULTING PSYCHOLOGY, 1963, 27, 228-235.
                    (CORRELATES:PSYCHOLOGICAL, DEMOGRAPHIC; FACTOR ANALYSIS; 6 STUDIES:
                    N=4098 MALES & 3572 FEMALES, 300 UNDERGRADUATES, 57 MALE & 18 FEMALE
                    UNDERGRADUATES, 64 HIGH SCHOOL COUNSELORS, 250 MALE COLLEGE FRESHMEN,
                    88 FEMALE & 58 MALE PSYCHIATRIC PATIENTS)
        @APPLICATION 1963 G-22 S-33 D-45 E-2 G-26 R-31 L-39 G-21

1801   CROOKES, T. G., & HUTT, S. J.
            SCORES OF PSYCHOTIC PATIENTS ON THE MAUDSLEY PERSONALITY INVENTORY.
            JOURNAL OF CONSULTING PSYCHOLOGY, 1963, 27, 243-247.
                (VALIDITY:CRITERION; CORRELATES:PSYCHOLOGICAL; USED AS CRITERION;
                NORMATIVE DATA; N=80 MALE AND FEMALE PSYCHIATRIC PATIENTS)
        @APPLICATION 1963 E-5

1802   JOHANNSEN, W. J., FRIEDMAN, S. H., LEITSCHUH, T. H., & AMMONS, H.
            A STUDY OF CERTAIN SCHIZOPHRENIC DIMENSIONS AND THEIR RELATIONSHIP TO
            DOUBLE ALTERNATION LEARNING.
            JOURNAL OF CONSULTING PSYCHOLOGY, 1963, 27, 375-382.
                (RELIABILITY:INTERRATER; CORRELATES:PSYCHOLOGICAL; USED AS CRITERION;
                N=52 PATIENTS)
        @APPLICATION 1963 P-32 K-51

1803   TIMMONS, E. O., & NOBLIN, C. D.
            THE DIFFERENTIAL PERFORMANCE OF ORALS AND ANALS IN A VERBAL
            CONDITIONING PARADIGM.
            JOURNAL OF CONSULTING PSYCHOLOGY, 1963, 27, 383-386.
                (CORRELATES:BEHAVIORAL, PSYCHOLOGICAL; USED AS CRITERION;
                N=90 COLLEGE STUDENTS, 15 ORAL AND 15 ANAL S'S SELECTED)
        @APPLICATION 1963 B-176

1804   WALLACE, J., & SECHREST, L.
            FREQUENCY HYPOTHESIS AND CONTENT ANALYSIS OF PROJECTIVE TECHNIQUES.
            JOURNAL OF CONSULTING PSYCHOLOGY, 1963, 27, 387-393.
                (RELIABILITY:INTERRATER; VALIDITY:CRITERION; CORRELATES:BEHAVIORAL,
                PSYCHOLOGICAL; N=72 NURSING STUDENTS)
        @APPLICATION 1963 R-30 M-20 R-31

1805   RASKIN, A., & CLYDE, D. J.
            FACTORS OF PSYCHOPATHOLOGY IN THE WARD BEHAVIOR OF ACUTE SCHIZOPHRENICS.
            JOURNAL OF CONSULTING PSYCHOLOGY, 1963, 27, 420-425.
                (FACTOR ANALYSIS; N=417 PSYCHIATRIC PATIENTS)
        @APPLICATION 1963 L-39 B-86

1806   BENTLER, P. M.
            INTERPERSONAL ORIENTATION IN RELATION TO HYPNOTIC SUSCEPTIBILITY.
            JOURNAL OF CONSULTING PSYCHOLOGY, 1963, 27, 426-431.
                (DESCRIPTION; CORRELATES:PSYCHOLOGICAL, DEMOGRAPHIC; FACTOR ANALYSIS;
                3 SAMPLES: N=37 FEMALE UNDERGRADUATES, N=47 FEMALE UNDERGRADUATES,
                N=43 MALE UNDERGRADUATES)
        @APPLICATION 1963 L-35 W-31

1807   SILLER, J., & CHIPMAN, A.
            RESPONSE SET PARALYSIS: IMPLICATIONS FOR MEASUREMENT AND CONTROL.
            JOURNAL OF CONSULTING PSYCHOLOGY, 1963, 27, 432-438.
                (CORRELATES:PSYCHOLOGICAL; FACTOR ANALYSIS; BIAS:RESPONSE; N=284
                STUDENTS)
        @APPLICATION 1963 S-86 S-87 Y-1 C-27 E-1 C-23 F-34 G-125 W-8 W-41 B-5 Z-7
        @Z-13 B-10 G-21 M-50

1808   HARTUP, W. W., & MOORE, S. G.
            AVOIDANCE OF INAPPROPRIATE SEX-TYPING BY YOUNG CHILDREN.
            JOURNAL OF CONSULTING PSYCHOLOGY, 1963, 27, 467-473.
                (CORRELATES:BEHAVIORAL, PSYCHOLOGICAL, DEMOGRAPHIC; N=69 BOYS AND 78
                GIRLS AGES 3-8)
        @APPLICATION 1963 B-35

1809   KAPLAN, M. F., & SINGER, E.
            DOGMATISM AND SENSORY ALIENATION: AN EMPIRICAL INVESTIGATION.
            JOURNAL OF CONSULTING PSYCHOLOGY, 1963, 27, 486-491.
                (VALIDITY:CONSTRUCT; CORRELATES:BEHAVIORAL, PHYSIOLOGICAL;
                USED AS CRITERION; NORMATIVE DATA; N=40, 13 DOGMATIC AND 13
                NONDOGMATIC S'S SELECTED)
        @APPLICATION 1963 R-8

1810   DEMPSEY, P.
            THE DIMENSIONALITY OF THE MMPI CLINICAL SCALES AMONG NORMAL SUBJECTS.
            JOURNAL OF CONSULTING PSYCHOLOGY, 1963, 27, 492-497.
                (FACTOR ANALYSIS; N=40 MALE AND 40 FEMALE STUDENTS)
        @APPLICATION 1963 D-45

1811   ELVEKROG, M. O., & VESTRE, N. D.
            THE EDWARDS SOCIAL DESIRABILITY SCALES AS A SHORT FORM OF THE MMPI.
            JOURNAL OF CONSULTING PSYCHOLOGY, 1963, 27, 503-507.
                (VALIDITY:CRITERION; CORRELATES:PSYCHOLOGICAL; N=76 SCHIZOPHRENICS,
                102 MENTAL PATIENTS AND 78 NURSES)
        aAPPLICATION 1963 D-45 E-1

1812   LEVY, B. I., LOMAX, J. V., JR., & MINSKY, R.
            AN UNDERLYING VARIABLE IN THE CLINICAL EVALUATION OF DRAWINGS OF HUMAN
            FIGURES.
            JOURNAL OF CONSULTING PSYCHOLOGY, 1963, 27, 508-512.
                (RELIABILITY:INTERRATER; CORRELATES:PSYCHOLOGICAL, INTELLIGENCE; N=36
                MALE AND FEMALE CLINICAL PSYCHOLOGISTS)
        aAPPLICATION 1963 L-94

1813   WALLACH, M. S.
            DREAM REPORT AND SOME PSYCHOLOGICAL CONCOMITANTS.
            JOURNAL OF CONSULTING PSYCHOLOGY, 1963, 27, 549.
                (CORRELATES:BEHAVIORAL, PSYCHOLOGICAL; N=332 MALE STUDENTS)
        aAPPLICATION 1963 D-45

1814   ROSENZWEIG, S.
            VALIDITY OF THE ROSENZWEIG PICTURE-FRUSTRATION STUDY WITH FELONS AND
            DELINQUENTS.
            JOURNAL OF CONSULTING PSYCHOLOGY, 1963, 27, 535-536.
                (REVIEW ARTICLE; VALIDITY:CRITERION; CORRELATES:BEHAVIORAL,
                PSYCHOLOGICAL)
        aAPPLICATION 1963 R-12 M-20

1815   CHAPMAN, L. J.
            THE PROBLEM OF SELECTING DRUG FREE SCHIZOPHRENICS FOR RESEARCH.
            JOURNAL OF CONSULTING PSYCHOLOGY, 1963, 27, 540-542.
                (CORRELATES:BEHAVIORAL, PSYCHOLOGICAL; N=38 MENTAL PATIENTS)
        aAPPLICATION 1963 B-271
        aC-20

1816   WALKER, J. N.
            SOCIAL DESIRABILITY: A REPLY TO WIGGINS.
            JOURNAL OF CONSULTING PSYCHOLOGY, 1963, 27, 458.
                (MENTION; REVIEW ARTICLE; VALIDITY:CONSTRUCT)
        aAPPLICATION 1963 W-14 E-1

1817   WILLINGHAM, W. W., & AMBLER, R. K.
            THE RELATION OF THE GORDON PERSONAL INVENTORY TO SEVERAL EXTERNAL CRITERIA.
            JOURNAL OF CONSULTING PSYCHOLOGY, 1963, 27, 460.
                (RELIABILITY:INTERRATER; VALIDITY:CRITERION; CORRELATES:BEHAVIORAL,
                PSYCHOLOGICAL; N=208 NAVAL CADETS)
        aAPPLICATION 1963 G-12

1818   HEBERLEIN, M., & MARCUSE, F. L.
            PERSONALITY VARIABLES IN THE DAP.
            JOURNAL OF CONSULTING PSYCHOLOGY, 1963, 27, 461.
                (CORRELATES:PSYCHOLOGICAL; N=80 MALE AND 80 FEMALE UNDERGRADUATES)
        aAPPLICATION 1963 E-2 G-78

1819   ROTHSTEIN, R., & EPSTEIN, S.
            UNCONSCIOUS SELF-EVALUATION AS A FUNCTION OF AVAILABILITY OF CUES.
            JOURNAL OF CONSULTING PSYCHOLOGY, 1963, 27, 480-485.
                (MENTION; CORRELATES:PSYCHOLOGICAL; N=20 FEMALE STUDENTS)
        aAPPLICATION 1963 D-45 E-45 H-129

1820   SIDLE, A.
            ORIGINALITY IN PROBLEM SOLVING AS A FUNCTION OF ANXIETY AND WITHDRAWAL IN
            SCHIZOPHRENICS.
            JOURNAL OF CONSULTING PSYCHOLOGY, 1963, 27, 550.
                (CORRELATES:PSYCHOLOGICAL; N=50 MALE SCHIZOPHRENICS)
        aAPPLICATION 1963 M-138 H-65

1821   BERNSTEIN, L., & DANA, R. H.
            EFFECT OF ORDER OF PRESENTATION OF TAT CARDS.
            JOURNAL OF CONSULTING PSYCHOLOGY, 1963, 27, 533-535.
                (MENTION; CORRELATES:PSYCHOLOGICAL, DEMOGRAPHIC; BIAS:RESPONSE; N=67)
        aAPPLICATION 1963 M-20

1822   MEER, B., & AMON, A. H.
            PHOTOS PREFERENCE TEST (PPT) AS A MEASURE OF MENTAL STATUS FOR
            HOSPITALIZED PSYCHIATRIC PATIENTS.
            JOURNAL OF CONSULTING PSYCHOLOGY, 1963, 27, 283-293.
                (CORRELATES:PSYCHOLOGICAL, DEMOGRAPHIC; N=490 PATIENTS AND 369
                NORMALS)
        @APPLICATION 1963 D-45 G-78

1823   KURZ, R. B.
            RELATIONSHIP BETWEEN TIME IMAGERY AND RORSCHACH HUMAN MOVEMENT RESPONSE.
            JOURNAL OF CONSULTING PSYCHOLOGY, 1963, 27, 273-276.
                (CORRELATES:PSYCHOLOGICAL; NORMATIVE DATA; N=46 FEMALE
                UNDERGRADUATES)
        @APPLICATION 1963 K-14 H-123

1824   MURSTEIN, B. I.
            THE RELATIONSHIP OF EXPECTANCY OF REWARD TO ACHIEVEMENT PERFORMANCE ON AN
            ARITHMETIC AND THEMATIC TEST.
            JOURNAL OF CONSULTING PSYCHOLOGY, 1963, 27, 394-399.
                (RELIABILITY:INTERRATER; CORRELATES:PSYCHOLOGICAL, ENVIRONMENTAL;
                NORMATIVE DATA; N=56 COLLEGE MEN)
        @APPLICATION 1963 M-7

1825   WIMSATT, W. R., & VESTRE, N. D.
            EXTRAEXPERIMENTAL EFFECTS IN VERBAL CONDITIONING.
            JOURNAL OF CONSULTING PSYCHOLOGY, 1963, 27, 400-404.
                (CORRELATES:PSYCHOLOGICAL; USED AS CRITERION; N=74 MALE PSYCHIATRIC
                PATIENTS)
        @APPLICATION 1963 D-45 G-26 L-70

1826   HIGASHIMACHI, W. H.
            THE CONSTRUCT VALIDITY OF THE PROGRESSIVE MATRICES AS A MEASURE OF SUPER-
            EGO STRENGTH IN JUVENILE DELINQUENTS.
            JOURNAL OF CONSULTING PSYCHOLOGY, 1963, 27, 413-419.
                (CORRELATES:BEHAVIORAL, PSYCHOLOGICAL, INTELLIGENCE; USED AS
                CRITERION; NORMATIVE DATA; N=24 DELINQUENT BOYS SELECTED FROM 48)
        @APPLICATION 1963 T-70 R-158

1827   MEDINNUS, G. R., & CURTIS, F. J.
            THE RELATION BETWEEN MATERNAL SELF-ACCEPTANCE AND CHILD ACCEPTANCE.
            JOURNAL OF CONSULTING PSYCHOLOGY, 1963, 27, 542-544.
                (CORRELATES:PSYCHOLOGICAL; N=56 MOTHERS OF NURSERY CHILDREN)
        @APPLICATION 1963 B-18

1828   NICKOLS, J.
            RORSCHACH Z SCORES ON DISTURBED SUBJECTS.
            JOURNAL OF CONSULTING PSYCHOLOGY, 1963, 27, 544-545.
                (CORRELATES:BEHAVIORAL, PSYCHOLOGICAL, INTELLIGENCE; N=12 DISTURBED
                CHILDREN AND 75 PSYCHIATRIC ADULTS)
        @APPLICATION 1963 R-30 G-78

1829   RASKIN, A., & SULLIVAN, P. D.
            FACTORS ASSOCIATED WITH INTERRATER DISCREPANCIES ON A PSYCHIATRIC RATING
            SCALE.
            JOURNAL OF CONSULTING PSYCHOLOGY, 1963, 27, 547.
                (RELIABILITY:INTERRATER; CORRELATES:PSYCHOLOGICAL, DEMOGRAPHIC;
                N=87 MALE AND FEMALE PSYCHIATRIC PATIENTS AND 55 RATER PAIRS)
        @APPLICATION 1963 L-39

1830   NEIGER, S., & PAPASTERGIOU, C.
            THE RELATIONSHIP BETWEEN DEPRESSIVE PERSONALITY CHARACTERISTICS AND
            RORSCHACH CARD PREFERENCE: A REPLY TO T. E. SMITH.
            JOURNAL OF CONSULTING PSYCHOLOGY, 1963, 27, 463.
                (MENTION; CORRELATES:PSYCHOLOGICAL; N=100 NORMALS AND 50 NEUROTICS)
        @APPLICATION 1963 R-30 D-45

1831   NORMAN, R. P.
            NEED FOR SOCIAL APPROVAL AS REFLECTED ON THE TAT.
            JOURNAL OF CONSULTING PSYCHOLOGY, 1963, 27, 464.
                (RELIABILITY:INTERRATER; VALIDITY:CONSTRUCT; CORRELATES:BEHAVIORAL,
                PSYCHOLOGICAL; USED AS CRITERION; N=21 HIGH AND 17 LOW SD
                UNDERGRADUATE FEMALES)
        @APPLICATION 1963 M-20 C-27

1832   GOLDSTEIN, I. B.
            A COMPARISON BETWEEN TAYLOR'S AND FREEMAN'S MANIFEST ANXIETY SCALES.
            JOURNAL OF CONSULTING PSYCHOLOGY, 1963, 27, 466.
                    (CORRELATES:PSYCHOLOGICAL; N=80 FEMALE STUDENTS)
        @APPLICATION 1963 T-2 G-26 ?F-139

1833   WINTER, W. D., FERREIRA, A. J., & RANSOM, R.
            TWO MEASURES OF ANXIETY: A VALIDATION.
            JOURNAL OF CONSULTING PSYCHOLOGY, 1963, 27, 520-524.
                    (VALIDITY:CRITERION; CORRELATES:PSYCHOLOGICAL, PHYSIOLOGICAL,
                    ENVIRONMENTAL; N=13 MALE AND 6 FEMALE UNDERGRADUATES)
        @APPLICATION 1963 Z-13 T-2

1834   RAMER, J.
            THE RORSCHACH BARRIER SCORE AND SOCIAL BEHAVIOR.
            JOURNAL OF CONSULTING PSYCHOLOGY, 1963, 27, 525-531.
                    (RELIABILITY:INTERRATER; CORRELATES:BEHAVIORAL, PSYHCOLOGICAL; N=96
                    FEMALE STUDENTS)
        @APPLICATION 1963 R-30 F-75

1835   SILVERMAN, J.
            THE VALIDITY OF THE BARRON EGO STRENGTH SCALE IN AN INDIVIDUAL FORM.
            JOURNAL OF CONSULTING PSYCHOLOGY, 1963, 27, 532-533.
                    (MODIFICATION; RELIABILITY:RETEST; VALIDITY:CONSTRUCT;
                    CORRELATES:PSYCHOLOGICAL; NORMATIVE DATA; N=36 HOSPITALIZED NORMALS
                    AND 32 CHRONIC SCHIZOPHRENICS)
        @APPLICATION 1963 B-5 D-45

1836   NEURINGER, C.
            RIGID THINKING IN SUICIDAL INDIVIDUALS.
            JOURNAL OF CONSULTING PSYCHOLOGY, 1964, 28, 54-58.
                    (VALIDITY:CRITERION; CORRELATES:PSYCHOLOGICAL; N=15 SUICIDAL
                    PATIENTS, 15 PSYCHOSOMATIC PATIENTS, AND 15 HOSPITALIZED NORMAL
                    SUBJECTS)
        @APPLICATION 1964 A-5 R-88

1837   CONNERS, C. K., EISENBERG, L., & SHARPE, L.
            EFFECTS OF METHYLPHENIDATE (RITALIN) ON PAIRED-ASSOCIATE LEARNING AND
            PORTEUS MAZE PERFORMANCE IN EMOTIONALLY DISTURBED CHILDREN.
            JOURNAL OF CONSULTING PSYCHOLOGY, 1964, 28, 14-22.
                    (CORRELATES:BEHAVIORAL, PHYSIOLOGICAL, INTELLIGENCE; N=81
                    DEPRIVED AND EMOTIONALLY DISTURBED CHILDREN)
        @APPLICATION 1964 C-55 S-133 P-22 S-192

1838   DUNN, J. A.
            FACTOR STRUCTURE OF THE TEST ANXIETY SCALE FOR CHILDREN.
            JOURNAL OF CONSULTING PSYCHOLOGY, 1964, 28, 92.
                    (FACTOR ANALYSIS; N=633 ELEMENTARY SCHOOL CHILDREN)
        @APPLICATION 1964 S-35

1839   VELDMAN, D. J., & PIERCE-JONES, J.
            SEX DIFFERENCES IN FACTOR STRUCTURE FOR THE CALIFORNIA PSYCHOLOGICAL
            INVENTORY.
            JOURNAL OF CONSULTING PSYCHOLOGY, 1964, 28, 93.
                    (CORRELATES:DEMOGRAPHIC; FACTOR ANALYSIS; N=266 MALE, 1049 FEMALE
                    COLLEGE STUDENTS)
        @APPLICATION 1964 G-22

1840   LAWTON, M. P.
            CORRELATES OF THE OPINIONS ABOUT MENTAL ILLNESS SCALE.
            JOURNAL OF CONSULTING PSYCHOLOGY, 1964, 28, 94.
                    (CORRELATES:PSYCHOLOGICAL; N=72 PSYCHIATRIC AIDES)
        @APPLICATION 1964 C-69 L-35 E-2

1841   KNAPP, R. H., & HOLZBERG, J. D.
            CHARACTERISTICS OF COLLEGE STUDENTS VOLUNTEERING FOR SERVICE TO MENTAL
            PATIENTS.
            JOURNAL OF CONSULTING PSYCHOLOGY, 1964, 28, 82-85.
                    (CORRELATES:BEHAVIORAL, PSYCHOLOGICAL; NORMATIVE DATA; N=85 COLLEGE
                    MALES VOLUNTEERING FOR SERVICE TO MENTAL PATIENTS, 85 CONTROLS)
        @APPLICATION 1964 E-2 D-45 A-7

1842   MATSUSHIMA, J.
            AN INSTRUMENT FOR CLASSIFYING IMPULSE CONTROL AMONG BOYS.
            JOURNAL OF CONSULTING PSYCHOLOGY, 1964, 28, 87-90.
                (RELIABILITY:INTERNAL CONSISTENCY; VALIDITY:CRITERION; NORMATIVE
                DATA; N=192 ELEMENTARY SCHOOL BOYS)
        @APPLICATION 1964 M-51

1843   HIMELSTEIN, P.
            FURTHER EVIDENCE ON THE EGO STRENGTH SCALE AS A MEASURE OF PSYCHOLOGICAL
            HEALTH.
            JOURNAL OF CONSULTING PSYCHOLOGY, 1964, 28, 90-91.
                (VALIDITY:CRITERION; NORMATIVE DATA; N=23 CLINICAL AND 25
                NONCLINICAL COLLEGE STUDENTS)
        @APPLICATION 1964 B-5 D-45

1844   JOHNSTON, R. & MCNEAL, B. F.
            COMBINED MMPI AND DEMOGRAPHIC DATA IN PREDICTING LENGTH OF NEUROPSYCHIATRIC
            HOSPITAL STAY.
            JOURNAL OF CONSULTING PSYCHOLOGY, 1964, 28, 64-70.
                (VALIDITY:CRITERION, CROSS-VALIDATION; CORRELATES:PSYCHOLOGICAL,
                DEMOGRAPHIC; 3 SAMPLES: N=241, 316, AND 352 PSYCHIATRIC PATIENTS)
        @APPLICATION 1964 D-45 B-5 C-150 M-137 M-249 A-32 G-201

1845   DIERS, C. J.
            SOCIAL DESIRABILITY AND ACQUIESCENCE IN RESPONSE TO PERSONALITY ITEMS.
            JOURNAL OF CONSULTING PSYCHOLOGY, 1964, 28, 71-77.
                (CORRELATES:PSYCHOLOGICAL; BIAS:RESPONSE; N=146 COLLEGE MALES AND
                81 FEMALES)
        @APPLICATION 1964 D-45

1846   PRESTON, C. E.
            ACCIDENT-PRONENESS IN ATTEMPTED SUICIDE AND IN AUTOMOBILE ACCIDENT VICTIMS.
            JOURNAL OF CONSULTING PSYCHOLOGY, 1964, 28, 79-82.
                (CORRELATES:BEHAVIORAL; NORMATIVE DATA; N=58 SUICIDAL PATIENTS AND
                30 ACCIDENT VICTIM DRIVERS, 30 CONTROL DRIVERS)
        @APPLICATION 1964 R-12

1847   SPEISMAN, J. C., LAZARUS, R. S., DAVISON, L., & MORDKOFF, A. M.
            EXPERIMENTAL ANALYSIS OF A FILM USED AS A THREATENING STIMULUS.
            JOURNAL OF CONSULTING PSYCHOLOGY, 1964, 28, 23-33.
                (CORRELATES:PSYCHOLOGICAL, PHYSIOLOGICAL, DEMOGRAPHIC; N=12 COLLEGE
                MALES, 12 COLLEGE FEMALES)
        @APPLICATION 1964 D-45 B-91 L-93 N-5

1848   GARMIZE, L. M., & RYCHLAK, J. F.
            ROLE-PLAY VALIDATION OF A SOCIOCULTURAL THEORY OF SYMBOLISM.
            JOURNAL OF CONSULTING PSYCHOLOGY, 1964, 28, 107-115.
                (RELIABILITY:INTERRATER; VALIDITY:CONSTRUCT; N=344 STUDENTS)
        @APPLICATION 1964 R-30 R-90

1849   VOGEL, W., LAUTERBACH, C. G., LIVINGSTON, M., & HOLLOWAY, H.
            RELATIONSHIPS BETWEEN MEMORIES OF THEIR PARENTS' BEHAVIOR AND
            PSYCHODIAGNOSIS IN PSYCHIATRICALLY DISTURBED SOLDIERS.
            JOURNAL OF CONSULTING PSYCHOLOGY, 1964, 28, 126-132.
                (CORRELATES:PSYCHOLOGICAL; N=80 NEUROPSYCHIATRIC SOLDIER PATIENTS
                AND 117 NORMALS)
        @APPLICATION 1964 S-8

1850   BROVERMAN, D. M.
            GENERALITY AND BEHAVIORAL CORRELATES OF COGNITIVE STYLES.
            JOURNAL OF CONSULTING PSYCHOLOGY, 1964, 28, 487-500.
                (CORRELATES:BEHAVIORAL, PSYCHOLOGICAL; FACTOR ANALYSIS; 3 SAMPLES:
                N=32 AND 65 ADULT MALES, AND 206 ADOLESCENT MALE AND FEMALE TWINS)
        @APPLICATION 1964 S-61 G-78 W-19 P-22

1851   QUERY, J. M. N., & QUERY, W. T., JR.
            PROGNOSIS AND PROGRESS: A FIVE-YEAR STUDY OF FORTY-EIGHT SCHIZOPHRENIC MEN.
            JOURNAL OF CONSULTING PSYCHOLOGY, 1964, 28, 501-505.
                (VALIDITY:CRITERION; CORRELATES:DEMOGRAPHIC, INTELLIGENCE; N=48
                MALE SCHIZOPHRENICS)
        @APPLICATION 1964 P-32

1852   MURRAY, J. E., & JACKSON, D. N.
            IMPULSIVITY AND COLOR-FORM ABSTRACTION.
            JOURNAL OF CONSULTING PSYCHOLOGY, 1964, 28, 518-522.
                    (CORRELATES:BEHAVIORAL, PSYCHOLOGICAL; N=57 COLLEGE MALES AND 44
                    COLLEGE FEMALES)
        @APPLICATION 1964 H-37

1853   SUINN, R. M., & HILL, H.
            INFLUENCE OF ANXIETY ON THE RELATIONSHIP BETWEEN SELF-ACCEPTANCE AND
            ACCEPTANCE OF OTHERS.
            JOURNAL OF CONSULTING PSYCHOLOGY, 1964, 28, 116-119.
                    (CORRELATES:PSYCHOLOGICAL; N=92 STUDENTS)
        @APPLICATION 1964 T-2 S-5 P-19 S-203?

1854   PERKINS, J. E., & GOLDBERG, L. R.
            CONTEXTUAL EFFECTS ON THE MMPI.
            JOURNAL OF CONSULTING PSYCHOLOGY, 1964, 28, 133-140.
                    (VALIDITY:CONTENT; NORMATIVE DATA; BIAS:RESPONSE; N=475 STUDENTS,
                    108 NEUROTICS, AND 54 PARANOID SCHIZOPHRENICS)
        @APPLICATION 1964 D-45 W-14 W-25 W-8 W-41

1855   WILCOCK, K. D.
            NEUROTIC DIFFERENCES BETWEEN INDIVIDUALIZED AND SOCIALIZED CRIMINALS.
            JOURNAL OF CONSULTING PSYCHOLOGY, 1964, 28, 141-145.
                    (CORRELATES:BEHAVIORAL, PSYCHOLOGICAL; NORMATIVE DATA; N=45 PRISON
                    INMATES)
        @APPLICATION 1964 D-45 G-22

1856   BLATT, S. J.
            AN ATTEMPT TO DEFINE MENTAL HEALTH.
            JOURNAL OF CONSULTING PSYCHOLOGY, 1964, 28, 146-153.
                    (VALIDITY:CONSTRUCT; CORRELATES:PSYCHOLOGICAL; N=116 RESEARCH
                    SCIENTISTS AND 7 GRADUATE STUDENTS)
        @APPLICATION 1964 S-204 B-5 T-2 F-35 S-205 S-206 S-207? B-176 S-209 L-162

1857   EASTER, L. V., & MURSTEIN, B. I.
            ACHIEVEMENT FANTASY AS A FUNCTION OF PROBABILITY OF SUCCESS.
            JOURNAL OF CONSULTING PSYCHOLOGY, 1964, 28, 154-159.
                    (RELIABILITY:INTERRATER; CORRELATES:PSYCHOLOGICAL; N=90 MALE
                    COLLEGE STUDENTS)
        @APPLICATION 1964 M-7

1858   CHAPMAN, L. J., & KNOWLES, R. R.
            THE EFFECTS OF PHENOTHIAZINE ON DISORDERED THOUGHT IN SCHIZOPHRENIA.
            JOURNAL OF CONSULTING PSYCHOLOGY, 1964, 28, 165-169.
                    (CORRELATES:PHYSIOLOGICAL; N=24 MALE CHRONIC SCHIZOPHRENICS)
        @APPLICATION 1964 C-1 C-20

1859   MARLOWE, D., & GOTTESMAN, I. I.
            THE EDWARDS SD SCALE: A SHORT FORM OF THE MMPI?
            JOURNAL OF CONSULTING PSYCHOLOGY, 1964, 28, 181-182.
                    (VALIDITY:CRITERION; NORMATIVE DATA; N=5035 STUDENTS)
        @APPLICATION 1964 E-1 D-45

1860   EDWARDS, A. L.
            PREDICTION OF MEAN SCORES ON MMPI SCALES.
            JOURNAL OF CONSULTING PSYCHOLOGY, 1964, 28, 183-185.
                    (VALIDITY:CRITERION; NORMATIVE DATA; N=150 MALE STUDENTS)
        @APPLICATION 1964 E-1 D-45

1861   MARLOWE, D., & GOTTESMAN, I. I.
            PREDICTION OF MEAN SCORES ON MMPI SCALES: A REPLY.
            JOURNAL OF CONSULTING PSYCHOLOGY, 1964, 28, 185-186.
                    (MENTION: VALIDITY:CRITERION; NORMATIVE DATA)
        @APPLICATION 1964 E-1 D-45

1862   SPIVACK, G., LEVINE, M., & GRAZIANO, A.
            ANXIETY AND SET IN THE RORSCHACH TEST.
            JOURNAL OF CONSULTING PSYCHOLOGY, 1964, 28, 189.
                    (CORRELATES:PSYCHOLOGICAL, DEMOGRAPHIC; BIAS:RESPONSE; N=36 MALE AND
                    FEMALE COLLEGE STUDENTS)
        @APPLICATION 1964 R-30 L-26

1863   SCHWAB, J. R., & IVERSON, M. A.
              RESISTANCE OF HIGH-ANXIOUS SUBJECTS UNDER EGO THREAT TO PERCEPTION OF
              FIGURAL DISTORTION.
              JOURNAL OF CONSULTING PSYCHOLOGY, 1964, 28, 191-198.
                   (CORRELATES:PSYCHOLOGICAL; USED AS CRITERION; N=40 COLLEGE STUDENTS)
         @APPLICATION 1964 C-136

1864   JUDSON, A. J., & KATAHN, M.
              LEVELS OF PERSONALITY ORGANIZATION AND PRODUCTION OF ASSOCIATIVE
              SEQUENCES IN PROCESS-REACTIVE SCHIZOPHRENIA.
              JOURNAL OF CONSULTING PSYCHOLOGY, 1964, 28, 208-213.
                   (RELIABILITY:INTERRATER; CORRELATES:PSYCHOLOGICAL; USED AS CRITERION;
                   N=40 SCHIZOPHRENIC PATIENTS)
         @APPLICATION 1964 W-44 R-30 B-94

1865   WALKER, R. E., & SPENCE, J. T.
              RELATIONSHIP BETWEEN DIGIT SPAN AND ANXIETY.
              JOURNAL OF CONSULTING PSYCHOLOGY, 1964, 28, 220-223.
                   (CORRELATES:INTELLIGENCE; NORMATIVE DATA; N=51 MALE, 59 FEMALE
                   COLLEGE STUDENTS)
         @APPLICATION 1964 T-2 S-5

1866   STELMACHERS, Z. T., & MCHUGH, R. B.
              CONTRIBUTION OF STEREOTYPED AND INDIVIDUALIZED INFORMATION TO PREDICTIVE
              ACCURACY.
              JOURNAL OF CONSULTING PSYCHOLOGY, 1964, 28, 234-242.
                   (VALIDITY:CRITERION; N=112 CLINICIANS AND NURSING STUDENTS, JUDGED 4
                   SUBJECTS)
         @APPLICATION 1964 D-45 G-21 E-1

1867   WINSLOW, C. N., & RAPERSAND, I.
              POSTDICTION OF THE OUTCOME OF SOMATIC THERAPY FROM THE RORSCHACH RECORDS
              OF SCHIZOPHRENIC PATIENTS.
              JOURNAL OF CONSULTING PSYCHOLOGY, 1964, 28, 243-247.
                   (VALIDITY:CRITERION; N=60 SCHIZOPHRENIC PATIENTS)
         @APPLICATION 1964 R-30

1868   GOLDMAN, I. J.
              EFFECTIVENESS OF THE FORCED-CHOICE METHOD IN MINIMIZING SOCIAL
              DESIRABILITY INFLUENCE.
              JOURNAL OF CONSULTING PSYCHOLOGY, 1964, 28, 289.
                   (BIAS:RESPONSE; N=89 COLLEGE MALES, 73 COLLEGE FEMALES)
         @APPLICATION 1964 G-131

1869   HANDLER, L., & REYHER, J.
              THE EFFECTS OF STRESS ON THE DRAW-A-PERSON TEST.
              JOURNAL OF CONSULTING PSYCHOLOGY, 1964, 28, 259-264.
                   (RELIABILITY:INTERRATER; CORRELATES:PSYCHOLOGICAL; N=57 MALE
                   STUDENTS)
         @APPLICATION 1964 M-58

1870   GARD, J. G., & BENDIG, A. W.
              A FACTOR ANALYTIC STUDY OF EYSENCK'S AND SCHUTZ'S PERSONALITY DIMENSIONS
              AMONG PSYCHIATRIC GROUPS.
              JOURNAL OF CONSULTING PSYCHOLOGY, 1964, 28, 252-258.
                   (VALIDITY:CRITERION; FACTOR ANALYSIS; N=20 SCHIZOPHRENICS, 12
                   NEUROTICS, AND 20 NORMALS)
         @APPLICATION 1964 E-5 S-11 H-22 G-132

1871   VAN DE CASTLE, R. L.
              EFFECT OF TEST ORDER UPON RORSCHACH HUMAN CONTENT.
              JOURNAL OF CONSULTING PSYCHOLOGY, 1964, 28, 286-288.
                   (RELIABILITY; CORRELATES:PSYCHOLOGICAL; N=22 GRADUATE STUDENTS)
         @APPLICATION 1964 M-58 R-30 M-2C

1872   ROE, E. E., & KOGAN, W. S.
              EFFECT OF SOCIAL DESIRABILITY INSTRUCTIONS ON SEVERAL MMPI MEASURES OF
              SOCIAL DESIRABILITY.
              JOURNAL OF CONSULTING PSYCHOLOGY, 1964, 28, 248-251.
                   (VALIDITY:CRITERION, CROSS-VALIDATION; BIAS:RESPONSE; N=105
                   PSYCHIATRIC MALE PATIENTS)
         @APPLICATION 1964 E-1 W-14 C-58 D-45

1873 DISTLER, L. S., MAY, P. R. A., & TUMA, A. H.
ANXIETY AND EGO STRENGTH AS PREDICTORS OF RESPONSE TO TREATMENT IN
SCHIZOPHRENIC PATIENTS.
JOURNAL OF CONSULTING PSYCHOLOGY, 1964, 28, 170-177.
(VALIDITY:CONSTRUCT, CRITERION; CORRELATES:DEMOGRAPHIC; N=50 MALE
AND 50 FEMALE SCHIZOPHRENICS)
@APPLICATION 1964 B-5 T-2 L-101 J-39

1874 MCNAIR, D. M., & LORR, M.
AN ANALYSIS OF PROFESSED PSYCHOTHERAPEUTIC TECHNIQUES.
JOURNAL OF CONSULTING PSYCHOLOGY, 1964, 28, 265-271.
(REVISION; CLUSTER ANALYSIS; N=192 MALE, 73 FEMALE
PSYCHOTHERAPISTS)
@APPLICATION 1964 S-202

1875 LAXER, R. M.
SELF-CONCEPT CHANGES OF DEPRESSIVE PATIENTS IN GENERAL HOSPITAL TREATMENT.
JOURNAL OF CONSULTING PSYCHOLOGY, 1964, 28, 214-219.
(USED AS CRITERION; N=37 NEUROTIC DEPRESSIVES, 37 PARANOIDS AND
67 OTHER PATIENTS AND 41 NORMAL STUDENTS)
@APPLICATION 1964 E-20 O-16

1876 BENNETT, V. D. C.
DOES SIZE OF FIGURE DRAWING REFLECT SELF-CONCEPT?
JOURNAL OF CONSULTING PSYCHOLOGY, 1964, 28, 285-286.
(VALIDITY:CRITERION; CORRELATES:PSYCHOLOGICAL, INTELLIGENCE; N=198
SIXTH GRADERS)
@APPLICATION 1964 M-58

1877 SCHAEFFER, R. W.
CLINICAL PSYCHOLOGISTS' ABILITY TO USE THE DRAW-A-PERSON TEST AS AN
INDICATOR OF PERSONALITY ADJUSTMENT.
JOURNAL OF CONSULTING PSYCHOLOGY, 1964, 28, 383.
(RELIABILITY:INTERRATER; VALIDITY:CRITERION; N=10 NORMAL AND 20
HOSPITALIZED FEMALE PSYCHIATRIC PATIENTS, 17 CLINICIANS, 17
CLINICAL TRAINEES, 5 NON-PSYCHOLOGISTS)
@APPLICATION 1964 M-58

1878 LORR, M.
A SIMPLEX OF PARANOID PROJECTION.
JOURNAL OF CONSULTING PSYCHOLOGY, 1964, 28, 378-380.
(VALIDITY:CONTENT, CRITERION; N=296 AND 566 PSYCHOTICS IN 47 AND 44
HOSPITALS, RESP.)
@APPLICATION 1964 L-39

1879 LEWINSOHN, P. M.
RELATIONSHIP BETWEEN HEIGHT OF FIGURE DRAWINGS AND DEPRESSION IN
PSYCHIATRIC PATIENTS.
JOURNAL OF CONSULTING PSYCHOLOGY, 1964, 28, 380-381.
(CORRELATES:PSYCHOLOGICAL; NORMATIVE DATA; 2 STUDIES: N=100
DEPRESSED AND NON-DEPRESSED PATIENTS, N=50 MALE, 60 FEMALE
PSYCHIATRIC PATIENTS)
@APPLICATION 1964 L-39 M-58

1880 ENDICOTT, N. A., & ENDICOTT, J.
PREDICTION OF IMPROVEMENT IN TREATED AND UNTREATED PATIENTS USING THE
RORSCHACH PROGNOSTIC RATING SCALE.
JOURNAL OF CONSULTING PSYCHOLOGY, 1964, 28, 342-348.
(VALIDITY:CRITERION; CORRELATES:PSYCHOLOGICAL, ENVIRONMENTAL;
NORMATIVE DATA; N=61 TREATED AND UNTREATED PSYCHIATRIC PATIENTS)
@APPLICATION 1964 K-13 R-30 D-45 M-250

1881 LOREI, T. W.
PREDICTION OF LENGTH OF STAY OUT OF THE HOSPITAL FOR RELEASED PSYCHIATRIC
PATIENTS.
JOURNAL OF CONSULTING PSYCHOLOGY, 1964, 28, 358-363.
(VALIDITY:CRITERION; CORRELATES:PSYCHOLOGICAL; N=104 RELEASED
PSYCHIATRIC PATIENTS)
@APPLICATION 1964 G-22 C-69 P-8C

1882   SASSENRATH, J. M.
            A FACTOR ANALYSIS OF RATING-SCALE ITEMS ON THE TEST ANXIETY QUESTIONNAIRE.
            JOURNAL OF CONSULTING PSYCHOLOGY, 1964, 28, 371-377.
                    (DESCRIPTION; FACTOR ANALYSIS; N=77 COLLEGE MALES AND 125 COLLEGE
                    FEMALES)
        @APPLICATION 1964 M-4

1883   COHEN, J., & STRUENING, E. L.
            OPINIONS ABOUT MENTAL ILLNESS: HOSPITAL SOCIAL ATMOSPHERE PROFILES AND
            THEIR RELEVANCE TO EFFECTIVENESS.
            JOURNAL OF CONSULTING PSYCHOLOGY, 1964, 28, 291-298.
                    (VALIDITY:CRITERION; CORRELATES:ENVIRONMENTAL; NORMATIVE DATA;
                    N=12 HOSPITALS WITH 3148 EMPLOYEES, 1304 PATIENTS)
        @APPLICATION 1964 C-69

1884   HOLZBERG, J. D., GEWIRTZ, H., & EBNER, E.
            CHANGES IN MORAL JUDGMENT AND SELF-ACCEPTANCE IN COLLEGE STUDENTS AS A
            FUNCTION OF COMPANIONSHIP WITH HOSPITALIZED MENTAL PATIENTS.
            JOURNAL OF CONSULTING PSYCHOLOGY, 1964, 28, 299-303.
                    (MODIFICATION; VALIDITY:CRITERION; N=56 COLLEGE MALES)
        @APPLICATION 1964 E-2 L-81

1885   DAVIDS, A., & TALMADGE, M.
            UTILITY OF THE RORSCHACH IN PREDICTING MOVEMENT IN PSYCHIATRIC CASEWORK.
            JOURNAL OF CONSULTING PSYCHOLOGY, 1964, 28, 311-316.
                    (VALIDITY:CRITERION; N=50 MOTHERS OF EMOTIONALLY DISTURBED
                    CHILDREN)
        @APPLICATION 1964 R-30

1886   BARBER, T. X., & CALVERLEY, D. S.
            COMPARATIVE EFFECTS ON "HYPNOTIC-LIKE" SUGGESTIBILITY OF RECORDED AND
            SPOKEN SUGGESTIONS.
            JOURNAL OF CONSULTING PSYCHOLOGY, 1964, 28, 384.
                    (CORRELATES:ENVIRONMENTAL; 2 STUDIES: N=84 FEMALE NURSES, 66 MALE
                    STUDENTS)
        @APPLICATION 1964 B-3

1887   SILVERMAN, J.
            SCANNING-CONTROL MECHANISM AND "COGNITIVE FILTERING" IN PARANOID AND
            NONPARANOID SCHIZOPHRENIA.
            JOURNAL OF CONSULTING PSYCHOLOGY, 1964, 28, 385-393.
                    (USED AS CRITERION; NORMATIVE DATA; N=55 MALE PARANOID AND
                    NONPARANOID SCHIZOPHRENICS)
        @APPLICATION 1964 P-7

1888   COAN, R. W.
            FACTORS IN MOVEMENT PERCEPTION.
            JOURNAL OF CONSULTING PSYCHOLOGY, 1964, 28, 394-402.
                    (CORRELATES:BEHAVIORAL, PSYCHOLOGICAL; FACTOR ANALYSIS; N=50
                    COLLEGE MALES AND 50 COLLEGE FEMALES)
        @APPLICATION 1964 C-10 W-72

1889   GRACE, D. P.
            PREDICTING PROGRESS OF SCHIZOPHRENICS IN A WORK-ORIENTED REHABILITATION
            PROGRAM.
            JOURNAL OF CONSULTING PSYCHOLOGY, 1964, 28, 560.
                    (VALIDITY:CRITERION; N=60 MALE SCHIZOPHRENICS)
        @APPLICATION 1964 B-5 M-141 D-45

1890   FORD, L. H., JR.
            A FORCED-CHOICE, ACQUIESCENCE-FREE, SOCIAL DESIRABILITY (DEFENSIVENESS)
            SCALE.
            JOURNAL OF CONSULTING PSYCHOLOGY, 1964, 28, 475.
                    (REVISION; VALIDITY:CONSTRUCT; CORRELATES:PSYCHOLOGICAL; 7 SAMPLES
                    OF MALE AND FEMALE COLLEGE STUDENTS, MEDIAN N=118)
        @APPLICATION 1964 C-27 H-30

1891   DEAN, R. B., & RICHARDSON, H.
            ANALYSIS OF MMPI PROFILES OF FORTY COLLEGE-EDUCATED OVERT MALE HOMOSEXUALS.
            JOURNAL OF CONSULTING PSYCHOLOGY, 1964, 28, 483-486.
                    (CORRELATES:BEHAVIORAL; NORMATIVE DATA; N=40 MALE HOMOSEXUALS, 40
                    HETEROSEXUAL CONTROLS)
        @APPLICATION 1964 D-45

1892   SILBER, L. D., & GREBSTEIN, L. C.
           REPRESSION-SENSITIZATION AND SOCIAL DESIRABILITY RESPONDING.
           JOURNAL OF CONSULTING PSYCHOLOGY, 1964, 28, 559.
                   (CORRELATES:PSYCHOLOGICAL; BIAS:RESPONSE; 3 SAMPLES: N=59 AND 75
                   MEDICAL STUDENTS, 74 COLLEGE STUDENTS)
       @APPLICATION 1964 B-46 C-27

1893   HAFNER, A. J., QUAST, W., SPEER, D. C., & GRAMS, A.
           CHILDREN'S ANXIETY SCALES IN RELATION TO SELF, PARENTAL, AND PSYCHIATRIC
           RATINGS OF ANXIETY.
           JOURNAL OF CONSULTING PSYCHOLOGY, 1964, 28, 555-558.
                   (CORRELATES:PSYCHOLOGICAL; NORMATIVE DATA; N=40 PEDIATRIC, 40
                   PSYCHIATRIC PREADOLESCENT BOYS AND GIRLS AND THEIR PARENTS)
       @APPLICATION 1964 C-55 S-133

1894   LAXER, R. M.
           RELATION OF REAL SELF-RATING TO MOOD AND BLAME AND THEIR INTERACTION IN
           DEPRESSION.
           JOURNAL OF CONSULTING PSYCHOLOGY, 1964, 28, 538-546.
                   (CORRELATES:PSYCHOLOGICAL; USED AS CRITERION; N=72 PSYCHIATRIC
                   PATIENTS, 132 COLLEGE STUDENTS)
       @APPLICATION 1964 W-52 D-16

1895   LOWE, C. M.
           THE EQUIVALENCE OF GUILT AND ANXIETY AS PSYCHOLOGICAL CONSTRUCTS.
           JOURNAL OF CONSULTING PSYCHOLOGY, 1964, 28, 553-554.
                   (RELIABILITY:INTERNAL CONSISTENCY; VALIDITY:CONSTRUCT;
                   CORRELATES:PSYCHOLOGICAL; N=70 PSYCHIATRIC PATIENTS AND 140
                   PSYCHIATRIC AIDE APPLICANTS)
       @APPLICATION 1964 T-2 D-45

1896   BOE, E. E.
           ACQUIESCENCE SET IN EDWARDS' SD SCALE: AN EVALUATION OF THE ADAMS AND
           KIRBY PAPER.
           JOURNAL OF CONSULTING PSYCHOLOGY, 1964, 28, 472-473.
                   (VALIDITY:CONTENT; BIAS:RESPONSE; NO SAMPLE)
       @APPLICATION 1964 E-1

1897   KANFER, F. H., & MARSTON, A. R.
           CHARACTERISTICS OF INTERACTIONAL BEHAVIOR IN A PSYCHOTHERAPY ANALOGUE.
           JOURNAL OF CONSULTING PSYCHOLOGY, 1964, 28, 456-467.
                   (CORRELATES:BEHAVIORAL, PSYCHOLOGICAL; USED AS CRITERION;
                   3 STUDIES: N=50, 48, AND 30 MALE AND FEMALE UNDERGRADUATES)
       @APPLICATION 1964 D-45 C-27 B-83

1898   SAPOLSKY, A.
           AN EFFORT AT STUDYING RORSCHACH CONTENT SYMBOLISM: THE FROG RESPONSE.
           JOURNAL OF CONSULTING PSYCHOLOGY, 1964, 28, 469-472.
                   (VALIDITY:CONTENT; N=31 PSYCHIATRIC PATIENTS GIVING FROG
                   RESPONSES ON RORSCHACH, 30 MATCHED CONTROLS)
       @APPLICATION 1964 R-30

1899   LIBERTY, P. G., JR., LUNNEBORG, C. E., & ATKINSON, G. C.
           PERCEPTUAL DEFENSE, DISSIMULATION, AND RESPONSE STYLES.
           JOURNAL OF CONSULTING PSYCHOLOGY, 1964, 28, 529-537.
                   (MENTION; VALIDITY:CONSTRUCT; CORRELATES:PSYCHOLOGICAL; FACTOR
                   ANALYSIS; BIAS:RESPONSE; N=150 MALE COLLEGE STUDENTS)
       @APPLICATION 1964 D-45 C-23 C-27 B-46 E-1 U-4 C-58 T-2 W-8 B-5 F-13 W-41 W-14
       @G-127 H-122 G-19 G-36 G-121 W-123 E-79

1900   MCKEEVER, M. F., & MAY, P. R. A.
           THE MACC SCALE AS A PREDICTOR OF LENGTH OF HOSPITALIZATION FOR
           SCHIZOPHRENIC PATIENTS.
           JOURNAL OF CONSULTING PSYCHOLOGY, 1964, 28, 474.
                   (VALIDITY:CRITERION; CORRELATES:DEMOGRAPHIC; N=47 MALE AND 53
                   FEMALE PSYCHIATRIC PATIENTS)
       @APPLICATION 1964 E-20

1901   GRAY, D. M., & PEPITONE, A.
           EFFECT OF SELF-ESTEEM ON DRAWINGS OF THE HUMAN FIGURE.
           JOURNAL OF CONSULTING PSYCHOLOGY, 1964, 29, 452-455.
                   (CORRELATES:PSYCHOLOGICAL; N=25 LOW, 25 HIGH SELF ESTEEM COLLEGE
                   STUDENTS, 38 CONTROLS)
       @APPLICATION 1964 M-58

1902   SUTHERLAND, B. V., & SPILKA, B.
            SOCIAL DESIRABILITY, ITEM-RESPONSE TIME, AND ITEM SIGNIFICANCE.
            JOURNAL OF CONSULTING PSYCHOLOGY, 1964, 28, 447-451.
                    (VALIDITY:CONTENT; CORRELATES:DEMOGRAPHIC, ENVIRONMENTAL;
                    NORMATIVE DATA; BIAS:RESPONSE; N=125 COLLEGE MALES AND FEMALES)
        @APPLICATION 1964 M-50

1903   GOLDEN, M.
            SOME EFFECTS OF COMBINING PSYCHOLOGICAL TESTS ON CLINICAL INFERENCES.
            JOURNAL OF CONSULTING PSYCHOLOGY, 1964, 28, 440-446.
                    (VALIDITY:CRITERION; CORRELATES:PSYCHOLOGICAL; N=5 PSYCHIATRIC
                    PATIENTS)
        @APPLICATION 1964 D-45 R-30 M-20 L-52

1904   CARSON, R. C., HARDEN, J. A., & SHOWS, W. D.
            A-B DISTINCTION AND BEHAVIOR IN QUASI-THERAPEUTIC SITUATIONS.
            JOURNAL OF CONSULTING PSYCHOLOGY, 1964, 28, 426-433.
                    (REVISION; CORRELATES:BEHAVIORAL, PSYCHOLOGICAL; USED AS CRITERION;
                    2 STUDIES: N=60 AND 32 COLLEGE MALES)
        @APPLICATION 1964 W-91 O-16 K-78

1905   MCDAVID, J. W.
            IMMEDIATE EFFECTS OF GROUP THERAPY UPON RESPONSE TO SOCIAL REINFORCEMENT
            AMONG JUVENILE DELINQUENTS.
            JOURNAL OF CONSULTING PSYCHOLOGY, 1964, 28, 409-412.
                    (CORRELATES:PSYCHOLOGICAL; USED AS CRITERION; N=89 ADOLESCENT MALE
                    DELINQUENTS)
        @APPLICATION 1964 M-65

1906   JONES, N. F., & KAHN, M. W.
            PATIENT ATTITUDES AS RELATED TO SOCIAL CLASS AND OTHER VARIABLES CONCERNED
            WITH HOSPITALIZATION.
            JOURNAL OF CONSULTING PSYCHOLOGY, 1964, 28, 403-408.
                    (CORRELATES:PSYCHOLOGICAL, DEMOGRAPHIC, ENVIRONMENTAL; N=54
                    PSYCHIATRIC PATIENTS)
        @APPLICATION 1964 K-99

1907   SIEGELMAN, M.
            COLLEGE STUDENT PERSONALITY CORRELATES OF EARLY PARENT-CHILD RELATIONSHIP.
            JOURNAL OF CONSULTING PSYCHOLOGY, 1965, 29, 558-564.
                    (RELIABILITY:INTERNAL CONSISTENCY; CORRELATES:PSYCHOLOGICAL,
                    DEMOGRAPHIC; N=57 MALES, 97 FEMALES)
        @APPLICATION 1965 R-41 C-10

1908   STURM, I. E.
            OVERINCLUSION AND CONCRETENESS AMONG PATHOLOGICAL GROUPS.
            JOURNAL OF CONSULTING PSYCHOLOGY, 1965, 29, 9-18.
                    (MODIFICATION; DESCRIPTION; RELIABILITY:INTERNAL CONSISTENCY;
                    VALIDITY:CONSTRUCT; CORRELATES:DEMOGRAPHIC, INTELLIGENCE;
                    NORMATIVE DATA; N=40 TUBERCULOUS, 40 BRAIN DAMAGED, AND 45
                    SCHIZOPHRENIC PATIENTS)
        @APPLICATION 1965 E-38

1909   LIBERTY, P. G., JR.
            METHODOLOGICAL CONSIDERATIONS IN THE ASSESSMENT OF ACQUIESCENCE IN THE MA
            AND SD SCALE.
            JOURNAL OF CONSULTING PSYCHOLOGY, 1965, 29, 37-42.
                    (VALIDITY:CONSTRUCT; BIAS:RESPONSE; 2 STUDIES: N=50, 70 COLLEGE
                    MALES)
        @APPLICATION 1965 E-1 T-2 D-45

1910   MURSTEIN, B. I.
            PROJECTION OF HOSTILITY ON THE TAT AS A FUNCTION OF STIMULUS, BACKGROUND,
            AND PERSONALITY VARIABLES.
            JOURNAL OF CONSULTING PSYCHOLOGY, 1965, 29, 43-48.
                    (MENTION; RELIABILITY:INTERRATER; CORRELATES:BEHAVIORAL,
                    PSYCHOLOGICAL, DEMOGRAPHIC, ENVIRONMENTAL; N=48 MALE AND 48 FEMALE
                    COLLEGE STUDENTS)
        @APPLICATION 1965 M-20 H-73 M-134

1911   MENDELSOHN, G. A., & GELLER, M. H.
            STRUCTURE OF CLIENT ATTITUDES TOWARD COUNSELING AND THEIR RELATION TO
            CLIENT-COUNSELOR SIMILARITY.
            JOURNAL OF CONSULTING PSYCHOLOGY, 1965, 29, 63-72.
                    (DESCRIPTION; CORRELATES:BEHAVIORAL; CLUSTER ANALYSIS; 2 STUDIES:
                    N=72 UNDERGRADUATES, 178 UNDERGRADUATES AND GRADUATES, 15
                    COUNSELORS)
            @APPLICATION 1965 M-22

1912   SCHMEIDLER, G. R.
            VISUAL IMAGERY CORRELATED TO A MEASURE OF CREATIVITY.
            JOURNAL OF CONSULTING PSYCHOLOGY, 1965, 29, 78-80.
                    (MODIFICATION; CORRELATES:PSYCHOLOGICAL, DEMOGRAPHIC)
            @APPLICATION 1965 B-4

1913   GREENBERGER, E.
            FANTASIES OF WOMEN CONFRONTING DEATH.
            JOURNAL OF CONSULTING PSYCHOLOGY, 1965, 29, 252-260.
                    (CORRELATES:PSYCHOLOGICAL; N=25 FEMALE CANCER PATIENTS AND 25 FEMALES
                    WITH MILD DISEASES)
            @APPLICATION 1965 M-20

1914   EDWARDS, A. L.
            CORRELATION OF "A UNIDIMENSIONAL DEPRESSION SCALE FOR THE MMPI" WITH THE
            SD SCALE.
            JOURNAL OF CONSULTING PSYCHOLOGY, 1965, 29, 271-273.
                    (RELIABILITY:INTERNAL CONSISTENCY; CORRELATES:PSYCHOLOGICAL;
                    NORMATIVE DATA; BIAS:RESPONSE; 3 SAMPLES: N=155 MALES, 150 MALES,
                    163 FEMALES)
            @APPLICATION 1965 D-3 E-1 D-45

1915   MASLING, J.
            DIFFERENTIAL INDOCTRINATION OF EXAMINERS AND RORSCHACH RESPONSES.
            JOURNAL OF CONSULTING PSYCHOLOGY, 1965, 29, 198-201.
                    (RELIABILITY:INTERRATER; BIAS:TESTER; N=14 GRADUATE STUDENTS)
            @APPLICATION 1965 R-30

1916   SHORE, M. F., MASSIMO, J. L., & MACK, R.
            CHANGES IN THE PERCEPTION OF INTERPERSONAL RELATIONSHIPS IN SUCCESSFULLY
            TREATED ADOLESCENT DELINQUENT BOYS.
            JOURNAL OF CONSULTING PSYCHOLOGY, 1965, 29, 213-217.
                    (RELIABILITY:INTERRATER; CORRELATES:BEHAVIORAL, INTELLIGENCE; N=20
                    ANTISOCIAL ADOLESCENT BOYS)
            @APPLICATION 1965 T-20 E-43

1917   BLATT, S. J., ALLISON, J., & BAKER, B. L.
            THE WECHSLER OBJECT ASSEMBLY SUBTEST AND BODILY CONCERNS.
            JOURNAL OF CONSULTING PSYCHOLOGY, 1965, 29, 223-230.
                    (CORRELATES:PHYSIOLOGICAL, INTELLIGENCE; N=40 PSYCHIATRIC PATIENTS)
            @APPLICATION 1965 R-30

1918   HOLLENBECK, G. P.
            CONDITIONS AND OUTCOMES IN THE STUDENT-PARENT RELATIONSHIP.
            JOURNAL OF CONSULTING PSYCHOLOGY, 1965, 29, 237-241.
                    (CORRELATES:PSYCHOLOGICAL, DEMOGRAPHIC, INTELLIGENCE; N=50 MALE AND
                    50 FEMALE COLLEGE STUDENTS)
            @APPLICATION 1965 B-50 S-193

1919   PORRO, C. R.
            PERCEPTION OF MATERNAL CHILD REARING ATTITUDES BY SCHIZOPHRENIC MALES,
            THEIR NORMAL MALE SIBLINGS, AND NORMAL MALES WHOSE SIBLINGS ARE NORMAL.
            JOURNAL OF CONSULTING PSYCHOLOGY, 1965, 29, 242-246.
                    (CORRELATES:PSYCHOLOGICAL, DEMOGRAPHIC; N=14 SCHIZOPHRENIC PATIENTS,
                    14 NORMAL MALE SIBLINGS OF SCHIZOPHRENIC PATIENTS, 14 NORMAL MALE
                    SIBLINGS OF NORMALS)
            @APPLICATION 1965 M-136

1920   DEMPSEY, P.
            DEPRESSION OR SOCIAL DESIRABILITY: COMMENT ON EDWARDS' APPRAISAL OF THE
            D30 SCALE.
            JOURNAL OF CONSULTING PSYCHOLOGY, 1965, 29, 274-276.
                    (VALIDITY:CONTENT, CONSTRUCT; BAIS:RESPONSE; N=40 PEACE CORPS
                    TRAINEES)
            @APPLICATION 1965 D-3 E-1

1921   MUZEKARI, L. H.
            THE MMPI IN PREDICTING TREATMENT OUTCOME IN ALCOHOLISM.
            JOURNAL OF CONSULTING PSYCHOLOGY, 1965, 29, 281.
                    (VALIDITY:CRITERION, CROSS-VALIDATION; CORRELATES:BEHAVIORAL;
                    N=86 CONVERTED ALCOHOLICS, 94 RELAPSED ALCOHOLICS)
        @APPLICATION 1965 D-45

1922   BARBER, T. X., & CALVERLEY, D. S.
            EMPIRICAL EVIDENCE FOR A THEORY OF HYPNOTIC BEHAVIOR: EFFECTS ON
            SUGGESTIBILITY OF FIVE VARIABLES TYPICALLY INCLUDED IN HYPNOTIC INDUCTION
            PROCEDURES.
            JOURNAL OF CONSULTING PSYCHOLOGY, 1965, 29, 98-107.
                    CORRELATES:PSYCHOLOGICAL, ENVIRONMENTAL; 3 STUDIES: N=136 FEMALE
                    STUDENTS, 74 COLLEGE STUDENTS, 48 MALE COLLEGE UNDERGRADUATES)
        @APPLICATION 1965 B-3

1923   QUAY, H. C., & HUNT, W. A.
            PSYCHOPATHY, NEUROTICISM, AND VERBAL CONDITIONING: A REPLICATION AND
            EXTENSION.
            JOURNAL OF CONSULTING PSYCHOLOGY, 1965, 29, 283.
                    (CORRELATES:BEHAVIORAL, PSYCHOLOGICAL; USED AS CRITERION; N=458
                    MILITARY PRISONERS)
        @APPLICATION 1965 E-5 P-31

1924   HARRIS, J. G., JR., & BAXTER, J. C.
            AMBIGUITY IN THE MMPI.
            JOURNAL OF CONSULTING PSYCHOLOGY, 1965, 29, 112-118.
                    (VALIDITY:CONSTRUCT; CORRELATES:PSYCHOLOGICAL; N=56 MALE AND 56
                    FEMALE COLLEGE STUDENTS)
        @APPLICATION 1965 D-45 B-5 T-2 W-8 W-41

1925   TRUAX, C. B., & CARKHUFF, R. R.
            EXPERIMENTAL MANIPULATION OF THERAPEUTIC CONDITIONS.
            JOURNAL OF CONSULTING PSYCHOLOGY, 1965, 29, 119-124.
                    (CORRELATES:BEHAVIORAL, PSYCHOLOGICAL; N=3 FEMALE PSYCHIATRIC
                    PATIENTS)
        @APPLICATION 1965 T-37 T-24 T-69 T-89

1926   MUELLER, W. J., & GRATER, H. A.
            AGGRESSION CONFLICT, ANXIETY, AND EGO STRENGTH.
            JOURNAL OF CONSULTING PSYCHOLOGY, 1965, 29, 130-134.
                    (CORRELATES:PSYCHOLOGICAL, DEMOGRAPHIC; USED AS CRITERION; N=86 MALE
                    AND 95 FEMALE COLLEGE STUDENTS)
        @APPLICATION 1965 D-45 B-5 T-2 O-16

1927   FISHER, S.
            BODY SENSATION AND PERCEPTION OF PROJECTIVE STIMULI.
            JOURNAL OF CONSULTING PSYCHOLOGY, 1965, 29, 135-138.
                    (CORRELATES:PSYCHOLOGICAL, PHYSIOLOGICAL; 2 STUDIES: N=52 MALE AND 50
                    FEMALE COLLEGE STUDENTS, AND 51 MALE AND 42 FEMALE COLLEGE STUDENTS)
        @APPLICATION 1965 R-30

1928   MAUPIN, E. W.
            INDIVIDUAL DIFFERENCES IN RESPONSE TO A ZEN MEDITATION EXERCISE.
            JOURNAL OF CONSULTING PSYCHOLOGY, 1965, 29, 139-145.
                    (VALIDITY:CRITERION; CORRELATES:PSYCHOLOGICAL; N=28 COLLEGE MALES)
        @APPLICATION 1965 R-30 K-155

1929   ELSTEIN, A. S.
            BEHAVIORAL CORRELATES OF THE RORSCHACH SHADING DETERMINANT.
            JOURNAL OF CONSULTING PSYCHOLOGY, 1965, 29, 231-236.
                    (VALIDITY:CRITERION; CORRELATES:BEHAVIORAL; N=20 MALE
                    PSYCHIATRIC PATIENTS)
        @APPLICATION 1965 R-30

1930   BYRNE, D., GOLIGHTLY, C., & SHEFFIELD, J.
            THE REPRESSION-SENSITIZATION SCALE AS A MEASURE OF ADJUSTMENT: RELATIONSHIP
            WITH THE CPI.
            JOURNAL OF CONSULTING PSYCHOLOGY, 1965, 29, 586-589.
                    (VALIDITY:CONSTRUCT; CORRELATES:PSYCHOLOGICAL; N=43 MALE, 48
                    FEMALE COLLEGE STUDENTS)
        @APPLICATION 1965 B-46 G-22

1931   AMIR, Y., KOHEN-RAZ, R., & RABINOVITZ, G.
            GROUP RORSCHACH TECHNIQUE FOR SCREENING ARMY OFFICERS.
            JOURNAL OF CONSULTING PSYCHOLOGY, 1965, 29, 598.
                (RELIABILITY:INTERNAL CONSISTENCY; VALIDITY:CRITERION; N=275)
        @APPLICATION 1965 K-98

1932   MUTHARD, J. E.
            MMPI FINDINGS FOR CEREBRAL PALSIED COLLEGE STUDENTS.
            JOURNAL OF CONSULTING PSYCHOLOGY, 1965, 29, 599.
                (CORRELATES:PHYSIOLOGICAL, DEMOGRAPHIC; N=48 MALE AND 28 FEMALE
                COLLEGE STUDENTS)
        @APPLICATION 1965 D-45 W-8 W-41 B-5 G-19 K-138 D-57

1933   HELSON, R.
            CHILDHOOD INTEREST CLUSTERS RELATED TO CREATIVITY IN WOMEN.
            JOURNAL OF CONSULTING PSYCHOLOGY, 1965, 29, 352-361.
                (CORRELATES:PSYCHOLOGICAL; USED AS CRITERION; 3 SAMPLES: N=135
                FEMALE COLLEGE STUDENTS AND 139 FEMALE COLLEGE STUDENTS, 100
                COLLEGE MALES AND 100 COLLEGE FEMALES)
        @APPLICATION 1965 D-45 G-22 M-22 B-78 B-6 B-4 G-52 G-53

1934   NUTTALL, R. L., & SOLOMON, L. F.
            FACTORIAL STRUCTURE AND PROGNOSTIC SIGNIFICANCE OF PREMORBID ADJUSTMENT
            IN SCHIZOPHRENIA.
            JOURNAL OF CONSULTING PSYCHOLOGY, 1965, 29, 362-372.
                (VALIDITY:CRITERION; CORRELATES:PSYCHOLOGICAL; NORMATIVE DATA;
                FACTOR ANALYSIS; N=291 MALE SCHIZOPHRENIC PATIENTS)
        @APPLICATION 1965 P-32 B-275

1935   MEDINNUS, G. R.
            ADOLESCENTS' SELF-ACCEPTANCE AND PERCEPTIONS OF THEIR PARENTS.
            JOURNAL OF CONSULTING PSYCHOLOGY, 1965, 29, 150-154.
                (CORRELATES:PSYCHOLOGICAL, DEMOGRAPHIC; N=26 FEMALE AND 18 MALE
                COLLEGE STUDENTS)
        @APPLICATION 1965 B-18 R-41 O-16

1936   MOSHER, D. L.
            INTERACTION OF FEAR AND GUILT IN INHIBITING UNACCEPTABLE BEHAVIOR.
            JOURNAL OF CONSULTING PSYCHOLOGY, 1965, 29, 161-167.
                (RELIABILITY:INTERRATER; CORRELATES:BEHAVIORAL, PSYCHOLOGICAL;
                NORMATIVE DATA; N=80 MALE COLLEGE STUDENTS)
        @APPLICATION 1965 M-16

1937   KNAPP, R. R.
            RELATIONSHIP OF A MEASURE OF SELF-ACTUALIZATION TO NEUROTICISM AND
            EXTRAVERSION.
            JOURNAL OF CONSULTING PSYCHOLOGY, 1965, 29, 168-172.
                (VALIDITY:CRITERION; CORRELATES:PSYCHOLOGICAL; USED AS CRITERION;
                NORMATIVE DATA; N=136 COLLEGE STUDENTS)
        @APPLICATION 1965 E-6 S-21

1938   RESNICK, J. H., & DEAN, S. J.
            METHODOLOGICAL DETERMINANTS OF PECULIAR PERSONAL CONSTRUCTS.
            JOURNAL OF CONSULTING PSYCHOLOGY, 1965, 29, 178-180.
                (VALIDITY:CONSTRUCT; N=122 FEMALE COLLEGE STUDENTS)
        @APPLICATION 1965 K-23

1939   WHITAKER, L., JR.
            THE RORSCHACH AND HOLTZMAN AS MEASURES OF PATHOGNOMIC VERBALIZATION.
            JOURNAL OF CONSULTING PSYCHOLOGY, 1965, 29, 181-183.
                (RELIABILITY:INTERRATER; VALIDITY:CONSTRUCT; CORRELATES:BEHAVIORAL,
                INTELLIGENCE; N=45 PSYCHIATRIC PATIENTS)
        @APPLICATION 1965 R-30 H-37

1940   JAMES, W. H., WOODRUFF, A. B., & WERNER, W.
            EFFECT OF INTERNAL AND EXTERNAL CONTROL UPON CHANGES IN SMOKING BEHAVIOR.
            JOURNAL OF CONSULTING PSYCHOLOGY, 1965, 29, 184-186.
                (VALIDITY:CONSTRUCT; CORRELATES:BEHAVIORAL; N=272 FEMALE AND 185
                MALE SMOKING AND NON-SMOKING COLLEGE STUDENTS)
        @APPLICATION 1965 R-18

1941   DUNN, J. A.
            STABILITY OF THE FACTOR STRUCTURE OF THE TEST ANXIETY SCALE FOR CHILDREN
            ACROSS AGE AND SEX GROUPS.
            JOURNAL OF CONSULTING PSYCHOLOGY, 1965, 29, 187.
                    (VALIDITY:CRITERION; CORRELATES:DEMOGRAPHIC; FACTOR ANALYSIS; N=449
                    BOYS AND 417 GIRLS)
        @APPLICATION 1965 S-35

1942   LORR, M., & KLETT, C. J.
            CONSTANCY OF PSYCHOTIC SYNDROMES IN MEN AND WOMEN.
            JOURNAL OF CONSULTING PSYCHOLOGY, 1965, 29, 309-313.
                    (VALIDITY:CONSTRUCT; FACTOR ANALYSIS; N=375 MALE AND 448 FEMALE
                    PSYCHOTICS)
        @APPLICATION 1965 L-39

1943   CARKHUFF, R. R., & TRUAX, C. B.
            TRAINING IN COUNSELING AND PSYCHOTHERAPY: AN EVALUATION OF AN INTEGRATED
            DIDACTIC AND EXPERIMENTAL APPROACH.
            JOURNAL OF CONSULTING PSYCHOLOGY, 1965, 29, 333-336.
                    (RELIABILITY:INTERRATER; CORRELATES:PSYCHOLOGICAL; N=5 LAY HOSPITAL
                    WORKERS, 12 GRADUATE STUDENT THERAPISTS, 18 EXPERIENCED THERAPISTS)
        @APPLICATION 1965 T-24 T-69 T-105

1944   KURZ, R. B., COHEN, R., & STARZYNSKI, S.
            RORSCHACH CORRELATES OF TIME ESTIMATION.
            JOURNAL OF CONSULTING PSYCHOLOGY, 1965, 29, 379-382.
                    (RELIABILITY:INTERRATER; CORRELATES:PSYCHOLOGICAL; N=26 COLLEGE
                    MALES, 25 COLLEGE FEMALES)
        @APPLICATION 1965 R-30

1945   ZIMMERMAN, I. L.
            RESIDUAL EFFECTS OF BRAIN DAMAGE AND FIVE MMPI ITEMS.
            JOURNAL OF CONSULTING PSYCHOLOGY, 1965, 29, 394.
                    (VALIDITY:CROSS-VALIDATION; CORRELATES:PHYSIOLOGICAL; N=85
                    VETERANS 7 YEARS AFTER BRAIN DAMAGE)
        @APPLICATION 1965 D-45 H-215

1946   WAGMAN, M.
            DAYDREAMING FREQUENCY AND SOME PERSONALITY MEASURES.
            JOURNAL OF CONSULTING PSYCHOLOGY, 1965, 29, 395.
                    (CORRELATES:PSYCHOLOGICAL; N=104 MALE AND 100 FEMALE COLLEGE
                    STUDENTS)
        @APPLICATION 1965 S-82 W-8 W-41 D-45

1947   CLEMES, S. R., & D'ANDREA, V. J.
            PATIENTS' ANXIETY AS A FUNCTION OF EXPECTATION AND DEGREE OF INITIAL
            INTERVIEW AMBIGUITY.
            JOURNAL OF CONSULTING PSYCHOLOGY, 1965, 29, 397-404.
                    (CORRELATES:BEHAVIORAL, PSYCHOLOGICAL, ENVIRONMENTAL; N=85
                    PSYCHIATRIC PATIENTS, 9 THERAPISTS)
        @APPLICATION 1965 D-27 H-215

1948   HAAN, N.
            COPING AND DEFENSE MECHANISMS RELATED TO PERSONALITY INVENTORIES.
            JOURNAL OF CONSULTING PSYCHOLOGY, 1965, 29, 373-378.
                    (CORRELATES:PSYCHOLOGICAL; N=49 MEN AND 50 WOMEN)
        @APPLICATION 1965 D-45 G-22 W-8 B-91 E-1

1949   GYNTHER, M. D., & SHIMKUNAS, A. M.
            AGE, INTELLIGENCE, AND MMPI F SCORES.
            JOURNAL OF CONSULTING PSYCHOLOGY, 1965, 29, 383-388.
                    (CORRELATES:DEMOGRAPHIC, INTELLIGENCE; NORMATIVE DATA; N=214 MALE,
                    193 FEMALE PSYCHIATRIC PATIENTS)
        @APPLICATION 1965 D-45

1950   ADAMS, D. K., & HORN, J. L.
            NONOVERLAPPING KEYS FOR THE MMPI SCALES.
            JOURNAL OF CONSULTING PSYCHOLOGY, 1965, 29, 284.
                    (MENTION; VALIDITY:CONTENT; NO SAMPLE USED)
        @APPLICATION 1965 D-45

1951   SCHECHTER, N., SCHMEIDLER, G. R., & STAAL, M.
            DREAM REPORTS AND CREATIVE TENDENCIES IN STUDENTS OF THE ARTS, SCIENCES,
            AND ENGINEERING.
            JOURNAL OF CONSULTING PSYCHOLOGY, 1965, 29, 415-421.
                (VALIDITY:CRITERION; CORRELATES:PSYCHOLOGICAL; N=105 STUDENTS OF
                ART, SCIENCES, AND ENGINEERING)
        @APPLICATION 1965 B-4 S-194

1952   PHILLIPS, F. L., RAIFORD, A., & EL-BATRAWI, S.
            THE Q SORT REEVALUATED.
            JOURNAL OF CONSULTING PSYCHOLOGY, 1965, 29, 422-425.
                (VALIDITY:CRITERION; N=55 MALE, 24 FEMALE HIGH SCHOOL AND COLLEGE
                STUDENTS)
        @APPLICATION 1965 B-60

1953   CARKHUFF, R. P., & TRUAX, C. B.
            LAY MENTAL HEALTH COUNSELING: THE EFFECTS OF LAY GROUP COUNSELING.
            JOURNAL OF CONSULTING PSYCHOLOGY, 1965, 29, 426-431.
                (MENTION; VALIDITY:CRITERION; N=80 HOSPITALIZED MENTAL PATIENTS
                IN EXPERIMENTAL LAY COUNSELING, 70 PATIENT CONTROLS)
        @APPLICATION 1965 D-45 B-60 C-243

1954   STRASSBURGER, F., & STRASSBURGER, Z.
            MEASUREMENT OF ATTITUDES TOWARD ALCOHOL AND THEIR RELATION TO PERSONALITY
            VARIABLES.
            JOURNAL OF CONSULTING PSYCHOLOGY, 1965, 29, 440-445.
                (CORRELATES:BEHAVIORAL, PSYCHOLOGICAL; 2 SAMPLES: N=92 COLLEGE
                STUDENTS, 102 COLLEGE STUDENTS)
        @APPLICATION 1965 H-12

1955   BUTCHER, J. N.
            MANIFEST AGGRESSION: MMPI CORRELATES IN NORMAL BOYS.
            JOURNAL OF CONSULTING PSYCHOLOGY, 1965, 29, 446-454.
                (MODIFICATION; CORRELATES:BEHAVIORAL, PSYCHOLOGICAL; USED AS
                CRITERION; NORMATIVE DATA; N=234 WHITE RURAL JUNIOR HIGH SCHOOL
                STUDENTS)
        @APPLICATION 1965 D-45 E-44

1956   HARSCH, O. H., & ZIMMER, H.
            AN EXPERIMENTAL APPROXIMATION OF THOUGHT REFORM.
            JOURNAL OF CONSULTING PSYCHOLOGY, 1965, 29, 475-479.
                (RELIABILITY:INTERRATER; USED AS CRITERION; N=62 MALE, 34 FEMALE
                COLLEGE STUDENTS)
        @APPLICATION 1965 Z-14

1957   WEATHERLEY, D.
            SOME PERSONALITY CORRELATES OF THE ABILITY TO STOP SMOKING.
            JOURNAL OF CONSULTING PSYCHOLOGY, 1965, 29, 483-485.
                (CORRELATES:BEHAVIORAL; N=182 MALE UNDERGRADUATES)
        @APPLICATION 1965 E-2

1958   LEWINSOHN, P. M.
            PSYCHOLOGICAL CORRELATES OF OVERALL QUALITY OF FIGURE DRAWINGS.
            JOURNAL OF CONSULTING PSYCHOLOGY, 1965, 29, 504-512.
                (RELIABILITY:INTERRATER; VALIDITY:CRITERION; CORRELATES:BEHAVIORAL,
                PSYCHOLOGICAL, DEMOGRAPHIC, INTELLIGENCE; USED AS CRITERION; N=75
                FEMALE AND 62 MALE PSYCHIATRIC PATIENTS)
        @APPLICATION 1965 M-58 L-39 L-35 C-10 M-66 C-148 D-45 C-136 R-31 S-124 G-83
        @L-153 L-154

1959   SCHONBAR, R. A.
            DIFFERENTIAL DREAM RECALL FREQUENCY AS A COMPONENT OF "LIFE STYLE."
            JOURNAL OF CONSULTING PSYCHOLOGY, 1965, 29, 468-474.
                (CORRELATES:BEHAVIORAL, PSYCHOLOGICAL; USED AS CRITERION; N=83
                GRADUATE STUDENTS)
        @APPLICATION 1965 S-88 B-162 W-19 R-18 S-89 L-91

1960   SCHAEFER, E. S.
            A CONFIGURATIONAL ANALYSIS OF CHILDREN'S REPORTS OF PARENT BEHAVIOR.
            JOURNAL OF CONSULTING PSYCHOLOGY, 1965, 29, 552-557.
                (DESCRIPTION; FACTOR ANALYSIS; 3 SAMPLES: N=166 SCHOOL CHILDREN,
                154 ARMY PERSONNEL, 108 ARMY PATIENTS AND PERSONNEL)
        @APPLICATION 1965 S-8

1961   HILGARD, E. R., LAUER, L. W., & CUCA, J. M.
           ACQUIESCENCE, HYPNOTIC SUSCEPTIBILITY, AND THE MMPI.
           JOURNAL OF CONSULTING PSYCHOLOGY, 1965, 29, 489.
                (VALIDITY:CRITERION; CORRELATES:PSYCHOLOGICAL; N=50 MALE AND 50
                FEMALE SUBJECTS)
        @APPLICATION 1965 W-31 D-45

1962   DREIBLATT, I. S., & WEATHERLEY, D.
           AN EVALUATION OF THE EFFICACY OF BRIEF-CONTACT THERAPY WITH HOSPITALIZED
           PSYCHIATRIC PATIENTS.
           JOURNAL OF CONSULTING PSYCHOLOGY, 1965, 29, 513-519.
                (MODIFICATION; USED AS CRITERION; 2 STUDIES: N=44 PSYCHIATRIC
                PATIENTS, 76 PSYCHIATRIC PATIENTS)
        @APPLICATION 1965 S-30 H-57 W-8 C-149 M-236

1963   COLON, F.
           A STUDY OF RESPONSE TO ACHROMATIC AND CHROMATIC STIMULI.
           JOURNAL OF CONSULTING PSYCHOLOGY, 1965, 29, 571-576.
                (CORRELATES:PSYCHOLOGICAL; USED AS CRITERION; N=200 COLLEGE
                STUDENTS, 45 SELECTED)
        @APPLICATION 1965 D-45

1964   DUFF, F. L.
           ITEM SUBTLETY IN PERSONALITY INVENTORY SCALES.
           JOURNAL OF CONSULTING PSYCHOLOGY, 1965, 29, 565-570.
                (VALIDITY:CONTENT, CRITERION; N=541 NORMAL STUDENTS AND 184
                PSYCHIATRIC PATIENTS, 2 SAMPLES OF 33, 25 CLINICIAN JUDGES)
        @APPLICATION 1965 D-45

1965   DANET, B. N.
           PREDICTION OF MENTAL ILLNESS IN COLLEGE STUDENTS ON THE BASIS OF
           "NONPSYCHIATRIC" MMPI PROFILES.
           JOURNAL OF CONSULTING PSYCHOLOGY, 1965, 29, 577-580.
                (VALIDITY:CRITERION; N=70 COLLEGE STUDENTS, SOME HAVING PSYCHIATRIC
                HISTORY, 34 CLINICIANS, 7 INEXPERIENCED STUDENTS)
        @APPLICATION 1965 D-45

1966   MEDINNUS. G. R.
           DELINQUENTS' PERCEPTIONS OF THEIR PARENTS.
           JOURNAL OF CONSULTING PSYCHOLOGY, 1965, 29, 592-593.
                (CORRELATES:BEHAVIORAL: N=30 DELINQUENTS, 30 NONDELINQUENTS)
        @APPLICATION 1965 R-41

1967   ZUCKERMAN, M., LUBIN, B., & ROBINS, S.
           VALIDATION OF THE MULTIPLE AFFECT ADJECTIVE CHECK LIST IN CLINICAL
           SITUATIONS.
           JOURNAL OF CONSULTING PSYCHOLOGY, 1965, 29, 594.
                (VALIDITY:CONSTRUCT, CRITERION; N=266 PSYCHIATRIC PATIENTS AND
                275 NORMALS)
        @APPLICATION 1965 D-45 Z-4

1968   MURSTEIN, B. I.
           SCALING OF THE TAT FOR ACHIEVEMENT.
           JOURNAL OF CONSULTING PSYCHOLOGY, 1965, 29, 286.
                (RELIABILITY:INTERNAL CONSISTENCY; VALIDITY:CRITERION; N=92 COLLEGE
                STUDENTS)
        @APPLICATION 1965 M-20 M-7

1969   WACHTEL, P. L., & BLATT, S. J.
           ENERGY DEPLOYMENT AND ACHIEVEMENT.
           JOURNAL OF CONSULTING PSYCHOLOGY, 1965, 29, 302-308.
                (CORRELATES:PSYCHOLOGICAL, INTELLIGENCE; N=188 COLLEGE STUDENTS)
        @APPLICATION 1965 F-35 B-177

1970   SUINN, R. M.
           ANXIETY AND INTELLECTUAL PERFORMANCE: A PARTIAL FAILURE TO REPLICATE.
           JOURNAL OF CONSULTING PSYCHOLOGY, 1965, 29, 81-82.
                (CORRELATES:PSYCHOLOGICAL, INTELLIGENCE; NORMATIVE DATA; N=55
                COLLEGE STUDENTS AND 70 COLLEGE STUDENTS)
        @APPLICATION 1965 S-5 T-2

1971   LOMONT, J. F.
        THE REPRESSION-SENSITIZATION DIMENSION IN RELATION TO ANXIETY RESPONSES.
        JOURNAL OF CONSULTING PSYCHOLOGY, 1965, 29, 84-86.
            (CORRELATES:PSYCHOLOGICAL; N=24 HOSPITALIZED ACUTE SCHIZOPHRENICS
            AND 11 HOSPITALIZED NONPSYCHOTIC PATIENTS)
        @APPLICATION 1965 C-151 B-46

1972   COSTA, L. D., COX, M., & KATZMAN, R.
        RELATIONSHIP BETWEEN MMPI VARIABLES AND PERCENTAGE AND AMPLITUDE OF EEG
        ALPHA ACTIVITY.
        JOURNAL OF CONSULTING PSYCHOLOGY, 1965, 29, 90.
            (CORRELATES:PHYSIOLOGICAL; N=72 MEDICAL STUDENTS)
        @APPLICATION 1965 D-45

1973   LEVITT, H., & FELLNER, C.
        MMPI PROFILES OF THREE OBESITY SUBGROUPS.
        JOURNAL OF CONSULTING PSYCHOLOGY, 1965, 29, 91.
            (CORRELATES:PHYSIOLOGICAL; N=28 OBESE FEMALES)
        @APPLICATION 1965 D-45

1974   HILER, E. W., & NESVIG, D.
        AN EVALUATION OF CRITERIA USED BY CLINICIANS TO INFER PATHOLOGY FROM
        FIGURE DRAWINGS.
        JOURNAL OF CONSULTING PSYCHOLOGY, 1965, 29, 520-529.
            (MENTION; VALIDITY:CRITERION, CROSS-VALIDATION; N=30 DISTURBED
            CHILDREN AND 30 NORMALS)
        @APPLICATION 1965 M-58 R-30

1975   DERMEN, D. & LONDON, P.
        CORRELATES OF HYPNOTIC SUSCEPTIBILITY.
        JOURNAL OF CONSULTING PSYCHOLOGY, 1965, 29, 537-545.
            (CORRELATES:BEHAVIORAL, PSYCHOLOGICAL; N=80 MALE AND 97 FEMALE
            COLLEGE STUDENTS)
        @APPLICATION 1965 G-40 L-90 S-90

1976   KLETT, C. J., & MOSELEY, E. C.
        THE RIGHT DRUG FOR THE RIGHT PATIENT.
        JOURNAL OF CONSULTING PSYCHOLOGY, 1965, 29, 546-551.
            (MENTION)
        @APPLICATION 1965 L-39

1977   DICKSTEIN, L. S., & BLATT, S. J.
        DEATH CONCERN, FUTURITY, AND ANTICIPATION.
        JOURNAL OF CONSULTING PSYCHOLOGY, 1966, 30, 11-17.
            (CORRELATES:PSYCHOLOGICAL; N=76 MALE UNDERGRADUATES)
        @APPLICATION 1966 W-109

1978   GARFIELD, S. L., & SUNDLAND, D. M.
        PROGNOSTIC SCALES IN SCHIZOPHRENIA.
        JOURNAL OF CONSULTING PSYCHOLOGY, 1966, 30, 18-24.
            (RELIABILITY:INTERRATER; VALIDITY:CRITERION;
            CORRELATES:PSYCHOLOGICAL, DEMOGRAPHIC; N=65 FEMALE SCHIZOPHRENIC
            PATIENTS)
        @APPLICATION 1966 P-32 K-51 W-44

1979   MOSHER, D. L.
        THE DEVELOPMENT AND MULTITRAIT-MULTIMETHOD MATRIX ANALYSIS OF THREE
        MEASURES OF THREE ASPECTS OF GUILT.
        JOURNAL OF CONSULTING PSYCHOLOGY, 1966, 30, 25-29.
            (VALIDITY:CRITERION; CORRELATES:PSYCHOLOGICAL; N=95 COLLEGE MALES)
        @APPLICATION 1966 M-64 M-16 M-17 T-2 F-1 C-152

1980   HANDLER, L., & REYHER, J.
        RELATIONSHIP BETWEEN GSR AND ANXIETY INDEXES IN PROJECTIVE DRAWINGS.
        JOURNAL OF CONSULTING PSYCHOLOGY, 1966, 30, 60-67.
            (RELIABILITY:INTERRATER; CORRELATES:PHYSIOLOGICAL; N=96 MALE COLLEGE
            STUDENTS)
        @APPLICATION 1966 M-58

1981   DEWOLFE, A. S., BARRELL, R. P., & CUMMINGS, J. W.
        PATIENT VARIABLES IN EMOTIONAL RESPONSE TO HOSPITALIZATION FOR PHYSICAL
        ILLNESS.
        JOURNAL OF CONSULTING PSYCHOLOGY, 1966, 30, 68-72.
            (REVISION; MODIFICATION; CORRELATES:PSYCHOLOGICAL, DEMOGRAPHIC,
            INTELLIGENCE; N=517 LONG TERM MEDICAL PATIENTS)
        @APPLICATION 1966 P-32 M-142 C-151 V-45 H-220 B-290

1982   BORDIN, E. S.
PERSONALITY AND FREE ASSOCIATION.
JOURNAL OF CONSULTING PSYCHOLOGY, 1966, 30, 30-38.
(VALIDITY:CONSTRUCT; CORRELATES:PSYCHOLOGICAL; 2 STUDIES: N=40
MALE COLLEGE STUDENTS, 60 COLLEGE STUDENTS)
aAPPLICATION 1966 D-45 B-91 E-5 R-30 K-13

1983   COHEN, J., GUREL, L., & STUMPF, J. C.
DIMENSIONS OF PSYCHIATRIC SYMPTOM RATINGS DETERMINED AT THIRTEEN TIMEPOINTS
FROM HOSPITAL ADMISSION.
JOURNAL OF CONSULTING PSYCHOLOGY, 1966, 30, 39-44.
(FACTOR ANALYSIS; SAMPLES OF PSYCHOTIC PATIENTS: N RANGES 329 TO
1,274)
aAPPLICATION 1966 J-38

1984   HEILBRUN, A. B., JR., ORR, H. K., & HARRELL, S. N.
PATTERNS OF PARENTAL CHILDREARING AND SUBSEQUENT VULNERABILITY TO
COGNITIVE DISTURBANCE.
JOURNAL OF CONSULTING PSYCHOLOGY, 1966, 30, 51-59.
(CORRELATES:PSYCHOLOGICAL; 2 SAMPLES: N=63 MALE COLLEGE STUDENTS,
74 MALE COLLEGE STUDENTS)
aAPPLICATION 1966 S-9 H-66

1985   SCARR, S.
THE ADJECTIVE CHECK LIST AS A PERSONALITY ASSESSMENT TECHNIQUE WITH
CHILDREN.
JOURNAL OF CONSULTING PSYCHOLOGY, 1966, 30, 122-128.
(VALIDITY:CONSTRUCT; CORRELATES:PSYCHOLOGICAL; FACTOR ANALYSIS;
N=MOTHERS OF 52 PAIRS OF GRADE-SCHOOL TWIN GIRLS)
aAPPLICATION 1966 G-21 G-78 M-20 M-36 D-7 R-89

1986   PALMER, R. D.
BIRTH ORDER AND IDENTIFICATION.
JOURNAL OF CONSULTING PSYCHOLOGY, 1966, 30, 129-135.
(CORRELATES:DEMOGRAPHIC; N=55 UNDERGRADUATE MALES)
aAPPLICATION 1966 S-199

1987   GOUGH, H. G.
A CROSS-CULTURAL ANALYSIS OF THE CPI FEMININITY SCALE.
JOURNAL OF CONSULTING PSYCHOLOGY, 1966, 30, 136-141.
(CROSS-CULTURAL APPLICATION; NORMATIVE DATA; N=1388 MALES, 845
FEMALES IN FRANCE, ITALY, VENEZUELA, AND TURKEY)
aAPPLICATION 1966 G-20

1988   ROBINSON, B. W.
A STUDY OF ANXIETY AND ACADEMIC ACHIEVEMENT.
JOURNAL OF CONSULTING PSYCHOLOGY, 1966, 30, 165-167.
(CORRELATES:DEMOGRAPHIC, INTELLIGENCE; N=54 HIGH HONORS STUDENTS
AND 131 HONORS STUDENTS)
aAPPLICATION 1966 D-45 W-8

1989   PHILLIPS, B. N.
DEFENSIVENESS AS A FACTOR IN SEX DIFFERENCES IN ANXIETY.
JOURNAL OF CONSULTING PSYCHOLOGY, 1966, 30, 167-169.
(CORRELATES:PSYCHOLOGICAL, DEMOGRAPHIC; N=120'COLLEGE MALES, 116
COLLEGE FEMALES)
aAPPLICATION 1966 T-2 S-110

1990   HILER, E. W.
PROGNOSTIC INDICATORS FOR CHILDREN IN A PSYCHIATRIC HOSPITAL.
JOURNAL OF CONSULTING PSYCHOLOGY, 1966, 30, 169-171.
(VALIDITY:CRITERION; CORRELATES:INTELLIGENCE; N=34 PSYCHIATRIC
HOSPITALIZED CHILDREN)
aAPPLICATION 1966 G-78 H-125

1991   ROSEN, A.
STABILITY OF NEW MMPI SCALES AND STATISTICAL PROCEDURES FOR EVALUATING
CHANGES AND DIFFERENCES IN PSYCHIATRIC PATIENTS.
JOURNAL OF CONSULTING PSYCHOLOGY, 1966, 30, 142-145.
(RELIABILITY:RETEST; NORMATIVE DATA; N=40 MALE PSYCHIATRIC PATIENTS)
aAPPLICATION 1966 D-45

1992   DOBBS, D. D., & GRIFFITH, R. M.
            AN EXPERIMENTAL MANIPULATION OF RORSCHACH FORM: THE EFFECT OF MAKING
            INDISTINCT THE AMBIGUOUS.
            JOURNAL OF CONSULTING PSYCHOLOGY, 1966, 30, 151-157.
                (VALIDITY:CONSTRUCT; N=40 STUDENTS)
        aAPPLICATION 1966 R-30

1993   LITTLE, L. K.
            EFFECTS OF THE INTERPERSONAL INTERACTION ON ABSTRACT THINKING
            PERFORMANCE IN SCHIZOPHRENICS.
            JOURNAL OF CONSULTING PSYCHOLOGY, 1966, 30, 158-164.
                (RELIABILITY:INTERRATER; VALIDITY:CROSS-VALIDATION;
                CORRELATES:PSYCHOLOGICAL, DEMOGRAPHIC, ENVIRONMENTAL; N=72
                SCHIZOPHRENICS)
        aAPPLICATION 1966 W-44 K-123

1994   SILVERMAN, L. H.
            A TECHNIQUE FOR THE STUDY OF PSYCHODYNAMIC RELATIONSHIPS: THE EFFECTS OF
            SUBLIMINALLY PRESENTED AGGRESSIVE STIMULI ON THE PRODUCTION OF PATHOLOGICAL
            THINKING IN A SCHIZOPHRENIC POPULATION.
            JOURNAL OF CONSULTING PSYCHOLOGY, 1966, 30, 103-111.
                (CORRELATES:PSYCHOLOGICAL; N=32 HOSPITALIZED MALE SCHIZOPHRENICS)
        aAPPLICATION 1966 H-117 R-30

1995   LOEB, J., & PRICE, J. R.
            MOTHER AND CHILD PERSONALITY CHARACTERISTICS RELATED TO PARENTAL MARITAL
            STATUS IN CHILD GUIDANCE CASES.
            JOURNAL OF CONSULTING PSYCHOLOGY, 1966, 30, 112-117.
                (CORRELATES:PSYCHOLOGICAL, DEMOGRAPHIC; N=44 DIVORCED OR SEPARATED
                MOTHERS AND 44 CONTINUOUSLY MARRIED MOTHERS)
        aAPPLICATION 1966 D-45

1996   GYNTHER, M. D., & SHIMKUNAS, A. M.
            AGE AND MMPI PERFORMANCE.
            JOURNAL OF CONSULTING PSYCHOLOGY, 1966, 30, 118-121.
                (CORRELATES:DEMOGRAPHIC, INTELLIGENCE; N=420 HOSPITALIZED
                PSYCHIATRIC PATIENTS)
        aAPPLICATION 1966 D-45

1997   VESTRE, N. D.
            VALIDITY DATA ON THE PSYCHOTIC REACTION PROFILE.
            JOURNAL OF CONSULTING PSYCHOLOGY, 1966, 30, 84-85.
                (RELIABILITY:INTERRATER; VALIDITY:CRITERION; N=4 GROUPS OF
                HOSPITALIZED PSYCHOTICS, TOTAL N=196)
        aAPPLICATION 1966 L-70

1998   ULMER, R. A., & TIMMONS, E. O.
            AN APPLICATION OF THE MINIMAL SOCIAL BEHAVIOR SCALE (MSBS): A SHORT
            OBJECTIVE, EMPIRICAL, RELIABLE MEASURE OF PERSONALITY FUNCTIONING.
            JOURNAL OF CONSULTING PSYCHOLOGY, 1966, 30, 86.
                (CORRELATES:PSYCHOLOGICAL; N=27 MALE, 28 FEMALE HOSPITALIZED
                PSYCHOTIC PATIENTS)
        aAPPLICATION 1966 F-1

1999   WELSH, G. S.
            COMPARISON OF D-48, TERMAN CMT AND ART SCALE SCORES OF GIFTED
            ADOLESCENTS.
            JOURNAL OF CONSULTING PSYCHOLOGY, 1966, 30, 88.
                (CORRELATES:INTELLIGENCE; NORMATIVE DATA; N=368 GIFTED HIGH SCHOOL
                STUDENTS)
        aAPPLICATION 1966 W-9

2000   HARE, R. D.
            DENIAL OF THREAT AND EMOTIONAL RESPONSE TO IMPENDING PAINFUL STIMULATION.
            JOURNAL OF CONSULTING PSYCHOLOGY, 1966, 30, 359-361.
                (CORRELATES:PSYCHOLOGICAL, PHYSIOLOGICAL; N=14 FEMALE, 17 MALE
                COLLEGE STUDENTS)
        aAPPLICATION 1966 B-46 W-8

2001   LEVINSON, R. B., & KITCHENER, H. L.
            TREATMENT OF DELINQUENTS:COMPARISON OF FOUR METHODS FOR ASSIGNING INMATES
            TO COUNSELORS.
            JOURNAL OF CONSULTING PSYCHOLOGY, 1966, 30, 364.
                (MENTION; MODIFICATION)
        aAPPLICATION 1966 E-2

2002　LICHTENSTEIN, E., & BRYAN, J. H.
　　　　SHORT-TERM STABILITY OF MMPI PROFILES.
　　　　JOURNAL OF CONSULTING PSYCHOLOGY, 1966, 30, 172-174.
　　　　　　(RELIABILITY:RETEST; N=42 HOSPITAL WORKERS, 40 HOSPITALIZED
　　　　　　PSYCHIATRIC PATIENTS)
　　　@APPLICATION 1966 D-45

2003　MOSHER, D. L.
　　　　SOME CHARACTERISTICS OF HIGH- AND LOW-FREQUENCY "CANNOT SAY" ITEMS ON THE
　　　　MMPI.
　　　　JOURNAL OF CONSULTING PSYCHOLOGY, 1966, 30, 177.
　　　　　　(VALIDITY:CONSTRUCT; N=74 MALE STUDENTS)
　　　@APPLICATION 1966 D-45

2004　GOLDBERG, L. R., & WERTS, C. E.
　　　　THE RELIABILITY OF CLINICIANS' JUDGMENTS: A MULTITRAIT-MULTIMETHOD
　　　　APPROACH.
　　　　JOURNAL OF CONSULTING PSYCHOLOGY, 1966, 30, 199-206.
　　　　　　(RELIABILITY:RETEST, INTERRATER: VALIDITY:CONSTRUCT;
　　　　　　CORRELATES:PSYCHOLOGICAL, INTELLIGENCE; N=4 GROUPS OF 10
　　　　　　PSYCHIATRIC OUTPATIENTS EACH)
　　　@APPLICATION 1966 D-45 R-30

2005　STRICKLAND, L. H., & LEWICKI, R. J.
　　　　NEED FOR SOCIAL APPROVAL AND EVALUATION OF MILITARY DEPORTMENT.
　　　　JOURNAL OF CONSULTING PSYCHOLOGY, 1966, 30, 462.
　　　　　　(CORRELATES:BEHAVIORAL; USED AS CRITERION; N=108 UNDERGRADUATES)
　　　@APPLICATION 1966 C-27

2006　MEGARGEE, E. I.
　　　　THE RELATION OF RESPONSE LENGTH TO THE HOLTZMAN INKBLOT TECHNIQUE.
　　　　JOURNAL OF CONSULTING PSYCHOLOGY, 1966, 30, 415-419.
　　　　　　(FACTOR ANALYSIS; 2 STUDIES: N=84 COLLEGE STUDENTS AND 75 MALE
　　　　　　JUVENILE DELINQUENTS, N=319 COLLEGE STUDENTS)
　　　@APPLICATION 1966 H-37

2007　SHIPE, D., CROMWELL, R. L., & DUNN, L. M.
　　　　RESPONSES OF EMOTIONALLY DISTURBED AND NONDISTURBED RETARDATES TO PPVT
　　　　ITEMS OF HUMAN VERSUS NONHUMAN CONTENT.
　　　　JOURNAL OF CONSULTING PSYCHOLOGY, 1966, 30, 439-443.
　　　　　　(USED AS CRITERION; N=40 INSTITUTIONALIZED RETARDED CHILDREN)
　　　@APPLICATION 1966 S-201

2008　LEFCOURT, H. M.
　　　　REPRESSION-SENSITIZATION: A MEASURE OF THE EVALUATION OF EMOTIONAL
　　　　EXPRESSION.
　　　　JOURNAL OF CONSULTING PSYCHOLOGY, 1966, 30, 444-449.
　　　　　　(VALIDITY:CONSTRUCT; USED AS CRITERION; NORMATIVE DATA; 2 STUDIES:
　　　　　　N=28 UNDERGRADUATES, 96 STUDENTS)
　　　@APPLICATION 1966 B-46 M-20 B-182 K-113

2009　MOSHER, D. L.
　　　　DIFFERENTIAL INFLUENCE OF GUILT ON THE VERBAL OPERANT CONDITIONING OF
　　　　HOSTILE AND "SUPEREGO" VERBS.
　　　　JOURNAL OF CONSULTING PSYCHOLOGY, 1966, 30, 280.
　　　　　　(CORRELATES:PSYCHOLOGICAL; N=105 FEMALE COLLEGE STUDENTS)
　　　@APPLICATION 1966 M-16

2010　BREGER, L.
　　　　FURTHER STUDIES OF THE SOCIAL DESIRABILITY SCALE.
　　　　JOURNAL OF CONSULTING PSYCHOLOGY, 1966, 30, 281.
　　　　　　(VALIDITY:CONSTRUCT; CORRELATES:BEHAVIORAL, PSYCHOLOGICAL;
　　　　　　USED AS CRITERION; 3 STUDIES: N=79 FEMALE SUBJECTS, 57 AND 61
　　　　　　SUBJECTS)
　　　@APPLICATION 1966 C-27 M-20 A-5 B-32

2011　LICHTENSTEIN, E.
　　　　PERSONALITY SIMILARITY AND THERAPEUTIC SUCCESS: A FAILURE TO REPLICATE.
　　　　JOURNAL OF CONSULTING PSYCHOLOGY, 1966, 30, 282.
　　　　　　(CORRELATES:PSYCHOLOGICAL; N=14 MALE, 40 FEMALE PSYCHIATRIC PATIENTS)
　　　@APPLICATION 1966 D-45 W-8 W-41

2012   TRUAX, C. B., WARGO, D. G., FRANK, J. D., IMBER, S. D., BATTLE, C. C.,
        HOEHN-SARIC, R., NASH, E. H., & STONE, A. R.
            THERAPIST EMPATHY, GENUINENESS, AND WARMTH AND PATIENT THERAPEUTIC
            OUTCOME.
            JOURNAL OF CONSULTING PSYCHOLOGY, 1966, 30, 395-401.
                (RELIABILITY:INTERRATER; CORRELATES:PSYCHOLOGICAL, ENVIRONMENTAL;
                N=40 PSYCHONEUROTIC PATIENTS WITH GOOD AND BAD THERAPY PROSPECTS)
        @APPLICATION 1966 T-24 T-69 T-89

2013   SIGAL, J. J., & DORKEN, H.
            WORD-ASSOCIATION COMMONALITY: A STANDARDIZED TEST AND A THEORY.
            JOURNAL OF CONSULTING PSYCHOLOGY, 1966, 30, 402-407.
                (RELIABILITY:RETEST; VALIDITY:CRITERION, CROSS-VALIDATION; N=575
                NORMAL EMPLOYED ADULTS. 100 WORKING, 100 NONWORKING PSYCHIATRIC
                PATIENTS, 15 PSYCHIATRIC OUTPATIENTS, AND 44 REJECTED ARMY
                VOLUNTEERS)
        @APPLICATION 1966 L-98

2014   CORTES, J. B., & GATTI, F. M.
            PHYSIQUE AND MOTIVATION.
            JOURNAL OF CONSULTING PSYCHOLOGY, 1966, 30, 408-414.
                (CORRELATES:PHYSIOLOGICAL: N=100 DELINQUENT AND 100 NONDELINQUENT
                BOYS)
        @APPLICATION 1966 M-7 V-4 C-242

2015   PEARSON, P. H., & MADDI, S. R.
            THE SIMILES PREFERENCE INVENTORY: DEVELOPMENT OF A STRUCTURED MEASURE OF
            THE TENDENCY TOWARD VARIETY.
            JOURNAL OF CONSULTING PSYCHOLOGY, 1966, 30, 301-308.
                (MODIFICATION; CORRELATES:PSYCHOLOGICAL, INTELLIGENCE; 3 STUDIES:
                N=50 GRADUATE STUDENTS. 40 UNDERGRADUATES, 69 MALE NAVY MEDICAL
        @APPLICATION 1966 M-20 M-127 M-124 C-27 G-129 S-56
        @M-261

2016   SHERWOOD, J. J.
            SELF-REPORT AND PROJECTIVE MEASURES OF ACHIEVEMENT AND AFFILIATION.
            JOURNAL OF CONSULTING PSYCHOLOGY, 1966, 30, 329-337.
                (MODIFICATION; RELIABILITY:INTERRATER; VALIDITY:CONSTRUCT,
                CRITERION; CORRELATES:BEHAVIORAL, PSYCHOLOGICAL; NORMATIVE DATA;
                2 STUDIES: N=37 COLLEGE MALES, 30 COLLEGE FEMALES; 80 COLLEGE MALES)
        @APPLICATION 1966 M-20 M-7 S-19

2017   MORGAN, D. W.
            WAIS 'ANALYTIC INDEX' AND REHOSPITALIZATION OF SCHIZOPHRENIC SERVICEMEN.
            JOURNAL OF CONSULTING PSYCHOLOGY, 1966, 30, 267-269.
                (CORRELATES:PSYCHOLOGICAL, DEMOGRAPHIC, INTELLIGENCE; N=98 DISCHARGED
                SCHIZOPHRENIC SERVICEMEN)
        @APPLICATION 1966 W-19 W-72 R-30 D-45 W-73

2018   JOHNSON, M. H.
            VERBAL ABSTRACTING ABILITY AND SCHIZOPHRENIA.
            JOURNAL OF CONSULTING PSYCHOLOGY, 1966, 30, 275-277.
                (CORRELATES:PSYCHOLOGICAL; USED AS CRITERION; N=3 GROUPS OF 40
                SUBJECTS EACH: REACTIVE SCHIZOPHRENICS, PROCESS SCHIZOPHRENICS,
                AND NORMALS)
        @APPLICATION 1966 P-32 B-94

2019   NORMAN, R. P.
            DOGMATISM AND PSYCHONEUROSIS IN COLLEGE WOMEN.
            JOURNAL OF CONSULTING PSYCHOLOGY, 1966, 30, 278.
                (CORRELATES:PSYCHOLOGICAL; USED AS CRITERION; N=130 FEMALE
                COLLEGE STUDENTS)
        @APPLICATION 1966 R-8 D-45 T-2 B-5 S-208

2020   STEWART, L., & LIVSON, N.
            SMOKING AND REBELLIOUSNESS: A LONGITUDINAL STUDY FROM CHILDHOOD TO
            MATURITY.
            JOURNAL OF CONSULTING PSYCHOLOGY, 1966, 30, 225-229.
                (CORRELATES:BEHAVIORAL, DEMOGRAPHIC; NORMATIVE DATA; N=83 MALE, 82
                FEMALE SMOKERS AND NONSMOKERS)
        @APPLICATION 1966 G-22

2021   SIEGMAN, A. W., & POPE, B.
            AMBIGUITY AND VERBAL FLUENCY IN THE TAT.
            JOURNAL OF CONSULTING PSYCHOLOGY, 1966, 30, 239-245.
                (CORRELATES:PSYCHOLOGICAL; N=30 FEMALE NURSING STUDENTS)
        @APPLICATION 1966 M-20 H-22 P-81 E-48 M-35

2022   EHRLICH, H. J., & BAUER, M. L.
            THE CORRELATES OF DOGMATISM AND FLEXIBILITY IN PSYCHIATRIC HOSPITALIZATION.
            JOURNAL OF CONSULTING PSYCHOLOGY, 1966, 30, 253-259.
                (RELIABILITY:RETEST, INTERNAL CONSISTENCY; CORRELATES:PSYCHOLOGICAL,
                DEMOGRAPHIC: NORMATIVE DATA; N=20 PSYCHIATRIC RESIDENTS, 390
                PSYCHIATRIC PATIENTS)
        @APPLICATION 1966 R-8 G-22

2023   GORDON, C. M.
            SOME EFFECTS OF INFORMATION, SITUATION, AND PERSONALITY ON DECISION
            MAKING IN A CLINICAL SETTING.
            JOURNAL OF CONSULTING PSYCHOLOGY, 1966, 30, 219-224.
                (CORRELATES:PSYCHOLOGICAL, ENVIRONMENTAL; USED AS CRITERION; N=40
                GRADUATE STUDENTS)
        @APPLICATION 1966 G-43

2024   TRUAX, C. B., WARGO, D. G., CARKHUFF, R. R., KODMAN, F., JR., & MOLES, E. A.
            CHANGES IN SELF-CONCEPTS DURING GROUP PSYCHOTHERAPY AS A FUNCTION OF
            ALTERNATE SESSIONS AND VICARIOUS THERAPY PRETRAINING IN INSTITUTIONALIZED
            MENTAL PATIENTS AND JUVENILE DELINQUENTS.
            JOURNAL OF CONSULTING PSYCHOLOGY, 1966, 30, 309-314.
                (MODIFICATION; CORRELATES:PSYCHOLOGICAL; NORMATIVE DATA;
                N=40 INSTITUTIONALIZED JUVENILE DELINQUENTS AND 40 HOSPITALIZED
                MENTAL PATIENTS)
        @APPLICATION 1966 B-60 L-99

2025   GOLDFRIED, M. R.
            ON THE DIAGNOSIS OF HOMOSEXUALITY FROM THE RORSCHACH.
            JOURNAL OF CONSULTING PSYCHOLOGY, 1966, 30, 338-349.
                (DESCRIPTION; REVIEW; RELIABILITY; VALIDITY)
        @APPLICATION 1966 W-113

2026   SCARR, S.
            THE ORIGINS OF INDIVIDUAL DIFFERENCES IN ADJECTIVE CHECK LIST SCORES.
            JOURNAL OF CONSULTING PSYCHOLOGY, 1966, 30, 354-357.
                (CORRELATES:ENVIRONMENTAL; N=61 PAIRS OF IDENTICAL AND NON-IDENTICAL
                TWINS)
        @APPLICATION 1966 G-21

2027   MUELLER, W. J., & GRATER, H. A.
            A STABILITY STUDY OF THE AGGRESSION CONFLICT SCALE.
            JOURNAL OF CONSULTING PSYCHOLOGY, 1966, 30, 357-359.
                (RELIABILITY:RETEST; FACTOR ANALYSIS; N=207 UNDERGRADUATE FEMALES)
        @APPLICATION 1966 M-144

2028   APFELDORF, M., SCHEINKER, J. L., & WHITMAN, G. L.
            MMPI RESPONSES OF AGED DOMICILED VETERANS WITH DISCIPLINARY RECORDS.
            JOURNAL OF CONSULTING PSYCHOLOGY, 1966, 30, 362.
                (VALIDITY:CRITERION; N=22 VETERAN OFFENDERS AND 39 NONOFFENDERS)
        @APPLICATION 1966 M-20

2029   KATAHN, M., STRENGER, S., & CHERRY, N.
            GROUP COUNSELING AND BEHAVIOR THERAPY WITH TEST-ANXIOUS COLLEGE STUDENTS.
            JOURNAL OF CONSULTING PSYCHOLOGY, 1966, 30, 544-549.
                (USED AS CRITERION; N=43 COLLEGE STUDENTS)
        @APPLICATION 1966 S-5

2030   LOEB, J.
            THE PERSONALITY FACTOR IN DIVORCE.
            JOURNAL OF CONSULTING PSYCHOLOGY, 1966, 30, 562.
                (CORRELATES:BEHAVIORAL, PSYCHOLOGICAL, DEMOGRAPHIC; N=22 DIVORCED
                EX-STUDENTS, 22 CONTINUOUSLY MARRIED EX-STUDENTS)
        @APPLICATION 1966 D-45

2031   SKOLNICK, A.
            MOTIVATIONAL IMAGERY AND BEHAVIOR OVER TWENTY YEARS.
            JOURNAL OF CONSULTING PSYCHOLOGY, 1966, 30, 463-478.
                (RELIABILITY:INTERRATER; VALIDITY:CONSTRUCT, CRITERION;
                CORRELATES:PSYCHOLOGICAL, DEMOGRAPHIC, INTELLIGENCE; LONGITUDINAL
                STUDY: N=44 MEN AND 47 WOMEN)
        @APPLICATION 1966 M-20 G-22 M-7

2032   MCCLELLAND, D. C.
            LONGITUDINAL TRENDS IN THE RELATION OF THOUGHT TO ACTION.
            JOURNAL OF CONSULTING PSYCHOLOGY, 1966, 30, 479-483.
                (REVIEW ARTICLE; VALIDITY:CONSTRUCT, CRITERION)
        @APPLICATION 1966 M-20 M-7

2033   LAZARUS, R. S.
            STORY TELLING AND THE MEASUREMENT OF MOTIVATION: THE DIRECT VERSUS
            SUBSTITUTIVE CONTROVERSY.
            JOURNAL OF CONSULTING PSYCHOLOGY, 1966, 30, 483-487.
                (REVIEW ARTICLE; VALIDITY:CONSTRUCT, CRITERION)
        @APPLICATION 1966 M-20 M-7

2034   BUTCHER, J. N., & TELLEGEN, A.
            OBJECTIONS TO MMPI ITEMS.
            JOURNAL OF CONSULTING PSYCHOLOGY, 1966, 30, 527-534.
                (VALIDITY:CONTENT; N≈139 COLLEGE STUDENTS)
        @APPLICATION 1966 D-45

2035   GAYLIN, N. L.
            PSYCHOTHERAPY AND PSYCHOLOGICAL HEALTH: A RORSCHACH FUNCTION AND STRUCTURE
            ANALYSIS.
            JOURNAL OF CONSULTING PSYCHOLOGY, 1966, 30, 494-500.
                (CORRELATES:PSYCHOLOGICAL; USED AS CRITERION; N=30 MALE, 27
                FEMALE PSYCHOTHERAPY APPLICANTS)
        @APPLICATION 1966 R-30 B-60

2036   HELLER, K., DAVIS, J. D., & MYERS, R. A.
            THE EFFECTS OF INTERVIEWER STYLE IN A STANDARDIZED INTERVIEW.
            JOURNAL OF CONSULTING PSYCHOLOGY, 1966, 30, 501-508.
                (CORRELATES:BEHAVIORAL, PSYCHOLOGICAL; USED AS CRITERION; N=69
                COLLEGE MALES, 51 COLLEGE FEMALES)
        @APPLICATION 1966 L-35 D-45 M-172

2037   KEMP, D. E.
            CORRELATES OF THE WHITEHORN-BETZ AB SCALE IN A QUASI-THERAPEUTIC
            SITUATION.
            JOURNAL OF CONSULTING PSYCHOLOGY, 1966, 30, 509-516.
                (MODIFICATION; CORRELATES:PSYCHOLOGICAL; USED AS CRITERION; N=72 MALE
                COLLEGE STUDENTS)
        @APPLICATION 1966 W-91

2038   HARRISON, R.
            COGNITIVE CHANGE AND PARTICIPATION IN A SENSITIVITY-TRAINING LABORATORY.
            JOURNAL OF CONSULTING PSYCHOLOGY, 1966, 30, 517-520.
                (RELIABILITY:INTERRATER; CORRELATES:PSYCHOLOGICAL, ENVIRONMENTAL;
                N=79 MEN AND 36 WOMEN FROM GOVERNMENT, INDUSTRY, AND OTHER
                ORGANIZATIONS)
        @APPLICATION 1966 K-23

2039   EISENMAN, R.
            BIRTH ORDER, ANXIETY, AND VERBALIZATICNS IN GROUP PSYCHOTHERAPY.
            JOURNAL OF CONSULTING PSYCHOLOGY, 1966, 30, 521-526.
                (CORRELATES:PSYCHOLOGICAL, DEMOGRAPHIC, ENVIRONMENTAL; USED AS
                CRITERION: 2 STUDIES: N=24 PSYCHOTHERAPY PATIENTS EACH)
        @APPLICATION 1966 F-1 T-2 W-10

2040   ZUCKER, R. A., & MANOSEVITZ, M.
            MMPI PATTERNS OF OVERT MALE HOMOSEXUALS: REINTERPRETATION AND COMMENT ON
            DEAN AND RICHARDSON'S STUDY.
            JOURNAL OF CONSULTING PSYCHOLOGY, 1966, 30, 555-557.
                (CORRELATES:BEHAVIORAL, PSYCHOLOGICAL; N=40 OVERT HCMOSEXUALS AND 40
                MALE GRADUATE STUDENT CONTROLS)
        @APPLICATION 1966 D-45

2041   DEAN, R. B., & RICHARDSON, H.
            ONE MMPI HIGH-POINT CODES OF HOMOSEXUAL VERSUS HETEROSEXUAL MALES.
            JOURNAL OF CONSULTING PSYCHOLOGY, 1966, 30, 558-560.
                    (CORRELATES:BEHAVIORAL, PSYCHOLOGICAL; N=40 COLLEGE EDUCATED
                    HOMOSEXUALS, 31 LESS EDUCATED HOMOSEXUALS AND 40 COLLEGE EDUCATED
                    CONTROLS)
        @APPLICATION 1966 D-45

2042   KATKIN, E. S.
            SEX DIFFERENCES AND THE RELATIONSHIP BETWEEN THE MARLOWE-CROWNE SOCIAL
            DESIRABILITY SCALE AND MMPI INDEXES OF PSYCHOPATHOLOGY.
            JOURNAL OF CONSULTING PSYCHOLOGY, 1966, 30, 564.
                    (CORRELATES:PSYCHOLOGICAL, DEMOGRAPHIC; N=66 FEMALE AND 53 MALE
                    STUDENTS)
        @APPLICATION 1966 E-1 D-45 T-2 W-8 C-27

2043   ENGEL, I. M.
            A FACTOR-ANALYTIC STUDY OF ITEMS FROM FIVE MASCULINITY-FEMININITY TESTS.
            JOURNAL OF CONSULTING PSYCHOLOGY, 1966, 30, 565.
                    (FACTOR ANALYSIS; N=50 MALE, 50 FEMALE GRADUATE STUDENTS)
        @APPLICATION 1966 D-45 T-3 G-20 F-11 S-33

2044   MEGARGEE, E. I.
            THE EDWARDS SD SCALE: A MEASURE OF ADJUSTMENT OR DISSIMULATION?
            JOURNAL OF CONSULTING PSYCHOLOGY, 1966, 30, 566.
                    (VALIDITY:CONSTRUCT; N=41 COLLEGE STUDENTS, 21 PEACE CORPS
                    TRAINEES AND 65 DISTURBED CRIMINALS)
        @APPLICATION 1966 E-1 D-45

2045   ERICKSON, R. V., & ROBERTS, A. H.
            A COMPARISON OF TWO GROUPS OF INSTITUTIONALIZED DELINQUENTS ON PORTEUS
            MAZE TEST PERFORMANCE.
            JOURNAL OF CONSULTING PSYCHOLOGY, 1966, 30, 567.
                    (VALIDITY:CRITERION; CORRELATES:BEHAVIORAL; 2 STUDIES: N=20
                    INSTITUTIONALIZED DELINQUENT BOYS, 28 INSTITUTIONALIZED DELINQUENTS)
        @APPLICATION 1966 P-22

2046   SHRY, S. A.
            RELATIVE SIZE OF SAME AND OPPOSITE SEX DRAWINGS ON THE DAP AS AN INDEX OF
            DOMINANCE-SUBMISSIVENESS.
            JOURNAL OF CONSULTING PSYCHOLOGY, 1966, 30, 568.
                    (VALIDITY:CONSTRUCT; CORRELATES:PSYCHOLOGICAL; N=45 FRATERNITY AND
                    45 SORORITY MEMBERS)
        @APPLICATION 1966 M-58 L-35 C-10

2047   CARSON, R. C., & LLEWELLYN, C. E., JR.
            SIMILARITY IN THERAPEUTIC DYADS: A REEVALUATION.
            JOURNAL OF CONSULTING PSYCHOLOGY, 1966, 30, 458.
                    (VALIDITY:CRITERION; N=65 PSYCHIATRIC OUTPATIENTS, 22 THERAPISTS)
        @APPLICATION 1966 D-45

2048   FOX, J.
            SOCIAL DESIRABILITY AND THE PREDICTION OF MMPI SCORES.
            JOURNAL OF CONSULTING PSYCHOLOGY, 1966, 30, 460.
                    (VALIDITY:CROSS-VALIDATION; N=46 PSYCHIATRIC TECHNICIAN TRAINEES)
        @APPLICATION 1966 D-45 E-1

2049   WEISS, R. L.
            "ACQUIESCENCE" RESPONSE SET AND BIRTH ORDER.
            JOURNAL OF CONSULTING PSYCHOLOGY, 1966, 30, 365.
                    (CORRELATES:DEMOGRAPHIC; BIAS:RESPONSE; 2 SAMPLES: N=792 COLLEGE
                    FRESHMEN, 75 COLLEGE FRESHMEN)
        @APPLICATION 1966 G-22 W-72

2050   COWEN, E. L., ZAX, M., IZZO, L. D., & TROST, M. A.
            PREVENTION OF EMOTICNAL DISORDERS IN THE SCHOOL SETTING: A FURTHER
            INVESTIGATION.
            JOURNAL OF CONSULTING PSYCHOLOGY, 1966, 30, 381-387.
                    (CORRELATES:PSYCHOLOGICAL, INTELLIGENCE; USED AS CRITERION; N=103
                    EXPERIMENTAL AND 136 CONTROL THIRD GRADERS)
        @APPLICATION 1966 C-55 B-144 B-145 C-159

2051   PURCELL, K., & CLIFFORD, E.
            BINOCULAR RIVALRY AND THE STUDY OF IDENTIFICATION IN ASTHMATIC AND
            NONASTHMATIC BOYS.
            JOURNAL OF CONSULTING PSYCHOLOGY, 1966, 30, 388-394.
                (CORRELATES:PSYCHOLOGICAL, PHYSICAL; N=26 ASTHMATIC AND 29
                NONASTHMATIC BOYS)
        @APPLICATION 1966 R-11 M-143 C-158

2052   HARDYCK, C. D., CHUN, K., & ENGEL, B. T.
            PERSONALITY AND MARITAL-ADJUSTMENT DIFFERENCES IN ESSENTIAL FUNCTIONS.
            JOURNAL OF CONSULTING PSYCHOLOGY, 1966, 30, 459.
                (VALIDITY:CROSS-VALIDATION; CORRELATES:PHYSICAL; 2 STUDIES: N=42
                FEMALE HYPERTENSIVE PATIENTS AND 44 CONTROL SUBJECTS, 89 FEMALE
                HYPERTENSIVE PATIENTS)
        @APPLICATION 1966 D-45 T-4

2053   SECHREST, L., GALLIMORE, R., & HERSCH, P. D.
            FEEDBACK AND ACCURACY OF CLINICAL PREDICTIONS.
            JOURNAL OF CONSULTING PSYCHOLOGY, 1967, 31, 1-11.
                (MENTION; USED AS CRITERION; N=60 NURSING STUDENT PROTOCOLS AND
                96 MALE UNDERGRADUATE JUDGES)
        @APPLICATION 1967 R-31 D-45

2054   TOMLINSON, J. R.
            SITUATIONAL AND PERSONALITY CORRELATES OF PREDICTIVE ACCURACY.
            JOURNAL OF CONSULTING PSYCHOLOGY, 1967, 31, 19-22.
                (CORRELATES:PSYCHOLOGICAL, DEMOGRAPHIC, ENVIRONMENTAL; N=60 MALE,
                60 FEMALE UNDERGRADUATES)
        @APPLICATION 1967 G-21

2055   DAVIDS, A., & HAINSWORTH, P. K.
            MATERNAL ATTITUDES ABOUT FAMILY LIFE AND CHILD REARING AS AVOWED BY
            MOTHERS AND PERCEIVED BY THEIR UNDERACHIEVING AND HIGH-ACHIEVING SONS.
            JOURNAL OF CONSULTING PSYCHOLOGY, 1967, 31, 29-37.
                (DESCRIPTION; CORRELATES:PSYCHOLOGICAL, INTELLIGENCE; NORMATIVE DATA;
                N=55 UNDERACHIEVING BOYS, 48 MOTHERS, 31 HIGH ACHIEVING BOYS AND
                29 MOTHERS)
        @APPLICATION 1967 S-9

2056   WELKOWITZ, J., COHEN, J., & ORTMEYER, D.
            VALUE SYSTEM SIMILARITY: INVESTIGATION OF PATIENT-THERAPIST DYADS.
            JOURNAL OF CONSULTING PSYCHOLOGY, 1967, 31, 48-55.
                (CORRELATES:PSYCHOLOGICAL; N=38 THERAPISTS, 44 PATIENTS)
        @APPLICATION 1967 S-33 M-22

2057   GORHAM, D. R.
            VALIDITY AND RELIABILITY STUDIES OF A COMPUTER-BASED SCORING SYSTEM FOR
            INKBLOT RESPONSES.
            JOURNAL OF CONSULTING PSYCHOLOGY, 1967, 31, 65-70.
                (RELIABILITY:INTERNAL CONSISTENCY, INTERRATER; VALIDITY:CRITERION,
                CROSS-VALIDATION; FACTOR ANALYSIS; NORMATIVE DATA; 4 STUDIES: N=145
                STUDENTS, 50 COLLEGE STUDENTS, 100 COLLEGE STUDENTS, 85 COLLEGE
                STUDENTS)
        @APPLICATION 1967 H-37

2058   BOTWINICK, J., & THOMPSON, L. W.
            DEPRESSIVE AFFECT, SPEED OF RESPONSE, AND AGE.
            JOURNAL OF CONSULTING PSYCHOLOGY, 1967, 31, 106.
                (CORRELATES:PSYCHOLOGICAL, DEMOGRAPHIC; N=23 ELDERLY MEN, 28
                ELDERLY WOMEN, 37 YOUNG MEN, AND 20 YOUNG WOMEN)
        @APPLICATION 1967 D-45

2059   SATTLER, J. M., & BRANDON, R. A.
            EARLY RECOLLECTIONS RELATED TO ANXIETY AND INTROVERSION-EXTROVERSION.
            JOURNAL OF CONSULTING PSYCHOLOGY, 1967, 31, 107.
                (RELIABILITY:INTERRATER; CORRELATES:PSYCHOLOGICAL; USED AS CRITERION;
                N=84 COLLEGE STUDENTS)
        @APPLICATION 1967 T-2 G-39

2060   GARFIELD, S. L.
            A FURTHER NOTE ON "PROGNOSTIC SCALES IN SCHIZOPHRENIA."
            JOURNAL OF CONSULTING PSYCHOLOGY, 1967, 31, 99.
                (MENTION; VALIDITY)
        @APPLICATION 1967 W-44 P-32 K-51

2061   WATSON, D. L.
            INTROVERSION, NEUROTICISM, RIGIDITY, AND DOGMATISM.
            JOURNAL OF CONSULTING PSYCHOLOGY, 1967, 31, 105.
                 (CORRELATES:PSYCHOLOGICAL; USED AS CRITERION; N=194 STUDENTS)
        @APPLICATION 1967 E-5

2062   KAHN, P.
            TIME SPAN AND RORSCHACH HUMAN MOVEMENT RESPONSES.
            JOURNAL OF CONSULTING PSYCHOLOGY, 1967, 31, 92-93.
                 (CORRELATES:PSYCHOLOGICAL; N=44 CHILDREN AGES 8-11)
        @APPLICATION 1967 R-30 L-57

2063   LANYON, R. I.
            SIMULATION OF NORMAL AND PSYCHOPATHIC MMPI PERSONALITY PATTERNS.
            JOURNAL OF CONSULTING PSYCHOLOGY, 1967, 31, 94-97.
                 (USED AS CRITERION; BIAS:RESPONSE; N=37 WELL ADJUSTED, 42
                 MALADJUSTED MALE UNDERGRADUATES)
        @APPLICATION 1967 D-45

2064   FARINA, A.
            A NOTE ON "PROGNOSTIC SCALES IN SCHIZOPHRENIA."
            JOURNAL OF CONSULTING PSYCHOLOGY, 1967, 31, 98.
                 (MENTION; VALIDITY)
        @APPLICATION 1967 W-44 P-32 K-51

2065   DOWNING, R. W., & RICKELS, K.
            SELF-REPORT OF HOSTILITY AND THE INCIDENCE OF SIDE REACTIONS IN NEUROTIC
            OUTPATIENTS TREATED WITH TRANQUILIZING DRUGS AND PLACEBO.
            JOURNAL OF CONSULTING PSYCHOLOGY, 1967, 31, 71-76.
                 (CORRELATES:PHYSIOLOGICAL, ENVIRONMENTAL; N=47 NEGRO FEMALE
                 PSYCHIATRIC OUTPATIENTS)
        @APPLICATION 1967 B-44

2066   WAGNER, E. E., & DOBBINS, R. D.
            MMPI PROFILES OF PARISHIONERS SEEKING PASTORAL COUNSELING.
            JOURNAL OF CONSULTING PSYCHOLOGY, 1967, 31, 83-84.
                 (VALIDITY:CRITERION; NORMATIVE DATA; N=40 PARISHIONERS SEEKING
                 COUNSELING HELP, AND 40 NOT SEEKING IT)
        @APPLICATION 1967 D-45

2067   FRIBERG, R. R.
            MEASURES OF HOMOSEXUALITY: CROSS-VALIDATION OF TWO MMPI SCALES AND
            IMPLICATIONS FOR USAGE.
            JOURNAL OF CONSULTING PSYCHOLOGY, 1967, 31, 88-91.
                 (VALIDITY:CRITERION; CROSS-VALIDATION; CORRELATES:DEMOGRAPHIC,
                 INTELLIGENCE; NORMATIVE DATA; N=19 HOMOSEXUALS, 16 SEXUAL DEVIANTS,
                 67 GENERAL ABNORMALS, AND 50 NORMALS)
        @APPLICATION 1967 D-45 P-15

2068   KATAHN, M., HARRIS, J. H., & SWANSON, R. T.
            PRODUCTION OF ASSOCIATIVE SEQUENCES IN PROCESS-REACTIVE SCHIZOPHRENIC AND
            NONSCHIZOPHRENIC GROUPS.
            JOURNAL OF CONSULTING PSYCHOLOGY, 1967, 31, 104.
                 (CORRELATES:PSYCHOLOGICAL; N=52 SCHIZOPHRENICS AND NONSCHIZOPHRENICS)
        @APPLICATION 1967 P-32

2069   TEMPONE, V. J., & LAMB, W.
            REPRESSION-SENTIZATION AND ITS RELATION TO MEASURES OF ADJUSTMENT AND
            CONFLICT.
            JOURNAL OF CONSULTING PSYCHOLOGY, 1967, 31, 131-136.
                 (CORRELATES:PSYCHOLOGICAL; NORMATIVE DATA; N=459 COLLEGE STUDENTS,
                 AND 175 MENTAL HEALTH OUTPATIENTS)
        @APPLICATION 1967 R-31 B-46

2070   WATSON, C. G.
            RELATIONSHIP OF DISTORTION TO DAP DIAGNOSTIC ACCURACY AMONG PSYCHOLOGISTS
            AT THREE LEVELS OF SOPHISTICATION.
            JOURNAL OF CONSULTING PSYCHOLOGY, 1967, 31, 142-146.
                 (VALIDITY:CRITERION; N=24 CLINICAL PSYCHOLOGISTS, 48 PSYCHIATRIC
                 PATIENTS)
        @APPLICATION 1967 M-58 G-78

2071   STEIN, K. B., & CHU, C.
            DIMENSIONALITY OF BARRON'S EGO STRENGTH SCALE.
            JOURNAL OF CONSULTING PSYCHOLOGY, 1967, 31, 153-161.
                    (VALIDITY:CONSTRUCT, CROSS-VALIDATION; CLUSTER ANALYSIS; NORMATIVE
                    DATA; 2 STUDIES: N=220 MALE PSYCHIATRIC PATIENTS AND 90 NORMALS,
                    100 NORMALS AND 100 PSYCHIATRIC PATIENTS)
            @APPLICATION 1967 B-5

2072   HUPLEY, J. R.
            PARENTAL MALEVOLENCE AND CHILDREN'S INTELLIGENCE.
            JOURNAL OF CONSULTING PSYCHOLOGY, 1967, 31, 199-204.
                    (CORRELATES:PSYCHOLOGICAL, DEMOGRAPHIC, INTELLIGENCE; NORMATIVE
                    DATA; N=206 3RD GRADE GIRLS, 245 BOYS AND THEIR PARENTS)
            @APPLICATION 1967 E-51 Z-7

2073   TAGGART, M.
            CHARACTERISTICS OF PARTICIPANTS AND NONPARTICIPANTS IN INDIVIDUAL TEST-
            INTERPRETATION INTERVIEWS.
            JOURNAL OF CONSULTING PSYCHOLOGY, 1967, 31, 213-215.
                    (CORRELATES:BEHAVIORAL: NORMATIVE DATA; N=96 COLLEGE STUDENTS
                    PARTICIPATING IN INDIVIDUAL TEST-INTERPRETATION INTERVIEWS, 35
                    NONPARTICIPANTS)
            @APPLICATION 1967 D-45 B-5 W-8 W-41 D-115 O-33

2074   BLATT, S. J., & QUINLAN, P.
            PUNCTUAL AND PROCRASTINATING STUDENTS: A STUDY OF TEMPORAL PARAMETERS.
            JOURNAL OF CONSULTING PSYCHOLOGY, 1967, 31, 169-174.
                    (VALIDITY:CONSTRUCT, CRITERION; CORRELATES:BEHAVIORAL, PSYCHOLOGICAL;
                    N=14 PUNCTUAL, 15 PROCRASTINATING MALE COLLEGE STUDENTS)
            @APPLICATION 1967 S-61 B-186 D-64 A-5 G-129 G-194

2075   GOLDBERG, S. C., & MATTSSON, N.
            SYMPTOM CHANGES ASSOCIATED WITH IMPROVEMENT IN SCHIZOPHRENIA.
            JOURNAL OF CONSULTING PSYCHOLOGY, 1967, 31, 175-180.
                    (VALIDITY:CRITERION; CORRELATES:PSYCHOLOGICAL; 2 STUDIES: N=250, 460
                    PSYCHIATRIC PATIENTS)
            @APPLICATION 1967 L-39 B-86

2076   DUNTEMAN, G. H., & WOLKING, W. D.
            RELATIONSHIP BETWEEN MARITAL STATUS AND THE PERSONALITY OF MOTHERS OF
            DISTURBED CHILDREN.
            JOURNAL OF CONSULTING PSYCHOLOGY, 1967, 31, 220.
                    (VALIDITY:CRITERION; CORRELATES:DEMOGRAPHIC; N=44 DIVORCED, 44
                    MARRIED MOTHERS OF DISTURBED CHILDREN)
            @APPLICATION 1967 D-45

2077   NORMINGTON, C. J.
            TIME ESTIMATION IN PROCESS-REACTIVE SCHIZOPHRENIA.
            JOURNAL OF CONSULTING PSYCHOLOGY, 1967, 31, 222.
                    (RELIABILITY: INTERRATER; CORRELATES:PSYCHOLOGICAL; USED AS
                    CRITERION; N=45 SCHIZOPHRENICS, 15 NORMALS)
            @APPLICATION 1967 B-242

2078   CICHETTI, D. V., & FARINA, A.
            RELATIONSHIP BETWEEN REPORTED AND OBSERVED DOMINANCE AND CONFLICT AMONG
            PARENTS OF SCHIZOPHRENICS.
            JOURNAL OF CONSULTING PSYCHOLOGY, 1967, 31, 223.
                    (CORRELATES:PSYCHOLOGICAL; USED AS CRITERION; N=11 PARENTS OF
                    POOR PREMORBID SCHIZOPHRENICS, 12 PARENTS OF GOOD PREMORBID
                    SCHIZOPHRENICS, 12 PARENTS OF MEDICAL PATIENT CONTROLS)
            @APPLICATION 1967 S-9 P-32

2079   FARLEY, F., & FARLEY, S. V.
            EXTROVERSION AND STIMULUS-SEEKING MOTIVATION.
            JOURNAL OF CONSULTING PSYCHOLOGY, 1967, 31, 215-216.
                    (VALIDITY:CONSTRUCT; CORRELATES:PSYCHOLOGICAL; NORMATIVE DATA;
                    N=100 ADULT MALES)
            @APPLICATION 1967 E-6 Z-3

2080   STORMS, L. H., BROEN, W. E., JR., & LEVIN, I. P.
           VERBAL ASSOCIATIVE STABILITY AND COMMONALITY AS A FUNCTION OF STRESS IN
           SCHIZOPHRENICS, NEUROTICS, AND NORMALS.
           JOURNAL OF CONSULTING PSYCHOLOGY, 1967, 31, 181-187.
                   (USED AS CRITERION; N=40 SCHIZOPHRENIC PATIENTS, 32 NEUROTIC
                   PATIENTS, 27 NORMALS)
       @APPLICATION 1967 D-45 P-32

2081   RASKIN, A., SCHULTERBRANDT, J., REATIG, N., & RICE, C. E.
           FACTORS OF PSYCHOTHERAPY IN INTERVIEW, WARD BEHAVIOR AND SELF REPORT
           RATINGS OF HOSPITALIZED DEPRESSIVES.
           JOURNAL OF CONSULTING PSYCHOLOGY, 1967, 31, 270-278.
                   (REVISION; FACTOR ANALYSIS; N=42 MALE, 82 FEMALE DEPRESSED
                   PATIENTS)
       @APPLICATION 1967 F-84 B-86

2082   PIORKOWSKI, G. K.
           ANXIETY-REDUCING EFFICACY OF DISTRACTION, CATHARSIS, AND RATIONALIZATION
           IN TWO PERSONALITY TYPES.
           JOURNAL OF CONSULTING PSYCHOLOGY, 1967, 31, 279-285.
                   (MODIFICATION; CORRELATES:PSYCHOLOGICAL, PHYSIOLOGICAL; USED AS
                   CRITERION; N=40 REPRESSOR, 40 SENSITIZER HIGH SCHOOL BOYS)
       @APPLICATION 1967 B-46 A-26

2083   FANCHER, R. E., JR.
           ACCURACY VERSUS VALIDITY IN PERSON PERCEPTION.
           JOURNAL OF CONSULTING PSYCHOLOGY, 1967, 31, 264-269.
                   (DESCRIPTION; RELIABILITY:INTERRATER; VALIDITY:CRITERION;
                   CORRELATES:PSYCHOLOGICAL; N=24 STUDENTS, 72 STUDENTS)
       @APPLICATION 1967 K-23 F-85

2084   WECKOWICZ, T. E., MUIR, W., & CROPLEY, A. J.
           A FACTOR ANALYSIS OF THE BECK INVENTORY OF DEPRESSION.
           JOURNAL OF CONSULTING PSYCHOLOGY, 1967, 31, 23-28.
                   (USED AS CRITERION; FACTOR ANALYSIS; N=180 FEMALE, 74 MALE
                   DEPRESSED PATIENTS)
       @APPLICATION 1967 B-8

2085   WILCOX, R.; & KRASNOFF, A.
           INFLUENCE OF TEST-TAKING ATTITUDES ON PERSONALITY INVENTORY SCORES.
           JOURNAL OF CONSULTING PSYCHOLOGY, 1967, 31, 188-194.
                   (CORRELATES:PSYCHOLOGICAL, ENVIRONMENTAL; BIAS:RESPONSE; N=50
                   PSYCHIATRIC PATIENTS)
       @APPLICATION 1967 C-27 R-31 D-45 E-1 C-58 H-122 G-127 L-93 L-103 W-14 H-123
       @G-202

2086   WALKER, C. E., & TAHMISIAN, J.
           BIRTH ORDER AND STUDENT CHARACTERISTICS: A REPLICATION.
           JOURNAL OF CONSULTING PSYCHOLOGY, 1967, 31, 219.
                   (CORRELATES:DEMOGRAPHIC, INTELLIGENCE; N=142 COLLEGE MALES AND
                   FEMALES)
       @APPLICATION 1967 B-46 C-27

2087   MASLING, J., RABIE, L., & BLONDHEIM, S. H.
           OBESITY, LEVEL OF ASPIRATION, AND RORSCHACH AND TAT MEASURES OF ORAL
           DEPENDENCE.
           JOURNAL OF CONSULTING PSYCHOLOGY, 1967, 31, 233-239.
                   (CORRELATES:PHYSICAL; N=20 OBESE SUBJECTS, 18 CONTROLS)
       @APPLICATION 1967 R-30 M-20

2088   BUXBAUM, J.
           EFFECT OF NURTURANCE ON WIVES' APPRAISAL OF THEIR MARITAL SATISFACTION AND
           THE DEGREE OF THEIR HUSBANDS' APHASIA.
           JOURNAL OF CONSULTING PSYCHOLOGY, 1967, 31, 240-243.
                   (REVISION; MODIFICATION; CORRELATES:PSYCHOLOGICAL; USED AS CRITERION;
                   N=47 MIDDLE CLASS WHITE FEMALES, WIVES OF MEN WHO HAD HAD STROKES)
       @APPLICATION 1967 L-15 K-100 E-2 K-97

2089   MARWIT, S. J., & MARCIA, J. E.
           TESTER BIAS AND RESPONSE TO PROJECTIVE INSTRUMENTS.
           JOURNAL OF CONSULTING PSYCHOLOGY, 1967, 31, 253-258.
                   (BIAS:TESTER; N=36 STUDENT EXPERIMENT SUBJECTS AND 53 STUDENT
                   SUBJECTS)
       @APPLICATION 1967 H-37

2090   KIESLER, D. J., MATHIEU, P. L., & KLEIN, M. H.
        PATIENT EXPERIENCING LEVEL AND INTERACTION-CHRONOGRAPH VARIABLES IN
        THERAPY INTERVIEW SEGMENTS.
        JOURNAL OF CONSULTING PSYCHOLOGY, 1967, 31, 224.
               (RELIABILITY:INTERRATER; CORRELATES:BEHAVIORAL, PSYCHOLOGICAL;
               N=16 PSYCHIATRIC PATIENTS, 8 NORMALS)
        @APPLICATION 1967 R-95 M-147

2091   PARKER, G. V. C.
        SOME CONCOMITANTS OF THERAPIST DOMINANCE IN THE PSYCHOTHERAPY INTERVIEW.
        JOURNAL OF CONSULTING PSYCHOLOGY, 1967, 31, 313-318.
               (MENTION; RELIABILITY:INTERRATER; CORRELATES:BEHAVIORAL,
               PSYCHOLOGICAL, DEMOGRAPHIC; USED AS CRITERION; NORMATIVE DATA; N=32
               STUDENTS AND NONSTUDENT COUNSELING CLIENTS, 16 THERAPISTS)
        @APPLICATION 1967 G-21 H-216 S-341 F-144

2092   JOHNSON, M. H., & RIES, H. A.
        VALIDATIONAL STUDY OF THE SELF-REPORT SCALE FOR PROCESS-REACTIVE
        SCHIZOPHRENIA.
        JOURNAL OF CONSULTING PSYCHOLOGY, 1967, 31, 321-322.
               (VALIDITY:CRITERION; N=91 MALE SCHIZOPHRENICS)
        @APPLICATION 1967 U-5 P-32

2093   CRUMPTON, E., GRAYSON, H. M., & KEITH-LEE, P.
        WHAT KINDS OF ANXIETY DOES THE TAYLOR MA MEASURE?
        JOURNAL OF CONSULTING PSYCHOLOGY, 1967, 31, 324-326.
               (VALIDITY:CONSTRUCT; CORRELATES:PSYCHOLOGICAL; N=159 HOSPITALIZED
               CHRONIC PSYCHIATRIC PATIENTS)
        @APPLICATION 1967 T-2 C-162

2094   GUREL, L.
        DIMENSIONS OF PSYCHIATRIC PATIENT WARD BEHAVIOR.
        JOURNAL OF CONSULTING PSYCHOLOGY, 1967, 31, 328-331.
               (FACTOR ANALYSIS; N=1274 FUNCTIONAL PSYCHOTICS)
        @APPLICATION 1967 P-83

2095   PAUL, G. L.
        INSIGHT VERSUS DESENSITIZATION IN PSYCHOTHERAPY TWO YEARS AFTER
        TERMINATION.
        JOURNAL OF CONSULTING PSYCHOLOGY, 1967, 31, 333-348.
               (RELIABILITY:INTERNAL CONSISTENCY; VALIDITY:CONSTRUCT, CRITERION;
               CORRELATES:PSYCHOLOGICAL; USED AS CRITERION; NORMATIVE DATA; N=45
               STUDENTS UNDERGOING PSYCHIATRIC TREATMENTS OF DIFFERING SORTS, 44
               UNTREATED CONTROLS)
        @APPLICATION 1967 C-136 E-16 B-84 P-82 B-182

2096   LOREI, T. W.
        PREDICTION OF COMMUNITY STAY AND EMPLOYMENT FOR RELEASED PSYCHIATRIC
        PATIENTS.
        JOURNAL OF CONSULTING PSYCHOLOGY, 1967, 31, 349-357.
               (MODIFICATION; VALIDITY:CRITERION; CORRELATES:PSYCHOLOGICAL,
               ENVIRONMENTAL; FACTOR ANALYSIS; N=215 MALE PSYCHIATRIC PATIENTS,
               TREATED AND RELEASED)
        @APPLICATION 1967 S-72 U-1

2097   ZUCKERMAN, M., SCHULTZ, D. P., & HOPKINS, T. R.
        SENSATION SEEKING AND VOLUNTEERING FOR SENSORY DEPRIVATION AND HYPNOSIS
        EXPERIMENTS.
        JOURNAL OF CONSULTING PSYCHOLOGY, 1967, 31, 358-363.
               (CORRELATES:PSYCHOLOGICAL; 3 STUDIES: N=127 COLLEGE FEMALES, 121
               COLLEGE MALES, 54 COLLEGE MALES AND 55 FEMALES)
        @APPLICATION 1967 D-45 T-2 Z-3

2098   GRISSO, J. T., & MEADOW, A.
        TEST INTERFERENCE IN A RORSCHACH-WAIS ADMINSTRATION SEQUENCE.
        JOURNAL OF CONSULTING PSYCHOLOGY, 1967, 31, 382-386.
               (CORRELATES:PSYCHOLOGICAL, INTELLIGENCE; BIAS:RESPONSE; N=36 COLLEGE
               FEMALES, 24 COLLEGE MALES)
        @APPLICATION 1967 R-30

2099   NEWBERRY, L. A.
            DEFENSIVENESS AND NEED FOR APPROVAL.
            JOURNAL OF CONSULTING PSYCHOLOGY, 1967, 31, 396-400.
                    (CORRELATES:PSYCHOLOGICAL; USED AS CRITERION; N=29 MALE AND 31
                FEMALE COLLEGE STUDENTS)
        @APPLICATION 1967 C-27 D-45 G-21 R-31

2100   FEDER, C. Z.
            RELATIONSHIP OF REPRESSION-SENSITIZATION TO ADJUSTMENT STATUS, SOCIAL
            DESIRABILITY, AND ACQUIESCENCE RESPONSE SET.
            JOURNAL OF CONSULTING PSYCHOLOGY, 1967, 31, 401-406.
                    (VALIDITY:CONSTRUCT; CORRELATES:PSYCHOLOGICAL; USED AS CRITERION;
                BIAS:RESPONSE; N=83 HOSPITALIZED MALE MEDICAL/SURGICAL PATIENTS,
                78 HOSPITALIZED MALE PSYCHIATRIC PATIENTS)
        @APPLICATION 1967 C-27 W-10 B-46 C-23 S-124

2101   OETTING, E. R., & COLE, C. W.
            USE OF THE MINIMAL SOCIAL BEHAVIOR SCALE IN A NONPSYCHIATRIC POPULATION.
            JOURNAL OF CONSULTING PSYCHOLOGY, 1967, 31, 407-408.
                    (VALIDITY:CRITERION; CORRELATES:INTELLIGENCE; N=37 NONHOSPITALIZED
                ADULT MALES OF LOW INTELLIGENCE)
        @APPLICATION 1967 F-1

2102   MORAN, G.
            ORDINAL POSITION AND APPROVAL MOTIVATION.
            JOURNAL OF CONSULTING PSYCHOLOGY, 1967, 31, 319-320.
                    (CORRELATES:DEMOGRAPHIC; N=80 FIRST, 110 LATTER BORN MALES AND 67
                FIRST, 92 LATTER BORN FEMALES)
        @APPLICATION 1967 C-27

2103   HARWOOD, B. T.
            SOME INTELLECTUAL CORRELATES OF SCHIZOID INDICATORS: WAIS AND MMPI.
            JOURNAL OF CONSULTING PSYCHOLOGY, 1967, 31, 218.
                    (CORRELATES:INTELLIGENCE; USED AS CRITERION; OUT OF 533, N=23 COLLEGE
                MALES SCORING HIGH ON MMPI SCHIZOPHRENIA SCALE, 28 CONTROLS)
        @APPLICATION 1967, D-45

2104   COWDEN, J. E., & PACHT, A. R.
            PREDICTING INSTITUTIONAL AND POSTRELEASE ADJUSTMENT OF DELINQUENT BOYS.
            JOURNAL OF CONSULTING PSYCHOLOGY, 1967, 31, 377-381.
                    (VALIDITY:CRITERION, CROSS-VALIDATION; 2 SAMPLES: N=72 DELINQUENT
                BOYS, 72 DELINQUENT BOYS)
        @APPLICATION 1967 B-44 B-11

2105   HOLMES, D. S.
            MALE-FEMALE DIFFERENCES IM MMPI EGO STRENGTH: AN ARTIFACT.
            JOURNAL OF CONSULTING PSYCHOLOGY, 1967, 31, 408-410.
                    (VALIDITY:CONSTRUCT; CORRELATES:DEMOGRAPHIC; N=21 MALE, 17 FEMALE
                PSYCHIATRIC PATIENTS)
        @APPLICATION 1967 D-45 B-5

2106   BRIGHAM, J. C., RICKETTS, J. L., & JOHNSON, R. C.
            REPORTED MATERNAL AND PATERNAL BEHAVIORS OF SOLITARY AND SOCIAL
            DELINQUENTS.
            JOURNAL OF CONSULTING PSYCHOLOGY, 1967, 31, 420-422.
                    (MODIFICATION; CORRELATES:BEHAVIORAL, PSYCHOLOGICAL, ENVIRONMENTAL;
                N=59 DELINQUENTS)
        @APPLICATION 1967 R-41

2107   BERGMAN, P., MALASKY, C., & ZAHN, T. P.
            RELATION OF SUCKING STRENGTH TO PERSONALITY VARIABLES.
            JOURNAL OF CONSULTING PSYCHOLOGY, 1967, 31, 426-428.
                    (CORRELATES:BEHAVIORAL, PHYSIOLOGICAL, DEMOGRAPHIC; N=44 MALES AND
                33 FEMALES)
        @APPLICATION 1967 D-45 W-8 W-41 B-5

2108   DOMHOFF, B., & GERSON, A.
            REPLICATION AND CRITIQUE OF THREE STUDIES ON PERSONALITY CORRELATES OF
            DREAM RECALL.
            JOURNAL OF CONSULTING PSYCHOLOGY, 1967, 31, 431.
                    (CORRELATES:PSYCHOLOGICAL; N=84 MALE AND 104 FEMALE COLLEGE STUDENTS)
        @APPLICATION 1967 B-5 W-8 W-41 J-40

2109   HUNTER, C. G., & GOODSTEIN, L. D.
            EGO STRENGTH AND TYPES OF DEFENSIVE AND COPING BEHAVIOR.
            JOURNAL OF CONSULTING PSYCHOLOGY, 1967, 31, 432.
                    (CORRELATES:PSYCHOLOGICAL; USED AS CRITERION; N=40 COLLEGE STUDENTS
                    HIGH OR LOW ON EGO STRENGTH)
        @APPLICATION 1967 B-5

2110   JACOBSON, H. A., & HANDLER, L.
            EXTROVERSION-INTROVERSION AND THE EFFECTS OF STRESS ON THE DRAW-A-PERSON
            TEST.
            JOURNAL OF CONSULTING PSYCHOLOGY, 1967, 31, 433.
                    (CORRELATES:PSYCHOLOGICAL; USED AS CRITERION; N=40 INTROVERTED AND
                    40 EXTRAVERTED COLLEGE STUDENTS)
        @APPLICATION 1967 E-5 G-78

2111   WATSON, C. G.
            INTERRELATIONSHIPS OF SIX OVERINCLUSION MEASURES.
            JOURNAL OF CONSULTING PSYCHOLOGY, 1967, 31, 517-520.
                    (VALIDITY:CONSTRUCT; CORRELATES:BEHAVIORAL, PSYCHOLOGICAL; N=100
                    MALE SCHIZOPHRENICS)
        @APPLICATION 1967 E-38 B-94

2112   WOLKING, W. D., DUNTEMAN, G. H., & BAILEY, J. P., JR.
            MULTIVARIATE ANALYSIS OF PARENTS' MMPI'S BASED ON THE PSYCHIATRIC DIAGNOSES
            OF THEIR CHILDREN.
            JOURNAL OF CONSULTING PSYCHOLOGY, 1967, 31, 521-524.
                    (NORMATIVE DATA; N=793 PARENTS OF PSYCHIATRICALLY DIAGNOSED CHILDREN)
        @APPLICATION 1967 D-45

2113   GREBSTEIN, L. C.
            DEFENSIVE BEHAVIOR IN AN INTERPERSONAL SITUATION.
            JOURNAL OF CONSULTING PSYCHOLOGY, 1967, 31, 529-535.
                    (CORRELATES:BEHAVIORAL, PSYCHOLOGICAL; USED AS CRITERION; N=57
                    COLLEGE MALES)
        @APPLICATION 1967 B-46

2114   FEIRSTEIN, A.
            PERSONALITY CORRELATES OF TOLERANCE FOR UNREALISTIC EXPERIENCES.
            JOURNAL OF CONSULTING PSYCHOLOGY, 1967, 31, 387-395.
                    (CORRELATES:PSYCHOLOGICAL; N=20 MALE UNDERGRADUATES)
        @APPLICATION 1967 R-30

2115   FELD, S., & LEWIS, J.
            FURTHER EVIDENCE ON THE STABILITY OF THE FACTOR STRUCTURE ON THE TEST
            ANXIETY SCALE FOR CHILDREN.
            JOURNAL OF CONSULTING PSYCHOLOGY, 1967, 31, 434.
                    (MODIFICATION; FACTOR ANALYSIS; N=3867 BOYS AND 3684 GIRLS)
        @APPLICATION 1967 S-35

2116   BOYD, H. S., & SISNEY, V. V.
            IMMEDIATE SELF-IMAGE CONFRONTATION AND CHANGES IN SELF CONCEPT.
            JOURNAL OF CONSULTING PSYCHOLOGY, 1967, 31, 291-294.
                    (CORRELATES:PSYCHOLOGICAL; N=14 MALE PSYCHIATRIC PATIENTS)
        @APPLICATION 1967 L-35

2117   VAN DER VEEN, F.
            BASIC ELEMENTS IN THE PROCESS OF PSYCHOTHERAPY: A RESEARCH STUDY.
            JOURNAL OF CONSULTING PSYCHOLOGY, 1967, 31, 295-303.
                    (MODIFICATION; CORRELATES:BEHAVIORAL, PSYCHOLOGICAL; N=15 INDIVIDUAL
                    THERAPY CASES)
        @APPLICATION 1967 R-30 M-20 D-45 B-50 H-131 T-38

2118   KROGER, R. O.
            EFFECTS OF ROLE DEMANDS AND TEST-CUE PROPERTIES UPON PERSONALITY TEST
            PERFORMANCE.
            JOURNAL OF CONSULTING PSYCHOLOGY, 1967, 31, 304-312.
                    (MODIFICATION; CORRELATES:PSYCHOLOGICAL, ENVIRONMENTAL; N=100 ROTC
                    CADETS AND UNDERGRADUATES)
        @APPLICATION 1967 W-9 S-33

2119   ANTROBUS, J. S., COLEMAN, R., & SINGER, J. L.
            SIGNAL-DETECTION PERFORMANCE BY SUBJECTS DIFFERING IN PREDISPOSITION TO DAY
            DREAMING.
            JOURNAL OF CONSULTING PSYCHOLOGY, 1967, 31, 487-491.
                (CORRELATES:BEHAVIORAL, PSYCHOLOGICAL; USED AS CRITERION; N=20
                COLLEGE MALES AND FEMALES SCORING HIGH AND LOW ON DAYDREAMING AND
                THOUGHTFULNESS)
        @APPLICATION 1967 G-26

2120   ROSENFELD, J. M.
            SOME PERCEPTUAL AND COGNITIVE CORRELATES OF STRONG APPROVAL MOTIVATION.
            JOURNAL OF CONSULTING PSYCHOLOGY, 1967, 31, 507-512.
                (CORRELATES:BEHAVIORAL, PSYCHOLOGICAL; USED AS CRITERION; N=50
                COLLEGE MALES)
        @APPLICATION 1967 C-27 W-19 W-72

2121   GOLDSCHMID, M. L., & DOMINO, G.
            DIFFERENTIAL PATIENT PERCEPTION AMONG VARIOUS PROFESSIONAL DISCIPLINES.
            JOURNAL OF CONSULTING PSYCHOLOGY, 1967, 31, 548-550.
                (RELIABILITY:INTERRATER; N=48 PROFESSIONAL HOSPITAL STAFF MEMBERS
                RATING 4 PSYCHIATRIC PATIENTS)
        @APPLICATION 1967 D-67

2122   KAPLAN, M. F.
            INTERVIEW INTERACTION OF REPRESSORS AND SENSITIZERS.
            JOURNAL OF CONSULTING PSYCHOLOGY, 1967, 31, 513-516.
                (CORRELATES:BEHAVIORAL; USED AS CRITERION; N=120 COLLEGE MALE
                REPRESSORS AND SENSITIZERS)
        @APPLICATION 1967 B-46 M-147

2123   HARRISON, R. H., & KASS, E. H.
            DIFFERENCES BETWEEN NEGRO AND WHITE PREGNANT WOMEN ON THE MMPI.
            JOURNAL OF CONSULTING PSYCHOLOGY, 1967, 31, 454-463.
                (CORRELATES:DEMOGRAPHIC; FACTOR ANALYSIS; NORMATIVE DATA; N=772 BLACK
                AND WHITE PREGNANT WOMEN)
        @APPLICATION 1967 D-45 B-5 T-2

2124   ZUCKERMAN, M., PERSKY, H., & LINK, K.
            RELATION OF MOOD AND HYPNOTIZABILITY: AN ILLUSTRATION OF THE IMPORTANCE
            OF THE STATE VERSUS TRAIT DISTINCTION.
            JOURNAL OF CONSULTING PSYCHOLOGY, 1967, 31, 464-470.
                (CORRELATES:PSYCHOLOGICAL; USED AS CRITERION; BIAS:RESPONSE; N=112
                ADULT MALES)
        @APPLICATION 1967 Z-4 S-9C T-2 D-45 S-208 S-24

2125   GORDON, C. M.
            SOME EFFECTS OF CLINICIAN AND PATIENT PERSONALITY ON DECISION MAKING IN A
            CLINICAL SETTING.
            JOURNAL OF CONSULTING PSYCHOLOGY, 1967, 31, 477-480.
                (MODIFICATION; CORRELATES:BEHAVIORAL, PSYCHOLOGICAL; USED AS
                CRITERION; N=44 CLINICAL PSYCHOLOGISTS AND TRAINEES)
        @APPLICATION 1967 G-43 G-130

2126   GILBERT, J. G., & LOMBARDI, D. N.
            PERSONALITY CHARACTERISTICS OF YOUNG MALE NARCOTICS ADDICTS.
            JOURNAL OF CONSULTING PSYCHOLOGY, 1967, 31, 536-538.
                (CORRELATES:BEHAVIORAL; NORMATIVE DATA; N=45 MALE NARCOTIC
                ADDICTS AND 45 NONADDICTS)
        @APPLICATION 1967 D-45 B-5 B-184 E-1

2127   WEINSTOCK, A. R.
            LONGITUDINAL STUDY OF SOCIAL CLASS AND DEFENSE PREFERENCES.
            JOURNAL OF CONSULTING PSYCHOLOGY, 1967, 31, 539-541.
                (RELIABILITY:INTERRATER; CORRELATES:DEMOGRAPHIC; N=39 ADULT MALES)
        @APPLICATION 1967 H-1

2128   MCCARTHY, D., SCHIRO, F. M., & SUDIMACK, J. P.
            COMPARISON OF WAIS M-F INDEX WITH TWO MEASURES OF MASCULINITY-FEMININITY.
            JOURNAL OF CONSULTING PSYCHOLOGY, 1967, 31, 639-640.
                (CORRELATES:DEMOGRAPHIC, INTELLIGENCE; N=40 COLLEGE MALES AND
                40 COLLEGE FEMALES)
        @APPLICATION 1967 G-40 T-3

2129   GRAVITZ, M. A.
           FREQUENCY AND CONTENT OF TEST ITEMS NORMALLY OMITTED FROM MMPI SCALES.
           JOURNAL OF CONSULTING PSYCHOLOGY, 1967, 31, 642.
                (N=7149 MALE AND 4816 FEMALE JOB APPLICANTS)
       @APPLICATION 1967 D-45

2130   DATTA, L.
           DRAW-A-PERSON TEST AS A MEASURE OF INTELLIGENCE IN PRESCHOOL CHILDREN
           FROM VERY LOW INCOME FAMILIES.
           JOURNAL OF CONSULTING PSYCHOLOGY, 1967, 31, 626-630.
                (VALIDITY:CONSTRUCT: CORRELATES:INTELLIGENCE, DEMOGRAPHIC;
                N=456 CHILDREN FROM LOW INCOME FAMILIES)
       @APPLICATION 1967 M-58

2131   THORNTON, C. L., & BARRETT, G. V.
           METHODOLOGICAL NOTE ON N ACHIEVEMENT AND FIELD INDEPENDENCE COMPARISONS.
           JOURNAL OF CONSULTING PSYCHOLOGY, 1967, 31, 631-632.
                (MENTION; CORRELATES:PSYCHOLOGICAL, DEMOGRAPHIC)
       @APPLICATION 1967 W-19 M-7 W-72 W-73

2132   KORNER, I. N., & BUCKWALTER, M. M.
           EFFECTS OF AGE AND INTELLIGENCE ON THE OPERATION OF SUPPRESSION.
           JOURNAL OF CONSULTING PSYCHOLOGY, 1967, 31, 637-639.
                (CORRELATES:DEMOGRAPHIC, INTELLIGENCE; N=60 ELEMENTARY SCHOOL
                CHILDREN)
       @APPLICATION 1967 K-48

2133   DILLING, C. A., & RABIN, A. I.
           TEMPORAL EXPERIENCE IN DEPRESSIVE STATES AND SCHIZOPHRENIA.
           JOURNAL OF CONSULTING PSYCHOLOGY, 1967, 31, 604-608.
                (MODIFICATION; DESCRIPTION; RELIABILITY:INTERRATER;
                CORRELATES:PSYCHOLOGICAL; NORMATIVE DATA; N=20 SCHIZOPHRENICS,
                20 DEPRESSIVES, AND 20 NORMALS)
       @APPLICATION 1967 W-109 B-186 L-57

2134   HERSCH, P. D., & SCHEIBE, K. E.
           RELIABILITY AND VALIDITY OF INTERNAL-EXTERNAL CONTROL AS A PERSONALITY
           DIMENSION.
           JOURNAL OF CONSULTING PSYCHOLOGY, 1967, 31, 609-613.
                (RELIABILITY:RETEST; VALIDITY:CONSTRUCT; CORRELATES:PSYCHOLOGICAL,
                INTELLIGENCE; NORMATIVE DATA; N=446 COLLEGE STUDENTS)
       @APPLICATION 1967 R-18 R-31 G-21 G-22 D-45

2135   WHITELEY, J. M., & BLAINE, G. B., JR.
           RORSCHACH IN RELATION TO OUTCOME IN PSYCHOTHERAPY WITH COLLEGE STUDENTS.
           JOURNAL OF CONSULTING PSYCHOLOGY, 1967, 31, 595-599.
                (VALIDITY:CONSTRUCT, CRITERION; USED AS CRITERION; N=50 COLLEGE MALES
                IN PSYCHOTHERAPY)
       @APPLICATION 1967 K-13

2136   BOOR, M., & SCHILL, T.
           DIGIT SYMBOL PERFORMANCE OF SUBJECTS VARYING IN ANXIETY AND DEFENSIVENESS.
           JOURNAL OF CONSULTING PSYCHOLOGY, 1967, 31, 600-603.
                (DESCRIPTION; RELIABILITY:INTERNAL CONSISTENCY; CORRELATES:
                BEHAVIORAL, DEMOGRAPHIC; USED AS CRITERION; NORMATIVE DATA;
                N=159 COLLEGE MALES AND 187 COLLEGE FEMALES)
       @APPLICATION 1967 T-2 C-27

2137   SNELBECKER, G. E.
           INFLUENCE OF THERAPEUTIC TECHNIQUES ON COLLEGE STUDENTS' PERCEPTIONS
           OF THERAPISTS.
           JOURNAL OF CONSULTING PSYCHOLOGY, 1967, 31, 614-618.
                (CORRELATES:PSYCHOLOGICAL; USED AS CRITERION; NORMATIVE DATA;
                N=168 COLLEGE MALES, 70 COLLEGE FEMALES)
       @APPLICATION 1967 B-50

2138   LEWINSOHN, P. M.
           FACTORS RELATED TO IMPROVEMENT IN MENTAL HOSPITAL PATIENTS.
           JOURNAL OF CONSULTING PSYCHOLOGY, 1967, 31, 588-594.
                (RELIABILITY:INTERRATER; VALIDITY:CRITERION; CORRELATES:DEMOGRAPHIC,
                INTELLIGENCE; USED AS CRITERION; NORMATIVE DATA; N=165 PSYCHIATRIC
                PATIENTS)
       @APPLICATION 1967 L-39 C-136 G-83

2139   HILL, A. H.
             USE OF A STRUCTURED AUTOBIOGRAPHY IN THE CONSTRUCT VALIDATION OF
             PERSONALITY SCALES.
             JOURNAL OF CONSULTING PSYCHOLOGY, 1967, 31, 551-556.
                   (VALIDITY:CONSTRUCT; N=352 COLLEGE MALES)
       @APPLICATION 1967 G-22

2140   GOLIN, S., HERRON, E. W., LAKOTA, R., & REINECK, L.
             FACTOR ANALYTIC STUDY OF THE MANIFEST ANXIETY, EXTRAVERSION, AND
             REPRESSION-SENSITIZATION SCALES.
             JOURNAL OF CONSULTING PSYCHOLOGY, 1967, 31, 564-569.
                   (CORRELATES:PSYCHOLOGICAL; FACTOR ANALYSIS; NORMATIVE DATA;
                   N=226 COLLEGE STUDENTS)
       @APPLICATION 1967 T-2 B-46 B-5 C-23 E-5 A-5 S-5 B-7 S-24 G-18 W-11 D-45
       @E-6

2141   MEISELS, M.
             TEST ANXIETY, STRESS, AND VERBAL BEHAVIOR.
             JOURNAL OF CONSULTING PSYCHOLOGY, 1967, 31, 577-582.
                   (RELIABILITY:INTERRATER; CORRELATES:BEHAVIORAL, PSYCHOLOGICAL;
                   USED AS CRITERION; N=391 COLLEGE FEMALES, 80 SELECTED)
       @APPLICATION 1967 M-4 M-20 G-6 M-35

2142   LAPLACE, R., STEIN, D. D., & WEISSMAN, H. N.
             CLINICAL EXPERIENCE AND THE PERCEPTION OF THE SCHIZOPHRENIC PATIENT.
             JOURNAL OF CONSULTING AND CLINICAL PSYCHOLOGY, 1968, 32, 134-139.
                   (CORRELATES:PSYCHOLOGICAL, ENVIRONMENTAL; N=39 STAFF MEMBERS OF
                   PSYCHIATRIC HOSPITAL WARD)
       @APPLICATION 1968 G-21

2143   EISENMAN, R.
             PERSONALITY AND DEMOGRAPHY IN COMPLEXITY-SIMPLICITY.
             JOURNAL OF CONSULTING AND CLINICAL PSYCHOLOGY, 1968, 32, 140-143.
                   (MODIFICATION; CORRELATES:PSYCHOLOGICAL, DEMOGRAPHIC; N=123 COLLEGE
                   MALES, 82 COLLEGE FEMALES)
       @APPLICATION 1968 T-2 B-4 B-118

2144   HOUTS, P. S., & WITTNER, W. K.
             PATIENTS' RECOGNITION MEMORY FOR STATEMENTS MADE IN WARD COMMUNITY
             MEETINGS.
             JOURNAL OF CONSULTING AND CLINICAL PSYCHOLOGY, 1968, 32, 130-133.
                   (CORRELATES:PSYCHOLOGICAL; N=16 ACUTE PSYCHIATRIC PATIENTS)
       @APPLICATION 1968 H-136

2145   KASMAR, J. V., GRIFFIN, W. V., & MAURITZEN, J. H.
             EFFECT OF ENVIRONMENTAL SURROUNDINGS ON OUTPATIENTS' MOOD AND PERCEPTION
             OF PSYCHIATRISTS.
             JOURNAL OF CONSULTING AND CLINICAL PSYCHOLOGY, 1968, 32, 223-226.
                   (CORRELATES:PSYCHOLOGICAL, ENVIRONMENTAL; FACTOR ANALYSIS;
                   N=56 MALE, 59 FEMALE PSYCHIATRIC OUTPATIENTS)
       @APPLICATION 1968 L-17 L-43 V-46

2146   JONES, M. C.
             PERSONALITY CORRELATES AND ANTECEDENTS OF DRINKING PATTERNS IN ADULT MALES.
             JOURNAL OF CONSULTING AND CLINICAL PSYCHOLOGY, 1968, 32, 2-12.
                   (CORRELATES:BEHAVIORAL, PSYCHOLOGICAL; N=66 MIDDLE-AGED MEN IN
                   LONGITUDINAL STUDY)
       @APPLICATION 1968 B-126

2147   TRUAX, C. B., SCHULDT, W. J., & WARGO, D. G.
             SELF-IDEAL CONCEPT CONGRUENCE AND IMPROVEMENT IN GROUP PSYCHOTHERAPY.
             JOURNAL OF CONSULTING AND CLINICAL PSYCHOLOGY, 1968, 32, 47-53.
                   (VALIDITY:CONSTRUCT, CRITERION; CORRELATES:PSYCHOLOGICAL; N=86
                   HOSPITALIZED MENTAL PATIENTS, 50 NEUROTIC OUTPATIENTS AND 73
                   INSTITUTIONALIZED JUVENILE DELINQUENTS)
       @APPLICATION 1968 D-45 T-36 B-60 B-11 E-1 B-5 W-8

2148   LIPP, L., KOLSTOE, R., JAMES, W., & RANDALL, H.
             DENIAL OF DISABILITY AND INTERNAL CONTROL OF REINFORCEMENT: A STUDY USING A
             PERCEPTUAL DEFENSE PARADIGM.
             JOURNAL OF CONSULTING AND CLINICAL PSYCHOLOGY, 1968, 32, 72-75.
                   (CORRELATES:PSYCHOLOGICAL, PHYSICAL; NORMATIVE DATA; N=30 DISABLED
                   AND 30 NORMAL PERSONS, AGE 15-70)
       @APPLICATION 1968 J-6

2149   VACCHIANO, R. B., STRAUSS, P. S., & SCHIFFMAN, D. C.
              PERSONALITY CORRELATES OF DOGMATISM.
              JOURNAL OF CONSULTING AND CLINICAL PSYCHOLOGY, 1968, 32, 83-85.
                    (CORRELATES:PSYCHOLOGICAL; FACTOR ANALYSIS; N=53 MALE, 29 FEMALE
                    COLLEGE STUDENTS)
        @APPLICATION 1968 E-2 F-7 G-2 C-10 R-8

2150   LEFCOURT, H. M.
              SERENDIPITOUS VALIDITY STUDY OF GOUGH'S SOCIAL MATURITY INDEX.
              JOURNAL OF CONSULTING AND CLINICAL PSYCHOLOGY, 1968, 32, 85-86.
                    (VALIDITY:CRITERION; CORRELATES:BEHAVIORAL; N=66 STUDENTS OF
                    PERSONALITY THEORY)
        @APPLICATION 1968 G-140

2151   MASLING, J., WEISS, L., & ROTHSCHILD, B.
              RELATIONSHIPS OF ORAL IMAGERY TO YIELDING BEHAVIOR AND BIRTH ORDER.
              JOURNAL OF CONSULTING AND CLINICAL PSYCHOLOGY, 1968, 32, 89-91.
                    (RELIABILITY:INTERRATER; CORRELATES:BEHAVIORAL, DEMOGRAPHIC;
                    N=23 CONFORMING, 21 NON-CONFORMING MALE UNDERGRADUATES)
        @APPLICATION 1968 R-30 M-148

2152   LIEBERMAN, L. R.
              EFFECTS OF INSTRUCTIONAL SET ON THE SIMILES PREFERENCE INVENTORY.
              JOURNAL OF CONSULTING AND CLINICAL PSYCHOLOGY, 1968, 32, 96-97.
                    (VALIDITY:CONSTRUCT; NORMATIVE DATA; BIAS:RESPONSE; N=50 MALE AND
                    50 FEMALE COLLEGE STUDENTS)
        @APPLICATION 1968 P-2

2153   RALPH, D. E.
              ATTITUDES TOWARD MENTAL ILLNESS AMONG TWO GROUPS OF COLLEGE STUDENTS IN
              A NEUROPSYCHIATRIC HOSPITAL SETTING.
              JOURNAL OF CONSULTING AND CLINICAL PSYCHOLOGY, 1968, 32, 98.
                    (CORRELATES:BEHAVIORAL, ENVIRONMENTAL; N=56 FEMALE COLLEGE STUDENTS)
        @APPLICATION 1968 G-31

2154   BLOOMBAUM, M., YAMAMOTO, J., & JAMES, Q.
              CULTURAL STEREOTYPING AMONG PSYCHOTHERAPISTS.
              JOURNAL OF CONSULTING AND CLINICAL PSYCHOLOGY, 1968, 32, 99.
                    (VALIDITY:CRITERION; N=16 PRACTICING PSYCHOTHERAPISTS)
        @APPLICATION 1968 B-58

2155   ROSEN, G. M., & ROSS, A. O.
              RELATIONSHIP OF BODY IMAGE TO SELF-CONCEPT.
              JOURNAL OF CONSULTING AND CLINICAL PSYCHOLOGY, 1968, 32, 100.
                    (MODIFICATION; CORRELATES:PSYCHOLOGICAL; N=82 UNDERGRADUATES)
        @APPLICATION 1968 G-21

2156   SHAPIRO, J. G.
              RELATIONSHIPS BETWEEN EXPERT AND NEOPHYTE RATINGS OF THERAPEUTIC
              CONDITIONS.
              JOURNAL OF CONSULTING AND CLINICAL PSYCHOLOGY, 1968, 32, 87-89.
                    (RELIABILITY:INTERRATER; N=18 NAIVE STUDENTS AND 13 TRAINED RATERS)
        @APPLICATION 1968 T-89 T-74 T-75

2157   ELLSWORTH, R. B., FOSTER, L., CHILDERS, B., ARTHUR, G., & KROEKER, D.
              HOSPITAL AND COMMUNITY ADJUSTMENT AS PERCEIVED BY PSYCHIATRIC PATIENTS,
              THEIR FAMILIES, AND STAFF.
              JOURNAL OF CONSULTING AND CLINICAL PSYCHOLOGY MONOGRAPH SUPPLEMENT, 1968,
              32, NO. 2, PART 2, 1-41.
                    (RELIABILITY:INTERNAL CONSISTENCY; VALIDITY:CRITERION; CORRELATES:
                    PSYCHOLOGICAL; N=178 PSYCHIATRIC PATIENTS)
        @APPLICATION 1968 E-20 J-38

2158   HUNDLEBY, J. D., & CONNOR, W. H.
              INTERRELATIONSHIPS BETWEEN PERSONALITY INVENTORIES: THE 16 PF, THE MMPI,
              AND THE MPI.
              JOURNAL OF CONSULTING AND CLINICAL PSYCHOLOGY, 1968, 32, 152-157.
                    (VALIDITY:CONTENT, CONSTRUCT; CORRELATES:PSYCHOLOGICAL; FACTOR
                    ANALYSIS; N=267 AIRMEN)
        @APPLICATION 1968 C-10 D-45 E-5

2159   WILLIAMS, G. J., NAHINSKY, I. D., HALL, D. M., & ABRAMSON, Y.
        FREQUENCY OF THE RORSCHACH HUMAN MOVEMENT RESPONSE IN NEGRO AND WHITE
        EMOTIONALLY DISTURBED CHILDREN.
        JOURNAL OF CONSULTING AND CLINICAL PSYCHOLOGY, 1968, 32, 158-163.
            (CORRELATES:DEMOGRAPHIC; NORMATIVE DATA; N=197 NEGRO AND 196 WHITE
            EMOTIONALLY DISTURBED CHILDREN)
        @APPLICATION 1968 R-30

2160   LIEBERMAN, L. R., & WALTERS, W. M., JR.
        EFFECT OF BACKGROUND ITEMS ON RESPONSES TO PERSONALITY INVENTORY ITEMS.
        JOURNAL OF CONSULTING AND CLINICAL PSYCHOLOGY, 1968, 32, 230-232.
            (BIAS:RESPONSE; N=270 COLLEGE STUDENTS)
        @APPLICATION 1968 D-45

2161   VARBLE, D. L.
        RELATIONSHIP BETWEEN THE THERAPISTS' APPROACH-AVOIDANCE REACTIONS TO
        HOSTILITY AND CLIENT BEHAVIOR IN THERAPY.
        JOURNAL OF CONSULTING AND CLINICAL PSYCHOLOGY, 1968, 32, 237-242.
            (MODIFICATION; RELIABILITY:INTERRATER; CORRELATES:BEHAVIORAL,
            PSYCHOLOGICAL; N=10 FEMALE, 6 MALE PSYCHOTHERAPY CLIENTS)
        @APPLICATION 1968 B-22

2162   FONTANA, A. F., & KLEIN, E. B.
        SELF-PRESENTATION AND THE SCHIZOPHRENIC "DEFICIT."
        JOURNAL OF CONSULTING AND CLINICAL PSYCHOLOGY, 1968, 32, 250-256.
            (REVISION; CORRELATES:BEHAVIORAL; USED AS CRITERION; N=103
            SCHIZOPHRENICS AND 10 HOSPITAL EMPLOYEES)
        @APPLICATION 1968 S-123 E-1

2163   PIVIK, T., & FOULKES, D.
        NREM MENTATION: RELATION TO PERSONALITY, ORIENTATION TIME, AND TIME
        OF NIGHT.
        JOURNAL OF CONSULTING AND CLINICAL PSYCHOLOGY, 1968, 32, 144-151.
            (CORRELATES:PSYCHOLOGICAL; N=20 YOUNG ADULT MALES)
        @APPLICATION 1968 F-88 G-22 B-46 B-5 F-89

2164   LEIBOWITZ, G.
        COMPARISON OF SELF-REPORT AND BEHAVIORAL TECHNIQUES OF ASSESSING
        AGGRESSION.
        JOURNAL OF CONSULTING AND CLINICAL PSYCHOLOGY, 1968, 32, 21-25.
            (VALIDITY:CONSTRUCT; CORRELATES:BEHAVIORAL, PSYCHOLOGICAL; N=38
            COLLEGE MALES)
        @APPLICATION 1968 B-44 C-27 B-187

2165   MCKEACHIE, W. J., ISAACSON, R. L., MILHOLLAND, J. E., & LIN, Y.
        STUDENT ACHIEVEMENT MOTIVES, ACHIEVEMENT CUES, AND ACADEMIC ACHIEVEMENT.
        JOURNAL OF CONSULTING AND CLINICAL PSYCHOLOGY, 1968, 32, 26-29.
            (RELIABILITY:INTERRATER; VALIDITY:CONSTRUCT, CRITERION;
            CORRELATES:PSYCHOLOGICAL, INTELLIGENCE, DEMOGRAPHIC, ENVIRONMENTAL;
            NORMATIVE DATA; 3 STUDIES: N=825, 754, 510 COLLEGE STUDENTS)
        @APPLICATION 1968 M-7 V-23 M-251 I-9 V-23

2166   WINTER, S. K., GRIFFITH, J. C., & KOLB, D. A.
        CAPACITY FOR SELF-DIRECTION.
        JOURNAL OF CONSULTING AND CLINICAL PSYCHOLOGY, 1968, 32, 35-41.
            (CORRELATES:PSYCHOLOGICAL; N=55 MASTER'S DEGREE CANDIDATES)
        @APPLICATION 1968 R-8

2167   WOLKON, G. H.
        BIRTH ORDER AND DESIRE FOR AND PARTICIPATION IN PSYCHIATRIC
        POSTHOSPITAL SERVICES.
        JOURNAL OF CONSULTING AND CLINICAL PSYCHOLOGY, 1968, 32, 42-46.
            (CORRELATES:BEHAVIORAL, PSYCHOLOGICAL, DEMOGRAPHIC; N=540 PSYCHIATRIC
            PATIENTS UPON RELEASE)
        @APPLICATION 1968 S-209

2168   SMITH, J., & LANYON, R. I.
        PREDICTION OF JUVENILE PROBATION VIOLATORS.
        JOURNAL OF CONSULTING AND CLINICAL PSYCHOLOGY, 1968, 32, 54-58.
            (VALIDITY:CRITERION; CORRELATES:BEHAVIORAL; N=287 MALE JUVENILE
            DELINQUENTS)
        @APPLICATION 1968 D-45

2169   NEURINGER, C.
            DIVERGENCIES BETWEEN ATTITUDES TOWARDS LIFE AND DEATH AMONG SUICIDAL,
            PSYCHOSOMATIC, AND NORMAL HOSPITALIZED PATIENTS.
            JOURNAL OF CONSULTING AND CLINICAL PSYCHOLOGY, 1968, 32, 59-63.
                (CORRELATES:BEHAVIORAL, PSYCHOLOGICAL; N=45 PATIENTS HOSPITALIZED
                FOR SUICIDE ATTEMPTS)
        @APPLICATION 1968 O-16

2170   PARSONS, L. B., & PARKER, G. V. C.
            PERSONAL ATTITUDES, CLINICAL APPRAISALS, AND VERBAL BEHAVIOR OF TRAINED
            AND UNTRAINED THERAPISTS.
            JOURNAL OF CONSULTING AND CLINICAL PSYCHOLOGY, 1968, 32, 64-71.
                (DESCRIPTION; MODIFICATION; CORRELATES:BEHAVIORAL, PSYCHOLOGICAL;
                NORMATIVE DATA; N=55 PSYCHIATRISTS OR PSYCHIATRIC TRAINEES, 30 SENIOR
                MEDICAL STUDENTS AND 120 MALE COLLEGE STUDENTS)
        @APPLICATION 1968 G-21 W-114

2171   JOHNSON, S. M., & SECHREST, L.
            COMPARISON OF DESENSITIZATION AND PROGRESSIVE RELAXATION IN TREATING
            TEST ANXIETY.
            JOURNAL OF CONSULTING AND CLINICAL PSYCHOLOGY, 1968, 32, 280-286.
                (USED AS CRITERION; 41 TEST ANXIOUS COLLEGE STUDENTS)
        @APPLICATION 1968 A-8

2172   BAXTER, J. C., & MORRIS, K. L.
            ITEM AMBIGUITY AND ITEM DISCRIMINATION IN THE MMPI.
            JOURNAL OF CONSULTING AND CLINICAL PSYCHOLOGY, 1968, 32, 309-313.
                (VALIDITY:CONTENT; SAMPLES OF COLLEGE STUDENTS FROM PREVIOUS
                STUDIES USED, NO SAMPLE SIZE GIVEN)
        @APPLICATION 1968 D-45 B-46

2173   BIELIAUSKAS, V. J., MIRANDA, S. B., & LANSKY, L. M.
            OBVIOUSNESS OF TWO MASCULINITY-FEMININITY TESTS.
            JOURNAL OF CONSULTING AND CLINICAL PSYCHOLOGY, 1968, 32, 314-318.
                (RELIABILITY:INTERRATER; VALIDITY:CONTENT, CRITERION; NORMATIVE
                DATA; N=90 MALE, 90 FEMALE COLLEGE STUDENTS)
        @APPLICATION 1968 G-20 F-11

2174   FONTANA, A. F., KLEIN, E. B., LEWIS, E., & LEVINE, L.
            PRESENTATION OF SELF IN MENTAL ILLNESS.
            JOURNAL OF CONSULTING AND CLINICAL PSYCHOLOGY, 1968, 32, 110-119.
                (VALIDITY:CRITERION; CORRELATES:BEHAVIORAL, PSYCHOLOGICAL; USED AS
                CRITERION; NORMATIVE DATA; 3 STUDIES: 130, 60, AND 57 MENTAL
                PATIENTS)
        @APPLICATION 1968 G-138 R-18 C-27 S-123

2175   MILLER, J. P., BOHN, S. E., GILDEN, J. B., & STEVENS, E.
            ANXIETY AS A FUNCTION OF TAKING THE MMPI.
            JOURNAL OF CONSULTING AND CLINICAL PSYCHOLOGY, 1968, 32, 120-124.
                (CORRELATES:PSYCHOLOGICAL, ENVIRONMENTAL; N=44 COLLEGE STUDENTS)
        @APPLICATION 1968 D-45

2176   STRAUSS, M. E.
            EXAMINER EXPECTANCY: EFFECTS ON RORSCHACH EXPERIENCE BALANCE.
            JOURNAL OF CONSULTING AND CLINICAL PSYCHOLOGY, 1968, 32, 125-129.
                (RELIABILITY:INTERRATER; BIAS:TESTER; N=30 FEMALE STUDENT
                SUBJECTS, 5 STUDENT EXPERIMENTERS)
        @APPLICATION 1968 R-30

2177   DUBLIN, J. E.
            PERCEPTION OF AND REACTION TO AMBIGUITY BY REPRESSORS AND SENSITIZERS: A
            CONSTRUCT-VALIDITY STUDY.
            JOURNAL OF CONSULTING AND CLINICAL PSYCHOLOGY, 1968, 32, 198-205.
                (VALIDITY:CONSTRUCT, CRITERION; N=116 COLLEGE FRESHMEN)
        @APPLICATION 1968 B-46 R-30 H-37

2178   TOLOR, A., & JALOWIEC, J. E.
            BODY BOUNDARY, PARENTAL ATTITUDES, AND INTERNAL-EXTERNAL EXPECTANCY.
            JOURNAL OF CONSULTING AND CLINICAL PSYCHOLOGY, 1968, 32, 206-209.
                (VALIDITY:CONSTRUCT; CORRELATES:PSYCHOLOGICAL; N=68 MALE
                FRESHMEN)
        @APPLICATION 1968 R-30 R-18 S-9 C-27

2179   JOHNSON, R. C., ACKERMAN, J. M., FRANK, H., & FIONDA, A. J.
            RESISTANCE TO TEMPTATION, GUILT FOLLOWING YIELDING, AND PSYCHOPATHOLOGY.
            JOURNAL OF CONSULTING AND CLINICAL PSYCHOLOGY, 1968, 32, 169-175.
                (MODIFICATION; RELIABILITY:INTERRATER; CORRELATES:PSYCHOLOGICAL,
                DEMOGRAPHIC; 3 STUDIES: N=12 SCHIZOPHRENICS AND CONTROLS, 21
                PSYCHIATRIC AND 24 PHYSICAL COMPLAINTS, AND 107 STUDENTS)
        @APPLICATION 1968 R-18 E-6 J-15 A-14 A-71

2180   TURNER, R., & TRIPODI, T.
            COGNITIVE COMPLEXITY AS A FUNCTION OF TYPE OF STIMULUS OBJECTS JUDGED AND
            AFFECTIVE STIMULUS VALUE.
            JOURNAL OF CONSULTING AND CLINICAL PSYCHOLOGY, 1968, 32, 182-185.
                (CORRELATES:PSYCHOLOGICAL; NORMATIVE DATA; N=20 FEMALE AND 16 MALE
                GRADUATE SOCIAL WORK STUDENTS)
        @APPLICATION 1968 K-23 T-13 B-97

2181   GALBRAITH, G. G., HAHN, K., & LEIBERMAN, H.
            PERSONALITY CORRELATES OF FREE-ASSOCIATIVE SEX RESPONSES TO
            DOUBLE-ENTENDRE WORDS.
            JOURNAL OF CONSULTING AND CLINICAL PSYCHOLOGY, 1968, 32, 193-197.
                (VALIDITY:CONSTRUCT; CORRELATES:PSYCHOLOGICAL; NORMATIVE DATA;
                N=71 MALE STUDENTS)
        @APPLICATION 1968 M-64 E-2 C-27

2182   PERKINS, C. W.
            PATIENT MANIFEST-NEED HIERARCHIES: THERAPISTS' FORMULATIONS AND EPPS
            RESULTS COMPARED.
            JOURNAL OF CONSULTING AND CLINICAL PSYCHOLOGY, 1968, 32, 221-222.
                (VALIDITY:CRITERION; CORRELATES:PSYCHOLOGICAL; N=15 PSYCHIATRIC
                PATIENTS)
        @APPLICATION 1968 E-2

2183   FARLEY, F. H.
            MODERATING EFFECTS OF INTELLIGENCE ON THE INDEPENDENCE OF EXTRAVERSION
            AND NEUROTICISM.
            JOURNAL OF CONSULTING AND CLINICAL PSYCHOLOGY, 1968, 32, 226-228.
                (CORRELATES:INTELLIGENCE; N=215 MALE TRADE APPRENTICES)
        @APPLICATION 1968 F-6

2184   OKEL, E., & MOSHER, D. L.
            CHANGES IN AFFECTIVE STATES AS A FUNCTION OF GUILT OVER AGGRESSIVE
            BEHAVIOR.
            JOURNAL OF CONSULTING AND CLINICAL PSYCHOLOGY, 1968, 32, 265-270.
                (DESCRIPTION; VALIDITY:CONSTRUCT; CORRELATES:BEHAVIORAL,
                PSYCHOLOGICAL; USED AS CRITERION; N=60 COLLEGE STUDENTS)
        @APPLICATION 1968 N-17 M-64

2185   KLETT, W. G., & VESTRE, N. D.
            DEMOGRAPHIC AND PROGNOSTIC CHARACTERISTICS OF PSYCHIATRIC PATIENTS
            CLASSIFIED BY GROSS MMPI MEASURES.
            JOURNAL OF CONSULTING AND CLINICAL PSYCHOLOGY, 1968, 32, 271-275.
                (CORRELATES:DEMOGRAPHIC; USED AS CRITERION; N=400 PSYCHIATRIC
                PATIENTS)
        @APPLICATION 1968 D-45

2186   FISLER, R. M.
            THEMATIC EXPRESSION OF SEXUAL CONFLICT UNDER VARYING STIMULUS CONDITIONS.
            JOURNAL OF CONSULTING AND CLINICAL PSYCHOLOGY, 1968, 32, 216-220.
                (CORRELATES:PSYCHOLOGICAL; USED AS CRITERION; N=SELECTION FROM 380
                MALE STUDENTS)
        @APPLICATION 1968 D-45 L-105

2187   KULIK, J. A., STEIN, K. B., & SARBIN, T. R.
            DIMENSIONS AND PATTERNS OF ADOLESCENT ANTISOCIAL BEHAVIOR.
            JOURNAL OF CONSULTING AND CLINICAL PSYCHOLOGY, 1968, 32, 375-382.
                (CORRELATES:BEHAVIORAL, PSYCHOLOGICAL; N=505 HIGH SCHOOL BOYS AND
                391 DELINQUENT INSTITUTIONALIZED BOYS)
        @APPLICATION 1968 B-181

2188   ZUCKERMAN, M., & LINK, K.
          CONSTRUCT VALIDITY FOR THE SENSATION-SEEKING SCALE.
          JOURNAL OF CONSULTING AND CLINICAL PSYCHOLOGY, 1968, 32, 420-426.
              (VALIDITY:CONSTRUCT; CORRELATES:PSYCHOLOGICAL; FACTOR ANALYSIS;
              2 STUDIES: N=268 MALE, 277 FEMALE UNDERGRADUATES, 40 UNDERGRADUATE
              MALES)
       @APPLICATION 1968 Z-3 D-45 E-2 G-21 E-6 W-72 W-19 Z-4

2189   INSEL, S. A., REESE, C. S., & ALEXANDER, B. B.
          SELF-PRESENTATIONS IN RELATION TO INTERNAL AND EXTERNAL REFERENTS.
          JOURNAL OF CONSULTING AND CLINICAL PSYCHOLOGY, 1968, 32, 389-395.
              (DESCRIPTION; CORRELATES:PSYCHOLOGICAL, DEMOGRAPHIC; USED AS
              CRITERION; N=2 CRITERION GROUPS (54 EACH) FROM POPULATION OF 204
              SUBJECTS)
       @APPLICATION 1968 M-22 S-11 B-39

2190   BERZINS, J. I., & SEIDMAN, E.
          SUBJECTIVE REACTIONS OF A AND B QUASI-THERAPISTS TO SCHIZOID AND NEUROTIC
          COMMUNICATIONS: A REPLICATION AND EXTENSION.
          JOURNAL OF CONSULTING AND CLINICAL PSYCHOLOGY, 1968, 32, 342-347.
              (REVISION; VALIDITY:CONSTRUCT; CORRELATES:PSYCHOLOGICAL; USED AS
              CRITERION; N=72 UNTRAINED QUASI THERAPISTS)
       @APPLICATION 1968 W-91 K-78

2191   MURSTEIN, B. I.
          EFFECT OF STIMULUS, BACKGROUND, PERSONALITY, AND SCORING SYSTEM ON THE
          MANIFESTATION OF HOSTILITY ON THE TAT.
          JOURNAL OF CONSULTING AND CLINICAL PSYCHOLOGY, 1968, 32, 355-365.
              (CORRELATES:PSYCHOLOGICAL, DEMOGRAPHIC; N=48 MALE, 48 FEMALE
              COLLEGE STUDENTS)
       @APPLICATION 1968 M-134 P-138 H-73

2192   LESSLER, K., & ERICKSON, M. T.
          RESPONSE TO SEXUAL SYMBOLS BY ELEMENTARY SCHOOL CHILDREN.
          JOURNAL OF CONSULTING AND CLINICAL PSYCHOLOGY, 1968, 32, 473-477.
              (MODIFICATION; CORRELATES:PSYCHOLOGICAL, DEMOGRAPHIC; NORMATIVE DATA;
              N=142 MALE, 162 FEMALE FIRST-SIXTH GRADE CHILDREN)
       @APPLICATION 1968 L-92

2193   MAGARO, P. A.
          A VALIDITY AND RELIABILITY STUDY OF THE PROCESS-REACTIVE SELF-REPORT SCALE.
          JOURNAL OF CONSULTING AND CLINICAL PSYCHOLOGY, 1968, 32, 482-485.
              (DESCRIPTION; RELIABILITY:RETEST, INTERNAL CONSISTENCY;
              VALIDITY:CRITERION; CORRELATES:PSYCHOLOGICAL; N=70 MALE PSYCHIATRIC
              PATIENTS)
       @APPLICATION 1968 P-32 U-5

2194   FEFFER, M., & JAHELKA, M.
          IMPLICATIONS OF THE DECENTERING CONCEPT FOR THE STRUCTURING OF PROJECTIVE
          CONTENT.
          JOURNAL OF CONSULTING AND CLINICAL PSYCHOLOGY, 1968, 32, 434-441.
              (RELIABILITY:INTERRATER; VALIDITY:CONSTRUCT;
              CORRELATES:PSYCHOLOGICAL; 2 STUDIES: N=50 COLLEGE STUDENTS,
              70 COLLEGE STUDENTS)
       @APPLICATION 1968 F-76 M-20

2195   BERGER, C. R.
          SEX DIFFERENCES RELATED TO SELF-ESTEEM FACTOR STRUCTURE.
          JOURNAL OF CONSULTING AND CLINICAL PSYCHOLOGY, 1968, 32, 442-446.
              (MODIFICATION; VALIDITY:CONSTRUCT; CORRELATES:DEMOGRAPHIC; FACTOR
              ANALYSIS; 2 STUDIES: N=149 MALE, 149 FEMALE UNDERGRADUATES,
              196 MALE, 78 FEMALE UNDERGRADUATES)
       @APPLICATION 1968 J-7 E-53

2196   PALMER, R. D., & FIELD, P. B.
          VISUAL IMAGERY AND SUSCEPTIBILITY TO HYPNOSIS.
          JOURNAL OF CONSULTING AND CLINICAL PSYCHOLOGY, 1968, 32, 456-461.
              (MODIFICATION; VALIDITY:CONSTRUCT; CORRELATES:PSYCHOLOGICAL,
              DEMOGRAPHIC; N=43 COLLEGE MALES, 41 COLLEGE FEMALES)
       @APPLICATION 1968 W-31 F-87

2197   HEILBURN, A. B., JR.
            COUNSELING READINESS AND THE PROBLEM-SOLVING BEHAVIOR OF CLIENTS.
            JOURNAL OF CONSULTING AND CLINICAL PSYCHOLOGY, 1968, 32, 396-399,
                (CORRELATES:BEHAVIORAL, DEMOGRAPHIC; USED AS CRITERION; N=32 MALE
                AND 19 FEMALE PSYCHOLOGY CENTER CLIENTS)
        @APPLICATION 1968 G-21

2198   YULIS, S., & KIESLER, D. J.
            COUNTERTRANSFERENCE RESPONSE AS A FUNCTION OF THERAPIST ANXIETY AND
            CONTENT OF PATIENT TALK.
            JOURNAL OF CONSULTING AND CLINICAL PSYCHOLOGY, 1968, 32, 413-419.
                (RELIABILITY:INTERRATER; CORRELATES:PSYCHOLOGICAL; USED AS CRITERION;
                N=24 THERAPISTS)
        @APPLICATION 1968 G-6

2199   ZAX, M., COWEN, E. L., RAPPAPORT, J., BEACH, D. R., & LAIRD, J. D.
            FOLLOW-UP STUDY OF CHILDREN IDENTIFIED EARLY AS EMOTIONALLY DISTURBED.
            JOURNAL OF CONSULTING AND CLINICAL PSYCHOLOGY, 1968, 32, 369-374.
                (VALIDITY:CRITERION; CORRELATES:BEHAVIORAL, PSYCHOLOGICAL,
                INTELLIGENCE; N=43 NONDISTURBED, 23 DISTURBED, 36 DISTURBED AND 16
                NONDISTURBED CHILDREN)
        @APPLICATION 1968 C-55 C-159 B-144 B-145

2200   HEILBRUN, A. B., JR.
            COGNITIVE SENSITIVITY TO AVERSIVE MATERNAL STIMULATION IN LATE-ADOLESCENT
            MALES.
            JOURNAL OF CONSULTING AND CLINICAL PSYCHOLOGY, 1968, 32, 326-332.
                (CORRELATES:PSYCHOLOGICAL; USED AS CRITERION; NORMATIVE DATA; N=2
                CRITERION GROUPS OF 20 COLLEGE MALES FROM INITIAL POOL OF 100)
        @APPLICATION 1968 S-9 H-66 D-45 S-61

2201   SCHNEIDER, J. M.
            SKILL VERSUS CHANCE ACTIVITY PREFERENCE AND LOCUS OF CONTROL.
            JOURNAL OF CONSULTING AND CLINICAL PSYCHOLOGY, 1968, 32, 333-337.
                (VALIDITY:CONSTRUCT; CORRELATES:PSYCHOLOGICAL, DEMOGRAPHIC;
                NORMATIVE DATA; N=40 MALE, 43 FEMALE COLLEGE STUDENTS)
        @APPLICATION 1968 R-18

2202   CRAGO, M., & THARP, R. G.
            PSYCHOPATHOLOGY AND MARITAL ROLE DISTURBANCE: A TEST OF THE THARP-OTIS
            DESCRIPTIVE HYPOTHESIS.
            JOURNAL OF CONSULTING AND CLINICAL PSYCHOLOGY, 1968, 32, 338-341.
                (CORRELATES:PSYCHOLOGICAL, DEMOGRAPHIC; N=35 PSYCHIATRIC
                PATIENTS AND SPOUSES, 67 NORMAL SUBJECTS AND THEIR SPOUSES)
        @APPLICATION 1968 T-42

2203   PETZEL, T. P., & GYNTHER, M. D.
            TASK PERFORMANCE OF REPRESSORS AND SENSITIZERS UNDER EGO-ORIENTED VERSUS
            TASK-ORIENTED INSTRUCTIONS.
            JOURNAL OF CONSULTING AND CLINICAL PSYCHOLOGY, 1968, 32, 486-487.
                (CORRELATES:BEHAVIORAL; USED AS CRITERION; N=100 MALE COLLEGE
                STUDENTS)
        @APPLICATION 1968 B-46

2204   SCHOENINGER, D. W., KLEIN, M. H., & MATHIEU, P. L.
            COMPARISON OF TWO METHODS FOR TRAINING JUDGES TO RATE PSYCHOTHERAPY
            RECORDINGS.
            JOURNAL OF CONSULTING AND CLINICAL PSYCHOLOGY, 1968, 32, 499.
                (RELIABILITY:INTERRATER; N=8 JUDGES AND 32 THERAPY CLIENTS)
        @APPLICATION 1968 R-95

2205   KULIK, J. A., STEIN, K. B., & SARBIN, T. R.
            DISCLOSURE OF DELINQUENT BEHAVIOR UNDER CONDITIONS OF ANONYMITY AND
            NONANONYMITY.
            JOURNAL OF CONSULTING AND CLINICAL PSYCHOLOGY, 1968, 32, 506-509.
                (RELIABILITY:INTERNAL CONSISTENCY; VALIDITY:CRITERION;
                CORRELATES:BEHAVIORAL, PSYCHOLOGICAL, ENVIRONMENTAL; NORMATIVE DATA;
                N=245 MALE HIGH SCHOOL STUDENTS AND 137 INSTITUTIONALIZED
                DELINQUENTS)
        @APPLICATION 1968 K-49 K-50 G-22 K-115

2206   REHM, L. P., & MARSTON, A. R.
           REDUCTION OF SOCIAL ANXIETY THROUGH MODIFICATION OF SELF-REINFORCEMENT: AN
           INSTIGATION THERAPY TECHNIQUE.
           JOURNAL OF CONSULTING AND CLINICAL PSYCHOLOGY, 1968, 32, 565-574.
               (MODIFICATION; CORRELATES:PSYCHOLOGICAL; N=24 COLLEGE MALES)
       @APPLICATION 1968 T-2 G-21 W-37

2207   NEURINGER, C., & ORR, S. G.
           PREDICTION OF PATHOLOGY FROM MAKE-A-PICTURE STORY (MAPS) TEST FIGURES.
           JOURNAL OF CONSULTING AND CLINICAL PSYCHOLOGY, 1968, 32, 491-493.
               (VALIDITY:CRITERION; N=67 MAPS FIGURES, 4 CLINICAL JUDGES,
               24 NORMALS, 24 SCHIZOPHRENICS, 24 NEUROTIC MALES)
       @APPLICATION 1968 S-97

2208   RAPPAPORT, H., REZNIKOFF, M., GLUECK, B. C., JR., HONEYMAN, M. S., &
       EISENBERG, H.
           SMOKING BEHAVIOR IN OFFSPRING OF HEART DISEASE PATIENTS: A RESPONSE TO
           COGNITIVE DISSONANCE.
           JOURNAL OF CONSULTING AND CLINICAL PSYCHOLOGY, 1968, 32, 494-496.
               (CORRELATES:BEHAVIORAL: N=433 OFFSPRING OF HEART DISEASE PATIENTS
               AND 893 CONTROLS)
       @APPLICATION 1968 D-45

2209   SCHALON, C. L.
           EFFECT OF SELF-ESTEEM UPON PERFORMANCE FOLLOWING FAILURE STRESS.
           JOURNAL OF CONSULTING AND CLINICAL PSYCHOLOGY, 1968, 32, 497.
               (CORRELATES:PSYCHOLOGICAL, INTELLIGENCE; USED AS CRITERION; N=220
               MALE COLLEGE STUDENTS)
       @APPLICATION 1968 F-7

2210   KROGER, R. O.
           EFFECTS OF IMPLICIT AND EXPLICIT TASK CUES UPON PERSONALITY TEST
           PERFORMANCE.
           JOURNAL OF CONSULTING AND CLINICAL PSYCHOLOGY, 1968, 32, 498.
               (MODIFICATION; CORRELATES:ENVIRONMENTAL; N=64 MALE COLLEGE STUDENTS)
       @APPLICATION 1968 W-9 S-33

2211   BARNARD, P. G.
           INTERACTION EFFECTS AMONG CERTAIN EXPERIMENTER AND SUBJECT CHARACTERISTICS
           ON A PROJECTIVE TEST.
           JOURNAL OF CONSULTING AND CLINICAL PSYCHOLOGY, 1968, 32, 514-521.
               (RELIABILITY:INTERRATER; USED AS CRITERION; BIAS:TESTER; N=16 MALE
               UNDERGRADUATE EXPERIMENTERS AND 160 UNDERGRADUATE STUDENT SUBJECTS)
       @APPLICATION 1968 S-36 S-217 H-139

2212   DEVRIES, D. L.
           EFFECTS OF ENVIRONMENTAL CHANGE AND OF PARTICIPATION ON THE BEHAVIOR OF
           MENTAL PATIENTS.
           JOURNAL OF CONSULTING AND CLINICAL PSYCHOLOGY, 1968, 32, 532-536.
               (MODIFICATION; DESCRIPTION; RELIABILITY:INTERRATER;
               CORRELATES:ENVIRONMENTAL; N=390 MENTAL PATIENTS)
       @APPLICATION 1968 H-67

2213   GOLDSTEIN, G., NEURINGER, C., REIFF, C., & SHELLY, C. H.
           GENERALIZABILITY OF FIELD DEPENDENCY IN ALCOHOLICS.
           JOURNAL OF CONSULTING AND CLINICAL PSYCHOLOGY, 1968, 32, 560-564.
               (VALIDITY:CONSTRUCT; CORRELATES:PSYCHOLOGICAL, INTELLIGENCE; FACTOR
               ANALYSIS; NORMATIVE DATA; N=30 ALCOHOLIC PATIENTS)
       @APPLICATION 1968 E-2 D-45 C-27 B-7 C-23 W-72 G-40 L-35

2214   FREDE, M. C., GAUTNEY, D. B., & BAXTER, J. C.
           RELATIONSHIPS BETWEEN BODY IMAGE BOUNDARY AND INTERACTION PATTERNS ON THE
           MAPS TEST.
           JOURNAL OF CONSULTING AND CLINICAL PSYCHOLOGY, 1968, 32, 575-578.
               (CORRELATES:PSYCHOLOGICAL; N=32 MALE COLLEGE STUDENTS)
       @APPLICATION 1968 H-37 S-97

2215   POPE, B., & SIEGMAN, A. W.
           INTERVIEWER WARMTH IN RELATION TO INTERVIEWEE VERBAL BEHAVIOR.
           JOURNAL OF CONSULTING AND CLINICAL PSYCHOLOGY, 1968, 32, 588-595.
               (MODIFICATION; CORRELATES:BEHAVIORAL, ENVIRONMENTAL; N=32 JUNIOR AND
               SENIOR NURSING STUDENTS)
       @APPLICATION 1968 L-95 M-35

2216   EDWARDS, C. N.
            CULTURAL DISSONANCE AND DISSIMULATION: A STUDY IN ROLE CONFLICT.
            JOURNAL OF CONSULTING AND CLINICAL PSYCHOLOGY, 1968, 32, 607-610.
                (CORRELATES:PSYCHOLOGICAL; N=572 FEMALE NURSING AND TEACHING
                STUDENTS)
        @APPLICATION 1968 G-22

2217   HARMATZ, M. G.
            THE TEST-ANXIOUS SUBJECT IN THE ROLE OF A TEACHER: THE USE OF PUNISHMENT.
            JOURNAL OF CONSULTING AND CLINICAL PSYCHOLOGY, 1968, 32, 623-627.
                (CORRELATES:BEHAVIORAL; USED AS CRITERION; N=54 FEMALE COLLEGE
                STUDENTS)
        @APPLICATION 1968 S-5

2218   KISH, G. B., & BUSSE, W.
            CORRELATES OF STIMULUS-SEEKING: AGE, EDUCATION, INTELLIGENCE, AND
            APTITUDES.
            JOURNAL OF CONSULTING AND CLINICAL PSYCHOLOGY, 1968, 32, 633-637.
                (VALIDITY:CONSTRUCT; CORRELATES:PSYCHOLOGICAL, DEMOGRAPHIC,
                INTELLIGENCE; NORMATIVE DATA; 3 STUDIES: N=53 MALE ALCOHOLICS AND 98
                MALE HOSPITAL EMPLOYEES, 60 HOSPITALIZED ALCOHOLIC PATIENTS, 157
                COLLEGE MALES AND FEMALES)
        @APPLICATION 1968 Z-3

2219   VINGOE, F. J.
            ROGERS' SELF THEORY AND EYSENCK'S EXTRAVERSION AND NEUROTICISM.
            JOURNAL OF CONSULTING AND CLINICAL PSYCHOLOGY, 1968, 32, 618-620.
                (MODIFICATION; CORRELATES:PSYCHOLOGICAL; USED AS CRITERION; NORMATIVE
                DATA; N=66 FRESHMEN WOMEN)
        @APPLICATION 1968 G-22 E-6 S-161

2220   WOLFF, W. M.
            PERSONALITY PATTERNS OF PRIVATE CLIENTS.
            JOURNAL OF CONSULTING AND CLINICAL PSYCHOLOGY, 1968, 32, 621.
                (CORRELATES:DEMOGRAPHIC; N=416 TERMINATED PSYCHOTHERAPY CLIENTS)
        @APPLICATION 1968 D-45

2221   GALBRAITH, G. G.
            RELIABILITY OF FREE ASSOCIATIVE SEXUAL RESPONSES.
            JOURNAL OF CONSULTING AND CLINICAL PSYCHOLOGY, 1968, 32, 622.
                (RELIABILITY:RETEST, INTERNAL CONSISTENCY, INTERRATER; NORMATIVE
                DATA; SAMPLES OF N=30, 31, 41, 45, AND 65 COLLEGE MALES)
        @APPLICATION 1968 G-105

2222   THORNE, D. E., & BEIER, E. G.
            HYPNOTIST AND MANNER OF PRESENTATION EFFECTS ON A STANDARDIZED
            HYPNOTIC SUSCEPTIBILITY TEST.
            JOURNAL OF CONSULTING AND CLINICAL PSYCHOLOGY, 1968, 32, 610-612.
                (CORRELATES:ENVIRONMENTAL; BIAS:TESTER; N=111 MALES, 109 FEMALE
                COLLEGE STUDENTS)
        @APPLICATION 1968 S-90

2223   JACOB, T., & LEVINE, D.
            A-B DISTINCTION AND PREDICTION OF INTERVIEWEE SELF DESCRIPTIONS BASED ON A
            QUASI-THERAPEUTIC INTERACTION.
            JOURNAL OF CONSULTING AND CLINICAL PSYCHOLOGY, 1968, 32, 613-615.
                (CORRELATES:PSYCHOLOGICAL, ENVIRONMENTAL; USED AS CRITERION; N=250
                MALE UNDERGRADUATES)
        @APPLICATION 1968 W-91 R-75

2224   GYNTHER, M. D., & BRILLIANT, P. J.
            THE MMPI K PROFILE: A REEXAMINATION.
            JOURNAL OF CONSULTING AND CLINICAL PSYCHOLOGY, 1968, 32, 616-617.
                (CORRELATES:DEMOGRAPHIC, INTELLIGENCE; N=1155 PSYCHIATRIC PATIENT
                PROFILES)
        @APPLICATION 1968 D-45

2225   KENYON, F. E.
            STUDIES IN FEMALE HOMOSEXUALITY-PSYCHOLOGICAL TEST RESULTS.
            JOURNAL OF CONSULTING AND CLINICAL PSYCHOLOGY, 1968, 32, 510-513.
                (VALIDITY:CRITERION; CORRELATES:BEHAVIORAL, PSYCHOLOGICAL; NORMATIVE
                DATA; N=123 FEMALE HOMOSEXUALS, 123 CONTROLS)
        @APPLICATION 1968 B-127 E-5

2226   VAN ATTA, R. E.
            RELATIONSHIP OF PERSONALITY CHARACTERISTICS TO PERSISTANCE IN
            PSYCHOTHERAPY.
            JOURNAL OF CONSULTING AND CLINICAL PSYCHOLOGY, 1968, 32, 731-733.
                    (CORRELATES:BEHAVIORAL: NORMATIVE DATA; N=28 PAIRS OF SUBJECTS WITH
                    LONG AND SHORT TERM COUNSELING CASES)
            @APPLICATION 1968 E-2

2227   PAYNE, F. D., & WIGGINS, J. S.
            EFFECTS OF RULE RELAXATION AND SYSTEM COMBINATION ON CLASSIFICATION RATES
            IN TWO MMPI 'COOKBOOK' SYSTEMS.
            JOURNAL OF CONSULTING AND CLINICAL PSYCHOLOGY, 1968, 32, 734-736.
                    (NORMATIVE DATA; N=294 MALE, 247 FEMALE PSYCHIATRIC INPATIENTS)
            @APPLICATION 1968 D-45 M-255 G-203

2228   VINGOE, F. J.
            NOTE ON THE VALIDITY OF THE CALIFORNIA PSYCHOLOGICAL INVENTORY.
            JOURNAL OF CONSULTING AND CLINICAL PSYCHOLOGY, 1968, 32, 725-727.
                    (VALIDITY:CRITERION; CORRELATES:PSYCHOLOGICAL; N=66 FRESHMEN WOMEN)
            @APPLICATION 1968 G-22 E-6

2229   GALBRAITH, G. G.
            EFFECTS OF SEXUAL AROUSAL AND GUILT UPON FREE ASSOCIATIVE SEXUAL
            RESPONSES.
            JOURNAL OF CONSULTING AND CLINICAL PSYCHOLOGY, 1968, 32, 707-711.
                    (MODIFICATION; RELIABILITY:INTERRATER; CORRELATES:PSYCHOLOGICAL;
                    USED AS CRITERION; N=84 STUDENT MALES)
            @APPLICATION 1968 M-16 R-57

2230   HOLMES, D. S., & TYLER, J. D.
            DIRECT VERSUS PROJECTIVE MEASUREMENT OF ACHIEVEMENT MOTIVATION.
            JOURNAL OF CONSULTING AND CLINICAL PSYCHOLOGY, 1968, 32, 712-717.
                    (VALIDITY:CRITERION; CORRELATES:PSYCHOLOGICAL; N=72 MALE
                    UNDERGRADUATES)
            @APPLICATION 1968 M-7

2231   RIES, H. A.
            COMMONALITY OF WORD ASSOCIATIONS AND LENGTH OF HOSPITALIZATION IN
            NEUROTICS AND SCHIZOPHRENICS.
            JOURNAL OF CONSULTING AND CLINICAL PSYCHOLOGY, 1968, 32, 722-724.
                    (VALIDITY:CRITERION; CORRELATES:BEHAVIORAL; NORMATIVE DATA; N=240
                    NEWLY HOSPITALIZED MALE AND FEMALE NEUROTICS AND SCHIZOPHRENICS)
            @APPLICATION 1968 R-27

2232   MOSHER, D. L.
            MEASUREMENT OF GUILT IN FEMALES BY SELF-REPORT INVENTORIES.
            JOURNAL OF CONSULTING AND CLINICAL PSYCHOLOGY, 1968, 32, 690-695.
                    (VALIDITY:CONSTRUCT, CRITERION; FACTOR ANALYSIS; N=62 FEMALE
                    STUDENTS)
            @APPLICATION 1968 C-27 E-1 M-16

2233   ARMSTRONG, H. E., JR.
            RELATIONSHIP BETWEEN A DIMENSION OF BODY IMAGE AND TWO MEASURES OF
            CONDITIONING.
            JOURNAL OF CONSULTING AND CLINICAL PSYCHOLOGY, 1968, 32, 696-700.
                    (CORRELATES:PHYSIOLOGICAL; USED AS CRITERION; N=150 MALE
                    UNDERGRADUATE STUDENTS)
            @APPLICATION 1968 R-30 F-75

2234   ERICKSON, M. T.
            MMPI COMPARISONS BETWEEN PARENTS OF YOUNG EMOTIONALLY DISTURBED AND
            ORGANICALLY RETARDED CHILDREN.
            JOURNAL OF CONSULTING AND CLINICAL PSYCHOLOGY, 1968, 32, 701-706.
                    (CORRELATES:PSYCHOLOGICAL; NORMATIVE DATA; N = PARENTS OF 12
                    EMOTIONALLY DISTURBED CHILDREN AND 12 ORGANICALLY RETARDED
                    CHILDREN)
            @APPLICATION 1968 D-45

2235   TUDDENHAM, R. D., BLUMENKRANTZ, J., & WILKIN, W. R.
            AGE CHANGES ON AGCT: A LONGITUDINAL STUDY OF AVERAGE ADULTS.
            JOURNAL OF CONSULTING AND CLINICAL PSYCHOLOGY, 1968, 32, 659-663.
                    (CORRELATES:DEMOGRAPHIC, INTELLIGENCE; N=164 MEN ENTERING AND
                    RETIRING FROM THE ARMY)
            @APPLICATION 1968 B-127

2236   JONES, S. C., & SHRAUGER, J. S.
            LOCUS OF CONTROL AND INTERPERSONAL EVALUATION.
            JOURNAL OF CONSULTING AND CLINICAL PSYCHOLOGY, 1968, 32, 664-668.
                (CORRELATES:BEHAVIORAL, PSYCHOLOGICAL, ENVIRONMENTAL; USED AS
                CRITERION; N=21 MALE AND 21 FEMALE UNDERGRADUATE STUDENTS)
        @APPLICATION 1968 R-18 C-71

2237   DUNN, J. A.
            ANXIETY, STRESS, AND THE PERFORMANCE OF COMPLEX INTELLECTUAL TASKS: A NEW
            LOOK AT AN OLD QUESTION.
            JOURNAL OF CONSULTING AND CLINICAL PSYCHOLOGY, 1968, 32, 669-673.
                (CORRELATES:INTELLIGENCE, ENVIRONMENTAL; NORMATIVE DATA; N=176
                COLLEGE MALES AND FEMALES)
        @APPLICATION 1968 M-234

2238   LEVINE, F. J.
            COLOR-WORD TEST PERFORMANCE AND DRIVE REGULATION IN THREE VOCATIONAL
            GROUPS.
            JOURNAL OF CONSULTING AND CLINICAL PSYCHOLOGY, 1968, 32, 642-647.
                (RELIABILITY:INTERRATER; CORRELATES:PSYCHOLOGICAL; USED AS
                CRITERION; NORMATIVE DATA; N=76 UNIVERSITY MALES AND 26
                MATHEMATICIANS, 25 MEDICAL STUDENTS AND 24 CREATIVE WRITERS)
        @APPLICATION 1968 S-61 M-20 P-28 D-68 K-113 K-114

2239   MORDKOFF, A. M., & RAND, M. A.
            PERSONALITY AND ADAPTATION TO CORONARY ARTERY DISEASE.
            JOURNAL OF CONSULTING AND CLINICAL PSYCHOLOGY, 1968, 32, 648-653.
                (CORRELATES:PSYCHOLOGICAL; NORMATIVE DATA; N=31 CORONARY DISEASE
                PATIENTS, 31 CONTROLS)
        @APPLICATION 1968 D-45 H-37 C-16 S-61 L-45 S-171 W-8 W-41 B-5 G-139 Z-38

2240   JOHNSON, D. T.
            TRAIT ANXIETY, STATE ANXIETY, AND THE ESTIMATION OF ELAPSED TIME.
            JOURNAL OF CONSULTING AND CLINICAL PSYCHOLOGY, 1968, 32, 654-658.
                (CORRELATES:PSYCHOLOGICAL, PHYSIOLOGICAL; N=46 MALE HOSPITALIZED
                PSYCHIATRIC PATIENTS)
        @APPLICATION 1968 Z-13 T-2

2241   CATTELL, R. B., & BOLTON, L. S.
            WHAT PATHOLOGICAL DIMENSIONS LIE BEYOND THE NORMAL DIMENSIONS OF THE 16PF?
            A COMPARISON OF MMPI AND 16PF FACTOR DOMAINS.
            JOURNAL OF CONSULTING AND CLINICAL PSYCHOLOGY, 1969, 33, 18-29.
                (VALIDITY:CRITERION; CORRELATES:PSYCHOLOGICAL; FACTOR ANALYSIS; N=217
                NORMAL, 40 ABNORMAL ADULT AIR FORCE MEN)
        @APPLICATION 1969 C-10 D-45

2242   VELDMAN, D. J., & BOWN, O. H.
            PERSONALITY AND PERFORMANCE CHARACTERISTICS ASSOCIATED WITH
            CIGARETTE-SMOKING AMONG COLLEGE FRESHMEN.
            JOURNAL OF CONSULTING AND CLINICAL PSYCHOLOGY, 1969, 33, 109-119.
                (DESCRIPTION; CORRELATES:BEHAVIORAL, PSYCHOLOGICAL, DEMOGRAPHIC;
                N=401 SMOKING COLLEGE STUDENTS, 401 NON-SMOKERS)
        @APPLICATION 1969 B-30 V-28

2243   WATSON, C. G., & LOGUE, P. E.
            INTERRELATIONSHIPS OF SEVERAL PROCESS-REACTIVE MEASURES.
            JOURNAL OF CONSULTING AND CLINICAL PSYCHOLOGY, 1969, 33, 120-122.
                (CORRELATES:PSYCHOLOGICAL; FACTOR ANALYSIS; N=94 SCHIZOPHRENIC
                PATIENTS)
        @APPLICATION 1969 B-5 P-32 B-82 U-5

2244   EFRAN, J. S., & KORN, P. R.
            MEASUREMENT OF SOCIAL CAUTION: SELF-APPRAISAL, ROLE PLAYING, AND
            DISCUSSION BEHAVIOR.
            JOURNAL OF CONSULTING AND CLINICAL PSYCHOLOGY, 1969, 33, 78-83.
                (CORRELATES:BEHAVIORAL, PSYCHOLOGICAL; N=99 COLLEGE MALES)
        @APPLICATION 1969 W-16

2245   ZILLER, R. C., HAGEY, J., SMITH, M. D. C., & LONG, B. H.
            SELF-ESTEEM: A SELF-SOCIAL CONSTRUCT.
            JOURNAL OF CONSULTING AND CLINICAL PSYCHOLOGY, 1969, 33, 84-95.
                (REVIEW ARTICLE; VALIDITY:CONSTRUCT; CORRELATES:PSYCHOLOGICAL,
                DEMOGRAPHIC; N=33 MALES AND 53 FEMALES)
        @APPLICATION 1969 C-38 B-18 D-69

2246   LEFCOURT, H. M.
            NEED FOR APPROVAL AND THREATENED NEGATIVE EVALUATION AS DETERMINANTS OF
            EXPRESSIVENESS IN A PROJECTIVE TEST.
            JOURNAL OF CONSULTING AND CLINICAL PSYCHOLOGY, 1969, 33, 96-102.
                (RELIABILITY:INTERRATER; CORRELATES:PSYCHOLOGICAL; USED AS
                CRITERION; NORMATIVE DATA; N=71 CANADIAN COLLEGE MALES, 62 COLLEGE
                FEMALES)
            @APPLICATION 1969 C-27 B-46 B-162 G-22

2247   HERSCH, P. D., KULIK, J. A., & SCHEIBE, K. E.
            PERSONAL CHARACTERISTICS OF COLLEGE VOLUNTEERS IN MENTAL HOSPITALS.
            JOURNAL OF CONSULTING AND CLINICAL PSYCHOLOGY, 1969, 33, 30-34.
                (CORRELATES:BEHAVIORAL, DEMOGRAPHIC; NORMATIVE DATA; N=41 MALE AND
                110 FEMALE COLLEGE HOSPITAL VOLUNTEERS, 66 FEMALE, 76 MALE
                COLLEGE STUDENT CONTROLS)
            @APPLICATION 1969 G-22 G-21 R-18 C-27 S-33

2248   TULKIN, S. R., MULLER, J. P., & CONN, L. K.
            NEED FOR APPROVAL AND POPULARITY: SEX DIFFERENCES IN ELEMENTARY SCHOOL
            STUDENTS.
            JOURNAL OF CONSULTING AND CLINICAL PSYCHOLOGY, 1969, 33, 35-39.
                (CORRELATES:PSYCHOLOGICAL, DEMOGRAPHIC, INTELLIGENCE; NORMATIVE DATA;
                N=192 ELEMENTARY SCHOOL CHILDREN)
            @APPLICATION 1969 C-42

2249   MURRAY, E. J., SEAGULL, A., & GEISINGER, D.
            MOTIVATIONAL PATTERNS IN THE FAMILIES OF ADJUSTED AND MALADJUSTED BOYS.
            JOURNAL OF CONSULTING AND CLINICAL PSYCHOLOGY, 1969, 33, 337-342.
                (RELIABILITY:INTERRATER; CORRELATES:PSYCHOLOGICAL, DEMOGRAPHIC;
                N=20 FAMILIES WITH A MALADJUSTED BOY AND 20 MATCHED FAMILIES WITH
                ADJUSTED BOY)
            @APPLICATION 1969 H-22 T-20 M-235 P-129

2250   BUSH, M., HATCHER, R., & MAYMAN, M.
            REALITY ATTENTIVENESS-INATTENTIVENESS AND EXTERNALIZATION-INTERNALIZATION
            IN DEFENSE STYLE.
            JOURNAL OF CONSULTING AND CLINICAL PSYCHOLOGY, 1969, 33, 343-350.
                (DESCRIPTION: RELIABILITY:INTERNAL CONSISTENCY;
                CORRELATES:BEHAVIORAL, PSYCHOLOGICAL; N=83 FEMALE COLLEGE
                STUDENTS)
            @APPLICATION 1969 B-189

2251   FOX, E., & BLATT, S. J.
            AN ATTEMPT TO TEST ASSUMPTIONS ABOUT SOME INDICATIONS OF NEGATIVISM ON
            PSYCHOLOGICAL TESTS.
            JOURNAL OF CONSULTING AND CLINICAL PSYCHOLOGY, 1969, 33, 365-366.
                (CORRELATES:PSYCHOLOGICAL, INTELLIGENCE: N=21 MALE, 21 FEMALE
                SUBJECTS)
            @APPLICATION 1969 R-30

2252   HOFFNUNG, R. J.
            CONDITIONING AND TRANSFER OF AFFECTIVE SELF-REFERENCES IN A ROLE-PLAYED
            COUNSELING INTERVIEW.
            JOURNAL OF CONSULTING AND CLINICAL PSYCHOLOGY, 1969, 33, 527-531.
                (CORRELATES:BEHAVIORAL, PSYCHOLOGICAL; N=72 FEMALE STUDENTS)
            @APPLICATION 1969 M-20

2253   DOMINO, G.
            MATERNAL PERSONALITY CORRELATES OF SONS' CREATIVITY.
            JOURNAL OF CONSULTING AND CLINICAL PSYCHOLOGY, 1969, 33, 180-183.
                (CORRELATES:PSYCHOLOGICAL, ENVIRONMENTAL; USED AS CRITERION;
                NORMATIVE DATA; N=76 COLLEGE MALES AND 64 MOTHERS)
            @APPLICATION 1969 M-29 G-22 W-118

2254   THELEN, M. H.
            REPRESSION-SENSITIZATION: ITS RELATION TO ADJUSTMENT AND SEEKING
            PSYCHOTHERAPY AMONG COLLEGE STUDENTS.
            JOURNAL OF CONSULTING AND CLINICAL PSYCHOLOGY, 1969, 33, 161-165.
                (CORRELATES:PSYCHOLOGICAL; NORMATIVE DATA; N=63 THERAPY-SEEKING
                COLLEGE MALES AND FEMALES, 112 NON-THERAPY SEEKING COLLEGE MALES AND
                FEMALES)
            @APPLICATION 1969 B-46 G-22

2255   MASLING, J., & HARRIS, S.
             SEXUAL ASPECTS OF TAT ADMINISTRATION.
             JOURNAL OF CONSULTING AND CLINICAL PSYCHOLOGY, 1969, 33, 166-169.
                 (BIAS:TESTER; N=20 MALE AND 6 FEMALE GRADUATE STUDENT EXAMINERS)
         @APPLICATION 1969 M-20

2256   PETTIT, T. F.
             ANALITY AND TIME.
             JOURNAL OF CONSULTING AND CLINICAL PSYCHOLOGY, 1969, 33, 170-174.
                 (MODIFICATION; RELIABILITY:INTERNAL CONSISTENCY;
                 CORRELATES:PSYCHOLOGICAL; N=91 COLLEGE MALES AND FEMALES)
         @APPLICATION 1969 G-43

2257   WANDERER, Z. W.
             VALIDITY OF CLINICAL JUDGMENTS BASED ON HUMAN FIGURE DRAWINGS.
             JOURNAL OF CONSULTING AND CLINICAL PSYCHOLOGY, 1969, 33, 143-150.
                 (VALIDITY:CRITERION; N=20 JUDGES, 25 DIAGNOSED PSYCHIATRIC CASES
                 AND NORMALS)
         @APPLICATION 1969 M-58

2258   HAMMER, E. F.
             DAP: BACK AGAINST THE WALL?
             JOURNAL OF CONSULTING AND CLINICAL PSYCHOLOGY, 1969, 33, 151-156.
                 (MENTION; REVIEW ARTICLE; VALIDITY:CRITERION)
         @APPLICATION 1969 M-58

2259   EISENMANN, R.
             CREATIVITY, AWARENESS, AND LIKING.
             JOURNAL OF CONSULTING AND CLINICAL PSYCHOLOGY, 1969, 33, 157-160.
                 (VALIDITY:CONSTRUCT; CORRELATES:PSYCHOLOGICAL; N=302 COLLEGE
                 STUDENTS)
         @APPLICATION 1969 B-76

2260   HSIEH, T. T., SHYBUT, J., & LOFSOF, E. J.
             INTERNAL VERSUS EXTERNAL CONTROL AND ETHNIC GROUP MEMBERSHIP: A CROSS-
             CULTURAL COMPARISON.
             JOURNAL OF CONSULTING AND CLINICAL PSYCHOLOGY, 1969, 33, 122-124.
                 (MODIFICATION; RELIABILITY:RETEST; CORRELATES:DEMOGRAPHIC;
                 CROSS-CULTURAL APPLICATION; NORMATIVE DATA; N=343 CHINESE, 239
                 ANGLO-AMERICANS, 80 AMERICAN BORN CHINESE)
         @APPLICATION 1969 R-18

2261   KLEIN, E. B., GOULD, L. J., & COREY, M.
             SOCIAL DESIRABILITY IN CHILDREN: AN EXTENSION AND REPLICATION.
             JOURNAL OF CONSULTING AND CLINICAL PSYCHOLOGY, 1969, 33, 128.
                 (MODIFICATION; VALIDITY:CONSTRUCT; CORRELATES:DEMOGRAPHIC; N=1008
                 CHILDREN, AGED 7 TO 14)
         @APPLICATION 1969 C-42

2262   EVANS, R. B.
             CHILDHOOD PARENTAL RELATIONSHIPS OF HOMOSEXUAL MEN.
             JOURNAL OF CONSULTING AND CLINICAL PSYCHOLOGY, 1969, 33, 129-135.
                 (MODIFICATION; VALIDITY:CRITERION; NORMATIVE DATA; N=43 HOMOSEXUAL
                 AND 142 HETEROSEXUAL ADULT MALES)
         @APPLICATION 1969 B-193

2263   MAGARO, P. A., & HANSON, B. A.
             PERCEIVED MATERNAL NURTURANCE AND CONTROL OF PROCESS SCHIZOPHRENICS,
             REACTIVE SCHIZOPHRENICS, AND NORMALS.
             JOURNAL OF CONSULTING AND CLINICAL PSYCHOLOGY, 1969, 33, 507.
                 (CORRELATES:PSYCHOLOGICAL; USED AS CRITERION; N=198 COLLEGE MALES,
                 66 SCHIZOPHRENIC PATIENTS)
         @APPLICATION 1969 P-32 S-9 H-66

2264   MORRIS, L. W., & LIEBERT, R. M.
             EFFECTS OF ANXIETY ON TIMED AND UNTIMED INTELLIGENCE TESTS.
             JOURNAL OF CONSULTING AND CLINICAL PSYCHOLOGY, 1969, 33, 240-244.
                 (MODIFICATION; CORRELATES:INTELLIGENCE; USED AS CRITERION; N=48
                 COLLEGE STUDENTS)
         @APPLICATION 1969 T-2

2265   NEALE, J. M., & CROMWELL, R. L.
            PREFERENCE FOR COMPLEXITY IN ACUTE SCHIZOPHRENICS.
            JOURNAL OF CONSULTING AND CLINICAL PSYCHOLOGY, 1969, 33, 245-246.
                (CORRELATES:PSYCHOLOGICAL; USED AS CRITERION; N=38 SCHIZOPHRENIC
                PATIENTS)
        @APPLICATION 1969 P-32

2266   FONTANA, A. F., & GESSNER, T.
            PATIENTS' GOALS AND THE MANIFESTATION OF PSYCHOPATHOLOGY.
            JOURNAL OF CONSULTING AND CLINICAL PSYCHOLOGY, 1969, 33, 247-253.
                (RELIABILITY:INTERNAL CONSISTENCY; CORRELATES:PSYCHOLOGICAL;
                USED AS CRITERION; NORMATIVE DATA; N=75 MALE PSYCHIATRIC PATIENTS)
        @APPLICATION 1969 R-18 D-45 A-32 F-43

2267   STREISSGUTH, A. P., WAGNER, N. N., & WECHSLER, J. C.
            EFFECTS OF SEX, ILLNESS, AND HOSPITALIZATION ON DAYDREAMING.
            JOURNAL OF CONSULTING AND CLINICAL PSYCHOLOGY, 1969, 33, 218-225.
                (CORRELATES:PSYCHOLOGICAL, DEMOGRAPHIC; NORMATIVE DATA; N=200 MALE
                AND FEMALE PSYCHIATRIC IN- AND OUTPATIENTS, MEDICAL PATIENTS AND
                CONTROLS)
        @APPLICATION 1969 S-83

2268   ASHEM, B. A.
            USE OF SPEECH IN THE INHIBITORY CONTROL OF MOTORIC BEHAVIOR OF
            SCHIZOPHRENIC PATIENTS.
            JOURNAL OF CONSULTING AND CLINICAL PSYCHOLOGY, 1969, 33, 226-234.
                (CORRELATES:BEHAVIORAL, PSYCHOLOGICAL; USED AS CRITERION; N=48
                SCHIZOPHRENICS, 48 CONTROLS)
        @APPLICATION 1969 U-5 P-45

2269   HARROW, M., FOX, D. A., & DETRE, T.
            SELF-CONCEPT OF THE MARRIED PSYCHIATRIC PATIENT AND HIS MATE'S
            PERCEPTION OF HIM.
            JOURNAL OF CONSULTING AND CLINICAL PSYCHOLOGY, 1969, 33, 235-239.
                (MODIFICATION; VALIDITY:CRITERION; NORMATIVE DATA; N=26 PSYCHIATRIC
                PATIENTS AND SPOUSES)
        @APPLICATION 1969 B-60

2270   VESTRE, N. D., & ZIMMERMAN, R.
            VALIDITY OF INFORMANTS' RATINGS OF THE BEHAVIOR AND SYMPTOMS OF PSYCHIATRIC
            PATIENTS.
            JOURNAL OF CONSULTING AND CLINICAL PSYCHOLOGY, 1969, 33, 175-179.
                (DESCRIPTION; VALIDITY:CRITERION; CORRELATES:PSYCHOLOGICAL; FACTOR
                ANALYSIS; N=159 PSYCHIATRIC PATIENTS)
        @APPLICATION 1969 L-70 K-58

2271   HALVERSON, C. F., JR., & SHORE, R. E.
            SELF-DISCLOSURE AND INTERPERSONAL FUNCTIONING.
            JOURNAL OF CONSULTING AND CLINICAL PSYCHOLOGY, 1969, 33, 213-217.
                (VALIDITY:CONSTRUCT; CORRELATES:PSYCHOLOGICAL, INTELLIGENCE; N=53
                PEACE CORPS TRAINEES)
        @APPLICATION 1969 J-15 S-41 T-76 S-130

2272   CANCRO, R.
            ABSTRACTION ON PROVERBS IN PROCESS-REACTIVE SCHIZOPHRENIA.
            JOURNAL OF CONSULTING AND CLINICAL PSYCHOLOGY, 1969, 33, 267-270.
                (CORRELATES:PSYCHOLOGICAL, DEMOGRAPHIC, INTELLIGENCE; USED AS
                CRITERION; N=51 MALE SCHIZOPHRENIC PATIENTS)
        @APPLICATION 1969 B-94 P-32

2273   CROSS, H. J.
            COLLEGE STUDENTS' MEMORIES OF THEIR PARENTS: A FACTOR ANALYSIS OF THE
            CRPBI.
            JOURNAL OF CONSULTING AND CLINICAL PSYCHOLOGY, 1969, 33, 275-278.
                (MODIFICATION; FACTOR ANALYSIS; N=119 FEMALE AND 99 MALE COLLEGE
                STUDENTS)
        @APPLICATION 1969 S-3

2274   LEFF, S., & LAMB, N.
         EXPERIMENTAL APPROACH TO DEFINING THE ROLE OF SOCIAL DESIRABILITY IN
         PERSONALITY ASSESSMENT: IS THERE ONE RESPONSE PROCESS OR TWO?
         JOURNAL OF CONSULTING AND CLINICAL PSYCHOLOGY, 1969, 33, 287-291.
             (VALIDITY:CONSTRUCT; CORRELATES:PSYCHOLOGICAL, ENVIRONMENTAL;
             BIAS:RESPONSE; N=60 WHITE MALE UNDERGRADUATES)
         @APPLICATION 1969 C-27 L-35

2275   HOLMES, D. S.
         SENSING HUMOR: LATENCY AND AMPLITUDE OF RESPONSE RELATED TO MMPI PROFILES.
         JOURNAL OF CONSULTING AND CLINICAL PSYCHOLOGY, 1969, 33, 296-301.
             (CORRELATES:PSYCHOLOGICAL; USED AS CRITERION; N=48 MALE PSYCHIATRIC
             TECHNICIANS)
         @APPLICATION 1969 D-45 T-2 S-124

2276   WILSON, G. D., & PATTERSON, J. R.
         CONSERVATISM AS A PREDICTOR OF HUMOR PREFERENCES.
         JOURNAL OF CONSULTING AND CLINICAL PSYCHOLOGY, 1969, 33, 271-274.
             (CORRELATES:PSYCHOLOGICAL; USED AS CRITERION; N=75 FEMALE, 64 MALE
             HIGH SCHOOL STUDENTS)
         @APPLICATION 1969 W-87 E-6

2277   HOCKING, J., & ROBERTSON, M.
         SENSATION SEEKING SCALE AS A PREDICTOR OF NEED FOR STIMULATION DURING
         SENSORY RESTRICTION.
         JOURNAL OF CONSULTING AND CLINICAL PSYCHOLOGY, 1969, 33, 367-369.
             (CORRELATES:PSYCHOLOGICAL; USED AS CRITERION; N=214 MALE
             UNDERGRADUATES, 30 SELECTED)
         @APPLICATION 1969 Z-3

2278   SMITH, J. J.
         PSYCHIATRIC HOSPITAL EXPERIENCE AND ATTITUDES TOWARD "MENTAL ILLNESS".
         JOURNAL OF CONSULTING AND CLINICAL PSYCHOLOGY, 1969, 33, 302-306.
             (CORRELATES:ENVIRONMENTAL; USED AS CRITERION; NORMATIVE DATA; N=129
             SUBJECTS WITH PSYCHIATRIC HOSPITAL EXPERIENCE AND 103 CONTROL
             SUBJECTS)
         @APPLICATION 1969 C-69

2279   MISKIMINS, R. W., & WILSON, L. T.
         REVISED SUICIDE POTENTIAL SCALE.
         JOURNAL OF CONSULTING AND CLINICAL PSYCHOLOGY, 1969, 33, 258.
             (DESCRIPTION; REVISION; VALIDITY:CRITERION; N=15 SUICIDES, 30
             CONTROLS)
         @APPLICATION 1969 M-155 M-233

2280   DOSTER, J. A., & STRICKLAND, B. R.
         PERCEIVED CHILD-REARING PRACTICES AND SELF-DISCLOSURE PATTERNS.
         JOURNAL OF CONSULTING AND CLINICAL PSYCHOLOGY, 1969, 33, 382.
             (CORRELATES:PSYCHOLOGICAL, DEMOGRAPHIC; N=110 PARENTS AND 80
             COLLEGE STUDENTS)
         @APPLICATION 1969 C-27 H-66 J-15

2281   ARBUTHNOT, J., & GRUENFELD, L.
         FIELD INDEPENDENCE AND EDUCATIONAL-VOCATIONAL INTERESTS.
         JOURNAL OF CONSULTING AND CLINICAL PSYCHOLOGY, 1969, 33, 631.
             (VALIDITY:CONSTRUCT; CORRELATES:PSYCHOLOGICAL, INTELLIGENCE; N=55
             MALE FRESHMAN)
         @APPLICATION 1969 W-19 G-26 F-21 W-188

2282   MACDONALD, A. P., JR., & HALL, J.
         PERCEPTION OF DISABILITY BY THE NONDISABLED.
         JOURNAL OF CONSULTING AND CLINICAL PSYCHOLOGY, 1969, 33, 654-660.
             (CORRELATES:PSYCHOLOGICAL; N=30 MALE, 20 FEMALE GRADUATE STUDENTS)
         @APPLICATION 1969 R-18

2283   SPIEGEL, D.
         SPI DISCRIMINATION AMONG 4 PSYCHOLOGICAL HEALTH-SICKNESS LEVELS.
         JOURNAL OF CONSULTING AND CLINICAL PSYCHOLOGY, 1969, 33, 750-756.
             (DESCRIPTION; VALIDITY:CRITERION; USED AS CRITERION; NORMATIVE DATA;
             N=87 HOSPITALIZED PSYCHIATRIC PATIENTS AND 145 NORMAL ADULTS)
         @APPLICATION 1969 D-45 S-111

2284   SMITH, G. M.
         RELATIONS BETWEEN PERSONALITY AND SMOKING BEHAVIOR IN PREADULT SUBJECTS.
         JOURNAL OF CONSULTING AND CLINICAL PSYCHOLOGY, 1969, 33, 710-715.
              (VALIDITY:CROSS-VALIDATION; CORRELATES:BEHAVIORAL; FACTOR ANALYSIS;
              N=562 HIGH AND JUNIOR HIGH SCHOOL STUDENTS)
         @APPLICATION 1969 S-212

2285   VESPRANI, G. J.
         PERSONALITY CORRELATES OF ACCURATE EMPATHY IN A COLLEGE COMPANION PROGRAM.
         JOURNAL OF CONSULTING AND CLINICAL PSYCHOLOGY, 1969, 33, 722-727.
              (VALIDITY:CROSS-VALIDATION; CORRELATES:PSYCHOLOGICAL; NORMATIVE DATA;
              N=33 FEMALE COLLEGE STUDENTS)
         @APPLICATION 1969 E-2 D-45 T-24

2286   DUBLIN, J. E., ELTON, C. F., & BERZINS, J. I.
         SOME PERSONALITY AND APTITUDINAL CORRELATES OF THE "A-B" THERAPIST SCALE.
         JOURNAL OF CONSULTING AND CLINICAL PSYCHOLOGY, 1969, 33, 739-735.
              (CORRELATES:PSYCHOLOGICAL, DEMOGRAPHIC, INTELLIGENCE; FACTOR
              ANALYSIS; NORMATIVE DATA; N= OVER 2400 MALE AND FEMALE STUDENTS)
         @APPLICATION 1969 W-91 H-12

2287   MOSHER, D. L., & GREENBERG, I.
         FEMALES' AFFECTIVE RESPONSES TO READING EROTIC LITERATURE.
         JOURNAL OF CONSULTING AND CLINICAL PSYCHOLOGY, 1969, 33, 472-477.
              (RELIABILITY:INTERNAL CONSISTENCY; CORRELATES:PSYCHOLOGICAL,
              ENVIRONMENTAL; N=72 FEMALE STUDENTS)
         @APPLICATION 1969 M-86 N-17 C-27 E-1

2288   WILLIAMS, C. B., & NICKELS, J. B
         INTERNAL-EXTERNAL CONTROL DIMENSION AS RELATED TO ACCIDENT AND SUICIDE
         PRONENESS.
         JOURNAL OF CONSULTING AND CLINICAL PSYCHOLOGY, 1969, 33, 485-494.
              (CORRELATES:PSYCHOLOGICAL, DEMOGRAPHIC; NORMATIVE DATA; N=114
              COLLEGE MALES, 121 COLLEGE FEMALES)
         @APPLICATION 1969 R-18 D-15 F-137

2289   GRANLUND, E., & KNOWLES, L.
         CHILD-PARENT IDENTIFICATION AND ACADEMIC UNDERACHIEVEMENT.
         JOURNAL OF CONSULTING AND CLINICAL PSYCHOLOGY, 1969, 33, 495-496.
              (CORRELATES:PSYCHOLOGICAL, INTELLIGENCE; N=48 MALE CHILDREN)
         @APPLICATION 1969 B-281

2290   SMITH, R. E.
         BRIEF REPORTS: MOTIVATIONAL PROPERTIES OF PERSONALITY CONFLICT.
         JOURNAL OF CONSULTING AND CLINICAL PSYCHOLOGY, 1969, 33, 506.
              (CORRELATES:PSYCHOLOGICAL; USED AS CRITERION; NORMATIVE DATA;
              N=28 MALE COLLEGE STUDENTS SELECTED)
         @APPLICATION 1969 M-7 H-137

2291   KRESTRICK, J. L., & GORLOW, L.
         EFFECT OF INFORMATION, SUBJECT AGE, AND INSTRUCTIONAL SET ON PREDICTIVE
         JUDGMENTS.
         JOURNAL OF CONSULTING AND CLINICAL PSYCHOLOGY, 1969, 33, 691-698.
              (USED AS CRITERION; N=120 MALE STUDENT JUDGES, 2 SUBJECTS)
         @APPLICATION 1969 S-213

2292   CARLSON, R.
         RORSCHACH PREDICTION OF SUCCESS IN CLINICAL TRAINING: A SECOND LOOK.
         JOURNAL OF CONSULTING AND CLINICAL PSYCHOLOGY, 1969, 33, 699-704.
              (VALIDITY:CRITERION; N=155 CLINICAL PSYCHOLOGY TRAINEES)
         @APPLICATION 1969 R-30 S-33

2293   FAZIO, A. F.
         VERBAL AND OVERT-BEHAVIORAL ASSESSMENT OF A SPECIFIC FEAR.
         JOURNAL OF CONSULTING AND CLINICAL PSYCHOLOGY, 1969, 33, 705-709.
              (CORRELATES:BEHAVIORAL, ENVIRONMENTAL; N=56 FEMALE, 14 MALE COLLEGE
              STUDENTS)
         @APPLICATION 1969 W-37

2294 TAYLOR, D. A., ALTMAN, I., WHEELER, L., & KUSHNER, E. N.
PERSONALITY FACTORS RELATED TO RESPONSE TO SOCIAL ISOLATION AND
CONFINEMENT.
JOURNAL OF CONSULTING AND CLINICAL PSYCHOLOGY, 1969, 33, 411-419.
(CORRELATES:PSYCHOLOGICAL, ENVIRONMENTAL; NORMATIVE DATA; N= APPROX.
160 NAVAL TRAINEES)
aAPPLICATION 1969 D-45 H-37 E-2 L-22

2295 EISENTHAL, S., & SHERMAN, L. J.
PSYCHOLOGICAL CHARACTERISTICS OF NEIGHBORHOOD YOUTH CORPS ENROLLEES.
JOURNAL OF CONSULTING AND CLINICAL PSYCHOLOGY, 1969, 33, 420-424.
(DESCRIPTION; CORRELATES:DEMOGRAPHIC; NORMATIVE DATA; N=111 MALE,
150 FEMALE NEIGHBORHOOD YOUTH CORPS ENROLLEES)
aAPPLICATION 1969 G-22

2296 HODGES, W. F., & SPIELBERGER, C. D.
DIGIT SPAN: AN INDICANT OF TRAIT OR STATE ANXIETY?
JOURNAL OF CONSULTING AND CLINICAL PSYCHOLOGY, 1969, 33, 430-434.
(CORRELATES:INTELLIGENCE; ENVIRONMENTAL; N=72 COLLEGE MALES)
aAPPLICATION 1969 T-2 Z-13

2297 TRAUX, C. B., & WARGO, D. G.
EFFECTS OF VICARIOUS THERAPY PRETRAINING AND ALTERNATE SESSIONS ON
OUTCOME IN GROUP PSYCHOTHERAPY WITH OUTPATIENTS.
JOURNAL OF CONSULTING AND CLINICAL PSYCHOLOGY, 1969, 33, 440-447.
(CORRELATES:PSYCHOLOGICAL; N=80 PATIENTS IN PSYCHOTHERAPY)
aAPPLICATION 1969 T-37 D-45 B-5 W-8 E-1 F-45 B-60 W-57 T-38

2298 VAN DE MARK, S. N., & NEURINGER, C.
EFFECT OF PHYSICAL AND COGNITIVE SOMATIC AROUSAL ON RORSCHACH RESPONSES:
AN EXPERIMENT TEST OF THE ASSUMPTION THAT BODY IMAGE INFLUENCES THE
PERCEPTUAL ORGANIZATION OF UNSTRUCTURED STIMULI.
JOURNAL OF CONSULTING AND CLINICAL PSYCHOLOGY, 1969, 33, 458-465.
(RELIABILITY:INTERRATER; CORRELATES:PSYCHOLOGICAL, PHYSIOLOGICAL;
NORMATIVE DATA; 2 SAMPLES: N=48 COLLEGE STUDENTS, N=120 COLLEGE
STUDENTS)
aAPPLICATION 1969 F-75 R-30 S-93 F-33 F-135

2299 RAVENSBORG, M. R., & FOSS, A.
SUICIDE AND NATURAL DEATH IN A STATE HOSPITAL POPULATION: A COMPARISON OF
ADMISSION COMPLAINTS, MMPI PROFILE AND SOCIAL COMPETENCE FACTORS.
JOURNAL OF CONSULTING AND CLINICAL PSYCHOLOGY, 1969, 33, 466-471.
(DESCRIPTION; CORRELATES:BEHAVIORAL, DEMOGRAPHIC; N=23 SUICIDES, 23
PATIENTS HAVING NATURAL DEATHS, 23 PSYCHIATRIC PATIENTS)
aAPPLICATION 1969 D-45 Z-28 F-137

2300 GIEBINK, J. W., & STOVER, D. O.
ADJUSTMENT, MENTAL HEALTH OPINIONS, AND PROFICIENCY OF CHILD CARE
PERSONNEL.
JOURNAL OF CONSULTING AND CLINICAL PSYCHOLOGY, 1969, 33, 532-535.
(CORRELATES:BEHAVIORAL, PSYCHOLOGICAL; FACTOR ANALYSIS; N=52 CHILD
CARE PERSONNEL)
aAPPLICATION 1969 D-45 N-25

2301 COTTLE, T. J.
TEMPORAL CORRELATES OF THE ACHIEVEMENT VALUE AND MANIFEST ANXIETY.
JOURNAL OF CONSULTING AND CLINICAL PSYCHOLOGY, 1969, 33, 541-550.
(CORRELATES:PSYCHOLOGICAL, DEMOGRAPHIC, INTELLIGENCE; NORMATIVE DATA;
N=332 MEN, 98 WOMEN FROM NAVAL TRAINING STATION)
aAPPLICATION 1969 T-2 S-131 O-16 C-155 C-154 C-166 C-164 C-156

2302 PLACKBURN, R.
SENSATION SEEKING, INPULSIVITY, AND PSYCHOPATHIC PERSONALITY.
JOURNAL OF CONSULTING AND CLINICAL PSYCHOLOGY, 1969, 33, 571-574.
(VALIDITY:CONSTRUCT; CORRELATES:PSYCHOLOGICAL; N=83 MALE PSYCHIATRIC
OFFENDERS)
aAPPLICATION 1969 Z-3 D-45 W-41 W-8 B-188 F-86 G-137

2303 ANDERSON, L. M.
PERSONALITY CHARACTERISTICS OF PARENTS OF NEUROTIC, AGGRESSIVE, AND
NORMAL PREADOLESCENT BOYS.
JOURNAL OF CONSULTING AND CLINICAL PSYCHOLOGY, 1969, 33, 575-581.
(CORRELATES:DEMOGRAPHIC; USED AS CRITERION; N=29 PARENTS OF
AGGRESSIVE, 23 PARENTS OF NEUROTIC, AND 50 NORMAL PARENTS OF NORMAL
BOYS)
aAPPLICATION 1969 D-45 A-59

2304   HARROW, M., & FERRANTE, A.
                LOCUS OF CONTROL IN PSYCHIATRIC PATIENTS.
                JOURNAL OF CONSULTING AND CLINICAL PSYCHOLOGY, 1969, 33, 582-589.
                      (RELIABILITY:RETEST; CORRELATES:DEMOGRAPHIC; NORMATIVE DATA; N=128
                      PSYCHIATRIC INPATIENTS)
         @APPLICATION 1969 R-18

2305   HOWARD, K. I., KRAUSE, M. S., & ORLINSKY, D. E.
                DIRECTION OF AFFECTIVE INFLUENCE IN PSYCHOTHERAPY.
                JOURNAL OF CONSULTING AND CLINICAL PSYCHOLOGY, 1969, 33, 614-620.
                      (DESCRIPTION; CORRELATES:PSYCHOLOGICAL, DEMOGRAPHIC; N=45
                      PATIENT-THERAPIST PAIRS)
         @APPLICATION 1969 O-12

2306   COWDEN, J. E.
                PREDICTION ENHANCEMENT THROUGH THE USE OF MODERATOR VARIABLES.
                JOURNAL OF CONSULTING AND CLINICAL PSYCHOLOGY, 1969, 33, 621-624.
                      (VALIDITY:CRITERION, CROSS-VALIDATION; N=152 INSITUTIONALIZED
                      DELINQUENT BOYS)
         @APPLICATION 1969 B-11

2307   CALLENS, C. J., & MELTZER, M. L.
                EFFECT OF INTELLIGENCE, ANXIETY, AND DIAGNOSIS ON ARITHMETIC AND DIGIT
                SPAN PERFORMANCE ON THE WAIS.
                JOURNAL OF CONSULTING AND CLINICAL PSYCHOLOGY, 1969, 33, 630.
                      (CORRELATES:INTELLIGENCE; USED AS CRITERION; N=80 MALE PSYCHIATRIC IN
                      PATIENTS)
         @APPLICATION 1969 W-8

2308   BERRY, K. L., & MISKIMINS, R. W.
                CONCEPT OF SELF AND POSTHOSPITAL VOCATIONAL ADJUSTMENT.
                JOURNAL OF CONSULTING AND CLINICAL PSYCHOLOGY, 1969, 33, 103-108.
                      (DESCRIPTION; VALIDITY:CRITERION; NORMATIVE DATA; N=104 PSYCHIATRIC
                      PATIENTS AND NORMALS)
         @APPLICATION 1969 M-112

2309   NORMAN, R. P.
                EXTREME RESPONSE TENDENCY AS A FUNCTION OF EMOTIONAL ADJUSTMENT AND
                STIMULUS AMBIGUITY.
                JOURNAL OF CONSULTING AND CLINICAL PSYCHOLOGY, 1969, 33, 406-410.
                      (CORRELATES:PSYCHOLOGICAL; USED AS CRITERION; N=115 STUDENTS)
         @APPLICATION 1969 W-41 W-8 D-45 M-20 R-30 O-16

2310   GREENBERG, R. P.
                EFFECTS OF PRESESSION INFORMATION ON PERCEPTION OF THE THERAPIST AND
                RECEPTIVITY TO INFLUENCE IN A PSYCHOTHERAPY ANALOGUE.
                JOURNAL OF CONSULTING AND CLINICAL PSYCHOLOGY, 1969, 33, 425-429.
                      (DESCRIPTION; CORRELATES:ENVIRONMENTAL; N=112 STUDENTS)
         @APPLICATION 1969 A-48 G-136

2311   HAGEBAK, R. W., & PARKER, G. V. C.
                THERAPIST DIRECTIVENESS, CLIENT DOMINANCE, AND THERAPY RESISTANCE.
                JOURNAL OF CONSULTING AND CLINICAL PSYCHOLOGY, 1969, 33, 536-540.
                      (CORRELATES:BEHAVIORAL, PSYCHOLOGICAL; USED AS CRITERION; N=240 MALE
                      STUDENTS)
         @APPLICATION 1969 G-21

2312   DICKEN, C.
                PREDICTING THE SUCCESS OF PEACE CORPS COMMUNITY DEVELOPMENT WORKERS.
                JOURNAL OF CONSULTING AND CLINICAL PSYCHOLOGY, 1969, 33, 597-606.
                      (VALIDITY:CRITERION; CORRELATES:BEHAVIORAL, PSYCHOLOGICAL,
                      DEMOGRAPHIC, INTELLIGENCE; FACTOR ANALYSIS; NORMATIVE DATA; N=55
                      PEACE CORPS VOLUNTEERS)
         @APPLICATION 1969 D-45 G-20 G-19 G-36 G-82 B-5

2313   COHEN, D. B.
                FREQUENCY OF DREAM RECALL ESTIMATED BY THREE METHODS AND RELATED TO
                DEFENSE PREFERENCE AND ANXIETY.
                JOURNAL OF CONSULTING AND CLINICAL PSYCHOLOGY, 1969, 33, 661-667.
                      (CORRELATES:PSYCHOLOGICAL; USED AS CRITERION; N=86 COLLEGE MALES)
         @APPLICATION 1969 G-30 C-136

2314   LEVITZ, L. S., & ULLMANN, L. P.
            MANIPULATION OF INDICATIONS OF DISTURBED THINKING IN NORMAL SUBJECTS.
            JOURNAL OF CONSULTING AND CLINICAL PSYCHOLOGY, 1969, 33, 633-341.
                (RELIABILITY:INTERRATER; CORRELATES:ENVIRONMENTAL; N=500 MALE
                COLLEGE STUDENTS)
        @APPLICATION 1969 H-37 R-27

2315   SULLIVAN, P. F., & ROBERTS, L. K.
            RELATIONSHIP OF MANIFEST ANXIETY TO REPRESSION-SENSITIZATION ON THE MMPI.
            JOURNAL OF CONSULTING AND CLINICAL PSYCHOLOGY, 1969, 33, 763-764.
                (VALIDITY:CONTENT, CONSTRUCT; CORRELATES:PSYCHOLOGICAL; NORMATIVE
                DATA; N=386 MALE PSYCHOTHERAPY APPLICANTS)
        @APPLICATION 1969 B-46 T-2

2316   MELNICK, B., & HURLEY, J. R.
            DISTINCTIVE PERSONALITY ATTRIBUTES OF CHILD-ABUSING MOTHERS.
            JOURNAL OF CONSULTING AND CLINICAL PSYCHOLOGY, 1969, 33, 746-749.
                (RELIABILITY:INTERRATER; CORRELATES:BEHAVIORAL, PSYCHOLOGICAL;
                NORMATIVE DATA; N=10 ABUSIVE AND 10 CONTROL MOTHERS)
        @APPLICATION 1969 T-25 V-12 H-135 M-150 M-20

2317   DICKSTEIN, L. S.
            PROSPECTIVE SPAN AS A COGNITIVE ABILITY.
            JOURNAL OF CONSULTING AND CLINICAL PSYCHOLOGY, 1969, 33, 757-760.
                (RELIABILITY:INTERNAL CONSISTENCY; CORRELATES:INTELLIGENCE;
                NORMATIVE DATA; N=51 MALE COLLEGE STUDENTS)
        @APPLICATION 1969 E-13 M-20

2318   HENDRICK, C., & PAGE, H. A.
            SELF-ESTEEM, ATTITUDE SIMILARITY, AND ATTRACTION.
            JOURNAL OF PERSONALITY, 1970, 38, 588-601.
                (MODIFICATION; CORRELATES:PSYCHOLOGICAL; USED AS CRITERION; N=90
                COLLEGE STUDENTS)
        @APPLICATION 1970 P-88

2319   FEATHER, N. T.
            BALANCING AND POSITIVITY EFFECTS IN SOCIAL RECALL.
            JOURNAL OF PERSONALITY, 1970, 38, 602-628.
                (CORRELATES:PSYCHOLOGICAL, DEMOGRAPHIC; 3 STUDIES:
                N=53 MALE AND 67 FEMALE UNDERGRADUATES, N=50 MALE UNDERGRADUATES,
                N=50 MALE AND 79 FEMALE UNDERGRADUATES)
        @APPLICATION 1970 R-8 B-37

2320   REISMAN, S., INSKO, C. A., & VALINS, S.
            TRIADIC CONSISTENCY AND FALSE HEART-RATE FEEDBACK.
            JOURNAL OF PERSONALITY, 1970, 38, 629-640.
                (CORRELATES:PHYSIOLOGICAL, ENVIRONMENTAL; N=77 MALE UNDERGRADUATES)
        @APPLICATION 1970 R-30

2321   WACHTEL, P. L., & SCHIMEK, J. G.
            AN EXPLORATORY STUDY OF THE EFFECTS OF EMOTIONALLY TONED INCIDENTAL
            STIMULI.
            JOURNAL OF PERSONALITY, 1970, 38, 467-481.
                (CORRELATES:PSYCHOLOGICAL, ENVIRONMENTAL; 2 STUDIES: N=60 MALE
                COLLEGE STUDENTS, N=20 MALE COLLEGE STUDENTS)
        @APPLICATION 1970 M-20

2322   EAGLY, A. H.
            LEADERSHIP STYLE AND ROLE DIFFERENTIATION AS DETERMINANTS OF GROUP
            EFFECTIVENESS.
            JOURNAL OF PERSONALITY, 1970, 38, 509-524.
                (CORRELATES:BEHAVIORAL, PSYCHOLOGICAL; N=456 UNDERGRADUATES)
        @APPLICATION 1970 F-48

2323   MATCHOTKA, P.
            EGO DEFENSE AND AESTHETIC DISTORTION: EXPERIMENTER EFFECTS.
            JOURNAL OF PERSONALITY, 1970, 38, 560-580.
                (CORRELATES:BEHAVIORAL, PSYCHOLOGICAL; USED AS CRITERION;
                BIAS:TESTER; N=124 MALE AND FEMALE COLLEGE STUDENTS)
        @APPLICATION 1970 C-75 C-57 B-4 B-46 D-45 S-80

2324   NOONAN, J. R., BARRY, J. R., & DAVIS, H. C.
            PERSONALITY DETERMINANTS IN ATTITUDES TOWARD VISIBLE DISABILITY.
            JOURNAL OF PERSONALITY, 1970, 38, 1-15.
                (VALIDITY:CROSS-VALIDATION; CORRELATES:PSYCHOLOGICAL; BIAS:RESPONSE;
                N=240 COLLEGE FEMALES)
        @APPLICATION 1970 B-7 B-5 A-5 S-15 Y-1 C-27 B-61 G-85 S-93

2325   LEVENTHAL, H., & MACE, W.
            THE EFFECT OF LAUGHTER ON EVALUATION OF A SLAPSTICK MOVIE.
            JOURNAL OF PERSONALITY, 1970, 38, 16-30.
                (MODIFICATION; RELIABILITY; CORRELATES:BEHAVIORAL, DEMOGRAPHIC;
                2 STUDIES: N=72 CHILDREN, N=49 HIGH SCHOOL SOPHOMORES)
        @APPLICATION 1970 R-40 Z-40

2326   EZEKIEL, R. S.
            AUTHORITARIANISM, ACQUIESCENCE, AND FIELD BEHAVIOR.
            JOURNAL OF PERSONALITY, 1970, 38, 31-42.
                (REVIEW ARTICLE; CORRELATES:BEHAVIORAL, PSYCHOLOGICAL; USED AS
                CRITERION; N=49 PEACE CORPS VOLUNTEERS)
        @APPLICATION 1970 B-126 S-102 C-81

2327   CRANDALL, J. E.
            PREDICTIVE VALUE AND CONFIRMABILITY OF TRAITS AS DETERMINANTS OF JUDGED
            TRAIT IMPORTANCE.
            JOURNAL OF PERSONALITY, 1970, 38, 77-90.
                (CORRELATES:PSYCHOLOGICAL; N=20 MALE, 25 FEMALE UNDERGRADUATES)
        @APPLICATION 1970 L-35

2328   HAMILTON, D. L.
            PERSONALITY ATTRIBUTES RELATED TO RESPONSE PREFERENCES IN RESOLVING
            INCONSISTENCY.
            JOURNAL OF PERSONALITY, 1970, 38, 134-145.
                (CORRELATES:PSYCHOLOGICAL; USED AS CRITERION; N=161 MALE
                UNDERGRADUATES)
        @APPLICATION 1970 B-46 C-27 R-8
        @L-35

2329   MARTUZA, V. R.
            AN INVESTIGATION OF THE EFFECTS OF STRATEGY AVAILABILITY, BANKROLL, AND
            SEX ON RISK-TAKING BEHAVIOR MEASURED IN A PSYCHOMETRIC CONTEXT.
            JOURNAL OF PERSONALITY, 1970, 38, 146-160.
                (CORRELATES:BEHAVIORAL, DEMOGRAPHIC; USED AS CRITERION; NORMATIVE
                DATA; N=68 MALE, 82 FEMALE HIGH SCHOOL STUDENTS)
        @APPLICATION 1970 C-27 A-8 K-94

2330   COTLER, S., & PALMER, R. J.
            THE EFFECTS OF TEST ANXIETY, SEX OF SUBJECT, AND TYPE OF VERBAL
            REINFORCEMENT ON MAZE PERFORMANCE OF ELEMENTARY SCHOOL CHILDREN.
            JOURNAL OF PERSONALITY, 1970, 38, 216-234.
                (MENTION: CORRELATES:BEHAVIORAL, PSYCHOLOGICAL, DEMOGRAPHIC,
                INTELLIGENCE, ENVIRONMENTAL; USED AS CRITERION; N=90 4TH, 5TH, AND
                6TH GRADERS)
        @APPLICATION 1970 C-55 S-133 S-35

2331   OSTROM, T. M., & UPSHAW, H. S.
            RACE DIFFERENCES IN THE JUDGMENT OF ATTITUDE STATEMENTS OVER A THIRTY-FIVE
            YEAR PERIOD.
            JOURNAL OF PERSONALITY, 1970, 38, 235-248.
                (REVIEW ARTICLE; CORRELATES:PSYCHOLOGICAL, ENVIRONMENTAL;
                4 STUDIES: N=250 BLACK, 200 WHITE; 175 WHITE; 40 BLACK, 43 WHITE;
                38 BLACK, 54 WHITE SUBJECTS)
        @APPLICATION 1970 T-23

2332   MARCIA, J. E., & FRIEDMAN, M. L.
            EGO IDENTITY STATUS IN COLLEGE WOMEN.
            JOURNAL OF PERSONALITY, 1970, 38, 249-263.
                (RELIABILITY:INTERRATER; VALIDITY:CRITERION;
                CORRELATES:PSYCHOLOGICAL, INTELLIGENCE; USED AS CRITERION; NORMATIVE
                DATA; N=49 SENIOR COLLEGE WOMEN)
        @APPLICATION 1970 A-5 L-45 D-14 S-124 W-8

2333   GORDON, A., & GLASS, D. C.
            CHOICE AMBIGUITY, DISSONANCE, AND DEFENSIVENESS.
            JOURNAL OF PERSONALITY, 1970, 38, 264-272.
                (CORRELATES:BEHAVIORAL, PHYSIOLOGICAL, ENVIRONMENTAL; USED AS
                CRITERION; N=109 PAID FEMALE VOLUNTEERS)
        @APPLICATION 1970 B-46

2334   THOMAS, L. E.
            THE I-E SCALE, IDEOLOGICAL BIAS, AND POLITICAL PARTICIPATION.
            JOURNAL OF PERSONALITY, 1970, 38, 273-286.
                (VALIDITY:CONSTRUCT; NORMATIVE DATA; N=60 FAMILIES, IN WHICH 1 PARENT
                AND 1 COLLEGE AGE CHILD INTERVIEWED)
        @APPLICATION 1970 R-18 A-5 C-109

2335   LUDWIG, L. D.
            INTRA- AND INTERINDIVIDUAL RELATIONSHIPS BETWEEN ELATION-DEPRESSION AND
            DESIRE FOR EXCITEMENT.
            JOURNAL OF PERSONALITY, 1970, 38, 167-176.
                (CORRELATES:PSYCHOLOGICAL, ENVIRONMENTAL; USED AS CRITERION;
                BIAS:RESPONSE; N=45 COLLEGE STUDENTS)
        @APPLICATION 1970 W-52 J-27

2336   HELSON, R., & CRUTCHFIELD, R. S.
            CREATIVE TYPES IN MATHEMATICS.
            JOURNAL OF PERSONALITY, 1970, 38, 177-197.
                (MODIFICATION; MENTION; RELIABILITY:INTERNAL CONSISTENCY, INTERRATER;
                CORRELATES:BEHAVIORAL, PSYCHOLOGICAL, DEMOGRAPHIC; FACTOR ANALYSIS;
                N=34 MATHEMATICIANS)
        @APPLICATION 1970 G-22 G-90 D-45 M-22 S-33 K-14 H-89 G-21 A-7 G-53 B-78

2337   DIENSTBIER, R. A.
            POSITIVE AND NEGATIVE PREJUDICE: INTERACTIONS OF PREJUDICE WITH RACE AND
            SOCIAL DESIRABILITY.
            JOURNAL OF PERSONALITY, 1970, 38, 198-215.
                (CORRELATES:PSYCHOLOGICAL; USED AS CRITERION; N=80 MALE HIGH SCHOOL
                JUNIORS)
        @APPLICATION 1970 S-55 R-8 T-12 B-65

2338   STRICKLAND, B. R.
            INDIVIDUAL DIFFERENCES IN VERBAL CONDITIONING, EXTINCTION, AND AWARENESS.
            JOURNAL OF PERSONALITY, 1970, 38, 364-378.
                (RELIABILITY:RETEST; CORRELATES:BEHAVIORAL, PSYCHOLOGICAL;
                NORMATIVE DATA; N=187 FEMALE UNDERGRADUATES)
        @APPLICATION 1970 C-27 R-18

2339   SMITH, C. P., & WINTERBOTTOM, M. T.
            PERSONALITY CHARACTERISTICS OF COLLEGE STUDENTS ON ACADEMIC PROBATION.
            JOURNAL OF PERSONALITY, 1970, 38, 379-391.
                (MODIFICATION; CORRELATES:BEHAVIORAL, PSYCHOLOGICAL, INTELLIGENCE;
                2 STUDIES: N=27 STUDENTS ON PROBATION, 27 CONTROLS,
                22 STUDENTS ON PROBATION, 22 CONTROLS)
        @APPLICATION 1970 H-12 M-4 E-1 L-22

2340   SCHRAUGER, J. S., & ROSENBERG, S. E.
            SELF-ESTEEM AND THE EFFECTS OF SUCCESS AND FAILURE FEEDBACK ON PERFORMANCE.
            JOURNAL OF PERSONALITY, 1970, 38, 404-417.
                (MODIFICATION; CORRELATES:BEHAVIORAL, PSYCHOLOGICAL; USED AS
                CRITERION; N=36 MALE UNDERGRADUATES)
        @APPLICATION 1970 C-96

2341   PEABODY, D.
            SYMMETRY AND ASYMMETRY IN INTERPERSONAL RELATIONS WITH IMPLICATIONS FOR
            THE CONCEPT OF PROJECTION.
            JOURNAL OF PERSONALITY, 1970, 38, 426-434.
                (MENTION; NO SAMPLE DATA)
        @APPLICATION 1970 L-35 D-48

2342   CENTERS, R., SHOMER, R. W., & RODRIGUES, A.
            A FIELD EXPERIMENT IN INTERPERSONAL PERSUASION USING AUTHORITATIVE
            INFLUENCE.
            JOURNAL OF PERSONALITY, 1970, 38, 392-403.
                (CORRELATES:PSYCHOLOGICAL; N=1275 ADULTS)
        @APPLICATION 1970 S-146

2343   KUUSINEN, S.
            EVIDENCE FOR A CURVILINEAR RELATIONSHIP BETWEEN COMPLEXITY AND ORIGINALITY.
            JOURNAL OF PERSONALITY, 1970, 38, 329-343.
                    (CORRELATES:BEHAVIORAL, PSYCHOLOGICAL; NORMATIVE DATA; N=80 MALE
                    UNDERGRADUATES)
        @APPLICATION 1970 H-12

2344   HENDRICK, C., & LILLY, R. S.
            THE STRUCTURE OF MOOD: A COMPARISON BETWEEN SLEEP DEPRIVATION AND NORMAL
            WAKEFUL CONDITIONS.
            JOURNAL OF PERSONALITY, 1970, 38, 453-465.
                    (CORRELATES:ENVIRONMENTAL; FACTOR ANALYSIS; NORMATIVE DATA; N=126
                    STUDENTS)
        @APPLICATION 1970 N-5

2345   MYERS, D. G., MURDOCH, P., & SMITH, G. F.
            RESPONSIBILITY DIFFUSION AND DRIVE ENHANCEMENT EFFECTS ON RISKY SHIFT.
            JOURNAL OF PERSONALITY, 1970, 38, 418-425.
                    (CORRELATES:PSYCHOLOGICAL, ENVIRONMENTAL; USED AS CRITERION;
                    2 STUDIES: N= OVER 400 UNDERGRADUATES, 75 SELECTED; N= OVER 1200
                    UNDERGRADUATES, 215 SELECTED)
        @APPLICATION 1970 W-2 C-27 A-8 T-2

2346   COTTLE, T. J., EDWARDS, C. N., & PLECK, J.
            THE RELATIONSHIP OF SEX, ROLE, IDENTITY AND SOCIAL AND POLITICAL ATTITUDES.
            JOURNAL OF PERSONALITY, 1970, 38, 435-452.
                    (CORRELATES:BEHAVIORAL, PSYCHOLOGICAL, DEMOGRAPHIC; USED AS
                    CRITERION; FACTOR ANALYSIS; NORMATIVE DATA; N=85 MALE AND 80
                    FEMALE MIDDLE, UPPER TO MIDDLE AND UPPER CLASS RESPONDENTS)
        @APPLICATION 1970 F-11 G-20 C-247

2347   SHEARD, J. L.
            INTRASUBJECT PREDICTION OF PREFERENCES FOR ORGANIZATION TYPES.
            JOURNAL OF APPLIED PSYCHOLOGY, 1970, 54, 248-252.
                    (VALIDITY:CRITERION; CORRELATES:BEHAVIORAL; N=382 COLLEGE STUDENTS)
        @APPLICATION 1970 V-21

2348   BARRETT, G. V., THORNTON, C. L., & CABE, P. A.
            CUE CONFLICT RELATED TO PERCEPTUAL STYLE.
            JOURNAL OF APPLIED PSYCHOLOGY, 1970, 54, 258-264.
                    (VALIDITY:CRITERION; CORRELATES:PSYCHOLOGICAL, PHYSIOLOGICAL; USED AS
                    CRITERION; N=25 MALE AEROSPACE EMPLOYEES)
        @APPLICATION 1970 W-19 W-188

2349   DODD, W. E., WOLLOWICK, H. B., & MCNAMARA, W. J.
            TASK DIFFICULTY AS A MODERATOR OF LONG-RANGE PREDICTION.
            JOURNAL OF APPLIED PSYCHOLOGY, 1970, 54, 265-270.
                    (VALIDITY:CRITERION; CORRELATES:BEHAVIORAL, INTELLIGENCE;
                    USED AS CRITERION; N=396 MAINTENANCE TECHNICIANS, 103 SALES TRAINEES)
        @APPLICATION 1970 G-70 S-33

2350   GRUENFELD, L. W., & WEISSENBERG, P.
            FIELD INDEPENDENCE AND ARTICULATION OF SOURCES OF JOB SATISFACTION.
            JOURNAL OF APPLIED PSYCHOLOGY, 1970, 54, 424-426.
                    (CORRELATES:PSYCHOLOGICAL; USED AS CRITERION; N=96 MALE
                    SUPERVISORS)
        @APPLICATION 1970 W-81 W-142

2351   SHOTLAND, R. L., & BERGER, W. G.
            BEHAVIORAL VALIDATION OF SEVERAL VALUES FROM THE ROKEACH VALUE SCALE AS AN
            INDEX OF HONESTY.
            JOURNAL OF APPLIED PSYCHOLOGY, 1970, 54, 433-435.
                    (VALIDITY:CRITERION; CORRELATES:BEHAVIORAL, PSYCHOLOGICAL; N=131
                    FEMALE LINE WORKERS)
        @APPLICATION 1970 R-119

2352   SILVER, H. A., & BARNETTE, W. L., JR.
            PREDICTIVE AND CONCURRENT VALIDITY OF THE MINNESOTA VOCATIONAL INTEREST
            INVENTORY FOR VOCATIONAL HIGH SCHOOL BOYS.
            JOURNAL OF APPLIED PSYCHOLOGY, 1970, 54, 436-440.
                    (VALIDITY:CRITERION; CORRELATES:BEHAVIORAL, INTELLIGENCE; N=223
                    SENIOR BOYS IN VOCATIONAL HIGH SCHOOLS)
        @APPLICATION 1970 C-52

2353   SHIMP, T. A., DONNELLY, J. H., & IVANCEVICH, J. M.
            STUDY OF CONSUMER POLITICAL ORIENTATIONS AND STORE PATRONAGE.
            JOURNAL OF APPLIED PSYCHOLOGY, 1970, 54, 470-472.
                (CORRELATES:BEHAVIORAL: N=106 COLLEGE FRESHMEN)
        @APPLICATION 1970 M-175

2354   GOODMAN, P. S., ROSE, J. H., & FURCON, J. E.
            COMPARISON OF MOTIVATIONAL ANTECEDENTS OF THE WORK PERFORMANCE OF
            SCIENTISTS AND ENGINEERS.
            JOURNAL OF APPLIED PSYCHOLOGY, 1970, 54, 491-495.
                (VALIDITY:CRITERION; CORRELATES:BEHAVIORAL, PSYCHOLOGICAL; N=78
                EMPLOYEES IN GOVERNMENT RESEARCH LABORATORY)
        @APPLICATION 1970 L-128

2355   DISTEFANO, M. K., JR., & PRYER, M. W.
            PREDICTING VOCATIONAL OUTCOME OF PSYCHIATRIC PATIENTS WITH THE EDWARDS
            PERSONAL PREFERENCE SCHEDULE.
            JOURNAL OF APPLIED PSYCHOLOGY, 1970, 54, 552-554.
                (CORRELATES:BEHAVIORAL, PSYCHOLOGICAL; USED AS CRITERION; N=47 MALE
                AND 64 FEMALE PSYCHIATRIC PATIENTS)
        @APPLICATION 1970 E-2

2356   ARSENIAN, S.
            CHANGE IN EVALUATIVE ATTITUDES DURING TWENTY-FIVE YEARS.
            JOURNAL OF APPLIED PSYCHOLOGY, 1970, 54, 302-304.
                (USED AS CRITERION; NORMATIVE DATA; N=54 MALES IN 25 YEAR
                LONGITUDINAL STUDY)
        @APPLICATION 1970 A-7

2357   HERMANS, H. J. M.
            A QUESTIONNAIRE MEASURE OF ACHIEVEMENT MOTIVATION.
            JOURNAL OF APPLIED PSYCHOLOGY, 1970, 54, 353-363.
                (RELIABILITY:INTERRATER; CORRELATES:BEHAVIORAL, PSYCHOLOGICAL,
                INTELLIGENCE; N=32 COLLEGE MALES)
        @APPLICATION 1970 M-7

2358   SOLIMAN, H. M.
            MOTIVATION-HYGIENE THEORY OF JOB ATTITUDES: AN EMPIRICAL INVESTIGATION AND
            AN ATTEMPT TO RECONCILE BOTH THE ONE- AND THE TWO-FACTOR THEORIES OF JOB
            ATTITUDES.
            JOURNAL OF APPLIED PSYCHOLOGY, 1970, 54, 452-461.
                (MODIFICATION; CORRELATES:PSYCHOLOGICAL; N=150 EMPLOYEES--TEACHERS,
                CLERICAL, SEMIPROFESSIONALS & PROFESSIONALS)
        @APPLICATION 1970 M-70 P-49 B-215

2359   MORGAN, B. S., BLONSKY, M. R., & ROSEN, H.
            EMPLOYEE ATTITUDES TOWARD A HARD-CORE HIRING PROGRAM.
            JOURNAL OF APPLIED PSYCHOLOGY, 1970, 54, 473-478.
                (CORRELATES:BEHAVIORAL, PSYCHOLOGICAL; NORMATIVE DATA; N=214
                EMPLOYEES IN UTILITY COMPANY)
        @APPLICATION 1970 R-120

2360   CLARK, A. W., & MCCABE, S.
            LEADERSHIP BELIEFS OF AUSTRALIAN MANAGERS.
            JOURNAL OF APPLIED PSYCHOLOGY, 1970, 54, 1-6.
                (DESCRIPTION; USED AS CRITERION; CROSS-CULTURAL APPLICATION;
                NORMATIVE DATA; N=1339 AUSTRALIAN MANAGERS)
        @APPLICATION 1970 H-81

2361   MATARAZZO, J. D., WIENS, A. N., JACKSON, R. H., & MANAUGH, T. S.
            INTERVIEWEE SPEECH BEHAVIOR UNDER DIFFERENT CONTENT CONDITIONS.
            JOURNAL OF APPLIED PSYCHOLOGY, 1970, 54, 15-26.
                (VALIDITY:CROSS-VALIDATION; CORRELATES:BEHAVIORAL, ENVIRONMENTAL;
                NORMATIVE DATA; N=90 ADULT MALES)
        @APPLICATION 1970 W-78 T-2 R-30 D-45

2362   KORMAN, A. K.
            TOWARD AN HYPOTHESIS OF WORK BEHAVIOR.
            JOURNAL OF APPLIED PSYCHOLOGY, 1970, 54, 31-41.
                (VALIDITY:CRITERION; CORRELATES:BEHAVIORAL, PSYCHOLOGICAL,
                ENVIRONMENTAL; NORMATIVE DATA; N=85 HIGH SCHOOL, 76 AND 173 COLLEGE
                STUDENTS)
        @APPLICATION 1970 G-59 W-79

2363   NOLTING, E., JR.
            VOCATIONAL INTERESTS OF WOMEN: A LONGITUDINAL STUDY OF THE STRONG
            VOCATIONAL INTEREST BLANK.
            JOURNAL OF APPLIED PSYCHOLOGY, 1970, 54, 120-127.
                (RELIABILITY:RETEST; CORRELATES:BEHAVIORAL; NORMATIVE DATA; N=390
                COLLEGE FEMALES)
        @APPLICATION 1970 S-33

2364   SALVENDY, G., SEYMOUR, W. D., & CORLETT, E. N.
            COMPARATIVE STUDY OF STATIC VERSUS DYNAMIC SCORING OF PERFORMANCE TESTS
            FOR INDUSTRIAL OPERATORS.
            JOURNAL OF APPLIED PSYCHOLOGY, 1970, 54, 135-139.
                (CORRELATES:BEHAVIORAL: N=158 ADULT FEMALE EMPLOYEES)
        @APPLICATION 1970 E-6

2365   MULLER, H. P.
            RELATIONSHIP BETWEEN TIME-SPAN OF DISCRETION, LEADERSHIP BEHAVIOR, AND
            FIEDLER'S LPC SCORES.
            JOURNAL OF APPLIED PSYCHOLOGY, 1970, 54, 140-144.
                (CORRELATES:BEHAVIORAL: N=78 COLLEGE STUDENTS)
        @APPLICATION 1970 S-117 F-38 F-48 F-36 F-60

2366   KAVANAGH, M. J., MACKINNEY, A. C., & WOLINS, L.
            SATISFACTION AND MORALE OF FOREMEN AS A FUNCTION OF MIDDLE MANAGER'S
            PERFORMANCE.
            JOURNAL OF APPLIED PSYCHOLOGY, 1970, 54, 145-156.
                (VALIDITY:CRITERION, CROSS-VALIDATION; CORRELATES:BEHAVIORAL,
                ENVIRONMENTAL; N=658 MANAGERS)
        @APPLICATION 1970 M-49

2367   BRAUNSTEIN, D. N.
            INTERPERSONAL BEHAVIOR IN A CHANGING ORGANIZATION.
            JOURNAL OF APPLIED PSYCHOLOGY, 1970, 54, 184-191.
                (CORRELATES:BEHAVIORAL, PSYCHOLOGICAL; N=250 HOSPITAL STAFF
                PERSONNEL)
        @APPLICATION 1970 G-13 T-43

2368   MCBRIDE, R. S.
            PREDICTION OF DRIVING BEHAVIOR FOLLOWING A GROUP DRIVER IMPROVEMENT
            SESSION.
            JOURNAL OF APPLIED PSYCHOLOGY, 1970, 54, 45-50.
                (VALIDITY:CRITERION; CORRELATES:BEHAVIORAL, DEMOGRAPHIC; N=75
                NEGLIGENT DRIVERS IN TRAINING COURSE)
        @APPLICATION 1970 G-70

2369   LICHTMAN, C. M.
            SOME INTRAPERSONAL RESPONSE CORRELATES OF ORGANIZATIONAL RANK.
            JOURNAL OF APPLIED PSYCHOLOGY, 1970, 54, 77-80.
                (MODIFICATION; RELIABILITY:INTERRATER; CORRELATES:PSYCHOLOGICAL;
                NORMATIVE DATA; N=95 MANAGERS, SUPERVISORS AND WORKERS)
        @APPLICATION 1970 J-6 H-82 F-20 K-71 R-18 I-5

2370   MITCHELL, V. F.
            NEED SATISFACTION OF MILITARY COMMANDERS AND STAFF.
            JOURNAL OF APPLIED PSYCHOLOGY, 1970, 54, 282-287.
                (CORRELATES:DEMOGRAPHIC, ENVIRONMENTAL; N=675 AIR FORCE OFFICERS)
        @APPLICATION 1970 P-49

2371   BRAATZ, G. A.
            PREFERENCE INTRANSITIVITY AS A INDICATOR OF COGNITIVE SLIPPAGE IN
            SCHIZOPHRENIA.
            JOURNAL OF ABNORMAL PSYCHOLOGY, 1970, 75, 1-6.
                (VALIDITY:CONSTRUCT; CORRELATES:PSYCHOLOGICAL; N=30 PSYCHIATRIC
                NONSCHIZOPHRENICS, 30 MEDICAL PATIENTS)
        @APPLICATION 1970 D-45 B-5

2372   KLINGER, B.
            EFFECT OF PEER MODEL RESPONSIVENESS AND LENGTH OF INDUCTION PROCEDURE ON
            HYPNOTIC RESPONSIVENESS.
            JOURNAL OF ABNORMAL PSYCHOLOGY, 1970, 75, 15-18.
                (CORRELATES:PSYCHOLOGICAL, ENVIRONMENTAL; NORMATIVE DATA; N=68
                FEMALE UNDERGRADUATES)
        @APPLICATION 1970 B-3

2373   SCHUHAM, A. I.
              POWER RELATIONS IN EMOTIONALLY DISTURBED AND NORMAL FAMILY TRIADS.
              JOURNAL OF ABNORMAL PSYCHOLOGY, 1970, 75, 30-37.
                       (RELIABILITY:INTERRATER; CORRELATES:BEHAVIORAL, PSYCHOLOGICAL; N=14
                       NORMAL & 14 DISTURBED FAMILY TRIADS: FATHER, MOTHER, CHILD)
              ƏAPPLICATION 1970 B-2

2374   MURSTEIN, B. I., & WOLF, S. R.
              EMPIRICAL TEST OF THE "LEVELS" HYPOTHESIS WITH FIVE PROJECTIVE TECHNIQUES.
              JOURNAL OF ABNORMAL PSYCHOLOGY, 1970, 75, 38-44.
                       (RELIABILITY:INTERRATER; VALIDITY:CONSTRUCT, CRITERION;
                       CORRELATES:BEHAVIORAL, PSYCHOLOGICAL, INTELLIGENCE; NORMATIVE DATA;
                       N=11 FEMALE, 9 MALE NORMALS (AGE 16-20) AND 11 FEMALE, 9 MALE
                       HOSPITALIZED PATIENTS)
              ƏAPPLICATION 1970 M-58 R-31 R-30 M-47

2375   BUTTERFIELD, E. C., & ZIGLER, E.
              PREINSTITUTIONAL SOCIAL DEPRIVATION AND IQ CHANGES AMONG INSTITUTIONALIZED
              RETARDED CHILDREN.
              JOURNAL OF ABNORMAL PSYCHOLOGY, 1970, 75, 83-89.
                       (RELIABILITY:INTERRATER; CORRELATES:PSYCHOLOGICAL, INTELLIGENCE;
                       N=110 RETARDED CHILDREN)
              ƏAPPLICATION 1970 Z-18

2376   STEWART, D. J., & RESNICK, J. H.
              VERBAL CONDITIONING OF PSYCHOPATHS AS A FUNCTION OF EXPERIMENTER-SUBJECT
              SEX DIFFERENCES.
              JOURNAL OF ABNORMAL PSYCHOLOGY, 1970, 75, 90-92.
                       (CORRELATES:BEHAVIORAL, DEMOGRAPHIC, INTELLIGENCE; USED AS
                       CRITERION; N=965 UNDERGRADUATES, 48 MALES AND 48 FEMALES SELECTED)
              ƏAPPLICATION 1970 D-45

2377   BOURDON, K. H., & SILBER, D. E.
              PERCEIVED PARENTAL BEHAVIOR AMONG STUTTERERS AND NONSTUTTERERS.
              JOURNAL OF ABNORMAL PSYCHOLOGY, 1970, 75, 93-97.
                       (CORRELATES:BEHAVIORAL; N=24 STUTTERERS, 24 NONSTUTTERERS FROM
                       PUBLIC SCHOOLS)
              ƏAPPLICATION 1970 S-8

2378   SHEEHAN, P. W.
              ANALYSIS OF THE TREATMENT EFFECTS OF SIMULATION INSTRUCTIONS IN THE
              APPLICATION OF THE REAL SIMULATING MODEL OF HYPNOSIS.
              JOURNAL OF ABNORMAL PSYCHOLOGY, 1970, 75, 98-103.
                       (RELIABILITY:INTERRATER; CORRELATES:PSYCHOLOGICAL, ENVIRONMENTAL;
                       USED AS CRITERION; N=15 MALES, 9 FEMALES)
              ƏAPPLICATION 1970 S-90 R-31 C-27 W-31 E-29

2379   HOROWITZ, S. L.
              STRATEGIES WITHIN HYPNOSIS FOR REDUCING PHOBIC BEHAVIOR.
              JOURNAL OF ABNORMAL PSYCHOLOGY, 1970, 75, 104-112.
                       (CORRELATES:BEHAVIORAL, PSYCHOLOGICAL, ENVIRONMENTAL; USED AS
                       CRITERION; NORMATIVE DATA; N=36 ADULT FEMALE SNAKE PHOBICS)
              ƏAPPLICATION 1970 W-31 B-184

2380   JACKSON, N. L. P., JR.
              SEX AND DOMINANCE CUES IN GOOD-POOR PREMORBID SCHIZOPHRENIA.
              JOURNAL OF ABNORMAL PSYCHOLOGY, 1970, 75, 78-82.
                       (MODIFICATION; CORRELATES:BEHAVIORAL, PSYCHOLOGICAL, ENVIRONMENTAL;
                       USED AS CRITERION; N=60 POOR PREMORBID SCHIZOPHRENICS, 60 GOOD
                       PREMORBID SCHIZOPRHENICS, 60 CONTROLS)
              ƏAPPLICATION 1970 P-32 O-16

2381   DRAGUNS, J. G., PHILLIPS, L., BROVERMAN, I. K., & CAUDILL, W.
              SOCIAL COMPETENCE AND PSYCHIATRIC SYMPTOMATOLOGY IN JAPAN: A CROSS-
              CULTURAL EXTENSION OF EARLIER AMERICAN FINDINGS.
              JOURNAL OF ABNORMAL PSYCHOLOGY, 1970, 75, 68-73.
                       (CORRELATES:PSYCHOLOGICAL, DEMOGRAPHIC; CROSS-CULTURAL
                       APPLICATION; N=238 MALE AND 269 FEMALE JAPANESE PSYCHIATRIC
                       PATIENTS)
              ƏAPPLICATION 1970 P-51 B-45

2382   SMITH, R. E.
        CHANGES IN LOCUS OF CONTROL AS A FUNCTION OF LIFE CRISIS RESOLUTION.
        JOURNAL OF ABNORMAL PSYCHOLOGY, 1970, 75, 329-332.
                (VALIDITY:CRITERION; CORRELATES:ENVIRONMENTAL; N=60 MENTAL PATIENTS)
        @APPLICATION 1970 R-18

2383   KRAPEL, J. E., & NAWAS, M. M.
        DIFFERENTIAL ORDERING OF STIMULUS PRESENTATION IN SYSTEMATIC
        DESENSITIZATION.
        JOURNAL OF ABNORMAL PSYCHOLOGY, 1970, 75, 333-337.
                (CORRELATES:BEHAVIORAL, PSYCHOLOGICAL, ENVIRONMENTAL; USED AS
                CRITERION; N=50 SNAKE-PHOBIC FEMALE UNDERGRADUATES)
        @APPLICATION 1970 L-24 G-41

2384   O'CONNELL, D. N., SHOR, R. E., & ORNE, M. T.
        HYPNOTIC AGE REGRESSION: AN EMPIRICAL AND METHODOLOGICAL ANALYSIS.
        JOURNAL OF ABNORMAL PSYCHOLOGY, 1970, 76, 1-32.
                (CORRELATES:BEHAVIORAL, PSYCHOLOGICAL; USED AS CRITERION; N=10
                DEEPLY HYPNOTIZABLE UNDERGRADUATES)
        @APPLICATION 1970 W-31

2385   NACE, E. P., & ORNE, M. T.
        FATE OF AN UNCOMPLETED POSTHYPNOTIC SUGGESTION.
        JOURNAL OF ABNORMAL PSYCHOLOGY, 1970, 75, 278-285.
                (CORRELATES:BEHAVIORAL, PSYCHOLOGICAL; N=50 MALE UNDERGRADUATES)
        @APPLICATION 1970 W-31 W-19

2386   SMART, R. G., & JONES, D.
        ILLICIT LSD USERS: THEIR PERSONALITY CHARACTERISTICS AND PSYCHOPATHOLOGY.
        JOURNAL OF ABNORMAL PSYCHOLOGY, 1970, 75, 286-292.
                (CORRELATES:BEHAVIORAL, PSYCHOLOGICAL, DEMOGRAPHIC, INTELLIGENCE;
                N=100 LSD USERS, 46 NON-USERS)
        @APPLICATION 1970 B-5 B-123 H-92 C-98 M-89 D-45

2387   DINNERSTEIN, A. J., & HALM, J.
        MODIFICATION OF PLACEBO EFFECTS BY MEANS OF DRUGS: EFFECTS OF ASPIRIN
        AND PLACEBOS ON SELF-RATED MOODS.
        JOURNAL OF ABNORMAL PSYCHOLOGY, 1970, 75, 308-314.
                (CORRELATES:PHYSIOLOGICAL, ENVIRONMENTAL; USED AS CRITERION; N=80
                MALE UNDERGRADUATES)
        @APPLICATION 1970 C-16 W-19

2388   TART, C. T.
        INCREASES IN HYPNOTIZABILITY RESULTING FROM A PROLONGED PROGRAM FOR
        ENHANCING PERSONAL GROWTH.
        JOURNAL OF ABNORMAL PSYCHOLOGY, 1970, 75, 260-266.
                (CORRELATES:BEHAVIORAL: BIAS:TESTER; N=15 ESALEN FELLOWS)
        @APPLICATION 1970 S-90 W-31

2389   HOWARD, K. I., ORLINSKY, D. E., & HILL, J. A.
        AFFECTIVE EXPERIENCE IN PSYCHOTHERAPY.
        JOURNAL OF ABNORMAL PSYCHOLOGY, 1970, 75, 267-275.
                (CORRELATES:BEHAVIORAL, PSYCHOLOGICAL; FACTOR ANALYSIS; N=118 FEMALE
                PATIENTS AND 17 THERAPISTS)
        @APPLICATION 1970 O-12

2390   HIGGINS, J.
        PERSONALITY CORRELATES OF THE GOODMAN SOCIO-SEXUAL ADJUSTMENT SCALE.
        JOURNAL OF ABNORMAL PSYCHOLOGY, 1970, 75, 276-277.
                (CORRELATES:BEHAVIORAL, PSYCHOLOGICAL; NORMATIVE DATA; N=71 MALE
                UNDERGRADUATES)
        @APPLICATION 1970 G-100 H-12

2391   HOLZMAN, P. S., & ROUSEY, C.
        MONITORING, ACTIVATION, AND DISINHIBITION: EFFECTS OF WHITE NOISE MASKING
        ON SPOKEN THOUGHT.
        JOURNAL OF ABNORMAL PSYCHOLOGY, 1970, 75, 227-241.
                (RELIABILITY:INTERRATER; CORRELATES:BEHAVIORAL, PSYCHOLOGICAL,
                DEMOGRAPHIC, ENVIRONMENTAL; 2 STUDIES: N=20 MEN, 20 WOMEN AND N=20
                MEN, 20 WOMEN)
        @APPLICATION 1970 H-37 M-20

2392   BUCKEY, H. M., MUENCH, G. A., & SJOBERG, B. M.
        EFFECTS OF A COLLEGE STUDENT VISITATION PROGRAM ON A GROUP OF CHRONIC
        SCHIZOPHRENICS.
        JOURNAL OF ABNORMAL PSYCHOLOGY, 1970, 75, 242-244.
            (CORRELATES:PSYCHOLOGICAL; N=76 MENTAL PATIENTS)
        @APPLICATION 1970 S-11 R-27

2393   TRATTNER, J. H., & HOWARD, K. I.
        A PRELIMINARY INVESTIGATION OF COVERT COMMUNICATION OF EXPECTANCIES TO
        SCHIZOPHRENICS.
        JOURNAL OF ABNORMAL PSYCHOLOGY, 1970, 75, 245-247.
            (CORRELATES:PSYCHOLOGICAL; USED AS CRITERION; BIAS:TESTER; 2 STUDIES:
            N=28 MENTAL HOSPITAL MALE ATTENDANTS, 50 MALE PATIENTS; N=13 MALE
            UNDERGRADUATES)
        @APPLICATION 1970 K-78 P-32

2394   SILVERSTEIN, A. B., MCLAIN, R. E., & MOHAN, P. J.
        DIMENSIONS OF CONCEPTUAL BEHAVIOR.
        JOURNAL OF ABNORMAL PSYCHOLOGY, 1970, 75, 217-220.
            (RELIABILITY:INTERRATER; N=110 CLINICAL PSYCHOLOGISTS)
        @APPLICATION 1970 R-58

2395   SHRAUGER, J. S., & KATKIN, E. S.
        THE USE OF NONSPECIFIC UNDERLYING MOTIVATIONAL FACTORS IN THE SYSTEMATIC
        DESENSITIZATION OF SPECIFIC MARITAL AND INTERPERSONAL FEARS: A CASE STUDY.
        JOURNAL OF ABNORMAL PSYCHOLOGY, 1970, 75, 221-226.
            (CORRELATES:BEHAVIORAL, PSYCHOLOGICAL; N=1 FEMALE PSYCHIATRIC
            PATIENT)
        @APPLICATION 1970 D-45

2396   SPOHN, H. E., THETFORD, P. E., & WOODHAM, F. L.
        SPAN OF APPREHENSION AND AROUSAL IN SCHIZOPHRENIA.
        JOURNAL OF ABNORMAL PSYCHOLOGY, 1970, 75, 113-123.
            (CORRELATES:BEHAVIORAL, PHYSIOLOGICAL, INTELLIGENCE; USED AS
            CRITERION; N=32 MALE SCHIZOPHRENICS, 16 MALE CONTROLS)
        @APPLICATION 1970 P-32 L-39

2397   MCALLISTER, L. W.
        MODIFICATION OF PERFORMANCE ON THE ROD-AND-FRAME TEST THROUGH TOKEN
        REINFORCEMENT PROCEDURES.
        JOURNAL OF ABNORMAL PSYCHOLOGY, 1970, 75, 124-130.
            (CORRELATES:BEHAVIORAL, PSYCHOLOGICAL, ENVIRONMENTAL; NORMATIVE DATA;
            2 STUDIES: N=60 MALE SCHIZOPHRENICS, N=20 MALE SCHIZOPHRENICS)
        @APPLICATION 1970 W-188

2398   JORDAN, B. T., & KEMPLER, B.
        HYSTERICAL PERSONALITY: AN EXPERIMENTAL INVESTIGATION OF SEX-ROLE CONFLICT.
        JOURNAL OF ABNORMAL PSYCHOLOGY, 1970, 75, 172-176.
            (CORRELATES:BEHAVIORAL, PHYSIOLOGICAL, ENVIRONMENTAL; USED AS
            CRITERION; BIAS:TESTER: N=39 HYSTERICS, 39 NONHYSTERICS)
        @APPLICATION 1970 E-2 G-26 O-7

2399   EPSTEIN, S., & FENZ, W. D.
        HABITUATION TO A LOUD SOUND AS A FUNCTION OF MANIFEST ANXIETY.
        JOURNAL OF ABNORMAL PSYCHOLOGY, 1970, 75, 189-194.
            (CORRELATES:PHYSIOLOGICAL; USED AS CRITERION; N=40 UNDERGRADUATES,
            20 SELECTED)
        @APPLICATION 1970 F-42

2400   LENOX, J. R.
        EFFECT OF HYPNOTIC ANALGESIA ON VERBAL REPORT AND CARDIOVASCULAR
        RESPONSES TO ISCHEMIC PAIN.
        JOURNAL OF ABNORMAL PSYCHOLOGY, 1970, 75, 199-206.
            (CORRELATES:BEHAVIORAL, PHYSIOLOGICAL; USED AS CRITERION; N=5 HIGH
            SCHOOL AND 3 COLLEGE STUDENTS)
        @APPLICATION 1970 W-31

2401   WERNER, M., STABENAU, J. R., & POLLIN, W.
        THEMATIC APPERCEPTION TEST METHOD FOR THE DIFFERENTIATION OF FAMILIES OF
        SCHIZOPHRENICS, DELINQUENTS, AND "NORMALS."
        JOURNAL OF ABNORMAL PSYCHOLOGY, 1970, 75, 139-145.
            (VALIDITY:CRITERION; CORRELATES:PSYCHOLOGICAL; 2 STUDIES: N= PARENTS
            OF 10 SCHIZOPHRENICS, 10 DELINQUENTS, 10 NORMALS; N=20 MOTHERS OF
            SCHIZOPHRENICS, 20 MOTHERS OF NORMALS)
        @APPLICATION 1970 M-20

2402   BERNSTEIN, A. S.
            PHASIC ELECTRODERMAL ORIENTING RESPONSE IN CHRONIC SCHZIOPHRENICS: II.
            RESPONSE TO AUDITORY SIGNALS OF VARYING INTENSITY.
            JOURNAL OF ABNORMAL PSYCHOLOGY, 1970, 75, 146-156.
                    (CORRELATES:PHYSIOLOGICAL; USED AS CRITERION; NORMATIVE DATA; N=48
                    NORMAL MALES, 72 CLEAR AND 72 CONFUSED MALE CHRONIC SCHIZOPHRENICS)
        @APPLICATION 1970 R-37

2403   FARINA, A., & HOLZBERG, J. D.
            ANXIETY LEVEL OF SCHIZOPHRENIC AND CONTROL PATIENTS AND THEIR PARENTS.
            JOURNAL OF ABNORMAL PSYCHOLOGY, 1970, 75, 157-163.
                    (RELIABILITY:INTERRATER; CORRELATES:PSYCHOLOGICAL, ENVIRONMENTAL;
                    N=24 GOOD AND 24 POOR SCHIZOPHRENICS, 24 NONPSYCHIATRIC PATIENTS)
        @APPLICATION 1970 M-35 P-32

2404   PAYNE, R. W., HOCHBERG, A. C., & HAWKS, D. V.
            DICHOTIC STIMULATION AS A METHOD OF ASSESSING DISORDER OF ATTENTION IN
            OVERINCLUSIVE SCHIZOPHRENIC PATIENTS.
            JOURNAL OF ABNORMAL PSYCHOLOGY, 1970, 76, 185-193.
                    (VALIDITY: CRITERION; CORRELATES:BEHAVIORAL, PSYCHOLOGICAL; USED AS
                    CRITERION; NORMATIVE DATA; N=24 SCHIZOPHRENICS, 12 NORMAL CONTROLS)
        @APPLICATION 1970 B-94 P-103 H-171 P-108

2405   CREGO, C. A.
            A PATTERN ANALYTIC APPROACH TO THE MEASURE OF MODES OF EXPRESSION OF
            PSYCHOLOGICAL DIFFERENTIATION.
            JOURNAL OF ABNORMAL PSYCHOLOGY, 1970, 76, 194-198.
                    (CORRELATES:PSYCHOLOGICAL; USED AS CRITERION; NORMATIVE DATA; N=99
                    FEMALE UNDERGRADUATES)
        @APPLICATION 1970 B-46 R-18 W-19 J-17

2406   KAMIL, L. J.
            PSYCHODYNAMIC CHANGES THROUGH SYSTEMATIC DESENSITIZATION.
            JOURNAL OF ABNORMAL PSYCHOLOGY, 1970, 76, 199-205.
                    (RELIABILITY:INTERRATER; VALIDITY:CRITERION; CORRELATES:BEHAVIORAL,
                    PSYCHOLOGICAL; USED AS CRITERION; N=20 SNAKE PHOBICS, 10 GENERAL
                    PHOBICS, 10 NORMALS)
        @APPLICATION 1970 W-37 S-256 R-30 M-20 S-317

2407   HAGGARD, E. A., AS, A., & BORGEN, C. M.
            SOCIAL ISOLATES AND URBANITES IN PERCEPTUAL ISOLATION.
            JOURNAL OF ABNORMAL PSYCHOLOGY, 1970, 76, 1-9.
                    (CORRELATES:BEHAVIORAL, PSYCHOLOGICAL, PHYSIOLOGICAL; FACTOR
                    ANALYSIS; N=10 ISOLATES, 10 CONTROLS)
        @APPLICATION 1970 R-27 R-30

2408   FENZ, W. D., & VELNER, J.
            PHYSIOLOGICAL CONCOMITANTS OF BEHAVIORAL INDICES IN SCHIZOPHRENIA.
            JOURNAL OF ABNORMAL PSYCHOLOGY, 1970, 76, 27-35.
                    (CORRELATES:PSYCHOLOGICAL, PHYSIOLOGICAL; NORMATIVE DATA; N=28
                    PSYCHIATRIC PATIENTS AND 14 NORMAL MALES)
        @APPLICATION 1970 P-32

2409   SHEVRIN, H., SMITH, W. H., & FRITZER, D. E.
            SUBLIMINALLY STIMULATED BRAIN AND VERBAL RESPONSES OF TWINS DIFFERING IN
            REPRESSIVENESS.
            JOURNAL OF ABNORMAL PSYCHOLOGY, 1970, 76, 39-46.
                    (RELIABILITY:INTERRATER; CORRELATES:PSYCHOLOGICAL, PHYSIOLOGICAL;
                    USED AS CRITERION; N=12 PAIRS OF TWINS)
        @APPLICATION 1970 R-30   '

2410   POWELL, B. J.
            ROLE OF VERBAL INTELLIGENCE IN THE FIELD APPROACH OF SELECTED GROUPS OF
            PSYCHOTICS.
            JOURNAL OF ABNORMAL PSYCHOLOGY, 1970, 76, 47-49.
                    (CORRELATES:BEHAVIORAL, PSYCHOLOGICAL, INTELLIGENCE; NORMATIVE DATA;
                    N=72 HOSPITALIZED PSYCHOTICS AND 24 HOSPITAL EMPLOYEES)
        @APPLICATION 1970 W-19 W-72

2411   JACOBSON, G. R., PISCERI, V. D., & BERENBAUM, H. L.
            TEMPORAL STABILITY OF FIELD DEPENDENCE AMONG HOSPITALIZED ALCOHOLICS.
            JOURNAL OF ABNORMAL PSYCHOLOGY, 1970, 76, 10-12.
                    (CORRELATES:PSYCHOLOGICAL; N=37 CHRONIC ALCOHOLICS)
        @APPLICATION 1970 W-72

2412   RICE, J. K.
              DISORDERED LANGUAGE AS RELATED TO AUTONOMIC RESPONSIVITY AND THE
              PROCESS-REACTIVE DISTINCTION.
              JOURNAL OF ABNORMAL PSYCHOLOGY, 1970, 76, 50-54.
                    (CORRELATES:PSYCHOLOGICAL, PHYSIOLOGICAL, INTELLIGENCE; USED AS
                    CRITERION; NORMATIVE DATA; N=37 SCHIZOPHRENICS)
        @APPLICATION 1970 P-51

2413   SUTCLIFFE, J. P., PERRY, C. W., & SHEEHAN, P. W.
              RELATION OF SOME ASPECTS OF IMAGERY AND FANTASY TO HYPNOTIC SUSCEPTIBILITY.
              JOURNAL OF ABNORMAL PSYCHOLOGY, 1970, 76, 279-287.
                    (VALIDITY:CRITERION; CORRELATES:PSYCHOLOGICAL; 3 STUDIES: N=53 MALE,
                    42 FEMALE UNDERGRADUATES; N=140 MALES, 140 FEMALES; N=95
                    UNDERGRADUATES)
        @APPLICATION 1970 W-31 B-226

2414   MCFALL, R. M., & MARSTON, A. R.
              AN EXPERIMENTAL INVESTIGATION OF BEHAVIOR REHEARSAL IN ASSERTIVE TRAINING.
              JOURNAL OF ABNORMAL PSYCHOLOGY, 1970, 76, 295-303.
                    (CORRELATES:BEHAVIORAL, PSYCHOLOGICAL, PHYSIOLOGICAL, ENVIRONMENTAL;
                    USED AS CRITERION; N=48 MALE, 24 FEMALE NONASSERTIVE COLLEGE
                    STUDENTS)
        @APPLICATION 1970 W-37 T-2 W-146

2415   TART, C. T., & DICK, L.
              CONSCIOUS CONTROL OF DREAMING: I. THE POSTHYPNOTIC DREAM.
              JOURNAL OF ABNORMAL PSYCHOLOGY, 1970, 76, 304-315.
                    (VALIDITY:CONSTRUCT; CORRELATES:PSYCHOLOGICAL; USED AS CRITERION;
                    N=4 MALE, 9 FEMALE UNDERGRADUATES HIGHLY HYPNOTIZABLE)
        @APPLICATION 1970 W-31 D-45 W-103 T-93 T-94

2416   LANG, P. J., MELAMED, B. G., & HART, J.
              A PSYCHOPHYSIOLOGICAL ANALYSIS OF FEAR MODIFICATION USING AN AUTOMATED
              DESENSITIZATION PROCEDURE.
              JOURNAL OF ABNORMAL PSYCHOLOGY, 1970, 76, 220-234.
                    (CORRELATES:BEHAVIORAL, PSYCHOLOGICAL, PHYSIOLOGICAL, ENVIRONMENTAL;
                    USED AS CRITERION; 2 STUDIES: N=29 FEMALE UNDERGRADUATE SNAKE
                    PHOBICS; 5 MALE AND 15 FEMALE OTHER PHOBICS)
        @APPLICATION 1970 L-46 W-135 D-45 L-135 L-24

2417   TRUAX, C. B., WARGO, D. G., & VOLKSDORF, N. R.
              ANTECEDENTS TO OUTCOME IN GROUP COUNSELING WITH INSTITUTIONALIZED JUVENILE
              DELINQUENTS: EFFECTS OF THERAPEUTIC CONDITIONS, PATIENT SELF-EXPLORATION,
              ALTERNATE SESSIONS, AND VICARIOUS THERAPY PRETRAINING.
              JOURNAL OF ABNORMAL PSYCHOLOGY, 1970, 76, 235-242.
                    (VALIDITY:CRITERION; CORRELATES:BEHAVIORAL, PSYCHOLOGICAL,
                    ENVIRONMENTAL; NORMATIVE DATA; N=40 MALE, 40 FEMALE DELINQUENTS)
        @APPLICATION 1970 T-69 T-89 T-24 F-45 T-35 T-36 T-38 B-60

2418   SCHMAUK, F. J.
              PUNISHMENT, AROUSAL, AND AVOIDANCE LEARNING IN SOCIOPATHS.
              JOURNAL OF ABNORMAL PSYCHOLOGY, 1970, 76, 325-335.
                    (CORRELATES:BEHAVIORAL, PSYCHOLOGICAL, PHYSIOLOGICAL, ENVIRONMENTAL;
                    USED AS CRITERION; NORMATIVE DATA; N=90 MALE PRISONERS AND
                    PSYCHIATRIC PATIENTS)
        @APPLICATION 1970 L-22 D-45 T-2 W-8

2419   LONDON, P., & MCDEVITT, R. A.
              EFFECTS OF HYPNOTIC SUSCEPTIBILITY AND TRAINING ON RESPONSES TO STRESS.
              JOURNAL OF ABNORMAL PSYCHOLOGY, 1970, 76, 336-348.
                    (CORRELATES:PSYCHOLOGICAL, PHYSIOLOGICAL, ENVIRONMENTAL; USED AS
                    CRITERION; N=64 MALE COLLEGE STUDENTS)
        @APPLICATION 1970 W-31 S-90

2420   CARR, J. E.
              DIFFERENTIATION SIMILARITY OF PATIENT AND THERAPIST AND THE OUTCOME OF
              PSYCHOTHERAPY.
              JOURNAL OF ABNORMAL PSYCHOLOGY, 1970, 76, 361-369.
                    (VALIDITY:CRITERION; CORRELATES:PSYCHOLOGICAL, DEMOGRAPHIC,
                    INTELLIGENCE; USED AS CRITERION; N=24 ADULT PSYCHIATRIC OUTPATIENTS)
        @APPLICATION 1970 W-10 C-77 D-45 W-8 W-41 B-5

2421   HARE, R. D., & THORVALDSON, S. A.
            PSYCHOPATHY AND RESPONSE TO ELECTRICAL STIMULATION.
            JOURNAL OF ABNORMAL PSYCHOLOGY, 1970, 76, 370-374.
                (CORRELATES:PSYCHOLOGICAL, PHYSIOLOGICAL; USED AS CRITERION; N=14
                PSYCHOPATHIC AND 14 NONPSYCHOPATHIC PRISONERS AND 14 MEN)
        @APPLICATION 1970 D-45 C-189

2422   STEWART, D. J., & RESNICK, J. H.
            VERBAL CONDITIONING AND DEPENDENCY BEHAVIOR IN DELINQUENTS.
            JOURNAL OF ABNORMAL PSYCHOLOGY, 1970, 76, 375-377.
                (VALIDITY:CRITERION; CORRELATES:BEHAVIORAL, PSYCHOLOGICAL; N=33
                DELINQUENT BOYS)
        @APPLICATION 1970 D-45 G-22 C-27 K-66

2423   SCHMID, A. C.
            SUSCEPTIBILITY TO SOCIAL INFLUENCE AND RETENTION OF OPINION CHANGE IN TWO
            TYPES OF DELINQUENTS.
            JOURNAL OF ABNORMAL PSYCHOLOGY, 1970, 76, 123-129.
                (CORRELATES:BEHAVIORAL, ENVIRONMENTAL; USED AS CRITERION; N=142
                DELINQUENT BOYS)
        @APPLICATION 1970 H-98 C-245

2424   WICKRAMASEKERA, I.
            EFFECTS OF SENSORY RESTRICTION ON SUSCEPTIBILITY TO HYPNOSIS: A HYPOTHESIS
            AND MORE PRELIMINARY DATA.
            JOURNAL OF ABNORMAL PSYCHOLOGY, 1970, 76, 69-75.
                (CORRELATES:BEHAVIORAL, PSYCHOLOGICAL; N=45 MALE PRISONERS)
        @APPLICATION 1970 W-31

2425   SUTKER, P. B.
            VICARIOUS CONDITIONING AND SOCIOPATHY.
            JOURNAL OF ABNORMAL PSYCHOLOGY, 1970, 76, 380-386.
                (CORRELATES:PSYCHOLOGICAL, PHYSIOLOGICAL; USED AS CRITERION; N=12
                MALE SOCIOPATHS AND 12 NORMAL COLLEGE STUDENTS)
        @APPLICATION 1970 D-45

2426   GRISSO, J. T.
            VERBAL BEHAVIOR AND THE ACTION-THOUGHT DIMENSION.
            JOURNAL OF ABNORMAL PSYCHOLOGY, 1970, 76, 265-269.
                (VALIDITY:CROSS-VALIDATION; CORRELATES:BEHAVIORAL, PSYCHOLOGICAL,
                DEMOGRAPHIC; USED AS CRITERION; 2 STUDIES: N=91 COLLEGE STUDENTS,
                N=60 MALE PSYCHIATRIC PATIENTS)
        @APPLICATION 1970 M-20 Z-28 P-51

2427   HAURI, P.
            EVENING ACTIVITY, SLEEP MENTATION, AND SUBJECTIVE SLEEP QUALITY.
            JOURNAL OF ABNORMAL PSYCHOLOGY, 1970, 76, 270-275.
                (CORRELATES:BEHAVIORAL, PHYSIOLOGICAL; N=15 PAID YOUNG MALES)
        @APPLICATION 1970 H-151 H-170

2428   MILLER, R. J., LUNDY, R. M., & GALBRAITH, G. G.
            EFFECTS OF HYPNOTICALLY INDUCED HALLUCINATION OF A COLD FILTER.
            JOURNAL OF ABNORMAL PSYCHOLOGY, 1970, 76, 316-319.
                (CORRELATES:PSYCHOLOGICAL; USED AS CRITERION; N=93 UNDERGRADUATES,
                10 SELECTED)
        @APPLICATION 1970 W-31

2429   FAZIO, A. F.
            TREATMENT COMPONENTS IN IMPLOSIVE THERAPY.
            JOURNAL OF ABNORMAL PSYCHOLOGY, 1970, 76, 211-219.
                (MODIFICATION; CORRELATES:BEHAVIORAL, PSYCHOLOGICAL, ENVIRONMENTAL;
                USED AS CRITERION; 2 STUDIES: N=18 FEMALE UNDERGRADUATES, 29 FEMALE
                UNDERGRADUATES)
        @APPLICATION 1970 W-37 E-16 D-45 F-109 P-104 F-110

2430   ZUCKERMAN, M., PERSKY, H., MILLER, L., & LEVINE, B.
            SENSORY DEPRIVATION VERSUS SENSORY VARIATION.
            JOURNAL OF ABNORMAL PSYCHOLOGY, 1970, 76, 76-82.
                (CORRELATES:PSYCHOLOGICAL, PHYSIOLOGICAL; NORMATIVE DATA; N=22 MALE
                COLLEGE STUDENTS)
        @APPLICATION 1970 Z-4 D-45 M-94

2431   WEISS, L., & MASLING, J.
            FURTHER VALIDATION OF A RORSCHACH MEASURE OF ORAL IMAGERY.
            JOURNAL OF ABNORMAL PSYCHOLOGY, 1970, 76, 83-87.
                    (CORRELATES:BEHAVIORAL, PSYCHOLOGICAL; NORMATIVE DATA; N=81
                    PSYCHIATRIC OUTPATIENTS, 70 CONTROLS)
        @APPLICATION 1970 R-30

2432   NOLAN, J. D., MATTIS, P. R., & HOLLIDAY, W. C.
            LONG-TERM EFFECTS OF BEHAVIOR THERAPY: A 12 MONTH FOLLOW-UP.
            JOURNAL OF ABNORMAL PSYCHOLOGY, 1970, 76, 88-92.
                    (CORRELATES:BEHAVIORAL, PSYCHOLOGICAL; USED AS CRITERION; N=19
                    FEMALES)
        @APPLICATION 1970 L-46 D-49 D-5C D-51

2433   SIMAL, F. J., & HERR, V. V.
            AUTONOMIC RESPONSES TO THREATENING STIMULI IN RELATION TO THE REPRESSION-
            SENSITIZATION DIMENSION.
            JOURNAL OF ABNORMAL PSYCHOLOGY, 1970, 76, 106-109.
                    (CORRELATES:BEHAVIORAL, PHYSIOLOGICAL; USED AS CRITERION; NORMATIVE
                    DATA; N=300 MALE UNDERGRADUATES, 40 SELECTED)
        @APPLICATION 1970 B-46 M-20

2434   TURNER, R. J., DOPKEEN, L. S., & LABPRECHE, G. P.
            MARITAL STATUS AND SCHIZOPHRENIA: A STUDY OF INCIDENCE AND OUTCOME.
            JOURNAL OF ABNORMAL PSYCHOLOGY, 1970, 76, 110-116.
                    (RELIABILITY:INTERRATER; CORRELATES:BEHAVIORAL, PSYCHOLOGICAL,
                    DEMOGRAPHIC; N=213 MALE SCHIZOPHRENICS)
        @APPLICATION 1970 H-15

2435   MCDANIEL, J. W., & SEXTON, A. W.
            PSYCHOENDOCRINE STUDIES OF PATIENTS WITH SPINAL CORD LESIONS.
            JOURNAL OF ABNORMAL PSYCHOLOGY, 1970, 76, 117-122.
                    (MODIFICATION; CORRELATES:PSYCHOLOGICAL, PHYSIOLOGICAL; N=22 SPINAL
                    CORD LESION PATIENTS, 9 CONTROLS)
        @APPLICATION 1970 B-129

2436   NEWTON, P. M.
            RECALLED DREAM CONTENT AND THE MAINTENANCE OF BODY IMAGE.
            JOURNAL OF ABNORMAL PSYCHOLOGY, 1970, 76, 134-139.
                    (RELIABILITY:INTERRATER; CORRELATES:BEHAVIORAL, PSYCHOLOGICAL; N=27
                    PARALYZED AND 29 NORMAL MALES)
        @APPLICATION 1970 H-37

2437   YATES, A. J., & KORBOOT, P.
            SPEED OF PERCEPTUAL FUNCTIONING IN CHRONIC NONPARANOID SCHIZOPHRENICS.
            JOURNAL OF ABNORMAL PSYCHOLOGY, 1970, 76, 453-461.
                    (CORRELATES:BEHAVIORAL, PSYCHOLOGICAL, INTELLIGENCE; USED AS
                    CRITERION; N=60 PSYCHIATRIC PATIENTS)
        @APPLICATION 1970 F-10

2438   WOLLERSHEIM, J. P.
            EFFECTIVENESS OF GROUP THERAPY BASED UPON LEARNING PRINCIPLES IN THE
            TREATMENT OF OVERWEIGHT WOMEN.
            JOURNAL OF ABNORMAL PSYCHOLOGY, 1970, 76, 462-474.
                    (CORRELATES:BEHAVIORAL, PSYCHOLOGICAL, ENVIRONMENTAL; USED AS
                    CRITERION; NORMATIVE DATA; N=79 OBESE FEMALES)
        @APPLICATION 1970 B-84 C-136 E-16

2439   CALHOUN, J. F.
            EFFECTS OF PERFORMANCE PAYOFF AND CUES ON RECALL BY HOSPITALIZED
            SCHIZOPHRENICS.
            JOURNAL OF ABNORMAL PSYCHOLOGY, 1970, 76, 485-491.
                    (CORRELATES:BEHAVIORAL, INTELLIGENCE; USED AS CRITERION;
                    N=162 MALE VETERAN SCHIZOPHRENICS)
        @APPLICATION 1970 U-5 W-199

2440   HIGGS, W. J.
            EFFECTS OF GROSS ENVIRONMENTAL CHANGE UPON BEHAVIOR OF SCHIZOPHRENICS: A
            CAUTIONARY NOTE.
            JOURNAL OF ABNORMAL PSYCHOLOGY, 1970, 76, 421-422.
                    (USED AS CRITERION; N=193 SCHIZOPHRENIC PATIENTS)
        @APPLICATION 1970 O-22

2441   SHIMKUNAS, A. M.
           RECIPROCAL SHIFTS IN SCHIZOPHRENIC THOUGHT PROCESSES.
           JOURNAL OF ABNORMAL PSYCHOLOGY, 1970, 76, 423-426.
               (CORRELATES:PSYCHOLOGICAL, INTELLIGENCE; USED AS CRITERION;
               NORMATIVE DATA; N=36 SCHIZOPHRENIC PATIENTS)
       @APPLICATION 1970 N-39 G-83

2442   SCHUCMAN, H., & THETFORD, W. N.
           A COMPARISON OF PERSONALITY TRAITS IN ULCERATIVE COLITIS AND MIGRAINE
           PATIENTS.
           JOURNAL OF ABNORMAL PSYCHOLOGY, 1970, 76, 443-452.
               (DESCRIPTION; CORRELATES:PHYSIOLOGICAL, INTELLIGENCE; N=271 ADULT
               HOSPITAL PATIENTS AND NONHOSPITALIZED CONTROLS)
       @APPLICATION 1970 S-265

2443   PERSONS, R. W., & MARKS, P. A.
           SELF-DISCLOSURE WITH RECIDIVISTS: OPTIMUM INTERVIEWER-INTERVIEWEE
           MATCHING.
           JOURNAL OF ABNORMAL PSYCHOLOGY, 1970, 76, 387-391.
               (CORRELATES:PSYCHOLOGICAL; USED AS CRITERION; N=81 MALE REFORMATORY
               INMATES & 3 COLLEGE STUDENTS)
       @APPLICATION 1970 D-45 M-17 T-2 T-48

2444   MANOSEVITZ, M.
           EARLY SEXUAL BEHAVIOR IN ADULT HOMOSEXUAL AND HETEROSEXUAL MALES.
           JOURNAL OF ABNORMAL PSYCHOLOGY, 1970, 76, 396-402.
               (CORRELATES:PSYCHOLOGICAL, DEMOGRAPHIC; NORMATIVE DATA; N=28
               HOMOSEXUAL & 22 HETEROSEXUAL MALES)
       @APPLICATION 1970 D-45

2445   GREENBERG, I. M.
           CLINICAL CORRELATES OF FOURTEEN- AND SIX-CYCLES-PER-SECOND POSITIVE EEG
           SPIKING AND FAMILY PATHOLOGY.
           JOURNAL OF ABNORMAL PSYCHOLOGY, 1970, 76, 403-412.
               (CORRELATES:BEHAVIORAL, PHYSIOLOGICAL, DEMOGRAPHIC, INTELLIGENCE,
               ENVIRONMENTAL; USED AS CRITERION; N=48 PSYCHIATRIC PATIENTS)
       @APPLICATION 1970 G-167

2446   BAILES, D. W., & GULLER, I. B.
           DOGMATISM AND ATTITUDES TOWARDS THE VIETNAM WAR.
           SOCIOMETRY, 1970, 33, 140-146.
               (CORRELATES:PSYCHOLOGICAL; NORMATIVE DATA; N=150 MALE UNDERGRADUATES)
       @APPLICATION 1970 R-8

2447   TURNER, J. H.
           ENTREPRENEURIAL ENVIRONMENTS AND THE EMERGENCE OF ACHIEVEMENT MOTIVATION
           IN ADOLESCENT MALES.
           SOCIOMETRY, 1970, 33, 147-165.
               (CORRELATES:BEHAVIORAL, DEMOGRAPHIC; N=639 MALE HIGH SCHOOL STUDENTS)
       @APPLICATION 1970 M-7

2448   CLOUD, J., & VAUGHAN, G. M.
           USING BALANCED SCALES TO CONTROL ACQUIESCENCE.
           SOCIOMETRY, 1970, 33, 193-202.
               (MENTION; CORRELATES:PSYCHOLOGICAL; CROSS-CULTURAL APPLICATION;
               BIAS:RESPONSE; N=183 UNDERGRADUATES)
       @APPLICATION 1970 W-87 C-23 B-14

2449   LEVINGER, G., SENN, D. J., & JORGENSEN, B. W.
           PROPERTIES TOWARD PERMANENCE IN COURTSHIP: A TEST OF THE KERCKHOFF-DAVIS
           HYPOTHESIS.
           SOCIOMETRY, 1970, 33, 427-443.
               (MODIFICATION; VALIDITY:CRITERION; CORRELATES:BEHAVIORAL,
               DEMOGRAPHIC; 2 STUDIES: N=234 DATING COUPLES, 214 DATING COUPLES)
       @APPLICATION 1970 S-11 B-195 F-143

2450   ALEXANDER, C. N., JR., ZUCKER, L. G., & BRODY, C. L.
           EXPERIMENTAL EXPECTATIONS AND AUTOKINETIC EXPERIENCES: CONSISTENCY
           THEORIES AND JUDGMENTAL CONVERGENCE.
           SOCIOMETRY, 1970, 33, 108-122.
               (CORRELATES:BEHAVIORAL, PSYCHOLOGICAL, ENVIRONMENTAL; N=20--NO
               SAMPLE DESCRIPTION)
       @APPLICATION 1970 G-21

2451   COOK, T. D., BURD, J. R., & TALBERT, T. L.
           COGNITIVE, BEHAVIORAL AND TEMPORAL EFFECTS OF CONFRONTING A BELIEF WITH
           ITS COSTLY ACTION IMPLICATIONS.
           SOCIOMETRY, 1970, 33, 358-369.
               (CORRELATES:BEHAVIORAL, ENVIRONMENTAL; N=81 UNDERGRADUATES)
       @APPLICATION 1970 G-22

2452   DRAKE, D. M.
           PERCEPTUAL CORRELATES OF IMPULSIVE AND REFLECTIVE BEHAVIOR.
           DEVELOPMENTAL PSYCHOLOGY, 1970, 2, 202-214.
               (CORRELATES:BEHAVIORAL, DEMOGRAPHIC; USED AS CRITERION; N=22
               THIRD GRADE CHILDREN AND 6 FEMALE, 10 MALE UNDERGRADUATES)
       @APPLICATION 1970 K-60

2453   HOLLANDER, E. P., & MARCIA, J. F.
           PARENTAL DETERMINANTS OF PEER-ORIENTATION AND SELF ORIENTATION AMONG
           PREADOLESCENTS.
           DEVELOPMENTAL PSYCHOLOGY, 1970, 2, 292-302.
               (CORRELATES:BEHAVIORAL, PSYCHOLOGICAL, DEMOGRAPHIC, ENVIRONMENTAL;
               N=30 BOYS AND 22 GIRLS)
       @APPLICATION 1970 B-133

2454   VAN DEN DAELE, L. D.
           CONTINUITY IN THE DEVELOPMENT OF CONCEPTUAL BEHAVIOR IN PRESCHOOL CHILDREN:
           A REJOINDER.
           DEVELOPMENTAL PSYCHOLOGY, 1970, 2, 303-305.
               (MENTION: REVIEW ARTICLE)
       @APPLICATION 1970 R-58

2455   VOGEL, S. R., BORVERMAN, I. K., BORVERMAN, D. M., CLARKSON, F. E., &
       ROSENCRANTZ, P. S.
           MATERNAL EMPLOYMENT AND PERCEPTION OF SEX ROLES AMONG COLLEGE STUDENTS.
           DEVELOPMENTAL PSYCHOLOGY, 1970, 3, 384-391.
               (VALIDITY:CRITERION; CORRELATES:DEMOGRAPHIC; N=120 COLLEGE STUDENTS,
               47 WITH NON-WORKING & 73 WITH WORKING MOTHERS)
       @APPLICATION 1970 R-72

2456   REALI, N., & HALL, V.
           EFFECT OF SUCCESS AND FAILURE ON THE REFLECTIVE AND IMPULSIVE CHILD.
           DEVELOPMENTAL PSYCHOLOGY, 1970, 3, 392-402.
               (CORRELATES:BEHAVIORAL, PSYCHOLOGICAL; USED AS CRITERION; N=167 3RD
               GRADE BOYS)
       @APPLICATION 1970 K-60

2457   RICHARD, H. C., ELLIS, N. R., BARNHART, S., & HOLT, M.
           SUBJECT-MODEL SEXUAL STATUS AND VERBAL IMITATIVE PERFORMANCE IN
           KINDERGARTEN CHILDREN.
           DEVELOPMENTAL PSYCHOLOGY, 1970, 3, 405.
               (MODIFICATION; RELIABILITY:INTERRATER; CORRELATES:PSYCHOLOGICAL;
               BIAS:TESTER; N= MIDDLE-CLASS KINDERGARTEN CHILDREN)
       @APPLICATION 1970 B-223

2458   LIBBY, W. L., JR.
           REACTION TIME AND REMOTE ASSOCIATION IN TALENTED MALE ADOLESCENTS.
           DEVELOPMENTAL PSYCHOLOGY, 1970, 3, 285-297.
               (CORRELATES:PSYCHOLOGICAL, INTELLIGENCE; USED AS CRITERION;
               NORMATIVE DATA; N=32 TALENTED HIGH SCHOOL STUDENTS)
       @APPLICATION 1970 M-29

2459   EISENMAN, R.
           CREATIVITY CHANGE IN STUDENT NURSES: A CROSS-SECTIONAL AND LONGITUDINAL
           STUDY.
           DEVELOPMENTAL PSYCHOLOGY, 1970, 3, 320-325.
               (VALIDITY:CRITERION; CORRELATES:DEMOGRAPHIC; NORMATIVE DATA; N=266
               FEMALE NURSING STUDENTS)
       @APPLICATION 1970 E-22 E-64

2460   MUSSEN, P., HARRIS, S., RUTHERFORD, E., & KEASEY, C. B.
           HONESTY AND ALTRUISM AMONG PREADOLESCENTS.
           DEVELOPMENTAL PSYCHOLOGY, 1970, 3, 169-194.
               (MODIFICATION; VALIDITY:CONSTRUCT; CORRELATES:BEHAVIORAL,
               PSYCHOLOGICAL, DEMOGRAPHIC, INTELLIGENCE; N=46 BOYS, 49 GIRLS IN
               THREE 6TH GRADE SCHOOL CLASSES)
       @APPLICATION 1970 P-17 B-233 C-38 G-141

2461   DUSEK, J. B., & HILL, K. T.
            PROBABILITY LEARNING AS A FUNCTION OF SEX OF THE SUBJECT, TEST ANXIETY, AND
            PERCENTAGE OF REINFORCEMENT.
            DEVELOPMENTAL PSYCHOLOGY, 1970, 3, 195-207.
                  (CORRELATES:PSYCHOLOGICAL, DEMOGRAPHIC, INTELLIGENCE, ENVIRONMENTAL;
                  USED AS CRITERION; N=64 BOYS AND 76 4TH AND 5TH GRADE CHILDREN)
        @APPLICATION 1970 S-35 S-79 S-263

2462   GROSS, R. B., & MARSH, M.
            AN INSTRUMENT FOR MEASURING CREATIVITY IN YOUNG CHILDREN: THE GROSS
            GEOMETRIC FORMS.
            DEVELOPMENTAL PSYCHOLOGY, 1970, 3, 267.
                  (CORRELATES:PSYCHOLOGICAL, DEMOGRAPHIC, INTELLIGENCE; N=67 LOWER TO
                  MIDDLE CLASS NEGRO CHILDREN, 103 UPPER MIDDLE CLASS WHITE SUBJECTS)
        @APPLICATION 1970 B-231 B-232

2463   CONNELL, D. M., & JOHNSON, J. E.
            RELATIONSHIP BETWEEN SEX-ROLE IDENTIFICATION AND SELF-ESTEEM IN EARLY
            ADOLESCENTS.
            DEVELOPMENTAL PSYCHOLOGY, 1970, 3, 268.
                  (CORRELATES:PSYCHOLOGICAL; USED AS CRITERION; NO SAMPLE SIZE GIVEN,
                  EARLY ADOLESCENT WHITE CATHOLIC MALES & FEMALES)
        @APPLICATION 1970 C-38 G-20

2464   PALMER, F. H.
            SOCIOECONOMIC STATUS AND INTELLECTIVE PERFORMANCE AMONG NEGRO PRESCHOOL
            BOYS.
            DEVELOPMENTAL PSYCHOLOGY, 1970, 3, 1-9.
                  (CORRELATES:DEMOGRAPHIC, INTELLIGENCE; N=310 MALE NEGRO BOYS)
        @APPLICATION 1970 H-22

2465   HEILBRUN, A. B., JR., & NORBERT, N.
            MATERNAL CHILD-REARING EXPERIENCE AND SELF-REINFORCEMENT EFFECTIVENESS.
            DEVELOPMENTAL PSYCHOLOGY, 1970, 3, 81-87.
                  (CORRELATES:BEHAVIORAL, ENVIRONMENTAL; USED AS CRITERION; NORMATIVE
                  DATA; N=109 STUDENTS)
        @APPLICATION 1970 H-66 S-9

2466   BOWLES, S., & WRIGHT, L.
            PERSONALITY INTEGRATION IN PREADOLESCENT MALES.
            DEVELOPMENTAL PSYCHOLOGY, 1970, 2, 151.
                  (CORRELATES:PSYCHOLOGICAL; USED AS CRITERION; N=32 ELEMENTARY SCHOOL
                  BOYS)
        @APPLICATION 1970 D-9

2467   DOHERTY, A.
            INFLUENCE OF PARENTAL CONTROL ON THE DEVELOPMENT OF FEMININE SEX ROLE AND
            CONSCIENCE.
            DEVELOPMENTAL PSYCHOLOGY, 1970, 2, 157-158.
                  (CORRELATES:PSYCHOLOGICAL; N=93 COLLEGE FEMALES AND THEIR PARENTS)
        @APPLICATION 1970 S-8 G-20

2468   SCHNEIDER, B., & OLSON, L. K.
            EFFORT AS A CORRELATE OF ORGANIZATIONAL REWARD SYSTEM AND INDIVIDUAL
            VALUES.
            PERSONNEL PSYCHOLOGY, 1970, 23, 313-326.
                  (CORRELATES:PSYCHOLOGICAL; NORMATIVE DATA; N=146 REGISTERED NURSES)
        @APPLICATION 1970 P-49 M-109

2469   RITCHIE, J. B., & MILES, R. E.
            AN ANALYSIS OF QUANTITY AND QUALITY OF PARTICIPATION AS MEDIATING
            VARIABLES IN THE PARTICIPATIVE DECISION MAKING PROCESS.
            PERSONNEL PSYCHOLOGY, 1970, 23, 347-359.
                  (CORRELATES:BEHAVIORAL, PSYCHOLOGICAL; USED AS CRITERION; NORMATIVE
                  DATA; N=330 MANAGERS)
        @APPLICATION 1970 M-110 B-142 R-71

2470   HARRELL, T. W.
            THE PERSONALITY OF HIGH EARNING MBA'S IN SMALL BUSINESS.
            PERSONNEL PSYCHOLOGY, 1970, 23, 369-375.
                  (CORRELATES:BEHAVIORAL, PSYCHOLOGICAL, INTELLIGENCE; USED AS
                  CRITERION; N=299 GRADUATE STUDENTS)
        @APPLICATION 1970 G-26 G-59 A-5 M-7 S-33 D-45 F-38

2471   TOSI, H.
                A REEXAMINATION OF PERSONALITY AS A DETERMINANT OF THE EFFECTS OF
                PARTICIPATION.
                PERSONNEL PSYCHOLOGY, 1970, 23, 91-99.
                        (CORRELATES:BEHAVIORAL, PSYCHOLOGICAL; N=488 MANAGERS)
        @APPLICATION 1970 V-16 V-17 V-18 V-19 V-20

2472   IVANCEVICH, J. M., DONNELLY, J. M., & LYON, H. L.
                A STUDY OF THE IMPACT OF MANAGEMENT BY OBJECTIVES ON PERCEIVED NEED
                SATISFACTION.
                PERSONNEL PSYCHOLOGY, 1970, 23, 139-151.
                        (CORRELATES:BEHAVIORAL: USED AS CRITERION; N=166 MANAGERS)
        @APPLICATION 1970 P-49 P-20

2473   FLEISHMAN, E. A., & SIMMONS, J.
                RELATIONSHIP BETWEEN LEADERSHIP PATTERNS AND EFFECTIVENESS RATINGS AMONG
                ISRAELI FOREMEN.
                PERSONNEL PSYCHOLOGY, 1970, 23, 169-172.
                        (CORRELATES:BEHAVIORAL: CROSS-CULTURAL APPLICATION; N=318 FOREMEN)
        @APPLICATION 1970 F-61

2474   PAYNE, R.
                FACTOR ANALYSIS OF A MASLOW-TYPE NEED SATISFACTION QUESTIONNAIRE.
                PERSONNEL PSYCHOLOGY, 1970, 23, 251-268.
                        (CORRELATES:BEHAVIORAL: FACTOR ANALYSIS; N=113 FEMALE OPERATORS IN
                        CIGARETTE FACTORY)
        @APPLICATION 1970 E-6 P-49

2475   GORDON, L. V.
                MEASUREMENT OF BUREAUCRATIC ORIENTATION.
                PERSONNEL PSYCHOLOGY, 1970, 23, 1-11.
                        (DESCRIPTION; VALIDITY:CRITERION, CONSTRUCT;
                        CORRELATES:PSYCHOLOGICAL, DEMOGRAPHIC; NORMATIVE DATA; 2 STUDIES:
                        N=172 AIR FORCE CADETS, N=472 MILITARY ACADEMY SENIORS)
        @APPLICATION 1970 G-11

2476   HORNADAY, J. A., & BUNKER, C. S.
                THE NATURE OF THE ENTREPRENEUR.
                PERSONNEL PSYCHOLOGY, 1970, 23, 47-54.
                        (USED AS CRITERION; N=20 "SUCCESSFUL" ENTREPRENEURS IN BUSINESS)
        @APPLICATION 1970 G-13 E-2 K-72

2477   STEELE, F. I., ZAND, D. E., & ZALKIND, S. S.
                MANAGERIAL BEHAVIOR AND PARTICIPATION IN A LABORATORY TRAINING PROCESS.
                PERSONNEL PSYCHOLOGY, 1970, 23, 77-90.
                        (CORRELATES:BEHAVIORAL, ENVIRONMENTAL; USED AS CRITERION; NORMATIVE
                        DATA; N=56 MANAGERS)
        @APPLICATION 1970 H-85

2478   BONS, P. M., BASS, A. R., & KOMORITA, S. S.
                CHANGES IN LEADERSHIP STYLE AS A FUNCTION OF MILITARY EXPERIENCE AND
                TYPE OF COMMAND.
                PERSONNEL PSYCHOLOGY, 1970, 23, 551-568.
                        (MODIFICATION; CORRELATES:BEHAVIORAL, PSYCHOLOGICAL,
                        ENVIRONMENTAL; N=596 MALE CADETS)
        @APPLICATION 1970 F-50 F-38 F-48 H-217

2479   GHISELLI, E. E., & JOHNSON, D. A.
                NEED SATISFACTION, MANAGERIAL SUCCESS, AND ORGANIZATIONAL STRUCTURE.
                PERSONNEL PSYCHOLOGY, 1970, 23, 569-576.
                        (CORRELATES:PSYCHOLOGICAL, ENVIRONMENTAL: N=413 MANAGERS)
        @APPLICATION 1970 P-49

2480   WOOD, M. T., & SOBEL, R. S.
                EFFECTS OF SIMILARITY OF LEADERSHIP STYLE AT TWO LEVELS OF MANAGEMENT ON
                THE JOB SATISFACTION OF THE FIRST LEVEL MANAGER.
                PERSONNEL PSYCHOLOGY, 1970, 23, 577-590.
                        (CORRELATES:BEHAVIORAL, PSYCHOLOGICAL; N=48 FIRST LEVEL, & 24 SECOND
                        LEVEL MANAGERS)
        @APPLICATION 1970 F-48 K-7

2481   SCHUSTER, J. R., & CLARK, B.
              INDIVIDUAL DIFFERENCES RELATED TO FEELINGS TOWARD PAY.
              PERSONNEL PSYCHOLOGY, 1970, 23, 591-604.
                    (CORRELATES:BEHAVIORAL, DEMOGRAPHIC; N=575 FIRM EMPLOYEES)
       @APPLICATION 1970 P-85

2482   HOLMES, D. S., & APPELBAUM, A. S.
              NATURE OF PRIOR EXPERIMENTAL EXPERIENCE AS A DETERMINANT OF PERFORMANCE
              IN A SUBSEQUENT EXPERIMENT.
              JOURNAL OF PERSONALITY AND SOCIAL PSYCHOLOGY, 1970, 14, 195-202.
                    (CORRELATES:BEHAVIORAL, INTELLIGENCE, ENVIRONMENTAL; N=132
                    UNDERGRADUATES)
       @APPLICATION 1970 M-30 M-20 D-45

2483   SILVERMAN, I., SHULMAN, A. D., & WIESENTHAL, D. L.
              EFFECTS OF DECEIVING AND DEBRIEFING PSYCHOLOGICAL SUBJECTS ON PERFORMANCE
              IN LATER EXPERIMENTS.
              JOURNAL OF PERSONALITY AND SOCIAL PSYCHOLOGY, 1970, 14, 203-212.
                    (RELIABILITY:INTERRATER; CORRELATES:BEHAVIORAL, PSYCHOLOGICAL,
                    DEMOGRAPHIC, INTELLIGENCE, ENVIRONMENTAL; N=69 MALE AND 63 FEMALE
                    UNDERGRADUATES)
       @APPLICATION 1970 G-21 R-31 C-67 J-50

2484   GOLDING, S. L., & LICHTENSTEIN, E.
              CONFESSION OF AWARENESS AND PRIOR KNOWLEDGE OF DECEPTION AS A FUNCTION
              OF INTERVIEW SET AND APPROVAL MOTIVATION.
              JOURNAL OF PERSONALITY AND SOCIAL PSYCHOLOGY, 1970, 14, 213-223.
                    (CORRELATES:BEHAVIORAL, PSYCHOLOGICAL, PHYSIOLOGICAL, ENVIRONMENTAL;
                    NORMATIVE DATA: N=65 MALE UNDERGRADUATES)
       @APPLICATION 1970 C-27

2485   BOWERS, K. S., & VANDERMEULEN, S. J.
              EFFECT OF HYPNOTIC SUSCEPTIBILITY ON CREATIVITY TEST PERFORMANCE.
              JOURNAL OF PERSONALITY AND SOCIAL PSYCHOLOGY, 1970, 14, 247-256.
                    (RELIABILITY:INTERRATER; CORRELATES:BEHAVIORAL, PSYCHOLOGICAL; USED
                    AS CRITERION: N=90 COLLEGE STUDENTS)
       @APPLICATION 1970 S-90 G-5 W-31 H-37 G-80

2486   RENNER, V.
              EFFECTS OF MODIFICATION OF COGNITIVE STYLE ON CREATIVE BEHAVIOR.
              JOURNAL OF PERSONALITY AND SOCIAL PSYCHOLOGY, 1970, 14, 257-262.
                    (CORRELATES:BEHAVIORAL, PSYCHOLOGICAL, ENVIRONMENTAL; USED AS
                    CRITERION; N=60 UNDERGRADUATES)
       @APPLICATION 1970 G-80 W-72 T-28 M-237

2487   LAO, R. C.
              INTERNAL-EXTERNAL CONTROL AND COMPETENT AND INNOVATIVE BEHAVIOR AMONG
              NEGRO COLLEGE STUDENTS.
              JOURNAL OF PERSONALITY AND SOCIAL PSYCHOLOGY, 1970, 14, 263-270.
                    (MODIFICATION; CORRELATES:BEHAVIORAL, PSYCHOLOGICAL, ENVIRONMENTAL;
                    FACTOR ANALYSIS; N=1493 BLACK MALE UNDERGRADUATES)
       @APPLICATION 1970 R-18 G-87

2488   LOTT, A. J., BRIGHT, M. A., WEINSTEIN, P., & LOTT, B. E.
              LIKING FOR PERSONS AS A FUNCTION OF INCENTIVE AND DRIVE DURING ACQUISITION.
              JOURNAL OF PERSONALITY AND SOCIAL PSYCHOLOGY, 1970, 14, 66-76.
                    (CORRELATES:BEHAVIORAL, PSYCHOLOGICAL, ENVIRONMENTAL; USED AS
                    CRITERION; NORMATIVE DATA; 2 STUDIES: N=30 MALE AND 30 FEMALE 1ST
                    GRADERS, N=31 UNDERGRADUATES)
       @APPLICATION 1970 L-29 B-65 O-16

2489   HICKS, J. M., & WRIGHT, J. H.
              CONVERGENT-DISCRIMINANT VALIDATION AND FACTOR ANALYSIS OF FIVE SCALES OF
              LIBERALISM-CONSERVATISM.
              JOURNAL OF PERSONALITY AND SOCIAL PSYCHOLOGY, 1970, 14, 114-120.
                    (VALIDITY:CRITERION; CORRELATES:INTELLIGENCE; FACTOR ANALYSIS;
                    BIAS:RESPONSE; N=149 MALE, 106 FEMALE UNDERGRADUATES)
       @APPLICATION 1970 C-7 A-29 C-64 K-12 A-5 C-27 E-1 C-23 W-23

2490   JONES, R. A.
          VOLUNTEERING TO HELP: THE EFFECTS OF CHOICE, DEPENDENCE, AND ANTICIPATED
          DEPENDENCE.
          JOURNAL OF PERSONALITY AND SOCIAL PSYCHOLOGY, 1970, 14, 121-129.
              (CORRELATES:BEHAVIORAL, ENVIRONMENTAL; USED AS CRITERION; N=129 MALE
              UNDERGRADUATES)
       @APPLICATION 1970 B-83 J-7 R-18

2491   ADERMAN, D., & BERKOWITZ, L.
          OBSERVATIONAL SET, EMPATHY, AND HELPING.
          JOURNAL OF PERSONALITY AND SOCIAL PSYCHOLOGY, 1970, 14, 141-148.
              (CORRELATES:BEHAVIORAL, PSYCHOLOGICAL; N=120 UNDERGRADUATE MALES)
       @APPLICATION 1970 N-5

2492   WALLACH, M. A., & MABLI, J.
          INFORMATION VERSUS CONFORMITY IN THE EFFECTS OF GROUP DISCUSSION ON RISK
          TAKING.
          JOURNAL OF PERSONALITY AND SOCIAL PSYCHOLOGY, 1970, 14, 149-156.
              (CORRELATES:BEHAVIORAL, DEMOGRAPHIC, ENVIRONMENTAL; USED AS
              CRITERION; NORMATIVE DATA; N=447 MALES AND 335 FEMALES)
       @APPLICATION 1970 W-2

2493   ELLIOTT, R., BANKART, B., & LIGHT, T.
          DIFFERENCES IN THE MOTIVATIONAL SIGNIFICANCE OF HEART RATE AND PALMAR
          CONDUCTANCE.
          JOURNAL OF PERSONALITY AND SOCIAL PSYCHOLOGY, 1970, 14, 166-172.
              (CORRELATES:BEHAVIORAL, PSYCHOLOGICAL, PHYSIOLOGICAL,
              ENVIRONMENTAL; N=60 MALE UNDERGRADUATES)
       @APPLICATION 1970 S-61

2494   FOLKINS, C. H.
          TEMPORAL FACTORS AND THE COGNITIVE MEDIATORS OF STRESS REACTION.
          JOURNAL OF PERSONALITY AND SOCIAL PSYCHOLOGY, 1970, 14, 173-184.
              (MODIFICATION; RELIABILITY:INTERRATER; CORRELATES:BEHAVIORAL,
              PHYSIOLOGICAL, ENVIRONMENTAL; FACTOR ANALYSIS; N=90 MALE
              UNDERGRADUATES)
       @APPLICATION 1970 Z-13 W-12

2495   EDELMAN, R. I.
          SOME VARIABLES AFFECTING SUSPICION OF DECEPTION.
          JOURNAL OF PERSONALITY AND SOCIAL PSYCHOLOGY, 1970, 15, 333-337.
              (CORRELATES:BEHAVIORAL, PSYCHOLOGICAL, INTELLIGENCE, ENVIRONMENTAL;
              2 STUDIES: N=48 MALE & 12 FEMALE UNDERGRADUATES; 72 MALE & 18
              FEMALE UNDERGRADUATES)
       @APPLICATION 1970 G-12 B-7 D-45

2496   LAMIN, H., TROMMSDORFF, G., & KOGAN, N.
          PESSIMISM-OPTIMISM AND RISK TAKING IN INDIVIDUAL AND GROUP CONTEXTS.
          JOURNAL OF PERSONALITY AND SOCIAL PSYCHOLOGY, 1970, 15, 366-374.
              (MODIFICATION; CORRELATES:PSYCHOLOGICAL, ENVIRONMENTAL;
              CROSS-CULTURAL APPLICATION; N=130 MALE GERMAN COLLEGE STUDENTS)
       @APPLICATION 1970 W-2

2497   JELLISON, J. M., & RISKIND, J.
          A SOCIAL COMPARISON OF ABILITIES INTERPRETATION OF RISK-TAKING BEHAVIOR.
          JOURNAL OF PERSONALITY AND SOCIAL PSYCHOLOGY, 1970, 15, 375-390.
              (CORRELATES:BEHAVIORAL; USED AS CRITERION; 4 STUDIES: N=218, 29, 54
              AND 82 UNDERGRADUATES)
       @APPLICATION 1970 W-2 A-12

2498   SHOMER, R. W., & CENTERS, R.
          DIFFERENCES IN ATTITUDINAL RESPONSES UNDER CONDITIONS OF IMPLICITLY
          MANIPULATED GROUP SALIENCE.
          JOURNAL OF PERSONALITY AND SOCIAL PSYCHOLOGY, 1970, 15, 125-132.
              (CORRELATES:PSYCHOLOGICAL, DEMOGRAPHIC, ENVIRONMENTAL;
              NORMATIVE DATA; N=214 UNDERGRADUATES)
       @APPLICATION 1970 S-9 K-11

2499   PETRONKO, M. R., & PERIN, C. T.
          A CONSIDERATION OF COGNITIVE COMPLEXITY AND PRIMACY-RECENCY EFFECTS IN
          IMPRESSION FORMATION.
          JOURNAL OF PERSONALITY AND SOCIAL PSYCHOLOGY, 1970, 15, 151-157.
              (CORRELATES:BEHAVIORAL, PSYCHOLOGICAL; USED AS CRITERION;
              N=106 UNDERGRADUATES)
       @APPLICATION 1970 T-13.

2500   GEEN, R. G., & PIGG, R.
             ACQUISITION OF AN AGGRESSIVE RESPONSE AND ITS GENERALIZATION TO VERBAL
             BEHAVIOR.
             JOURNAL OF PERSONALITY AND SOCIAL PSYCHOLOGY, 1970, 15, 165-170.
                    (RELIABILITY:INTERRATER; CORRELATES:BEHAVIORAL, PSYCHOLOGICAL,
                    ENVIRONMENTAL; N=40 MALE UNDERGRADUATES)
        @APPLICATION 1970 G-63

2501   WEINER, B., & KUKLA, A.
             AN ATTRIBUTIONAL ANALYSIS OF ACHIEVEMENT MOTIVATION.
             JOURNAL OF PERSONALITY AND SOCIAL PSYCHOLOGY, 1970, 15, 1-20.
                    (CORRELATES:PSYCHOLOGICAL; N=258 BOYS & 127 GIRLS)
        @APPLICATION 1970 C-25 M-4 M-13 M-7

2502   KATES, S. L., & BARRY, W. T.
             FAILURE AVOIDANCE AND CONCEPT ATTAINMENT.
             JOURNAL OF PERSONALITY AND SOCIAL PSYCHOLOGY, 1970, 15, 21-27.
                    (MODIFICATION; CORRELATES:BEHAVIORAL; USED AS CRITERION; NORMATIVE
                    DATA; N=633 UNDERGRADUATES)
        @APPLICATION 1970 S-76

2503   RAYNOR, J. O.
             RELATIONSHIPS BETWEEN ACHIEVEMENT-RELATED MOTIVES, FUTURE ORIENTATION,
             AND ACADEMIC PERFORMANCE.
             JOURNAL OF PERSONALITY AND SOCIAL PSYCHOLOGY, 1970, 15, 28-33.
                    (CORRELATES:BEHAVIORAL, PSYCHOLOGICAL, INTELLIGENCE; USED AS
                    CRITERION; 2 STUDIES: N=69 MALE AND 52 FEMALE UNDERGRADUATES,
                    N=189 MALE UNDERGRADUATES)
        @APPLICATION 1970 M-7 M-4

2504   SHIMKUNAS, A. M.
             ANXIETY AND EXPECTANCY CHANGE: THE EFFECTS OF FAILURE AND UNCERTAINTY.
             JOURNAL OF PERSONALITY AND SOCIAL PSYCHOLOGY, 1970, 15, 34-42.
                    (VALIDITY:CONSTRUCT; CORRELATES:BEHAVIORAL, PSYCHOLOGICAL,
                    ENVIRONMENTAL; USED AS CRITERION; NORMATIVE DATA; N=80
                    UNDERGRADUATES)
        @APPLICATION 1970 T-2

2505   MILBURN, T. W., BELL, N., & KOESKE, G. F.
             EFFECT OF CENSURE OR PRAISE AND EVALUATIVE DEPENDENCE ON PERFORMANCE IN A
             FREE-LEARNING TASK.
             JOURNAL OF PERSONALITY AND SOCIAL PSYCHOLOGY, 1970, 15, 43-47.
                    (CORRELATES:PSYCHOLOGICAL, DEMOGRAPHIC, ENVIRONMENTAL; USED AS
                    CRITERION; NORMATIVE DATA; 2 STUDIES: N=48 MALE, 38 FEMALE
                    UNDERGRADUATES, N=24 MALE, 24 FEMALE UNDERGRADUATES)
        @APPLICATION 1970 C-27

2506   JACOBSON, L. I., BERGER, S. E., & MILLHAM, J.
             INDIVIDUAL DIFFERENCES IN CHEATING DURING A TEMPTATION PERIOD WHEN
             CONFRONTING FAILURE.
             JOURNAL OF PERSONALITY AND SOCIAL PSYCHOLOGY, 1970, 15, 48-56.
                    (VALIDITY:CONSTRUCT; CORRELATES:BEHAVIORAL, PSYCHOLOGICAL,
                    DEMOGRAPHIC; USED AS CRITERION; NORMATIVE DATA; N=276 UNDERGRADUATES)
        @APPLICATION 1970 C-27 E-1

2507   PREALE, I., AMIR, Y., & SHARAN, S.
             PERCEPTUAL ARTICULATION AND TASK EFFECTIVENESS IN SEVERAL ISRAEL
             SUBCULTURES.
             JOURNAL OF PERSONALITY AND SOCIAL PSYCHOLOGY, 1970, 15, 190-195.
                    (RELIABILITY:INTERNAL CONSISTENCY, INTERRATER;
                    CORRELATES:PSYCHOLOGICAL, DEMOGRAPHIC, INTELLIGENCE; CROSS-CULTURAL
                    APPLICATION; NORMATIVE DATA; 2 STUDIES: N=88 MIDDLE-EASTERN AND 112
                    WESTERN MALES, 145 KIBBUTZ AND 145 WESTERN MALES)
        @APPLICATION 1970 W-19

2508   SHALIT, B.
             ENVIRONMENTAL HOSTILITY AND HOSTILITY IN FANTASY.
             JOURNAL OF PERSONALITY AND SOCIAL PSYCHOLOGY, 1970, 15, 171-174.
                    (CORRELATES:PSYCHOLOGICAL, ENVIRONMENTAL; CROSS-CULTURAL APPLICATION;
                    N=200 NATIONAL SERVICE RECRUITS IN ISRAEL)
        @APPLICATION 1970 M-20 H-37

2509   HOCHREICH, D. J., & ROTTER, J. B.
           HAVE COLLEGE STUDENTS BECOME LESS TRUSTING?
           JOURNAL OF PERSONALITY AND SOCIAL PSYCHOLOGY, 1970, 15, 211-214.
                   (CORRELATES:PSYCHOLOGICAL, DEMOGRAPHIC, ENVIRONMENTAL; USED AS
                   CRITERION; NORMATIVE DATA; N=4605 UNDERGRADUATES)
       @APPLICATION 1970 R-16 C-27

2510   JESSOR, R., BOUTOURLINE YOUNG, H., YOUNG, E. B., & TESI, G.
           PERCEIVED OPPORTUNITY, ALIENATION AND DRINKING BEHAVIOR AMONG ITALIAN AND
           AMERICAN YOUTH.
           JOURNAL OF PERSONALITY AND SOCIAL PSYCHOLOGY, 1970, 15, 215-222.
                   (RELIABILITY:INTERNAL CONSISTENCY; CORRELATES:BEHAVIORAL;
                   CROSS-CULTURAL APPLICATION; N=79 BOSTONIANS, 94 MALE YOUTHS FROM
                   PALERMO AND 108 MALE YOUTHS FROM ROME)
       @APPLICATION 1970 J-28 J-29 J-70

2511   ANDREW, J. M.
           RECOVERY FROM SURGERY, WITH AND WITHOUT PREPARATORY INSTRUCTION, FOR THREE
           COPING STYLES.
           JOURNAL OF PERSONALITY AND SOCIAL PSYCHOLOGY, 1970, 15, 223-226.
                   (CORRELATES:PSYCHOLOGICAL, INTELLIGENCE; USED AS CRITERION; N=59
                   HOSPITALIZED VETERANS)
       @APPLICATION 1970 G-10

2512   GRIFFITT, W.
           ENVIRONMENTAL EFFECTS ON INTERPERSONAL AFFECTIVE BEHAVIOR: AMBIENT
           EFFECTIVE TEMPERATURE AND ATTRACTION.
           JOURNAL OF PERSONALITY AND SOCIAL PSYCHOLOGY, 1970, 15, 240-244.
                   (RELIABILITY:INTERNAL CONSISTENCY; CORRELATES:PSYCHOLOGICAL,
                   ENVIRONMENTAL; N=40 UNDERGRADUATES)
       @APPLICATION 1970 N-17 B-46 B-65

2513   STEIN, K. B., & LENROW, P.
           EXPRESSIVE STYLES AND THEIR MEASUREMENT.
           JOURNAL OF PERSONALITY AND SOCIAL PSYCHOLOGY, 1970, 16, 656-664.
                   (MENTION; VALIDITY:CONSTRUCT; CORRELATES:BEHAVIORAL, PSYCHOLOGICAL;
                   N=91 MALE & 96 FEMALE COLLEGE STUDENTS: 133 FEMALE & 116 MALE COLLEGE
                   STUDENTS)
       @APPLICATION 1970 S-11 C-57 C-59 C-75 C-74 C-73

2514   ROUBERTOUX, P.
           PERSONALITY VARIABLES AND INTEREST IN ART.
           JOURNAL OF PERSONALITY AND SOCIAL PSYCHOLOGY, 1970, 16, 665-668.
                   (MODIFICATION; CORRELATES:PSYCHOLOGICAL; CROSS-CULTURAL APPLICATION;
                   N=81 FRENCH HIGH SCHOOL STUDENTS)
       @APPLICATION 1970 G-26 C-136 C-10

2515   BERKOWITZ, L.
           AGGRESSIVE HUMOR AS A STIMULUS TO AGGRESSIVE RESPONSES.
           JOURNAL OF PERSONALITY AND SOCIAL PSYCHOLOGY, 1970, 16, 710-717.
                   (MODIFICATION; CORRELATES:BEHAVIORAL, PSYCHOLOGICAL; N=80 FEMALE
                   UNDERGRADUATES)
       @APPLICATION 1970 N-17

2516   SUNDBERG, N. D., ROHILA, P. K., & TYLER, L. E.
           VALUES OF INDIAN AND AMERICAN ADOLESCENTS.
           JOURNAL OF PERSONALITY AND SOCIAL PSYCHOLOGY, 1970, 16, 374-397.
                   (DESCRIPTION; RELIABILITY:RETEST; VALIDITY:CRITERION; CROSS-CULTURAL
                   APPLICATION; NORMATIVE DATA; N=48 AMERICAN, 48 INDIAN 9TH GRADERS)
       @APPLICATION 1970 T-90 T-91

2517   LEVENTHAL, G. S.
           INFLUENCE OF BROTHERS AND SISTERS ON SEX-ROLE BEHAVIOR.
           JOURNAL OF PERSONALITY AND SOCIAL PSYCHOLOGY, 1970, 16, 452-465.
                   (RELIABILITY:INTERNAL CONSISTENCY; CORRELATES:PSYCHOLOGICAL,
                   DEMOGRAPHIC; USED AS CRITERION; NORMATIVE DATA; 4 STUDIES: MEDIAN
                   N=APPROX. 300 COLLEGE MALES)
       @APPLICATION 1970 G-22 E-5 C-136 D-45 B-46 W-8

2518   SCHNEIDER, F. W.
           CONFORMING BEHAVIOR OF BLACK AND WHITE CHILDREN.
           JOURNAL OF PERSONALITY AND SOCIAL PSYCHOLOGY, 1970, 16, 466-471.
                   (MODIFICATION; RELIABILITY:RETEST; CORRELATES:BEHAVIORAL,
                   PSYCHOLOGICAL, DEMOGRAPHIC; N=96 MALE AND FEMALE, BLACK AND WHITE
                   7TH AND 8TH GRADERS)
       @APPLICATION 1970 M-180

2519   MARTENS, R., & LANDERS, D. M.
            MOTOR PERFORMANCE UNDER STRESS: A TEST OF THE INVERTED-U HYPOTHESIS.
            JOURNAL OF PERSONALITY AND SOCIAL PSYCHOLOGY, 1970, 16, 29-37.
                (CORRELATES:BEHAVIORAL, PHYSIOLOGICAL, ENVIRONMENTAL; USED AS
                CRITERION; N=1000 JUNIOR HIGH SCHOOL BOYS)
        @APPLICATION 1970 C-55 D-45

2520   BYRNE, D., ERVIN, C. R., & LAMBERTH, J.
            CONTINUITY BETWEEN THE EXPERIMENTAL STUDY OF ATTRACTION AND REAL-LIFE
            COMPUTER DATING.
            JOURNAL OF PERSONALITY AND SOCIAL PSYCHOLOGY, 1970, 16, 157-165.
                (CORRELATES:BEHAVIORAL, PSYCHOLOGICAL, ENVIRONMENTAL; N=88
                UNDERGRADUATES)
        @APPLICATION 1970 B-65

2521   LOTT, A. J., LOTT, B. E., REED, T., & CROW, T.
            PERSONALITY-TRAIT DESCRIPTIONS OF DIFFERENTIALLY LIKED PERSONS.
            JOURNAL OF PERSONALITY AND SOCIAL PSYCHOLOGY, 1970, 16, 284-290.
                (CORRELATES:PSYCHOLOGICAL; NORMATIVE DATA; N=49 MALE AND 61 FEMALE
                UNDERGRADUATES)
        @APPLICATION 1970 A-12

2522   SCHWARTZ, S. H., & CLAUSEN, G. T.
            RESPONSIBILITY, NORMS, AND HELPING IN AN EMERGENCY.
            JOURNAL OF PERSONALITY AND SOCIAL PSYCHOLOGY, 1970, 16, 299-310.
                (MODIFICATION; CORRELATES:BEHAVIORAL, DEMOGRAPHIC; USED AS
                CRITERION; N=189 UNDERGRADUATES)
        @APPLICATION 1970 S-42 W-12

2523   FITCH, G.
            EFFECTS OF SELF-ESTEEM, PERCEIVED PERFORMANCE, AND CHOICE ON CAUSAL
            ATTRIBUTIONS.
            JOURNAL OF PERSONALITY AND SOCIAL PSYCHOLOGY, 1970, 16, 311-315.
                (CORRELATES:PSYCHOLOGICAL, ENVIRONMENTAL; USED AS CRITERION; N=135
                UNDERGRADUATES)
        @APPLICATION 1970 F-7 R-18

2524   MCARTHUR, L. A.
            LUCK IS ALIVE AND WELL IN NEW HAVEN: A SERENDIPITOUS FINDING ON PERCEIVED
            CONTROL OF REINFORCEMENT AFTER THE DRAFT LOTTERY.
            JOURNAL OF PERSONALITY AND SOCIAL PSYCHOLOGY, 1970, 16, 316-318.
                (VALIDITY:CONSTRUCT; CORRELATES:ENVIRONMENTAL; N=23 UNDERGRADUATES)
        @APPLICATION 1970 R-18

2525   CARLSON, R., & LEVY, N.
            SELF, VALUES, AND AFFECTS: DERIVATIONS FROM TOMKINS' POLARITY THEORY.
            JOURNAL OF PERSONALITY AND SOCIAL PSYCHOLOGY, 1970, 16, 338-345.
                (DESCRIPTION; MODIFICATION; RELIABILITY:INTERNAL CONSISTENCY;
                CORRELATES:PSYCHOLOGICAL, DEMOGRAPHIC; USED AS CRITERION; 3 STUDIES:
                N=202 BLACK COLLEGE STUDENTS, N=40 BLACK COLLEGE STUDENTS, N=20
                STUDENTS)
        @APPLICATION 1970 T-70 T-76 C-3

2526   EVANS, R. I., ROZELLE, R. M., LASATER, T. M., DEMBROSKI, T. M., & ALLEN, B. P.
            FEAR AROUSAL, PERSUASION, AND ACTUAL VERSUS IMPLIED BEHAVIORAL CHANGE:
            NEW PERSPECTIVE UTILIZING A REAL-LIFE DENTAL HYGIENE PROGRAM.
            JOURNAL OF PERSONALITY AND SOCIAL PSYCHOLOGY, 1970, 16, 220-227.
                (CORRELATES:BEHAVIORAL, ENVIRONMENTAL; N=394 JUNIOR HIGH SCHOOL
                CHILDREN)
        @APPLICATION 1970 R-8 R-18 C-27

2527   BETTINGHAUS, E., MILLER, G., & STEINFATT, T.
            SOURCE EVALUATION, SYLLOGISTIC CONTENT, AND JUDGMENTS OF LOGICAL VALIDITY
            BY HIGH- AND LOW-DOGMATIC PERSONS.
            JOURNAL OF PERSONALITY AND SOCIAL PSYCHOLOGY, 1970, 16, 238-244.
                (CORRELATES:PSYCHOLOGICAL; USED AS CRITERION; NORMATIVE DATA; N=191
                COLLEGE STUDENTS, 31 NON-STUDENTS)
        @APPLICATION 1970 T-18

2528   MENDELSOHN, G. A., & GALL, M. D.
          PERSONALITY VARIABLES AND THE EFFECTIVENESS OF TECHNIQUES TO FACILITATE
          CREATIVE PROBLEM SOLVING.
          JOURNAL OF PERSONALITY AND SOCIAL PSYCHOLOGY, 1970, 16, 346-351.
                 (CORRELATES:PSYCHOLOGICAL, DEMOGRAPHIC, ENVIRONMENTAL;
                 USED AS CRITERION; BIAS:TESTER; N=54 MALE AND 45
                 FEMALE SUBJECTS)
          @APPLICATION 1970 W-8 W-41 G-21 A-8 M-29

2529   RUBIN, Z.
          MEASUREMENT OF ROMANTIC LOVE.
          JOURNAL OF PERSONALITY AND SOCIAL PSYCHOLOGY, 1970, 16, 265-273.
                 (CORRELATES:BEHAVIORAL, PSYCHOLOGICAL, DEMOGRAPHIC; BIAS:RESPONSE;
                 N=158 DATING COLLEGE COUPLES)
          @APPLICATION 1970 C-27 W-2

2530   HOUSTON, B. K., & HODGES, W. F.
          SITUATIONAL DENIAL AND PERFORMANCE UNDER STRESS.
          JOURNAL OF PERSONALITY AND SOCIAL PSYCHOLOGY, 1970, 16, 726-730.
                 (CORRELATES:BEHAVIORAL, PSYCHOLOGICAL, PHYSIOLOGICAL, INTELLIGENCE,
                 ENVIRONMENTAL; USED AS CRITERION; N=54 HIGH- AND 54 LOW-ANXIETY
                 MALE UNDERGRADUATES)
          @APPLICATION 1970 T-2 Z-13

2531   MAUSNER, B., & GRAHAM, J.
          FIELD DEPENDENCE AND PRIOR REINFORCEMENT AS DETERMINANTS OF SOCIAL
          INTERACTION IN JUDGMENT.
          JOURNAL OF PERSONALITY AND SOCIAL PSYCHOLOGY, 1970, 16, 486-493.
                 (RELIABILITY:INTERRATER; CORRELATES:BEHAVIORAL, PSYCHOLOGICAL; USED
                 AS CRITERION; NORMATIVE DATA; N=132 MALE HIGH SCHOOL STUDENTS, 74
                 SELECTED)
          @APPLICATION 1970 H-37 F-56

2532   MACNEIL, L. W., & RULE, B. G.
          EFFECTS OF CONCEPTUAL STRUCTURE ON INFORMATION PREFERENCE UNDER SENSORY-
          DEPRIVATION CONDITIONS.
          JOURNAL OF PERSONALITY AND SOCIAL PSYCHOLOGY, 1970, 16, 530-535.
                 (CORRELATES:BEHAVIORAL, ENVIRONMENTAL; USED AS CRITERION; N=40 MALE
                 UNDERGRADUATES)
          @APPLICATION 1970 T-16

2533   GOSS, A., & MOROSKO, T. E.
          RELATION BETWEEN A DIMENSION OF INTERNAL-EXTERNAL CONTROL AND THE MMPI
          WITH AN ALCOHOLIC POPULATION.
          JOURNAL OF CONSULTING AND CLINICAL PSYCHOLOGY, 1970, 34, 189-192.
                 (VALIDITY:CROSS-VALIDATION; CORRELATES:PSYCHOLOGICAL; N=200 MALE AND
                 62 FEMALE ALCOHOLICS)
          @APPLICATION 1970 R-18 D-45

2534   LEFCOURT, H. M., & STEFFY, R. A.
          LEVEL OF ASPIRATION, RISK-TAKING BEHAVIOR, AND PROJECTIVE TEST PERFORMANCE:
          A SEARCH FOR COHERENCE.
          JOURNAL OF CONSULTING AND CLINICAL PSYCHOLOGY, 1970, 34, 193-198.
                 (MODIFICATION; CORRELATES:BEHAVIORAL, PSYCHOLOGICAL; NORMATIVE DATA;
                 N=37 STUDENT NURSES)
          @APPLICATION 1970 R-18 R-17 M-20

2535   PEARSON, P. H.
          RELATIONSHIPS BETWEEN GLOBAL AND SPECIFIED MEASURES OF NOVELTY SEEKING.
          JOURNAL OF CONSULTING AND CLINICAL PSYCHOLOGY, 1970, 34, 199-204.
                 (CORRELATES:PSYCHOLOGICAL; NORMATIVE DATA; N=70 AIRMEN)
          @APPLICATION 1970 Z-3 E-30 S-56 J-1 M-244

2536   EVANS, R. B.
          SIXTEEN PERSONALITY FACTOR QUESTIONNAIRE SCORES OF HOMOSEXUAL MEN.
          JOURNAL OF CONSULTING AND CLINICAL PSYCHOLOGY, 1970, 34, 212-215.
                 (CORRELATES:BEHAVIORAL, PSYCHOLOGICAL; NORMATIVE DATA; N=44
                 HOMOSEXUAL AND 111 HETEROSEXUAL MEN)
          @APPLICATION 1970 C-10

2537   MIRELS, H. L.
           DIMENSIONS OF INTERNAL VERSUS EXTERNAL CONTROL.
           JOURNAL OF CONSULTING AND CLINICAL PSYCHOLOGY, 1970, 34, 226-228.
               (CORRELATES:DEMOGRAPHIC; FACTOR ANALYSIS; N=159 MALE, 157 FEMALE
               COLLEGE STUDENTS)
       @APPLICATION 1970 R-18

2538   EDWARDS, A. L., CONE, J. D., JR., & ABBOTT, R. D.
           ANXIETY, STRUCTURE, OR SOCIAL DESIRABILITY?
           JOURNAL OF CONSULTING AND CLINICAL PSYCHOLOGY, 1970, 34, 236-238.
               (RELIABILITY:INTERNAL CONSISTENCY; VALIDITY:CONSTRUCT;
               CORRELATES:PSYCHOLOGICAL, DEMOGRAPHIC; NORMATIVE DATA;
               N=148 MALE, 197 FEMALE UNDERGRADUATES)
       @APPLICATION 1970 T-2 K-75 D-45

2539   BROVERMAN, I. K., BROVERMAN, D. M., CLARKSON, F. E., ROSENCRANTZ, P. S., &
       VOGEL, S. R.
           SEX-ROLE STEREOTYPES AND CLINICAL JUDGMENTS OF MENTAL HEALTH.
           JOURNAL OF CONSULTING AND CLINICAL PSYCHOLOGY, 1970, 34, 1-7.
               (CORRELATES:PSYCHOLOGICAL, ENVIRONMENTAL; NORMATIVE DATA; N=79
               CLINICALLY TRAINED PSYCHOLOGISTS)
       @APPLICATION 1970 R-72

2540   SINGER, M. I.
           COMPARISON OF INDICATORS OF HOMOSEXUALITY ON THE MMPI.
           JOURNAL OF CONSULTING AND CLINICAL PSYCHOLOGY, 1970, 34, 15-18.
               (VALIDITY:CONSTRUCT; N=97 MALE PSYCHIATRIC OUTPATIENTS)
       @APPLICATION 1970 P-15 A-1 D-45

2541   CLEMENT, P. W.
           ELIMINATION OF SLEEP WALKING IN A 7-YEAR OLD BOY.
           JOURNAL OF CONSULTING AND CLINICAL PSYCHOLOGY, 1970, 34, 22-26.
               (MENTION; N=1 BOY)
       @APPLICATION 1970 A-76

2542   BROWN, W. P.
           INDIVIDUAL DIFFERENCES IN ASSOCIATING TO NEUTRAL AND EMOTIONAL WORDS.
           JOURNAL OF CONSULTING AND CLINICAL PSYCHOLOGY, 1970, 34, 33-36.
               (CORRELATES:BEHAVIORAL, PSYCHOLOGICAL; N=100 UNIVERSITY STUDENTS)
       @APPLICATION 1970 E-5

2543   STEINHELBER, J. C.
           BIAS IN THE ASSESSMENT OF PSYCHOTHERAPY.
           JOURNAL OF CONSULTING AND CLINICAL PSYCHOLOGY, 1970, 34, 37-42.
               (USED AS CRITERION; NORMATIVE DATA; BIAS:TESTER; N=54 MALE VETERAN
               PSYCHIATRIC OUTPATIENTS)
       @APPLICATION 1970 L-49

2544   HAASE, R. F., & IVEY, A. E.
           INFLUENCE OF CLIENT PRETESTING ON COUNSELING OUTCOME.
           JOURNAL OF CONSULTING AND CLINICAL PSYCHOLOGY, 1970, 34, 128.
               (CORRELATES:PSYCHOLOGICAL; NORMATIVE DATA; N=27 STUDENTS AT
               COUNSELING CLINIC)
       @APPLICATION 1970 D-45 L-76 A-48

2545   COWEN, E. L., HUSEN, J., BEACH, D. R., & RAPPAPORT, J.
           PARENTAL PERCEPTIONS OF YOUNG CHILDREN AND THEIR RELATION TO INDEXES OF
           ADJUSTMENT.
           JOURNAL OF CONSULTING AND CLINICAL PSYCHOLOGY, 1970, 34, 97-103.
               (RELIABILITY:RETEST, INTERNAL CONSISTENCY; CORRELATES:PSYCHOLOGICAL,
               INTELLIGENCE; NORMATIVE DATA; N=395 PARENTS OF SCHOOL CHILDREN)
       @APPLICATION 1970 C-55 L-77 P-66 B-145 B-144

2546   LUNNEBORG, P. W.
           STEREOTYPIC ASPECT IN MASCULINITY-FEMININITY MEASUREMENT.
           JOURNAL OF CONSULTING AND CLINICAL PSYCHOLOGY, 1970, 34, 113-118.
               (VALIDITY:CONSTRUCT; N=204 MALE AND 194 FEMALE UNDERGRADUATES)
       @APPLICATION 1970 E-2

2547   SILVERMAN, J., & KING, C.
           PSEUDO PERCEPTUAL DIFFERENTIATION.
           JOURNAL OF CONSULTING AND CLINICAL PSYCHOLOGY, 1970, 34, 119-123.
               (CORRELATES:PSYCHOLOGICAL, DEMOGRAPHIC; 2 STUDIES: N=13 MALES AND 11
               FEMALES, N=10 MALE AND 13 FEMALE ACUTE SCHIZOPHRENICS)
       @APPLICATION 1970 W-188

2548   EISENMAN, R., & SCHUSSEL, N. R.
              CREATIVITY, BIRTH ORDER, AND PREFERENCE FOR SYMMETRY.
              JOURNAL OF CONSULTING AND CLINICAL PSYCHOLOGY, 1970, 34, 275-280.
                   (MODIFICATION; VALIDITY:CONSTRUCT; CORRELATES:PSYCHOLOGICAL,
                   DEMOGRAPHIC; NORMATIVE DATA; N=450 COLLEGE STUDENTS)
         @APPLICATION 1970 E-22 E-64

2549   CROSS, H. J., & ALLEN, J. G.
              EGO IDENTITY STATUS, ADJUSTMENT, AND ACADEMIC ACHIEVEMENT.
              JOURNAL OF CONSULTING AND CLINICAL PSYCHOLOGY, 1970, 34, 288.
                   (CORRELATES:BEHAVIORAL, INTELLIGENCE; N=81 MALES IN COLLEGE)
         @APPLICATION 1970 7-4

2550   EVANS, M. B., & PAUL, G. L.
              EFFECTS OF HYPNOTICALLY SUGGESTED ANALGESIA AND PHYSIOLOGICAL AND
              SUBJECTIVE RESPONSES TO COLD STRESS.
              JOURNAL OF CONSULTING AND CLINICAL PSYCHOLOGY, 1970, 35, 362-371.
                   (MODIFICATION; CORRELATES:BEHAVIORAL, PSYCHOLOGICAL, PHYSIOLOGICAL;
                   USED AS CRITERION; N=64 FEMALE UNDERGRADUATES)
         @APPLICATION 1970 S-90

2551   HETTICH, P. I., & WALKER, R. E.
              EFFECTS OF EXPERIMENTAL ABSENCE AND SUBJECTIVE BRIEFING ON SOCIAL
              DESIRABILITY SCALE SCORES.
              JOURNAL OF CONSULTING AND CLINICAL PSYCHOLOGY, 1970, 35, 372-375.
                   (CORRELATES:ENVIRONMENTAL; NORMATIVE DATA; N=200 MALE COLLEGE
                   STUDENTS)
         @APPLICATION 1970 C-27

2552   KROGER, R. O., & TURNBULL, W.
              EFFECTS OF ROLE DEMANDS AND TEST-CUE PROPERTIES ON PERSONALITY TEST
              PERFORMANCE: REPLICATION AND EXTENSION.
              JOURNAL OF CONSULTING AND CLINICAL PSYCHOLOGY, 1970, 35, 381-387.
                   (RELIABILITY:INTERRATER; CORRELATES:ENVIRONMENTAL; NORMATIVE DATA;
                   BIAS:RESPONSE; N=44 COLLEGE MALES)
         @APPLICATION 1970 S-33 T-2 W-9

2553   BAXTER, J. C., & DEAROVICH, B. F.
              ANXIETY AROUSING EFFECTS OF INAPPROPRIATE CROWDING.
              JOURNAL OF CONSULTING AND CLINICAL PSYCHOLOGY, 1970, 35, 174-178.
                   (CORRELATES:PSYCHOLOGICAL, ENVIRONMENTAL; N=48 FEMALE STUDENTS)
         @APPLICATION 1970 S-97 G-21

2554   TAYLOR, G. P., JR.
              MODERATOR-VARIABLE EFFECT ON PERSONALITY TEST-ITEM ENDORSEMENTS OF
              PHYSICALLY DISABLED PATIENTS.
              JOURNAL OF CONSULTING AND CLINICAL PSYCHOLOGY, 1970, 35, 183-188.
                   (VALIDITY:CONTENT; CORRELATES:BEHAVIORAL; NORMATIVE DATA; N=28
                   SPINAL INJURED PATIENTS AND 28 NON-INJURED MEN)
         @APPLICATION 1970 D-45

2555   HOGAN, R.
              A DIMENSION OF MORAL JUDGMENT.
              JOURNAL OF CONSULTING AND CLINICAL PSYCHOLOGY, 1970, 35, 205-212.
                   (CORRELATES:PSYCHOLOGICAL, INTELLIGENCE; N=95 MALE, 54 FEMALE
                   UNDERGRADUATES AND 48 MEN AND WOMEN AND OTHER SIMILAR SAMPLES)
         @APPLICATION 1970 E-1 A-5 R-8 G-22 G-21 M-22

2556   BOROOVEC, T. D.
              AUTONOMIC REACTIVITY TO SENSORY STIMULATION IN PSYCHOPATHIC, NEUROTIC, AND
              NORMAL JUVENILE DELINQUENTS.
              JOURNAL OF CONSULTING AND CLINICAL PSYCHOLOGY, 1970, 35, 217-222.
                   (MODIFICATION; CORRELATES:PHYSIOLOGICAL; USED AS CRITERION; N=19
                   PSYCHOPATHIC, 21 NEUROTIC, 25 NORMAL DELINQUENTS)
         @APPLICATION 1970 Q-8 L-22

2557   KHAN, S. B.
              DIMENSIONS OF MANIFEST ANXIETY AND THEIR RELATIONSHIP TO COLLEGE
              ACHIEVEMENT.
              JOURNAL OF CONSULTING AND CLINICAL PSYCHOLOGY, 1970, 35, 223-228.
                   (VALIDITY:CRITERION; CORRELATES:DEMOGRAPHIC, INTELLIGENCE; FACTOR
                   ANALYSIS; N=152 MALE 107 FEMALE COLLEGE STUDENTS)
         @APPLICATION 1970 T-2

2558   MATELL, M. S., & SMITH, R. E.
            APPROVAL MOTIVE AND ACADEMIC BEHAVIORS.
            JOURNAL OF CONSULTING AND CLINICAL PSYCHOLOGY, 1970, 35, 229-232.
                (CORRELATES:BEHAVIORAL, ENVIRONMENTAL; NORMATIVE DATA;
                N=60 UNDERGRADUATES)
        @APPLICATION 1970 C-27

2559   SARBIN, T. R., & MANCUSO, J. C.
            FAILURE OF A MORAL ENTERPRISE: ATTITUDES OF THE PUBLIC TOWARD MENTAL
            ILLNESS.
            JOURNAL OF CONSULTING AND CLINICAL PSYCHOLOGY, 1970, 35, 159-173.
                (MENTION; DESCRIPTION; REVIEW ARTICLE; NO SAMPLE SIZE)
        @APPLICATION 1970 N-32 K-99 F-112 C-209 P-105 C-208 B-229 G-164 O-16 S-305

2560   POPE, B., SIEGMAN, A. W., & BLASS, T.
            ANXIETY AND SPEECH IN THE INITIAL INTERVIEW.
            JOURNAL OF CONSULTING AND CLINICAL PSYCHOLOGY, 1970, 35, 233-238.
                (RELIABILITY:INTERRATER; CORRELATES:BEHAVIORAL, PSYCHOLOGICAL,
                ENVIRONMENTAL; N=32 JUNIOR AND SENIOR NURSING STUDENTS)
        @APPLICATION 1970 T-2 M-187

2561   ROSENZWEIG, S. P., & HARFORD, T.
            CORRELATES OF THE PSYCHOTIC REACTION PROFILE IN AN OUTPATIENT PSYCHIATRIC
            SAMPLE.
            JOURNAL OF CONSULTING AND CLINICAL PSYCHOLOGY, 1970, 35, 244-247.
                (RELIABILITY:INTERRATER; CORRELATES:PSYCHOLOGICAL, INTELLIGENCE;
                USED AS CRITERION; NORMATIVE DATA; N=73 MALE PSYCHIATRIC PATIENTS)
        @APPLICATION 1970 D-7 L-70 H-37 S-61

2562   CHANDLER, M. J.
            SELF-AWARENESS AND ITS RELATION TO OTHER PARAMETERS OF THE CLINICAL
            INFERENCE PROCESS.
            JOURNAL OF CONSULTING AND CLINICAL PSYCHOLOGY, 1970, 35, 258-264.
                (RELIABILITY:RETEST, INTERRATER; VALIDITY:CRITERION; BIAS:TESTER;
                N=30 PROFESSIONAL AND STUDENT PSYCHOLOGISTS)
        @APPLICATION 1970 E-20 D-45

2563   BERZINS, J. I., ROSS, W. F., & COHEN, D. I.
            SKILL VERSUS CHANCE ACTIVITY PREFERENCES AS ALTERNATIVE MEASURES OF
            LOCUS OF CONTROL: AN ATTEMPTED CROSS-VALIDATION.
            JOURNAL OF CONSULTING AND CLINICAL PSYCHOLOGY, 1970, 35, 18-20.
                (RELIABILITY:INTERNAL CONSISTENCY; NORMATIVE DATA; N=97 MALE ADDICT
                PATIENTS)
        @APPLICATION 1970 R-18 S-159 E-1 D-45 M-230

2564   MCCLAIN, E.
            FURTHER VALIDATION OF THE PERSONAL ORIENTATION INVENTORY: ASSESSMENT OF
            SELF-ACTUALIZATION OF SCHOOL COUNSELORS.
            JOURNAL OF CONSULTING AND CLINICAL PSYCHOLOGY, 1970, 35, 21-22.
                (CORRELATES:PSYCHOLOGICAL; N=30 COUNSELORS)
        @APPLICATION 1970 S-21

2565   BAUGH, J. R., PASCAL, G. R., & COTTRELL, T. B.
            RELATIONSHIP OF REPORTED MEMORIES OF EARLY EXPERIENCES WITH PARENTS ON
            INTERVIEW BEHAVIOR.
            JOURNAL OF CONSULTING AND CLINICAL PSYCHOLOGY, 1970, 35, 23-29.
                (RELIABILITY:INTERRATER; VALIDITY:CRITERION; N=22 FEMALE COLLEGE
                STUDENTS)
        @APPLICATION 1970 P-63

2566   PARSONS, O. A., SCHNEIDER, J. M., & HANSEN, A. S.
            INTERNAL-EXTERNAL LOCUS OF CONTROL AND NATIONAL STEREOTYPES IN DENMARK
            AND THE UNITED STATES.
            JOURNAL OF CONSULTING AND CLINICAL PSYCHOLOGY, 1970, 35, 30-37.
                (VALIDITY:CROSS-VALIDATION: CORRELATES:DEMOGRAPHIC; CROSS-CULTURAL
                APPLICATION; NORMATIVE DATA; 3 STUDIES: N=57 MALES, 58 FEMALES; 67
                MALES, 82 FEMALES; 116 MALES, 108 FEMALES, ALL STUDENTS)
        @APPLICATION 1970 R-18

2567   SCHILL, T., EMANUEL, G., PEDERSEN, V., SCHNEIDER, L., & WACHOWIAK, D.
            SEXUAL RESPONSIVITY OF DEFENSIVE AND NON-DEFENSIVE SENSITIZERS AND
            REPRESSORS.
            JOURNAL OF CONSULTING AND CLINICAL PSYCHOLOGY, 1970, 35, 44-47.
                (VALIDITY:CRITERION; USED AS CRITERION; NORMATIVE DATA; BIAS:TESTER;
                N=166 MALE COLLEGE STUDENTS)
        @APPLICATION 1970 C-27 B-46 G-105

2568   DOMINO, G.
            IDENTIFICATION OF POTENTIALLY CREATIVE PERSONS FROM THE ADJECTIVE CHECK
            LIST.
            JOURNAL OF CONSULTING AND CLINICAL PSYCHOLOGY, 1970, 35, 48-51.
                (VALIDITY:CRITERION, CROSS-VALIDATION; USED AS CRITERION;
                NORMATIVE DATA; N=141 MALE STUDENTS)
        @APPLICATION 1970 G-21 B-76 M-29 G-50

2569   RESH, M. G.
            ASTHMA OF UNKNOWN ORIGIN AS A PSYCHOLOGICAL GROUP.
            JOURNAL OF CONSULTING AND CLINICAL PSYCHOLOGY, 1970, 35, 429.
                (CORRELATES:PHYSIOLOGICAL; N=30 ADOLESCENT & ADULT MEDICAL PATIENTS)
        @APPLICATION 1970 D-45

2570   NEVA, E., & HICKS, R. A.
            A NEW LOOK AT AN OLD ISSUE: MANIFEST ANXIETY SCALE VALIDITY.
            JOURNAL OF CONSULTING AND CLINICAL PSYCHOLOGY, 1970, 35, 406-408.
                (VALIDITY:CRITERION; CORRELATES:PHYSIOLOGICAL, INTELLIGENCE; N=24
                MALE AND 24 FEMALE UNDERGRADUATES)
        @APPLICATION 1970 B-184

2571   BURHENNE, D., & MIRELS, H. L.
            SELF-DISCLOSURE IN SELF-DESCRIPTIVE ESSAYS.
            JOURNAL OF CONSULTING AND CLINICAL PSYCHOLOGY, 1970, 35, 409-413.
                (RELIABILITY:INTERRATER; VALIDITY:CONSTRUCT;
                CORRELATES:PSYCHOLOGICAL; N=56 COLLEGE FEMALES)
        @APPLICATION 1970 J-14 C-27

2572   MCCARTHY, D., ANTHONY, R. J., & DOMINO, G.
            A COMPARISON OF THE CPI, FRANCK, MMPI, AND WAIS MASCULINITY-FEMININITY
            INDEXES.
            JOURNAL OF CONSULTING AND CLINICAL PSYCHOLOGY, 1970, 35, 414-416.
                (RELIABILITY:INTERRATER; VALIDITY:CONSTRUCT, CRITERION;
                CORRELATES:DEMOGRAPHIC; NORMATIVE DATA; N=31 MALE AND 29 FEMALE
                COLLEGE STUDENTS)
        @APPLICATION 1970 G-22 D-45 F-11 W-5

2573   CHINSKY, J. M., & RAPPAPORT, J.
            ATTITUDE CHANGE IN COLLEGE STUDENTS AND CHRONIC PATIENTS.
            JOURNAL OF CONSULTING AND CLINICAL PSYCHOLOGY, 1970, 35, 388-394.
                (CORRELATES:BEHAVIORAL, PSYCHOLOGICAL; NORMATIVE DATA; N=15 MALE AND
                15 FEMALE UNDERGRADUATES)
        @APPLICATION 1970 G-21 O-16

2574   MANOSEVITZ, M.
            ITEM ANALYSIS OF THE MMPI MF SCALE USING HOMOSEXUAL AND HETEROSEXUAL MALES.
            JOURNAL OF CONSULTING AND CLINICAL PSYCHOLOGY, 1970, 35, 395-399.
                (CORRELATES:PSYCHOLOGICAL; N=89 HETEROSEXUALS & 89 HOMOSEXUALS)
        @APPLICATION 1970 D-45

2575   DIXON, T. R.
            EXPERIMENTER APPROVAL, SOCIAL DESIRABILITY, AND STATEMENTS OF SELF-
            PREFERENCE.
            JOURNAL OF CONSULTING AND CLINICAL PSYCHOLOGY, 1970, 35, 400-405.
                (CORRELATES:PSYCHOLOGICAL, ENVIRONMENTAL; BIAS:TESTER; N=80 FEMALE
                UNDERGRADUATES)
        @APPLICATION 1970 C-27

2576   SIEGELMAN, E., BLOCK, J., & VONDERLIPPE, A.
            ANTECEDENTS OF OPTIMAL PSYCHOLOGICAL ADJUSTMENT.
            JOURNAL OF CONSULTING AND CLINICAL PSYCHOLOGY, 1970, 35, 283-289.
                (RELIABILITY:INTERNAL CONSISTENCY; VALIDITY:CONSTRUCT;
                CORRELATES:DEMOGRAPHIC, ENVIRONMENTAL; USED AS CRITERION; N=171
                ADULTS IN THEIR MID-30'S)
        @APPLICATION 1970 B-126

2577   DIES, R. R.
            NEED FOR SOCIAL APPROVAL AND BLAME ASSIGNMENT.
            JOURNAL OF CONSULTING AND CLINICAL PSYCHOLOGY, 1970, 35, 311-316.
                (CORRELATES:PSYCHOLOGICAL; USED AS CRITERION; N=80 FEMALE
                PSYCHIATRIC NURSING STUDENTS)
        @APPLICATION 1970 C-27

2578   PARSONS, O. A., & KLEIN, H. P.
            CONCEPT FORMATION AND PRACTICE IN BRAIN DAMAGED AND PROCESS-REACTIVE
            SCHIZOPHRENIC GROUPS.
            JOURNAL OF CONSULTING AND CLINICAL PSYCHOLOGY, 1970, 35, 317-323.
                 (CORRELATES:BEHAVIORAL, PSYCHOLOGICAL, PHYSIOLOGICAL; USED AS
                 CRITERION; N=15 BRAIN DAMAGED PATIENTS, 15 PROCESS AND 15 REACTIVE
                 SCHIZOPHRENICS, AND 15 CONTROLS)
        @APPLICATION 1970 H-163 K-51

2579   MORRIS, L. W., & LIEBERT, R. M.
            RELATIONSHIP OF COGNITIVE AND EMOTIONAL COMPONENTS OF TEST ANXIETY TO
            PHYSIOLOGICAL AROUSAL AND ACADEMIC PERFORMANCE.
            JOURNAL OF CONSULTING AND CLINICAL PSYCHOLOGY, 1970, 35, 332-337.
                 (VALIDITY:CONSTRUCT; CORRELATES:PSYCHOLOGICAL, PHYSIOLOGICAL,
                 INTELLIGENCE; 2 STUDIES: N=95 UNDERGRADUATES, N=91 HIGH SCHOOL
                 SENIORS)
        @APPLICATION 1970 M-4

2580   ROGERS, L. S., YOUNG, H. H., COHEN, I. H., DWORIN, J., & LIPETZ, M. E.
            MARITAL STABILITY, MENTAL HEALTH, AND MARITAL SATISFACTION.
            JOURNAL OF CONSULTING AND CLINICAL PSYCHOLOGY, 1970, 35, 342-348.
                 (MODIFICATION; CORRELATES:PSYCHOLOGICAL, DEMOGRAPHIC; NORMATIVE DATA;
                 N=50 STABLE AND 50 SEEKING-HELP COUPLES)
        @APPLICATION 1970 L-3 T-2 B-5 G-26 L-133

2581   WOGAN, M.
            EFFECT OF THERAPIST-PATIENT PERSONALITY VARIABLES ON THERAPEUTIC OUTCOME.
            JOURNAL OF CONSULTING AND CLINICAL PSYCHOLOGY, 1970, 35, 356-361.
                 (CORRELATES:PSYCHOLOGICAL; FACTOR ANALYSIS; N=82 PSYCHIATRIC
                 INPATIENTS: 55 WOMEN, 27 MEN)
        @APPLICATION 1970 D-45 W-8 W-41

2582   SZABO, M., & FELDHUSEN, J. F.
            PERSONALITY AND INTELLECTIVE PREDICTORS AND ACADEMIC SUCCESS IN AN
            INDEPENDENT STUDY SCIENCE COURSE AT THE COLLEGE LEVEL.
            PSYCHOLOGICAL REPORTS, 1970, 26, 493-494.
                 (CORRELATES:BEHAVIORAL, PSYCHOLOGICAL, INTELLIGENCE; N=630
                 UNDERGRADUATES)
        @APPLICATION 1970 G-26

2583   DECKNER, C. W., & CROMWELL, R. L.
            COMMONALITY OF WORD ASSOCIATION RESPONSE IN SCHIZOPHRENIA AS A FUNCTION OF
            PREMORBID ADJUSTMENT, CHRONICITY, AND PARANOID STATUS.
            PSYCHOLOGICAL REPORTS, 1970, 26, 503-509.
                 (CORRELATES:PSYCHOLOGICAL, DEMOGRAPHIC; USED AS CRITERION; N=102
                 MALE SCHIZOPHRENIC PATIENTS AGES 19-54 YEARS OLD)
        @APPLICATION 1970 U-5 R-27

2584   KLAVETTER, R. E., MOGAR, R. E., & WATT, J.
            CHANGES ON THE MYERS-BRIGG FOLLOWING PSYCHEDELIC THERAPY: A PILOT STUDY.
            PSYCHOLOGICAL REPORTS, 1970, 26, 510.
                 (CORRELATES:ENVIRONMENTAL; N=12 NEUROTIC PATIENTS)
        @APPLICATION 1970 M-22

2585   BATES, G. L., PARKER, H. J., & MCCOY, J. F.
            VOCATIONAL REHABILITANTS' PERSONALITY AND WORK ADJUSTMENT: A TEST OF
            HOLLAND'S THEORY OF VOCATIONAL CHOICE.
            PSYCHOLOGICAL REPORTS, 1970, 26, 511-516.
                 (VALIDITY:CONSTRUCT; CORRELATES:PSYCHOLOGICAL, DEMOGRAPHIC; USED AS
                 CRITERION; N=124 MALE, 76 FEMALE VOCATIONAL REHABILITATION CLIENTS,
                 59 UNEMPLOYED)
        @APPLICATION 1970 W-158 W-159 H-21

2586   ROTTER, J. B.
            COMMENT ON FITZGERALD, PASEWORK, AND NOAH'S STUDY OF VALIDITY OF THE
            INTERPERSONAL TRUST SCALE.
            PSYCHOLOGICAL REPORTS, 1970, 26, 517-518.
                 (REVIEW; VALIDITY:CONSTRUCT, CRITERION)
        @APPLICATION 1970 R-16

2587   NOE, F. P.
        A DENOTATIVE DIMENSION OF MEANING FOR THE MENTALLY ILL-HEALTHY ROLE IN
        SOCIETY.
        PSYCHOLOGICAL REPORTS, 1970, 26, 519-531.
                (RELIABILITY:INTERNAL CONSISTENCY; CORRELATES:PSYCHOLOGICAL,
                ENVIRONMENTAL; BIAS:RESPONSE; N=66 UNDERGRADUATES)
        @APPLICATION 1970 O-16 N-45

2588   LESTER, D.
        ANOMIE AND THE SUICIDAL INDIVIDUAL.
        PSYCHOLOGICAL REPORTS, 1970, 26, 532.
                (CORRELATES:BEHAVIORAL, PSYCHOLOGICAL; USED AS CRITERION;
                N=6 STUDENTS WHO HAD ATTEMPTED SUICIDE, 8 WHO HAD THREATENED & 28
                WHO HAD NEVER CONSIDERED IT)
        @APPLICATION 1970 J-48 D-15 S-28

2589   JUAN, I. R., & HALEY, H. B.
        HIGH AND LOW LEVELS OF DOGMATISM IN RELATION TO PERSONALITY, INTELLECTUAL,
        AND ENVIRONMENTAL CHARACTERISTICS OF MEDICAL STUDENTS.
        PSYCHOLOGICAL REPORTS, 1970, 26, 535-544.
                (CORRELATES:PSYCHOLOGICAL, DEMOGRAPHIC; USED AS CRITERION;
                NORMATIVE DATA; N=514 ENTERING MEDICAL STUDENTS, 141 SELECTED)
        @APPLICATION 1970 R-8 A-7 H-176 G-13

2590   HJELLE, L. A., & CLOUSER, R.
        INTERNAL-EXTERNAL CONTROL OF REINFORCEMENT IN SMOKING BEHAVIOR.
        PSYCHOLOGICAL REPORTS, 1970, 26, 562.
                (CORRELATES:BEHAVIORAL; USED AS CRITERION; N=49 FEMALE, 75 MALE
                COLLEGE STUDENTS)
        @APPLICATION 1970 R-18

2591   GORDON, L. V.
        BUREAUCRATIC VALUES AND ROTC RE-ENROLLMENT.
        PSYCHOLOGICAL REPORTS, 1970, 26, 570.
                (VALIDITY:CONSTRUCT; CORRELATES:BEHAVIORAL; NORMATIVE DATA; N=337
                COLLEGE STUDENTS IN ROTC)
        @APPLICATION 1970 G-11

2592   CRAIG, R. J.
        SIGNIFICANT INTERCORRELATIONS AMONG MEASURES OF OVERINCLUSIVE THINKING.
        PSYCHOLOGICAL REPORTS, 1970, 26, 571-574.
                (CORRELATES:PSYCHOLOGICAL; N=40 SCHIZOPHRENICS, 40 PSYCHIATRIC
                ATTENDANTS)
        @APPLICATION 1970 P-108 B-94

2593   HANSON, D. J.
        VALIDITY TEST OF THE DOGMATISM SCALE.
        PSYCHOLOGICAL REPORTS, 1970, 26, 585-586.
                (VALIDITY:CONSTRUCT; CORRELATES:PSYCHOLOGICAL; N=301 COLLEGE
                STUDENTS)
        @APPLICATION 1970 R-8 S-130

2594   WARD, C. D., HIGGS, W. J., & PARK, G. D.
        ISSUE SALIENCY AND CORRESPONDENCE BETWEEN MEASURES OF ATTITUDE.
        PSYCHOLOGICAL REPORTS, 1970, 26, 587-593.
                (VALIDITY:CONSTRUCT; CORRELATES:PSYCHOLOGICAL; USED AS CRITERION;
                NORMATIVE DATA; N=180 COLLEGE STUDENTS)
        @APPLICATION 1970 O-16 T-23

2595   LUCK, J. I., & GRUNER, C. R.
        ANOTHER NOTE ON POLITICAL CANDIDATE PREFERENCE AND AUTHORITARIANISM.
        PSYCHOLOGICAL REPORTS, 1970, 26, 594.
                (CORRELATES:BEHAVIORAL; N=110 UNDERGRADUATES)
        @APPLICATION 1970 A-5

2596   STACEY, B. G.
        AN EVALUATION OF AN ETHNOCENTRISM SCALE WITH REFERENCE TO ITEM CONTENT AND
        RESPONSE STYLE.
        PSYCHOLOGICAL REPORTS, 1970, 26, 595-602.
                (RELIABILITY:INTERNAL CONSISTENCY; VALIDITY:CONSTRUCT;
                CORRELATES:DEMOGRAPHIC; FACTOR ANALYSIS; N=230 WOMEN IN GLASGOW,
                SCOTLAND)
        @APPLICATION 1970 W-157

2597   GANNON, D. R., & TYLER, D. W.
        EFFECTS OF PARAPHRASING CLINICAL INTERVIEW ITEMS ON STRUCTURED RESPONSES.
        PSYCHOLOGICAL REPORTS, 1970, 26, 631-635.
            (MODIFICATION; BIAS:TESTER; N=6 PARAPHRASING OF MMPI ITEMS, 33 VA
            PATIENTS)
        @APPLICATION 1970 D-45

2598   LESTER, D., & ORLOFF, L. F.
        PERSONALITY CORRELATES OF THE DURATION OF THE MENSES.
        PSYCHOLOGICAL REPORTS, 1970, 26, 650.
            (CORRELATES:BEHAVIORAL, PHYSIOLOGICAL; N=56 COLLEGE FEMALES)
        @APPLICATION 1970 M-197 L-35

2599   OAKLAND, J. A.
        TEST-RETEST RELIABILITY AND THE SIGNIFICANCE OF DOUBTFUL RESPONSES
        IN THE EDWARDS PERSONALITY INVENTORY.
        PSYCHOLOGICAL REPORTS, 1970, 26, 659-664.
            (RELIABILITY:RETEST, INTERNAL CONSISTENCY; BIAS:RESPONSE; N=16 MALE
            & 29 FEMALE COLLEGE STUDENTS)
        @APPLICATION 1970 E-30

2600   FITZGERALD, B. J., PASEWARK, R. A., & NOAH, S.
        INTERPERSONAL TRUST AND DELINQUENCY: A REPLY TO ROTTER.
        PSYCHOLOGICAL REPORTS, 1970, 26, 665-666.
            (REVIEW; VALIDITY:CONSTRUCT; NO SAMPLE USED)
        @APPLICATION 1970 R-16

2601   BLOUNT, H. P., & PEDERSEN, D. M.
        EFFECTS OF VIDEO PLAYBACK OF A PERSON ON HIS SELF-CONCEPT.
        PSYCHOLOGICAL REPORTS, 1970, 26, 667-670.
            (CORRELATES:PSYCHOLOGICAL, ENVIRONMENTAL; NORMATIVE DATA; N=20 MALE
            & 30 FEMALE COLLEGE STUDENTS)
        @APPLICATION 1970 S-15 S-282 P-48 G-21

2602   SCHWAB, D. P.
        COUNTERBALANCING AND FAKABILITY OF THE GORDON PERSONAL INVENTORY AND
        PROFILE.
        PSYCHOLOGICAL REPORTS, 1970, 26, 671-675.
            (VALIDITY:CONSTRUCT; CORRELATES:ENVIRONEMNTAL; BIAS:RESPONSE; N=74
            COLLEGE STUDENTS)
        @APPLICATION 1970 G-12 G-70

2603   FRACCHIA, J., FIORENTINO, D., SHEPPARD, C., & MERLIS, S.
        RAVEN PROGRESSIVE MATRICES ABOIDABLE ERRORS AS A MEASURE OF
        PSYCHOPATHOLOGICAL IDEATIONAL INFLUENCES UPON REASONING ABILITY.
        PSYCHOLOGICAL REPORTS, 1970, 26, 359-362.
            (CORRELATES:BEHAVIORAL, INTELLIGENCE; USED AS CRITERION; NORMATIVE
            DATA; N=88 HEROIN ADDICTS)
        @APPLICATION 1970 D-45

2604   WATSON, C. G., KLETT, W. G., & LOREI, T. W.
        TOWARD AN OPERATIONAL DEFINITION OF ANHEDONIA.
        PSYCHOLOGICAL REPORTS, 1970, 26, 371-376.
            (REVISION; VALIDITY:CONSTRUCT; CORRELATES:PSYCHOLOGICAL; FACTOR
            ANALYSIS; N=70 HOSPITALIZED MALE SCHIZOPHRENIC VETERANS)
        @APPLICATION 1970 D-45 G-172 B-242 K-34 L-69 W-152 W-153 W-154 W-155 W-156

2605   KERLINGER, F. N.
        A SOCIAL ATTITUDE SCALE: EVIDENCE ON RELIABILITY AND VALIDITY.
        PSYCHOLOGICAL REPORTS, 1970, 26, 379-383.
            (RELIABILITY:RETEST, INTERNAL CONSISTENCY; VALIDITY:CONSTRUCT,
            CROSS-VALIDATION; CORRELATES:PSYCHOLOGICAL, INTELLIGENCE; FACTOR
            ANALYSIS; NORMATIVE DATA; 2 STUDIES: 6 SAMPLES--N=190, 206, 97, 64,
            227, 263 AND N=161 EDUCATION GRADUATE STUDENTS IN SECOND STUDY)
        @APPLICATION 1970 R-8 A-5 C-23 B-7 G-76 E-1 K-80

2606   KANEKAR, S., & DOLKE, A. M.
        SMOKING, EXTRAVERSION, AND NEUROTICISM.
        PSYCHOLOGICAL REPORTS, 1970, 26, 384.
            (VALIDITY:CONSTRUCT; CORRELATES:BEHAVIORAL; N=25 MALE INDIANS, 25-35
            YEARS, HAVING AT LEAST COMPLETED HIGH SCHOOL)
        @APPLICATION 1970 E-6

2607   BROWN, W. P., & MACKAY, C. K.
       COMPARISON OF TWO METHODS FOR ASSESSING ATTITUDE TOWARD CONSCIENCE AND
       SUCCESS.
       PSYCHOLOGICAL REPORTS, 1970, 26, 386.
          (DESCRIPTION; CORRELATES:PSYCHOLOGICAL; 2 STUDIES: N=32; & 31
          GRADUATE TRAINEE TEACHERS)
     @APPLICATION 1970 K-14 O-16

2608   TORRANCE, E. P.
       INFLUENCE OF DYADIC INTERACTION ON CREATIVE FUNCTIONING.
       PSYCHOLOGICAL REPORTS, 1970, 26, 391-394.
          (CORRELATES:ENVIRONMENTAL; NORMATIVE DATA; 2 STUDIES: N=40 COLLEGE
          JUNIORS AND SENIORS; 46 5-YEAR-OLD KINDERGARTENERS)
     @APPLICATION 1970 T-39

2609   ROTHSCHILD, B. H., & HOROWITZ, I. A.
       EFFECT OF INSTRUCTIONS AND INTERNAL-EXTERNAL CONTROL OF REINFORCEMENT ON A
       CONDITIONED FINGER-WITHDRAWAL RESPONSE.
       PSYCHOLOGICAL REPORTS, 1970, 26, 395-400.
          (VALIDITY:CONSTRUCT; CORRELATES:BEHAVIORAL, PSYCHOLOGICAL,
          ENVIRONMENTAL; NORMATIVE DATA; N=40 MALE UNDERGRADUATES)
     @APPLICATION 1970 R-18

2610   MARTIN, W. T.
       TRANSPARENCY OR PSEUDO-TRANSPARENCY ON THE SUBSCALES OF THE
       SELF-PERCEPTION INVENTORY.
       PSYCHOLOGICAL REPORTS, 1970, 26, 401-402.
          (REVIEW; VALIDITY:CONSTRUCT; CORRELATES:PSYCHOLOGICAL;
          BIAS:RESPONSE; NO SAMPLE USED)
     @APPLICATION 1970 M-196

2611   SACHSON, A. D., RAPPOPORT, L., & SINNETT, E. R.
       THE ACTIVITY RECORD: A MEASURE OF SOCIAL ISOLATION-INVOLVEMENT.
       PSYCHOLOGICAL REPORTS, 1970, 26, 413-414.
          (CORRELATES:BEHAVIORAL; N=94 EMOTIONALLY DISTURBED, 87 NORMAL
          COLLEGE STUDENTS)
     @APPLICATION 1970 D-45

2612   PERSONS, R. W.
       INTERMITTENT REINFORCEMENT, GUILT, AND CRIME.
       PSYCHOLOGICAL REPORTS, 1970, 26, 421-422.
          (VALIDITY:CONSTRUCT; CORRELATES:BEHAVIORAL; N=75 MALE YOUTHS, AGES
          16-19, IN MAXIMUM SECURITY REFORMATORY)
     @APPLICATION 1970 M-64

2613   LACKS, P. B., LANDSBAUM, J. B., & STERN, M. R.
       WORKSHOP IN COMMUNICATION FOR MEMBERS OF A PSYCHIATRIC TEAM.
       PSYCHOLOGICAL REPORTS, 1970, 26, 423-430.
          (CORRELATES:ENVIRONMENTAL; USED AS CRITERION; N=33 MEMBERS ON STAFF
          OF CHILDREN'S PSYCHIATRIC UNIT)
     @APPLICATION 1970 G-31 O-16

2614   MINTON, H. L., & MILLER, A. G.
       GROUP RISK-TAKING AND INTERNAL-EXTERNAL CONTROL OF GROUP MEMBERS.
       PSYCHOLOGICAL REPORTS, 1970, 26, 431-436.
          (CORRELATES:BEHAVIORAL, PSYCHOLOGICAL, DEMOGRAPHIC; USED AS
          CRITERION: N=156 MALE AND 156 FEMALE COLLEGE STUDENTS)
     @APPLICATION 1970 R-18 K-87

2615   SKINNER, N. F., HOWARTH, E., & BROWNE, J. A.
       NOTE ON THE ROLE OF NEUROTICISM AND EXRRAVERSION IN THE "NICE PERSONALITY"
       STEREOTYPE.
       PSYCHOLOGICAL REPORTS, 1970, 26, 445-446.
          (VALIDITY:CONSTRUCT; CORRELATES:PSYCHOLOGICAL, ENVIRONMENTAL;
          BIAS:RESPONSE; NORMATIVE DATA; N=70 ADULTS AGES 18-53 YEARS)
     @APPLICATION 1970 E-6

2616   POMERANZ, D. M., & GOLDFRIED, M. R.
       AN INTAKE REPORT OUTLINE FOR BEHAVIOR MODIFICATION.
       PSYCHOLOGICAL REPORTS, 1970, 26, 447-450.
          (REVIEW; MENTION; NO SAMPLE)
     @APPLICATION 1970 G-41 C-213

2617   HOFFMAN, H.
          PERSONALITY PATTERN OF DEPRESSION AND ITS RELATION TO ACQUIESCENCE.
          PSYCHOLOGICAL REPORTS, 1970, 26, 459-464.
               (CORRELATES:PSYCHOLOGICAL; USED AS CRITERION; BIAS:RESPONSE;
               NORMATIVE DATA; N=35 DEPRESSIVE PSYCHIATRIC PATIENTS, 37 NORMALS)
       @APPLICATION 1970 J-1

2618   REITER, H. H.
          SIMILARITIES AND DIFFERENCES IN SCORES ON CERTAIN PERSONALITY SCALES
          AMONG ENGAGED COUPLES.
          PSYCHOLOGICAL REPORTS, 1970, 26, 465-466.
               (CORRELATES:PSYCHOLOGICAL; USED AS CRITERION; N=19 WHITE MIDDLE-CLASS
               ENGAGED COUPLES)
       @APPLICATION 1970 E-2

2619   WHITE, W. F., & PORTER, J. L.
          MULTIVARIATE ANALYSIS OF ATTITUDES AND PERSONALITY CHARACTERISTICS AMONG
          60 YOUTHFUL OFFENDERS.
          PSYCHOLOGICAL REPORTS, 1970, 26, 487-491.
               (MODIFICATION; CORRELATES:BEHAVIORAL, PSYCHOLOGICAL; FACTOR ANALYSIS;
               N=60 WHITE MALE DELINQUENTS, AGES 14-17 YEARS)
       @APPLICATION 1970 C-89 O-16

2620   PLATT, J. J., EISENMAN, R., & DARBES, A.
          SELF-ESTEEM AND INTERNAL-EXTERNAL CONTROL: A VALIDATION STUDY.
          PSYCHOLOGICAL REPORTS, 1970, 26, 162.
               (VALIDITY:CONSTRUCT; CORRELATES:PSYCHOLOGICAL; N=24 MILITARY
               COLLEGE MALES, 36 COLLEGE MALES, 31 COLLEGE FEMALES)
       @APPLICATION 1970 Z-6 R-18

2621   FITZGERALD, B. J., PASEWORK, R. A., & NOAH, S. J.
          VALIDITY OF ROTTER'S INTERPERSONAL TRUST SCALE: A STUDY OF DELINQUENT
          ADOLESCENTS.
          PSYCHOLOGICAL REPORTS, 1970, 26, 163-166.
               (VALIDITY:CRITERION; NORMATIVE DATA; N=41 FEMALE, 51 MALE ADOLESCENT
               DELINQUENTS, 41 FEMALE, 51 MALE ADOLESCENT NONDELINQUENTS)
       @APPLICATION 1970 R-16

2622   VERINIS, J. S.
          INHIBITION OF HUMOR ENJOYMENT: EFFECTS OF SEXUAL CONTENT AND INTROVERSION-
          EXTRAVERSION.
          PSYCHOLOGICAL REPORTS, 1970, 26, 167-170.
               (CORRELATES:PSYCHOLOGICAL; N=34 FEMALES, 21-56 YEARS OLD, AND 12
               FEMALE AND 20 MALE UNDERGRADUATES)
       @APPLICATION 1970 E-6

2623   DINOFF, M., FINCH, A. J., JR., CLEMENTS, C. B., & HODO, G. L.
          TESTING CLINICAL JUDGMENT DURING A CRISIS.
          PSYCHOLOGICAL REPORTS, 1970, 26, 181-182.
               (VALIDITY:CRITERION; NORMATIVE DATA; N=30 NEUROPSYCHIATRIC PATIENTS)
       @APPLICATION 1970 F-1

2624   HAYNES, J. R., & CARLEY, J. W.
          RELATION OF SPATIAL ABILITIES AND SELECTED PERSONALITY TRAITS.
          PSYCHOLOGICAL REPORTS, 1970, 26, 214.
               (CORRELATES:PSYCHOLOGICAL; USED AS CRITERION; N=106 UNDERGRADUATES)
       @APPLICATION 1970 C-10

2625   HOFMAN, J. E.
          DIMENSIONALITY (STRUCTURE) OF EDUCATIONAL ATTITUDE REFERENTS: NOTE ON
          VALIDITY OF A CRITERIAL REFERENTS THEORY OF ATTITUDES.
          PSYCHOLOGICAL REPORTS, 1970, 26, 215-217.
               (USED AS CRITERION; FACTOR ANALYSIS; N=79 COLLEGE FRESHMEN, 95
               GRADUATE STUDENTS, 56 PROFESSORS)
       @APPLICATION 1970 O-16

2626   WEST, L. W.
          SEX DIFFERENCES IN THE EXERCISE OF CIRCUMSPECTION IN SELF-DISCLOSURE
          AMONG ADOLESCENTS.
          PSYCHOLOGICAL REPORTS, 1970, 26, 226.
               (CORRELATES:DEMOGRAPHIC; N=271 NINTH GRADE CANADIANS)
       @APPLICATION 1970 W-148

2627   BLUM, D. M.
        MMPI CHARACTERISTICS OF MALES IN A PRIVATE HOSPITAL POPULATION.
        PSYCHOLOGICAL REPORTS, 1970, 26, 234.
            (VALIDITY:CRITERION: N=90 MALE PSYCHIATRIC PATIENTS)
    @APPLICATION 1970 D-45

2628   HOGAN, R., & MANKIN, D.
        DETERMINANTS OF INTERPERSONAL ATTRACTION: A CLARIFICATION.
        PSYCHOLOGICAL REPORTS, 1970, 26, 235-238.
            (CORRELATES:PSYCHOLOGICAL; N=34 MALE UNDERGRADUATES)
    @APPLICATION 1970 G-22 H-132

2629   WARD, W. D., & DAY, C. R.
        MANIFEST ANXIETY AS RELATED TO PERCEIVED SIMILARITY TO PEERS.
        PSYCHOLOGICAL REPORTS, 1970, 26, 247-250.
            (CORRELATES:PSYCHOLOGICAL, DEMOGRAPHIC; USED AS CRITERION; N=40
            MALE, 40 FEMALE COLLEGE STUDENTS)
    @APPLICATION 1970 T-2 K-23

2630   CRAIG, R. J.
        RELATIONSHIP BETWEEN SEVERITY OF ILLNESS AND OVERINCLUSIVE THINKING IN
        SCHIZOPHRENIA.
        PSYCHOLOGICAL REPORTS, 1970, 26, 251-254.
            (RELIABILITY:INTERRATER; VALIDITY:CRITERION; CORRELATES:
            PSYCHOLOGICAL; USED AS CRITERION; N=20 MALE, 20 FEMALE
            HOSPITALIZED CHRONIC SCHIZOPHRENICS)
    @APPLICATION 1970 E-38 B-94 P-108 L-70

2631   EISENMAN, R., & PLATT, J. J.
        AUTHORITARIANISM, CREATIVITY, AND OTHER CORRELATES OF THE FAMOUS SAYINGS
        TEST.
        PSYCHOLOGICAL REPORTS, 1970, 26, 267-271.
            (MODIFICATION; CORRELATES:PSYCHOLOGICAL; N=59 COLLEGE STUDENTS)
    @APPLICATION 1970 B-81 A-5 E-65 C-128 E-66 E-31

2632   JOHNSON, G. R., MARTIN, P. L., & VOGLER, R. E.
        PREDICTION OF REHOSPITALIZATION OF FAMILY-CARE PATIENTS USING THE MMPI.
        PSYCHOLOGICAL REPORTS, 1970, 26, 273-274.
            (VALIDITY:CRITERION: CORRELATES:PSYCHOLOGICAL; N=29 FEMALE, 11 MALE
            SCHIZOPHRENIC PATIENTS ABOUT TO BE PLACED IN FAMILY-CARE HOMES)
    @APPLICATION 1970 P-107 D-45

2633   LEVINE, D., & WITTENBORN, J. R.
        RELATION OF EXPRESSED ATTITUDES TO IMPROVEMENT IN FUNCTIONAL PSYCHOTICS.
        PSYCHOLOGICAL REPORTS, 1970, 26, 275-277.
            (VALIDITY:CONSTRUCT; CORRELATES:PSYCHOLOGICAL: FACTOR ANALYSIS; N=120
            FUNCTIONALLY PSYCHOTIC PATIENTS)
    @APPLICATION 1970 L-137

2634   RAVENSBORG, M. R.
        EMPIRICAL VALIDATION OF AUTOMATED NURSING NOTES: INFORMATIONAL UTILITY.
        PSYCHOLOGICAL REPORTS, 1970, 26, 279-282.
            (VALIDITY:CONSTRUCT, CRITERION; CORRELATES:BEHAVIORAL, PSYCHOLOGICAL;
            N=2 OBSERVERS, 4 MALE, 4 FEMALE ADOLESCENT PSYCHIATRIC PATIENTS)
    @APPLICATION 1970 R-130

2635   OZEHOSKY, J. R., MCCARTHY, J. B., & CLARK, E. T.
        MANIFEST NEEDS AMONG ROTC AND NON-ROTC UNDERGRADUATES.
        PSYCHOLOGICAL REPORTS, 1970, 26, 299-301.
            (CORRELATES:BEHAVIORAL, DEMOGRAPHIC; USED AS CRITERION; N=20 ROTC,
            20 NON-ROTC UNDERGRADUATES)
    @APPLICATION 1970 E-2

2636   FIORENTINO, D., SHEPPARD, C., & MERLIS, S.
        EMOTIONS PROFILE INDEX (EPI) PATTERN FOR PARANOID PERSONALITY TYPES:
        CROSS-VALIDATION AND EXTENSION.
        PSYCHOLOGICAL REPORTS, 1970, 26, 303-308.
            (VALIDITY:CROSS-VALIDATION; CORRELATES:PSYCHOLOGICAL; NORMATIVE DATA;
            N=20 ACUTE PARANOID SCHIZOPHRENICS, 23 NARCOTIC USERS)
    @APPLICATION 1970 O-22 D-45 P-43

2637   MIKESELL, R. H., CALHOUN, L. G., LOTTMAN, T. J.
        INSTRUCTIONAL SET AND THE COOPERSMITH SELF-ESTEEM INVENTORY.
        PSYCHOLOGICAL REPORTS, 1970, 26, 317-318.
            (CORRELATES:ENVIRONMENTAL; BIAS:RESPONSE; NORMATIVE DATA; N=21 MALE,
            8 FEMALE HIGH SCHOOL SOPHOMORES)
        @APPLICATION 1970 C-38

2638   HJELLE, L. A.
        INTERNAL-EXTERNAL CONTROL AS A DETERMINANT OF ACADEMIC ADJUSTMENT.
        PSYCHOLOGICAL REPORTS, 1970, 26, 326.
            (CORRELATES:BEHAVIORAL, INTELLIGENCE: USED AS CRITERION; N=107 MALE,
            32 FEMALE COLLEGE STUDENTS)
        @APPLICATION 1970 R-18

2639   OHNMACHT, F. W.
        PERSONALITY AND COGNITIVE REFERENTS OF CREATIVITY: A SECOND LOOK.
        PSYCHOLOGICAL REPORTS, 1970, 26, 336-338.
            (CORRELATES:PSYCHOLOGICAL, INTELLIGENCE: N=90 UNDERGRADUATES)
        @APPLICATION 1970 C-10 B-6 M-22 G-50

2640   SPEIGLER, M. D., & LIEBERT, R. M.
        SOME CORRELATES OF SELF-REPORTED FEAR.
        PSYCHOLOGICAL REPORTS, 1970, 26, 691-695.
            (RELIABILITY:INTERNAL CONSISTENCY; CORRELATES:DEMOGRAPHIC; BIAS:
            RESPONSE; N=160 MALES & 189 FEMALES)
        @APPLICATION 1970 W-37

2641   VON SINGER, R., & PEDERSON, M. G.
        BEHAVIORAL CORRELATES OF THE ACL HETEROSEXUAL SCALE.
        PSYCHOLOGICAL REPORTS, 1970, 26, 719-722.
            (CORRELATES:BEHAVIORAL: USED AS CRITERION; N=36 MALE UNDERGRADUATES)
        @APPLICATION 1970 G-21

2642   GORMAN, B. S.
        16 PF CORRELATES OF SENSATION-SEEKING.
        PSYCHOLOGICAL REPORTS, 1970, 26, 741-742.
            (CORRELATES:PSYCHOLOGICAL: N=39 FEMALE, 25 MALE UNDERGRADUATES)
        @APPLICATION 1970 Z-3 C-10

2643   MEHRYAR, A. H., & SHAPURIAN, R.
        SOME NORMATIVE DATA ON A PERSIAN FARM OF THE NEW JUNIOR MAUDSLEY INVENTORY.
        PSYCHOLOGICAL REPORTS, 1970, 26, 743-746.
            (CROSS-CULTURAL APPLICATION; NORMATIVE DATA; BIAS:RESPONSE; N=274
            MALE AND 318 FEMALE SCHOOLGOING PERSIAN CHILDREN)
        @APPLICATION 1970 F-111

2644   ZUNICH, M.
        ATTITUDES OF LOWER- AND MIDDLE-CLASS FAMILIES CONCERNING PERSONAL
        ADJUSTMENT.
        PSYCHOLOGICAL REPORTS, 1970, 26, 750.
            (CORRELATES:DEMOGRAPHIC; N=242 ADULTS)
        @APPLICATION 1970 B-227

2645   HOOD, R. W., JR., & GINSBURG, G. P.
        CULTURAL AVAILABILITY: A CROSS-CULTURALLY STABLE DETERMINANT OF PERFORMANCE
        ON REMOTE ASSOCIATES TEST ITEMS.
        PSYCHOLOGICAL REPORTS, 1970, 26, 755-758.
            (CORRELATES:PSYCHOLOGICAL, DEMOGRAPHIC; N=138 UNDERGRADUATES)
        @APPLICATION 1970 M-29

2646   WIENER, D. J.
        FAILURE OF PERSONALITY VARIABLES TO MEDIATE INTERPERSONAL ATTRACTION.
        PSYCHOLOGICAL REPORTS, 1970, 26, 784-786.
            (CORRELATES:BEHAVIORAL, PSYCHOLOGICAL, ENVIRONMENTAL; N=543
            UNDERGRADUATES)
        @APPLICATION 1970 B-195 B-65 C-27 E-2 D-3 L-35 M-4

2647   MACDONALD, A. P., JR.
        REVISED SCALE FOR AMBIGUITY TOLERANCE: RELIABILITY AND VALIDITY.
        PSYCHOLOGICAL REPORTS, 1970, 26, 791-798.
            (MENTION: DESCRIPTION: MODIFICATION; RELIABILITY:RETEST,
            INTERNAL CONSISTENCY; VALIDITY:CONSTRUCT, CROSS-VALIDATION;
            CORRELATES:BEHAVIORAL, PSYCHOLOGICAL; 3 STUDIES: N=74 FEMALE
            UNDERGRADUATES; 341 MALE AND 448 FEMALE UNDERGRADUATES; 24 MALE
            UNDERGRADUATES)
        @APPLICATION 1970 R-128 G-22 B-4 R-8 G-76 M-185 C-27

2648 URBINA, S., HARRISON, J. P., SCHAEFER, C. E., & ANASTASI, A.
        RELATIONSHIP BETWEEN MASCULINITY-FEMININITY AND CREATIVITY AS MEASURED BY
        THE FRANCK DRAWING COMPLETION TEST.
        PSYCHOLOGICAL REPORTS, 1970, 26, 799-804.
            (CORRELATES:PSYCHOLOGICAL, DEMOGRAPHIC; N=240 HIGH SCHOOL STUDENTS)
        @APPLICATION 1970 F-11

2649 ALLON, R., & GRAHAM, J. R.
        INTERCORRELATIONS OF FACTOR SCORES FROM THE OPINIONS ABOUT MENTAL ILLNESS
        SCALE.
        PSYCHOLOGICAL REPORTS, 1970, 26, 805-806.
            (VALIDITY:CONTENT; CORRELATES:PSYCHOLOGICAL; N=31 PSYCHIATRISTS &
            PSYCHIATRIC RESIDENTS, 29 NURSES & 97 NURSING AIDES)
        @APPLICATION 1970 C-69

2650 KNOTT, P. D.
        A FURTHER METHODOLOGICAL STUDY OF THE MEASUREMENT OF INTERPERSONAL
        AGGRESSION.
        PSYCHOLOGICAL REPORTS, 1970, 26, 807-809.
            (CORRELATES:BEHAVIORAL, PSYCHOLOGICAL; USED AS CRITERION; NORMATIVE
            DATA; N=110 MALE UNDERGRADUATES, 18 SELECTED)
        @APPLICATION 1970 B-44

2651 ADAMS, H. L., MASON, E. P., & BLOOD, D. F.
        PERSONALITY CHARACTERISTICS OF AMERICAN AND ENGLISH, BRIGHT AND AVERAGE
        COLLEGE FRESHMEN.
        PSYCHOLOGICAL REPORTS, 1970, 26, 831-834.
            (CORRELATES:PSYCHOLOGICAL, DEMOGRAPHIC; CROSS-CULTURAL APPLICATION;
            N=STUDENTS IN 3 U.S. COLLEGES & 1 ENGLISH GRAMMAR SCHOOL)
        @APPLICATION 1970 G-21 A-7 B-39

2652 SUTKER, P. B., SUTKER, L. W., & KILPATRICK, D. G.
        RELIGIOUS PREFERENCE, PRACTICE, AND PERSONAL SEXUAL ATTITUDES AND BEHAVIOR.
        PSYCHOLOGICAL REPORTS, 1970, 26, 835-841.
            (CORRELATES:BEHAVIORAL, PSYCHOLOGICAL, DEMOGRAPHIC; N=253 MALE & 256
            FEMALE UNDERGRADUATES)
        @APPLICATION 1970 K-140

2653 GOLIGHTLY, C., & REINEHR, R. C.
        AUTHORITARIANISM AND CHOICE OF A MILITARY MILIEU.
        PSYCHOLOGICAL REPORTS, 1970, 26, 854.
            (MODIFICATION; CORRELATES:PSYCHOLOGICAL, DEMOGRAPHIC; NORMATIVE DATA;
            N=77 STUDENTS--55 "CIVILIANS" AND 22 CADET CORPS MEMBERS)
        @APPLICATION 1970 A-5

2654 MOORE, C. H., & ASCOUGH, J. C.
        SELF-ACCEPTANCE AND ADJUSTMENT REVISITED: A REPLICATION.
        PSYCHOLOGICAL REPORTS, 1970, 26, 855-858.
            (MODIFICATION; CORRELATES:PSYCHOLOGICAL, DEMOGRAPHIC; USED AS
            CRITERION; N=102 UNDERGRADUATES)
        @APPLICATION 1970 T-25 T-113

2655 WEISSMAN, H. N., & RITTER, K.
        OPENNSS TO EXPERIENCE, EGO STRENGTH AND SELF-DESCRIPTION AS A FUNCTION OF
        REPRESSION AND SENSITIZATION.
        PSYCHOLOGICAL REPORTS, 1970, 26, 859-864.
            (VALIDITY:CONSTRUCT; CORRELATES:PSYCHOLOGICAL, INTELLIGENCE; USED AS
            CRITERION: NORMATIVE DATA; N=62 MALE AND 62 FEMALE UNDERGRADUATES,
            30 UNDERGRADUATES)
        @APPLICATION 1970 B-46 G-21 B-5 F-19

2656 HUNDAL, P. S., SINGH, A., & SINGH, M.
        FACTOR ANALYTICAL STUDY OF TESTS OF ANXIETY.
        PSYCHOLOGICAL REPORTS, 1970, 26, 875-878.
            (RELIABILITY:INTERNAL CONSISTENCY; VALIDITY:CROSS-VALIDATION;
            CORRELATES:PHYSIOLOGICAL, INTELLIGENCE; FACTOR ANALYSIS;
            CROSS-CULTURAL APPLICATION; NORMATIVE DATA; N=200 INDIAN MALE
            GRADUATES)
        @APPLICATION 1970 T-2 E-5 C-136 D-80 S-262

2657   KILBURN, K. L., MCDOLE, G., & SMITH, R. E.
        THE STRONG VOCATIONAL INTEREST BLANK AS A MEASURE OF SUCCESS IN THE
        TRAINING OF PSYCHIATRIC TECHNICIANS.
        PSYCHOLOGICAL REPORTS, 1970, 26, 883-886.
            (CORRELATES:BEHAVIORAL, INTELLIGENCE; NORMATIVE DATA; N=162
            PSYCHIATRIC TECHNICIAN TRAINEES)
        @APPLICATION 1970 G-22 S-33

2658   HOFFMAN, H., & ABBOTT, D.
        EMOTIONAL SELF-DESCRIPTION OF ALCOHOLIC PATIENTS AFTER TREATMENT.
        PSYCHOLOGICAL REPORTS, 1970, 26, 892.
            (CORRELATES:BEHAVIORAL, PSYCHOLOGICAL; N=122 ALCOHOLICS,
            97 UNDERGRADUATES)
        @APPLICATION 1970 E-2 C-27

2659   TEMPLER, D. I., & DOTSON, E.
        RELIGIOUS CORRELATES OF DEATH ANXIETY.
        PSYCHOLOGICAL REPORTS, 1970, 26, 895-897.
            (CORRELATES:PSYCHOLOGICAL, DEMOGRAPHIC; NORMATIVE DATA; N=109 FEMALE,
            104 MALE UNDERGRADUATES)
        @APPLICATION 1970 T-96

2660   EVANS, D. A., & ALEXANDER, S.
        SOME PSYCHOLOGICAL CORRELATES OF CIVIL RIGHTS ACTIVITY.
        PSYCHOLOGICAL REPORTS, 1970, 26, 899-906.
            (RELIABILITY:INTERNAL CONSISTENCY; CORRELATES:PSYCHOLOGICAL,
            DEMOGRAPHIC; NORMATIVE DATA; N=52 CIVIL RIGHTS & 40 MALE AND 18
            FEMALE BLACK NON-CIVIL RIGHTS UNDERGRADUATES)
        @APPLICATION 1970 B-46 B-5 C-27 R-18

2661   SCHNEIDER, N. G., & HOUSTON, J. P.
        SMOKING AND ANXIETY.
        PSYCHOLOGICAL REPORTS, 1970, 26, 941-942.
            (CORRELATES:BEHAVIORAL, PSYCHOLOGICAL; N=460)
        @APPLICATION 1970 T-2

2662   MOON, W. H., & LAIR, C. V.
        MANIFEST ANXIETY, INDUCED ANXIETY AND DIGIT SYMBOL PERFORMANCE.
        PSYCHOLOGICAL REPORTS, 1970, 26, 947-950.
            (CORRELATES:PSYCHOLOGICAL, INTELLIGENCE, ENVIRONMENTAL; USED AS
            CRITERION; NORMATIVE DATA; N=144 FEMALE UNDERGRADUATES)
        @APPLICATION 1970 T-2

2663   WOLKON, G. H.
        EGO STRENGTH, ROLE POSITION SALIENCE AND COMMUNE BY TENURE OF THE
        PSYCHIATRIC PATIENT.
        PSYCHOLOGICAL REPORTS, 1970, 26, 951-953.
            (CORRELATES:BEHAVIORAL, PSYCHOLOGICAL, INTELLIGENCE; USED AS
            CRITERION; N=178 PSYCHIATRIC PATIENTS)
        @APPLICATION 1970 B-5 S-31

2664   DUSEWICZ, R. A.
        EARLY CHILDHOOD EDUCATION FOR DISADVANTAGED TWO-YEAR OLDS.
        PSYCHOLOGICAL REPORTS, 1970, 26, 954.
            (CORRELATES:PSYCHOLOGICAL, INTELLIGENCE, ENVIRONMENTAL; NORMATIVE
            DATA; N=10 DISADVANTAGED NEGRO 2 YEAR OLDS)
        @APPLICATION 1970 D-7

2665   WATSON, R. L., PASEWARK, R. A., & FITZGERALD, B. J.
        USE OF THE EDWARDS' PERSONAL PREFERENCE SCHEDULE WITH DELINQUENTS.
        PSYCHOLOGICAL REPORTS, 1970, 26, 963-965.
            (VALIDITY:CRITERION; N=49 MALE AND 46 FEMALE DELINQUENTS AND
            MATCHED NONDELINQUENTS)
        @APPLICATION 1970 E-2

2666   LESTER, D.
        ANIMISM AND INTOLERANCE OF AMBIGUITY.
        PSYCHOLOGICAL REPORTS, 1970, 26, 966.
            (CORRELATES:PSYCHOLOGICAL; USED AS CRITERION; N=39 FEMALE STUDENTS)
        @APPLICATION 1970 B-37 D-81

2667   BONE, R. N., & MONTGOMERY, D. D.
            EXTRAVERSION, NEUROTICISM, AND SENSATION SEEKING.
            PSYCHOLOGICAL REPORTS, 1970, 26, 974.
                (CORRELATES:PSYCHOLOGICAL; N=123 FEMALE AND 137 MALE UNDERGRADUATES)
        aAPPLICATION 1970 E-5 Z-3

2668   FINCH, A. J., JR., WELSH, D. K., HANEY, J. R., & DINOFF, M.
            COMPARISON OF TWO VERSIONS OF A MINIMAL SOCIAL BEHAVIOR SCALE.
            PSYCHOLOGICAL REPORTS, 1970, 26, 985-986.
                (MODIFICATION; VALIDITY:CONSTRUCT; CORRELATES:PSYCHOLOGICAL;
                NORMATIVE DATA; N=16 GERIATRIC PATIENTS)
        aAPPLICATION 1970 F-1

2669   CLAUSER, R. A., & HJELLE, L. A.
            RELATIONSHIP BETWEEN LOCUS OF CONTROL AND DOGMATISM.
            PSYCHOLOGICAL REPORTS, 1970, 26, 1006.
                (CORRELATES:PSYCHOLOGICAL; N=116 MALE AND 125 FEMALE UNDERGRADUATES)
        aAPPLICATION 1970 R-18 R-8

2670   GERJUOY, H., & AARONSON, B. S.
            MULTIDIMENSIONAL SCALING OF TERMS USED TO DESCRIBE PERSONALITY.
            PSYCHOLOGICAL REPORTS, 1970, 26, 3-8.
                (FACTOR ANALYSIS; N=22 PSYCHOLOGISTS)
        aAPPLICATION 1970 B-131

2671   MILLER, A. R., WOO-SAM, J., ZAVOS. H., & BARKER, B.
            AN OBJECTIVE MEASURE OF INDUCED AGGRESSION.
            PSYCHOLOGICAL REPORTS, 1970, 26, 11-14.
                (MENTION; CORRELATES:BEHAVIORAL, ENVIRONMENTAL; N=67 COLLEGE
                STUDENTS)
        aAPPLICATION 1970 D-45 M-20 R-30

2672   KILPATRICK, D. G., SUTKER, L. W., & SUTKER, P. B.
            DOGMATISM, RELIGION, AND RELIGIOSITY, A REVIEW AND RE-EVALUATION.
            PSYCHOLOGICAL REPORTS, 1970, 26, 15-22.
                (CORRELATES:BEHAVIORAL, PSYCHOLOGICAL, DEMOGRAPHIC; N=188 MALE, 178
                FEMALE SOUTHERN COLLEGE STUDENTS; 57 MALE AND 72 FEMALE SOUTHERN
                CATHOLIC COLLEGE STUDENTS)
        aAPPLICATION 1970 R-8

2673   HOFFMANN, H.
            DEPRESSION AND DEFENSIVENESS IN SELF-DESCRIPTIVE MOODS OF ALCOHOLICS.
            PSYCHOLOGICAL REPORTS, 1970, 26, 23-26.
                (MODIFICATION; RELIABILITY:INTERNAL CONSISTENCY;
                CORRELATES:PSYCHOLOGICAL; NORMATIVE DATA; N=61 MALE HOSPITALIZED
                ALCHOLICS)
        aAPPLICATION 1970 E-1 C-27 D-45 C-16 D-3

2674   JONES, K. J., & JONES, P. P.
            CONTRIBUTION OF THE RORSCHACH TO DESCRIPTION OF PERSONALITY STRUCTURE
            DEFINED BY SEVERAL OBJECTIVE TESTS.
            PSYCHOLOGICAL REPORTS, 1970, 26, 35-45.
                (VALIDITY:CONSTRUCT; CORRELATES:PSYCHOLOGICAL, INTELLIGENCE;
                NORMATIVE DATA; N=178 HIGH SCHOOL JUNIORS)
        aAPPLICATION 1970 K-34 G-26 R-30

2675   LIEBERMAN, L. R.
            ATTITUDES TOWARD THE MENTALLY ILL, KNOWLEDGE OF MENTAL ILLNESS, AND
            PERSONAL ADJUSTMENT.
            PSYCHOLOGICAL REPORTS, 1970, 26, 47-52.
                (CORRELATES:PSYCHOLOGICAL, DEMOGRAPHIC; FACTOR ANALYSIS; NORMATIVE
                DATA: 2 STUDIES: N=121 COLLEGE STUDENTS, 67 MALE COLLEGE FRESHMEN)
        aAPPLICATION 1970 C-69 N-25 D-45

2676   TREADWELL, Y.
            HUMOR AND CREATIVITY.
            PSYCHOLOGICAL REPORTS, 1970, 26, 55-58.
                (RELIABILITY:INTERNAL CONSISTENCY, INTERRATER;
                CORRELATES:PSYCHOLOGICAL; N=83 SCIENCE AND ENGINEERING
                UNDERGRADUATES)
        aAPPLICATION 1970 M-29 G-107 M-20
        aM-244

2677   SERUM, C. S., & MYERS, D. G.
            NOTE ON PREJUDICE AND PERSONALITY.
            PSYCHOLOGICAL REPORTS, 1970, 26, 65-66.
                (CORRELATES:PSYCHOLOGICAL; USED AS CRITERION; N=101 HIGH SCHOOL
                STUDENTS)
        @APPLICATION 1970 W-41 W-8 S-266

2678   RAINA, M. K.
            CREATIVITY AND TEACHING SUCCESS.
    •   PSYCHOLOGICAL REPORTS, 1970, 26, 70.
                (CORRELATES:PSYCHOLOGICAL; N=55 INDIAN EDUCATION STUDENTS)
        @APPLICATION 1970 T-39

2679   BRAUN, J. R., & TINLEY, J. J.
            FAKING STUDY OF SCORES ON THE SELF-PERCEPTION INVENTORY.
            PSYCHOLOGICAL REPORTS, 1970, 26, 118.
                (VALIDITY:CONSTRUCT; NORMATIVE DATA; BIAS:RESPONSE; N=37 COLLEGE
                STUDENTS)
        @APPLICATION 1970 M-196

2680   VERINIS, J. S., & ROLL, S.
            PRIMARY AND SECONDARY MALE CHARACTERISTICS: THE HAIRINESS AND LARGE PENIS
            STEREOTYPES.
            PSYCHOLOGICAL REPORTS, 1970, 26, 123-126.
                (CORRELATES:PSYCHOLOGICAL; N=53 MALE AND 44 FEMALE COLLEGE STUDENTS)
        @APPLICATION 1970 O-16

2681   DEMILLE, R.
            LOGICAL AND EMPIRICAL OPPOSITENESS IN VALUE RESPONSES.
            PSYCHOLOGICAL REPORTS, 1970, 26, 143-154.
                (MENTION; CORRELATES:PSYCHOLOGICAL; N=555 SS IN 16 DOMESTIC AND
                FOREIGN SAMPLES)
        @APPLICATION 1970 B-235 B-237

2682   PROPPER, M. M., KIAUNE, V., & MURRAY, J. B.
            ALIENATION SYNDROME AMONG MALE ADOLESCENTS IN PRESTIGE CATHOLIC AND
            PUBLIC HIGH SCHOOLS.
            PSYCHOLOGICAL REPORTS, 1970, 27, 311-315.
                (RELIABILITY:INTERRATER; CORRELATES:PSYCHOLOGICAL, DEMOGRAPHIC,
                INTELLIGENCE; NORMATIVE DATA; N=40 CATHOLIC AND 80 PUBLIC HIGH
                SCHOOL MALES)
        @APPLICATION 1970 D-46 D-47 D-37

2683   KING, D. J.
            NOTE ON SUGGESTIBILITY AND CLUSTERING.
            PSYCHOLOGICAL REPORTS, 1970, 27, 316.
                (CORRELATES:BEHAVIORAL: N=50 COLLEGE STUDENTS)
        @APPLICATION 1970 S-90

2684   MEHRYAR, A. H.
            AUTHORITARIANISM, RIGIDITY, AND EYSENCK'S E AND N DIMENSIONS IN AN
            AUTHORITARIAN CULTURE.
            PSYCHOLOGICAL REPORTS, 1970, 27, 326.
                (CORRELATES:PSYCHOLOGICAL: CROSS-CULTURAL APPLICATION; N=108
                IRANIAN COLLEGE STUDENTS)
        @APPLICATION 1970 A-5 R-8 E-6

2685   MACDONALD, A. P., JR.
            INTERNAL-EXTERNAL LOCUS OF CONTROL AND THE PRACTICE OF BIRTH CONTROL.
            PSYCHOLOGICAL REPORTS, 1970, 27, 206.
                (CORRELATES:BEHAVIORAL: USED AS CRITERION; N=508 FEMALE COLLEGE
                STUDENTS, 212 SELECTED)
        @APPLICATION 1970 R-18

2686   LEWINSOHN, P. M., FLIPPO, J. R., & BERGQUIST, W. H.
            LEVELING-SHARPENING: ITS RELATION TO REPRESSION-SENSITIZATION AND MEMORY.
            PSYCHOLOGICAL REPORTS, 1970, 27, 211-214.
                (CORRELATES:PSYCHOLOGICAL; USED AS CRITERION; N=500 COLLEGE STUDENTS,
                48 SELECTED)
        @APPLICATION 1970 B-46 L-26

2687   WALL, J. B.
            RELATIONSHIP OF LOCUS OF CONTROL TO SELF-ACTUALIZATION.
            PSYCHOLOGICAL REPORTS, 1970, 27, 282.
                    (VALIDITY:CONSTRUCT; CORRELATES:PSYCHOLOGICAL; N=113 COLLEGE
                    STUDENTS)
        @APPLICATION 1970 R-18 S-21

2688   EISENMAN, R., & FOULKS, E. F.
            USEFULNESS OF MUSSEN'S TAT SCORING SYSTEM: I. DIFFERENCES AMONG
            GUATEMALAN INDIANS, LADINOS, AND MENGALAS ON A MODIFIED TAT; II. ATTITUDES
            TOWARD THE PHYSICALLY DISABLED AS RELATED TO NURTURANCE AND DEFERENCE.
            PSYCHOLOGICAL REPORTS, 1970, 27, 179-185.
                    (MODIFICATION; CORRELATES:DEMOGRAPHIC; CROSS-CULTURAL APPLICATION;
                    2 STUDIES: N=57 GUATEMALANS (34 INDIANS, 17 LADINOS, 6 MANGALAS),
                    N=40 COLLEGE STUDENTS)
        @APPLICATION 1970 M-100 M-20

2689   HOFFMANN, H., & PETERSON, D.
            ANALYSIS OF MOODS IN PERSONALITY DISORDERS.
            PSYCHOLOGICAL REPORTS, 1970, 27, 187-190.
                    (FACTOR ANALYSIS; NORMATIVE DATA; N=95 PSYCHIATRIC PATIENTS)
        @APPLICATION 1970
        @R-93

2690   KRAUSS, H. H., & BLANCHARD, E. B.
            LOCUS OF CONTROL IN ETHICAL RISK TAKING.
            PSYCHOLOGICAL REPORTS, 1970, 27, 142.
                    (CORRELATES:BEHAVIORAL, PSYCHOLOGICAL; USED AS CRITERION; N=56 MALE
                    AND 56 FEMALE COLLEGE STUDENTS)
        @APPLICATION 1970 R-18 R-26

2691   HOFFMANN, H.
            PERSONALITY CHARACTERISTICS OF ALCOHOLICS IN RELATION TO AGE.
            PSYCHOLOGICAL REPORTS, 1970, 27, 167-171.
                    (CORRELATES:DEMOGRAPHIC; NORMATIVE DATA; N=377 HOSPITALIZED MALE
                    ALCOHOLICS AND 62 CONTROLS)
        @APPLICATION 1970 J-1

2692   FRAAS, L. A.
            SEX OF FIGURE DRAWING IN IDENTIFYING PRACTICING MALE HOMOSEXUALS.
            PSYCHOLOGICAL REPORTS, 1970, 27, 172-174.
                    (CORRELATES:PSYCHOLOGICAL; 2 STUDIES: N=9 HOMOSEXUALS, 9 OTHER
                    MENTAL PATIENTS; 73 PATIENTS)
        @APPLICATION 1970 G-22 D-45

2693   WALKER, M., & HOLBERT, W.
            PERCEIVED ACCEPTANCE AND HELPFULNESS IN A MARATHON GROUP.
            PSYCHOLOGICAL REPORTS, 1970, 27, 83-90.
                    (CORRELATES:BEHAVIORAL; N=15 T-GROUP ADULT MEMBERS)
        @APPLICATION 1970 B-136

2694   HANEY, J. R., WELSH, D. K., FINCH, A. J., JR., & DINOFF, M.
            COMPARISON OF AGE MATCHED REGRESSED PATIENTS ON THE MINIMAL SOCIAL
            BEHAVIOR SCALE.
            PSYCHOLOGICAL REPORTS, 1970, 27, 104.
                    (CORRELATES:PSYCHOLOGICAL; NORMATIVE DATA; N=30 AGED MENTAL
                    PATIENTS)
        @APPLICATION 1970 F-1

2695   SMART, M. S., & SMART, R. C.
            SELF-ESTEEM AND SOCIAL-PERSONAL ORIENTATION OF INDIAN 12- AND 18-YEAR-OLDS.
            PSYCHOLOGICAL REPORTS, 1970, 27, 107-115.
                    (CORRELATES:BEHAVIORAL, PSYCHOLOGICAL, DEMOGRAPHIC; CROSS-CULTURAL
                    APPLICATION; NORMATIVE DATA; N=200 ADOLESCENT INDIAN MALES AND
                    FEMALES)
        @APPLICATION 1970 C-88

2696   WOHL, J., HOROWITZ, I. A., TAPINGKAE, A., & PARDTHAISONG, T.
            SOME PERSONALITY CHARACTERISTICS OF THAI AND AMERICAN UNIVERSITY STUDENTS.
            PSYCHOLOGICAL REPORTS, 1970, 27, 45-46.
                    (CORRELATES:DEMOGRAPHIC; CROSS-CULTURAL APPLICATION; NORMATIVE DATA;
                    N=193 FEMALE AND 87 MALE THAI AND 126 MALE AND 113 FEMALE AMERICAN
                    COLLEGE STUDENTS)
        @APPLICATION 1970 C-101

2697   WEBB, W. B., & FRIEL, J.
              CHARACTERISTICS OF "NATURAL" LONG AND SHORT SLEEPERS: A PRELIMINARY REPORT.
              PSYCHOLOGICAL REPORTS, 1970, 27, 63-66.
                    (CORRELATES:BEHAVIORAL; N=32 COLLEGE STUDENTS)
        @APPLICATION 1970 G-22 Z-5 B-127 D-45

2698   LIEBERMAN, L. R.
              LIFE SATISFACTION IN THE YOUNG AND OLD.
              PSYCHOLOGICAL REPORTS, 1970, 27, 75-79.
                    (CORRELATES:PSYCHOLOGICAL; NORMATIVE DATA; 2 STUDIES: N=101 AGED;
                    44 MALE AND 34 FEMALE COLLEGE STUDENTS)
        @APPLICATION 1970 N-9 T-51

2699   LEVIN, J., & BLACK, H.
              PERSONAL APPEARANCE AS A REFLECTION OF SOCIAL ATTITUDES: STEREOTYPE OR
              REALITY?
              PSYCHOLOGICAL REPORTS, 1970, 27, 338.
                    (CORRELATES:BEHAVIORAL; N=91 MALE AND 102 FEMALE COLLEGE STUDENTS)
        @APPLICATION 1970 K-80

2700   WILLIS, J., WILSON, W., & WILLIS, J.
              RELIGIONS ORIENTATION OF THREE SAMPLES OF GRADUATE STUDENTS IN CLINICAL
              PSYCHOLOGY, SOCIAL WORK, AND COUNSELING AND GUIDANCE.
              PSYCHOLOGICAL REPORTS, 1970, 26, 623-630.
                    (CORRELATES:BEHAVIORAL, PSYCHOLOGICAL, DEMOGRAPHIC; USED AS
                    CRITERION; NORMATIVE DATA; N=100 STUDENTS)
        @APPLICATION 1970 E-62 D-85 D-84

2701   KUDER, F.
              SOME PRINCIPLES OF INTEREST MEASUREMENT.
              EDUCATIONAL AND PSYCHOLOGICAL MEASUREMENT, 1970, 30, 205-226.
                    (MENTION; REVIEW ARTICLE)
        @APPLICATION 1970 K-72 S-33

2702   TUPES, E. C., & MADDEN, H. L.
              RELATIONSHIPS BETWEEN COLLEGE CHARACTERISTICS AND LATER PERFORMANCE OF
              COLLEGE GRADUATES.
              EDUCATIONAL AND PSYCHOLOGICAL MEASUREMENT, 1970, 30, 273-282.
                    (DESCRIPTION; VALIDITY:CRITERION; CORRELATES:BEHAVIORAL; N=172
                    COLLEGES WITH AIR FORCE ROTC ATTACHMENTS)
        @APPLICATION 1970 A-18

2703   ROTTER, G. S., & TINKLEMAN, V.
              ANCHOR EFFECTS IN THE DEVELOPMENT OF BEHAVIOR RATING SCALES.
              EDUCATIONAL AND PSYCHOLOGICAL MEASUREMENT, 1970, 30, 311-318.
                    (CORRELATES:PSYCHOLOGICAL; USED AS CRITERION; BIAS:RESPONSE; N=56
                    COLLEGE MALES)
        @APPLICATION 1970 C-27

2704   KOSON, D., KITCHEN, C., KOCHEN, M., & STODOLSKY, D.
              PSYCHOLOGICAL TESTING BY COMPUTER: EFFECT ON RESPONSE BIAS.
              EDUCATIONAL AND PSYCHOLOGICAL MEASUREMENT, 1970, 30, 803-810.
                    (CORRELATES:PSYCHOLOGICAL, ENVIRONMENTAL; BIAS:RESPONSE; NORMATIVE
                    DATA; N=68 UNDERGRADUATE AND GRADUATE STUDENTS)
        @APPLICATION 1970 D-45

2705   BORUCH, R. F., LARKIN, J. D., WOLINS, L., & MACKINNEY, A. C.
              ALTERNATIVE METHODS OF ANALYSIS: MULTITRAIT-MULTIMETHOD DATA.
              EDUCATIONAL AND PSYCHOLOGICAL MEASUREMENT, 1970, 30, 833-853.
                    (VALIDITY:CRITERION; CORRELATES:PSYCHOLOGICAL; FACTOR ANALYSIS;
                    2 STUDIES: N=111 SUPERVISORS, 222 WORKERS, 124 MANAGERS)
        @APPLICATION 1970 U-6 H-141 W-121

2706   KOPPEL, M. A., & SECHREST, L.
              A MULTITRAIT-MULTIMETHOD MATRIX ANALYSIS OF SENSE OF HUMOR.
              EDUCATIONAL AND PSYCHOLOGICAL MEASUREMENT, 1970, 30, 77-85.
                    (VALIDITY:CONSTRUCT, CRITERION; CORRELATES:PSYCHOLOGICAL,
                    INTELLIGENCE; N=62 MALE COLLEGE STUDENTS)
        @APPLICATION 1970 E-5

2707   HENDEL, D. D., & WEISS, D. J.
            INDIVIDUAL INCONSISTENCY AND RELIABILITY OF MEASUREMENT.
            EDUCATIONAL AND PSYCHOLOGICAL MEASUREMENT, 1970, 30, 579-593.
                (RELIABILITY:RETEST, INTERNAL CONSISTENCY; 9 SAMPLES: MEDIAN N=73
                MALES AND FEMALES (RANGE 27-283))
        @APPLICATION 1970 W-97

2708   HALL, R. F.
            AN APPLICATION OF UNFOLDING THEORY TO THE MEASUREMENT OF ATTITUDES.
            EDUCATIONAL AND PSYCHOLOGICAL MEASUREMENT, 1970, 30, 621-637.
                (FACTOR ANALYSIS; N=52, SAMPLE DESCRIPTION NOT AVAILABLE)
        @APPLICATION 1970 T-23

2709   HOFSTEE, W. K. B.
            COMPARATIVE VERSUS ABSOLUTE JUDGMENTS OF TRAIT DESIRABILITY.
            EDUCATIONAL AND PSYCHOLOGICAL MEASUREMENT, 1970, 30, 639-646.
                (MODIFICATION; CROSS-CULTURAL APPLICATION; BIAS:RESPONSE;
                N=16,300 DUTCH MALES)
        @APPLICATION 1970 H-109

2710   WRIGHT, L., & DUNN, T.
            FACTOR STRUCTURE OF THE EXPANDED SOCIOMETRIC DEVICE: A MEASURE OF
            PERSONAL EFFECTIVENESS.
            EDUCATIONAL AND PSYCHOLOGICAL MEASUREMENT, 1970, 30, 319-326.
                (CORRELATES:DEMOGRAPHIC, ENVIRONMENTAL; FACTOR ANALYSIS; 2 STUDIES:
                N=256 COLLEGE STUDENTS, 393 COLLEGE STUDENTS)
        @APPLICATION 1970 W-22

2711   STEWART, R. G.
            SOME EFFECTS OF REVERSING CERTAIN ITEMS IN THE ROKEACH DOGMATISM SCALE.
            EDUCATIONAL AND PSYCHOLOGICAL MEASUREMENT, 1970, 30, 327-336.
                (MODIFICATION; RELIABILITY:INTERNAL CONSISTENCY; VALIDITY:CONTENT,
                CONSTRUCT; NORMATIVE DATA; BIAS:RESPONSE; N=134 COLLEGE STUDENTS)
        @APPLICATION 1970 R-8

2712   ROMINE, B. H., DAVIS, J. A., & GEHMAN, W. S.
            THE INTERACTION OF LEARNING, PERSONALITY TRAITS, ABILITY, AND ENVIRONMENT:
            A PRELIMINARY STUDY.
            EDUCATIONAL AND PSYCHOLOGICAL MEASUREMENT, 1970, 30, 337-347.
                (VALIDITY:CRITERION; CORRELATES:PSYCHOLOGICAL, ENVIRONMENTAL; USED
                AS CRITERION; N=250 COLLEGE FEMALES)
        @APPLICATION 1970 P-67 P-68

2713   LUNNEBORG, P. W.
            EPPS PATTERNS AND ACADEMIC ACHIEVEMENT IN COUNSELING CLIENTS.
            EDUCATIONAL AND PSYCHOLOGICAL MEASUREMENT, 1970, 30, 393-398.
                (VALIDITY:CRITERION, CROSS-VALIDATION; CORRELATES:BEHAVIORAL;
                2 SAMPLES: N=600 COUNSELING CLIENTS, N=189 COUNSELING CLIENTS)
        @APPLICATION 1970 E-2

2714   CENTRA, J. A., HARNETT, R. T., & PETERSON, R. E.
            FACULTY VIEWS OF INSTITUTIONAL FUNCTIONING: A NEW MEASURE OF COLLEGE
            ENVIRONMENTS.
            EDUCATIONAL AND PSYCHOLOGICAL MEASUREMENT, 1970, 30, 405-416.
                (DESCRIPTION; VALIDITY:CONSTRUCT, CRITERION; CORRELATES:
                PSYCHOLOGICAL, ENVIRONMENTAL; USED AS CRITERION; N= BETWEEN 20 AND 60
                COLLEGES)
        @APPLICATION 1970 P-67 P-61

2715   GRAFF, R. W., BRADSHAW, H. E., DANISH, S. J., AUSTIN, B. A., & ALTEKRUSE, M.
            THE POI: A VALIDITY CHECK.
            EDUCATIONAL AND PSYCHOLOGICAL MEASUREMENT, 1970, 30, 429-432.
                (VALIDITY:CRITERION; CORRELATES:BEHAVIORAL, PSYCHOLOGICAL; N=71
                MALE COLLEGE DORMITORY ASSISTANTS)
        @APPLICATION 1970 S-21

2716   NEILL, J. A., & JACKSON, D. N.
            AN EVALUATION OF ITEM SELECTION STRATEGIES IN PERSONALITY SCALE
            CONSTRUCTION.
            EDUCATIONAL AND PSYCHOLOGICAL MEASUREMENT, 1970, 30, 647-661.
                (RELIABILITY:INTERNAL CONSISTENCY; CORRELATES:PSYCHOLOGICAL;
                BIAS:RESPONSE; N=264 STUDENTS)
        @APPLICATION 1970 J-1

2717   CLEMÉNS, B., LINDEN, J., & SHERTZER, B.
            ENGINEERS' INTEREST PATTERNS: THEN AND NOW.
            EDUCATIONAL AND PSYCHOLOGICAL MEASUREMENT, 1970, 30, 675-685.
                (VALIDITY:CRITERION; USED AS CRITERION; 2 SAMPLES: N=229 MALE
                ENGINEERS, N=210 MALE ENGINEERING STUDENTS)
        @APPLICATION 1970 S-33

2718   BEZDEK, W., & STRODTBECK, F. L.
            SEX-ROLE IDENTITY AND PRAGMATIC ACTION.
            AMERICAN SOCIOLOGICAL REVIEW, 1970, 35, 491-502.
                (MODIFICATION; VALIDITY:CRITERION; CORRELATES:ENVIRONMENTAL;
                NORMATIVE DATA; N=174 MALES AND FEMALES)
        @APPLICATION 1970 G-20 F-11

2719   PHILLIPS, D. L., & CLANCY, K. J.
            RESPONSE BIASES IN FIELD STUDIES OF MENTAL ILLNESS.
            AMERICAN SOCIOLOGICAL REVIEW, 1970, 35, 503-515.
                (VALIDITY:CONSTRUCT; CORRELATES:PSYCHOLOGICAL, DEMOGRAPHIC;
                BIAS:RESPONSE; N=115 ADULTS)
        @APPLICATION 1970 L-1

2720   CAIN, G. C., & WATTS, H. W.
            PROBLEMS IN MAKING POLICY INFERENCES FROM THE COLEMAN REPORT.
            AMERICAN SOCIOLOGICAL REVIEW, 1970, 35, 228-241.
                (MENTION; REVIEW ARTICLE)
        @APPLICATION 1970 C-107

2721   SNYDER, C. R., & KATAHN, M.
            THE RELATIONSHIP OF STATE ANXIETY, FEEDBACK, AND ONGOING SELF-REPORTED
            AFFECT TO PERFORMANCE IN COMPLEX VERBAL LEARNING.
            AMERICAN JOURNAL OF PSYCHOLOGY, 1970, 83, 237-247.
                (CORRELATES:BEHAVIORAL; USED AS CRITERION; N=90 COLLEGE MALES
                SELECTED)
        @APPLICATION 1970 S-147

2722   GURIN, P.
            MOTIVATION AND ASPIRATIONS OF SOUTHERN NEGRO COLLEGE YOUTH.
            AMERICAN JOURNAL OF SOCIOLOGY, 1970, 75, 607-631.
                (CORRELATES:PSYCHOLOGICAL; N=980 NEGRO COLLEGE STUDENTS)
        @APPLICATION 1970 R-18 M-7 M-4

2723   NEAL, A. G., & GROAT, H. T.
            ALIENATION CORRELATES OF CATHOLIC FERTILITY.
            AMERICAN JOURNAL OF SOCIOLOGY, 1970, 76, 460-473.
                (CORRELATES:PHYSIOLOGICAL, DEMOGRAPHIC; N=687 MOTHERS INCLUDING 269
                CATHOLICS)
        @APPLICATION 1970 G-158

2724   REHBERG, R. A., SINCLAIR, J., & SCHAFER, W. E.
            ADOLESCENT ACHIEVMENT BEHAVIOR, FAMILY AUTHORITY STRUCTURE, AND PARENTAL
            SOCIALIZATION PRACTICES.
            AMERICAN JOURNAL OF SOCIOLOGY, 1970, 75, 1012-1034.
                (CORRELATES:PSYCHOLOGICAL; N=1455 FRESHMEN MALE HIGH SCHOOL STUDENTS)
        @APPLICATION 1970 H-22

2725   ZEISSET, R. M.
            SENSITIZATION AND RELAXATION IN THE MODIFICATION OF PSYCHIATRIC PATIENTS'
            INTERVIEW BEHAVIOR.
            JOURNAL OF ABNORMAL PSYCHOLOGY, 1968, 73, 18-24.
                (MENTION; MODIFICATION; RELIABILITY:INTERRATER;
                CORRELATES:BEHAVIORAL, PSYCHOLOGICAL, ENVIRONMENTAL; N=48 MALE
                PSYCHIATRIC PATIENTS)
        @APPLICATION 1968 W-41 W-8 D-45 U-5 W-37 M-11 P-82 Z-33 E-62 E-29

2726   PALMER, R. D.
            PATTERNS OF DEFENSIVE RESPONSE TO THREATENING STIMULI: ANTECEDENTS AND
            CONSISTENCY.
            JOURNAL OF ABNORMAL PSYCHOLOGY, 1968, 73, 30-36.
                (MODIFICATION; RELIABILITY:INTERNAL CONSISTENCY;
                CORRELATES:BEHAVIORAL, PSYCHOLOGICAL; N=35 COLLEGE MALES)
        @APPLICATION 1968 T-2 D-45 G-21 B-176 G-157 H-139

2727   NEALE, J. M., & CROMWELL, R. L.
            SIZE ESTIMATION IN SCHIZOPHRENICS AS A FUNCTION OF STIMULUS PRESENTATION
            TIME.
            JOURNAL OF ABNORMAL PSYCHOLOGY, 1968, 73, 44-48.
                (CORRELATES:BEHAVIORAL: USED AS CRITERION; N=15 GOOD PREMORBID ACUTE
                PARANOID SCHIZOPHRENICS, 15 POOR PREMORBID ACUTE NONPARANOID
                SCHIZOPHRENICS AND 15 HOSPITAL AIDES)
        @APPLICATION 1968 P-32

2728   BURDOCK, E. I., & HARDESTY, A. S.
            PSYCHOLOGICAL TEST FOR PSYCHOPATHOLOGY.
            JOURNAL OF ABNORMAL PSYCHOLOGY, 1968, 73, 62-69.
                (DESCRIPTION; RELIABILITY:RETEST, INTERNAL CONSISTENCY, INTERRATER;
                VALIDITY:CONTENT; N=870 INPATIENTS)
        @APPLICATION 1968 B-41 B-86

2729   WIGGINS, N., & HOFFMAN, P. J.
            THREE MODELS OF CLINICAL JUDGMENT.
            JOURNAL OF ABNORMAL PSYCHOLOGY, 1968, 73, 70-77.
                (VALIDITY:CROSS-VALIDATION; USED AS CRITERION; BIAS:TESTER;
                7 SAMPLES: MEDIAN N=103 AND N=29 JUDGES)
        @APPLICATION 1968 D-45

2730   KATZ, M. M., WASKOW, I. E., & OLSSON, J.
            CHARACTERIZING THE PSYCHOLOGICAL STATE PRODUCED BY LSD.
            JOURNAL OF ABNORMAL PSYCHOLOGY, 1968, 73, 1-14.
                (VALIDITY:CRITERION; CORRELATES:PHYSIOLOGICAL; 2 STUDIES: N=44
                PRISON INMATES, N=36 PRISON INMATES)
        @APPLICATION 1968 C-16 N-5

2731   CICCHETTI, D. V., & ORNSTON, P. S.
            RELIABILITY OF REPORTED PARENT-CHILD RELATIONSHIPS AMONG NEUROPSYCHIATRIC
            PATIENTS.
            JOURNAL OF ABNORMAL PSYCHOLOGY, 1968, 73, 15.
                (RELIABILITY:INTERNAL CONSISTENCY; N=66 HOSPITALIZED WHITE MALE
                NEUROPSYCHIATRIC PATIENTS)
        @APPLICATION 1968 G-55

2732   CARR, J. E., & WHITTENBAUGH, J. A.
            VOLUNTEER AND NONVOLUTEER CHARACTERISTICS IN AN OUTPATIENT POPULATION.
            JOURNAL OF ABNORMAL PSYCHOLOGY, 1968, 73, 16-17.
                (CORRELATES:BEHAVIORAL, PSYCHOLOGICAL; N=21 MALE AND 57 FEMALE
                OUTPATIENTS)
        @APPLICATION 1968 D-45

2733   FISHER, S.
            BODY BOUNDARY AND PERCEPTUAL VIVIDNESS.
            JOURNAL OF ABNORMAL PSYCHOLOGY, 1968, 73, 392-396.
                (CORRELATES:BEHAVIORAL, PSYCHOLOGICAL; 2 STUDIES: N=70 MALES & 39
                FEMALES)
        @APPLICATION 1968 R-30

2734   MARKS, J., SONODA, B., & SCHALOCK, R.
            REINFORCEMENT VERSUS RELATIONSHIP THERAPY FOR SCHIZOPHRENICS.
            JOURNAL OF ABNORMAL PSYCHOLOGY, 1968, 73, 397-402.
                (DESCRIPTION; CORRELATES:BEHAVIORAL, PSYCHOLOGICAL, INTELLIGENCE;
                USED AS CRITERION; N=22 CHRONIC SCHIZOPHRENIC MALES)
        @APPLICATION 1968 M-66 C-203 G-21 R-27 M-58 S-61

2735   MOSHER, D. L., MORTIMER, R. L., & GREBEL, M.
            VERBAL AGGRESSIVE BEHAVIOR IN DELINQUENT BOYS.
            JOURNAL OF ABNORMAL PSYCHOLOGY, 1968, 73, 454-460.
                (CORRELATES:BEHAVIORAL, DEMOGRAPHIC; NORMATIVE DATA; 2 STUDIES: N=80
                DELINQUENT BOYS, N=128 DELINQUENT BOYS)
        @APPLICATION 1968 M-64

2736   WEISS, B. W., KATKIN, E. S., & RUBIN, B. M.
            RELATIONSHIP BETWEEN A FACTOR ANALYTICALLY DERIVED MEASURE OF A SPECIFIC
            FEAR AND PERFORMANCE AFTER RELATED FEAR INDUCTION.
            JOURNAL OF ABNORMAL PSYCHOLOGY, 1968, 73, 461-463.
                (MODIFICATION; CORRELATES:BEHAVIORAL, PSYCHOLOGICAL, INTELLIGENCE,
                ENVIRONMENTAL; USED AS CRITERION; N=22 SELECTED COLLEGE FEMALES)
        @APPLICATION 1968 G-41

2737   COOKE, G.
            EVALUATION OF THE EFFICACY OF THE COMPONENTS OF RECIPROCAL INHIBITION
            PSYCHOTHERAPY.
            JOURNAL OF ABNORMAL PSYCHOLOGY, 1968, 73, 464-467.
                (CORRELATES:BEHAVIORAL: USED AS CRITERION; N=484 FEMALE
                UNDERGRADUATES, 50 SELECTED)
        @APPLICATION 1968 G-41

2738   FOULKES, D., PIVIK, T., AHRENS, J. B., & SWANSON, E. M.
            EFFECTS OF "DREAM DEPRIVATION" ON DREAM CONTENT: AN ATTEMPTED CROSS-NIGHT
            REPLICATION.
            JOURNAL OF ABNORMAL PSYCHOLOGY, 1968, 73, 403-415.
                (VALIDITY:CRITERION; CORRELATES:BEHAVIORAL, PHYSIOLOGICAL; USED AS
                CRITERION; N=16 COLLEGE MALES)
        @APPLICATION 1968 G-21 B-46

2739   GOTTHEIL, E., PAREDES, A., & EXLINE, R. V.
            PARENTAL SCHEMATA IN EMOTIONALLY DISTRUBED WOMEN.
            JOURNAL OF ABNORMAL PSYCHOLOGY, 1968, 73, 416-419.
                (MODIFICATION; CORRELATES:PSYCHOLOGICAL; NORMATIVE DATA; N=30
                FEMALE PSYCHIATRIC PATIENTS AND 20 FEMALE UNDERGRADUATES)
        @APPLICATION 1968 D-45 G-56 B-5

2740   STORY, R. I.
            EFFECTS ON THINKING OF RELATIONSHIPS BETWEEN CONFLICT AROUSAL AND
            ORAL FIXATION.
            JOURNAL OF ABNORMAL PSYCHOLOGY, 1968, 73, 440-448.
                (MODIFICATION; CORRELATES:BEHAVIORAL; NORMATIVE DATA; N=60 MALES)
        @APPLICATION 1968 G-57

2741   PRICE, R. H.
            ANALYSIS OF TASK REQUIREMENTS IN SCHIZOPHRENIC CONCEPT-IDENTIFICATION
            PERFORMANCE.
            JOURNAL OF ABNORMAL PSYCHOLOGY, 1968, 73, 285-293.
                (CORRELATES:BEHAVIORAL: USED AS CRITERION; N=72 MALE HOSPITALIZED
                VETERANS)
        @APPLICATION 1968 A-20

2742   FEDER, C. Z.
            RELATIONSHIP BETWEEN SELF-ACCEPTANCE AND ADJUSTMENT, REPRESSION-
            SENSITIZATION, AND SOCIAL COMPETENCE.
            JOURNAL OF ABNORMAL PSYCHOLOGY, 1968, 73, 317-322.
                (CORRELATES:PSYCHOLOGICAL, INTELLIGENCE; N=80 MALE PATIENTS)
        @APPLICATION 1968 S-124 C-23 C-27 C-24 B-46 D-45 Z-28

2743   OLIVER, W. A., & MOSHER, D. L.
            PSYCHOPATHOLOGY AND GUILT IN HETEROSEXUAL AND SUBGROUPS OF HOMOSEXUAL
            REFORMATORY INMATES.
            JOURNAL OF ABNORMAL PSYCHOLOGY, 1968, 73, 323-329.
                (RELIABILITY:INTERNAL CONSISTENCY; VALIDITY:CRITERION;
                CORRELATES:PSYCHOLOGICAL; USED AS CRITERION; NORMATIVE DATA; N=75
                PRISON INMATES)
        @APPLICATION 1968 D-45 M-16 M-64

2744   MOSSMAN, III., B. M., & ZILLER, R. C.
            SELF-ESTEEM AND CONSISTENCY OF SOCIAL BEHAVIOR.
            JOURNAL OF ABNORMAL PSYCHOLOGY, 1968, 73, 363-367.
                (DESCRIPTION; RELIABILITY:INTERNAL CONSISTENCY; VALIDITY:CONSTRUCT;
                CORRELATES:BEHAVIORAL, PSYCHOLOGICAL; N=76 VA PSYCHIATRIC PATIENTS)
        @APPLICATION 1968 L-74

2745   MORDKOFF, A. M., & GOLAS, R. M.
            CORONARY ARTERY DISEASE AND RESPONSE TO THE ROSENZWEIG PICTURE-FRUSTRATION
            STUDY.
            JOURNAL OF ABNORMAL PSYCHOLOGY, 1968, 73, 381-386.
                (CORRELATES:PHYSIOLOGICAL, DEMOGRAPHIC; N=30 WHITE MALES WITH
                CORONARY ARTERY DISEASE & 30 HEALTHY CONTROLS)
        @APPLICATION 1968 R-12

2746   KRISTOFFERSON, M. W.
            EFFECT OF ALCOHOL ON PERCEPTUAL FIELD DEPENDENCE.
            JOURNAL OF ABNORMAL PSYCHOLOGY, 1968, 73, 387-391.
                (CORRELATES:PHYSIOLOGICAL; USED AS CRITERION; NORMATIVE DATA; N=48
                COLLEGE MALES)
        @APPLICATION 1968 W-188

2747   SAVICKI, V., SCHUMER, H., & STANFIELD, R. E.
            STUDENT ROLE ORIENTATIONS AND COLLEGE DROPOUTS.
            JOURNAL OF COUNSELING PSYCHOLOGY, 1970, 17, 559-566.
                (VALIDITY:CRITERION; CORRELATES:BEHAVIORAL; NORMATIVE DATA; N=382
                COLLEGE MALES AND FEMALES)
        aAPPLICATION 1970 S-270

2748   DUA, P. S.
            COMPARISON OF THE EFFECTS OF BEHAVIORALLY ORIENTED ACTION AND PSYCHOTHERAPY
            REEDUCATION ON INTROVERSION-EXTRAVERSION, EMOTIONALITY, AND INTERNAL-
            EXTERNAL CONTROL.
            JOURNAL OF COUNSELING PSYCHOLOGY, 1970, 17, 567-572.
                (CORRELATES:PSYCHOLOGICAL, ENVIRONMENTAL; USED AS CRITERION;
                NORMATIVE DATA; N=30 COLLEGE FEMALES)
        aAPPLICATION 1970 B-84 R-18

2749   HARMON, L. W.
            STRONG VOCATIONAL INTEREST BLANK PROFILES OF DISADVANTAGED WOMEN.
            JOURNAL OF COUNSELING PSYCHOLOGY, 1970, 17, 519-521.
                (VALIDITY:CRITERION; CORRELATES:DEMOGRAPHIC, ENVIRONMENTAL; N=25
                DISADVANTAGED WOMEN)
        aAPPLICATION 1970 S-33

2750   BANDUCCI, R.
            ACCURACY OF OCCUPATIONAL STEROTYPES OF GRADE-TWELVE BOYS.
            JOURNAL OF COUNSELING PSYCHOLOGY, 1970, 17, 534-539.
                (CORRELATES:PSYCHOLOGICAL, DEMOGRAPHIC; N=679 12TH GRADE BOYS)
        aAPPLICATION 1970 H-21 A-2

2751   HANSON, G. R., & TAYLOR, R. G.
            INTERACTION OF ABILITY AND PERSONALITY: ANOTHER LOOK AT THE DROP-OUT
            PROBLEM IN AN INSTITUTE OF TECHNOLOGY.
            JOURNAL OF COUNSELING PSYCHOLOGY, 1970, 17, 540-545.
                (DESCRIPTION; CORRELATES:BEHAVIORAL, INTELLIGENCE; N=408
                ENGINEERING STUDENTS)
        aAPPLICATION 1970 B-11

2752   TSENG, M. S.
            LOCUS OF CONTROL AS A DETERMINANT OF JOB PROFICIENCY, EMPLOYABILITY, AND
            TRAINING SATISFACTION OF VOCATIONAL REHABILITATION CLIENTS.
            JOURNAL OF COUNSELING PSYCHOLOGY, 1970, 17, 487-491.
                (CORRELATES:PSYCHOLOGICAL; USED AS CRITERION; NORMATIVE DATA; N=95
                MALE, 45 FEMALE VOCATIONAL REHABILITATION CLIENTS)
        aAPPLICATION 1970 R-18 C-55 E-2 C-10

2753   GRAFF, R. W., & BRADSHAW, H. E.
            RELATIONSHIP OF A MEASURE OF SELF-ACTUALIZATION TO DORMITORY ASSISTANT
            EFFECTIVENESS.
            JOURNAL OF COUNSELING PSYCHOLOGY, 1970, 17, 502-505.
                (VALIDITY:CRITERION; CORRELATES:PSYCHOLOGICAL; N=71 MALE DORMITORY
                ASSISTANTS)
        aAPPLICATION 1970 S-21

2754   TAYLOR, R. G., & HANSON, G. R.
            INTEREST AND PERSISTENCE.
            JOURNAL OF COUNSELING PSYCHOLOGY, 1970, 17, 506-509.
                (VALIDITY:CRITERION; CORRELATES:BEHAVIORAL; N=485 MALE
                UNDERGRADUATES)
        aAPPLICATION 1970 S-33

2755   ZIEGLER, D. J.
            SELF CONCEPT, OCCUPATIONAL MERITS CONCEPT, AND OCCUPATIONAL INTEREST
            AREA RELATIONSHIPS IN MALE COLLEGE STUDENTS.
            JOURNAL OF COUNSELING PSYCHOLOGY, 1970, 17, 133-136.
                (CORRELATES:BEHAVIORAL, PSYCHOLOGICAL; N=428 STUDENTS)
        aAPPLICATION 1970 G-21

2756   GUINAR, J. F., & FOULDS, M. L.
            MARATHON GROUP: FACILITATOR OF PERSONAL GROWTH?
            JOURNAL OF COUNSELING PSYCHOLOGY, 1970, 17, 145-149.
                (CORRELATES:ENVIRONMENTAL; NORMATIVE DATA; N=6 MALE AND 4 FEMALE
                COLLEGE STUDENTS)
        aAPPLICATION 1970 S-21

2757   TSENG, M. S., & CARTER, A. R.
          ACHIEVEMENT MOTIVATION AND FEAR OF FAILURE AS DETERMINANTS OF VOCATIONAL
          CHOICE, VOCATIONAL ASPRRATION, AND PERCEPTION OF VOCATIONAL PRESTIGE.
          JOURNAL OF COUNSELING PSYCHOLOGY, 1970, 17, 150-156.
             (CORRELATES:PSYCHOLOGICAL; USED AS CRITERION; N=228 ADOLESCENT BOYS)
       @APPLICATION 1970 M-7 H-26 M-4 N-46

2758   WALSH, W. B., & LACEY, D. W.
          FURTHER EXPLORATION OF PERCEIVED CHANGE AND HOLLANDS THEORY.
          JOURNAL OF COUNSELING PSYCHOLOGY, 1970, 17, 189-190.
             (CORRELATES:ENVIRONMENTAL; USED AS CRITERION; N=157 COLLEGE FEMALES)
       @APPLICATION 1970 H-47

2759   JONES, G. B., & KRUMBOLTZ, J. D.
          STIMULATING VOCATIONAL EXPLORATION THROUGH FILM-MEDIATED PROBLEMS.
          JOURNAL OF COUNSELING PSYCHOLOGY, 1970, 17, 107-114.
             (CORRELATES:PSYCHOLOGICAL, DEMOGRAPHIC, ENVIRONMENTAL; USED AS
             CRITERION; N=270 HIGH SCHOOL STUDENTS)
       @APPLICATION 1970 F-64

2760   SHAFFER, W. F.
          EXPERIMENT WHICH CASTS DOUBT ON THE FINDINGS OF THE STANFORD MOBILITY
          STUDY.
          JOURNAL OF COUNSELING PSYCHOLOGY, 1970, 17, 299-305.
             (MODIFICATION; CORRELATES:PSYCHOLOGICAL, DEMOGRAPHIC; NORMATIVE DATA;
             N=108 HIGH SCHOOL STUDENTS, 3 SAMPLES)
       @APPLICATION 1970 T-2 S-155 K-23 S-154

2761   LIN, Y. G., & MCKEACHIE, W. J.
          APTITUDE, ANXIETY, STUDY HABITS, AND ACADEMIC ACHIEVEMENT.
          JOURNAL OF COUNSELING PSYCHOLOGY, 1970, 17, 306-309.
             (MODIFICATION; CORRELATES:BEHAVIORAL, PSYCHOLOGICAL; NORMATIVE DATA;
             N=APPROX. 208 MALE AND FEMALE COLLEGE STUDENTS, 2 SAMPLES)
       @APPLICATION 1970 A-8 B-74 V-23

2762   WILLIS, C. H., HARFORD, T., & EDDY, B.
          COMPARISON OF SAMPLES OF AMPUTEE AND NONAMPUTEE SUBJECTS ON THE STRONG
          VOCATIONAL INTEREST BLANK.
          JOURNAL OF COUNSELING PSYCHOLOGY, 1970, 17, 310-312.
             (CORRELATES:PSYCHOLOGICAL; NORMATIVE DATA; N=50 MALE AMPUTEES, 213
             MALE NONAMPUTEES)
       @APPLICATION 1970 S-33

2763   VITALO, R. L.
          EFFECTS OF FACILITATIVE INTERPERSONAL FUNCTIONING IN A CONDITIONING
          PARADIGM.
          JOURNAL OF COUNSELING PSYCHOLOGY, 1970, 17, 141-144.
             (CORRELATES:PSYCHOLOGICAL; USED AS CRITERION; N=4 MALE GRADUATE
             STUDENTS, 14 UNDERGRADUATES)
       @APPLICATION 1970 T-74 T-69 T-89

2764   JOHNSON, D. E.
          PERSONALITY CHARACTERISTICS IN RELATION TO COLLEGE PERSISTENCE.
          JOURNAL OF COUNSELING PSYCHOLOGY, 1970, 17, 162-167.
             (CORRELATES:BEHAVIORAL; NORMATIVE DATA; N=3554 STUDENTS)
       @APPLICATION 1970 B-11

2765   WARNER, R. W., JR., & HANSEN, J. C.
          VERBAL-REINFORCEMENT AND MODEL-REINFORCEMENT GROUP COUNSELING WITH
          ALIENATED STUDENTS.
          JOURNAL OF COUNSELING PSYCHOLOGY, 1970, 17, 168-172.
             (CORRELATES:ENVIRONMENTAL; USED AS CRITERION; NORMATIVE DATA; N=180
             9TH GRADERS)
       @APPLICATION 1970 D-13

2766   GALLESSICH, J.
          AN INVESTIGATION OF CORRELATES OF ACADEMIC SUCCESS OF FRESHMEN ENGINEERING
          STUDENTS.
          JOURNAL OF COUNSELING PSYCHOLOGY, 1970, 17, 173-176.
             (VALIDITY:CROSS-VALIDATION; CORRELATES:PSYCHOLOGICAL, INTELLIGENCE;
             N=164 ENGINEERING FRESHMEN)
       @APPLICATION 1970 E-2 B-74 L-1 P-8 T-50 B-270 D-88

2767   CICIRELLI, V. G., & CICIRELLI, J. S.
            COUNSELORS' CREATIVE ABILITY AND ATTITUDE IN RELATION TO COUNSELING
            BEHAVIOR WITH DISADVANTAGED COUNSELEES.
            JOURNAL OF COUNSELING PSYCHOLOGY, 1970, 17, 177-183.
                (CORRELATES:PSYCHOLOGICAL; NORMATIVE DATA; N=52 COUNSELORS OF
                SOCIALLY DISADVANTAGED)
        @APPLICATION 1970 M-29 T-39

2768   ROSSMANN, J. E., & KIRK, B. A.
            COMPARISON OF COUNSELING SEEKERS AND NONSEEKERS.
            JOURNAL OF COUNSELING PSYCHOLOGY, 1970, 17, 184-188.
                (CORRELATES:PSYCHOLOGICAL, DEMOGRAPHIC, INTELLIGENCE; NORMATIVE DATA;
                N=1648 MALE AND 1243 FEMALE FRESHMEN)
        @APPLICATION 1970 H-12

2769   HARMON, L. W.
            ANATOMY OF CAREER COMMITMENT IN WOMEN.
            JOURNAL OF COUNSELING PSYCHOLOGY, 1970, 17, 77-80.
                (CORRELATES:BEHAVIORAL, PSYCHOLOGICAL; USED AS CRITERION; N=169 ADULT
                WOMEN)
        @APPLICATION 1970 S-33

2770   STRONG, S. R., & SCHMIDT, L. D.
            EXPERTNESS AND INFLUENCE IN COUNSELING.
            JOURNAL OF COUNSELING PSYCHOLOGY, 1970, 17, 81-87.
                (CORRELATES:PSYCHOLOGICAL, ENVIRONMENTAL; N=49 MALE COLLEGE STUDENTS)
        @APPLICATION 1970 E-2 P-53

2771   MEGARGEE, E. I., PRICE, A. C., FROHWIRTH, R., & LEVINE, R.
            TIME ORIENTATION OF YOUTHFUL PRISON INMATES.
            JOURNAL OF COUNSELING PSYCHOLOGY, 1970, 17, 8-14.
                (CORRELATES:BEHAVIORAL; NORMATIVE DATA; N=60 PRISONERS)
        @APPLICATION 1970 R-47

2772   HIGGINS, W. H., IVEY, A. E., & UHLEMANN, M. R.
            MEDIA THERAPY: A PROGRAMMED APPROACH TO TEACHING BEHAVIORAL SKILLS.
            JOURNAL OF COUNSELING PSYCHOLOGY, 1970, 17, 20-26.
                (MODIFICATION; CORRELATES:BEHAVIORAL; N=30 PAIRS OF ADULTS)
        @APPLICATION 1970 K-73 I-3 O-16

2773   SIESS, T. F., & JACKSON, D. N.
            VOCATIONAL INTERESTS AND PERSONALITY: AN EMPIRICAL INTEGRATION.
            JOURNAL OF COUNSELING PSYCHOLOGY, 1970, 17, 27-35.
                (CORRELATES:PSYCHOLOGICAL; FACTOR ANALYSIS; N=212 MALE COLLEGE
                STUDENTS)
        @APPLICATION 1970 J-1 S-33

2774   LEFKOWITZ, D. M.
            COMPARISON OF THE STRONG VOCATIONAL INTEREST BLANK AND THE KUDER
            OCCUPATIONAL INTEREST SURVEY SCORING PROCEDURES.
            JOURNAL OF COUNSELING PSYCHOLOGY, 1970, 17, 357-363.
                (VALIDITY:CONSTRUCT; NORMATIVE DATA; N=600 MALE PROFESSIONAL
                ENGINEERS)
        @APPLICATION 1970 S-33 K-72

2775   BODDEN, J. R.
            COGNITIVE COMPLEXITY AS A FACTOR IN APPROPRIATE VOCATIONAL CHOICE.
            JOURNAL OF COUNSELING PSYCHOLOGY, 1970, 17, 364-368.
                (MODIFICATION; CORRELATES:PSYCHOLOGICAL; NORMATIVE DATA; N=87 MALE
                AND 113 FEMALE COLLEGE STUDENTS)
        @APPLICATION 1970 B-97 K-23 H-21

2776   PALLONE, N. J., RICKARD, F. S., HURLEY, R. B., & TIRMAN, R. J.
            WORK VALUES AND SELF-MEANING.
            JOURNAL OF COUNSELING PSYCHOLOGY, 1970, 17, 376-377.
                (CORRELATES:PSYCHOLOGICAL; N=531 BLACK & WHITE HIGH SCHOOL MALES &
                FEMALES)
        @APPLICATION 1970 S-59 O-16

2777   EDWARDS, B. C., & EDGERLY, J. W.
            EFFECTS OF COUNSELOR-CLIENT COGNITIVE CONGRUENCE ON COUNSELING OUTCOME IN
            BRIEF COUNSELING.
            JOURNAL OF COUNSELING PSYCHOLOGY, 1970, 17, 313-318.
                (MODIFICATION; N=34 MALE AND 14 FEMALE COLLEGE STUDENTS)
        @APPLICATION 1970 O-16
        @B-60

2778   BUCK, C. W.
          CRYSTALLIZATION OF VOCATIONAL INTERESTS AS A FUNCTION OF VOCATIONAL
          EXPLORATION IN COLLEGE.
          JOURNAL OF COUNSELING PSYCHOLOGY, 1970, 17, 347-351.
                (RELIABILITY:RETEST; CORRELATES:PSYCHOLOGICAL; USED AS CRITERION;
                NORMATIVE DATA; N=120 MALE COLLEGE STUDENTS)
       @APPLICATION 1970 S-33 G-22

2779   POSTHUMA, A. B., & NAVRAN, L.
          RELATION OF CONGRUENCE IN STUDENT-FACULTY INTERESTS TO ACHIEVEMENT IN
          COLLEGE.
          JOURNAL OF COUNSELING PSYCHOLOGY, 1970, 17, 352-356.
                (CORRELATES:PSYCHOLOGICAL, INTELLIGENCE; N=121 MILITARY SCHOOL
                CADETS)
       @APPLICATION 1970 H-21 E-2 S-33

2780   NIDORF, L. J., & ARGABRITE, A. H.
          AESTHETIC COMMUNICATION: I. MEDIATING ORGANISMIC VARIABLES.
          JOURNAL OF GENERAL PSYCHOLOGY, 1970, 82, 179-193.
                (CORRELATES:BEHAVIORAL: USED AS CRITERION; N=172 UNDERGRADUATES)
       @APPLICATION 1970 B-5 C-76 0-16

2781   GRAVITZ, M. A.
          LARGE SCALE NORMAL ADULT BASE RATES FOR MMPI "PRIVACY" ITEMS: I. SEXUAL
          ATTITUDES AND EXPERIENCES.
          JOURNAL OF GENERAL PSYCHOLOGY, 1970, 82, 153-156.
                (BIAS:RESPONSE; N=6686 NORMAL MALES AND 4717 NORMAL FEMALES)
       @APPLICATION 1970 D-45

2782   SCHWENDIMAN, G., LARSEN, K. S., & PARKS, C.
          BIRTH ORDER, AGGRESSION TRAINING AND AUTHORITARIANISM.
          PSYCHOLOGICAL RECORD, 1970, 20, 69-71.
                (RELIABILITY:RETEST: CORRELATES:PSYCHOLOGICAL, DEMOGRAPHIC; N=17
                PAIRS OF FIRST AND SECOND BORN CHILDREN)
       @APPLICATION 1970 R-8 A-5 L-63

2783   EISENMAN, R.
          TEACHING ABOUT THE AUTHORITARIAN PERSONALITY: EFFECT ON MORAL JUDGMENT.
          PSYCHOLOGICAL RECORD, 1970, 20, 33-40.
                (DESCRIPTION; CORRELATES:PSYCHOLOGICAL, DEMOGRAPHIC; USED AS
                CRITERION; NORMATIVE DATA; N=200 UNDERGRADUATES)
       @APPLICATION 1970 E-31

2784   WINETT, R. A.
          ATTRIBUTION OF ATTITUDE AND BEHAVIOR CHANGE AND ITS RELEVANCE TO BEHAVIOR
          THERAPY.
          PSYCHOLOGICAL RECORD, 1970, 20, 17-32
                (MENT-ION)
       @APPLICATION 1970 R-18

2785   MCBAIN, W. N., FOX, W., KIMURA, S., NAKANISHI, M., & TIRADO, J.
          QUASI-SENSORY COMMUNICATION: AN INVESTIGATION USING SEMANTIC MATCHING AND
          ACCENTUATED AFFECT.
          JOURNAL OF PERSONALITY AND SOCIAL PSYCHOLOGY, 1970, 14, 281-291.
                (CORRELATES:BEHAVIORAL, PSYCHOLOGICAL; N=22 MALE AND FEMALE
                UNDERGRADUATES)
       @APPLICATION 1970 W-31 0-16

2786   LEVY, L. H., & HOUSE, W. C.
          PERCEIVED ORIGINS OF BELIEFS AS DETERMINANTS OF EXPECTANCY OF THEIR CHANGE.
          JOURNAL OF PERSONALITY AND SOCIAL PSYCHOLOGY, 1970, 14, 329-334.
                (CORRELATES:PSYCHOLOGICAL; N=57 MALE AND 43 FEMALE UNDERGRADUATES)
       @APPLICATION 1970 A-12

2787   COOP, R. H., & BROWN, L. D.
          EFFECTS OF COGNITIVE STYLE AND TEACHING METHOD ON CATEGORIES OF
          ACHIEVEMENT.
          JOURNAL OF EDUCATIONAL PSYCHOLOGY, 1970, 61, 400-405.
                (CORRELATES:BEHAVIORAL, PSYCHOLOGICAL, ENVIRONMENTAL; USED AS
                CRITERION; NORMATIVE DATA; N=80 SELECTED UNDERGRADUATES)
       @APPLICATION 1970 S-254

2788   ACHENBACH, T. M.
            THE CHILDREN'S ASSOCIATIVE RESPONDING TEST: A POSSIBLE ALTERNATIVE TO GROUP
            IQ TESTS.
            JOURNAL OF EDUCATIONAL PSYCHOLOGY, 1970, 61, 340-348.
                (VALIDITY:CONSTRUCT, CROSS-VALIDATION; CORRELATES:INTELLIGENCE; USED
                AS CRITERION; NORMATIVE DATA; 2 STUDIES: N=158, 126 FIFTH GRADERS)
        @APPLICATION 1970 A-73

2789   EGELAND, B., HUNT, D. E., & HARDT, R. H.
            COLLEGE ENROLLMENT OF UPWARD BOUND STUDENTS AS A FUNCTION OF ATTITUDE AND
            MOTIVATION.
            JOURNAL OF EDUCATIONAL PSYCHOLOGY, 1970, 61, 375-379.
                (CORRELATES:PSYCHOLOGICAL, DEMOGRAPHIC, INTELLIGENCE; N=304 UPWARD
                BOUND COLLEGE, AND 108 UPWARD BOUND NONCOLLEGE STUDENTS)
        @APPLICATION 1970 R-114 H-167 R-18 S-251 S-28 R-10

2790   GANDRY, E., & SPIELBERGER, C. D.
            ANXIETY AND INTELLIGENCE IN PAIRED-ASSOCIATE LEARNING.
            JOURNAL OF EDUCATIONAL PSYCHOLOGY, 1970, 61, 386-391.
                (CORRELATES:BEHAVIORAL, INTELLIGENCE; USED AS CRITERION;
                CROSS-CULTURAL APPLICATION; NORMATIVE DATA; N=72 AUSTRALIAN COLLEGE
                STUDENTS)
        @APPLICATION 1970 T-2

2791   ACUFF, G., & ALLEN, D.
            HIATUS IN "MEANING:" DISENGAGEMENT FOR RETIRED PROFESSORS.
            JOURNAL OF GERONTOLOGY, 1970. 25, 126-128.
                (DESCRIPTION; CORRELATES:PSYCHOLOGICAL, DEMOGRAPHIC, ENVIRONMENTAL;
                USED AS CRITERION; N=188 MALE COLLEGE PROFESSORS)
        @APPLICATION 1970 C-235

2792   TORRANCE, E. P., GOWAN, J. C., WU, J. J., & ALIOTTI, N. C.
            CREATIVE FUNCTIONING OF MONOLINGUAL AND BILINGUAL CHILDREN IN SINGAPORE.
            JOURNAL OF EDUCATIONAL PSYCHOLOGY, 1970, 61, 72-75.
                (CORRELATES:BEHAVIORAL: CROSS-CULTURAL APPLICATION; NORMATIVE DATA;
                N=1063 ELEMENTARY SCHOOL CHILDREN IN SINGAPORE)
        @APPLICATION 1970 T-39

2793   MARKS, E.
            COGNITIVE AND INCENTIVE FACTORS INVOLVED IN WITHIN-UNIVERSITY TRANSFER.
            JOURNAL OF EDUCATIONAL PSYCHOLOGY, 1970, 61, 1-9.
                (CORRELATES:BEHAVIORAL, PSYCHOLOGICAL, INTELLIGENCE; N=1443 MALE
                COLLEGE STUDENTS)
        @APPLICATION 1970 J-1 M-257

2794   RYAN, F. L., & MACMILLAN, D. L.
            EFFECTS OF INTERRUPTION DURING SOCIAL STUDIES INSTRUCTION ON LEARNING
            EFFECTIVENESS AND EFFICIENCY.
            JOURNAL OF EDUCATIONAL PSYCHOLOGY, 1970, 61, 27-32.
                (CORRELATES:ENVIRONMENTAL; USED AS CRITERION; NORMATIVE DATA; N=96
                ELEMENTARY SCHOOL CHILDREN)
        @APPLICATION 1970 S-35

2795   BERK, L. E., ROSE, M. H., & STEWART, D.
            ATTITUDES OF ENGLISH AND AMERICAN CHILDREN TOWARD THEIR SCHOOL
            EXPERIENCE.
            JOURNAL OF EDUCATIONAL PSYCHOLOGY, 1970, 61, 33-40.
                (CORRELATES:PSYCHOLOGICAL, DEMOGRAPHIC, INTELLIGENCE; CROSS-CULTURAL
                APPLICATION; NORMATIVE DATA; N=787 AMERICAN ELEMENTARY SCHOOL
                CHILDREN)
        @APPLICATION 1970 L-64

2796   RINGNESS, T. A.
            IDENTIFYING FIGURES, THEIR ACHIEVEMENT VALUES, AND CHILDREN'S VALUES AS
            RELATED TO ACTUAL AND PREDICTED ACHIEVEMENT.
            JOURNAL OF EDUCATIONAL PSYCHOLOGY, 1970, 61, 174-185.
                (CORRELATES:BEHAVIORAL, PSYCHOLOGICAL, INTELLIGENCE; FACTOR ANALYSIS;
                NORMATIVE DATA; N=267 8TH GRADE GIRLS)
        @APPLICATION 1970 R-67

2797   AHAMMER, I. M., & SCHAIE, K. W.
            AGE DIFFERENCES IN THE RELATIONSHIP BETWEEN PERSONALITY QUESTIONNAIRE
            FACTORS AND SCHOOL ACHIEVEMENT.
            JOURNAL OF EDUCATIONAL PSYCHOLOGY, 1970, 61, 193-197.
                 (VALIDITY:CRITERION; CORRELATES:PSYCHOLOGICAL, INTELLIGENCE;
                 N=104 THIRD GRADERS, 114 SIXTH GRADERS)
         @APPLICATION 1970 C-89 C-102 P-62

2798   FREEBERG, N. E.
            ASSESSMENT OF DISADVANTAGED ADOLESCENTS: A DIFFERENT APPROACH TO RESEARCH
            AND EVALUATION MEASURES.
            JOURNAL OF EDUCATIONAL PSYCHOLOGY, 1970, 61, 229-240.
                 (RELIABILITY:INTERNAL CONSISTENCY; VALIDITY:CRITERION;
                 CORRELATES:DEMOGRAPHIC: FACTOR ANALYSIS; N=123 MALE AND 133 FEMALE
                 DISADVANTAGED ADOLESCENTS)
         @APPLICATION 1970 B-15 R-12 S-160

2799   MARKS, E.
            INDIVIDUAL DIFFERENCES IN PERCEPTIONS OF THE COLLEGE ENVIRONMENT.
            JOURNAL OF EDUCATIONAL PSYCHOLOGY, 1970, 61, 270-279.
                 (CORRELATES:PSYCHOLOGICAL, INTELLIGENCE, ENVIRONMENTAL; FACTOR
                 ANALYSIS; N=100 MALE COLLEGE STUDENTS)
         @APPLICATION 1970 J-1

2800   MARX, D. J.
            INTENTIONAL AND INCIDENTAL CONCEPT FORMATION AS A FUNCTION OF CONCEPTUAL
            COMPLEXITY, INTELLIGENCE, AND TASK COMPLEXITY.
            JOURNAL OF EDUCATIONAL PSYCHOLOGY, 1970, 61, 297-304.
                 (CORRELATES:PSYCHOLOGICAL, INTELLIGENCE; USED AS CRITERION; N=144
                 FEMALE HIGH SCHOOL STUDENTS)
         @APPLICATION 1970 S-41

2801   RICHARDS, J. M., JR., SELIGMAN, R., & JONES, P. K.
            FACULTY AND CURRICULUM AS MEASURES OF COLLEGE ENVIRONMENT.
            JOURNAL OF EDUCATIONAL PSYCHOLOGY, 1970, 61, 324-332.
                 (VALIDITY:CONSTRUCT, CRITERION; CORRELATES:ENVIRONMENTAL; NORMATIVE
                 DATA; N=142 COLLEGES IN 1968, 51 IN 1948)
         @APPLICATION 1970 A-31 P-67

2802   LAHADERNE, H. M., & JACKSON, P. W.
            WITHDRAWAL IN THE CLASSROOM: A NOTE ON SOME EDUCATIONAL CORRELATES OF
            SOCIAL DESIRABILITY AMONG SCHOOL CHILDREN.
            JOURNAL OF EDUCATIONAL PSYCHOLOGY, 1970, 61, 97-101.
                 (RELIABILITY:INTERNAL CONSISTENCY; CORRELATES:BEHAVIORAL,
                 PSYCHOLOGICAL, DEMOGRAPHIC, INTELLIGENCE; NORMATIVE DATA; N=62 BOYS
                 AND 63 GIRLS IN 6TH GRADE)
         @APPLICATION 1970 C-42

2803   WALLS, R. T., & SMITH, T. S.
            DEVELOPMENT OF PREFERENCE FOR DELAYED REINFORCEMENT IN DISADVANTAGED
            CHILDREN.
            JOURNAL OF EDUCATIONAL PSYCHOLOGY, 1970, 61, 118-123.
                 (MODIFICATION: CORRELATES:BEHAVIORAL, PSYCHOLOGICAL, DEMOGRAPHIC;
                 N=45 DISADVANTAGED, 45 CONTROL 2ND AND 3RD GRADE CHILDREN)
         @APPLICATION 1970 B-115 H-29 S-89

2804   TAFT, R., & GILCHRIST, M. B.
            CREATIVE ATTITUDES AND CREATIVE PRODUCTIVITY: A COMPARISON OF TWO
            ASPECTS OF CREATIVITY AMONG STUDENTS.
            JOURNAL OF EDUCATIONAL PSYCHOLOGY, 1970, 61, 136-143.
                 (CORRELATES:BEHAVIORAL, PSYCHOLOGICAL; N=112 FEMALE AND 81 MALE
                 STUDENTS)
         @APPLICATION 1970 G-21 E-6 E-8 T-54 Z-21

2805   WEINER, B., & POTEPAN, P. A.
            PERSONALITY CHARACTERISTICS AND AFFECTIVE REACTIONS TOWARD EXAMS OF
            SUPERIOR AND FAILING COLLEGE STUDENTS.
            JOURNAL OF EDUCATIONAL PSYCHOLOGY, 1970, 61, 144-151.
                 (MODIFICATION; VALIDITY:CRITERION; CORRELATES:PSYCHOLOGICAL,
                 DEMOGRAPHIC; N=107 COLLEGE STUDENTS)
         @APPLICATION 1970 M-4 M-13 C-25

2806   SIEBER, J. E., KAMEYA, L. I., & PAULSON, F. L.
            EFFECT OF MEMORY SUPPORT ON THE PROBLEM SOLVING ABILITY OF TEXT-ANXIOUS
            CHILDREN.
            JOURNAL OF EDUCATIONAL PSYCHOLOGY, 1970, 61, 159-168.
                (CORRELATES:BEHAVIORAL, PSYCHOLOGICAL, INTELLIGENCE; USED AS
                CRITERION; 2 STUDIES: N=20 MALE, 20 FEMALE 5TH AND 6TH GRADE
                CHILDREN, 48 MALE, 48 FEMALE 5TH AND 6TH GRADERS)
        @APPLICATION 1970 W-94

2807   SMITH, K. H.
            CONFORMITY AS RELATED TO MASCULINITY, SELF, AND OTHER DESCRIPTIONS,
            SUSPICION, AND ARTISTIC PREFERENCE BY SEX GROUPS.
            JOURNAL OF SOCIAL PSYCHOLOGY, 1970, 80, 79-88.
                (RELIABILITY:INTERNAL CONSISTENCY; CORRELATES:PSYCHOLOGICAL; FACTOR
                ANALYSIS; N=45 FEMALE AND 41 MALE COLLEGE STUDENTS)
        @APPLICATION 1970 G-40 B-76 O-16

2808   MITCHELL, T. R.
            THE CONSTRUCT VALIDITY OF THREE DIMENSIONS OF LEADERSHIP RESEARCH.
            JOURNAL OF SOCIAL PSYCHOLOGY, 1970, 80, 89-94.
                (MODIFICATION; VALIDITY:CONSTRUCT; CORRELATES:PSYCHOLOGICAL; N=105
                MALE COLLEGE STUDENTS)
        @APPLICATION 1970 H-97 F-63

2809   DUSTIN, D. S., & DAVIS, H. P.
            EVALUATIVE BIAS IN GROUP AND INDIVIDUAL COMPETITION.
            JOURNAL OF SOCIAL PSYCHOLOGY, 1970, 80, 103-108.
                (MODIFICATION; CORRELATES:BEHAVIORAL, PSYCHOLOGICAL; N=138 MALE
                COLLEGE STUDENTS)
        @APPLICATION 1970 W-89

2810   MEHRYAR, A. H.
            AN ATTEMPT TO CROSS-VALIDATE EYSENCK'S HYPOTHESIS REGARDING THE
            RELATIONSHIP BETWEEN EXTRAVERSION AND TOUGH-MINDEDNESS.
            JOURNAL OF SOCIAL PSYCHOLOGY, 1970, 80, 109-110.
                (MENTION; VALIDITY:CROSS-VALIDATION; CROSS-CULTURAL APPLICATION;
                N=69 STUDENTS)
        @APPLICATION 1970 E-6 A-7

2811   PAPAGEORGIS, D.
            EFFECTS OF DISGUISED AND PERSUASION CONTEXTS ON BELIEFS.
            JOURNAL OF SOCIAL PSYCHOLOGY, 1970, 80, 43-48.
                (CORRELATES:ENVIRONMENTAL; N=100 UNDERGRADUATES)
        @APPLICATION 1970 M-225

2812   ANTLER, L.
            CORRELATES OF HOME AND HOST COUNTRY ACQUAINTANCESHIP AMONG FOREIGN MEDICAL
            RESIDENTS IN THE UNITED STATES.
            JOURNAL OF SOCIAL PSYCHOLOGY, 1970, 80, 49-57.
                (RELIABILITY:INTERNAL CONSISTENCY; CORRELATES:BEHAVIORAL,
                PSYCHOLOGICAL, DEMOGRAPHIC; N=170 FOREIGN MEDICAL RESIDENTS)
        @APPLICATION 1970 G-70

2813   CHEMERS, M. M.
            THE RELATIONSHIP BETWEEN BIRTH ORDER AND LEADERSHIP STYLE.
            JOURNAL OF SOCIAL PSYCHOLOGY, 1970, 80, 243-244.
                (CORRELATES:DEMOGRAPHIC; N=350 COLLEGE STUDENTS)
        @APPLICATION 1970 F-48

2814   HOUSTON, B. K.
            DOGMATISM AND INTOLERANCE FOR SENSORY DISCREPANCY.
            JOURNAL OF SOCIAL PSYCHOLOGY, 1970, 80, 245-246.
                (CORRELATES:BEHAVIORAL; N=51 MALE COLLEGE STUDENTS)
        @APPLICATION 1970 R-8

2815   LANDERS, D. M.
            SIBLING-SEX-STATUS AND ORDINAL POSITION EFFECTS ON FEMALES' SPORT
            PARTICIPATION AND INTERESTS.
            JOURNAL OF SOCIAL PSYCHOLOGY, 1970, 80, 247-248.
                (CORRELATES:BEHAVIORAL, ENVIRONMENTAL; N=202 COLLEGE STUDENTS)
        @APPLICATION 1970 G-20 D-45

2816   EISENMAN, R., & CHERRY, H. O.
               CREATIVITY, AUTHORITARIANISM, AND BIRTH ORDER.
               JOURNAL OF SOCIAL PSYCHOLOGY, 1970, 80, 233-235.
                      (MODIFICATION; CORRELATES:PSYCHOLOGICAL, DEMOGRAPHIC; N=263 COLLEGE
                      STUDENTS)
        @APPLICATION 1970 A-5 E-22 C-45

2817   HORNE, W. C.
               GROUP INFLUENCE ON ETHICAL RISK TAKING: THE INADEQUACY OF TWO HYPOTHESES.
               JOURNAL OF SOCIAL PSYCHOLOGY, 1970, 80, 237-238.
                      (VALIDITY:CONSTRUCT; CORRELATES:BEHAVIORAL, PSYCHOLOGICAL; N=36
                      COLLEGE STUDENTS)
        @APPLICATION 1970 R-26

2818   HOGAN, H. W.
               A SYMBOLIC MEASURE OF AUTHORITARIANISM: A REPLICATION.
               JOURNAL OF SOCIAL PSYCHOLOGY, 1970, 80, 241-242.
                      (RELIABILITY:INTERNAL CONSISTENCY; CORRELATES:PSYCHOLOGICAL,
                      DEMOGRAPHIC; N=72 COLLEGE STUDENTS AND 52 PRISON GUARDS)
        @APPLICATION 1970 A-5 H-108

2819   YUKL, G.
               LEADER LPC SCORES: ATTITUDE DIMENSIONS AND BEHAVIORAL CORRELATES.
               JOURNAL OF SOCIAL PSYCHOLOGY, 1970, 80, 207-212.
                      (MENTION; CORRELATES:BEHAVIORAL, PSYCHOLOGICAL; FACTOR ANALYSIS;
                      N=116 BUSINESS AND STUDENT LEADERS)
        @APPLICATION 1970 H-141 B-2
        @F-48

2820   LUDWIG, D. J.
               EVIDENCE OF CONSTRUCT AND CRITERION-RELATED VALIDITY FOR THE SELF-CONCEPT.
               JOURNAL OF SOCIAL PSYCHOLOGY, 1970, 80, 213-223.
                      (VALIDITY:CONSTRUCT, CRITERION; CORRELATES:PSYCHOLOGICAL; N=179 MALE
                      HIGH SCHOOL STUDENTS)
        @APPLICATION 1970 R-12 M-106

2821   STEININGER, M.
               APTITUDE, DOGMATISM, AND COLLEGE PRESS AS CODETERMINANTS OF ACADEMIC
               ACHIEVEMENT.
               JOURNAL OF SOCIAL PSYCHOLOGY, 1970, 80, 229-230.
                      (CORRELATES:BEHAVIORAL, PSYCHOLOGICAL; N=74 MALE AND 75 FEMALE
                      COLLEGE STUDENTS)
        @APPLICATION 1970 R-8

2822   WILLIAMS, R. L., & BYARS, H.
               THE EFFECT OF ACADEMIC INTEGRATION ON THE SELF-ESTEEM OF SOUTHERN NEGRO
               STUDENTS.
               JOURNAL OF SOCIAL PSYCHOLOGY, 1970, 80, 183-188.
                      (CORRELATES:PSYCHOLOGICAL, ENVIRONMENTAL; N=94 SOUTHERN NEGRO HIGH
                      SCHOOL STUDENTS)
        . @APPLICATION 1970 F-7

2823   STIMPSON, D. V.
               THE INFLUENCE OF COMMITMENT AND SELF-ESTEEM ON SUSCEPTIBILITY TO
               PERSUASION.
               JOURNAL OF SOCIAL PSYCHOLOGY, 1970, 80, 189-195.
                      (CORRELATES:BEHAVIORAL, PSYCHOLOGICAL; N=79 MALE COLLEGE STUDENTS)
        @APPLICATION 1970 J-7

2824   CHESON, B. D., STRICKER, G., & FRY, C. L.
               THE REPRESSION-SENSITIZATION SCALE AND MEASURES OF PREJUDICE.
               JOURNAL OF SOCIAL PSYCHOLOGY, 1970, 80, 197-200.
                      (CORRELATES:BEHAVIORAL, PSYCHOLOGICAL; N=56 MALE COLLEGE STUDENTS)
        @APPLICATION 1970 B-46 A-37 G-18

2825   LINDGREN, H. C., & MARRASH, J.
               A COMPARATIVE STUDY OF INTERCULTURAL INSIGHT AND EMPATHY.
               JOURNAL OF SOCIAL PSYCHOLOGY, 1970, 80, 135-141.
                      (RELIABILITY:RETEST; CROSS-CULTURAL APPLICATION; N=317 MIXED
                      NATIONALITY STUDENTS IN LEBANON)
        @APPLICATION 1970 E-12

2826   KATZELL, R. A., MILLER, C. E., ROTTER, N. G., & VENET, T. G.
           EFFECTS OF LEADERSHIP AND OTHER INPUTS ON GROUP PROCESSES AND OUTPUTS.
           JOURNAL OF SOCIAL PSYCHOLOGY. 1970, 80, 157-169.
               (CORRELATES:BEHAVIORAL, PSYCHOLOGICAL; N=76 COLLEGE STUDENTS)
       @APPLICATION 1970 B-2

2827   YANG, K.
           AUTHORITARIANISM AND EVALUATION OF APPROPRIATENESS OF ROLE BEHAVIOR.
           JOURNAL OF SOCIAL PSYCHOLOGY. 1970, 80, 171-181.
               (CROSS-CULTURAL APPLICATION; FACTOR ANALYSIS; N=227 MALE CHINESE
               COLLEGE STUDENTS)
       @APPLICATION 1970 A-5 T-12

2828   OSKAMP, S., & THOMPSON, G.
           INTERNAL CONSISTENCY IN THE STEREOPATHY-ACQUIESCENCE SCALES: A WARNING
           NOTE.
           JOURNAL OF SOCIAL PSYCHOLOGY. 1970, 81, 73-77.
               (VALIDITY:CONSTRUCT; CORRELATES:BEHAVIORAL, PSYCHOLOGICAL; N=91
               COLLEGE STUDENTS AND MOTHERS)
       @APPLICATION 1970 S-9 S-130 T-2 M-50

2829   ZIMMERMAN, S. F., SMITH, K. H., & PEDERSEN, D. M.
           THE EFFECT OF ANTICONFORMITY APPEALS ON CONFORMITY BEHAVIOR.
           JOURNAL OF SOCIAL PSYCHOLOGY. 1970, 81, 93-103.
               (CORRELATES:BEHAVIORAL, PSYCHOLOGICAL; N=121 COLLEGE STUDENTS)
       @APPLICATION 1970 C-23 R-8 B-76 G-13 S-21 S-68

2830   ORPEN, C.
           AUTHORITARIANISM IN AN "AUTHORITARIAN" CULTURE: THE CASE OF
           AFRIKAANS-SPEAKING SOUTH AFRICA.
           JOURNAL OF SOCIAL PSYCHOLOGY. 1970, 81, 119-120.
               (CROSS-CULTURAL APPLICATION; N=100 AFRICAN COLLEGE STUDENTS)
       @APPLICATION 1970 A-5 A-17 C-23 C-31

2831   HOLMES, J. S., & CURETON, E. E.
           GROUP THERAPY INTERACTION WITH AND WITHOUT THE LEADER.
           JOURNAL OF SOCIAL PSYCHOLOGY. 1970, 81, 127-128.
               (CORRELATES:ENVIRONMENTAL; N=24 PSYCHIATRIC PATIENTS)
       @APPLICATION 1970 H-87

2832   NOTTINGHAM, J., GORSUCH, R., & WRIGHTSMAN, L.
           FACTORIAL REPLICATION OF THE THEORETICALLY DERIVED SUBSCALES ON THE
           PHILOSOPHIES OF HUMAN NATURE SCALE.
           JOURNAL OF SOCIAL PSYCHOLOGY. 1970, 81, 129-130.
               (FACTOR ANALYSIS; N=400 FEMALES, 307 MALES)
       @APPLICATION 1970 W-24

2833   BAGLEY, C. B., WILSON, G. D., & BOSHIER, R.
           THE CONSERVATISM SCALE: A FACTOR-STRUCTURE COMPARISON OF ENGLISH, DUTCH,
           AND NEW ZEALAND SAMPLES.
           JOURNAL OF SOCIAL PSYCHOLOGY. 1970, 81, 267-268.
               (CROSS-CULTURAL APPLICATION; FACTOR ANALYSIS; N=200 (LONDON SAMPLE),
               200 (DUTCH SAMPLE), 357 (NEW ZEALAND SAMPLE))
       @APPLICATION 1970 W-87

2834   WILKINSON, A. L.
           RELATIONSHIP BETWEEN MEASURES OF INTELLECTUAL FUNCTIONING AND EXTREME
           RESPONSE STYLE.
           JOURNAL OF SOCIAL PSYCHOLOGY. 1970, 81, 271-272.
               (CORRELATES:PSYCHOLOGICAL, INTELLIGENCE; N=131 ALCOHOLICS)
       @APPLICATION 1970 W-21

2835   KENNEDY, J. J., COOK, P. A., & BREWER, R. R.
           THE EFFECTS OF THREE SELECTED EXPERIMENTER VARIABLES IN VERBAL
           CONDITIONING RESEARCH.
           JOURNAL OF SOCIAL PSYCHOLOGY. 1970, 81, 167-175.
               (USED AS CRITERION; N=80 UNDERGRADUATES)
       @APPLICATION 1970 W-24

2836   LONG, H. B.
            RELATIONSHIPS OF SELECTED PERSONAL AND SOCIAL VARIABLES IN CONFORMING
            JUDGMENT.
            JOURNAL OF SOCIAL PSYCHOLOGY, 1970, 81, 177-182.
                    (CORRELATES:BEHAVIORAL, DEMOGRAPHIC, INTELLIGENCE; N=109 PRISON
                    INMATES, 55 BLACK, 54 WHITE)
        @APPLICATION 1970 R-8 C-23

2837   GEEN, R. G.
            PERCEIVED SUFFERING OF THE VICTIM AS AN INHIBITOR OF ATTACK-INDUCED
            AGGRESSION.
            JOURNAL OF SOCIAL PSYCHOLOGY, 1970, 81, 209-215.
                    (CORRELATES:BEHAVIORAL: N=48 MALE STUDENTS)
        @APPLICATION 1970 G-101

2838   GORDON, L. V., & KIKUCHI, A.
            THE COMPARABILITY OF THE FORCED-CHOICE AND Q SORT MEASUREMENT APPROACHES:
            ANOTHER CULTURAL STUDY.
            JOURNAL OF SOCIAL PSYCHOLOGY, 1970, 81, 137-144.
                    (MODIFICATION; RELIABILITY:INTERNAL CONSISTENCY;
                    CROSS-CULTURAL APPLICATION; N=73 JAPANESE COLLEGE STUDENTS)
        @APPLICATION 1970 G-13

2839   SINGH, N. P.
            N/ACH AMONG AGRICULTURAL AND BUSINESS ENTREPRENEURS IN DELHI.
            JOURNAL OF SOCIAL PSYCHOLOGY, 1970, 81, 145-150.
                    (CORRELATES:PSYCHOLOGICAL, DEMOGRAPHIC: CROSS-CULTURAL APPLICATION;
                    N=80 AGRICULTURAL ENTREPRENEURS, 80 BUSINESS ENTREPRENEURS)
        @APPLICATION 1970 V-23

2840   BECKER, G.
            SITUATIONAL DISCRIMINATION IN REPRESSOR-TYPE AND SENSITIZER-TYPE APPROVAL
            SEEKERS AND THE BIRTH ORDER BY SUBJECT SEX INTERACTION.
            JOURNAL OF SOCIAL PSYCHOLOGY, 1970, 82, 81-97.
                    (CORRELATES:PSYCHOLOGICAL; USED AS CRITERION; N=71
                    UNDERGRADUATES)
        @APPLICATION 1970 C-27 M-8

2841   MCLAUGHLIN, B.
            INCIDENTAL LEARNING AND MACHIAVELLIANISM.
            JOURNAL OF SOCIAL PSYCHOLOGY, 1970, 82, 109-116.
                    (USED AS CRITERION; N=200)
        @APPLICATION 1970 C-14

2842   HOGAN, H. W.
            A SYMBOLIC MEASURE OF AUTHORITARIANISM: AN EXPLORATORY STUDY.
            JOURNAL OF SOCIAL PSYCHOLOGY, 1970, 82, 215-219.
                    (VALIDITY:CONSTRUCT, CRITERION; CORRELATES:PSYCHOLOGICAL; N=40 MALE,
                    31 FEMALE STUDENTS)
        @APPLICATION 1970 A-5

2843   DELHEES, K. H., CATTELL, R. B., & SWENEY, A. B.
            THE STRUCTURE OF PARENTAL INTRAFAMILIAL ATTITUDES AND SENTIMENTS MEASURED
            BY OBJECTIVE TESTS AND A VECTOR MODEL.
            JOURNAL OF SOCIAL PSYCHOLOGY, 1970, 82, 231-252.
                    (REVIEW)
        @APPLICATION 1970 B-1 R-89 S-13 S-9 R-41 B-219 I-6

2844   HJELLE, L. A., & ABOUD, J., JR.
            SOME PERSONALITY DIFFERENCES BETWEEN SEMINARIANS AND NONSEMINARIANS.
            JOURNAL OF SOCIAL PSYCHOLOGY, 1970, 82, 279-280.
                    (CORRELATES:DEMOGRAPHIC; N=57 MALE CATHOLIC UNDERGRADUATES, 33
                    SEMINARIANS)
        @APPLICATION 1970 E-2

2845   HORTON, M., & KNAUCIUNAS, R.
            MINNESOTA MULTIPHASIC PERSONALITY INVENTORY DIFFERENCES BETWEEN
            TERMINATORS AND CONTINUERS IN YOUTH COUNSELING.
            JOURNAL OF COUNSELING PSYCHOLOGY, 1970, 17, 98-101.
                    (CORRELATES:PSYCHOLOGICAL; N=60 ADOLESCENTS FROM COUNSELING SERVICE)
        @APPLICATION 1970 D-45 L-68 L-71

2846   WALLS, R. T., & MILLER, J. J.
            DELAY OF GRATIFICATION IN WELFARE AND REHABILITATICN CLIENTS.
            JOURNAL OF COUNSELING PSYCHOLOGY, 1970, 17, 383-384.
                (CORRELATES:BEHAVIORAL: N=14 REHABILITATION AND 11 WELFARE CLIENTS)
        @APPLICATION 1970 E-2 R-18

2847   BEDNAR, R. L.
            THERAPEUTIC RELATIONSHIP OF A-B THERAPISTS AS PERCEIVEC BY CLIENT AND
            THERAPIST.
            JOURNAL OF COUNSELING PSYCHOLOGY, 1970, 17, 119-122.
                (USED AS CRITERION: N=47 THERAPISTS AND 47 CLINICAL PATIENTS)
        @APPLICATION 1970 W-91 T-48 S-156

2848   YOUNG, E. R., & JACOBSON, L. I.
            EFFECTS OF TIME-EXTENDED MARATHON GROUP EXPERIENCES ON PERSONALITY
            CHARACTERISTICS.
            JOURNAL OF COUNSELING PSYCHOLOGY, 1970, 17, 247-251.
                (CORRELATES:PSYCHOLOGICAL; N=14 COLLEGE STUDENTS)
        @APPLICATION 1970 E-1 C-27 S-21

2849   JOURARD, S. M., & JAFFE, P. E.
            INFLUENCE OF AN INTERVIEWER'S DISCLOSURE ON THE SELF-DISCLOSING BEHAVIOR OF
            INTERVIEWEES.
            JOURNAL OF COUNSELING PSYCHOLOGY, 1970, 17, 252-257.
                (CORRELATES:BEHAVIORAL, ENVIRONMENTAL; N=80 FEMALE UNDERGRADUATES,
                40 SELECTED)
        @APPLICATION 1970 J-15

2850   SHARF, R.
            JOURNAL OF COUNSELING PSYCHOLOGY, 1970, 17, 258-262.
            RELATIVE IMPORTANCE OF INTEREST AND ABILITY IN VOCATIONAL DECISION MAKING.
                (MODIFICATION; CORRELATES:BEHAVIORAL; NORMATIVE DATA; N=274 MALE
                UNDERGRADUATES, 76 SELECTED)
        @APPLICATION 1970 S-33

2851   STRONG, S. R., & SCHMIDT, L. D.
            TRUSTWORTHINESS AND INFLUENCE IN COUNSELING.
            JOURNAL OF COUNSELING PSYCHOLOGY, 1970, 17, 197-204.
                (CORRELATES:BEHAVIORAL, PSYCHOLOGICAL; N=54 COLLEGE STUDENTS)
        @APPLICATION 1970 E-2 P-53

2852   HEDQUIST, F. J., & WEINHOLD, B. K.
            BEHAVIORAL GROUP COUNSELING WITH SOCIALLY ANXIOUS AND UNASSERTIVE COLLEGE
            STUDENTS.
            JOURNAL OF COUNSELING PSYCHOLOGY, 1970, 17, 237-242.
                (USED AS CRITERION; N=20 COLLEGE STUDENTS)
        @APPLICATION 1970 G-26 E-16

2853   MEDVENE, A. M.
            PERSON-ORIENTED AND NON-PERSON-ORIENTED OCCUPATIONS IN PSYCHOLOGY.
            JOURNAL OF COUNSELING PSYCHOLOGY, 1970, 17, 243-246.
                (CORRELATES:BEHAVIORAL, PSYCHOLOGICAL; N=470 MALE GRADUATE STUDENTS)
        @APPLICATION 1970 B-135 R-64

2854   TOSI, D. J.
            DOGMATISM WITHIN THE COUNSELOR-CLIENT DYAD.
            JOURNAL OF COUNSELING PSYCHOLOGY, 1970, 17, 284-288.
                (RELIABILITY:INTERNAL CONSISTENCY; CORRELATES:PSYCHOLOGICAL; N=12
                MALE COUNSELORS AND N=40 MALE AND 29 FEMALE UNDERGRADUATE CLIENTS)
        @APPLICATION 1970 R-8 B-50

2855   MARTINSON, W. D., & ZERFACE, J. P.
            COMPARISON OF INDIVIDUAL COUNSELING AND A SOCIAL PROGRAM WITH NONDATERS.
            JOURNAL OF COUNSELING PSYCHOLOGY, 1970, 17, 36-40.
                (CORRELATES:BEHAVIORAL: N=24 MALE COLLEGE STUDENTS)
        @APPLICATION 1970 W-86 W-135

2856   ROSSMAN, J. E., & KIRK, B. A.
            FACTORS RELATED TO PERSISTENCE AND WITHDRAWAL AMONG UNIVERSITY STUDENTS.
            JOURNAL OF COUNSELING PSYCHOLOGY, 1970, 17, 56-62.
                (CORRELATES:BEHAVIORAL, INTELLIGENCE; N=APPRCX. 1500 MALE AND FEMALE
                COLLEGE STUDENTS)
        @APPLICATION 1970 H-12

2857   HUDESMAN, J.
            PREDICTIVE VALIDITY OF THE STRONG VOCATIONAL INTEREST BLANK APPLIED TO
            ACCOUNTING STUDENTS IN AN URBAN TWO-YEAR COLLEGE.
            JOURNAL OF COUNSELING PSYCHOLOGY, 1970, 17, 67-69.
                (VALIDITY:CRITERION; N=56 MALE COLLEGE STUDENTS)
        @APPLICATION 1970 S-33

2858   MAYNARD, P. E., & HANSEN, J. C.
            VOCATIONAL MATURITY AMONG INNER-CITY YOUTHS.
            JOURNAL OF COUNSELING PSYCHOLOGY, 1970, 17, 400-404.
                (CORRELATES:PSYCHOLOGICAL, INTELLIGENCE; N=450 EIGHTH GRADE BOYS)
        @APPLICATION 1970 C-26

2859   SOUTHWORTH, A. J., & MORNINGSTAR, M. E.
            PERSISTENCE OF OCCUPATIONAL CHOICE AND PERSONALITY CONGRUENCE.
            JOURNAL OF COUNSELING PSYCHOLOGY, 1970, 17, 409-412.
                (CORRELATES:BEHAVIORAL; N=102 ENGINEERING STUDENTS)
        @APPLICATION 1970 H-21

2860   CARKHUFF, R. R., & BANKS, G.
            TRAINING AS A PREFERRED MODE OF FACILITATING RELATIONS BETWEEN RACES AND
            GENERATIONS.
            JOURNAL OF COUNSELING PSYCHOLOGY, 1970, 17, 413-418.
                (CORRELATES:PSYCHOLOGICAL; N=14 WHITE TEACHERS, 10 BLACK PARENTS)
        @APPLICATION 1970 C-105 C-106

2861   BAILEY, S. T.
            INDEPENDENCE AND FACTOR STRUCTURE OF SELF-CONCEPT METADIMENSIONS.
            JOURNAL OF COUNSELING PSYCHOLOGY, 1970, 17, 425-430.
                (VALIDITY:CONSTRUCT; FACTOR ANALYSIS; N=50 MEN AGES 18-35)
        @APPLICATION 1970 K-23

2862   LAXER, R. M., & WALKER, K.
            COUNTERCONDITIONING VERSUS RELAXATION IN THE DESENSITIZATION OF TEST
            ANXIETY.
            JOURNAL OF COUNSELING PSYCHOLOGY, 1970, 17, 431-436.
                (CORRELATES:PSYCHOLOGICAL, INTELLIGENCE, ENVIRONMENTAL; N=300
                SECONDARY SCHOOL STUDENTS, 119 SELECTED)
        @APPLICATION 1970 A-8 T-2

2863   JOHANSSON, C. B.
            STRONG VOCATIONAL INTEREST BLANK INTROVERSION-EXTRAVERSION AND
            OCCUPATIONAL MEMBERSHIP.
            JOURNAL OF COUNSELING PSYCHOLOGY, 1970, 17, 451-455.
                (RELIABILITY:RETEST; VALIDITY:CONTENT, CROSS-VALIDATION; USED AS
                CRITERION; 2 SAMPLES: N=486 MALE UNDERGRADUATES, N=200 MALE
                UNDERGRADUATES)
        @APPLICATION 1970 S-33 D-45 J-31

2864   ADINOLFI, A. A.
            CHARACTERISTICS OF HIGHLY ACCEPTED, HIGHLY REJECTED, AND RELATIVELY UNKNOWN
            UNIVERSITY FRESHMEN.
            JOURNAL OF COUNSELING PSYCHOLOGY, 1970, 17, 456-464.
                (CORRELATES:PSYCHOLOGICAL; N=297 MALE, 325 FEMALE UNDERGRADUATES)
        @APPLICATION 1970 J-1 R-18 S-33 S-11 S-162 P-65

2865   RESNICK, H., FAUBLE, M. L., & OSIPOW, S. H.
            VOCATIONAL CRYSTALLIZATION AND SELF-ESTEEM IN COLLEGE STUDENTS.
            JOURNAL OF COUNSELING PSYCHOLOGY, 1970, 17, 465-467.
                (CORRELATES:PSYCHOLOGICAL; USED AS CRITERION; N=114 MALE, 102 FEMALE
                STUDENTS)
        @APPLICATION 1970 K-34 F-7

2866   UHES, M. J., & SHAVER, J. P.
            DOGMATISM AND DIVERGENT-CONVERGENT ABILITIES.
            JOURNAL OF PSYCHOLOGY, 1970, 75, 3-11.
                (CORRELATES:PSYCHOLOGICAL; N=165 MALES, 151 FEMALES)
        @APPLICATION 1970 R-8 G-50

2867   PROPPER, M. M., & CLARK, E. T.
            ALIENATION: ANOTHER DIMENSION OF UNDERACHIEVEMENT.
            JOURNAL OF PSYCHOLOGY, 1970, 75, 13-18.
                (CORRELATES:PSYCHOLOGICAL; N=80 MALE HIGH SCHOOL STUDENTS)
        @APPLICATION 1970 D-46 D-47 D-37 M-20 R-31

2868   NORMAN, R. D., & FENSON, J. N.
            FURTHER ASPECTS OF CONSTRUCT VALIDITY OF THE ZUCKERMAN SENSATION-SEEKING
            SCALE.
            JOURNAL OF PSYCHOLOGY, 1970, 74, 131-140.
                (VALIDITY:CONSTRUCT; CORRELATES:PSYCHOLOGICAL; N=104 MALE, 102 FEMALE
                COLLEGE STUDENTS)
        @APPLICATION 1970 Z-3 B-76 T-2

2869   HOUNTRAS, P. T., & SCHARF, M. C.
            MANIFEST ANXIETY AND LOCUS OF CONTROL OF LOW-ACHIEVING COLLEGE MALES.
            JOURNAL OF PSYCHOLOGY, 1970, 74, 95-100.
                (CORRELATES:PSYCHOLOGICAL, INTELLIGENCE; N=60 LOW-ACHIEVING COLLEGE
                STUDENTS)
        @APPLICATION 1970 R-18 H-51

2870   NEUMANN, J.
            SEX DIFFERENCES IN ANXIETY SCORES FOR COLLEGE FRESHMEN AND SOPHOMORES.
            JOURNAL OF PSYCHOLOGY, 1970, 74, 113-115.
                (CORRELATES:DEMOGRAPHIC; N=50 COLLEGE STUDENTS)
        @APPLICATION 1970 C-97

2871   BORGATTA, E. F., & FORD, R. N.
            A NOTE ON TASK AND SITUATIONAL FACTORS IN WORK ORIENTATION AND
            SATISFACTION.
            JOURNAL OF PSYCHOLOGY, 1970, 74, 125-130.
                (CORRELATES:ENVIRONMENTAL; NORMATIVE DATA; N=APPROX 1500 EMPLOYEES,
                5 SAMPLES)
        @APPLICATION 1970 B-110

2872   SCHLUDERMANN, S., & SCHLUDERMANN, E.
            GENERALIZABILITY OF CALIFORNIA PERSONALITY INVENTORY FACTORS.
            JOURNAL OF PSYCHOLOGY, 1970, 74, 43-50.
                (CORRELATES:DEMOGRAPHIC; FACTOR ANALYSIS; N=328 COLLEGE STUDENTS)
        @APPLICATION 1970 G-22

2873   HORROCKS, J. E., & WEINBERG, S. A.
            PSYCHOLOGICAL NEEDS AND THEIR DEVELOPMENT DURING ADOLESCENCE.
            JOURNAL OF PSYCHOLOGY, 1970, 74, 51-69.
                (CORRELATES:DEMOGRAPHIC; NORMATIVE DATA; N=330 BOYS, 324 GIRLS,
                GRADES 7-12)
        @APPLICATION 1970 L-21

2874   SCHLUDERMAN, S., & SCHLUDERMAN, E.
            PERSONALITY CORRELATIONS OF ADOLESCENT SELF-CONCEPTS AND
            SECURITY-INSECURITY.
            JOURNAL OF PSYCHOLOGY, 1970, 74, 85-90.
                (CORRELATES:PSYCHOLOGICAL, DEMOGRAPHIC; FACTOR ANALYSIS; N=328
                COLLEGE STUDENTS)
        @APPLICATION 1970 G-22 M-50 W-21

2875   SHEPPARD, C., O'NEILL, C., FRACCIA, J., & MERLIS, S.
            LEVELS OF PERSONAL CONFLICT DERIVED FROM RESPONSE TO THE EMOTION PROFILE
            INDEX.
            JOURNAL OF PSYCHOLOGY, 1970, 74, 143-148.
                (VALIDITY:CROSS-VALIDATION; CORRELATES:BEHAVIORAL, PSYCHOLOGICAL,
                INTELLIGENCE; USED AS CRITERION; NORMATIVE DATA; N=68 PATIENTS
                HOSPITALIZED FOR DRUG ABUSE AND 31 CHRONIC SCHIZOPHRENIC
                PATIENTS)
        @APPLICATION 1970 S-68 T-2 B-5 D-45 K-77

2876   DAHLEN, N. W.
            YOUNG AMERICANS' REPORTED PERCEPTIONS OF THEIR PARENTS.
            JOURNAL OF PSYCHOLOGY, 1970, 74, 187-194.
                (VALIDITY:CROSS-VALIDATION; N=151 COLLEGE STUDENTS, 147 UNIVERSITY
                STUDENTS, 87 HIGH SCHOOL STUDENTS)
        @APPLICATION 1970 B-122

2877   CARLSON, J. S.
            A NOTE ON THE RELATIONSHIPS BETWEEN THE DRAW-A-MAN TEST, THE PROGRESSIVE
            MATRICES TEST, AND CONSERVATION.
            JOURNAL OF PSYCHOLOGY, 1970, 74, 231-235.
                (CORRELATES:BEHAVIORAL, PSYCHOLOGICAL, INTELLIGENCE; N=221 CHILDREN,
                KINDERGARTEN TO GRADE 3)
        @APPLICATION 1970 G-78

2878   MCCARTHY, B. W., & BRODSKY, S. L.
            THE EFFECTS OF MARLOWE-CROWNE AND INSTRUCTIONAL SOCIAL DESIRABILITY SETS ON
            THE SELF-CONCEPT SCALE.
            JOURNAL OF PSYCHOLOGY, 1970, 74, 237-238.
                (CORRELATES:PSYCHOLOGICAL; USED AS CRITERION; N=40 FEMALE UNIVERSITY
                STUDENTS)
        @APPLICATION 1970 C-27 B-60

2879   SWEENEY, C. J., SMOUSE, A. D., RUPIPER, O., & MUNZ, D. C.
            A TEST OF THE INVERTED-U HYPOTHESIS RELATING ACHIEVEMENT ANXIETY AND
            ACADEMIC TEST PERFORMANCE.
            JOURNAL OF PSYCHOLOGY, 1970, 74, 267-273.
                (VALIDITY:CONSTRUCT; CORRELATES:PSYCHOLOGICAL, INTELLIGENCE; USED AS
                CRITERION; N=120 UNIVERSITY STUDENTS)
        @APPLICATION 1970 A-8

2880   HOUNTRAS, P. T., GRADY, W. E., & VRAA, C. W.
            MANIFEST ANXIETY AND ACADEMIC ACHIEVEMENT OF AMERICAN AND CANADIAN COLLEGE
            FRESHMEN.
            JOURNAL OF PSYCHOLOGY, 1970, 76, 3-8.
                (CORRELATES:PSYCHOLOGICAL, INTELLIGENCE; USED AS CRITERION; N=23
                AMERICAN, 25 CANADIAN MALE COLLEGE FRESHMEN)
        @APPLICATION 1970 T-2

2881   SHERIDAN, K., & SHACK, J. R.
            PERSONALITY CORRELATES OF THE UNDERGRADUATE VOLUNTEER SUBJECT.
            JOURNAL OF PSYCHOLOGY, 1970, 76, 23-26.
                (CORRELATES:BEHAVIORAL, PSYCHOLOGICAL; N=81 UNDERGRADUATES)
        @APPLICATION 1970 S-21 S-168

2882   GILLEY, H. M., & SUMMERS, C. S.
            SEX DIFFERENCES IN THE USE OF HOSTILE VERBS.
            JOURNAL OF PSYCHOLOGY, 1970, 76, 33-37.
                (CORRELATES:BEHAVIORAL; N=50 MALE UNDERGRADUATES, 50 FEMALE
                UNDERGRADUATES)
        @APPLICATION 1970 B-44

2883   HOGAN, H. W.
            RELIABILITY AND CONVERGENT VALIDITY OF A SYMBOLIC TEST FOR
            AUTHORITARIANISM.
            JOURNAL OF PSYCHOLOGY, 1970, 76, 39-43.
                (RELIABILITY:INTERNAL CONSISTENCY; VALIDITY:CONSTRUCT; CORRELATES:
                PSYCHOLOGICAL; N=72 STUDENTS)
        @APPLICATION 1970 A-5 H-108 O-16

2884   SCHLUDERMANN, S., & SCHLUDERMANN, E.
            CONCEPTUALIZATION OF MATERNAL BEHAVIOR.
            JOURNAL OF PSYCHOLOGY, 1970, 75, 205-215.
                (FACTOR ANALYSIS; N=293 FEMALE COLLEGE STUDENTS)
        @APPLICATION 1970 S-9

2885   SHERMAN, R.
            CULTURE AND STRATEGIC CHOICE.
            JOURNAL OF PSYCHOLOGY, 1970, 75, 227-230.
                (CORRELATES:PSYCHOLOGICAL; CROSS-CULTURAL APPLICATION; N=57 BRITISH
                U. STUDENTS, 20 AMERICAN U. STUDENTS)
        @APPLICATION 1970 K-87 S-139 P-47

2886   BRESKIN, S., GORMAN, B. S., & HOCHMAN, S. H.
            NONVERBAL RIGIDITY AND PERSEVERATION.
            JOURNAL OF PSYCHOLOGY, 1970, 75, 239-242.
                (CORRELATES:PSYCHOLOGICAL; USED AS CRITERION; N=34 UNIVERSITY
                STUDENTS AND 42 FEMALE UNIVERSITY STUDENTS)
        @APPLICATION 1970 S-171 B-155 S-61

2887   KIRTLEY, D., & HARKLESS, R.
            STUDENT POLITICAL ACTIVITY IN RELATION TO PERSONAL AND SOCIAL
            ADJUSTMENT.
            JOURNAL OF PSYCHOLOGY, 1970, 75, 253-256.
                (CORRELATES:PSYCHOLOGICAL; N=61 STUDENTS)
        @APPLICATION 1970 D-45 A-29 B-58 W-79 T-18

2888   EISENMAN, R.
            BIRTH ORDER, SEX, SELF-ESTEEM, AND PREJUDICE AGAINST THE PHYSICALLY
            DISABLED.
            JOURNAL OF PSYCHOLOGY, 1970, 75, 147-155.
                (CORRELATES:PSYCHOLOGICAL, DEMOGRAPHIC; USED AS CRITERION; N=278 AND
                300 COLLEGE STUDENTS)
        aAPPLICATION 1970 E-32

2889   OZEHOSKY, R. J., & CLARK, E. T.
            CHILDREN'S SELF-CONCEPT AND KINDERGARTEN ACHIEVEMENT.
            JOURNAL OF PSYCHOLOGY, 1970, 75, 185-192.
                (RELIABILITY:INTERRATER; CORRELATES:PSYCHOLOGICAL; USED AS
                CRITERION; N=1042 KINDERGARTEN CHILDREN)
        aAPPLICATION 1970 W-99 C-113

2890   SCHLUDERMANN, S., & SCHLUDERMANN, E.
            CONCEPTUAL FRAMES OF PARENTAL ATTITUDES OF FATHERS.
            JOURNAL OF PSYCHOLOGY, 1970, 75, 193-204.
                (MODIFICATION; FACTOR ANALYSIS; N=269 MALE STUDENTS)
        aAPPLICATION 1970 S-9

2891   PIERCE, R. A.
            NEED SIMILARITY AND COMPLEMENTARITY AS DETERMINANTS OF FRIENDSHIP CHOICE.
            JOURNAL OF PSYCHOLOGY, 1970, 76, 231-238.
                (CORRELATES:PSYCHOLOGICAL; N=208 COLLEGE FRESHMEN)
        aAPPLICATION 1970 J-1

2892   SCHLUDERMANN, E., & SCHLUDERMANN, S.
            REPLICABILITY OF FACTORS IN CHILDREN'S REPORT OF PARENT BEHAVIOR (CRBI).
            JOURNAL OF PSYCHOLOGY, 1970, 76, 239-249.
                (FACTOR ANALYSIS; TOTAL N=317 MALE, 375 FEMALE COLLEGE STUDENTS)
        aAPPLICATION 1970 S-8

2893   SOPCHAK, A. L.
            ANXIETY INDICATORS ON THE DRAW-A-PERSON TEST FOR CLINIC AND NONCLINIC BOYS
            AND THEIR PARENTS.
            JOURNAL OF PSYCHOLOGY, 1970, 76, 251-260.
                (MODIFICATION; VALIDITY:CRITERION; N=20 FAMILIES WITH CHILD ATTENDING
                PSYCHIATRIC CLINIC, 20 NONCLINIC FAMILIES)
        aAPPLICATION 1970 M-58 R-30 M-20 H-168

2894   HARTNETT, J. J., BAILEY, K. G., & GIBSON, F. W., JR.
            PERSONAL SPACE AS INFLUENCED BY SEX AND TYPE OF MOVEMENT.
            JOURNAL OF PSYCHOLOGY, 1970, 76, 139-144.
                (CORRELATES:BEHAVIORAL, PSYCHOLOGICAL; N=32 MALE, 32 FEMALE COLLEGE
                STUDENTS)
        aAPPLICATION 1970 E-2

2895   SCHLUDERMANN, S., & SCHLUDERMANN, E.
            A METHODOLOGICAL NOTE ON CONCEPTUAL FRAMES OF PARENTAL ATTITUDES OF
            FATHERS (PARI).
            JOURNAL OF PSYCHOLOGY, 1970, 76, 145-148.
                (MODIFICATION; FACTOR ANALYSIS; N=369 MALE COLLEGE STUDENTS)
        aAPPLICATION 1970 S-9

2896   PETERS, D. R.
            SELF-IDEAL CONGRUENCE AS A FUNCTION OF HUMAN RELATIONS TRAINING.
            JOURNAL OF PSYCHOLOGY, 1970, 76, 199-207.
                (CORRELATES:PSYCHOLOGICAL; N=57 PARTICIPANTS IN INTENSIVE 2-WEEK
                RESIDENT LABORATORY)
        aAPPLICATION 1970 P-102 B-225

2897   BARTOL, G. H., & DUERFELDT, P. H.
            SELF-REINFORCING BEHAVIOR: THE EFFECTS OF BASE RATE AND DEPENDENCY.
            JOURNAL OF GENERAL PSYCHOLOGY, 1970, 83, 151-161.
                (CORRELATES:BEHAVIORAL, PSYCHOLOGICAL; USED AS CRITERION; N=44
                COLLEGE STUDENTS)
        aAPPLICATION 1970 E-2 T-2 M-4

2898   MACKAY, C. K., & BROWN, W. P.
            METAPHOR PREFERENCE VS. SEMANTIC RATINGS AS MEASURES OF ATTITUDE TOWARD
            TIME.
            JOURNAL OF GENERAL PSYCHOLOGY, 1970, 83, 207-212.
                (CORRELATES:PSYCHOLOGICAL; N=31 COLLEGE STUDENTS)
        aAPPLICATION 1970 K-14

2899   LAKE, A. E., III, & TEDFORD, W. H., JR.
        INFLUENCE OF CREATIVITY ON FORMATION OF SUBJECTIVE UNITS.
        JOURNAL OF GENERAL PSYCHOLOGY, 1970, 83, 227-237.
            (USED AS CRITERION; N=95 COLLEGE STUDENTS)
        aAPPLICATION 1970 H-37 G-50

2900   DRUCKMAN, D.
        DOUBLE AGREEMENT WITH REVERSED ITEMS: THE PLAUSIBILITY OF AN ALTERNATIVE
        EXPLANATION TO RESPONSE BIAS.
        JOURNAL OF GENERAL PSYCHOLOGY, 1970, 82, 63-75.
            (VALIDITY:CONSTRUCT; CORRELATES:PSYCHOLOGICAL; BIAS:RESPONSE;
            N=325 UNDERGRADUATES)
        aAPPLICATION 1970 C-27 R-8

2901   PETZEL, T. P., & GYNTHER, M. D.
        EFFECTS OF INTERNAL-EXTERNAL LOCUS OF CONTROL AND SKILL OR CHANCE
        INSTRUCTIONAL SETS ON TASK PERFORMANCE.
        JOURNAL OF GENERAL PSYCHOLOGY, 1970, 82, 87-93.
            (CORRELATES:BEHAVIORAL; N=98 MALE COLLEGE STUDENTS)
        aAPPLICATION 1970 R-18

2902   WEISSMAN, H. N.
        DISPOSITION TOWARD INTELLECTUALITY: ITS COMPOSITION AND ITS
        ASSESSMENT.
        JOURNAL OF GENERAL PSYCHOLOGY, 1970, 82, 99-107.
            (CORRELATES:PSYCHOLOGICAL; FACTOR ANALYSIS; N=72 MALE COLLEGE
            STUDENTS)
        aAPPLICATION 1970 H-12 B-76 G-21 W-79 G-50

2903   KREBS, D. L.
        ALTRUISM--AN EXAMINATION OF THE CONCEPT AND A REVIEW OF THE LITERATURE.
        PSYCHOLOGICAL BULLETIN, 1970, 73, 258-302.
            (REVIEW; VALIDITY:CONSTRUCT; CORRELATES:BEHAVIORAL, PSYCHOLOGICAL)
        aAPPLICATION 1970 A-7 T-55 E-2 F-14 M-102 B-54 C-27 C-42 S-161 R-70 R-18

2904   BLOCK, J.
        AMENDATION TO COHEN'S CAUTIONS REGARDING THE MEASUREMENT OF PROFILE
        SIMILARITY.
        PSYCHOLOGICAL BULLETIN, 1970, 73, 307-308.
            (MENTION)
        aAPPLICATION 1970 D-45

2905   GRAEN, G., ALVARES, K., ORRIS, J. B., & MARTELLA, J. A.
        CONTINGENCY MODEL OF LEADERSHIP EFFECTIVENESS: ANTECEDENT AND EVIDENTIAL
        RESULTS.
        PSYCHOLOGICAL BULLETIN, 1970, 74, 285-296.
            (CORRELATES:BEHAVIORAL, PSYCHOLOGICAL; CROSS-CULTURAL APPLICATION;
            N=228 BELGIAN NAVY PERSONNEL)
        aAPPLICATION 1970 F-48

2906   CHINSKY, J. M., & RAPPAPORT, J.
        BRIEF CRITIQUE OF THE MEANING AND RELIABILITY OF "ACCURATE EMPATHY"
        RATINGS.
        PSYCHOLOGICAL BULLETIN, 1970, 73, 379-382.
            (RELIABILITY:INTERRATER; VALIDITY:CONSTRUCT; BIAS:RATER; N=8 RATERS)
        aAPPLICATION 1970 T-36

2907   WARD, A. J.
        EARLY INFANTILE AUTISM: DIAGNOSIS, ETIOLOGY, AND TREATMENT.
        PSYCHOLOGICAL BULLETIN, 1970, 73, 350-362.
            (MENTION)
        aAPPLICATION 1970 P-54

2908   SATTLER, J. M.
        RACIAL "EXPERIMENTER EFFECTS" IN EXPERIMENTATION, TESTING,
        INTERVIEWING, AND PSYCHOTHERAPY.
        PSYCHOLOGICAL BULLETIN, 1970, 73, 137-160.
            (MENTION)
        aAPPLICATION 1970 M-20 M-4

2909   SIMONS, H. W., MOYER, R. J., & BERKOWITZ, N. N.
        SIMILARITY, CREDIBILITY, AND ATTITUDE CHANGE: A REVIEW AND A THEORY.
        PSYCHOLOGICAL BULLETIN, 1970, 73, 1-16.
            (MENTION)
        @APPLICATION 1970 B-65 W-21

2910   DAMARIN, F.
        A LATENT-STRUCTURE MODEL FOR ANSWERING PERSONAL QUESTIONS.
        PSYCHOLOGICAL BULLETIN, 1970, 73, 23-40.
            (REVIEW; CORRELATES:BEHAVIORAL, PSYCHOLOGICAL; FACTOR ANALYSIS;
            BIAS:RESPONSE)
        @APPLICATION 1970 D-45 W-8 W-41 W-64 C-27 C-58 E-1 W-14

2911   BARRY, W. E.
        MARRIAGE RESEARCH AND CONFLICT: AN INTEGRATIVE REVIEW.
        PSYCHOLOGICAL BULLETIN, 1970, 73, 41-54.
            (REVIEW; CORRELATES:BEHAVIORAL, PSYCHOLOGICAL)
        @APPLICATION 1970 B-99 T-49 D-45 A-5 L-35

2912   DELLAS, M., & GAIER, E. L.
        IDENTIFICATION OF CREATIVITY: THE INDIVIDUAL.
        PSYCHOLOGICAL BULLETIN, 1970, 73, 55-73.
            (MENTION; REVIEW; RELIABILITY:INTERNAL CONSISTENCY;
            VALIDITY:CONSTRUCT; CORRELATES:BEHAVIORAL, PSYCHOLOGICAL,
            INTELLIGENCE)
        @APPLICATION 1970 G-50 G-80 T-28 T-35 W-72 W-9 T-39 M-20 H-37 M-22 G-26 H-20
        @C-10 M-29 L-67 G-22 W-26 S-157 R-30 V-24.M-101 P-64

2913   MUELLER, E. F., KASL, S. V., BROOKS, G. W., & COBB, S.
        PSYCHOSOCIAL CORRELATES OF SERUM URATE LEVELS.
        PSYCHOLOGICAL BULLETIN, 1970, 73, 238-257.
            (MENTION; REVIEW; CORRELATES:PSYCHOLOGICAL, PHYSIOLOGICAL)
        @APPLICATION 1970 B-139 C-10 M-20

2914   HARRIS, S., & MASLING, J.
        EXAMINER SEX, SUBJECT SEX, AND RORSCHACH PRODUCTIVITY.
        JOURNAL OF CONSULTING AND CLINICAL PSYCHOLOGY, 1970, 34, 60-63.
            (CORRELATES:DEMOGRAPHIC; BIAS:TESTER; N=29 MALE, 35 FEMALE SUBJECTS
            AND 32 MALE, 9 FEMALE CLINICAL TRAINEES)
        @APPLICATION 1970 R-30

2915   HOLTZMAN, W. H., SWARTZ, J. D., & SANDERS, J. L.
        EFFECTS OF STIMULUS VARIATION ON RESPONSES TO THE GROUP VERSION OF THE
        HOLTZMAN INKBLOT TECHNIQUE.
        JOURNAL OF CONSULTING AND CLINICAL PSYCHOLOGY, 1970, 34, 64-66.
            (MODIFICATION; NORMATIVE DATA; N=60 FEMALE, 20 MALE UNDERGRADUATES)
        @APPLICATION 1970 H-37

2916   GALBRAITH, G. G., & MOSHER, D. L.
        EFFECTS OF SEX GUILT AND SEXUAL STIMULATION ON THE RECALL OF WORD
        ASSOCIATIONS.
        JOURNAL OF CONSULTING AND CLINICAL PSYCHOLOGY, 1970, 34, 67-71.
            (CORRELATES:PSYCHOLOGICAL, ENVIRONMENTAL; USED AS CRITERION;
            NORMATIVE DATA; N=84 MALE COLLEGE STUDENTS)
        @APPLICATION 1970 M-64 G-105

2917   LEFF, H. S., NYDEGGER, R. V., & BUCK, M.
        EFFECT OF NURSES' MODE OF DRESS ON BEHAVIOR OF PSYCHIATRIC PATIENTS
        DIFFERING IN INFORMATION-PROCESSING COMPLEXITY.
        JOURNAL OF CONSULTING AND CLINICAL PSYCHOLOGY, 1970, 34, 72-79.
            (CORRELATES:BEHAVIORAL, PSYCHOLOGICAL; USED AS CRITERION; N=20 VA
            PATIENTS)
        @APPLICATION 1970 L-35 S-41

2918   HALVERSON, C. F.
        INTERPERSONAL PERCEPTION: COGNITIVE COMPLEXITY AND TRAIT IMPLICATION.
        JOURNAL OF CONSULTING AND CLINICAL PSYCHOLOGY, 1970, 34, 86-90.
            (RELIABILITY:INTERRATER; CORRELATES:PSYCHOLOGICAL, INTELLIGENCE;
            USED AS CRITERION; N=180 MALE UNDERGRADUATES, 96 SELECTED)
        @APPLICATION 1970 S-41

2919   HOFFMAN, H.
            USE OF AVOIDANCE AND VIGILANCE BY REPRESSORS AND SENSITIZERS.
            JOURNAL OF CONSULTING AND CLINICAL PSYCHOLOGY, 1970, 34, 91-96.
                (VALIDITY:CONSTRUCT; CORRELATES:PSYCHOLOGICAL, ENVIRONMENTAL;
                USED AS CRITERION; N=90 MALE COLLEGE STUDENTS)
        @APPLICATION 1970 B-46 S-68

2920   PHILIP, A. E., & MCCULLOUCH, J. W.
            TEST-RETEST CHARACTERISTICS OF A GROUP OF ATTEMPTED SUICIDE PATIENTS.
            JOURNAL OF CONSULTING AND CLINICAL PSYCHOLOGY, 1970, 34, 144-147.
                (RELIABILITY:RETEST; CORRELATES:PSYCHOLOGICAL, DEMOGRAPHIC;
                NORMATIVE DATA; N=37 WOMEN, 15 MEN WHO ATTEMPTED SUICIDE)
        @APPLICATION 1970 S-10 F-10

2921   DEROGATIS, L. R., LIPMAN, R. S., COVI, L., RICKELS, K., & UHLENHUTH, E. H.
            DIMENSIONS OF OUTPATIENT NEUROTIC PATHOLOGY: COMPARISON OF A CLINICAL
            VERSUS AN EMPIRICAL ASSESSMENT.
            JOURNAL OF CONSULTING AND CLINICAL PSYCHOLOGY, 1970, 34, 164-171.
                (MODIFICATION; FACTOR ANALYSIS; N=837 NEUROTIC PATIENTS, 20
                CLINICIANS AS ITEM RATERS, 34 PSYCHIATRISTS RATING S'S)
        @APPLICATION 1970 P-58

2922   HARTLAGE, L. C.
            SUBPROFESSIONAL THERAPISTS' USE OF REINFORCEMENT VERSUS TRADITIONAL
            PSYCHOTHERAPEUTIC TECHNIQUES WITH SCHIZOPHRENICS.
            JOURNAL OF CONSULTING AND CLINICAL PSYCHOLOGY, 1970, 34, 181-183.
                (CORRELATES:ENVIRONMENTAL; N=44 CHRONIC SCHIZOPHRENIC WOMEN)
        @APPLICATION 1970 M-66 H-90 K-162

2923   BEERY, J. W.
            THERAPISTS' RESPONSES AS A FUNCTION OF LEVEL OF THERAPIST EXPERIENCE AND
            ATTITUDE OF THE PATIENT.
            JOURNAL OF CONSULTING AND CLINICAL PSYCHOLOGY, 1970, 34, 239-243.
                (RELIABILITY:INTERRATER; CORRELATES:PSYCHOLOGICAL, ENVIRONMENTAL;
                N=16 EXPERIENCED, 16 INEXPERIENCED MALE THERAPISTS)
        @APPLICATION 1970 S-143

2924   HELSON, R., & CRUTCHFIELD, R. S.
            MATHEMATICIANS: THE CREATIVE RESEARCHER AND THE AVERAGE PHD.
            JOURNAL OF CONSULTING AND CLINICAL PSYCHOLOGY, 1970, 34, 250-257.
                (CORRELATES:PSYCHOLOGICAL; NORMATIVE DATA; N=56 MALE MATHEMATICIANS)
        @APPLICATION 1970 G-22 G-21 B-76 S-33 A-7 H-89 B-78 D-45

2925   WAGNER, M. K., & BRAGG, R. A.
            COMPARING BEHAVIOR MODIFICATION APPROACHES TO HABIT DECREMENT--SMOKING.
            JOURNAL OF CONSULTING AND CLINICAL PSYCHOLOGY, 1970, 34, 258-263.
                (CORRELATES:BEHAVIORAL; N=28 FEMALE, 26 MALE ADULTS)
        @APPLICATION 1970 G-21 G-28

2926   IRVIN, F. S., & JOHNSON, M. L.
            EFFECT OF DIFFERENTIAL INSTRUCTIONAL SET ON SENTENCE COMPLETION RESPONSES.
            JOURNAL OF CONSULTING AND CLINICAL PSYCHOLOGY, 1970, 34, 319-322.
                (MODIFICATION; RELIABILITY:INTERRATER; CORRELATES:ENVIRONMENTAL;
                NORMATIVE DATA; N=100 MALE HIGH SCHOOL GRADUATES, AGES 16-18)
        @APPLICATION 1970 I-4

2927   HODGES, W. F., & FELLING, J. P.
            TYPES OF STRESSFUL SITUATIONS AND THEIR RELATION TO TRAIT ANXIETY AND SEX.
            JOURNAL OF CONSULTING AND CLINICAL PSYCHOLOGY, 1970, 34, 333-337.
                (CORRELATES:PSYCHOLOGICAL; N=141 MALE, 87 FEMALE UNDERGRADUATES)
        @APPLICATION 1970 S-147

2928   GYNTHER, M. D., GRAY, B. G., & STRAUSS, M. E.
            EFFECTS OF RELIGIOUS AFFILIATION, RELIGIOUS INVOLVEMENT, AND SEX ON THE
            SOCIAL DESIRABILITY RATINGS OF MMPI RELIGION ITEMS.
            JOURNAL OF CONSULTING AND CLINICAL PSYCHOLOGY, 1970, 34, 338-342.
                (CORRELATES:BEHAVIORAL, PSYCHOLOGICAL, DEMOGRAPHIC; N=90 COLLEGE
                STUDENTS)
        @APPLICATION 1970 D-45

2929   KESTENBAUM, J. M., & WEINER, B.
          ACHIEVEMENT PERFORMANCE RELATED TO ACHIEVEMENT MOTIVATION AND TEST
          ANXIETY.
          JOURNAL OF CONSULTING AND CLINICAL PSYCHOLOGY, 1970, 34, 343-344.
             (CORRELATES:PSYCHOLOGICAL, INTELLIGENCE; N=43 MALE, 36 FEMALE 7TH AND
             8TH GRADE HEBREW ACADEMY STUDENTS)
       @APPLICATION 1970 S-133 W-74

2930   HAYNES, J. R.
          FACTOR-ANALYTIC STUDY OF PERFORMANCE ON THE BENDER-GESTALT.
          JOURNAL OF CONSULTING AND CLINICAL PSYCHOLOGY, 1970, 34, 345-347.
             (CORRELATES:PSYCHOLOGICAL, INTELLIGENCE; FACTOR ANALYSIS; N=106
             UNDERGRADUATES)
       @APPLICATION 1970 C-10

2931   ALLEN, G. J.
          EFFECT OF THREE CONDITIONS OF ADMINISTRATION ON "TRAIT" AND "STATE"
          MEASURES OF ANXIETY.
          JOURNAL OF CONSULTING AND CLINICAL PSYCHOLOGY, 1970, 34, 355-359.
             (RELIABILITY:RETEST; CORRELATES:PHYSIOLOGICAL, INTELLIGENCE,
             ENVIRONMENTAL; NORMATIVE DATA; N=15 FEMALE, 10 MALE COLLEGE
             STUDENTS)
       @APPLICATION 1970 A-8 S-5 S-147
       @A-26

2932   KARST, T. O., & TREXLER, L. D.
          INITIAL STUDY USING FIXED-ROLE AND RATIONAL-EMOTIVE THERAPY IN
          TREATING PUBLIC-SPEAKING ANXIETY.
          JOURNAL OF CONSULTING AND CLINICAL PSYCHOLOGY, 1970, 34, 360-366.
             (RELIABILITY:INTERRATER; CORRELATES:ENVIRONMENTAL; N=15 FEMALE, 7
             MALE COLLEGE STUDENTS)
       @APPLICATION 1970 R-62 P-147 P-148 K-161

2933   RAPPAPORT, J., & CHINSKY, J. M.
          BEHAVIOR RATINGS OF CHRONIC HOSPITALIZED PATIENTS: CROSS-SITUATIONAL AND
          CROSS-RATER AGREEMENT.
          JOURNAL OF CONSULTING AND CLINICAL PSYCHOLOGY, 1970, 34, 394-397.
             (RELIABILITY:RETEST; CORRELATES:ENVIRONMENTAL; N=86 MALE AND 64
             FEMALE PSYCHIATRIC PATIENTS, 16 MALE AND 14 FEMALE UNDERGRADUATES,
             16 MALE AND 10 FEMALE ATTENDANTS)
       @APPLICATION 1970 E-20

2934   SHARMA, S.
          MANIFEST ANXIETY AND SCHOOL ACHIEVEMENT OF ADOLESCENTS.
          JOURNAL OF CONSULTING AND CLINICAL PSYCHOLOGY, 1970, 34, 403-407.
             (CORRELATES:INTELLIGENCE; NORMATIVE DATA; N=362 BOY AND 338 GIRL
             INDIANS, AGES 15-17)
       @APPLICATION 1970 S-148

2935   GASSNER, S. M.
          RELATIONSHIP BETWEEN PATIENT-THERAPIST COMPATIBILITY AND TREATMENT
          EFFECTIVENESS.
          JOURNAL OF CONSULTING AND CLINICAL PSYCHOLOGY, 1970, 34, 408-414.
             (CORRELATES:PSYCHOLOGICAL; USED AS CRITERION; NORMATIVE DATA;
             N=22 MALE, 2 FEMALE THEOLOGICAL CLINICAL TRAINEES)
       @APPLICATION 1970 S-11 E-20 D-45 A-48

2936   BERNHARDSON, C. S., & FISHER, R. J.
          PERSONALITY CORRELATES OF DOGMATISM: METHODOLOGICAL PROBLEMS.
          JOURNAL OF CONSULTING AND CLINICAL PSYCHOLOGY, 1970, 34, 449.
             (CORRELATES:PSYCHOLOGICAL; BIAS:RESPONSE; N=68 UNDERGRADUATES)
       @APPLICATION 1970 E-2 R-8 C-27 C-10

2937   LACKS, P. B.
          FURTHER INVESTIGATION OF THE MINI-MULT.
          JOURNAL OF CONSULTING AND CLINICAL PSYCHOLOGY, 1970, 35, 126-127.
             (VALIDITY:CONSTRUCT; CORRELATES:PSYCHOLOGICAL; N=94 INPATIENTS)
       @APPLICATION 1970 D-45 K-82

2938   POPE, B., BLASS, T., SIEGMAN, A. W., & RAHER, J.
          ANXIETY AND DEPRESSION IN SPEECH.
          JOURNAL OF CONSULTING AND CLINICAL PSYCHOLOGY, 1970, 35, 128-133.
             (RELIABILITY:INTERRATER; CORRELATES:BEHAVIORAL, PSYCHOLOGICAL;
             N=6 PSYCHOSOMATIC PATIENTS)
       @APPLICATION 1970 B-129

2939   KIESLER, D. J.
        COMPARISON OF EXPERIENCING SCALE RATINGS OF NAIVE VERSUS CLINICALLY
        SOPHISTICATED JUDGES.
        JOURNAL OF CONSULTING AND CLINICAL PSYCHOLOGY, 1970, 35, 134.
             (RELIABILITY:INTERRATER; USED AS CRITERION; N=8 JUDGES)
        @APPLICATION 1970 K-83

2940   KING, M., WALDER, L. O., & PAVEY, S.
        PERSONALITY CHANGE AS A FUNCTION OF VOLUNTEER EXPERIENCE IN A PSYCHIATRIC
        HOSPITAL.
        JOURNAL OF CONSULTING AND CLINICAL PSYCHOLOGY, 1970, 35, 423-425.
             (CORRELATES:BEHAVIORAL, PSYCHOLOGICAL; USED AS CRITERION;
             N=416 COLLEGE STUDENTS)
        @APPLICATION 1970 H-164 H-165

2941   BRAUCHT, G. N., & WILSON, L. T.
        PREDICTIVE UTILITY OF THE REVISED SUICIDE POTENTIAL SCALE.
        JOURNAL OF CONSULTING AND CLINICAL PSYCHOLOGY, 1970, 35, 426.
             (VALIDITY:CRITERION; N=63 FATAL SUICIDES, 324 NONFATAL SUICIDE
             ATTEMPTERS, AND 95 NONSUICIDAL CONTROLS)
        @APPLICATION 1970 M-155

2942   KOPFSTEIN, J. H.
        SOCIAL DESIRABILITY, EXPECTANCY AND SUCCESS-FAILURE-ORIENTED BEHAVIOR IN
        CHILDREN.
        JOURNAL OF CONSULTING AND CLINICAL PSYCHOLOGY, 1970, 35, 428.
             (CORRELATES:BEHAVIORAL, PSYCHOLOGICAL; USED AS CRITERION; N=87
             SCHOOLGOING BOYS)
        @APPLICATION 1970
        @E-21

2943   ANZEL, A. S.
        A-B TYPING AND PATIENT SOCIO-ECONOMIC AND PERSONALITY CHARACTERISTICS IN A
        QUASI-THERAPEUTIC SITUATION.
        JOURNAL OF CONSULTING AND CLINICAL PSYCHOLOGY, 1970, 35, 102-115.
             (CORRELATES:PSYCHOLOGICAL, DEMOGRAPHIC; USED AS CRITERION; NORMATIVE
             DATA; N=70 THERAPISTS AND 226 MALE UNDERGRADUATES)
        @APPLICATION 1970 B-126 W-91

2944   DARBY, J. A.
        ALTERATION OF SOME BODY IMAGE INDEXES IN SCHIZOPHRENICS.
        JOURNAL OF CONSULTING AND CLINICAL PSYCHOLOGY, 1970, 35, 116-121.
             (RELIABILITY:INTERRATER; CORRELATES:BEHAVIORAL, PSYCHOLOGICAL;
             NORMATIVE DATA; N=75 MALE SCHIZOPHRENICS)
        @APPLICATION 1970 H-37

2945   OBERLANDER, M. I., FRAUENFELDER, K. J., & HEATH, H.
        ORDINAL POSITION, SEX OF SIBLING, SEX, AND PERSONAL PREFERENCES IN A GROUP
        OF EIGHTEEN-YEAR-OLDS.
        JOURNAL OF CONSULTING AND CLINICAL PSYCHOLOGY, 1970, 35, 122-125.
             (CORRELATES:PSYCHOLOGICAL, DEMOGRAPHIC; N=93 MALE, 124 FEMALE 18-YEAR
             OLDS)
        @APPLICATION 1970 K-34

2946   FISCHER, E. H., & TURNER, J. LEB.
        ORIENTATIONS TO SEEKING PROFESSIONAL HELP: DEVELOPMENT AND RESEARCH
        UTILITY OF AN ATTITUDE SCALE.
        JOURNAL OF CONSULTING AND CLINICAL PSYCHOLOGY, 1970, 35, 79-90.
             (CORRELATES:PSYCHOLOGICAL; FACTOR ANALYSIS; N=492 FEMALE AND 468
             MALE STUDENTS)
        @APPLICATION 1970 C-27 C-31 R-16 R-18

2947   MCNEAL, B. F., JOHNSTON, R., & ASPROMONTE, V. A.
        EFFECT OF ACCURATE FORECASTS ON LENGTH OF HOSPITAL STAY OF PSYCHIATRIC
        PATIENTS.
        JOURNAL OF CONSULTING AND CLINICAL PSYCHOLOGY, 1970, 35, 91-94.
             (CORRELATES:ENVIRONMENTAL; USED AS CRITERION; N=200 MALE PSYCHIATRIC
             PATIENTS)
        @APPLICATION 1970 D-45

2948   BRAUCHT, G. N.
            IMMEDIATE EFFECTS OF SELF-CONFRONTATION ON THE SELF-CONCEPT.
            JOURNAL OF CONSULTING AND CLINICAL PSYCHOLOGY, 1970, 35, 95-101.
                    (RELIABILITY:INTERRATER; CORRELATES:PSYCHOLOGICAL, ENVIRONMENTAL;
                    BIAS:TESTER; N=73 PATIENTS)
        @APPLICATION 1970 S-147 M-112

2949   HOGAN, R., MANKIN, D., CONWAY, J., & FOX, S.
            PERSONALITY CORRELATES OF UNDERGRADUATE MARIJUANA USE.
            JOURNAL OF CONSULTING AND CLINICAL PSYCHOLOGY, 1970, 35, 58-63.
                    (CORRELATES:BEHAVIORAL, PSYCHOLOGICAL; N=148 MALE UNDERGRADUATES)
        @APPLICATION 1970 G-22 G-140

2950   FISH, J. M.
            EMPATHY AND THE REPORTED EMOTIONAL EXPERIENCES OF BEGINNING
            PSYCHOTHERAPISTS.
            JOURNAL OF CONSULTING AND CLINICAL PSYCHOLOGY, 1970, 35, 64-69.
                    (RELIABILITY:INTERRATER, INTERNAL CONSISTENCY;
                    CORRELATES:PSYCHOLOGICAL; N=43 THERAPISTS AND 57 CLIENTS)
        @APPLICATION 1970 B-50 W-95 B-148

2951   LAPUC, P. S., & HARMATZ, M. G.
            VERBAL CONDITIONING AND THERAPEUTIC CHANGE.
            JOURNAL OF CONSULTING AND CLINICAL PSYCHOLOGY, 1970, 35, 70-78.
                    (RELIABILITY:INTERRATER; CORRELATES:PSYCHOLOGICAL, ENVIRONMENTAL;
                    N=27 NEUROPSYCHIATRIC PATIENTS)
        @APPLICATION 1970 L-70 T-2 O-16

2952   STONE, L. A.
            MASCULINITY-FEMININITY AS REFLECTED BY THE STERN ACTIVITIES INDEX--A BRIEF.
            JOURNAL OF COUNSELING PSYCHOLOGY, 1963, 10, 87.
                    (CORRELATES:DEMOGRAPHIC; CLUSTER ANALYSIS; N=1568 FRESHMEN COLLEGE
                    MALES AND FEMALES)
        @APPLICATION 1963 S-56

2953   LODATO, F. J., & SOKOLOFF, M. A.
            GROUP COUNSELING FOR SLOW LEARNERS.
            JOURNAL OF COUNSELING PSYCHOLOGY, 1963, 10, 95-96.
                    (CORRELATES:BEHAVIORAL, PSYCHOLOGICAL, INTELLIGENCE; USED AS
                    CRITERION; N=10 LOW ACHIEVING 8TH GRADERS)
        @APPLICATION 1963 B-175 M-58

2954   SIEGEL, L.
            TEST REVIEW: OMNIBUS PERSONALITY INVENTORY, FORM C.
            JOURNAL OF COUNSELING PSYCHOLOGY, 1963, 10, 99-101.
                    (DESCRIPTION; REVIEW ARTICLE)
        @APPLICATION 1963 H-12

2955   LUCKEY, E. B.
            IMPLICATIONS FOR MARRIAGE COUNSELING OF SELF PERCEPTIONS AND SPOUSE
            PERCEPTIONS.
            JOURNAL OF COUNSELING PSYCHOLOGY, 1960, 7, 3-9.
                    (MODIFICATION; CORRELATES:PSYCHOLOGICAL; USED AS CRITERION; N=594
                    MARRIED FORMER STUDENTS)
        @APPLICATION 1960 L-35 L-15

2956   ROMANO, R. L.
            THE USE OF THE INTERPERSONAL SYSTEM OF DIAGNOSIS IN MARITAL COUNSELING.
            JOURNAL OF COUNSELING PSYCHOLOGY, 1960, 7, 10-18.
                    (CORRELATES:BEHAVIORAL, PSYCHOLOGICAL; N=3 MARRIED COUPLES UNDER
                    COUNSELING)
        @APPLICATION 1960 L-35 M-20

2957   LEARY, T.
            COMMENT.
            JOURNAL OF COUNSELING PSYCHOLOGY, 1960, 7, 19.
                    (MENTION; NO SAMPLE SIZE)
        @APPLICATION 1960 L-35

2958   BARCLAY, J. R.
            EFFECTING BEHAVIOR CHANGE IN THE ELEMENTARY CLASSROOM.
            JOURNAL OF COUNSELING PSYCHOLOGY, 1967, 14, 240-247.
                    (MODIFICATION; CORRELATES:PSYCHOLOGICAL, DEMOGRAPHIC,
                    ENVIRONMENTAL; USED AS CRITERION; N=3 5TH GRADE CITY SCHOOL CLASSES)
        @APPLICATION 1967 H-21 O-16

2959   LOWE, C. M.
         PREDICTION OF POSTHOSPITAL WORK ADJUSTMENT BY THE USE OF PSYCHOLOGICAL
         TESTS.
         JOURNAL OF COUNSELING PSYCHOLOGY, 1967, 14, 248-252.
                 (VALIDITY:CRITERION, CROSS-VALIDATION; CORRELATES:BEHAVIORAL,
                 INTELLIGENCE; NORMATIVE DATA; N=34 EMPLOYED, 35 UNEMPLOYED
                 PSYCHIATRIC PATIENTS)
         aAPPLICATION 1967 R-30 D-45

2960   NADLER, E. B., & FINK, S. L.
         IMPACT OF LABORATORY TRAINING ON SOCIOPOLITICAL IDEOLOGY.
         JOURNAL OF APPLIED BEHAVIORAL SCIENCE, 1970, 6, 79-92.
                 (MODIFICATION; CORRELATES:PSYCHOLOGICAL, ENVIRONMENTAL; N=41 COLLEGE
                 STUDENTS)
         aAPPLICATION 1970 A-5 A-17 N-4 N-8

2961   JENKS, R. S.
         AN ACTION-RESEARCH APPROACH TO ORGANIZATIONAL CHANGE.
         JOURNAL OF APPLIED BEHAVIORAL SCIENCE, 1970, 6, 131-150.
                 (REVISION; MENTION)
         aAPPLICATION 1970 S-11 H-161 W-144

2962   DEBUS, R. L.
         EFFECTS OF BRIEF OBSERVATION OF MODEL BEHAVIOR ON CONCEPTUAL TEMPO OF
         IMPULSIVE CHILDREN.
         DEVELOPMENTAL PSYCHOLOGY, 1970, 2, 22-32.
                 (CORRELATES:BEHAVIORAL, PSYCHOLOGICAL; USED AS CRITERION;
                 CROSS-CULTURAL APPLICATION; NORMATIVE DATA; N=320 AUSTRALIAN
                 ELEMENTARY SCHOOL CHILDREN)
         aAPPLICATION 1970 K-60 K-163

2963   LIEBERMAN, M. A., & COPLAN, A. S.
         DISTANCE FROM DEATH AS A VARIABLE IN THE STUDY OF AGING.
         DEVELOPMENTAL PSYCHOLOGY, 1970, 2, 71-84.
                 (MODIFICATION; RELIABILITY:RETEST, INTERRATER, INTERNAL CONSISTENCY;
                 CORRELATES:PSYCHOLOGICAL, DEMOGRAPHIC; N=80 AGED MALES AND FEMALES)
         aAPPLICATION 1970 C-10 N-9 S-28 R-65 L-35 D-68 O-16 M-20 L-165

2964   ROTHENBERG, B. B.
         CHILDREN'S SOCIAL SENSITIVITY AND THE RELATIONSHIP TO INTERPERSONAL
         COMPETENCE, INTERPERSONAL COMFORT, AND INTELLECTUAL LEVEL.
         DEVELOPMENTAL PSYCHOLOGY, 1970, 2, 335-350.
                 (MODIFICATION; CORRELATES:PSYCHOLOGICAL; USED AS CRITERION; N=108
                 3RD AND 5TH GRADE CHILDREN)
         aAPPLICATION 1970 R-89 S-79 C-254

2965   DAVIDS, A., & HOLDEN, R. H.
         CONSISTENCY OF MATERNAL ATTITUDES AND PERSONALITY FROM PREGNANCY TO
         8 MONTHS FOLLOWING CHILDBIRTH.
         DEVELOPMENTAL PSYCHOLOGY, 1970, 2, 364-366.
                 (MODIFICATION; RELIABILITY:RETEST; CORRELATES:PSYCHOLOGICAL,
                 INTELLIGENCE; N=42 PREGNANT WOMEN)
         aAPPLICATION 1970 S-9

2966   WEISBROTH, S. P.
         MORAL JUDGMENT, SEX, AND PARENTAL IDENTIFICATION IN ADULTS.
         DEVELOPMENTAL PSYCHOLOGY, 1970, 2, 396-402.
                 (RELIABILITY:INTERRATER; CORRELATES:PSYCHOLOGICAL, DEMOGRAPHIC;
                 NORMATIVE DATA; N=37 MALE, 41 FEMALE WHITE MIDDLE CLASS ADULTS)
         aAPPLICATION 1970 K-27 O-16 D-16

2967   FATERSON, H. F., & WITKIN, H. A.
         LONGITUDINAL STUDY OF DEVELOPMENT OF THE BODY CONCEPT.
         DEVELOPMENTAL PSYCHOLOGY, 1970, 2, 429-438.
                 (RELIABILITY:RETEST, INTERRATER; CORRELATES:DEMOGRAPHIC,
                 INTELLIGENCE; 2 LONGITUDINAL GROUPS: N=30 BOYS, 30 GIRLS IN AGE 10-24
                 GROUP, 26 BOYS, 22 GIRLS IN 8-13 YEAR GROUP)
         aAPPLICATION 1970 W-19 W-73 W-20 G-78 W-188

2968   CONSTANTINOPLE, A.
         SOME CORRELATES OF AVERAGE LEVEL OF HAPPINESS AMONG COLLEGE STUDENTS.
         DEVELOPMENTAL PSYCHOLOGY, 1970, 2, 447.
                 (CORRELATES:PSYCHOLOGICAL, DEMOGRAPHIC; N=48 MALES, 40 FEMALES IN
                 LONGITUDINAL STUDY)
         aAPPLICATION 1970 C-37 C-205 C-206

2969   WALLS, R. J., & DIVESTA, F. J.
            COGNITIVE FACTORS IN THE CONDITIONING OF CHILDREN'S PREFERENCES.
            DEVELOPMENTAL PSYCHOLOGY, 1970, 2, 318-324.
                    (CORRELATES:PSYCHOLOGICAL; USED AS CRITERION; N=108 1ST GRADE PUBLIC
                    SCHOOL CHILDREN)
        @APPLICATION 1970 N-38

2970   MAW, W. H., & MAW, E. W.
            NATURE OF CREATIVITY IN HIGH- AND LOW-CURIOSITY BOYS.
            DEVELOPMENTAL PSYCHOLOGY, 1970, 2, 325-329.
                    (CORRELATES:PSYCHOLOGICAL; FACTOR ANALYSIS; N=224 WHITE 5TH GRADE
                    BOYS)
        @APPLICATION 1970 T-25 G-62 C-212 M-258

2971   SUMMERS, D. L., & FELKER, D. W.
            USE OF THE IT SCALE FOR CHILDREN IN ASSESSING SEX-ROLE PREFERENCE IN
            PRESCHOOL NEGRO CHILDREN.
            DEVELOPMENTAL PSYCHOLOGY, 1970, 2, 330-334.
                    (VALIDITY:CONSTRUCT; CORRELATES:DEMOGRAPHIC; NORMATIVE DATA; N=15
                    MALE, 15 FEMALE NEGRO PRESCHOOL CHILDREN)
        @APPLICATION 1970 B-35

2972   WACHS, T. D.
            REPORT ON THE UTILITY OF A PIAGET-BASED INFANT SCALE WITH OLDER RETARDED
            CHILDREN.
            DEVELOPMENTAL PSYCHOLOGY, 1970, 2, 449.
                    (CORRELATES:INTELLIGENCE; N=16 RETARDED PRESCHOOL CHILDREN)
        @APPLICATION 1970 U-7

2973   JORDAN, T. E.
            THE INFLUENCE OF AGE AND SOCIAL CLASS ON AUTHORITARIAN FAMILY IDEOLOGY.
            MULTIVARIATE BEHAVIORAL RESEARCH, 1970, 5, 193-201.
                    (CORRELATES:DEMOGRAPHIC; NORMATIVE DATA; N=438 MOTHERS)
        @APPLICATION 1970 L-72

2974   COMREY, A. L., & BACKER, T. E.
            CONSTRUCT VALIDATION OF THE COMREY PERSONALITY SCALES.
            MULTIVARIATE BEHAVIORAL RESEARCH, 1970, 5, 469-477.
                    (RELIABILITY:INTERRATER; VALIDITY:CONSTRUCT; CORRELATES:BEHAVIORAL,
                    PSYCHOLOGICAL, DEMOGRAPHIC; N=86 MALE, 123 FEMALE COLLEGE STUDENTS)
        @APPLICATION 1970 C-19

2975   EDWARDS, A. L., KLOCKARS, A. J., & ABBOTT, R. D.
            SOCIAL DESIRABILITY AND THE TSC-MMPI SCALE.
            MULTIVARIATE BEHAVIORAL RESEARCH, 1970, 5, 153-156.
                    (FACTOR ANALYSIS; N=468 MALE COLLEGE STUDENTS)
        @APPLICATION 1970 E-1 W-41 T-56 D-45

2976   CAVE, R. L.
            A COMBINED FACTOR ANALYSIS OF CREATIVITY AND INTELLIGENCE.
            MULTIVARIATE BEHAVIORAL RESEARCH, 1970, 5, 177-192.
                    (RELIABILITY:INTERRATER; VALIDITY:CONSTRUCT;
                    CORRELATES:PSYCHOLOGICAL, INTELLIGENCE; NORMATIVE DATA; FACTOR
                    ANALYSIS; N=477 HIGH SCHOOL STUDENTS)
        @APPLICATION 1970 T-39 M-29 G-129 G-62

2977   STEIN, K. B.
            THE T.S.C. SCALES: SOCIAL UNDESIRABILITY OR PERSONAL MALADJUSTMENT?
            A REPLY TO EDWARDS, KLOCKARS, AND ABBOTT.
            MULTIVARIATE BEHAVIORAL RESEARCH, 1970, 5, 157-158.
                    (MENTION; REVIEW ARTICLE)
        @APPLICATION 1970 T-56 D-45 E-1

2978   VELDMAN, D. J., & PARKER, G. V. C.
            ADJECTIVE RATING SCALES FOR SELF-DESCRIPTION.
            MULTIVARIATE BEHAVIORAL RESEARCH, 1970, 5, 295-302.
                    (REVISION; VALIDITY:CONSTRUCT, CRITERION; CORRELATES:PSYCHOLOGICAL;
                    FACTOR ANALYSIS; N=779 COLLEGE STUDENTS, N=713 FEMALE TEACHER
                    TRAINEES)
        @APPLICATION 1970 B-30 G-21 V-25

2979   EDWARDS, A. L., ABBOTT, R. D., & KLOCKARS, A. J.
            SOCIAL DESIRABILITY AND THE TSC SCALES: A REPLICATION AND REPLY TO STEIN.
            MULTIVARIATE BEHAVIORAL RESEARCH, 1970, 5, 325-327.
                    (MENTION; REVIEW ARTICLE)
        @APPLICATION 1970 T-56 E-1 W-41 D-45

2980   SELLS, S. B., DEMAREE, R. G., & WILL, D. G., JR.
            DIMENSIONS OF PERSONALITY: I. CONJOINT FACTOR STRUCTURE OF GUILFORD AND
            CATTELL TRAIT MARKERS.
            MULTIVARIATE BEHAVIORAL RESEARCH, 1970, 5, 391-422.
                    (REVIEW; FACTOR ANALYSIS; N=2011 MALE AIR FORCE RECRUITS)
        @APPLICATION 1970 C-10 G-26

2981   HILL, J. A., HOWARD, K. I., & ORLINSKY, D. E.
            THE THERAPIST'S EXPERIENCE OF PSYCHOTHERAPY: SOME DIMENSIONS AND
            DETERMINANTS.
            MULTIVARIATE BEHAVIORAL RESEARCH, 1970, 5, 435-451.
                    (FACTOR ANALYSIS; N=17 THERAPISTS, 31 FEMALE PATIENTS)
        @APPLICATION 1970 O-12

2982   SNYDER, F. W., & WIGGINS, N.
            AFFECTIVE MEANING SYSTEMS: A MULTIVARIATE APPROACH.
            MULTIVARIATE BEHAVIORAL RESEARCH, 1970, 5, 453-468.
                    (REVIEW; FACTOR ANALYSIS)
        @APPLICATION 1970 O-16